فضائلِ اعمال

FAZA'IL-E-A'MAAL

Vol. 1

Revised Translation of
TABLIGHI NISAAB

By
Shaikhul Hadeeth Maulana
Muhammad Zakariyya Kandhalwi (Rah.)

idara
ادارہ اشاعتِ دینیات (پرائیویٹ) لمیٹڈ
IDARA ISHA'AT-E-DINIYAT (P) LTD.

Faza'il-E-A'maal

By

Shaikhul Hadeeth Maulana

Muhammad Zakariyya Kandhalwi (Rah.)

Edition: 2004

ISBN: 81-7101-016-4 (VOLUME-1)
ISBN: 81-7101-009-7 (SET)

Published by
IDARA ISHA'AT-E-DINIYAT (P) LTD.
168/2, Jha House, Hazrat Nizamuddin
New Delhi-110 013 (India)
Tel.: 26926832/33, 55658575
Fax: +91-11-26322787
Email: **sales@idara.com**
Visit us at: **www.idara.com**

Typesetted at: **DTP Division**
IDARA ISHA'AT-E-DINIYAT (P) LTD.
P.O. Box 9795, Jamia Nagar, New Delhi-110025 (India)

Stories of the SAHAABAH

Stories of the Sahaabah

Revised translation of
the Urdu book Hikayaat-e-Sahaabah

حکایات صحابہ

By:-
Shaikhul Hadith Maulana Muhammad Zakariyyah Kaandhlawi (Rah)

translated by
Abdul Rashid Arshad

ادارہ اشاعتِ دینیات (پرائیویٹ) لمیٹڈ
idara.com
IDARA ISHA'AT-E-DINIYAT (P) LTD.

"Translator's Note'

The original Arabic names and terms which are understood all over the Muslim world, have been retained untranslated. These are often printed within 'Commas' and have been explained in the Appendix (Glossary), so as to facilitate their correct pronunciation.

The symbol (') used in such words as 'Ja'far, ka'abah' stands for the Arabic Alphabet (ع). The symbol(') stands for prolonged 'a' sound as in 'Qur'an'.

CONTENTS

STEADFASTNESS IN THE FACE OF HARDSHIPS

CHAPTER II

FEAR OF ALLAH

CHAPTER III

ABSTENENCE AND SELF-DENIAL OF THE SAHABAH

Page No.

CHAPTER IV

PIETY AND SCRUPULOUSNESS

CHAPTER V

DEVOTION TO SALAAT

CHAPTER VI

SYMPATHY AND SELF SACRIFICE

CHAPTER VII

VALOUR AND HEROISM

CHAPTER VIII

MISCELLANEOUS STORIES ABOUT ZEAL FOR KNOWLEDGE

CHAPTER IX

PLEASING THE PROPHET

CHAPTER X

THE WOMEN'S COURAGE AND SPIRIT FOR ISLAM

CHAPTER XI

THE CHILDREN – THEIR DEVOTION TO ISLAM

CHAPTER XII

LOVE FOR THE PROPHET

بِسْمِ اللّٰهِ الرَّحْمٰنِ الرَّحِيْمِ

AUTHOR'S FOREWORD

نَحْمَدُهٗ وَنُصَلِّيْ وَنُسَلِّمُ عَلٰى رَسُوْلِهِ الْكَرِيْمِ وَاٰلِهٖ وَصَحْبِهٖ
وَاَتْبَاعِهٖ الْحُمَاةِ لِلدِّيْنِ الْقَوِيْمِ۔

We glorify Allah and ask blessings and salutations of peace for the noble Prophet (Sallallaho alaihe wasallam) and his companions and those who follow him in upholding the cause of the right religion.

It was in the year 1353 A.H. that an eminent Sheikh, who is my patron and for whom I have every respect, enjoined me to compile a book containing stories of the companions of the Holy Prophet (Sallallaho alaihe wasallam), with special reference to the Faith and Practices of the women and children of his time. The main idea underlying this behest was that Muslim mothers, while going to bed at night, instead of telling myths and fables to their children, may narrate to them such real and true tales of the golden age of Islam that would create in them an Islamic spirit of love and esteem for Sahabah, and thereby improve their 'Imaan'; and the proposed book may, thus, be a useful substitute for the current story books. It became essential for me to comply with the desire of the Sheikh, for, besides being under moral debt and obligation to him for his immense beneficence, I consider the goodwill of such godly people to be the source of success in this world and the Hereafter. I knew my shortcomings and difficulties and, therefore, had been postponing the execution of this work for four years, when in Safar 1357 A.H., it so happened that I was advised by the doctors to suspend my regular duty of teaching for some time. I decided to utilize this period of rest for complying with the long-standing desire of the Sheikh, with the belief that even if my attempt did not come up to his expectation, it would anyhow be a pleasant engagement for me and one likely to bring me spiritual blessings, in addition.

FOREWORD

It is an admitted fact that the stories of the godly people deserve to be studied rather deeply, in order to derive proper benefit from them. This is more important in case of Sahabah, who were chosen by Allah for the company of His beloved and our dear Prophet (Sallallaho alaihe wasallam). Their stories not only serve as a beacon of Faith and Practice but also cause Allah's blessings and mercy to descend on the readers. Junaid Baghdadi (Rahmatullah alaih), a head of the Sufees, once said:

> "Stories of the pious and godly are Allah's special devices, which encourage the hearts of those who strive in His Path."

Somebody inquired of Junaid (Rahmatullah alaih) if he could cite something in support of his statement. He replied:

"Yes. Allah has said in His Book—

وَكُلًّا نَّقُصُّ عَلَيْكَ مِنْ أَنبَاءِ الرُّسُلِ مَا نُثَبِّتُ بِهِ فُؤَادَكَ وَجَاءَكَ فِي هَٰذِهِ الْحَقُّ
وَمَوْعِظَةٌ وَذِكْرَىٰ لِلْمُؤْمِنِينَ (هود - ١٢٠)

> "And all that we relate unto thee of the stories of the messengers is in order that thereby We may make the heart firm. And herein hath come unto thee the Truth and an exhortation and a reminder for believers."
> (XI: 120)

One cannot lay too much stress on the point that whether these be the sayings of the Holy Prophet (Sallallaho alaihe wasallam) or the stories of other God-fearing people, or the books on Islamic practices, or the epistles and written discourses of the saints, it is not enough to go through them once only, but they have to be studied over and over again in order to derive proper benefit from them. Abu Sulaiman Darani (Rahmatullah alaih), a famous Saint, writes:

> "I attended a discourse by a Sheikh at his residence. It had some effect on me, but only till the time that I rose from the meeting. I went to his audience for the second time to listen to his discourse, and this time the effect remained with me till I reached my home. When I visited him for the third time, the effect of his discourse

stayed with me even after reaching home. Then I broke the shackles that had kept me away from Allah, and set out on His path to seek His pleasure.''

Such is the case with religious books. A cursory reading of these seldom produces the desired effect, and a frequent and thorough study thereof is therefore necessary.

For the convenience of the readers, and to interest them, I have divided this book into the following twelve chapters together with an epilogue.

Chapter I Steadfastness in the face of hardships.

Chapter II Fear of Allah.

Chapter III Abstinence and Contentment.

Chapter IV Piety and Scrupulousness.

Chapter V Devotion to Salaat.

Chapter VI Sympathy and Self-sacrifice and spending in the path of Allah.

Chapter VII Valour and Heroism.

Chapter VIII Zeal for knowledge.

Chapter IX Ready Compliance with the Prophet's Wishes.

Chapter X The Women's love of Faith and their Courage.

Chapter XI The Children's Devotion to Islam.

Chapter XII Love and Devotion for the Prophet (Sallallaho alaihe wasallam).

The Epilogue: Sahabah's Virtues and Privileges.

CHAPTER I

STEADFASTNESS IN THE FACE OF HARDSHIPS

It is really very hard for the Muslims of to-day to imagine, and much less to endure or even to attempt to endure, the hardships that were borne by the Prophet (Sallallaho alaihe wasallam) and his illustrious companions in the path of Allah. Books of history are full of stories of their sufferings. It is a pity that we are so indifferent to those events and our knowledge is so poor in this regard. I open this chapter with a story about the Prophet (Sallallaho alaihe wasallam) himself to get the blessings of Allah, which are sure to attend his auspicious mention.

1. The Prophet's (Sallallaho alaihe Wasallam) Journey to Taif

For nine years, since his selection by Allah for His mission, the Prophet (Sallallaho alaihe wasallam) had been delivering the message of Allah in Mecca and making all-out efforts to guide and reform his community. Excepting a few persons who had either embraced Islam or who helped him though not accepting his creed, all the rest in Mecca left no stone unturned in persecuting and deriding him and his followers. His uncle Abu Talib was one of those good-hearted people who helped him, in spite of his not entering into the fold of Islam.

The following year, on the death of Abu Talib, the Qureysh got a free hand and therefore accelerated their sinister pursuits without check and hindrance. At Taif, the second biggest town of Hijaz, there lived Banu Thaqif, a clan strong in number. The Prophet (Sallallaho alaihe wasallam) left for Taif with the hope of winning them over to Islam, thus giving quarter to Muslims from the persecution of the Qureysh, and also establishing a base for the future propagation of Islam. On reaching Taif he visited the three chieftains of the clan separately, and placed before each of them the message of Allah, and called upon them to stand by his Prophet's (Sallallaho alaihe wasallam) side. Instead of accepting his message, they refused even to listen to him and, notwithstanding the proverbial Arab hospitality, each of them treated him most contemptuously and rudely. They plainly told him that they did not like his stay in their town. The Prophet (Sallallaho alaihe wasallam) had expected a civil, even a cordial treatment and due courtesy in speech from them, as they were the heads of the clan. But one of them sneered:

"Hey, Allah has made you a Prophet!"

The other exclaimed with derision:

"Could Allah not lay His hand on anyone else, beside you to make him His Prophet?"

The third one gibed at him:

"I do not want to talk to you, for if you are in fact a Prophet, then to oppose you is to invite trouble, and if you only pretend to be one, why should I talk with an impostor?"

The Prophet (Sallallaho alaihe wasallam), who was a rock of steadfastness and perseverance, did not lose heart over this check from the chieftains, and tried to approach the common people; but nobody would listen to him. Instead they asked him to clear off from their own town and go wherever else he liked. When he realised that further efforts were in vain, he decided to leave the town. But they would not let him depart in peace, and set the street urchins after him to hiss, to hoot, to jeer at, and to stone him. He was so much pelted at with stones that his whole body was covered with blood, and his shoes were clogged to his feet. He left the town in this woeful plight. When he was far out of the town, and safe from the rabble, he prayed to Allah thus:

اَللّٰهُمَّ اِلَيْكَ اَشْكُوْا ضُعْفَ قُوَّتِىْ وَقِلَّةَ حِيْلَتِيْ وَهَوَانِىْ عَلَى النَّاسِ يَاأَرْحَمَ
الرَّاحِمِيْنَ ، اَنْتَ رَبُّ الْمُسْتَضْعَفِيْنَ وَاَنْتَ رَبِّىْ اِلٰى مَنْ تَكِلُنِىْ اِلٰى بَعِيْدٍ
يَّتَجَهَّمُنِىْ اَمْ اِلٰى عَدُوٍّ مَلَّكْتَهُ اَمْرِىْ اِنْ لَمْيَكُنْ بِكَ عَلَىَّ غَضَبٌ فَلَااُبَالِىْ وَلٰكِنْ
عَافِيَتُكَ ، هِىَ اَوْسَعُ لِىْ اَعُوْذُ بِنُوْرِ وَجْهِكَ الَّذِيْ اَشْرَقَتْ لَهُ الظُّلُمَاتُ وَصَلَحَ
عَلَيْهِ اَمْرُ الدُّنْيَا وَالْاٰخِرَةِ مِنْ اَنْ تُنَزِّلَ بِىْ غَضَبَكَ اَوْ يَحِلَّ عَلَىَّ سَخَطُكَ لَكَ
الْعُتْبٰى حَتّٰى تَرْضٰى وَلَا حَوْلَ وَلَا قُوَّةَ اِلَّا بِكَ

"O, my Allah! To Thee I complain of the feebleness of my strength, of my lack of resources and my being unimportant in the eyes of people. O, Most Merciful of all those capable of showing mercy! Thou art the Lord of the weak, and Thou art my own Lord. To whom art Thou to entrust me; to an unsympathetic foe who would sullenly frown at me, or to an alien to whom Thou hast given control over my affairs? Not in the least do I care for anything except that I may have Thy protection for myself. I seek shelter in Your light–the light which illuminates the Heavens and dispels all sorts of darkness, and which controls all affairs in this world as well as in the Hereafter. May it never be that I should incur Thy wrath, or that Thou should be displeased with me. I must remove the cause of Thy displeasure till Thou art pleased. There is no strength nor power but through Thee."

The Heavens were moved by the prayer, and Jibrail (Alayhis salaam) appeared before the Prophet (Sallallaho alaihe wasallam), greeting him with Assalamu Alaikum and said:

> "Allah knows all that has passed between you and these people. He has deputed an angel in charge of the mountains to be at your command."

Saying this, Jibrail (Alayhis salam) ushered the angel before the Prophet (Sallallaho alaihe wasallam). The angel greeted the Prophet (Sallallaho alaihe wasallam) and said:

> "O, Prophet of Allah! I am at your service. If you wish, I can cause the mountains overlooking this town on both sides to collide with each other, so that all the people therein would be crushed to death, or you may suggest any other punishment for them."

The merciful and noble Prophet (Sallallaho alaihe wasallam) said:

> "Even if these people do not accept Islam, I do hope from Allah that there will be persons from among their progeny who would worship Allah and serve His cause."

Behold the conduct of our noble Prophet (Sallallaho alaihe wasallam), whom we profess to follow! We get so much irritated over a little trouble or a mere abuse from somebody that we keep on torturing and taking our revenge throughout our lives in every possible manner. Does it become people who claim to follow the magnanimous

Prophet (Sallallaho alaihe wasallam)? Look, even after so much suffering at the hands of the Taif mob, he neither curses them nor does he work for any revenge, even when he has the full opportunity to do so.

2. Martyrdom of Hadhrat Anas bin Nadhr (Radhiyallaho anho):

Hadhrat Anas bin Nadhr (Radhiyallaho anho) was one of the Sahabah who could not take part in the campaign of Badr. He very much regretted to have missed the honour of participating in the first and the most illustrious battle for Islam. He longed for a chance wherein he could make amends for Badr. He did not have to wait for long. The battle of Uhud came about in the following year. He joined the army with the most determined zeal. Despite heavy odds, the Muslims were gaining the upper hand, when some people made a blunder and the Muslims had to suffer a reverse. The Prophet (Sallallaho alaihe wasallam) had posted a band of fifty archers to guard a pass in the rear against the enemy cavalry. They had definite instructions not to move from their position till further orders from him. But when they saw the Muslims gaining victory and the enemy in full flight, they left their position in the belief that the battle was over and it was time to join in the pursuit and get on to the booty. The leader of the band tried his utmost to check them by reminding them of the Prophet's (Sallallaho alaihe wasallam) command and solicited them to stay on, but no more than ten persons would listen to him, arguing that the orders given by the Prophet (Sallallaho alaihe wasallam) were only for the duration of the actual fight. The enemy cavalry then noticed the unguarded pass in the rear, made a flank movement, forced a passage through it, and fell right on the rear of the Muslims, who were pre-occupied with the booty. It was in this state of affairs that Hadhrat Anas (Radhiyallaho anho) saw Hadhrat Sa'ad bin Ma'az (Radhiyallaho anho) passing in front of him. He shouted to him:

> "O, Sa'ad! where are you going? By Allah! I smell the fragrance of Paradise coming from Mount Uhud."

Saying this, he threw himself into the very thick of the enemy, and fought tooth and nail till he met his martyrdom

After the battle, it was found that his body had been mauled and mutilated to such an extent that only his sister could identify him, and that barely from the finger tips. No less than eighty wounds of arrows and swords were counted on his body.

Those who strive in the path of Allah with sincerity and devotion taste the pleasures of Paradise even in this world, and so did Anas (Radhiyallaho anho) smell the fragrance of Paradise.

3. The Truce of Hudeybiah and Story of Hadhrat Abu Jandal and Hadhrat Abu Basir (Radhiyallaho anhuma)

In the 6th year of Hijrah, the Prophet (Sallallaho alaihe wasallam) along with his companions left for Mecca to perform Umrah. The Qureysh heard of the news and decided to resist his entry into Mecca even as a pilgrim, and so he had to encamp at Hudeybiah. The devoted Sahabah, 1 400 in number, were however determined to enter, even if it involved an open fight; but the Prophet (Sallallaho alaihe wasallam) viewed the matter differently and in spite of the Sahabah's eagerness to fight, entered into a treaty with the Qureysh, accepting their conditions in full.

This one-sided and seemingly ungraceful truce was a very bitter pill for the Sahabah to swallow, but their devotion to the Prophet (Sallallaho alaihe wasallam) would not allow them to demur, and even the most valiant man like Hadhrat Umar (Radhiyallaho anho) could not but submit to his decision. According to one of the articles of the treaty, converts to Islam during the period of the truce were to be returned, but not so the deserters from Muslims to Qureysh.

Hadhrat Abu Jandal (Radhiyallaho anho) a Muslim in Mecca, was suffering great persecution at the hands of Qureysh. They kept him constantly in chains. On hearing about the arrival of the Prophet (Sallallaho alaihe wasallam) in Hudeybiah, he escaped somehow and managed to reach the Muslim camp at a time when the truce was about to be signed. His father, Suhail (till then a non-Muslim) was the envoy of Qureysh in the negotiations for the truce. He smote Hadhrat Abu Jandal (Radhiyallaho anho) on his face and insisted on taking him back to Mecca. The Prophet (Sallallaho alaihe wasallam) represented that, since the truce had not till then been written, its application in Abu Jandal's case was premature. Suhail, however, would not listen to any argument and was not inclined to leave his son with the Muslims even at the personal request of the Prophet (Sallallaho alaihe wasallam), and would have forgone the truce even. Abu Jandal (Radhiyallaho anho) counting his hardships remonstrated at the top of his voice but, much to the grief of the Sahabah, the Prophet (Sallallaho alaihe wasallam) agreed to his return. He however enjoined patience on him saying:

> "Do not be distressed, Hadhrat Abu Jandal (Radhiyallaho anho), Allah will shortly open a way for you."

After the truce was signed and the Prophet (Sallallaho alaihe wasallam) had returned to Madinah, another Meccan Muslim Hadhrat Abu Basir (Radhiyallaho anho) escaped to Madinah and besought the Prophet's (Sallallaho alaihe wasallam) protection. The Prophet (Sallallaho alaihe wasallam) refused to accept his implorations and, in deference to the truce condition, handed him over to the two persons who had been deputed by the Qureysh to claim him. He, however, advised him as he had advised Hadhrat Abu Jandal (Radhiallaho anho) to be patient and to hope for the help of Allah. When Hadhrat Abu Basir (Radhiyallaho anho) and his escort were on their way back to Mecca, Hadhrat Abu Basir (Radhiyallaho anho) said to one of them:

> "Friend, your sword is extremely fine."

The man was flattered and took it out from the sheath and said:

> "Yes it is really very fine, and I have tried it on so many persons. You can have a look at it."

Most foolishly he made over the sword to Abu Basir (Radhiyallaho anho), who immediately 'tried' it on its owner and killed him. The other man took to his heels and reached Madinah to report to the Prophet (Sallallaho alaihe wasallam). In the meantime Abu Basir (Radhiyallaho anho) also arrived. He said to the Prophet (Sallallaho alaihe wasallam):

> "O, Prophet of Allah, you once returned me and absolved yourself of the truce obligations. I had no obligations to fulfil and I managed my escape from them by this trick, as I was afraid of their forcing me to forsake my faith."

The Prophet (Sallallaho alaihe wasallam) remarked:

"You are a war-monger. I wish you could be helped."

Hadhrat Abu Basir (Radhiyallaho anho) came to understand from this that he would be returned to Qureysh again when they demanded him. He therefore left Madinah and fled to a place in the desert on the sea shore. Abu Jandal (Radhiyallaho anho) also managed his escape and joined him there. More Muslims of Mecca followed, and in a few days quite a small group of such fugitives gathered in the wilderness. They had to undergo untold sufferings in the desert, where there was neither habitation nor vegetation. They, however, being bound by no treaty proved a great nuisance for the Qureysh by dealing blows after blows on their caravans passing that way. This compelled the Qureysh to approach the Prophet (Sallallaho alaihe wasallam) and beseech him to intervene and call the fugitives to Madinah, so that they might be bound by the terms of the treaty like other Muslims, and the caravans might pass in safety. It is said that Hadhrat Abu Basir (Radhiyallaho anho) was on his death bed when the letter sent by the Prophet (Sallallaho alaihe wasallam) permitting his return to Madinah reached him. He died while holding the Prophet's (Sallallaho alaihe wasallam) letter in his hand.

No power on the earth can make a person forsake his faith, provided it is a true faith. Moreover, Allah has given an assurance to help those who are genuine Muslims.

4. Hadhrat Bilal (Radhiyallaho anho) and his Sufferings:

Hadhrat Bilal (Radhiyallaho anho) is one of the best known of the galaxy of Sahabah as moazzin of the Prophet's (Sallallaho alaihe wasallam) masjid. He was an Abyssinian slave of a disbeliever in Mecca. His conversion to Islam was, naturally, not liked by his master and he was, therefore, persecuted mercilessly. Ummayah bin Khalaf, who was the worst enemy of Islam, would make him lie down on the burning sand at midday and would place a heavy stone on his breast, so that he could not even move a limb. He would then say to him:

"Renounce Islam or swelter and die."

Even under these afflictions, Bilal (Radhiyallaho anho) would exclaim:–

"Ahad"–The One (Allah). "Ahad"–The One (Allah).

He was whipped at night and with the cuts thus received, made to lie on the burning ground during the day to make him either forsake Islam or to die a lingering death from wounds. The torturers would get tired and take turns (Abu Jahl, Umayyah and others) and vie with one another in afflicting more and more painful punishment, but Hadhrat Bilal (Radhiyallaho anho) would not yield. At last Abu Bakr (Radhiyallaho anho) bought his freedom, and he became a free Muslim.

As Islam taught implicitly the oneness of the Almighty Creator, while the idolaters of Mecca believed in many gods and goddesses with minor godlings, therefore Bilal (Radhiyallaho anho) repeated:

"Ahad (The One), Ahad (The One)."

This shows his love and devotion to Allah. Allah was so dear to him that no amount of persecution could distract him from reciting His Holy name. It is said that the urchins of Mecca would drag him in the streets, with his words "Ahad!, Ahad!" ringing in their wake.

Look how Allah rewarded his steadfastness! He was to have the honour of becoming the Prophet's moazzin. He was always to remain with him at home and abroad to call out the Azaan for his Salaat. After the Prophet's death it became very hard for him to continue his stay in Madinah where he would miss him at every step and in every corner. He therefore left Madinah, and decided to pass the rest of his life striving in the path of Allah. Once he beheld the Prophet (Sallallaho alaihe wasallam) in his dream saying to him:

"O, Bilal! How is it that you never visit me."

No sooner did he get up than he set out for Madinah. On reaching there, Hadhrat Hasan and Hadhrat Husain (Radhiyallaho anhuma) (The Prophet's (Sallallaho alaihe wasallam) grandsons) requested him to call out the Azaan. He could not refuse them, for they were very dear to him. But as soon as the Azaan was called, the people of Madinah cried openly out of their anguish at the memory of the happy old days of the Prophet's (Sallallaho alaihe wasallam) time. Even the women came out of their houses weeping. Hadhrat Bilal (Radhiyallaho anho) left Madinah again after a few days and died in Damascus in 20 A.H.

5. Hadhrat Abuzar Ghifari's (Radhiyallaho anho) Conversion to Islam:

Hadhrat Abuzar Ghifari (Radhiyallaho anho) is very famous among the Sahabah for his piety and knowledge. Hadhrat Ali (Radhiyallaho anho) used to say:

> "Abuzar is the custodian of such knowledge as other people are incapable of acquiring."

When he first got news of the Prophet's (Sallallaho alaihe wasallam) mission, he deputed his brother to go to Mecca and make investigations regarding 'the person' who claimed to be the recipient of Divine revelation. His brother returned after necessary enquiries, and informed him that he found Muhammad (Sallallaho alaihe wasallam) to be a man of good habits and excellent conduct, and that his wonderful revelations were neither poetry nor sooth-sayings. This report did not satisfy him, and he decided to set out for Mecca and find out the facts for himself. On reaching Mecca, he went straight to the Haram. He did not know the Prophet (Sallallaho alaihe wasallam) and he did not consider it advisable (under the circumstances prevailing at that time) to enquire about him from anybody. When it became dark, Hadhrat Ali (Radhiyallaho anho) noticed him and seeing in him a stranger, could not ignore him, as hospitality and care for the travellers, the poor and the strangers, were the Sahabah's second nature. He, therefore, took him to his place. He did not ask him about the purpose of his visit to Mecca, nor did Abuzar (Radhiyallaho anho) himself disclose it. Next day, he again went to the Haram and stayed there till nightfall without being able to learn who the Prophet (Sallallaho alaihe wasallam) was. In fact everybody knew that the Prophet (Sallallaho alaihe wasallam) and his companions were being persecuted in Mecca, and Abuzar (Radhiyallaho anho) might have had misgivings about the result of his quest for the Prophet (Sallallaho alaihe wasallam). Hadhrat Ali (Radhiyallaho anho) again took him home for the night, but again did not have any talk with him about the purpose of his visit to the city. On the third night, however, after Hadhrat Ali (Radhiyallaho anho) had entertained him as on the two previous nights, he asked him:

> "Brother, what brings you to this town?"

Before replying, Hadhrat Abuzar (Radhiyallaho anho) took

an undertaking from Hadhrat Ali (Radhiyallaho anho) that he would speak the truth, and then he enquired from him about Muhammad (Sallallaho alaihe wasallam). Hadhrat Ali (Radhiyallaho anho) replied:

> "He is verily the Prophet of Allah. You accompany me tomorrow and I shall take you to him. But you have to be very careful, lest people come to know of your association with me, and you get into trouble. When on our way I apprehend some trouble, I shall get aside pretending some necessity or adjusting my shoes, and you will proceed ahead without stopping so that the people may not connect us."

The next day, he followed Hadhrat Ali (Radhiyallaho anho), who took him before the Prophet (Sallallaho alaihe wasallam). In the very first meeting, he embraced Islam. The Prophet (Sallallaho alaihe wasallam), fearing that the Qureysh might harm him, enjoined upon him not to make an open declaration of his Islam, and bade him to go back to his clan and return when Muslims had gained the upper hand. Hadhrat Abuzar (Radhiyallaho anho) replied:

> "O, Prophet of Allah! By Him who is the master of my soul, I must go and recite the Kalimah in the midst of these unbelievers."

True to his word, he went straight to the Haram and, right in the midst of the crowd and at the pitch of his voice, recited Shahadah viz:

اَشْهَدُ اَنْ لَّآاِلٰهَ اِلَّا اللّٰهُ وَاَشْهَدُ اَنَّ مُحَمَّدًا رَّسُوْلُ اللّٰهِ

> "I bear witness that there is no god save Allah, and I bear witness that Muhammad (Sallallaho alaihe wasallam) is the Prophet of Allah."

People fell upon him from all sides, and would have beaten him to death if Abbas (the Prophet's uncle, who had not till then embraced Islam) had not shielded him and saved him from death. Abbas said to the mob:

> "Do you know who he is? He belongs to the Ghifar clan, who live on the way of our caravans to Syria. If he is killed, they will waylay us and we shall not be able to trade with that country."

This appealed to their prudence and they left him alone.

The next day, Hadhrat Abuzar (Radhiyallaho anho) repeated his perilous confession of Imaan and would have surely been beaten to death by the crowd, had not Abbas intervened once again and saved him for the second time.

The action of Hadhrat Abuzar (Radhiyallaho anho) was due to his extraordinary zeal for proclaiming Kalimah among the disbelievers, and the prohibition by the Prophet (Sallallaho alaihe wasallam) was due to the soft corner in his heart for Hadhrat Abuzar (Radhiyallaho anho), lest he be put to hardships that might prove too much for him. There is not the least shadow of disobedience in this episode. Since the Prophet (Sallallaho alaihe wasallam) himself was undergoing all sorts of hardships in spreading the message of Islam, Abuzar (Radhiyallaho anho) also thought it fit to follow his example rather than to avail of his permission to avoid danger. It was this spirit of Sahabah that took them to the heights of material and spiritual progress. When a person once recited the Kalimah and entered the fold of Islam, no power on earth could turn him back and no oppression or tyranny could stop him from Tabligh.

6. The Afflictions of Hadhrat Khabbab bin Alarat (Radhiyallaho anho):

Hadhrat Khabbab (Radhiyallaho anho) is also one of those blessed persons who offered themselves for sacrifice and suffering for the cause of Allah. He was the sixth or seventh person to embrace Islam and, therefore, he suffered long. He was made to put on steel armour and lie in the sun to sweat and swelter. Very often he was made to lie flat on burning sand, which caused the flesh on his back to waste away. He was the slave of a woman. When she came to know that he was visiting the Prophet (Sallallaho alaihe wasallam), she used to brand his head with a hot iron rod. Hadhrat 'Umar (Radhiyallaho anho) during his caliphate once inquired of him about the details of his sufferings after embracing Islam. He showed him his back, seeing which Hadhrat 'Umar (Radhiyallaho anho) remarked, "I have never seen such a back before." He said, "My body was dragged over heaps of smouldering charcoal, and the blood and fat coming out of my back put out the fire." It is said that, when Islam spread and the Muslims conquered all the surrounding territory, he used to weep and say:

> "Allah seems to be compensating us in this world for all our sufferings, and perhaps nothing would be left for us as reward in the Hereafter."

Hadhrat Khabbab (Radhiyallaho anho) narrates:

"The Prophet (Sallallaho alaihe wasallam) once performed an unusually long rakaat while leading a Salaat. When the Sahabah mentioned it to him, he said, "This was a Salaat of yearning and humility. I asked three boons from Allah. I besought Him:

'O, Allah! Let not my Ummat perish by famine; let not my Ummat be annihilated by an enemy gaining an upper hand on them; and let not my Ummat fight among themselves.'

Allah granted the first two prayers, but not the third one."

Hadhrat Khabbab (Radhiyallaho anho) died in 37 A.H. He was the first of the Sahabah to be buried at Koofah. Hadhrat Ali (Radhiyallaho anho) once passing his grave said:

"May Allah bless and show mercy on Hadhrat Khabbab (Radhiyallaho anho). He embraced Islam willingly. He emigrated with great pleasure in Allah's path, and spent his whole life in striving and suffering for Islam. Blessed is the person who is mindful of the Day of Judgement, prepares for his reckoning, remains contented with very little of this world, and is able to please his Lord."

To be able to please Allah, was really, the Sahabah's greatest achievement, for this was the sole purpose of their life.

7. Hadhrat Ammaar (Radhiyallaho anho) and His Parents:

Hadhrat Ammaar (Radhiyallaho anho) and his parents were also subjected to the severest afflictions. They were tormented on the scorching sands of Mecca. The Prophet (Sallallaho alaihe wasallam) while passing by them would enjoin patience giving them glad tidings about paradise. Ammaar's father Yasir (Radhiyallaho anho) died after prolonged sufferings at the hands of persecutors, and his mother Sumayya (Radhiyallaho anha) was killed by Abu Jahl, who put his spear through the most private part of her body, causing her death. She had refused to renounce Islam in the face of terrible torture in her old age. The blessed lady was the first to meet martyrdom in the cause of Islam. The first mosque in Islam was built by Ammaar (Radhiyallaho anho).

When the Prophet (Sallallaho alaihe wasallam) emigrated to Madinah, Ammaar (Radhiyallaho anho) offered to build a structure for him where he could sit, take rest in the afternoon, and say his Salaat under its roof. He first collected the stones and then built the musjid in Quba. He fought against the enemies of Islam with great zeal and courage. Once he was fighting in a battle when he said rejoicingly:

> "I am to meet my friends very soon, I am to meet Muhammad (Sallallaho alaihe wasallam) and his companions."

He then asked for water. He was offered some milk. He took it and said:

> "I heard the Prophet (Sallallaho alaihe wasallam) saying to me, "Milk shall be the last drink of your worldly life."

He then fought till he met his coveted end. He was then aged about ninety-four.

8. Hadhrat Sohaib's (Radhiyallaho anho) coming into Islam:

Hadhrat Sohaib and Hadhrat Ammaar (Radhiyallaho anhuma) became Muslims at the same time. The Prophet (Sallallaho alaihe wasallam) was staying at Arqam's (Radhiyallaho anho) place, when they both came separately with the same intention of embracing Islam and met each other at the door of the house. Sohaib (Radhiyallaho anho) also suffered very much at the hands of his persecutors, like other poor Muslims of that time. At last he decided to emigrate to Madinah. The Qureysh would not tolerate this and, soon after his departure, a party went in pursuit to bring him back to Mecca. As the party drew near, he shouted to them:

> "You know that I am a better archer than all of you. So long as I have a single arrow left with me, you will not be able to approach me and, when I finish all my arrows, I shall fight you with my sword, as long as it is in my hand. If you like you can get my money which I have left in Mecca and my two women slaves, in lieu of me."

And they agreed. He told them the whereabouts of his money, and they allowed him to proceed to Madinah. At this, Allah revealed the following verse of the Qur'an to the Prophet (Sallallaho alaihe wasallam):

وَمِنَ النَّاسِ مَنْ يَّشْرِىْ نَفْسَهُ ابْتِغَآءَ مَرْضَاتِ اللهِ ، وَاللهُ رَءُوْفٌ م بِالْعِبَادِ (بقره ، ٢٠٧)

"And of mankind is he who would sell himself, seeking the pleasure of Allah, and Allah has compassion on His bondsmen."

The Prophet (Sallallaho alaihe wasallam) was at that time at Quba. When he saw Hadhrat Sohaib (Radhiyallaho anho) coming, he remarked:

"A good bargain, Sohaib!"

Sohaib (Radhiyallaho anho) narrates:

"The Prophet (Sallallaho alaihe wasallam) was eating dates at that time. I also joined him in eating. One of my eyes was sore." He said, "Sohaib! you are taking dates when your eye is sore." 'But I am taking them by the side of the other eye, which is not sore, O, Prophet of Allah,' I replied. The Prophet (Sallallaho alaihe wasallam) was much amused with my retort."

Hadhrat Sohaib (Radhiyallaho anho) was very generous and he spent his money on others most lavishly. 'Umar (Radhiyallaho anho) once told him that he was rather extravagant. He replied:

"But I spend only where it is right."

When Hadhrat 'Umar (Radhiyallaho anho) was about to die, he expressed the wish that his funeral service be led by Hadhrat Sohaib (Radhiyallaho anho).

9. Hadhrat 'Umar (Radhiyallaho anho) coming into Islam.

Hadhrat 'Umar (Radhiyallaho anho), of whom all the Muslims are justly proud, and the disbelievers still dread, was most adamant in opposing the Prophet (Sallallaho alaihe wasallam) and very prominent in persecuting the Muslims before he embraced Islam. One day, the Qureysh in a meeting called for somebody to volunteer himself for the assassination of the Prophet (Sallallaho alaihe wasallam). 'Umar (Radhiyallaho anho) offered himself for this job, at which everybody exclaimed:

"Surely, you can do it, 'Umar!"

With sword hanging from his neck, he set out straight away on his sinister errand. On his way he met Sa'ad bin Abi Waqqas of the Zuhrah clan. Sa'ad inquired:

"Whither! 'Umar?"

'Umar: "I am after finishing Muhammad."

Sa'ad: "But do not you see that Banu Hashim, Banu Zuhrah and Banu Abde Munaf are likely to kill you in retaliation?"

'Umar (upset at the warning):

"It seems that you also have renounced the religion of your forefathers. Let me settle with you first."

So saying, Umar drew out his sword. Sa'ad announcing his Islam, also took out his sword. They were about to start a duel when Sa'ad said:

"You had better first set your own house in order. Your sister and brother-in-law both have accepted Islam."

Hearing this, Umar flew into a towering rage and turned his steps towards his sister's house. The door of the house was bolted from inside and both husband and wife were receiving lessons in the Qur'an from Hadhrat Khabbab (Radhiyallaho anho). 'Umar knocked at the door and shouted for his sister to open it. Hadhrat Khabbab (Radhiyallaho anho) hearing the voice of 'Umar, hid himself in some inner room, forgetting to take the manuscript pages of the Holy Qur'an with him. When the sister opened the door, 'Umar hit her on the head, saying:

"O, enemy of yourself. You too have renounced your religion."

Her head began to bleed. He then went inside and inquired, "What were you doing? And who was the stranger I heard from outside?" His brother-in-law replied, "We were talking to each other." 'Umar said to him, "Have you also forsaken the creed of your forefathers and gone over to the new religion?" The brother-in-law replied, "But what if the new religion be the better and the true one?" 'Umar got beside himself with rage and fell on him, pulling his beard and beating him most savagely. When the sister intervened, he smote her so violently on her face that it bled most profusely. She was, after all, 'Umar's sister; she burst out:

> "'Umar! we are beaten only because we have become Muslims. Listen! we are determined to die as Muslims. You are free to do whatever you like."

When 'Umar had cooled down and felt a bit ashamed over his sister's bleeding, his eyes fell on the pages of the Qur'an left behind by Hadhrat Khabbab (Radhiyallaho anho). He said, "Alright show me, what are these?" "No," said the sister, "you are unclean and no unclean person can touch the Scripture." He insisted, but the sister was not prepared to allow him to touch the leaves unless he washed his body. 'Umar at last gave in. He washed his body and then began to read the leaves. It was Surah "Taha". He started from the beginning of the Surah, and he was a changed man altogether when he came to the verse:

إِنَّنِىْ أَنَا اللّٰهُ لَآ إِلٰهَ إِلَّآ أَنَا فَاعْبُدْنِىْ وَأَقِمِ الصَّلٰوةَ لِذِكْرِىْ (طٰهٰ ، ١٤)

> "Lo! I, indeed I am Allah. There is none worthy of worship save Me. So serve me and establish Salaat for My remembrance."

He said: "Alright, take me to Muhammad (Sallallaho alaihe wasallam)."

On hearing this, Hadhrat Khabbab (Radhiyallaho anho) came out from inside and said:

> "O, 'Umar! Glad tidings for you. Yesterday (on Thursday night) the Prophet (Sallallaho alaihe wasallam) prayed to Allah, 'O, Allah strengthen Islam with either 'Umar or Abu Jahl, whomsoever Thou likest'. It seems that his prayer has been answered in your favour."

'Umar then went to the Prophet (Sallallaho alaihe wasallam) and embraced Islam on Friday morning. 'Umar's Islam was a terrible blow to the morale of the unbelievers, but still the Muslims were few in number and the whole country was against them. The disbelievers intensified their efforts for the complete annihilation of Muslims and the extinction of Islam. With 'Umar (Radhiyallaho anho) on their side, the Muslims now started saying their Salaat in the Haram. Abdullah bin Mas'ood (Radhiyallaho anho) says:

> "'Umar's Islam was a big triumph, his emigration to Madinah a tremendous reinforcement, and his accession to the Caliphate a great blessing for the Muslims."

10. The Flight to Abyssinia and Ostracism in the Gorge of Ibn-Abi Talib:

The hardships and sufferings borne by the Muslims were ever on the increase. The Prophet (Sallallaho alaihe wasallam) at last permitted them to emigrate to some other place. Abyssinia at that time was ruled by a Christian King (who later on embraced Islam), famous for his mercy and equity. In Rajab of the fifth year of the Mission, the first group emigrated to Abyssinia. The group comprised about twelve men and five women. The Qureysh pursued them to the port to capture them, but their vessels had left the shore. When the group reached Abyssinia, they heard the rumour that the whole tribe of the Qureysh had accepted Islam. They were naturally very much pleased at the news and returned to their country. On approaching Mecca, they learnt that the rumour was false and the persecutions were going on unabated. Some of them decided to return to Abyssinia and the rest entered Mecca, seeking the protection of a few influential people. This is known as the first migration to Abyssinia. Later on, a bigger group of eighty-three men and eighteen women emigrated to Abyssinia (separately). This is called the second emigration to that country. Some Sahabah took part in both the migrations. The Qureysh did not like the emigrations, and the thought of peace enjoyed by the fugitives gave them no rest. They sent a delegation to Abyssinia with handsome presents for the king, his courtiers and the clergy. The delegation first met the chiefs and the priests and, by offering them presents, succeeded in winning the court officials to their side. Having thus made their way to the royal court, they prostrated themselves before the king and then presenting the gifts put their case before him. They said:

> "O, king! A few foolish lads of our community have renounced their ancestral faith, and have joined an absolutely new religion, which is opposed to our as well as your religions. They have come and settled in your country. The nobility of Mecca, their own parents

and kith and kin have sent us to take them back to their country. We beseech you to make them over to us."

The king replied:

"We cannot make over the people who have sought our shelter, without proper investigation. Let us call them to our presence, and hear them out. If your charge of apostasy against them is genuine, we shall make them over to you."

The king thereupon summoned the Muslims to his court. They were at first greatly distressed and did not know what to do, but Allah gave them courage, and they decided to go and place the true facts before the king. On appearing before him, they greeted him with 'Salaam'. Someone from the courtiers objected that they had not prostrated before the king according to the rules of the land. They explained:

"Our Prophet (Sallallaho alaihe wasallam) has forbidden us from prostrating before any one except Allah."

The king then asked them to submit what defence they could make to the charges brought against them. Ja'far (Radhiyallaho anho) rose and addressed the king thus:

"O, king! we were an ignorant people. We neither knew Allah nor His Prophets A.S. We worshipped stones. We used to eat carrion and commit all sorts of undesirable and disgraceful acts. We did not make good our obligations to our relatives. The strong among us would thrive at the expense of the weak. Till at last, Allah raised a Prophet (Sallallaho alaihe wasallam) for our reformation. His noble descent, up-right conduct, integrity of purpose, and pure life are only too well known amongst us. He called upon us to worship Allah, and exhorted us to give up idolatry and stone-worship. He enjoined upon us right conduct, and forbade us from indecency. He taught us to tell the truth, to make good our trust, to have regard for our kith and kin, and to do good to our neighbours. From him we learnt to observe Salaat, Fasting, Zakaat and good conduct; and to shun everything foul, and to avoid bloodshed. He forbade adultery, lewdness telling of lies, misappropriating the orphan's heritage, bringing false accusations against others, and all other indecent things of that sort. He taught us the Qur'an, the won-

> derful book of Allah. So we believed in him, followed him and acted up to his teachings. Thereupon our people began to persecute us, and to subject us to tortures, thinking that we might abjure our faith and revert to idolatry. When, however, their cruelties exceeded all bounds, we took shelter in your country by the permission of our Prophet (Sallallaho alaihe wasallam)."

The king said:

> "Let us hear something of the Qur'an that your Prophet (Sallallaho alaihe wasallam) has taught you."

Hadhrat Ja'far (Radhiyallaho anho) recited a few verses from the beginning of Surah "Maryam", which touched the hearts of the king and the priestly class so much that tears flowed down their cheeks and wetted their beards. The king remarked:

> "By Allah, these words and the words revealed to Moosa ('Alayhis Salam) are the rays of one and the same light,"

and he told the Qureysh embassy that he would by no means hand over the refugees to them. Then, disappointed and disgraced, they held a counsel. One of them said:

> "I have hit upon a plan that is sure to draw the king's wrath upon their heads."

Although the others did not agree to such a drastic step (for after all they were their own flesh and blood), yet he would not listen. The next day, they excited the king by telling him that those heretics denounced 'Isa ('Alayhis Salam) and did not believe in his Divinity. The Muslims were again summoned to the court. They were much more distressed this time. When the king inquired about their belief in 'Isa ('Alayhis Salam), they said:

> "We believe in what Allah has revealed about him to our Prophet (Sallallaho alaihe wasallam), i.e. he is a servant and Prophet of Allah, and is His word, which He conveyed to the virgin and pure Maryam."

Negus said: "'Isa ('Alayhis Salam) himself does not say anything beyond that."

The priests then began to murmur in protest, but the king, would not listen to them. He returned to the delegation the presents they had brought for him, and said to the Muslims:

> "Go and live in peace. If anybody ill-treats you, he will have to pay heavily for it."

A royal declaration was also issued to that effect. This enhanced the prestige of the Muslims in the country, and the Qureysh delegation had to return crestfallen.

This failure of the Qureysh embassy to Abyssinia, and the triumph of Muslims over them, led to an increase in the exasperation of the idolaters; the conversion of 'Umar (Radhiyallaho anho) to Islam added fuel to fire. They grew more and more embittered, till things came to such a pass that a large number of the Qureysh chiefs conspired to kill Muhammad (Sallallaho alaihe wasallam) outright and deal summarily with the whole affair. But this was not so easy. Banu Hashim to which clan the Prophet (Sallallaho alaihe wasallam) belonged, were strong in number and still stronger in influence. Although all of them were not Muslims, yet even the non-Muslims among them would not agree to, or tolerate the murder of the Prophet (Sallallaho alaihe wasallam). The Qureysh, therefore, decided to place a social ban on the Banu Hashim, and their chiefs drew up a document to the effect that none of them or their clans would associate with, buy from or sell to those who sided with the Banu Hashim, unless and until they surrendered Muhammad (Sallallaho alaihe wasallam) for the death penalty. All of them signed this document on 1st Moharram of 7th year of the Mission, and the scroll was hung up in the Ka'abah in order to give it full sanctity. Then, for three long years, the Prophet (Sallallaho alaihe wasallam) was shut up with all his kinsfolk in the glen, which was a sub-section of one of the gorges that run down to Mecca. For three long years, nobody could see them nor could they see anybody. They could not purchase anything in Mecca nor from any trader coming from outside. If any person was found outside this natural prison, he was beaten mercilessly and if he asked for anything it was flatly refused. Soon their stock of food was exhausted and they were reduced to famine rations. Their women and, more specially, the children and suckling babies would cry with hunger, and this was harder on them than their own starvation. During the last part of this period, their sole subsistence was the little food that the husbands of Hashimite women married into other clans managed to smuggle into the glen in the darkness of night.

At last by the Grace of Allah, after three years the scroll was eaten up by white ants and the ban was removed. The severity of the afflictions, which they bore during this period of ostracism, cannot be imagined. But the Sahabah not only remained steadfast in their faith, but also kept busy in spreading the light of Islam amongst their comrades in distress.

Look! How much the Sahabah have suffered in the path of Allah and for the cause of Islam. We claim to follow their footsteps, and dream of the material progress and spiritual elevation which was theirs, but how much have we suffered in the true cause? what sacrifice have we offered for the sake of Allah in His path? Success is always proportionate to the sacrifice. We wish to live in luxury and comfort, and are too eager to race shoulder to shoulder with the non-Muslims in enjoying the good things of this world, forgetting the Hereafter, and then at the same time we expect to receive the same help from Allah which the Sahabah received in their time. We cannot beguile anybody but ourselves by working like this. As the Poet has said,

ترسم نرسی بکعبہ اے اعرابی
کیں راہ کہ تو میروی بترکستان است

'I am afraid, O wayfarer, that you will not reach the Ka'aba because the path that you are following goes (in the opposite direction) to Turkistan.'

CHAPTER II

FEAR OF ALLAH

Coupled with the remarkable spirit of sacrifice, the Sahabah had genuine and deep-rooted fear of Allah in their hearts. I wish today's Muslims could have an iota of that fear of Allah. Here are a few stories about this aspect of their lives.

1. The Prophet's (Sallallaho alaihe wasallam) Apprehensions at the time of a storm.

Hadhrat Aishah (Radhiyallaho anha) relates that whenever a strong wind bringing dense clouds started blowing, the Prophet's (Sallallaho alaihe wasallam) face turned pale with the fear of Allah. He became restive and would go in and out with perturbation, and would recite the following prayer:

اَللّٰهُمَّ اِنِّىْ اَسْئَلُكَ خَيْرَهَا وَخَيْرَ مَافِيْهَا وَخَيْرَ مَاۤاَرْسَلْتَ بِهِ وَاَعُوْذُبِكَ مِنْ شَرِّهَا

وَشَرِّ مَا فِيْهَا وَشَرِّ مَا اَرْسَلْتَ بِهِ

> "O, my Allah! I ask of Thee the good out of this wind, the good out of that which is in this wind, and the good out of that which is the outcome of this wind. I seek refuge in Thee from the evil of this wind, from the evil out of that which is in this wind, and from the evil out of that which is the outcome of this wind."

She says:

> "And further when it began to rain, signs of delight appeared on his face. I said to him once, 'O, Prophet of Allah when clouds appear everybody is happy as they foretell rain, but why is it that I see you so much perturbed at that time?' He replied, 'O, 'Aishah! How can I feel secure that this wind does not portend Allah's wrath? The people of A'ad were punished with the wind. They were happy when they beheld the gathering dense clouds, believing that they brought rain; but actually those clouds brought no rain but utter destruction to 'A'ad."

The Prophet (Sallallaho alaihe wasallam) was, obviously, referring to the following verses of the Qur'an:

فَلَمَّا رَاَوْهُ عَارِضًا مُّسْتَقْبِلَ اَوْدِيَتِهِمْ قَالُوْا هٰذَا عَارِضٌ مُّمْطِرُنَا ، بَلْ هُوَ مَاسْتَعْجَلْتُمْ بِهٖ ، رِيْحٌ فِيْهَا عَذَابٌ اَلِيْمٌ ، تُدَمِّرُ كُلَّ شَيْءٍۢ بِاَمْرِ رَبِّهَا فَاَصْبَحُوْا لَايُرٰى اِلَّا مَسٰكِنُهُمْ ، كَذٰلِكَ نَجْزِى الْقَوْمَ الْمُجْرِمِيْنَ (احقاف ٢٤ ، ٢٥)

"Then, when they (A'ad) beheld a dense cloud coming toward their valleys, they said: "Here is a cloud bringing us rain." Nay, but it is that very calamity which you did seek to hasten, a wind wherein is grievous penalty, destroying all things by commandment of its Lord. And morning found them so that naught could be seen, save their dwellings. Thus we treat the guilty folk." (XLVI: 24 & 25)

Look at the fear of Allah in the heart of a person who is the best of all creation (Sallallaho alaihe wasallam). In spite of a clear verse in the Qur'an that Allah would not punish the people so long as the Prophet (Sallallaho alaihe wasallam) was with them (Al-Qur'an VIII: 33), he has so much fear of Allah in him that a strong wind reminds him of the punishment awarded to the people in the past. Now let us peep into our own hearts for a moment. Although we are fully saturated with sins, yet none of the unusual phenomena viz: earthquake, lightning, etc., arouses the least fear of Allah in our hearts and, instead of resorting to Istighfaar or Salaat at such times, we only indulge in absurd investigations.

2. What Hadhrat Anas (Radhiyallaho anho) used to do when a storm approached:

Hadhrat Nadhr-bin-Abdullah relates:

"One day while Hadhrat Anas (Radhiyallaho anho) was alive, it became very dark during the day time. I went to him and said, "Did you ever see much a thing in the Prophet's time?" He replied, "I seek refuge in Allah! In those days if the breeze grew a little stronger than normal, we would hasten towards the musjid, fearing the approach of the Last Day."

Hadhrat Abu Darda (Radhiyallaho anho) narrates:

"Whenever there was a storm, the Prophet (Sallallaho

alaihe wasallam) would get perturbed and would go to the musjid."

Who thinks of going to musjid, now-a-days, even at the time of the worst of calamities? Leave aside the common people, even those who regard themselves as good and practising Muslims do not practise this Sunnat. What a deterioration!

3. The action of Prophet (Sallallaho alaihe wasallam) at the Time of Solar Eclipse.

The Sun once was in eclipse in the Prophet's (Sallallaho alaihe wasallam) time. The Sahabah left their jobs. Even the young boys, practising archery, hastened towards the musjid to know what the Prophet (Sallallaho alaihe wasallam) would do at that time. The Prophet (Sallallaho alaihe wasallam) started Salaat of two rakaat, which were so long that some people fainted and fell down. He wept in his Salaat and said:

> "O, My Lord! Thou has said that Thou wouldst not punish them as long as I am with them and so long as they seek Thy forgiveness."

This refers to a verse in the Qur'an wherein Allah says:

وَمَاكَانَ اللهُ لِيُعَذِّبَهُمْ وَاَنْتَ فِيهِمْ ، وَمَا كَانَ اللهُ مُعَذِّبَهُمْ وَهُمْ يَسْتَغْفِرُوْن

> "But Allah would not punish them while Thou art with them, nor will He punish them while they seek forgiveness." (VIII–33)

He then addressed the people saying:

> "You should hasten for Salaat whenever you happen to find the Sun or the Moon in eclipse. If you happen to know the signs of the Last Day as I do, then surely you would weep more and laugh less. In all such happenings, repair to Salaat; pray to Allah and distribute alms to the poor."

4. The Prophet's weeping the whole night:

The Prophet once (Sallallaho alaihe wasallam) kept weeping the whole night through, repeating again and again the following verse:

اِنْ تُعَذِّبْهُمْ فَاِنَّهُمْ عِبادُكَ ، وَاِنْ تَغْفِرْلَهُمْ فَاِنَّكَ اَنْتَ الْعَزِيْزُ الْحَكِيْمْ

"If Thou punish them, they art Thy slaves; and if Thou forgive them, Thou only art the Mighty, the Wise."
(V: 118)

It is said about Imam Abu Hanifah (Rahmatullah alaih) that he also once wept the whole night, reciting the following verse of the Qur'an in Tahajjud:

وَامْتَازُوا الْيَوْمَ اَيُّهَا الْمُجْرِمُوْنَ (يٰسين ٥٨)

"But avaunt ye, O, ye guilty, this day." (XXXVI: 58)

This verse means that on the Day of Judgement, the guilty will be asked to separate themselves from the good, and will not be allowed to mix with them as they were doing in the worldly life. Why should not the people with fear of Allah in their hearts weep in anxiety regarding which class they will belong to on that Day?

5. Hadhrat Abu Bakr (Radhiyallaho anho) and The Fear of Allah:

According to our belief, Abu Bakr (Radhiyallaho anho) is the most exalted person after the Prophets (may peace be on all of them). The Prophet (Sallallaho alaihe wasallam) himself conveyed to him the glad tidings of his being the head of a group of persons in Paradise. The Prophet (Sallallaho alaihe wasallam) once remarked:

"Abu Bakr's name shall be called out from all the gates of Paradise, and he will be the first of my followers to enter it."

With all these virtues and privileges, Abu Bakr (Radhiyallaho anho) used to say:

"I wish I were a tree that would be cut and done away with."

Sometimes he would say:

"I wish I were a blade of grass, whose life ended with the grazing by some beast."

He also said: "I wish I were a hair on the body of a Mo'min."

Once he went to a garden, where he saw a bird singing. He sighed deeply and said:

> "O, bird! How lucky you are! You eat, you drink and fly under the shade of the trees, and you fear no reckoning of the Day of Judgement. I wish I were just like you."

Hadhrat Rabiah Aslami (Radhiyallaho anho) narrates:

> "Once I had some argument with Abu Bakr (Radhiyallaho anho), during which he uttered a word that I did not like. He realized it immediately and said to me 'Brother, please say that word back to me in retaliation.' I refused to do so. He persisted, and even spoke of referring the matter to the Prophet (Sallallaho alaihe wasallam), but I did not agree to utter that word. He got up and left me. A few people of my clan remarked, 'Look! How strange! The person does wrong to you and, on the top of that, he threatens to complain to the Prophet (Sallallaho alaihe wasallam)'. I said, 'Do you know who he is. He is Abu Bakr (Radhiyallaho anho). To displease him is to displease the Prophet (Sallallaho alaihe wasallam) and to displease the Prophet (Sallallaho alaihe wasallam) is to displease Allah, and if Allah is displeased then who can save Rabiah from ruin?' I went to the Prophet (Sallallaho alaihe wasallam) and narrated the whole story to him. He said, 'You were quite right in refusing to utter that word. But you could have said this much in reply: 'O, Abu Bakr, (Radhiyallaho anho) May Allah forgive you!"

Look at the fear of Allah in Hadhrat Abu Bakr (Radhiyallaho anho)! He is so anxious to clear his accounts in this world that no sooner has a slightly unpleasant word been addressed by him to a person, than he regrets it and requests him to say that word back to him in retaliation. He is so particular in this that he threatens to have the retaliation done through the intervention of the Prophet (Sallallaho alaihe wasallam). We are in the habit of saying offensive words to others, but we fear neither the retaliation nor the reckoning in the Hereafter.

6. Hadhrat 'Umar (Radhiyallaho anho) and the Fear of Allah.

Umar (Radhiyallaho anho) would often hold a straw in his hand and say:

> "I wish I were a straw like this."

Sometimes he would say:

> "I wish my mother had not given birth to me."

Once he was busy with some important work when a person came to him and, complaining about some petty grievance, requested for its redress. Hadhrat Umar (Radhiyallaho anho) laid a lash across his shoulders, saying:

> "When I sit for that purpose, you do not come to me but when I am engaged in other important work you come with your grievances to interrupt me."

The person walked away. But Hadhrat 'Umar (Radhiyallaho anho) sent for him and, handing his whip over to him, said:

> "You now lash me to even the matter."

He said: "I forgive you for the sake of Allah."

Hadhrat Umar (Radhiyallaho anho) went home, prayed a Salaat of two rakaats in repentance and upbraided himself saying:

> "O, Umar! You were low but Allah elevated you. You were wandering astray but Allah guided you. You were base but Allah ennobled you and gave you sovereignty over His people. Now one of them comes and asks you for redress of the wrong done to him, and you beat him? What answer have you to give before Allah?"

He kept on chiding himself thus for a very long time.

Once Hadhrat Umar (Radhiyallaho anho) was going on his usual round towards Harrah (a suburb of Madinah) with his slave Aslam, when he saw a distant fire in the desert. He said:

> "There seems to be a camp. Perhaps, it is a caravan that could not enter the town due to night fall. Let's go and look after them and arrange for their protection during the night."

When he reached there, he found a woman and some children. The children were crying. The woman had a pan of water over the fire. Hadhrat 'Umar (Radhiyallaho anho) greeted her with salaam and, with her permission, went near her.

Umar:	"Why are these children crying?"
The Woman:	"Because they are hungry."
Umar:	"What is in the pan?"
The Woman:	"Only water to soothe the children, so that they may go to sleep in the belief that food is being prepared for them. Ah! Allah will judge between Umar (Radhiyallaho anho) and me, on the Day of Judgement, for neglecting me in my distress."
'Umar (weeping):	"May Allah have mercy on you! How can Umar know of your distress?"
The Woman:	"When he is our Amir, he must keep himself informed about us."

Hadhrat 'Umar (Radhiyallaho anho) returned to the town and straightway went to Baitul-Mal to fill a sack with flour, dates, fat and clothes, and also drew some money. When the sack was ready, he said to Aslam:

"Now put this sack on my back, Aslam."

Aslam: "No please, Amir-ul-Mo'mineen! I shall carry this sack."

'Umar refused to listen to Aslam, even on his persistant requests to allow him to carry the sack, and remarked:

"What! Will you carry my load on the Day of Judgement? I must carry this bag, for it is I who would be questioned (in the Hereafter) about this woman."

Aslam most reluctantly placed the bag on Umar's (Radhiyallaho anho) back, who carried it with a swift pace right to the woman's tent. Aslam followed at his heels. He put a little flour and some dates and fat in the pan and began to stir. He blew (with his mouth) into the fire to kindle it. Aslam says:

"I saw the smoke passing through his thick beard."

After some time, the pottage was ready. He himself served it to the family. When they had eaten to their fill, he made over to them the little that was left for their next meal. The children were very happy after their meal and began to play about merrily. The woman felt very grateful and remarked:

> "May Allah reward you for your kindness! In fact you deserve to take the place of Khalifah instead of 'Umar."

'Umar consoled her and said:

> "When you come to see the Khalifah, you will find me there."

He sat for a while at a place close by and kept on watching the children. He then returned to Madinah. On his way back, he said to Aslam:

> "Do you know why I sat there, Aslam? I had seen them weeping in distress; I liked to see them laughing and happy for some time."

It is said that Hadhrat Umar (Radhiyallaho anho) while leading Fajr Salaat used to recite 'Kahf', 'Taha' and other such Soorahs in his Salaat, and would weep so much that his crying could be heard way back to several rows. Once he was reciting Surah 'Yusuf' in Fajr. When he came to the verse:

اِنَّمَآ اَشْكُوْا بَثِّىْ وَحُزْنِىْ اِلَى اللهِ

"I only plead for my distress and anguish unto Allah,"
(XII: 86)

he wept so much that he could not recite any further. In Tahajjud, he would sometimes fall to the ground and would get indisposed with excessive weeping.

Such was the fear of Allah in Hadhrat Umar (Radhiyallaho anho) whose name struck terror in the hearts of the mightiest monarchs of his time. Even today, the people are filled with awe when they read about him. Is there any person in power today who is prepared to show such kindness to the people in his charge?

7. An Admonition by Hadhrat Abdullah bin Abbas (Radhiyallaho anho).

Wahab bin Munabbah says:

> "Abdullah bin Abbas (Radhiyallaho anho) lost his eyesight in his old age. I once led him to the Haram in Mecca, where he heard a group of people exchanging

hot words among themselves. He asked me to lead him to them. He greeted them with 'Assalamu Alaikum.' They requested him to sit down, but he refused and said: 'May I tell you about people whom Allah holds in high esteem? These are those whom His fear has driven to absolute silence, even though they are neither helpless nor dumb. Rather they are possessors of eloquence and have power to speak and sense to understand. But constant glorification of Allah's name has so over-powered their wits that their hearts are overawed and their lips sealed. When they get established in this state, they hasten towards righteousness. Whither have you people deviated from this course? After this admonition, I never saw an assembly of even two persons in the Haram."

It is said that Hadhrat Ibne Abbas (Radhiyallaho anho) used to weep so much with Allah's fear that the tears streaming down his cheeks had left permanent marks on them.

In this story, Hadhrat Abdullah bin Abbas (Radhiyallaho anho) has prescribed a very easy way to righteousness. This is to meditate over the greatness of Allah. If this is done, it becomes very easy to perform all other acts of righteousness with full sincerity. Is it so very difficult to devote a few minutes, out of the twenty four hours of a day at one's disposal, to this spiritual meditation?

8. The Prophet's (Sallallaho alaihe wasallam) passing near the ruins of Thamud during Tabuk expedition:

The Tabuk expedition is one of the major campaigns of the Prophet (Sallallaho alaihe wasallam), and the last one in which he personally took part. When he received the news that the Caesar (of Rome) had mustered a large force to crush the power of Islam and was on his way (through Syria) to invade Madinah, he decided to lead the Sahabah to check him on his way. On Thursday the 5th of Rajab, 9 A.H., the devoted band marched out of Madinah. As the weather was hot and the fighting was expected to be very tough, the Prophet (Sallallaho alaihe wasallam) made an open declaration that the Muslims should gather in strength and prepare fully to face the forces of the Roman Empire. He also exhorted them to contribute towards the equipment of the expedition. It was on this occasion that Hadhrat Abu Bakr (Radhiyallaho anho) contributed all his belongings. When he was questioned by the Prophet (Sallallaho alaihe wasallam) as to what he had left for his family, he replied:

"I have left Allah and His Prophet (Sallallaho alaihe wasallam) for them."

Hadhrat Umar (Radhiyallaho anho) contributed half of his belongings and Hadhrat 'Usman (Radhiyallaho anho) provided for the equipment of one-third of the whole army. Although everybody. contributed beyond his means, yet the equipment fell far short of the requirements. Only one camel was available for each group of ten persons, who were to ride it in turn. This is why this campaign is known as: "The campaign of hardship."

The journey was long and the weather hot and dry. The orchards were laden with ripe dates (the staple crop of Madinah) and it was just the time for harvesting, when all of a sudden the Sahabah were required to start on this campaign. It was really an acid test of their Imaan. They visualised the long and arduous journey, the scorching heat, the formidable enemy opposed to them and, to top all, the prospective loss of the year's crop, but they could not even dream of evading the call to arms, and that solely on account of the deep-rooted fear of Allah in their hearts. Except the women, children (who were excusable), those who were ordered to stay behind by the Prophet (Sallallaho alaihe wasallam) himself, and the munafiqin, nearly everybody joined the expedition. Also among those left behind were such persons as could neither arrange conveyance for themselves, nor was the Prophet (Sallallaho alaihe wasallam) able to provide them with any. It is about such people that Allah says in his Book:

تَوَلَّوْا وَّاَعْيُنُهُمْ تَفِيْضُ مِنَ الدَّمْعِ حَزَنًا اَلَّا يَجِدُوْا مَا يُنْفِقُوْنَ (التوبة ، ٩٢)

"They turned back with eyes flowing with tears in sorrow that they could not find means to spend."

(IX: 92)

Of the true believers, those who stayed behind without any excuse whatsoever were three in number. Their story would be presently related. On their way to Syria when the expedition reached the habitation of Thamud, the Prophet (Sallallaho alaihe wasallam) covered his face with his shirt and quickened the pace of his camel. He also instructed the

Sahabah to do the same, since that was the scene of Thamud's destruction. They were advised to pass there weeping and fearing lest Allah should punish them as he had punished the Thamud.

The dearest and the most beloved Prophet of Allah and his privileged companions pass by the ruins of the punished people in fear and tears, lest they meet the same fate; on the other hand today, if any place is struck with an earthquake, it becomes a place of sightseeing for us and, if we come across any ruins, our eyes remain dry and our hearts unaffected. What a change of attitude!

9. Hadhrat Ka'ab's (Radhiyallaho anho) Failure to Join the Tabuk Expedition:

Among the Munafiqin who did not join the Tabuk expedition, there were more than eighty persons from among the Ansar and an equal number from amongst the nomadic Arabs and a large number from the out-stations. Not only did they stay behind themselves, but they induced others to do so saying:

لَاتَنْفِرُوْا فِىْ الْحَرِّ (التوبة ٨١)

"Go not forth in the heat."

Allah's reply to this was:

قُلْ نَارُ جَهَنَّمَ اَشَدُّ حَرًّا (التوبة ٨١)

"Say the fire of Hell is of more intense heat."

From amongst the faithful, there were only three persons who failed to rally to the Prophet's call. They were Murarah bin Rabi, Hilal bin Umayyah and Ka'ab bin Malik (Radhiyallaho anhum). Murarah had orchards of dates, laden with fruit. He persuaded himself to lag behind with the plea:

> "I have taken part in all the campaigns so far. What possible harm would befall the Muslims, if I miss this one?"

He feared the loss of his entire crop in his absence, and this prevented him from going out. But when he realised his folly, he gave away in charity the whole crop and garden, too, that had caused him to tarry behind the Prophet (Sallallaho alaihe wasallam). Hilal's case was different. Some of his kinsfolk who had been away for a long time had just returned to Madinah. It was for the sake of their company that he did not join the expedition. He also had participated in all the campaigns previously and thought (like Murarah) that it would not matter much if he missed just that one campaign. When he came to know of the seriousness of his default, he made up his mind to sever all his connections with those relatives who had been the cause of that blunder. Ka'ab himself gives his account in detail, which is quoted in all books of Hadith. He says:

"I had never been financially so well off as I was at the time of Tabuk. I had two dromedaries of my own. I had never possessed this number before. It was a habit with the Prophet (Sallallaho alaihe wasallam) that he never disclosed the destination of his expeditions, but he would keep enquiring about the conditions prevailing elsewhere. But this time in view of the distance, the hot season, and the strength of the enemy, he had declared his destination, so that preparations could be made thorough and complete. The number of the participants was so large that it was difficult to note down their names even, so much so, that absentees could hardly be detected in the large host. The gardens of Madinah were full of fruit. I intended every morning to make preparation for the journey but, somehow or other, the days passed by and I made no progress. I was satisfied that I had all the necessary means at my disposal and that I would be ready in no time if I once did decide to do so. I was still in this state of indecision when I learnt that the Prophet (Sallallaho alaihe wasallam) had left with his companions. The idea still lingered in my mind that I would take a day or two to get ready and overtake the party. This procrastination continued till the time for the Prophet's arrival in Tabuk drew very near. I then tried to get ready but again, somehow or other, I did not do so. Now, when I came to look at the people left behind, I realised that there was none in Madinah except those who had been condemned as Munafiqin or had been specially exempted from going for certain reasons. The Prophet (Sallallaho alaihe wasallam) on reaching Tabuk inquired as well, 'How is it that I do not see Ka'ab?' Somebody said, 'O, Prophet of Allah: His pride in wealth and ease has caused him to stay behind.' Ma'az interrupted and said, No, this is wrong. As far as our knowledge goes, he is a true Muslim.' The Prophet (Sallallaho alaihe wasallam) however, kept quiet."

Ka'ab (Radhiyallaho anho) says:

"After a few days I heard the news of the Prophet's return. I was struck with grief and remorse. Good excuses one after the other entered my mind, and I was sure that I could escape the Prophet's wrath with one of them for the time being, and later on I could pray for forgiveness to Allah. I also sought advice of the wise men of my family in the matter. But when I knew that the Prophet (Sallallaho alaihe wasallam) had actually arrived, I was convinced that nothing but the truth would save me; so I decided to speak out the plain truth. It was a habit with the Prophet (Sallallaho alaihe wasallam) that whenever he returned from a journey he would repair to the musjid, first of all, say two rakaat 'Tahiyyatul musjid' and then stay there for a while to meet visitors. Now also, as he sat in the musjid, the Munafiqin came and placed before him on solemn oaths, their excuses for failing to accompany him on the campaign. He took them at their words, leaving the rest to Allah. Just then I came and greeted him with 'salaam'. He turned his face with a sardonic smile. I besought him with the words: 'O, Prophet of Allah! You turn your face from me. By Allah! I am neither a Munafiq, nor have I the least doubt in my faith.' He asked me to draw near and I did so. He then said to me: 'What prevented you from going out? Had you not purchased the dromedaries? I made a reply: 'O, Prophet of Allah: If I were dealing with a worldly man, I am sure I would escape his displeasure through (seemingly) reasonable excuses, for Allah has endowed me with the gift of the gab. But in your case I am sure that if I appease you with a false statement, Allah would be displeased with me. And, on the other hand, I am sure that if I displease you by confessing the simple truth, then Allah would very soon blow away your displeasure. I, therefore, make bold to speak the very truth. By Allah, I had no excuse at all. I had never been so well to do as I was at that time.' The Prophet (Sallallaho alaihe wasallam) remarked: 'He is speaking the truth.' He then said to me: 'You go away, Allah will decide about you. When I left the musjid, many a man of my clan blamed me and admonished me thus; 'Never before you had committed any wrong; if after making some good excuse for once, you had requested the Prophet (Sallallaho alaihe wasallam) to pray for your goodness, surely his prayer would have sufficed you.' I inquired of them if there were any more people like me. They informed me that there were two other persons viz. Hilal bin Umayyah and Murarah bin Rabi, who also had admitted their faults like me and received the same reply from the Prophet (Sallallaho alaihe wasallam). I knew that both of them were very good Muslims and had participated in the campaign of Badr. The Prophet (Sallallaho alaihe wasallam) issued instructions that none was to speak with the three of us.'

It is a common principle that displeasure is shown where some attachment exists, and a reprimand is given when there is hope for correction. A reprimand to an incorrigible person would be a futile effort.

Ka'ab (Radhiyallaho anho) continues:

"Under the instructions of the Prophet (Sallallaho alaihe wasallam), the Sahabah completely boycotted us. Nobody was prepared to mix with or even speak to us. It seemed as if I was living in a strange land altogether. My own birth-place looked like a foreign locality and my bosom friends behaved like strangers. 'The earth, vast as it is, was straightened' (Al–Qur'an IX: 113) for me. The thing that worried me most was that, if I died in this condition, the Prophet (Sallallaho alaihe wasallam) would not lead my funeral prayer, and if the Prophet (Sallallaho alaihe wasallam) died in the meantime, I would be doomed for ever, with none to talk to me and with none to pray at my funeral. The other two companions of mine confined themselves to their houses. I was the most daring of the three; I would go to the market, and join the Jamaat for Salaat, but nobody would talk to me. I would approach the Prophet (Sallallaho alaihe wasallam) and say 'Assalamo alaikum' and would watch eagerly to see if his lips moved in reply. After Fardh, I used to complete the Salaat by standing close to him, and I would look at him from the corner of my eye to learn if he ever cast a single glance at me. I noticed that when I was engaged in Salaat he did glance at me, but when I was out of it, he would avert his face from me."

Ka'ab (Radhiyallaho anho) continues:

"When this complete social boycott became too hard for me to bear, I, one day, climbed up the wall of Qatadah, my dear cousin, and greeted him with 'Assalamo-alaikum'. He did not return my greetings. I said to him, 'For Allah's sake, do answer me one question. Do not you know that I love Allah and His Prophet (Sallallaho alaihe wasallam)?' He kept quiet. Again I repeated my request, but again he would not speak. When I inquired for the third time, he simply said, 'Allah and His Prophet (Sallallaho alaihe wasallam) know best.' At this, tears welled out of my eyes and he left me alone."

"Once; I was passing through a street of Madinah, when I noticed a Coptic Christian, who had come from Syria to sell his grain, inquiring about Káab-bin-Malik. When people pointed me out to him, he came and made over a letter to me from the Christian King of Ghassan. Thus it read: 'We have come to know that your master has ill-treated you. Allah may not keep you in abasement and in disgrace. You had better come to us. We shall extend all help to you.' When I read this letter, I uttered "Inna-lillahi-wa-Inna-ilaihi-raaji-oon" To Allah we belong and to Him is our return; and said; 'So my state of affairs (had) reached such an ebb that even the Kafirs were aspiring to draw me away from Islam.' I could not imagine a calamity worse than that. I went and threw the letter into an oven. Thereafter I presented myself to the Prophet (Sallallaho alaihe wasallam) and exclaimed: 'O, Prophet of Allah! Your indifference towards me has lowered me to such an extent that even the Kafirs are building up their hopes over me."

When forty days had passed in this condition, a messenger of the Prophet (Sallallaho alaihe wasallam) brought me this mandate: 'Be separated from your wife' I inquired, 'Am I to divorce her?' He replied: 'No, only be separated.' A similar message was delivered to my other two companions as well. I consequently said to my wife: 'Go to your parents and wait till Allah decides my case.' Hilal's wife went to the Prophet (Sallallaho alaihe wasallam) and said; 'O, Prophet of Allah! Hilal is an old man and there is nobody else to look after him. If I go away from him, he will perish. If it is not very serious, kindly permit me to keep attending to him.' The Prophet (Sallallaho alaihe wasallam) replied; 'There is no harm, provided you don't indulge in cohabitation with each other.' She remarked! 'O, Prophet of Allah: He has no urge for such a thing; since the day his ordeal has started, he has been spending his entire time in weeping.''

Ka'ab (Radhiyallaho anho) says:

"It was suggested to me that I might also request the Prophet (Sallallaho alaihe wasallam) for permission to keep my wife with me for service, but I said; 'Hilal is old, while I am young. I do not know what reply I shall get and, as such, I have no courage to make the request.' Another ten days passed and now our ordeal had lasted for a full fifty days. On the morning of the fiftieth day, when I had said my 'Fajr' prayer and was sitting on the roof of my house stricken with grief, and the earth had 'straightened' for me and the life had become dismal for me, I heard a crier's cry from over the top of the mount Sula; 'Happy tidings to you, O, Káab.' The moment I heard this, I fell prostrate on the ground and tears of joy rolled down my cheeks, as I understood that the ordeal was now over. In fact, the Prophet (Sallallaho alaihe wasallam) had announced the Divine forgiveness for all three of us after the Salaat that morning. At this, a person ran up the top of the mountain and yelled out the cry that had reached me. Thereafter, a rider came galloping to deliver the same happy news to me. I gave away as a gift the clothes, I was wearing, to the messenger of glad tidings. I swear by Allah I had no other clothes in my possession at that time. I dressed up by borrowing clothes from some friend and went to the Prophet (Sallallaho alaihe wasallam). As I entered the musjid, the people in the audience of the Prophet (Sallallaho alaihe wasallam) ran to congratulate me. Abu Talha (Radhiyallaho anho) was the first to approach me. He shook my hand with a warmth that I shall never forget. Thereafter I offered my salutation to the Prophet (Sallallaho alaihe wasallam). I found his face beaming and radiant like

> the full moon. This was usual with him at times of extreme joy. I said to him, 'O, Prophet of Allah! I propose to give away in charity all that I possess as thanks for the acceptance of my Taubah.' He said: 'This will be too much for you. Keep a portion with you.' I agreed to keep my share of the booty that fell in our hands in the Khaiber campaign."

He says:

> "It is the truth that brought me salvation, and as such I am determined to speak nothing but the truth in future."

The above story brings out the following salient characteristics of the Muslims of that time:—

(1) The importance of striving in the path of Allah. Even the persons who had hitherto faithfully participated in every expedition, had to bear the brunt of the Prophet's (Sallallaho alaihe wasallam) anger when they failed to respond to Allah's call even though for the first time in their lives.

(2) Their devotion and obedience to the Prophet (Sallallaho alaihe wasallam). For full fifty days the whole Muslim community, even their nearest and dearest, would not speak to the three persons, in obedience to the Prophet's (Sallallaho alaihe wasallam) orders. The three persons themselves went most steadfastly through the ordeal imposed on them.

(3) Their strong faith. Káab was so much perturbed when he received the letter from the Christian King, exciting him against the Prophet (Sallallaho alaihe wasallam). His words and his action at that time are a testimony to the strong faith in his heart.

Let us search our hearts and see how much devotion we have in them for the observance of the duties we owe to Islam. Leaving aside Zakaat and Hajj, which involve the sacrifice of money, take the case of Salaat alone, which is the most important pillar of Islam after Imaan. How many of us are particular about it?

10. The Prophet's (Sallallaho alaihe wasallam) reprimand on the Sahabah's Laughing:

Once, the Prophet (Sallallaho alaihe wasallam) came to the musjid for Salaat, where he noticed some people laughing and giggling. He remarked:

> "If you remembered your death, I would not see you like this. Think of your death often. Not a single day passes when the grave does not call out: 'I am a wilderness', I am a place of dust, I am a place of worms'. When a Mo'min is laid in the grave, it says; 'Welcome to you. It is good of you to have come into me. Of all the people walking on the earth, I liked you best. Now that you have come into me, you will see how I entertain you'. It then expands as far as the occupant can see. A door from Paradise is opened for him in the grave and, through this door, he gets the fresh and fragrant air of Paradise. But when an evil man is laid in the grave it says; 'No word of welcome for you. Your coming into me is very bad for you. Of all the persons walking on the earth, I disliked you most. Now that you have been made over to me, you will see how I treat you!' It then closes upon him so much that his ribs of one side penetrate into the ribs of the other. As many as seventy serpents are then set upon him, to keep biting him till the Day of Resurrection. These serpents are so venomous that if one of them happened to spurt its venom upon the earth, not a single blade of grass would ever grow."

After this, the Prophet (Sallallaho alaihe wasallam) said:

> "The grave is either a garden of Paradise or a pit of Hell."

Fear of Allah is the basic and essential qualification of a Muslim. The Prophet (Sallallaho alaihe wasallam) advised the believers to remember death, off and on, and to keep the fear of Allah ever present in their hearts.

11. Hadhrat Hanzlah's (Radhiyallaho anho) Fear of Nifaq:

Hadhrat Hanzalah (Radhiyallaho anho) says:

> "We were once with the Prophet (Sallallaho alaihe wasallam) when he delivered a sermon. Our hearts

became tender, our eyes were flowing with tears, and we realised where we stood. I left the Prophet and returned home. I sat with my wife and children and cracked jokes with my wife, and I felt that the effect of the Prophet's sermon had completely vanished from my heart. Suddenly, it occurred to me that I was not what I had been, and I said to myself; 'O, Hanzalah! You are a Munafiq'. I was striken with grief and I left my house repeating these words in sorrow; 'Hanzlah has turned Munafiq'. I saw Abu Bakr (Radhiyallaho anho) coming towards me and I said to him; 'Hanzalah has turned Munafiq.' He said; 'Subhanallah' What are you saying? Hanzalah can never be a Munafiq'. I explained to him: 'When we are with the Prophet (Sallallaho alaihe wasallam) and listen to his discourses about Paradise and Hell, we feel as if both are present before our very eyes but when we return home and are absorbed in our domestic and family affairs, we forget all about the Hereafter. Abu Bakr (Radhiyallaho anho) said: 'My case is exactly the same.' We both went to the Prophet (Sallallaho alaihe wasallam) and I said; 'I have turned Munafiq, O Prophet of Allah!' He inquired about the matter, and I repeated what I had said to Abu Bakr (Radhiyallaho anho). Thereupon the Prophet (Sallallaho alaihe wasallam) remarked: 'By Him Who controls my life, if you could keep up for all times the fervour aroused in you when you are with me, angels would greet you in your walks and in your beds. But, O, Hanzlah! This is rare! This is rare!"

We have to attend to our personal and impersonal worldly affairs, and therefore we cannot be contemplating the Hereafter for all the twenty-four hours of the day. According to what has been said by the Prophet (Sallallaho alaihe wasallam), complete absorption in the Hereafter is rare, and it should not be expected by all. It is only for the angels to remain in the same state for ever. In case of men, the state of their mind changes with circumstances and environments. But we can see from this story how anxious the Sahabah were about the condition of their Imaan. Hanzlah (Radhiyallaho anho) suspects Nifaq in himself when he feels that the condition of his mind at home is not the same as it is when he is with the Prophet (Sallallaho alaihe wasallam).

12. A Few Miscellaneous Stories about the Fear of Allah:

It is very difficult to cover all that is said in the Qur'an and the Hadith about the importance of fear of Allah. It may, however, be understood that fear of Allah is an essential step towards all spiritual advancement. The Prophet (Sallallaho alaihe wasallam) said:

"Fear of Allah is the root of all wisdom"

Hadhrat Ibn 'Umar (Radhiyallaho anho) used to weep so much with the fear of Allah that he lost his eyesight. He said to somebody watching him:

"You wonder at my weeping. Even the sun weeps with the fear of Allah."

On another occasion, he is reported to have said:

"Even the moon weeps with His fear."

The Prophet (Sallallaho alaihe wasallam) once passed by one of the Sahabah who was reciting the Qur'an. When he came to the verse:

فَإِذَا انْشَقَّتِ السَّمَآءُ فَكَانَتْ وَرْدَةً كَالدِّهَانِ (الرحمٰن ، ٣٧)

"And when the heaven splitteth asunder and becometh rosy like red hide" (LV: 37)

the hair of his body stood on end, and he was nearly choked, with excessive weeping. He would cry and say:

"Alas; what will happen to me on the day when even the Heaven splitteth asunder. Woe is me!"

The Prophet (Sallallaho alai-he-wasallam) said to him:

"Your crying has made even the angels weep".

Once an Ansari sat and wept after Tahajjud, saying:

"I cry to Allah for protection from the fire of Hell".

The Prophet (Sallallaho alaihe wasallam) said to him:

"You have made the angels weep today".

Hadhrat Abdullah bin Rawahah (Radhiyallaho anho) was once weeping. His wife also began to weep on seeing him in this condition. He enquired of her:

"Why are you weeping?"

She replied: "Whatever makes you weep makes me weep too".

He said: "The idea that I have to cross the bridge of Siraat across Hell makes me weep. I don't know whether I shall be able to cross over or fall into Hell".

Zurarah bin Aufa was leading the Salaat in a musjid. When he recited the verse:

فَإِذَا نُقِرَ فِى النَّاقُوْرِ ، فَذٰلِكَ يَوْمَئِذٍ يَّوْمٌ عَسِيْرٌ (المدثر ٩ ، ٨)

"For when the Trumpet shall sound; Surely that day will be a day of anguish"! (LXXIV: 8 & 9)

he fell down and expired. People carried his body to his house.

Khulaid was saying his Salaat. During his Qiraat, when he reached the verse:

كُلُّ نَفْسٍ ذَآئِقَةُ الْمَوْتِ (العنكبوت ٥٧)

"Every soul will taste of death" (III: 185)

he began to repeat it again and again. He heard a voice from a corner of the room saying:

"How often are you going to repeat this verse? Your recitation has already caused the death of four Jinns".

It is reported about another Sheikh that (while reciting the Qur'an) when he reached the verse:

ثُمَّ رُدُّوْٓا اِلَى اللهِ مَوْلٰهُمُ الْحَقِّ ، اَلَا لَهُ الْحُكْمُ (الانعام ٦٢)

"Then are they returned unto Allah, their Lord, the Just, is not His the Command?" (VI:62)

he gave out a cry, shivered and breathed his last.

There are many stories of this type. Fudhail, a famous Sheikh, says:

"Fear of Allah leads to everything that is good".

Shibli, another Sheikh of high position, says:

"Whenever I have felt Allah's fear in me, I have found a fresh door of knowledge and wisdom opened for me".

In a Hadith, it is said:

"Allah says; 'I do not impose two fears on my slave. If he does not fear me in this world, I shall give him fear in the next, and if he fears me in this world I shall save him from all fears in the Hereafter".

The Prophet (Sallallaho alaihe wasallam) says:

"All things fear a person who fears Allah, while everything is a source of fear to him who fears somebody other than Allah."

Yahya bin Ma'az (Rahmatullah alaih) says:

"If a man fears Hell as much as he is afraid of poverty then he may enter into Paradise."

Abu Sulaiman Daarani (Rahmatullah alaih) says:

"There is nothing but ruin for a heart that is devoid of fear of Allah."

The Prophet (Sallallaho alaihe wasallam) says:

"The face that gets wet with the smallest drop of tear from the fear of Allah is safe from entrance into the fire of Hell."

He also said:

"When a Muslim shivers with the fear of Allah, his sins fall away from him like the falling leaves of a tree."

The dear Prophet (Sallallaho alaihe wasallam) has said:

"A person weeping with fear of Allah cannot go to Hell until milk goes back into the teats (which is an impossibility)".

Hadhrat Uqbah bin Amir (Radhiyallaho anho) once inquired of the Prophet (Sallallaho alaihe wasallam).

"What is the way to salvation?".

He replied: "Hold your tongue, stay indoors and cry over your sins."

Hadhrat A'ishah (Radhiyallaho anha) once inquired of the Prophet (Sallallaho alaihe wasallam).

"Is there anybody among your followers who will go to Paradise without reckoning?"

"Yes," replied the Prophet, "the person who often cries over his sins."

There is another Hadith, in which my dear Master, Muhammad (Sallallaho alaihe wasallam) has said:

> "No drop is more dear to Allah than two drops; a drop of tear shed in the fear of Allah, and a drop of blood shed in the path of Allah."

It is said in a Hadith that seven persons would be under the shade of the Arsh on the day of judgement. One of them would be the person who remembered Allah when all alone by himself, and tears flowed from his eyes with awe of Allah and in repentence for his sins.

Hadhrat Abu Bakr (Radhiyallaho anho) says:

> "One who can weep should do so, and one who cannot should make the appearance of a weeping person."

It is reported of Muhammad bin Munkadir (Radhiyallaho anho) that, when he wept, he smeared his tears over his face and beard saying:

> "I have heard that the fire of Hell does not touch the place touched by these tears."

Thabit Banani was suffering from a disease of the eyes. His doctor said to him:

> "Your eyes would be all right, provided you do not weep in future."

He replied: "What is the good of an eye if it cannot shed tears."

Yazid bin Maisarah (Rahmatullah alaih) says:

> 'There can be seven reasons for weeping viz., extreme joy, insanity, extreme pain, horror, artifice, intoxication and fear of Allah. A single tear shed in the fear of Allah is sufficient to quench oceans of fire (of Hell)."

Hadhrat Ka'ab Ahbar (Radhiyallaho anho) says:

> "By Him who holds my life in His (hands), I love to weep for fear of Allah, with tears flowing down my cheeks, rather than spend a mountain of gold in charity"

There are numerous other sayings of the Saints and other pious people, indicating that weeping because of the fear of Allah, and over one's sins, is very effective and beneficial in attaining spiritual elevation. We should not, however, lose hope in Allah. His Mercy is all-embracing. Hadhrat 'Umar (Radhiyallaho anho) says:

"If it be announced on the Day of Judgement that all except one individual shall go to Hell, my expectation of the Mercy of Allah would make me hope that I may be that chosen one. Again, if it be announced on that day that all except one individual shall go to Paradise, then my sins would make me fear that I may be that condemned one."

It is therefore necessary that we should combine fear and hope together in our hearts. Especially when the time of death is approaching, we should have more hope than fear. The Prophet (Sallallaho alaihe wasallam) says:

"None of you should die, except with a strong hope in the Mercy of Allah."

When Imaam Ahmad bin Hanbal (Radhiyallaho anho) approached his end, he sent for his son and asked him to read to him the Ahaadith that induce hope in Allah and His Mercy.

CHAPTER III

ABSTINENCE AND SELF-DENIAL OF THE SAHABAH

There is such a wealth of Ahadith about this aspect of the Prophet's life that it is really difficult to chose a few examples. He said:

"Abstinence is an asset of a Mo'min."

1. The Prophet's (Sallallaho alaihe wasallam) Dislike for gold:

The Prophet (Sallallaho alaihe wasallam) said:

"My Lord offered to turn the mounts of Mecca into gold for me. But my supplication to Him was; 'O, Allah! I like to eat one day and feel hungry the next, so that I may cry before Thee and remember Thee when I am hungry; and be grateful to Thee and glorify Thee when my hunger is gone!"

Thus said our Prophet (Sallallaho alaihe wasallam). We profess to follow him and are proud of being in the fold of his Ummat. Isn't it incumbent upon us to follow him in practice also?

2. The Prophet's (Sallallaho alaihe wasallam) Life of Abstinence:

Once, the Prophet (Sallallaho alaihe wasallam) decided to stay away from his wives for one month, as he was displeased with them on some account. He lived for that one month in a separate room in the upper storey. A rumour that the Prophet (Sallallaho alaihe wasallam) had divorced his wives got afloat among the Sahabah. When 'Umar heard of this, he came running to the musjid and found the Sahabah sitting in groups, struck with grief over the Prophet's suffering. He went to his daughter Hafsah (Radhiyallaho anha), who was a wife of the Prophet, and found her weeping in her room. He said to her:

"Why are you weeping now? Have I not been warning you all these times to refrain from any act likely to cause the Prophet's displeasure?"

He returned to the musjid and found some of the Sahabah sitting near the pulpit and weeping. He sat there for some time, but could not sit for long due to his excessive grief. He went towards the room where the Prophet (Sallallaho alaihe wasallam) was staying. He found Rabah (Radhiyallaho anho), a slave, sitting on the steps. He asked him to go and inquire of the Prophet (Sallallaho alaihe wasallam) if he could allow 'Umar (Radhiyallaho anho) to see him. Rabah went inside and came back to inform him that the Prophet (Sallallaho alaihe wasallam) held his peace and said nothing. 'Umar (Radhiyallaho anho) returned to the musjid and sat near the pulpit. Again the anguish eating his heart would not allow him any rest, and he requested Rabah to convey his request to the Prophet a second time. The Prophet (Sallallaho alaihe wasallam) did not make any answer this time too. After tarrying near the pulpit for some time more, 'Umar (Radhiyallaho anho) craved permission to see the Prophet (Sallallaho alaihe wasallam) for the third time. This time, his request was acceded to. When he was ushered in, he saw the Prophet (Sallallaho alaihe wasallam) lying on a date leaf matting. The crossed pattern of the matting could easily be seen imprinted on his handsome body. He had a leather bag filled with the bark of the datepalm as his pillow.

Hadhrat 'Umar (Radhiyallaho anho) says:

"I greeted him with Assalamo alaikum and inquired: 'Have you divorced your wives, O, Prophet of Allah?" He answered in the negative. Much relieved, then I made bold to remark, a bit amusingly; 'O, Prophet of Allah! we the Qureysh have always been having the upper hand over our women, but in case of the Ansar of Madinah, it is the women who have the upper hand. Our women have also got influenced by the women over here'. I said a few more similar things which made him smile. I noticed that the contents of his room consisted of only three pieces of tanned skin and a handful of barley lying in a corner. I looked about, but I failed to find anything else. I began to weep. He said; 'Why are you weeping?' I replied: 'O, Prophet of Allah! why should I not weep? I can see the mat's pattern imprinted on your body, and I am also beholding all that you have got in this room. O, Prophet of Allah! Pray that Allah may grant ample provisions for us. The Persians and the Romans who have no true faith and who worship not Allah but their kings–Caesar and Chosroes–presently live in gardens with streams running in their midst, but the chosen Prophet and the accepted slave of Allah does live in such a dire poverty!' The Prophet (Sallallaho alaihe wasallam) was resting against his pillow, but when he heard me talk like this, he sat up and said; 'O, 'Umar! are you still in doubt about this matter? Ease and comfort in the Hereafter are much better than ease and comfort in this world. The unbelievers are enjoying their share of the good things in this very world, whereas we have all such things in store for us in the next. I implored him: 'O, Prophet of Allah! Ask forgiveness for me. I was really in the wrong"

Look at the household effects of the sovereign in this world and in the hereafter, and the beloved Prophet of Allah. See how he rebukes 'Umar when he asks him to pray for some relief and comfort.

Somebody inquired of A'ishah (Radhiyallaho anha) about the bedding of the Prophet (Sallallaho alaihe wasallam) in her house. She said:

"It consisted of a skin filled with the bark of date-palm."

The same question was put to Hafsah (Radhiyallaho anha); she said:

"It consisted of a piece of canvas, which I spread doublefolded under him. Once I laid it fourfold in an effort to make it more comfortable. The next morning he asked me: 'What did you spread under me last night?' I replied: 'The same canvas, but I had four-folded it instead of the customary double fold.' He said: 'Keep it as it was before. The additional softness stands in the way of getting up for Tahajjud.'"

Now let us look around and survey the furniture of our bedrooms. We, who live in so much comfort, never hesitate to complain of hard times, instead of being grateful and more obedient to Allah for his bounties.

3. Hadhrat Abu Hurairah (Radhiyallaho anho) in a State of Hunger

Once, Hadhrat Abu Hurairah (Radhiyallaho anho) after wiping his nose with piece of fine linen remarked to himself:

"Look at Abu Hurairah (Radhiyallaho anho)! He cleans his nose with fine linen, today. I remember the time when he used to lie down between the pulpit and the Prophet's house. People took him to be suffering from epilepsy and put their feet on his neck. But there was no other malady with him, other than spasms of hunger."

Hadhrat Abu Hurairah (Radhiyallaho anho) had to remain hungry for days together. At times, he was overpowered with hunger so much that he fell unconscious, and people mistook this as attacks of epilepsy. It seems that in those days they treated epilepsy by placing a foot on the neck of the patient. Hadhrat Abu Hurairah (Radhiyallaho anho) is one of those people who suffered from extremes of want and poverty in the early days of Islam. He however, saw better days in later years when Muslim conquests followed in succession. He was very pious, and loved very much to say the Nafl Salaat. He had with him a bag full of date-stones. He used these stones for his Zikr. When the bag was exhausted, his maid filled it again with date-stones. Somebody was always busy in Salaat in his house during the night; his wife and his servant taking turns with him in the prayers.

4. Hadhrat Abu Bakr's (Radhiyallaho anho) Daily Allowance from the Bait-ul Mal

Hadhrat Abu Bakr (Radhiyallaho anho) was a cloth merchant and lived by that trade. On the death of the Prophet (Sallallaho alaihe wasallam), people selected him as the Khalifah. Next day with some cloth slung on his arms, he was proceeding to the market as usual when 'Umar (Radhiyallaho anho) met him in the way.

'Umar: "Where are you going to, Abu Bakr?"

Abu Bakr: "To the market".

'Umar: "If you get busy with your trade, who will carry out the duties of the caliphate?"

Abu Bakr: "How am I to feed my family then?"

'Umar: "Let's go to Abu 'Ubaidah (In charge of Bait-ul-Mal), who will fix some daily allowance for you from the Bait-ul-Mal."

They both went to Abu 'Ubaidah (Radhiyallaho anho).

He fixed for Abu Bakr an allowance equal to that usually paid to an average Muhajir.

Once Abu Bakr's (Radhiyallaho anho) wife said to him:

"I would like to have a sweet dish."

Abu Bakr: "I have no money to arrange for the dish."

His wife: "If you permit, I shall try to save something daily from our allowance, which will some day make enough to enable us to prepare the sweet dish."

He agreed. A little money was saved in many days. When his wife brought him the money to make purchases for the sweet dish, he said:

"It seems that we have received so much over and above our needs."

He deposited the saving in the Bait-ul-Mal and for the future got his allowance cut down by the amount saved by his wife.

Hadhrat A'ishah (Radhiyallaho anha) narrates:

"When Abu Bakr (Radhiyallaho anho) was selected as Khalifah, he said to the people: 'You well know that I live by trade, and my income therefrom is sufficient to meet my expenses. Now I have to devote my full time to the affairs of the state and therefore my family allowance shall be paid from the 'Bait-ul-Mal.'"

Hadhrat A'ishah (Radhiyallaho anha) says:

"At the time of his death, Abu Bakr (Radhiyallaho anho) directed me to hand over to his successor all that was issued to him from the Bait-ul-Mal for his household needs.

It is said that Hadhrat Abu Bakr (Radhiyallaho anho) left no cash after him. Anas (Radhiyallaho anho) says:

"Abu Bakr (Radhiyallaho anho) left a milch she-camel, a bowl and a servant."

According to some other narrators, he left a bedding also. When all these were made over to 'Umar (Radhiyallaho anho), his successor, he remarked:

"May Allah be merciful to Abu Bakr! He has set a precedent for his successors which is very hard to follow."

5. Hadhrat 'Umar's (Radhiyallaho anho) Daily Allowance:

Hadhrat 'Umar (Radhiyallaho anho) also lived by trade. When he was made Khalifah after Hadhrat Abu Bakr (Radhiyallaho anho), he assembled the people and said to them:

> "I earned my living through trade. As you people have engaged me as Khalifah, I cannot attend to my business. Now, what about my living?"

Different amounts of daily allowance from the Bait-ul-Mal were suggested by different people. Hadhrat Ali (Radhiyallaho anho) did not speak. 'Umar inquired of him:

> "Oh Ali! what is your suggestion?"

He replied:

> "I suggest that you should take such amount as may be on average be sufficient for your family."

Hadhrat Umar (Radhiyallaho anho) accepted his suggestion and a moderate amount was fixed as his daily allowance.

Later on, some people including Hadhrat Ali, Hadhrat Usman, Hadhrat Zubair and Hadhrat Talhah (Radhiyallaho anhum) once proposed that Hadhrat Umar's (Radhiyallaho anho) allowance might be increased, as it was hardly sufficient for him, but nobody dared to suggest that to Hadhrat 'Umar (Radhiyallaho anho). People approached Ummul-momineen Hadhrat Hafsah (radhiyallaho anha), his daughter, and requested her to ascertain 'Umar's (Radhiyallaho anho) reaction to the suggestion without mentioning their names to him. When Hadhrat Hafsah (Radhiyallaho anha) talked about it to Hadhrat Umar (Radhiyallaho anho), he became angry and said:

> "Who are the persons making this suggestion?"

Hadhrat Hafsah (Radhiyallaho anha):

> "Let me first know your opinion."

Hadhrat 'Umar (Radhiyallaho anho):

> "If I knew them, I would smite them on their faces Hafsah! just tell me what was the Prophet's best dress in your house?"

Hadhrat Hafsah (Radhiyallaho anha):

> "It was a pair of reddish brown clothes, which the Prophet (Sallallaho alaihe wasallam) wore on Friday or while receiving some envoy."

Hadhrat 'Umar (Radhiyallaho anho):

"What was the best of food that the Prophet (Sallallaho alaihe wasallam) ever took at your house?"

Hadhrat Hafsah (Radhiyallaho anha):

"Simple barley bread was the only food we used to take. One day I anointed a piece of bread with the sediments from an empty butter tin, and he ate it with relish and offered it to others as well."

Hadhrat 'Umar (Radhiyallaho anho):

What was the best bedding that the Prophet ever used in your house?"

Hadhrat Hafsah (Radhiyallaho anha):

"It was a piece of thick cloth. In the summer it was spread in four layers, and in the winter in two, half he spread underneath and with the other half he covered himself."

Hadhrat 'Umar (Radhiyallaho anho):

"Hafsah! Go and tell these people that the Prophet (Sallallaho alaihe wasallam) has set a standard by his personal example. I must follow him. My example and that of my other two companions viz., the Prophet (Sallallaho alaihe wasallam) and Abu Bakr (Radhiyallaho anho) is like that of three men travelling on the same road. The first man started with a provision and reached the goal. The second followed the first and joined him. Now the third is on his way. If he follows their way, he will also join them, otherwise he can never reach them."

Such is the life of the person who was a dread for the monarchs of the world. What a simple life he lived! Once he was reciting the Khutbah when it was noticed that his lower cloth had as many as twelve patches, including one of leather. Once he came late for his Jumu'ah prayer and told the congregation:

"Excuse me, people! I got late because I was washing my clothes and had no other clothes to put on."

Once he was having his meal when 'Utbah bin Abi Farqad (Radhiyallaho anho) asked permission to see him.

He allowed him in and invited him to share the food with him. 'Utbah (Radhiyallaho anho) started eating, but the bread was so coarse that he could not swallow it. He said:

"Why don't you use fine flour for your bread, 'Umar?"

He said: "Can every Muslim afford fine flour for his bread?"

'Utbah replied, "No. Everybody cannot afford it."

He remarked, "Alas! You wish to fulfill all my pleasures while I am in this world."

There are thousands of such stories about the illustrious Sahabah. Everybody should not try to imitate them, for we lack the physical strength of those people; and that is why the Sufi Sheikhs of our time do not recommend such exercise, which tax the body too much, as the people are already low in physical strength. We should however keep the life of the Sahabah as an ideal before us, so that we may at least give up some of our luxuries and lead a simpler life (judged by modern standards). With the Sahabah's lives as an ideal, we can at least feel ashamed when vieing with one another in running after the luxuries of this world.

6. Bilal's (Radhiyallaho anho) story about the Prophet:

Someone inquired of Bilal (Radhiyallaho anho) how the Prophet (Sallallaho alaihe wasallam) met his expenses. He replied:

"He never kept back anything for future use. I arranged money for him. Whenever a needy person, whether hungry or naked, came to him, he would make him over to me and I would then arrange for his needs by borrowing money from somebody. This is what usually happened. Once a Mushrik came to me and said: 'Look here! I have a lot of money to spare. Don't borrow money from anybody else. Whenever you need it, come straight to me.' I exclaimed: 'This is indeed fine.' I began to borrow money from him to meet the needs of the Prophet (Sallallaho alaihe wasallam). One day, after I had taken my Wudhu and was about to call Azaan, the same Mushrik accompanied by some people came and shouted, 'O, Negro!' When I attended to him, he began to abuse me, using filthy language and said: 'How many days are left of this month? 'I said: 'It is about to finish. 'He said most insolently: 'Look here! there are only four days left of this month. If you fail to clear up your debts by the end of the month, I shall take you as my slave for my money and then you will be grazing sheep as you have been doing before.' After saying this he went away. I remained melancholy and full of grief throughout the day. After Isha when the Prophet (Sallallaho alaihe wasallam) was alone, I went and narrated the story to him, saying: 'O, Prophet of Allah! you have nothing with you, nor can I arrange any money from somewhere so quickly. I am afraid the Mushrik will disgrace me. I therefore intend to keep away for such time as you get sufficient money to clear the debts.' I went home, took my sword, shield, and shoes, and waited for the morning to make for some other place. Just before dawn, somebody came to me and said, 'Hurry up. The Prophet (Sallallaho alaihe wasallam) wants you.' I hurried to the musjid and found four loaded camels sitting near the Prophet. He said: 'Good news, Bilal. Allah has made arrangements for clearing your debts. Take these camels with their load. The Chief of Fidak has sent them as a gift to me.' I thanked Allah and took the camels and cleared up all the debts. In the meantime, the Prophet (Sallallaho alaihe wasallam) kept sitting in the musjid. When I returned, I said: 'Alhamdulillah.' All the debts are now clear, O, Prophet of Allah' He inquired: 'Is there anything left from the gift?" I said, "Yes, something is still left." He said, "Go and spend that as well. I shall not go home until the whole lot is spent.' The Prophet kept sitting in the musjid all day long. After Isha he inquired again if everything had been spent. I said: 'Something is still left unspent. A few of the poor have not turned up so far.' He slept in the musjid that night. Next day after Isha'a he again called me to him and said: 'Bilal! Is everything finished now?" I said: 'Yes, Allah has blessed you with peace. Everything is now spent and gone.' The Prophet (Sallallaho alaihe wasallam) began to hymn the Glory of Allah over this news, for he did not like death to overtake him while any of the riches were in his possession. He then went home and met his family."

It is common with pious people that they do not like to keep any wealth with them. How could the Prophet (Sallallaho alaihe wasallam), being the fountain-head of all piety, like to keep anything in his possession? It is said of Maulana Abdur Rahim (May Allah have mercy on him), a Saint of our time, that all that he received as gifts from the people was immediately spent by him and he did not keep anything for himself. A few days before his death, he gave over all his clothes to one of his attendants and said:

> "If I need to wear any clothes in my life, I shall borrow them from you."

And I also know about my late father, who whenever had any money left after Maghrib, would give it to someone of his creditors (he was several thousand rupees in debt) and would say 'I would not like to keep this source of trouble with me for the night.'

7. Another Story of Hadhrat Abu Hurairah's (Radhiyallaho anho) Hunger:

Hadhrat Abu Hurairah (Radhiyallaho anho) says:

"I wish you had seen some of us living on a starvation diet for several days, successively, so much so that we could not even stand erect. On account of spasms of hunger, I would lie on my belly and press my stomach against the ground or keep a stone tied to my abdomen. Once, I intentionally sat in wait for some notable people to pass that way. As Hadhrat Abu Bakr (Radhiyallaho anho) came along, I joined in conversation with him, intending to continue the talk till we reach his home, where I expected him to invite me to share his meals, as was his wont. But his answer was brief, and my plan did not work. The same thing happened with Hadhrat Umar, (Radhiyallaho anho) when he chanced that way. The Prophet (Sallallaho alaihe wasallam) himself was the next to come. A smile spread on his face when he saw me, for he at once divined why I was sitting there. 'Come with me, Abu Hurairah', he said, and I accompanied him to his house. He took me in, where a bowl of milk was brought before him. He asked, 'Who brought this milk?" and was told that somebody had sent it as a present. He bade me to go and invite all the Suffah friends. The Suffah people were treated as everyone's guests by all the Muslims. They were such persons who had neither hearth nor home of their own, nor any other means of livelihood.

Their number varied with time. But at this particular juncture, they mustered seventy in all. The Prophet (Sallallaho alaihe wasallam) would send them in groups of two or four each to the well-to-do Sahabah as guests. He himself would pass on to them all that came to him as 'Sadaqah', and would share the gifts too with them."

Hadhrat Abu Hurairah (Radhiyallaho anho) says:

"When the Prophet (Sallallaho alaihe wasallam) asked me to invite all these persons, I naturally had some misgivings, for the milk was so little that it could hardly suffice a single person. Also, I was aware that the Prophet (Sallallaho alaihe wasallam) would ask myself to serve the milk to the others first, and a server is always the last and, more often than not, gets the least of the lot. Anyway, out I went, and fetched them all. The Prophet (Sallallaho alaihe wasallam) said to me: Hadhrat 'Abu Hurairah (Radhiyallaho anho), do serve the milk to them.' I took the bowl to each person in turn, and he drank the contents to his heart's desire, and returned the same to me, till all of them were served. The Prophet (Sallallaho alaihe wasallam) then held the goblet in his own hand, smiled at me, and remarked; 'Only two of us are left now!' 'Quite so', I replied. 'Then take it,' he said. I needed no second bidding, and took enough. He exhorted me to have more, and I had my fill; till I declared that I had no room for any more. He then took hold of the bowl, and drained the still remaining milk."

8. The Prophet's (Sallallaho alaihe wasallam) opinion about two persons:

Some people were sitting with the Prophet (Sallallaho alaihe wasallam) when a person passed that way. The Prophet (Sallallaho alaihe wasallam) asked of the company:

"What do you think of this person?"

They replied:

"O, Prophet of Allah! He is the scion of a good family. By Allah, he is such that if he seeks in marriage the hand of a woman of the most illustrious family, he would not be rejected. If he recommends anybody, his recommendation would be readily accepted."

Thereupon the Prophet (Sallallaho alaihe wasallam) held his peace. A little later, another person happened to pass that way, and the Prophet (Sallallaho alaihe wasallam) put the same question to his companions about that person also. They replied:

> "O, Prophet of Allah! He is a very poor Muslim. If he is betrothed somewhere, chances are that he will not get married. If he happens to recommend anybody, his recommendation is not likely to be accepted. If he talks, few would listen to him."

Thereupon the Prophet (Sallallaho alaihe wasallam) remarked:

> "This latter person is better than a whole lot of such persons as the former."

Belonging to a good family carries absolutely no weight with Allah. A poor Muslim, who is of little esteem and who commands but little respect in this world, is far nearer to Allah than hundreds of the so-called noblemen who, though respected and attended upon by the wordly people, are far from the path of Allah. It is said in Hadith:

> "It will be the end of this world when there remains not a single soul to hymn the name of Allah. It is by the holy name of Allah that the system of this universe is running."

9. Privations go with love for the Prophet (Sallallaho alaihe wasallam)

A person came to the Prophet (Sallallaho alaihe wasallam) and said:

> "O Prophet of Allah! I love you so much."

The Prophet (Sallallaho alaihe wasallam):

> "Think well before you say this."

The person:

> "I have already given thought. I love you very much O, Prophet of Allah."

The Prophet (Sallallaho alaihe wasallam): "Think once again before you declare such a thing."

The person:

> "I still love you very much, O, Prophet of Allah."

The Prophet (Sallallaho alaihe wasallam):

> "Well, if you are sincere in what you say, then be prepared to face privation and want coming to you from all directions, for it pursues all those who love me, as swiftly as water running down-stream."

That is why we find the Sahabah living mostly a life of poverty. Similarly the eminent Muhaddithin, Sufi's and theologians lived hand to mouth throughout their life.

10. The Al-Ambar Expedition:

The Prophet (Sallallaho alaihe wasallam) despatched towards the sea-shore an expedition of three hundred men, under the command of Hadhrat Abu Ubaidah (Radhiyallaho anho) in 8 A.H. He gave them a bag full of dates for their rations. They had been hardly out for fifteen days when they ran short of rations. In order to provide the contingent with food, Hadhrat Qais (Radhiyallaho anho) began buying three camels daily from his own men, to feed the Mujahideen, with a promise to pay on return to Madinah. The Amir seeing that the slaughter of camels would deprive the party of their only means of transport, prohibited him to do so. He collected the dates that had been left with each person and stored them in a bag. He would issue one date to each man as his daily ration. When Hadhrat Jabir (Radhiyallaho anho) later on narrated this story to the people, one of his audience inquired:

> "How did you manage to live upon one date only for the whole day?"

He replied:

> "We longed even for that one date, when the whole stock was exhausted. We were on the verge of starvation. We moistened the dry tree-leaves with water and ate them."

When they reached this stage, Allah had mercy on them, for He always brings ease after every hardship, provided it is endured patiently. A big fish known as "Ambar" was thrown out of the sea for them. The fish was so big that they lived on it for eighteen days altogether. They also filled their satchels with the remaining portion, which lasted them right up to Madinah. When the episode was narrated to the Prophet (Sallallaho alaihe wasallam), he said:

> "The fish was a provision arranged for you by Allah."

Difficulties and hardships are not uncommon in this world to the people of Allah; these are bound to come. The Prophet (Sallallaho alaihe wasallam) says:

> "The worst trials in this world are reserved for the Prophets, then for those who are next to them, and then for those who are best of the rest."

The trial of a person is proportionate to his position near Allah, and He bestows solace and comfort by His Grace and Mercy after each trial. Look how much our ancestors in Islam have suffered in the path of Allah. They had to live on leaves of trees, starve and shed their blood in the service of the true faith, which we now fail to preserve.

CHAPTER IV

PIETY AND SCRUPULOUSNESS

The habits and traits of character of the Sahabah, as a whole, are worth following, as they were the people specially chosen and selected by Allah to be the companions of His beloved Prophet (Sallallaho alaihe wasallam). The Prophet (Sallallaho alaihe wasallam) says:

> "I have been sent in the best period of human history."

The time of the Prophet (Sallallaho alaihe wasallam) was itself a blessed period, and the people favoured with his company were really the cream of that age.

1. The Prophet (Sallallaho alaihe wasallam) accepts a woman's invitation:

The Prophet (Sallallaho alaihe wasallam) was once returning from a funeral, when a woman invited him to partake of some food at her house. He went in with some of his Sahabah. When the food was served, it was noticed that the Prophet (Sallallaho alaihe wasallam) was trying to chew a morsel, but it would simply not go down his throat. He said:

> "It seems that the animal has been slaughtered without the permission of its owner."

The woman said:

> "O, Prophet of Allah! I had asked a man to purchase a goat for me from the market, but he could not obtain one. My neighbour also had recently purchased a goat. So I sent the man thither with some money to buy the same from him: My neighbour was out and his wife made over the goat to my man."

The Prophet (Sallallaho alaihe wasallam) directed her to go and serve the meat to the captives.

It has been noted of pious and saintly Muslims that food obtained from doubtful sources would simply not go down their throats. So this is not such a surprising thing in the case of the Prophet (Sallallaho alaihe wasallam), who is the fountain-head of all piety.

2. The Prophet's (Sallallaho alaihe wasallam) Sleepless Night:

Once the Prophet (Sallallaho alaihe wasallam) spent a sleepless night. He would turn from side to side and could not sleep. His wife asked him:

"O, Prophet of Allah! Why can you not sleep?"

He responded:

"A date was lying about. I took it up and ate it, lest it should be wasted. Now I am troubled lest it might be from Sadaqah."

Most probably the date belonged to the Prophet himself, but because people sent him their 'Sadaqah' as well (for distribution), he could not sleep with the apprehension that it might be of Sadaqah. This is the last word in scruples from the master himself, that he could not sleep because of a suspicion in his mind. How would it go with those who claim themselves to be the slaves of that very master but indulge in usury, corruption, theft, plunder and every other type of 'haraam' business without the least scruple.

3. Hadhrat Abu Bakr (Radhiyallaho anho) and a soothsayer's food:

Hadhrat Abu Bakr (Radhiyallaho anho) had a slave who used to give him a portion of his daily income as the master's share. Once he brought him some food, and Hadhrat Abu Bakr (Radhiyallaho anho) took a morsel out of it. Then the slave remarked:

"You always enquire about the source of what I bring to you, but today you have not done so."

He replied:

"I was feeling so hungry that I failed to do that. Tell me now, how did you come by this food?"

The slave said:

"Before I embraced Islam, I practised sooth-saying. During those days I came across some people for whom I practised some of my charms. They promised to pay me for that later on. I happened to pass by those people today, while they were engaged in a marriage ceremony, and they gave me this food."

Hadhrat Abu Bakr (Radhiyallaho anho) exclaimed:

'Ah! you would have surely killed me?"

Then he tried to vomit the morsel he had swallowed, but could not do so, as his stomach had been quite empty. Somebody suggested to him to take water to his fill and then try to vomit. He sent for a goblet of water and kept on taking water and forcing it out, till the morsel was vomited out. Somebody remarked:

"May Allah have mercy on you! You put yourself to such trouble for one single morsel."

To this he made reply:

"I would have thrust it out even if I had to lose my life. I have heard the Prophet (Sallallaho alaihe wasallam) saying. 'The flesh nourished by haraam food, is destined for the fire of Hell.' I, therefore, made haste to vomit this morsel, lest any portion of my body should receive nourishment from it."

Many stories of this nature have been reported about Hadhrat Abu Bakr (Radhiyallaho anho). As he was very scrupulous and would not taste anything but that about which he was perfectly sure, even the slightest doubt about its being 'halal' would make him vomit what he had taken.

4. Hadhrat Umar (Radhiyallaho anho) vomits out milk of Sadaqah:

A person once brought some milk for Hadhrat Umar (Radhiyallaho anho). When he took it, he noted its queer taste, and asked the person as to how he had come in possession of the milk. He replied:

"The camels given in Sadaqah were grazing in the desert, and the attendants gave me this milk out of what they got from them."

Upon this, Hadhrat Umar (Radhiyallaho anho) put his hand in his throat and vomited all that he had taken.

These God-fearing people not only totally abstained from 'haraam' food, but were most anxious to avoid any doubtful morsel finding its way inside them. They could not dare taking anything that was 'haraam', which is so usual these days.

5. Hadhrat Abu Bakr (Radhiyallaho anho) gives his garden to Bait-ul-Maal:

Ibn-Seereen writes:

"When Hadhrat Abu Bakr (Radhiyallaho anho) was about to die, he said to his daughter, Hadhrat Aishah (Radhiyallaho anha), 'I did not like to take anything from the Bait-ul-Maal, but Hadhrat Umar (Radhiyallaho anho) insisted on it, to relieve me of my occupation, and to enable me to devote my full time to the duties of the 'Khilafat; and I was left no choice. Now make over that garden of mine to my successor, in lieu of what I have received from the Bait-ul-maal'.

When Hadhrat Abu Bakr (Radhiyallaho anho) died, Aishah (Radhiyallaho anha) asked Hadhrat Umar (Radhiyallaho anho) to take over that garden, as desired by her late father. Hadhrat Umar (Radhiyallaho anho) remarked:

"May Allah bless your father! He has left no chance for anybody to open his lips against him."

Hadhrat Abu Bakr (Radhiyallaho anho) received his subsistence allowance from the Bait-ul-maal in the interest of all the Muslims, and that too at the request of the most prominent Sahabah. Again the amount taken was almost the minimum possible, and hardly sufficient for him, as we have already seen in the story (in the last chapter) about his wife's inability to cook one sweet dish during the whole month. In spite of all this he was so scrupulous that he made over his garden to the Bait-ul-maal in lieu of what he had received from the public funds.

6. The story of Ali bin Ma'bad: (Rahmatullah alaih)

Ali bin Ma'bad (Rahmatullah alaih) is a Mohaddith. He says:

"I was living in a rented house. Once I wrote something which I wanted to dry up quickly. The house walls were of mud and I intended to scrape a little mud from there to dry up the ink. But I thought: 'This house is not mine, and I cannot scrape the walls without the owner's permission.' After a moment I reflected: 'After all what difference does it make? It is only a very little mud that I am using.' So, I scraped a little mud from a wall and used it. That night, while asleep, I saw a person in my dream, admonishing me: 'Perchance tomorrow, on the Day of Judgement, you may rue that saying of yours: (It is, only a very little mud that I am using)'"

The dictates of piety are different with different persons. The high rank of the Mohaddith demanded that he should have been scrupulous even about a small quantity of mud, though for a common man it was insignificant and therefore within permissible limits.

7. Hadhrat Ali (Radhiyallaho anho) passes by a grave:

Hadhrat Kumail (Radhiyallaho anho) says:

"I was with Ali (Radhiyallaho anho) once on a journey, when he reached an uninhabited place; he approached a grave and said: 'O you dwellers of the graves! O you who live amongst ruins! O you who live in the wilderness and solitude! How fare you in the other world? How has it gone with you there?' He continued: 'The news from our side is that all you did leave of the wealth and riches here, has long been distributed; your children are orphans; your widows have long since remarried. Now let us hear about you.' He then turned to me: 'O Kumail! If they could speak, they would have informed us that the best provision for the Hereafter is Taqwa.' Tears welled out of his eyes, as he added: 'O Kumail! The grave is a container of the deeds; but one realizes it only after death."

Our good or bad actions are stored up in our graves. It is said in a Hadith that every person meets his good deeds in the grave in the person of an agreeable companion who befriends and consoles him there. But his wicked deeds assume hideous shapes emitting bad smells, which add to his misery. In another Hadith it is said:

"Three things accompany a person to his grave viz: His wealth (as was the prevalent custom among the Arabs of the time), his relatives, and his deeds. His wealth and his relatives turn back after his burial, but his actions go in and stay with him in the grave."

Once the Prophet (Sallallaho alaihe wasallam) asked the Sahabah:

"Do you know in what relation your relatives, your wealth, and your deeds stand to you?"

The Sahabah expressed their desire to know about it. He replied:

"It can be likened to a person having three brothers. When he is about to die, he calls one of his brothers to him, and asks him: 'Brother! You know what plight is mine? What help can you render me at this juncture?' That brother replies: 'I shall call the doctor to you, nurse you and attend upon you. And when you are dead, I shall bathe you, enshroud you, and carry you to the grave. Then I shall pray for you after you are buried. This brother is his kith and kin. He puts the same question to the second brother, who delivers himself like this: 'I shall remain with you as long as you are alive. No sooner you are dead than I shall betake myself to someone else.' This brother is his wordly wealth. He then questions the last brother in the same strain, who makes response: 'I shall not forsake you even in your grave; and I shall accompany you into that place of utter solitude. When your deeds are weighed in the balance. I shall forthwith lend my weight to the scale of your good deeds and weigh it down.' This brother is the personification of his good deeds. Now, tell me, which of the brothers you regard to be the most useful to the person?' The Sahabah replied: 'O, Prophet of Allah! The last brother is really the most useful to him. There is no doubt about it. The other two brothers were of no avail."

8. The Prophet's (Sallallaho alaihe wasallam) verdict about haraam food:

The Prophet (Sallallaho alaihe wasallam) once said:

"As Allah Himself is above all blemishes, likewise, He blesses with His grace only the unblemished things. He enjoins upon the Muslims, what He has laid down for His Prophets. He says in His Holy Book:

يَآيُّهَا الرُّسُلُ كُلُوْا مِنَ الطَّيِّبٰتِ وَاعْمَلُوْا صَالِحًا ، اِنِّى بِمَا تَعْمَلُوْنَ عَلِيْمٌ (المومنون ٥١)

"O, Prophets! Eat of the good things and do right. Lo! I am aware of what ye do." (XXIII: 51).

يَآيُّهَا الَّذِيْنَ اٰمَنُوْا كُلُوْا مِنْ طَيِّبٰتِ مَارَزَقْنٰكُمْ (البقره ١٧٢)

"O Ye who believe Eat of the good things where-with we have provided you." (II: 172)

Then the Prophet (Sallallaho alaihe wasallam) did mention of a person who is a way-farer with dishevelled hair and dusty clothes; raising his hands towards the heaven, he calls out: "O, Allah! O, Allah!" but his food, drink and dress all were from haraam sources. So, Allah would never listen to him and answer his prayers, even though his outward condition showed him deserving.

People wonder why the prayers of the Muslims are not always fulfilled by Allah; the reason is easy enough to understand in the light of the above Hadith. Though Allah does sometimes grant the prayers of even a Kafir (not to mention the prayer or requests of a sinful Muslim), but it is particularly the prayer of a pious person that is seldom rejected. That is the reason why people generally seek the prayers of such persons for themselves. It follows that those who wish to have their prayers often granted must abstain from haraam. No wise person would like to run the risk of his prayers being rejected.

9. Hadhrat Umar (Radhiyallaho anho) does not like his wife to weigh musk:

Hadhrat Umar (Radhiyallaho anha) once received some musk from Bahrain. He said:

"I want someone to weigh it, so that it may be equally distributed among the Muslims.'

His wife said: "I shall weigh it."

Hadhrat Umar (Radhiyallaho anho) kept quiet. A little later he again asked for someone to weigh the musk, and again his wife volunteered to do so. But he kept quiet this time too. When she repeated her offer for the third time, he said:

"I do not like your touching the musk with your hands (while weighing it) and rubbing those hands on your body afterwards, as that would amount to something over and above my legitimate share."

Any other person weighing the musk would, for that matter, have had the same advantage, but Hadhrat Umar (Radhiyallaho anha) did not like this preference particularly for any member of his own family. Look at this scrupulous anxiety to avoid charge of selfishness.

A similar story is related about Hadhrat Umar bin Abdul Aziz (Rahmatullah alaih) (who is known as the second Umar). While he was holding the reins of the Khilafat, musk belonging to the Bait ul-Maal was being weighed. He closed his own nostrils, with the remark:

"The use of musk is to smell it."

These were the scruples of the Sahabah, and their successors, and our elders in Islam.

10. Hadhrat Umar-bin-Abdul Aziz (Rahmatullah alaih) dismisses a governor:

Hadhrat Umar-bin-Abdul Aziz (Rahmatullah alaih) appointed a person as governor of a province. Somebody remarked that this person had held the same post under Hajjaj-bin-Yusuf (the notorious blood shedder) also. Hadhrat Umar bin Abdul Aziz (Rahmatullah alaih) immediately issued orders of his dismissal. The man protested:

"I had been with Hajjaj only for a very short time."

To this, the Khalifa replied:

"His company for a day or even less is sufficient to render a man unfit for public service."

"A man is known by the company he keeps." The company of pious people leaves an imperceptible impression of piety on the character, and likewise evil company has its evil influence. That is why association with bad people is always discouraged. Even the company of animals is not without its own effect. The Prophet (Sallallaho alaihe wasallam) said:

"Pride and arrogance are prone to be found in those who own camels and horses, while meekness and humility characterise those who tend sheep and goats."

The Prophet (Sallallaho alaihe wasallam) is reported to have said:

"A person who associates with a pious man is like one who sits with a musk-seller. Even if he does not receive any musk from the latter still the pleasant smell would be a source of pleasure to him. But bad company may be likened to a furnace; a man sitting near one cannot escape the smoke and the fumes, even if a spark does not fall on him."

CHAPTER V

DEVOTION TO SALAAT

Salaat is the most important of all forms of worship. It is, in fact, the first and foremost item to be reckoned with on the Day of Judgement. The Prophet (Sallallaho alaihe wasallam) is reported to have said:

> "Salaat is the only line of demarcation between Kufr and Islam."

There are many Ahadith about Salaat, which I have collected in a separate book.

1. Blessings of Nafl (non-obligatory) Prayers:

The Prophet (Sallallaho alaihe wasallam) reported that Allah told him:

> "My wrath descends upon a person who bears ill-will towards My friends. And only those are blessed with My love who implicitly carry out Fardh (obligatory) injunctions. A person keeps on advancing in my esteem through 'Nafl'; till I choose him as 'My beloved'. I then become his ear by which he listens, his eye by which he looks, his hands by which he holds, and his feet by which he walks (i.e his listening, looking, holding and walking are all in perfect accord with My injunctions, and he would never even dream of employing any part of his body in any action contrary to My commands). If such a person prays for anything, I grant it to him and if he seeks My protection I do protect him."

Those people are really blessed who, after performing their Fardh, are in the habit of observing Nafl profusely. May Allah give me and all my friends the strength to earn this blessing.

2. The Propet (Sallallaho alaihe wasallam) spends the whole night in Salaat:

A certain person asked A'ishah (Radhiyallaho anha):

"Tell me something noteworthy concerning the Prophet (Sallallaho alaihe wasallam)."

She answered:

> "There was nothing which was not unusual about him. Everything he did was noteworthy. One night he came and lay down with me. After sometime, he got up saying, 'Now let me pray to my Lord, the Sustainer."

With this, he stood up in Salaat, humbling himself before his Creator with such sincerity that tears rolled down his cheeks to his beard and on to his breast. He then bowed for Ruku' and Sajdah, and his tears flowed down as fast as before and after raising his head from his Sajdah, he continued weeping in this manner till Hadhrat Bilal (Radhiyallaho anha) announced the approach of Fajr. I pleaded with him:

> "O, Prophet of Allah! you are sinless, as Allah has in His munificence forgiven your each and every sin (even if committed) in the past and which may happen in the life to come (XLVIII: 2) and still you grieve so much". He replied: Why, then, should I not be a grateful slave of Allah? Then he added, 'Why should I not be praying like this when Allah has today revealed to me these verses?'

اِنَّ فِىْ خَلْقِ السَّمٰوٰتِ وَالْاَرْضِ وَاخْتِلَافِ الَّيْلِ وَالنَّهَارِ لَاٰيٰتٍ لِّاُولِى الْاَلْبَابِ ،
اَلَّذِيْنَ يَذْكُرُوْنَ اللّٰهَ قِيَامًا وَّقُعُوْدًا وَّعَلٰى جُنُوْبِهِمْ (آل عمران ١٩٠-١٩١)

> 'Lo! in the creation of the Heavens and the Earth, and in the difference of night and day, are tokens (of His Sovereignty) for men of understanding, such as remember Allah, standing, sitting and reclining . . .
> (III: 190–191)'"

It has been reported in many Ahadith that the Prophet's feet would get swollen because of his very long rakaats in Salaat; people tried to reason with him:

> "O, Prophet of Allah! You are sinless and still you labour so hard!"

He would reply: "Should I not be a grateful slave of my Allah, then?"

3. The Prophet's (Sallallaho alaihe wasallam) recitation of the Qur'an in Salaat:

Hadhrat 'Auf (Radhiyallaho anho) narrates:

"I was once with the Prophet (Sallallaho alaihe wasallam). He brushed his teeth with a Miswak, performed his Wudhu and stood up for Salaat. I also availed of the opportunity to join him. He recited surah 'Baqarah' in his first rakaat; he would pray for mercy when he recited any verse extolling the Grace of Allah, and would supplicate for Divine forgiveness when reciting any verse referring to His wrath. He took as much time in Ruku' and Sajdah each as he had taken in Qiyaam. In Ruku' he recited:

سُبْحَانَ ذِیْ الْجَبَرُوْتِ وَالْمَلَكُوْتِ وَالْعَظْمَةِ

'Glory to Allah the Lord of Majesty, sovereignty and magnificence.'

He recited the next three successive Soorahs in the remaining three rakaats, and each rakaat was of about the same length as the first one."

Hadhrat Huzaifah (Radhiyallaho anho) has also narrated a similar story about his Salaat with the Prophet (Sallallaho alaihe wasallam.)

The Qiraat (recitation) of the Qur'an by the Prophet (Sallallaho alaihe wasallam) in the above mentioned four rakaats amounts to more than one-fifth of he whole Qur'an. And the Prophet (Sallallaho alaihe wasallam) recited the Qur'an with proper intonation (Tajweed), and would also pray and seek forgiveness after relevant verses. Again his Ruku' and Sajdah also would last as long as his Qiyaam. We can thus have a fair idea of how much time he must have taken to say his Salaat. This can only be possible when Salaat is a source of great inner satisfaction and spiritual ecstasy. That is why the Prophet (Sallallaho alaihe wasallam) has often been quoted as saying:

"The comfort of my eyes lies in Salaat."

4. Salaat of a Few Eminent Sahabah:

Hadhrat Mujahid (Radhiyallaho anho), describing the Salaat of Hadhrat Abu Bakr (Radhiyallaho anho), and that of Hadhrat Abdullah bin Zubair (Radhiyallaho anho) says:

"They stood in Salaat motionless like pieces of wood stuck in the ground."

'Ulama agree that Hadhrat Abdullah bin Zubair (Radhiyallaho anho) learnt to say his Salaat from Hadhrat Abu Bakr

(Radhiyallaho anho), who in turn learnt it direct from the Prophet (Sallallaho alaihe wasallam).

It is said about Hadhrat Abdullah bin Zubair (Radhiyallaho anho) that he remained in Sajdah for so long, and kept so motionless therein, that birds would come and perch on his back. He would sometimes remain in Sajdah or Ruku' all night long. During an attack against him, a missile came and hit the wall of the musjid wherein he was saying his Salaat. A piece of masonry flew from the wall and passed in between his beard and throat. He neither cut short his Salaat, nor was he the least perturbed. Once he was saying his Salaat while his son Hashim was sleeping near him. A snake fell from the ceiling and coiled round the child. The child woke up and shrieked, and the whole household gathered round him. They killed the snake after a great hue and cry. Ibne Zubair (Radhiyallaho anho), calm and quiet, remained engaged in his Salaat all the while. When he had finished it, he said to his wife: "I heard some noise during my Salaat; what was that?"

His wife exclaimed:

> "May Allah have mercy on you! The child's life was in danger, and you took least notice of it."

His answer was:

> "Had I turned my attention to anything else, what would have remained of the Salaat?"

Hadhrat 'Umar (Radhiyallaho anho) was stabbed at the close of his career, and this same wound caused his death. He bled profusely and remained unconscious for long intervals. But when he was informed of the time of Salaat, he would perform it in that very condition, and say:

> "There is no portion in Islam for the person who discards Salaat."

Hadhrat Uthman (Radhiyallaho anho) would remain in Salaat all night long, finishing the whole of the Qur'an in one rakaat.

It is reported about Hadhrat Ali (Radhiyallaho anho) that he would turn pale and tremble at the time of Salaat. Somebody asked him the reason, and he said:

> "It is the time to discharge that trust which Allah offered to the Heavens and the Earth and the hills, but they shrank from bearing it, and I have assumed it."

Somebody asked Khalaf-bin-Ayub:

"Do not the flies annoy you in your Salaat?"

His answer was:

"Even the sinful persons patiently bear the lashes of the government, to boast of their endurance afterwards. Why should I be made to skip about by mere flies when standing in the presence of my Lord?"

Muslim bin Yasaar when he stood up for Salaat, said to members of his family:

"You may keep on talking, I shall not be knowing what you talk."

Once he was saying his Salaat in the Jaami' musjid of Basrah. A portion of the musjid wall fell down with a crash; and every body ran pell mell for safety, but he never even heard the noise.

Somebody asked Haatim Asam as to how did he say his Salaat.

He replied:

"When the time for Salaat comes, I perform my Wudhu and go to the place where I have to say my Salaat. I sit down for some time, till all the parts of my body are relaxed. Then I stand up for Salaat, visualising the Ka'bah in front of me, imagining my feet upon the Bridge of Siraat, with Paradise to my right, and Hell to my left, and Izraa-eel close behind me, and thinking that it may be my last Salaat. Then I say my Salaat with full sincerity and devotion. And I finish my Salaat between fear and hope about its acceptance.

5. Salaat of a Muhajir and an Ansari keeping watch:

While returning from a campaign, the Prophet (Sallallaho alaihe wasallam) happened to halt for the night at some place. He inquired:

"Who would keep watch over the camp this night?"

Hadhrat Ammar bin Yasir (Radhiyallaho anho) of the Muhajirin and Hadhrat Abbaad bin Bishr (Radhiyallaho anho) of the Ansar offered their services. Both of them were posted to watch from a hill-top against any possible night attack by the enemy.

Abbaad (Radhiyallaho anho) said to Ammar (Radhiyallaho anho):

> "Let us keep watch and sleep turn by turn. In the first half of the night I shall keep awake, while you go to sleep. In the next half, you may keep watch while I go to sleep."

Hadhrat Ammar (Radhiyallaho anho) agreed and went to sleep, and Hadhrat Abbaad (Radhiyallaho anho) started his Salaat. But an enemy scout made him out in the dark from a distance, and let fly an arrow at him. Seeing that he made no movement, he shot another and still another arrow at him. Hadhrat Abbaad (Radhiyallaho anho) drew out and threw away each arrow as it struck him, and at last awakened his companion. The enemy fled when he saw them both together, fearing that there might be many more of them. Hadhrat Ammar (Radhiyallaho anho) noticed Abbaad (Radhiyallaho anho) bleeding from three places. He said:

> "Subhanallah! why did you not awake me earlier?"

Abbaad replied:

> "I had started reciting Surah 'Kahf' in my Salaat. I did not like to cut it short, but when I was struck by the third arrow, I was greatly concerned that my death might jeopardise the safety of the Prophet (Sallallaho alaihe wasallam). I therefore finished the Salaat and awakened you. But for this fear, I would not have gone to Ruku' before finishing the Surah even if I had been killed."

Look at the devotion of the Sahaba to Salaat. One arrow after another is piercing Hadhrat Abbaad's (Radhiyallaho anho) body and he is bleeding profusely, but is not prepared to sacrifice the pleasure of reciting the Qur'an in his Salaat. On the other hand, the bite of a wasp, nay of a mosquito, is sufficient to distract us from our Salaat.

According to the Hanafiyyah school of jurisprudence, Wudhu breaks with bleeding, while according to the Shafi'iyyah it does not. It is just possible that Abbaad might be having the latter view, or that this point might not have been brought to an issue till then.

6. Hadhrat Abu Talha (Radhiyallaho anho) and his Salaat:

Hadhrat Abu Talha (Radhiyallaho anho) was once saying his Salaat in his garden. His attention was drawn towards a bird that flitted about, but could not find a way out of the dense foliage. For a short moment, he followed the bird with his eyes, and forgot the number of his rakaat. Upon this mishap, his sorrow knew no bounds. He repaired to the Prophet's (Sallallaho alaihe wasallam) presence straightway and submitted thus:

> "O Prophet of Allah, this garden of mine has been the cause of a diversion in my Salaat. I give it away in the cause of Allah. Kindly spend it as may appear proper to you."

A similar chance befell one of the Ansaar in the time of Hadhrat Usman (Radhiyallaho anho). He was saying his Salaat in his garden. The branches of the trees were weighed down with ripe juicy dates, luxurious abundance, which caught his eyes, and he felt pleased with it. This made him forget the number of his rakaat. He was so much stricken with grief that he decided to part with the garden that had distracted him from his Salaat. He approached Usman (Radhiyallaho anho) and made over the garden to him for utilising it in the path of Allah. Usman (Radhiyallaho anho) had the garden sold for fifty thousand dirhams and spent the money as desired. This shows the value the Sahaba set on their faith; and Hadhrat Abu Talha (Radhiyallaho anho) could give away his orchard worth fifty thousand dirhams because it had interfered with his Salaat. According to Shah Waliullah, the Sufis give preference to obedience to Allah over anything that distracts from it.

7. Hadhrat Ibn Abbas (Radhiyallaho anho) and his Salaat:

Hadhrat Abdullah bin Abbas (Radhiyallaho anho) suffered from cataract of the eye. A doctor told him:

> "A treatment is possible, provided you are willing to take precautions. For five days, it will be essential for you to avoid prostrating yourself on the ground. You can, however, use a wooden desk for performing Sajdah."

He said: "This cannot be so. I would not say a single rakaat like that. I have heard the Prophet (Sallallaho alaihe wasallam) saying, "A person who intentionally foregoes a single Salaat shall have to face Divine wrath on the Day of Judgement."

Although it is quite permissible to perform Salaat in the way advised by the doctors, and it involves no direct transgression of the Law of Allah, yet due to his utter devotion to Salaat and implicit regard for the Prophet's warning, he was ready to lose his eyesight rather than allow the slightest modification in the Salaat as performed by the Prophet (Sallallaho alaihe wasallam) himself. In fact, the Sahabah would sacrifice the whole world for their Salaat. We may dub it as 'fanaticism', or make any other remark about that devoted band, but the verdict in the Hereafter would prove, beyond doubt, that they were the personages who really feared and loved their Creator above everything else in this world.

8. Sahabah's suspending trade at the time of Salaat:

Hadhrat Abdullah bin 'Umar (Radhiyallaho anho) once visited the market. He noticed that at the time of Salaat, everybody closed his shop and flocked to the musjid. He remarked:

"These are people about whom Allah has remarked:

رِجَالٌ ، لَّاتُلْهِيْهِمْ تِجَارَةٌ وَّلَابَيْعٌ عَنْ ذِكْرِ اللهِ وَاِقَامِ الصَّلٰوةِ وَاِيْتَآءِ الزَّكٰوةِ ، يَخَافُوْنَ يَوْمًا تَتَقَلَّبُ فِيْهِ الْقُلُوْبُ وَالْاَبْصَارُ (النور ٣٧)

"Men whom neither merchandise nor sale beguileth from remembrance of Allah and constancy in Salaat and paying to the poor their due; who fear a day when hearts and eyeballs will be overturned. (XXIV: 37)"

Hadhrat Ibn Abbas (Radhiyallaho anho) says:

"These people were completely absorbed in their trade, but when they heard Azaan they left everything and hastened towards the musjid."

He once remarked: "By Allah, they were such traders whose trade did not hinder them from the remembrance of Allah."

Hadhrat Abdullah bin Masood (Radhiyallaho anho) once chanced to be in the market when Azaan was called out. He noticed everybody leaving his shop as it was, and proceeding to the musjid. He remarked:

"These are surely the persons of whom Allah says:

رِجَالٌ ، لَّاتُلْهِيْهِمْ تِجَارَةٌ وَّلَابَيْعٌ عَنْ ذِكْرِ اللهِ وَاِقَامِ الصَّلٰوةِ وَ اِيْتَآءِ الزَّكٰوةِ (النور ٣٧)

'Men whom neither merchandise nor sale beguileth from remembrance of Allah and constancy in Salaat and paying to the poor their due. (XXIV:37).'

Another Hadith has it:

"All the people shall be gathered on the Day of Judgement, when it will be asked, 'Who are those who glorified Allah in ease and adversity?" A group will arise and enter Paradise without any reckoning. Again it will be asked, 'who are those who kept away from their beds and passed their nights in worshipping their Creator.' Another group will arise and enter Paradise without any reckoning. The angel will ask yet again, 'where are those whom trade did not hinder from remembering Allah.' And yet another group will arise and enter Paradise without any reckoning. After these three groups have departed, and reckoning would commence for the people in general."

9. Martyrdom of Hadhrat Khubaib, Hadhrat Zaid and Hadhrat 'Asim (Radhiyallaho anhum):

The Qureysh writhed with fury and rage at the loss of some of their greatest men in Uhud. Sulaifah, whose two sons had fallen in action, had taken a solemn vow that she would drink wine in the skull of 'Asim (Radhiyallaho anho), who had killed both of them, if she could get possession of his head. She had proclaimed a prize of one hundred camels (a stupendous sum for the place and the time) for the person who brought 'Asim's head to her. Sufyan bin Khalid worked out a plan to secure the prize. He sent a few men of Adhal Waqarah to Madinah, who pretended to embrace Islam: they besought the Prophet (Sallallaho alaihe wasallam) to detail some persons to accompany them to their locality to preach Islam to the populace. They made a special request for 'Asim (Radhiyallaho anho) saying:

> "Our people will very much appreciate his mode of address."

The Prophet (Sallallaho alaihe wasallam) deputed ten (or six according to another report) of his companions to go with them, and 'Asim (Radhiyallaho anho) was of course included in these. They started satisfactorily from Madinah, but treachery awaited them on the way; they were attacked by not less than two hundred of the enemy, including one hundred crack selected archers. The Sahabah climbed up a hill called Fadfad. The enemy called out to them:

> "We do not want to kill you; we shall only take you to Mecca and sell you to the Qureysh."

The Sahabah (Radhiyallaho anhum) rejected this parley and chose to fight to the finish. When they ran short of arrows, they attacked the enemy with their spears. Hadhrat Asim (Radhiyallaho anho) called out to his companions:

> "No doubt you have been betrayed by these treacherous people, but you should not lose heart; because martyrdom is itself the acme of your aspirations. Allah, the most beloved, is with you, and your celestial spouses are this minute waiting for you."

With these words, he rushed into the very thick of the enemy, and when his spear broke he fought on with his sword. Thus he fell fighting to the last. His last prayer was:

> "O, Allah! inform the Prophet (Sallallaho alaihe wasallam) about our fate."

Allah, in His compassion, answered his prayer by revealing the news to the Prophet (Sallallaho alaihe wasallam). As 'Asim (Radhiyallaho anho) had come to know about Sulafah's vow to drink wine in his skull, he also prayed:

> "O, Allah! I have laid down my life in Thy cause; O, Allah, do save my head from the sacriligeous hands of these unbelievers."

This prayer was also granted. After his death, a swarm of bees (or wasps according to another report) settled upon his body, and foiled all attempts of the enemy to sever his head. They left the body alone, intending to do their dirty job during the night, when the bees would have gone. But during the night, there was a cloud-burst, which washed the body away.

To return to the fight, when seven out of the ten Sahabah (Radhiyallaho anhum) had attained martyrdom and the remaining three, Khubaib, Zaid bin Wathnah and Abdullah bin Tariq (Radhiyallaho anhum) were still sticking to their position on the hill-top, the enemy again called out to them:

> "You three should come down the hill; of course we would do no harm to you."

The three trusted them and came down the hill, but the enemy immediately pounced upon them, and pinioned them with the gutstrings of their bows. Upon this, Abdullah bin Tariq (Radhiyallaho anho) protested:

> "So this is the very first breach of your solemn promise. I would rather join my martyred brothers than go alive with you."

He then refused to follow them in captivity. They tried their best to make him walk, but could not, and ultimately perceiving that he would on no account budge an inch from the spot, despatched him there and then. The two remaining captives were taken by them to Mecca and sold to the Qureysh. Safwan bin Umayyah paid fifty camels for Zaid bin Wathna (Radhiyallaho anho) to kill him in revenge for the death of his father Umayyah in 'Uhud', and Hujair bin Abi Ahaab bought Khubaib (Radhiyallaho anho) for one hundred camels to avenge the fall of his father in the same battle.

Safwan made over Hadhrat Zaid (Radhiyallaho anho) to his slave to be killed outside the limits of the Haram. A crowd followed them to watch Hadhrat Zaid (Radhiyallaho anho) meet his end, and Abu Sufyan (Radhiyallaho anho) also happened to be one of the spectators. When Zaid (Radhiyallaho anho) stood prepared to meet his doom, Abu Sufyan asked him thus:

> "Don't you wish Muhammad (Sallallaho alaihe wasallam) to be in your place today, and you be let off to enjoy life with your family?"

Zaid's (Radhiyallaho anho) reply amazed them all:

> "By Allah!" he said, "the very thought of enjoying life with my family is unbearable to me, if the Prophet (Sallallaho alaihe wasallam) were even to suffer a thorn-prick in his foot for that."

The Qureysh simply could not understand this reply, and Abu Sufyan (Radhiyallaho anho) remarked:

"There is absolutely no parallel, anywhere in the world, to the love that the companions of Muhammad (Sallallaho alaihe wasallam) bear him."

Hadhrat Zaid (Radhiyallaho anho) was then martyred.

Hadhrat Khubaib (Radhiyallaho anho) remained in the captivity of Hujair for a long time. A woman slave of Hujair (who later embraced Islam) says:

"When Hadhrat Khubaib (Radhiyallaho anho) was in captivity with us, I noticed one day that he was eating grapes from a bunch as big as a human head, though it was not the season of grapes in Mecca at that time. When the day for his execution drew near, he asked for a razor, which was handed over to him. Meanwhile a child of the house, in his play, went close to Hadhrat Khubaib (Radhiyallaho anho). All the inmates of the house got alarmed at the sight. Hadhrat Khubaib (Radhiyallaho anho) having been marked for death, they thought there was nothing to prevent him from killing the child with the razor. But to remove their fears on observing their alarm, Hadhrat Khubaib (Radhiyallaho anho) remarked: 'Do you think that I would stoop to the killing of an innocent child? This heinous crime is simply not possible for me.'"

When he was brought to the gallows, and asked to make his last wish, if any, he requested:

"Allow me to say two rakaat of Salaat, for it is time for me to leave the world and meet my Allah."

They let him say his Salaat. On finishing the two rakaat most calmly, he said:

"But for your thinking that I was afraid of death, I would have said another two rakaats."

He was then tied to the gallows. At that time he said:

"O, Allah! There is nobody to convey my last Salaam to Thy Prophet (Sallallaho alaihe wasallam)."

And Allah sent his Salaam to the Prophet (Sallallaho alaihe wasallam) through an angel. The Prophet (Sallallaho alaihe wasallam) answered:

"Wa alaikumus salaam! O Khubaib,"

and observed to the Sahabah:

"Khubaib has been martyred by the Qureysh."

At the gallows, forty of the Querysh speared him simultaneously. One of those teased him:

Say by Allah, if you now wish Muhammad (Sallallaho alaihe wasallam) to be in your place and you to be let off."

He replied: "By Allah the Most Magnificent, I will not tolerate a thorn pricking the Prophet (Sallallaho alaihe wasallam) in ransom for my life."

Every word of this story is a lesson for us all. The devotion and love of the Sahabah narrated therein is really something to esteem and covet. They would lay down their very lives, but they would not tolerate even a thorn pricking the Prophet (Sallallaho alaihe wasallam). Again, look at Hadhrat Khubaib's (Radhiyallaho anho) last wish. He neither remembers his family members nor wishes to see any of them; what he wishes is to send his last Salaam to the Prophet (Sallallaho alaihe wasallam) and to say two last rakaats of Salaat.

10. Prophet's (Sallallaho alaihe wasallam) company in Paradise:

Rabee'ah (Radhiyallaho anho) narrates:

"I used to remain in attendance upon the Prophet (Sallallaho alaihe wasallam) at night. I would keep water, miswak, praying mat, etc., ready for his Tahajjud. Once he (being very pleased with my services) asked me, 'What would you wish most?' I submitted, 'O, Prophet of Allah, I wish your company in Paradise.' He asked me if there was anything else I wished for. But I replied. 'This is the only thing I long for.' Upon this, he remarked. 'All right. You should help me by prostrating in prayer frequently.'"

Here is a lesson for us. We should not depend on verbal prayers alone, but we should also make some practical efforts to gain our object. The best of all efforts is Salaat. Also, it would be wrong to depend entirely on the prayers of saints and pious people alone. This is a world of cause and effect; and, no doubt, Allah sometimes in His Wisdom and Might does bring into effect things for which there is no apparent and tangible cause, but this happens only on very rare occasions. For us, as in this world we make all possible efforts, and never depend on prayers alone nor rest contented with our lot, so in all gains pertaining to the Hereafter, we should try our best to conform to the conduct demanded by religious and ethical standards, and not regard verbal prayer as the only factor which counts, nor like a fatalist leave all to a ruthless destiny. No doubt, the prayers of pious people and lovers of Allah have their due effect, but they only go to augment our own sincere efforts, and even the Prophet (Sallallaho alaihe wasallam) asked Rabee'ah (Radhiyallaho anho) to "help" him by prostrating frequently (i.e., saying Salaat in his leisure hours too).

CHAPTER VI

SYMPATHY AND SELF-SACRIFICE

The Sahabah, as a class, were an embodiment of righteousness. They attained a standard that is rather difficult to emulate in a modern society. We would be fortunate if we really attain even a partial resemblance to their character. Some of their qualities are peculiarly their own, and self-sacrifice is one of these. Allah has made a mention of this in the Holy Qur'an in these words.

يُؤْثِرُوْنَ عَلٰى اَنْفُسِهِمْ وَلَوْ كَانَ بِهِمْ خَصَاصَةٌ (الحشر ٩)

"They prefer others above themselves, even though poverty become their lot. (LIX: 9)."

1. Feeding the guest in darkness:

A Sahabi came to the Prophet (Sallallaho alaihe wasallam) and complained of hunger and distress. Just then, the Prophet (Sallallaho alaihe wasallam) had nothing in hand, or in his home to feed him. He asked the Sahabah:

"Would anybody entertain him as a guest tonight on my behalf?"

One of the Ansaar said:

"O, Prophet of Allah, I will do that."

The Ansari took the person to his house and instructed his wife:

"Look here, this man is a guest of the Prophet (Sallallaho alaihe wasallam). We will entertain him as best as we can, and won't spare anything in doing so."

The wife replied:

"By Allah! I have got no food in the house, except a very little—something just enough for the children."

The Ansari said:

"You lull the children to sleep without feeding them, while I sit with the guest over the meagre meal. When we start eating, put out the lamp pretending to set it right, so that the guest may not become aware of my not sharing the meal with him."

The scheme worked out nicely, and the whole family, including the children, stayed hungry to enable the guest to eat to his fill. It was over this incident that Allah revealed the verse:

يُؤْثِرُوْنَ عَلٰى اَنْفُسِهِمْ وَلَوْ كَانَ بِهِمْ خَصَاصَةٌ (الحشر ٩)

"They prefer others above themselves, even though poverty become their lot (LIX: 9)."

There are quite a number of similar incidents about the Sahabah. The following is one of these.

2. Feeding a fasting Sahabi:

One of the Sahabah was keeping fast after fast, as he could not get anything to eat. Hadhrat Thabit (Radhiyallaho anho) came to know of this. He told his wife:

"I shall bring a guest tonight. When we sit at the meal, put out the lamp, pretending to set it right, and you are not to eat anything until the guest has taken his fill."

The scheme worked out as in the last story. The husband and wife sat with the guest and the simple soul never suspected in the least that neither of them had partaken at all of the food, though their hands and jaws seemed to be moving all right. When Hadhrat Thabit (Radhiyallaho anho) repaired to the Prophet's (Sallallaho alaihe wasallam) presence next morning, he was greeted with the happy news;

"O, Thabit! Allah has very much appreciated your entertainment of the guest last night."

3. Overpayment of Zakaat:

Hadhrat Ubay bin Kaab (Radhiyallaho anho) says: "The Prophet (Sallallaho alaihe wasallam) once deputed me to collect Zakaat dues from a locality. I went to a person there, and asked about the details of his possessions. A baby camel one year old was due from him in Zakaat. When he heard this, he exclaimed, 'Of what use is a baby camel, one year old? You can neither milk it, nor ride it. Here is a fine grown-up she-camel. You had better take this instead.' I replied, 'My commission does not permit me to take more than what is actually due from you. I, therefore, cannot accept what you offer. The Prophet (Sallallaho alaihe wasallam) is visiting this locality, and tonight he will be camping at a place not very far from here. It is better you should go and place your offer before him. If he does not object, I would gladly accept your offer, otherwise you shall have to give me exactly what is due from you.' Thereupon, he took the she-camel to the Prophet (Sallallaho alaihe wasallam) and besought him thus: 'O, Prophet of Allah! Your deputy came to receive Zakaat from me. By Allah! before this time, I have never had the honour of paying anything to the Prophet (Sallallaho alaihe wasallam) or his deputy. I therefore placed everything that I possessed before him. He decided that a baby camel one year old was due from me. Now, O, Prophet of Allah! This baby camel is of no use. It can neither yield milk nor carry a load. I, therefore, pressed him to accept a fine grown-up she-camel in-stead; which he refused to accept without your permission. I have now come to you with the she-camel. The Prophet (Sallallaho alaihe wasallam) observed, 'No doubt only that much is due from you which he has worked out, but if you are willing to give more than that, of your own accord, it would be accepted.' I then presented the she-camel to the Prophet (Sallallaho alaihe wasallam), which he accordingly accepted and sought Allah's blessings for the donor."

Look, with what magnanimity of heart the Sahabah parted with their best things for the sake of Allah. On the other hand, we too claim to be the true followers of Islam, and ardent devotees of the Prophet (Sallallaho alaihe wasallam) but, leaving apart the bestowing of alms in general to the poor and the needy, we are most reluctant to pay the actual obligatory dues. Zakaat, as a pillar of Islam, is not even known to our upper classes. Of the middle classes, only the religiously conscious strata keep up a form of paying Zakaat, in as much as even the expenditure incurred on their own relatives and acquaintances, and all other charitable donations squeezed out of them by the force of circumstances and face-savings are debited to this account.

4. Hadhrat 'Umar (Radhiyallaho anho) trying to emulate Hadhrat Abu Bakr (Radhiyallaho anho):

Hadhrat 'Umar (Radhiyallaho anho) narrates:

"Once the Prophet (Sallallaho alaihe wasallam) asked for contributions in the path of Allah. In those days, I was in possession of some wealth. I mused thus, 'Time and again Abu Bakr (Radhiyallaho anho) has surpassed me in spending for the sake of Allah. I shall by the Grace of Allah surpass him this time, because I have just now some wealth with me to spend'. I went home buoyant with the idea. I divided my whole property into two exactly equal parts. One I left for my family, and with the other I rejoined the Prophet (Sallallaho alaihe wasallam), who accosted me thus:

The Prophet (Sallallaho alaihe wasallam):

'Did you leave anything for your family, 'Umar?'

'Umar (Radhiyallaho anho):

'Yes, O Prophet of Allah.'

The Prophet (Sallallaho alaihe wasallam):

'How much?'

'Umar (Radhiyallaho anho):

'Exactly one-half.'

By and by, Hadhrat Abu Bakr (Radhiyallaho anho) came along with his load. It transpired that he had brought everything that he possessed.

This is what I heard:

The Prophet (Sallallaho alaihe wasallam):

'What did you leave for your family, Abu Bakr?'

Hadhrat Abu Bakr (Radhiyallaho anho):

'I have left Allah and his Prophet for them.'

Hadhrat 'Umar (Radhiyallaho anho) says that on that day he admitted to himself that he could never hope to surpass Hadhrat Abu Bakr (Radhiyallaho anho).

Allah says in his Holy Book,

"Vie one with another in good works (V:48)."

Such healthy emulation in sacrifice is therefore quite

desirable and welcome. This incident happened at the time of Tabuk, when the Sahabah in response to the Prophet's (Sallallaho alaihe wasallam) appeal for help contributed beyond their means. This has already been mentioned in Chapter II. May Allah grant them best rewards on behalf of all the Muslims!

جَزَاهُمُ اللهُ عَنَّا وَ عَنْ سَآئِرِ الْمُسْلِمِيْنَ اَحْسَنَ الْجَزَآءِ

5. Sahabah dying thirsty for others:

Hadhrat Abu-Jahm-bin-Huzaifah (Radhiyallaho anho) narrates:

> "During the battle of Yarmuk, I went out in search of my cousin, who was in the forefront of the fight. I also took some water with me for him. I found him in the very thick of battle in the last throes of death. I advanced to help him with the little water I had. But, soon, another sorely wounded soldier beside him gave a groan, and my cousin averted his face, and beckoned me to take the water to that person first. I went to this other person with the water. He turned out to be Hishaam bin Abil Aas (Radhiyallaho anho). But I had hardly reached him, when there was heard the groan of yet another person lying not very far off. Hisham (Radhiyallaho anho) too motioned me in his direction. Alas, before I could approach him, he had breathed his last. I made all haste back to Hishaam and found him dead as well. Thereupon, I hurried as fast as I could to my cousin, and, lo! in the meantime he had also joined the other two.
>
> اِنَّا لِلّٰهِ وَاِنَّا اِلَيْهِ رَاجِعُوْنَ

Many an incident of such self-denial and heroic sacrifice is recorded in the books of Hadith. This is the last word in self-sacrifice, that each dying person should forego slaking his own thirst in favour of his other needy brother. May Allah bless their souls with His choicest favours for their sacrifice for others even at the time of death, when a person has seldom the sense to make a choice.

6. Hadhrat Hamzah's (Radhiyallaho anho) shroud:

The Prophet's (Sallallaho alaihe wasallam) dear uncle, and one of his earliest supporters, Hadhrat Hamzah (Radhiyallaho anho) fell in Uhud, and the ruthless enemy brutally cut off his nose, ears and vitals. He was ripped open, and his heart, lungs and liver were torn out; and the whole body was thoroughly mutilated. While the Prophet (Sallallaho alaihe wasallam) was making arrangements for the burial of the dead, he caught sight of Hadhrat Hamzah's (Radhiyallaho anho) body, and was shocked to find it in that condition. He covered the body with a sheet of cloth. Presently, Hadhrat Hamzah's (Radhiyallaho anho) sister Safiyyah (Radhiyallaho anha) also came to see her martyred brother for the last time. The Prophet (Sallallaho alaihe wasallam) feared that the sight might be too much for her to bear, bade her son Hadhrat Zubair (Radhiyallaho anho) to dissuade her from seeing the body. She however, rejoined:

> "Yes, I have heard that the wretches have mutilated my dear brother's body. It is not too much in the path of Allah, and we should be resigned to it. I will bear all this patiently, and may Allah in His Grace have mercy on us all."

Hadhrat Zubair (Radhiyallaho anho) informed the Prophet (Sallallaho alaihe wasallam) of his mother's resolve, and he gave his assent to her seeing the body. When she beheld what they had done to it, she simply exclaimed, 'Inna lillahi wa inna ilaihi raaji-oon' and offered a prayer for his soul."

In another Hadith, Hadhrat Zubair (Radhiyallaho anho) himself narrates the incident. He says:

> "We made out a woman drawing near the place where the martyrs of Uhud had been gathered. On her close approach, I recognised her to be my own mother. I advanced to stop her, but she proved to be too strong for me. She thrust me aside, with the words, 'Leave me alone,' When I told her that the Prophet (Sallallaho alaihe wasallam) had prohibited her from seeing the dead body, she at once desisted from her purpose and explained, "Hearing the news of my brother's death, I have brought a couple of sheets for his shroud. Take these sheets and make use of them.' We took the sheets and had begun to enshroud the body, when the dead body of an Ansari named Hadhrat Suhail (Radhiyallaho anho) caught our eyes. It was also lying close by in the same condition. We considered it a shame to enshroud Hadhrat Hamzah (Radhiyallaho anho) in two sheets, while the body of another Muslim brother lay bare. We, therefore, decided to use one sheet each for

the two bodies. Now, one sheet was bigger than the other, so we drew lots, and the bigger sheet came to the lot of Hadhrat Suhail (Radhiyallaho anho) and the smaller one to that of Hadhrat Hamzah (Radhiyallaho anho). We found that the sheet meant for Hadhrat Hamzah (Radhiyallaho anho), being too small, would not cover his body: if we covered the head the feet remained uncovered, and when we pulled it down to cover the feet, the head was exposed. The Prophet (Sallallaho alaihe wasallam) said, "Cover the head with the sheet, and the feet with tree leaves."

This is how the body of Hadhrat Hamzah (Radhiyallaho anho), the dear uncle of him (Sallallaho alaihe wasallam) who wore the crown of perfection, was buried. Look at the spirit of the Sahabah, who could not tolerate Hadhrat Hamzah (Radhiyallaho anho) being enshrouded in two sheets and another Muslim brother remaining without a shroud at all. Again, although Hadhrat Hamzah (Radhiyallaho anho) deserved preferential treatment due to his exalted position, his body was covered with a smaller sheet that had fallen to his lot. Can there be a better example of sympathy, equality and self-sacrifice? Is it not shameful on our part that we, who call ourselves the followers of these illustrious people, do not possess any of these qualities.

7. The Story of the Goat's Head:

Hadhrat Ibn Umar (Radhiyallaho anho) says:

> "One of the Sahabah received a goat's head as a present. He thought of a neighbour who had a larger family and was in greater need of it than himself, and presented the same to him. This brother, on receipt of the present, recollected yet another person whom he considered even more deserving than himself, and sent on the head to him. The goat's head is, thus, said to have changed hands no less than seven times, and at last came back to the original person from whom the circulation had started."

We learn from the story how poor and needy the Sahabah usually were, and yet how they indeed preferred others above themselves.

8. Hadhrat 'Umar's (Radhiyallaho anho) wife acts as a midwife:

Amir-ul-Mominin Hadhrat 'Umar (Radhiyallaho anho), during the time of his Khilafat, used to patrol the streets and suburbs of Madinah himself during the night to keep a watch. During one of his night-patrols, he noticed a camel-hair tent pitched in an open space. He had never seen this particular tent before. Approaching the tent, he found an individual sitting outside, and heard a sort of groan coming out of the tent. Hadhrat 'Umar (Radhiyallaho anho) greeted the stranger with "Assalaam-o-alaikum" and sat down beside him.

Hadhrat 'Umar (Radhiyallaho anho):
"Whence brother?"

The person:
"I am from the desert, and a stranger to this place. I have come to request Amir-ul-Momnin for some help in my need."

Hadhrat 'Umar (Radhiyallaho anho):
"Who is there groaning like this inside the tent?"

The person:
"Please mind your own business."

Hadhrat 'Umar (Radhiyallaho anho):
"Do tell me please. May be that I can help you."

The person:
"If you must know, inside there is my wife groaning with labour pains."

Hadhrat 'Umar (Radhiyallaho anho):
"Is there anybody else to attend her?"

The person:
"No one."

Hadhrat 'Umar (Radhiyallaho anho), thereupon, got up and hurried homewards. He broached the subject to his wife Hadhrat Umme-Kulsum (Radhiyallaho anha) thus:

"Allah has brought you an opportunity to receive great blessings."

Wife:
"What is it, O, Amir-ul-Mominin?"

Hadhrat 'Umar (Radhiyallaho anho):

"Yonder, a poor woman of the desert is in child birth, with none to attend her."

Wife:

"I am ready to attend her, if it may please you so."

Hadhrat Umme-Kulsum (Radhiyallaho anho) was after all the daughter of Hadhrat Fatimah (Radhiyallaho anho), and grand-daughter of the Prophet; how could she hesitate at the time of such need of a forlorn sister, such a service and a devotion which Allah loves best?

Hadhrat 'Umar (Radhiyallaho anho):

"Then you should make all due haste. Also take a pan, some butter, provisions and other things needed during the child birth."

Hadhrat Umme-Kulsum (Radhiyallaho anho) did as she was bidden and left for the place where the tent was pitched. Hadhrat 'Umar (Radhiyallaho anho) followed her close. She entered the tent, while Hadhrat 'Umar (Radhiyallaho anho) made a fire and occupied himself with cooking something which those people could eat. After some time, Hadhrat Umme-Kulsum (Radhiyallaho anha) called out from inside the tent,

"Amir-ul-Mominin, congratulate your friend on the birth of a son."

The person was much embarrassed when he heard the address of 'Amir-ul-Mominin' and realized the position of the person who had been serving him. But Hadhrat 'Umar (Radhiyallaho anho) put all his fears to rest, saying:

"That is all right, there is nothing to worry about."

He then placed the pan near the tent, asking his wife to take it and feed the woman. She fed her and returned the pan. Then Hadhrat U'mar (Radhiyallaho anho) asked the bedouin to partake of the food, as he had kept awake the whole night.

Having rendered this service, Hadhrat U'mar (Radhiyallaho anho) returned home with his wife, telling the person "Come to me tomorrow, and I shall see what I can do for you."

Is there any king, nay a petty chief, or even an ordinary middle class person of our time, who will thus take his wife out at the dead of night, and out in the wilderness, to attend a poor strange woman, while he himself gladly engages in making a fire and cooking food. Leave the worldly rich aside, how many of the religious people would do that? We should realize that unless we really follow in the footsteps of those God-fearing people whom we profess to look up to as our models, we cannot deserve and wish for the special blessings that Allah bestowed on them.

9. Hadhrat Abu Talhah (Radhiyallaho anho) gives his garden to Allah:

Hadhrat Anas (Radhiyallaho anho) says, "Abu Talhah owned the best gardens in Madinah, and they were more numerous than those of any other Ansari. One of his gardens was known by the name of Bir Há, and this was his most favourite resort. It was close to the Prophet's (Sallallaho alaihe wasallam) musjid and the water of its well was sweet and abundant. The Prophet (Sallallaho alaihe wasallam) often visited that garden, and drank of the water. When Allah revealed the verse,

لَنْ تَنَالُوْا الْبِرَّ حَتّٰى تُنْفِقُوْا مِمَّا تُحِبُّوْنَ (آل عمران ٩٢)

"You will not attain unto piety until you spend of that which Ye love (III: 92)."

Hadhrat Abu Talhah (Radhiyallaho anho) repaired to the Prophet's presence and thus opened his heart,

"O, Prophet of Allah! I love Bir Há very much. As Allah wants us to spend precisely that which we love, I make over that garden to be spent in the path of Allah as you please."

The Prophet (Sallallaho alaihe wasallam) was very much pleased, and remarked:

"What a fine present (to Allah)! I think it would be best utilized if you distribute it among your own heirs."

Hadhrat Abu Talhah (Radhiyallaho anho) went and acted upon the Prophet's advice.

Are we prepared to part with any of our dear things for the sake of Allah so quickly, after reading a verse of the Qur'an or listening to a well-delivered sermon?

Even when we wish to make a charitable endowment, usually we do it only for our death-beds or else when we are so displeased with some relatives that we decide to disinherit them. But, when an occasion of public spending like marriage comes round, we are eager to win popularity even if we have to take a loan on interest.

10. Hadhrat Abuzar (Radhiyallaho anho) reprimands his servant:

Hadhrat Abuzar Ghifari (Radhiyallaho anho) was well known for his piety and abstinence. He kept no money with him, and likewise did not like others to hoard it. He was always fighting against the moneyed class. Hadhrat Usman, (Radhiyallaho anho), therefore, during his caliphate advised him to shift to Rabzah (a small village in the desert). He had a few camels to live on, and an old servant to look after them. A tribesman from Banu Sulaim once presented himself with a request:

> "I wish to stay with you to benefit from your knowledge of Allah's commandments and the Prophet's (Sallallaho alaihe wasallam) ways and habits; I shall also help your servant in looking after the camels."

Hadhrat Abuzar (Radhiyallaho anho) replied:

> "I cannot keep with me a person who does not comply with my wishes; but if you can always do as bidden you may remain with me, else I wish good-bye to you."

The person asked:

> "In what way do you like me to carry out your wishes."

Hadhrat Abuzar (Radhiyallaho anho) replied:

> "When I ask you to spend from my belongings, you are required to spend the best of them."

The person says, "I accepted Hadhrat Abuzar's (Radhiyallaho anho) condition and stayed on with him. One day, somebody informed him that there were some poor folk camping near the spring close-by and were in dire need of food. He asked me to fetch a camel. Accordingly, I went and intended to select the best of the lot, as I had pledged to do. It was a very fine and submissive animal and good for riding, so I decided to let it be, and selected the second best, as after all it was only to be slaughtered and eaten and, for this purpose, just as good as the other.

The other one was very good for riding and much more useful to Hadhrat Abuzar (Radhiyallaho anho) and his family, while the poor would find the one as tasty as the other. I, therefore, led the other camel to Hadhrat Abuzar (Radhiyallaho anho). He retorted:

"So, after all you have broken your pledge."

Knowing well what he meant, I turned back and fetched the best camel instead. He addressed the people about him,

"I want two persons to do a job for Allah."

As two persons volunteered themselves, he bade them go and slaughter the camel, and distribute the meat equally among the families camping near the water, including his own, saying, "My family will also share equally with the rest." The volunteers carried out his instructions. He then sent for me and asked:

'Did you intentionally ignore my instructions about spending the best out of my belongings, or you just happened to forget about it.'

I: 'I did not forget you instructions, but thought it better to preserve the one for transport duties, while the other was as good for eating.'

Abuzar: 'Was it for my personal need that you left it?'

I: 'Yes.'

Hadhrat Abuzar (Radhiyallaho anho):

'Come, let me tell you the occasion of my needs. That is the day when I shall be laid all alone in the solitude of the grave. Remember, there are three partners in your wealth, viz. (1) Your destiny; which does not wait to take away its share. Good or bad it would take away all that it has to take. (2) Your heirs, who are waiting for the day of your death, so that they may take over their share, and (3) Yourself. If you can manage, don't be the most helpless of the three partners. Take your full share, while you can. Allah says:

لَنْ تَنَالُوْا الْبِرَّ حَتّٰى تُنْفِقُوْا مِمَّا تُحِبُّوْنَ (آل عمران ٩٢)

'Ye will not attain unto piety until you spend of that which you love. (III: 92). I, therefore, think it advisable to send in advance the things which I love best, so that they may be in safe deposit for me there.'

That man is the worst loser of the three partners who does not spend his wealth in the path of Allah, and keeps postponing the event till at last destiny takes it away from him, or he dies and his heirs appropriate it. It is very seldom that the heirs give away in the path of Allah the wealth inherited from another person, so that his soul may benefit by it. The Prophet (Sallallaho alaihe wasallam) once remarked:

> "Man cherishes his worldly belongings, hugging them to his soul, and gloating, 'my wealth, my wealth,' but in reality only that much of it is his wealth, which he either enjoys in the form of food or dress or spends in the path of Allah to be stored up for him in the Hereafter. What is left of his wealth belongs to others; he is only acting as a custodian."

In another Hadith, it is reported that once the Prophet (Sallallaho alaihe wasallam) inquired of the Sahabah.

> "Which of you would rather like to see his wealth in the hands of his heirs than keep it with himself?"

They replied: "Who would like to be such a person, O Prophet of Allah? (Sallallaho alaihe wasallam)"

Thereupon the Prophet (Sallallaho alaihe wasallam) explained:

> "Whatever you send in advance by spending it in the path of Allah is yours, and whatever is left behind belongs to your heirs."

11. The Story of Hadhrat Abdullah bin Ja'far and Hadhrat Abdullah Bin Zubair (Radhiyallaho anhuma):

Hadhrat Ja'far Tayyar (Radhiyallaho anho) is a cousin of the Prophet (Sallallaho alaihe wasallam) and a brother of Hadhrat Ali (Radhiyallaho anho). His whole family is renowned for magnanimity, generosity, valour and heroism, but Hadhrat Ja'far (Radhiyallaho anho) had a special love for the poor and often mingled and associated with them. He emigrated to Abyssinia with the other Muslims at the time of the persecution by Qureysh, and he was the spokesman who so successfully defended the emigrants in the court of the Negus. This story we have already given in Chapter I. After returning from Abyssinia, he emigrated to Madinah and was martyred in the expedition of Mootah.

On receiving the news of his death, the Prophet (Sallallaho alaihe wasallam) went to his house to condole with his family. He called his sons Abdullah, Aun and Muhammad (Radhiyallaho anhum), consoled them and blessed them with his prayers. All his sons were cast in the mould of their father, but Hadhrat Abdullah (Radhiyallaho anho) was so generous and large-hearted that people called him "Qutbus Sakha" (the chief of the generous). He embraced Islam at the hands of the Prophet (Sallallaho alaihe wasallam) when he was barely seven. Once on his recommendation, his uncle Hadhrat Ali (Radhiyallaho anho) helped some person in his need. The person sent four thousand dirhams as a present to Hadhrat Abdullah (Radhiyallaho anho), but he returned the whole lot saying:

"We people don't sell our good deeds."

Upon another occasion, somebody sent him two thousand dirhams as a present; and he spent all of them in charity there and then. A trader once happened to bring a large quantity of sugar for sale in the market, but as chance would have it, there was no demand for the commodity just then and this grieved him very much. Hadhrat Abdullah (Radhiyallaho anho) purchased the whole lot through his agent, and distributed it (free) among the people. He always acted as a host to all the strangers who were stranded in the city during the night.

Hadhrat Zubair (Radhiyallaho anho), when participating in his last battle, called his son Hadhrat Abdullah (Radhiyallaho anho) to his side and confided to him that he had a premonition that this was going to be his last fight, in which he was destined to fall, adding that if it turned out to be so, Hadhrat Abdullah (Radhiyallaho anho) was to clear all his debts. He further admonished his son to call upon his 'Master' if he encountered any difficulty in doing so. His son, a bit puzzled, inquired as to who his Master was? "Allah," replied Hadhrat Zubair (Radhiyallaho anho). The same day he met his fate. When Hadhrat Abdullah bin Zubair (Radhiyallaho anho) checked the accounts of his father, he discovered debts that amounted to no less than two million dirhams. Having the reputation of being as honest and trustworthy a person as any that ever breathed, people flocked to him for the safe deposit of their money. He invariably address them like this:

"Dear brethren, I posses no vaults for the safe-keeping of your deposits. I will treat them as loans to me, and you may take the same back when you please."

He would then spend the money on the poor and the needy. By and by, Hadhrat Abdullah bin Zubair (Radhiyallaho anho) cleared all the debts of his father. He says:

"Whenever I experienced any difficulty, I would pray (to Allah) 'O, Master of Zubair help me,' and the difficulty would be removed."

He narrates an incident with Hadhrat Abdullah bin Ja'far (Radhiyallaho anho) to whom he had gone on business.

Abdullah bin Zubair (Radhiyallaho anho):
"I find from the accounts of my father that you owe him one million dirham."

Abdullah bin Ja'far (Radhiyallaho anho):
"All right. You can have the money when you please."

On checking the accounts once again, however, he found that it was his mistake, and in fact this much money was due to Hadhrat Abdullah bin Ja'far (Radhiyallaho anho) from his father. He therefore went to him again and said:

Abdullah bin Zubair (Radhiyallaho anho):
"Excuse me. It was my mistake. In fact my father owed you that much money."

Abdullah bin Ja'far (Radhiyallaho anho):
"If that is the case, I remit the debt."

Abdullah bin Zubair (Radhiyallaho anho):
"No, I must pay it."

Abdullah bin Ja'far (Radhiyallaho anho):
"All right. You may pay it at your convenience."

Abdullah bin Zubair (Radhiyallaho anho):
"Will you accept some land in lieu thereof? (He had received some land as his share of booty, and he wanted to dispose of it.")

Abdullah bin Ja'far (Radhiyallaho anho):
"Yes, if it suits you."

Abdullah bin Zubair (Radhiyallaho anho) says, "I made over to him a piece of waterless land. He asked his slave to go and spread his prayer-mat in that land. He then went and said two rakaats of Salaat, spending a long time in Sajdah. On finishing the Salaat, he pointed out a certain spot to his slave, and ordered him to dig at that particular place. After a little digging, water gushed forth from the pit."

The qualities of the Sahabah mentioned in this Chapter, were part of their every-day life. In fact, these things were not considered to be anything unusual.

CHAPTER VII

VALOUR AND HEROISM

Fear of death was unknown to the Sahabah. They were therefore most fearless and valorous. A person who can look death in the face can meet all situations. There is left for him no attraction in the wealth of this world, and no fear of an enemy. I wish I could inherit this quality from these true heroes.

1. Ibn Jahsh (Radhiyallaho anho) and Sa'd (Radhiyallaho anho) Pray for Each Other:

On the eve of Uhud, Abdullah bin Jahsh (Radhiyallaho anho) said to Sa'd bin Abi Waqqaas (Radhiyallaho anho):

"O, Sa'd! come, let us pray together. Let each pray to Allah for the grant of his sole desire, and the other would say Ameen to it. This way, the prayers are more likely to be answered by Allah."

Sa'd (Radhiyallaho anho) agreed, and they both went to a corner to pray.

Sa'd (Radhiyallaho anho) was first to pray, saying:

"O, Allah, when the battle rages tomorrow, let me face a very strong and fierce enemy. Let him attack me with might and main, and let me repulse him with all my strength. Then O, Allah, let me be triumphant by killing him for your sake, and allow me to have his possessions as booty."

Abdullah (Radhiyallaho anho) said: "Ameen ."

Then Abdullah (Radhiyallaho anho) started his prayer, saying:

"O, Allah, let me face one of the toughest fighters among the enemy tomorrow. Let him attack me with full fury and let me attack him with my full strength. Then let him have the upper hand and kill me. He may cut my nose and ears from my body. And when I appear before You on the day of Judgement, You may ask me, 'How did you lose your nose and ears, O, Abdullah!,' to which I may reply, 'These were lost in the way of Allah and His Prophet (Sallallaho alaihe wasallam).' Then You will say, 'Yes! surely these were lost in My way.'"

Sa'd (Radhiyallaho anho) said: "Ameen."

In the battle field next day, both of the Sahabah saw their prayers answered exactly as they had asked. Sa'd (Radhiyallaho anho) says:

"Abdullah's prayer was better than mine. In the evening I noticed his ears and nose strung in a thread."

This story on the one hand depicts great chivalry and valour on the part of Sahabah, in as much as they were anxious to face the brave and the strong amongst the enemy, and on the other hand it shows their devotion and love for Allah. Abdullah (Radhiyallaho anho) wishes Allah to confirm on the Day of Judgement that his sacrifice was really for Allah's cause. What an excellent wish!

2. Hadhrat Ali's (Radhiyallaho anho) valour in Uhud:

Neglect of the Prophet's orders changed the victory at Uhud into a defeat, the details of which we have already seen in Chapter I. That was a very hard time for the Muslims. They were simply caught between the two groups of the enemy, and many were killed. The Prophet (Sallalaho alaihe wasallam) was surrounded by the enemy, who spread the rumour that he had died. Most of the Sahabah lost their balance of mind at this rumour, and that was the main cause of their confusion.

Hadhrat Ali (Radhiyallaho anho) says:

"We were surrounded by the enemy, and I could not see the Prophet (sallalaho alaihe wasallam). I first searched for him among the living and then among the dead, but I could not find him. I said to myself, 'It is impossible for him to fly from the battle-field. It seems that Allah is angry with us due to our sins, and He has lifted him up to the heavens. There is no way left for me except to jump into the enemy lines and fight till I am killed.' I therefore attacked the enemy, clearing them with my sword till I caught sight of the Prophet (Sallallaho alaihe wasallam); I was very happy and was sure that Allah had been protecting him through His angels. I approached him and stood by his side. Meanwhile an enemy contingent advanced to attack the Prophet (Sallallaho alaihe wasallam). He said to me, 'Ali go and check them.' I fought and repulsed them single-handed, killing quite a few of them. After this, yet another group came to attack him. He again called out, 'Ali go and check them.' I fought with that group again single-handed and put them to their heels.'"

It was on this occasion that Hadhrat Jibrail (Alaihe salaam) came and praised Hadhrat Ali (Radhiyallaho anho) for his valour and his devotion to the Prophet. The Prophet (Sallallaho alaihe wasallam) said:

اِنَّهُ مِنِّىْ وَاَنَا مِنْهُ

"Ali belongs to me and I belong to him."

At this, Hadhrat Jibrail (Alaihis salaam) remarked:

وَاَنَا مِنْكُمَا

"I belong to you both."

Look at the valour of Hadhrat Ali (Radhiyallaho anho). He jumps into the enemy lines singlehanded, when he is unable to find the Prophet (Sallallaho alaihe wasallam). This also shows his extreme love and devotion to the Prophet (Sallallaho alaihe wasallam).

3. Hadhrat Hanzalah (Radhiyallaho anho) is martyred

When the battle of Uhud started, Hadhrat Hanzalah (Radhiyallaho anho) had just been wedded and therefore did not join the battle from the beginning. It is said that he had just left the bed of his wife and had hardly started taking his bath, when he heard somebody breaking the news about the defeat. He postponed the bath and, with sword in hand, rushed towards the battle-field. He jumped into the enemy concentration, fighting and penetrating till he was killed. Now the body of the person killed in the path of Allah is not washed, unless a bath has been incumbent on him before his death. Not knowing his failure to take the bath incumbent on him, the Sahabah buried him without a wash. Just before his burial, the Prophet (Sallallaho alaihe wasallam) said:

"I see the angels washing Hanzalah's body."

Hadhrat Abu Saeed Sa'di (Radhiyallaho anho) says:

> "On hearing this from the Prophet (Sallallaho alaihe wasallam), I went to have a look at Hanzalah's face and I noticed drops of water trickling down his hair."

When the Prophet (Sallallaho alaihe wasallam) returned to Madinah, he made queries and the facts of Hadhrat Hanzalah's (Radhiyallaho anho) postponing his bath came to light.

This, again, shows the valour of those people. A brave person cannot tolerate any delay and jumps into the jaws of death. Hadhrat Hanzalah (Radhiyallaho anho) also could not wait to finish the bath incumbent on him.

4. Hadhrat 'Amr bin Jamooh's (Radhiyallaho anho) desire for martyrdom.

'Amr bin Jamooh (Radhiyallaho anho) was lame. He had four sons, who often remained in the company of the Prophet (Sallallaho alaihe wasallam) and took part in the campaigns. In Uhud, Amr (Radhiyallaho anho) desired very much to join the battle. People said to him:

> "You are excusable, as you are lame. You need not go to the battle."

He replied: "How sad! that my sons go to Paradise, and I stay behind."

His wife also wanted him to fight and get martyred, so that she might have the honour of being the widow of a martyr. To exhort him, she said to him:

> "I do not believe that people have stopped you from going. It seems that you are yourself afraid to go to the battlefield."

Hearing this, Hadhrat 'Amr (Radhiyallaho anho) equipped himself with arms and, facing Qiblah, prayed to Allah:

اللّٰهُمَّ لاتَرُدَّنِیْ اِلٰی اَهْلِی

"O, Allah! Let me not come back to my family again."

He then went to the Prophet (Sallallaho alaihe wasallam) and said:

> "I had always wished for martyrdom, but my people have always been stopping me from going into the

> battle. O, Prophet of Allah! I cannot resist my desire any more. Do permit me to join the battle. I hope to walk in Paradise with my lame foot."

The Prophet (Sallallaho alaihe wasallam) said to him:

> "You have an excuse. There is no harm if you stay behind."

But he still insisted, and at last the Prophet (Sallallaho alaihe wasallam) permitted him to fight. Hadhrat Abu Talha (Radhiyallaho anho) says:

> "I saw 'Amr (Radhiyallaho anho) fighting. He walked proudly and said, 'By Allah! I am fond of Paradise'. One of his sons was following him at his heels. The father and the son fought till both of them were killed."

His wife on hearing of the death of her husband and son, came with a camel to fetch their bodies. It is said that when the bodies were loaded on the camel, it refused to stand up. When it was made to stand up after great beating, it would not go to Madinah and would turn towards Uhud, again and again. When the Prophet (Sallallaho alaihe wasallam) was informed of this, he said:

> "The camel is charged to do that. Did 'Amr (Radhiyallaho anho) say anything at the time of leaving his home?"

His wife informed the Prophet (Sallallaho alaihe wasallam) that he had prayed to Allah, facing Qiblah:

اَللّٰهُمَّ لَاتَرُدَّنِىْ اِلٰى اَهْلِىْ

"O, Allah! Let me not come back to my family again."

The Prophet (Sallallaho alaihe wasallam) said:

> "This is why the camel is refusing to go toward his home."

Look at Hadhrat 'Amr's (Radhiyallaho anho) desire to die in the path of Allah. It was their love and devotion for Allah and His Prophet that led the Sahabah to the height of such attainment. Even after death, 'Amr (Radhiyallaho anho) wants to remain in the battle-field, and the camel refused to take his body back to Madinah.

5. Hadhrat Mus‘ab bin ‘Umair (Radhiyallaho anho) gets martyred.

Hadhrat Mus‘ab bin ‘Umair (Radhiyallaho anho) had been brought up with great love and affection by his well-to-do parents. Before embracing Islam, he lived in luxury and comfort. It is said that he was the most well-dressed youth of Mecca. In fact his parents would buy a dress worth two hundred dirhams for him. He embraced Islam in its early days, without the knowledge of his parents. When, however, they came to know of it, they tied him with a rope and compelled him to stay at home. He got an opportunity to escape and emigrated to Abyssinia. On return from Abyssinia, he emigrated again to Madinah. So a person like him, brought up in luxury and comfort, was now living a life of abstinence and austerity. Once the Prophet (Sallallaho alaihe wasallam) was sitting when Mus‘ab (Radhiyallaho anho) passed in front of him. He had only one sheet of cloth to clothe his body, and this bore a number of patches, including one of leather. The Prophet (Sallallaho alaihe wasallam) with tears in his eyes mentioned Mus‘ab's life of luxury before Islam. In the battle of Uhud, Musab (Radhiyallaho anho) held the flag of Islam. When the Muslims on meeting defeat were dispersing in confusion, he held the flag and stood at his post like a rock. An enemy came and cut his hand with a sword, so that the flag might fall and the defeat might be accomplished. He at once took the flag in the other hand. The enemy then cut the other hand also. He held the flag to his bosom with the help of his bleeding arms. The enemy at last pierced his body with an arrow. He fell dead and, with him fell the flag that he had not allowed to fall while he was alive. Another Muslim ran and took over the flag. At the time of his burial, he had only one sheet to cover his body. This sheet was too short for his size. When it was drawn to cover the head, the feet would be exposed, and when it was drawn to cover the feet, the head would become uncovered. The Prophet (Sallallaho alaihe wasallam) said:

> "Cover his head with the sheet, and his feet with ‘Azkhar'leaves."

Such was the end of the youth who was brought up in luxury and comfort. The person who used to wear a dress worth two hundred dirhams does not have sufficient cloth to cover his dead body. Look! With what valour he tried to keep the flag up, and did not allow it to fall till he was dead. This is the miracle of Imaan. Once Imaan gets into a person, it makes him forget everything else, whether wealth, luxury or life itself.

6. Hadhrat Sa'd's (Radhiyallaho anho) epistle to Rustam.

In the Iraq expedition, Hadhrat 'Umar (Radhiyallaho anho) wanted to lead the army himself. There were, on several days, deliberations separately among the common people and among the chiefs, whether Amir-ul-Mominin should lead the expedition or stay in Madinah to direct the operations and arrange reinforcements from the headquarters. The common people were in favour of the former, and the chiefs in favour of the latter alternative. Somebody mentioned the name of Hadhrat Sa'd bin Abi Waqqaas (Radhiyallaho anho) as a substitute for Umar (Radhiyallaho anho) to command the expedition.

Both the groups agreed, and it was decided that Hadhrat Sa'd (Radhiyallaho anho) should lead the expedition and Hadhrat Umar (Radhiyallaho anho) should stay behind in Madinah. Hadhrat Sa'd (Radhiyallaho anho) was very brave and considered to be one of the heroes of Arabia. Iraq was a part of the Persian Empire and Yazdjard was the Emperor at that time. He sent for one of his best generals named Rustam and charged him with the task of checking the Muslim advance. Rustam tried to avoid going to the front, because of the fear of the Muslims, and requested the Emperor again and again to keep him back, saying:

> "I shall make arrangements for the despatch of reinforcements and shall be of use to your Majesty at the time of counsel."

But the Emperor did not agree, and he had to go to the battlefield.

When Hadhrat Sa'd (Radhiyallaho anho) was about to leave Madinah, Hadhrat Umar (Radhiyallaho anho) gave him the following instructions:

> "O, Sa'd! Let this fact not beguile you that you are one of the trusted companions of the Prophet (Sallallaho alaihe wasallam) and that people call you his uncle. Allah does not repel evil with evil, but He repels evil with good. Allah has no relation with His creation. All

men, high and low, are equal before Him, for all are His creation and He is their sole Lord. One can win His favours only through devotion to His service. Remember that the Sunnat of the Prophet (Sallallaho alaihe wasallam) is the only correct way of doing things. You are going on a very heavy task. This you can discharge only by following the truth. Inculcate good habits in yourself and your companions. Choose fear of Allah as your chief asset, for this will lead you to His obedience and prevent you from His disobedience. Obedience to Allah's command is the lot of those alone who hate this world and love the Hereafter."

Sa'd (Radhiyallaho anho) faced the heavy odds with full confidence in Allah. When both the armies were ready to fight, he sent an epistle to Rustam, which read:

فَإِنَّ مَعِى قَوْمًا يُّحِبُّوْنَ الْمَوْتَ كَمَا يُحِبُّوْنَ الْأَعَاجِمُ الْخَمْرَ

"Rustam! there are people with me to whom death (in the path of Allah) is more attractive than is wine to the people in your army."

Ask the people who are addicted to liquor, how much they love to taste it. The Sahabah loved to meet death in the Path of Allah even more. This was the chief cause of their success.

7. Hadhrat Wahb bin Qabus (Radhiyallaho anho) gets martyred.

Wahb bin Qabus (Radhiyallaho anho) was a shepherd and had been a Muslim for some time. He lived in his village in the desert. He came to Madinah to see the Prophet (Sallallaho alaihe wasallam). He was accompanied by his nephew and his herd of goats, which he had tied with a rope. He learnt that the Prophet (Sallallaho alaihe wasallam) was in Uhud. He left his goats and went to Uhud to fight by the side of the Prophet (Sallallaho alaihe wasallam). A group of the enemy was at that time advancing to attack the Prophet (Sallallaho alaihe wasallam). The Prophet announced:

"The person who disperses these people will be my companion in Paradise."

Hadhrat Wahb (Radhiyallaho anho) attacked them fiercely and repulsed all of them. A second and third group of the enemy tried to advance, and each time it was Hadhrat Wahb (Radhiyallaho anho) who fought them and put them to flight single handed. The Prophet (Sallallaho alaihe wasallam) gave him good tidings of Paradise. No sooner did he hear this, than he jumped into the enemy lines and fought till he was no more.

Hadhrat Sa'd bin Abi Waqqaas (Radhiyallaho anho) says:

"I have never seen a person fighting so bravely and fearlessly as Wahb did. I saw the Prophet (Sallallaho alaihe wasallam) standing beside his dead body, saying, 'O Wahb! You have pleased me. May Allah be pleased with you."

Although the Prophet (Sallallaho alaihe wasallam) himself was wounded in this battle, yet he buried Wahb's body with his own hands. Hadhrat Umar (Radhiyallaho anho) used to say:

"I never envied anybody more than Wahb (Radhiyallaho anho). I wish I could appear before Allah with a record as good as his."

What is it in the life of Hadhrat Wahb (Radhiyallaho anho) that makes an illustrious and exalted person like Hadhrat Umar (Radhiyallaho anho) to envy him. It is the same spirit of sacrifice for the sake of Allah and His Prophet (Sallallaho alaihe wasallam) even though Hadhrat 'Umar (Radhiyallaho anho) and other Sahabah have better deeds.

8. Tragedy of Bi'r Ma'oona.

In the tragedy of Bi'r Ma'oona, seventy Sahabah were massacred. All of them were Hafiz of Qur'an. Their Jama'at was called the Jama'at of Quraa and consisted mostly of Ansaar.

The Prophet (Sallallaho alaihe wasallam) loved them very much, for they engaged themselves in Zikr and recitation of the Qur'an during the night, and attended upon the Prophet (Sallallaho alaihe wasallam) and his family during the day. A person named Amir bin Malik and known as Abu Bara, belonging to Bani Amir clan of Najd, came to the Prophet (Sallallaho alaihe wasallam) and took this Jama'at with him for the Tabligh and the Ta'leem of his clan. The

Prophet (Sallallaho alaihe wasallam) expressed his apprehensions, saying:

"I fear some harm may come to my Sahabah."

But the person assured him that he was personally responsible for their safety. The Prophet (Sallallaho alaihe wasallam), after much hesitation, agreed to send the Jama'at of seventy Sahabah with him. He also gave them an epistle to 'Amir bin Tufail (the head of the clan), inviting him to Islam.

These Sahabah camped at Bi'r Ma'oona. Hadhrat 'Umar bin Umayyah (Radhiyallaho anho) and Hadhrat Munzir bin 'Umar (Radhiyallaho anho) took the camels for grazing and Hadhrat Haraam (Radhiyallaho anho) with two companions went to deliver the Prophet's epistle to 'Amir bin Tufail. On reaching near his place, Hadhrat Haraam (Radhiyallaho anho) said to his companions:

"You both stay here, I shall go alone to him. If I am safe, you may also come after me, but if I am betrayed you may return from here, as the loss of one is better than of three."

'Amir bin Tufail was the nephew of 'Amir bin Malik, who had brought the Jama'at. He was a bitter enemy of Islam and hated the Muslims to the core. When Hadhrat Haraam (Radhiyallaho anho) delivered the Prophet's (Sallallaho alaihe wasallam) epistle to him, he did not even care to read it and attacked Hadhrat Haraam (Radhiyallaho anho) with his spear, which pierced through the latter's body. Hadhrat Haraam (Radhiyallaho anho) uttered "By the Lord of the Ka'bah, I have triumphed," and died. The heartless person had no consideration for the guarantee given by his uncle, nor for the accepted tradition all over the world, that nobody would kill the envoy. He then assembled the people of his clan and exhorted them to kill all the Sahabah camping at Bi'r Ma'oona. The people hesitated, in view of the guarantee given by 'Amir bin Malik. He collected a large number of people from the neighbouring tribes and attacked the Muslims. They massacred each one of them, except Hadhrat Ka'b bin Zaid (Radhiyallaho anho), who had some life left in him and the enemy left him as dead. Hadhrat Munzir and Hadhrat Umar (Radhiyallaho anhuma), while grazing the camels, noticed vultures hovering in the air. They exclaimed. 'Something foul has happened, and returned to the camp. They saw from some distance that their companions were dead and the murderers were standing around their bodies with bloody swords in their hands. They stopped a while to think what they might do. Hadhrat 'Umar (Radhiyallaho anho) said:

> "Let us go back to Madinah and inform the Prophet (Sallallaho alaihe wasallam)."

Hadhrat Munzir (Radhiyallaho anho) did not agree. He said:

> "The Prophet (Sallallaho alaihe wasallam) will get the information sooner or later. I do not like to miss martyrdom and run away from the place where our companions are lying in their peaceful sleep. Let us go forward and meet them."

They both went and jumped into the thick of battle. Hadhrat Munzir (Radhiyallaho anho) was killed and Hadhrat 'Umar (Radhiyallaho anho) was captured. As 'Amir's mother had to set free a slave in connection with some vow that she had made, 'Amir set Hadhrat 'Umar (Radhiyallaho anho) free and let him go. 'Amir bin Fuhairah (Radhiyallaho anho), a slave of Abu Bakr (Radhiyallaho anho), was also among those who were killed at Bi'r Ma'oona. Jabbar bin Salmi, who killed him says:

> When I thrust my spear through him, he uttered, 'By Allah, I have triumphed and to my amazement I saw his body lifted upwards towards the sky. I made enquiries later on as to what was the triumph that 'Amir bin Fuhairah (Radhiyallaho anho) meant when he uttered, 'By Allah, I have triumphed.' I was told that it was that of entering into Paradise. This made me embrace Islam.

These are the illustrious people, of whom Islam is rightly proud. Death had really more attraction for them than wine for their enemies. As they did deeds which were sure to win Allah's pleasure, they felt most triumphant at the time of surrendering their souls

9. Hadhrat 'Umair (Radhivallaho anho) gives up Eating Dates.

In Badr, the Prophet (Sallallaho alaihe wasallam) was sitting in a tent. He exhorted the Sahabah to fight, saying:

"Rise up and race one with another for a Paradise as wide as are the Heavens and the Earth, prepared for the Muttaqin."

Hadhrat 'Umair ibnul Humaam (Radhiyallaho anho) was also listening to this. He exlaimed:

"Bakh! Bakh! (How wonderful)."

The Prophet (Sallallaho alaihe wasallam) asked Hadhrat 'Umair (Radhiyallaho anho) what he meant by that exclamation.

He said: "I wish to be one of those for whom this Paradise has been prepared."

The Prophet (Sallallaho alaihe wasallam) said:

"Rest assured, you are one of them."

Hadhrat 'Umair (Radhiyallaho anho) then took out a few dates from his bag and began to eat. While he was eating, he suddenly said:

"To wait till the dates finish will be a very long time. I cannot do that."

Saying this, he threw away the dates, and with sword in hand jumped into the battle-field and fought till he was killed.

In fact, these people appreciated the value of Paradise, for their Yaqeen was firm. If we too get that Yaqeen in our hearts, nothing will be too difficult or too much for us.

10. Hadhrat 'Umar's (Radhiyallaho anho) Emigration to Madinah.

Hadhrat Umar (Radhiyallaho anho) is well known for his valour and heroism by one and all. When the Muslims were very weak in the beginning, the Prophet (Sallallaho alaihe wasallam) prayed to Allah to strengthen the Muslims with Hadhrat 'Umar's (Radhiyallaho anho) Islam. This prayer was answered by Allah in no time, as we have seen in Chapter I. Hadhrat Abdullah bin Ma'sood (Radhiyallaho anho) says:

"We could not say our Salaat in the Haram till 'Umar had accepted Islam."

Hadhrat Ali (Radhiyallaho anho) says:

"Early emigrants to Madinah left Mecca quietly and secretly, due to the fear of Qureysh. But when Hadhrat 'Umar (Radhiyallaho anho) decided to emigrate, he hung his sword from his neck, held his bow in his hand and took a large number of arrows with him. He first went to Haram, performed Tawaf most confidently, said his Salaat most calmly and then went to the different groups of Quereysh, declaring before each of them, "Whoso does not mind his mother lamenting him, his wife becoming a widow and his children being rendered orphans, he may come out of Mecca and face me'. There was none to accept his challenge."

11. Expedition to Moota.

Of the epistles that the Prophet (Sallallaho alaihe wasallam) despatched to various kings, inviting them to Islam, one was sent to the King of Busra through Hadhrat Haris bin Umair Azdi. When Hadhrat Haris (Radhiyallaho anho) reached Moota, he was killed by Sharjeel Ghassani, one of the governors of Caesar. The murder of the envoy was against all laws of inter-tribal morality. The Prophet (Sallallaho alaihe wasallam) was naturally very much upset when the news reached him. He collected an army, 3 000-strong, to advance against the enemy. While nominating Hadhrat Zaid bin Harithah (Radhiyallaho anho) to command the army, the Prophet (Sallallaho alaihe wasallam) said:

> "If Zaid is killed, then Ja'far bin Abi Talib will be your Amir and if he is also martyred, then Abdullah bin Rawahah will take the command. If he also dies, then you can select a commander from among yourselves."

A Jew, who was listening to this, said:

> "All the three must die. This is exactly how the earlier Prophets used to prophesy."

The Prophet (Sallallaho alaihe wasallam) gave Hadhrat Zaid (Radhiyallaho anho) a white flag made by himself. He then accompanied the army for some distance out of Madinah and prayed for them saying:

> "May Allah bring you back safely and triumphantly. May He guard you against all evils."

At that moment, Hadhrat Abdullah bin Rawahah (Radhiyallaho anho), who was a poet too, recited three couplets, which meant:

"I only wish forgiveness of my sins and a sword to cause my blood to gush out like water from a fountain.

Or a spear to pierce me through my liver and my stomach. And when people pass my grave they say:

'May you, who have died for Allah's cause,

Triumph and prosper. You are really triumphant and prosperous."

Sharjeel received the intelligence about this army. He prepared himself to meet them with an army, 100 000-strong. When they proceeded further, they heard the rumour that the Caesar himself was coming with another army of 100 000-men to help Sharjeel. The Sahabah hesitated whether they should face such heavy odds or inform the Prophet (Sallallaho alaihe wasallam) for further instructions. At this Hadhrat Abdullah bin Rawahah (Radhiyallaho anho) called aloud:

"Friends! what are you bothering about? What are you here for? You are here to be martyred. We have never fought by dint of our strength in arms and numbers. We have always fought on the score of Islam, through which Allah has exalted us. You are sure of one of the two triumphs: Victory or Martyrdom."

Thus exhorted by Hadhrat Abdullah bin Rawahah (Radhiyallaho anho), the Sahabah decided to advance till they faced the Christian army in the battle-field of Moota. Hadhrat Zaid (Radhiyallaho anho) with flag in his hand directed the field operations. A fierce battle raged; Sharjeel's brother was killed in action. Sharjeel himself fled from the field and took shelter in a fort. He sent a message to the Caesar, who immediately despatched for his help and an army, which was 200 000-strong. The Muslims were fighting against very heavy odds. Hadhrat Zaid (Radhiyallaho anho) was killed and the flag was taken over by Hadhrat Ja'far (Radhiyallaho anho). He intentionally disabled his horse to dispel any idea of returning home from the battlefield. He then recited a few couplets, which meant:

"O, people! What a beautiful place is Paradise. And how happy is its approach! How fine and how cool is its water. The Roman's doom is at hand, I must finish them all."

With flag in one hand and sword in the other, he jumped into the enemy lines. The enemy cut his right hand, which held the flag. He at once transferred it to his left. When that was cut off, he held the flag in his teeth and supported it with his bleeding arms. His body was cut into two by somebody from behind and fell dead. He was thirty-three at that time.

Hadhrat Abdullah bin Umar (Radhiyallaho anho) says:

> "When we removed him from the battle-field, we counted as many as ninety wounds on his body—all on the front side."

When Hadhrat Ja'far (Radhiyallaho anho) was killed, Hadhrat Abdullah bin Rawahah (Radhiyallaho anho) was eating a piece of meat in a corner of the battle-field. He had been hungry for three days. On hearing about Hadhrat Ja'far's (Radhiyallaho anho) death, he threw away that piece of meat, saying to himself:

> "Abdullah! You are busy in eating, while Ja'far has reached Paradise."

He took the flag and began to fight. His finger was severely injured and hung loose. He put the hanging finger under his foot and tore it off from the hand, and then rushed forward. Knowing the Muslims were fighting against very overwhelming odds, and his own weakness, made him pause for a moment. He at once recovered from his despair and said to himself:

> "O, Heart! what makes you tarry now? Is it for the love of wife? If so, then I divorce her this very moment. Is it for the slaves? Then I set them all free. Is it for the garden? I give it over in Sadaqah. He then recited a few couplets, which meant: 'O, Abdullah! You have to go down after all; whether you do it willingly or unwillingly. You have had enough of peace. O, you, who are only a drop of dirty fluid! See how the disbelievers are assaulting the Muslims. Why does Paradise not entice you? Even if you are not killed in this battle, remember, you have to die one day."

He then got down from his horse. Meanwhile his cousin brought him a slice of meat, saying, "You have had neither sleep nor food for so many days. Eat this and take a little rest before you fight." He held the slice and was about to eat it when he heard an uproar of the enemy's assault from one direction. He threw away the slice and jumped into the crowd, striking with his sword till he was killed.

The history of the Sahabah is full of episodes, which show that worldly pleasures were most insignificant in their eyes, and their only concern was to get success in the Hereafter.

12. The Story of Saeed bin Jubair and Hajjaj Bin Yusuf.

We see the same spirit even in their successors (the Tabi'ees). I close this chapter with an account of Saeed bin Jubair, who is famous Tabi'ee. The Prophet (Sallallaho alaihe wasallam) has said:

اَفْضَلُ الْجِهَادِ كَلِمَةُ الْحَقِّ عِنْدَ سُلْطَانٍ جَآئِرٍ

"To utter truth in the face of a tyrant is the best Jihad."

This is a story of Jihad of that type. At that time, Hajjaj bin Yusuf, the notorious blood-shedder was in power. Hajjaj's harshness and tyranny are well known in human history. The rulers in those days, in spite of their shortcomings, never lagged behind in propagating the faith, yet we treat them as the worst among rulers because of the contrast with the just and God-fearing rulers. He was the viceroy of king Abdul Malik bin Marwan for Hijaz and Iraq. The king lived in Damascus and Hajjaj had his headquarters at Koofah. Saeed bin Jubair had fought against Hajjaj on the side of Ibnul Ash-ath. After the defeat, Saeed (Rahmatullah alaih) ran away and took asylum in Mecca. The Government posted a very stern person as the Governor of Mecca, with instructions to arrest Saeed. The Governor assembled all the people of Mecca and read before them the order of Abdul Malik, which said:

> "Any person who gives shelter to Hadhrat Saeed (Rahmatullah alaih) shall meet the same fate as Hadhrat Saeed (Rahmatullahi alaih) himself."

He then announced to the people:

> "By Allah, I must kill the person who gives shelter to Hadhrat Saeed (Rahmatullah alaih). His and his neighbours houses shall be razed to the ground."

Hadhrat Saeed (Rahmatullahi alaih) was arrested with great difficulty and sent to Koofah. When he was brought before Hajjaj, the following conversation took place:

Hajjaj: "What is your name?"

Hadhrat Saeed: "My name is Saeed (lit. auspicious)."

Hajjaj: "What is your father's name?"

Hadhrat Saeed: "Jubair (lit. Trimmed)."

Hajjaj: "No, you are in fact Shaqi (lit. wretched) son of Kusair (lit. a broken thing)."

Hadhrat Saeed: "My mother knew my name better than you do."

Hajjaj: "You are wretched and your mother is also wretched."

Hadhrat Saeed: "The Knower of the hidden things is someone else"

Hajjaj: "Look! I am putting you to sword."

Hadhrat Saeed: "Then my mother was right in giving me this name."

Hajjaj: "I shall send you to Hell."

Hadhrat Saeed: "If I knew that you had that power, I would have taken you as my god."

Hajjaj: "What is your belief about the Prophet (Sallallaho alaihe wasallam)?"

Hadhrat Saeed: "He was an apostle of Mercy and a Prophet of Allah, sent with the best Guidance for the whole creation."

Hajjaj: "What do you say about the Khalifas?"

Hadhrat Saeed: "I am not a warder over them. Everybody is responsible for his own actions."

Hajjaj: "Who is the most exalted of the four Khalifahs?"

Hadhrat Saeed: "The one who had been able to please Allah more than the rest."

Hajjaj: "Which of them had been able to please Allah more than the rest?"

Hadhrat Saeed: "This is known only to Him Who knows what is hidden in the bosoms and what the hearts conceal."

Hajjaj: "Is Ali in Paradise or in Hell?"

Hadhrat Saeed: "I can answer only after I visit the two places and meet their dwellers."

Hajjaj: "How shall I fare on the Day of Judgement?"

Hadhrat Saeed: "I am not fit to receive the knowledge of the unseen?"

Hajjaj: "You do not intend to tell me the truth."

Hadhrat Saeed: "But I did not tell a lie either."

Hajjaj: "Why do you never laugh?"

Hadhrat Saeed: "I do not see anything to laugh at; and indeed why should one laugh, who is created from dust, who has to appear on the Day of Judgement, and is always surrounded by tribulations.

Hajjaj: "But I do laugh."

Hadhrat Saeed: "Allah has created us with different temperaments."

Hajjaj: "I am now going to kill you."

Hadhrat Saeed: "The time and mode of my death have already been decreed."

Hajjaj: "Allah has preferred me to you."

Hadhrat Saeed: "Nobody can be proud of his relation with Allah, unless he knows his position; and Allah is the only knower of the unseen."

Hajjaj: "Why should I not be proud of my relation with Allah, when I am with the Amir-ul-Mominin and you are with the rebels."

Hadhrat Saeed: "I am with the other Muslims. I myself shun mischief, but nobody can change the decree of Allah."

Hajjaj: "What do you say about what we collect for Amir-ul-Mominin?"

Hadhrat Saeed: "I do not know what you collect for him."

Hajjaj sent for gold, silver and dresses from the treasury and showed these to Saeed.

Hadhrat Saeed: "These are useful, provided you are able to obtain with them the things that may provide you peace on the Day of Consternation (i.e Day of Judgement), when every nursing mother will forget her nursing, and every pregnant one will be delivered of her burden, and when nothing but good will be of any avail."

Hajjaj: "Are our collections not good?"

Hadhrat Saeed: "You have collected them, and you are the best judge."

Hajjaj: "Do you like any of these things for yourself?"

Hadhrat Saeed: "I only like the things which Allah likes."

Hajjaj: "Woe to you!"

Hadhrat Saeed: "Woe is for the person who is deprived of Paradise and is made to enter Hell."

Hajjaj: (Annoyed): "Say how should I kill you?"

Hadhrat Saeed: "As you would like to be killed."

Hajjaj: "Should I forgive you?"

Hadhrat Saeed: "Allah's forgiveness is real. Your aforgiveness is of no value."

Hajjaj: (To the executioner): "Kill this man."

Hadhrat Saeed laughed while he was being taken for execution. Hajjaj was informed of this. He called him back.

"What made you laugh?"

Hadhrat Saeed: "Your boldness with Allah, and His clemency to you."

Hajjaj: "I am killing a person who has caused dissent among the Muslims. (To the executioner) Kill him in front of me."

Hadhrat Saeed: "Let me say my Salaat of two rakaats."

After finishing Salaat, he faced Qiblah and recited:

اِنِّیْ وَجَّهْتُ وَجْهِیَ لِلَّذِیْ فَطَرَ السَّمٰوٰتِ وَالْاَرْضَ حَنِیْفًا وَّمَآ اَنَا مِنَ الْمُشْرِکِیْنَ

(الْانعام ۸۰)

"Verily, I have turned my face toward Him Who created the heavens and earth, as one by nature upright, and I am not of the idolaters" (VI: 80).

Hajjaj: "Turn him from our Qiblah and let him face the Qiblah of the Christians, who also caused dissension and dispute among their community."

His face was immediately turned to the other direction.

Hadhrat Saeed:

اَیْنَمَا تُوَلُّوْا فَثَمَّ وَجْهُ اللهِ (البقرة ۱۱۵)

"And wither-so-ever you turn, there is Allah's countenance" (II: 115), Who is knower of the hidden thoughts.

Hajjaj: "Make him lie on his face. We are only responsible for appearance."

Hadhrat Saeed (Rahmatullahi alaih) was made to lie on his face.
Saeed:

مِنْهَا خَلَقْنٰكُمْ وَفِيْهَا نُعِيْدُكُمْ وَمِنْهَا نُخْرِجُكُمْ تَارَةً اُخْرٰى (طٰهٰ ۵۵)

"Thereof We created you, and thereunto We return you, and thence We bring you forth a second time." (XX: 55).

Hajjaj: "Kill him"

Hadhrat Saeed: I call you to witness what I recite:

اَشْهَدُ اَنْ لَّاۤ اِلٰهَ اِلَّا اللهُ وَحْدَهٗ لَاشَرِيْكَ لَهٗ وَاَشْهَدُ اَنَّ مُحَمَّدًا عَبْدُهٗ وَرَسُوْلُهٗ

"I bear witness that there is no god except Allah, who is all alone and Who has no partner and I bear witness that Muhammad (Sallallaho alaihe wasallam) is His slave and His Prophet."

He was then beheaded (Inna lillahi wa inna ilaihi raaj-oon).

اِنَّا لِلّٰهِ وَاِنَّآ اِلَيْهِ رَاجِعُوْنَ

After the execution, too much blood came out from Hadhrat Saeed's (Rahmatullahi alaih) body. Hajjaj himself marvelled greatly at it. He inquired the reason from his doctors, who said:—

> "His tranquillity and composure at the time of death had kept his blood in its original form. Generally, people to be executed are so much scared and afraid of death that their blood curdles and does not flow profusely."

There are many such incidents in the annals of the Taabi'een. Hadhrat Imam Abu Hanifa, Hadhrat Imam Malik, Hadhrat Imam Ahmad bin Hambal and other divines had to undergo trials and tribulations because of their truthfulness; but they remained steadfast in the righteous path.

CHAPTER–VIII

ZEAL FOR KNOWLEDGE

The Kalimah is the essence of Islam and the basis for all achievements. No good action is acceptable with out belief in Kalimah. The Sahabah, therefore, devoted most of their energy, specially in the early days of Islám, to the propagation of the Kalimah and to fighting with the forces that resisted it. Although their engagements left them very little time to drink deep from the ocean of learning with the single-mindedness demanded thereof, yet their zeal even in this direction has left us a legacy in the form of knowledge about the Qur'an and Hadith, which is quite highly creditable and a glaring example. When Sahabah got a little leisure from the work that kept them engaged in the beginning of Islam, and also when the number of people in Islam grew considerably, Allah revealed the following verse in the Qur'an:

وَمَا كَانَ الْمُؤْمِنُوْنَ لِيَنْفِرُوْا كَآفَّةً ، فَلَوْ لَانَفَرَ مِنْ كُلِّ فِرْقَةٍ مِّنْهُمْ طَآئِفَةٌ لِّيَتَفَقَّهُوْا
فِى الدِّيْنِ وَلِيُنْذِرُوْا قَوْمَهُمْ اِذَا رَجَعُوْآ اِلَيْهِمْ لَعَلَّهُمْ يَحْذَرُوْنَ (التوبة ١٢٢)

"And the believers should not all go out (in the path of Allah). Of every group of them, a party only should go forth that they (who are left behind) may gain sound knowledge in religion and that they may warn their folk when they come to them, so that they may beware."
(IX: 122).

Hadhrat Abdullah bin Abbas (Radhiyallaho anho) says:

"The verses of the Qur'an which were revealed in the beginning of Islam, demanding every Muslim to move out in the path of Allah; for example:

اِلَّا تَنْفِرُوا يُعَذِّبْكُمْ عَذَابًا اَلِيْمًا (التوبة ٣٩)

"If you go not forth, He will afflict you with a painful doom;
(IX: 39)"

اِنْفِرُوْا خِفَافًا وَّثِقَالًا وَّجَاهِدُوْا بِاَمْوَالِكُمْ وَاَنْفُسِكُمْ فِىْ سَبِيْلِ اللهِ (التوبة ٤١)

'Go forth, light and heavily armed, and strive with your wealth and your lives in the way of Allah;

(IX: 41).'

These verses were later on superceded by the foregoing verse, which advised only a party from each group to leave their places.

وَمَا كَانَ الْمُؤْمِنُوْنَ لِيَنْفِرُوْا كَآفَّةً ، فَلَوْ لَانَفَرَ مِنْ كُلِّ فِرْقَةٍ مِّنْهُمْ طَآئِفَةٌ لِّيَتَفَقَّهُوْا فِى الدِّيْنِ وَلِيُنْذِرُوْا قَوْمَهُمْ اِذَا رَجَعُوْآ اِلَيْهِمْ لَعَلَّهُمْ يَحْذَرُوْنَ (التوبة ١٢٢)

The Sahabah, very few in number as they were, had to assume the responsibilities of Islam in all fields. Allah therefore endowed them with the versatility that was theirs. After the Sahabah, the Islam spread far and wide and the Muslims swelled in number. Again, the later people lacked the versatility of the Sahabah. Allah then caused different people to specialize in different branches of Islamic learning. Mohaddithin were to devote themselves to the collection and propagation of Hadith. Similarly the Fuqaha (jurists) Soofia (Experts in Zikr), Qurraa (Experts in recitation of Qur'an), Mujahidin (Fighters in the path of Allah), etc, each own group had its own field to take up as a whole-time task. This was very necessary at that time, for otherwise different branches of Islamic learning would not have developed so nicely, as it is difficult for one man to specialize in all the branches. The Prophets (alaihimus salaam), and specially Muhammad (Sallallaho alaihe wasallam) the chief among them, were specially endowed with such a capacity. This will explain why the stories of other eminent personalities, besides the Sahabah have also been narrated in this chapter.

1. Sahabah's Panel for Fatwa.

Although all the Sahabah, along with their engagement in Jihad and propagation of faith, were devoted to acquiring and further spreading of knowledge, yet there was a panel of Sahabah who were exclusively entrusted with Fatwa, even during the life time of the Prophet (Sallallaho alaihe wasallam). The panel comprised the following Sahabah:—

Hadhrat Abu Bakr, Hadhrat 'Umar, Hadhrat Usman, Hadhrat Ali, Hadhrat Abdur Rahman bin 'Auf. Hadhrat

Ubayy bin Kaab, Hadhrat Abdullah bin Mas'ood, Hadhrat Ma'aaz bin Jabal, Hadhrat Ammaar bin Yaasir, Hadhrat Huzaifah, Hadhrat Salman Farsi, Hadhrat Zaid bin Thabit, Hadhrat Abu Musa, Hadhrat Abu Darda (Radhiyallaho anhum).

To give Fatwa during the lifetime of the Prophet (Sallallaho alaihe wasallam) was a big privilege for these Sahabah, and speaks of their deep and dependable knowledge.

2. Hadhrat Abu Bakr (Radhiyallaho anho) burns his collections:

Hadhrat Aishah (Radhiyallaho anha) says:

> "My father (Hadhrat Abu Bakr) (Radhiyallaho anho) had a collection of five hundred Hadiths. One night I noticed that he was very restless. He was tossing about in the bed and could not sleep. I got worried over this and inquired, 'Are you suffering from any trouble or worried about anything.' But he did not speak and remained restless throughout the night. Next morning he called me and said, 'Bring the collection of Hadith that I gave you to keep.' I brought the book and he set fire to it, till it was burnt. He said, 'The collection contained many Hadiths that I had heard from other people. I thought if I died and left behind a Hadith accepted as authentic by me, but really not so, then I should have to answer for that."

It was Hadhrat Abu Bakr's (Radhiyallaho anho) zeal for knowledge, that caused him to compile a book of five hundred Hadiths. But it was due to his extreme cautiousness that he burnt the collection.

The Sahabah were very careful and cautious about Hadith. That is why you find very few Hadiths narrated by eminent Sahabah; those people who do not hesitate to quote Hadith (without authority) in their sermons from the pulpit should take a lesson from this story. Hadhrat Abu Bakr (Radhiyallaho anho) remained in the Prophet's company for most of his time; many Sahabah say:

> Hadhrat "Abu Bakr (Radhiyallaho anho) was the most learned amongst us;"

Hadhrat 'Umar (Radhiyallaho anho) says:

"After the death of the Prophet (Sallallaho alaihe wasallam), when the Khalifah's selection was under consideration, Hadhrat Abu Bakr (Radhiyallaho anho) addressed the people quoting all those verses of the Qur'an and all such Hadiths of the Prophet (Sallallaho alaihe wasallam) which dealt with the virtues and privileges of the Ansar."

This shows how much knowledge of the Qu'ran he had, and how many Hadiths he remembered. In spite of all this, there are very few Ahadith that have been narrated by Hadhrat Abu Bakr (Radhiyallaho anho). For similar reasons, Imam Abu Hanifah (Rahmatullah alaih) too was not so liberal in reporting Hadith.

3. Hadhrat Mu'sab bin Umair (Radhiyallaho anho) Carries out Tabligh.

A story about Hadhrat Mus'ab bin Umair (Radhiyallaho anho) has already been given in Chapter VII. When the first group of people from Madinah embraced Islam in Mina, the Prophet (Sallallaho alaihe wasallam) deputed Hadhrat Mus'ab bin Umair (Radhiyallaho anho) to go with them to teach Islam and preach to others. He remained busy all the time in teaching the Qur'an and other Islamic practices to the people. He stayed with Hadhrat As'ad bin Zararah (Radhiyallaho anho) and was known as 'Muqree' (the teacher).

Sa'd bin Ma'az and Usaid bin Hudhairiyah, who were among the chiefs of Madinah, did not like Mus'ab's activities. Sa'd said to Usaid:

> You go to As'ad and tell that we do not like his having brought a stranger with him to Madinah, who misleads the poor and simple folk of the town."

Usaid went to Hadhrat As'ad (Radhiyallaho anho) and talked to him very harshly. Hadhrat As'ad (Radhiyallaho anho) said to him:

> "You first listen to him; if you like his teachings, you may accept them; if not, you have every right to denounce and stop him."

Usaid agreed to it. Hadhrat Mus'ab (Radhiyallaho anho) explained the virtues of Islam and recited a few verses of the Qur'an before him. Usaid said:

"These teachings are very fine and these verses are simply beautiful. How do you admit a person to your faith?"

He said: "You take a bath, put on clean clothes and recite the Kalimah."

Usaid immediately complied with all these formalities and embraced Islam. He then went to Sa'd and brought him to Mus'ab (Radhiyallaho anho) to listen to his Tabligh. Sa'd also embraced Islam. No sooner had Sa'd accepted Islam than he went to people of his clan (Banu Ash-hal) and said to them:

"What type of person do you think I am?"

They replied: "You are the best and the noblest of the clan."

He then said: "I have vowed not to talk to your men and women until you all embrace Islam and believe in Muhammad (Sallallaho alaihe wasallam)."

All the men and women of Banu Ash-hal embraced Islam then and there. Hadhrat Mus'ab (Radhiyallaho anho) began to teach them and train them in Islam.

No sooner did anybody embrace Islam than he began to preach it. Everyone of them considered it incumbent upon him to preach and teach to others what he know about Islam. His trade, farm or occupation was no barrier to Tabligh.

4. Hadhrat 'Ubayy bin Ka'ab (Radhiyallaho anho) Teaches Hadith.

Hadhrat Ubayy bin Ka'ab (Radhiyallaho anho) is one of the most eminent Sahabah and was an expert in the recitation of the Qur'an. Very few Arabs were literate before Islam, and he was one of these. The Prophet (Sallallaho alaihe wasallam) used to dictate the revealed Qur'an to him. He memorised the Qur'an during the life time of the Prophet (Sallallaho alaihe wasallam) and had thorough understanding of it. The Prophet (Sallallaho alaihe wasallam) is reported to have said:

"Hadhrat Ubayy bin Ka'ab (Radhiyallaho anho) is the greatest Qari of my Ummat."

He used to finish the Qur'an once in Tahajjud in eight nights. Once the Prophet (Sallallaho alaihe wassalam) said to him:

> "Allah has commanded me to recite the Qur'an to you."

He said: "O, Prophet of Allah! Did Allah mention me by my name?"

The Prophet (Sallallaho alaihe wasallam) replied:

> "Yes, He mentioned you by your name."

Tears began to roll down his cheeks with excessive joy.

Hadhrat Jundub bin Abdullah (Radhiyallaho anho) says:

> "When I went to Madinah to acquire knowledge, I found that people were sitting in groups, and each group was entrusted to a teacher. In one of the groups I saw a person teaching Hadith, clad in two sheets of cloth and looking like a traveller. I asked the people, 'Who is this person?' They said, 'He is our esteemed Imam, Hadhrat Ubayy bin Ka'ab (Radhiyallaho anho).' When he finished teaching, I followed him to his house. He was staying in a very old and dilapidated building, with little or no furniture. I noticed Hadhrat Ubayy (Radhiyallaho anho) living in a very simple and ascetic life.'

Hadhrat Ubayy (Radhiyallaho anho) says:

> "Once the Prohet (Sallallaho alaihe wasallam) tested me in my knowledge of the Qur'an. He asked me, 'Ubayy, which is the most august verse of the Qur'an?' I said, 'Allah and His Prophet (Sallallaho alaihe wasallam) know best.' He again asked my the same question and I gave the same modest and respectful reply. When he put the same question once again, I replied, 'The most august verse in the Qur'an is Ayatul Kursi (II: 255).' My reply made him very happy. He said, 'May Allah bless you through your knowledge.'

Once the Prophet (Sallallaho alaihe wasallam) was leading Salaat when he missed one verse. Ubayy (Radhiyallaho anho) pointed out the correction from behind. On finishing Salaat, the Prophet (Sallallaho alaihe wasallam) inquired 'Who corrected me?' He was told that it was Hadhrat Ubayy

(Radhiyallaho anho). He remarked, 'I also thought that it was he.''

In spite of his devotion to knowledge and his special job of writing the Qur'an, he took part in all the battles by the side of the Prophet (Sallallaho alaihe wasallam). He did not miss a single campaign or expedition led by the Prophet (Sallallaho alaihe wasallam).

5. Hadhrat Huzaifah's (Radhiyallaho anho) Anxiety Regarding Tribulations.

Hadhrat Huzaifah (Radhiyallaho anho) is one of the well-known Sahabah. He is known as 'Keeper of Secrets.' The Prophet (Sallalaho alaihe wasallam) had confided to him the names of Munafiqin, and had informed him in chronological order all the tribulations which the Muslims were to face till the last day. He gave him full details (viz. the name of the mischief maker, his parents' names, his community, etc.) about the incidents that were going to affect three hundred or more people. Hadhrat Huzaifah (Radhiyallaho anho) says:

> "Other people used to ask the Prophet (Sallallaho alaihe wasallam) about good things, while I always asked him about the adverse events, so that I might guard against them."

He then narrated the following conversation with the Prophet:

Huzaifah: "O, Prophet of Allah! Shall we revert to evil, after the good that you have brought us?"

The Prophet: "Yes. The evil is coming."

Huzaifah: "Shall we have good again after that evil?"

The Prophet: "Huzaifah! Go and read the Qur'an, meditate on its meaning and follow its commandments."

But Huzaifah anxiety grew more and more, and he continued his queries about evils that were to befall the Muslims.

Huzaifah: "O, Prophet of Allah! Tell me if good will come after that evil?"

The Prophet: "Yes, good will come again, but the hearts of the people will not be so clear as before."

Huzaifah: "And will there by any evil coming after this good?"

The Prophet: "Yes, There will be such persons who will misguide the people and take them to Hell."

Huzaifah: "What should I do if I witness that time?"

The Prophet: "If there be a group of Muslims united under one Amir, then join them, otherwise dissociate yourself from all such factions and be secluded in a corner, or take refuge under a tree (i.e., in the forest) and be there till you die."

As the Prophet (Sallallaho alaihe wasallam) had disclosed to him the identities of the Munafiqin of that time, Hadhrat Umar (Radhiyallaho anho) used to ask him:

"Is there any Munafiq among my deputies?"

He once replied: "Yes. There is one, but I shall not disclose his name."

Hadhrat Umar (Radhiyallaho anho) dismissed the man, probably by his own discernment.

Whenever somebody died, Hadhrat Umar (Radhiyallaho anho) would inquire if Hadhrat Huzaifah (Radhiyallaho anho) was participating in the funeral prayer. If Huzaifah (Radhiyallaho anho) did not do so, then Hadhrat Umar (Radhiyallaho anho) would also absent himself from that funeral:

When Hadhrat Huzaifah (Radhiyallaho anho) was about to die, he wept in anxiety and uneasiness. People said to him:–

"Are you weeping over your departure from this world?"

He said: "No. I am not weeping over that. I love to die. I weep because I do not know whether, at this time of my departure from this world, Allah is pleased with me or not."

He then prayed: "O, Allah, these are the last moments of

> my life. You know that I have always loved Thee. Bless my meeting with Thee."

6. Hadhrat Abu Hurairah's (Radhiyallaho anho) Memory for Hadith.

Hadhrat Abu Hurairah (Radhiyallaho anho) is another eminent Sahabi. No other person has narrated as many Ahadith as he has done. He embraced Islam in 7 A.H. and, as the Prophet (Sallallaho alaihe wasallam) died in 11 A.H., he had been with him for four years only. People used to marvel how he could remember so many Ahadith in such a short period. He explains this himself, saying:

> "People wonder how I narrate so many Ahadith. The fact is that my Muhajir brothers remained busy in trade and my Ansar brothers did their farming, while I was always with the Prophet (Sallallaho alaihe wasallam). I was among the people of Suffah. I never cared to earn my living; I was contented with the little food that the Prophet (Sallallaho alaihe wasallam) could give me. I would be with the Prophet (Sallallaho alaihe wasallam) at times when no one else was there. I once complained to the Prophet (Sallallaho alaihe wasallam) about my poor memory. He said, 'Spread your shawl!' I did so. He made some signs on the shawl with his own hands and said, 'Now wrap this shawl around you.' I wrapped it around my breast. Since then, I never have forgotten anything that I have wished to remember."

The people of Suffah were residents in the Prophet's mosque. They had no regular source of income. They were the guests of the Prophet (Sallallaho alaihe wasallam), who transferred to them the Sadaqah and shared with them the gifts that he received. Abu Hurairah (Radhiyallaho anho) was one of them. He would, sometimes, go without food for days together and sometimes would behave like a lunatic, due to excessive hunger, as we have already seen in Chapter III. In spite of such difficulties, he was all the time occupied in memorising the sayings of the Prophet.

This enabled him to narrate such a large number of Ahadith Imaam Ibn Jauzi (Rahmatullahi alaih) has attributed as many as 5 374 Ahadith to him. Once he narrated the following Hadith:–

"A person participating in a funeral gets one Qeeraat of reward if he returns after the funeral service, but gets two Qeeraats of reward if he remains there till the burial is over, and one Qeeraat is weightier than mount Uhud."

Hadhrat Abdullah bin 'Umar (Radhiyallaho anho) heard this and doubted authenticity of the Hadith, saying:

"O, Abu Hurairah! Think before you speak."

Hadhrat Abu Hurairah (Radhiyallaho anho) got upset over this and took Hadhrat Abdullah bin Umar (Radhiyallaho anho) to Hadhrat 'Aishah (Radhiyallaho anha), and said to her:

"O, Ummul-Mo'minin, I request you to say by Allah if you have heard from the Prophet (Sallallaho alaihe wasallam) the Hadith regarding Qeeraats of reward?"

She said: "Yes. I have heard this Hadith."

Hadhrat Abu Hurairah (Radhiyallaho anho) then said to Hadhrat Abdullah bin Umar (Radhiyallaho anho):

"During the Prophet's time, I had no tree to plant in the orchard and no merchandise to sell in the market. I was always with the Prophet. My only job was to memorise what the Prophet said, and to eat only what he gave me."

Hadhrat Abdullah bin Umar (Radhiyallaho anho) said:

"No doubt. Of us all, you were the most constant in attendance to him and therefore most informed about the Prophet (Sallallaho alaihe wasallam)."

With all these achievements, Hadhrat Abu Hurairah (Radhiyallaho anho) says:

"I recite Istighfar 12000 time daily."

He had a piece of thread with 1000 knots. He would not go to sleep until he had said Subhanallah on all of these knots.

7. Death of Musailamah and Compilation of Qur'an.

Musailamah was an imposter who called himself a Prophet, even during the life time of the Prophet (Sallallaho alaihe wasallam). After the death of the Prophet (Sallallaho alaihe wasallam), people of the weak faith, especially among wandering Arabs, began to desert Islam and become renegades. Musailamah took advantage of the situation and succeeded in causing a large number of people to fall a prey to his seduction. Abu Bakr (Radhiyallaho anho) decided to put a stop to this onslaught on Islam. A fierce battle was fought with him, in which the Muslims triumphed with the help of Allah, and Musailamah was killed. A good number of Sahabah, including many Huffaz, however, lost their lives. After this battle, Hadhrat Umar (Radhiyallaho anho) went to Hadhrat Abu Bakr (Radhiyallaho anho) and said:

> "Many Huffaz gave been slain in this battle. I am afraid we are likely to lose a good portion of the Qur'an if we fight a few more battles and suffer loss of Hufaaz at this rate. I, therefore, suggest that the Qur'an may be compiled and preserved in the form of one complete book."

Hadhrat Abu Bakr (Radhiyallaho anho) remarked:

> "How can I venture on a thing that was not done in the life of the Prophet (Sallallaho alaihe wasallam)?"

But Hadhrat Umar (Radhiyallaho anho) pressed his point so much that Hadhrat Abu Bakr (Radhiyallaho anho) agreed to it. He sent for Hadhrat Zaid bin Thabit (Radhiyallaho anho) and informed him of what had passed between him and Umar (Radhiyallaho anho), and then said:

> "You are young and intelligent. Everybody considers you trustworthy. Moreover you were charged by the Prophet (Sallallaho alaihe wasallam) with the writing of the Qur'an during his life time. I, therefore, request you to go to the people and collect the Qur'an from them and compile it in the form of a book."

Hadhrat Zaid (Radhiyallaho anho) says:

> "By Allah, if Abu Bakr (Radhiyallaho anho) had asked me to shift a mountain from one place to another, it would not have been so hard for me as the compilation of the Qur'an. I said, 'How do you both dare to take up a thing which was not done by the Prophet (Sallallaho

alaihe wasallam)?" They explained to me their point, till Allah made the truth dawn on me, and I also was convinced of the importance of the task. I then started going to the people and collecting the Qur'an from those who had written it and from those who had learnt it by heart, till the final collection was ready."

Look at the spirit of the Sahabah as regards their strictly following the Prophet (Sallallaho alaihe wasallam). Shifting of a mountain from its position was not so difficult for them as doing a thing that they had not seen the Prophet (Sallallaho alaihe wasallam) doing. Allah gave them the honour of doing the greatest service to Islam by compiling the Qur'an, which is the source-book of Islam. Hadhrat Zaid (Radhiyallaho anho) was so particular and cautious that he would accept the fragments only when these were proved to be written during the Prophet's time and after they were duly corroborated by the recitation of those who had preserved the Qur'an in their hearts. No doubt, he had to go from door to door and person to person, but Allah caused, thanks to his labours, every word revealed by Him to be collected and compiled. He was constantly assisted by Hadhrat Ubayy bin Ka'ab (Radhiyallaho anho), whom the Prophet (Sallallaho alaihe wasallam) had declared a great expert in Qur'anic knowledge. The Muslims of all times are highly indebted to the Sahabah for their marvellous achievement.

8. Hadhrat Ibn Mas'ood's (Radhiyallaho anho) Cautiousness About Hadith:

Hadhrat Abdullah bin Mas'ood (Radhiyallaho anho) is one of those eminent Sahabah who were entrusted with the task of issuing Fatwa, even during the Prophet's (Sallallaho alaihe wasallam) time. He had been in the fold of Islam since its advent and was one of the emigrants to Abyssinia. He accompanied the Prophet (Sallallaho alaihe wasallam) in all his campaigns and worked as his attendant. He carried the shoes of the Prophet (Sallallaho alaihe wasallam), provided him with a pillow when he needed one, and brought him water for his Wudhu. He was therefore called "The Keeper of the shoes", "The Keeper of Pillow" and "The Manager for Wudhu". The Prophet (Sallallaho alaihe wasallam) once said:

"Abdullah bin Mas'ood (Radhiyallaho anho) is the

only person whom I can safely appoint as an Amir without consulting anybody."

He was permitted by the Prophet (Sallallaho alaihe wasallam) to visit him at all times. The Prophet (Sallallaho alaihe wasallam) is reported to have said:

(1) "If you want to recite the Qur'an as it was revealed to me, then copy the recitation of Abdullah bin Mas'ood."

(2) "Believe in what Abdullah bin Mas'ood (Radhiyallaho anho) narrates about me."

Hadhrat Abu Moosa Ash'ari (Radhiyallaho anho) says:

"Abdullah bin Masood (Radhiyallaho anho) and his mother visited the Prophet's (Sallallaho alaihe wasallam) house so often and were so at home there that the people of Yemen, who had come to see the Prophet (Sallallaho alaihe wasallam), took him as one of the Ahlul Bait (family member.)" Though he was so near to the Prophet (Sallallaho alaihe wasallam), yet he was very cautious about narrating the words of the Prophet (Sallallaho alaihe wasallam). Hadhrat Abu 'Amir Shaibani (Radhiyallaho anho) says:

"I stayed with Abdullah bin Mas'ood (Radhiyallaho anho) for one year. I never heard him attributing any words direct to the Prophet (Sallallaho alaihe wasallam). Whenever he intended doing so, he would shiver with fear."

Hadhrat 'Amr bin Maimoon (Radhiyallaho anho) says:

"I have been visiting Abdullah bin Mas'ood (Radhiyallaho anho) every Thursday for one year: I never heard him attributing any words direct to the Prophet (Sallallaho alaihe wasallam). Once he was narrating Hadith. When he uttered the words 'The Prophet (Sallallaho alaihe wasallam) said so,' then his body began to shiver, his eyes became full of tears, his forehead sweated, his veins swelled and he said 'Insha-Allah' the Prophet said so, or something like that, it might be something less or something more."

Look at the Sahabah's caution and care about Hadith.

The Prophet (Sallallaho alaihe wasallam) said:

"A person who attributes anything to me, which I have not said, is making his abode in the Hell."

This is why the Sahabah, though speaking and doing everything according to the instructions and example of the Prophet (Sallallaho alaihe wasallam), were afraid of attributing any words to the Prophet (Sallallaho alaihe wasallam), lest they should be different from what the Prophet (Sallallaho alaihe wasallam) had actually uttered. On the other hand, we go on quoting Ahadith without being sure of their authenticity and fear not the serious consequences of attributing wrongly anything to the Prophet (Sallallaho alaihe wasallam). It may be mentioned that the Fiqah Hanifiyah is based mostly on the Ahadith narrated by Hadhrat Abdullah bin Mas'ood (Radhiyallaho anho).

9. A Person Travels from Madinah to Damascus For One Hadith.

Kathir bin Qais narrates:

"I was sitting with Hadhrat Abu Darda (Radhiyallaho anho) in a musjid in Damascus, when a person came to him and said, 'O, Hadhrat Abu Darda (Radhiyallaho anho), I have come all the way from Madinah to learn one Hadith from you, as I understand you have heard it directly from the Prophet (Sallallaho alaihe wasallam)."

Hadhrat Abu Darda (Radhiyallaho anho):

"Have you any other business in Damascus?"

The person:

"No."

Hadhrat Abu Darda (Radhiyallaho anho):

"Are you sure that you have no other work in Damascus?"

The person:

"I have come to this place with the sole purpose of learning this Hadith."

Hadhrat Abu Darda (Radhiyallaho anho):

"Listen. I have heard the Prophet (Sallallaho aliahe wasallam) saying, 'Allah eases the way to Paradise for one who traverses some distance to seek knowledge. The angels spread their wings under his feet, and all things in heavens and earth (even the fish in the water) pray for his forgiveness. The superiority of a person possessing knowledge over a person doing worship is as the superiority of the moon over the stars. The Ulama are the inheritors of the Prophet (Sallallaho alaihe wassallam). The legacy of Prophets (Alaihimus-salaam) is neither gold nor silver. Their legacy is knowledge. A person who acquires knowledge acquires a great wealth."

Hadhrat Abu-Darda (Radhiyallaho anho) is foremost among the Sahabah who possessed very sound knowledge in religion. He is called 'Hakim-ul-Ummah' (The Sage of Islam). He once said:

"Before Islam, I lived on trade. After accepting Islam, I tried to combine the service of Allah with my business, but I could not do so. I therefore gave up business and devoted myself solely to the service of Allah. Now if I have a shop at the gate of a musjid and have no fear of losing a single Salaat thereby, and even if the shop gives me a daily profit of 40 dinars to spend the whole lot in the path of Allah, even then I am not willing to turn to business."

Somebody inquired the reason. He replied:—

"Because of the fear of reckoning."

He used to say: "I love death, so that I may meet Allah. I love destitution, so that I be meek. I love sickness, so that I be pardoned my sins."

In this story, we find a person travelling all the way from Madinah to Damascus for the sake of one Hadith. This was not at all hard for those people. Hadhrat Sha'abi (Rahmatullahi alaih) is a famous Muhaddith of Koofa. He once narrated a Hadith to one of his students and said:

"You are listening to this Hadith while sitting in your home town. People had to travel all their way to Madinah for even less important things, because Madinah was the only of seat learning in those days."

Saeed ibnul Musayyab (Rahmatullahi alaih) is a famous Tabi'ee. He says:

"For each Hadith that I have learnt, I had to travel on foot for days and nights together."

Imam Bukhari (Rahmatullahi alaih) was born in Shawwal 194 A.H. He started learning Hadith in 205 A.H. i.e., when he was only eleven. He had memorised all the books written by Abdullah bin Mubarak (Rahmatullahi alaih) while he was in his early teens. After collecting Ahadith from all the learned men of his own locality, he set out in 216 A.H. in search of further knowledge. His father died and he could not leave his widowed mother alone. He therefore took her with him on his long and strenuous journey to Balkh, Baghdad, Mecca, Basra, Koofah, Asqalan, Hims and Damascus. He collected all the available Ahadith from these seats of learning. He was accepted as an expert in Hadith, while he had not a single hair on his chin. He writes:

I was eighteen when I compiled the Fatwah of the Sahabah and Tabi'ees."

Hashad (Rahmatullahi alaihe) and one of his companions say:–

"Bukhari and we two used to go together to the same teacher. We noted down all the Ahadith that we learnt, but he wrote nothing. After many days we said to him, 'Bukhari, you are wasting your time.' He kept quiet. When we admonished him again and again, he said, 'You are now annoying me too much. Bring your notes.' We brought our notes, which covered about 15,000 Ahadith. He, to our utter amazement, recited all those Ahadith by heart."

10. Hadhrat Ibn Abbas's (Radhiyallaho anho) Thirst For Knowledge.

Hadhrat Abdullah bin Abbas (Radhiyallaho anho) says:

"After the passing away of the Prophet (Sallallaho alaihe wasallam), I said to an Ansari friend of mine. The Prophet (Sallallaho alaihe wasallam) is not now with us. But a large number of Sahabah are still among us. Let us go to them and get knowledge of the Islamic practices". He said. 'Who is going to approach you for learning a regulation in the presence of these eminent Sahabah?' I was not discouraged. I kept up my quest for knowledge and approached every person who was supposed to have heard something from the Prophet (Sallallaho alaihe wasallam). I managed to gather substantial information from the Ansar. If on my visit to someone of the Sahabah, I found him asleep, I spread my shawl at the gate and sat waiting. Sometimes my face and body would get covered with dust, but I kept sitting till they woke and I was able to contact them. Some of them said: 'Abdullah you are the cousin of the Prophet (Sallallaho alaihe wasallam); you could have sent for us. Why did you take the trouble of coming to our places?' I said to them: 'I must come to you, for I am a student and you are my teachers.' Some people for whom I had waited said: 'Since when have you been waiting for us?' I informed them that I had been sitting there for a pretty long time. They said: 'What a pity! You could have awakened us from our sleep.' I said: 'I did not like to disturb you for my own sake.' I thus carried on my pursuits, till there came a time when people began to flock to me for learning. My Ansari friend realised this at that time and remarked. 'This boy has surely proved himself more sensible than us.''

It was this devotion to knowledge, which caused Hadhrat Abdullah bin Abbas (Radhiyallaho anho) to be known as Hibr-ul-Ummat (the most learned man of Islam) and Bahrul Ulum (ocean of knowledge) in his time. At the time of his death, he was in Taif. Hadhrat Muhammad bin Ali (Radhiyallaho anho) led the funeral service and said:

"Today we have lost our godly leader."

Hadhrat Abdullah bin Umar (Radhiyallaho anho) says:

"Abdullah bin Abbas (Radhiyallaho anho) is noted for his knowledge of the occasions when various verses of the Qur'an were revealed."

According to Hadhrat Umar (Radhiyallaho anho) Hadhrat Ibne Abbas (Radhiyallaho anho) is one of the most eminent Ulama of Islam. This is all due to his hard labour in acquiring knowledge. Had he considered himself a member of the Prophet's family (Sallallaho alaihe wasallam), and as such demanded respect from the people instead of going to them for knowledge, he could not have attained this position. The Prophet (Sallallaho alaihe wasallam) has said:

"Be most humble and respectful to persons from whom you receive knowledge."

Mujahid says: "A proud or shy student cannot gain much."

Hadhrat Ali (Radhiyallaho anho) says:

"I am a slave to the person who has taught me even a single word. He may sell me or set me free."

Hadhrat Yahya bin Kathir (Rahmatullahi alaih) says:

"Knowledge and easy living cannot go hand in hand."

Hadhrat Imam Shaf'i (Rahmatullah alaih) says:

"A student who learns half-heartedly and ungratefully can never succeed. A student who is humble and hard-living often reaches his goal."

Mughirah says: "We feared our teacher Hadhrat Ibrahim (Rahmatullah alaih) more than even the kings of our times."

Hadhrat Bukhari (Rahmatullah alaih) writes about Yahya bin Ma'een, the famous Mohaddith:

"I have never seen a person more respectful to the Muhaddithin than Yahya."

Imam Abu Yusuf (Rahmatullah alaih) says:

"I have heard from eminent people that a student who does not respect his teacher is never successful."

This story shows that Hadhrat Abdullah bin Abbas (Radhiyallaho anho) was very humble and respectful to those from whom he learnt Islam. It also shows his devotion to knowledge. He did not mind any amount of labour or inconvenience in going to persons who had some knowledge of Hadith. In fact, nothing can be achieved without inconvenience. As the Arabic proverb goes

مَنْ طَلَبَ الْعُلٰى سَهِرَ اللَّيَالِىْ

"A person who wishes to excell others must burn the midnight oil."

It is said about Hadhrat Harith bin Yazid, Hadhrat Ibn Shubrumah, Hadhrat Qa'qaa, and Hadhrat Mughirah (Rahmatullahi alaihim) that they held discussions over religious matters among themselves after Isha and would not disperse before Azaan of Fajr. Hadhrat Laith bin Sa'eed (Rahmatullah alaih) says:

> "Imam Zuhri (Rahmatullah alaih) sat after Isha with Wudhu and continued his discussion on Hadith till it was Fajr."

Darawardi says:

> "I saw Imam Abu Hanifa and Imam Malik in the Prophet's musjid after Isha, discussing some religious point very calmly and without offending each other. They dispersed only after performing Fajr Salaat."

Ibn Furat Baghdadi (Rahmatullah alaih)—a Muhaddith, left on his death, eighteen boxes full of books. Most of these books were written in his own hand. He is famous among Muhaddithin for his authentic and systematic record.

Ibn Jauzi (Rahmatullah alaih) is another famous Muhaddith. He was brought up as an orphan, as he lost his father when he was only three. He was so studious that he would not leave his house except for Jum'uah prayer. He once declared from the pulpit, pointing to his fingers:

> "With these fingers I have written or copied no less than two thousand books."

He was himself the author of more than two hundred and fifty books. It is said that he never remained idle. He used to write four parts of a book daily. His lessons were so popular that as many as 100000 students at a time listened to him. The kings, their ministers and chiefs would also attend his lectures. He himself says:

> "As many as 100000 disciples have pledged devotion to me, and not less than 20000 disbelievers have accepted Islam at my hands."

He also had to suffer much at the hands of Shiahs, who were in power those days. While mending his reed pen, he preserved the chips, and at the time of his death expressed the desire that those chips be used for warming the water for washing his dead body. It is said that not only the preserved stock was sufficient for warming water, but a part was still left unused.

Yahya bin Ma'een (Rahmatullah alaih) is a famous shaikh of Ahadith. He says:

> "I have written one million Ahadith with my own hand"

Ibn Jarir Tabari (Rahmatullah alaih) is a historian of great fame. He is an authority on the history of the Sahabah and Tabien. For forty years, he wrote 80 pages daily. After his death, his output in written work (since his maturity) was calculated to come to 28 pages daily. The book on history written by him which is generally available is very famous and popular. When he planned to write this book, he said to the people round him:

> "You will be pleased to learn that I intend writing a book on world history.

They inquired: "How big will that book be?"

He said: "About 30 000 leaves."

They remarked: "Who will live to finish this book?"

He said: "Inna lillahi wa inna ilaihi raaji-oon. People have become so unaspiring."

He then decided to condense the material, which still covered 6 000 pages. The same story is reported about his book on the meaning and commentary of the Qu'ran. This is also a very famous and popular book.

Daaraqutni (Rahmatullah alaih) is a famous writer on Hadith. He travelled to Baghdad, Basrah, Koofah, Wasit, Egypt and Syria for learning Hadith. Once he was attending the class of his teacher. During the teacher's lecture he was once seen copying from a certain book. One of the fellow students admonished him saying:

> "How can you listen to the Shaikh while doing that work?"

He said: "There is a difference in my listening and yours. Tell me how many Hadiths has the Shaikh recited so far?"

The student began to think. Daaraqutni (Rahmatullah alaih) said:

> "Now let me tell you. The Shaikh has so far recited eighteen Hadiths and these are . . ."

He then repeated all the eighteen Ahadiths that the Shaikh had recited in the same order, quoting the chain of narration in each case.

Hafiz Athram (Rahmatullah alaih) is a Muhaddith. He had a wonderful capacity for memorising Ahadith. Once he was in Mecca for Hajj. Two reputed Shaikhs from Khurasan were holding their lectures on Hadith in the Haram separately, and a large number of people were listening to each Shaikh. He sat between the two groups and noted down the lectures of both the Shaikhs at one and the same time.

Abdullah bin Mubarak (Rahmatullah alaih) is a Mohaddith of great fame. His labours and efforts in collecting Hadiths are known to everybody. He says:

"I have learnt Hadith from four thousand teachers."

Ali bin Hasan (Rahmatullah alaih) says:

"It was a very cold night when I and Ibn Mubarak stepped out from the musjid after Isha. We continued discussion on a Hadith while standing there, till we heard the Azaan for Fajr."

Humaidi (Rahmatullah alaih) is a Muhaddith, who has combined Bukhari and Muslim in one compilation. It is said that he wrote throughout the night. When it was very hot, he would write while sitting in a tub of water. He also wrote poetry. The following verses have been written by him:—

لِقَآءُ النَّاسِ لَيْسَ يُفِيْدُ شَيْئًا سِوَى الْهَذْيَانِ مِنْ قِيْلٍ وَّقَالِ

فَاَقْلِلْ مِنْ لِقَاءِ النَّاسِ اِلَّا لِاَخْذِ الْعِلْمِ اَوْ اِصْلَاحِ حَالِ

Mixing with people does not benefit
Beyond waste of time in gossip;
Don't go to the people, except
For acquiring knowledge and piety

Imam Tabrani (Rahmatullah alaih) is a reputed Muhaddith and author of numerous books. Somebody inquired:

"How could you write so many books, Shaikh?"

He replied: "I have been on my mat for thirty years."

Abul Abbas Shirazi (Rahmatullah alaih) says:

"I have learnt 300000 Ahadith from Tabrani."

Imam Abu Hanifa (Rahmatullah alaih) laboured very hard in going deep into those Ahadiths which contradicted some others. Koofah was the centre of Islamic learning in those days. He had collected Hadith from all the Muhaddithin of that place. Whenever a Muhaddith from outside came to Koofah, he sent his students to him to ascertain if he knew any such Hadith that was not known to him. The Imam had established a circle where scholars of Hadith, Fiqah, and Philology gathered together. They had discussions on regulations about Islamic practices. Sometimes the discussions continued for one month before a point was agreed upon, and written in the book of regulations for the people of his school of thought.

Imam Tirmizi (Rahmatullah alaih) is known to one and all. He was unique in his capacity for memorising and retaining Ahadith. His memory was marvellous. Some Muhaddithin once tested his memory. They recited before him forty-one Hadiths. Imam Tirmizi (Radmatullah alaih) immediately repeated all of them. He himself writes:

> "On my way to Mecca, I copied two parts from the collections of Hadith by a Shaikh. I happened to come across that Shaikh personally. I said to him, 'I have copied two parts of your collections. I wish to compare those Hadiths by listening to them directly from you.' The Shaikh agreed. While going to his place I, by mistake, took a blank book instead of the note book in which I had copied the Hadiths. The Shaikh started reciting the Hadiths, while I held the blank book in my hand. When he noticed it, he was very angry with me. I explained to him how that had happened, and said, 'Shaikh, your time is not wasted. I remember everything that you have said.' He did not believe me and asked me to repeat all that he had recited. I repeated all the Ahadith. He thought I had memorised them before I came to him. I said, 'You may recite some other Hadiths.' He recited forty new Hadiths. I repeated all of them without any error."

It is very difficult to work and labour as hard as these Muhaddithin did in collecting, memorising and propagating Hadith. It is difficult even to cover all such stories. Qartamah (Rahmatullah alaih) is a Muhaddith who is not very famous. One of his students, Daud, says:

> "People speak about the memory of Abu Hatim (Rahmatullah alaih). I have never seen a person with better memory than Qartamah. Once he said to me, "Pick any of the books from my library. I shall recite it from my memory." I picked up 'Kitabul-Ashribah.' He recited the whole book in the reverse order i.e., reading from the end to the beginning of each chapter."

Abu Zur'ah (Rahmatullahi alaih) says:

> "Imam Ahmad bin Hambal (Rahmatullah alaih) remembered one million Ahadith by heart. I have collected 100 000 Ahadith and I know 30 000 of them by heart."

Khafaf (Rahmatullah alaih) says:

> 'Ishaq (Rahmatulla alaih) once dictated to us 11000 Ahadith from his memory. He then repeated all of them in the same order, with no error at all."

Abu Sa'd Isbahani, (Rahmatullah alaih) when he was only sixteen, left from Baghdad to learn Hadith from Abu Nasr (Rahmatullah alaih). He heard about his death on the way. He cried bitterly like a child, and would say:

> "How shall I know the chain of narrators of his Hadiths?"

Such crying is not possible without love and devotion. He knew the 'Muslim' collection of Ahadith by heart and taught the book to his puplis from memory.

Abu Umar Dharir (Rahmatullah alaih) was blind by birth, but is counted among the Huffaaz of Hadith. He was an expert in History, Fiqah, Law of inheritance and mathematics.

Abul Husain Isfahani (Rahmatullah alaih) remembered the Bukhari and Muslim compilations both by heart. Bukhari was so deeply fixed in his memory that he would give the chain of narrators for any text or vice versa.

Shaikh Taqi-ud-Din Ba'albakki (Rahmatullah alaih) memorised the 'Muslim' in four months. He was also Hafiz of Hadith common in Muslim's and Bukhari's compilations. He was a saint, and many miracles are attributed to him. He had also memorised the Qur'an. It is said that Soorah Al-An'aam was memorised by him in one day.

Ibnus-Sunni (Rahmatullah alaih) is a famous pupil of Imam Nasai (Rahmatullah alaih). He was writing Hadith even upto the last moments of his life. His son says:

"My father was writing Hadith when he put aside the pen, raised his hands in prayer and breathed his last."

Allamah Saaji (Rahmatullah alaih) mastered Fiqah in his teens. Then he began to acquire knowledge about Hadith. He stayed in Herat for ten years and wrote the whole of 'Tirmizi' six times during that stay. His teacher Ibn Mandah (Rahmatullah alaih) died while teaching him 'Gharaib Sho'bah' after Isha.

Abu-Umar Khafaf (Rahmatullah alaih) remembered 100 000 hadiths by heart. More than 100 000 persons attended the lectures of Asim bin Ali (Rahmatullah alaih) (Shaikh of Imam Bukhari) when he was in Baghdad. One day, an audience of 120 000 was estimated during his lecture. The words uttered by him were relayed a number of times, before these could be heard by all the people. The words "Al-Laith (Rahmatullah alaih) reported to me," uttered by him, once had to be relayed fourteen times.

Abu Muslim Basri (Rahmatullah alaih) on reaching Baghdad took his class to a big ground. Seven hundred men were relaying his lecture. 40 000 ink-pots, used for taking down his lecture, were counted in one lecture. There were many more who simply listened. In the lectures by Faryabi (Rahmatullah alaih) there used to be 316 persons who would relay his words to enable people to write these down. It was this labour and devotion which has caused the sacred knowledge to live upto our time.

Imam Bukhari (Rahmatullah alaih) says:

"I compiled my collection of 7 275 Ahadith by selection from 600 000. I have been saying Salaat of 2 rakaats before writing each Hadith".

When Imaam Bukhari (Rahmatullah alaih) came to Baghdad, the Muhaddithin tested his knowledge. Ten persons were nominated for the test. Each of these persons selected ten Ahadith of his choice and, after making some changes in the wording, recited each Hadith before Imam Bukhari (Rahmatullah alaih). On each recital, he would say:

"I do not know such Hadith."

When all had finished, he addressed each man saying:

"Brother, the first Hadith you recited as such (reciting as the man had done), but actually it is such (reciting the correct wording) . . . and so on."

He repeated all the hundred Ahadith first in the form in which those men had recited, and again in the correct form in that very order.

Imam Muslim (Rahmatullah alaih) started learning Hadith when he was fourteen, and remained engaged in that till his death. He says:

"I have compiled my book of 12 000 after selecting from 300 000 Ahadith."

Abu Daud (Rahmatullah alaih) says:

"I had collected 500 000 Ahadith, but I selected only 4 800 for inclusion in my book."

Yusuf Muzi (Rahmatullah alaih) is a famous Muhadith. He is an Imam in the science of Asmaa-ur Rijaal (classification of reporting persons). After learning Fiqh and Hadith from the teachers in his own town he went to Mecca, Madinah, Halb, Hamat Ba'albak etc, in search of further knowledge. He is the writer of many books. 'Tahzib-ul-Kamal' is in 200 parts and 'Kitab-ul-Atraaf' has more than 80 parts. He often kept quiet and spoke very little. Most of the time, he was engaged in reading or writing. He suffered at the hands of his enemies, who were jealous of him, but he never retaliated.

It is really very difficult to cover all the stories of other illustrious people about their service to knowledge. The details of their toils cannot be covered even in several volumes. What has been written above is only meant to give a few glimpses of the pains that our elders in Islam have taken in the development of knowledge about Hadith and leaving it to us in such an accomplished form. Let those people who profess to seek knowledge see for themselves what sacrifices they are really making in this field. It is futile to hope that the knowledge about the Prophet (Sallalaho alaihe wasallam), which has thus reached us, will be spread and brought into practice while we remain absorbed in our luxuries, comforts, pleasures and other worldly engagements.

CHAPTER IX

PLEASING THE PROPHET (SALLALLAHO ALAIHE WASALLAM)

As we have already seen from the stories in previous chapters, obedience to Allah and His Prophet (Sallallaho alaihe wasallam) was the guiding factor in the Sahabah's life. Stories given exclusively in this chapter are to enable us to examine our way of living and see how far we are prepared to please Allah and His Prophet (Sallallaho alihe wasallam), in order to deserve the necessary progress and other blessings, which the Sahabah received. If we are desirous of similar results, we shall have to live the way they lived.

1. Hadhrat Ibn Amr (Radhiyallaho anho) Burns His Sheet.

Hadhrat Abdullah bin Amr ibnul Aas (Radhiyallaho anho) says:

> "Once we were accompanying the Prophet (Sallallaho alaihe wasallam) on a journey. I went to see him and I was wearing a saffron coloured sheet. He said to me, 'What is this that you are wearing?' I felt that he did not like my wearing a dress of that colour. When I reached home, I found a fire burning in the hearth. I threw my garment into the fire. The next day when I went to the Prophet (Sallallaho alaihe wasallam), he inquired, 'Where is that sheet?' I told him what I had done with it. He remarked, "You could have given it to one of the ladies in your house, women are permitted to wear clothes of that colour."

In fact, Abdullah was so much perturbed at the Prophet (Sallallaho alaihe wasallam's) displeasure that he did not hesitate to avail of the first opportunity of doing away with the sheet that caused the displeasure. He did not even think of making any other use of that garment. If we had been in his place, we would have thought of some excuse or the other for keeping it, or at least finding some other use for it.

2. An Ansari razes a building to the ground.

The Prophet (Sallallaho alaihe wasallam) was once passing through a street of Madinah when he saw a building with a dome. He inquired of the companions, "What is this?" They informed him that it was a new building built by one of the Ansar. The Prophet (Sallallaho alaihe wasallam) ramained silent. At some other time, the Ansari who had built that house came to the Prophet (Sallallaho alaihe wasallam) and greeted him with 'Assalamo alaikum'. The Prophet (Sallallaho alaihe wasallam) turned his face from him. He repeated the greetings, but the Prophet (Sallallaho alaihe wasallam) again gave him the cold shoulder. He was very much shocked to notice the Prophet's aversion for him. When he investigated, he was given the account of the Prophet's inquring about his new building. He immediately went and razed the new building to the ground, and did not even inform the Prophet (Sallallaho alaihe wasallam) about his action. The Prophet (Sallallaho alaihe wasallam) happened to pass that way again. He inquired:

> "Where is that building with a dome that I saw at this spot last time?"

The Sahabah informed him of Ansari's razing it to the ground, as it had been the likely cause of the Prophet's displeasure. He remarked.

> "Every new structure is a sinful burden for its owner, except that which is absolutely essential."

This is a matter of love and devotion. The Sahabah could not bear the displeasure of the Prophet (Sallallaho alaihe wasallam) and, no sooner did they smell such a thing, than they removed the cause thereof at all costs. Again the person does not even inform the Prophet (Sallallaho alaihe wasallam) of his drastic action in removing the cause of his displeasure, till he himself happened to notice it. The Prophet (Sallallaho alaihe wasallam) had a special aversion for the people wasting their money on buildings. His own house was a temporary structure of date palm, with mats serving the purpose of walls to secure privacy. Once, during his absence from Madinah, Ummul Mo'minin Umme Salma (Radhiallaho anha) who had some money in hand, erected walls of unbaked bricks for her house. When the Prophet (Sallallaho alaihe wasallam) returned from his journey, he asked her:

"Why did you do this?"

She replied: "O, Prophet of Allah. This is only to have better privacy."

The Prophet (Sallallaho alaihe wasallam) remarked:

"The worst use of money is to spend it in raising up buildings."

Hadhrat Abdullah bin Amr (Radhiyallaho anho) narrates:

"I and my mother were once repairing a wall of our house. The Prophet (Sallallaho alaihe wasallam) happened to see us working and remarked: 'Your own fall (death) is more at hand than the fall of this wall."

3. Sahabah's Discard of Red Sheets of Saddle Cloth.

Hadhrat Rafe' (Radhiyallaho anho) says:

"We were once with the Prophet (Sallallaho alaihe wasallam) on a journey. The sheets that we had spread on our camels were decorated with red thread work on the borders. The Prophet (Sallallaho alaihe wasallam) said, 'I notice that the red colour has begun to catch your fancy.' We stood up and dispersed in confusion at this rebuke; so much so that our camels seeing our bewilderment began to run about. We immediately removed the sheets from their backs."

We are surprised on hearing such stories about Sahabah, as we are living in a different atmosphere with quite a different frame of mind. When the Truce of Hudeybiyah was being negotiated, Urwah bin Mas'ood (Radhiyallaho anho) an envoy of Qureysh, had an opportunity of studying very carefully the behaviour of Sahabah. When he returned to his people, he said to them:

"I have been to the courts of great kings and monarchs as an envoy. I have met the Emperors of Persia, Rome and Abyssinia. Nowhere have I seen people around a sovereign so respectful to him as I saw the companions of Muhammad (Sallallaho alaihe wasallam). When he spits, his sputum is not allowed to fall on the ground.

It is taken by somebody in his hands to anoint his face and body therewith. When he issues some order, every person hastens to carry it out. When he makes Wudhu, his companions race one with another to snatch the water trickling down from his limbs, in such a way that an observer would think they are going to fight over that water. When he speaks, everybody is silent as if they were dumb. Nobody raises his eyes to look at him, out of respect for him."

4. Hadhrat Waa'il (Radhiyallaho anho) Has His Hair Cut.

Hadhrat Waa'il bin Hajar (Radhiyallaho anho) says:

> "I once visited the Prophet (Sallallaho alaihe wasallam) when the hair on my head was long. While I was sitting with him, he uttered the words. 'Zubab, Zubab' (Meaning something evil or ominous). I though he was referring to my hair. I returned home and had my hair cut. Next day when I again went to him, he said, 'I never referred to your hair when I uttered those words yesterday. Any how, it is good that you had your hair cut."

This shows the frame of mind of those people. They tolerated no delay in acting upon the wishes of the Prophet (Sallallaho alaihe wasallam), whether they understood it rightly or wrongly. They never thought it necessary to further inquire or clarify.

In the early years, talking in Salaat was permissible. Once Hadhrat Abdullah bin Mas'ood (Radhiyallaho anho) visited the Prophet (Sallallaho alaihe wasallam) while he was saying his Salaat. He greated him with "Assallamo'a-laikum" but received no reply, as to talk in Salaat had meanwhile been forbidden. He says:

> "For receiving no reply, all sorts of explanations began to haunt my mind. I thought perhaps he is displeased with me, or he is angry with me on such and such account, and so on.' At last when the Prophet (Sallallaho alaihe wasallam) finished his Salaat and informed me that Allah had forbidden talking in Salaat I heaved a sigh of relief."

5. Hadhrat Khuraim Asadi (Radhiyallaho anho) gives up what is not liked by the Prophet:

Hadhrat Suhail bin Hanzalah (Radhiyallaho anho) was living a life of seclusion in Damascus. He did not mix with people, nor did he go anywhere. He was either busy in Salaat or in Zikr throughout the day. While going to musjid, he would pass by Hadhrat Abu Darda (Radhiyallaho anho), one of the eminent Sahabah. Abu Darda (Radhiyallaho anho) would say to him:

> "O, Suhail! Let us hear some good words from you. We shall gain much, though you will lose nothing."

Hadhrat Suhail (Radhiyallaho anho) would then relate something that he had heard from the Prophet (Sallallaho alaihe wasallam), or some event that he had seen in his life time. Once on Hadhrat Abu Darda (Radhiyallaho anho's) request as usual, he said:

> "Once the Prophet (Sallallaho alaihe wasallam) made a mention of Hadhrat Khuraim Asadi (Radhiyallaho anho) and said, "He is a good man except for two habits, viz, he keeps the hair of his head too long and he allows his izaar to go below his ankles. When Khuraim learnt this, he immediately cut the hair up to his ears and began to keep his izaar up to the middle of the calf of his leg."

6. Hadhrat Ibn Umar (Radhiyallaho anho) gives up speaking with his son.

Hadhrat Abdullah bin Umar (Radhiyallaho anho) once said:

> "I have heard the Prophet (Sallallaho alaihe wasallam) saying, 'Allow your women to go to the musjid.'"

One of his sons remarked:

> "We cannot allow our women to go to the musjid, as this may lead to corruption later on."

Hadhrat Ibn Umar (Radhiyallaho anho) became very angry and rebuked his son, saying:

> "When I tell you that the Prophet (Sallallaho alaihe wasallam) has allowed our women folk to go to musjid, how dare you say that you cannot allow them."

He then, refused to speak to him throughout his life.

Hadhrat Ibn Umar (Radhiyallaho anho's) son obviously had no intention of disobeying the Prophet (Sallallaho alaihe wasallam). He feared corruption in allowing the women-folk of that time to go to the musjid. For the same reason, Hadhrat Aishah (Radhiyallaho anha) is reported to have said:

> "If the Prophet (Sallallaho alaihe wasallam) had seen the women of our time, he would have stopped them from going to the musjid."

Now, Hadhrat Aishah (Radhiyallaho anha) said this not very long after the death of the Prophet (Sallallaho alaihe wasallam). Notwithstanding all this, Hadhrat Ibn Umar (Radhiyallaho anho) could not tolerate his son refusing to do something which the Prophet (Sallallaho alaihe wasallam) had desired to be done, and he gave up talking to him for the rest of his life. The Sahabah sometimes found themselves faced with a dilemma regarding the women visiting the musjid. On the one hand, there was the explicit desire of the Prophet (Sallallaho alaihe wasallam) in favour of permitting them to go to the musjid, and on the other there was the possibility of looseness in society (the signs of which were becoming visible) that demanded an immediate check on this permission. Hadhrat 'Atikah (Radhiyallaho anha) the wife of Hadhrat Umar (Radhiyallaho anho) went to musjid regularly but Umar (Radhiyallaho anho) did not like it. Somebody told her that Hadhrat Umar (Radhiyallaho anho) did not like her going to the musjid. She said:

> "Why does he not prevent me from doing it then?"

After the death of Hadhrat Umar (Radhiyallaho anho) Hadhrat 'Atikah (Radhiyallaho anha) was married to Hadhrat Zubair (Radhiyallaho anho). He also did not like her going to musjid, but could not check her for the above obvious reason. Once he sat in her way to musjid and, as she passed by him, he teased her. In the dark, she could not make out who it was. After this incident, she stopped going to musjid. When Zubair inquired of her:

> "Why do not you go to the musjid now?"

She replied: "Times have changed."

7. Hadhrat Ibn Umar (Radhiyallaho anho) Replies to a Question.

Somebody said to Hadhrat Ibn Umar (Radhiyallaho anho):

"Allah has said in the Qur'an something about Salaat in peace and Salaat in fear, but He has not said anything about Salaat during a journey."

He replied: "O, my nephew! Allah sent Muhammad (Sallallaho alaihe wasallam) as his Apostle to us, when we were ignorant and knew nothing. We must do what we have seen him doing."

This shows that it is not necessary that each and every regulation should be explicitly mentioned in the Qur'an. The acts of the Prophet (Sallallaho alaihe wasallam) is a very good guide for our practice. The Prophet (Sallallaho alaihe wasallam) says:

"I have been given the Qur'an and also other commandments. Beware of the time, which is coming shortly, when carefree people sitting on their couches will say, 'Stick to the Qur'an only. Carry out only the commandments contained therein.'"

Such corrupted views are generally inspired by arrogance due to wealth, and perhaps that is why the word "carefree" is used for such people.

8. Hadhrat Ibn Mughaffal (Radhiyallaho anho) Discontinues Relations With His Nephew.

A young nephew of Hadhrat Abdullah-bin-Mughaffal (Radhiyallaho allaho anho) was playing 'Khazaf'. He said to him:

"O nephew! Stop doing that. The Prophet (Sallallaho alaihe wasallam) has prohibited this play. It can neither shoot a bird nor harm an enemy. It is likely to injure somebody's eye or tooth.

The boy stopped playing but, after some time when he thought that his uncle was not watching him, he started doing it again Hadhrat Ibne-Mughaffal (Radhiyallaho anha) was very angry and said:

"How dare you do a thing after knowing that the Prophet (Sallallaho alaihe wasallam) has forbidden it?

By Allah! I will never speak to you again. I will never visit you when you are sick, nor join your funeral if you die during my life time."

'Khazaf' is a game in which a pebble is placed on the thumb and then thrown with the force of other fingers. Children are fond of playing such games. Hadhrat Ibn Mughaffal (Radhiyallaho anho) could not tolerate his nephew's ignoring the words of the Prophet (Sallallaho alaihe wasallam). Do we not know the instructions of the Prophet (Sallallaho alaihe wasallam) about many things we are wont to do from morning till evening? How much regard do we have in our hearts for his verdict? Let everybody ponder over it himself and answer.

9. Hadhrat Ibn Hizam (Radhiyallaho anho) Gives up Begging.

Hadhrat Hakim bin Hizam (Radhiyallaho anho) came to the Prophet (Sallallaho alaihe wasallam) and begged him for help. He gave him something. Next time he came and asked for something. The Prophet (Sallallaho alaihe wasallam) gave him something this time also. When he came to beg the third time, the Prophet (Sallallaho alaihe wasallam), after giving him something, said:

"Hakim! Money has a deceptive appearance. It appears to be very sweet (but it is really not so). It is a blessing when earned with contentment of heart, but there is no satisfaction in it when it is got with greed."

Hakim said: "O, Prophet of Allah, I will not bother anybody after this."

Hadhrat Abu Bakr (Radhiyallaho anho) in the time of his Khilafat offered to help Hakim from Baitul Mal, but he refused. Again Umar (Radhiyallaho anho) as Amir-ul-Mominin requested Hakim many times to accept something from him, but he did not agree.

Our greed and avarice know no bounds; this is why we find no blessings in what we earn.

10. Hadhrat Huzaifah (Radhiyallaho anho) Goes For Spying.

Hadhrat Huzaifah (Radhiyallaho anho) narattes:

"In the war of the Trench, we were facing a very big

army of the enemy, comprising of non-believers from Mecca and other such groups. At the same time, the Jews of Banu Quraizah in Madinah were preparing to stab us in the back, and we apprehended their plundering our houses and families, for all of us were outside defending Madinah against the invaders. The Munafiqin started asking permission from the Prophet (Sallallaho alaihe wasallam) to go back to Madinah, on the pretext of their homes being unattended and open to the enemy. He permitted every one of them. During those days of trial, one night it was unusually very dark and windy, It was so dark that one could not see one's own hand, and the wind was blowing wildly. The Munafiqin were returning to their homes. We, three hundred strong, were sticking to our posts. The Prophet (Sallallaho alaihe wasallam) approached every one and made enquiries about him. I had no arms to defend myself, nor clothes to resist the cold. I had only one small sheet, which belonged to my wife and was lent to me. I wrapped it round my loins and sat with my knees clinging to the ground. When the Prophet (Sallallaho alaihe wasallam) passed by me, he said, 'Who are you? I said, 'Huzaifah!' I could not stand up due to severe cold and I clung to the ground more tightly with shame. He said, 'Huzaifah, stand up and go to the enemy camp and bring us their news.' Of all the Sahabah, I was the most ill-equipped, both against the enemy and against the cold that night, but as soon as I got the order I stood up and left for the enemy camp. As I was going, the Prophet (Sallallaho alaihe wasallam) prayed for me saying, 'O Allah! Protect him from all directions.' Immediately after his prayer, I was completely relieved of my fear and cold. I felt as if I were walking in a warm and peaceful atmosphere. The Prophet (Sallallaho alaihe wasallam) warned me thus, 'Return immediately after observing what they are doing. Do not take any other step.' When I reached the enemy camp, I found a fire burning and people sitting round it. Each person warmed his hands before the fire and then rubbed them over his abdomen. The shouts of retreat were heard from all directions. Every one was shouting to the people of his clan to pack up and go back. The wind was causing the stones to fly and strike against their tents. The guy ropes of the tents were breaking and the animals were dying. I found Abu

Sufyan, the Commander-in-Chief of the enemy forces, sitting near the fire warming himself. I thought of finishing him off. I had actually taken out an arrow from my quiver and placed it in my bow, when I remembered the directive of the Prophet (Sallallaho alaihe wasallam). I put the arrow back into the quiver. While I was among them, they seemed to become aware of my presence. They shouted, 'There is a spy among us. Every one of us should catch the hand of the person next to him I immediately caught the hand of a person and shouted, 'Who are you? 'He said, 'Subhanallah! you do not know me. I am so and so. 'I then returned to my camp. While I was on my way back, I met twenty horsemen with turbans on their heads. They said to me, 'Tell your master that Allah has dealt with his enemy and that he has nothing to worry about now.' When I reached my camp, I found the Prophet (Sallallaho alaihe wasallam) saying his Salaat with a small shawl around him. Whenever he faced a difficulty, he immediately turned towards Salaat. When he had finished, I reported to him what I had seen in the enemy camp. When I narrated how I escaped their 'search for the spy', I could see his beautiful teeth shining. He then asked me to lie down near his feet and put a corner of his shawl over my body. I lay down and pressed my breast against the soles of his feet."

Look at their spirit of carrying out the orders of the Prophet (Sallallaho alaihe wasallam) under very adverse and trying conditions. May Allah favour us with such spirit of obedience, even though we do not deserve it. Aameen!

CHAPTER–X

THE WOMEN'S COURAGE AND SPIRIT OF ISLAM

The lap of the mother is admitted to be the best field of instruction. Mothers imbued with the religious spirit are more likely to bring up children who will have similar aptitudes. Alas! our children are brought up in surroundings that draw them away from Islam or at least make them indifferent to the duties they owe therein; the results are obvious.

1. Hadhrat Fatimah (Radhiyallaho anha's) Tasbih:

Hadhrat Ali (Radhiyallaho anho) once said to one of his pupils:

"Shall I tell you the story of Hadhrat Fatimah (Radhiyallaho anha), the dearest and the most loved daughter of the Prophet (Sallallaho alaihe wasallam)?"

When the pupil replied in the affirmative, he said:

"Hadhrat Fatimah (Radhiyallaho anha) used to grind the grain herself, which caused corns on her hands. She carried water for the house in a leather bag, which left a mark on her breast. She cleaned the house herself, which made her clothes dirty. Once some war-captives were brought to Madinah. I said to her, 'Go to the Prophet (Sallallaho alaihe wasallam) and request him for an assistant to help you in your house-work.' She went to him, but found many people round him. As she was very modest, she could not be bold enough to request the Prophet (Sallallaho alaihe wasallam) in the presence of other people. Next day the Prophet (Sallalaho alaihe wasallam) came to our house and said, "Fatimah! what made you come to me yesterday?" She felt shy and kept quiet. I said, "O, Prophet of Allah! Fatimah has developed callusses on both her hands and breast, on account of grinding and carrying water. She is constantly busy in cleaning the house and in other domestic jobs, causing her clothes to remain dirty. I informed her about the captives and advised her to go to you and make a request for a servant.' It has also been reported that Hadhrat Fatimah (Radhiyallaho anha) made a request, 'I and Ali own only one bedding and that also is a skin of a goat. We use it in the morning to put the feed of the camel.' The Prophet (Sallallaho alaihe wasallam) said, "Fatimah! Be patient. The Prophet Moses (Alayhis Salam) and his wife owned only one bedding, which was the cloak of Moses. Fear Allah; acquire Taqwa and keep doing your service to Allah and attend to your domestic jobs. When you go to bed, recite Subhanallah 33 times, Alhamdulillah 33 times and Allahoakbar 34 times. You will find this more helpful than an assistant.' Hadhrat Fatimah (Radhiyallaho anha) remarked, 'I am happy with what Allah and His Prophet (Sallallaho alaihe wasallam) would be pleased with."

Look! This is the life of the Prophet's dear daughter. In moderately rich families of our times, the ladies think it below their dignity to attend to domestic work. They need assistance in each and every thing, even in their bathroom! What a difference!

In this Hadith, the prescribed Zikr is before sleep. In other Ahadith, the Prophet (Sallallaho alaihe wasallam) is reported to have advised Hadhrat Fatimah (Radhiyallaho anha) to recite after every Salaat, Subhanallah 33 times, Alhamdulillah 33 times, Allahoakbar 33 times and Lailaha-illallaho wahdahu-lasharikalahu-lahulmulku walahulhamdu-wahuwa-ala-kulli-sha-in-Qadir, once,

لَآاِلٰهَ اِلَّا اللّٰهُ وَحْدَهٗ لَاشَرِيْكَ لَهٗ لَهُ الْمُلْكُ وَلَهُ الْحَمْدُ وَهُوَ عَلٰى كُلِّ شَيْءٍ قَدِيْرٌ

2. Hadhrat Aishah (Radhiyallaho anha's) Spending In the Path of Allah.

Once Aishah (Radhiyallaho anha) received a gift of two bags containing one lakh (100,000) Dirhams. She started distributing these among the poor, till by the evening not a single dirham was left with her. She was fasting that day. Her maid servant brought her a loaf of bread and a little olive oil for Iftar, and remarked, "I wish we had kept one dirham for ourselves to get some meat for Iftaar." Aishah said:

"Do not be sorry now. If you had told me at that time I would have perhaps spared one dirham."

Gifts of this nature were often received by Hadhrat Aishah (Radhiyallaho anha) from Amir Muawiah, Hadhrat Abdullah bin Zubair (Radhiyallaho anhuma) and others, for that was the time of ease and plenty for the Muslims as territory after territory fell into their hands. In spite of this abundance, Hadhrat Aishah (Radhiyallaho anha) led a life of abstention. Look! She distributes 100 000 dirhams to the poor, but she does not remember to get some meat for her own Iftar. In our own atmosphere today, such stories seem to be impossible but, to the people who have understood the Sahabah's frame of mind, hundreds of such incidents are quite credible. There are many stories of this nature reported about Aishah (Radhiyallaho anha). Once she was fasting and had nothing for her Iftar except one piece of bread. A poor man came and begged for some food. She asked her maid to give him that piece of bread. The maid said:

> "If I give him the piece of bread, there will be nothing left for your Iftar".

She said: "Never mind. Let him have the piece".

Once she killed a snake. She saw a vision in her dream, saying: "Aishah (Radhiyallaho anha) you killed a Muslim".

She replied: "How could a Muslim come into the house of the Prophet's widow?"

The vision rejoined: "But he had come in Purdah (disguise)".

She abruptly got up from her sleep and at once spent 12 000 dirhams in Sadaqah, which was the blood-money fixed for a Muslim killed by mistake. Hadhrat Urwah (Radhiyallaho anho) says:

> "I once saw Hadhrat Aishah (Radhiyallaho anha) spending 70 000 dirhams in charity, while she herself was wearing a dress with patches."

3. Hadhrat Aishah (Radhiyallaho anha) Gets Angry With Hadhrat Ibn Zubair (Radhiyallaho anho):

Hadhrat Abdullah bin Zubair (Radhiyallaho anho) was Hadhrat Aishah's (Radhiyallaho anha) nephew. He was very dear to her, as she had brought him up. He did not like her spending so much in charity, while she herself lived in want and poverty. He mentioned this to somebody and said:

"I must stop my aunt from doing that".

She learnt about this and was so much displeased that she swore not to speak to Hadhrat Abdullah for the rest of her life. Hadhrat Abdullah bin Zubair (Radhiyallaho anho) was very much shocked by her oath. He deputed many people to speak to her for him, but she told them, "I have taken an oath and I am not prepared to violate it." He, at last, took two persons from the family of the Prophet's mother to her house to intercede for him. Aishah (Radhiyallaho anha) allowed the persons to enter the house and to speak to her from behind a curtain. Ibn Zubair (Radhiyallaho anho) also stealthily got in with these persons. When these persons started talking, he could not control himself and crossed the curtain and clung to his aunt, crying and entreating her for pardon. The two persons also interceded and reminded her of the Prophet's forbidding a Muslim from forswearing speech with another Muslim. When she heard this Hadith, she got frightened of Allah's displeasure and the result thereof, and began to weep very bitterly. She forgave Hadhrat Zubair (Radhiyallaho anho) and began to speak with him. She then began liberating slave after slave in expiation of her oath, till 40 slaves had been set free by her. Even later on, whenever she thought of the violation of her oath, she wept so much that her shawl would become wet with her tears.

How much do we worry about the oaths we take from morning till evening? It is for every one to examine his own self and answer. Come and see the people who had real reverence for Allah and His name; how deeply did they feel when they were unable to fulfil an oath. We see Hadhrat Aishah (Radhiyallaho anha) weeping so much whenever she remembered that incident about the violation of her oath.

4. Hadhrat Aishah (Radhiyallaho anha) and Fear of Allah:

Who does not know about the love that the Prophet (Sallallaho alaihe wasallam) had for his dear wife Hadhrat Aishah (Radhiyallaho anha)? It is said that when he was asked whom he loved most, he replied, "Aishah". She was so well-versed in Islamic jurisprudence that many eminent Sahabah would go to her for solving their problems in this field. Jibrail used to greet her with 'Assalamo alaikum'. The Prophet once told her that she would be his wife in the Paradise. When she was slandered by the Munafiqin, Allah exonerated her from the slander and confirmed her innocence by revealing verses in the Qur'an.

According to Hadhrat Ibn Sa'd (Radhiyallaho anho) Hadhrat Aishah (Radhiyallaho anha) once enumerated as many as ten special virtues that Allah had given her over the other wives of the Prophet (Sallallaho alaihe wasallam). Her spending in the path of Allah has already been narrated in the previous stories. In spite of all these privileges and virtues, she feared Allah so much that she was often heard saying;

> "I wish I was a tree, so that I could be always busy in Allah's tasbih and be absolved of reckoning on the Day of Judgment".
>
> "I wish I had been a stone or a clod of earth".
>
> "I wish I had been a leaf of tree or a blade of grass".
>
> "I wish I had not been born at all".

The stories about the awe and fear of Allah, which Sahabah had in their hearts, have already been given in Chapter II. This was the guiding factor of their lives.

5. Story of Hadhrat Umme Salmah (Radhiyallaho anha):

Ummul-Momineen Hadhrat Umme Salmah (Radhiyallaho anha) was first married to Abu Salmah (Radhiyallaho anho). The husband and wife were very much attached to each other. Once Umme Salmah said to her husband:

> "I have heard that if a husband does not marry another woman during the life or after the death of his wife, and also if the wife does not remarry after the death of her husband, the couple when admitted to paradise is allowed to live there as husband and wife. Give me your word that you will not marry after my death, and I too pledge that I will not marry again if you happen to die before me".

Hadhrat Abu Salmah (Radhiyallaho anho) said: "Will you do as I say?"
She replied: "Of course".

He said: "I want you to take a husband after my death".

He then prayed, saying, "O, Allah! Let Umme Salmah be married after my death to a husband better than I. May he give her no trouble whatsoever"

In the beginning, the couple emigrated to Abyssinia. After their return, they again emigrated to Madinah Hadhrat Umme Salmah (Radhiyallaho anha) says:

> "When my husband made up his mind to emigrate to Madinah, he loaded the camel with the luggage. He then made me and our son Salmah ride the camel. He led the camel out of the town, holding the string in his hand. The people of my father's clan (Banu Mughirah) happened to see us leaving. They came and snatched the string from Hadhrat Abu Salmah (Radhiyallaho anho's) hand saying, 'You can go wherever you like but we cannot allow our girl to go and perish with you.' They forcibly took me and my son back to their clan. When the people of my husband's clan (Banu Abdul Asad) learnt this, they came to Banu Mughirah and began to argue with them saying, "You can keep your girl if you like, but you have no claim over the child who belongs to our clan. Why should we allow him to stay in your clan, when you have not allowed your girl to go with her husband". They forcibly took the boy away. Hadhrat Abu Salmah (Radhiyallaho anho) had already gone to Madinah. All the members of the family were thus separated from each other. Daily, I would go out in the desert and weep there from morning till night. I lived in this condition for one full year, separated from my husband and my son. One day, one of my cousins taking pity on me said to the people of the clan, 'You have separated this poor woman from her husband and son. Why don't you have mercy on her and let her go? Due to the humanitarian efforts of this cousin of mine, the people of Banu Mughirah agreed to let me go and join my husband. Banu Abdul Asad also made over my son to me. I got a camel ready and, with my son in my lap, I sat on its back and set off for Madinah all alone. I had hardly gone four miles, when 'Hadhrat Usman-bin-Talhah (Radhiyallaho anho) met me at Tan'eem. He inquired, 'Where are you going?' I said, 'To Madinah! He remarked, 'With none accompanying you!, I said 'No, I

have nobody except Allah to accompany me.' He took the rope of my camel and began to lead. By Allah, I have never come across a person more noble than Hadhrat Usman (Radhiyallaho anho). When I had to get down, he would make the camel sit and himself go behind a bush and when I had to climb up he would bring the camel and make it sit close to me. He would then hold the rope and lead the animal. Thus we reached Quba (a suburb of Madinah). He informed me that Hadhrat Abu Salmah (Radhiyallaho anho) was staying there. He then made us over to my husband and then returned all the way back to Mecca. By Allah, no one else could bear the hardships that I bore during that single year".

Look at Hadhrat Umme Salmah (Radhiyallaho anha's) faith and trust in Allah. She set out on a long and hazardous journey all alone. See how Allah sent His help to her. No doubt Allah can depute anybody to render help to those who place trust in Him, for the hearts of all people are in His control.

As a rule, a lady is not permitted to travel alone on a long journey, except in the event of obligatory emigration for the sake of Allah.

6. Ladies in the Khaibar Campaign:

Shoulder to shoulder with their menfolk, the ladies of those times, imbued with the same spirit of sacrifice, were striving heart and soul in the path of Allah, and no service in this connection was too much for them.

Hadhrat Umme Ziyad (Radhiyallaho anha) says:

"In the Khaibar campaign, I along with other five women reached the battle-field. The Prophet (Sallalaho alaihe wasallam), having learnt this, sent for us. He said with anger, 'Who permitted you to come over here? Who brought you to this place?' We said, 'O, Prophet of Allah! we know knitting and we have some medicines with us. We shall help the Mujahidin by supplying them with arrows, by attending them when they are sick, and by preparing food for them.' The Prophet (Sallallaho alaihe wasallam) permitted us to stay."

The women of that time were blessed with the spirit

which even the men of our times do not possess. Look at the courage of these women who reached the battle-field on their own accord, and who offered to attend to different jobs in the field.

Hadhrat Umme Salim (Radhiyallaho anha) joined the Huneyn campaign in the state of pregnancy. She kept a dagger on her person. The Prophet (Sallallaho alaihe wasallam) inquired:

"What is this dagger for, O, Umme Salim?"

She replied: "I shall run it through the belly of any Kafir approaching me".

She had also taken part in the battle of Uhud, wherein she tended the wounds of the fighting men. Anas (Radhiyallaho anho) says:

"I saw Hadhrat Aishah and Hadhrat Umme Salim (Radhiyallaho anhuma) running to and fro in the battle-field, carrying water for the wounded"

7. Hadhrat Umme Haram (Radhiyallaho anha) in the battle for Cyprus:

Umme Haram (Radhiyallaho anha) was an aunt of Anas (Radhiyallaho anha). The Prophet (Sallallaho alaihe wasallam) often visited her and sometimes had his afternoon nap at her place. Once he was sleeping in her house, when he woke up smiling.

Hadhrat Umme Haram (Radhiyallaho anha) said:

"O, Prophet (Sallallaho alaihe wasallam)! You are dearer to me than my parents, tell me what made you smile"

He said:

"I saw in my dream a few of my followers going for Jihad across the sea. They, in their barges, looked like kings sitting on their thrones".

Hadhrat Umme Haram (Radhiyallaho anha) said:

"O, Prophet of Allah! Pray that I may also be one among those people"

He replied: "Rest assured, you will be one of them"

He went to sleep again, and got up smiling for the second

time. On Hadhrat Haram (Radhiyallaho anha's) query he said:

> "I again saw some more people going for Jihad across the sea".

Hadhrat Umme Haram (Radhiyallaho anha) requested him to pray for her joining them also, he said:

> "No, you are with the first group only."

During the Khilafat of Hadhrat Usman (Radhiyallaho anho) Amir Muawiyah, the Governor of Syria, sought permission to send an expeditionary force to Cyprus Island. This permission was granted by Hadhrat Usman (Radhiyallaho anho). Hadhrat Umme Haram (Radhiyallaho anha), with her husband Hadhrat Ubadah (Radhiyallaho anho), was in that force. While returning from the island she fell from her mule, broke her neck and died. She was buried in Cyprus.

Look at the spirit of Hadhrat Umme Haram (Radhiyallaho anha). She wanted to join both the expeditions. As she was destined to die during the first expedition, the Prophet (Sallallaho alaihe wasallam) did not pray for her participation in the second one.

8. Story of Hadhrat Umme Sulaim (Radhiyallaho anha):

Umme Sulaim (Radhiyallaho anha) was the mother of Hadhrat Anas (Radhiyallaho anho). After the death of her husband, she remained a widow for some time with a view to devoting herself to the proper upbringing of her son. She was then married to Hadhrat Abu Talhah (Radhiyallaho anho) and got a son named Abu Umair from him. The Prophet (Sallallaho alaihe wasallam) used to go to her house and play with the child.

One day, Abu Umair was ill and Hadhrat Abu Talhah (Radhiyallaho anho) was fasting. While Hadhrat Abu Talhah (Radhiyallaho anho) was out on his job, the child died. She washed and enshrouded the dead body and laid it on the cot. She then herself took a bath changed her clothes and made her toilet. When the husband returned home and had his Iftar he asked her:

> "How is the child?"

She replied: "He is now in peace."

He was satisfied. The couple shared the bed for the night.

When they got up in the morning, they had the following conversation.

Hadhrat Umme Sulaim (Radhiyallaho anha):

"I have a question to ask you."

Hadhrat Abu Talhah (Radhiyallaho anho):

"What is that?"

Hadhrat Umme Sulaim (Radhiyallaho anha):

"Suppose a person is entrusted with something. Should he deliver up on demand that which is entrusted to him or not?"

Hadhrat Abu Talhah (Radhiyallaho anho):

"He must deliver up. He has no right to hold it back".

Hadhrat Umme Sulaim (Radhiyallaho anha):

"Abu Umair was entrusted to us by Allah. He has taken him back."

Hadhrat Abu Talhah (Radhiyallaho anho) was filled with grief. He simply said:

"But why did you not inform me before?"

He went to the Prophet (Sallallaho alaihe wasallam) and narrated the story to him. He prayed for him and said:

"Allah is likely to bless your sharing the bed with your wife last night."

One of the Sahabah says:

"I lived to see the effect of the Prophet's blessing. As a result of his union with his wife on that night, Hadhrat Abu Talhah (Radhiyallaho anho) got a son named Abdullah. This Abdullah had nine sons, all of whom were Qaris."

It needs much courage and patience to do what Hadhrat Umme Sulaim (Radhiyallaho anha) did at the death of her son. She did not like her husband to know about the death of the child while he was fasting and while he needed food and rest.

9. Hadhrat Umme Habibah (Radhiyallaho anha's) Behaviour With Her Father:

Hadhrat Ummul Mominin Umme Habibah (Radhiyallaho anha) was previously married to Ubaidullah bin Jahsh. She emigrated with her husband to Abyssinia. The husband turned renegade and died there as a Kafir. The Prophet (Sallallaho alaihe wasallam) sent his offer to marry her through king Negus, while she was still passing her days in Abyssinia as a widow. She accepted the offer and came to Madinah to live with the Prophet (Sallallaho alaihe wasallam). During the period of truce between the Muslims and the idolaters of Mecca, her father Hadhrat Abu Sufyan (Radhiyallaho anho) once came to Madinah for negotiations in connection with reinforcing the truce. He went to see Umme Habibah. As he was about to sit on the bedding in her room, she removed it from under him. He was surprised over her behaviour and said:

"Was the bedding unfit for me or I unfit for the bedding?"

She replied: "This bedding is meant for the dear and holy Prophet (Sallallaho alaihe wasallam), while you are an idolater and therefore unclean. How can I allow you to sit on this bedding?"

Abu Sufyan was full of grief and remarked:

"Since you left us, you have developed bad manners."

In the face of the great reverence that she had for the Prophet (Sallallaho alaihe wasallam), she could not tolerate an unclean mushrik (though he be her own father) to sit on the Prophet's bedding.

Once she came to know from the Prophet (Sallallaho alaihe wasallam) about the virtues of twelve rakaats of Chasht. Since that time, she kept on offering this Salaat regularly.

Her father Hadhrat Abu Sufyan (Radhiyallaho anha) later embraced Islam. On the third day of his death, she sent for some perfume and used it saying:

"I neither need nor like the perfume. I have heard the Prophet (Sallallaho alaihe wasallam) saying, 'A woman is not permitted to mourn the death of any person (except her husband's) for more than three days. (The mourning period in case of husband's death is however four months and ten days.) I am using the perfume simply to show that I am not mourning the death of my father any longer."

When she was about to die, she sent for Hadhrat Aishah (Radhiyallaho anha) and said:

"We have been rivals in sharing the love of the Prophet (Sallallaho alaihe wasallam). It is just possible that we might have offended each other. I forgive you. Please forgive me too."

Hadhrat Aishah (Radhiyallaho anha) said:

"I forgive you by all means. May Allah forgive you too."

She remarked:

"O, Aishah, you have made me very happy. May Allah keep you happy."

Similarly, she sent for Hadhrat Umme Salmah (Radhiyallaho anha) and secured her forgiveness.

The tension between two rival wives is natural and proverbial. Hadhrat Umme Habibah (Radhiyallaho anha) wanted to be forgiven by people before she appeared before Allah. Her reverence and love for the Prophet (Sallallaho alaihe wasallam) can be judged from her behaviour towards her own father.

10. The Story of Hadhrat Zainab (Radhiyallaho anha)

Hadhrat Ummul Mominin Zainab (Radhiyallaho anha) was a cousin of the Prophet (Sallallaho alaihe wasallam). She accepted Islam soon after its advent. In the beginning, she was married to Hadhrat Zaid (Radhiyallaho anho), who was a liberated slave and the adopted son of the Prophet (Sallallaho alaihe wasallam). He was therefore, known as Hadhrat Zaid bin Muhammad (Radhiyallaho anho). Hadhrat Zaid (Radhiyallaho anho) could not pull on smoothly with Zainab and at last divorced her. Now, according to the pre-Islamic customs, an adopted son was treated as a real son, so much so that his widow or divorced wife could not be married to his adopted father. The Prophet (Sallallaho alaihe wasallam), with a view to break this unjustified custom, communicated to Hadhrat Zainah (Radhiyallaho anha) his proposal for marriage. When Hadhrat Zainab (Radhiyallaho anha) received the proposal, she said:

"Let me consult my Lord!"

She then performed Wudhu and stood up in her Salaat. Her action was so much blessed by Allah that the following verse was revealed to the Prophet (Sallallaho alaihe wasallam):

فَلَمَّا قَضٰى زَيْدٌ مِّنْهَا وَطَرًا زَوَّجْنٰكَهَا لِكَىْ لَايَكُوْنَ عَلَى الْمُؤْمِنِيْنَ حَرَجٌ فِىْ
اَزْوَاجِ اَدْعِيَآئِهِمْ اِذَا قَضَوْا مِنْهُنَّ وَطَرًا ، وَكَانَ اَمْرُ اللهِ مَفْعُوْلًا (الاحزاب ٣٧)

"So when Zaid had performed the necessary formality (of divorce) from her, we gave her unto thee in marriage, so that (hence forth) there may be no sin for believers in respect of the wives of their adopted sons, when the latter have performed necessary formality (of release) from them. The commandment of Allah must be fulfilled."

When Hadhrat Zainab (Radhiyallaho anha) was informed of the good news that Allah had given her in the Prophet's marriage and had revealed a verse to that effect, she made over to the reporter in gratification all her jewellery that she was wearing at that time. Then she fell down in Sajdah and vowed to keep fast for two months. She was justly proud of the fact that, while every other wife of the Prophet (Sallallaho alaihe wasallam) was given in the marriage to him by her relations, she was given by Allah, as mentioned in Qur'an. As Hadhrat Aishah (Radhiyallaho anha) was also proud of being the most beloved wife of the Prophet (Sallallaho alaihe wasallam), there was always some rivalry between the two. In spite of all this, when the Prophet (Sallallaho alaihe wasallam) asked Hadhrat Zainab (Radhiyallaho anha's) opinion about Hadhrat Aishah (Radhiyallaho anha) in the matter of the slander against Hadhrat Aishah (Radhiyallaho anha), she said:

"I find everything good in Aishah."

Look at her integrity and strong character. Had she wished, she could have harmed the reputation of her rival and lowered her, in the eyes of their common husband, who loved Hadhrat Aishah (Radhiyallaho anha) so much. On the other hand, she praised her in very strong words.

Hadhrat Zainab (Radhiyallaho anha) was a very pious lady. She fasted very often and would say her Nafl Salaat very frequently. She earned by working with her hands, and spent all that she earned in the path of Allah.

At the time of the Prophet's death, his wives asked him:

"Which of us will join you first?"

He said: "The one with long arms."

They began to measure their arms with a stick. They, however, came to know later that long hands symbolised lavish spending in charity. Hadhrat Zainab (Radhiyallaho anha) was indeed the first to die after the Prophet (Sallallaho alaihe wasallam).

Hadhrat Barazah (Radhiyallaho anho) narrates:

> Hadhrat "Umar (Radhiyallaho anho) decided to pay an annual allowance to the Ummahat-ul-Mominin from the Baitul Maal. He sent 12 000 dirhams to Hadhrat Zainab (Radhiyallaho anha) through me as her share. She thought that it was for all of them, and said to me, 'Umar should have asked somebody else to distribute this money.' I said, 'It is the annual share for you alone.' She asked me to throw it in the corner of a room and cover it with a piece of cloth. Then she mentioned the names of some poor persons, widows and her relatives, and asked me to give one handful to each of them. After I had distributed as desired, some money was still left under the cloth. I expressed a desire to have something for myself. She said, 'You take the rest.' I counted the money. It was eighty four dirhams. Then she lifted her hands in prayer and said, 'O, Allah keep this money away from me, for it brings temptation.' She died before the allowance for the next year could be paid to her. When Hadhrat Umar (Radhiyallaho anho) came to know of what she had done with the money, he sent her another 1 000 dirhams for her personal needs but even those she spent in no time. Although during the last portion of her life, the Muslims were conquering territory after territory, and wealth was pouring into Madinah, yet she left no money or other wealth after her, except the house where she lived. She was called Ma'wal Masaakeen,

(refuge of the poor), due to her lavish spending in charity."

A woman narrates:

"I and Hadhrat Zainab (Radhiyallaho anha) were dyeing our clothes with red ochre. The Prophet (Sallallaho alaihe wasallam) came in, but went out again when he saw us engaged in dyeing. Hadhrat Zainab (Radhiyallaho anha) felt that the Prophet (Sallallaho alaihe wasallam) had perhaps not liked our dyeing in that colour. She immediately washed all the dyed clothes till their colour was gone."

Everybody knows the love and liking of women for money and colours. But look at these ladies, who would push away the money coming to them and who were prepared to discard any colour on receiving the least hint of the Prophet's disapproval.

11. Hadhrat Khansa (Radhiyallaho anha) Exhorts Her Sons to Bravery.

Hadhrat Khansa (Radhiyallaho anha) was a famous poetess. She embraced Islam in Madinah, along with some others of her clan. Ibn Athir writes:

"All masters of literature are unanimous in declaring Hadhrat Khansa (Radhiyallaho anha) as the best woman poet in Arabic. No woman in history has ever written such poetry as Hadhrat Khansa (Radhiyallaho anha)."

During the time of 'Hadhrat Umar (Radhiyallaho anho) in 16 A.H, the famous battle of Qadisiyyah was fought between the Muslims and the Persians. Hadhrat Khansa (Radhiyallaho anha), along with her four sons, took part in this battle. On the eve of the battle, she exhorted all her four sons, saying:

"O, My sons! You embraced Islam and emigrated of your own free will. By Allah, beside Whom there is no God, you all are the sons of the same father, just as you are the sons of the same mother. I never betrayed your father, nor defamed your maternal uncle. I never allowed a blot to come on your high birth nor polluted your pedigree. You know what rewards Allah has promised for those who fight against the disbelievers in His path. You must remember that the everlasting life of the Hereafter is far better than the transitory life of this world. Allah has said in His Holy Book:

يٰٓاَيُّهَا الَّذِيْنَ اٰمَنُوْا اصْبِرُوْا وَصَابِرُوْا وَرَابِطُوْا ، وَاتَّقُوْا اللهَ لَعَلَّكُمْ تُفْلِحُوْنَ

(آل عمران ٢٠٠)

"O, Ye who believe! Endure, outdo all others in endurance, be ready and observe your duty to Allah, in order that Ye may succeed. (III:200)"

When you get up tomorrow morning, be prepared to contribute your best in the battle. Go ahead into the enemy lines, seeking help from Allah. When you see the flames of war rising high, get right into the centre and face the enemy chiefs. Inshallah you will get your abode in paradise with honour and success."

Next day, when the battle was in full swing, all the four sons advanced towards the enemy lines. One by one, they attacked the enemy, reciting the words of their mother in verses and fought till all of them were martyred. When the mother got the news, she said:

"Alhamdulillah. Glory to Allah Who has honoured me with their martyrdom. I hope that Allah will unite me with them under the shade of His Mercy."

Here is a mother of that time. She exhorts her sons to jump into the flames of battle and, when all the sons are killed in quick succession, she glorifies Allah and thanks Him.

12. Hadhrat Safiyyah (Radhiyallaho anha) Kills A Jew

Hadhrat Safiyyah (Radhiyallaho anha) was the aunt of the Prophet (Sallallaho alaihe wasallam) and a real sister of Hadhrat Hamzah (Radhiyallaho anho). She took part in the battle of Uhud. When the Muslims were defeated and some of them began to flee from the battle, she would smite their faces with her spear and excite them to go back and fight.

In the war of the Khandaq (Trench), the Prophet (Sallallaho alaihe wasallam) had collected all the Muslim women in a fortress and had deputed Hadhrat Hassaan bin Thabit (Radhiyallaho anho) to look after them. The Jews, who were always on the look-out for such opportunities for doing mischief, surrounded the place and sent one of them to find out if there were any men with the ladies. Hadhrat Safiyyah (Radhiyallaho anha) happened to see the Jew approaching the fort. She said to Hadhrat Hassaan (Radhiyallaho anho):

> "There is a Jew coming to spy on us. You go out and kill him."

Hadhrat Hassaan (Radhiyallaho anho) was a weak person. He did not make bold to do the job. Safiyyah (Radhiyallaho anha) got hold of a tent peg and went outside the fortress and gave a blow on the head of the Jew that killed him on the spot. She came back and said to Hassaan:

> "The man is dead. I have not removed the clothes and arms from his body for reasons of modesty. Now you go and remove everything from his body. Also bring his head after severing it from the body."

Hadhrat Hassaan (Radhiyallaho anho) was too weak-hearted to do that even. She herself went again and brought his head, and threw it over the wall amidst the Jews. When they saw this, they said:

> "We were wondering how Muhammad (Sallallaho alaihe wasallam) could keep the womenfolk alone in this fort. Surely, there are men inside to guard the ladies."

Safiyyah died in 20 A.H. at the age of seventy three. The war of the Trench was fought in 5 A.H. She was, therefore, 58 then. These days, a lady of that age is hardly able to do her domestic work. But look how Saffiyyah (Radhiyallaho anha) goes and kills a Jew all alone.

13. Hadhrat Asma (Radhiyallaho anha's) Interview With the Prophet (Sallallaho alaihe wasallam) Regarding the Reward for Women.

Hadhrat Asma bintYazid Ansari (Radhiyallaho anha) came to the Prophet (Sallallaho alaihe wasallam) and said:

> "O, Prophet of Allah! You are dearer to me than my parents. My Muslim women have deputed me as their representative to talk to you on their behalf. Verily you are the Prophet of Allah for both men and women. We stay for most part of our time within the four walls of our houses. We remain pinned to our duties of fulfilling the sexual desires of men, bearing children for

them and looking after their homes. Notwithstanding all this, men excel us in getting rewards for things which we are unable to do. They go and say their daily Salaat and weekly Jumu'ah in the musjid, visit the sick, attend the funerals, perform Hajj after Hajj and, above all, fight in the way of Allah. When they go for Hajj or Jehad, we look after their property, bring up their children and weave cloth for them. Do we not share their rewards with them?"

The Prophet (Sallallaho alaihe wasallam) addressing the Sahabah sitting round him, said:

"Did you ever hear a woman asking a better question?"

Sahabah replied: "O, Prophet of Allah! We never thought that a woman could ever put such a question."

The Prophet (Sallallaho alaihe wasallam) addressing Asma said:

"Listen attentively, and then go and tell the ladies who have sent you that when a woman seeks the pleasure of her husband and carries out her domestic functions to his satisfaction, she gets the same reward as the men get for all their services to Allah."

Hadhrat Asma (Radhiyallaho anha) returned very happily after getting this reply to her question.

Obedience to and good behaviour towards husbands is a very great asset for the women, provided they know its value.

The Sahabah once said to the Prophet (Sallallaho alaihe wasallam):

"In foreign countries, people prostrate before their kings and chiefs. You deserve such reverence much more."

He said, "No. If it were permissible to prostrate before anybody besides Allah, I would asked the women to prostrate before their husbands."

He then said,

"By him Who has my life in His hand, a woman cannot do what she owes to Allah until she has done what she owes to her husband."

It is reported in a Hadith that once a camel bowed in prostration before the Prophet (Sallallaho alaihe wasallam). The Sahabah on seeing this, said:

"When this animal prostrates before you, why should we not have this honour too?"

He replied:

"Never. If I could make somebody prostrate before anybody besides Allah, I would ask the wives to prostrate before their husbands."

The following is reported to have been said by the Prophet (Sallallaho alaihe wasallam) in this connection:

(1) "A woman whose husband is pleased with her at the time of her death goes straight into Paradise."

(2) "A woman is cursed by the angels if her husband is displeased with her, and she stays away from him in anger for the night."

(3) "The Salaat of two persons hardly rises beyond their heads in its flight to heaven. These two persons are a run-away slave and a disobedient wife."

14. The Story of Hadhrat Umme Ammarah (Radhiyallaho anha).

Hadhrat Umme Ammarah (Radhiyallaho anha) is one of those Ansar who embraced Islâm in the very beginning. She was among the group that vowed allegience to the Prophet (Sallallaho alaihe wasallam) at Al-Aqabah. Al-Aqabah in Arabic means a narrow Mountain Pass. In the early days of Islam, the new Muslims were persecuted by Qureysh very badly. They would put all hurdles in the way of Tabligh. The Prophet (Sallallaho alaihe wasallam), therefore, carried on his mission quietly and secretly. People from Madinah who used to come to Mecca for Hajj usually embraced Islam secretly in a mountain pass near Mina, so that Qureysh might not see them. She was in the third such group from Madinah. She participated in most of the battles that were fought after emigration. She took prominent part in Uhud, Hudeybiah, Khaiber, Umratul Qadha, Huneyn and Yamamah.

In the battle of Uhud, she was forty-three. Her husband and two sons were also fighting in the battle. She took a leather bottle full of water and headed for Uhud. In the beginning, the Muslims had an upper hand, but the tables were turned in another moment and the enemy were in the winning position. She had reached the Prophet (Sallallaho alaihe wasallam), when wave after wave of enemy troops rushed to attack and kill him. She shielded the Prophet (Sallallaho alaihe wasallam) whenever anybody approached him. She had a cloth-belt round her waist full of pieces of lint. She tended the wounded. She herself got about twelve wounds, one of which was very serious. Hadhrat Umme Sa'eed (Radhiyallaho anha) says:

> "I once saw a very deep cut on the shoulder of Hadhrat Umme Ammarah (Radhiyallaho anha). I inquired how she had got that. She said, 'I got it in Uhud. When people were running about in confusion, I saw Ibn Qumiah coming towards us and shouting, 'where is Muhammad (Sallallaho alaihe wasallam). Let somebody tell me his whereabouts. If he is saved today, I am no more.' I, Hadhrat Mus'ab bin Umair (Radhiyallaho anho) and some others intercepted him. He gave me this deep cut on my shoulder. I also attacked him, but he escaped on account of the double coat of mail that he was wearing."

In spite of a year's treatment, the wound would not heal. In the meantime, the Prophet (Sallallaho alaihe wasallam) decided about the expedition to Hamra-ul-Asad. Hadhrat Umme Ammarah (Radhiyallaho anha) also got ready to join the expedition. But as her wound was still unhealed, she could not participate. When the Prophet (Sallallaho alaihe wasallam) returned from the expedition, he straight away went to visit Hadhrat Umme Ammarah (Radhiyallaho anha). He was very happy to find her better.

She says:

> "In fact, we were very much handicapped in Uhud. The enemy had very strong cavalry, while we fought on foot. There would have been a fair fight if they too had been on foot. When somebody came riding on his horse to attack me, I stopped his sword on my shield and when he turned about, I attacked his horse from the rear and cut its leg. This caused the horse as well as the rider to fall on the ground. As soon as this happened, the Prophet (Sallallaho alaihe wasallam) would

shout to my son, who would run to my help and then we both finished the man in no time."

Her son Hadhrat Abdullah bin Zaid (Radhiyallaho anho) says:

"I had a wound on my left arm, which would not stop bleeding. The Prophet (Sallallaho alaihe wasallam) said to my mother, 'Put a bandage over it.' My mother took out a bandage from her belt and after bandaging my wound, said, 'Now, son! go and fight again with the idolaters.' The Prophet (Sallallaho alaihe wasallam) was watching us. He said, 'O, Umme Ammarah, who can have courage like yours?"

The Prophet (Sallallaho alaihe wasallam) at that time prayed again and again for Hadhrat Umme Ammarah (Radhiyallaho anha) and her family. Hadhrat Umme Ammarah (Radhiyallaho anha) says:

"I was standing with the Prophet (Sallallaho alaihe wasallam), when one of the enemy passed in front of me. The Prophet (Sallallaho alaihe wasallam) said to me, Umme Ammarah! He is the man who wounded your son.' I jumped at him and hit his leg. It made him fall down. We then went forward and finished him. The Prophet (Sallallaho alaihe wasallam) smiled and said, 'Umme Ammarah has avenged her son.' When the Prophet (Sallallaho alaihe wasallam) was praying for us, I said to him, 'O, Prophet of Allah! Pray for my company with you in Paradise.' He favoured me with this prayer too, and after that I cared little for what happened to me in this life."

As has already been said, she also participated in many other battles with the same zeal and spirit. After the death of the Prophet (Sallallaho alaihe wasallam), she took part in the fierce battle of Yamamah, which was fought with the renegades. She lost one of her arms and received eleven other wounds in this battle. She was forty-three in Uhud and fifty-two in Yamamah. Her heroism in these battles at that age was really miraculous.

15. Story of Hadhrat Umme Hakim (Radhiyallaho anha).

Hadhrat Umme Hakim (Radhiyallaho anha) was the wife of Ikramah bin Abi Jahl. She participated in Uhud on the enemy side. She embraced Islam on the fall of Mecca.

She loved her husband very much, who would not become a Muslim on account of his father, who was the worst enemy of Islam. After the fall of Mecca, her husband fled to Yemen. She secured pardon for him from the Prophet (Sallallaho alaihe wasallam) and went to Yemen and induced her husband to return to his home. She told him:

> "You can be safe from the sword of Muhammad (Sallallaho alaihe wasallam) only when you put yourself in his lap."

She returned with him to Madinah, where Ikramah embraced Islam and the couple began to live together happily. They both participated in the Syrian war during the caliphate of Hadhrat Abu Bakr (Radhiyallaho anho). Ikramah was killed in a battle. She was then married to another Mujahid, Hadhrat Khalid bin Sa'eed (Radhiyallaho anho). It was at a place called Marja-us-Safr that her husband wanted to meet her. She said:

> "We have enemy concentrating on all fronts. We shall meet after they are done away with."

He said: "I am sure I shall not survive this battle."

They then shared the bed for the first time in a tent at that place. Next day, Hadhrat Khalid bin Sa'eed (Radhiyallaho anho) was arranging for the Walimah when the enemy attacked with full force and he was killed in the battle. Hadhrat Umme Hakim (Radhiyallaho anha) packed up her tent and other luggage, and, with a tent-peg in her hand, fought the enemy till she had killed seven of them.

In war times, not to speak of a woman, no man would like to get married under such circumstances. Look at her marriage in the battle-field and her fight with the enemy! Instead of mourning the loss of her husband on the day of his death, she rushes in to the battle-field and kills seven of the enemy soldiers single-handed. Is this not enough to show the wonderful strength of Iman in women of that time?

16. Martyrdom of Hadhrat Sumayyah (Radhiyallaho anha).

Hadhrat Sumayyah (Radhiyallaho anha) is the mother of 'Hadhrat Ammar (Radhiyallaho anho), whose story we have already read in Chapter V. Just like 'Hadhrat Ammar (Radhiyallaho anho) her son, and Yasir her husband, she patiently bore the hardships in various forms in the cause of Islam. She would not weaken in her love for and devotion to Islam in spite of all these afflictions. One day, Hadhrat Sumayyah (Radhiyallaho anha) was standing when Abu Jahl passed that way. He flung all sorts of dirty words at her and then put his spear through her private parts. She died on account of the wound. She is the first to meet martyrdom for the cause of Islam.

Patience, perseverence and sacrifice of these ladies are really enviable. No affliction is too much when a person blessed with the spirit of Islam is determined to bear it. We hear about hundreds of persons dying for one cause or the other. It is only dying for the cause of Allah that brings eternal happiness and comfort in the life to come. Persons losing their lives for material gains really lose twice, i.e., in this world as well as in the Hereafter.

17. The story of Hadhrat Asma bint Abu Bakr (Radhiyallaho anha).

Hadhrat Asma bint Abu Bakr (Radhiyallaho anha) is the daughter of Hadhrat Abu Bakr (Radhiyallaho anho), mother of Hadhrat Abdullah bin Zubair (Radhiyallaho anho) and step-sister of Hadhrat Aishah (Radhiyallaho anha). She is one of the famous women of her time. She was the eighteenth person to embrace Islam. She was twenty-seven years old at the time of the Hijrat. After the migration from Mecca, when the Prophet (Sallallaho alaihe wasallam) and Hadhrat Abu Bakr (Radhiyallaho anho) reached Madinah safely, they sent Hadhrat Zaid (Radhiyallaho anho) and some other Sahabah to bring their families from Mecca. Hadhrat Asma (Radhiyallaho anho) came to Madinah with Hadhrat Abu Bakr (Radhiyallaho anho's) family. When she reached Quba, she gave birth to Hadhrat—Abdullah bin-Zubair (Radhiyallaho anho), the first Muslim baby born since the Hijrat. She says:

> "When I was married to Hadhrat Zubair (Radhiyallaho anho), he had neither money nor property of any kind. He had only one camel for carrying water and one horse. I would bring fodder for the animals and date-stones to feed them in lieu of grass, bring water from the well, mend bucket myself when needed, and attend to other domestic duties. Attending to the horse was the most difficult of all jobs. I was not good at baking and, therefore, after kneading the flour, I would

take it to Ansar women in my neighbourhood, who would bake bread for me. When we arrived in Madinah, the Prophet (Sallallaho alaihe wasallam) alloted a piece of land to Hadhrat Zubair (Radhiyallaho anho) two miles away from the town. I would bring date stones from there on my head. One day when I was coming in this fashion, I met the Prophet (Sallallaho alaihe wasallam) with a group of Ansar in the way. He stopped his camel. From his gesture, I understood that he intended to give me a lift. I felt shy of going with men, and I also remembered that Hadhrat Zubair (Radhiyallaho anho) was very sensitive in this matter. The Prophet (Sallallaho alaihe wasallam) understood my hesitation and left me alone. When I reached home, I narrated the story to Hadhrat Zubair (Radhiyallaho anho) and told him that, due to my own shyness and his sensitiveness, I did not avail of the offer of the Prophet (Sallallaho alaihe wasallam). He said, 'By Allah I am more sensitive about your carrying the load over such a long distance, but I cannot help it. (In fact, Sahabah remained occupied in striving in the path of Allah and all other such jobs had to be done by their womenfolk. Sometime later, Hadhrat Abu Bakr (Radhiyallaho anho) transferred to us a servant that the Prophet (Sallallaho alaihe wasallam) had given to him. I was therefore relieved of attending to the horse, which had been really very hard for me."

18. Hadhrat Asma (Radhiyallaho anha) Pacifies her Grandfather.

When Hadhrat Abu Bakr (Radhiyallaho anho) emigrated to Madinah in the company of the Prophet (Sallallaho alaihe wasallam), he took with him all his money, thinking that the Prophet might need it. It was about 6 000 dirhams. After his departure, his father Abu Quhafah (who was blind and who had not till then accepted Islam) came to express his sympathy with his granddaughters.

Hadhrat Asma (Radhiyallaho anha) says:

"Our grandfather came to us and said, 'Your father has shocked you with his migration to Madinah, and seems to have put you to further hardship by taking all his money with him.' I said, 'No grandfather, do not worry. He has left a lot of money for us.' I collected some pebbles and deposited them in the recess where my father used to keep his money; I covered it with a cloth. I then took my grandfather to the place and placed his hand over the cloth. He thought that the recess was really full of dirhams. He remarked: 'It is good that he has left something for you to live on.' By Allah, my father had not left a single dirham for us: I played this trick simply to pacify my grandfather."

Look at this brave Muslim girl. Strictly speaking, the girls needed more consolation than their grandfather. Judged by normal course of things, they should have complained of their destitution to their grandfather to win his sympathy, as there was nobody else in Mecca to extend them any sympathy or help. But Allah had given such a frame of mind to Muslim men and women of those days that everything they did was really wonderful and worthy of emulation.

Hadhrat Abu Bakr (Radhiyallaho anho) was quite a well-to-do person in the beginning, but he always spent liberally in the path of Allah. At the time of Tabuk, he contributed all that he possessed (This we have already read in Chapter VI). The Prophet (Sallallaho alaihe wasallam) once said:

"No body's wealth has benefited me so much as that of Hadhrat Abu Bakr (Radhiyallaho anho). I have compensated everybody for the good done to me, except Hadhrat Abu Bakr (Radhiyallaho anho). He shall be compensated by Allah Himself."

19. Hadhrat Asma (Radhiyallaho anha's) Spending in Charity.

Hadhrat Asma (Radhiyallaho anha) had a very large heart for spending in the path of Allah. In the beginning, she used to spend carefully with measure and weight. Once the Prophet (Sallallaho alaihe wasallam) said to her:

"O, Asma, do not put by and be calculating; spend in the path of Allah liberally."

After this, she started spending most generously. She would advise her daughters and house maids:

"Don't wait for any surplus or excess of requirements before spending in the path of Allah. As the requirements go on increasing in the chances of having something, excess will become more and more remote, and the time for spending in the path of Allah will never come. Remember that you will not lose by spending in charity."

Although these people were poor and lived hand to mouth, yet they were liberal in spending and generous of heart. The Muslims today complain of their poverty, but there will be hardly any group op people among them who are so poor and needy as the Sahabah used to be. We have already read how they had to go without food for several days together, and how some of them had to keep stones tied on their bellies to relieve their pangs of hunger.

20. The Story of the Prophet Sallallaho alaihe wasallam's Daughter Hadhrat Zainab (Radhiyallaho anha):

Hadhrat Zainab (Radhiyallaho anha) was born after five years of the Prophet's (Sallallaho alaihe wasallam) marriage to Hadhrat Khadijah (Radhiyallaho anha), when the Prophet (Sallallaho alaihe wasallam) was thirty years of age. She came of age and then accepted Islam. She was married to her cousin Abul Aas bin Rabi. Her husband fought in Badr for Qureysh and fell a captive to the Muslims.

When the Qureysh were paying ransom to secure release of their prisoners, Hadhrat Zainab (Radhiyallaho anha) gave over as ransom for her husband the necklace she had received in dowry from her mother Hadhrat Khadijah (Radhiyallaho anha). When the Prophet (Sallallaho alaihe wasallam) saw the necklace, the memories of Hadhrat Khadijah (Radhiyallaho anha) came to his mind and tears were in his eyes. After consultation with Sahabah, he returned the necklace to Hadhrat Zainab (Radhiyallaho ahna) and released her husband without ransom on the condition that he would send Hadhrat Zainab (Radhiyallaho anha) to Madinah on his return to Mecca. Two men were sent to stay outside Mecca and bring Hadhrat Zainab (Radhiyallaho anha) safely to Madinah, when she was made over to them. Her husband asked his brother Kinanah to take Hadhrat Zainab (Radhiyallaho anha) outside Mecca and make her over to the Muslim escort. As Hadhrat Zainab (Radhiyallaho anha) and Kinanah were moving out of the town on camel's back, the Qureysh sent a party to intercept them. Her own cousin Habar bin Aswad flung a spear at her, which wounded her and made her fall from the camel. As she was pregnant, she had an abortion. Kinanah started sending arrows towards the interceptors, when Abu Sufyan said to him:

> "We cannot tolerate the daughter of Muhammad leaving Mecca so openly. Let her go back and you can send her secretly after a few days."

Kinanah agreed. Hadhrat Zainab (Radhiyallaho anha) was despatched after a few days. She suffered from this wound for a long time, till at last she died of the same in 8 A. H. The Prophet said at the time of her death:

> "She was my best daughter, for she has suffered much on my account."

The Prophet (Sallallaho alaihe wasallam) buried her with his own hands. As he went into the grave to lay her down, he looked very sorrowful but, when he came out of the grave, he was quite composed. On the query by the Sahabah, he said:

> "In view of the feebleness of Zainab, I prayed to Allah to remove from her the tortures of the grave, and this prayer has been answered by Allah."

Just imagine, even the daughter of the Prophet who sacrificed her life for Islam needed a prayer from the Prophet (Sallallaho alaihe wasallam) for protection from difficulties in the grave. What about us people who are so much steeped in sins? It is but necessary that we should always seek protection from the difficulties in the grave. The Prophet (Sallallaho alaihe wasallam) would often seek refuge in Allah from the horrors of the grave. This was all for the instruction of his followers. (O, Allah! protect us from the horrors of the grave by Thy special Favour, Grace and Bounty).

اَللّٰهُمَّ احْفَظْنَا مِنْهُ بِمَنِّكَ وَكَرَمِكَ وَفَضْلِكَ

21. Hadhrat Rubayyi (Radhiyallaho anha's) High-mindedness:

Rubayyi-bint-Mu'awiz (Radhiyallaho anha) was a woman of Ansar, who had participated in many battles, by the side of the Prophet (Sallallaho alaihe wasallam). She nursed the wounded and carried the dead bodies during the battle. She had accepted Islam before the Prophet emigrated to Madinah. She was married when the Prophet was in Madinah. He graced her marriage with his presence. He heard some girls singing an epic poem about the battle of Badr at her place. One of them sang a verse, which meant:

وَفِيْنَا نَبِىٌّ يَّعْلَمُ مَا فِىْ غَدٍ

> "We have among us the Prophet (Sallallaho alaihe wasallam), who knows what is to happen tomorrow."

He stopped her from saying such things , because nobody except Allah knows what is going to happen in future.

It was Hadhrat Rubayyi (Radhiyallaho anha's) father Hadhrat Mu'awiz (Radhiyallaho anho) who was one of those who killed Abu Jahl in Badr. Abu Jahl, as we know, was one of the big chiefs of Qureysh and the worst enemy of Islam. There was a woman named Asma who used to sell perfumes to the ladies. She once came to Hadhrat Rubayyi (Radhiyallaho anha) to sell perfume. When Hadhrat Rubayyi (Radhiyallaho anha) was introduced to her as the daughter of Hadhrat Mu'awiz (Radhiyallaho anha), she remarked:

> "So you are the daughter of him who killed his chief."

Hadhrat Rubayyi (Radhiyallaho anha's) high mind could not tolerate the wretched person like Abu Jahl to be mentioned as the chief of her father. She, therefore, retorted:

> "No. I am the daughter of one who killed his slave."

Asma did not like this epithet for Abu Jahl, and said with anger:

> "It is haram for me to sell perfume to you."

Hadhrat Rubayyi (Radhiyallaho anha) said, in the same strain,

> "It is haram for me to buy perfume from you. I have never found stink in any perfume except yours."

Hadhrat Rubayyi (Radhiyallaho anha) says:

> "I had used the last words simply to provoke her."

Look at her sensitiveness and feeling for Islam. She could not tolerate an enemy of Islam being mentioned as a chief. We hear from the lips of Muslims most flowery and high sounding epithets being used for the open enemies of Islam. When they are reminded, they call it narrow-mindedness. The Prophet (Sallallaho alaihe wasallam) says:

"Don't call a Munafiq a chief. You displease Allah when you take him as a chief."

22. Life Sketches of Ummuhat-ul-Momineen:

Every Muslim likes to know (and he must know) about the members of the family of the Prophet (Sallallaho alaihe wasallam). A very brief account of their lives is, therefore, given in the following pages. The Muhaddithin and historians all agree that eleven ladies had the honour of being the wives of the Prophet (Sallallaho alaihe wasallam).

(1) Hadhrat Khadijah (Radhiyallaho anha) was the first among them. At the time of her marriage, she was 40 years old and the Prophet (Sallallaho alaihe wasallam) was twenty-five. She begot all his children, except a son, Ibrahim.

She was first to be married to Waraqah bin Naufal, but this marriage could not take place. Her first husband was Atiq bin Aa'iz. She had a daughter from him, whose name was Hind. Hind grew up and embraced Islam, and she was the mother of many children. On the death of Atiq, Khadijah (Radhiyallaho anha) was married to Abu Halah and got two children from him viz. Hind and Halah. Hind lived up to the time of Ali's Caliphate. On the death of Abu Halah, the Prophet (Sallallaho alaihe wasallam) married her as his first wife. She died in Ramadhan of the 10th year of the mission at the age of sixty-five. He loved her very much and did not marry any other woman during her life time. She was popularly called Tahirah (Clean and pure) even before Islam. Her children from other husbands are therefore known as Banu Tahirah. Her virtues and privileges have been mentioned extensively (in Hadith). The Prophet (Sallallaho alaihe wasallam) laid her in the grave with his own hands. The funeral service had not till then been enjoined.

(2) Hadhrat Sauda (Radhiyallaho anha):

Hadhrat Sauda bint Zam'ah bin Qais (Radhiyallaho anha) was previously married to her cousin Hadhrat Sukran bin 'Amor (Radhiyallaho anho). The couple embraced Islam and emigrated to Abysinnia. Hadhrat Sukran

(Radhiyallaho anho) died in Abyssinia. Hadhrat Saudah (Radhiyallaho anha), now a widow, returned to Mecca. The Prophet (Sallallaho alaihe wasallam), on the death of Hadhrat Khadijah (Radhiyallaho anha) (in Shawwal of the same year), married Hadhrat Saudah (Radhiyallaho anha). We know the devotion of the Prophet (Sallallaho alaihe wasallam) in his salaat. Once Hadhrat Saudah (Radhiyallaho anha) stood after him in Tahajjud. The next day she said to him:

> "O, Prophet of Allah! Last night you took so long in your Ruk'u that I apprehended bleeding from my nose."

(As she was bulky, the strain might have been too much for her).

The Prophet (Sallallaho alaihe wasallam) once intended to divorce her. As meanwhile Hadhrat Aishah (Radhiyallaho anha) had also been married to the Prophet (Sallallaho alaihe wasallam), she said:

> "O, Prophet of Allah! I am ready to forego my turn in favour of Hadhrat Aishah (Radhiyallaho anha), but I don't like to be divorced (by you). I wish to be in Paradise as one of your wives."

The Prophet (Sallallaho alaihe wasallam) agreed to this suggestion. She died in about 55 A. H. towards the end of the Khilafat of Hadhrat Umar (Radhiyallaho anho).

There was another Qureysh woman of the same name. She was also a widow having about six children. The Prophet offered to marry her, but she said:

> "O, Prophet of Allah! You are dearer to me than any other person in this world. I do not like my children to be a nuisance to you."

He appreciated this, and withdrew the offer.

(3) Hadhrat Aishah (Radhiyallaho anha):

Hadhrat Aishah (Radhiyallaho anha) too was married to the Prophet (Sallallaho alaihe wasallam) in Swawwal of the 10th year of the Nubuwwat. She was born in the 4th year of Nubuwwat and was married when she was six, but was actually sent by her parents to live with the Prophet (Sallallaho alaihe wasallam) after his emigration to Madinah, when she was nine. She was eighteen at the time of the Prophet Sallallaho alaihe wasallam's death. She died on the night of Tuesday, the 17th Ramadhan, 57 A. H., at the age of sixty-six. She desired at the time of her death that she might be buried, along with other Ummahat-ul-Momineen, in the public graveyard, though she could be buried by the side of the Prophet's grave, which was in her house. She was the only wife of the Prophet who had not been married previously. All the remaining wives had either been widowed or divorced (some quite a few times) before they became Ummuhat-ul-Momineen. To be married in Shawwal was considered a bad omen among the Arab women. Hadhrat Aishah (Radhiyallaho anha) says:

> "I was married in Shawwal. It was also Shawwal when I was sent to live with the Prophet (Sallallaho alaihe wasallam). Which of the Prophet (Sallallaho alaihe wasallam's) wives has been more blessed with his love and Allah's other favours than me?"

On the death of Hadhrat Khadijah (Radhiyallaho anha), Hadhrat Khaulah bint Hakim (Radhiyallaho anha) came to the Prophet (Sallallaho alaihe wasallam) and said:

"O, Prophet of Allah! Don't you like to marry again?"

The Prophet (Sallallaho alaihe wasallam):
"Whom can I marry?"

Khaylah:
"I know one virgin and one widow."

The Prophet (Sallallaho alaihe wasallam):
"Name them."

Khaulah:
"The virgin is Aishah, (Radhiyallaho anha) the daughter of your bosom friend Abu Bakr (Radhiyallaho anho), and the widow is Saudah bint Zam'ah."

The Prophet (Sallallaho alaihe wasallam):
"All right! You may make the proposal."

Hadhrat Khaulah (Radhiyallaho anha) then went to Hadhrat Aisha (Radhiyallaho anha's) mother Hadhrat Umme-Rooman (Radhiyallaho anha) and said to her:

"I have come with good tidings for your family."

Hadhrat Umme Rooman (Radhiyallaho anha):
"What is that?"

Hadhrat Khaulah (Radhiyallaho anha):

"The Prophet (Sallallaho alaihe wasallam) has sent me to seek Hadhrat Aishah (Radhiyallaho anha's) hand for him"

Hadhrat Umme Rooman (Radhiyallaho anha):

"But 'Hadhrat Aishah (Radhiyallaho anha) is like his niece. How can she be married to him? Let me consult her father."

Hadhrat Abu Bakr (Radhiyallaho anho) was not at home at that time. When he came, the proposal was placed before him, and he expressed the same difficulty. Hadhrat Khaulah (Radhiyallaho anho) returned to the Prophet (Sallallaho alaihe wasallam) and apprised him of their difficulty. The Prophet (Sallallaho alaihe wasallam) said:

"Abu Bakr is my bosom friend and brother-in-Islam, but this does not forbid my marrying his daughter."

Hadhrat Khaulah (Radhiyallaho anho) went and informed Hadhrat Abu Bakr (Radhiyallaho anho) accordingly. Abu Bakr (Radhiyallaho anho) was extremely glad to call the Prophet (Sallallaho alaihe wasallam) to his home and perform Aishah's (Radhiyallaho anha) Nikah with him. A few months later, when the Prophet (Sallallaho alaihe wasallam) had emigrated to Madinah, Hadhrat Abu Bakr (Radhiyallaho anho) said to the Prophet:

"Why don't you have your wife Hadhrat Aishah (Radhiyallaho anho) to live with you?"

He said: "I have to make some preparations, etc., before I do that."

Hadhrat Abu Bakr (Radhiyallaho anho) presented him with some money, with which necessary things were arranged. Hadhrat Aishah (Radhiyallaho anho) then started living with the Prophet from Shawwal of 1 or 2 A. H. She shared the bed with the Prophet (Sallallaho alaihe wasallam) for the first time in Hadhrat Abu Bakr (Radhiyallaho anho's) house.

These are the three marriages, which the Prophet (Sallallaho alaihe wasallam) had before Hijrah. All the remaining wives were taken by him in Madinah.

(4) Hadhrat Hafsah (Radhiyallaho anho):

Hafsah was the daughter of 'Hadhrat Umar (Radhiyallaho anho) who was born in Mecca five years before the Nubuwwat. She was first married to Hadhrat Khunais bin Huzaifah (Radhiyallaho anho), who was one of the very early Muslims. He first emigrated to Abyssinia and then to Madinah. He participated in Badr, and was fatally wounded in Badr (or in Uhud) and died of the wound in the year 1 or 2 A. H. Hadhrat Hafsah (Radhiyallaho anho) had also emigrated to Madinah with her husband. When her husband died, Hadhrat Umar (Radhiyallaho anho) went to Hadhrat Abu Bakr (Radhiyallaho anho) and said:

> "I want to give Hafsah in marriage to you."

Hadhrat Abu Bakr (Radhiyallaho anho) kept quiet and said nothing. Meanwhile Ruqayyah (Radhiyallaho anho) the daughter of the Prophet (Sallallaho alaihe wasallam) and the wife of 'Hadhrat Usman (Radhiyallaho anho) died. 'Hadhrat Umar (Radhiyallaho anho) went to Hadhrat Usman (Radhiyallaho anho) and offered Hadhrat Hafsah (Radhiyallaho anho's) hand to him. He declined by saying, "I have no mind to marry for the present." 'Hadhrat Umar (Radhiyallaho anho) complained of this to the Prophet. The Prophet said:

> "I tell you of a husband for Hafsah better than 'Usman, and of a wife for 'Usman better than Hafsah."

He then took Hadhrat Hafsah (Radhiyallaho anho) as his next wife, and gave his own daughter Hadhrat Umme Kulsum (Radhiyallaho anha) in marriage to 'Hadhrat (Radhiyallaho anho) Usman. Hadhrat Abu Bakr (Radhiyallaho anho) later said to 'Hadhrat 'Usman Umar (Radhiyallaho anho):

> "When you offered Hafsah's hand to me, I kept quiet as the Prophet had expressed to me his intention of marrying her. I could neither accept your offer nor disclose the Prophet's secret to you. I, therefore, kept quiet. If the Prophet (Sallallaho alaihe wasallam) had changed his mind, I would have gladly married her."

'Hadhrat Umar (Radhiyallaho anho) says:

> "Abu Bakr's silence over the offer was in fact more shocking to me than 'Usman's rejection."

Hadhrat Hafsah (Radhiyallaho anha) was a very pious woman, and very much devoted to Salaat. She would often fast during the day and spend the night in prayers. Once the Prophet (Sallallaho alaihe wasallam), for some reason, was displeased with Hafsah and even pronounced the first divorce to her. 'Hadhrat Umar (Radhiyallaho anho) was naturally very much shocked over this. Jibra-eel Alayhis came to the Prophet (Sallal Salaam laho alaihe wasallam) and said:

> "Allah wants you to take Hafsah back, as she is fasting often and spending her nights in Salaat, and also Allah wants it for Hadhrat Umar's (Radhiyallaho anho) sake."

The Prophet (Sallallaho alaihe wasallam) therefore took her back She died in Jamadil oola, 45 A. H., at the age of 63.

(5) Hadhrat Zainab bint Khuzaimah (Radhiyallaho anha):

Hadhrat Zainab (Radhiyallaho anha) was the next to be married to the Prophet (Sallallaho alaihe wasallam). There are divergent reports about her previous husbands. According to one report, she was first married to Hadhrat Abdullah bin Jahsh (Radhiyallaho anho) who was killed in Uhud, as we have already seen in his story in chapter VII. According to another report, she was first married to Tufail ibnul al Harith and when divorced by him was remarried to his brother Ubaidah ibnul Harith, who was killed in Badr. The Prophet (Sallallaho alaihe wasallam) married her in Ramadhan, 3 A. H. She lived with the Prophet (Sallallaho alaihe wasallam) for eight months only, as she died in Rabi-ul-Akhir, 4 A. H. Hadhrat Zainab and Hadhrat Khadijah (Radhiyallaho anhuma) are the two wives of the Prophet who died during his life time. All the other wives lived on after him and died later. Hadhrat Zainab (Radhiyallaho anha) spent very liberally on the poor, and was known as 'Ummul Masakin' (mother of the poor) even before Islam.

After her death, the Prophet (Sallallaho alaihe wasallam) married Hadhrat Umme Salmah (Radhiyallaho anha).

(6) Hadhrat Umme Salamah (Radhiyallaho anha):

She was the daughter of Hadhrat Abu Ummayyah. (Radhiyallaho anho). She was first married to her cousin Hadhrat Abdullah bin Abdul Asad known as Abu Salamah (Radhiyallaho anho). The couple embraced Islam in the very beginning and emigrated to Abyssinia, due to the persecutions of Qureysh. A son was born to them in exile, who was named Salamah. After returning from Abyssinia, the family emigrated to Madinah. Hadhrat Umme Salamah's (Radhiyallaho anha) story about her journey to Madinah has been already given in the early part of the chapter. After reaching Madinah, Hadhrat Umme Salmah (Radhiyallaho anha) got another son 'Umar and two daughters, Durrah and Zainab (Radhiyallaho anhum). Hadhrat Abu Salamah (Radhiyallaho anho) was the eleventh man to embrace Islam. He participated in the battle of Badr as well as in Uhud. He got a severe wound in Uhud, which did not heal for a long time. He was sent by the Prophet (Sallallaho alaihe wasallam) in an expedition in Safar, 4 A. H. When he returned from the expedition, the old wound again started giving trouble and at last he died of the same on 8th Jamadil-Akhir, 4 A. H. Hadhrat Umme Salamah (Radhiyallaho anha) was pregnant at the time. Zainab was born to her after the death of her husband. After she had completed her Iddat (waiting period), Hadhrat Abu Bakr (Radhiyallaho anho) proposed to marry her, but she declined.

Later, the Prophet (Sallallaho alaihe wasallam) offered to marry her. She said:

> "O, Prophet of Allah! I have quite a few children with me and I am very sensitive by nature. Moreover, all my people are in Mecca, and their permission for getting remarried is necessary."

The Prophet (Sallallaho alaihe wasallam) said:

> "Allah will look after your children and your sensitiveness will vanish in due course. None of your people will dislike the proposed marriage".

She then asked her (eldest) son Hadhrat Salamah (Radhiyallaho anho) to serve as her guardian and give her in marriage to the Prophet (Sallallaho alaihe wasallam). She was married in the end of Shawwal, 4 A. H.

She says: "I had heard from the Prophet (Sallallaho alaihe wasallam) that a person struck with a calamity should recite this prayer:

اَللّٰهُمَّ اَجِرْنِى فِى مُصِيْبَتِى وَاخْلُفْنِى خَيْرًا مِّنْهَا

"O, Allah! Recompense me for this affliction by giving me something better than what I have lost: then Allah would accept his prayer." I had been reciting this prayer since the death of Hadhrat Abu Salamah (Radhiyallaho anho), but I could not imagine a husband better than he, till Allah arranged my marriage with the Prophet (Sallallaho alaihe wasallam)."

Hadhrat Aishah (Radhiyallaho anha) says:

"Umme Salamah (Radhiyallaho anha) was famous for her beauty. Once I contrived to see her. I found her much more beautiful than I had heard. I mentioned this to Hafsah who said. "In my opinion, she is not as beautiful as people say."

She was the last of the Prophet (Sallallaho alaihe wasallam's) wives to die. It was in 59 or 62 A. H. She was 84 at the time of her death, and as such she was born 9 years before Nubuwwat.

As has already been said, the Prophet (Sallallaho alaihe wasallam) married her after the death of Hadhrat Zainab bint Khuzaimah (Radhiyallaho anha). She therefore lived in Hadhrat Zainab (Radhiyallaho anha's) house. She found a hand-mill, a kettle and some barley in an earthen jar, lying in the house. She milled some barley and after putting some fat cooked a preparation, which she served to the Prophet (Sallallaho alaihe wasallam) on the very first day of her marriage with him.

(7) Hadhrat Zainab bint Jahsh (Radhiyallaho anha):

She was the Prophet (Sallallaho alaihe wasallam's) cousin. She was first given in marriage by the Prophet (Sallallaho alaihe wasallam) to his adopted son Hadhrat Zaid bin Harithah (Radhiyallaho anho). When Hadhrat Zaid (Radhiyallaho anho) divorced her, she was married to the Prophet (Sallallaho alaihe wasallam) by command of Allah, as mentioned in Soorah Al Ahzab. This took place in 5 A. H; at that time, she was 35. She was therefore born 17 years before Nabuwat. She was always proud of the fact that, while all the other wives were given in marriage to the Prophet by their guardians, it was Allah Himself Who did this for her. When Hadhrat Zaid (Radhiyallaho anho) divorced her and she had completed her Iddat, the Prophet (Sallallaho alaihe wasallam) sent the proposal to her. She said:

"I cannot say anything until I have consulted my

Allah." She performed Wudhu, said two rakaat of Salaat, and prayed to Allah:

"O, Allah! Thy Prophet proposes to marry me. If I am fit for the honour, then give me in his marriage."

Allah answered her prayer by revealing the following verse to the Prophet (Sallallaho alaihe wasallam):

فَلَمَّا قَضٰى زَيْدٌ مِّنْهَا وَطَرًا زَوَّجْنٰكَهَا لِكَىْ لَايَكُوْنَ عَلَى الْمُؤْمِنِيْنَ حَرَجٌ فِىْ
أَزْوَاجِ أَدْعِيَآئِهِمْ اِذَا قَضَوْا مِنْهُنَّ وَطَرًا ، وَكَانَ اَمْرُ اللّٰهِ مَفْعُوْلًا (الاحزاب ٣٧)

"So when Zaid had performed the necessary formality (of divorce) from her, we gave her unto thee in marriage, so that (henceforth) there may be no sin for believers in respect of the wives of their adopted sons, when the latter have performed the necessary formality (of release) from them. The Commandment of Allah must be fulfilled." (XXXIII: 37)

When she received the good news about this revelation, she prostrated before Allah in thanksgiving. The Prophet (Sallallaho alaihe wasallam) arranged a big feast of Walimah for this marriage. A goat was slaughtered and mutton-curry with bread was served to the guests. People came in groups, and were served till all of them were fed.

Hadhrat Zainab (Radhiyallaho anha) had a very large heart for spending in the way of Allah. She earned by working with her hands and spent all her earnings in charity. It was about her that the Prophet (Sallallaho alaihe wasallam) prophesied:

"My wife with long hands will be the first to meet me after my death."

The wives took this to mean the physical length of arms and began to measure their hands with a stick. The hands of Hadhrat Saudah (Radhiyallaho anha) came out to be the longest by measurement. But when Hadhrat Zainab (Radhiyallaho anha) died first, the meaning of the metaphor used by the Prophet (Sallallaho alaihe wasallam) dawned upon them. She fasted very often. She died in 20 A. H. and Umar (Radhiyallaho anho) led the funeral service. She was fifty at the time of her death.

(8) Hadhrat Juwairiah bintul Harith (Radhiyallaho anha):

Hadhrat Juwairiah (Radhiyallaho anha) was the daughter of Harith, the chief of Banu Mustaliq and was married to Musafe' bin Safwan.

She was one of the large number of captives who fell into Muslim hands after the battle of Muraisee', and she was given to Hadhrat Thabit bin Qais (Radhiyallaho anho). He offered to release her for 360 Dirhams. She came to the Prophet (Sallallaho alaihe wasallam) and said:

> "O, Prophet of Allah! I am the daughter of Harith who is the chief of the tribe, and you know my story. The ransom demanded by Hadhrat Thabit (Radhiyallaho anho) is too much for me. I have come to seek your help in the matter."

The Prophet (Sallallaho alaihe wasallam) agreed to pay her ransom, set her free, and offered to take her as his wife. She was very glad to accept this offer. She was married to the Prophet in 5 A. H. and as a consequence of this marriage, the prisoners of Banu Mustaliq (Juwairiah's tribe), about a hundred families, were all set free by the Muslims. "The tribe which was so honoured by the Prophet's relationship," they said, "should not remain in slavery."

Such were the noble expediences in all the marriages of the Prophet. Hadhrat Juwairiah (Radhiyallaho anha) was very pretty, her face was very attractive. Three days before her falling captive in the battle, she had seen in her dream the moon coming out from Madinah and falling into her lap. She says:

> "When I was captured, I began to hope that my dream would come true."

She was 20 at the time of her marriage with the Prophet (Sallallaho alaihe wasallam). She died in Rabi-ul-Awwal, 50 A. H., in Madinah at the age of 65.

(9) Hadhrat Umme Habibah (Radhiyallaho anha):

She was the daughter of Abu Sufyan, and was first married to Ubaidullah bin Jahsh in Mecca. The couple embraced Islam, and then emigrated to Abyssinia due to persecution by the Qureysh. One night she saw her husband (in a dream) in the most ugly and obnoxious form. The next day she came to know that he had turned Christian. She, however, remained a Muslim and was therefore separated from him. She was now all alone in exile. But Allah soon recompensed her loss. The Prophet (Sallallaho alaihe wasallam) sent her an offer of marriage through the King Negus, who sent a woman named Abrahah to her with the message. She was so happy with the good news that she made over the bracelets and other jewellery that she was wearing to the woman in gratification. King Negus represented the Prophet (Sallallaho alaihe wasallam) in the Nikah ceremony, and gave her 400 dinars as her portion and many other things in dowry from himself. He also gave a feast and dinars as gift to all those who were present in the ceremony. The Negus then despatched her to Madinah with her dowry and other gifts such as perfume, etc. This marriage took place in 7 A. H. (Her father was not a Muslim then). She most probably died in 44 A. H.

(10) Hadhrat Safiyyah (Radhiyallaho anha):

She was the daughter of Hayi, who was a descendant of Hadhrat Harun (Alaihis salaam) the brother of Hadhrat Moosa (Alaihis salaam). She was first married to Salam bin Mishkam and then to Kinanah bin Abi Huqaiq at the time of Kheybar. Kinanah was killed in the battle and she was captured by the Muslims. Hadhrat Dahya Kalbi (Radhiyallaho anho) requested for a maid, and the Prophet made her over to him. At this, the other Sahabah approached the Prophet (Sallallaho alaihe wasallam) and said:

> "O, Prophet of Allah! Banu Nazir and Banu Quraizah (the Jewish tribes of Madinah) will feel offended to see the daughter of a Jewish chief working as a maid. We therefore suggest that she may be taken as your own wife."

The Prophet paid a reasonable sum of money to Hadhrat Dahya (Radhiyallaho anho) as ransom, and said to Safiyyah:

> "You are now free; if you like you can go back to your tribe or can be my wife."

She said: "I longed to be with you while I was a Jew. How can I leave you now, when I am a Muslim?"

This is probably a reference to the fact that she once saw in her dream a portion of the moon falling into her lap. When she mentioned her dream to Kinanah, he smote her face so severely that she developed a mark on her eye. He said:

"You seem to be desiring to become the wife of the King of Madinah."

Her father is also reported to have treated her similarly when she related the same or similar dream to him. She again saw (in her dream) the sun lying on her breast. When she mentioned this to her husband, he remarked:

"You seem to be wishing to become the Queen of Madinah."

She says: "I was seventeen when I was married to the Prophet (Sallallaho alaihe wasallam).

She came to live with the Prophet (Sallallaho alaihe wasallam) when he was camping at the first stage from Khaiber. Next morning, he said to the Sahabah:

"Let everybody bring whatever he has got to eat."

They brought their own dates, cheese, butter, etc. A long leather sheet was spread and all sat round it to share the food among themselves. This was the Walimah for the marriage.

She died in Ramadhan, 50 A. H., when she was about 60.

(11) Hadhrat Maimoonah (Radhiyallaho anha):

She was the daughter of Harith bin Hazan. Her original name was Barrah, but she was later renamed Maimoonah by the Prophet (Sallallaho alaihe wasallam). She was first married to Abu Rahm bin Abdul Uzza. According to some reports, she was married twice before she became Ummul Mominin. She had been widowed lately when the Prophet (Sallallaho alaihe wasallam) married her at Saraf, a place lying on his journey to Mecca for 'Umrah in Zul Qa'dah 7 A. H. He had intended to start living with her when in Mecca after performing 'Umrah but, as Qureysh did not allow him to enter Mecca, he called her over to him in the same place on his return journey. Many years later she died and was buried exactly at the same place in 51 A. H. (when she was 81). This is a strange coincidence that at a certain place during one journey she is married, at the same place on the return journey she starts living with the Prophet, (Sallallaho alaihe wasallam) and at the very place during another journey she dies and is buried.

Hadhrat Aishah (Radhiyallaho anha) says:

"Maimoonah was the most pious, and the most mindful of her kith and kin, among the Prophet's wives."

Hadhrat Yazid bin Asam (Radhiyallaho anho) says:

"She was seen either engaged in Salat or in domestic work. When she was doing neither, she was busy in Miswak."

She was the last woman to be married by the Prophet (Sallallaho alaihe wasallam). Certain Muhaddithin have, however, mentioned one or two other marriages contracted by the Prophet (Sallallaho alaihe wasallam).

Appendix:
The Sons of The Prophet (Sallallaho alaihe wasallam):

The Prophet (Sallallaho alaihe wasallam) had three sons and four daughters. All the children were born from Hadhrat Khadija (Radhiyallaho anha), except the son Ibrahim. Qasim was his first son, born to him before Nubuwwat. He died when he was two. Abdullah, the second son, was born after Nubuwwat. He was, hence, called Tayyab and Taahir. He also died in his childhood. At the time of his death, the Qureysh rejoiced and said:

"Muhammad is without a son, and will therefore be without posterity. His name will also die out with his death."

It was on this occasion that Soorah Al-Kauthar was revealed by Allah. It said:

إِنَّآ أَعْطَيْنٰكَ الْكَوْثَرَ ، فَصَلِّ لِرَبِّكَ وَانْحَرْ ، إِنَّ شَانِئَكَ هُوَ الْأَبْتَرُ

(الكوثر ١، ٢، ٣)

"Lo! We have given thee Abundance. So pray unto thy Lord, and sacrifice. Lo! it is thy detractor (not thou) who is without posterity." (XVIII: 1 to 3)

Even after more than thirteen hundred years, today there are millions who are proud to be connected to him in love and devotion.

Ibrahim, the third son and last child, was born in Madinah in 8 A. H. The Prophet (Sallallaho alaihe wasallam's) woman slave Mariah begot this for him. The Prophet (Sallallaho alaihe wasallam) performed the Aqiqah ceremony on the seventh day of his birth. Two lambs were slaughtered, the child's head was shaved by Hadhrat Abu Hind Bayazi (Radhiyallaho anho), silver equal in weight to his hair was spent in charity, and the hair was buried. The Prophet (Sallallaho alaihe wasallam) said:

> "I am naming my child after the name of my forefather Ibrahim (Alaihis salaam)."

This son also died, on 10th of Rabi-ul-Awwal, 10 A. H., when he was only 18 months old. The Prophet (Sallallaho alaihe wasallam) then remarked:

> "Allah has appointed a heavenly nurse to tend to Ibrahim in the gardens of Paradise."

The Daughters of the Prophet (Sallallaho alaihe wasallam):

(1) Hadhrat Zainab (Radhiyallaho anha):

She was the eldest daughter of the Prophet (Sallallaho alaihe wasallam) and was born in the fifth year of his first marriage, when he was thirty. She embraced Islam and was married to her cousin Abul Aas bin Rabi. The story of her emigration to Madinah and her getting wounded by the Qureysh has already been given in the early part of this chapter. She suffered long from that wound, and at last died of it in the beginning of 8 A. H. Her husband also embraced Islam later and joined her in Madinah. She had a son Ali (Radhiyallaho anho), and a daughter Amamah. Ali died during the life time of the Prophet (Sallallaho alaihe wasallam). This same Ali (Radhiyallaho anho) was the person who sat with the Prophet (Sallallaho alaihe wasallam) on the camel's back at the time of his triumphal entry into Mecca. We read frequently in Hadith about a little girl riding on the back of the Prophet (Sallallaho alaihe wasallam) as he prostrated in Salaat; this was Amamah, Zainab's (Radhiyallaho anha) daughter. She lived long after the death of the Prophet (Sallallaho alaihe wasallam). Ali (Radhiyallaho anho) married her on the death of Fatima (Radhiyallaho anha)—his first wife. It is said that Fatimah (Radhiyallaho anha) at the time of her death had expressed a desire for this union. She had no issue from Ali (Radhiyallaho anho). After Hadhrat Ali's (Radhiyallaho anho) death she was again married to Hadhrat Mughirah bin Naufal (Radhiyallaho anho), from whom she probably got one son named Yahya. She died in 50 A. H.

(2) Hadhrat Ruqayyah (Radhiyallaho anha):

She was born three years after the birth of Hadhrat Zainab (Radhiyallaho anha), when the Prophet (Sallallaho alaihe wasallam) was 33. She was married to Utbah, son of Abu Lahab, the Prophet's (Sallallaho alaihe wasallam) uncle, but had not yet started living with him when Soorah Al-Lahab was revealed. Abu Lahab called his sons Utbah and Utaibah (to whom Umme Kulsum, another daughter of the Prophet (Sallallaho alaihe wassallam) was married), and said to them:

> "Unless you both divorce the daughters of Muhammad, I am not going to see your faces."

They divorced their wives. Later, upon the fall of Mecca, Utbah embraced Islam. Hadhrat Ruqayyah (Radhiyallaho anha) after this divorce was married to Hadhrat 'Usman (Radhiyallaho anho). The couple emigrated to Abyssinia twice, as we have already seen in chapter I.

Since the Prophet (Sallallaho alaihe wasallam) had announced to the Sahabah that he was expecting to receive Allah's command for emigration to Madinah any time, they started shifting to Madinah even before the Prophet's (Sallallaho alaihe wassallam) Hijrat. Hadhrat Usman (Radhiyallaho anho) and Hadhrat Ruqayyah (Radhiyallaho anha) had also emigrated to Madinah before the Prophet (Sallallaho alaihe wasallam) arrived in the town. At the time of Badr, Ruqayyah was ill (she died subsequently of this illness). 'Usman (Radhiyallaho anho) was, therefore, asked by the Prophet (Sallallaho alaihe wasallam) to stay in Madinah and look after her. The news about the victory in Badr was received in Madinah when people were returning from Ruqayyah's funeral. The Prophet (Sallallaho alaihe wasallam) was, therefore, not present at her burial.

A son was born to Hadhrat Ruqayyah (Radhiyallaho anha) in Abyssinia. He was named Abdullah and survived his mother, but died in 4 A. H. when he was six years old

(3) Hadhrat Umme Kulsum (Radhiyallaho anha):

She is the third daughter of the Prophet (Sallallaho alaihe wasallam). She was married to Utaibah son of Abu Lahab, but had not yet started living with him when Utaibah divorced her after the revelation of Soorah Al-Lahab, as has already been mentioned. After divorcing her, Utaibah came to the Prophet (Sallallaho alaihe wasallam) and used most insolent words to him. The Prophet (Sallallaho alaihe wasallam) cursed him by praying:

"O, Allah! depute one of Thy dogs to punish him."

Abu Talib, who had also not embraced Islam, was alarmed at the curse and said to Utaibah:

"You have no way out now."

Once Utaibah was accompanying Abu Lahab in a caravan going to Syria. Abu Lahab, in spite of his disbelief, said to the people:

"I am afraid of Muhammad's curse. Everybody should be very careful of my son."

They happened to camp at a place which was inhabited by lions. The people piled up all their luggage and Utaibah was made to sleep on top of the pile, while the rest of the people slept around the pile. A lion came at night; it smelt all the people sleeping round the pile. Then it jumped over the people and reached Utaibah. He gave out a shriek, but meanwhile the lion had severed his head from his body. It is very necessary that we avoid offending the people dear to Allah. The Prophet (Sallallaho alaihe wasallam) has reported Allah as saying:

مَنْ عَادٰى لِىْ وَلِيًّا فَقَدْ اٰذَنْتُهٗ بِالْحَرْبِ

"I give a challenge of war to one who offends My friends."

After the death of Hadhrat Ruqayyah (Radhiallaho anha), Hadhrat Umme Kulsum (Radhiyallaho anha) was also married to Hadhrat 'Usman (Radhiyallaho anho) in Rabi-ul-Awwal, 3 A. H. The Prophet (Sallallaho alaihe wasallam) said:

"I have given Umme Kulsum in marriage to Usman by Allah's command."

She died issueless in Shaaban, 9 A. H. After her death, the Prophet (Sallallaho alaihe wasallam) is reported to have remarked:

"Even if I had one hundred daughters, I would have given all of them in marriage to 'Usman (one after the other), if each one had died."

(4) Hadhrat Fatimah (Radhiyallaho anha):

Hadhrat Fatimah (Radhiyallaho anha) the fourth and the youngest daughter of the Prophet (Sallallaho alaihe wasallam), and the "head of the ladies in Paradise" was born in the 1st year of Nubuwwat, when he was 41. It is said that the name Fatimah (lit: safe from fire) was revealed by Allah. She was married to Ali (Radhiyallaho anho) in 2 A. H. and she began to live with him seven and a half months later. She was about fifteen and Ali was 21 at the time of their union. Of all the daughters, she was the most loved by the Prophet (Sallallaho alaihe wasallam); whenever he went out on a journey, she was the last one to part with and when he returned home she was the first one to meet him. When Ali (Radhiyallaho anho) intended to marry Abu Jahal's daughter, she was very much grieved and expressed her grief to the Prophet (Sallallaho alaihe wasallam). The Prophet (Sallallaho alaihe wasallam) said to Ali (Radhiyallaho anho):

> "Fatimah is a part of my body. Whoever grieves her, grieves me."

Ali (Radhiyallaho anho) gave up the idea of the second marriage during her life time. After her death, he married her niece Amamah (Radhiyallaho anha), as we have already seen in the previous pages.

It was about six months after the death of the Prophet (Sallallaho alaihe wasallam) that Fatimah fell ill. One day, she said to her maid:

> "I want to take a bath. Arrange some water for me."

She took a bath and changed her clothes. She then desired her bed to be placed in the middle of the room. She laid herself down on the bedding, with her face towards Qiblah, and her right hand under her right cheek, and said:

> "I am now going to die."

The next moment she was no more. The Prophet's (Sallallaho alaihe wasallam) progeny continued and shall continue (inshallah) through her children. She had three sons and three daughters. Hasan (Radhiyallaho anho) and Hussain (Radhiyallaho anho) were born in the second and the third year after the marriage, respectively. Muhassan (Radhiyallaho anho), the third son, was born in 4 A. H., but died in childhood.

Ruqayyah, her first daughter, died in infancy and has, therefore, not been mentioned much in history. Her second daughter Umme Kulsum was first married to Hadhrat Umar (Radhiyallaho anho), begetting one son Zaid and one daughter Hadhrat Ruqayyah. On Hadhrat 'Umar (Radhiyallaho anho's) death, Hadhrat Umme Kulsum (Radhiyallaho anha) was married to Aun bin Ja'far, but had no issue from him. After his death, his brother Muhammad bin Ja'far married her. A daughter was born to them, who died in childhood. Even Muhammad (Radhiyallaho anho) died in her lifetime and she was again married to the third brother, Abdullah bin Ja'far (Radhiyallaho anho), from whom she had no issue. She died as Abdullah's wife. Her son Zaid also died the same day, and both were carried for burial at the same time. Abdullah, 'Aun and Muhammad (Radhiyallaho anhum) have already been mentioned as sons of Ja'far (Radhiyallaho anho) and nephews of Ali (Radhiyallaho anho) in chapter VI.

Zainab, Hadhrat Fatima's (Radhiyallaho anha) third daughter, was married to Abdullah bin Ja'far and had two sons Abdullah and Aun from him. It was after her death that he married her sister Hadhrat Umme Kulsum (Radhiyallaho anha). Hadhrat Ali (Radhiyallaho anho) had many other children from his wives after Fatimah. It is stated that he had as many as thirty-two issues. Hasan (Radhiyallaho anho) had fifteen sons and eight daughters, while Husain (Radhiyallaho anho) was the father of six sons and three daughters.

رَضِیَ اللّٰہُ تَعَالٰی عَنْھُمْ وَاَرْضَاھُمْ اَجْمَعِیْنَ وَجَعَلْنَا بِھَدْیِھِمْ مُتَّبِعِیْنَ وَاللّٰہُ اَعْلَمُ
وَعِلْمُهٗ اَتَمُّ (ملخص من الخميس والزرقانى على المواهب والتلقيح والاصابة واسد الغابه)

CHAPTER XI

THE CHILDREN – THEIR DEVOTION TO ISLAM

The true spirit of Islam that we find in the children of Sahabah's time was the fruit of the upbringing which they received at the hands of their parents. The parents and guardians of our times spoil the children by over fondling them. If, instead, they inculcated in their young hearts the importance of Islamic practices, these could easily become their habits when they grow up. When we see a child doing something undesirable, we simply brush it off by saying, 'He is but a child.' We have seen some parents even feeling happy over their darling (child) having sufficient grown up to do such unseemly things. We deceive ourselves when we say, on seeing a child doing something un-Islamic, that he will be all right when he grows up.

How can a bad seed grow up into a good plant? If you really wish your child to be a good Muslim when he is grown up, you have to sow the seed of Iman and Islam in his heart right from his childhood. The Sahabah were very particular about training their children in Islamic practices, and they kept a watchful eye on their doings.

In Hadhrat 'Umar's (Radhiyallaho anho) time, a person was arrested by the police for drinking in Ramadhan. When he was brought before Hadhrat 'Umar (Radhiyallaho anho), he said to him:

> "Woe to you! Even our children are keeping fast in this month."

He was punished with eighty lashes and was banished from Madinah for ever.

1. Children keep fast.

Hadhrat Rubbayi' bint Mu'awwaz (Radhiyallaho anha) (who was mentioned in the last chapter) says:

> "Once the Prophet (Sallallaho alaihe wasallam) enjoined on us to fast on the 10th of Muharram. Since then we have always been fasting on that day. Even the children were made to fast with us. When they cried

out in hunger, we diverted them with toys made of cotton flakes till the time of Iftaar."

We learn from Hadith that the nursing mothers of those days would not feed their infants during the fast. No doubt they could bear all this, as their general health and endurance were decidedly of much higher standard than ours. But, are we really doing even what we can easily bear? Surely, we should not impose on our children what they cannot stand, but we must tax them with what they can easily endure.

2. Hadhrat Aishah's (Radhiyallaho anha) Zeal for Knowledge.

Hadhrat Aishah (Radhiyallaho anha) was given in Nikah when she was six. She started living with the Prophet (Sallallaho alaihe wasallam) when she was nine. She was only 18 at the time of the Prophet's passing away. Notwithstanding her age, she is responsible for innumerable Ahadiths and regulations of Islamic practices. Masrooq (Rahmatullah alaih) says:

> "I saw many eminent Sahabah coming to Aishah (Radhiyallaho anha) for seeking knowledge about Islamic jurisprudence."

'Ata (Rahmatullah alaih) says:

> "Aishah (Radhiyallaho anha) was more learned than any of the men of her time."

Hadhrat Abu Moosa (Radhiyallaho anho) says:

> "With the help of Hadhrat Aishah (Radhiyallaho anha), a solution was found to each and every problem we had to face in the field of religious knowledge."

The books of Hadith contain as many as 2 210 Ahadith narrated by Hadhrat Aishah (Radhiyallaho anha). She says:

> "I was a child and playing with my playmates in Mecca when the verse,

بَلِ السَّاعَةُ مَوْعِدُهُمْ وَالسَّاعَةُ اَدْهٰى وَاَمَرُّ (القمر ٤٦)

> (Nay, but the Hour is their appointed tryst, and the Hour will be more wretched and more bitter–LIV: 46), was revealed to the Prophet (Sallallaho alaihe wasallam)."

We know she emigrated to Madinah when she was only eight. She would have been much younger at the revelation of this early Meccan verse. This clearly shows her great zeal and devotion for Islamic knowledge right from her childhood.

3. Hadhrat 'Umair (Radhiyallaho anho) goes to Battle.

Hadhrat Umair (Radhiyallaho anho) was a slave of Abil Lahm (Radhiyallaho anho) and of very tender age. Every soul in those days, irrespective of age, was eager to strive in the Path of Allah, 'Umair (Radhiyallaho anho) requested the Prophet (Sallallaho alaihe wasallam) to permit him to fight in the battle of Khaiber. His master also recommended him very strongly. The Prophet (Sallallaho alaihe wasallam) permitted him and gave him a sword, which 'Umair (Radhiyallaho anho) hung round his neck. Now the sword was too big for his size, and he had to drag it with him. He fought in the battle till it ended in victory. As he was a minor and a slave, he was not entitled to full share in the booty. The Prophet (Sallallaho alaihe wasallam), however, allotted him a share as a very special case.

Although 'Umair (Radhiyallaho anho) knew that he was not going to get any share from the spoils of war, yet he was so eager to fight in the battle and sought recommendations for it. What could be his motive other than the reward of the Hereafter, as promised by Allah and reported by the Prophet (Sallallaho alaihe wasallam).

4. Hadhrat 'Umair bin Abi Waqqaas (Radhiyallaho anho) hides himself.

Hadhrat 'Umair bin Abi Waqqaas (Radhiyallaho anho) was a Sahabi of tender age, who had embraced Islam in its early days. He was a brother of Hadhrat Sa'd bin Abi Waqqaas (Radhiyallaho anha) the famous Muslim general. Hadhrat Sa'd (Radhiyallaho anho) narrates:

> "At the time when we were preparing to march for Badr, I noticed 'Umair (Radhiyallaho anho) trying somehow to hide himself. This surprised me. I said to him, 'What has happened to you? What makes you hide like this?' He replied, 'I am afraid the Prophet (Sallallaho alaihe wasallam) may stop me from taking part in the battle on account of my young age, though I

am yearning to go and get martyred in the path of Allah."

Hadhrat 'Umair's (Radhiyallaho anho) fear proved just true. The Prophet (Sallallaho alaihe wasallam) detected him and then stopped him from going with the army. Hadhrat 'Umair (Radhiyallaho anho) could not bear this and began to cry. When the Prophet (Sallallaho alaihe wasallam) was informed of this eagerness and disappointment, he permitted him to go. He fought in the battle till he was killed.

Hadhrat Sa'd (Radhiyallaho anho), Umair's brother, says:

"The sword of Umair (Radhiyallaho anho) was too big for his size. I had to put a number of knots in the belt, so that it might not touch the ground."

5. Two Youngsters of the Ansar Kill Abu Jahl.

Hadhrat Abdur Rahman bin 'Auf (Radhiyallaho anho), one of the most eminent Sahabah, narrates:

"In the battle of Badr, I was standing in the fighting line when I noticed two Ansar youngsters, one on either side. I thought it would have been better if I had been between strong men who could then help me in need. Suddenly, one of the boys caught my hand and said, 'Uncle, do you know Abu Jahl?' I said, 'Yes, but what do you mean by this?' He said, 'I have come to know that the wretched man reviles the Prophet (Sallallaho alaihe wasallam). By Him who holds my life in His hand, if I see him, I will not leave him until I kill him or I am killed.' His words left me wonderstruck. Then the other boy had a similar talk with me. I happened to notice Abu Jahl dashing about in the battlefield on the back of his horse. I said to the boys, 'There is the object of your quest.' Both of them immediately darted towards him and started attacking him with their swords, till I saw him fall from the horse's back."

These boys were Hadhrat Ma'az bin Amr bin Jamooh and Ma'az bin Afra (Radhiyallaho anhuma). Ma'az bin Amr bin Jamooh says:

"I had heard the people say, 'No one can kill Abu Jahl. He is very well guarded'. At that time, I took upon myself to finish him."

Abu Jahl was arranging his lines for assault, when he

was spotted by Hadhrat Abdur Rahman bin Auf (Radhiyallaho anho). The boys were on foot, while Abu Jahl was on horse back. One of the boys hit a leg of the horse and the other that of Abu Jahl. This caused both to fall down and Abu Jahl was unable to get up. The boys left him in this condition. Mu'awwaz bin Afra brother of Hadhrat Ma'az bin Afra (Radhiyallaho anho) then went and further disabled him with his sword, so that he might not drag himself to his camp. Hadhrat Abdullah bin Masood (Radhiyallaho anho), last of all, attacked him and severed his head from the body."

Hadhrat Ma'az bin Amr bin Jamooh (Radhiyallaho anho) says:

"When I hit Abu Jahl with my sword, his son Ikramah was with him. He attacked me on my shoulder and cut my arm, leaving it hanging by the skin only. I threw the broken arm over my shoulder and kept fighting with one hand. But when I found it too cumbersome, I severed it from my body, by placing it under my foot and pulling myself up, and threw it away."

6. A Contest Between Rafe' and Samurah.

Whenever an army of Mujahidin moved out from Madinah for a campaign, the Prophet (Sallallaho alaihe wasallam) inspected them at some distance outside to ensure that nothing was lacking in men and equipment. It was here that he usually returned to Madinah all those tender-aged boys who had come out with the army in their zeal to fight for Islam. While setting out for Uhud, the Prophet (Sallallaho alaihe wasallam) carried out this inspection just outside Madinah. He ordered the young boys to go back. Among them were Abdullah bin 'Umar, Zaid bin Thabit, Usamah bin Zaid, Zaid bin Arqam, Bara bin Azib, Amr bin Hazam, Usaid bin Zubair, 'Urabah bin Aus, Abu Sa'eed Khudri, Samurah bin Jundub and Rafe' bin Khudaij (Radhiyallaho anhum). All of them had just entered their teens. Khudaij said to the Prophet (Sallallaho alaihe wasallam):

"O, Prophet of Allah! My son Rafe' is a very good archer."

Hadhrat Rafe' (Radhiyallaho anho) too, stood on his toes to show himself taller than he actually was. The Prophet (Sallallaho alaihe wasallam) permitted him to stay on. When

Samurah bin Jundub learnt about this, he complained to his step-father Murrah bin Sanan saying:

> "The Prophet (Sallallaho alaihe wasallam) has permitted Rafe' and rejected me, while I am sure to beat him in a wrestling contest and, therefore, I was more deserving of the Prophet's (Sallallaho alaihe wasallam) favour."

This was reported to the Prophet (Sallallaho alaihe wasallam), who allowed Samrah to prove his claim by wrestling with Rafe': Samurah did actually beat Rafe' in the bout and he too was permitted to stay in the army. A few more boys made similar efforts to stay on, and some of them did succeed. Meanwhile it became dark. The Prophet (Sallallaho alaihe wasallam) made necessary arrangements for the watch and ward of the camp during the night, and then inquired:

> "Now, who is going to guard my tent during the night?"

A person (standing at his place):

> "I, O Prophet of Allah!"

The Prophet (Sallallaho alaihe wasallam):

> "What is your name?"

The person:

> "Zakwan."

The Prophet (Sallallaho alaihe wasallam):

> "All right. You take your seat."

He again inquired:

> "Who else is volunteering to guard my tent for tonight?"

A voice:

> "I, O Prophet of Allah!"

The Prophet (Sallallaho alaihe wasallam):

> "Who are you?"

A voice:

> "Abu Saba' (father of Saba')."

The Prophet (Sallallaho alaihe wasallam):

"All right. Sit down."

He enquired for the third time:

"Who will be the third man to guard my tent, tonight?"

Again came a voice from the crowd:

"I, O Prophet of Allah!"

The Prophet (Sallallaho alaihe wasallam):

"Your name?"

The voice:

"Ibn Abdulqais (son of Abdul Qais)."

The Prophet (Sallallaho alaihe wasallam):

"All right. You also sit down."

Then the Prophet (Sallallaho alaihe wasallam) bade all the three volunteers to come to him. Only one person came forward.

The Prophet (Sallallaho alaihe wasallam):

"Where are your other two comrades?"

The Person:

"O Prophet of Allah! It was I who stood up all the three times.

The Prophet (Sallallaho alaihe wasallam) blessed him with his prayers, and allowed him to guard his tent. He kept watching the tent all night long.

Just look! How eager the Sahabah were to face death for the sake of Allah and His Prophet (Sallallaho alaihe wasallam). The children and adults, young and old, men and women, all were intoxicated with the same spirit of sacrifice and devotion.

Rafé bin Khudaij had offered to fight in Badr too, but he was not permitted. In Uhud, however, he was allowed to fight for the first time. Since then, he had been participating in almost all the campaigns. In Uhud the enemy's arrow struck him in his chest. When it was drawn out, a small remnant remained inside his body. This caused a wound, which eventually proved fatal in his old age.

7. Hadhrat Zaid (Radhiyallaho anho) Gets Preference for His Qur'an.

Hadhrat Zaid bin Thabit (Radhiyallaho anho) was six when he lost his father. He was eleven at the time of Hijrah.

He offered himself for the battle of Badr, but was rejected on account of his tender age. He again volunteered for Uhud. This time also he was not permitted, as we saw in the last story. He had since then been participating in all the campaigns. While the Mujahidin were marching towards Tabuk, the flag of Banu Malik clan was held by Ammarah. The Prophet (Sallallaho alaihe wasallam) bade him make over the flag to Zaid. Ammarah (Radhiyallaho anho) thought that perhaps somebody had made a complaint against him, which had displeased the Prophet (Sallallaho alaihe wasallam). He therefore said:

"O, Prophet of Allah! Is it due to somebody complaining against me?"

The Prophet (Sallallaho alaihe wasallam) said:

"No. But Zaid knows more Qur'an than you do. His Qur'an has given him preference."

It was common with the Prophet (Sallallaho alaihe wasallam) that he gave preference to the people in accordance with their virtues. Although this was an occasion of battle, and a knowledge of the Qur'an had no direct bearing on the issue, yet the Prophet (Sallallaho alaihe wasallam) gave preference to Zaid (Radhiyallaho anho) for his Qur'an. This distinction we find on other occasions as well. When a number of dead persons had to be accommodated in one grave (as in Uhud), they were buried in the order of their knowledge of the Qur'an, priority being given to those who knew more of it.

8. Hadhrat Abu Saeed Khudri's (Radhiyallaho anho) Restraint.

Abu Sa'eed Khudri (Radhiyallaho anho) says, "I was presented to the Prophet (Sallallaho alaihe wasallam) by my father for fighting at Uhud, when I was thirteen. My father recommended me saying:

'O, Prophet of Allah! He has a very good body. His bones are very well-developed."

The Prophet (Sallallaho alaihe wasallam) looked at me again and again, and finally rejected me due to my young age. My father, however, participated in the battle and was killed. He left me nothing to live on. I went to the Prophet (Sallallaho alaihe wasallam) to seek some financial help from him. Before I could express myself, he addressed me saying:

> 'Abu Saeed! Whoso seeks endurance from Allah! gets it; Whoso seeks chastity from Him, gets it; And whoso seeks contentment from Him will surely get it.'

After hearing this, I returned home without making any request to him. On this, Allah blessed him with such an exalted position that, among the younger Sahabah, there is nobody endowed with so much knowledge and learning as Hadhrat Abu Sa'eed (Radhiyallaho anho).

Look at the restraint of Abu Sa'eed at such a young age. As we know, in Uhud he had lost his father who had left him nothing to live on and therefore he fully deserved all help; yet a few words of the Prophet (Sallallaho alaihe wasallam) stopped him from talking of his distress and seeking a favour. Can a person much older than him show such a strength of character? In fact, the persons selected by Allah for the company of his dear Prophet (Sallallaho alaihe wasallam) did really deserve that honour. That is why the Prophet (Sallallaho alaihe wasallam) had said:

> "Allah has preferred my companions over all other men."

9. Hadhrat Salmah bin Akwah (Radhiyallaho anho) faces the Bandits.

Ghabah was a small village at four or five miles from Madinah. The Prophet's (Sallallaho alaihe wasallam) camels were sent to that place for grazing. Abdur Rahman Fazari, with the help of a few disbelievers, killed the person looking after the camels and took them away. The bandits were riding their horses, and all of them were armed. Salmah bin Akwah (Radhiyallaho anho) was going on foot in the morning with his bow and arrows, when he happened to see the bandits. He was only a boy but he ran very fast. It is said that he could beat the fastest horse in race. He was also a very good archer. No sooner did he see the bandits than he climbed up a hill and shouted towards

Madinah to raise an alarm. He then chased the bandits and, on approaching near them, started sending arrows one after the other. He did this so swiftly and incessantly that the bandits thought they were being chased by a large number of people. If any of the bandits happened to turn his horse towards him, he hid behind a tree and inflicted wounds on the animal with his arrow. The bandits at once retreated at full speed to escape from being captured. Salmah (Radhiyallaho anho) says:

> "I kept on chasing the bandits till all the camels taken away by them were behind me. Besides, in their flight they left behind 30 spears and 30 sheets of cloth of their own. Meanwhile, Uyainah bin Hisn (another bandit) and his party arrived on the scene to reinforce the bandits. They had meanwhile come to know that I was all alone. They now chased me in large concentration and I was compelled to climb up a hill. As they were about to approach me I shouted, 'Stop. First listen to me. Do you know who am I? I am Ibnul Akwah. By Him who has given glory to Muhammad (Sallallaho alaihe wasallam), if anyone of you chases me, he cannot catch me. On the other hand, if I run after any of you he cannot escape me.' I kept on talking to them in that strain to beguile them till, I thought, help would reach me from Madinah. I looked anxiously through the trees, as I talked to them when at last, I noticed a group of riders headed by Akhram Asadi (Radhiyallaho anho) coming towards me. As Akhram approached the bandits, he attacked Abdur Rahman and cut one leg of his horse. Abdur Rahman, as he fell down from the horse, attacked Akhram and killed him. Abu Qatadah (Radhiyallaho anho) had meanwhile arrived. In the combat that ensued, Abdur Rahman lost his life and Abu Qatadah his horse."

It is written in some books of history that, when Akhram was going to attack Abdur Rahman, Salmah advised him to wait till the rest of his people had joined him. But he did not wait, saying:

> "I wish to die as a martyr in the path of Allah."

He was the only person killed from among the Muslims. The bandits lost a good number of their men. Then more reinforcement reached the Muslims, and the bandits took to their heels. Salmah (Radhiyallaho anho) sought the

Prophet's (Sallallaho alaihe wasallam) permission to pursue them saying:

"O, Prophet of Allah! Let me have one hundred men, I shall teach them a lesson."

But the Prophet (Sallallaho alaihe wasallam) said:

"No. They would have by now reached their bases."

Most of the historians say that Salmah (Radhiyallaho anha) was hardly 12 or 13 at that time. Look how a boy of such a small age was able to chase so many bandits single-handed. He recovered all the plunder and besides took a considerable booty from them. This was the outcome of Iman and Ikhlas, with which Allah had imbued the hearts of those blessed people.

10. Hadhrat Bara's (Radhiyallaho anho) eagerness to Join in Badr.

Badr was the most gallant and illustrious battle ever fought by the Muslims, who were faced with very heavy odds. There were 313 men, 3 horses, seventy camels, six or nine coats of arms and eight swords with the Prophet (Sallallaho alaihe wasallam), while the Qureysh had about 1000 men, 100 horses, 700 camels, and were armed to their teeth. The Qureysh were so sure of their victory that they had brought with them musical instruments and songstresses to celebrate the victory. The Prophet (Sallallaho alaihe wasallam) was very anxious because of the heavy odds against him. He prayed to Allah saying:

"O, Allah! Thy faithful slaves are barefooted; Thou and only Thou can provide them with animals to ride upon. They are naked; Thou and only Thou can clothe them. They are poor; Thou and only Thou can sustain them."

Allah granted his prayer and gave the most glorious victory to the Muslims.

In spite of knowing the strength of the Qureysh, Abdullah bin 'Umar and Bara bin Azib (Radhiyallaho anhuma), in eagerness to join the battle, had come out with the Mujahidin. The Prophet (Sallallaho alaihe wasallam), however, in consideration of their tender age, did not permit them to proceed to the battle-field.

As we have already seen, both these boys were also rejected for the same reason at the time of Uhud, which took place one year after Badr. Look at the wonderful spirit of the youngsters of that time that they were anxious to obtain permission for participating in every battle.

11. Hadhrat Abdullah bin Abdullah bin Ubayy (Radhiyallaho anha) disgraces his Munafiq Father

During the famous campaign of Banul Mustaliq in 5 A. H., a Muhajir had a strife with Ansari over some trifling matter. Each of them called his own people for help, and there was a serious danger of a fight among the two groups of the Muslims but, through the efforts of some sane people, this was averted. Abdullah bin Ubayy was the chief of Munafiqin. He was a very bitter enemy of Islam. As he posed to be a Muslim, he was treated as such by the other Muslims. When he came to know of this incident, he used some insolent words for the Prophet (Sallallaho alaihe wasallam) and, exploiting the situation, addressed his people thus:

> "All this is the outcome of the seed that you people have sown with your own hands. You provided refuge to these strangers (meaning Muhajirin) in your town and shared your wealth equally with them. If you withdraw your help from them, they will be obliged to go back."

He further said:

> "By Allah! On return to Madinah, we, the respected people, shall drive out these mean people from there."

Hadhrat Zaid bin Arqam (Radhiyallaho anho), an Ansari boy was listening to him. He could not tolerate these words and at once retorted by saying to him:

> "By Allah! You yourself are wretched. Even your own people look down upon you, and nobody will support you. Muhammad (Sallallaho alaihe wasallam) is most honoured. He is exalted by Rahman and revered by his followers."

Abdullah bin Ubayy said:

> "All right. Do not mention it to anybody. It was only a jest; I was not serious in what I said."

Hadhrat Zaid (Radhiyallaho anho) however went straight to the Prophet (Sallallaho alaihe wasallam) and narrated to him what the Munafiq had said. 'Umar (Radhiyallaho anho) sought the Prophet's (Sallallaho alaihe wasallam) permission to kill Abdullah bin Ubayy, but the Prophet refused. When Abdullah bin Ubayy learnt that the Prophet (Sallallaho alaihe wasallam) had received the report about his insolent talk, he came to him and swore by Allah saying:

> "I never said such a thing. Zaid is a liar; he has given you false report."

A few of the Ansars were also sitting with the Prophet (Sallallaho alaihe wasallam). They also pleaded his case by saying:

> "O, Prophet of Allah! He is chief of his clan and is a big man. His statement is more reliable than the report by a mere boy. It is just possible that Zaid might have misheard or misunderstood him."

The Prophet (Sallallaho alaihe wasallam) accepted his statement and took no action against him. When Zaid (Radhiyallaho anho) came to know that the Munafiq had succeeded in beguiling the Prophet (Sallallaho alaihe wasallam) through false oaths, he would not come out for shame of being considered a liar by the people. He would not even go to the Prophet (Sallallaho alaihe wasallam). At last, Allah revealed Soorah Al Munafiqoon, in which the report of Zaid (Radhiyallaho anho) was confirmed and the Munafiq was exposed. After this, all people began to honour Zaid and look down upon the Munafiq.

Now the Munafiq (Abdullah bin Ubayy) had a son. His name was also Abdullah and he was a very sincere Muslim. When the Mujahidin were about to reach Madinah, he drew out his sword and stood just outside the town and, in a challenging tone, said to his Munafiq father:

> "I will not allow you to enter Madinah, until you admit with your own tongue that it is you who is mean and Muhammad (Sallallaho alaihe wasallam) is most exalted."

This surprised him very much, as the son had always been very respectful to him, but now he was prepared to kill him, his own father, for the honour of the Prophet (Sallallaho alaihe wasallam). The Munafiq had to declare:

> "By Allah! I am mean, and Muhammad (Sallallaho alaihe wasallam) is most exalted."

He was then allowed to enter the town.

12. Hadhrat Jabir's (Radhiyallaho anho) Eagerness to Fight.

When the battle of Uhud was over, the remnant of Sahabah returned to Madinah, most tired and broken. When the Qureysh, on their way back to Mecca, were camping at a place called Hamra-ul Asad, their chief, Abu Sufyan, sat in council with his lieutenants. They said among themselves:

> "The Muslims are defeated in Uhud. Their morale must be very low. This is the best time to finish Muhammad."

They, therefore, decided to return and attack Madinah. When the Prophet (Sallallaho alaihe wasallam) received intelligence about this council, he ordered all those Sahabah who had participated in Uhud, and who had just returned from the battle, to move out of Madinah and meet the enemy on the way.

Jabir (Radhiyallaho anho) came to the Prophet (Sallallaho alaihe wasallam) and said:

> "O, Prophet of Allah! I was very eager to fight in Uhud, but my father prevented me from going, on the plea that there was no other member in the house to look after my seven sisters and only one of us could join the campaign. As he had made up his mind to go, he bade me stay back with the family. He met the most coveted end (i.e., martyrdom) in Uhud. Now I am very eager to go with you this time and fight the Qureysh."

The Prophet (Sallallaho alaihe wasallam) allowed him to go. He was the only person in that campaign who had not fought in Uhud.

Hadhrat Jabir's (Radhiyallaho anho) father was martyred in Uhud. He left Jabir a big family to look after and large debts to clear, with nothing to live on. The debts were due to one of the Jews, who as we know seldom have any soft corner in their hearts for their debtors. Also his seven sisters for whose sake he was not allowed to go to Uhud– were still there to be looked after. Now look! inspite of all these difficulties, Jabir (Radhiyallaho anho) requests the Prophet (Sallallaho alaihe wasallam) for permission to go to the battle. His spirit is really wonderful!

13. Hadhrat Ibn Zubair's (Radhiyallaho anho) Valour against the Romans.

In 26 A.H., 'Usman (Radhiyallaho anho), the then Khalifah, appointed Abdullah bin Abi Sarah (Radhiyallaho anho) as the Governor of Egypt in place of Amr bin Aas (Radhiyallaho anho). Abdullah (Radhiyallaho anho), with 20 000 Mujahidin, advanced to meet the Roman Army numbering 200 000. It was a very fierce battle. The Roman commander Jarjir made a proclamation saying:

> "The person who kills Abdullah will get my daughter's hand in marriage and also 100 000 dinars in prize."

Some of the Muslims grew anxious over this proclamation. When Abdullah bin Zubair was informed of this, he said:

> "There is nothing to worry about. We may also announce that the person killing Jarjir will get Jarjir's daughter in marriage, 100 000 dinars in prize, and also governorship over the area now ruled by him."

The fight was very tough and went on for a long time. Ibn Zubair (Radhiyallaho anho) succeeded in spotting Jarjir seated behind his forces, under an umbrella of peacock feathers held by two maids. Ibn Zubair (Radhiyallaho anho), all at once, outskirted the Roman troops and approached him. He attacked Jarjir with his sword and severed his head from his body. He then fixed the head on the point of his spear and returned to his camp, to the utter amazement of both the armies at his matchless valour.

When the Sahabah emigrated to Madinah, no son was borne to any of the emigrants for one year after the emigration. The Jews of Madinah said:

> "We have cast a spell on the emigrants. They cannot have male issue."

Abdullah bin Zubair (Radhiyallaho anho) was the first male child born to the Muhajirin. The Muslims were, naturally, very happy over his birth. The Prophet (Sallallaho alaihe wasallam) would not generally allow the children to take oath of allegiance to him. But Abdullah bin Zubair

(Radhiyallaho anho) had the honour of pledging allegiance to the Prophet (Sallallaho alaihe wasallam) when he was only seven. During this battle, he was barely in his early twenties. To go single-handed and kill the commander, after hoodwinking his army of 200 000 men, at this age is really marvellous.

14. Hadhrat Amr bin Salamah (Radhiyallaho anho) Leads in Salaat.

Hadhrat Amr bin Salamah (Radhiyallaho anho) says:

"We lived with our father at a place on the caravan route to Madinah. When a caravan from Madinah passed our village, we asked the people therein about Muhammad (Sallallaho alaihe wasallam). They would tell us that he claimed to be receiving revelations from Allah, and they would also recite a few verses of the Qur'an before us to give us an idea about his claim. Then I immediately used to commit those verses to memory. In this way, I remembered a good portion of the Qur'an, even before I embraced Islam. All the desert tribes were waiting for Mecca to fall to the Prophet (Sallallaho alaihe wasallam) before they embraced Islam. On his victorious entry into Mecca, deputations from all the tribes began to come to the Prophet (Sallallaho alaihe wasallam) in order to accept Islam. My father headed the group who went to the Prophet (Sallallaho alaihe wasallam) to pledge allegiance to him on behalf of our tribe. The Prophet (Sallallaho alaihe wasallam) taught them the basic regulations about Salaat and other Islamic practices. He said to them, "The person who knows more Qur'an is entitled to lead in Salaat. Now it so happened that none in my tribe knew so much Qur'an as I did. They searched for an Imam, but they could not find a person knowing more Qur'an than me. I was, therefore, made Imam. At that time, I was only seven. I led the congregational Salaat and funeral service if any."

It was his natural inclination and affinity towards Islam that made him remember so much of the Qur'an when he was only a boy and he had not even embraced Islam.

15. Hadhrat Abdullah bin Abbas (Radhiyallaho anho) Teaches His Slave.

Ikramah the slave of Abdullah bin Abbas (Radhiyallaho anho) is one of the eminent ulama. He says:

> "During my learning the Qur'an and Hadith, I was kept in chains by my master, so that I might not go anywhere and devote full time to my lessons."

In fact, real knowledge can only be acquired when one is totally devoted to it. The students who are in the habit of wasting their time in roaming about and enjoying themselves can seldom acquire deep knowledge. It was the result of this labour that Ikramah was later on called. "The ocean of knowledge" and "The most learned man of the Ummat." Qatadah says:

> "There are four most learned men among the Tabi'ees, and Ikramah is one of them."

16. Hadhrat Ibn Abbas (Radhiyallaho anho) Memorises the Qur'an in His Childhood.

Hadhrat Abdullah bin Abbas (Radhiyallaho anho) used to say to the people:

> "Come to me for your difficulties in understanding the Qur'an. I memorised it while I was only a child."

In another Hadith, he is reported to have said:

> "I had completed my reading of the Qur'an when I was only ten."

The reading of the Qur'an by Sahabah was not done like the reading by the non-Arabs of today. Whatever they read, they read with full meaning and explanation. As the impression of something memorised in childhood is very deep and permanent, so Abdullah bin Abbas (Radhiyallaho anho) is accepted as Imam in Tafsir. None of the Sahabah has narrated more Ahadith explaining the meaning of Qur'an than was done by Ibn Abbas. Abdullah bin Mas'ood (Radhiyallaho anho) says:

> "Abdullah bin Abbas (Radhiyallaho anho) is the best commentator of the Qur'an."

Abu Abdur Rahman (Rahmatullah alaih), on the authority of Sahabah who taught him the Qur'an, says:

"The Sahabah learnt ten verses of the Qur'an from the Prophet (Sallallaho alaihe wasallam) at a time. They would not take the next lesson until they had mastered the knowledge and acted upon those ten verses."

Abdullah bin Abbas (Radhiyallaho anho) was 13 at the time of the Prophet's death. It is miracle that he knew so much of the Qur'an and Hadith at such a young age. Many eminent Sahabah used to come to him to solve their difficulties about the interpretation of the Qur'an. This was, however, all due to the blessing of the Prophet (Sallallaho alaihe wasallam), who once coming out from the closet had found water lying ready for his use and inquired:

"Who put this water here?"

Somebody said: "Ibn Abbas."

The Prophet (Sallallaho alaihe wasallam) appreciated the service and prayed for Ibn Abbas:

"O, Allah! Give him the knowledge and understanding of the Qur'an and practices of Islam."

On another occasion, the Prophet (Sallallaho alaihe wasallam) was saying his Salaat. Ibn Abbas (Radhiyallaho anho) joined him in Salaat by standing behind him. The Prophet caught him by the hand and drew him to his side. (When there is only one follower in Salaat with Jamaat, he stands by the side of Imam and not after him). While the Prophet (Sallallaho alaihe wasallam) was busy in Salaat, he moved back a little distance. When the Salaat was over, the Prophet (Sallallaho alaihe wasallam) asked him:

"What made you recede from your place?"

He said: "You are the Prophet of Allah!. How could I stand with you."

On this occasion too, the Prophet (Sallallaho alaihe wasallam) prayed for his knowledge and understanding.

17. Abdullah bin Amr bin Aas Notes Down Ahadith:

Abdullah bin Amr bin Aas (Radhiyallaho anho) was one of the most pious Sahabah. Daily he used to fast during the day, and finish one Qur'an during the night. The Prophet (Sallallaho alaihe wasallam) restrained him from this excessive devotion and said:

"You will get weak by daily fasting, and your eye-sight will suffer by keeping awake very night. You owe some obligation to your body, the members of your family, and those who come to visit you."

He says: "The Prophet (Sallallaho alaihe wasallam) then advised me to take not less than a month to finish one Qur'an. I said, "O, Prophet of Allah! This is too little. Let me make full use of my strength while I am still young." He then reduced the period to 20 days. I kept on repeating my words and the Prophet (Sallallaho alaihe wasallam) continued reducing the period, till finally I was permitted to take three days in finishing one reading of the Qur'an."

He had a collection of the Hadith compiled by him, which he had named "Sadiqah (True)". He says:

"I used to put down all that I heard from the Prophet (Sallalaho alaihe wasallam). People once said to me, 'The Prophet (Sallalaho alaihe wasallam) is after all a human being and many words uttered by him in anger or humour are actually not meant by him. You should not write each and every thing spoken by him.' I accepted the advice. On my once mentioning this to the Prophet (Sallallaho alaihe wasallam), he said, 'You keep doing as before. By Him who holds my life in His hand, my lips do not utter anything except the truth, even in anger or joy."

Abu Hurairah (Radhiyallaho anho) says:

"No one has narrated about the Prophet (Sallallaho alaihe wasallam) more than me, except Abdullah bin Amr. This is because he used to note down what he heard, while I relied on my memory."

This is really wonderful, especially when we know that most of his time was reading the Qur'an and other acts of piety.

18. Zaid bin Thabit Memorises the Qur'an.

Zaid bin Thabit (Radhiyallaho anho) is one of those eminent Sahabah who are considered to be most learned and whose words in religious matters carry much weight. He was an expert in regulations regarding obligatory practices. It is said that he was among the top ranking jurists, judges and Qaris. He was only 11 when the Prophet (Sallallaho alaihe wasallam) emigrated to Madinah. That is why, in spite of his eagerness, he was not allowed to participate in the early battles like Badr, etc. He had lost his father when he was six. When the Prophet (Sallallaho alaihe wasallam) arrived in Madinah, people brought their children to him to receive his blessing. Zaid was also brought to him for the same purpose. He says:

> "When I was presented to the Prophet (Sallallaho alaihe wasallam), he was informed that I had then memorised seventeen soorahs of the Qur'an. In order to test me, he bade me to recite some of these. I recited Surah Qaaf. He rewarded me with his words of appreciation."

The Prophet (Sallallaho alaihe wasallam), when writing letters to the Jews outside Madinah, used to utilise the services of the local Jews. Once he said to Zaid:

> "I am not satisfied with what the Jews write and read for me. I apprehend mischief from them in miswriting or misreading. I desire you to learn the Jewish language."

Zaid (Radhiyallaho anho) says:

> "In fifteen days, I mastered Hebrew and after that I started doing all such correspondence for him."

According to another Hadith, Zaid (Radhiyallaho anho) is reported to have similarly mastered the Syriac language at the instance of the Prophet (Sallallaho alaihe wasallam). He managed this within the short period of 17 days only.

19. Hasan's Knowledge of Islam.

The head of Sayyids, Hasan (Radhiyallaho anho) was born in Ramadhan, 3 A. H. He was thus a little over seven years old at the time of the Prophet's death. In spite of his tender age, quite a few Ahadith have been narrated by him. Abul Howraa once asked him:

> "Do you remember any saying of the Prophet (Sallallaho alaihe wasallam)?"

He said:

> "Yes. Once I was going with him. On the way I saw a large quantity of dates of Sadaqah piled up at one

place. I took a date from the pile and put it into my mouth. The Prophet (Sallallaho alaihe wasallam) exclaimed, 'Kakh! Kakh!' (exclamation of disapproval) and then he took out the date from my mouth with the help of his finger, saying: 'Eating the Sadaqah is not permissible for us (i.e. family of the Prophet)'. The Prophet (Sallallaho alaihe wasallam) had taught me how to say my five times daily Salaat."

Hasan (Radhiyallaho anho) says:

"The Prophet (Sallallaho alaihe wasallam) advised me to recite the following prayer for my Witr:

اَللّٰهُمَّ اهْدِنِي فِيْمَنْ هَدَيْتَ وَعَافِنِي فِيْمَنْ عَافَيْتَ وَتَوَلَّنِي فِيْمَنْ تَوَلَّيْتَ وَبَارِكْ لِيْ فِيْمَا اَعْطَيْتَ وَقِنِى شَرَّ مَا قَضَيْتَ فَإِنَّكَ تَقْضِي وَلَايُقْضٰي عَلَيْكَ اِنَّهُ لَايَذِلُّ مَنْ وَّالَيْتَ تَبَارَكْتَ رَبَّنَا وَتَعَالَيْتَ

"O, Allah! Guide me along with those whom Thou hast guided. Keep me in ease along with those whom Thou hast kept in ease. Be my protecting friend along with those whose protecting friend Thou has been. Bless me in what Thou hast granted me. Grant me protection against the ill-effects of what may have been ordained for me, for Thy decision is final and nobody can decide against Thy will. He who has Thee as the protecting Friend cannot be abased. O, Our Lord! Thou art blessed and Thou art the Highest."

Hasan (Radhiyallaho anho) narrates that he heard the Prophet (Sallallaho alaihe wasallam) saying:

"The person who keeps sitting till sunrise at the place where he said his Fajr prayers shall be saved from the Hell."

Hasan (Radhiyallaho anho) performed his Hajj many times by covering the distance from Madinah to Mecca on foot and, when asked about his reasons for undergoing such hardships, he remarked:

"I feel ashamed to face Allah (after my death) without having gone to Mecca on foot for pilgrimage to his House."

Hasan is reputed for his piety and mildness. He is responsible for narrating many Ahadith, collected by Imaam

Ahmad in his Musnad. The author of 'Talqih' has included Hasan (Radhiyallaho anho) among those who have reported as many as 13 Ahadith. To have remembered so many Ahadith at the age of 7 shows his devotion to Islam and his remarkable memory. On the other hand, our children at this age generally do not know even the elements of Islam.

20. Husain's Zeal for Knowledge.

Husain (Radhiyallaho anho) was one year junior to Hasan (Radhiyallaho anha), his brother. He was a little over 6 at the time of the Prophet's death. Nothing much can be expected from a child of this age, but there are quite a few Ahadith narrated by Husain (Radhiyallaho anho). Muhaddithin count him among those Sahabah who are responsible for giving us at least 8 Ahadith.

The following Ahadith are among those narrated by Husain (Radhiyallaho anho):

1. "Each time a person recites 'Inna-lillahi-wa-inna-Ilaihi-raaji-oon' when he recalls or is otherwise reminded of an adversity previously met by him, he receives a reward from Allah as good as he would have had at the time of actual infliction."

2. "A Muslim gets immunity from drowning while crossing a river if, at the time of embarking, he recites:

   بِسْمِ اللهِ مَجْرِيْهَا وَمُرْسَاهَا اِنَّ رَبِّىْ لَغَفُوْرٌ رَّحِيْمٌ (هود ٤١)

   (In the name of Allah be its course and its mooring. Lo! My Lord is, surely, most Forgiving, most Merciful!)."

3. "To shun vain things makes one a good Muslim."

Rabee'ah (Radhiyallaho anho) says:

"I once asked Husain (Radhiyallaho anho) if he remembered any incident in the life of the Prophet (Sallallaho alaihe wasallam). He said, 'Yes. Once I managed to get on to a few dates lying near a window and put one of them into my mouth. The Prophet (Sallallaho alaihe wasallam) bade me take out and throw away the date, as we (i.e. his family members) were not permitted to eat anything from Sadaqah."

Husain (Radhiyallaho anho) had gone on foot 25 times for pilgrimage to Mecca. He was very punctual in fasting, saying Nafl and spending on the poor.

We find quite a few Sahabah narrating many sayings, which they had heard from the Prophet (Sallallaho alaihe wasallam) in their childhood. Mahmood bin Rab-ee' (Radhiyallaho anho) was only five at the time of the Prophet's death. He says:

> "Once the Prophet (Sallallaho alaihe wasallam) came to our house. We had a well inside the house. He filled some water in his mouth from that well and then squirted it on my face. I shall never forget this incident."

We are in the habit of engaging our children in vain talk, confusing their minds by telling them fictitious stories and frightening them with the giants and the Jinns. If, instead, we induce them to read the lives of great men of Islam, narrate to them stories of the pious people and warn them of the consequences of Allah's disobedience, they may be greatly benefited in their life in this world and in the Hereafter. In childhood the memory is at its best. Anything memorised at that time is seldom forgotten. If children are made to memorise the Qur'an, they will be able to do so very easily and quickly. I have heard very frequently from the elderly ladies of my family and from my respected father himself that he had memorised one fourth of the thirtieth part of the Qur'an even before he was weaned, and he had finished memorising the whole Qur'an and, on the top of that, he had read a few standard books in Persian literature (the latter of his own accord) while he was only seven. He once narrated to me:

> "When I had finished memorising the Qur'an, my father required me to repeat (from memory) the full Qur'an once daily, and permitted me to play for the rest of the day. I used to sit on the roof of the house (being summer) and start reciting the Qur'an just after Fajr. I would finish the whole of it in about seven hours. I then had my lunch. In the evening, I used to have lessons in Persian, though it was not compulsory for me. To this routine I stuck for full six months."

It is not an ordinary thing for a child of seven to recite the Qur'an once daily for full six months, along with learning other things. As a result, he would never forget or commit an error when reciting the Qur'an from memory. Apparently, he earned his livelihood by trade in books. He was found reciting the Qur'an with his lips, even when his hands were engaged in his job. Sometimes he would even teach the boys (who wanted to learn from him after the school hours), while himself reciting the Qur'an and doing his job. He thus attended to three things at a time. But his way of teaching his students was different from that adopted currently in the schools, where the entire burden is on the teachers. He simply listened to the student reading, translating and explaining the meaning. If the student was correct, he simply said, '"Go ahead," but if the student made some error or needed some further explanation, then he only would correct or explain as the case might be. Now, this story is not of ancient times; this has happened only recently. It is therefore wrong to presume that the Muslims of today, being of poor physical strength, cannot try to follow the footsteps of their ancestors in Islam.

CHAPTER XII

LOVE FOR THE PROPHET

What we have hitherto read about the achievement of the Sahabah in their time was in fact the result of their love for Allah and for His Prophet (Sallallaho alaihe wasallam). Love, as a matter of fact, was a great dynamic force in the Sahabah's career. It was this force that made them forego their luxuries, forget their lives, give up all their desires for wealth, ignore all afflictions, and have no fear of death even. There is no room for any other consideration (except that of beloved) in the heart saturated with love. May Allah through His Grace grant us His own love and that of His Prophet (Sallallaho alaihe wasallam), so that we may be blessed with devotion in His worship and have sense of comfort in all difficulties faced in His service.

1. Abu Bakr's (Radhiyallaho anho) Sufferings for Islam.

In the beginning, those who embraced Islam had to keep their faith secret, as far as possible. As the Muslims were being constantly persecuted by the Qureysh, even the Prophet (Sallallaho alaihe wasallam) advised all new converts to practise Islam secretly, so that they might not have to suffer at the hands of Qureysh. When, however, the number of Muslims reached 39, Abu Bakr (Radhiyallaho anho) made a suggestion for the open preaching and practising of Islam. The Prophet (Sallallaho alaihe wasallam) would not agree, but, when Abu Bakr (Radhiyallaho anho) insisted, he gave his consent and so all of them went to Haram for Tabligh. Abu Bakr (Radhiyallaho anho) began to speak, and the Khutbah given by him was the first ever delivered in the annals of Islam. Hamzah (Radhiyallaho anho) the Prophet's uncle and the Chief of Martyrs embraced Islam on that very day, while 'Umar (Radhiyallaho anho) came into the Muslim fold on the third day of this address. No sooner did Abu Bakr (Radhiyallaho anho) start speaking than the idolaters and disbelievers from amongst the Qureysh fell upon the Muslims from all sides. Despite the fact that he was considered to be the noblest and most respectable of all the people in Mecca, Abu Bakr (Radhiyallaho anho) was beaten to such an extent that his nose and ears and his entire face were besmeared with blood. He was kicked, thrashed with shoes, trampled under feet and handled most roughly and savagely. He became unconscious and half-dead; none hoped that he would ever survive this brutal onslaught. Banu Teem, the people of his clan, came and carried him to his house. They also announced in the Haram that if Abu Bakr succumbed to the injuries, they would in retaliation take the life of Utbah bin Rabee'ah, who had taken the most active part in the attack. Abu Bakr (Radhiyallaho anho) remained unconscious the whole day. People round him shouted his name again and again to know if he was in senses, but he would not speak. Late in the evening however he opened his eyes and showed signs of consciousness. As soon as he was able to speak, he enquired:

"How is the Prophet (Sallallaho alaihe wasallam)?"

The people were most disappointed with him and they said:

> "How is it that, despite all this calamity and after virtually remaining in the jaws of death all day long on account of the Prophet, (Sallallaho alaihe wasallam), as soon as he has come back to consciousness he has nothing else to talk about, but the Prophet himself."

They left Abu Bakr (Radhiyallaho anho), much disgusted at his devotion for the Prophet (Sallallaho alaihe wasallam), while they were satisfied that he was out of danger. They advised Umme Khair, his mother, to give him something to eat. But least minding his food, Abu Bakr (Radhiyallaho anho) would incessantly and impatiently ask his mother the same question again and again i.e.

"How is the Prophet (Sallallaho alaihe wasallam)?'

On her showing ignorance about the welfare of the Prophet (Sallallaho alaihe wasallam), Abu Bakr entreated her to go to Umme Jamil (Umar's sister) and find out from her the latest news about the Prophet (Sallalaho alaihe wasallam). The mother could not refuse the request of her son in this pitiable condition, and hurried to Umme Jamil's (Radhiyallaho anha) house to enquire about the welfare of Muhammad (Sallallaho alaihe wasallam). Like other Muslims of that time, Umme Jamil (Radhiyallah anha) was also keeping her faith secret. She therefore concealed her knowledge about the Prophet (Sallallaho alaihe wasallam), saying:

"Who is Muhammad and who is Abu Bakr? Why should I know anything about them? I am however sorry to learn about the condition of your son; if you like, I can go with you to see him."

Umme Khair agreed and they both came to Abu Bakr. On seeing Abu Bakr (Radhiyallaho anho) in that miserable condition, Umme Jamil (Radhiyallaho anha) could not control herself and began to cry, saying:

"Woe to the ruffians for what they have done to a man like Abu Bakr. May Allah punish them for their misconduct."

Regardless of what Umme Jamil (Radhiyallaho anha) said, Abu Bakr (Radhiyallaho anho) had the same words on his lips viz:

"How is the Prophet (Sallallaho alaihe wasallam)?"

Umme Jamil (pointing towards Umme Khair):

"Is it safe to say anything in her presence?"

Abu Bakr: "Do not worry about her. Tell me quickly how is the Prophet (Sallallaho alaihe wasallam)?"

Umme Jamil: "He is quite well."

Abu Bakr: "Where is he at this moment."

Umme Jamil: "He is at Arqam's place."

Abu Bakr: "By Allah! I will not eat anything until I have looked at him."

Now, his mother was very anxious to feed him. She knew that when he had sworn by Allah he would not break his oath and, therefore, would not eat under any circumstances. She therefore agreed to take him to Arqam's place. She had to wait till the street was least-frequented by the people and she was able to take him to that place undetected by Qureysh. When they both reached Arqam's place, Abu Bakr (Radhiyallaho anho) saw the Prophet (Sallallaho alaihe wasallam) and clung to him weeping profusely. The Prophet (Sallallaho alaihe wasallam) reciprocated, and all the Muslims who were present there also began to weep bitterly over the condition of Abu Bakr (Radhiyallaho anho). Abu Bakr (Radhiyallaho anho) then introduced his mother Umme Khair to the Prophet (Sallallaho alaihe wasallam), saying:

> "She is my mother, O, Prophet of Allah! Pray for her and induce her to accept Islam."

The prophet first prayed for her and then preached to her. She accepted Islam there and then.

Many people can claim to be lovers while in ease and comfort. But a lover is a real lover when he is able to prove his love even in the tribulation and adversity.

2. 'Umar's (Radhiyallaho anho) Grief at the Prophet's Death.

None can deny the proverbial valour, courage and strength of 'Umar (Radhiyallaho anho), over whose mention, even after the lapse of 1400 years, hearts are struck with awe and respect. Islam could not be professed and preached openly before 'Umar's coming into its fold. As soon as he embraced Islam, the Muslims started saying Salaat in the Haram, as none could dare harm them with 'Umar (Radhiyallaho anho) on their side. Notwithstanding all this, he could not bear the shock of the Prophet passing away. So much so that he stood with sword in his hand, utterly confused and bewildered, saying:

> "I shall behead the person who says that the Prophet (Sallallaho alaihe wasallam) has passed away. The Prophet (Sallallaho alaihe wasallam) has only gone to visit his Lord, just as Moosa (Alayhis salaam) had gone to Toor. He will shortly return and cut off the hands and feet of those who were spreading the false news of his death."

On the other hand, 'Usman (Radhiyallaho anho) was stunned with grief on this event. He could not utter a single word, even till the next day, and walked about as if bereft of speech. Ali (Radhiyallaho anho), too, was in terrible grief. He was still and motionless. Only Abu Bakr, (Radhiyallaho anho) for all his love of the Prophet (Sallallaho alaihe wasallam) as we have seen in the last story, stood firm as a rock against this terrible storm of grief and did not lose his mental composure. He calmly entered the Prophet's house, kissed his forehead and came back to the people. He called 'Umar (Radhiyallaho anho) to sit down, and began to address the people. He said:

> "Whoso worshipped Muhammad (Sallallaho alaihe wasallam), let him know that Muhammad is no more, and whoso worshipped Allah should know that Allah is Everliving and Eternal. He then recited the following verse of the Qur'an:

وَمَا مُحَمَّدٌ اِلَّا رَسُوْلٌ ، قَدْ خَلَتْ مِنْ قَبْلِهِ الرُّسُلُ ، اَفَائِنْ مَّاتَ اَوْقُتِلَ انْقَلَبْتُمْ عَلٰى اَعْقَابِكُمْ ، وَمَنْ يَّنْقَلِبْ عَلٰى عَقِبَيْهِ فَلَنْ يَّضُرَّ اللّٰهَ شَيْئًا ، وَسَيَجْزِى اللّٰهُ الشَّاكِرِيْنَ (اٰل عمران ١٤٤)

> "Muhammad is but a messenger; messengers, the like of those who have passed away before him. Will it be that when he dies or is slain, Ye will turn back on your heels. He who turneth back doth not hurt Allah, and Allah will reward those who recognise the Truth.
> (III: 144)."

As Abu Bakr (Radhiyallaho anho) was destined to be the Khalifah after the Prophet, (Sallalaho alaihe wasallam) it is significant that, unlike other Sahabah, he behaved with the composure and patience that were needed on an occasion like this. Again, it was Abu Bakr (Radhiyallaho anho) alone who knew better than anybody else about the regulations regarding the burial, inheritance, etc, of the Prophet (Sallalaho alaihe wasallam). When difference of opinion arose among the Sahabah whether the burial place of the Prophet (Sallallaho alaihe wasallam) be at Mecca or Madinah or Jerusalem, it was Abu Bakr (Radhiyallaho anho) who settled the difference by saying on the authority of the Prophet (Sallallaho alaihe wasallam) that the Prophets are buried where they have died. There were several other Ahadith known only to Abu Bakr (Radhiyallaho anho) that helped solve many of the other problems arising out of the death of the Prophet (Sallallaho alaihe wasallam). Some of these Ahadith were:

(1) "Prophets have no heirs. All that a Prophet leaves behind is Sadaqah."

(2) "Allah's curse is on the Amir who does not take proper interest and excercise proper care in the appointment of his deputies."

(3) "The state affairs shall remain in the custody of Qureysh."

3. An Ansari Woman's Anxiety About the Prophet.

In the battle of Uhud, the Muslims suffered heavy losses and quite a large number of them were killed. When the sensational news of their heavy casualties reached Madinah, the women came out of their houses eager to know the actual details of these casualties. On seeing the crowd of people at a place, a woman of the Ansar anxiously inquired:

"How is the Prophet (Sallallaho alaihe wasallam)?"

When told that her father was killed in the battle, she uttered 'Inna Lillah' and impatiently repeated the same question about the Prophet (Sallallaho alaihe wasallam), This time she was told that her husband was no more, her brother was dead and that her son too was slain. With ever-growing anxiety, she repeated the same question about the welfare of the Prophet (Sallallaho alaihe wasallam). She was told that he was safe and sound, but she would not rest contented, and insisted on seeing him herself. When at last she had satisfied her eyes with his sight, she said:

"O Prophet of Allah, every affliction is eased and every worry removed with the blessing of seeing you."

According to another version, she herself clung to the Prophet's robes and said:

"O Prophet of Allah! you are dearer to me than my parents. The death of my kinsmen has lost all its sting for me when I have seen you living."

There are several incidents of this kind that occurred after the battle of Uhud. It is, perhaps, for the large number of such incidents that different names have been reported by different narrators about these women. In fact, such incidents happened in large numbers with many women of that time.

4. The Behaviour of Sahabah at Hudeybiyah.

The campaign of Hudevbiyah took place in 6 A.H., when the Prophet (Sallallaho alaihe wasallam) with a large number of Sahabah was going to Mecca with the intention of performing 'Umrah. The Qureysh came to know of this and decided to prevent their entry into Mecca. They also decided to invite the neighbouring tribes of Mecca for help, and made large-scale preparations for battle. When the Prophet (Sallallaho alaihe wasallam) reached Zul Hulaifah, he sent a man to bring intelligence about the Qureysh. When the Prophet (Sallallaho alaihe wasallam) reached Asfan, the person returned from Mecca with the information that the Qureysh were equipped to the teeth to resist the Prophet's entry into Mecca and that the neighbouring tribes also were by their side. At this, the Prophet (Sallallaho alaihe wasallam) consulted the eminent Sahabah to consider the situation. One proposal was to attack the houses of the tribes who had sent their men to help the Qureysh (so that they might forsake Qureysh in order to protect their own homes), and the other was to march straight towards Mecca, Abu Bakr (Radhiyallaho anho) said:

> "O Prophet of Allah! We have come to perform 'Umrah. We have no intention of fighting with the Qureysh. Let us go ahead. If they stop us we shall fight, otherwise not."

The Prophet (Sallallaho alaihe wasallam) agreed to the proposal of Abu Bakr (Radhiyallaho anho) and decided to march ahead towards Mecca. When he reached Hudeybiyah, Budail bin Waraqa Khuza'i met him with a group of people. He said:

> "The Qureysh under no circumstances will permit your entry into Mecca. They are already drawn up in battle array."

At this, the Prophet (Sallallaho alaihe wasallam) replied:

> "We have come to perform 'Umrah only and have no intention to fight. Frequent battles have already inflicted heavy casualties on Qureysh. If, therefore, they agree, I am prepared to talk over a no-war pact with them, so that they do not fight with me and I may deal with others. If, however, Qureysh do not see their way to accepting this proposal, then by Him who holds my life in His hand, I will fight them till at last either Islam prevails or I am slain."

Budail returned to the Qureysh and conveyed to them what the Prophet had told him. But they did not agree to the peace proposal of the Prophet (Sallallaho alaihe wasallam). Parleys between the two sides however continued and, at one time, Urwah bin Mas'ood Thaqafi was sent by Qureysh as a plenipotentiary. Urwah had not then accepted Islam. The Prophet (Sallallaho alaihe wasallam) talked to him in the same strain as he had done to Budail. 'Urwah said:

> "O Muhammad (Sallallaho alaihe wasallam)! If you want to slay all the Arabs you cannot possibly do so, as none before you has ever succeeded in putting an end to all the Arabs. On the contrary if the Arabs get the upper hand, then take it from me that these persons round you will disappear in no time, leaving, you all alone, for I don't find any people of high birth among them. In fact they all come from a low stock drawn from all corners who will desert in trouble."

Abu Bakr (Radhiyallaho anho), standing close by, was infuriated at this statement, and resentfully told 'Urwah:

> "Go and faun upon your goddess 'Lat'! We will by no means flee away and leave the Prophet (Sallallaho alaihe wasallam) by himself."

'Urwah asked: "Who is he?"

The Prophet: "He is Abu Bakr."

'Urwah: "Abu Bakr! I am indebted to you for a good turn you have done to me in the past. But for this, I would have replied to your abuse."

'Urwah then resumed his deliberations with the Prophet (Sallallaho alaihe wasallam). 'Urwah occasionally touched the beard of the Prophet (according to the Arab custom) as he talked. The Sahabah could not tolerate this. Accordingly, 'Urwah's own nephew Mughirah bin Shu'bah (Radhiyallaho anho), who was standing armed near by, struck Urwah's hand with the handle of his sword and said:

"Keep your hand away."

'Urwah: "Who is he?"

The Prophet: (Sallallaho alaihe wasallam):

"He is Mughirah."

'Urwah: "O, you betrayer! How dare you maltreat your uncle, who is still suffering for your misbehaviour."

(Before Islam, Mughirah, (Radhiyallaho anho) had killed a few persons. Urwah paid the blood money on his behalf, and was referring to this incident). During his long discourse with the Prophet (Sallallaho alaihe wasallam), 'Urwah's had been quietly observing the behaviour of the Sahabah towards their Master; so when he returned to Qureysh he said to them:

"O, Qureysh! I have been an envoy to many great kings. I have seen the courts of Caesar, the Chosroes and the Negus. By Allah! Nowhere have I seen the people around a sovereign so respectful to him as I found the companions of Muhammad (Sallallaho alaihe wasallam). When Muhammad spits, they rush to receive the sputum in their hands before it touches the ground and anoint their faces with it. Hardly a word escapes his lips before all of them run to carry out his wish. When he makes Wudhu, they fight with one another to collect some drop of the used water before it falls on the ground. If any one fails to get that water, he touches the wet hands of the person who had got it and then rubs his own hands on the face. When they speak in his presence, they speak in low voice. They do not lift their gaze to look at his face, out of respect for him. A hair falling from his head or beard is preserved to get benediction from it and is looked upon as a sacred relic. In short, I have never seen any group of people so devoted to their master as I have seen the companions of Muhammad (Sallallaho alaihe wasallam) towards him."

At long last, 'Usman (Radhiyallaho anho) was commissioned by the Prophet (Sallallaho alaihe wasallam) to negotiate with the Qureysh, as he, in spite of his conversion to Islam, commanded respect with them. When 'Usman (Radhiyallaho anho) had left for Mecca, some of the Sahabah envied Usman's luck in (as they thought) being able to perform Tawaf of the house of Allah. The Prophet (Sallallaho alaihe wasallam) on the other hand remarked:

"I do not think he will ever like to do Tawaf without me."

However when 'Usman (Radhiyallaho anho) entered Mecca, Abaan bin Sa'eed took him in his protection and said to him:

"You roam where you like. Nobody can touch you."

'Usman (Radhiyallaho anho) carried on his negotiations with Abu Sufyan and other chiefs of Mecca on behalf of the Prophet (Sallallaho alaihe wasallam) and, when he was about to return, the Qureysh themselves said to him:

"Now when you are here at Mecca, you can perform Tawaf before you return."

He replied: "How can it be possible for me when the Prophet (Sallallaho alaihe wasallam) has been prevented by you people from entering Mecca."

This reply was most unpalatable for the Qureysh and they decided to detain 'Usman (Radhiyallaho anho) at Mecca. A news reached the Muslims that 'Usman (Radhiyallaho anho) had been martyred. On this news reaching the Prophet (Sallallaho alaihe wasallam), he took the oath of allegiance from all Sahabah to fight to the last drop of their blood. When the Qureysh learnt of this, they got frightened and immediately released 'Usman (Radhiyallaho anho).

In this story, Abu Bakr's (Radhiyallaho anho) insulting 'Urwah, Mughirah's (Radhiyallaho anho) treatment of his uncle, the Sahabah's behaviour towards the Prophet (Sallallaho alaihe wasallam) as evidenced by 'Urwah, and 'Usman's (Radhiyallaho anho) refusing to do 'Tawaf', all speak volumes, about the love and devotion of Sahabah for the Prophet (Sallallaho alaihe wasallam). The oath of allegiance mentioned in this story is known Bai'atush Shajarah (The Oath of allegiance beneath the tree) and is mentioned in the Quran (XLVIII: 18).

5. Ibn Zubair's (Radhiyallaho anho) disposal of blood.

Once the Prophet (Sallallaho alaihe wasallam) was bled by cupping. The blood was given to Abdullah bin Zubair (Radhiyallaho anho) to bury it somewhere. He returned and informed the Prophet (Sallallaho alaihe wasallam) that the blood had been disposed of. The Prophet (Sallallaho alaihe wasallam) inquired:

"What did you do with it?"

Ibn-Zubair said: "I have swallowed it."

The Prophet (Sallallaho alaihe wasallam) remarked:

> "The person who has my blood in his body cannot be touched by fire of Hell. But you will kill people and people will kill you."

Everything coming out of the Prophet's body is clean. No doubt, therefore, remains in understanding Ibn Zubair's action. The last words of the Prophet (Sallallaho alaihe wasallam), however, make prophesy about the battles for power, which Ibn Zubair (Radhiyallaho anho) had to fight with Yazid and Abdul Malik. In the later part of his life, Ibn Zubair (Radhiyallaho anho) was killed in one of these battles. Even at the time of Ibn Zubair's (Radhiyallaho anho) birth, the Prophet (Sallallaho alaihe wasallam) had remarked that he was a sheep among the cloaked wolves.

6. Abu 'Ubaidah (Radhiyallaho anho) loses His Teeth.

During the battle of Uhud, when at one time the Prophet (Sallallaho alaihe wasallam) was fiercely attacked by the enemy and two links of the helmet worn by him were struck deep into his head (or face), Abu Bakr and Abu 'Ubaidah (Radhiyallaho anhuma) ran to help him. Abu 'Ubaidah (Radhiyallaho anho) started pulling out the links with his teeth. By the time one of the links was out, he had lost one of his teeth. Without minding this, he again used his teeth to pull up the other link as well. He succeeded in taking out that one too, but he had to lose another tooth in the effort. When the links were drawn out, the blood began to ooze out from the Prophet's body. Malik bin Sinaan (Radhiyallaho anho), the father of Abu Sa'eed Khudri (Radhiyallaho anho), licked the blood with his lips. At this, the Prophet (Sallallaho alaihe wasallam) remarked:

> "The fire of Hell cannot touch the person who has my blood mixed with his."

7. Zaid (Radhiyallaho anho) Refuses to Go With His Father.

Once in pre-Islam days, Zaid (Radhiyallaho anho) was

travelling in a caravan, with his mother going to her father's town, when the caravan was way-laid by Banu Qais. They took Zaid (Radhiyallaho anho) as slave and sold him in Mecca. Hakim bin Hazam purchased him for his aunt Khadijah (Radhiyallaho anha), who offered him as a present to the Prophet (Sallallaho alaihe wasallam) at the time of her marriage with him. On the other hand, Zaid's (Radhiyallaho anho) father was in immense grief at the loss of the son. He roamed about in search of him, lamenting his separation in the following heart-rendering verses:

"I weep in memory of Zaid, while I know not whether he is alive (to be hoped for) or finished by death."

"O, Zaid, By Allah, no knowledge I have, whether you are killed on soft soil or on a rock."

"Ah, I wish I knew whether you would ever come back to me, for that is the only desire I am living for."

"I remember Zaid when the sun rises in the East. I remember him when the rain comes from the clouds."

"The blowing wind kindles the fire of his memory. Alas, my lengthening grief and unending distress."

"I shall run my swift camels in search of him. I shall search for him round the universe."

"The camels may get tired, but I shall not rest, till I die, for death is the end of every hope."

"I shall still enjoin on my sons and such and such people, to keep searching for Zaid even after my death."

Some people of his clan happened to meet Zaid (Radhiyallaho anho) during their pilgrimage to Mecca. They related to him the story of his father's grief and anguish, and recited to him the couplets which he sang in his memory. Zaid (Radhiyallaho anho) sent a letter to his father through these people. The letter consisted of three couplets addressed to his father assuring him that he was quite well and happy in the present environments with his noble master. When the people went back, they informed his father of his whereabouts and delivered him Zaid's (Radhiyallaho anho) message. On receiving the letter, his father and his uncle left for Mecca with sufficient money to ransom Zaid (Radhiyallaho anho). When they came to the Prophet (Sallallaho alaihe wasallam) they said:

"O, son of Hashim and the chief of Qureysh. You are the dweller of the Haram and the neighbour of Allah. You are known for freeing the captives and feeding the hungry. We have come to you in quest of our son. Accept the ransom money for Zaid and set him free. We are willing to pay even more than the ransom money. Pray, show mercy and be kind to us."

The Prophet: "What do you wish to do with Zaid?"

Zaid's father: "We want to take him with us to our place."

The Prophet: "Is that all? Allright, then call Zaid and ask him. If he wishes to go with you, I shall let him go without any ransom. But I shall not send him against his wishes."

Zaid's father: "You have shown us more favour than we deserve. We most gladly agree to what you say."

Zaid (Radhiyallaho anho) was presently sent for. The Prophet (Sallallaho alaihe wasallam) said to Zaid: "Do you know these men?"

Zaid: "Yes, I know them. This is my father and that is my uncle."

The Prophet: "And you know me too. They have come to take you back to your home. You have my full permission to go with them. If, on the other hand, you chose to stay on with me, you shall have your choice."

Zaid: "How can I prefer anybody else to you? You are everybody for me, including my father and my uncle."

Zaid's father and uncle:

"O, Zaid! Do you prefer to be a slave? How can you leave your own father, uncle and other members of your family, and remain a bondsman?"

Zaid: "Verily, I have seen something in my master that makes me prefer him to everybody else in the world."

On this, the Prophet (Sallallaho alaihe wasallam) took Zaid (Radhiyallaho anho) in his lap and said:

"From today, I adopt Zaid as my son."

The father and uncle were quite satisfied with the situation and gladly left Zaid (Radhiyallaho anho) with the Prophet (Sallallaho alaihe wasallam) and returned without him.

Zaid (Radhiyallaho anho) was only a child at that time. His preferring to remain a slave, and refusing to go with his own father giving up his home and kith and kin is an obvious tribute to his love for the Prophet (Sallallaho alaihe wasallam).

8. Anas bin Nadhr's (Radhiyallaho anho) Martyrdom in Uhud.

When the Muslims were facing defeat in Uhud, somebody started the rumour that the Prophet (Sallallaho alaihe wasallam) had been killed. You can imagine the Sahabah's grief and anguish over this tragic news. This, quite naturally, caused most of them to lose heart in despair. Anas bin Nadhr (Radhiyallaho anho) happened to see 'Umar and Talhah (Radhiyallaho anhuma) with a group of Muslims in a state of utter bewilderment. He said to them:

"Why am I seeing you all so bewildered?"

They said:

"The Prophet (Sallallaho alaihe wasallam) is slain."

Anas (Radhiyallaho anho) exclaimed:

"Then who will like to live after him? Come, let us go forward with our swords and join our dear Prophet."

No sooner did he utter these words than he plunged into the enemy lines and fought till he was martyred.

In fact, Anas (Radhiyallaho anho) had such an extreme love for the Prophet (Sallallaho alaihe wasallam) that he did not consider this life worth living without him.

9. Sa'd's (Radhiyallaho anho) Message For The Muslims.

During the battle of Uhud, the Prophet (Sallallaho alaihe wasallam) inquired:

"What about Sa'd bin Rabee'? I don't know how things have gone with him."

One of the Sahabah was despatched to search for him. He went to the spot where the bodies of martyrs lay in heaps. He shouted Sa'd's (Radhiyallaho anho) name to know if he was alive. At one place, while he was announcing that he was deputed by the Prophet to enquire about Sa'd bin Rabee' (Radhiyallaho anho), he heard a feeble voice coming from one direction. He turned to that direction and found that Sa'd (Radhiyallaho anho) was lying among the killed and was about to breathe his last. Sa'd (Radhiyallaho anho) was heard saying:

> "Convey my Salaam to the Prophet with my message, 'O Prophet of Allah! May Allah grant you on my behalf a reward more exalted and more handsome than the one Allah has ever granted a Prophet on behalf of any of his followers, and tell my Muslim brothers, 'Nothing will absolve you from blame, on the Day of Judgement, if the enemy succeeds in reaching the Prophet (Sallallaho alaihe wasallam) before all of you have fallen."

With these words, Sa'd (Radhiyallaho anho) drew his last breath and passed into the presence of Allah.

فَجَزَاهُ اللهُ عَنَّا اَفْضَلَ مَاجَزٰى صَحَابِيًّا عَنْ اُمَّةِ نَبِيِّهِ

As a matter of fact, the Sahabah have given a true proof of their devotion to the Prophet (Sallallaho alaihe wasallam). While they suffered wound after wound and were on their last breath, they had no complaint nor wish on their lips and could not think of anything else except about the safety and welfare of the Prophet. Would that a sinner like me be blessed with an atom of the love that the Sahabah bore for the Prophet (Sallallaho alaihe wasallam).

10. A Woman Dies On Seeing the Prophet's Grave.

A woman came to Aishah (Radhiyallaho anha) and said:

> "Take me to the grave of the Prophet (Sallallaho alaihe wasallam), so that I may be blessed with its sight."

Aishah (Radhiyallaho anha) opened the room that contained the grave of the Prophet (Sallallaho alaihe wasallam) and let her go inside. The woman on seeing the grave started crying in love and memory of the Prophet. In fact she wept so bitterly and incessantly that she swooned and expired there and then (May Allah bless her). The blessed lady recollected the happy days when the Prophet (Sallallaho alaihe wasallam) was alive, and then the pangs of separation proved fatal for her. Can the annals of history produce a parallel to such love and devotion?

11. Sahabah's Love For the Prophet (Sallallaho alaihe wasallam) and other Anecdotes.

Somebody asked Ali (Radhiyallaho anho):

"How much was the Sahabah's love for the Prophet (Sallallaho alaihe wasallam)."

He replied:

"By Allah! To us the Prophet (Sallallaho alaihe wasallam) was dearer than our riches, our children and our mothers, and was more cherishable than a drink of cold water at the time of severest thirst."

There is no exaggeration in Ali's (Radhiyallaho anho) statement. As a matter of fact, the Sahabah reached this state because of the perfection of their Iman. It could not be otherwise, in the face of what Allah has enjoined viz:

قُلْ اِنْ كَانَ اٰبَآؤُكُمْ وَاَبْنَاءُكُمْ وَاِخْوَانُكُمْ وَاَزْوَاجُكُمْ وَعَشِيْرَتُكُمْ
وَاَمْوَالُ نِ اقْتَرَفْتُمُوْهَا وَتِجَارَةٌ تَخْشَوْنَ كَسَادَهَا وَمَسٰكِنُ تَرْضَوْنَهَآ اَحَبَّ اِلَيْكُمْ
مِّنَ اللهِ وَرَسُوْلِهِ وَجِهَادٍ فِيْ سَبِيْلِهِ فَتَرَبَّصُوْا حَتّٰى يَاْتِيَ اللهُ بِاَمْرِهِ ، وَاللهُ لَايَهْدِى
الْقَوْمَ الْفٰسِقِيْنَ (التوبة ٢٤)

"Say! If your fathers and your sons and your brethren and your wives and your tribe and the wealth you have acquired and the merchandise, for which you fear that there will be no sale, and the dwellings you desire are dearer to you than Allah and His messenger and striving in His way, then wait till Allah bringeth His command to pass. Allah guideth not the wrong-doing folk." (IX: 24).

This verse sounds a note of warning against anything else becoming more attractive than the love of Allah and that of the Prophet (Sallallaho alaihe wasallam). Anas (Radhiyallaho anho) and Abu Hurairah (Radhiyallaho anho) report that the Prophet (Sallallaho alaihe wasallam) once said:

"None of you can be a Mo'min until his love for me is more than his love for his parents, children and all the people of the world."

'Ulama say that the love mentioned in this Hadith and others of its kind is the voluntary love and not instinctive love. If, however, it is taken to mean the natural and instinctive love, then the word Mo'min will denote the Iman of the highest degree, for instance that of Sahabah.

Anas (Radhiyallaho anho) says that he heard from the Prophet (Sallallaho alaihe wasallam), "There are three things which when found in a person enable him to taste the sweetness of real Iman. These are:

(1) When Allah and His Prophet (Sallallaho alaihe wasallam) are dearer to him than anything else in this world.

(2) When his love for anyone is solely for the pleasure of Allah, and

(3) When turning to 'Kufr' is as abhorrent to him as being flung into the fire."

12. Miscellaneous Stories About Sahabah's Love for the Prophet (Sallallaho alaihe wasallam).

(1) 'Umar (Radhiyallaho anho) once said to the Prophet (Sallallaho alaihe wasallam):

"O Prophet of Allah, you are dearer to me than anybody else in the world except my own self."

The Prophet: "No body can be a perfect Momin until I am dearer to him than even his own self."

'Umar: "Now you are dearer to me than my own self."

The Prophet: "Now, O'Umar."

The 'Ulama have given two meanings to the concluding words of the Prophet viz:

(i) "Now you have the real Iman."

(ii) "Why is it that it is only now that I am dearer to you than your own self? This should have been so long ago."

Suhail Tastari (Rahmatullah alaih) says:

"No one can have the relish of Sunnat until he takes

the Prophet (Sallallaho alaihe wasallam) as his Master and considers himself his (the Prophet's) slave."

(2) A person came to the Prophet (Sallallaho alaihe wasallam) and asked:

"When shall be the Day of Judgement? O, Prophet of Allah!"

The Prophet: "What preparations have you made for that Day?"

The person: "O, Prophet of Allah! I do not claim much Salaat, fast and Sadaqah to my credit, but I do have in my heart the love of Allah and that of His Prophet (Sallallaho alaihe wasallam)."

The Prophet: "On the Day of Judgement, you will surely be with him whom you love."

What the Prophet (Sallallaho alaihe wasallam) told the person in this story has also been narrated by several other Sahabah, namely Abdullah bin Mas'ood, Abu Moosa Ash'ari, Safwan, Abu Zar, (Radhiyallaho anhum) etc.

Anas (Radhiyallaho anho) says:

"Nothing did ever make Sahabah more happy than these words of the Prophet (Sallallaho alaihe wasallam)."

They had every reason to be happy when the love of the Prophet (Sallallaho alaihe wasallam) had gone deep into every tissue and fibre of their body.

(3) In the beginning, Fatimah's (Radhiyallaho anha) house was at some distance from the Prophet's. The Prophet (Sallallaho alaihe wasallam) once said to her:

"Would that you were living near me."

Fatimah:

"Harithah's house is close by. If you ask him to exchange his house with mine, he will very gladly do it."

The Prophet:

"He has already exchanged once on my request, I feel shy to request him again."

But Harithah (Radhiyallaho anho) somehow came to know that the Prophet (Sallallaho alaihe wasallam) likes Fatimah (Radhiyallaho anha) to live near him. He at once came to the Prophet (Sallallaho alaihe wasallam) and said:

"O, Prophet of Allah! I have come to know that you wish Fatimah to live near you. Here are my houses at your disposal. No other house is closer to yours than these. Fatimah can have her house exchanged with any of these. O, Prophet of Allah, what you accept from me is dearer to me than what you leave for me."

The Prophet (Sallallaho alaihe wasallam) accepted the offer, saying:

"I know you are quite sincere in what you say", and gave him his blessings.

(4) A person came to the Prophet (Sallallaho alaihe wasallam) and said:

"O, Prophet of Allah! You are dearer to me than my life, my wealth and my family. When I am at my house and happen to think of you, I become restless till I come and see you. O, Prophet of Allah, death is sure to come to both of us. After death, you will be in your exalted position as a Prophet, while I shall be somewhere else and perhaps I may not be able to see you. I am very anxious and distressed when I think of this separation from you."

The Prophet (Sallallaho alaihe wasallam) observed silence over this and he did not know what to say; then Jibra'eel (Alayhis Salaam) appeared and revealed the following verse:

وَمَنْ يُّطِعِ اللهَ وَالرَّسُوْلَ فَاُوْلٰٓئِكَ مَعَ الَّذِيْنَ اَنْعَمَ اللهُ عَلَيْهِمْ مِّنَ النَّبِيّٖنَ وَالصِّدِّيْقِيْنَ وَالشُّهَدَآءِ وَالصّٰلِحِيْنَ ، وَحَسُنَ اُوْلٰٓئِكَ رَفِيْقًا ، ذٰلِكَ الْفَضْلُ مِنَ اللهِ ، وَكَفٰى بِاللهِ عَلِيْمًا (النساء ٦٩ ، ٧٠)

"Whoso obeyeth Allah and the Prophet, they are with those unto whom Allah has shown favour among the Prophets and the Saints and the Martyrs and the Righteous. The best of company are they. Such is the bounty of Allah, and Allah, sufficeth, as knower. (IV: 69 & 70)"

These incidents were of frequent occurrence with the Sahabah. Such fears in the hearts of the lovers are quite natural. The Prophet (Sallallaho alaihe wasallam) recited these verses for their consolation.

A person once came to the Prophet (Sallallaho alaihe wasallam) and said:

> "O, Prophet of Allah, my love for you is such that when I think of you, I cannot rest till I run to see you, for I am sure I would die if I did not see you. Now I grow very anxious when I imagine that, even if I am able to enter Paradise, it will be very difficult for me to see you, for you will be in a position far above my reach."

The Prophet (Sallallaho alaihe wasallam) consoled him by reciting the foregoing verses in his reply.

The Prophet (Sallallaho alaihe wasallam) saw a person from the Ansar looking very much distressed. He inquired:

"What makes you look so distressed?"

The Person: "O, Prophet of Allah! I have a worry."

The Prophet: "What is it?"

The person:

> "O, Prophet of Allah! We come to you every morning and evening. We are blessed with your sight and delighted to be in your presence. But one day, we will be deprived of your company for you will be placed on heights inaccessible to us."

The Prophet (Sallallaho alaihe wasallam) observed silence over this, but when the foregoing verses were revealed he sent for that person and gave him the glad tidings contained therein.

According to another Hadith, a number of Sahabah had expressed similar fears until the Prophet (Sallallaho alaihe wasallam) recited these verses to them, and they were satisfied.

According to another version, the Sahabah once asked the Prophet (Sallallaho alaihe wasallam):

> "The Prophets on account of their ranks will surely be in much higher position than their followers. How will the followers be able to see them?"

The Prophet (Sallallaho alaihe wasallam) replied:

"Those in higher positions will come down to their friends in lower positions to sit with them and talk to them."

(5) The Prophet (Sallallaho alaihe wasallam) once said:

"Some of my followers coming after me will love me very much. They will wish that they could see me, even if they had to spend their wealth, forego their families and sacrifice all their possessions for it."

Khalid's daughter Abdah (Radhiyallaho anhuma) says:

"My father while in bed would talk about and remember the Prophet (Sallallaho alaihe wasallam) with love and eagerness for him. He would also remember each and every Muhajir and Ansari (by name) and would say, "They are my elders and they are my youngers. My heart is eager to meet them. O, Allah! Call me back soon, so that I may be able to meet all of them. He would keep on doing this till he would be overtaken by sleep."

(6) Abu Bakr (Radhiyallaho anho) once said to the Prophet (Sallallaho alaihe wasallam):

"I have a greater wish for your uncle Abu Talib to come into Islam than for my own father, as I know it would please you more."

'Umar (Radhiyallaho anho) similarly, once said to 'Abbas (The prophet's uncle):

"I was more pleased at your Islam that at that of my father, for that gave pleasure to the Prophet (Sallallaho alaihe wasallam)."

(7) One night, 'Umar (Radhiyallaho anho) was on his security patrol when he saw a light and heard a sound coming from a house. He peeped in to find an old lady spinning wool and singing a few couplets with the following meaning:

"May Allah accept the prayers Of the pious and the elect."

"Seeking blessings for Muhammad (Sallallaho alaihe wasallam)."

"O, Allah's Prophet! You worshipped each night. And you wept before the dawning of each day."

"I wish to know if I could be together with my beloved (Prophet)."

"For death comes in different states (of mind) And I do not know how I shall die."

'Umar (Radhiyallaho anho) on hearing these couplets, sat down weeping in love and memory of the Prophet (Sallallaho alaihe wasallam).

(8) The story of Bilal (Radhiyallaho anho) is known to all. At the time of his death, his wife sat by his side exclaiming in excessive grief:

"O, dear! Alas!"

He retorted: "Subhanallah! What a lovely thing it is to die and be able to meet Muhammad (Sallallaho alaihe wasallam) and his Sahabah."

(9) We have already read the story of Zaid (Radhiyallaho anho) in Chapter V. While he stood at the gallows, about to be executed, Abu Sufyan said to him:

"How would you like it if Muhammad (Sallallaho alaihe wasallam) be killed in your place and you be let off to enjoy life with your family."

Zaid (Radhiyallaho anho) replied:

"By Allah, it is unbearable for me to sit happily with my family while (even) a thorn is pricking the Prophet (Sallallaho alaihe wasallam)."

On this, Abu Sufyan remarked:

"There is no parallel anywhere in the world to the love which the companions of Muhammad (Sallallaho alaihe wasallam) have for him."

A note:

What is expected of those who claim to love the Prophet (Sallallaho alaihe wasallam)? The Ulama have given various answers to this question. Qaadhi Iyaadh writes:

"A lover prefers his beloved above all other things and persons. If this is not the case, the love is not sincere. It is, therefore, essential for those who claim to love the Prophet (Sallallaho alaihe wasallam) that they follow him in his words and deeds, carry out his commandments, give up everything that he has disliked and adopt his code of life (Sunnat) in ease and in adversity. Allah has said in His holy book:

قُلْ اِنْ كُنْتُمْ تُحِبُّوْنَ اللهَ فَاتَّبِعُوْنِى يُحْبِبْكُمُ اللهُ وَيَغْفِرْلَكُمْ ذُنُوْبَكُمْ ، وَاللهُ غَفُوْرٌ رَّحِيْمٌ (آل عمران ٣١)

Say (O, Prophet): If ye love Allah, follow me; Allah will love you and forgive you your sins. Allah is Forgiving, Merciful." (III: 31).

The Epilogue.

The stories given in the previous pages are meant to serve as specimens. In fact a detailed account of Sahabah's lives can not be covered even in big volumes. It is now quite a few months since I started writing this small book. My engagements in Madrasah and other matters needing immediate attention have already delayed this work. I, therefore, propose to finish the book at this stage, so that people may at least benefit from these pages. I have to write an important warning before I close. Just as we are today lacking in our other duties we owe to Islam, so are we very seriously neglectful in our respect and esteem of the Sahabah. Some negligent people go to the extent of even making adverse remarks against them. We must remember that the Sahabah are those people who laid the foundations of Islam. They are the pioneers in Tabligh. We can never be too grateful to them. May Allah shower His choicest blessings on their souls for their efforts in acquiring Islam from the Prophet (Sallallaho alaihe wasallam) and handing it down to their successors. I am reproducing below the translation of a chapter from "Shifa" by Qaadhi Iyaadh:

"If we claim to revere and honour the Prophet (Sallallaho alaihe wasallam), we must also respect his Sahabah. As Muslims, it is incumbent on us to appreciate what we owe to them, to follow them and to ask forgiveness of Allah for them. No doubt they had their differences, but we have no right to comment on them. We must beware of the stories forged by Shiahs, innovators or biased historians, whose mischievous motive is to slander some of the Sahabah and slight the others. We must never doubt the sincerity and honesty of Sahabah. When we come across any event in history which appears likely to lower their status in our eyes, we must explain it as far as we can in their favour and attribute it to sincere motives, for they really deserve this line of action. We should always speak of their virtues and must hold our tongue in uttering anything likely to slight them. The Prophet (Sallallaho alaihe wasallam) himself has said, "Observe silence in respect of my Sahabah (when they are mentioned with disrespect)."

There are many virtues and privileges of the Sahabah given in the Qur'an and Hadith. Allah says in His holy book:

مُحَمَّدٌ رَّسُوْلُ اللهِ ، وَالَّذِيْنَ مَعَهُ اَشِدَّآءُ عَلَى الْكُفَّارِ رُحَمَآءُ بَيْنَهُمْ تَرٰهُمْ رُكَّعًا سُجَّدًا يَّبْتَغُوْنَ فَضْلًا مِّنَ اللهِ وَرِضْوَانًا ، سِيْمَاهُمْ فِيْ وُجُوْهِهِمْ مِّنْ اَثَرِ السُّجُوْدِ ، ذٰلِكَ مَثَلُهُمْ فِي التَّوْرٰىةِ ، وَمَثَلُهُمْ فِي الْاِنْجِيْلِ ، كَزَرْعٍ اَخْرَجَ شَطْاَهُ فَاٰزَرَهُ فَاسْتَغْلَظَ فَاسْتَوٰى عَلٰى سُوْقِهِ يُعْجِبُ الزُّرَّاعَ لِيَغِيْظَ بِهِمُ الْكُفَّارَ وَعَدَ اللهُ الَّذِيْنَ اٰمَنُوْا وَعَمِلُوا الصّٰلِحٰتِ مِنْهُمْ مَّغْفِرَةً وَّاَجْرًا عَظِيْمًا (الفتح ٢٩)

"Muhammad is the Prophet of Allah. And those with him are hard against the disbelievers and merciful among themselves. Thou (O, Muhammad) see-est them bowing and falling prostrate (in Salaat), seeking bounty from Allah and (His) acceptance. On their faces there are marks, being the traces of their prostration. Such is their likeness in the Torah and their likeness in Gospel; like as sown corn that sendeth forth its shoot and strengthenth it and riseth firm upon it stalk, delighting the sowers-that He may enrage the disbelievers with (the sight of) them. Allah has promised, unto such of them as believe and do good works, His forgiveness and immense reward. (XLVIII 29)."

لَقَدْ رَضِىَ اللهُ عَنِ الْمُؤْمِنِيْنَ اِذْيُبَايِعُوْنَكَ تَحْتَ الشَّجَرَةِ فَعَلِمَ مَا فِىْ قُلُوْبِهِمْ فَاَنْزَلَ السَّكِيْنَةَ عَلَيْهِمْ وَاَثَابَهُمْ فَتْحًا قَرِيْبًا ، وَّمَغَانِمَ كَثِيْرَةً يَّاْخُذُوْنَهَا ، وَكَانَ اللهُ عَزِيْزًا حَكِيْمًا (الفتح ۱۸ ، ۱۹)

2) Allah was well-pleased with the believers when they swore allegiance unto thee beneath the tree, and He knew what was in their hearts, and He sent down peace and reassurance on them and rewarded them with a near victory. And much booty that they will capture. Allah is ever Mighty, Wise. (XLVIII: 18: 19)''

مِنَ الْمُؤْمِنِيْنَ رِجَالٌ صَدَقُوْا مَاعَاهَدُوا اللهَ عَلَيْهِ ، فَمِنْهُمْ مَّنْ قَضٰى نَحْبَهُ وَمِنْهُمْ مَّنْ يَّنْتَظِرُ ، وَمَابَدَّلُوْا تَبْدِيْلًا (الاحزاب ۲۳)

3) Of the believers are men who are true to what they covenanted with Allah. Some of them have paid their vow by death (in battle), and some of them are still waiting to receive their martyrdom; and they have not altered in the least. (XXXIII: 23).''

وَالسّٰبِقُوْنَ الْاَوَّلُوْنَ مِنَ الْمُهٰجِرِيْنَ وَالْاَنْصَارِ وَالَّذِيْنَ اتَّبَعُوْهُمْ بِاِحْسَانٍ ، رَّضِىَ اللهُ عَنْهُمْ وَرَضُوْا عَنْهُ وَاَعَدَّلَهُمْ جَنّٰتٍ تَجْرِىْ تَحْتَهَا الْاَنْهٰرُ خٰلِدِيْنَ فِيْهَآ اَبَدًا ، ذٰلِكَ الْفَوْزُ الْعَظِيْمُ (التوبة ۱۰۰)

4) And the first to lead the way (in accepting Islam) among the Muhajirin and the Ansar, and those who followed them in sincerity, Allah is well pleased with them and they are well pleased with Him; and He hath made ready for them Gardens underneath which rivers flow, wherein they will abide for ever. That is the supreme triumph. (IX: 100).''

In the above verses of the Qur'an, Allah has praised Sahabah and expressed His pleasure with them. Similarly the books of Hadith are full of their virtues e.g.:

(1) Follow Abu Bakr and 'Umar when I am no more with you.''

(2) My Sahabah are like (guiding) stars. Whomsoever you follow, you will be guided (on the right path):''

(3) "The likeness of my Sahabah (amongst mankind) is as the likeness of salt in food. There is no relish in the food without the salt."

(4) "Beware (of opening your tongue) in slighting my Sahabah. Do not make them the target of your calumny. Who loves them, loves them for his love for me, and who spites them spites them for his spite for me. Who annoys them, annoys me, and who annoys me annoys Allah. Allah will very soon seize the person who annoys Him."

(5) "Do not revile my Sahabah. If any of you (persons coming after Sahabah) has spent gold (in Sadaqah) equal in weight to Mount Uhud, he cannot get a reward equal to what my Sahabah get while spending one or half mudd of grain only."

(A mudd equals $1\frac{3}{4}$ lbs.)

(6) "On the person who reviles my Sahabah rests the curse of Allah and of angels and of men combined. Neither his Fardh no his Nafl is accepted by Allah."

(7) "After the Prophets, Allah has preferred my Sahabah above all His creation. He has again preferred four of my Sahabah over the rest of them. They are Abu Bakr, 'Umar, 'Usman and Ali (Radhiyallaho anhum)."

(8) "O, people! I am pleased with Abu Bakr. You should realize his rank. I am also pleased with 'Umar, Ali, 'Usman, Talhah, Zubair, Sa'd, Sa'eed, Abdur Rahman bin Auf and Abu Ubaidah (Radhiyallaho anhum). You should realize their rank. O, people! Allah has announced the forgiveness of all those who participated in Uhud and who swore allegiance at Hudeybiah. O, people! You should have regard for me while dealing with my Sahabah, especially those who are my kindred by marriage. Beware doing wrong to them, lest they complain against you on the Day of Judgement and you may not be pardoned."

(9) "Have regard for me in dealing with my Sahabah and my kindred in marriage. The person who has regard for me shall be in the protection of Allah on the Day of Judgement. Allah is free of any obliga-

tion to him who has no regard for me. He may seize him any time."

(10) "On the Day of Judgement, I shall be the guardian of those who have regard for me in their dealing with my Sahabah."

(11) "The person who has regard for me in his dealing with my Sahabah, shall be able to reach me, when I shall be at Kauthar; while the person who has no regard for me in his dealing with them shall not be able to approach me. He may have a look at me from a distance."

Ayub Sakhtiani (Rahmatullah alaih) says:

"Whoso loves Abu Bakr (Radhiyallaho anho), he establishes his faith. Whoso loves 'Umar (Radhiyallaho anho), he receives guidance on the right path. Whoso loves Usman (Radhiyallaho anho), he is illumined with the light of Allah. Whoso loves Ali (Radhiyallaho anho), he holds fast to the cable of Allah. Whoso honours Sahabah, can never be a Munafiq. Whoso reviles them, he is surely an innovator or Munafiq or anti-Sunnat. No good action of such person, I am afraid, will be accepted by Allah until he cleans his heart of their spite, and begins to love all of them."

Sahl bin Abdullah (Rahmatullah alaih) says:

"He, who does not honour Sahabah, has actually not believed in the Prophet (Sallallaho alaihe wasallam)."

May Allah save me, my friends, my patrons, my acquaintances, my Shaikhs, my pupils and all Muslims from His wrath and from His beloved Prophet's (Sallallaho alaihe wasallam) displeasure, and may He fill our hearts with the love for the Sahabah (Radhiyallaho anhum).

اٰمِيْن ، بِرَحْمَتِكَ يَاأَرْحَمَ الرَّاحِمِيْنَ

وَاٰخِرُ دَعْوَانَا اَنِ الْحَمْدُ لِلّٰهِ رَبِّ الْعَالَمِيْنَ وَالصَّلٰوةُ وَالسَّلَامُ الْاَتَمَّانِ الْاَكْمَلَانِ عَلٰى سَيِّدِ الْمُرْسَلِيْنَ وَعَلٰى اٰلِهٖ وَاَصْحَابِهِ الطَّيِّبِيْنَ الطَّاهِرِيْنَ وَعَلٰى اَتْبَاعِهِمْ حَمَلَةِ الدِّيْنِ الْمَتِيْنِ

Translated by:–Abdul Rashid Arshad

By MUHAMMAD ZAKARIYYA

12 Shawaal 1357 **(HIJRI)** **KANDHLAVI**

Virtues of the HOLY QUR'AAN

Virtues of the
Holy Qur'aan

**Revised translation of
the Urdu book Faza'il-e-Qur'aan**

فَضَائلِ قُرآن

By:-
Shaikhul Hadith Maulana Muhammad Zakariyyah Kaandhlawi (Rah)

**translated by
Aziz-ud-Din**

ادارہ اشاعتِ دینیات (پرائیویٹ) لمیٹڈ
idara.com
IDARA ISHA'AT-E-DINIYAT (P) LTD.

FAZA'IL-E-QUR'AN

By: Shaikhul Hadith
Maulana Muhammad Zakariyya Kaandhlawi (Rah)

Edition 2001

Published by:
IDARA ISHA'AT-E-DINIYAT (P) LTD.
168/2, Jha House, Hazrat Nizamuddin
New Delhi-110 013 (India)
Tel.: 6926832, 6926833
Fax: +91-11-6322787,4352786
Email: **sales@idara.com**
Visit us at: **www.idara.com**

Printed at:
Nice Printing Press, Delhi

CONTENTS

PART 1–FORTY AHADITH

Contents

Contents

Contents

بِسْمِ اللهِ الرَّحْمٰنِ الرَّحِيْمِ

In the name of Allah, the Most Benevolent, the Most Merciful

FOREWORD

اَلْحَمْدُ للهِ الَّذِىْ خَلَقَ الْاِنْسَانَ وَعَلَّمَهُ الْبَيَانَ وَاَنْزَلَ لَهُ الْقُرْآنَ وَجعَلَهُ مَوْعِظَةً وَّشِفَاءً وَّهُدًى وَّرَحْمَةً لِّذَوِى الْاِيْمَانِ لَارَيْبَ فِيْهِ وَلَمْ يَجْعَلْ لَّهُ عِوَجًا وَاَنْزَلَهُ قَيِّمًا حُجَّةً نُوْرًا لِذَوِى الْاِيْقَانِ وَالصَّلٰوةُ وَالسَّلَامُ الْاَتَمَّانِ الْاَكْمَلَانِ عَلٰى خَيْرِ الْخَلَائِقِ مِنَ الْاِنْسِ وَالْجَانِّ الَّذِىْ نَوَّرَ الْقَلْبَ وَالْقُبُوْرَ نُوْرُهُ وَ رَحْمَةٌ لِّلْعٰلَمِيْنَ ظُهُوْرُهُ وَعَلٰى اٰلِهِ وَصَحْبِهِ الَّذِىْ هُمْ نُجُوْمُ الْهِدَايَةِ وَنَاشِرُ الْفُرْقَانِ وَعَلٰى مَنْ تَبِعَهُمْ بِالْاِيْمَانِ وَبَعْدُ فَيَقُوْلُ الْمُفْتَقِرُ اِلٰى رَحْمَةِ رَبِّهِ الْجَلِيْلِ عَبْدُهُ الْمَدْعُوُّ بِزَكَرِيَّا بْنِ يَحْيٰى بْنِ اِسْمٰعِيْلَ هٰذِهِ الْعُجَالَةُ اَرْبَعُوْنَةٌ فِىْ فَضَائِلِ الْقُرْآنِ اَلَّفْتُهَا مُمْتَثِلًا لِاَمْرِ مَنْ اِشَارَتُهُ حُكْمٌ وَطَاعَتُهُ غُنْمٌ

All praise be to Allah Who created man, gave him the gift of expression and revealed for him the Holy Qur'an, which is a source of advice, healing guidance and mercy for those who have faith. The Qur'an contains nothing that is doubtful or crooked. It is absolutely straight, and authority and Nur (enlightenment) for the believers. Abundant and perfect salutation be on Muhammad Rasulullah (Sallallaho alaihe wasallam) (blessing and peace from Allah be upon him), the person who is the best of all creation, whose Nur illuminated the hearts of the living and their graves after death, whose appearance was a bounty for the whole universe. Peace be upon his descendants and Companions, who are the stars of guidance and propagators of the Holy Qur'an, and also upon those believers who are their followers in faith.

After this praise and salutation, I (the author), Zakariyya, son of Yahya, son of Isma'il, state that these hurriedly written pages contain forty ahadith (Plural of hadith–a saying of the Holy Prophet (Sallallaho alaihe wasallam)), which I have compiled on virtues of the Holy Qur'an, in obedience to such people whose words are law for me and following whom is most valuable to me. One of the special favours of Allah, the Sanctified and Pure, which have always descended upon the higher Madrasah (religious school) of Mazahir-ul-Ulum, Saharanpur, has been the annual gathering of this Madrasah for the purpose of briefly mentioning the progress of the institution. For this gathering at the Madrasah, not much effort is made to collect speakers, preachers and the famous people of India, but more attention is paid to invite men whose hearts are full of love for Allah and Masha'ikh (saintly people) who prefer to live unknown. Although those days have receded in the past when 'Hujjat-ul-Islam' (a title meaning a great authority on Islam) Maulana Mohammad Qasim Nanautvi Saheb (Rahmatullah alaih) and Qutbul Irshad (a title meaning a great savant) Hadhrat Maulana Rashid Ahmad Ganghoi Saheb (Nawwarallahu marqadahu) used to honour this gathering with their presence and illuminate the hearts of all who attended, and the scene has not yet disappeared from the eyes when the spiritual descendants of those revivalists of Islam–Hadhrat Shaikh-ul-Hind (Rahmatullah alaih), Hadhrat Shah Abdur Rahim (Rahmatullah alaih), Hadhrat Maulana Khalil Ahmad Saheb (Rahmatullah alaih), and Hadhrat Maulana Ashraf Ali Thanwi Saheb (Nawwarallahu marqadahu) used to assemble at the annual gathering of the Madrasah. Their presence was a fountain source of life and light for deadened souls and quenched the thirst of those who sought Divine love.

At present, though the annual gatherings do not have the illuminations of even such sources of guidance, their true spiritual descendants still honour these gatherings with their presence and enrich the audience with bounties and blessings. The people who attended the gathering this year are witnesses to this. Only those who possess eyes that see can experience the effulgence, but sightless beings like us can also feel something unusual.

At the annual gathering of this Madrasah, if a person comes to listen to polished speeches and forceful lectures, he will perhaps not return so much happy as one who seeks a balm for his heart.

فَلِلّٰهِ الْحَمْدُ وَالْمِنَّةُ

All praise and supplication is for Allah.

In the same connection, during this year on 27th Zil-qa'dah (name of the eleventh month of Islamic calendar), 1348 Hijri, Hadhrat Shah Hafiz Mohammad Yasin Naginwi (Rahmatullah alaih) visited the Madrasah. His coming was like a shower of affection and kindness, and I cannot adequately thank him for this. After knowing about him that he is one of the spiritual heirs of Hadhrat Gangohi (Rahmatullah alaih), there is no need of mentioning his fine qualities of devotion and piety, and the presence of Anwaar (Plural of 'Nur'–enlightenment and blessings) in his own person. When this gathering was over, he returned home and honoured me with a kind letter asking me to compile forty ahadith regarding the virtues of the Glorious Quran and send them to him along with their translations. He also wrote to me that, if I did not carry out his wishes, he would ask the successor to my Shaikh (teacher) and elderly uncle, Maulana Hafiz Alhaj Maulvi Mohammad Ilyas (Rahmatullah alaih), to confirm this order of his. He made it certain that he wanted me to do this job. Incidentally, I received that honoured message when I was out travelling and my uncle was present (at Saharanpur). On my return, my uncle gave this letter to me along with his own firm orders for compliance. Now there was no occasion for me for any excuse or to plead lack of ability. Although my occupation with the commentary of 'Mo'atta' (a book of Ahadith) of Imam Malik (Rahmatullah alaih) was a good excuse, I had to postpone that work for a few days and, in compliance with the urgent orders, produce my effort for his esteemed consideration. I beg to be excused for such shortcomings as are inevitable because of my incompetence.

رَجَاءَ الْحَشْرِ فِىْ سِلْكِ مَنْ قَالَ فِيْهِمُ النَّبِىُّ صَلَّى اللّٰهُ عَلَيْهِ وَسَلَّمَ مَنْ حَفِظَ عَلٰى
اُمَّتِىْ اَرْبَعِيْنَ حَدِيْثًا فِىْ اَمْرِ دِيْنِهَا بَعَثَهُ اللّٰهُ فَقِيْهاً وَكُنْتُ لَهُ يَوْمَ الْقِيٰمَةِ شَافِعًا وَّ
شَهِيْدًا ، قَالَ الْعَلْقَمِىُّ اَلْحِفْظُ ضَبْطُ الشَّىْءِ وَمَنْعُهُ مِنَ الضِّيَاعِ فَتَارَةً يَّكُوْنُ
حِفْظُ الْعِلْمِ بِالْقَلْبِ وَاِنْ لَّمْ يَكْتُبْ وَتَارَةً فِىْ الْكِتَابِ وَاِنْ لَّمْ يَحْفَظْهُ بِقَلْبِهِ فَلَوْ
حَفِظَ فِىْ كِتَابٍ ثُمَّ نَقَلَ اِلَى النَّاسِ دَخَلَ فِىْ وَعْدِ الْحَدِيْثِ وَقَالَ الْمُنَاوِىُّ قَوْلُهُ
مَنْ حَفِظَ عَلٰى اُمَّتِىْ اَىْ نَقَلَ اِلَيْهِمْ بِطَرِيْقِ التَّخْرِيْجِ وَالْاِسْنَادِ وَقِيْلَ مَعْنٰى حِفْظِهَا

اَنْ يَّنْقُلَهَا اِلَى الْمُسْلِمِيْنَ وَاِنْ لَمْ يَحْفَظْهَا وَلَاعَرَفَ مَعْنَاهَا وَقَوْلُهُ اَرْبَعِيْنَ حَدِيْثًا صِحَاحًا اَوْ حِسَانًا قِيْلَ اَوْ ضِعَافًا يُعْمَلُ بِهَا فِى الْفَضَائِلِ اهـ فَلِلّٰهِ دَرُّ الْاِسْلَامِ مَااَيْسَرَهُ وَلِلّٰهِ دَرُّ اَهْلِهٖ مَااَجْوَدَ مَااسْتَنْبَطُوْا رَزَقَنِى اللّٰهُ تَعَالٰى وَاِيَّاكُمْ كَمَالَ الْاِسْلَامِ وَمِمَّا لَابُدَّ مِنَ التَّنْبِيْهِ عَلَيْهِ اَنِّىْ اِعْتَمَدْتُّ فِى التَّخْرِيْجِ عَلَى الْمِشْكٰوةِ وَتَخْرِيْجِهٖ وَشَرْحِهِ الْمِرْقَاةِ وَشَرْحِ الْاِحْيَاءِ لِلسَّيِّدِ مُحَمَّدِنِ الْمُرْتَضٰى وَالتَّرْغِيْبِ لِلْمُنْذِرِىِّ وَمَا عَزَوْتُ اِلَيْهَا لِكَثْرَةِ الْاَخْذِ عَنْهَا وَمَا اَخَذْتُ عَنْ غَيْرِهَا عَزَوْتُهُ اِلٰى مَأْخِذِهٖ وَيَنْبَغِىْ لِلْقَارِىْ مُرَاعَاتُ اٰدَابِ التِّلَاوَةِ عِنْدَ الْقِرَائَةِ

I have done it in the hope of being raised together on the day of judgement together with such people as were referred by Rasulullah (Sallallaho alaihe wasallam) when he said: "Whoever will preserve for my Ummah (followers of the Prophet) forty 'Ahadith' concerning important matters of their faith, Almighty Allah will raise him, on the Day of Judgement, as an Alim (religious scholar) and I will intercede on his behalf and stand witness in his favour."

Alqami (Rahmatullah alaih) says that the word 'preserve' occurring in this hadith is used in the sense of securing something and guarding it against loss by either committing it to memory without recording it or by recording in black and white, without even memorizing it. So any one writing them in the form of a book and passing them on to others will also be covered by the blessings mentioned in this 'hadith.'

Munaawi (Rahmatullah alaih) is of the opinion that "preserve for my Ummat" means reporting of a hadith along with its authority. According to some, "preserve" includes even those who are reporting it to other Muslims without memorizing it or even without knowing its meanings. Also the expression "forty ahadith" has been used in general sense, i.e., these ahadith may be all sahih (authentic), hasan (correct) or even da'if (weak) to the degree that can be acted upon because of their virtues.

Allaho akbar! (How great Allah is!). Many are the facilities provided in Islam. And commendable indeed has been the role of scholars and theologians who took such pains to explain the subtleties of various expressions. May Almighty Allah bless us all with perfection in Islam.

It is important to note that whenever I have quoted a hadith without mentioning the name of the book, it should be deemed to have been taken from one of the five books, viz., 'Al-Mishkat', 'Tanqih-ur-Ruwat', 'Al-Mirqat'. 'Sharah-ul-Ihya' and 'At-Targhib' of Mundhiri, on which I have relied and from which I have drawn extensively. Whenever I have quoted from any other book, the source has been mentioned.

It is incumbent upon the reader of the Qur'an to observe the rules of reverence for its recitation.

Before proceeding further, it seems desirable to mention first some of the requirements of decorum for reading of the Holy Qur'an; because, as admitted.

بے ادب محروم گشت از فضل رب

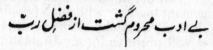

One who is devoid of reverence misses Allah's special favour.

In brief, the essence of all the rules of reverence is to consider the Glorious Qur'an as the words of Almighty Allah, Whom we worship, and as the Word of One Whom we love and seek.

Those who have ever experieced love, know how worthy of adoration is a letter or speech of the beloved. The ecstatic raptures caused by such a communication are beyond all rules of propriety because, as it is said.

محبت تجھ کو آداب محبت خود سکھا دے گی

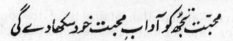

Love itself will teach one the rules of conduct in love.

So, while reading the Qur'an, if we attempt to visualise the real beauty and limitless bounty of our Beloved Allah, our hearts will be swayed by emotions of heavenly love. At the same tine, the Qur'an is the Word of the Master of masters and the commands of the Emperor of all kings. It is the law promulgated by the All-powerful Monarch, Who remains unequalled for ever. Those who have served at the courts of kings know by experience, while others can just visualise the extreme awe inspried by the king's orders.

The Qur'an is the word of our Beloved Lord, Who is also the Supreme Monarch. We should, therefore read the Qur'an with the emotions of love and awe.

It is said that whenever Hadhrat 'Ikramah (Radhiyallaho anho) (may Allah be pleased with him) opened the Book for recitation, he became unconscious and fell down. Then he would utter,

هٰذَا كَلَامُ رَبِّىْ هٰذَا كَلَامُ رَبِّىْ

"This is the Word of my Allah, this is the Word of my Allah."

The aforesaid contains briefly the spirit of the requirements of decorum as written in great detail by the Muslim scholars. It will further be explained in the following paragraphs. In short, a Muslim should read the book of Allah not just as a servant, but as a slave in the spirit of complete humility towards his Lord, Master and Benefactor. The Sufia (Plural of Sufi–mystic) have written that, if a person feels his shortcomings in exercising due respect and reverence while reciting the Qur'an, he will continue to progress along the path of nearness to Almighty Allah but a person who regards himself with approval or pride will not advance further.

Rules of Reverence for reading the Holy Qur'an

After cleaning the teeth with a miswak (a green twig of special varieties of trees used for brushing the teeth) and wudhu (ablution), one should sit in a quite place with grace and humility and face towards Qiblah (direction towards the Ka'bah in Mecca). Then, with an attentive heart, deep devotion and zest befitting the occasion, one should recite, imagining all the time that he is reciting it to Almighty Allah. If one understands the meaning, one should pause and reflect on ayaat (Plural of 'ayat'–a verse of the Qur'an) of promise and mercy and should beg for His forgiveness and compassion. On ayaat of punishment and admonition, one should seek His refuge, as except Him there is no Helper. On ayaat pertaining to His Majesty and Sanctity, one should say "Subhaanallah" (Glory to Allah). If one does not spontaneously shed tears while reading the Book, one must induce oneself to weep a little.

وَالَذُّ حَالاَتِ الْغَرَامِ لِمُغْرَمٍ   شَكْوَى الْهَوى بِالْمَدْمَعِ الْمُهْرَاقِ

For a lover, the moments of greatest pleasure are those when, in the presence of his beloved, he is full of self-reproach and shedding tears profusely.

One should not read fast unless one desires to memorize it. The Qu'ran should be placed in a slightly elevated position on a wooden stand or a pillow. One should not talk to others during recitation. If one is forced by necessity to speak to someone, it should be done after first closing the Book, and then recite 'Ta'awwudh' (seeking refuge of Allah against Satan), before reading again. If people nearby are occupied in their work, reading in a low voice is appreciated otherwise reading loudly is more rewarding.

The Masha'ikh have mentioned six external and six internal rules of reverence for reading the Holy Qu'ran, which are given below:

Rules of External Reverence

(1) Perform Wudhu and then sit facing Qiblah in an extremely dignified manner.

(2) Do not proceed fast, but read with measure and correct pronunciation.

(3) Try to weep, even if you have to compel yourself to do so.

(4) The response to ayaat of mercy or of punishment should be as explained above.

(5) Reading should be in a low voice, if insincerity is apprehended on your own part or disturbance is caused to others. Otherwise read in a loud voice.

(6) Read in a melodious voice, because there are numerous ahadith laying emphasis on this.

Rules of Internal Reverence

(1) The heart should be full of the glory of Qur'an i.e. realizing how sublime it is.

(2) Bear in the heart the Loftiness, Majesty and Magnificence of Almighty Allah, Whose Revelation the Qu'ran is.

(3) The heart should be free from distraction and doubts.

(4) Dwell upon the meanings and enjoy reading it.

Rasulullah (Sallallaho alaihe wasallam) once spent the whole night reading over and over again the following ayat:

اِنْ تُعَذِّبْهُمْ فَاِنَّهُمْ عِبَادُكَ وَاِنْ تَغْفِرْلَهُمْ فَاِنَّكَ اَنْتَ الْعَزِيْزُ الْحَكِيْمُ .

If Thou should chastise them, they are Thy servants, and if Thou should forgive them, Thou art the Mighty, the Wise (V: 118).

Once, Hadhrat Sa'eed ibn Jubair (Radhiyallaho anho) spent the whole night repeating the following ayat:

وَامْتَازُوْا الْيَوْمَ اَيُّهَا الْمُجْرِمُوْنَ

And withdraw aside today, O guilty ones! (XXXVI: 59).

(5) Submit your heart to the subject-matter of the verses you are reading. For instance, on ayaat containing a message of mercy, the heart should be filled with delight. And on ayaat of chastisement, the heart should tremble with awe.

(6) The ears should be made as attentive as if Almighty Allah Himself is speaking and the reader is listening to Him.

May Allah, out of His mercy and kindness, grant all of us the ability to read the Qu'ran according to these rules of reverence.

A Religious Principle

The memorizing of that much of the Glorious Qu'ran as is necessary for the offering of salaat is obligatory for every Muslim, whereas memorizing the whole of the Holy Qur'an is Fard Kifayah, i.e. an act obligatory on all, but which may suffice if performed by an adequate number. If there were not a single hafiz (may Allah forbid) all the Muslims would be held responsible for this sin. Mulla'Ali Qari (Rahmatullah alaih) has further reported from Zarkashi (Rahmatullah alaih) that if, in a town or a village, there were no person to read the Holy Qur'an, all the Muslim inhabitants of that place would be considered sinful. In this age of darkness and ignorance when the Muslims have become misguided in respect of many aspects of Islam, it is generally considered useless and stupid to memorize the Qur'an and a sheer waste of time and mental energy to repeat its words without understanding their meaning. If this were the only case of our aversion to faith, something in detail could be written about it. But today all our acts are erring and all our thoughts are leading us astray. For how many should one wail and about how many should one complain.

فَإِلَى اللهِ الْمُشْتَكىٰ وَاللهُ الْمُسْتَعَانُ

So to Allah do we complain and from Him do we seek help.

PART I

FORTY AHADITH

Hadith–1

(١) عَنْ عُثْمَانَ رَضِىَ اللهُ عَنْهُ قَالَ قَالَ رَسُوْلُ اللهِ ﷺ خَيْرُكُمْ مَّنْ تَعَلَّمَ الْقُرْآنَ وَعَلَّمَهُ (رواه البخارى وأبو داود والترمذى والنسائى وابن ماجه هذا فى الترغيب وعزاه إلى مسلم أيضاً لكن حكى الحافظ فى الفتح عن أبى العلاء اَنَّ مسلماً سكت عنه)

Hadhrat Uthman (Radhiyallaho anha) narrates that Rasulullah (Sallallaho alaihe wasallam) said: "The best amongst you is he who learns the Qur'an and teaches it." In most of the books, this hadith is quoted with the word 'and' between 'learns' and 'teaches' as above. Thus the greatest reward would be for him who learns the Holy Qur'an and thereafter teaches it to others. But in some of the books this 'hadith's is narrated with the word 'or', in which case the meaning would be: "The best amongst you is he who learns the Qur'an or teaches it."

According to this version, the reward is general, i.e., equally great whether one learns himself or teaches to others. Thus there would be equal virtue for both.

The Qur'an is the basis of the religion of Islam, and on the preservation and propagation of the Qur'an depends the very existence of this faith. Hence the virtue of learning and teaching the Qur'an is self-evident and does not need further elucidation.

There are, however, various degrees of excellence. The highest is to learn the Qur'an along with its meanings and purport, and the least is to learn its words only.

The hadith mentioned above is supported also by another saying of Rasulullah (Sallallaho alaihe wasallam) as reported by Hadhrat Sa'eed ibn Saleem (Radhiyallaho anho): "If a person who has acquired knowledge of the Holy Qur'an considers another person who has been gifted with something else to be more fortunate than himself, he has shown disrespect to the blessings of Allah bestowed on him on account of his learning the Qur'an.'' It is evident that since the Qur'an, being the Word of Allah, is superior to all other discourses as mentioned in some of the ahadith quoted later, its reading and teaching must be superior to everything else.

Mulla Ali Qari quotes from another hadith that whoever acquires the knowledge of Holy Qur'an stores the knowledge of prophethood in his forehead.

Sahl Tastari (Rahmatullah alaih) says that the proof of love for Allah is the existence of love for the Word of Allah in one's heart.

In 'Sharhul Ihya', the list of people who will be given shelter in the shade of the Arsh (Throne of Allah) on the fearful Day of Judgement includes those persons who teach the Qur'an to the children of Muslims and also those who learn the Holy Qur'an in their childhood and are devoted to its recitation when grown up.

HADITH–2

(٢) عَنْ اَبِىْ سَعِيْدٍ رَضِىَ اللّٰهُ عَنْهُ قَالَ قَالَ رَسُوْلُ اللّٰهِ ﷺ يَقُوْلُ الرَّبُّ تَبَارَكَ وَتَعَالٰى مَنْ شَغَلَهُ الْقُرْآنُ عَنْ ذِكْرِىْ وَمَسْئَلَتِىْ اَعْطَيْتُهُ اَفْضَلَ مَا اُعْطِى السَّائِلِيْنَ وَفَضْلُ كَلَامِ اللّٰهِ عَلٰى سَائِرِ الْكَلَامِ كَفَضْلِ اللّٰهِ عَلٰى خَلْقِهٖ (رواه الترمذى والدارمى والبيهقى فى الشعب)

Hadhrat Abu Sa'eed (Radhiyallaho anho) narrates that Rasulullah (Sallallaho alaihe wasallam) said: "Almighty Allah says; "If anybody finds no time for My remembrance and for begging favours of Me, because of his remaining busy with the Holy Qur'an, I shall give him more than what I give to all those who beg favours of Me. The superiority of the Word of Allah over all other words is like the superiority of Allah over the entire creation.''

In other words, compared to those who are begging favours of Allah, He will surely confer some better reward on a person who remains so occupied with committing the Qur'an to memory or learning and understanding it that he hardly gets time for du'a (prayer).

It is commonly known that when a man distributes sweets, or something else amongst others, a share is set aside for the person who cannot attend the function because of the task of distribution given to him by the distributor himself. In another hadith, in the same context, it is mentioned that Allah would give such a person a better reward than what He would give to His ever grateful servants.

HADITH–3

(٣) عَنْ عُقْبَةَ بْنِ عَامِرٍ رَضِىَ اللّٰهُ عَنْهُ قَالَ خَرَجَ رَسُوْلُ اللّٰهِ ﷺ وَنَحْنُ فِى الصُّفَّةِ فَقَالَ اَيُّكُمْ اَنْ يَّغْدُوَ كُلَّ يَوْمٍ اِلٰى بُطْحَانَ اَوِ الْعَقِيْقِ فَيَاْتِىَ بِنَاقَتَيْنِ كَوْمَاوَيْنِ فِىْ غَيْرِ اِثْمٍ وَّلَاقَطِيْعَةِ رَحْمٍ فَقُلْنَا يَارَسُوْلَ اللّٰهِ كُلُّنَا نُحِبُّ ذٰلِكَ قَالَ اَفَلَا يَغْدُوْ اَحَدُكُمْ اِلَى الْمَسْجِدِ فَيَعْلَمُ اَوْ يَقْرَاُ اٰيَتَيْنِ مِنْ كِتَابِ اللّٰهِ خَيْرٌ لَّهُ مِنْ نَاقَتَيْنِ وَثَلٰثٌ خَيْرٌ لَّهُ مِنْ ثَلٰثٍ وَّاَرْبَعٌ خَيْرٌ لَّهُ مِنْ اَرْبَعٍ وَمِنْ اَعْدَادِهِنَّ مِنَ الْاِبِلِ

(رواه مسلم وأبوداود)

Hadhrat 'Uqbah ibn Aamir (Radhiyallaho anho) has said: "Rasulullah (Sallallaho alaihe wasallam) came to us while we were sitting on the Suffah and asked if any one of us would like to go to the market of But-haan or Aqeeq and fetch from there two she-camels of the finest breed without commiting any sin or severing a tie of kinship. We replied that everyone of us would love to do so. Rasulullah (Sallallaho alaihe wasallam) then said that going to the musjid and reciting or teaching two ayaat of the Qur'an is more precious than two she-camels, three ayaat are most precious than three she-camels, and that similarly reciting or teaching of four ayaat is better than four she-camels and an equal number of camels."

"Suffah" is the name of a particular raised platform in the Mosque of the Holy Prophet (Sallallaho alaihe wasallam) in Medina. It used to be occupied by the poor Muslim muhajirin (Plural of muhajir-emigrant from Mecca to Medina) who are known as "Ashab-us-Suffah" (Men of Suffah). The number of these men varied from time to time: 'Allamah Suyuti (Rahmatullah alaih) has listed one hundred and one names and also written an independent booklet about their names.

But-han and Aqeeq were the two market-places for camels near Medina. The camel, more particularly a she-camel having a fat hump, was a favourite of the Arabs.

The expression "without sin" is significant. A thing can be acquired without labour either by extortion, through illegal inheritance (by forcefully taking over the property of some relative) or by theft. Rasullullah (Sallallaho alaihe wasallam) thus ruled out all such acquisitions. Acquiring a thing without any sin is certainly preferred by all, but much more valuable is the learning of a few ayaat.

It is a clear fact that let alone one or two camels, even if one acquires the kingdom of all the seven continents one will be forced to leave it, if not today surely tomorrow (at the time of death), but the reward of one ayat will be everlasting. We see even in this life that a man feels happier when he is given only one rupee (without the condition of returning it), rather than if he is given one thousand rupees for keeping in his safe custody for a while only. In the latter case, he is merely burdened with a trust without getting any benefit out of it. In fact, this hadith implies an admonition not to compare something temporary with something eternal. Whether in action or at rest, a man should consider if his efforts are being wasted on acquiring the temporary gains of this world, or, are directed towards achieving the everlasting ones. Woe be to the waste of effort for which we earn eternal misery. The last phrase of the hadith "superior to an equal number of camels" contains three meanings. First, upto the number four, the reward has been mentioned in detail. Beyond this, it is briefly mentioned that the more ayaat a person acquires, the greater will be their superiority over the number of camels. In this case, the word "camels" at the end refers to the species–either he-camels or she-camels–and the number implied is more than four because, upto the number four, the reward has been mentioned in detail. The second meaning is that the numbers mentioned are the same as referred to earlier, the significance being that inclinations are always different; some are fond of she-camels, others prefer a he-camel. Therefore Rasulullah (Sallallaho alaihe wasallam) has used this expression to signify that every ayat is superior to a she-camel, and if one prefers a he-camel, an ayat is also superior to a he-camel. The third meaning is that the numbers mentioned are the same as referred to before and not more than four. According to the second meaning, the explanation that an ayat is superior to a she-camel or he-camel does not hold good, but it implies a collection, i.e., one ayat is superior to a he-camel and a she-camel considered together, and likewise every ayat is superior to the combination of an equal number of he-camels or she-camels. Thus a single ayat has been compared to a pair or couple (of camels). My late father (May Allah bless his grave with Divine light) has preferred the latter interpretation because it points to a superior virtue. This however, does not mean that the reward of an ayat can be equalled to a camel or two camels. All this is for inducement and illustration. It has been clearly written before that an ayat whose reward is permanent and enduring is superior and preferable even to a kingdom over the seven continents, which is bound to disintegrate.

Mulla 'Ali Qari has written an account of a pious Shaikh who went to Mecca for Hajj on the 9th day of Dhul Hijjah—the 12th month of the Islamic calendar. When he landed at Jiddah, some of his friends in business requested him to prolong his stay in Jiddah, so that they could earn more profit for their merchandise by virtue of his blessed presence. In fact they wanted that some of the servants of the Shaikh be benefited by the profits of their business. At first the Shaikh expressed his inability to prolong his stay, but when they insisted the Shaikh asked them as to the maximum profit that they would earn for their goods. They explained that the profit was not the same in all cases; but the maximum that they could expect was hundred per cent. The Shaikh said, "You have taken all this trouble for such a petty gain; for such an insignificant gain. I cannot miss the salaat in the respected Haram (the most Sacred Mosque), where the reward of salaat gets multiplied one hundred thousand times." In fact, we Muslims should consider how, for petty worldly gains, we sometimes sacrifice great spiritual benefits.

HADITH—4

(٤) عَنْ عَائِشَةَ رَضِىَ اللّٰهُ تَعَالٰى عَنْهَا قَالَتْ قَالَ رَسُوْلُ اللّٰهِ ﷺ اَلْمَاهِرُ بِالْقُرْآنِ مَعَ السَّفَرَةِ الْكِرَامِ الْبَرَرَةِ وَالَّذِىْ يَقْرَاُ الْقُرْآنَ وَيَتَتَعْتَعُ فِيْهِ وَهُوَ عَلَيْهِ شَاقٌّ لَهٗ اَجْرَانِ (رواه البخارى ومسلم وأبوداود والترمذى والنسائى وابن ماجه)

Hadhrat 'Aa'ishah (Radhiyallaho anha) narrates that Rasulullah (Sallallaho alaihe wasallam) once said, "One who is well versed in the Qur'an will be in the company of those angels who are scribes, noble and righteous; and one who falters in reading the Qur'an, and has to exert hard for learning, gets double the reward."

"One who is well versed in the Qur'an" means one who is proficient in memorizing as well as in reciting it. It is highly praiseworthy if one masters its meaning and significance as well. "To be with the angels" means that, like the angels who transferred the Qur'an from the, Lowhul Mahfooz' (Protected Tablet in the Heavens), he also conveys it to others through its recitation and, therefore, both have the same occupation; or that he will join the company of such angels on the Day of Judgement. One who falters will get double reward–one for his reading and the other for his effort in reading the Qur'an, in spite of faltering again and again. It does not mean that his reward will exceed that of a well-versed person. The reward that is mentioned for a well-versed person is far greater, so much so that he will be in the company of special angels. The explanation is that the labour involved in faltering and the difficulties in the reading of the Qur'an carry an independent reward. As such, reading of the Qur'an should not be given up, even though faltering may be an excuse.

Mulla 'Ali Qari has reproduced from the riwayat of Tabrani and Baihaqi that one who cannot memorize the Qur'an well and yet persists in learning it by heart gets double reward. Similarly, one who cherishes a longing for memorizing it and does not possess the ability to do so, but does not give up his efforts, will be reckoned by Almighty Allah among the huffaaz (Plural of hafiz–one who has learnt the whole Qur'an by heart) on the Day of Resurrection.

HADITH–5

(٥) عَنِ ابْنِ عُمَرَ رَضِىَ للهُ عَنْهُمَا قَالَ قَالَ رَسُوْلُ اللهِ ﷺ لَاحَسَدَ اِلَّا عَلٰى اِثْنَيْنِ رَجُلٌ اٰتَاهُ اللهُ الْقُرْآنَ فَهُوَ يَقُوْمُ بِهٖ اٰنَآءَ اللَّيْلِ وَاٰنَآءَ النَّهَارِ وَرَجُلٌ اٰتَاهُ اللهُ مَالًا فَهُوَ يُنْفِقُ مِنْهُ اٰنَآءَ اللَّيْلِ وَاٰنَآءَ النَّهَارِ (رواه البخارى والترمذى والنسائى)

Hadhrat Ibn Umar (Radhiyallaho anho) narrates that Rasulullah (Sallallaho alaihe wasallam) said, "Hasad (jealousy) is not permitted except in respect of two persons–one whom Allah blesses with recitation of Qur'an and he remains engaged in it day and night, and the other who is given a lot of wealth by Allah and he spends it day and night."

On the authority of many ayaat of the Qur'an and numerous ahadith, hasad is an evil and is absolutely forbidden. This hadith, however, appears to permit hasad in respect of two persons. Because there are many well-known traditions dealing with hasad, the Ulama (Plural of aalim–religious scholar) have interpreted this hadith in two ways. Firstly, hasad as denoted by the Arabic word 'ghibtah', is taken here in the sense of emulation. There is a difference between jealousy and emulation. Hasad is a desire that one possessing a blessing should be deprived of it; whether the person who feels jealous acquires it or not, while emulation signifies a desire to possess a thing, whether the actual owner is deprived of it or not. Since hasad is haram (religiously unlawful) under Ijma (consensus of opinion), the Ulama have translated, by way of metaphor, this word hasad as ghibtah, meaning emulation. Ghibtah is permissible in worldly affairs and commendable in religious matters.

The second interpretation is that the term hasad has been used in a hypothetical sense, i.e., if hasad were permissible it would have been so with regard to the two persons mentioned above.

HADITH–6

(٦) عَنْ اَبِىْ مُوْسٰى رَضِىَ اللّٰهُ عَنْهُ قَالَ قَالَ رَسُوْلُ اللّٰهِ ﷺ مَثَلُ الْمُؤْمِنِ الَّذِىْ يَقْرَأُ
الْقُرْآنَ مَثَلُ الْاُتْرُجَّةِ رِيْحُهَا طَيِّبٌ وَطَعْمُهَا طَيِّبٌ وَمَثَلُ الْمُؤْمِنِ الَّذِىْ لَايَقْرَأُ
الْقُرْآنَ مَثَلُ التَّمْرَةِ لَارِيْحَ لَهَا وَطَعْمُهَا حُلْوٌ وَمَثَلُ الْمُنَافِقِ الَّذِىْ لَايَقْرَأُ الْقُرْآنَ
كَمَثَلِ الْحَنْظَلَةِ لَيْسَ لَهَا رِيْحٌ وَطَعْمُهَا مُرٌّ وَمَثَلُ الْمُنَافِقِ الَّذِىْ يَقْرَأُ الْقُرْآنَ مَثَلُ
الرَّيْحَانَةِ رِيْحُهَا طَيِّبٌ وَطَعْمُهَا مُرٌّ (رواه البخارى ومسلم والنسائى وابن ماجه)

Hadhrat Abu Musa (Radhiyallaho anho) narrated that Rasulullah (Sallallaho alaihe wasallam) said:

> "The example of a mo'min (believer) who reads the Qur'an is like that of citron which has a pleasant smell and a sweet taste. The example of a mo'min who does not read the Qur'an is like that of a date, which has no smell, though its taste is sweet. The munafiq (hypocrite) who does not read the Qur'an is like a wild gourd, which has a bitter taste and no smell, and the munafiq who reads the Qur'an is like a raihan (sweet-smelling flower), which is fragrant but has a bitter taste."

In this hadith an abstract quality of reading the Glorious Qur'an, has been compared to concrete objects in order to illustrate the difference between reading and not reading the Holy Qur'an. Otherwise it is obvious that material objects of this world like citrons and dates cannot match the sweetness and perfume of the Qur'an. There are, however, special points in this similitude, which pertain to the deep knowledge of the Prophets and testify to the vast understanding of Rasulullah (Sallallaho alaihe wasallam). Consider, for example, the citron, which gives flavour to the mouth, cleans the stomach and stimulates digestion. These are the qualities specially associated with the reading of the Qur'an since, fragrance in the mouth, internal purity and spiritual strength result from reading the Qur'an. It is also said that if there is citron in the house, no jinn can enter it. If it is true, then such is the speciality of the Qur'an. Some physicians say that citron strengthens the memory and it is reported in 'Ihya' by Hadhrat Ali (Radhiyallaho anho) that three things, i.e., cleaning the teeth with miswak, fasting and reading the Holy Qur'an strengthen the memory.

In the book of Abu Dawood, it is mentioned at the conclusion of the hadith given above that a good companion is like a person having musk. Even if you do not get musk, you will at least enjoy its fragrance. An evil companion is like a person with a furnace, near whom, even if you do not get blackened, you certainly cannot avoid the smoke. It is, therefore, important that one should be very careful in choosing his companions, with whom he has to mix generally.

HADITH-7

(٧) عَنْ عُمَرَ بْنِ الْخَطَّابِ رَضِىَ اللّٰهُ عَنْهُ قَالَ قَالَ رَسُوْلُ اللّٰهِ ﷺ اِنَّ اللّٰهَ يَرْفَعُ بِهٰذَا الْكِتَابِ اَقْوَامًا وَيَضَعُ بِهِ اٰخَرِيْنَ (رواه مسلم)

Hadhrat 'Umar (Radhiyallaho anho) narrates that Rasullullah (Sallallaho alaihe wasallam) said: "Allah exalts many people by means of this Book (the Holy Qu'ran), and He also degrades and disgraces many others by means of the same."

People who believe in the Holy Book and act upon it are given by Allah position of honour and respect, both in this life as well as in the Hereafter, while those who do not act upon it are disgraced by Allah. This principle is also borne out by the various ayaat of the Holy Qur'an. At one place it reads:

يُضِلُّ بِهٖ كَثِيْرًا وَّيَهْدِىْ بِهٖ كَثِيْرًا

"He misleads many by this Book and guides many thereby."

At another place we come across:

وَنُنَزِّلُ مِنَ الْقُرْاٰنِ مَاهُوَ شِفَآءٌ وَّرَحْمَةٌ لِّلْمُؤْمِنِيْنَ وَلَايَزِيْدُ الظّٰلِمِيْنَ اِلَّا خَسَارًا

"And We send down in the Qur'an that which is a healing and mercy for believers, though it increases for the evil-doers naught save ruin."

The Prophet (Sallallaho alaihe wasallam) is also reported to have said: "Many hypocrites of this Ummat will be the qurraa, i.e., those who recite the Qur'an correctly." In 'Ihya-ul-Ulum' it is reported from some Mashaa'ikh, "As soon as a man starts reading a surah (chapter of the Holy Qur'an), the Angels start invoking mercy for him and they continue to do so till he stops reading; on the contrary another person starts reading a surah and the Angels start cursing him and they continue to do so till he completes the reading."

Some scholars have stated that sometimes a man reads the Holy Qur'an and invokes curses on himself without even knowing it. For instance, he reads in the Holy Qur'an:

اَلَا لَعْنَةُ اللهِ عَلَى الظّٰلِمِيْنَ

"Beware, the curse of Allah is on the wrong-doers" and he exposes himself to this warning because of his wrong-doings.

In the like manner, he reads in the Qur'an:

لَعْنَةُ اللهِ عَلَى الْكٰذِبِيْنَ

"The curse of Allah is upon the liars".

In fact he exposes himself to the warning by reason of his being himself a liar.

'Aamir ibn Waathilah (Radhiyallaho anho) says that Hadhrat 'Umar (Radhiyallaho anho) had appointed Naafi' ibn Abdul Harith as the Governor of Mecca. Once he asked the latter as to whom he had appointed as the administrator of forests. "Ibn Abzi" replied Naafi'. "Who is Ibn-e-Abzi?" said Hadhrat 'Umar (Radhiyallaho anho). "He is one of our slaves" was the reply. "Why have you appointed a slave the ameer (leader)?" objected Hadhrat 'Umar (Radhiyallaho anho). "Because he recites the Book of Allah" said Naafi'. At this, Hadhrat 'Umar (Radhiyallaho anho) narrated the hadith that it had been said by Rasullullah (Sallallaho alaihe wasallam) that, because of this Book, Allah elevates many people and degrades many.

HADITH-8

(٨) عَنْ عَبْدِ الرَّحْمٰنِ بْنِ عَوْفٍ رَضِىَ اللّٰهُ تَعَالٰى عَنْهُ عَنِ النَّبِىِّ ﷺ قَالَ ثَلٰثٌ تَحْتَ الْعَرْشِ يَوْمَ الْقِيٰمَةِ الْقُرْاٰنُ يُحَاجُّ الْعِبَادَ لَهُ ظَهْرٌ وَّبَطْنٌ وَّالْاَمَانَةُ وَالرَّحْمُ تُنَادِىْ اَلَا مَنْ وَّصَلَنِىْ وَصَلَهُ اللّٰهُ وَمَنْ قَطَعَنِىْ قَطَعَهُ اللّٰهُ (رواه فى شرح السنة)

Hadhrat 'Abdur Rahman ibn 'Auf (Radhiyallaho anho) narrates that Rasulullah (Sallallaho alaihe wasallam) said, "On the Day of Judgement, three things will be under the shade of the Arsh (Allah's Throne). One, the Holy Qur'an which will argue with men–the Qur'an has both an exterior and an interior. The second will be amaanat (trust). The third will be kinship, which shall proclaim, 'O, Allah! have mercy on the person who upheld me, and deprive him of Your mercy whosoever severed me.'"

"Three things will be under the shade of the 'Arsh" signifies their utmost nearness in the sublime presence of Allah. "The Qur'an will argue" means that it will plead the cause of those people who read it, respect it and act upon its commandments. It will intercede on their behalf and solicit the upgrading of their rank. Mulla 'Ali Qari has narrated on the authority of 'Tirmizi' (a book of Hadith) that, in the presence of Almighty Allah, the Holy Qur'an will beg Allah to grant an apparel to its reader. Almighty Allah will give him a crown of honour. The Qur'an will again beg for additional favours for him. Thereupon Almighty Allah will award the reader a complete robe of honour. The Qur'an will again beseech Allah to be pleased with him, and Almighty Allah will express His pleasure to him.

We find in this life that the pleasure of the beloved is considered to be the most coveted gift. Similarly in the life Hereafter, no bounty shall stand comparison with the pleasure of our Beloved Almighty Allah. And in case of those who ignore their duty towards the Qur'an, it will challenge them saying, "Did you care for me? Did you fulfil your obligations towards me?"

It has been reported on the authority of Imam Abu Hanifa (Rahmatullah alaih) in 'Ihya' that it is the due right of the Qur'an that it should be read completely twice a year. Those of us who never care to read the Qur'an should first consider how they will defend themselves against such a strong plaintiff. Death is inevitable and there can be no escape from it.

The meaning of the expression "exterior and interior of the Qur'an" is evident. The Qur'an has an apparent meaning which can be understood by all, but the deeper spiritual significance is not understood by everybody. It is in this connection that Rasulullah (Sallallaho alaihe wasallam) has said: "Whosoever expresses his personal opinion in respect of anything in the Qur'an commits a mistake, even if he be right in his opinion."

Some scholars hold that the word 'exterior', refers to its words, which can be recited properly by everybody and the word 'interior', i.e., spirit, refers to its meanings, and its underlying ideas, the understanding of which varies with the ability of the readers.

Hadhrat Ibn Mas'ood (Radhiyallaho anho) said, "It you seek knowledge, you should meditate on the meanings of the Qur'an, because it embodies the history of former as well as of latter times." It is, however, essential to observe the pre-requisites for interpreting the Qur'an. An unbecoming present-day fashion is that even those who possess little or no knowledge of Arabic vocabulary offer their personal opinion on the basis of vernacular translations of the Qur'an. Specialists have laid down that any one attempting a commentary of the Holy Qur'an should be well versed in fifteen subjects. These, as briefly given below, will show that it is not possible for everybody to understand the underlying significance and real meanings of the Holy Qur'an.

(1) *Lughat*, i.e., philology of language, which helps in understanding the appropriate meanings of words. Mujahid (Rahmatullah alaih) says, "one who believes in Allah and the Day of Judgement should not open his lips in respect of the Qur'an, unless he is thoroughly conversant with the philology of the Arabic language. Quite often an Arabic word has several meanings. A person may be knowing only one or two of them, though in a given context the actual meaning may be quite different."

(2) *Nahw*, i.e., syntax, a branch of grammar, which helps in understanding the relation of a sentence with another and also of I'raab (vowel sounds) of the letters of a word. A change in I'raab often means a change in the meaning.

(3) *Sarf*, i.e., etymology, a branch of grammar, which helps in knowing the root words and conjugations. The meaning of a word changes with the change in the root and with a change in its conjugation.

Ibn Faris (Rahmatullah alaih) says, "One who loses the knowledge of etymology loses a great deal." 'Allamah Zamakhshari (Rahmatullah alaih) mentions that, when a certain person set to translate the ayat–

يَوْمَ نَدْعُوْا كُلَّ اُنَاسٍۭ بِاِمَامِهِمْ

On the day that We shall call each and every people after their leader, he ignorantly rendered it thus: "On the day that We shall call each people after their mothers." He supposed that the singular Arabic word 'imam' (leader) was the plural of the Arabic word 'umm' (mother). If he had been conversant with etymology, he would have known that the plural of 'umm' is not 'imam'.

(4) *Ishtiqaaq*, i.e., derivatives. It is necessary to have the knowledge of derivatives and their root words, because if a word has been derived from two different root words, it will have two different meanings, e.g., the word 'maseeh' is derivable from 'masah' which means to touch or to move wet hands over, and also from 'masaahah' which means measurement.

(5) *Ilmul Ma'aani*, i.e., knowledge of semantics, because phrase constructions are understood from their meanings.

(6) *Ilmul Bayaan*, i.e., knowledge of figures of speech, like similes and metaphors, due to which expressions or shades of meaning or similes and metaphors become known.

(7) *Ilmul Badee'*, i.e., knowledge of rhetoric, the knowledge which reveals the beauty of language and its implications.

The last three are the branches of Ilmul Balaaghah (knowledge of oratory), and are considered very important subjects, which a commentator should master, because the Glorious Qur'an is a perfect miracle and its amazing constructions can only be understood after mastering these subjects.

(8) *Ilmul Qiraa'ah*, i.e., knowledge of the art of pronunciation, because different methods of recitation sometimes convey different meanings, and sometimes one meaning is to be preferred over the other.

(9) *Ilmul Aqaa'id*, i.e., knowledge of the fundamentals of faith. This is necessary to explain certain analogies. The literal meaning of certain ayaat referring to Almighty Allah is not the correct one. For example, the analogy in the ayat–

يَدُ اللهِ فَوْقَ اَيْدِيْهِمْ

(The hand of Allah is over their hands)

will have to be explained because Allah has no physical hands.

(10) *Usoolul Fiqh* i.e., Principles of Islamic Jurisprudence. These are necessary for reasoning out and finding arguments in the basic support of statements.

(11) *Asbaabun Nuzool*, i.e., the particular circumstances which caused revelation. The meaning of an ayat will be better understood if we know how and when it had been revealed. Sometimes the true meaning of an ayat is understood only if we know the circumstances in which the ayat had been revealed.

(12) *An Naasikh wal Mansookh*, i.e., knowledge of commandments that have subsequently been abrogated or changed, so that abrogated commandments may be distinguished from the standing ones.

(13) *Ilmul Fiqh*, i.e., knowledge of Islamic Jurisprudence, because it is only through this knowledge that we arrive at a complete understanding of general principles.

(14) Knowledge of such ahadith that happen to be commentary on certain brief verses of the Qur'an.

(15) The last but most important is the Wahbi ilm, or the gifted understanding, bestowed by Almighty Allah upon His selected ones, as is referred in the hadith–

مَنْ عَمِلَ بِمَا عَلِمَ وَرَّثَهُ اللهُ عِلْمَ مَالَمْ يَعْلَمْ

Whosoever acts upon what he knows, Almighty Allah bestows upon him the knowledge of things not known to him.

It is this special understanding that was implied in the reply of Hadhrat 'Ali (Karramallaahu wajhahu) (may Allah be kind to him) when he was asked by the people if he had received from Rasulullah (Sallallaho alaihe wasallam) any special knowledge or instructions which were not received by others. Hadhrat Ali (Radhiyallaho anho) said, "I swear by Him Who made the Paradise and created life that I possess nothing special, except the clear understanding which Almighty Allah bestows upon a person in respect of the Qur'an."

Ibn Abid Dunyaa (Rahmatullah alaih) says that the knowledge of the Holy Qur'an and that which can be derived out of it are as vast as a boundless ocean.

The branches of knowledge described above are like tools, i.e. essential pre-requisite for a commentator. A commentary written by a person who is not thoroughly acquainted with these branches of knowledge will be based on his personal opinion, which is prohibited. The Sahabah (Companions of the Holy Prophet (Sallallaho alaihe wasallam) already had Arabic language as their mother-tongue, and they reached the depth of the rest of the knowledge by means of their illuminating contact that they had with Rasulullah (Sallallaho alaihe wasallam).

'Allamah Suyuti says that those who think that it is beyond the capacity of a man to acquire Wahbi ilm, or gifted understanding, are not right. To get this knowledge from Allah, one should adopt the means to this end, e.g., acting upon the knowledge that one has acquired, and disinclination towards the world.

It is stated in 'Keemiyaa-e-Sa'aadat' that three persons are not blessed with complete understanding of the Qur'an. First, one who is not well versed in Arabic, secondly, one who persists in committing a major sin or indulges in act of religious innovation, because these actions blacken his heart, which in turn prevents him from understanding the Qur'an. Thirdly, one who is a rationalist, even in the matter of faith, and feels embarassed when he reads an ayat of the Qur'an which he is not able to fully rationalize.

اَللّٰهُمَّ احْفَظْنَا مِنْهُمْ

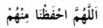

May Allah protect us from all such sins and evils.

HADITH 9

(٩) عَنْ عَبْدِ اللهِ بْنِ عَمْرٍو رَضِىَ اللهُ عَنْهُ قَالَ قَالَ رَسُوْلُ اللهِ ﷺ يُقَالُ لِصَاحِبِ الْقُرْآنِ اِقْرَأْ وَارْتَقِ وَرَتِّلْ كَمَا كُنْتَ تُرَتِّلُ فِى الدُّنْيَا فَاِنَّ مَنْزِلَكَ عِنْدَ اٰخِرِ اٰيَةٍ تَقْرَأُهَا (رواه أحمد والترمذى وأبوداود و النسائى وابن ماجه وابن حبان فى صحيحه)

Hadhrat 'Abdullah ibn Amr (Radhiyallaho anho) reports that Rasulullah (Sallallaho alihe wasallam) said: "On the Day of Judgement, it will be said to the Man devoted to the Qur'an, 'Go on reciting the Qur'an and continue ascending the storeys of Jannat (Paradise) and recite in the slow manner you had been reading in worldly life; your final abode will be where you reach at the time of the last ayat of your recitation."

"The man of Qur'an" apparently means a hafiz. Mulla 'Ali Qari has explained it fully that this honour is reserved for a hafiz, and that this hadith does not apply to one who reads by looking into the Holy Book. First, because the words "Man of Qur'an" point towards a hafiz and secondly there is a tradition in Musnad Ahmad–

حَتّٰى يَقْرَأَ شَيْئًا مَّعَهُ

Till he reads of whatever Qur'an is with him.

This word more clearly refers to a hafiz, although a reader who remains very often engaged in reciting the Qur'an may also be implied.

It is written in 'Mirqaat' that this hadith does not apply to a reader who is accursed by the Qur'an. This is with reference to the hadith that there are many readers of the Qur'an who read the Qur'an but the Qur'an invokes curses upon them. Therefore, the reading of Qur'an by a person who does not adhere to the correct tenets does not constitute an argument that he is acceptable to Allah. Many Ahadith of this type relate to the Khawarij (a sect who were opposed to Hadhrat 'Ali (Radhiyallaho anho).

In this commentary, Shah Abdul Aziz (Rahmatullah alaih) has written that 'tarteel' literally means reading with good and clear pronunciation, while according to Islamic principles it means reading in accordance with certain rules as follows:

(1) The letters of the alphabets should be correctly uttered to ensure their correct pronunciation so that '(طا)' is not read as '(تا)' and '(ضا)' and so on.

(2) Stopping correctly at the pauses, so that the joining or finishing of the verses may not take place at inappropriate places.

(3) The correct pronunciation of the vowel sounds.

(4) Raising the voice slightly so that the words of Qur'an uttered by the mouth may reach the ears and thus influence the heart.

(5) Setting the sound in a way that it may become full of pathos and may affect the heart quickly, because a pathetic voice influences the heart at once, moves and strengthens the soul more affectively.

The physicians are of the opinion that if a medicine is required to affect the heart quickly, it should be given a sweet smell by means of a perfume, for the heart is sensitive to sweet smell and if the medicine is required to affect the liver, it should be sweetened with sugar because the liver likes sweet things. Therefore, if a perfume is used at the time of recitation, it will have a better influence on the heart.

(6) Tashdeed ((نّ)) (doubling of letters) and madd ((نٓ)) (prolongation of letters) should be fully pronounced because this reveals the grandeur of the Qur'an and adds to its effectiveness.

(7) As stated earlier, the reader's heart should respond to the ayat indicating mercy of Allah or chastisement by Him.

The above-mentioned seven rules constitute the correct way of reciting the Qur'an, which is called tarteel, and the sole object of all this is to reach the correct understanding and grasp of the deeper meaning of the Holy Qur'an.

Hadhrat Umm-e-Salamah (Radhiyallaho anha) was once asked by someone as to how Rasulullah (Sallallaho alaihe wasallam) used to recite Qur'an. She said, "In a way that all vowel sounds were clear and the pronunciation of each letter was distinct." It is desirable to recite the Qur'an with propriety even if one may not understand the meaning. Ibn Abbas (Radhiyallaho anho) said that he preferred to recite with propriety, short surahs like Al-Qaari'ah (اَلْقَارِعَةُ) or Izaa zulzilah (اِذَا زُلْزِلَتِ) rather than to recite (otherwise long) surahs like Aal-e-Imran (اٰلِ عِمْرَانَ) without it.

The commentators and learned scholars explain the above-mentioned hadith to mean that, for each ayat recited, the reciter will be elevated to a higher level in Paradise. From other ahadith, it appears that there are as many levels in Paradise as the number of ayaat in the Holy Qur'an. Therefore, the status of a person will be raised by as many levels in Paradise as the number of ayaat in which he is well versed. As such, the one best versed in the whole Qur'an will reach the highest level in Paradise.

According to Mulla 'Ali Qari, it is mentioned in a hadith that there is no level in Jannat higher than that given to the reader of the Qur'an. So the readers will ascend in proportion to the number of ayaat recited by them in the world. 'Allamah Daani (Rahmatullah alaih) says that authorities agree that there are six thousand ayaat in the Qur'an. But there is some difference of opinion about the numbers over and above six thousand. These are variously reported to be 204, 14, 19, 25, 36.

It is written in 'Sharhul-Ihya' that each ayat corresponds to a higher level in Paradise. So a reader will be asked to ascend according to his recitation. One who reads the whole of the Qur'an will attain the highest level in Paradise. And one who knows only a part of the Qur'an will rise up to the proportionate level. In brief, the stage or level reached will be fixed by the number of ayaat recited.

According to my understanding, the above hadith has a different meaning—

فَاِنْ كَانَ صَوَابًا فَمِنَ اللّٰهِ وَاِنْ كَانَ خَطأً فَمِنِّىْ وَمِنَ الشَّيْطٰنِ وَاللّٰهُ وَرَسُوْلُهٗ مِنْهُ بَرِيْئَانِ

(If my interpretation is corect, it is from Allah and, if it is wrong, it is from me and from Satan, and Allah and His Prophet are free from it.)

I think that the elevation implied in this hadith is not that which can be determined by the number of ayat to be recited, i.e., when one ayat be recited, the status will be raised by one step, whether it be read with propriety or without. But this hadith points to another kind of elevation which is a type of an inner experience and is related to the recitation being with propriety or without it. So a person will be able to read in the same way as he reads in this worldly life. Mullah 'Ali Qari (Rahmatullah alaih) has quoted from one hadith that, if a person reads the Qur'an very often in this life, he will remember it in the life Hereafter, otherwise he will forget it. May Allah help us there. There are many among us who memorized the Qur'an in their childhood through the religious zeal of their parents, but through sheer carelessness and negligence on their own part, have forgotten this capability in the later part of this very life. It is mentioned in other ahadith that one who dies while labouring and working hard to commit the Glorious Qur'an to memory, will be reckoned amongst the huffaaz. Allah's bounty has no limits. We should only seek it. As a poet says:

اس کے الطاف تو ہیں عام شہیدی سب پر
تجھ سے کیا ضد تھی اگر تو کسی قابل ہوتا

O' Shaheedi! His bounties are common for all, You could not be denied (these bounties), if you were all worthy.

HADITH 10

(١٠) عَنِ ابْنِ مَسْعُوْدٍ رَضِىَ اللّٰهُ عَنْهُ قَالَ قَالَ رَسُوْلُ اللّٰهِ ﷺ مَنْ قَرَأَ حَرْفًا مِّنْ كِتَابِ اللّٰهِ فَلَهُ بِهٖ حَسَنَةٌ وَّالْحَسَنَةُ بِعَشْرِ اَمْثَالِهَا لَآ اَقُوْلُ الٓمّٓ حَرْفٌ اَلِفٌ حَرْفٌ وَّلَامٌ حَرْفٌ وَّمِيْمٌ حَرْفٌ (رواه الترمذى وقال هذا حديث صحيح غريب إسنادا والدارمى)

Hadhrat Ibn Mas'ood (Radhiyallaho anho) narrates that Rasullullah (Sallallaho alaihe wasallam) said, "Whosoever reads one letter of the Book of Allah is credited with one blessing and one blessing is equal to tenfold the like thereof in its reward. I do not say that الٓمّٓ (Alif Laam Meem) is one letter, but '(ا)' (alif) is one letter, '(ل)' (laam) is one letter, and '(م)' (meem) is one letter."

The hadith affirms that whereas, ordinarily for the purpose of reward an act as a whole is taken into account but in the case of Qur'an it is not so, parts also count. Thus, in reading each letter is counted as one good deed. And the reward of each good deed will be increased ten times, as promised by Almighty Allah.

مَنْ جَآءَ بِالْحَسَنَةِ فَلَهُ عَشْرُ اَمْثَلِهَا

"One who brings a good deed, for him will be tenfold the like thereof."

Ten times, however, is the minimum increase.

وَاللّٰهُ يُضَاعِفُ لِمَنْ يَّشَآءُ

Allah multiplies the reward for whomsoever He desires.

That each letter of the Holy Qur'an, when read, amounts to a good deed, has been illustrated by Rasulullah (Sallallaho alaihe wasallam) by saying that 'الٓمٓ' (Alif Laam Meem) is not one letter, but '(ا)' (alif), '(ل)' (laam) and '(م)' (meem) are three separate letters, so it will comprise thirty blessings. There is a difference of opinion among scholars whether 'الم' (alif, laam, meem) is the beginning of Surah Baqarah or of Surah Feel. If it is the beginning of Surah Baqarah, and only three letters are counted, as they are written, then the blessings will be thirty. And if it is the beginning of Surah Feel, then '(ا)' (alif), '(ل)' (laam) and '(م)' (meem), which is the beginning of Surah Baqarah will be nine letters. Therefore, its reward will be ninety blessings.

Baihaqi (Rahmatullah alaih) has reported another hadith similar to this portion of the above-mentioned hadith, viz., "I do not say that '(بسم الله)' (Bismillah) is one letter, but uphold that '(ب)' (ba) '(س)' (sin) and '(م)' (meem), etc, are separate letters."

HADITH—11

(١١) عَنْ مُعَاذِنِ الْجُهَنِيِّ رَضِىَ اللّٰهُ عَنْهُ قَالَ قَالَ رَسُوْلُ اللّٰهِ ﷺ مَنْ قَرَأَ الْقُرْآنَ وَعَمِلَ بِمَا فِيْهِ اُلْبِسَ وَالِدَاهُ تَاجًا يَوْمَ الْقِيٰمَةِ ضَوْئُهُ اَحْسَنُ مِنْ ضَوْءِ الشَّمْسِ فِى بُيُوْتِ الدُّنْيَا لَوْ كَانَتْ فِيْكُمْ فَمَا ظَنُّكُمْ بِالَّذِىْ عَمِلَ بِهٰذَا (رواه أحمد وأبوداود وصححه الحاكم)

Hadhrat Mu'aaz Juhani (Radhiyallaho anho) reports that Rasulullah (Sallallaho alaihe wasallam) said,

"Whoever reads the Qur'an and acts upon what is contained in it, his parents will be made to wear a crown on the Day of Judgement, the brilliance of which will excel that of the sun, if the same were within your wordly houses. So, what do you think about the person who himself acts upon it?"

Thus, it is through the virtues of his reading the Qur'an and acting upon it that the parents of the leader will be honoured with a crown, the brilliance of which will far excel the light of the sun even if the sun were within one's own house. The sun is at a great distance from us and even then its light is so bright. If the sun comes down into one's house, its light and brilliance will surely increase manifold. The light of the crown to be worn by the parents of the reader will be still more brilliant. When this is in store for the parents, what will be the reward of the reader himself? Surely if the beneficiaries get so much, the reward of the person who is the real cause should be much more. The parents get this reward solely because they were the cause of the reader coming into being, or were responsible for his education.

In addition to the fact that the light of the sun will be far greater if it were in one's own house, this simile implies yet another delicate point. Attachment and liking for a thing increase when it always remains with a person. Therefore, the feeling of strangeness for the sun due to distance will give place to attachment, because of its close nearness all the time. Thus, in addition to describing the brilliance of the crown, the hadith implies this attachment with the crown and also the great satisfaction that it belongs to oneself. Everybody gets benefited by the sun, but if it were to be given entirely to a person, how very proud he would feel.

Haakim (Rahmatullah alaih) has reported from Buraidah, (Radhiyallaho anho) saying of Rasulullah (Sallallaho alaihe wasallam); "One who recites the Qur'an and acts upon it will be made to wear a crown woven with noor, and his parents will be made to wear garments, which will be more valuable than the entire world. They will say, 'Almighty Allah! what is it that we are being given these garments for?' 'In lieu of the reading of Qur'an by your child', will be the reply."

It is given in Jam'ul Fawaa'id by Tabrani (Rahmatullah

alaih) that Hadhrat Anas (Radhiyallaho anho) had reported the saying of Rasulullah (Sallallaho alaihe wasallam) "Whoever teaches the reading of Qur'an to his son (without memorizing it), all his sins, whether previous or subsequent, will be forgiven; and whoever makes his child memorize the Qur'an will be raised on the Day of Judgement in the semblance of a full moon; and his son will be asked to start reciting, and for every ayat read by the child, the status of the parent will be raised to the next higher grade of Jannat, till the recitation of the Holy Qur'an is completed."

Such are the blessings for teaching the Qur'an to your children. This is not all. There is another point. God forbid, if you deprive your child of the knowledge of (deen) (religion) for the sake of a few coppers, not only shall you be deprived of eternal reward but you shall be held answerable before Allah. Is it not a fact that you are depriving your dear child of reading the Qur'an for fear that mullahs and huffaaz, after memorizing the Qur'an become dependent on others for their living? Please remember that not only do you expose your children to eternal misery, but carry on your shoulders a very heavy accountability. The hadith that–

كُلُّكُمْ رَاعٍ وَكُلُّكُمْ مَسْئُوْلٌ عَنْ رَعِيَّتِهٖ

> Each one of you is a guardian, and will be questioned about those under his control

means that everyone shall be questioned about his subordinates and dependents as to what extent he taught (deen) to them. Surely one should guard himself and his dependents against these shortcomings. But (as the proverb goes) "should one discard clothes for fear of lice?" Nay, one should surely try to keep his clothes clean. If you impart religious education to your child, you will be free from your responsibilities. As long as the child lives, and whatever good deed he does and salaat he performs and forgiveness that he seeks from Allah for you, will elevate your position in Paradise. If for the sake of this life and for the lust of a few coppers, you keep him ignorant of (deen), not only will you have to suffer for this misdeed but whatever evil and misdeeds he does, your account will not be free from their burden. For God's sake, have pity on yourselves. This life is only a passing phase and death will put an end to all its hardships, however great, but the sufferings for which there is no end, will be everlasting.

HADITH NO–12

(١٢) عَنْ عُقْبَةَ بْنِ عَامِرٍ رَضِىَ للهُ عَنْهُ قَالَ سَمِعْتُ رَسُوْلَ اللهِ ﷺ يَقُوْلُ لَوْ جُعِلَ الْقُرْآنُ فِىْ اِهَابٍ ثُمَّ اُلْقِىَ فِى النَّارِ مَااحْتَرَقَ (رواه الدارمى)

'Uqbah ibn 'Aamir (Radhiyallaho anho) narrated that Rasulullah (Sallallaho alaihe wasallam) said, "If the Qur'an is placed in a skin and then put in the fire, it will not get burnt."

The scholars of hadith have interpreted this hadith in two ways. Some of them take the words 'skin' and 'fire' in the literal sense. In this case the hadith refers to a miracle which was particular in the lifetime of Rasulullah (Sallallaho alaihe wasallam) in the same way as the miracles of other prophets were specific to their lifetime. In the second case, the word 'skin' is interpreted to mean the human skin and the word 'fire' means the fire of Hell. Thus the application of the hadith is general and not confined to any particular period. It means that if any hafiz of Qur'an were cast in due to any crime on his part, the fire of Hell will not affect him. In another hadith it is said that the fire will not even touch him. The second interpretation of the abovementioned hadith is also supported by another hadith reported by Abu Umaamah (Radhiyallaho anho) and also given in the book Sharhus Sunnah, by Mulla Ali Qari, which says, "Learn the Qur'an by heart, because Almighty Allah does not punish the heart which contains the Qur'an ." In its meanings this hadith is clear and confirmed by the Qur'an. Those who regard memorizing the Qur'an as useless should, for God's sake, ponder over these merits. The last-mentioned one alone should prompt everybody to dedicate his life to learning the Qur'an by heart, because there is no one who has not committed sins and does not deserve the fire of Hell.

In Sharhul Ihya there is a list of those people who will rest in the shade of Allah's mercy (protection) on the horrible Day of Judgement. It is mentioned therein that, according to a hadith reported from Hadhrat Ali (Radhiyallaho anho) by Dailami that the custodians of Qur'an, in other words those who learn the Qur'an by heart, will be in the shade of Allah, in the company of the Prophets and other virtuous people.

HADITH–13

(١٣) عَنْ عَلِيٍّ رَضِىَ اللّٰهُ عَنْهُ قَالَ قَالَ رَسُوْلُ اللّٰهِ ﷺ مَنْ قَرَأَ الْقُرْآنَ فَاسْتَظْهَرَهُ فَاَحَلَّ حَلَالَهُ وَحَرَّمَ حَرَامَهُ اَدْخَلَهُ اللّٰهُ الْجَنَّةَ وَشَفَّعَهُ فِىْ عَشَرَةٍ مِّنْ اَهْلِ بَيْتِهِ كُلُّهُمْ قَدْ وَجَبَتْ لَهُ النَّارُ رواه أحمد والترمذى وقال هذا حديث غريب وحفص بن سليمان الراوى ليس هو بالقوى يضعف فى الحديث ورواه ابن ماجه والدارمى

Hadhrat Ali (Radhiyallaho anho) says that Rasulullah (Sallallaho alaihe wasallam) said, "Whoever reads Qur'an and learns it by heart, and regards what it makes lawful as lawful and its unlawful as forbidden, will be admitted into Jannat by the Almighty Allah who will also accept his intercession in respect of ten such persons of his family who shall have been doomed to Hell."

By the grace of Allah, entry into Jannat is ensured for every believer though it may come after his being punished for his misdeeds. The hafiz will, however, be favoured with this entry right from the beginning. The ten persons in whose favour his intercession will be accepted will be those sinful and disobedient Muslims who are guilty of major sins. There can be no intercession, however, for the unbelievers. Almighty Allah has said:

مَنْ يُشْرِكْ بِاللّٰهِ فَقَدْ حَرَّمَ اللّٰهُ عَلَيْهِ الْجَنَّةَ وَمَأْوَاهُ النَّارُ وَمَا لِلظَّالِمِيْنَ مِنْ اَنْصَارٍ

Whosoever ascribes partners unto Allah, for him Allah has forbidden Jannat, and their place is Hell – and for evil-doers there will be none amongst the helpers.

It is also said in the Qur'an:

مَاكَانَ لِلنَّبِىِّ وَالَّذِيْنَ آمَنُوْآ اَنْ يَّسْتَغْفِرُوْا لِلْمُشْرِكِيْنَ (الآية)

The Prophet and the believers are not allowed to pray for the forgiveness of 'mushrikin' (Plural of mushrik one who ascribes partners unto Allah) the polytheists even if they are their relatives.

The Qur'anic ayat clearly say that polytheists will never be forgiven. The intercession of huffaaz will, therefore, be for those Muslims whose entry into Hell has been determined by their sins.

Those who are not huffaaz and cannot memorize the Qur'an should at least make one of their relatives a hafiz, so that by His grace they may be saved from their own evildoings.

Allah be thanked for this gracious favour on the person whose father, uncles and grandfathers both maternal and paternal, were all huffaaz. (This applies to the author May Allah bless him with more favours).

HADITH–14

(١٤) عَنْ اَبِىْ هُرَيْرَةَ رَضِىَ اللّٰهُ عَنْهُ قَالَ قَالَ رَسُوْلُ اللّٰهِ ﷺ تَعَلَّمُوْا الْقُرْآنَ
فَاقْرَأُوْهُ فَاِنَّ مَثَلَ الْقُرْآنِ لِمَنْ تَعَلَّمَ فَقَرَاَ وَقَامَ بِهٖ كَمَثَلِ جِرَابٍ مَحْشُوٍّ مِسْكًا
تَفُوْحُ رِيْحُهٗ كُلَّ مَكَانٍ وَمَثَلُ مَنْ تَعَلَّمَهٗ فَرَقَدَ وَهُوَ فِىْ جَوْفِهٖ كَمَثَلِ جِرَابٍ اُوْكِىَ
عَلٰى مِسْكٍ (رواه الترمذى والنسائى وابن ماجه وابن حبان)

Hadhrat Abu Hurairah (Radhiyallaho anho) narrated that Rasulullah (Sallallaho alaihe wasallam) said, "Learn the Qur'an and recite it, because the example of one who learns the Qur'an, reads it and recites it in Tahajjud (salaat late after midnight) is like an open bag full of musk, the fragrance whereof spreads over the entire place, and a person who has learnt the Qur'an but sleeps while the Qur'an is in his heart, is like a bag full of musk but with its mouth closed."

It means that the example of one who learns the Quran and cares for it and recites it in Tahajjud salaat is like that of a musk-container which, if opened, fills the whole house with its sweet smell. In the same way, the entire house is lit up with divine light and blessings due to the recitation by the hafiz. Even if the hafiz remains asleep or does not recite through his negligence, the Qur'an in his heart is in any case the musk. This negligence resulted in the loss that others were deprived of the blessings of Qur'an, but his heart does, in any case, contain the musk of Qur'an.

HADITH NO–15

(١٥) عَنِ ابْنِ عَبَّاسٍ رَضِىَ اللّٰهُ عَنْهُمَا قَالَ قَالَ رَسُوْلُ اللّٰهِ ﷺ اِنَّ الَّذِىْ لَيْسَ فِىْ جَوْفِهٖ شَىْءٌ مِّنَ الْقُرْاٰنِ كَالْبَيْتِ الْخَرِبِ (رواه الترمذى وقال هذا حديث صحيح ورواه الدارمى والحاكم وصححه)

Hadhrat Abdullah ibn Abbas (Radhiyallaho anho) has narrated the saying of Rasulullah (Sallallaho alaihe wasallam): "He in whose heart there is no part of the Qur'an is like a deserted house."

The allusion to a deserted house has a subtle meaning, which is expressed by the proverb that "an idle man's brain is the devil's workshop (literally the demon gets hold of an empty house). Similarly a heart, devoid of Qur'an, gets more and more possessed by Satan. What an emphasis is there in this hadith for memorizing the Holy Qur'an, that the heart which has not secured it has been likened to a deserted house.

Hadhrat Abu Hurairah (Radhiyallaho anho) says: "In the house where the Qur'an is read, the household members increase, virtues and blessings multiply, angels descend upon them and Satan quits the house. Whereas the house in which Qur'an is not recited, life therein becomes straitened and devoid of blessings, angels leave the house and Satan ravages it."

Hadhrat Ibn Mas'ood (Radhiyallaho anho) and some others have reported Rasulullah (Sallallaho alaihe wasallam) to have said that a deserted house is one in which the Holy Qur'an is not recited.

HADITH–16

(١٦) عَنْ عَائِشَةَ رَضِىَ اللّٰهُ عَنْهَا اَنَّ النَّبِىَّ ﷺ قَالَ قِرَاءَةُ الْقُرْاٰنِ فِى الصَّلٰوةِ اَفْضَلُ مِنْ قِرَاءَةِ الْقُرْاٰنِ فِىْ غَيْرِ الصَّلٰوةِ وَقِرَاءَةُ الْقُرْاٰنِ فِىْ غَيْرِ الصَّلٰوةِ اَفْضَلُ مِنَ التَّسْبِيْحِ وَالتَّكْبِيْرِ وَالتَّسْبِيْحُ اَفْضَلُ مِنَ الصَّدَقَةِ وَالصَّدَقَةُ اَفْضَلُ مِنَ الصَّوْمِ وَالصَّوْمُ جُنَّةٌ مِّنَ النَّارِ (رواه البيهقى فى شعب الإيمان)

Hadhrat 'Aa'ishah (Radhiyallaho anha) says that Rasulullah (Sallallaho alaihe wasallam) said, "Recitation of the Qur'an in salaat is more rewarding than the recitation outside salaat; recitation outside salaat is preferable to tasbeeh and takbeer (repeating words of Praise for Allah); tasbeeh is superior to sadaqah (alms); sadaqah to sowm (fasting) and sowm is protection against Fire."

The superiority of recitation of the Qur'an over zikr (glorification and remembrance of Allah) is evident because Qur'an is the Word of Allah. As mentioned earlier, the superiority of the Word of Allah over the speech of others is like His superiority over His creation. The superiority of zikr over sadaqah has been stressed in other ahadith as well. But the superiority of sadaqah over sowm as given in this hadith, seems contrary to that given in some other ahadith where sowm is said to be better than sadaqah.' This difference is due to the variations in the type of people and their conditions of life.

According to this hadith sowm comes last in the order of merit. When sowm is protection against the Fire of Hell, we can imagine numerous blessing of the recitation of Qur'an.

The author of 'Ihya' reports on the authority of Hadhrat' Ali (Radhiyallaho anho) that for every letter recited there are hundred blessings for one who reads the Qur'an while standing in salaat, fifty blessings for one who reads while sitting in salaat, twenty-five blessings for one who reads in the state of wudhu outside salaat, ten blessings for one who reads without wudhu, and one blessing for him who does not read himself but listens eagerly to the reader.

HADITH–17

(۱۷) عَنْ اَبِیْ هُرَیْرَةَ رَضِیَ اللّٰهُ عَنْهُ قَالَ قَالَ رَسُوْلُ اللّٰهِ ﷺ اَیُحِبُّ اَحَدُكُمْ اِذَا رَجَعَ اِلٰی اَهْلِهِ اَنْ یَّجِدَ فِیْهِ ثَلَاثَ خَلِفَاتٍ عِظَامٍ سِمَانٍ قُلْنَا نَعَمْ قَالَ فَثَلَاثُ اٰیَاتٍ یَقْرَأُ بِهِنَّ فِیْ صَلَاتِهٖ خَیْرٌ لَهٗ مِنْ ثَلَاثِ خَلِفَاتٍ عِظَامٍ سِمَانٍ (رواه مسلم)

Hadhrat Abu Hurairah (Radhiyallaho anho) says: "Rasulullah (Sallallaho alaihe wasallam) asked us, 'Does any one of you like that when he returns home, he should find three she-camels, pregnant and fat.' We said, 'We would love to do so.' Then Rasulullah (Sallallaho alaihe wasallam) said, "Three ayaat which one of you may recite in his salaat are better than three big pregnant and fat she-camels."

A similar subject-matter has been described in hadith 3. In this hadith there is a reference to recitation of the Qur'an inside salaat which is more virtuous than recitation outside salaat. That is why a comparison has been made to pregnant she-camels. Because, just as in one case, there is a reference to two virtues, that is salaat and recitation, in the other case there is a reference to two things that is a she-camel and her pregnancy. It has been mentioned under hadith 3 that ahadith of this kind are only for the purpose of a simile, otherwise the everlasting reward of one ayat is more valuable than thousands of mortal she-camels.

HADITH–18

(١٨) عَنْ عُثْمَانَ بْنِ عَبْدِ اللهِ بْنِ اَوْسٍ الثَّقْفِيِّ رَضِيَ اللهُ عَنْهُ عَنْ جَدِّهٖ قَالَ قَالَ رَسُوْلُ اللهِ ﷺ قِرَاءَةُ الرَّجُلِ الْقُرْآنَ فِيْ غَيْرِ الْمُصْحَفِ اَلْفُ دَرَجَةٍ وَقِرَاءَتُهٗ فِي الْمُصْحَفِ تَضْعَفُ عَلٰى ذَالِكَ اِلٰى اَلْفَيْ دَرَجَةٍ (رواه البيهقى فى شعب الإيمان)

Hazrat Uthman bin Abdullah bin Aus Thaqafi (Radhiyallaho anhum) narrates from his grand-father that Rasulullah (Sallallaho alaihe wasallam) said, "Reciting the Qur'an from memory carries one thousand degrees of spiritual reward, while reading the Qur'an from the Book increases it up to two thousand degrees."

Many virtues of being a hafiz have been mentioned before. In this hadith, however, preference is shown to reading from the Holy Book as compared to reciting it from memory, because reading from the Book is not only conducive to deeper understanding and meditation but also includes several other devotional acts, such as looking into the Qur'an and touching it, etc. The difference in the apparent meanings of the various ahadith has led to a difference of opinion among the scholars of hadith as to whether reading from the Holy Book is better than reciting it from memory. By reason of the above hadith, and because reading from the Book safeguards against making mistakes and includes the virtuous act of looking at the Holy Book, some scholars give preference to reading by looking into the Book. By reason of other ahadith, and because reciting from memory is conducive to greater devotion and is free from riyaa' (dissimulation) and because this was the way of recitation of Rasulullah (Sallallaho alaihe wasallam) himself, some scholars consider that reciting from memory is preferable. Imam Nawawi (Rahmatullah alaih) has decided that the preference between the two depends upon the individuals. Some people concentrate and meditate better while reading from the Book, while others do so, reciting from memory. Therefore, reading from the Book is preferable for some and reciting from memory for others. Hafiz Ibn Hajar (Rahmatullah alaih) also has favoured this interpretation in his book 'Fat-hul Baari.'

It is said that on account of excessive reading by Hadhrat Uthman (Radhiyallaho anho) two scripts of the Holy Qur'an tore. Amr ibn Maimoon (Rahmatullah alaih) has mentioned in 'Sharhul Ihya', that one who opens the Holy Qur'an after Fajr (dawn) salaat and reads a hundred ayaat gets a reward as large as the entire world. Reading the Qur'an by looking into it is reported to be beneficial for eyesight. Hadhrat Abu Ubaidah (Radhiyallaho anho) has narrated a lengthy hadith in which each reporter says that he had some trouble with his eyes and that his teacher bade him to recite the Qur'an by looking into it. Hadhrat Imaam Shaafi'ee, (Rahmatullah alaih) often used to open the Qur'an after Ishaa (night) salaat and close it only a little before Fajr salaat.'

HADITH–19

(١٩) عَنِ ابْنِ عُمَرَ رَضِىَ اللهُ عَنْهُ قَالَ قَالَ رَسُوْلُ اللهِ ﷺ اِنَّ هٰذِهِ الْقُلُوْبَ تَصْدَأُ كَمَا يَصْدَأُ الْحَدِيْدُ اِذَا اَصَابَهُ الْمَاءُ قِيْلَ يَارَسُوْلَ اللهِ وَمَا جِلَاءُهَا قَالَ كَثْرَةُ ذِكْرِ الْمَوْتِ وَتِلَاوَةُ الْقُرْاٰنِ (رواه البيهقى فى شعب الإيمان)

Abdullah ibn Umar (Radhiyallaho anhuma) narrated:

"Rasulullah (Sallallaho alaihe wasallam) said, "The hearts get rusted as does iron with water. When someone asked, "What could cleanse hearts again?' Rasulullah (Sallallaho alaihe wasallam) said, "Frequent remembrance of death and recitation of Qur'an."

Excess of sins and negligence in the remembrance of Allah cause the hearts to rust, as water causes iron to rust.

The reading of Qur'an and the remembrance of death polish the rusted hearts. The heart is like a mirror. If it is not cleaned, it will not properly reflect the recognition of Allah. The more burnished and brighter it is, the better will it show from the enlightenment. Therefore, the more we indulge in sinful lust and devilish acts, the more are we deprived of the recognition of Almighty Allah. It is with a view to polishing the mirror of the heart that mashaa'ikh enjoin upon their disciples to devote themselves to self-discipline endeavours, spiritual occupation, incantation and remembrance of Allah.

It is mentioned in some ahadith that when a man commits a sin, a black dot stains his heart. If he repents in real earnest, this dot is removed, but if he commits another sin, another black dot appears. In this way, if he goes on committing sin after sin, his heart gets completely blackened. At this stage the heart becomes quite disinclined to do good, and keeps on turning to evil.

اَللّٰهُمَّ احْفَظْنَا مِنْهُ

May Allah save us from such a stage.

كَلَّا بَلْ ، رَانَ عَلٰى قُلُوْبِهِمْ مَّا كَانُوْا يَكْسِبُوْنَ

"Verily their evil deeds have covered their hearts with rust" refers to this blackening of the heart.

According to another hadith, Rasulullah (Sallallaho alaihe wasallam) said, "I leave two 'wu'aaz' (plural of waa'iz–preacher)–one speaking and the other silent. That which speaks is the Holy Qur'an and that which is silent is the remembrance of death."

Certainly the words of Rasulullah (Sallallaho alaihe wasallam) are worthy of loving acceptance. But only those who take proper heed derive benefit from a sermon. On the other hand, if we consider deen itself as being a useless occupation and an obstacle in the way of material progress, we will neither feel the need of spiritual advice nor act upon it.

Hadhrat Hasan Basri (Rahmatullah alaih) says, "People of earlier times believed the Holy Qur'an to be the Commandment of Allah, they contemplated over it throughout the night and acted upon it during the day. Whereas today you exercise particular care to pronounce its words and vowels correctly, but do not take it as the Commandment of Allah, and do not contemplate over it."

(٢٠) عَنْ عَائِشَةَ رَضِيَ اللهُ تَعَالٰى عَنْهَا قَالَتْ قَالَ رَسُوْلُ اللهِ ﷺ اِنَّ لِكُلِّ شَيْءٍ شَرَفًا يَتَبَاهَوْنَ بِهِ وَاِنَّ بَهَاءَ اُمَّتِيْ وَشَرَفَهَا الْقُرْآنُ (رواه في الحلية)

Hadhrat Aa'ishah (Radhiyallaho anha) reports that Rasulullah (Sallallaho alaihe wasallam) said, "Certainly there is always a thing in which people take pride. And that which is glory and pride for my Ummat is the Holy Qur'an."

People indicate their nobility and dignity by virtue of their lineage, their family and other similar things. The Qur'an is the source of nobility and pride for the Ummat in the sense that reading, memorizing and teaching it, as also acting upon it; in short, everything related to it, confers an honour upon them. Why should it not be so? After all, it is the Word of the Beloved and the Commandment of the Master. Its dignity excels all worldly honours, however great. The achievements of this worldly life, however splendid vanish sooner or later, while the splendour and dignity of the Qur'an is eternal and unbounded.

Even the minor attributes of the Glorious Qur'an are such as we should be proud of, let alone its excellence in other respects, for example, its beautiful composition, wonderful coherence, the right choice of words, the proper development of arguments, the narration of past events and prophecies about the future. Its assailing remarks concerning other people are such as cannot be contradicted, e.g., the remark about the Jews, that they profess their love for Allah, but they never long for death. The listener is impressed by its recitation and the reader never gets tired of reading it. It is usual that, however lovely a discourse may be, it may even be a letter from a beloved who has made one mad; we will become tired of reading it for the twentieth time if not the tenth; or the fortieth time, if not the twentieth. On the other hand, if we just memorize one section of the Qur'an, one may read it two hundred times or four hundred times or go on doing so for the whole life, but one shall never lose interest. And if something prevents us from enjoying it, that will be for a while only. In fact, the more we read the Qur'an, the greater will be our enjoyment and satisfaction. Even if a few of the above excellent qualities were to be found in any composition, we would be all praise for it. So, if all these qualities were present in a composition to a perfect degree, surely it would have to be regarded with the greatest honour and pride.

Now, we should just reflect on our own condition. How many of us feel really proud of having memorized the whole Qur'an? Does a hafiz command real respect in our eyes? Alas! our honour and pride lie in high university degrees, in big titles, in worldly pomp and show, and in the wealth which we will have to leave behind us on our death. O, Allah! have mercy upon us.

HADITH–21

(٢١) عَنْ اَبِىْ ذَرٍّ رَضِىَ اللهُ عَنْهُ قَالَ قُلْتُ يَارَسُوْلَ اللهِ اَوْصِنِىْ قَالَ عَلَيْكَ بِتَقْوَى اللهِ فَاِنَّهُ رَأْسُ الْاَمْرِ كُلِّهِ قُلْتُ يَارَسُوْلَ اللهِ زِدْنِىْ قَالَ عَلَيْكَ بِتَلَاوَةِ الْقُرْآنِ فَاِنَّهُ نُوْرٌ لَّكَ فِى الْاَرْضِ وَذُخْرٌ لَّكَ فِى السَّمَاءِ (رواه ابن حبان فى صحيحه فى حديث طويل)

Hadhrat Abu Zar (Radhiyallaho anho) says that he requested Rasulullah (Sallallaho alaihe wasallam) to give him some lasting advice. Rasulullah (Sallallaho alaihe wasallam) said, "Cultivate the fear and reverence of Allah in your heart, because this is the root of all virtuous deeds." I asked him to add something more and he said, "Stick to the reading of the Qur'an, because it is a noor in this life and a provision for the Hereafter."

The fear of Allah is the root of all good actions. A man whose heart is filled with fear of Allah, does neither commit any sin nor experience any difficulty.

وَمَنْ يَّتَّقِ اللهَ يَجْعَلْ لَّهُ مَخْرَجًا وَّيَرْزُقْهُ مِنْ حَيْثُ لَايَحْتَسِبْ

Whoever fears Allah, Allah will make a way for him out of every difficulty and provide from whence he has no expectation.

Some of the foregoing traditions also disclose that the Qur'an is illuminating. In Sharahul Ihya, Hadhrat Abu Na'eem (Rahmatullah alaih) states that Hadhrat Baasit (Radhiyallaho anho) has reported from Rasulullah (Sallallaho alaihe wasallam) that the houses in which the Holy

Qur'an is read shine unto the inhabitants of the Heaven as do the stars shine unto the inhabitants of the Earth.

This hadith, which has been quoted from 'At-Targhib', is only a part of a long hadith reported from Ibn Hibban by Mulla Ali Qari in detail and by Suyuti in brief. Although the above-mentioned part of the hadith is sufficient for the purpose of this book, yet the whole hadith includes many essential and useful subjects and, therefore, its subject-matter is given in the following paragraphs.

Hadhrat Abu Zar (Radhiyallaho anha) says that he inquired from Rasulullah (Sallallaho alaihe wasallam) about the number of books revealed by Almighty Allah. Rasulullah (Sallallaho alaihe wasallam) replied, "One hundred booklets and four books. Fifty booklets were revealed to Hadhrat Sheeth (Alaihis salaam) (peace be upon him), thirty to Hadhrat Idrees (Alaihis salaam), ten to Hadhrat Ibrahim (Alaihis salaam) and ten to Hadhrat Musa (Alaihis salaam) before the Torah. In addition, four books, i.e., the Torah, the Bible, the Psalms and the Holy Qur'an have been revealed by Almighty Allah." Hadhrat Abu Zar (Radhiyallaho anho) enquired about the contents of the booklets revealed to Hadhrat Ibrahim (Alaihis salaam). Rasulullah (Sallallaho alaihe wasallam) replied that they consisted of proverbs, e.g., "O, you strong and proud king! I did not appoint you to hoard wealth, but to prevent the complaint of the oppressed from reaching me by redressing it beforehand, because I do not reject the complaint of the oppressed person, even though he may be a disbeliever."

The author states that whenever Rasulullah (Sallallaho alaihe wasallam) deputed any of his Companions as an ameer or governor, in addition to giving other advice, he used to emphasize:

وَاتَّقِ دَعْوَةَ الْمَظْلُوْمِ فَإِنَّهُ لَيْسَ بَيْنَهَا وَبَيْنَ اللهِ حِجَابٌ

Beware of the invocation of the oppressed because between him and Allah there is no veil or intermediary.

As a Persian verse goes:

بترس از آہ مظلوماں کہ ہنگام دعا کردن
اجابت از در حق بہر استقبال می آید!

"Beware of the sigh of those oppressed, when they pray,

Divine acceptance readily greets them.

These booklets also mentioned that it is incumbent on a wise man, unless he is deprived of sanity, to divide his time in three parts: one for worship of his Lord; one for self-reckoning to consider what acts, good or bad, he did and one for his lawful earning of livelihood. It is also incumbent upon him to watch of his time and be thoughtful about improving his conditions and to guard his tongue against unnecessary and useless talk. Whoever keeps a check on his own speech, his tongue will indulge less in useless talk.

Also, a wise man should not travel except for three purposes. viz., for making provision for the life Hereafter, or in search of livelihood, or for such recreation as is permissible.

Hadhrat Abu Zar (Radhiyallaho anho) then enquired about the contents of the booklets revealed to Hadhrat Musa (Alaihis salaam). Rasulullah (Sallallaho alaihe wasallam) said, "They contained monitions only, such as 'I am astonished by one who finds pleasures in anything in spite of his faith in the certainty of death.' (Naturally when a person becomes sure of his sentence of hanging, and mounting the gallows, he can never find pleasure in anything). 'I am astonished by one who laughs in spite of his faith in certainty of death'. 'I am astonished by one who observes accidents, changes and revolutions of the world all the time, and still finds satisfaction in it.' 'I am astonished by one who believes in predestination, still suffers from grief and hardship.' 'I am astonished by one who believes that he will soon be required to render an account and still does no good deed."

Hadhrat Abu Zar (Radhiyallaho anho) goes on saying that he asked for more advice. Rasulullah (Sallallaho alaihe wasallam) advised that he should cultivate fear of Allah, because it is the root and basis of all spiritual actions. Hadhrat Abu Zar (Radhiyallaho anho) then begged for more advice. Rasulullah (Sallallaho alaihe wasallam) said, "Be consistent in recitation of Qur'an and remembrance of Allah, because it is a noor in this world and a provision in Heaven." Hadhrat Abu Zar (Radhiyallaho anho) again sought further advice and was told, "Abstain from too much of laughter, because it causes the heart to wither, and the face loses its lustre." (Too much of laughter is injurious both for the outward and inward disposition of man.)

Hadhrat Abu Zar (Radhiyallaho anho) sought further advice, whereupon Rasulullah (Sallallaho alaihe wasallam) said, "Stick to jihaad because this is the rahbaaniyyat of my ummat." (Rahbaan – singular raahib – were those people of previous ummats who severed all their worldly connections and turned towards Allah.)

Hadhrat Abu Zar (Radhiyallaho anho) asked for more advice and Rasulullah (Sallallaho alaihe wasallam) said, "Associate yourself with the poor and the needy, be friendly with them and sit in their company." When Hadhrat Abu Zar (Radhiyallaho anho) requested further advice, Rasulullah (Sallallaho alaihe wasallam) said, "Look towards those who rank below you (so that you may get used to being thankful) and do not look at those who rank above you, lest you should despise the favours of Allah upon you."

When Hadhrat Abu Zar (Radhiyallaho anho) again asked for more advice, Rasulullah (Sallallaho alaihe wasallam) said, "Let your own faults prevent you from criticizing others and do not try to find fault with others, because you commit those faults yourself. It is enough to prove you guilty that you should find in others such faults as you yourself possess, though you may not be aware of them, and that you should find in others such misdeeds as you yourself commit." After this, Rasulullah (Sallallaho alaihe wasallam) patted the chest of Abu Zar (Radhiyallaho anho) with his loving hand and said, "O, Abu Zar! there is no wisdom better than prudence, nor any piety better than refraining from the unlawful, nor any nobility better than polite manners."

(In stating the contents of this long hadith, the gist and meaning has been kept in view, in preference to the literal translation.)

HADITH – 22

(٢٢) عَنْ اَبِىْ هُرَيْرَةَ رَضِىَ اللّٰهُ عَنْهُ اَنَّ رَسُوْلَ اللّٰهِ ﷺ قَالَ مَااجْتَمَعَ قَوْمٌ فِىْ بَيْتٍ
مِنْ بُيُوْتِ اللّٰهِ يَتْلُوْنَ كِتَابَ اللّٰهِ وَيَتَدَارَسُوْنَهُ بَيْنَهُمْ اِلَّا نَزَلَتْ عَلَيْهِمُ السَّكِيْنَةُ
وَغَشِيَتْهُمُ الرَّحْمَةُ وَحَفَّتْهُمُ الْمَلٰئِكَةُ وَذَكَرَهُمُ اللّٰهُ فِيْمَنْ عِنْدَهُ (رواه مسلم وأبوداود)

Hadhrat Abu Hurairah (Radhiyallaho anho) narrates that Rasulullah (Sallallaho alaihe wasallam) said, "Never do a people collect in one of the houses of Allah (mosque) reciting the Qur'an and reading it out to one another, but sakeenah (tranquillity) descends upon them, rahmat (mercy) enshrouds them, the angels throng around them and Almighty Allah mentions them, in the assembly of angels."

This hadith describes the special virtues of religious schools and institutions. Acquisition of either reward mentioned above is so sublime that even if one devotes his whole life to acquire it, it will be worth while. But here there are so many rewards, especially the last one. Mention in the Court of Almighty Allah and remembrance in the company of the beloved are bounties that can hardly be surpassed.

Descending of sakeenah has been mentioned in many ahadith. The scholars of ahadith have interpreted its real significance in many ways. The various interpretations, however, do not contradict each other and can be meaningfully put together.

Hadhrat Ali (Radhiyallaho anho) has interpreted sakeenah as a special breeze, which has a face like that of a human being.

Allamah Suddi (Rahmatullah alaih) is reported to have said that it is the name of a large golden dish in Paradise used for washing the hearts of the Prophets (Alaihimus salam) (peace be upon them).

Some have said that it is a special form of mercy.

Tabari (Rahmatullah alaih) prefers the view that it means peace of heart. Some interpret it as grace, others consider it as dignity, and some take it to mean angels. There are other views as well. Hafiz has written in 'Fat-hul Baari' that sakeena includes all the above mentioned blessings. In the opinion of Nawawi (Rahmatullah alaih), it is a combination of tranquility, mercy, etc., and descends along with the angels. It is mentioned in the Qur'an as follows:

فَأَنْزَلَ اللّٰهُ سَكِيْنَتَهُ عَلَيْهِ

Then Allah caused His sakeenah to descend upon him.

هُوَ الَّذِىْ اَنْزَلَ السَّكِيْنَةَ فِىْ قُلُوْبِ الْمُومِنِيْنَ

It is He Who sent down sakeenah into the hearts of the believers (XLVIII: 4).

فِيْهِ سَكِيْنَةٌ مِّنْ رَّبِّكُمْ

Wherein is sakeenah from your Lord (II : 248).

Thus this happy blessing is mentioned in several ayaat of the Qur'an, and there are many ahadith containing tidings of this.

It is narrated in 'Ihya' that once Ibn Thauban (Radhiyallaho anho) had promised one of his relatives that he would break his fast with him, but reached the house of his relative next morning. When the host complained about the guest being so late, the guest said, "But for the promise that I owe you, I would never disclose what prevented me from coming to you. I just got late by chance until it was time of Ishaa salaat. I thought I should complete my Witr (compulsory salaat of three raka'at following Isha) as well, lest I should die during the night without offering this salaat, because there can be no surety against death. While I was reciting qunoot (a special invocation in Witr salaat), I saw a green garden of Paradise, which had all sorts of flowers. I was so absorbed in the vision that it was dawn." There have been hundreds of similar incidents in the lives of our righteous ancestors. Such things are, however, experienced only when there is complete separation from everyone besides Allah, and perfect attention towards Him.

Similarly there are many ahadith mentioning enshrouding by the angels. A detailed story about Usaid ibn Hudhair (Radhiyallaho anho) is given in the books of Hadith. It is said that while he was reciting the Holy Qur'an, he felt a sort of cloud spread over himself. The Prophet (Sallallaho alaihe wasallam) informed him that these were angels who had gathered to listen to the recitation of the Qur'an. Due to their great throng they appeared like a cloud.

Once a Sahabi felt a sort of cloud over himself. Rasulullah (Sallallaho alaihe wasallam) told him that it was sakeenah, which was sent down by reason of the recitation of the Qur'an.

In Muslim Sharif, this hadith is given in greater detail. The concluding sentence is–

مَنْ بَطَّأَ بِهِ عَمَلُهُ لَمْ يُسْرِعْ بِهِ نَسَبُهُ

One whose evil deeds drive him away from the mercy of Allah, the superiority of his lineage or nobility of his family cannot bring him near it.

Thus a person who has a continuous noble pedigree, but indulges in disobedience and impiety, cannot be equal in the presence of Allah to a Muslim who is of low birth and abject in humility, but otherwise God-fearing and devout.

اِنَّ اَكْرَمَكُمْ عِنْدَ اللهِ اَتْقَاكُمْ

Verily the noblest of you in the view of Allah is the one who is most God-fearing.

HADITH–23

(٢٣) عَنْ اَبِىْ ذَرٍّ رَضِىَ اللهُ عَنْهُ قَالَ قَالَ رَسُوْلُ اللهِ ﷺ اِنَّكُمْ لَاتَرْجِعُوْنَ اِلَى اللهِ بِشَىْءٍ اَفْضَلَ مِمَّا خَرَجَ مِنْهُ يَعْنِى الْقُرْآنَ (رواه الحاكم وصححه أبوداود فى مراسيله عن جبير بن نفير والترمذى عن أبى أمامة بمعناه)

Hadhrat Abu Zar (Radhiyallaho anho) reports that Rasulullah (Sallallaho alaihe wasallam) said, "You cannot turn to Allah and gain nearness to Him with anything superior to that which directly proceeded from Him, i.e., the Holy Qur'an."

It is evident from numerous ahadith that there is no better means of seeking nearness to the presence of Allah than recitation of the Qur'an. Imam Ahmad ibn Hambal (Rahmatullah alaih) says, "I saw Almighty Allah in a dream and asked Him what was the best means for seeking nearness to His presence. Allah said, 'O, Ahmad! It is My Word (i.e. the Qur'an).' I enquired whether it is only reading while understanding the meaning, or reading without understanding. Allah said 'Whether by understanding the meaning or without understanding, it is a means of nearness either way.'"

That the reading of the Qur'an is the best means of getting access to Almighty Allah is explained in the commentary of Maulana Shah Abdul Aziz Dehlavi (Nawwarallaho marqadahu), who is an authority for the prosterity. Its substance is that sulook ilallaah (the path of mystics towards Allah) which is also called the stage of Ihsaan can be attained in three ways:–

(1) 'Tasawwur', known as meditation in Sharee'at and muraqabah in the terminology of mystics.

(2) Remembrance of Allah by repeating words of praise for Him.

(3) Reading of the Holy Qur'an.

Since the first method is remembrance in the heart, so there remain in fact two ways only; first the remembrance by heart or by word of mouth, and secondly recitation of the Qur'an. The essence of zikr is that the word which is used for or refers to Almighty Allah should be repeated over and over again. This repetition helps the mudrakah (the faculty of understanding) in concentrating upon the person of the one being remembered. It would give rise to a feeling of immediate presence of that person. Constancy in this state is called 'ma'iyyat' (togetherness), which is referred to in the hadith below:

لَايَزَالُ عَبْدِىْ يَتَقَرَّبُ اِلَیَّ بِالنَّوَافِلِ حَتّٰى اَحْبَبْتُهُ فَكُنْتُ سَمْعَهُ الَّذِىْ يَسْمَعُ بِهِ وَبَصَرَهُ الَّذِىْ يَبْصُرُ بِهِ وَيَدَهُ الَّتِىْ يَبْطِشُ بِهَا

My servant ceases not to seek nearness to Me through nafil (optional) deeds, until I make him My favourite, and thus I become his ears wherewith he hears, his eyes wherewith he sees, and his hands wherewith he holds, and his feet wherewith he walks.

It means that when a person, through excessive devotion becomes a favourite of Allah, Allah becomes a guardian of all the limbs of his body so that his eyes, ears, etc., all submit to His will. This blessing is said to be the result of constancy in nafil salaat, because fard (obligatory) salaat are specified and do not admit of excess, while nearness and close attachment demand constancy and concentration, as mentioned above.

But this mode of seeking nearness is exclusive for that

Pure and Beloved Being (Allah), and it is impossible to seek nearness to anybody else by remembering his name over and over again. This is because the one whose nearness is being sought must have two attributes. First, he should be omniscient, so that he comprehends the zikr of all the zaakireen, whether by word of mouth or by heart, irrespective of language, time and place. Secondly, he should have the power to illumine the understanding and fulfil the yearning of one who remembers, which is known as 'dunuww' (nearness), 'tadalli' (proximity), 'nuzul' (descent) and 'qurb' (nearness). Since these two prerequisites are possessed only by Allah, the abovementioned method of seeking nearness is effective only in respect of Him. The following hadith-e-qudsi (a revelation of Allah quoted by Rasulullah Sallallaho alaihe wasallam), points to this fact:

مَنْ تَقَرَّبَ اِلَیَّ شِبْرًا تَقَرَّبْتُ اِلَیْهِ ذِرَاعًا

> Whoever comes near Me by one span, I go near him by an arm's length; whoever comes near Me by one arm's length, I go near him by one 'baah' (stretch of both arms); whoever comes to Me walking, I go towards him running.

This similitude is only for illustration. Otherwise, Allah is above walking and running. It only means that those who remember and seek Him are helped and looked after by Almighty Allah in a measure far in excess of their own inner urge and efforts. This is so, because it behoves His Benevolence. So, the steadfastness of those who remember Him invokes constant attention and results in the descent of favours of Almighty Allah, the Glorious. The Qur'an altogether is zikr of Allah, in the sense that no ayat of the Qur'an is devoid of remembrance and attention towards Allah, and as such it bears characteristics of zikr as mentioned above. There is, however, another distinction of the Qur'an, which is the cause of increased nearness to Allah. And it is this: that every discourse carries the qualities and influencing traits of the speaker. It is obvious that recitation of the poetry of sinful and wicked people has its evil effects, while the verses of righteous people excercise a noble influence. It is for this reason that excessive study of knowledge of logic and philosophy produces pride and conceit, while excessive devotion to the study of hadith leads to humility. Although as languages, both English and

Persian are equal, they produce varying influences upon the readers due to the divergence in the beliefs and attitudes of the various authors. It can be concluded that repeated recitation of the Qur'an will result in the reader's being influenced by the qualities of the Originator of the verses and in developing a natural affinity for them. Moreover, if a person is devoted to the publications of an author, he naturally starts liking and favouring that person. In the same way, the reader of the Qur'an is sure to win Allah's abundant grace, which in turn promotes nearness to Him. May Allah bless us all with His favours.

HADITH-24

(٢٤) عَنْ اَنَسٍ رَضِىَ اللهُ عَنْهُ قَالَ قَالَ رَسُوْلُ اللهِ ﷺ اِنَّ لِلّٰهِ اَهْلِيْنَ مِنَ النَّاسِ قَالُوْا مَنْ هُمْ يَارَسُوْلَ اللهِ قَالَ اَهْلُ الْقُرْآنِ هُمْ اَهْلُ اللهِ وَخَاصَّتُهُ (رواه النسائى وابن ماجه والحاكم وأحمد)

Hadhrat Anas (Radhiyallaho anho) reports that Rasulullah (Sallallaho alaihe wasallam) said, "For Allah, from amongst the people, there are some who are those of His household." The Sahabah (Radhiyallaho anhum) (may Allah be pleased with them) asked, "Who are those people?" He replied "Men of the Qur'an. They are of the household of Allah, and are his favoured ones."

"Men of the Qur'an are those who always remain occupied with the Qur'an and have got a special attachment to it. That such people are of the household of Allah and His favourites is evident. It is, therefore, clear from the foregoing that, as long as such people always remain occupied with the Qur'an, special favours of Almighty Allah continue to be conferred upon them. Certainly those who live in constant company do become as one of the household. What a great honour it is to belong to His household, to be reckoned amongst the 'Men of Allah' and to become His favourites, with such little striving and endeavour. What sacrifices of comfort and money are not made by people for admittance to worldly courts or to be elected as members of an assembly. They flatter the voters and bear all sorts of humiliations; yet they consider all this worthwhile. But the endeavour for the Qur'an is considered as a waste of time and energy:

ببیں تفاوتِ رہ از کجاست تا بہ کجا

Look at the difference between the paths; what a great divergence!

HADITH–25

(۲۵) عَنْ اَبِیْ هُرَیْرَةَ رَضِیَ اللّٰهُ عَنْهُ قَالَ قَالَ رَسُوْلُ اللّٰهِ ﷺ مَااَذِنَ اللّٰهُ لِشَیْءٍ مَااَذِنَ لِنَبِیٍّ یَّتَغَنّٰی بِالْقُرْاٰنِ (رواه البخاری ومسلم)

Hadhrat Abu Hurairah (Radhiyallaho anho) narrates that Rasulullah (Sallallaho alaihe wasallam) said, "Almighty Allah never gives attention so much to anything as He does to the voice of a Prophet reading the Qur'an in a sweet tone."

It has been mentioned earlier that Almighty Allah devotes special attention to the recitation of Qur'an, which is His own Word. Since Prophets meticulously observe all the rules of reverence in reading the Qur'an, Allah's listening to them with greater attention is evident. And the sweetness of voice itself adds to the embellishment. As for people other than Prophets, their recitation attracts Divine attention according to the standard of its excellence.

HADITH–26

(۲٦) عَنْ فُضَالَةَ بْنِ عُبَیْدٍ رَضِیَ اللّٰهُ عَنْهُ قَالَ قَالَ رَسُوْلُ اللّٰهِ ﷺ اللّٰهُ اَشَدُّ اُذُنًا اِلٰی قَارِیِٔ الْقُرْاٰنِ مِنْ صَاحِبِ الْقَیْنَةِ اِلٰی قَیْنَتِهٖ (رواه ابن ماجه وابن حبان والحاكم كذا فی شرح الأحياء قلت وقال الحاكم صحيح على شرطهما وقال الذهبی منقطع)

Hadhrat Fudhaalah Ibn Ubaid (Radhiyallaho anho) narrates that Rasulullah (Sallallaho alaihe wasallam) said, "Almighty Allah listens to the voice of the reader of the Qur'an more eagerly than does a master to the song of his singing slave girl."

It is natural that singing should attract attention. But religious people do not listen to singing because of the restriction in Islam. However, Islam does not prohibit listening to the song of a slave woman in one's lawful possession, even though, this may attract the fullest attention.

It is, however, necessary that the Qur'an shall not be recited in a singing tone, because doing so is forbidden according to several ahadith. In one hadith it is said:

اِيَّاكُمْ وَلُحُوْنِ اَهْلِ الْعِشْقِ

> Beware of reciting the Qur'an in a musical tone, like that of lovers singing their love poems as musical compositions.

The mashaa'ikh say that one who reads the Glorious Qur'an like a musical song is a faasiq (evil-doer), and even a listener to such recitation commits a sin. It is, however, desirable to recite the Qur'an in a sweet voice without following the rules of singing. There are various ahadith containing exhortation for reading the Qur'an in a sweet voice. Rasulullah (Sallallaho alaihe wasallam) has said at one place, "Adorn the Qur'an with a good voice." In another hadith it is said, "A sweet voice makes the beauty of the Qur'an twice as beautiful."

Hadhrat Shaikh Abdul Qaadir Jilani (Rahmatullah alaih) has written in his book 'Ghunyah that once Hadhrat Abdullah ibn Mas'ood (Radhiyallaho anho) happened to pass a place in the vicinity of Kufa and saw a gathering of evil-doers in a house. A singer named Zaazaan was singing and playing his instrument. On hearing his voice, Ibn Mas'ood (Radhiyallaho anho) said, "What a sweet voice, only if it were used for reciting the Glorious Qur'an," and thus saying he covered his head with a piece of cloth and went his way. Zaazaan had seen him saying something. On enquiring from the people, he came to know that Ibn Mas'ood (Radhiyallaho anho) was a Sahabi who had passed saying those words. Zaazaan got very much perturbed by that remark and, to cut the story short, he broke all his musical instruments and became a follower of Ibn Mas'ood (Radhiyallaho anho) and thereafter rose to the position of a distinguished scholar of his time.

There are various ahadith that commend reading of the Holy Qur'an in a good voice and at the same time prohibit reading it in a voice resembling singing, as has been stated before.

Hadhrat Huzaifah (Radhiyallaho anho) reports that Rasulullah (Sallallaho alaihe wasallam) said, "Recite the Qur'an in the Arabic accent, do not recite it in the tone of lovers or in the voice of Jews and Christians. There will shortly arise a people who will recite the Qur'an with affectation like singers and mourners, and such reading will be of no advantage to them at all. They themselves will get into trouble, and so also those who admire their reading."

Taa'oos (Rahmatullah alaih) writes that someone asked Rasulullah (Sallalaho alaihe wasallam) "Who it was who read the Glorious Qur'an in the best voice?" Rasulullah (Sallallaho alaihe wasallam) replied, "It is he whom you hear and feel that he is under the fear of Allah, i.e., his voice shows his being overwhelmed with fear." This is, however, the extreme benevolence of Allah that He does not expect from a person anything beyond his capacity. There is a hadith that Allah has deputed an angel on a special duty. If there be somebody who recites the Qur'an, but is unable to do so as correctly, as it should be done, this angel corrects his recitation before he takes it up to the Heavens."

اَللّٰهُمَّ لَا اُحْصِىْ ثَنَاءً عَلَيْكَ

"Oh, Allah! I cannot enumerate the praises due to Thee.

HADITH—27

(٢٧) عَنْ عُبَيْدَةَ الْمُلَيْكِيِّ رَضِىَ اللهُ عَنْهُ قَالَ قَالَ رَسُوْلُ اللهِ ﷺ يَااَهْلَ الْقُرْاٰنِ لَاتَتَوَسَّدُوْا الْقُرْاٰنَ وَاتْلُوْهُ حَقَّ تِلَاوَتِهٖ مِنْ اٰنَآءِ الَّيْلِ وَالنَّهَارِ وَاَفْشُوْهُ وَتَغَنَّوْهُ وَتَدَبَّرُوْا مَافِيْهِ لَعَلَّكُمْ تُفْلِحُوْنَ وَلَاتَعْجَلُوْا ثَوَابَهٗ فَاِنَّ لَهٗ ثَوَابًا

(رواه البيهقى فى شعب الإيمان)

Hadhrat Ubaidah Mulaiki (Radhiyallaho anho) narrates that Rasulullah (Sallallaho alaihe wasallam) said, "O, you devotees of the Qur'an! do not use the Qur'an as a pillow, but read it properly day and night, as it ought to be read. Propagate the Holy Qur'an, read it in a good voice and ponder over its contents, so that you may succeed. Do not seek a reward for it (in this life), because it has got a magnificent reward (in the Hereafter)."

A few points in this hadith are as follows:

(1) It is said that the Qur'an should not be used as a pillow. Doing so is an act of disrespect towards the Holy Book. It has been written by Ibn Hajar (Rahmatullah alaih) that using the Qur'an as a pillow, stretching one's feet towards it, and trampling over it, are acts which are all forbidden. Secondly, the expression "using as a pillow" also implies showing neglect towards the Holy Qur'an. It serves no purpose to place it on a pillow, as it is sometimes found placed on a stand by the side of a grave in a shrine for barakah (blessings). This is utter disregard of the Holy Book. We owe it to the Holy Book that it should be read.

(2) The expression "Read it as it ought to be read" means that it should be read with the highest degree of reverence. Commandment to this effect is there in the Qur'an itself.

اَلَّذِيْنَ اٰتَيْنَاهُمُ الْكِتَابَ يَتْلُوْنَهٗ حَقَّ تِلَاوَتِهٖ

Those to whom We have given the Book, read it as it ought to be read.

The orders of a king are received with great respect, and a letter from the beloved is read with great fondness; similarly the Qur'an sould be read with great respect and fondness.

(3) The expression "propagate the Qur'an" means that we should do so by speech, by writing, by persuasion, by practising and by all other possible means.

Rasulullah (Sallallaho alaihe wasallam) ordered its propagation and spreading, but some of our bright thinkers consider it a vain task, and at the same time they claim that they have great love for Rasulullah (Sallallaho alaihe wasallam) and for Islam.

According to a Persian verse:

ترسم نہ رسی بکعبہ اے اعرابی
کیں رہ کہ تو می روی بترکستان است

I am afraid, O, Bedouin! you can never reach Ka'bah.
Because the path you are following leads to Turkistan.

Rasulullah (Sallallaho alaihe wasallam) has ordered spreading of the Qur'an, but we do not hesitate to put all sorts of hurdles in the way of its propagation. We make laws for compulsory secular education so that children, instead of learning the Qur'an, are forced to join primary schools. We are displeased with teachers in religious schools for spoiling the lives of children, and, therefore, we do not send our children to them. Even if this apprehension is correct, it does not absolve us of our responsibility. On the other hand, our responsibility becomes even greater because we are all duty-bound, individually and collectively, to propagate the Qur'an. The religious teacher is, no doubt, responsible for his shortcomings, but if, because of his defects, we prevent children from going to religious schools, get notices issued to their parents in the name of compulsory primary education, compelling them to deprive their children of learning the Qur'an, then this is like killing a tuberculosis patient by giving him poison. An attempt to justify our hostile conduct by the supposed omission on the part of the religious teacher is a lame excuse, and this argument will not avail in the court of Almighty Allah. We may consider it necessary to educate our children in subjects like elementary arithmetic, to make them fit for running a petty grocery shop or for getting employment with the country's rulers, but according to Almighty Allah the learning of the Qur'an is the most important.

(4) That recitation should be in a sweet voice has already been explained under the previous hadith.

(5) We are required to ponder over the meaning of the Qur'an. There is a quotation from the Torah in 'Ihya', in which Allah says, "My servant! are you not ashamed of your behaviour towards Me? If you receive a letter from a friend while you are going on a road you stop and sit at a suitable place and read it with full attention and try to understand every word therein. But in case of My Book, wherein I have explained everything and have repeatedly emphasized important matters, so that you may ponder over and understand them, you show an attitude of indifference. Do you consider Me inferior to your friend even? O, My servant!

some of your friends sit with you and talk to you; you pay them full attention. You listen to them and try to understand them. If anybody tries to interrupt you, you stop him with a gesture. I talk to you through My Book, but you pay no heed. Do you consider Me inferior to your friends?" The merits of meditation and contemplation on the contents of the Qur'an have already been mentioned in the Foreword of this book and again under hadith 8.

The expression "do not seek prompt reward" means that no wages should be accepted for reciting the Qur'an, because your recitation is going to fetch you a great reward in the Hereafter.

To accept reward for it in this life is just like being content with shells instead of money. Rasulullah (Sallallaho alaihe wasallam) said, "When my Ummat will attach more value to money, it will lose the dignity which Islam confers on it, and when it will give up enjoining good and forbidding evil, it will be deprived of the blessings of Divine Revelation, viz., the understanding of the Qur'an."

اَللّٰهُمَّ احْفَظْنَا مِنْهُ

O, Allah! guard us against this.

HADITH–28

(٢٨) عَنْ وَاثِلَةَ رَضِىَ اللّٰهُ عَنْهُ رَفَعَهُ اُعْطِيْتُ مَكَانَ التَّوْرَاةِ السَّبْعَ وَاُعْطِيْتُ مَكَانَ الزَّبُوْرِ الْمِئِيْنَ وَاُعْطِيْتُ مَكَانَ الْاِنْجِيْلِ اَلْمَثَانِىَ وَفُضِّلْتُ بِالْمُفَصَّلِ

(لأحمد والكبير كذا فى جمع الفوائد)

Hadhrat Waathilah (Radhiyallaho anho) narrates that Rasulullah (Sallallaho alaihe wasallam) said, "I have been given 'as-Sab'ut Tuwal' in lieu of the Torah, 'al-Mi'een' in lieu of the Psalms, 'al-Mathaani' in lieu of the Bible and al-Mufassal as a special favour to me."

The first seven surahs are called 'as-Sab'ut Tuwal' (the seven longest ones); the next eleven are called 'al-Mi'een' (surahs consisting of about a hundred ayaat each); the following twenty surahs are known as 'al-Mathaani' (the oft-repeated ones), while all the remaining surahs are called 'al-Mufassal' (the explicit ones). This division is according to a popular interpretation, but there is some difference of opinion as to whether a certain surah is included in 'as-Sab'ut Tuwal' or 'al-Mi'een'. Similarly there is a disagreement as to whether a surah falls under 'al-Mathaani' or 'al-Mufassal'. But this disagreement does not affect the meaning or purpose of this hadith. This hadith shows that the Holy Qur'aan contains the equivalents of all the important Heavenly Books that had been revealed earlier, and moreover contains 'al-Mufassal' as a special addition, the like of which is not to be found in the earlier books.

HADITH–29

٢٩) عَنْ اَبِیْ سَعِیْدِ نِ الْخُدْرِیِّ رَضِیَ اللّٰهُ عَنْهُ قَالَ جَلَسْتُ فِیْ عِصَابَةٍ مِّنْ ضُعَفَآءِ
لْمُهَاجِرِیْنَ وَاِنَّ بَعْضَهُمْ لَیَسْتَتِرُ بِبَعْضٍ مِّنَ الْعُرٰی وَقَارِیءٌ یَّقْرَأُ عَلَیْنَا اِذْ جَاءَ
سُوْلُ اللّٰهِ ﷺ فَقَامَ عَلَیْنَا فَلَمَّا قَامَ رَسُوْلُ اللّٰهِ ﷺ سَکَتَ الْقَارِیُٔ فَسَلَّمَ ثُمَّ قَالَ
ا کُنْتُمْ تَصْنَعُوْنَ قُلْنَا نَسْتَمِعُ اِلٰی کِتَابِ اللّٰهِ تَعَالٰی فَقَالَ الْحَمْدُ لِلّٰهِ الَّذِیْ جَعَلَ
نْ اُمَّتِیْ مَنْ اُمِرْتُ اَنْ اَصْبِرَ نَفْسِیْ مَعَهُمْ قَالَ فَجَلَسَ وَسْطَنَا لِیَعْدِلَ بِنَفْسِهِ فِیْنَا
مَّ قَالَ بِیَدِهِ هٰکَذَا فَتَحَلَّقُوْا وَبَرَزَتْ وَجُوْهُهُمْ لَهُ فَقَالَ اَبْشِرُوْا یَامَعْشَرَ
صَعَالِیْكِ الْمُهَاجِرِیْنَ بِالنُّوْرِ التَّامِّ یَوْمَ الْقِیٰمَةِ تَدْخُلُوْنَ الْجَنَّةَ قَبْلَ اَغْنِیَآءِ النَّاسِ
نِصْفِ یَوْمٍ وَذٰلِكَ خَمْسُ مِاَةِ سَنَةٍ (رواه أبوداود)

Hadhrat Abu Sa'eed Khudri (Radhiyallaho anho) narrates:

"Once I was sitting with a group of indigent muhajireen, who did not even have sufficient clothes to cover their whole body and as such some of them were hiding themselves behind others. A qaari (one who is well versed in reciting the Qur'an) was reciting the Glorious Qur'an. Suddenly Rasulullah (Sallallaho alaihe wasallam) came and stood near us. On his arrival the reader stopped reciting. He invoked peace upon us, and asked us what we had been doing. We replied that we had been listening to the Holy Qur'an. Then

Rasulullah (Sallallaho alaihe wasallam) said, "All praise is for Allah, Who created such people in my Ummat that I have been ordered to stay with them.' Rasulullah (Sallallaho alaihe wasallam) sat in our midst so as to be equidistant from all of us. Then he asked all of us to get closer to him. All of us sat with our faces towards him. Thereafter, Rasulullah (Sallallaho alaihe wasallam) said, 'O, you poor muhajireen, I give you glad tidings of perfect noor on the Day of Judgement, and you shall enter Paradise before wealthy people by half a day, and this half day will be equal to five hundred years."

That muhajireen did not even have sufficient clothes to cover their whole body apparently refers to the exposure of that part of the body which it is not obligatory to cover. But in public one feels shy at the exposure of even such parts. This is the reason why they were sitting behind one another.

They did not become aware of the arrival of Rasulullah (Sallallaho alaihe wasallam) as he came, because of their pre-occupation. They saw him when he had come very near to them and then, out of respect, the reader stopped reading.

Although Rasulullah (Sallallaho alaihe wasallam) had seen one of them reading the Qur'an, he inquired about what they had been doing. This enquiry was to express his pleasure over what he had seen them doing.

One day in the next life will be equal to one thousand years of this world, as is given in the Holy Qur'an:

وَاِنَّ يَوْمًا عِنْدَ رَبِّكَ كَاَلْفِ سَنَةٍ مِّمَّا تَعُدُّوْنَ

"Lo! a day with your Lord is as a thousand years of that ye reckon."

This is the reason why the Arabic word (غدًا) (ghadan) (tomorrow) is generally used while referring to the Day of Judgement. Even this will be the probable length of a day for the believers in general. As for the disbelievers, the Qur'an says that:

فِىْ يَوْمٍ كَانَ مِقْدَارُهٗ خَمْسِيْنَ اَلْفَ سَنَةٍ

"A day will be equal to fifty thousand years."

For true believers, this day will be shorter according to their status. It is reported that, for some true believers, it will be like the time spent in two rakaat of Fajr salaat.

The merits of reading the Qur'an are given in many ahadith. Similarly, the merits of listening to the Qur'an are also found in numerous ahadith. The act of listening to the recitation of the Qur'an is so virtuous that Rasulullah (Sallallaho alaihe wasallam) had been ordered to stay among those engaged in reading the Qur'an, as given in this hadith. Some learned scholars are of the opinion that listening to the Qur'an is more virtuous than reading it, because reading the Qur'an is nafl and listening fard, and fard act is always better than a nafl one.

From this hadith there is one more deduction, in respect of which the learned scholars differ in their opinion. There is disagreement as to whether a destitute but steadfast person, who conceals his poverty from others is better, or a wealthy person who is grateful to Allah and discharges his obligations. This hadith provides an argument in favour of the destitute one who is steadfast.

HADITH–30

(٣٠) عَنْ اَبِىْ هُرَيْرَةَ رَضِىَ اللهُ عَنْهُ قَالَ قَالَ رَسُوْلُ اللهِ ﷺ مَنِ اسْتَمَعَ اِلٰى اٰيَةٍ مِّنْ كِتَابِ اللهِ كُتِبَتْ لَهُ حَسَنَةٌ مُّضَاعَفَةٌ وَمَنْ تَلَاهَا كَانَتْ لَهُ نُوْرٌ يَوْمَ الْقِيٰمَةِ

(رواه أحمد عن عبادة بن ميسرة واختلف فى توثيقه عن الحسن عن أبى هريرة والجمهور على أن الحسن لم يسمع عن أبى هريرة)

Hadhrat Abu Hurairah (Radhiyallaho anho) reports that Rasulullah (Sallallaho alaihe wasallam) said, "Whoever listens to one ayat of the Holy Qur'an, there is written for him a twofold virtue, and whoever recites it (one ayat), it shall be noor for him on the Day of Judgement."

The scholars of hadith have questioned the above hadith with respect to its authority, but its subject-matter is also affirmed by various other traditions to the effect that even listening to the recitation of the Holy Qur'an carries great reward, so much so that according to some scholars, listening to the recitation of the Glorious Qur'an is more virtuous than its reading. Ibn Mas'ood (Radhiyallaho anho) narrates that once Rasulullah (Sallallaho alaihe wasallam), while sitting on the mimbar (pulpit), said to him, "Recite the Qur'an for me." Ibn Mas'ood (Radhiyallaho anho) said, "It does not behove me to read out the Qur'an to you, because it is you to whom it was revealed." Rasulullah (Sallallaho alaihe wasallam) said, "It is my heart's desire to listen." Ibn Mas'ood (Radhiyallaho anho) adds that when he recited the Qur'an, tears started flowing from the eyes of Rasulullah (Sallallaho alaihe wasallam). Once Saalim (Radhiyallaho anho), the freed slave of Huzaifah (Radhiyallaho anho) was reciting the Glorious Qur'an and Rasulullah (Sallallaho alaihe wasallam) stood by, listening to him for a long time. Once Rasulullah (Sallallaho alaihe wasallam) listened to recitation of the Glorious Qur'an by Abu Musa Ash'ari (Radhiyallaho anho) and admired his reading.

HADITH–31

(٣١) عَنْ عُقْبَةَ بْنِ عَامِرٍ رَضِىَ اللهُ عَنْهُ قَالَ قَالَ رَسُوْلُ اللهِ ﷺ اَلْجَاهِرُ بِالْقُرْآنِ كَالْجَاهِرِ بِالصَّدَقَةِ وَالْمُسِرُّ بِالْقُرْآنِ كَالْمُسِرِّ بِالصَّدَقَةِ (رواه الترمذى وأبوداود والنسائى والحاكم وقال على شرط البخارى)

Hadhrat 'Uqbah ibn Aamir (Radhiyallaho anho) reports that Rasulullah (Sallallaho alaihe wasallam) said, "One reading the Qur'an loudly is like one who gives alms openly, and one who reads silently is like one who gives alms secretly."

Sometimes it is more rewarding to give alms openly, when there is some good reason and the intention is to induce others by example. At other times, giving alms secretly is more virtuous, for instance, when the intention is to avoid show on one's own part or to save the recipient from humiliation.

In the same way, recitation of the Qur'an in a loud voice carries more reward when the intention is to induce others; besides, in this there is reward also for those who listen. At times it would be preferable to read silently, so as to avoid inconvenience to others or show on one's part. Thus the reading, either way, has independent virtue. Sometimes one mode is preferable, and sometimes the other.

Many people have argued on the basis of this hadith that reading in a low voice is more virtuous. Imam Baihaqi (Rahmatullah alaih) in his book, 'Kitabush Shu'ab', has written that Hadhrat 'Aa'ishah (Radhiyallaho anha) had reported that the reward of doing a good act secretly is seventy times more than that of doing it openly. But, according to the rules laid down by the muhadditheen (scholars of ahadith), this hadith is dha'eef (weak).

Hadhrat Jaabir (Radhiyallaho anho) reports that Rasulullah (Sallallaho alaihe wasallam) said, "Do not read in a loud voice, lest the voice of one should get mixed up with the other." Hadhrat Umar ibn Abdul Aziz (Radhiyallaho anho) found a person reading the Qur'an in a loud voice in Musjid-i-Nabawi and had stopped him. The reader, however, tried to argue, whereupon Hadhrat 'Umar ibn Abdul Aziz (Radhiyallaho anho) said, "If you read for the sake of Allah, read in a low voice and, if you read for the sake of men, then such reading is of no use."

Similarly an advice of Rasulullah (Sallallaho alaihe wasallam), for reading the Qur'an in a loud voice, has also been reported.

'Sharhul Ihya' contains both 'riwaayaat' (Plural of 'riwayat–Narrative tradition) and 'aathaar' (sayings of Sahabah) urging the reading of the Glorious Qur'an in a loud as well as in a low voice.

HADITH–32

(٣٢) عَنْ جَابِرٍ رَضِىَ اللّٰهُ عَنْهُ عَنِ النَّبِىِّ ﷺ اَلْقُرْآنُ شَافِعٌ مُّشَفَّعٌ وَّمَاحِلٌ مُصَدَّقٌ مَنْ جَعَلَهُ اَمَامَهُ قَادَهُ اِلَى الْجَنَّةِ وَمَنْ جَعَلَهُ خَلْفَ ظَهْرِهِ سَاقَطَهُ اِلَى النَّارِ

(رواه ابن حبان والحاكم مطولا وصححه)

Hadhrat Jaabir (Radhiyallaho anho) reports that Rasulullah (Sallallaho alaihe wasallam) said, "The Qur'an is such an interceder whose intercession is accepted, and a disputant whose dispute is upheld. Whoever keeps it in front of him, it draws him to Paradise, and whoever puts it behind his back, it hurls him into Hell."

This means that, if the Qur'an intercedes on behalf of anybody, its intercession is accepted by Almighty Allah.

The meaning of the "pleading of the Glorious Qur'an" has already been explained under hadith 8. The Qur'an pleads in the Court of Allah for increasing the status of those who abide by it, and takes to task those who neglect it. If one keeps it in front of him, i.e., follows it and acts upon its commands throughout his life, it leads him to Paradise. And if one turns his back towards it, i.e., does not follow it, he will, no doubt, fall into the pit of Hell. According to the author, indifference to the Qur'an can also amount to putting it behind the back. In many ahadith there are several warnings for those who neglect the Word of Allah. In the book of Sahihul Bukhari' there is a long hadith, according to which Rasulullah (Sallallaho alaihe wasallam) was once made by Almighty Allah to view some of the punishments given to the sinful ones. He was shown a person on whose head a stone was being struck with such force that the head was crushed. On the enquiry of Rasulullah (Sallallaho alaihe wasallam) it was said that Allah had taught His Glorious Word to that person, but he neither recited it during the night nor acted upon it during the day, so now this treatment for him will continue till the Day of Judgement. May Allah through His grace save us from His chastisement. In fact, the Holy Qur'an is such a great blessing that any indifference to it certainly deserves the severest punishment.

HADITH–33

(٣٣) عَنْ عَبْدِ اللهِ بْنِ عَمْرٍو رَضِيَ اللهُ عَنْهُ قَالَ قَالَ رَسُوْلُ اللهِ ﷺ اَلصِّيَامُ وَالْقُرْآنُ يَشْفَعَانِ لِلْعَبْدِ يَقُوْلُ الصِّيَامُ رَبِّ اِنِّىْ مَنَعْتُهُ الطَّعَامَ وَالشَّرَابَ فِى النَّهَارِ فَشَفِّعْنِىْ فِيْهِ وَيَقُوْلُ الْقُرْآنُ رَبِّ مَنَعْتُهُ النَّوْمَ بِاللَّيْلِ فَشَفِّعْنِىْ فِيْهِ فَيُشَفَّعَانِ

(رواه أحمد وابن أبى الدنيا والطبرانى فى الكبير والحاكم وقال صحيح على شرط مسلم)

Hadhrat 'Abdullah ibn Amr (Radhiyallaho anho) reports that Rasulullah (Sallallaho alaihe wasallam) said, "The sowm (fast) and the Qur'an both intercede for the obedient person. The fast submits, 'O Allah! I prevented him from eating and drinking during the day, so You accept my intercession on his behalf, and the Holy Qur'an says, 'O, Allah! I denied him sleep at night, so You accept my intercession for him.' Consequently, the intercession of both of them is accepted."

In the book 'Targhib', the hadith mentions the words

'ta'aam' and 'sharaab' i.e. food and drink, as translated above, but in the book of Haakim we find the word 'shahawaat' (passions) in place of 'sharaab', i.e. fasting prevented a person from eating and indulging in his passions. It is implied here that one should abstain even from such acts of physical pleasure which are permissible e.g. kissing and embracing (one's own wife). It is given in some ahadith that the Holy Qur'an will appear in the semblance of a youth and will say, "It is I who kept you awake during the night and thirsty during the day."

This hadith implies that a hafiz should recite the Qur'an in nafl salaat at night, as explained already in detail under hadith 27. In the Holy Qur'an itself at various places there are encouragements to this effect. Some verses are given below:

وَمِنَ الَّيْلِ فَتَهَجَّدْ بِهِ نَافِلَةً لَّكَ

(1) And keep awake some part of the night for reciting it in Tahajjud salaat.

وَمِنَ الَّيْلِ فَاسْجُدْ لَهُ وَسَبِّحْهُ لَيْلًا طَوِيْلًا

(2) And worship Him in a portion of the night and glorify Him during the long night.

يَتْلُوْنَ اٰيَاتِ اللهِ اٰنَاءَ الَّيْلِ وَهُمْ يَسْجُدُوْنَ

(3) They recite verses revealed by Allah during the night and they fall in sajdah (prostration) before Him.

وَالَّذِيْنَ يَبِيْتُوْنَ لِرَبِّهِمْ سُجَّدًا وَّقِيَامًا

(4) And who spend the night before their Lord, prostrate and standing.

Consequently, Rasulullah (Sallallaho alaihe wasallam) and his Sahabah (Radhiyallaho anhum) sometimes spent the whole night in reciting the Holy Qur'an. It is reported about Hadhrat 'Uthman (Radhiyallaho anho) that sometimes he recited the whole of Qur'an in a single rak'at of hi Witr salaat. In the same way, 'Abdullah ibn Zubair (Radhiyallaho anho) used to recite the whole Qur'an in a single night. Sa'eed ibn Jubair (Rahmatullah alaih) read out the whole Qur'an in two rakaats inside the Ka'bah. Thabit Banaani (Rahmatullah alaih) used to read out the whole Qur'an in one day and night, and so was also the case with Abu Hurairah (Radhiyallaho anho). Abu Shaikh Hannaa'i (Rahmatullah alaih) said, "I read the whole Qur'an twice, and ten parts in addition, in a single night. If I wanted, I could have completed the third reading as well." In the course of his journey for the Haj pilgrimage, Salih ibn Kaisaan (Radhiyallaho anho) often used to complete two readings of the Qur'an each night. Mansoor ibn Zaazaan (Rahmatullah alaih) completed one reading during nafl salaat before noon, and the second reading in the interval between Zuhr (afternoon) and Asr (late afternoon) salaat, and he spent the whole night in offering nafl salat, weeping so much that the end of his turban would become wet. Similar had been the case with many others, as described by Muhammad ibn Nasr (Rahmatullah alaih) in his book 'Qiyaamul Lail'

It is written in 'Sharhul Ihya' that our ancestors in deen differed from one another in their practices of completing the reading of the whole Qur'an. Some of them completed one reading of the whole Qur'an every day, as was the practice of Imam Shaafi'ee (Rahmatullah alaih) in months other than Ramadhan; and some completed two readings everyday, as was also done by Imam Shaafi'ee (Rahmatullah alaih) during the month of Ramadhan. Such was also the practice of Aswad, Salih bin Kaisaan, Sa'eed bin Jubair and of many others. Some used to complete three readings every day. This was the practice of Sulaim ibn Atar, who was an eminent Taabi'ee (the follower of a Sahabi). He had taken part in the conquest of Egypt during the regime of Hadhrat 'Umar (Radhiyallaho anho) and was also appointed ruler of Qasas by Hadhrat Ameer Mu'aawiyah (Radhiyallaho anho). He used to complete three readings of the whole Qur'an every night.

Imam Nawawi writes in 'Kitabul Azkar' that the maximum daily recitation reported is of Ibnul Kaatib who used to complete eight readings of the Holy Qur'an during each day and night. Ibn Quddamah has reported that, according to Imam Ahmad (Rahmatullah alaih), there is no limitation in this respect and that it entirely depends on the zest of the reader. Historians have stated that Imam Abu Hanifah (Rahmatullah alaih) used to complete sixty-one readings in the month of Ramadhan–once everyday, once everynight, and one reading was completed in Taraweeh salaat.

On the other hand, Rasulullah (Sallallaho alaihe wasallam) has said that one who completes one reading of the Qur'an in less than three days cannot meditate upon it. For this reason, Ibn Hazm (Rahmatullah alaih) and some others are of the opinion that reading the whole Qur'an in less than three days is forbidden. According to the author, this hadith refers to the capacity of the readers in general, otherwise completion of one reading of the Holy Qur'an in less than three days by a group of Sahabah has been reported. Similarly, according to the opinion of the Jamhur (general body of 'ulama), there is no limitation on the maximum period in which one reading should be completed. The reading should be completed within such time as is convenient. But some 'ulama say that the maximum period should not exceed forty days. This means that at least three-fourth of a part should be read daily and if, for any reason, this much of reading is not done on any day, the missed portion should also be covered on the next day, so that the whole reading is completed within forty days. According to the consensus of opinion, this is not obligatory but, in view of the belief of some 'ulama, it is better that the daily reading should not be less than this. This view is supported by some ahadith. The author of Majma' has reported in one hadith:

مَنْ قَرَأَ الْقُرْآنَ فِىْ اَرْبَعِيْنَ لَيْلَةً فَقَدْ عَزَّبَ

Whoever completed the reading of the whole Qur'an in forty nights, delayed the matter.

Some 'ulama are of the opinion that the whole reading should be completed once every month, though it is preferable to complete one reading every week, as was the practice of the most of the Sahabah. One should start on Friday and read one manzil (halting stage) daily, thus to complete on Thursday. It has already been stated that, according to Imam Abu Hanifah (Rahmatullah alaih), we owe it to the Qur'an that it must be read at least twice a year. Therefore, under no circumstances should one do less than this.

There is a hadith according to which, if the reading of the whole Qur'an is completed in the beginning of the day, the angels invoke mercy for the reader throughout the rest of the day and for rest of a night if done in the beginning of the night. Some mashaa'ikh have, therefore, concluded that the reading of the whole Qur'an should be completed preferably in the early part of the day during the summer season and in the early part of the night during winter, so that the reader is benefited for a longer period by the prayers of the angels.

HADITH–34

(٣٤) عَنْ سَعِيْدِ بْنِ سُلَيْمٍ رَضِىَ اللهُ عَنْهُ مُرْسَلًا قَالَ قَالَ رَسُوْلُ اللهِ ﷺ مَامِنْ شَفِيْعٍ اَفْضَلُ مَنْزِلَةً عِنْدَ اللهِ يَوْمَ الْقِيٰمَةِ مِنَ الْقُرْاٰنِ لَانَبِيٌّ وَّلَامَلَكٌ وَّلَاغَيْرُهٗ

(قال العراق رواه عبدالملك بن حبيب كذا فى شرح الاحياء)

Hadhrat Sa'eed bin Sulaim (Radhiyallaho anho) has reported that Rasulullah (Sallallaho alaihe wasallam) said, "On the Day of Judgement, before Allah, no other intercessor will have a greater status than the Qur'an, neither a Prophet nor an angel, etc."

It has been learnt from several other ahadith that the Holy Qur'an is an intercessor–such an intercessor whose intercession will be accepted. May Almighty Allah make the Qur'an intercede for us all, and may He not make it an opponent or a complainant against us.

In 'La'aali Masnoo'ah' it is reported from the riwaayat of Bazzaar, which is not considered as concocted, "When a man dies and his relatives are busy in funeral rites, there stands an extremely handsome man by his head. When the dead body is shrouded, that man gets in between the shroud and the chest of the deceased. When, after the burial, the people return home, two angels, Munkar and Nakeer (names of two special Angels), come in the grave and try to separate this handsome man so that they may be able to interrogate the dead man in privacy about his faith. But the handsome man says, "He is my companion, he is my friend. I will not leave him alone in any case. If you are appointed for interrogation, do your job. I cannot leave him until I get him admitted into Paradise." Thereafter he turns to his dead companion and says, "I am the Qur'an, which you used to read, sometimes in a loud voice and sometimes in a low voice. Do not worry. After the interrogation of Munkar and Nakeer, you will have no grief." When the interrogation is over, the handsome man arranges for him from al-Mala'ul A'laa (the angels in Heaven) a silk bedding filled with musk. May Allah bestow this favour on all of us.

This hadith in its complete form contains a description of many virtues and has not been quoted in full for the sake of brevity.

HADITH–35

(٣٥) عَنْ عَبْدِ اللهِ بْنِ عَمْرٍو رَضِىَ اللهُ عَنْهُ اَنَّ رَسُوْلَ اللهِ ﷺ قَالَ مَنْ قَرَأَ الْقُرْآنَ فَقَدْ اِسْتَدْرَجَ النُّبُوَّةَ بَيْنَ جَنْبَيْهِ غَيْرَ اَنَّهُ لَايُوْحىٰ اِلَيْهِ لَايَنْبَغِىْ لِصَاحِبِ الْقُرْآنِ اَنْ يَّجِدَ مَعَ مَنْ وَّجَدَ وَلَا يَجْهَلَ مَعَ مَنْ جَهِلَ وَفِىْ جَوْفِهِ كَلَامُ اللهِ

(رواه الحاكم وقال صحيح الإسناد)

Hadhrat 'Abdullah bin 'Amr (Radhiyallaho anho) reports that Rasulullah (Sallalaho alaihe wasallam) said, "Whoever reads the Qur'an secures the knowledge of prophethood within his ribs (bosom), though Divine Revelation is not sent upon him. It does not befit one endowed with the Qur'an that he should be indignant with those in anger, nor should he indulge in any act of ignorance with those who are ignorant, while the Qur'an is there in his bosom."

Since the chain of wahi (revelation) ended with Rasulullah (Sallallaho alaihe wasallam), further wahi cannot come. But since the Qur'an is the Word of the Almighty Allah, it doubtlessly contains the knowledge of 'Nubuwwat (prophethood) and if anybody is blessed with this knowledge, it is incumbent upon him that he should display the best conduct, and should refrain from bad manners. Fudhail bin Iyaadh (Rahmatullah alaih) has stated that a hafiz of the Qur'an is a bearer of the banner of Islam, and as such it does not behove him to join those who indulge in frivolous pursuits, or associate with the neglectful, or mix with the indolent.

HADITH–36

(٣٦) عَنِ ابْنِ عُمر رضى اللهُ عَنْهُمَا قال قال رَسُوْلُ اللهِ ﷺ ثلاثةٌ لايَهُوْلُهُمُ الْفزعُ الْاَكْبَرُ ولا ينالُهُمُ الْحِسابُ هُمْ على كثيبٍ مِّنْ مِّسْكٍ حَتّٰى يُفْرغَ مِنْ حِسابِ الْخلائقِ رَجُلٌ قرأَ الْقُرْآن ابْتِغاءَ وَجْهِ اللهِ وَامَّ بِهٖ قَوْمًا وَهُمْ بِهٖ رَاضُوْنَ

وَدَاعٍ يَّدْعُوْ اِلَى الصَّلٰوتِ اِبْتِغَاءَ وَجْهِ اللهِ وَرَجُلٌ اَحْسَنَ فِيْمَا بَيْنَهُ وَبَيْنَ رَبِّهٖ
وَفِيْمَا بَيْنَهُ وَبَيْنَ مَوَالِيْهِ (رواه الطبرانى فى المعاجم الثلاثة)

Hadhrat Ibn 'Umar (Radhiyallaho anho) reports that Rasulullah (Sallallaho alaihe wasallam) said, "Three persons are such as will have no fear of the horrors of the Day of Judgement, nor will they be required to render any account. They will stroll merrily on mounds of musk until the people are relieved of rendering their account. One is a person who learnt the Qur'an, merely seeking Allah's pleasure and therewith leads people in salaat in a manner that they are pleased with him; the second person is one who invites men to salaat for the pleasure of Allah alone. The third person is one who has fair dealings between him and his master, as well as between himself and his subordinates."

The severity, the horror, the dread and the miseries of the Day of Judgement are so great that a true Muslim is neither unmindful nor unaware of them. To be relieved of those worries in any way, on the Day of Judgement, is a favour that surpasses thousands of blessings and millions of pleasures. Those who will then be made to relax and rejoice will be the fortunate ones indeed. Utter ruin and loss is the lot of those insensible persons who consider the reading of the Qur'an as useless and waste of time.

In 'Mu'jam Kabeer', it is written about this hadith that its reporter, Hadhrat 'Abdullah bin 'Umar (Radhiyallaho anho), who was a Sahabi of Rasulullah (Sallallaho alaihe wasallam) said, "If I had not heard this hadith from Rasulullah (Sallallaho alaihe wasallam) once, once again and once again (he repeated it seven times), I would never have reported it."

HADITH–37

(٣٧) عَنْ اَبِىْ ذَرٍّ رَضِىَ اللهُ عَنْهُ قَالَ قَالَ رَسُوْلُ اللهِ ﷺ يَااَبَاذَرٍّ لَاَنْ تَغْدُوَ فَتَعَلَّمَ اٰيَةً مِّنْ كِتَابِ اللهِ خَيْرٌ لَّكَ مِنْ اَنْ تُصَلِّىَ مِائَةَ رَكْعَةٍ وَلَاَنْ تَغْدُوَ فَتَعَلَّمَ بَابًا مِّنَ الْعِلْمِ عُمِلَ بِهٖ اَوْ لَمْ يُعْمَلْ بِهٖ خَيْرٌ مِّنْ اَنْ تُصَلِّىَ اَلْفَ رَكْعَةٍ

(رواه ابن ماجه بإسناد حسن)

Hadhrat Abu Zar (Radhiyallaho anho) reports that Rasulullah (Sallallaho alaihe wasallam) said, "O, Abu Zar if you go in the morning and learn one ayat from the Book of Allah, it will be better for you than your offering one hundred rakaat of nafl salaat, and if you learn one chapter of knowledge, which may or may not be practised at that time will be better for you than your offering one thousand rakaat of nafl salaat.

It is mentioned in many ahadith that acquiring knowledge of religion is more virtuous than worship. There are so many traditions on the virtues of learning that they cannot all be mentioned here. Rasulullah (Sallallaho alaihe wasallam) said, "The superiority of an aalim over an aabid (worshipper) is like my superiority over the lowest among you." He is also reported to have said that a single faqeeh (jurist) is harder against Satan than one thousand worshippers.

HADITH–38

(٣٨) عَنْ اَبِیْ هُرَيْرَةَ رَضِیَ اللّٰهُ عَنْهُ قَالَ قَالَ رَسُوْلُ اللّٰهِ ﷺ مَنْ قَرَأَ عَشْرَ آيَاتٍ فِیْ لَيْلَةٍ لَمْ يُكْتَبْ مِنَ الْغَافِلِيْنَ (رواه الحاكم وقال صحيح على شرط مسلم)

Hadhrat Abu Hurairah (Radhiyallaho anho) reports that Rasulullah (Sallallaho alaihe wasallam) said, "Whoever recites ten ayaat in a night, is not reckoned amongst the neglectful."

It takes only a few minutes to recite ten ayaat. Doing so saves a man from being included in the list of the neglectful, for that night. It is really a great reward.

HADITH.–39

(٣٩) عَنْ اَبِیْ هُرَيْرَةَ رَضِیَ اللّٰهُ عَنْهُ قَالَ قَالَ رَسُوْلُ اللّٰهِ ﷺ مَنْ حَافَظَ عَلٰی هٰؤُلَآءِ الصَّلَوَاتِ الْمَكْتُوْبَاتِ لَمْ يُكْتَبْ مِنَ الْغَافِلِيْنَ وَمَنْ قَرَأَ فِیْ لَيْلَةٍ مِّائَةَ آيَةٍ كُتِبَ مِنَ الْقَانِتِيْنَ (رواه ابن خزيمه فى صحيحه والحاكم وقال صحيح على شرطهما)

Hadhrat Abu Hurairah (Radhiyallaho anho) narrates that Rasulullah (Sallallaho alaihe wasallam) said, "Whoever remains steadfast in the five salaat will not be written amongst the neglectful; and whoever reads one hundred ayaat in a night will be written among the qaaniteen (the obedient)."

Hadhrat Hasan Basri (Rahmatullah alaih) reports that Rasulullah (Sallallaho alaihe wasallam) said, "Whoever reads one hundred ayaat in a night will be exempted from the demands of the Qur'an, and one who reads two hundred ayaat will get a reward for offering salaat throughout the night and one who recites five hundred to one thousand ayaat will get one qintaar. The Sahabah asked, "What is meant by a qintaar?" Rasulullah (Sallallaho alaihe wasallam) replied, "It is equal to twelve thousand daraahim or danaaneer (Plural of dirham and deenaar, respectively—unit of currency used in Hijaaz in the Holy Prophet's (Sallallaho alaihe wasallam) days)."

HADITH—40

(٤٠) عَنِ ابْنِ عَبَّاسٍ رَضِيَ اللّٰهُ عَنْهُ قَالَ نَزَلَ جِبْرَئِيْلُ عَلَيْهِ السَّلَامُ عَلٰى رَسُوْلِ اللّٰهِ ﷺ فَاَخْبَرَهُ اَنَّهُ سَتَكُوْنُ فِتَنٌ قَالَ فَمَا الْمَخْرَجُ مِنْهَا يَاجِبْرَئِيْلُ قَالَ كِتَابُ اللّٰهِ

(رواه رزين كذا فى الرحمة المهداة)

Hadhrat Ibn Abbas (Radhiyallaho anho) has reported, "Hadhrat Jibra'eel (Alayhis salaam) once informed Rasulullah (Sallallaho alaihe wasallam) that many fitnahs will certainly appear. Rasulullah (Sallallaho alaihe wasallam) asked, 'What will be the way out, O, Jibra'eel?' He replied, 'The Book of Allah."

To act upon the Book of Allah serves as a safeguard against fitnahs, and its blessed recitation is a means of relief from the evils. It has already been mentioned in hadith 22 that if the Qur'an is recited in a house, peace and mercy descend upon it and Satan quits the place. The 'ulama interpret fitnahs to mean the coming of Dajjaal (Islamic Anti-Christ), the invasion by the Tatars, and like incidents. A long riwaayat from Hadhrat Ali (Radhiyallaho anho) also includes the subject-matter of this hadith.

It is mentioned in this riwaayat of Hadhrat 'Ali (Radhiyallaho anho) that Hadhrat Yahya (Alayhis salaam) told the Israelites: "Allah orders you to read His Book, and if you do so, you will be like the people protected in a fort, so that on whichever side the enemy wants to attack you, he will find there the Word of Allah as a guard to repulse him."

PART 2

CONCLUDING SECTION

فِىْ عِدَّةِ رِوَايَاتٍ زَائِدَةٍ عَلَى الْاَرْبَعِيْنَةِ لَابُدَّ مِنْ ذِكْرِهَا لِاَغْرَاضٍ تُنَاسِبُ الْمُقَامَ

There are a few ahadith over and above the forty already narrated, which certainly need to be mentioned, being appropriate for this place.

In this section, some special virtues of certain surahs are narrated. These surahs are short, but excel in virtues and rewards. In addition, there are one or two important matters, about which the readers of the Qur'an need to be warned.

HADITH–1

(١) عَنْ عَبْدِ الْمَلِكِ بْنِ عُمَيْرٍ رضى اللهُ عَنْهُ مُرْسَلًا قَالَ قَالَ رَسُوْلُ اللهِ ﷺ فِىْ فَاتِحَةِ الْكِتَابِ شِفَآءٌ مِّنْ كُلِّ دَآءٍ (رواه الدارمى والبيهقى فى شعب الإيمان)

Hadhrat 'Abdul Malik bin Umair (Radhiyallaho anho) reports that Rasulullah (Sallallaho alaihe wasallam) said, "In surah Fatihah there is a cure for all ailments."

The virtues of surah Fatihah are found in many ahadith. It is reported in one hadith, "a Sahabi was offering nafl salaat; Rasulullah (Sallallaho alaihe wasallam) called him, but since he was offering salaat he did not respond. After completing the salaat he went to Rasulullah (Sallallaho alaihe wasallam), who asked him why he did not respond as soon as he was called. He submitted that he could not do so because he was offering salaat. Rasulullah (Sallallaho alaihe wasallam) asked if he dit not read the following verse in Qur'an:

يَآاَيُّهَا الَّذِيْنَ آمَنُوْا اسْتَجِيْبُوْا لِلّٰهِ وَلِلرَّسُوْلِ اِذَا دَعَاكُمْ

Respond to the call of Allah and His Messenger whenever They call you.

Then Rasulullah (Sallallaho alaihe wasallam) said, "I tell you of a surah which is the greatest, the most virtuous in the Holy Qur'an. It is surah Al-Hamd (The first surah of the Qur'an), which has seven ayaat. These are the 'Sab'ul Mathaani' and represent the Grand Qur'an." It is said by some Sufia that whatever there was in the earlier Divine Books is condensed in the Glorious Qur'an, and the contents of Qur'an are condensed into 'surah Fatihah; and that which is in surah Fatihah is found in Bismillaah and that which is in Bismillah is to be found in its first letter ب (ba). It is explained that ب (ba) is a co-ordinating conjunction and stands for uniting. Surely the ultimate aim is to effect union of a devotee with Almighty Allah. Some 'Sufia' have gone still further and have said that whatever there is in ب (ba) is to be found in its dot, which signifies the Unity of Allah–a thing which is indivisible as a dot.

Some scholars are reported to have said that the verse–

اِيَّاكَ نَعْبُدُ وَاِيَّاكَ نَسْتَعِيْنُ

"We worship Thee and we seek Thy help", is prayer for fulfilment of all our objectives, both worldly and spiritual. According to another hadith, Rasulullah (Sallallaho alaihe wasallam) is reported to have said, "By Him Who is in possession of my life, a surah like this one has neither been revealed in the Torah nor in the Bible nor in the Psalms, nor even in the rest of the Qur'an.

The Mashaa'ikh have stated that the reading of surah Fatihah with firm belief and faith cures all maladies, whether spiritual or worldly, external or internal. To use its writing as an amulet, and also licking its writing is useful in the treatment of diseases. It occurs in Sihaah (the six authentic books of Hadith) that the Sahabah used to read surah Fatihah and blow upon those bitten by a snake or a scorpion, and even on the epileptic and on the mentally deranged. Rasulullah (Sallallaho alaihe wasallam) had also approved of this. There is another riwaayat to the effect that Rasulullah (Sallallaho alaihe wasallam) recited this surah and blew on Saa'ib bin Yazeed and applied his saliva on the spot (where some pain was felt by the latter). According to another hadith, it is said that if, at the time of going to sleep, one reads surah Fatihah and surah Ikhlaas and blows on himself he will be immune from all dangers except death.

According to one riwaayat, surah Fatihah is equivalent to two-thirds of the Qur'an in reward. It is also reported that Rasulullah (Sallallaho alaihe wasallam) has said, "I have been given four things from the special treasure of the Arsh, from which nothing has ever been given to any one before. These are surah Fatihah, Aayatul Kursi, the concluding ayaat of surah Baqarah and Surah Kowthar." Hadhrat Hasan Basri (Rahmatullah alaih) reports the saying of Rasulullah (Sallallaho alaihe wasallam) that whoever reads surah Fatihah is like one who reads the Torah, the Gospel, the Psalms and the Glorious Qur'an.

It is reported in one hadith that the devil lamented, wept and threw dust on his head on four occasions; first, when he was cursed; secondly when he was cast out of Heaven unto the earth; thirdly when Hadhrat Muhammad (Sallallaho alaihe wasallam) was given the Prophethood, and fourthly when surah Fatihah was revealed.

It is reported from Sha'bi (Rahmatullah alaih) that once a man came to him and complained of pain in his kidney. Sha'bi (Rahmathulla alaih) advised him to read Asaasul Qur'an (the foundation of the Qur'an) and blow on the aching spot. When he inquired what was meant by "Asaasul Qur'an", Sha'bi replied, "Surah Fatihah."

It is written in the established practices of mashaa'ikh that surah Fatihah is the Isme A'zam (اسم اعظم), the Most Glorious Name of Allah, and it should be read for the achievement of all our objectives. There are two ways of reading it:

One method is to read this surah forty-one times for forty days, in the interval between the sunnat (a practice of the Holy Prophet) (Sallallaho alaihe wasallam) and fardh rak'aats of the Fajr salaat. The meem of بسم الله الرحمن الرحيم (Bismillaahir rahmaanir raheem) should be read jointly with the laam of الحَمْدُ لله (Alhamdu lillaahi). Whatever the objective may be, it will, insha-Allah (if Allah wills), be fulfilled. In the treatment of a patient or of one who is bewitched, it should be recited and blown on water to be used for drinking.

The second method is to read it seventy times between the sunnat and the fardh rak'aat of the Fajr salaat on the first Sunday of a new moon, after which the number is reduced by ten every day until the course ends with a reading of ten times on the seventh day. Then this weekly course should be repeated, so as to complete four weeks. If the purpose is achieved at the end of the first month, well and good, otherwise this course should be repeated for the second and, if necessary, for the third month.

The surah is also written with water of roses, musk and saffron, on a porcelain dish, then the writing is washed off and the wash-water is given to the patient for drinking for forty days. This is a sure treatment of chronic diseases. To read it seven times and then blow on the patient is similarly an accepted treatment for toothache, headache and pain in the stomach.

All these points have been briefly quoted from the book 'Mazaahir-e-Haq."

'Muslim Sharif' contains a hadith in which Ibn 'Abbas (Radhiyallaho anho) narrates that once Rasulullah (Sallallaho alaihe wasallam) was sitting among us and said, "In Heaven a door has been opened today which was never opened before, and out of it has descended an angel who had never descended before. The angel said to me, "Receive the good news of two 'anwaar' which have not been bestowed upon anyone else before. One is surah Fatihah and the other the concluding portion of surah Baqarah, i.e. its last 'ruku' (section of the Qur'an)'." These two surahs have been called 'noor', because on the Day of Judgement these will travel in front of their readers (illuminating their path).

HADITH—2

(٢) عَنْ عَطَاءِ بْنِ اَبِىْ رَبَاحٍ رَضِىَ اللهُ عَنْهُ قَالَ بَلَغَنِىْ اَنَّ رَسُوْلَ اللهِ ﷺ قَالَ مَنْ قَرَأَ يٰسٓ فِىْ صَدْرِ النَّهَارِ قُضِيَتْ حَوَائِجُهُ (رواه الدارمى)

Hadhrat 'Ataa' bin Abi Ribaah, (Radhiyallaho anho) says that Rasulullah (Sallallaho alaihe wasallam) is reported to have said, "Whoever reads surah Yaaseen in the beginning of the day, all his needs for that day are fulfilled."

Many merits of surah Yaaseen are mentioned in ahadith. It is said in one hadith, "Everything has a heart, and the heart of the Glorious Qur'an is surah Yaaseen. Whoever reeds surah Yaaseen, Almighty Allah records for him a reward equal to that of reading the whole Qur'an ten times."

According to another Hadith Almighty Allah recited surah Yaaseen and surah Taahaa one thousand years before the creation of Heaven and Earth, and on hearing this the angels said, "Blessing is for the ummat unto whom the Qur'an will be sent down, blessing is for the hearts that will bear, i.e. memorize it, and blessing is for the tongues that will recite it."

There is other riwaayat like this, "Whoever reads surah Yaaseen for the pleasure of Allah only, all his earlier sins are forgiven. Therefore make a practice of reading this surah over your dead."

According to one hadith, surah Yaaseen is named in, Torah as mun'imah (giver of good things), because it contains benefits for its reader in this life as well as in the Hereafter; it removes from him the afflictions of this world and the next; and takes away the dread of the next life.

This 'surah' is also known as 'Raafi'ah Khaafidhaah', i.e., that which exalts the status of the believers and degrades the unbelievers. According to a riwaayat, Rasulullah (Sallallaho alaihe wasallam) said, "My heart desires that surah Yaaseen should be present in the heart of everyone of my ummat." According to another hadith, if anybody recites surah Yaaseen every night and then dies, he dies as shaheed (martyr).

It is reported in another hadith "Whoever reads surah Yaaseen, is forgiven; whoever reads it in hunger, is satisfied; whoever reads it having lost his way finds the way; whoever reads it on losing an animal finds the same. And when one reads it apprehending that his food will run short, that food becomes sufficient. And if one reads it beside a person who is in the throes of death, the same are made easy for him. And if anyone reads it on a woman experiencing difficulty in child-birth, her delivery becomes easy."

Maqri (Rahmatullah alaih) said, "If surah Yaaseen is read by one who fears the ruler or an enemy, he gets rid of this fear." According to another hadith, if somebody reads surah Yaaseen and surah Was-Saaffaat on Friday and begs of Allah something, his prayer is granted. (Most of the above has been drawn from Mazaahir-e-Haq, though the scholars of hadith have questioned some of the riwaayaat).

HADITH–3

(٣) عَنِ ابْنِ مَسْعُوْدٍ رَضِىَ اللّٰهُ عَنْهُ قَالَ قَالَ رَسُوْلُ اللّٰهِ ﷺ مَنْ قَرأَ سُوْرَةَ الْوَاقِعَةِ فِىْ كُلِّ لَيْلَةٍ لَمْ تُصِبْهُ فَاقَةٌ اَبَدًا وَكَانَ ابْنُ مَسْعُوْدٍ يَاْمُرُ بَنَاتَهُ يَقْرأْنَ بِهَا كُلَّ لَيْلَةٍ (رواه البيهقى فى الشعب)

Ibn Mas'ood (Radhiyallaho anho) reports that Rasulullah (Sallallaho alaihe wasallam) said, "Whoever reads surah Al-Waaqi'ah every night, starvation shall never afflict him."

Ibn Mas'ood (Radhiyallaho anho) used to command his daughters to recite this surah every night.

The virtues of surah Al-Waaqi'ah are also reported in many ahadith. There is a riwaayat to the effect that whoever reads surahs al-Hadeed, Al-Waaqi'ah and Ar-Rahmaan, is reckoned amongst the dwellers of Jannat-ul-Firdaus (the highest level of Paradise). In another hadith, it is stated that surah Al-Waaqi'ah, is surah Al-Ghinaa. Read it and teach it to your children. Another riwaayat says: "Teach it to your wives." Hadhrat 'Aa'ishah (Radhiyallaho anha) is reported to have emphasized its reading. But it is low mentality on our part to read it only for sake of petty worldly gain. If instead, it is read for the contentment of the heart and for the sake of the next world, then worldly gains will come to us without the asking.

HADITH–4

(٤) عَنْ اَبِىْ هُرَيْرَةَ رَضِىَ اللّٰهُ عَنْهُ قَالَ قَالَ رَسُوْلُ اللّٰهِ ﷺ اِنَّ سُوْرَةً فِى الْقُرْآنِ ثَلٰثُوْنَ آيَةً شَفَعَتْ لِرَجُلٍ حَتّٰى غُفِرَ لَهُ وَهِىَ تَبَارَكَ الَّذِىْ بِيَدِهِ الْمُلْكُ

(رواه أبوداود وأحمد والنسائى وابن ماجه والحاكم وصححه وابن حبان فى صحيحه)

Hadhrat Abu Hurairah (Radhiyallaho anho) narrates that Rasulullah (Sallallaho alaihe wasallam) said, "There is in the Qur'an a surah of thirty ayaat which intercedes for a person (its reader) until he is forgiven. This is surah Tabarakal lazi."

About surah Tabarakal lazi, there is a riwaayat also that Rasulullah (Sallallaho alaihe wasallam) said, "My heart desires that this surah should be in the heart of every believer."

According to a hadith, one who reads surah Tabarakal lazi and Alif-Laam Meem-Sajdah, between the Maghrib (dusk) salaat and the Ishaa' salaat, is like a person who stands in Salaat throughout the night called Lailatul Qadr (27th night of Ramadhaan–the month of fasting and the 9th month of the Islamic calendar). It is also reported that if somebody reads these two surahs, seventy virtues are added to his account and seventy sins are condoned. According to another riwaayat, if one reads these two surahs, a reward equal to that of standing in salaat throughout Lailatul Qadr is written for him. This is also mentioned in Mazaahir.

Tirmidhi (Rahmatullah alaih) reports from Ibn Abbas (Radhiyallaho anho): "Some sahabah pitched a tent, at a place without knowing that there was a grave at that place. All of a sudden, those who were putting up the tent heard somebody reciting surah Tabarakal lazi. They reported the matter to Rasulullah (Sallallaho alaihe wasallam), who explained to them that this surah guards against Allah's chastisement and ensures deliverance."

Jaabir (Radhiyallaho anho) reports that Rasulullah (Sallallaho alaihe wasallam) would not go to sleep until he had recited the surahs Alif Laam Meem-Sajdah and Tabarakal lazi.

Khalid bin Ma'daan (Radhiyallaho anho) has said that he had heard it narrated, "There was a man who was a great sinner, but he used to recite surah Sajdah. He never read anything else. This surah spread its wings over that man and submitted to Allah, 'O, my Lord! this man used to recite me very frequently'. So the intercession of that surah was accepted. It was ordered that each sin in his account should be substituted by a virtue." Khalid bin Ma'daan (Radhiyallaho anho) has also reported, "This surah pleads for its reader in the grave and says, 'O, Allah! if I am contained in Thy Book, then accept my intercession, otherwise write me off from Thy Book. This surah appears in the form of a bird, spreads its wings over the dead and guards him against punishment in the grave." He has reported all these merits for surah Tabarakal lazi as well. He himself would never go to sleep unless he had read these two surahs.

Taa'oos (Rahmatullah alaih) has said, "These two

surahs carry sixty virtues in excess of those carried by any other surah."

The punishment in the grave is not an ordinary affair. After death, the first stage that one has to pass through is the grave. Whenever Hadhrat 'Usman (Radhiyallaho anho) stood by a grave, he used to weep so much that his beard would become wet with tears. Somebody asked him why he wept more at the mention of the grave than he did at the mention of Heaven and Hell. He replied, "I have heard from Rasulullah (Sallallaho alaihe wasallam) that the grave is the first stage towards the Hereafter. Whoever is saved from chastisement in it, for him the subsequent events become easy, and whoever is not saved from chastisement in it, for him the coming events will be harsher still. And I have also heard that no scene is more horrible than that of the grave.":

اَللّٰهُمَّ احْفَظْنَا مِنْهُ بِفَضْلِكَ وَمَنِّكَ

O, Allah! save us from this punishment through Thy Mercy and Grace.

HADITH–5

(٥) عَنِ ابْنِ عَبَّاسٍ رَضِىَ اللّٰهُ عَنْهُ اَنَّ رَجُلًا قَالَ يَارَسُوْلَ اللّٰهِ اَىُّ الْاَعْمَالِ اَفْضَلُ قَالَ الْحَالُ الْمُرْتَحِلُ قَالَ يَارَسُوْلَ اللّٰهِ مَاالْحَالُ الْمُرْتَحِلُ قَالَ صَاحِبُ الْقُرْآنِ يَضْرِبُ مِنْ اَوَّلِهِ حَتّٰى يَبْلُغَ آخِرَهُ وَمِنْ آخِرِهِ حَتّٰى يَبْلُغَ اَوَّلَهُ كُلَّمَا حَلَّ اِرْتَحَلَ

(رواه الترمذى كما فى الرحمة والحاكم وقال تفرد به صالح المرى وهو من زهاد أهل البصرة إلا أن الشيخين لم يخرجاه وقال الذهبى صالح متروك قلت هو من رواة أبى داود والترمذى)

Ibn Abbas (Radhiyallaho anho) says: "Somebody asked Rasulullah (Sallallaho alaihe wasallam) as to which of the acts is the most virtuous. Rasulullah (Sallallaho alaihe wasallam) replied الحال والمرتحل ('al-haal wal-murtahil'). The man inquired, 'O, Rasullulah (Sallallaho alaihe wasallam)! what is 'alah-al wal murtahil?' Rasulallah (Sallallaho alaihe wasallam) replied, "It is that particular reader of the Qur'an who starts reading from the beginning and continues till he reaches its end, and after the end, he starts at the beginning again. Wherever he stops, he proceeds further."

The Arabic word (الحال) ('al-haal) means one who reaches a halting place, and the word (المرتحل) ('al-murtahil') means one who departs. In other words, as soon as a reading of the Holy Qur'an is finished, one should start again. And it should not be that when one reading is finished the other may be taken up later on. The term (الحال والمرتحل) ('al-haal wal murtahil') is explained in a riwaayat in Kanzul-Ummaal to mean (الخاتم المفتاح) (al-khaatimatul miftaah) (one who concludes and opens), i.e. one who completes the whole reading of the Holy Qur'an and then immediately starts another. Probably this has led to the practice generally prevalent in our country, according to which the reader while finishing the whole Qur'an does not stop after reading the last surah but also reads from the beginning of the Qur'an up to مُفْلِحُوْن. Doing so has now become a mere ritual and the people do not care to continue further and complete the reading. This hadith teaches us that, as soon as one reading of the Glorious Qur'an is completed, a fresh reading should be taken up immediately and brought to completion. It is written in Sharhul Ihya as well as in Allamah Suyuti's Al-Itqan that according to Daarami whenever Rasulullah (Sallallaho alaihe wasallam) read surah an-Naas (the last surah), he would also read al-Baqarah up to مُفْلِحُوْن after which he would offer the du'a meant to be read on completion of a reading of the whole Qur'an.

HADITH–6

(٦) عَنْ اَبِىْ مُوسٰى الْاَشْعَرِىِّ رَضِىَ اللهُ عَنْهُ قَالَ قَالَ رَسُوْلُ اللهِ ﷺ تَعَاهَدُوْا الْقُرْآنَ فَوَالَّذِىْ نَفْسِىْ بِيَدِهٖ لَهُوَ اَشَدُّ تَفَصِّيًا مِّنَ الْاِبِلِ فِىْ عُقُلِهَا

(رواه البخارى ومسلم)

Abu Musa Ash'ari (Radhiyallaho anho) reports that Rasulullah (Sallallaho alaihe wasallam) said, "Be watchful towards the Qur'an. I swear by Him in Whose hands my life is, that the Qur'an is apt to escape from the hearts more rapidly than do the camels from their strings."

If a man becomes neglectful in looking after an animal, and the animal frees itself from the halter, it will bolt away. Similarly if the Holy Qur'an is not looked after, it will not be remembered and will be forgotten. The fact that the

Holy Qur'an gets committed to memory is a distinct miracle of the Book itself. Otherwise memorizing a book one-half or even one-third of its size is not only difficult but well-nigh impossible. Therefore, the fact that the Holy Qur'an gets committed to memory is mentioned by Almighty Allah as a Divine favour in surah al-Qamar, where it is repeated over and over—

وَلَقَدْ يَسَّرْنَا الْقُرْآنَ لِلذِّكْرِ فَهَلْ مِن مُّدَّكِرٍ

We have made the Qur'an easy for remembrance, So is there any one who will remember?

The author of al-Jalalain writes that the interrogatory clause in this ayat is in fact an imperative one. Thus Almighty Allah has stressed over and over again the importance of memorizing the Qur'an, but if we Muslims are so perverse as to think that this act is useless and wasteful of time and energy, this blunder on our part is sufficient to justify our destruction. It is a matter of surprise indeed that, when 'Uzair (Alayhis salaam) reproduced the Torah from memory he was exalted to be called the "Son of God;" poor indeed is the regard that we have for the blessing and favour of Allah, that He has made the memorizing of the Glorious Qur'an easy for all of us (and not only for an individual as in the case of Torah). It is for such people that the Qur'an says:

فَسَيَعْلَمُ الَّذِيْنَ ظَلَمُوْا اَىَّ مُنْقَلَبٍ يَّنْقَلِبُوْنَ

And those who do wrong will come to know by what a (Great) reverse they will be over-turned!

It is merely through the grace and blessing of Almighty Allah that the Qur'an gets memorized, but afterwards, if a person neglects it, he is made to forget it. There are severe admonitions for those who forget the Glorious Qur'an after having learnt it. Rasulullah (Sallallaho alaihe wasallam) is reported to have said, "The sins of my ummat were shown to me. I did not find any sin as great as that of forgetting the Holy Qur'an after having read it. "In another hadith it is said that any one who forgets Qur'an after having read it, will appear in the Court of Allah as a leper. According to a riwaayat of Razeen (Rahmatullah alaih) in 'Jam'ul-Fawaa'id', the following ayat refer to it:

وَمَنْ اَعْرَضَ عَنْ ذِكْرِىْ فَاِنَّ لَهُ مَعِيْشَةً ضَنْكًا وَّنَحْشُرُهُ يَوْمَ الْقِيٰمَةِ اَعْمٰى ، قَالَ رَبِّ لِمَ حَشَرْتَنِىْ اَعْمٰى وَقَدْ كُنْتُ بَصِيْرًا ، قَالَ كَذٰلِكَ اَتَتْكَ اٰيٰتُنَا فَنَسِيْتَهَا وَكَذٰلِكَ الْيَوْمَ تُنْسٰى

> But whosoever turns away from My Message, verily for him is a narrowed life and We shall raise him up blind on the Day of Judgement. He shall say: "My Lord, why hast Thou raised me blind, and I was a seeing one indeed." He will say, "Even so Our Commandments came to thee, but thou didst neglect them; even thus shalt thou be forsaken today." (XX: 126-6).

HADITH–7

(٧) عَنْ بُرَيْدَةَ رَضِىَ اللهُ عَنْهُ قَالَ قَالَ رَسُوْلُ اللهِ ﷺ مَنْ قَرَأَ الْقُرْآنَ يَتَأَكَّلُ بِهِ النَّاسَ جَاءَ يَوْمَ الْقِيٰمَةِ وَوَجْهُهُ عَظْمٌ لَيْسَ عَلَيْهِ لَحْمٌ (رواه البيهقى فى شعب الإيمان)

> Buraidah (Radhiyallaho anho) reports that Rasulullah (Sallallaho alaihe wasallam) said, "He who reads the Qur'an so that he might thereby get something to eat from the people, shall so appear on the Day of Judgement that his face will only be a bone, on which there will be no flesh.

This means that those who read the Glorious Qur'an in order to fulfil the needs of this world will get no share in the Hereafter. Rasulullah (Sallallaho alaihe wasallam) has said, "We read the Holy Qur'an. There are amongst us Arabs as well as non-Arabs. Go on reading the Qur'an as you do it now. Shortly, there will rise people who will set right the pronunciation of letters of the Qur'an as an arrow, i.e., they will work hard to adorn it and spend hours in improving the pronunciation of each and every letter. They will take great pains over phonetics. But all this will be with a worldly motive. They will be the least concerned with the Hereafter." This hadith further signifies that mere recitation in a pleasing voice is of no avail if there would be no sincerity and if the purpose is only to earn worldly benefit. "There will be no flesh" means that when a man makes the noblest of all things (i.e. the Qur'an) the means for earning the inferior things of this world, the noblest of all parts of the body, i.e. his face, will be deprived of its beauty.

Once 'Imraan bin Husain (Radhiyallaho anho) happened to pass by a preacher who recited the Glorious Qur'an and then begged of the people. He was grieved to see this painful sight and recited 'Innaa lillaahi wa innaailaihi raaji-oon' (verily we are from Allah and will return to Him). He said that he had heard from Rasulullah (Sallallaho alaihe wasallam) that whoever recites the Glorious Qur'an should beg whatever he needs only from Almighty Allah. Shortly, there will come into existence a people who will recite and then beg of the people. It is reported from some scholars that the "example of one who earns the gains of this world through the knowledge of deen is like that of one who cleans his shoes with his cheeks; the shoes will no doubt be cleaned, but the act is most stupid. It is such people who are referred to in the following ayat of the Glorious Qur'an:

أُولَٰئِكَ الَّذِينَ اشْتَرَوُا الضَّلَالَةَ بِالْهُدَىٰ - الآية

These are they who buy error at the price of guidance. So their commerce doth not prosper, neither are they guided.

Ubayy bin Ka'b (Radhiyallaho anho) has narrated, "I taught a surah of the Glorious Qur'an to a man who gave me a bow as a gift. I mentioned this to Rasulullah (Sallallaho alaihe wasallam), who said that I had accepted a bow from Hell." A similar incident has been mentioned about himself by 'Ubaadah bin Saamit (Radhiyallaho anho) in whose case Rasulullah (Sallallaho alaihe wasallam) he said, "You have hung between your shoulders a spark from Hell." According to another riwaayat Rasulullah (Sallallaho alaihe wasallam) had said, "If you are prepared to put a yoke of Hell round your neck, you may accept it."

Now a word for such huffaaz who are working in Qur'anic schools, only for the sake of money. It is humbly requested that they should give a thoughtful consideration to their status and responsibility. This unbecoming conduct on their part is being attacked and made an excuse by some people for stopping the reading or memorizing of the Glorious Qur'an. They alone are not responsible for the evil consequences, but such huffaaz also share the responsibility for stopping the teaching of the Glorious Qur'an. These huffaaz think that they are engaged in the propagation of the Qur'an, but in reality they are obstructing it, through their misconduct and bad intentions. The ulama have not permitted the acceptance of salary for teaching the Glorious Qur'an so that it becomes the primary motive. In fact, the real motive of the teachers should only be to promote the education and propagation of knowlegde of the Qur'an. No salary can be a return for the sublime act of teaching the Qur'an. Such remuneration is only for meeting personal needs and has been permitted when forced by circumstances, in case of dire necessity.

PART–3

FINAL NOTE

The purpose of describing the beauties and virtues of the Holy Qur'an in the foregoing pages is to cultivate a love for it. Love for the Holy Qur'an is needed for developing a love for Almighty Allah, and vice versa. Love for one leads to love for the other.

The creation of man in this world is only for the purpose of acquiring a realization of Allah, and all other creation is for the sake of man. As a Persian poet says:

ابر و باد و مہ و خورشید و فلک درکارند　　تا تو نانے بکف آری و بغفلت نخوری

ہمہ از بہر تو سرگشتہ و فرماں بردار　　شرط انصاف نہ باشد کہ تو فرماں نبری

The clouds, the winds, the moon, the sun and the sky are constantly at work,

So that you earn your living and do not eat in forgetfulness

The whole creation is involved in working for you in obedience,

The law of justice will not be fulfilled if you fail to obey (Allah).

So man should learn a lesson from their punctuality and obedience in their functions of rendering service to him.

Sometimes, as a warning, temporary changes are caused in their functions by Almighty Allah. There is no rain when it should rain; no wind blows when it should blow; similar changes are wrought in the moon and the sun through their eclipses. In short, everything is subject to some change for admonishing those who neglect their duty to their Creator. How astonishing indeed that all these things be made subservient to fulful man's needs, yet their obedience does not lead man to his own submission to the Creator. Love alone provides the best help for obedience and submission to Almighty Allah.

اِنَّ الْمُحِبَّ لِمَنْ يُحِبُّ مُطِيْعٌ

Verily, the lover submits to his beloved.

When a person falls in love with someone, submission and obedience to the beloved becomes his habit and second nature. Disobedience to the beloved becomes as hard as it unwilling obedience to one whom one does not love.

One way of developing love for someone is the observation of his beauty and excellence. This observation may be through the physical senses or through inner perception. If a look at a beautiful face can lead to spontaneous love, a sweet heart-captivating voice can also sometimes produce a magnetic effect. A Persian poet says:

نہ تنہا عشق از دیدار خیزد
بسا کیں دولت از گفتار خیزد

Looks alone do not inspire love;

Often this wealth is attained through charming words.

Sometimes it is the sweetness of voice which draws the heart unconsciously and sometimes it is the beauty and wisdom of expression which causes one to fall in love. Experienced men have suggested that in order to develop love, one should dwell upon the fine attributes of the beloved, and none other than the beloved should find a place in one's heart. It is true even in the case of earthly love that the sight of a beautiful face or a hand urges one to see the other parts of the body of the beloved, so that love may increase and the yearning of the heart may be satisfied, but the stage of satisfaction is never reached. As an Urdu poet says:

مرض بڑھتا گیا جوں جوں دوا کی

The disease worsened as the treatment progressed.

If after sowing the seeds in a field, one does not care to water it, no crop will grow there. Similarly, after falling in love involuntarily, if one does not pay attention to the beloved, this love will vanish in course of time. But if one keeps on visualizing the charming features, the stature as well as the gait and the manner of speaking of the beloved, love will go on increasing every moment.

مکتب عشق کے انداز نرالے دیکھے
اس کو چھٹی نہ ملی جس نے سبق یاد کیا

Unusual are the ways in the school of love, One who learns his lesson gets no leave.

If you forget the lesson of love, there is a riddance for you at once. But the more you learn it, the more you are entrapped. In the same way, if a man wants to develop love with someone worthy of love, he should find out the excellence, the charms and the valued attributes of the beloved and should not remain content with what he knows, but should always be eager to know more about them.

When, even in the case of mortal beloved, the lover is not satisfied with a partial view of the beloved, and is always on the lookout for more chances to see as much of the beloved as he can, then Almighty Allah, the Pure and Sanctified, Who is the fountainhead of all elegance and beauty, (and in fact there is no beauty in this world except His) is certainly such a beloved Whose loveliness and perfection knows no bounds and is limitless. One of the manifestations of His utmost excellence is the Glorious Quran, which is the Word of Allah Himself. What greater plasure can there be for a lover of the Divine, than the fact that the Qur'an is Allah's own Revelation. A poet says:

اے گل بتو خرسندم تو بوئے کسے داری

'O, flower! how pleased am I with you, You have the smell of someone (beloved).

Even if we leave aside the consideration that the Holy Qur'an has its origin in Allah and is His attribute, the relationship that the Qur'an has with Rasulullah (Sallallaho alaihe wasallam) is enough for a Muslim to adore it. Study of the Qur'an itself makes one realise that there is no excellence elsewhere that cannot be found in the Glorious Qur'an.

A poet says:

دامانِ نگہ تنگ و گلِ حسنِ تو بسیار
گل چینِ بہارِ تو زداماں گلہ دارد

The limits of sight are narrow and the flowers of your beauty numerous;
He who plucks the flowers of your spring complains of the inadequacy of his hold.

There is another verse to this effect:

فدا ہو آپ کی کس کس ادا پر
ادائیں لاکھ اور بیتاب دل ایک

How many of your graces can be adored;
Your charms are innumerable and my restless heart is one.

It is evident to the careful reader of the above ahadith, that there is hardly any important thing of this world to which attention has not been drawn. Whatever taste for love and beauty one may possess, its excellence and perfection will be found in the Qur'an. In the first hadith the excellence of the Glorious Qur'an has been established over the beauty, as a whole or in substance, that lies in all worldly things; against the infinite number of excellent attributes that one can imagine, the Glorious Qur'an is found to be superior and matchless in respect of all of them.

The Holy Qur'an is superior to all other lovable things, taken individually or collectively in every respect. If one loves somebody because of the innumerable benefits accruing from him, Almighty Allah has promised (hadith 2) that He will give to the reader of the Qur'an more than that begged of Him by all other persons.

If somebody is adored for his personal greatness, attainment or excellence, Almighty Allah has said (in the same hadith) that the superiority of the Qur'an over all other discourses is like the superiority of Allah Himself over His creation, of the master over his slaves and of the possessor over those possessed.

If anybody is fond of wealth, property, servants and animals, and loves to rear animals of a particular kind, he is warned (in hadith 3) that the knowledge of the Qur'an is far more valuable than any number of good animals acquired even without labour or crime.

If a mystic seeks piety and fear of Allah, and works hard to acquire them, Rasulullah (Sallallaho alaihe wasallam) has said (hadith 4) that those who become proficient in the study of the Qur'an, will be reckoned amongst the angels. The piety of the angels cannot be excelled by anybody, because they cannot pass even a moment in disobedience to Allah.

Also if anybody takes pride in getting double the reward or if he likes that his words should carry a double weight, he should consider how even the reader who falters in his recitation gets double the reward.

If any jealous person can delight only in evil conduct, and jealousy has become a part and parcel of his nature and he cannot give up this vice, he can be rightly jealous of a hafiz whose excellence is worth being jealous of, as said by Rasulullah (Sallallaho alaihe wasallam) (hadith 5).

Let one who relishes fruit and cannot live without it, know that the Qur'an is like citron. If anybody is fond of sweets, he should know that Qur'an is sweeter than dates. (Hadith 6 refers to this.)

If anybody is desirous of honour and dignity and cannot resist being a member of some council, he should know that the Qur'an exalts the rank of its reader, both in this world as well as in the Hereafter. (This is mentioned in hadith 7.)

If anybody wants a sincere and dedicated companion, who should be ready to defend him in every dispute, he should know that the Qur'an is ready to defend its devotee in the court of the Emperor of all emperors (as mentioned in hadith 8.)

If a seeker of subtleties devotes his life to the critical study of various subjects, and appreciation of a delicate point is sufficient to turn him away from the greatest pleasure of this world, he should know that the body of the Qur'an is a treasure full of subtleties (as described in hadith 9).

If somebody attaches importance to discovering hidden secrets, and considers that experience in the criminal investigation department is an accomplishment and devotes his life to acquiring it, he should know that the body of the Holy Qur'an reveals those mysteries whose depths are boundless and to which hadith 10 refers.

Also if one hankers after the construction of lofty buildings and wants his special abode to be on the seventh floor, then verily the Qur'an raises its devotee to the seven thousandth floor in Paradise.

If anybody desires to do business which should bring maximum profit with a minimum of labour, he should know that the recitation of each letter of the Holy Qur'an yields ten blessings (as referred to in Hadith 10).

If anybody hankers after a crown and a throne, and for their sake fights battles in this world, he should consider that the Qur'an gets for the parents of its devotees a crown whose brilliance has no parellel in this world. (This is mentioned in hadith 11.)

If there is any expert in feats of jugglery who can catch a burning coal in his hand or can put a burning match-stick in his mouth, he should realize that the Glorious Qur'an provides safety even against the fire of Hell. (For this see hadith 12.)

There are people who want to develop good relations with government officers and take pride in relating how, as a result of their recommendation to an officer, an accused had not been punished but had been set free. For finding access to these officers, they spend their time and money everyday in flatteries and arrange dinners and so on. Through the intercession of its devotees, the Glorious Qur'an arranges deliverance of ten people who shall have been condemned to Hell. (This is mentioned in hadith 13.)

Now let us consider hadith 14. If somebody is fond of flowers and gardens and loves sweet smells, he should realize that the Holy Qur'an has been compared to musk. If someone loves perfumes and wants to bathe in dried musk, then the example of the Glorious Qur'an is like a musk-vase. This is only for illustration, otherwise musk has no comparison with the fragance of the Holy Qur'an. The particles of this earth cannot be likened to the Heavenly ones. A Persian Poet says:

کارزلفِ تست مشک افشانی اما عاشقاں
مصلحت را تہمتے بر آہوئے چیں بستہ اند

That sprinkling of musk is in fact the act of your looks;
It is out of expediency that lovers accuse the Chinese deer (reported to yield musk).

A person who is often beaten and works for fear of punishment, and persuasion is of no avail to him, will be benefited to know that one whose heart is devoid of the Qur'an, is like a ruined house (as mentioned in hadith 15.)

If a devotee is in search of the best way of all worships and is careful to devote himself to those acts which brings maximum of reward, he should know that recitation of the Holy Qur'an is superior to all other forms of worship, and it is specially mentioned in hadith 16 that it is superior to nafl salaat, fasting, tasbeeh and tahleel' (acclamation).

Some people are deeply interested in pregnant animals, as they fetch more price than the ordinary ones. Rasulullah (Sallallaho alaihe wasallam) has specifically said that the recitation of the Glorious Qur'an is far more precious than such animals (see hadith 17.)

Many people are always worried about their health. They take exercise and bathe every day, they run or go out for a walk in the morning. There are others who are given to grief, worry and anxiety. Rasulullah (Sallallaho alaihe wasallam) has said that the surah Fatihah provides treatment for every disease and the Holy Qur'an cures the ailment of the hearts, as mentioned in hadith 19.

People take pride in so many things that it is difficult to enumerate all these, for example, some boast of their lineage or good habits, others of their popularity or foresight. In fact, a thing of real pride is the Glorious Qur'an, which possesses all beauty and perfection.

As a Persian verse goes:

آنچہ خوباں ہمہ دارند تو تنہا داری

"What all the other beloveds possess collectively, You alone possess all that." (For this see hadith 20.)

Many people are fond of accumulating wealth. For this purpose, they practise miserliness in their food and dress, undergo many hardships and develop a mania that is not satisfied by any amount of wealth. Rasulullah (Sallallaho alaihe wasallam) has advised us that the only thing that should be treasured as much as possible is the Holy Qur'an. No treasure of wealth is better than this. (Hadith 21 refers to this.)

Similarly if anybody is fond of illumination and uses ten electric bulbs to light up his room, he should know that the Holy Qur'an provides the best of lights.

People earnestly desire to receive presents, and they expect gifts from their friends every day. They increase their sphere of acquaintance only with this motive. If anyone of their friends does not send them their share of fruit from his garden, they complain of him. They should realise that the Holy Qur'an is the best giver of gifts. Peace descends on those who recite the Glorious Qur'an. If you are enamoured of someone because he sends you a present everyday, then you would be pleased to know that the attachment with the Glorious Qur'an will bring you precious gifts (see hadith 22).

Some people fawn on a minister, so that he may mention them in the court of the ruler, some flatter the subordinates so that they may praise him before the officer. Sometimes a person entreats others so that they may mention his name in the presence of his beloved. Let all such people learn how, through the Glorious Qur'an, they may make themselves worthy of being mentioned by the beloved Lord Himself. (We find this mentioned in hadith 23.)

If a person is always eager to know about the most favourite thing of the beloved, and he is prepared to perform even the most arduous task to procure it, he should know that there is nothing more lovable to Allah than the Glorious Qur'an.

Some people seek access to the court of the ruler and, with this end in view, they plan and struggle all their lives. Through the Holy Qur'an we can become the special favourites of Almighty Allah, before Whom the greatest of kings is completely helpless (see hadith 24.)

It is strange that in order to become a member of some council, or to join the hunting party of some man in authority, people make sacrifices of time, money and comfort. They use all sorts of mean tactics for approaching them and thereby spoil their own temporal as well as spiritual life, only for the sake of gaining some false honours. Is it then not necessary to make some effort to win the real honour, and become a courtier of the Almighty Lord? If they can spend their whole life for the vanity of this world, we must spend at least a part of our lives for pleasing the very One Who gave us this life.

If you are fond of 'Chistiyyat' and do not find solace except in gatherings of men devotees, you should know that gatherings for recitation of the Qur'an are far more enthralling and attract the ears of the most unmindful.

If you want to attract the attention of our Great Master, you must devote yourself to the recitation of the Glorious Qur'an (This is discussed in ahadith 25 and 26).

If we declare ourselves to be Muslims and also feel proud of Islam, then we should know that it is the command of Rasulullah (Sallallaho alaihe wasallam) that the Glorious Qur'an should be recited in a befitting manner. If our Islam is not a mere declaration and it has really something to do with obedience to Allah and His Prophet (Sallallaho alaihe wasallam), then we should realise that Almighty Allah and Rasulullah (Sallallaho alaihe wasallam) have commanded the recitation of the Qur'an.

If you are a staunch nationalist and love a Turkish cap because you consider it to be a part of Islamic dress, if you are interested in national culture and its propagation by all possible means, if you write articles in the newspapers for this purpose and pass resolutions in public meetings, you should know that Rasulullah (Sallallaho alaihe wasallam) has commanded us to do our best to propagate the Holy Qur'an (see hadith 27.)

At this stage, it will not be out of place to express disappointment about the attitude of our national leaders in respect of the Qur'an. They do not assist in its propagation but, in some ways, help in obstructing it. Learning the Qur'an is looked upon by them as useless and a waste of time and effort. It is also considered an act of mental waste and fruitless toil. It may be that some of them are not in favour of this attitude, but when a group of people are engaged in anti-Qur'anic propaganda, silence on the part of our national leaders is tantamount to helping them in the crime. An Urdu poet says:

ہم نے مانا کہ تغافل نہ کرو گے لیکن
خاک ہو جائیں گے ہم تم کو خبر ہونے تک

We admit, you will not disregard us, but
We will be reduced to dust, before you become aware.

There are many who argue that the institution of teaching and learning the Holy Qur'an is promoted by the religious teachers for earning their bread. This is a vehement attack on the intention of all such teachers. Those who make such accusations are responsible for this calumny, which will have to be proved in the Hereafter. Such people are humbly requested to consider the results of the efforts of these so-called "selfish teachers" and also the would-be results of their own unselfish proposals. Rasulullah (Sallallaho alaihe wasallam) has commanded us to propagate the Holy Book. They should judge for themselves how far they have personally contributed in carrying out the command of Rasulullah (Sallallaho alaihe wasallam). Their attention is drawn to another misconception. Some people might think that they are not a party to this anti-Quranic propaganda and therefore remain unconcerned, but this cannot save them from the wrath of Allah.

The Sahabah (Radhiyallaho anhum) said to Rasulullah (Sallallaho alaihe wasallam):

اَنَهْلِكُ وَفِيْنَا الصّٰلِحُوْنَ قَالَ نَعَمْ اِذَا كَثُرَ الْخُبْثُ

"Shall we be destroyed while there are righteous persons amongst us."

Rasulullah (Sallallaho alaihe wasallam) replied, "Yes (it will be so), when evil shall have overwhelmed." There is another hadith to the same effect, "Almighty Allah ordered that a certain village should be overturned. Jibraa'eel (Alayhis salaam) submitted that in that village there was a person who had never committed any sin. Almighty Allah said that it was true, but though he witnessed so much disobedience to Me (around him), there never did appear a frown on his face (in its disapproval)". In fact, it is because of these ahadith that the ulama do not hesitate to express their disapproval when they see any disobedience to Almighty Allah being committed. It is deplorable that some of our so-called enlightened people consider it to be narrowmindedness on the part of ulama. This so-called broad-mindedness on the part of such people does not absolve them of their responsibility. They should understand that it is not the duty of the ulama alone to check disobedience to the Commandments of Allah. But it is the duty of every Muslim who sees disobedience being committed and has the power to stop it. Bilaal bin Sa'd (Radhiyallaho anho) has said, "If evil deeds are committed secretly, only the evil-doers suffer for it, but if they are committed openly, and nobody prevents them, all the people are punished."

There are some who are fond of history, and travel to consult old books of history wherever they may find them. Such people had better devote themselves to the study of the Qur'an, in which they will find an equivalent to all the books that are admitted to be most authoritative on the past ages.

If you want to acquire such a lofty status that even Prophets be commanded to sit in your company and participate in your gathering, you can do so through the Holy Qur'an. (Hadith 29 refers to this.)

If you are so lazy that you cannot apply yourself to hard work, even then you can earn an honourable status without any labour by means of the Glorious Qur'an. You should sit down and keep on listening silently to children reciting the Qur'an in a school. Thereby you shall earn a lot of reward without any hard work on your part. (This is referred to in hadith 30.)

If you are fond of variety, you can find it in the various ideas and different subjects of the Holy Qur'an, some dealing with mercy, others with chastisement, some relating to different stories and others to various commandments, and so on. You can also change your mode of recitation, low at times and loud at others. (see hadith 31.)

If your sins have passed all limits and you believe, you are to die one day, ahadith 32 to 34 will exhort you to lose no time and start recitation of the Qur'an, because you can never find such an influential intercessor, whose intercession is certain to be accepted. On the other hand, if you are very respectful and your sense of respect and honour makes you avoid disputes with quarrelsome people, even at the cost of your valuable rights, you should try to avoid dispute with the Qur'an on the Day of Judgement, when it will be the strongest complainant, whose contention will be upheld and there will be nobody to defend the respondent.

If you are in need of a guide who would lead you to the house of your beloved, and one would pay any price for such a guidance, you should take to recitation of the Holy Qur'an. Again if you want to safeguard yourself against imprisonment, you have no way out except recitation of the Glorious Qur'an.

If you want to acquire the knowledge of the Prophets and you are its devotee, hadith 35 shows that you can specialize in it through study of the Qur'an. Similarly if you are keen to develop the best of character, you can do so through recitation of the Holy Qur'an.

If you are very fond of hilly places and they alone provide you with the best recreation and satisfaction, you should know that the Holy Qur'an will provide recreation for you on mounds of musk, even on the Day of Judgement, when all creatures will be in a state of terror. (Hadith 36 refers to this.)

If you want to excel in the worship of Almighty Allah by remaining busy in nafl salaat day and night, you should know that teaching and learning the Holy Qur'an is a better means of doing so. (See hadith 37.)

If you want to keep yourself away from all troubles and save yourself from all anxieties, you can do so simply by devoting yourself to the Holy Qur'an. (This is pointed out in hadith 40.)

If you need to consult a physician, you should know that surah Fatihah provides treatment of all diseases, vide hadith 1 of part 2–Concluding Section.

If your numerous daily needs remain unfulfilled, why should you not recite surah Yaaseen, vide hadith 2 of part 2–Concluding Section.

If you hanker after money, you had better read surah Waaqi'ah'. (hadith 3 under Part 2–Concluding Section, refers to this.)

If fear of chastisement in the grave haunts you, it can also be relieved by the Glorious Qur'an, vide hadith 4 of Part II–Concluding Section.

If you are looking for an occupation that will absorb all your time, you can find none better than the Holy Qur'an, vide hadith 5 of Part 2–Concluding Section.

If one has acquired the wealth of the Glorious Qur'an, he should carefully guard against its loss. To lose such blessing, after having got it, is a great tragedy. He should also abstain from such unworthy acts as might convert this blessing into a curse (vide ahadith 6 and 7 of Part 2–Concluding Section.)

I know that I am not competent enough to point out the beauties of the Glorious Qur'an. I have explained them according to my humble understanding. This has, however, opened up a field of contemplation for scholars of deep understanding. According to those who are well versed in the art of love, the following five qualities of the beloved incite love. First, it is the being of the beloved, which one loves. The vicissitudes of time have no effect on the form of the Glorious Qur'an; this guarantees its life and security. Secondly, there should be a natural relationship between the lover and the beloved. The Qur'an is the attribute of Almighty Allah. The relationship between the Creator and His creation, the Master and His servants, needs no explanation. A Persian poet says:

هست ربّ الناس را با جان ناس
اتصالِ بے تکیف و بے قیاس

The Creator of mankind has, with the life of Man, a connection that is incomprehensible and unimaginable.

An Urdu poet says:

سب سے ربطِ آشنائی ہے اسے
دل میں ہر اک کے رسائی ہے اسے

He has a relationship of friendliness with all; He reaches out to the heart of each and everyone.

The third, fourth and fifth qualities are beauty, perfection and benevolence, respectively.

If the foregoing ahadith are studied, keeping the above three qualities in view, scholars will not feel contented with what has been written by me, but they will themselves arrive at the natural conclusion that all considerations that promote love and liking, such as sense of respect and status, fondness and constancy, beauty and perfection, greatness and benevolence, peace and pleasure, wealth and property, in short all such things as promote love are pointed out by Rasulullah (Sallallaho alaihe wasallam) to be possessed in a superb way by the Glorious Qur'an. It is but natural that some of these virtues may be hidden, and may not be directly visible as is the case with most of the wordly valuables. We do not reject a delicious fruit because of its rough outer cover. Nobody starts hating his beloved lady because she wears a veil. He would try, by all possible means, that his lady love unveils herself, but if he does not succeed, the very sight of the veil will thrill him, provided he is sure that it is his beloved indeed behind it. No doubt, the Glorious Qur'an excels in all the virtues that induce love, but if, for any reason, we fail to understand and realize them, it will not be wise on our part to become indifferent and disappointed. We should attribute this failure to our own shortcomings and feel sorry at our loss. We should contemplate more and more upon the beauties of the Glorious Qur'an and become worthy of understanding the Divine Book.

'Uthman (Radhiyallaho anho) and Huzaifah (Radhiyallaho anho) have reported that, if hearts become clean of all filth, then one would never be satiated with reading the Holy Qur'an. Thaabit Banaani (Rahmatullah alaih) said, "I put in a labour of twenty years to learn the Qur'an and it has been giving me solace for these twenty years." Thus it is obvious that whoever repents over his sins, and then meditates upon the Glorious Qur'an, will find it to possess all beauties that all the beloveds collectively possess. I wish I were also such a person. I, however, request the readers that they should not look to the humble personality of the writer, lest it should prevent them from realizing their objective, but they should consider the subject-matter and its source. I am only a means of drawing their attention to these sublime matters.

At this stage, it is just possible that some reader of this book might be blessed by Almighty Allah with an urge to learn the Holy Qur'an by heart and become a hafiz. If anyone has a desire to make his child a hafiz, then no special effort is required because this tender age itself is most conducive to memorizing. But if some grown-up person desires to memorize the Holy Qur'an, I suggest that he should start with a special prayer, which was recommended by Rasulullah (Sallallaho alaihe wasallam) and has been found effective by many people. It has been reported by Tirmizi, Hakim and others as follows:—

Hadhrat Ibn 'Abbas (Radhiyallaho anho) reports that he was once in the company of Rasulullah (Sallallaho alaihe wasallam) when Hadhrat Ali (Radhiyallaho anho) came in and said "O, Prophet of Allah! you are dearer to me than my father and mother. I try to memorize the Qur'an but cannot do so, as it vanishes from my memory." Rasulullah (Sallallaho alaihe wasallam) said, "Shall I tell you of a method that will benefit you as well as those to whom it is conveyed by you? You will then be able to retain whatever you learn." At the request of Hadhrat Ali (Radhiyallaho anho) Rasulullah (Sallallaho alaihe wasallam) said, "When the night preceding Friday comes, rise up in its last third portion, if possible, for that would be excellent, because this is the best part of the night, as this is the time when angels descend and prayers are specially granted at this hour. It was for this time that Hadhrat Yaqub (Alayhis salaam) had been waiting when he had said to his sons that he would, in the near future, pray to his Lord for forgiveness for them. If it be difficult to get up at that time, then you should do so in the middle part of the night and if even that be not possible, offer the four rak'aat in the early part of the night. After reciting surah Fatihah in each rak'aat, surah Yaaseen should be recited in the first rak'at, surah Dukhaan in the second, surah Alif Laam Meem Sajdah in the third and surah Mulk in the fourth. After completing at-tahiyaat (glorification of Allah in the sitting posture in salat) you should praise and glorify Almighty Allah abundantly, invoke peace and blessings on me and on all the Prophets, and seek forgiveness for all believers and those Muslim brethern who have passed away before you, and then recite the following du'a."

Before the du'a it may be mentioned that several forms of 'hamd-o-thana' (praise and glorification), etc., which are required to be recited before this du'a are reported in other ahadith given in 'Shurooh-e-Hisn' and 'Munaajaat Maqbul'. Those who can consult these books should themselves find the details and thereby enrich their du'a. For the convenience of those who cannot read these books, brief extracts are given as under:

اَلْحَمْدُ لِلّٰهِ رَبِّ الْعٰلَمِيْنَ عَدَدَ خَلْقِهٖ وَرِضَا نَفْسِهٖ وَزِنَةَ عَرْشِهٖ وَمِدَادَ كَلِمَاتِهٖ ،
اَللّٰهُمَّ لَآاُحْصِىْ ثَنَاءً عَلَيْكَ اَنْتَ كَمَا اَثْنَيْتَ عَلٰى نَفْسِكَ اَللّٰهُمَّ صَلِّ وَسَلِّمْ
وَبَارِكْ عَلٰى سَيِّدِنَا مُحَمَّدِ النَّبِىِّ الْاُمِّىِّ الْهَاشِمِىِّ وَعَلٰى آلِهٖ وَاَصْحَابِهِ الْبَرَرَةِ
الْكِرَامِ وَعَلٰى سَائِرِ الْاَنْبِيَآءِ وَالْمُرْسَلِيْنَ وَالْمَلٰٓئِكَةِ الْمُقَرَّبِيْنَ رَبَّنَا اغْفِرْلَنَا
وَلِاِخْوَانِنَا الَّذِيْنَ سَبَقُوْنَا بِالْاِيْمَانِ وَلَاتَجْعَلْ فِىْ قُلُوْبِنَا غِلًّا لِّلَّذِيْنَ آمَنُوْا رَبَّنَا اِنَّكَ
رَءُوْفٌ رَّحِيْمٌ اَللّٰهُمَّ اغْفِرْلِىْ وَلِوَالِدَىَّ وَلِجَمِيْعِ الْمُؤْمِنِيْنَ وَالْمُؤْمِنَاتِ وَالْمُسْلِمِيْنَ
وَالْمُسْلِمَاتِ اِنَّكَ سَمِيْعٌ مُّجِيْبُ الدَّعْوَاتِ

All praise be to Allah, the Lord of Worlds, praise up to the (countless) number of His creatures, matching His pleasure, weighty as the weight of His Throne and expansive as the ink (needed) for the writing of His Words. O, Allah! I cannot comprehend the praise due to Thee. Thou art as Thou praisest Thyself. O, Allah! send Thy peace, blessings and prosperity upon our Chief, the Ummi (not taught by any one), the Hashimite Prophet Muhammad and upon all the Prophets and Apostles and upon Thy favourite angels. O, Allah! forgive us and our brethren who preceded us in faith, and place not in our hearts any rancour towards those who believe. O, our Lord! You are Most Compassionate and Most Merciful. O, Master of the Worlds! forgive me and my parents and all believers and Muslims, whether male or female. Verily, Thou art the Hearer and Granter of our supplications.

After this, the following du'a which was taught by Rasulullah (Sallallaho alaihe wasallam) to Hadhrat Ali (Radhiyallaho anho), as mentioned in the above hadith, should be read:

اَللّٰهُمَّ ارْحَمْنِىْ بِتَرْكِ الْمَعَاصِىْ اَبَدًا مَّا اَبْقَيْتَنِىْ وَارْحَمْنِىْ اَنْ اَتَكَلَّفَ مَالَا يَعْنِيْنِىْ
وَارْزُقْنِىْ حُسْنَ النَّظَرِ فِيْمَا يُرْضِيْكَ عَنِّىْ اَللّٰهُمَّ بَدِيْعَ السَّمٰوٰتِ وَالْاَرْضِ

ذَاالْجَلَالِ وَالْاِكْرَامِ وَالْعِزَّةِ الَّتِىْ لَاتُرَامُ اَسْئَلُكَ يَااَللّٰهُ يَارَحْمٰنُ بِجَلَالِكَ وَنُوْرِ
وَجْهِكَ اَنْ تُلْزِمَ قَلْبِىْ حِفْظَ كِتَابِكَ كَمَا عَلَّمْتَنِىْ وَارْزُقْنِىْ اَنْ اَقْرَأَهُ عَلَى النَّحْوِ
الَّذِىْ يُرْضِيْكَ عَنِّىْ اَللّٰهُمَّ بَدِيْعَ السَّمٰوَاتِ وَالْاَرْضِ ذَاالْجَلَالِ وَالْاِكْرَامِ وَالْعِزَّةِ
الَّتِىْ لَا تُرَامُ اَسْئَلُكَ يَااَللّٰهُ يَارَحْمٰنُ بِجَلَالِكَ وَنُوْرِ وَجْهِكَ اَنْ تُنَوِّرَ بِكِتَابِكَ
بَصَرِىْ وَاَنْ تُطْلِقَ بِهِ لِسَانِىْ وَاَنْ تُفَرِّجَ بِهِ عَنْ قَلْبِىْ وَاَنْ تَشْرَحْ بِهِ صَدْرِىْ وَاَنْ
تَغْسِلَ بِهِ بَدَنِىْ فَاِنَّهُ لَا يُعِيْنُنِىْ عَلَى الْحَقِّ غَيْرُكَ وَلَا يُؤْتِيْهِ اِلَّا اَنْتَ وَلَا حَوْلَ وَلَا
قُوَّةَ اِلَّا بِاللّٰهِ الْعَلِىِّ الْعَظِيْمِ

'O, Allah! have mercy upon me, so that I always abstain from sinful deeds as long as I am alive, be kind to me so that I do not toil in vain pursuits, and bless me with solace in that which pleases Thee. O, Allah! the Originator of Heavens and Earth, Master of Glory and Honour, Lord of such Majesty, attainment of which cannot even be conceived. O, Allah! the Most Beneficent, I pray in the name of Thy Majesty and Effulgence of Thy Countenance, to impose upon by heart the memorizing of Thy Book, as Thou hast taught me the same, and grant me such a manner of recitation as pleases Thee. O, Allah! the Originator of Heavens and Earth, Master of Glory and Honour, Lord of such Majesty, attainment of which cannot even be conceived! O, Allah, the Most Beneficent I pray in the name of Thy Majesty and Effulgence of Thy Countenance, to illumine my vision with the noor of Thy Book, bless my tongue with a flow in its reading, and through its blessing remove heaviness of my heart, open my mind, and wash away (the sins of) my body. Certainly there is none except Thee to support me in the cause of truth, and none except Thee can fulfil this desire of mine. There can be no safeguard (against evil) nor any power (over virtue) except with the help of Allah, the Most High, the Most Great.

Rasulullah (Sallallaho alaihe wasallam) further said to Hadhrat Ali (Radhiyallaho anho), "Repeat this act for three, five or seven Fridays. If Allah so wills, your prayer will certainly be granted. I swear by Him Who made me Prophet that acceptance of His prayer will never be missed by any believer."

Ibn 'Abbas (Radhiyallaho anho) reports that hardly had five or seven Fridays passed when Hadhrat 'Ali (Radhiyallaho anho) came to Rasulullah (Sallallaho alaihe wasallam) and said, "Previously I used to learn about four ayaat but I was not able to retain them, and now I learn about forty and I can remember them as clearly as if I have the Qur'an open before me. Previously when I heard a hadith and then repeated it I could not retain it, and now I hear ahadith and, when I narrate them to others, I do not miss a single word."

May Almighty Allah bless me and you with memorizing of the Glorious Qur'an and the 'ahadith' by the grace of His Prophet's beneficence.

وَصَلَّى اللّٰهُ تَبَارَكَ وَتَعَالٰى عَلٰى خَيْرِ خَلْقِهٖ سَيِّدِنَا وَمَوْلَانَا مُحَمَّدٍ وَّاٰلِهٖ وَصَحْبِهٖ وَسَلَّمَ بِرَحْمَتِكَ يَاۤاَرْحَمَ الرَّاحِمِيْنَ

O, Almighty Allah! by Thy Mercy, send Thy Peace and blessings on Mohammad (Sallallaho alaihe wasallam), the best of Thy creation and our Chief, and on his Family and on his Companions. Thou art the Most Compassionate of all the Most Merciful ones.

PART 4

COMPLEMENTARY NOTE

The forty ahadith given in the foregoing pages relate to a special subject-matter and as such it has not been possible to maintain brevity. These days, we have become easy-going and it is difficult to bear even slight hardships in the cause of religion. In view of this, I give here another set of forty ahadith, which are very brief and are reported at one place from Rasulullah (Sallallaho alaihe wasallam). The beauty about it is that it embraces all the vital teachings of Islam and is unique in this respect. It is given in 'Kanzul-Ummaal' and ascribed to a group of the earliest scholars of hadith. Of the scholars of later times, Maulana Qutbuddin Muhajir Makki (Rahmatullah alaih) has also mentioned it. Let those having a zeal for Islam commit at least this hadith to memory and earn a bounteous reward for doing so little. This hadith is given below:

عَنْ سَلْمَانَ رَضِیَ اللّٰهُ عَنْهُ قَالَ سَأَلْتُ رَسُوْلَ اللّٰهِ ﷺ عَنِ الْاَرْبَعِیْنَ حَدِیْثًا نِالَّتِیْ
قَالَ مَنْ حَفِظَهَا مِنْ اُمَّتِیْ دَخَلَ الْجَنَّةَ قُلْتُ وَمَا هِیَ یَارَسُوْلَ اللّٰهِ قَالَ:
اَنْ تُؤْمِنَ بِاللّٰهِ وَالْیَوْمِ الْاٰخِرِ وَالْمَلٰٓئِکَةِ وَالْکُتُبِ وَالنَّبِیّٖنَ وَالْبَعْثِ بَعْدَ الْمَوْتِ
وَالْقَدْرِ خَیْرِهٖ وَشَرِّهٖ مِنَ اللّٰهِ تَعَالٰی وَاَنْ تَشْهَدَ اَنْ لَّآاِلٰهَ اِلَّا اللّٰهُ وَاَنَّ مُحَمَّدًا رَّسُوْلُ
اللّٰهِ وَتُقِیْمَ الصَّلٰوةَ بِوُضُوْءٍ سَابِغٍ کَامِلٍ لِوَقْتِهَا وَتُؤْتِیَ الزَّکٰوةَ وَتَصُوْمَ رَمْضَانَ
وَتَحُجَّ الْبَیْتَ اِنْ کَانَ لَکَ مَالٌ وَتُصَلِّیَ اثْنَتَیْ عَشَرَةَ رَکْعَةً فِیْ یَوْمٍ وَلَیْلَةٍ وَالْوِتْرَ
لَاتَتْرُکْهُ فِیْ کُلِّ لَیْلَةٍ وَلَاتُشْرِکْ بِاللّٰهِ شَیْئًا وَلَاتَعُقَّ وَالِدَیْکَ وَلَاتَأْکُلْ مَالَ الْیَتِیْمِ
ظُلْمًا وَلَاتَشْرَبِ الْخَمْرَ وَلَاتَزْنِ وَلَاتَحْلِفْ بِاللّٰهِ کَاذِبًا وَلَاتَشْهَدْ شَهَادَةَ زُوْرٍ
وَلَاتَعْمَلْ بِالْهَوٰی وَلَاتَغْتَبْ اَخَاکَ الْمُسْلِمَ وَلَاتَقْذِفِ الْمُحْصَنَةَ وَلَاتَغُلَّ اَخَاکَ
الْمُسْلِمَ وَلَاتَلْعَبْ وَلَاتَلْهُ مَعَ اللَّاهِیْنَ وَلَاتَقُلْ لِلْقَصِیْرِ یَاقَصِیْرُ تُرِیْدُ عَیْبَهٗ
وَلَاتَسْخَرْ بِاَحَدٍ مِّنَ النَّاسِ وَلَاتَمْشِ بِالنَّمِیْمَةِ بَیْنَ الْاَخَوَیْنِ وَاشْکُرِ اللّٰهَ تَعَالٰی
عَلٰی نِعْمَتِهٖ وَاصْبِرْ عَلَی الْبَلَاءِ وَالْمُصِیْبَةِ وَلَاتَأْمَنْ مِنْ عِقَابِ اللّٰهِ وَلَاتَقْطَعْ

اَقْرِبَآءَكَ وَصِلْهُمْ وَلَاتَلْعَنْ اَحَدًا مِّنْ خَلْقِ اللهِ وَاَكْثِرْ مِنَ التَّسْبِيْحِ وَالتَّكْبِيْرِ
وَالتَّهْلِيْلِ وَلَاتَدَعْ حُضُوْرَ الْجُمُعَةِ وَالْعِيْدَيْنِ وَاعْلَمْ اَنَّ مَآاَصَابَكَ لَمْ يَكُنْ
لِيُخْطِئَكَ وَمَا اَخْطَأَكَ لَمْ يَكُنْ لِّيُصِيْبَكَ وَلَاتَدَعْ قِرَاءَةَ الْقُرْآنِ عَلٰى كُلِّ حَالٍ

(رواه الحافظ أبوالقاسم بن عبدالرحمن بن محمد بن إسحاق بن مندة والحافظ أبوالحسن علي بن أبى القاسم بن بابويه الرازى فى الأربعين وابن عساكر والرافعى عن سلمان)

Salman (Radhiyallaho anha) narrates that he had asked Rasulullah (Sallallaho alaihe wasallam) about the forty 'ahadith' concerning which he had said that, if anyone from amongst his Ummat memorized them, he would enter Paradise. I asked which ahaadith are they? Rasulullah (Sallallaho alaihe wasallam) replied: "You should believe:

(1) In Allah, i.e. in His Person and Attributes; and

(2) The Last Day; and

(3) The Angels; and

(4) The earlier Divine Books; and

(5) All the Prophets; and

(6) The rising after death; and

(7) The destiny, i.e. all that is good or bad is from Allah; and

(8) That you bear witness that there is none worthy of worship except Allah, and that Mohammad (Sallallaho alaihe wasallam) is His Messenger; and

(9) That at the time of each salaat you make good salaat at its proper time after performing a perfect wudhu; and perfect wudhu is one performed with due regard even to adaab (due respects) and mustahabbaat (plural of mustahab–desirable action). Wudhu should preferably be performed afresh at the time of each salaat, although the previous wudhu subsists, and this is mustahab. To make good salaat means to be mindful of its component parts like fardh, sunnat and mustahab. In another hadith, it is said that during salaat the rows should be straight, i.e. the rows should not be curved and there should be no unoccupied space between them. This is also included in the meaning of establishing salaat.

إِنَّ تَسْوِيَةَ الصُّفُوْفِ مِنْ اِقَامَةِ الصَّلٰوةِ

(10) Pay the Zakaat (obligatory charity on wealth exceeding a prescribed limit) and

(11) Fast during the month of Ramadhan; and

(12) Perform Hajj if you have wealth;

The availability of wealth has particularly been mentioned, because want of wealth is generally made an excuse for non-performance of Hajj. Otherwise it is evident that the other prerequisites that make the Hajj obligatory should also exist.

(13) You should perform the twelve raka'aat sunnat-e-mu'akkadah salaat' every day; (According to other ahadith these twelve raka'aat are detailed as two raka'aat before the two fardh raka'aat of Fajr salaat, four before and two raka'aat after the four fardh raka'aat of Zohr, two after the three fardh raka'aat of Maghrib, and two after the four fardh raka'aat of Ishaa'.).

(14) You should never miss the Witr salaat at night; Witr salaat is waajib (compulsory, but less than fardh and more important than sunnat) and is, therefore, specially emphasized.

(15) You should ascribe no partners unto Allah;

(16) You should not disobey your parents;

(17) You should not devour the property of orphans unjustly; (Unjustly implies that there is no harm in using the belongings of an orphan in a lawful manner, as is the case under certain circumstances.)

(18) You should not drink wine;

(19) You should not commit adultery;

(20) You should not indulge in false oaths;

(21) You should not give false evidence;

(22) You should not yield to your base desires;

(23) You should not backbite on a Muslim brother;

(24) You should not bring a false charge against a chaste woman (or a chaste man);

(25) You should not bear ill-will towards your Muslim brethren;

(26) You should not indulge in useless amusements;

(27) You should not join the idle spectators;

(28) You should not call a short-statured person "O, you short-statured one!" with the intention of finding fault with him; (there is no harm if a person is called by a derogatory nickname which has become associated with him, provided the nickname is used neither as a taunt nor as a term of abuse. But using it as a taunt is not permissible.)

(29) You should not indulge in jokes at the cost of others;

(30) You should not indulge in slanders among Muslims;

(31) You should be ever grateful to Allah for His bounties;

(32) You should be steadfast in suffering and calamity;

(33) You should not be heedless of chastisement by Allah;

(34) You should not sever your ties of kinship with your relatives;

(35) You should discharge your obligations to your relatives;

(36) You should not curse any creature of Allah;

(37) You should remember and glorify Allah by repeating سُبْحَانَ اللهِ (Subhaanallaah), اَلْحَمْدُ لِلّٰهِ (Alhamdulillaah) (all praise is for Allah), لَا اِلٰهَ اِلَّا اللهُ (Laa ilaaha illallaah) (there is no god but Allah) and اَللهُ اَكْبَرُ (Allaahu akbar) frequently;

(38) You should not miss the Friday and Eid Salaat

(39) You should believe that whatever good or bad lot befalls you was predestined and could not be avoided, and whatever you have missed, you were ordained to do so; and

(40) You should not give up the recitation of the Qur'an under any circumstances."

Salmaan (Radhiyallaho anho) says that he asked Rasulullah (Sallallaho alaihe wasallam): "What reward would be given to one who memorizes these ahaadith?" Rasulullah (Sallallaho alaihe wasallam) said, "Allah will raise him up in the company of the Prophets and the ulama."

May Almighty Allah, through His sheer Grace, forgive all our sins and include us in the company of His obedient servants by His mercy alone. This is not beyond His generous grace. The readers are humbly requested to remember this sinner in their prayers.

وَمَا تَوْفِيْقِىْ اِلَّا بِاللّٰهِ عَلَيْهِ تَوَكَّلْتُ وَاِلَيْهِ اُنِيْبُ

MOHAMMAD ZAKARIYA KANDHLAVI,
Mazahir-ul-Ulum, Saharanpur.
29 Zilhaj 1348 HIJRI.

Virtues of SALAAT

Revised translation of the Urdu book Faza'il-e-Namaaz

Virtues of Salaat

فَضَائِلِ نماز

By:-

Shaikhul Hadith Maulana Muhammad Zakariyyah Kaandhlawi (Rah)

translated by

Abdul Rashid Arsahd

ادارہ اشاعتِ دینیات (پرائیویٹ) لمیٹڈ

idara.com

IDARA ISHA'AT-E-DINIYAT (P) LTD.

VRITUES OF SALAAT

By: Shaikhul Hadith
Maulana Muhammad Zakariyya Kaandhlawi (Rah)

Edition 2001

ISBN:- 81-7101-327-9

Published by:
IDARA ISHA'AT-E-DINIYAT (P) LTD.
168/2, Jha House, Hazrat Nizamuddin
New Delhi-110 013 (India)
Tel.: 6926832, 6926833
Fax: +91-11-6322787,4352786
Email: **sales@idara.com**
Visit us at: **www.idara.com**

Printed at:
Nice Printing Press, Delhi

CONTENTS

PART II.—IMPORTANCE OF JAMAAT

CHAPTER I.—THE REWARD OF JAMAAT

CHAPTER II.—WARNING AND REPROACH ON DISCARDING OF JAMAAT

PART III.—IMPORTANCE OF SINCERITY AND DEVOTION IN SALAAT

CHAPTER I.—QUOTATIONS FROM THE HOLY QUR'AN

بِسْمِ اللهِ الرَّحْمٰنِ الرَّحِيْمِ

IN THE NAME OF ALLAH, THE MOST GRACIOUS, THE MOST MERCIFUL.

AUTHOR'S FOREWORD

نَحْمَدُهُ وَنُصَلِّىْ وَنُسَلِّمُ عَلٰى رَسُوْلِهِ الْكَرِيْمِ وَاٰلِهِ وَصَحْبِهِ وَاَتْبَاعِهِ الْحُمَاةِ لِلدِّيْنِ الْقَوِيْمِ

"We glorify Allah and ask blessings on and salute His noble Prophet, his companions and those who follow him in upholding the cause of the right religion."

The indifference of Muslims towards practising Islam these days is too well known. So much so that even Salaat, which is the most important pillar of Islam (after Imaan) and the first and the foremost thing to be reckoned on the Day of Judgement, is being badly neglected. Although every call to 'Islam', nowadays, seems to be only a cry in the wilderness, yet experience shows that efforts in this direction are not altogether fruitless. The glorious words of the Holy Prophet (Sallallaho alaihe wasallam) are sure to benefit those with a receptive and submissive frame of mind. With this idea in view and to comply with the long-standing request of some of my dear friends, I have taken upon myself to write this booklet, which is the second of the series on 'Tabligh', the first one being "Virtues of Tabligh."

وَمَا تَوْفِيْقِىْ اِلَّا بِاللهِ ، عَلَيْهِ تَوَكَّلْتُ وَاِلَيْهِ اُنِيْبُ

And my success can only come from Allah! And in Him I trust and unto Him I turn . . . . (XI:88)

FOREWORD

The present-day Muslims, in respect of their behaviour towards Salaat, can be divided into three groups. A large number among them is totally unmindful of Salaat. Quite a few observe their Salaat, but are not particular about Jamaat. Then there are those who are regular in their Salaat (with Jamaat), but their Salaat is devoid of the care and thoroughness which it demands. I have divided the book into three parts to suit the requirements of each group. In each part, the illustrious Ahaadith of the Holy Prophet (Sallallaho alaihe wasallam) are quoted with their simple translation. The translation is idiomatic and not literal. Explanatory notes have been added wherever necessary. The names of the books of Hadith from which the quotations are taken have also been mentioned for reference.

PART I

IMPORTANCE OF SALAAT

There are two Chapters in this part. The first one is on 'Importance of salaat, and the second of 'Warning and Reproach' for those who neglect or discard salaat.

CHAPTER I

THE REWARDS OF SALAAT

Hadith.—1

عَنِ ابْنِ عُمَرَ رَضِىَ اللّٰهُ عَنْهُ قَالَ قَالَ رَسُوْلُ اللّٰهِ ﷺ بُنِىَ الْاِسْلَامُ عَلٰى خَمْسٍ شَهَادَةِ اَنْ لَّا اِلٰهَ اِلَّا اللّٰهُ وَاَنَّ مُحَمَّدًا عَبْدُهٗ وَرَسُوْلُهٗ وَاِقَامِ الصَّلٰوةِ وَاِيْتَاءِ الزَّكٰوةِ وَالْحَجِّ وَصَوْمِ رَمَضَانَ (متفق عليه) وقال المنذري في الترغيب رواه البخاري ومسلم وغيرهما عن غير واحد من الصحابة

Hadhrat Abdullah bin Umar (Radhiyallaho anho) narrates that he heard the Prophet (Sallallaho alaihe wasallam) saying:

"Islam is founded on five pillars: bearing witness that there is no god but Allah, and Muhammad (Sallallaho alaihe wasallam) is His servant and apostle; establishment of salaat; paying of Zakaat; performance of Hajj; and fasting in Ramadhaan."

The Prophet (Sallallaho alaihe wasallam) has compared Islam to a canopy resting on five supports. The Kalimah is the central support and the other four pillars of Islam are, so to say, the remaining four supports, one at each corner of the canopy. Without the central support, the canopy cannot possibly stand, and if any one of the corner supports is missing a collapse will result in the defective corner. Now, let us judge for ourselves how far we have kept up the canopy of Islam. Is there really any pillar that is being held in its proper place?

The five pillars of Islam mentioned in this Hadith signify the most essential duties of a Muslim. Although a Muslim cannot do without any one of them, yet salaat in Islam occupies a position next only to Imaan. Hadhrat Abdullah bin Mas'ood (Radhiyallaho anho) says:

"Once, I inquired of the Holy Prophet (Sallallaho alaihe wasallam), which act (of man) was the dearest to Allah. The Prophet replied, 'salaat'. I then inquired which act came next (in order of merit) and the Prophet replied,

'Kindness to parents'. I again asked what was next and he answered 'Jihaad'."

Mulla Ali Qari (Rahmatullah alaih) has quoted this Hadith in support of the belief that salaat is the most important religious duty after Imaan. This is further corroborated by a hadith, in which the Holy Prophet (Sallallaho alaihe wasallam) is reported to have said:

اَلصَّلٰوةُ خَيْرُ مَوْضُوْعٍ

"Salaat is the best of all that has been ordained by Allah."

Hadith.—II

عَنْ اَبِي ذَرٍ رَضِيَ اللّٰهُ عَنْهُ اَنَّ النَّبِيَّ ﷺ خَرَجَ فِيْ الشِّتَاءِ وَالْوَرَقُ يَتَهَافَتُ فَاَخَذَ بِغُصْنٍ مِنْ شَجَرَةٍ قَالَ فَجَعَلَ ذٰلِكَ الْوَرَقُ يَتَهَافَتُ فَقَالَ يَااَبَا ذَرٍ قُلْتُ لَبَّيْكَ يَارَسُوْلَ اللّٰهِ قَالَ اِنَّ الْعَبْدَ الْمُسْلِمَ لَيُصَلِّى الصَّلَاةَ يُرِيْدُ بِهَا وَجْهَ اللّٰهِ فَتَهَافَتَ عَنْهُ ذُنُوْبُهُ كَمَا تَهَافَتَ هٰذَا الْوَرَقُ عَنْ هٰذِهِ الشَّجَرَةِ

(رواه احمد باسناد حسن كما فى الترغيب)

"Hadhrat Abu Zar (Radhiyallaho anho) narrates that once the Holy Prophet (Sallallaho alaihe wasallam) came out of his house. It was autumn and the leaves were falling off the trees. He caught hold of a branch of a tree and its leaves began to drop in large number. At this he remarked, 'O, Abu Zar! (Radhiyallaho anho) when a Muslim offers his salaat to please Allah, his sins are shed away from him just as these leaves are falling off this tree."

In autumn, usually, the leaves of the trees fall in large numbers, so much so that on some trees not a single leaf is left behind. The same is the effect of salaat performed with sincerity and devotion. All the sins of the person offering salaat are wiped off. It should, however, be remembered that according to the verdict of the theologians, it is only the saghaa'ir (minor sins) that are forgiven by the performance of salaat and other services. The kabaa'ir (major sins) are not pardoned without repentance. We should, therefore, in addition to saying salaat, be particular about doing taubah (repentance) and istighfaar (seeking forgiveness). Allah may, however, pardon, by His bountiful Grace, even the kabaa'ir of any person because of his salaat.

Hadith.—III

عَنْ اَبِيْ عُثْمَانَ رَضِيَ اللّٰهُ عَنْهُ قَالَ كُنْتُ مَعَ سَلْمَانَ تَحْتَ شَجَرَةٍ فَاَخَذَ غُصْنًا
مِنْهَا يَابِسًا فَهَزَّهٗ حَتّٰى تَحَاتَّ وَرَقُهٗ ثُمَّ قَالَ يَااَبَا عُثْمَانَ اَلَا تَسْاَلُنِيْ لِمَ اَفْعَلُ هٰذَا
قُلْتُ وَلِمَ تَفْعَلُهٗ قَالَ هٰكَذَا فَعَلَ بِيْ رَسُوْلُ اللّٰهِ ﷺ وَاَنَا مَعَهٗ تَحْتَ الشَّجَرَةِ فَاَخَذَ
مِنْهَا غُصْنًا يَابِسًا حَتّٰى تَحَاتَّ وَرَقُهٗ فَقَالَ يَاسَلْمَانُ اَلَا تَسْاَلُنِيْ لِمَ اَفْعَلُ هٰذَا قُلْتُ
وَلِمَ تَفْعَلُهٗ قَالَ اِنَّ الْمُسْلِمَ اِذَا تَوَضَّاَ فَاَحْسَنَ الْوُضُوْءَ ثُمَّ صَلَّى الصَّلٰوتِ
الْخَمْسَ تَحَاتَّتْ خَطَايَاهُ كَمَا تَحَاتَّ هٰذَا الْوَرَقُ
وَقَالَ اَقِمِ الصَّلٰوةَ طَرَفَيِ النَّهَارِ وَزُلَفًا مِّنَ اللَّيْلِ اِنَّ الْحَسَنَاتِ يُذْهِبْنَ السَّيِّاٰتِ
ذٰلِكَ ذِكْرٰى لِلذّٰكِرِيْنَ (رواه احمد والنسائی والطبرانی و رواة احمد محتج بہم فی الصحیح الا علی
بن زید کما فی الترغیب

Hadhrat Abu Uthman (Radhiyallaho anho) says: "I was once sitting under a tree with Hadhrat Salmaan (Radhiyallaho anho). He caught hold of a dry branch of the tree and shook it till all its leaves fell off. He then said to me, "O, Abu Uthman! (Radhiyallaho anho) Will you not ask me why I am doing this?" "Do tell me," I entreated. He said, "The Apostle of Allah had done exactly like this before me, while I was with him under a tree. He caught a dry branch of it and shook it, till all its leaves fell off". At this he said: 'O, Salmaan! (Radhiyallaho anho) will you not ask me why I am doing this?' I replied: 'Do tell me why you are doing this?' He remarked: "Verily when a Muslim takes wudhu properly and then observes his salaat five times a day, his sins fall off just as these leaves have fallen off. He then recited the following verse of the Holy Qur'an:

اَقِمِ الصَّلٰوةَ طَرَفَيِ النَّهَارِ وَزُلَفًا مِّنَ الَّيْلِ اِنَّ الْحَسَنَاتِ يُذْهِبْنَ السَّيِّاٰتِ ذٰلِكَ
ذِكْرٰى لِلذّٰكِرِيْنَ

"Establish salaat at the two ends of the day, and at the approaches of the night. Verily, good deeds annul ill deeds. This is a reminder for the mindful. (XI: 114)"

The behaviour of Hadhrat Salmaan (Radhiyallaho anho) in the above hadith displays the profound love which the Sahabah had for the Prophet (Sallallaho alaihe wasallam). They would often cherish the sweet memories of the time when the Prophet (Sallallaho alaihe wasallam) was living among them. They would, while quoting him, enact exactly what they had seen him doing at a particular moment.

It is really very difficult to cover all the traditions of the Holy Prophet (Sallallaho alaihe wasallam), which deal with the importance of salaat and which declare forgiveness for those who guard it. As had already been said before, the theologians restrict this declaration of forgiveness to saghaa'ir (minor sins) only, but in the text of the hadith there is no such restriction. My learned father gave me two reasons for this. Firstly, it does not really become a Muslim to commit any of the kabaa'ir (major sins). If perchance any such sins are committed by him, he cannot rest in peace (due to inherent fear of Allah in him) until he washes them with his tears of repentance in crying before Allah. Secondly, the person who performs his salaat with sincerity and thoroughness is very likely to do istighfaar quite a number of times daily. Look for instance at the closing prayer of salaat itself, viz:

اللّٰهُمَّ اِنِّیْ ظَلَمْتُ نَفْسِیْ ظُلْمًا كَثِيْرًا وَّلَايَغْفِرُ الذُّنُوْبَ اِلَّا اَنْتَ فَاغْفِرْلِیْ مَغْفِرَةً مِّنْ عِنْدِكَ وَارْحَمْنِیْ اِنَّكَ اَنْتَ الْغَفُوْرُ الرَّحِيْمُ

"O, My Lord! I have wronged my soul a great wrong, and none forgiveth sins save Thou alone. Then forgive me and have mercy on me. Verily, Thou art the Forgiving, the Merciful."

In the above hadith, mention is made of wudhu to be done properly. We should, therefore, be sure of the regulations about wudhu and try to observe all of these. For example, take the case of miswaak. It is sunnat of wudhu, but is very often neglected. It is said in a hadith that the salaat offered after doing miswaak is seventy times superior to the salaat without miswaak. In another hadith, use of miswaak has been enjoined very strongly, and the following benefits are attributed to it:—

"It cleanses and sweetens the mouth and checks its bad smell."

"It is a cause of Allah's pleasure and a blow to the Devil."

"Allah and his angels love the person doing miswaak."

"It strengthens the gums and improves eye-sight."

"It is a purge against bile and phlegm."

To crown all, "It is a sunnah i.e. the practice of our beloved Prophet (Sallallaho alaihe wasallam)."

As many as seventy virtues of the miswaak have been enumerated by the theologians. It is said that a person in the habit of miswaak dies with the Kalimah on his lips. The rewards of taking wudhu properly are very many. It is mentioned in ahaadith that the parts of body washed in wudhu shall glitter on the Day of Judgement and, by this (distinction), the Prophet (Sallallaho alaihe wasallam) will at once recognise his followers.

Hadith.—IV(a)

عَنْ اَبِيْ هُرَيْرَةَ رَضِىَ اللّٰهُ عَنْهُ قَالَ سَمِعْتُ رَسُوْلَ اللّٰهِ ﷺ يَقُوْلُ اَرَاَيْتُمْ لَوْ اَنَّ نَهْرًا بِبَابِ اَحَدِكُمْ يَغْتَسِلُ فِيْهِ كُلَّ يَوْمٍ خَمْسَ مَرَّاتٍ هَلْ بَقِىَ مِنْ دَرَنِهٖ شَيْءٌ قَالُوْا لَايَبْقٰى مِنْ دَرَنِهٖ شَيْءٌ قَالَ فَكَذٰلِكَ مَثَلُ الصَّلَوٰتِ الْخَمْسِ يَمْحُوْ اللّٰهُ بِهِنَّ الْخَطَايَا رواه البخاري ومسلم والترمذي والنسائى ورواه ابن ماجه من حديث عثمان

"Hadhrat Abu Hurairah (Radhiyallaho anho) narrates that once the Prophet (Sallallaho alaihe wasallam) asked his companions, 'Do you believe that dirt can remain on a person bathing five times a day in a brook running in front of his door?' 'No', replied the companions, 'No dirt can remain on his body.' The Prophet (Sallallaho alaihe wasallam) remarked: 'So, exactly similar is the effect of salaat offered five times a day. With the Grace of Allah, it washes away all the sins'."

Hadith.—IV(b)

عَنْ جَابِرٍ رَضِىَ اللّٰهُ عَنْهُ قَالَ قَالَ رَسُوْلُ اللّٰهِ ﷺ مَثَلُ الصَّلَوٰتِ الْخَمْسِ كَمَثَلِ نَهْرٍ جَارٍ غَمْرٍ عَلٰى بَابِ اَحَدِكُمْ يَغْتَسِلُ مِنْهُ كُلَّ يَوْمٍ خَمْسَ مَرَّاتٍ

رواه مسلم كذا فى الترغيب

"Hadhrat Jaabir (Radhiyallaho anho) narrates that he heard the Prophet (Sallallaho alaihe wasallam) saying:

> "The likeness of five times daily salaat is as the likeness of a deep brook running in front of the door of a person who bathes therein five times a day."

Running water is generally free from dirt, and the deeper it runs the cleaner and purer it is. A bath in such water surely removes dirt from the body and makes it clean. Salaat offered with due regard for its essentials likewise cleanses the soul of all sins. There are several ahaadith of the same meaning, though with slight variations in expression, narrated by different companions of the Prophet (Sallallaho alaihe wasallam). Hadhrat Abu Sa'eed Khudri (Radhiyallaho anho) narrates that he heard the Prophet (Sallallaho alaihe wasallam) saying:

> 'Each of the five salaats expiates the sins committed since the salaat preceding it. To explain, let us take the case of a person working in a factory. His job is such that his body gets covered with dust. But there are five streams of running water in between the factory and his house and, on his return from the job, he takes a bath in each stream. The effect of five times daily salaat is quite similar. Any sins of omission and commission between two salaats are forgiven on account of 'istighfaar and taubah in each salaat.'

The Prophet (Sallallaho alaihe wasallam) through such parables, aims at impressing that salaat has the wonderful power of removing the sins. If we fail to avail of Allah's mercy, surely we ourselves are the losers.

To err is human. We are likely to commit innumerable acts of displeasing Allah and deserve thereby. His wrath and punishment, but look how relenting our dear Allah is! He has most graciously shown us the way to earn His mercy and forgiveness. It is a great pity if we do not avail of this great favour. Our Allah is always eager to show us His mercy on very small grounds. It is said in a hadith, that if a person goes to bed with the intention of getting up for Tahajjud and perchance does not wake up, he receives the full reward for Tahajjud, although he has been enjoying his sleep at the time of Tahajjud. How boundless is the grace of Allah and what a tremendous loss and deprivation if we do not receive blessings from such a Giver.

Hadith.—V

عَنْ حُذَيْفَةَ رَضِىَ اللهُ عَنْهُ قَالَ كَانَ رَسُوْلُ اللهِ ﷺ اِذَا حَزَبَهُ اَمْرٌ فَزَعَ اِلَى الصَّلٰوةِ أخرج أحمد وأبو داود وابن جرير كذا فى الدر المنثور

"Hadhrat Huzaifah (Radhiyallaho anho) says that, whenever the Prophet (Sallallaho alaihe wasallam) happened to face any difficulty, he would at once resort to salaat."

Salaat is a great blessing of Allah. To resort to salaat at the time of worry is to hasten towards His mercy, and when Allah's mercy comes to rescue, there can remain no trace of any worry. There are many traditions concerning this practice of the Holy Prophet (Sallallaho alaihe wasallam). Similar was the practice of his companions, who followed him in the minutest detail. Hadhrat Abu Darda (Radhiyallaho anho) says: "Whenever a strong wind blew, the Prophet (Sallallaho alaihe wasallam) would immediately enter the musjid and would not leave until the wind had subsided. Similarly, at the time of a solar or lunar eclipse, the Prophet (Sallallaho alaihe wasallam) would at once start offering salaat. Hadhrat Suhaib (Radhiyallaho anho) was informed by the Prophet (Sallallaho alaihe wasallam) that all the previous Apostles of Allah (peace be upon them) also used to resort to salaat in all adversities.

Hadhrat Ibno Abbas (Radhiyallaho anho) was once on journey. On his way he got the news of the death of his son. He got down from his camel and offered two rakaat of salaat, praying in Tashahhud for a long time. He then recited 'Innaa lillaahi wa innaallaihi raaji-oon' and said, "I have done what Allah has ordered us to do in His Holy Book i.e.:

وَاسْتَعِيْنُوْا بِالصَّبْرِ وَالصَّلٰوةِ.

"Seek Allah's help with patience and salaat" (II: 45).

Another similar story is narrated about him. He was on a journey when he received the news about the death of his brother Quthum. He descended from his camel by the roadside, and performed two rakaats of salaat and kept praying in Tashahhud for a long time. After finishing his salaat, he rode his camel reciting the following verse of the Holy Qur'an:

وَاستَعِيْنُوْا بِالصَّبْرِ والصَّلٰوةِ وَاِنَّهَا لَكَبِيْرَةٌ اِلَّا عَلَى الْخَاشِعِيْنَ

"Seek Allah's help with patience and salaat, and truly it is indeed hard except to the humble minded."

(II: 45).

There is yet another story about him. On hearing of the death of a wife of the Holy Prophet (Sallallaho alaihe wasallam), he fell down prostrate. When somebody asked him the reason he said, "Our dear Prophet (Sallallaho alaihe wasallam) had enjoined on us to prostrate (in salaat) whenever a calamity were to befall us. What calamity can be greater than the death of the Ummul-Mo'mineen?"

When Hadhrat Ubaada (Radhiyallaho anho) was about to breathe his last, he said to the people around him, "I prohibit one and all from crying over me. When my soul departs, I ask every one to perform wudhu, observing all its essentials, and to go to the musjid and pray for my forgiveness, because our Gracious Allah has enjoined on us to "Seek help with patience and salaat." After that, lay me down in the pit of my grave."

Hadhrat Nadhr (Radhiyallaho anho) narrates, "Once it became very dark during the day in Madina. I hurriedly went to Hadhrat Anas (Radhiyallaho anho) to know if he had ever experienced similar conditions during the lifetime of the Holy Prophet (Sallallaho alaihe wasallam). He said to me, "M'aathallaah! During those blessed days, whenever the wind blew strong, we would hurry to the musjid lest it should be the approach of the Last Day."

Hadhrat Abdullah bin Salaam (Radhiyallaho anho) narrates that whenever the members of the Prophet's family were hardpressed in any way, the Prophet (Sallallaho alaihe wasallam) would enjoin upon them to say salaat, and would recite the following verse of the Holy Qur'an:

وَاْمُرْ اَهْلَكَ بِالصَّلٰوةِ وَاصْطَبِرْ عَلَيْهَا لَانَسْئَلُكَ رِزْقًا نَحْنُ نَرْزُقُكَ وَالْعَاقِبَةُ لِلتَّقْوٰى

"And enjoin salaat upon thy people and be thyself constant therein. We ask not of thee to provide sustenance. We provide it for thee. And the Hereafter is for the righteousness." (XX: 132).

It is said in a hadith that when somebody is confronted with a need, whether pertaining to this life or the Hereafter, or whether it concerns Allah or a mortal, he should perform a perfect wudhu, offer salaat of two rakaats, glorify Allah, then ask blessing for the Prophet (Sallallaho alaihe wasallam), and then pray as under:

لَا اِلٰهَ اِلَّا اللهُ الْحَلِيْمُ الْكَرِيْمُ سُبْحَانَ اللهِ رَبِّ الْعَرْشِ الْعَظِيْمِ الْحَمْدُ لِلّٰهِ رَبِّ
الْعٰلَمِيْنَ اَسْئَلُكَ مُوْجِبَاتِ رَحْمَتِكَ وَعَزَائِمَ مَغْفِرَتِكَ وَالْغَنِيْمَةَ مِنْ كُلِّ بِرٍّ
وَالسَّلَامَةَ مِنْ كُلِّ اِثْمٍ لَاتَدَعْ لِيْ ذَنْبًا اِلَّا غَفَرْتَهٗ وَلَاهَمًّا اِلَّا فَرَّجْتَهٗ وَلَاحَاجَةً
هِيَ لَكَ رِضًا اِلَّا قَضَيْتَهَا يَا اَرْحَمَ الرَّاحِمِيْنَ

"There is no god save Allah–the Clement–the Bountiful. Glorified be Allah, the Lord of the tremendous throne. Praise be to Allah, the Lord of the worlds. I ask Thee all that leadeth to Thy Mercy and deserveth Thy forgiveness. I ask Thee abundance in all that is good and refuge from all that is evil. Leave me no sin but Thou pardonest it, and no distress but Thou removest it, and no need but Thou fulfillest it. O, most Merciful of those who show mercy!"

Wahb bin Munabbih writes: "Have your needs fulfilled by Allah through salaat. In the good old time, if a calamity befell the people, they would hurry towards salaat." It is said that in Koofah there was a porter who was well known for his honesty. People trusted him with their valuables and money, which he carried from one place to another. Once he was on his usual errand when a person met him on the way and asked him about his destination. When the porter gave him the required information, he said, "I am also bound for the same destination. If I could walk, I would have accompanied you on foot. Will you kindly give me a lift on your mule for one dinaar?" The porter agreed and allowed him to share the mule with him. They came to a crossing on the way. The person said, 'Now, which road will you take?' 'The main road, of course,' replied the porter. The person said, 'No, brother. We should go by the other road which is a shortcut and there is plenty of grass enroute to feed the animal.' The porter said, 'I have never been on this path.' The person remarked, 'But I have travelled by this route quite often'. The porter believed him and put the animal on that path. After some distance, the path ended in a terrifying forest where a large number of dead bodies were lying about. All of a sudden the person jumped down from the mule and took out his knife with the intention of slaying the porter. 'Hold your hand', shouted the porter, 'Take the animal and its load, but do not kill me'. The person refused to listen to his entreaty and swore that he would first kill the porter and then take possession of the animal and the goods. Seeing that his entreaties fell on deaf ears and that his cruel heart would not melt, the porter said to him, 'All right if you must kill me, then permit to say my salaat of only two rakaats.' The person agreed and remarked, 'You can please yourself. All the dead you see over here made the same request, but their salaat was of no avail to them.' The porter started the salaat, but could not recollect any soorah to connect with the Fatihah, in spite of his best efforts. Meanwhile the person grew impatient and pressed him hard to hurry up with the salaat. All of a sudden the following verse flashed to his mind:

اَمَّنْ يُّجِيْبُ الْمُضْطَرَّ اِذَا دَعَاهُ وَيَكْشِفُ السُّوْءَ

'Is it not He Who answereth the wronged one when he crieth unto Him, and removeth the evil . . . (XXVII-62).

The porter was reciting the verse and the tears welled up in his eyes, when a horseman suddenly appeared on the scene. He was wearing a glittering helmet and held a spear in his hand. He pierced the body of the pitiless rogue with his spear and killed him there and then. A flame of fire rose from the spot where the dead body fell. The porter fell down prostrate and thanked Allah. After finishing his salaat he ran towards the horseman and requested him to disclose his identity. He replied, 'I am a slave to Him who answereth the wronged one. You are now safe and can go wherever you like.' Saying this, the horseman rode away and disappeared."

Indeed salaat is a tremendous asset. Besides pleasing Allah it often gets us deliverence from the calamities of this life and provides us with tranquility and peace of mind. Ibn Seereen writes: "If I be allowed to choose between Paradise and salaat of two rakaats, I would prefer salaat. The reason is quite clear. Paradise is for my own pleasure while salaat is for the pleasure of my dear Lord." The Holy Prophet (Sallallaho alaihe wasallam) has said: "Enviable is the lot of that Muslim who is with least encumbrance, whose main fortune is salaat, who remains content with humble provision throughout his life, who worships his Lord in a dutiful manner, who lives a nameless life and who dies an early death, with very little to bequeath and very few to mourn him." In another hadith, the Holy Prophet (Sallallaho alaihe wasallam) is reported to have said: 'Offer your salaat at your homes quite frequently, so that these may be blessed with Allah's Grace and Mercy."

Hadith.—VI

عَنْ اَبِيْ مُسْلِمِ ن التَّغْلِبِيِّ رَضِىَ اللّٰهُ عَنْهُ قَالَ دَخَلْتُ عَلٰى اَبِيْ اُمَامَةَ وَهُوَ فِى الْمَسْجِدِ فَقُلْتُ يَااَبَا اُمَامَةَ اِنَّ رَجُلًا حَدَّثَنِىْ مِنْكَ اَنَّكَ سَمِعْتَ رَسُوْلَ اللّٰهِ ﷺ يَقُوْلُ مَنْ تَوَضَّأَ فَاَسْبَغَ الْوُضُوْءَ فَغَسَلَ يَدَيْهِ وَوَجْهَهُ وَمَسَحَ عَلٰى رَاْسِهِ وَاُذُنَيْهِ ثُمَّ قَامَ اِلَى صَلٰوةٍ مَفْرُوْضَةٍ غَفَرَ اللّٰهُ لَهُ فِيْ ذٰلِكَ الْيَوْمَ مَامَشَتْ اِلَيْهِ رِجْلَاهُ وَقَبَضَتْ عَلَيْهِ يَدَاهُ وَسَمِعَتْ اِلَيْهِ اُذُنَاهُ وَنَظَرَتْ اِلَيْهِ عَيْنَاهُ وَحَدَّثَ بِهِ نَفْسُهُ مِنْ سُوْءٍ فَقَالَ وَاللّٰهِ لَقَدْ سَمِعْتُهُ مِنَ النَّبِيِّ ﷺ مِرَارًا رواه احمد والغالب على سنده الحسن

"Abu Muslim narrates: I went to see Abu Umaamah (Radhiyallaho anho) while he was in the musjid. I asked him if he had really heard the Holy Prophet (Sallallaho alaihe wasallam) saying, "When a person performs wudhu with right performance and then says his fardh salaat, Allah forgives him all the sins committed that day by his feet in going towards evil, by his hands in doing evil, by his ears in listening to evil, by his eyes in looking at evil and by his heart in thinking of evil.' He replied, 'By Allah, I have heard these words from the Holy Prophet (Sallallaho alaihe wasallam) again and again."

Many of the companions have narrated this Hadith with slight variations. Those endowed with the power of Kashf can even witness the sins being shed. It is said of

Imam Abu Haneefa (Rahmatullah alaih) that he could tell from the water falling down from the limbs of the person performing wudhu as to which sins had been washed off therewith. In a narration by Hadhrat Uthman (Radhiyallaho anho), the Holy Prophet (Sallallaho alaihe wasallam) is reported to have warned against being wrong-headed in committing sins in the hope of getting them redeemed through salaat. We have, really, no ground to behave as such on this account. After all, what is the quality of the salaat that we offer? If Allah merely absolves us of our obligation it is His very special favour and grace. Again it is the height of ingratitude to disobey Allah just because He is Clement, Merciful and Forgiving.

Hadith.—VII

عَنْ اَبِيْ هُرَيْرَةَ رَضِىَ اللّٰهُ عَنْهُ قَالَ كَانَ رَجُلَانِ مِنْ بَلِيٍّ حَيٍّ مِّنْ قُضَاعَةَ اَسْلَمَا
مَعَ رَسُوْلِ اللّٰهِ ﷺ فَاسْتُشْهِدَ اَحَدُهُمَا وَاُخِّرَ الْاٰخَرُ لِاٰخِرِ سَنَةٍ قَالَ طَلْحَةُ بْنُ
عُبَيْدِ اللّٰهِ فَرَاَيْتُ الْمُؤَخَّرَ مِنْهُمَا اُدْخِلَ الْجَنَّةَ قَبْلَ الشَّهِيْدِ فَتَعَجَّبْتُ لِذٰلِكَ
فَاَصْبَحْتُ وَذَكَرْتُ ذٰلِكَ لِلنَّبِيِّ ﷺ اَوْ ذُكِرَ لِرَسُوْلِ اللّٰهِ ﷺ فَقَالَ رَسُوْلُ اللّٰهِ
اَلَيْسَ قَدْ صَامَ بَعْدَهُ رَمَضَانَ وَصَلَّى سِتَّةَ اٰلَافِ رَكْعَةٍ وَكَذَا رَكْعَةً صَلٰوةَ سَنَةٍ
رواه أحمد باسناد حسن ورواه ابن ماجه

Hadhrat Abu Hurairah (Radhiyallaho anho) narrates, "Two persons of one clan came to Prophet (Sallallaho alaihe wasallam) and embraced Islam at one and the same time. One of these was martyred in a battle and the other died a year later, Hadhrat Talha bin Ubaidullah (Radhiyallaho anho) says that he saw in his dream that the person who had died later was admitted into Paradise before the martyr. This surprised him. I do not recollect whether it was he or somebody else who narrated this dream. The Prophet (Sallallaho alaihe wasallam) thereupon remarked: "Has not the person dying later fasted for one additional month of Ramadhaan, and has he not offered six thousand or odd rakaats of salaat more during the year he lived after the martyr?"

Really, we do not know how valuable salaat is! The Holy Prophet (Sallallaho alaihe wasallam) was often heard saying, "The comfort of my eyes is in salaat." This is an expression of his profound love for salaat. As such, what else can be more valuable than salaat?

Hadith.—VIII

عَنْ اِبْنِ مَسْعُوْدٍ رَضِىَ اللهُ عَنْهُ عَنْ رَسُوْلِ اللهِ ﷺ اَنَّهُ قَالَ يُبْعَثُ مُنَادٍ عِنْدَ
حَضْرَةِ كُلِّ صَلٰوةٍ فَيَقُوْلُ يَابَنِيْ اٰدَمَ قُوْمُوْا فَاطْفِئُوْا مَا اَوْقَدْتُمْ عَلٰى اَنْفُسِكُمْ
فَيَقُوْمُوْنَ فَيَتَطَهَّرُوْنَ وَيُصَلُّوْنَ الظُّهْرَ فَيُغْفَرُلَهُمْ مَّابَيْنَهُمَا فَاِذَا حَضَرَتِ الْعَصْرُ
فَمِثْلُ ذٰلِكَ فَاِذَا حَضَرَتِ الْمَغْرِبُ فَمِثْلُ ذٰلِكَ فَاِذَا حَضَرَتِ الْعَتَمَةُ فَمِثْلُ ذٰلِكَ
فَيَنَامُوْنَ فَمُدْلِجٌ فِيْ خَيْرٍ وَمُدْلِجٌ فِيْ شَرٍّ رواه الطبراني في الكبير كذا في الترغيب

Hadhrat Ibn Mas'ood (Radhiyallaho anho) narrates that he heard the Holy Prophet (Sallallaho alaihe wasallam) saying: "At the approach of the hour of a salaat, an Angel is deputed to proclaim, 'Arise, O Children of Aadam! and extinguish the fire that you have (by committing sins) kindled to burn yourselves. So, the people rise up, perform wudhu and offer their Zuhr prayer. This causes forgiveness of their sins committed since day-break. The same is repeated at Asr, Maghrib and Ishaa. After Ishaa people go to bed, but there are some who busy themselves in good, while some others in evil deeds.

Hadhrat Salmaan (Radhiyallaho anho) says, "After Ishaa the people get divided into three groups. There are some for whom the night is a source of blessing and gain. They are those who spend it in the worship of Allah, while other people are asleep. For them the night brings great reward from their Lord. There are others who turn their night into a burden and curse for themselves, for they indulge in various dark deeds in the dead of night. To them the night brings woe and misery. There is the third group of people who go to bed immediately after Ishaa; they neither gain nor lose."

Hadith.—IX

عَنْ اَبِيْ قَتَادَةَ بْنِ رَبْعِيٍّ رَضِىَ اللهُ عَنْهُ قَالَ قَالَ رَسُوْلُ اللهِ ﷺ قَالَ اللهُ تَبَارَكَ
وَتَعَالٰى اِنِّىْ افْتَرَضْتُ عَلٰى اُمَّتِكَ خَمْسَ صَلَوَاتٍ وَعَهِدْتُ عِنْدِىْ عَهْدًا اَنَّهُ مَنْ

حَافَظَ عَلَيْهِنَّ لِوَقْتِهِنَّ اَدْخَلْتُهُ الْجَنَّةَ فِيْ عَهْدِيْ وَمَنْ لَمْ يُحَافِظْ عَلَيْهِنَّ فَلَاعَهْدَ لَهُ عِنْدِىْ كذا في الدر المنثور برواية أبي داود وابن ماجه وفيه أيضا أخرج مالك وابن أبي شيبة وأحمد وأبوداود والنسائى وابن ماجه وابن حبان والبيهقي عن عبادة بن الصامت فذكر معنى حديث الباب مرفوعًا بأطول منه

Hadhrat Abu Qataadah bin Rab'iyy (Radhiyallaho anho) says, "He heard the Prophet (Sallallaho alaihe wasallam) saying, Allah has said, "O, Muhammad! I have ordained five times daily salaat for thy followers. I have made a covenant with myself that whosoever is regular in performing his salaat at its fixed hour, he shall be admitted into the Paradise. Those of thy followers who do not guard their salaat, are not included in this covenant."

In another hadith, it is said that Allah has ordained five times salaat and whosoever is mindful of his salaat, by doing wudhu properly and by praying at fixed hours with sincerity and devotion, is assured by Allah of his entry into Paradise; and whosoever does not guard his salaat, there is no such guarantee for him; he may–or may not be forgiven. salaat has indeed a tremendous value. It affords us an opportunity to receive Allah's guarantee for Paradise. When an honourable person of some financial standing or having executive power gives us a guarantee or stands surety for meeting any of our requirements of this world, we feel quite satisfied and happy and we consider it our duty to remain obliged and devoted to him. Here Allah the Absolute Sovereign of both the worlds, is giving the guarantee and is standing surety for the real success after death in return for five times daily salaat, which does not involve much effort on our part. If even then we do not avail of the opportunity, we shall have none to blame, but ourselves for the dreadful doom that awaits us.

Hadith.—X

عَنْ ابْنِ سَلْمَانَ رَضِىَ اللهُ عَنْهُ اِنَّ رَجُلًا مِّنْ اَصْحَابِ النَّبِيِّ ﷺ حَدَّثَهُ قَالَ لَمَّا فَتَحْنَا خَيْبَرَ اَخْرَجُوْا غَنَائِمَهُمْ مِنَ الْمَتَاعِ وَالسَّبِيِّ فَجَعَلَ النَّاسُ يَتَبَايَعُوْنَ غَنَآئِمَهُمْ فَجَاءَ رَجُلٌ فَقَالَ يَارَسُوْلَ اللهِ لَقَدْ رَبِحْتُ رِبْحًا مَّارَبِحَ الْيَوْمَ مِثْلَهُ اَحَدٌ مِنْ اَهْلِ الْوَادِيْ فَقَالَ وَيْحَكَ وَمَارَبِحْتَ قَالَ مَازِلْتُ اَبِيْعُ وَاَبْتَاعُ حَتّٰى رَبِحْتُ

ثَلٰثِماءَةِ اَوْقِيَةٍ فَقَالَ رَسُوْلُ اللهِ ﷺ اَنَا اُنَبِّئُكَ بِخَيْرِ رَجُلٍ رَبِحَ قَالَ مَاهُوَ يَارَسُوْلَ اللهِ قَالَ رَكْعَتَيْنِ بَعْدَ الصَّلٰوةِ أخرجه أبو داود وسكت عنه المنذري

Ibn Salmaan says that he heard one of the companions of the Holy Prophet (Sallallaho alaihe wasallam) narrating, "When we had won the battle of Khaibar, we began to buy and sell among ourselves the booty that had fallen to our lot. One of us went to Holy Prophet (Sallallaho alaihe wasallam) and said, 'O, Apostle of Allah, no one else has earned so much profit as I have obtained in today's trade.' 'How much did you earn? asked the Prophet (Sallallaho alaihe wasallam). He replied, 'I kept on selling and buying till I earned a net profit of three hundred 'Ooqiyyah' of silver.' The Prophet (Sallallaho alaihe wasallam) said, "Shall I inform you of something better than that?" He exclaimed, 'Do tell me, O, Prophet of Allah!' The Prophet (Sallallaho alaihe wasallam) remarked 'Two rakaats nafl after (fardh) salaat."

Three hundred Ooqiyyahs of silver come to about three thousand rupees. According to the Prophet (Sallallaho alaihe wasallam), the perishable gain of this world stands no comparison with the everlasting gain of the Hereafter. Our life will be pleasant and worth living if we develop our 'Imaan' to an extent where two rakaats of salaat, in our sight, are more valuable than all the riches of this world. salaat is really a great treasure and that is why the Prophet (Sallallaho alaihe wasallam) has called it 'the comfort of his eyes' and had been enjoining its observance right up to his last breath. Umme Salamah (Radhiyallaho anha) narrates that the last words of the Prophet (Sallallaho alaihe wasallam), which he could hardly utter, were about guarding the salaat and kindness towards the slaves. There is a similar hadith narrated by Hadhrat Ali (Radhiyallaho anho) as well.

The Prophet (Sallallaho alaihe wasallam) once deputed in Jihaad a Jamaat towards Najd. They returned victorious very soon with a handsome booty. When the Prophet (Sallallaho alaihe wasallam) saw the people envying them and wondering at their quick and lucrative return, he said to them, "Shall I inform you of a group of people who earn much more in a much shorter time? They are those who perform their Fajr with Jamaat and keep sitting after prayer till a little while after sunrise and then offer two rakaats of salaat." According to Shaqeeq Balkhi, a very famous Shaikh, five things could be acquired through five channels; an increase in provisions through 'Chaasht' a light in the grave through Tahajjud, a very satisfactory answer to Munkar and Nakeer through the recitation of the Qur'an; an easy crossing of Siraat through fasting and alms, and room under the shade of Allah's Throne on the Day of Judgement through seclusion (i.e. Zikr).

There are so many sayings of the Holy Prophet (Sallalaho alaihe wasallam) enjoining salaat and explaining its virtues that it is very difficult to cover all of them in this small book. A few quotations are, however, reproduced below as a benediction:

1. "Salaat was the first and the foremost thing ordained by Allah, and it shall be the first and the foremost thing to be reckoned for on the Day of Judgement."
2. "Fear Allah in the matter of salaat! Fear Allah in the matter of salaat! Fear Allah in the matter of salaat!.
3. "Salaat intervenes between man and Shirk."
4. "Salaat is the mark of Islam. A person who says his salaat at the fixed hours with sincerity and devotion, observing all its regulations including the Mustahabbaat, is surely a Mo'min."
5. "Of all things that have been ordained by Allah, Imaan and salaat are the most valued. If there were any other thing better than salaat, then Allah would have ordained it for His Angels, some of whom are always in ruku and others in sajdah."
6. "Salaat is the pillar of Islam."
7. "Salaat abases the Devil."
8. "Salaat is the light of a Mo'min."
9. "Salaat is the best Jihaad."
10. "Allah keeps relenting towards a person so long as he is engaged in salaat."
11. "When a calamity befalls us from the heaven,

people frequenting the musjid are spared and saved."

12. "If some major sins of a Muslim land him in Hell, the fire would not burn those parts of his body which have touched the ground while he was in sajdah during his salaat."
13. "Fire has been forbidden to touch those parts of the body which touch the ground while performing the sajdah."
14. "Of all the practices, salaat made at fixed hours is most loved by Allah."
15. "Allah likes most the posture of a person when he is in sajdah, pressing his forehead on the ground in humility."
16. "A person in sajdah is nearest unto Allah."
17. "Salaat is a key to Paradise."
18. "When a person stands in salaat the gates of Paradise are let open and all the veils between him and Allah are lifted (provided that he spoils not his salaat by coughing etc)."
19. "A person in salaat (so to say) knocks at the door of the sovereign Lord, and the door is always opened for him who knocks."
20. "The position of salaat in Islam is as the position of the head in a body."
21. "Salaat is the light of the heart. Let those who wish enlighten their hearts (through salaat)".
22. "If a person wishes to have his sins forgiven by Allah, he should perform the wudhu properly, offer with devotion two or four rak'aats of fardh or nafl and then pray to Allah. Allah will forgive him."
23. "Any strip of earth, on which Allah is remembered in salaat, takes pride over the rest of the Earth."
24. "Allah accepts the prayer of a person who prays to Him after performing two rakaats of salaat. Allah grants him what he prays for, sometimes immediately and sometimes (in his own interest) later."

25. "A person who performs two rakaats of salaat in seclusion, where nobody except Allah and His Angels see him, receives a writ of deliverance from the fire of hell."

26. "Grant of one prayer (wish) becomes due to a person from Allah after each fardh salaat performed by him."

27. "Fire of Hell is forbidden and the Paradise becomes due to a person who performs his wudhu properly and says his salaat conscientiously, according to its regulations."

28. "The Devil remains scared of a Muslim so long as he is particular about his salaat, but no sooner does he neglect it than the Devil gets a hold upon him and aspires for success in seducing him."

29. "Salaat at its early hours is the most excellent practice."

30. "Salaat is the offering of the pious."

31. "Salaat at its early hours is a practice most liked by Allah."

32. "At dawn, some people go to the musjid and some to the market. Those going to the musjid are the flag-bearers of Imaan and those leaving for the market are the flag-bearers of the Devil."

33. "The four rakaats before Zuhr have the same reward as the four rakaats of Tahajjud."

34. "The four rakaats before Zuhr are counted equal (in reward) to the four rakaats of Tahajjud."

35. "Mercy of Allah turns towards a person standing in salaat."

36. "Salaat at the dead of night is most valued, but there are very few who do it."

37. "Jibra-eel (Alayhis salaam) came to me and said, O, Muhammad (Sallallaho alaihe wasallam)! however long thou livest thou shalt die one day, and whoever, thou may love thou shalt depart from him one day. Surely, thou shalt receive the recompense of whatever (good or evil) thou dost. No

doubt the dignity of a Mo'min is in Tahajjud and his honour is in contentment and restraint."

38. "Two rakaats in the late hours of the night are more valuable than all the riches of this world. But for fear of hardship to my followers, I would have made these obligatory."

39. "Keep offering Tahajjud, for it is the path of the righteous and the means of approach to Allah. Tahajjud keeps one away from sins, causes forgiveness of sins and improves the health of the body."

40. "Allah says, 'O, son of Aadam! Do not be weak in offering four rakaats in the early part of the day, for I shall suffice thee in thy jobs in the rest of it."

Books of hadith are full of discourses on the virtues of salaat, enjoining its observance on all Muslims. The forty short hadiths given above can be memorised and thus the reward of knowing ahaadith in that number can be earned. In fact, salaat is really a big boon, but this is realised only by those who have enjoyed its taste. That is why the Prophet (Sallallaho alaihe wasallam) used to call it the comfort of his eyes and used to spend the major part of the night standing before Allah. For the very same reason, our dear Prophet (Sallallaho alaihe wasallam) even on his death-bed charged us and enjoined on us to be particular about salaat. It has been reported in many ahaadith that the Prophet (Sallallaho alaihe wasallam) would often say, "Fear Allah concerning salaat." Abdullah bin Mas'ood, (Radhiyallaho anho) narrates that he heard the Prophet (Sallallaho alaihe wasallam) saying, "Of all the practices, salaat is the dearest to me."

One of the Sahabah narrates, "One night I happened to go to the musjid. I found the Prophet (Sallallaho alaihe wasallam) in salaat. I felt an ardent desire to join him. I made my intention and stood behind him; he was reciting 'Baqarah' at that time. I thought that he would finish the qiraat and go for ruku at the end of the hundredth verse, but he did not do so. Then I thought he would perhaps go to ruku after finishing two hundred verses, but he did not stop even there. I was sure then that he would finish qiyaam with the end of the soorah. When the soorah ended he hymned, 'Allahumma Lakalhamd' (Allah! Thine is all Glory) a number of times and then started 'Aal Imraan'. On finishing that soorah he again hymned 'Allahumma Lakalhamd' three times and started 'al-Maa'idah'. He went into ruku only after finishing that soorah. In ruku and sajdah he recited tasbeeh and some other prayers, which I could not catch. In the second, rakaat he started 'al-An'aam' after 'Fatihah'. I could not continue with him any longer and broke away helplessly." What the Prophet (Sallallaho alaihe wasallam) recited in one rakaat comes to about one sixth of the whole Qur'an. Besides, the Prophet (Sallallaho alaihe wasallam) must be reciting at ease with proper Tajweed; we can well imagine how long the rakaat would have been. It was on this account that his feet would often get swollen. But no amount of strain and inconvenience in salaat is in the way of one whose heart is imbued with its sweetness.

Abu Ishaaq Subaihi is a famous muhaddith. He died a centenarian. He would often exclaim in his old age, "Alas! This infirmity and old age have deprived me of the delight of long salaat. I am now only able to recite 'Baqarah' and 'Aal-Imraan' in my salaat of two rakaats." These two soorahs comprise about one eighth of the whole Qur'an.

Muhammad bin Sammaak, the famous Soofi, writes, "My neighbour at Koofah had a son. The boy fasted during the day and kept praying and hymning during the night. This constant strain emaciated him so much that his body was reduced to a skeleton. His father requested me to admonish him. Once I was sitting at my door when the boy passed by. He greeted me with 'Assalaamu alaikum' and sat down. I had hardly said anything when he interrupted saying, 'Dear Uncle! Maybe you intend to admonish me to reduce my pursuits. Listen to my story first. I had a few friends in the locality. We decided among ourselves to vie with one another in worship and adoration of Allah. They all applied themselves so hard that they were soon sent for by Allah. They embraced death delightedly and peacefully. Now I am the only one left behind. What will they think of me when they know of my lagging behind? Dear Uncle! My friends really strived very hard and achieved their goal,' He then began to relate the pursuits and accomplishments of his departed friends, which astonished all the listeners. After this he left me. I heard a few days later that the boy too had died (May Allah bless him)."

Even in these days there are persons who remain engaged in salaat for the major portion of the night and devote the whole day to Tableegh, Ta'leem and other services in the path of Allah. Maulana Abdul Waahid Lahori (peace be upon him) was a famous saint who lived about two centuries ago. He sighed and wept when he learnt that there was no salaat in Paradise–being the place for recompense and not of labour. He remarked, "How shall we enjoy the Paradise without salaat!" Such people are really the salt of this Earth. May Allah give us their strength of Imaan and love for His worship! Aameen.

Before I finish this chapter, let me reproduce the following lovely Hadith from Munabbihaat by Ibn Hajar, "Once when the Prophet (Sallallaho alaihe wasallam) was sitting among his companions, he remarked, "Three things of this world are very dear to me: Perfume, Women and salaat–the comfort of my eyes." "Quite true" rejoined Abu Bakr (Radhiyallaho anho), "And I cherish three things: a look at thy face, spending of my wealth on thee and that my daughter is thy wife, O Prophet of Allah!" "Quite true", said Hadhrat Umar (Radhiyallaho anho), "And the three I love most are; enforcing that which is right, forbidding evil and wearing old clothes." "Quite true", said Hadhrat Uthman (Radhiyallaho anho), "And the three I love most are: feeding the hungry, clothing the naked and reciting the Qur'an." "Quite true", said Hadhrat Ali (Radhiyallaho anho). "And I love the three things most: serving a guest, fasting on a very hot day and smiting the enemy with my sword." At this, Jibra-eel (Alayhis salaam) appeared on the scene and said to the Prophet (Sallallaho alaihe wasallam), "Allah has sent me to tell you what I would love if I be one of the mortals." "Yes, do tell us, Jibra-eel", said the Prophet. Jibra-eel then replied, "If I had been like you, I would have loved three things: guiding the people gone astray, loving those who worship in poverty and helping the poor family men. And as for Allah, He loves three characteristics of His slaves: striving in His Path, crying at the time of repentance, and steadfastness in want and hunger."

Hafiz Ibn Qayyim writes: 'Salaat ensures daily bread, promotes health, drives out diseases, strengthens the heart, brings light and beauty on the face, pleases the soul, refreshes the body, cures indolence, relieves the mind, feeds the soul, illumines the heart and guarantees Allah's favour. It grants protection against Allah's Doom. It keeps the Devil away and brings us nearer to Allah. In short, salaat is a guarantee for all that is desirable and a protection against all that is undesirable for both body and soul, equally in this world and in the Hereafter."

CHAPTER.—II

WARNING AND REPROACH FOR NEGLECTING SALAAT

The books on hadith mention very severe punishment for those who neglect salaat. From many traditions on the subject, only a few are reproduced in this chapter. Although a single warning from the most truthful Prophet (Sallallaho alaihe wasallam) was enough, yet we find that, out of love and mercy for his followers, he has cautioned them again and again and in various manners lest they should neglect salaat and suffer the consequences. In spite of all this, alas! we are unmindful of salaat, and still we have the audacity to consider ourselves devotees of the Prophet (Sallallaho alaihe wasallam) and champions of Islam.

Hadith.—I

عَنْ جَابِرِ بْنِ عَبْدِ اللهِ رَضِىَ اللهُ عَنْهُ قَالَ قَالَ رَسُوْلُ اللهِ ﷺ بَيْنَ الرَّجُلِ وَبَيْنَ الْكُفْرِ تَرْكُ الصَّلٰوةِ رواه احمد ومسلم وقال بين الرجل و بين الشرك والكفر ترك الصلوة رواه ابو داود والنسائی ولفظه ليس بين العبد وبين الكفر الا ترك الصلوة والترمذي ولفظه قال بين الكفر والايمان ترك الصلوة وابن ماجه ولفظه وقال بين العبد وبين الكفر ترك الصلوة كذا في الترغيب للمنذري وقال السيوطي في الدر لحديث جابر وغيره

Hadhrat Jaabir bin Abdullah (Radhiyallaho anho) narrates that he heard the Prophet of Allah (Sallallaho alaihe wasallam) saying:

1. "To discard salaat is to be linked with Kufr."
2. "To discard salaat is to be linked with Kufr and Shirk."
3. "Discarding of salaat is the only partition between Imaan and Kufr."

There are a number of ahaadith on the subject. On one occasion, the Holy Prophet (Sallallaho alaihe wasallam) is reported to have said: "Hurry up with your salaat when it is cloudy (lest you should err and miss the correct time), for to discard salaat is to become a kaafir." What a stern warning against even missing the correct time of salaat, as (according to this quotation) to miss the correct time of salaat is to discard it. Although, according to the interpretation of the Ulama, the verdict of kufr is given against a person only when he rejects (and not simply neglects) salaat, yet the words of the Prophet (Sallallaho alaihe wasallam) occurring in these ahaadith should be very weighty for those who have any regard for him. It may, however, be noted that some of the very important companions of the Prophet (Sallallaho alaihe wasallam) like Umar, Abdullah bin Mas'ood, Abdullah bin Abbas (Radhiyallaho anhum), etc. and eminent jurists like Ahmad bin Hanbal, Ishaaq bin Raahwayh, Ibn Mubaarak, (Rahmatullah alaihim), etc. are definitely of the opinion that verdict of kufr can be given against the person who intentionally discards his salaat. May Allah save us!

Hadith.—II

عَنْ عُبَادَةَ بْنِ الصَّامِتِ رَضِيَ اللّٰهُ عَنْهُ قَالَ اَوْصَانِي خَلِيْلِي رَسُوْلُ اللّٰهِ ﷺ بِسَبْعِ
خِصَالٍ فَقَالَ لَاتُشْرِكُوْا بِاللّٰهِ شَيْئًا وَاِنْ قُطِعْتُمْ اَوْ حُرِّقْتُمْ اَوْ صُلِبْتُمْ وَلَاتَتْرُكُوْا
الصَّلٰوةَ مُتَعَمِّدِيْنَ فَمَنْ تَرَكَهَا مُتَعَمِّدًا فَقَدْ خَرَجَ مِنَ الْمِلَّةِ وَلَاتَرْكَبُوْا الْمَعْصِيَةَ
فَاِنَّهَا سَخَطُ اللّٰهِ وَلَاتَشْرَبُوْا الْخَمْرَ فَاِنَّهَا رَاْسُ الْخَطَايَا كُلِّهَا ، الحديث

رواه الطبراني ومحمد بن نصر في كتاب الصلوة باسنادين لابأس بهما كذا في الترغيب وهكذا ذكره
السيوطي في الدر المنثور وعزاه إليهما وفي المشكواة برواية ابن ماجة عن ابن أبي الدرداء نحوه

Hadhrat Ubaadah bin Saamit (Radhiyallaho anho) narrates. 'My dear friend the Prophet (Sallallaho alaihe wasallam) while enjoining upon me seven good practices said, "Do not ascribe anything as partner to Allah, though you may be cut into pieces or burnt alive or crucified; do not forego salaat intentionally, lest you should get out of the fold of Islam; do not perpetrate disobedience of Allah, lest you deserve His wrath; and do not take to drinking, for that is the mother of all evils'."

In another hadith, Hadhrat Abu Darda (Radhiyallaho anho) says, "My dear Prophet (Sallallaho alaihe wasallam) warned me saying, 'Do not ascribe anything as partner unto

Allah, though you may be cut into pieces or burnt alive or crucified; do not discard salaat intentionally, as Allah is free from any obligation to a person who knowingly neglects salaat; and do not take wine, for that is the key to all vices."

Hadith–III

عَنْ مُعَاذِ بْنِ جَبَلٍ رَضِىَ اللهُ عَنْهُ قَالَ اَوْصَانِيْ رَسُوْلُ اللهِ ﷺ بِعَشْرِ كَلِمَاتٍ قَالَ
لَاتُشْرِكْ بِاللهِ شَيْئًا وَّاِنْ قُتِلْتَ اَوْ حُرِّقْتَ وَلَاتَعُقَّنَّ وَالِدَيْكَ وَاِنْ اَمَرَاكَ اَنْ تَخْرُجَ
مِنْ اَهْلِكَ وَمَالِكَ وَلَاتَتْرُكَنَّ صَلٰوةً مَّكْتُوْبَةً مُتَعَمِّدًا فَاِنَّ مَنْ تَرَكَ صَلَاةً مَكْتُوْبَةً
فَقَدْ بَرِئَتْ مِنْهُ ذِمَّةُ اللهِ وَلَاتَشْرَبَنَّ خَمْرًا فَاِنَّهُ رَاْسُ كُلِّ فَاحِشَةٍ وَاِيَّاكَ وَالْمَعْصِيَةَ
فَاِنَّ بِالْمَعْصِيَةِ حَلَّ سَخَطُ اللهِ وَاِيَّاكَ وَالْفِرَارَ مِنَ الزَّحْفِ وَاِنْ هَلَكَ النَّاسُ وَاِنْ
اَصَابَ النَّاسَ مَوْتٌ فَاثْبُتْ وَاَنْفِقْ عَلٰى اَهْلِكَ مِنْ طَوْلِكَ وَلَاتَرْفَعْ عَنْهُمْ عَصَاكَ
اَدَبًا وَاَخِفْهُمْ فِى اللهِ رواه أحمد والطبراني في الكبير وغيرهم

Hadhrat Mu'aaz bin Jabal (Radhiyallaho anho) narrates: "The Prophet (Sallallaho alaihe wasallam) enjoined upon me ten things, viz, 'Do not ascribe anything as partner unto Allah, though you may be slain or burnt alive; do not disobey your parents, though you may have to part with your wife or your entire wealth; do not neglect fardh salaat, intentionally, for Allah is free from obligation to a person who neglects fardh salaat intentionally; do not take wine, for it is an evil habit; that is the root of every vice; do not commit disobedience of Allah, for that brings the wrath of Allah. Do not turn your back to the enemy in battle, though all your comrades may have fallen. Do not fly from the locality where an epidemic has broken out. Do spend on your family members according to your capacity; let your rod be hanging on them, as a warning and to chastise against neglect of their duties towards Allah."

According to this hadith, we should not spare the rod in checking the children from becoming reckless in doing anything they like. Sometimes it is necessary to use the rod. It is a pity that out of love we do not use the rod in the beginning and, when the children get spoilt, we cry and complain about them. To spare the rod and to spoil the child is no kindness at all. Who would like to save a child from a surgical operation under advice from a doctor for the simple reason that it would cause pain to him? The Prophet (Sallallaho alaihe wasallam) is reported to have said very often: "Enjoin salaat on your child when he is seven years old, and beat him if he neglects it after he reaches ten." Hadhrat Abdullah bin Mas'ood (Radhiyallaho anho) says, "Guard the salaat of your children and inculcate good habits in them". Luqmaan the wise used to say, "The use of the rod on a child is as indispensable as is water for the fields." The Prophet (Sallallaho alaihe wasallam) is reported to have said, "A person while admonishing his children earns more reward from Allah than when he is spending about seven pounds of grain in His path." In another hadith the Prophet (Sallallaho alaihe wasallam) has said, "May Allah bless a person who keeps a lash hanging in his house for the admonition of his house-folk." On another occasion he said, "No father can bestow anything better on his children than to teach them good manners."

Hadith–IV

عَنْ نَّوْفَلِ بْنِ مُعَاوِيَةَ رَضِىَ اللهُ عَنْهُ اَنَّ النَّبِيَّ ﷺ قَالَ مَنْ فَاتَتْهُ صَلوٰةٌ فَكَاَنَّمَا وُتِرَ اَهْلُهُ وَمَالُهُ رواه ابن حبان في صحيحه كذا في الترغيب زاد السيوطي في الدر والنسائى أيضا قلت ورواه أحمد في مسنده

Hadhrat Naufil bin Mu'aawiyah (Radhiyallaho anho) narrates that he heard the Prophet (Sallallaho alaihe wasallam) saying, "A person who has missed one salaat is like one who has lost all his family and wealth."

Salaat is missed usually when either a person is in the company of his family members or is in pursuit of money. According to this hadith, the ultimate loss sustained in missing a salaat is in no way less than the loss of the whole family and property. In other words, if we miss a salaat we should be as much grieved as when we lose all of our folk and entire belongings. If we are cautioned by some reliable person about the presence of gangsters on a certain road, where people are robbed and killed during the night, we need a lion's heart to ignore the caution and travel on that road even during the day time. Strange enough to note that we have been cautioned again and again by the Prophet (Sallalaho alaihe wasallam) and we do believe that he was really the true Messenger of Allah, yet we heed not the caution and go on missing salaat one after the other.

Hadith V

عَنْ ابْنِ عَبَّاسٍ رَضِىَ اللهُ عَنْهُ قَالَ قَالَ رَسُوْلُ اللهِ ﷺ مَنْ جَمَعَ بَيْنَ الصَّلٰوتَيْنِ
مِنْ غَيْرِ عُذْرٍ فَقَدْ اَتٰى بَابًا مِنْ اَبْوَابِ الْكَبَائِرِ رواه الحاكم

Ibn Abbas (Radhiyallaho anho) narrates that he heard the Prophet (Sallallaho alaihe wasallam) saying, "A person who combines two salaats without any strong excuse reaches one of the doors of kabaa'ir (major sins)."

Hadhrat Ali (Radhiyallaho anho) reports that the Prophet (Sallallaho alaihe wasallam) once said, "Do not delay in three things: salaat when its time has set in, burial when the bier is ready and marriage of a solitary woman when her match is found." Many persons who consider themselves as practical Muslims perform a number of their salaats in combination on returning home, on the very feeble excuses of travel, trade or occupation. To put salaat off till after its set time without a strong excuse (illness, etc) is a major sin. Although it is not so disastrous as neglecting salaat, yet it is quite serious.

Hadith VI

عَنْ عَبْدِ اللهِ بن عَمْرٍو رَضِىَ اللهُ عَنْهُ عَنِ النَّبِيِّ صَلَى اللهُ عَلَيْهِ وَسَلَّمْ اَنَّهُ ذَكَرَ
الصَّلٰوةَ يَوْمًا فَقَالَ مَنْ حَافَظَ عَلَيْهَا كَانَتْ لَهُ نُوْرًا وَبُرْهَانًا وَنجاةً يَوْمَ الْقِيَامَةِ
وَمَنْ لَمْ يُحَافِظْ عَلَيْهَا لَمْ يَكُنْ لَهُ نُوْرٌ وَلَابُرْهَانٌ وَلَانَجَاةٌ وَكَانَ يَوْمَ الْقِيَامَةِ مَعَ
فِرْعَوْنَ وَهَامَانَ وَاُبَيِّ بْنِ خَلْفٍ أخرجه أحمد وابن حبان

Abdullah bin Amr (Radhiyallaho anho) narrates that once the Prophet (Sallallaho alaihe wasallam) while talking about salaat said: "For its votary, salaat shall on the Day of Judgement, be a light for him, an argument in his favour, and a means of his deliverance. Whereas there will be no light, no defence and no deliverance from doom for him who does not guard his salaat, and he shall meet the fate of Pharoah, Haamaan and Ubbay bin Khalaf."

Everybody knows that Pharoah–the big disbeliever–had been so arrogant that he proclaimed himself 'Lord the Highest' and made his people worship him. Haamaan was his Chief Minister and accomplice. Ubbay bin Khalaf was the most active and severest enemy of Islam among the disbelievers of Mecaa. Before the Hijrah, he used to announce to the Prophet (Sallallaho alaihe wasallam) most insolently, "I have reared a horse, which I feed very well; I will slay you one day riding on its back." Once the Prophet (Sallallaho alaihe wasallam) replied to him, "Inshaa-allaah! you shall meet your end at my hands." In the battle of Uhud, he ran about in the field in search of the Prophet (Sallallaho alaihe wasallam) saying, "If Muhammad (Sallallaho alaihe wasallam) is not slain today, then I stand no chance of surviving." He at last found the Prophet (Sallallaho alaihe wasallam) and advanced to attack him. The Companions decided to finish him before he reached the Prophet, but the Prophet (Sallallaho alaihe wasallam) stopped them. When he came near, the Prophet (Sallallaho alaihe wasallam) took a spear from one of the companions and struck him with it, causing a little scratch on his neck. He staggered and fell down from his horse and then fled towards his camp crying, "By Allah, Muhammad (Sallallaho alaihe wasallam) has killed me!" His people tried to console him and told him that it was only a bruise and there was nothing to worry about, but he would say, "Muhammad (Sallallaho alaihe wasallam) had once announced to me in Mecca that he would kill me. By Allah, had he only spat at me, I would be no more." It is said that he cried like a bull. Abu Sufyan, who was very active on that day, put him to shame for crying in that manner over a slight wound, but he said, "Do you know who has inflicted this injury upon me? It was none other than Muhammad (Sallallaho alaihe wasallam). By Laat and Uzza! if my agony be distributed over all the people of Hijaaz, none of them would survive. Since the time he had declared that he would kill me, I was sure that I would meet my death at his hands. If he only spat at me after that declaration, I would be no more." So he died on his way back, at a day's journey from Mecca.

Look! a disbeliever like Ubbay bin Khalaf is so sure about the truth of the Prophet's words that he does not have the slightest doubt about his own death; but where do we stand? Although we believe in him as the greatest Prophet of Allah, consider his words to be most genuine and boast of our love for him, yet how far do we act upon his advice and how much do we fear the punishments about which he has warned us! It is for each one of us to ponder over and answer.

Ibn Hajar, while quoting this hadith, has also mentioned Qaaroon with Pharaoh and others. He writes: "Sharing the fate of these people on the Day of Judgement is due to the fact that it is often the pursuits specific to these guilty persons which cause neglect of salaat. If, therefore, a person neglects salaat due to a craving for wealth, he will meet the fate of Qaaroon; if due to love for power, then that of Pharaoh; if due to a yearning for attachment to a ruler, then that of Haamaan; and if due to occupation in trade then that of Ubbay Bin Khalaf." Meeting the same fate as theirs, explains fully the severest tortures in store for those who neglect salaat. Although the disbelievers shall have to suffer their doom forever, while the believers will be released after their period of punishment is over and will ultimately be allowed to enter Paradise, yet this period of punishment, who knows, may last for thousands of years.

Hadith VII

قَالَ بَعْضُهُمْ وَرَدَ فِيْ الْحَدِيْثِ اَنَّ مَنْ حَافَظَ عَلَى الصَّلٰوةِ اَكْرَمَهُ اللّٰهُ بِخَمْسِ خِصَالٍ يَرْفَعُ عَنْهُ ضِيْقَ الْعَيْشِ وَعَذَابَ الْقَبْرِ وَيُعْطِيْهِ اللّٰهُ كِتَابَهُ بِيَمِيْنِهٖ وَيَمُرُّ عَلَى الصِّرَاطِ كَالْبَرْقِ وَيَدْخُلُ الْجَنَّةَ بِغَيْرِ حِسَابٍ ، وَمَنْ تَهَاوَنَ عَنِ الصَّلٰوةِ عَاقَبَهُ اللّٰهُ بِخَمْسَ عَشَرَةَ عُقُوْبَةً خَمْسَةٌ فِى الدُّنْيَا وَثَلَاثٌ عِنْدَ الْمَوْتِ وَثَلٰثٌ فِيْ قَبْرِهٖ وَثَلٰثٌ عِنْدَ خُرُوْجِهٖ مِنَ الْقَبْرِ ، فَاَمَّا اللَّوَاتِيْ فِى الدُّنْيَا فَالْاُوْلٰى تُنْزَعُ الْبَرَكَةُ مِنْ عُمْرِهٖ وَالثَّانِيَةُ تُمْحٰى سِيْمَا الصَّالِحِيْنَ مِنْ وَجْهِهٖ وَالثَّالِثَةُ كُلُّ عَمَلٍ يَعْمَلُهُ لَايَاْجُرُهُ اللّٰهُ عَلَيْهِ وَالرَّابِعَةُ لَايُرْفَعُ لَهُ دُعَاءٌ اِلَى السَّمَاءِ وَالْخَامِسَةُ لَيْسَ لَهُ حَقٌّ فِيْ دُعَاءِ الصَّالِحِيْنَ ، وَاَمَّا الَّتِيْ تُصِيْبُهُ عِنْدَ الْمَوْتِ فَاِنَّهُ يَمُوْتُ ذَلِيْلًا وَالثَّانِيَةُ يَمُوْتُ جُوْعًا وَالثَّالِثَةُ يَمُوْتُ عَطْشَانًا وَلَوْ سُقِىَ بِحَارَ الدُّنْيَا مَا رَوِيَ مِنْ عَطْشِهٖ ، وَاَمَّا الَّتِيْ تُصِيْبُهُ فِيْ قَبْرِهٖ فَالْاُوْلٰى يَضِيْقُ عَلَيْهِ الْقَبْرُ حَتّٰى تَخْتَلِفَ اَضْلَاعُهُ وَالثَّانِيَةُ يُوْقَدُ عَلَيْهِ الْقَبْرُ نَارًا فَيَتَقَلَّبُ عَلَى الْجَمْرِ لَيْلًا وَنَهَارًا وَالثَّالِثَةُ يُسَلَّطُ

عَلَيْهِ فِيْ قَبْرِهٖ ثُعْبَانٌ اِسْمُهُ الشُّجَاعُ الْاَقْرَعُ عَيْنَاهُ مِنْ نَارٍ وَاَظْفَارُهٗ مِنْ حَدِيْدٍ
طُوْلُ كُلِّ ظُفْرٍ مَسِيْرَةُ يَوْمٍ يُكَلِّمُ الْمَيِّتَ فَيَقُوْلُ اَنَا الشُّجَاعُ الْاَقْرَعُ وَصَوْتُهٗ مِثْلُ
الرَّعْدِ الْقَاصِفِ يَقُوْلُ اَمَرَنِيْ رَبِّيْ اَنْ اَضْرِبَكَ عَلٰى تَضْيِيْعِ صَلٰوةِ الصُّبْحِ اِلٰى بَعْدِ
طُلُوْعِ الشَّمْسِ وَاَضْرِبَكَ عَلٰى تَضْيِيْعِ صَلٰوةِ الظُّهْرِ اِلٰى الْعَصْرِ وَاَضْرِبَكَ عَلٰى
تَضْيِيْعِ صَلٰوةِ الْعَصْرِ اِلَى الْمَغْرِبِ وَاَضْرِبَكَ عَلٰى تَضْيِيْعِ صَلٰوةِ الْمَغْرِبِ اِلَى
الْعِشَاءِ وَاَضْرِبَكَ عَلٰى تَضْيِيْعِ صَلٰوةِ الْعِشَاءِ اِلَى الْفَجْرِ فَكُلَّمَا ضَرَبَهٗ ضَرْبَةً
يَغُوْصُ فِي الْاَرْضِ سَبْعِيْنَ ذِرَاعًا وَلَايَزَالُ فِي الْقَبْرِ مُعَذَّبًا اِلٰى عِنْدَ خُرُوْجِهٖ مِنَ
الْقَبْرِ فِيْ مَوْقِفِ الْقِيٰمَةِ فَشِدَّةُ الْحِسَابِ وَسَخَطُ الرَّبِّ وَدُخُوْلُ النَّارِ وَفِيْ رِوَايَةٍ
فَاِنَّهٗ يَاْتِيْ يَوْمَ الْقِيَامَةِ وَعَلٰى وَجْهِهٖ ثَلَاثَةُ اَسْطُرٍ مَّكْتُوْبَاتٍ اَلسَّطْرُ الْاَوَّلُ يَامُضَيِّعَ
حَقِّ اللّٰهِ اَلسَّطْرُ الثَّانِيْ يَامَخْصُوْصًا بِغَضَبِ اللّٰهِ اَلثَّالِثُ كَمَا ضَيَّعْتَ فِي الدُّنْيَا
حَقَّ اللّٰهِ فَاٰيِسْ اَلْيَوْمَ اَنْتَ مِنْ رَحْمَةِ اللّٰهِ

It is said in a hadith that, Allah bestows five favours on a person who is mindful of his salaat, viz: His daily bread is made easy for him; he is saved from the punishments in the grave; he shall receive his record in his right hand on the Day of Judgement; he shall cross the Siraat with the speed of lightning and he shall enter Paradise without reckoning. As for him who neglects his salaat, he shall meet five types of punishments in this world, three at the time of death, three in the grave and three after resurrection.

Those in this world are: he is not blessed in life; he is deprived of the light with which the faces of the righteous are endowed; he receives no rewards for his good practices; his prayers are not answered; and he has no share in the prayers of the pious. Those at the time of death are: he dies disgracefully; he dies hungry; he dies in thirst; which the water in the oceans of the world cannot quench.

Those in the grave are: He is so squeezed there that the ribs of one side penetrate into the ribs of the other side; fire is burnt inside for him and he is rolled on cinders day and night; a serpent with fiery eyes and iron nails equal in length to a day's journey is let loose on him and shouts with a thundering voice, 'My Lord has charged me with thrashing you till sunrise for neglecting Fajr, till Asr for neglecting Zuhur, till sunset for neglecting Asr, till Ishaa for neglecting Maghrib and till dawn for neglecting Ishaa. The serpent will keep on thrashing him thus till the Last Day. Each blow pushes him to a depth of seventy arm's length. The punishments will last till the Day of Judgement.

Those after resurrection are: His reckoning will be a hard one; Allah will be angry with him; and he will be thrown into the Fire. According to one report, he will have following three lines inscribed on his forehead:

'O you who neglected Allah's duty'
'O you who has deserved Allah's wrath.'
'Now despair of Allah's mercy, as you neglected our duty to Allah.'

Eminent theologians like Ibn Hajr, Abu Laith Samarqandi (Rahmatullah alaihim), and others, have mentioned this hadith in their books. Although I have not been able to trace the text in original books on hadith, yet other hadiths, some of which have already been mentioned and some are to follow, corroborate its meaning. Neglect of salaat, as has been stated above, leads one to kufr; hence no punishment is too severe for this offence. But it should be borne in mind that even after the declaration of a person as being guilty, Allah is free to pardon him as and when he pleases. He says in His Holy Book:

اِنَّ اللّٰهَ لَایَغْفِرُ اَنْ یُّشْرَكَ بِهٖ وَیَغْفِرُ مَادُوْنَ ذٰلِكَ لِمَنْ یَّشَآءُ

"Lo! Allah pardoneth not that partners should be ascribed unto Him. Allah pardoneth all (save that) whom He will. (IV: 116)"

If then it pleases Allah to pardon anybody neglecting salaat, it will be most fortunate; but who can be sure of this fortune?

It is also stated in hadith that there will be three courts to be held by Allah on the Day of Judgement. The first will judge between kufr and islaam and there will be no pardon. The second will be to judge the duties and conduct of one towards another. All aggrieved shall be compensated there; compensation will either be realised from the aggressor or paid by Allah Himself, if He pleases to pardon anybody. The third will deal with duties towards Allah. Here the doors of Allah's mercy will be thrown wide-open and He shall pardon anybody He wills. In the light of all that has been said above, it must be clearly understood that we deserve the punishments that have been laid down for our commission of sins, but the All-embracing mercy of Allah overrides everything and knows no bounds.

It was a habit with the Prophet (Sallallaho alaihe wasallam) to enquire from the companions, just after Fajr, if anybody had seen any dream. He would then interpret the dream as related to him. One day, after enquiring from others as usual, the Prophet (Sallallaho alaihe wasallam) himself narrated a long dream in which two men came and took him with them. Besides others he reported certain events which he happened to see in his dream. He said: "I noticed the head of a person being crushed with a heavy stone. It was struck with such force that, after crushing the head, the stone rolled down over a long distance. The head would assume its normal shape by the time the stone was brought back for repeating the process. This continued incessantly. On inquiring from one of my companions, I was told that the person first learnt the Qur'an, but failed to practise upon it and also used to go to sleep without offering the fardh salaat." There is another similar narration, in which the Prophet (Sallallaho alaihe wasallam) is reported to have seen (in his dream) a group of people being treated likewise. Jibra-eel (Alayhis salaam) informed him on his query that those were the persons who used to neglect their salaat.

Mujahid (Rahmatullah alaih) says, "Allah blesses the people who guard their salaat, just as he blessed Hadhrat Ibrahim (Alayhis salaam) and his descendants."

Hadhrat Anas (Radhiyallaho anho) narrates that he heard the Prophet (Sallallaho alaihe wasallam) saying, "If a person dies with sincere Imaan, observing the commandments of Allah, performing salaat, and paying Zakaat, when he dies Allah is pleased with him."

Hadhrat Anas (Radhiyallaho anho) also narrates that he heard the Prophet (Sallallaho alaihe wasallam) saying, "Allah says, 'I hold back retribution, deserved by a locality, when I see therein some people who frequently visit the musjid, love one another for My sake, and pray for forgiveness in the hours of darkness."

Hadhrat Abu Darda (Radhiyallaho anho) wrote to Hadhrat Salmaan: "Spend most of your time in the musjid. I have heard the Prophet (Sallallaho alaihe wasallam) saying, "The musjid is the abode of the pious. Allah has taken upon Himself to bless the person who spends most of his time in the mosque. Allah shall keep him in comfort and shall make him cross the Siraat with great ease. Surely Allah is pleased with such a person."

Hadhrat Abdullah bin Mas'ood (Radhiyallaho anho) narrates that he heard the Prophet (Sallallaho alaihe wasallam) saying: "The masaajid are the Houses of Allah, and people coming therein are His visitors. When everybody treats his visitors kindly, why should Allah not be kind to His guests?"

Hadhrat Abu Sa'eed Khudri (Radhiyallaho anho) narrates that he heard the Prophet (Sallallaho alaihe wasallam) saying: "Allah loves the person who is attached to the musjid."

Hadhrat Abu Hurairah (Radhiyallaho anho) narrates that he heard the Prophet (Sallallaho alaihe wasallam) saying, "When a dead person is laid in the grave, even before the people present at his burial clear off, Munkar and Nakeer visit him. Then, if the person is a Mo'min, his good practices encircle him; salaat comes close to his head, Zakaat to his right, Fast to his left, and the remaining good deeds towards his feet, so that none can approach him. Even the angels do the necessary questioning while standing at a distance."

One of the companions reports that, when the inmates of the Prophet's house were hard-pressed in any way, he would enjoin salaat on them and recite the following verse:

وَاْمُرْ اَهْلَكَ بِالصَّلٰوةِ وَاصْطَبِرْ عَلَيْهَا لَانَسْئَلُكَ رِزْقًا نَحْنُ نَرْزُقُكَ وَالْعَاقِبَةُ لِلتَّقْوٰى

"And enjoin salaat upon thy people and be constant therein. We ask not of thee a provision, We provide for thee. And the Hereafter is for the righteousness."
(XX: 132).

Asma (Radhiyallaho anha) narrates that she heard the Prophet (Sallallaho alaihe wasallam) saying, "All the people will be gathered together on the Day of Judgement and they will all hear the voice of the announcing angel He will say, 'where are those who glorified Allah in ease and adversity?' A group will rise up and enter Paradise without reckoning. It will then be announced, 'where are those who forsook their beds and spent their nights in worship?' Another group will rise up and enter Paradise without reckoning. The angel will again announce, 'where are those whom trade and business did not distract from remembrance of Allah?" Yet another group will rise up and enter Paradise.' In another hadith, the same account is given, with the addition that in the beginning the angel will say. "All those gathered here will see today who are the honoured people", and with the modification that the angel at the time of third announcement will say, 'Where are those whom their engagement in trade and business did not distract from salaat and remembrance of Allah?"

Sheik Nasr Samarqandi (Rahmatullah alaih), after quoting this Hadith writes, "When all the three groups will have entered Paradise without reckoning, a monster with a long neck, shining eyes and most eloquent tongue will rise up from Hell and say, 'I have been deputed on all who are proud and ill-tempered.' It will then pick up all such persons from the crowd, as a fowl picks up grain and then it will fling them into the Hell. It will rise up again saying, 'This time I have been deputed on all who maligned Allah and His Apostle' (Sallallaho alaihe wassallam).' It will then pick up all such persons and throw them into the Hell; it will appear for the third time and will, in a similar manner, take away all those who made images and pictures. The reckoning will then commence after these three groups have been eliminated."

It is said that during the early times people could see Satan. A person approached him saying how could he be like him. Satan told him that had he never received such a request before and asked him what had prompted him to ask for it. The person told him that he wished it from his heart. Satan told him to neglect his salaat and to swear very frequently, not caring whether he was doing it truthfully. The person told Satan that he would swear by Allah never to give up salaat and swear falsely. Satan told him that never before he had been tricked by a human being to seek his advice. He was determined never to do so in future.

Hadhrat Ubayy (Radhiyallaho anho) narrates that he heard the Prophet (Sallallaho alaihe wasallam) saying, "Give glad tidings to the Muslims that they shall be honoured and exalted, and their religion shall prevail, but there is no portion in the Hereafter for those who exploit Islam for wordly gains."

The Prophet (Sallallaho alaihe wasallam) is reported to have said, "I saw Allah in His best form. He said to me, 'O Muhammad! what are the Highest Chiefs (Angels) arguing about?' I said, 'I have no knowledge about that.' Allah placed His gracious hand on my bosom. I felt its solacing coolness right through my heart, and the entire universe was revealed to me. I said, 'They are arguing about the things which exalt, the things which atone for the sins, the rewards for the paces taken while going for salaat (with Jamaat), the virtues of performing wudhu properly when it was very cold, and the blessings that a person deserves when after performing one salaat he keeps on sitting in musjid till the next salaat.' A person particular of these shall live a blessed life and shall die an enviable death."

The Prophet (Sallallaho alaihe wasallam) is reported (in many ahaadith) to have said, "Allah says, 'O, Son of Aadam! Say four rakaats of salaat in the early part of the day. I shall help thee in accomplishing all thy jobs during the rest of the day."

It is said in a hadith: "Salaat is the cause of Allah's pleasure, is loved by the Angels, is a tradition of the Prophets, gives enlightenment about Allah, causes the prayers to be granted, blesses the daily bread, is the root of Imaan, refreshes the body, is a weapon against the enemy, shall intercede for its adherent, is a light in the darkness and a companion in the loneliness of the grave, is a reply to the questioning of Angels, is a shade against the Sun on the Day of Judgement, is a protection against the fire of Hell, is a weight for the scales of good deeds, is a means of swift crossing over the Siraat and is a key to Paradise."

Hadhrat Uthman (Radhiyallaho anho) is reported to have said, "Allah bestows nine favours on a person who guards his salaat and is particular in performing it at its appointed hours: viz; He is loved by Allah, he enjoys good health, is constantly under the protection of angels, his home is blessed, the light of righteousness shines on his face, his heart is made soft, he shall cross the Siraat with the speed of lightning, he is saved from Hell, and his neighbours in Paradise are those about whom Allah has said,

لَاخَوْفٌ عَلَيْهِمْ وَلَا هُمْ يَحْزَنُوْنَ

'There shall be no fear come upon them, neither shall they grieve (II: 36).

The Prophet (Sallallaho alaihe wasallam) says, "Salaat is the Pillar of Islam and it has ten virtues, viz: It is a charm of the face, a light of the heart, health and refreshment for the body, a company in the grave, a means for the descent of Allah's Mercy, a key to the Heaven, a weight of the scales (of good deeds) a means of winning Allah's pleasure, a price of Paradise and a protection against the fire of Hell. A person who is particular of salaat, in fact, establishes deen and one who neglects it demolishes (so to say, the structure of) deen."

According to one hadith, there is healing in salaat. Once the Prophet (Sallallaho alaihe wasallam) saw Hadhrat Abu Hurairah (Radhiyallaho anho) lying on his stomach. He said to him, "Are you suffering from stomach pain?" He replied in the affirmative. The Prophet (Sallallaho alaihe wasallam) said, "Then get up and busy yourself in salaat, for that will heal you."

Once the Prophet (Sallallaho alaihe wasallam), in his dream, saw Paradise and heard the footsteps of Hadhrat Bilaal (Radhiyallaho anha) there. Next morning he said to Bilaal: What deed of yours helped you to follow me even to Paradise?" He replied: "When my wudhu breaks even at night, I take a fresh wudhu and say as many 'rakaats' of nafl salaat as I can."

Safeeri (Rahmatullah alaih) writes: "The Angels address a person who misses Fajr as 'O you wrongdoer', and one who neglects Zuhr as 'O you loser', and one who ignores Asr as 'O you transgressor', and one who omits Maghrib as 'O you kaafir', and one who does not say Ishaa as 'O you violator of Allah's commandments."

Alama Sha'raani (Rahmatullah alaih) writes: "It should be clearly understood that a calamity is drawn off from a locality the people of which are particular about salaat, whereas a locality the people of which neglect salaat is frequently visited by calamities. Earthquakes, thunderbolts and sinking of houses are not unexpected where people are not particular about salaat. Simply guarding one's own salaat is not enough, because when a calamity strikes, it does not befall the wrongdoers alone. It affects everybody in that locality. Once the Sahabah asked the Prophet (Sallallaho alaihe wasallam): "Can we perish while there are pious people among us?" the Prophet (Sallallaho alaihe wasallam) replied, "Yes, if vice becomes predominant." It is therefore necessary that other people should also be enjoined to stick to Allah's commandments and refrain from wrongdoing.

Hadith VIII

رُوِىَ اَنَّهُ عَلَيْهِ الصَّلٰوةُ وَالسَّلَامُ قَالَ مَنْ تَرَكَ الصَّلٰوةَ حَتّٰى مَضٰى وَقْتُهَا ثُمَّ
قَضٰى عُذِّبَ فِى النَّارِ حُقْبًا وَالْحُقْبُ ثَمَانُوْنَ سَنَةً وَالسَّنَةُ ثَلٰثُمِائَةٍ وَسِتُّوْنَ يَوْمًا
كُلُّ يَوْمٍ كَانَ مِقْدَارُهُ اَلْفَ سَنَةٍ كذا في مجالس الأبرار

The Prophet (Sallallaho alaihe wasallam) is reported to have said, "A person neglecting his salaat (even though he makes it up later) shall remain in Hell for a period of one Haqb. A Haqb is equal to eighty years of three hundred and sixty days each, and a day in the Hereafter shall equal one thousand years of this world."

Abul Laith Samarqandi (Rahmatullah alaih) is responsible for the hadith in which the Prophet (Sallallaho alaihe wasallam) is reported to have said, "The name of a person who neglects even a single fardh salaat intentionally is written on the gate of the Hell, which he must enter." Hadhrat Ibn Abbas (Radhiyallaho anho) narrates that once the Prophet (Sallallaho alaihe wasallam) said, "Pray, O Allah! cause not any one of us to be a wretched destitute." He then said: "Do you know who is a wretched destitute?" At the request of the companions, he explained to them saying, "A wretched destitute is he who neglects his salaat. In Islaam there is nothing for him." In another hadith it is said, "Allah will not care a bit for the person who has been neglecting salaat intentionally, and for him shall be an awful doom."

It is reported in a hadith that ten persons will be specially tormented, and one of them will be the person who neglects his salaat. It is said that his hands will be tied while the angels shall smite him on his face and back. Paradise will tell him, 'In me there is no room for you,' and Hell will say to him, 'Come to me. You are for me and I am for you.' It is also reported that there is a valley in Hell named Lamlam. This valley is infested with serpents as fat as the neck of a camel and as long as one month's journey. A person neglecting salaat shall be tormented in this valley. In another hadith, it is reported that there is a vale in the Hell, which is known as the Pit of Grief; it is infested with scorpions of the size of a mule. This place is also meant for tormenting the people who neglect salaat. Of course, there is nothing to worry if the most merciful Allah pardons the sins. But are we really prepared to ask for His pardon?

Ibn Hajar writes, "A woman died. Her brother was present at her burial. By chance his purse fell into the grave and was buried with the dead body. The brother realized this after he had returned home and was very sorry for the loss. He decided to dig up the grave secretly and take out the purse. When he dug it up, he saw that the pit was in flames. He returned home, stricken with grief, and related the story to his mother, and inquired if she knew why it was so. The mother informed him that his sister used to delay in salaat and offered it after its fixed hours. May Allah save us from these habits!

Hadith IX

عَنْ اَبِيْ هُرَيْرَةَ رَضِيَ اللّٰهُ عَنْهُ قَالَ قَالَ رَسُوْلُ اللّٰهِ ﷺ لَاسَهْمَ فِيْ الْاِسلَامِ لِمَنْ لَّاصَلٰوةَ لَهُ وَلَاصَلٰوةَ لِمَنْ لَاوُضُوْءَ لَهُ أخرجه البزار وأخرج الحاكم عن عائشة مرفوعًا وصححه ثلث احلف عليهن لايجعل الله من له سهم في الاسلام كمن لاسهم له وسهام الْاسلام الصوم والصلٰوة والصدقة الحديث وأخرج الطبراني في الأوسط عن ابن عمر مرفوعًا لادين لمن لاصلٰوة له إنما موضع الصلٰوة من الدين كموضع الراس من الجسد كذا في الدر المنثور

Hadhrat Abu Hurairah (Radhiyallaho anho) narrates that he heard the Prophet (Sallallaho alaihe wasallam) saying: "There is no place in Islaam for a person who does not say his salaat, and there is no salaat without wudhu." Hadhrat Abdullah bin Umar (Radhiyallaho anho) also heard the Prophet (Sallallaho alaihe wasallam) saying, "There is no Islaam in a person when there is no salaat by him. The position of salaat in Islaam is as the position of the head in a body."

Let those who do not offer salaat, and not only call themselves Muslims, but also boast of their being champions of the Muslim cause, ponder over these words of the Holy Prophet (Sallallaho alaihe wasallam). They dream of reviving the past glory of Islaam, but would not care to know how rigidly the people responsible for that glory stuck to the practices of Islaam.

Hadhrat Abdullah bin Abbas (Radhiyallaho anho) suffered from cataract of the eye. People told him that the disease could be treated, but he would have to miss his salaat for a few days. He said: "This is not possible; I have heard the Prophet (Sallallaho alaihe wasallam) saying, 'A person who does not say his salaat shall stand before Allah while Allah shall be angry with him." The companions of the Prophet would rather like to go blind than to forego salaat (though permissible under such circumstances) even for a few days. When on his last day Hadhrat Umar (Radhiyallaho anho) was stabbed by a Majoos, he often remained unconscious and eventually died due to excessive bleeding. While on his death-bed, he was made conscious of the approaching salaat hours and he performed salaat in that very condition, and would remark: "There is no lot in Islaam for a person who does not say his salaat." These days it is considered unkind and improper to induce the patient or even allow him to say his salaat. What a world of difference is there between the view-points and approach of the Muslims of these two ages!

Hadhrat Ali (Radhiyallaho anho) once requested the Prophet (Sallallaho alaihe wasallam) to give him a servant. The Prophet (Sallallaho alaihe wasallam) said "Here are three slaves; take any one you like." Hadhrat Ali (Radhiyallaho anho) said, "You may kindly choose one for me." The Prophet (Sallallaho alaihe wasallam) pointed towards a certain man and said, "Take this one; he is particular about his salaat. But you are not to beat him. We are forbidden to beat one who says salaat." We, on the other hand, mock at our servant and consider him a liability if he goes for salaat.

Sufyaan Thauri (Rahmatullah alaih), the famous Soofi once fell into a state of ecstasy. He remained in his house for seven days without sleep, food and drink. When his Shaikh was informed of his condition, he inquired if Sufyaan was observing the hours of his salaat. He was told that his salaat was quite regular and safe. At this, the Shaikh remarked, "Glory be to Allah, Who has not allowed the Devil to have an upper hand on him!"

PART II

IMPORTANCE OF JAMAAT

As has already been said in the foreword, there are many who say their salaat regularly but are not very particular about Jamaat. The Prophet (Sallallaho alaihe wasallam) is as emphatic in enjoining Jamaat as he is particular about salaat. This part also consists of two chapters. The first deals with the rewards of Jamaat and the second with the consequences of its neglect.

CHAPTER I

REWARDS OF JAMAAT

Hadith I

عَنْ اِبْنِ عُمَرَ رَضِىَ اللّٰهُ عَنْهُ اَنَّ رَسُوْلَ اللّٰهِ ﷺ قَالَ صَلٰوةُ الْجَمَاعَةِ اَفْضَلُ مِنْ صَلٰوةِ الْفَذِّ بِسَبْعٍ وَّعِشْرِيْنَ دَرَجَةً رواه مالك والبخاري ومسلم والترمذي كذا في الترغيب

Hadhrat Abdullah bin Umar (Radhiyallaho anha) narrates that he heard the Prophet (Sallallaho alaihe wasallam) saying: "A salaat with Jamaat is twenty-seven times superior to salaat performed individually."

When we offer our salaat for getting reward from Allah, then why should it not be done in the musjid, where the reward earned is twenty-seven times more. Nobody will be so unwise as to forego a profit twenty-seven times greater with simply a little extra labour. But we are so indifferent about the profits promised for our religious practices! This can be due to nothing but our disregard for deen and the rewards of it. It is a pity that we apply ourselves so hard to acquiring the trifling gains in this material world; but are so unmindful of the gains in the Hereafter, which yield twenty-seven times more with a little extra effort. We often argue that for going to the musjid for Jamaat we have to close the shop and will thus lose business. These pretexts and others of the kind cannot stand in the way of those who have perfect faith in the Greatness of Allah, and in His word; and who realize the value of the blessings and reward in the Hereafter. It is in respect of such people that Allah says:

رِجَالٌ لَّاتُلْهِيْهِمْ تِجَارَةٌ وَّلَابَيْعٌ عَنْ ذِكْرِ اللهِ وَاِقَامِ الصَّلٰوةِ

"Men, whom neither merchandise nor sale beguileth then from remembrance of Allah and constancy in salaat." (XXIV; 37).

It is said of Saalim Haddaad (Rahmatullah alaih) (a trader and a great Soofi) that on hearing Azaan he would turn pale and grow restless. He would stand up immediately, leaving his shop open and recite these couplets:—

1. "When Thy summoner stands up to summon, quickly I stand up.

   To respond to (the summons of) The Mighty Lord Who hath no peer."

2. "I reply to the summons with complete submission and cheer, 'Here am I, O Bountiful One."

3. "My face grows pale with awe and fear, and occupation in Thee distracts me from all other occupations."

4. "I swear by Thee, naught is dear to me save Thy remembrance.

   Nothing is more ravishing for me than Thy sweet name."

5. "O, will there be a time for us to be together?
   A lover is happy only when he is with his love."

6. "He whose eyes have seen the light of Thy Beauty Can never be solaced. He must die yearning for Thee."

It is said in a hadith: "People frequenting the musjid are its pegs (dwellers). Angels are their companions and visit them when they are sick and help them when they are at their jobs."

Hadith II

عَنْ اَبِيْ هُرَيْرَةَ رضِىَ اللهُ عَنْهُ قَالَ قَالَ رَسُوْلُ اللهِ ﷺ صَلٰوةُ الرَّجُلِ فِيْ جَمَاعَةٍ
تَضْعَفُ عَلٰى صَلٰوتِهِ فِيْ بَيْتِهِ وَفِيْ سُوْقِهِ خَمْسًا وَّعِشْرِيْنَ ضِعْفًا وَّذٰلِكَ اَنَّهُ اِذَا

تَوَضَّا فَاَحْسَنَ الْوُضُوْءَ ثُمَّ خَرَجَ اِلَى الْمَسْجِدِ لَايُخْرِجُهُ اِلَّا الصَّلٰوةُ لَمْ يَخْطُ خُطْوَةً اِلَّا رُفِعَتْ لَهُ بِهَا دَرَجَةٌ وَحُطَّ عَنْهُ بِهَا خَطِيْئَةٌ فَإِذَا صَلّٰى لَمْ تَزَلِ الْمَلٰئِكَةُ تُصَلِّى عَلَيْهِ اَللّٰهُمَّ ارْحَمْهُ وَلَايَزَالُ فِيْ صَلٰوةٍ مَاانْتَظَرَ الصَّلٰوةَ رواه البخاري واللفظ له ومسلم وأبوداود والترمذي وابن ماجه كذا في الترغيب

"Hadhrat Abu Hurairah (Radhiyallaho anho) narrates that he heard the Prophet (Sallallaho alaihe wasallam) saying, "Salaat with Jamaat is twenty-five times superior to salaat which is said in a house or in a shop. It is so because when a person performs wudhu in right earnest and walks on to the musjid, with the sole intention of performing salaat, each step he takes, adds one blessing to his account and wipes out one sin therefrom. Again, if he keeps sitting in the musjid (with wudhu of course) after the salaat is over, the angels keep on seeking Allah's blessing and forgiveness for him. And as long as he keeps sitting in the musjid waiting for salaat, he goes on earning rewards as if he is busy in salaat."

In Hadith No. I, the superiority of salaat with Jamaat over that offered individually is described as being twenty-seven times more, while this hadith mentions only twenty-five times. Various theologians have discussed at length this seeming inconsistency. The following are some of the explanations:

1. "This variation from twenty-five to twenty-seven is due to variation of ikhlaas (sincerity) in different individuals."

2. "In Sirri (quiet) salaat (i.e., Zuhr and Asr), it is twenty-five times, while in Jahri (loud) salaat (i.e., Fajr, Maghrib and Ishaa), it is twenty-seven times."

3. "In Fajr and Ishaa, when it is somewhat inconvenient to go out due to cold and darkness, it is twenty-seven times, but in other salaats it is twenty-five times."

4. "In the beginning it was twenty-five times, but subsequently Allah (by special favour on the followers of the Prophet (Sallallaho alaihe wasallam) raised the reward to twenty-seven times."

Some others have brought forward a still finer explanation. They say that the reward for salaat with Jamaat mentioned in this Hadith is not merely 25 times but a doubling (2 raised to the power) twenty-five times, which comes to 33,554,432 times. This is something not beyond the bountiful Mercy of Allah. When neglect of one salaat can cause punishment in Hell for one Huqb (as we have seen in the last chapter), so much reward for one salaat with Jamaat is quite conceivable.

The Prophet (Sallallaho alaihe wasallam) has also explained to us how the reward goes on increasing in the case of a person who, after performing wudhu, leaves his house with the sole intention of joining Jamaat for salaat in the musjid. Each step he takes, brings one reward as well as washes away one sin. Banu Salama, a clan in Madina, had their houses at some distance. They intended to shift close to the musjid. The Prophet (Sallallaho alaihe wasallam) however, advised them saying: "Stay where you are. Every step you take when coming to musjid is written in your account." It is said in a hadith: "The likeness of a person performing wudhu at home and then leaving for musjid is as the likeness of of a person who, after dressing in the ihraam (Hajj apparel) at his house, leaves for Hajj".

Further, in the same hadith, the Prophet (Sallallaho alaihe wasallam) points to another act of great value; i.e., as long as one remains sitting in musjid after the salaat is over, the angels pray for him asking for forgiveness and mercy. The angels are the innocent and holy creation of Allah. So, the effectiveness of their prayers is self-evident.

Muhammad bin Samaak (Rahmatullah alaih) is a famous theologian and Sheikh. He died at the age of one hundred and three. He used to perform two hundred rakaats of nafl salaat daily. He writes: "For forty years, I never missed the first takbeer of salaat with Jamaat, except once when my mother had died." The same Shaikh writes: "Once I missed the Jamaat. As I knew that salaat with Jamaat was twenty-five times superior, I repeated this salaat (individually) twenty-five times to make up the loss. I heard in my dream some one saying to me, 'Muhammad! You have repeated your salaat 25 times (in the hope of making good the loss), but what about the 'Aameen' by the Angels?" It is reported in many ahaadith that when the Imaam says 'Aameen' after Fatihah, the Angels also say Aameen and all the past sins of a person whose Ameen, coincides with that of the Angels are forgiven. This is possible only in a salaat with Jamaat, hence Maulana Abdul Hayy quoting this story about the Shaikh writes: "Even if a person goes on repeating his salaat (individually) a thousand times, he cannot get the collective blessing of a salaat with Jamaat." This is obvious. He not only loses 'Aameen' with the Angels, but also the blessings of the congregation and the prayers of the Angels after salaat, with many other spiritual benefits. This should also be borne in mind that the prayers of Angels can be deserved only when the salaat is a proper one. If the salaat of a person is not, as it should be (according to hadith) it is flung back like a dirty rag at his face, then how can the Angels pray for him?

Hadith III

عَنْ اِبْنِ مَسْعُوْدٍ رَضِىَ اللّٰهُ عَنْهُ قَالَ مَنْ سَرَّهُ اَنْ يَلْقَى اللّٰهَ غَدًا مُّسْلِمًا فَالْيُحَافِظْ عَلٰى هٰؤُلَآءِ الصَّلَوَاتِ حَيْثُ يُنَادٰى بِهِنَّ فَاِنَّ اللّٰهَ تَعَالٰى شَرَعَ لِنَبِيِّكُمْ ﷺ سُنَنَ الْهُدٰى وَاِنَّهُنَّ مِنْ سُنَنِ الْهُدٰى وَلَوْ اَنَّكُمْ صَلَّيْتُمْ فِيْ بُيُوْتِكُمْ كَمَا يُصَلِّىْ هٰذَا الْمُتَخَلِّفُ فِيْ بَيْتِهِ لَتَرَكْتُمْ سُنَّةَ نَبِيِّكُمْ وَلَوْ تَرَكْتُمْ سُنَّةَ نَبِيِّكُمْ لَضَلَلْتُمْ وَمَامِنْ رَجُلٍ يَتَطَهَّرُ فَيُحْسِنُ الطُّهُوْرَ ثُمَّ يَعْمَدُ اِلٰى مَسْجِدٍ مِنْ هٰذِهِ الْمَسَاجِدِ اِلَّا كَتَبَ اللّٰهُ لَهُ بِكُلِّ خُطْوَةٍ يَخْطُوْهَا حَسَنَةً وَيَرْفَعُهُ بِهَا دَرَجَةً وَيَحُطُّ عَنْهُ بِهَا سَيِّئَةً وَلَقَدْ رَاَيْتُنَا وَمَايَتَخَلَّفُ عَنْهَا اِلَّا مُنَافِقٌ مَّعْلُوْمُ النِّفَاقِ وَلَقَدْ كَانَ الرَّجُلُ يُؤْتٰى بِهَا يُهَادٰى بَيْنَ الرَّجُلَيْنِ حَتّٰى يُقَامَ فِى الصَّفِّ وَفِىْ رِوَايَةٍ لَقَدْ رَاَيْتُنَا وَمَايَتَخَلَّفُ عَنِ الصَّلٰوةِ اِلَّا مُنَافِقٌ قَدْ عُلِمَ نِفَاقُهُ اَوْ مَرِيْضٌ اِنْ كَانَ الرَّجُلُ لَيَمْشِىْ بَيْنَ الرَّجُلَيْنِ حَتّٰى يَاْتِيَ الصَّلٰوةَ وَقَالَ اِنَّ رَسُوْلَ اللّٰهِ ﷺ عَلَّمَنَا سُنَنُ الْهُدٰى وَاِنَّ مِنْ سُنَنِ الْهُدٰى الصَّلٰوةُ فِي الْمَسْجِدِ الَّذِيْ يُؤَذَّنُ فِيْهِ رواه مسلم وأبو داود

Hadhrat Abdullah bin Masood (Radhiyallaho anho) says: "If one wishes to meet Allah on the Day of Judgement as a Muslim, he must say his salaat at a place where Azaan is called out, viz., a musjid, as Allah has prescribed through His Prophet (Sallallaho alaihe wasallam) such practices which are nothing but guidance through and through: and salaat (with Jamaat) is one of them. If you start saying your salaat at your houses (as so and so is doing), then you will be discarding the Sunnah of the Prophet (Sallallaho alaihe wasallam) and no sooner you desert his Sunnah than you go astray. When a person performs wudhu correctly and then leaves for the musjid, at each step that he takes, he gets one blessing and has one sin wiped out. During the lifetime of the Prophet (Sallallaho alaihe wasallam) no one would miss Jamaat except an open munaafiq or a real invalid. Even the munaafiq dared not miss the Jamaat and a sick person who could be taken to the musjid with the help of two men would be helped to join Jamaat."

This shows the extreme vigilance of the Sahabah over their salaat with Jamaat. Even a sick person was brought to the musjid somehow or other, even though it needed two men to help him. This concern was quite natural when they found the Prophet (Sallallaho alaihe wasallam) himself so very particular about it. It is said that when the Prophet (Sallallaho alaihe wasallam) was on his deathbed, and he would frequently faint, he succeeded in making wudhu after several attempts and, though he could hardly stand, went to the musjid with the help of Hadhrat Abbas (Radhiyallaho anho) and another companion. Hadhrat Abu Bakr (Radhiyallaho anho) led the salaat at his instance, and he himself joined the Jamaat."

Hadhrat Abu Darda (Radhiyallaho anho) narrates that the Prophet (Sallallaho alaihe wasallam) once said to him, "Worship your Lord as if you see Him before you, count yourself among the dead, beware of the curse of the wronged ones and, even if you could crawl to the musjid, do not miss Ishaa and Fajr with Jamaat."

It is said in another hadith, "Ishaa and Fajr are very heavy on those who are munaafiq. If they knew the reward of the Jamaat, they would go to the musjid and join the Jamaat even if they had to crawl."

Hadith IV

عَنْ اَنَسِ ابْنِ مَالِكٍ رَضِىَ اللهُ عَنْهُ قَالَ قَالَ رَسُوْلُ اللهِ ﷺ مَنْ صَلّٰى لِلّٰهِ اَرْبَعِيْنَ يَوْمًا فِيْ جَمَاعَةٍ يُدْرِكُ التَّكْبِيْرَةَ الْاُوْلٰى كُتِبَ لَهٗ بَرَائَتَانِ بَرَآئَةٌ مِّنَ النَّارِ وَبَرَآئَةٌ مِّنَ النِّفَاقِ رواه الترمذي

Hadhrat Anas bin Maalik (Radhiyallaho anho) narrates that he heard the Prophet (Sallallaho alaihe wasallam)

saying, "A person who in all sincerity is constant in his salaat with Jamaat for forty days, without missing the first takbeer, recieves two awards: one for deliverance from Hell and the other for freedom from nifaaq."

If a person is regular in his salaat (with sincerity) for forty days and joins the Jamaat from the very start (i.e., when the Imaam calls out his first takbeer), then he shall neither be a munaafiq nor shall he go to Hell. A munaafiq is a person who feigns being a Muslim, but there is kufr in his heart. Genesis of man (according to hadith) takes place in periods of forty days. This seems to be the significance of forty days in this hadith, and so the Soofis attach importance to this period (called Chillah in Urdu) for purposes of spiritual discipline.

Lucky indeed are the persons who do not miss their first takbeer for years together.

Hadith V

عَنْ اَبِيْ هُرَيْرَةَ رَضِىَ اللّٰهُ عَنْهُ قَالَ قَالَ رَسُوْلُ اللّٰهِ ﷺ مَنْ تَوَضَّأَ فَاَحْسَنَ
وُضُوْءَهٗ ثُمَّ رَاحَ فَوَجَدَ النَّاسَ قَدْ صَلَّوْا اَعْطَاهُ اللّٰهُ مِثْلَ اَجْرِ مَنْ صَلَّاهَا
وَحَضَرَهَا لَايَنْقُصُ ذٰلِكَ مِنْ اُجُوْرِهِمْ شَيْئًا رواه أبو داود والنسائى والحاكم

Hadhrat Abu Hurairah (Radhiyallaho anho) narrates that he heard the Prophet (Sallallaho alaihe wasallam) saying, "A person who performs wudhu scrupulously, and then goes to the musjid and finds that Jamaat is over, receives a reward equal to that of Jamaat. This would not diminish anything from the reward of those who have actually performed their salaat with Jamaat."

This is indeed Allah's great favour and beneficence that the mere effort and a slight exertion is enough to entitle us to a reward of Jamaat, though actually we fail to join it. Who is the loser then if we ourselves get left, and miss the bounties of the most Bountiful?

This hadith also shows that we should not postpone going to the musjid in apprehension of the Jamaat being over. Even if we find on reaching the musjid that Jamaat is over, we will still get the reward thereof. If, however, we are certain that the Jamaat is already over, then there is of course no idea in going to the musjid for Jamaat.

Hadith VI

عَنْ قُبَاثِ بْنِ اَشْيَمَ اللَّيْثِيْ رَضِىَ اللّٰهُ عَنْهُ قَالَ قَالَ رَسُوْلُ اللّٰهِ ﷺ صَلٰوةُ الرَّجُلَيْنِ يَؤُمُّ اَحَدُهُمَا صَاحِبَهُ اَزْكٰى عِنْدَ اللّٰهِ مِنْ صَلٰوةِ اَرْبَعَةٍ تَتْرٰى وَصَلٰوةُ اَرْبَعَةٍ اَزْكٰى عِنْدَ اللّٰهِ مِنْ صَلٰوةِ ثَمَانِيَةٍ تَتْرٰى وَصَلٰوةُ ثَمَانِيَةٍ يَّؤُمُّهُمْ اَحَدُهُمْ اَزْكٰى عِنْدَ اللّٰهِ مِنْ صَلٰوةِ مِائَةٍ تَتْرٰى رواه البزار والطبراني

Hadhrat Qubaath bin Ashyam Allaithi (Radhiyallaho anho) narrates that he heard the Prophet (Sallallaho alaihe wasallam) saying, "Two persons performing salaat together with one as Imaam are liked by Allah more than four persons saying salaat individually. Similarly four persons performing salaat with Jamaat are liked by Allah more than eight persons saying it individually. Similarly again, eight persons performing salaat with Jamaat are liked by Allah more than one hundred persons saying it individually."

In another hadith it is said, "A big Jamaat is more prefered by Allah than a small Jamaat." Some people think that there is no harm in having a small Jamaat of their own at their houses or at their business premises. This is not correct, as in the first place they are deprived of the reward of saying salaat in the musjid and secondly, they lose the blessing of salaat with a big Jamaat. The bigger the congregation, the more pleasing it is to Allah. When our sole aim is to achieve the pleasure of Allah, why should we not adopt a manner more pleasing to Him. It is reported in a hadith that Allah is pleased to see three things, namely, a row of worshippers offering salaat with Jamaat, a person busy in salaat at the time of Tahajjud at the dead of night, and a person fighting in the way of Allah."

Hadith VII

عَنْ سَهْلِ بْنِ سَعْدِ نِ السَّاعِدِيِّ رَضِىَ اللّٰهُ عَنْهُ قَالَ قَالَ رَسُوْلُ اللّٰهِ ﷺ بَشِّرِ الْمَشَّآئِيْنَ فِىْ الظُّلَمِ اِلَى الْمَسَاجِدِ بِالنُّوْرِ التَّامِّ يَوْمَ الْقِيٰمَةِ رواه ابن ماجة

Hadhrat Sahl bin Sa'd (Radhiyallaho anho) narrates that he heard the Prophet (Sallallaho alaihe wasallam) saying, "Give glad tidings to those who go to the musjid frequently during hours of darkness, for they will have perfect light on the Day of Judgement."

The value of going to the musjid in the darkness of night shall be realised on the dreadful Day of Judgement, when everybody shall be in a very miserable plight. A person subjecting himself to inconvenience in the hours of darkness in this world shall be more than compensated in the next, as he shall carry with him a light more glorious than that of the sun. In a hadith it is reported that such persons shall occupy the pulpits of light, with no worry at all, while others will be in utter bewilderment. In another hadith it is said, "Allah will say on the Day of Judgement, Where are My neighbours?" The Angels will inquire, "Who are Thy neighbours, O Allah?'. Allah will reply, 'Those who used to frequent the mosques."

In a hadith it is said, "Of all the places on this Earth, the mosques are the dearest to Allah, and the markets are the most offensive to Him."

In another hadith, the 'masaajid' are called "The gardens of Paradise."

Hadhrat Abu Sa'eed (Radhiyallaho anho) narrates, "The Prophet (Sallallaho alaihe wasallam) once said, 'Bear testimony to the Imaan of the person frequenting the musjid, and then he recited the following verse of the Qur'an'

إِنَّمَا يَعْمُرُ مَسَاجِدَ اللهِ مَنْ اٰمَنَ بِاللهِ وَالْيَوْمِ الْاٰخِرِ

"He only shall tend Allah's musjid who believes in Allah and the Last Day." (IV: 18)."

The following are a few more ahaadith about the virtues of salaat with Jamaat:—

1. "Making wudhu when inconvenient, walking towards the musjid and sitting there (after one salaat), waiting for the next salaat, wipe out the sins."

2. "The farther a person lives from the 'musjid' the greater the blessing he receives." This is so because a person coming from a distance shall have to walk more and, as already mentioned, every step will fetch him a blessing. For this very reason some companions have been reported to be taking short steps in going to the musjid in order to earn more blessings.

3. "There are three things in this world for which

people would fight with one another if they come to know their rewards. These are: To call out the Azaan; to go to the musjid for Zuhr in the scorching heat of the sun; and to be in the first line while in salaat with Jamaat."

4. "Seven persons shall be accommodated under the shade of Allah's mercy on the Day of Judgement, when everybody will be most bewildered under the inconceivably intense heat of the sun. One of them will be the person whose heart remains attached to the musjid. He is anxious to return to the musjid if he leaves it on any account. Another hadith narrates that Allah loves those who love the musjid."

Each article of faith in Islam is a source of innumerable blessings and rewards from Allah, and carries boundless benefits showered on those who adhere to it. Besides, no commandment of Allah is without a deep significance. It is often difficult to understand the full benefits of Allah's commandments, as no one can encompass His Knowledge and Wisdom. Some of the sages of Islam have tried to explain the importance of salaat with Jamaat, but their explanations vary with the extent of their understanding and their power to probe into Divine secrets. Our respected Shaikh, Shah Waliullah Dehlawi (may Allah illumine his grave), in his famous Book 'Hujjatullahil Balighah' writes:—

"To save the people from the fatal effects that their own customs and rituals can bring them, there is nothing more useful than to make one of the religious services so common a custom and so public a ritual that it may be performed openly before everybody by any person, whether he be learned or illiterate. The town-folk and the countrymen should both be equally anxious to observe it. It should become a subject of rivalry and pride among all of them, and it should be so universally practised that it becomes part and parcel of their social set-up, so much so, that life without it may be worthless for them. If this is achieved, it will help in establishing the worship and obedience of Allah and will form a very useful substitute for those rituals and customs which could cause them serious harm. Since salaat is the only religious observance that surpasses all others in importance and universality, both in reason and authority, it becomes therefore absolutely necessary to get it established universally by propagating it and by arranging special congregations, where it can be performed with absolute unity of form and purpose."

"Further, in every community or religious society. There are a few who have the capacity to lead, while the rest simply follow. There are some others who can be corrected with a little counsel or reproach. Then there is a third grade of people who are very weak in faith and, if they are not made to worship in public, they are prone to discard it altogether. It is therefore in the best interests of the Islamic society that all its members perform the worship collectively and in congregation, so that the delinquents may be distinguished from the observers and the shirkers from the adherents. This will also cause the people with less knowledge to follow the Ulama, and make the ignorant to learn from the learned the specific requirements of worship. The worshipper will distinguish right from wrong and genuine from counterfeit, so that the right and the genuine may prevail and the wrong and the counterfeit may be suppressed."

"Besides, these congregations of people loving Allah, seeking His Mercy, constantly fearing Him and having their hearts and souls turned to Him alone, have the wonderful effect of causing His blessings and Mercy to descend from Heaven.

"Moreover, the Muslim community has been raised so that the word of Allah be held supreme and Islamic Order be paramount over all others. This object cannot be achieved unless all Muslims, big and small, the elite and the common, the town folk and the countrymen, perform alike the most sublime service and the most sacred ritual of Islam (i.e., salaat) by assembling together in one place. It is for this reason that the Sharee-at (Islamic Law) lays such special stress on Friday congregation and on salaat with jamaat, by explaining the blessings that accrue therefrom and punishments awarded for neglect thereof. For the open and conspicuous observance of this important service, two types of assemblies are required; one for people of a clan or a particular locality and the other for the people of the whole town. Since the assembly of the former at any hour is convenient and that of the latter comparatively difficult, so for the former, the gathering for salaat (with jamaat) five times daily, has been laid down and in the case of the latter gathering, the weekly Friday salaat has been devised and ordained."

CHAPTER II

REPROACH ON GIVING UP JAMAAT

Just as Allah has promised rewards and blessings for adhering to His commandments, so has He warned us of the woeful consequences and punishments for their neglect. We are in bondage to Allah and as such it is obligatory on us to obey Him. No compensation or reward is due to us for our obedience to Him. If He gives a reward, it is surely a matter of His extreme favour on us. Similarly no punishments can be too much for us if we disobey Him—our Lord, for their can be no greater crime for a bondsman than to disobey his Master. Hence no warning or premonition was required to be imparted. Yet Allah and His Holy Prophet (Sallallaho alaihe wasallam) have so very kindly cautioned us in various ways, warned us frequently of the consequences and explained to us again and again, just to save us from disaster. If even then, we don't take a lesson, who could there be to save us from the inevitable consequences?

Hadith I

عَنْ اِبْنِ عَبَّاسٍ رَضِىَ اللّٰهُ عَنْهُ قَالَ قَالَ رَسُوْلُ اللّٰهِ ﷺ مَنْ سَمِعَ النِّدَآءَ فَلَمْ يَمْنَعْهُ مِنَ اتِّبَاعِهِ عُذْرٌ قَالُوْا وَمَا الْعُذْرُ قَالَ خَوْفٌ اَوْ مَرْضٌ لَمْ تُقْبَلْ مِنْهُ الصَّلٰوةُ الَّتِيْ صَلّٰى رواه أبو داود وابن حبان وابن ماجه بنحوه كذا في الترغيب وفي المشكواة رواه أبوداود والدارقطني

Hadhrat Ibn Abbas (Radhiyallaho anho) narrates, "I heard the Prophet (Sallallaho alaihe wasallam) saying, "If a person in spite of hearing the azaan does not go to the musjid (and he prefers to say his salaat at home) without a strong excuse, then his salaat is not accepted. When the Companions inquired as to what could be a strong excuse, he replied, "Illness or fear."

It may perhaps appear from this Hadith that the salaat performed at home (after hearing the Azaan) is no salaat at all; the Hanafiyyah do not hold this view. According to them, though the reward and blessings promised for fardh salaat will not be awarded, yet the person saying the salaat at his place does absolve himself of the obligation. But in the opinion of some of the companions and their successors, salaat with jamaat (after hearing the Azaan) is fardh and its discard is haraam. According to many other theologians, such a person is not even absolved of the obligation in respect of salaat of that hour. Anyhow, he is surely committing the sin of discarding jamaat. In another hadith narrated by Hadhrat Ibn Abbas, it is stated that such a person is guilty of disobedience of Allah and his Apostle (Sallallaho alaihe wasallam). Hadhrat Ibn Abbas (Radhiyallaho anho) also says, "No good is done by, nor any good is done to, the person who does not join jamaat after hearing the Azaan. Hadhrat Abu Hurairah (Radhiyallaho anho) says, "It is more appropriate to pour molten-lead into the ears of a person who does not go to join jamaat."

Hadith—II

عَنْ مُعَاذِ بْنِ اَنَسٍ رَضِىَ اللهُ عَنْهُ عَنْ رَسُوْلِ اللهِ ﷺ اَنَّهُ قَالَ الْجَفَآءُ كُلُّ الْجَفَاءِ وَالْكُفْرُ وَالنِّفَاقُ مَنْ سَمِعَ مُنَادِيَ اللهِ يُنَادِىْ اِلَى الصَّلٰوةِ فَلَايُجِيْبُهُ رواه أحمد

Hadhrat Mu'aaz bin Anas (Radhiyallaho anho) narrates that he heard the Prophet (Sallallaho alaihe wasallam) saying, "A person who does not go for salaat after hearing the Azaan is committing a great wrong and is doing an act of kufr and nifaaq."

According to this hadith, not to join jamaat after hearing the Azaan is not becoming of a Muslim and is the practice of a kaafir or a munaafiq. What a strong reproof!

In another hadith, it is said, "Not to join jamaat after hearing the Azaan is sufficient to render a person most unfortunate and most wretched."

Hadhrat Sulaimaan bin Abi Hathmah (Radhiyallaho anho) is one of the eminent people of the early days of Islam. He was born during the lifetime of the Prophet (Sallallaho alaihe wasallam), but was too young then to have had the honour of listening to any hadith from him. During the Caliphate of Hadhrat Umar (Radhiyallaho anho) he was made in charge of the market. One day Hadhrat Umar (Radhiyallaho anha) found him missing in Fajr salaat. Hadhrat Umar (Radhiyallaho anho) went to his house and inquired from his mother why Sulaimaan was not present in Fajr. She replied, "He kept saying nafl salaat throughout the night, and sleep overpowered him at the time of Fajr." At this, Hadhrat Umar (Radhiyallaho anho) remarked "I would prefer my Fajr with jamaat to my offering nafl salaat all night long."

Hadith–III

عَنْ اَبِيْ هُرَيْرَةَ رَضِىَ اللّٰهُ عَنْهُ قَالَ قَالَ رَسُوْلُ اللّٰهِ ﷺ لَقَدْ هَمَمْتُ اَنْ اٰمُرَ فِتْيَتِي فَيَجْمَعُوْا لِيْ حَزْمًا مِّنْ حَطَبٍ ثُمَّ آتِيْ قَوْمًا يُصَلُّوْنَ فِيْ بُيُوْتِهِمْ لَيْسَتْ بِهِمْ عِلَّةٌ فَاحْرِقُهَا عَلَيْهِمْ رواه مسلم

Hadhrat Abu Hurairah (Radhiyallaho anho) narrates that he heard the Prophet (Sallallaho alaihe wasallam) saying, "I wish I could ask the boys to collect a huge quantity of firewood for me, and then I would go around and set fire to the dwellings of those who say their salaat at their own houses without any excuse."

The Prophet (Sallallaho alaihe wasallam), who was most kind and merciful towards his followers and was greatly pained to see them even in a little trouble, gets offended so much that he is ready to set fire to the houses of those who are content with saying salaat at their houses.

Hadith–IV

عَنْ اَبِيْ دَرْدَاءِ رَضِىَ اللّٰهُ عَنْهُ قَالَ سَمِعْتُ قَالَ رَسُوْلُ اللّٰهِ ﷺ يَقُوْلُ مَامِنْ ثَلٰثَةٍ فِيْ قَرْيَةٍ وَّلَابَدْوٍ لَاتُقَامُ فِيْهِمُ الصَّلٰوةُ اِلَّا اسْتَحْوَذَ عَلَيْهِمُ الشَّيْطَانُ فَعَلَيْكُمْ بِالْجَمَاعَةِ فَاِنَّمَا يَاْكُلُ الذِّئْبُ مِنَ الْغَنَمِ الْقَاصِيَةِ رواه أحمد

Hadhrat Abu Darda (Radhiyallaho anho) narrates that he heard the Prophet (Sallallaho alaihe wasallam) saying, "If there are (even) three persons in a village or in a desert, and they do not say their salaat with jamaat, then Satan gets hold of them. Remember that jamaat for salaat is very necessary for you. Surely a wolf devours a lonely sheep, and Satan is the wolf for men."

This shows that people busy in farming etc. should arrange to say their salaat with jamaat if they are three or more in number. Even if they are two, it is better to have jamaat. The farmers in our country are generally negligent of salaat and consider their occupation a sufficient excuse for their neglect, and even those who are considered pious prefer to perform their salaat individually. If the farmers working in the nearby fields get together at a place and perform prayers in jamaat, they can have quite a big gathering and thereby receive the wonderful blessings of Allah. Notwithstanding the sun, rain, heat and cold, they keep busy for a trifling worldly gain, but lose tremendous amount of Allah's reward by losing salaat. On the other hand, they can earn a reward fifty times more (as conveyed in another hadith) by offering their salaat with jamaat in the fields.

It is stated in a hadith, "When a shepherd calls out the Azaan at the foot of a hill (or in the fields) and starts his salaat, Allah is greatly pleased with him and says proudly to the Angels, 'Behold My slave! He has called out the Azaan and is offering his salaat. All this he does out of fear for Me. I therefore grant him forgiveness and declare his admittance into Paradise."

Hadith–V

عَنْ اِبْنِ عَبَّاسٍ رَضِىَ اللّٰهُ عَنْهُ اَنَّهُ سُئِلَ عَنْ رَّجُلٍ يَّصُوْمُ النَّهَارَ وَيَقُوْمُ اللَّيْلَ وَلَايَشْهَدُ الْجَمَاعَةَ وَلَاالْجُمُعَةَ فَقَالَ هٰذَا فِى النَّارِ رواه الترمذي

Somebody asked Ibn Abbas (Radhiyallaho anho), "What about a person who keeps fast all day and offers nafl salaat all night, but does not go to the musjid for jamaat and Jumu'ah?" "He is doomed to Hell", replied Hadhrat Ibn Abbas (Radhiyallaho anho).

Such a person, being a Muslim, may ultimately get freedom from Hell, but who knows after how long. The ignorant among the Soofis and Shaikhs are very particular about Zikr and nafl salaat and consider this an act of eminence in piety, while they are not particular about salaat with jamaat. It must be clearly borne in mind for all times that no person can achieve religious eminence except through complete adherence to the practices of the beloved Prophet (Sallallaho alaihe wasallam).

It is stated in a hadith that Allah curses three persons: An Imaam who insists on leading the people of a place in salaat, although they do not like him on some reasonable account, a woman who is under the displeasure of her husband; and a person who hears the Azaan but does not go to the musjid for salaat with Jamaat.

Hadith–VI

اَخْرَجَ اِبْنُ مَرْدَوَيْهِ عَنْ كَعْبِ ن الْحِبْرِ قَالَ وَالَّذِيْ اَنْزَلَ التَّوْرٰةَ عَلٰى مُوْسٰى وَالْاِنْجِيْلَ عَلٰى عِيْسٰى وَالزَّبُوْرَ عَلٰى دَاوُدَ وَالْفُرْقَانَ عَلٰى مُحَمَّدٍ اُنْزِلَتْ هٰذِهِ الْاٰيَاتُ فِىْ الصَّلَوَاتِ الْمَكْتُوْبَاتِ حَيْثُ يُنَادٰى بِهِنَّ يَوْمَ يُكْشَفُ عَنْ سَاقٍ اِلٰى قَوْلِهِ وَهُمْ سَالِمُوْنَ ، الصَّلَوَاتُ الْخَمْسُ اِذَا نُوْدِىَ بِهَا وأخرج البيهقى في الشعب عن سعيد بن جبير قال الصلوات في الجماعات وأخرج البيهقى عن ابن عباس قال رجل يسمع الْاذان فلايجيب الصلٰوة كذا في الدر المنثور قلت وتمام الْاية يَوْمَ يُكْشَفُ عَنْ سَاقٍ وَّيُدْعَوْنَ اِلَى السُّجُوْدِ فَلَايَسْتَطِيْعُوْنَ خَاشِعَةً اَبْصَارُهُمْ تَرْهَقُهُمْ ذِلَّةٌ وَقَدْ كَانُوْا يُدْعَوْنَ اِلَى السُّجُوْدِ وَهُمْ سَالِمُوْنَ

Ka'b Ahbaar says, "By Him who revealed the Torah to Moosa, the Injeel to Eesa, the Psalms to Dawood (Alayhimus salaam), and the Qur'an on Muhammad (Sallallaho alaihe wasallam), the following verses were revealed in respect of saying fardh salaat in those places (mosques) where the Azaan is said: "On the day when the glory of Saaq is revealed and they are ordered to prostrate themselves, but are not able, with eyes downcast, abasement stupifying them. And they had been summoned to prostrate themselves when they were quite hale and healthy." (LXVIII: 42 and 43).

The glory of Saaq is a particular type of glory to be displayed on the Day of Judgement. All Muslims will fall prostrate on seeing this glory, but there will be some whose backs will turn stiff and they will be unable to prostrate themselves. As to who these unlucky persons would be, different interpretations have been given by different commentators. According to this hadith, which is also corroborated by another narrated by Hadhrat Ibn Abbas (Radhiyallaho anho), those shall be the persons who were called for salaat with jamaat, but did not go for it.

A few other interpretations of the same are given below:—

1. Hadhrat Abu Sa'eed Khudri (Radhiyallaho anho) narrates on the authority of the Prophet (Sallallaho alaihe wasallam) that these shall be the persons who used to offer their salaat to be seen by other men.

2. These shall be infidels who did not say salaat at all.
3. These shall be the munaafiqeen. (Allah knows best and His knowledge is most perfect).

What a terrible thing to be so abased and disgraced on the Day of Judgement that, while all Muslims shall fall prostrate at seeing Allah's glory, those who neglected salaat with jamaat shall be singled out by their inability to do so.

Besides these, many other warnings have been given against the neglect of jamaat. But as a matter of fact, none is necessary for a good Muslim to whom the word of Allah and His Apostle (Sallallaho alaihe wasallam) is all important. And for one who has no regard for their word, all such warnings are meaningless. But a time will come when every soul shall be called to account, and punished for its misdeeds, and then no amount of penitence shall be of any avail.

PART III

IMPORTANCE OF SINCERITY AND DEVOTION IN SALAAT

There are many persons who offer their salaat and quite a lot of them are particular about jamaat as well, but they say it so imperfectly that, instead of earning blessings and reward for them, it is rejected forthwith. This, however, is not so bad as to discard salaat altogether, which as we have already learnt, is very serious. Although we are deprived of the rewards by saying a defective salaat, which is not accepted, yet we are saved from the insolence of neglecting and disobeying Allah's commandments. However, when we spend our time, leave our work and undergo inconvenience, then why should we not see that we get the best return for our time and labour by saying our salaat as best as we can?

This third part is divided into three chapters. In the first chapter, a few quotations from the Holy Qur'an about the people who are condemned for their bad salaat and those who are praised for their good salaat, are given. In the second Chapter, stories about the salaat of a few lovers of Allah are collected. The third chapter consists of the sayings of the Prophet (Sallallaho alaihe wasallam) on this subject.

CHAPTER I

QUOTATIONS FROM THE QUR'AN

Quotation–I

لَنْ يَّنَالَ اللهَ لُحُوْمُهَا وَلَادِمَاؤُهَا وَلٰكِنْ يَّنَالُهُ التَّقْوٰى مِنْكُمْ

"Their flesh and their blood reach not Allah, but devotion from you reacheth to Him." (XXII: 37)

Although this particular verse refers to the animal sacrifice, yet in principle it equally applies to all other rituals. It is sincerity and devotion in a service by which its acceptance would be judged by Allah. Hadhrat Mu'aaz (Radhiyallaho anho) says, "When the Prophet (Sallallaho alaihe wasallam) deputed me to Yemen, I requested him to give me some parting advice. He replied, 'Be sincere in all your services, as sincerity will magnify the value of an action, however insignificant it may be."

Hadhrat Thaubaan (Radhiyallaho anho) narrates that he heard the Prophet (Sallallaho alaihe wasallam) saying, "Blessed be the sincere ones, for they are the lamps of guidance. They cause the worst evils to be driven off through their sincerity." It is said in another hadith, "It it through the presence of the weak and due to their salaat and their sincerity that Allah's help comes to all the people.'

Quotation–II

فَوَيْلٌ لِلْمُصَلِّيْنَ الَّذِيْنَ هُمْ عَنْ صَلَاتِهِمْ سَاهُوْنَ الَّذِيْنَ هُمْ يُرَاءُوْنَ

"Woe unto worshippers who are heedless of their salaat, who want but to be seen at salaat." (CVII: 4–6)

"To be heedless" has been given the following different interpretations:

1. To be so careless as to miss the correct time of salaat.
2. To be inattentive in salaat.
3. To forget the number of rakaats.

Quotation–III

وَاِذَا قَامُوْا اِلَى الصَّلٰوةِ قَامُوْا كُسَالٰى يُرَاءُوْنَ النَّاسَ وَلَايَذْكُرُوْنَ اللهَ اِلَّا قَلِيْلًا

"When they (the hypocrites) stand up for salaat, they perform it without earnestness and want but to be seen by men and are mindful of Allah but little." (IV: 142)

Quotation–IV

فَخَلَفَ مِنْ بَعْدِهِمْ خَلْفٌ اَضَاعُوْا الصَّلٰوةَ وَاتَّبَعُوْا الشَّهَوَاتِ فَسَوْفَ يَلْقَوْنَ غَيًّا

"Now there hath succeeded them (Prophets) a later generation who have ruined salaat and have followed lusts. So they will meet Ghayy." (XIX: 59)

In the dictionary 'Ghayy,' is explained as deception, which points towards the awful doom and ruin in the hereafter. According to many commentators, Ghayy is a pit in Hell full of blood and pus. The persons who had ruined their salaat shall be thrown into this pit.

Quotation–V

وَمَا مَنَعَهُمْ اَنْ تُقْبَلَ مِنْهُمْ نَفَقَاتُهُمْ اِلَّا اَنَّهُمْ كَفَرُوْا بِاللهِ وَبِرَسُوْلِهٖ وَلَايَاْتُوْنَ
الصَّلٰوةَ اِلَّا وَهُمْ كُسَالٰى وَلَايُنْفِقُوْنَ اِلَّا وَهُمْ كَارِهُوْنَ

"And naught preventeth that their (the hypocrites) contributions should be accepted from them, save that they have disbelieved in Allah and in His Apostle, and they come not to worship, save as idlers, and pay not (their contribution) save reluctantly." (IV: 54)

Note: The quotations I to V above relate to those who ruin salaat. On the other hand, the following speak of those whom Allah praises for their good salaat.

Quotation–VI

قَدْ اَفْلَحَ الْمُؤْمِنُوْنَ الَّذِيْنَ هُمْ فِيْ صَلَاتِهِمْ خَاشِعُوْنَ ، وَالَّذِيْنَ هُمْ عَنِ اللَّغْوِ
مُعْرِضُوْنَ ، وَالَّذِيْنَ هُمْ لِلزَّكَاةِ فَاعِلُوْنَ ، وَالَّذِيْنَ هُمْ لِفُرُوْجِهِمْ حَافِظُوْنَ ، اِلَّا
عَلٰى اَزْوَاجِهِمْ اَوْمَا مَلَكَتْ اَيْمَانُهُمْ فَاِنَّهُمْ غَيْرُ مَلُوْمِيْنَ ، فَمَنِ ابْتَغٰى وَرَاءَ ذٰلِكَ
فَاُوْلٰئِكَ هُمُ الْعَادُوْنَ وَالَّذِيْنَ هُمْ لِاَمَانَاتِهِمْ وَعَهْدِهِمْ رَاعُوْنَ وَالَّذِيْنَ هُمْ عَلٰى
صَلَوٰتِهِمْ يُحَافِظُوْنَ اُوْلٰئِكَ هُمُ الْوَارِثُوْنَ الَّذِيْنَ يَرِثُوْنَ الْفِرْدَوْسَ هُمْ فِيْهَا خٰلِدُوْنَ

"Successful indeed are the believers who are humble in their salaat. And who shun vain conversation. And who are payers of the Zakaat. And who abstain from sex, save from their wives or the slaves that their right hand possess, for then they are not blameworthy but who craveth beyond that, such are transgressors–And who faithfully observe their pledges and their covenants. And who pay heed to their salaat. These are the heirs who will inherit Firdaus (Paradise). There they will abide." (XXIII: 1 to 11)

The Prophet (Sallallaho alaihe wasallam) says, "Firdaus is the apex and the best portion of Paradise, where-from all its rivers originate. Allah's throne will be placed there. When you pray for Paradise, always pray for Firdaus."

Quotation–VII

وَاِنَّهَا لَكَبِيْرَةٌ اِلَّا عَلَى الْخٰشِعِيْنَ الَّذِيْنَ يَظُنُّوْنَ اَنَّهُمْ مُّلٰقُوْا رَبِّهِمْ وَاَنَّهُمْ اِلَيْهِ رَاجِعُوْن

"And truly it (salaat) is hard save for the humble-minded; who know that they have to meet their Lord, and that unto Him they are returning." (II: 45–46)

Quotation–VIII

فِيْ بُيُوْتٍ اَذِنَ اللّٰهُ اَنْ تُرْفَعَ وَيُذْكَرَ فِيْهَا اسْمُهُ يُسَبِّحُ لَهُ فِيْهَا بِالْغُدُوِّ وَالْاٰصَالِ ، رِجَالٌ لَاتُلْهِيْهِمْ تِجَارَةٌ وَّلَابَيْعٌ عَنْ ذِكْرِ اللّٰهِ وَاِقَامِ الصَّلٰوةِ وَاِيْتَاءِ الزَّكَاةِ يَخَافُوْنَ يَوْمًا تَتَقَلَّبُ فِيْهِ الْقُلُوْبُ وَالْاَبْصَارُ ، لِيَجْزِيَهُمُ اللّٰهُ اَحْسَنَ مَاعَمِلُوْا وَيَزِيْدَهُمْ مِّنْ فَضْلِهِ ، وَاللّٰهُ يَرْزُقُ مَنْ يَّشَاءُ بِغَيْرِ حِسَابٍ

"In houses which Allah hath allowed to be exalted, and His name shall be remembered therein, do offer praise to Him at morning and evening, men whom neither merchandise nor sale beguileth from rememberance of Allah and establishment of salaat and paying Zakaat, who fear that Day when the hearts and the eyeballs will be overturned so that Allah may reward them for the best of what they did and increase reward for them out of His bounty. Allah giveth blessings without measure to whom He will."

(XXIV: 36 to 38)

Hadhrat Abdullah bin Abbas (Radhiyallaho anho) says, "Establishment of salaat means performance of ruku and sajdah properly and constant concentration in salaat with complete humility and submission." Hadhrat Qataadah (Radhiyallaho anho) says: "Wherever the words 'Establishment of salaat' occur in Qur'an, they mean to guard its hours, to perform wudhu in the right manner and to observe ruku and sajdah properly."

Quotation–IX

وَعِبَادُ الرَّحْمٰنِ الَّذِيْنَ يَمْشُوْنَ عَلَى الْاَرْضِ هَوْنًا وَّاِذَا خَاطَبَهُمُ الْجَاهِلُوْنَ قَالُوْا
سَلَامًا ، وَالَّذِيْنَ يَبِيْتُوْنَ لِرَبِّهِمْ سُجَّدًا وَّقِيَامًا

"The (faithful) slaves of Rahmaan (the Beneficent) are they who walk upon the earth modestly and when the foolish ever address them, they answer: Peace; and who spend the night before their Lord, prostrate and standing." (XXV: 63–64)

After describing a few more qualities of His faithful slaves, Allah says in the same context:

اُوْلٰئِكَ يُجْزَوْنَ الْغُرْفَةَ بِمَا صَبَرُوْا وَيُلَقَّوْنَ فِيْهَا تَحِيَّةً وَّسَلَامًا خَالِدِيْنَ فِيْهَا
حَسُنَتْ مُسْتَقَرًّا وَّمُقَامًا

"They will be awarded the high place for as much as they were steadfast, and they will meet therein with welcome and the word of peace. Abiding there for ever. Happy is it as abode and station." (XXV: 75–76)

Quotation–X

تَتَجَافٰى جُنُوْبُهُمْ عَنِ الْمَضَاجِعِ يَدْعُوْنَ رَبَّهُمْ خَوْفًا وَّطَمَعًا وَّمِمَّا رَزَقْنَاهُمْ
يُنْفِقُوْنَ فَلَا تَعْلَمُ نَفْسٌ مَّا اُخْفِيَ لَهُمْ مِنْ قُرَّةِ اَعْيُنٍ جَزَاءً بِمَا كَانُوْا يَعْمَلُوْنَ

"The believers in our revelations are those who forsake their beds, to cry unto their Lord in fear and hope, and spend of what We have bestowed on them. No soul knoweth what is kept hid for them of joy, as a reward for what they used to do." (XXXII: 16–17)

Quotation–XI

اِنَّ الْمُتَّقِيْنَ فِيْ جَنّٰتٍ وَّعُيُوْنٍ اٰخِذِيْنَ مَآ اٰتَاهُمْ رَبُّهُمْ اِنَّهُمْ كَانُوْا قَبْلَ ذٰلِكَ
مُحْسِنِيْنَ ، كَانُوْا قَلِيْلًا مِّنَ اللَّيْلِ مَا يَهْجَعُوْنَ وَبِالْاَسْحَارِ هُمْ يَسْتَغْفِرُوْنَ

"Lo! those who keep from evil will dwell amid gardens and water-springs, taking to that which their Lord

giveth them; for Lo! aforetime they were doers of good. They used to sleep but little in the night. And ere the dawning of each day, would seek forgiveness."
(LI: 15–18)

Quotation–XII

اَمَّنْ هُوَ قَانِتٌ اٰنَـآءَ اللَّيْلِ سَاجِدًا وَّقَآئِمًا يَّحْذَرُ الْاٰخِرَةَ وَيَرْجُوْا رَحْمَةَ رَبِّهٖ قُلْ هَلْ يَسْتَوِى الَّذِيْنَ يَعْلَمُوْنَ وَالَّذِيْنَ لَايَعْلَمُوْنَ اِنَّمَا يَتَذَكَّرُ اُوْلُو الْاَلْبَابِ

"Is he who worships devotedly in the hours of the night, prostrate or standing, afraid of the Hereafter and hoping for the mercy of his Lord (to be counted equal with a disbeliever)? Say (unto them, O Muhammad) (Sallallaho alaihe wasallam): "Can those who know be equal with those who know not? But only men of understanding will pay heed." (XXXIX: 9)

Quotation–XIII

وَالْمَلٰٓئِكَةُ يَدْخُلُوْنَ عَلَيْهِمْ مِّنْ كُلِّ بَابٍ ، سَلَامٌ عَلَيْكُمْ بِمَا صَبَرْتُمْ فَنِعْمَ عُقْبَى الدَّارِ

And angels would be entering through every door proclaiming: "Peace be upon you, as a reward for your perseverance on religious practices." Thus how splendid would be their end! (XIII: 22–23).

اِنَّ الْاِنْسَانَ خُلِقَ هَلُوْعًا اِذَا مَسَّهُ الشَّرُّ جَزُوْعًا وَاِذَا مَسَّهُ الْخَيْرُ مَنُوْعًا اِلَّا الْمُصَلِّيْنَ الَّذِيْنَ هُمْ عَلٰى صَلٰوتِهِمْ دَائِمُوْنَ

"Lo! man was created very impatient. Fretful when evil befalleth him. And niggardly when good befalleth him, save the worshippers who are constant at their salaat." (LXX: 19–23)

After giving some more qualities of these blessed people, Allah says in the same context,

وَالَّذِيْنَ هُمْ عَلٰى صَلَاتِهِمْ يُحَافِظُوْنَ ، اُوْلٰئِكَ فِىْ جَنّٰتٍ مُّكْرَمُوْنَ

"And those who guard their salaat. These will dwell in gardens, honoured." (LXX: 34–35).

Besides the quotations given above, there are many verses of the Holy Qur'an enjoining salaat and exalting and extolling those who say their salaat properly. Salaat is indeed a great boon. That is why Muhammad (Sallallaho alaihe wasallam) has called it 'the comfort of my eyes', and Ibrahim (Alayhis salaam) prayed to Allah,

رَبِّ اجْعَلْنِیْ مُقِیْمَ الصَّلٰوةِ وَمِنْ ذُرِّیَّتِیْ رَبَّنَا وَتَقَبَّلْ دُعَاءِ

"My Lord! make me to establish Salaat, and some of my posterity (also); our Lord! and accept the prayer." (XIV: 40)

Here the eminent Prophet of Allah, whom Allah has called 'Khaleel', is asking Allah to make him say his salaat properly and regularly. The Glorious Allah Himself is ordering His beloved Prophet (Sallallaho alaihe wasallam) thus:—

وَاْمُرْ اَهْلَكَ بِالصَّلٰوةِ وَاصْطَبِرْ عَلَیْهَا لَا نَسْئَلُكَ رِزْقًا نَحْنُ نَرْزُقُكَ وَالْعَاقِبَةُ لِلتَّقْوٰی

"And enjoin salaat upon the people and be constant therein. We ask not of thee a provision. We provide for thee. And the Hereafter is for righteousness." (XX: 132).

It is said in a hadith that whenever the housefolk of the Prophet (Sallallaho alaihe wasallam) were hard-pressed in any way, he enjoined salaat on them and used to recite this verse. All the Prophets of Allah (peace be upon them) are reported to have engaged themselves in salaat whenever they had any difficulty. But, alas! we are so unmindful and indifferent about salaat that, in spite of all that we proclaim about Islaam and Islamic practices, we pay no attention to it. But on the contrary, if anybody stands up to invite us and to draw our attention towards it, we cut jokes and sneer at him and oppose him, thereby harming none else but ourselves.

Even those who offer the salaat, often perform it in such a way that it will not be wrong to call it a mockery of salaat, as it lacks the proper observation of its requisites and also the devotion and submission obligatory therein. The practical example of the Holy Prophet (Sallallaho alaihe wasallam), as also the practices of his illustrious companions, should be the guiding factor in our lives. I have collected the stories about the salaat of the companions in a separate book, named "Stories of Sahabah," and I need not repeat them here. However, I am giving stories from the lives of a few pious persons in the following pages. The practices and the sayings of the Holy Prophet (Sallallaho alaihe wasallam) about this subject would appear in Chapter III.

CHAPTER II

A FEW STORIES FROM THE LIVES OF THE PIOUS

Story–I

Shaikh Abdul Waahid (Rahmatullah alaih) says, "One day I was so much overpowered by sleep that I went to bed before finishing my Zikr for the night. I saw in my dream a most beautiful girl dressed in green silk. All parts of her body and even her shoes were engaged in Zikr. She said to me 'Aspire to possess me; I love you." And then she recited a few couplets depicting the eagerness of a lover. When I woke up from the dream, I vowed not to sleep any more during the night. It is reported that for full forty years he never slept at night, and said Ishaa and Fajr salaats with the same wudhu.

Story–II

Shaikh Mazhar Sa'di (Rahmatullah alaih), the famous pious man, kept weeping for sixty years in love and eagerness for Allah. One night he saw in a dream a few damsels by the side of pearl trees with gold branches, on the bank of the brook brimming with fluid musk, pure and fragrant. The girls were hymning the glory of Allah. He asked their identity. In reply they recited two couplets, which meant, "We have been created by the Sustainer of mankind and Lord of Muhammad (Sallallaho alaihe wasallam) for those people who keep standing before Allah all night long and hymning in supplication to Him."

Story–III

Abu Bakr Dharir (Rahmatullah alaih) says, "There lived a young slave with me. He fasted all day and stood in Tahajjud all night long. One day he came to me and related: "Last night against my usual practice I went to sleep. I saw in my dream that the wall of the Mihraab was cracked, and from the crevice appeared a few damsels. One of them was very ugly. I asked one of the pretty damsels who they were. She replied that they were my previous nights and that the ugly one was this night."

Story–IV

An eminent Shaikh says: "One night I was in a deep sleep and could not get up for Tahajjud. I saw in my dream a girl of such beauty as I had never seen in my life. She was emitting such fragrance as I had never smelt before. She handed over to me a piece of paper on which were written three couplets, which meant, 'You were so enamoured of deep sleep that you have become unmindful of the high balconies of Paradise, where you have to abide for ever with no fear of death. Wake up! It is better to recite the Qur'an in Tahajjud than to sleep." since then, wherever I feel sleepy, these couplets come to my mind and the sleep goes away."

Story–V

Ataa (Rahmatullah alaih) writes, "I went to the market. A person had a slave girl to sell, who was said to be mad; I purchased her for seven dinaars and brought her to my house. After a portion of the night had passed, I noticed that she got up, performed wudhu and started her salaat. In her salaat she wept so much that I thought she would die of excessive crying. After finishing the salaat, she began to supplicate before Allah saying, 'O my Lord! By the love Thou bearest for me, show mercy on me.' I interrupted by telling her that she should rather say, 'By the love that I have for Thee . . ." She got irritated at this suggestion and said, 'By Allah Himself! Had He not loved me, I would not be standing here before Him while you are in your bed.' Then she fell prostrate and recited a few couplets purporting, 'I am growing more and more restless. How can one rest whose peace of mind is taken away by love, eagerness and constant anxiety? O, Allah! Show mercy and give some glad tidings.' Then she prayed in a loud voice thus, 'O Allah! So far the matter between me and Thee has been a secret. Now people have come to know of it. O, Allah! Call me back.' After saying this, she cried aloud and died on the spot."

Story–VI

A similar thing happened with Sirri (Rahmatullah alaih). He writes: "I bought a slave woman to attend on me.

She served me for some time, but I was in the dark about her state of affairs. She had a corner in the house reserved for her salaat. After finishing her job, she would go there and offer her salaat. One night, I noticed her performing salaat and then supplicating before Allah. While making her supplication, she said, 'By the love Thou hast for me, do such and such a thing for me.' I shouted out to her, 'O woman, say by the love that I have for Thee.' She retorted, 'My Master, if He had not loved me, He would not have made me stand for salaat and deprive you thereof.' Next morning I sent for her and said to her, 'You are a misfit in your present job. You are exclusively meant for Allah's service. I then gave her some gifts and set her free."

Story–VII

Sirri Saqti (Rahmatullah alaih) writes about another woman: "When she stood up for Tahajjud she would say, 'O Allah! Satan is but Thy creation. Thou hast full power over him. He sees me and I cannot see him. Thou see-est him and hast control over all his actions, while he has no control over Thee. O, Allah! repel the evil that he wishes to do me. Requit the wrong he may do to deceive me. I seek Thy refuge from his evil designs and with Thy help I cast him away.' Thereafter she would cry bitterly. And as a result thereof she lost the sight of one eye. People admonished her to stop excessive weeping, lest she should lose her other eye as well. She replied, "If it is destined to be an eye of Paradise, Allah will grant me better than this; but if it be that of Hell, then the sooner it is lost the better."

Story–VIII

Shaikh Abu Abdullah Jilaa says: "One day my mother asked my father to fetch some fish from the market. My father left for the market and I also accompanied him. The fish was bought and we needed a porter to carry it for us. We engaged a boy who was standing there and who had offered to do the job for us. He put the load on his head and followed us. While we were on our way, we happened to hear the Azaan. The boy abruptly spoke, 'Allah's summoner has summoned me; I have to take my wudhu too. I shall now carry the fish after salaat. If you like you may wait, otherwise here it is." Saying this he put the load down and left for the musjid. My father thought when the poor boy could place his trust in Allah so much, we must as well do so in a greater degree. He, therefore, left the fish there and took me to the musjid. When we three returned after saying salaat, we found the fish lying in the same place as we had left it. The boy then carried it to our house. My father related the strange story to my mother who insisted that the boy should be invited to eat some fish with us. When the invitation was extended to him, he said, 'Excuse me I am fasting.' My father then requested him to have iftaar at our place. To this he said, 'It is not possible for me to return once I am gone. Just possibly, I may stay in a musjid close to your place; if so, then I shall join you in your dinner.' Saying this he went to the musjid and returned after Maghrib. When the dinner was over, I showed him the room where he could rest in privacy. Now, there lived a crippled woman in our neighbourhood. We were surprised to see her walking quite hale and hearty. When we enquired from her how she got cured, she said, 'I prayed to Allah to heal me for the sake of the blessings that your guest carries. No sooner I prayed than I was healed.' When we went to find the boy in the room where we had left him, the door was shut and the boy was nowhere to be seen."

Story–IX

It is said of a pious man that once he had a sore on his foot. According to the opinion of the surgeons, if his foot was not amputated, the sore might prove fatal. His mother proposed that the operation should be done while he was absorbed in his salaat. This was done, and no pain was felt by him.

Story–X

Abu 'Aamir (Rahmatullah alaih) says, "I saw a slave woman on sale for a very small sum. She was very emaciated and her hair was dirty. I took pity on her and purchased her. I said to her, 'Come, woman, let us go and make purchases for Ramadhaan.' She remarked, 'Alhamdulillah, all the months are alike for me.' She fasted on all days and stood in salaat for all nights. When Eid drew near, I said to her, 'Woman! You will go with me tomorrow to make purchases for Eid. She remarked, 'My master! You are too much absorbed in this world.' She then went into her room and started her salaat. She was reciting Soorah Ibrahim and when she reached the 16th verse of the Soorah (viz.,

مِنْ وَّرَآئِهِ جَهَنَّمُ وَيُسْقٰى مِنْ مَّآءٍ صَدِيْدٍ

'Hell is before him and he is made to drink boiling fetid water', which described the doom of a disbeliever, she repeated it again and again, and then gave out a cry and fell dead."

Story–XI

Everybody knows Umar bin Abdul Aziz (Rahmatullah alaih). After the four Khulafaa-ur Raashideen he is the most eminent Khalifah. His wife says, "There may be other people more particular about wudhu and salaat; but I have never seen anybody fearing Allah more than my husband. After his daily Ishaa, he would sit at a place reserved for his salaat and raise his hands in supplication and keep crying before Allah till sleep overpowered him. Whenever he woke during the night, he would again start praying and crying before Allah."

It is said that since his becoming Khalifah he never shared the bed with his wife. His wife was the daughter of the great King Abdul Malik. Her father had given her much jewellery in dowry, which included a marvellous diamond. He said to his wife, "Either part with all your jewellery for the sake of Allah, so that I may deposit it in the Baitul Maal or be separated from me. I would not like to live in a house where there is so much wealth." His wife replied, "I can part with a thousand times more wealth, but I cannot leave you." She then deposited everything she had in the Baitul Maal. After the death of Umar bin Abdul Aziz, when Yazeed son of Abdul Malik succeeded him as Khalifa, he said to his sister, "If you like you may have your jewellery back from the Baitul Maal. She replied, "How can the wealth I discarded during my husband's lifetime, satisfy me after his death."

Umar bin Abdul Aziz was on his death-bed when he inquired from the persons round him about the cause of his disease. Someone said, "People think it is the effect of black magic." He said, "No, it is not magic." He then sent for a particular slave of his and said to him, "What made you poison me?" He replied, "One hundred dinaars and a promise of liberty." Umar bin Abdul Aziz (Rahmatullah alaih) took those dinaars from the slave and deposited them in the Baitul Maal, and advised him to run away to some distant place where he could not be seized.

Just before his death, Muslimah (Rahmatullah alaih) came to him and said, "Nobody has ever treated his children as you are doing. None of your thirteen sons has anything to live on." He sat up in his bed and said, 'I have not held back from my sons what they were entitled to. I have, of course, refused them what was actually due to others. If my sons are righteous, then Allah will surely be their guardian as He has said in His Book: He is the guardian of the righteous (VII:196)', but if they are wrong-doers, then why should I care for them?"

Story–XII

Muhammad bin Munkadir (Rahmatullah alaih) was a Hafiz of Hadith. One night, he wept excessively in his Tahajjud. When someone inquired about it, he said, "During Qiraat, I came across the following words of the Qur'an:

وَبَدَا لَهُمْ سَيِّاٰتِ مَاكَسَبُوْا وَحَاقَ بِهِمْ مَّاكَانُوْ بِهِ يَسْتَهْزِءُوْنَ

"And the evils that they earned will confront them; and they will be surrounded by what they used to scoff at." (XXXIX: 48)

He was very anxious and worried at the time of his death, and said that these same words of the Qur'an were looming before him.

Story–XIII

Thaabit Banaani (Rahmatullah alaih) is another Hafiz of Hadith. He used to cry a great deal while supplicating before Allah. Someone warned him that he would lose his eyesight if he did not stop weeping like that. He replied to him, "What use are these eyes if these do not weep before Allah."

He used to ask in his prayer, "O, Allah! Permit me to offer my salaat in my grave, if ever you grant this privilege to any of Thy slaves!" Abu Sanaan (Rahmatullah alaih) narrates, "By Allah! I was among those present at the burial of Thaabit Banaani. Just after he had been placed in his grave, one of the bricks from the side fell off. I peeped into the pit to find to my great amazement, that Thaabit was offering his salaat. I said to a person standing by my side, 'Look what is that.' He advised me to keep quiet. After the burial, we went to his daughter and inquired from her, 'What was the special practice of your father?' She wanted to know what made us put that question. We related to her the incident at the grave. She said, "He has been constant in Tahajjud for fifty years and prayed every morning before Allah to allow him to offer salaat in the grave if that privilege could be granted to anybody."

Before finishing this chapter, I give below the pursuits (as regards salaat) of some of our eminent Muslim ancestors:

1. Imaam Ahmad bin Hambal (Rahmatullah alaih) is the famous Imaam of one of the four schools of Muslim jurisprudence. Besides being engaged in his usual work, he used to offer daily three hundred rakaats of nafl salaat. After he was lashed by the king for refusal to submit to the royal edict, he became very weak and reduced his routine nafl salaat to one hundred and fifty rakaats. We should not forget that he was eighty at that time.

2. Imaam Shaafi'ee (Rahmatullah alaih) another eminent Imaam of Muslim jurisprudence, used to finish reciting the Qur'an sixty times in his salaat during Ramadhaan. A person narrates, "I remained with Imaam Shaafi'ee for several days and found him sleeping only for a while at night."

3. Imaam Abu Haneefa (Rahmatullah alaih) is famous for his vigil. It is said that for thirty, forty or fifty years (according to the information of different narrators) he offered his Fajr prayer with the wudhu for Ishaa. He would go to sleep only for a few minutes in the afternoon saying, "It is sunnat to sleep in the afternoon."

4. It is said about Sa'eed bin Musayyab (Rahmatullah alaih) that for fifty years he offered his Fajr salaat with the wudhu performed at Ishaa.

   Imaam Ghazzali (Rahmatullah alaih) on the authority of Abu Taalib Makki reported the same practice by no less than forty Taabi'ees, some of whom had been doing it for forty years continuously.

5. Muhammad bin Nasr (Rahmatullah alaih) is a famous Muhaddith. His devotion to salaat had no

parallel. Once while in salaat, he was stung on his forehead by a wasp and though blood came out, neither did he stir nor did he allow it to disturb his devotion in salaat. It is said that in salaat, he stood motionless like a stick planted in the ground.

6. It is reported about Baqi bin Mukhallid (Rahmatullah alaih) that he used to recite the complete Qur'an every night in thirteen rakaats of Tahajjud and Witr.

7. Hannaad (Rahmatullah alaih) is a Muhaddith. One of his pupils narrates, "Hannaad used to weep very much. One day after he had finished our lesson in the morning, he continued to offer nafl salaat till midday. He went to his place for a short interval and then returned for his Zuhr. He again engaged himself in nafl salaat till Asr. Between Asr and Maghrib, he recited the Qur'an. I left him after Maghrib. I said to one of his neighbours, 'Our Shaikh prays so much. It is really wonderful.' He said, "He had been doing this for the last seventy years. You will wonder still more if you see his prayers during the night.''

8. Masrooq (Rahmatullah alaih) is another Muhaddith. His wife narrates, "He used to offer such long rakaats that his legs would get swollen and I sat behind weeping in pity for him.''

9. Abu Itaab Sulami (Rahmatullah alaih) is reported to have been fasting during the day and weeping during the night for full forty years.

10. It is said about a Sayyid that continuously for twelve days he has been offering his salaat with the same wudhu. For fifteen years, his back had not touched the bed. He would also go without food for days together.

Besides the above, there are numerous records of the pious pursuits of the heroes of Islamic History. It is difficult to cover all of them in this book. All that has been said here is sufficient to serve as examples. May Allah, through His Grace, grant me and the readers of this book the strength to follow in the footsteps of these blessed people! Aameen!

CHAPTER–III

QUOTATIONS FROM HADITH

Hadith–I

عَنْ عَمَّارِ بْنِ يَاسِرٍ رَضِىَ اللّٰهُ عَنْهُ قَالَ سَمِعْتُ رَسُوْلَ اللّٰهِ ﷺ يَقُوْلُ اِنَّ الرَّجُلَ لَيَنْصَرِفُ وَمَا كُتِبَ لَهُ اِلَّا عُشْرُ صَلٰوتِهِ تُسْعُهَا ثُمْنُهَا سُبْعُهَا سُدُسُهَا خُمْسُهَا رُبْعُهَا ثُلُثُهَا نِصْفُهَا رواه أبوداود والنسائى

> Hadhrat Ammar bin Yaasir (Radhiyallaho anho) narrates that he heard the Prophet (Sallallaho alaihe wasallam) saying: "When a person finishes his salaat, he gets one tenth, one ninth, one eighth, one seventh, one sixth, one fifth, one fourth, one third or one half of the maximum reward (according to the quality of salaat performed by him)."

This shows that the reward is given in proportion to the sincerity and devotion with which salaat is performed. So much so, that some get only one tenth of the total reward. There are others who get a reward ranging from one tenth to one half of the maximum. It is also correct to say that there are some who receive the reward in full and there are others who get no reward at all.

It is stated in a hadith that Allah has a standard for fardh salaat. An account is kept of the measure by which a salaat falls short of that standard.

It is said in the hadith that devotion in salaat will be the first thing to be taken away from the world. A time will come when not a single person in the whole congregation will offer his salaat with proper devotion.

Hadith–II

رُوِيَ عَنْ اَنَسٍ رَضِىَ اللّٰهُ عَنْهُ قَالَ قَالَ رَسُوْلُ اللّٰهِ ﷺ فَمَنْ صَلَّى الصَّلٰوةَ لِوَقْتِهَا وَاَسْبَغَ لَهَا وُضُوْءَهَا وَاَتَمَّ لَهَا قِيَامَهَا وَخُشُوْعَهَا وَرُكُوْعَهَا وَسُجُوْدَهَا خَرَجَتْ وَهِىَ بَيْضَآءُ مُسْفِرَةٌ تَقُوْلُ حَفِظَكَ اللّٰهُ كَمَا حَفِظْتَنِىْ مَنْ صَلَّاهَا لِغَيْرِ وَقْتِهَا

وَلَمْ يُصْبِغْ لَهَا وُضُوْءَهَا وَلَمْ يُتِمَّ لَهَا خُشُوْعَهَا وَلَا رُكُوْعَهَا وَلَا سُجُوْدَهَا خَرَجَتْ وَهِيَ سَوْدَآءُ مُظْلِمَةٌ تَقُوْلُ ضَيَّعَكَ اللّٰهُ كَمَا ضَيَّعْتَنِيْ حَتّٰى اِذَا كَانَتْ حَيْثُ شَآءَ اللّٰهُ لُفَّتْ كَمَا يُلَفُّ الثَّوْبُ الْخَلِقُ ثُمَّ ضُرِبَ بِهَا وَجْهُهُ رواه الطبراني

Hadhrat Anas (Radhiyallaho anho) narrates that he heard the Holy Prophet (Sallallaho alaihe wasallam) saying, "When a person offers his salaat at its fixed hours with proper wudhu, with humility and submission and with qiyaam, ruku and sajdah done satisfactorily, then such a salaat rises up in a bright and beautiful form and blesses the person in words: 'May Allah guard you as you have guarded me.' On the other hand, if a person is not punctual with his salaat nor does he perform wudhu, qiyaam, ruku and sajdah properly, then salaat rises up in an ugly and dark shape and curses the person saying, "May Allah ruin you as you have ruined me!" Then it is flung back like a dirty rag at the face of the person."

Lucky are those whose salaat is so perfect in all respects that this most important worship of Allah would pray for them. But what to say about the salaat which most of the people are wont? They go into sajdah direct from ruku, and they hardly lift their head from the first sajdah when they go for the second like a crow pecking at something. The curse that such a person deserves is mentioned in this hadith. When the salaat is cursing us then what else can check our downfall? This is why the condition of the Muslims is deteriorating day by day in every nook and corner of the world.

The same description is given in another hadith, with the addition that a salaat offered by a person with sincerity and devotion rises up highly illuminated, the gates of Heaven are let open for its reception, and then it intercedes (before Allah) for His devotee.

The Prophet (Sallallaho alaihe wasallam) has said, "The likeness of a person not bowing fully in ruku is that of a pregnant woman aborting just before delivery."

In a hadith, it is stated, "There are many fasting persons who get nothing out of their fast except hunger and thirst, and there are many worshippers who keep a vigil but get nothing from their vigil except sleeplessness.

Hadhrat Aa'ishah (Radhiyallaho anha) narrates that

she heard the Prophet (Sallallaho alaihe wasallam) saying, "Allah has decided to save (from punishment of the Hereafter) a person coming before Him who has been offering salaat five times daily at its fixed hours, with due sincerity and devotion and with proper wudhu. As regards a person who does not so come before Allah, there is no guarantee for him. He may be forgiven by Allah's special Grace or taken to task.

Once the Prophet (Sallallaho alaihe wasallam) came to his companions and said, "Do you know what Allah has said?" The companions replied, "Allah and His Apostle know best." He repeated the question twice and the companions made the same reply each time. Then he said, "Allah says, 'By my Greatness and My Glory, I must bring into Paradise the person offering salaat five times daily at its fixed hours. As regards the person who does not ensure his salaat, I may forgive him by My mercy or take him to task.'"

Hadith–III

عَنْ اَبِيْ هُرَيْرَةَ رَضِىَ اللّٰهُ عَنْهُ قَالَ سَمِعْتُ رَسُوْلَ اللّٰهِ ﷺ يَقُوْلُ اِنَّ اَوَّلَ مَايُحَاسَبُ بِهِ الْعَبْدُ يَوْمَ الْقِيَامَةِ مِنْ عَمَلِهٖ صَلٰوتُهُ فَاِنْ صَلُحَتْ فَقَدْ اَفْلَحَ وَاَنْجَحَ وَاِنْ فَسَدَتْ خَابَ وَخَسِرَ وَاِنْ انْتَقَصَ مِنْ فَرِيْضَةٍ قَالَ الرَّبُّ اُنْظُرُوْا هَلْ لِعَبْدِىْ مِنْ تَطَوُّعٍ فَيُكْمَلُ بِهَا مَاانْتَقَصَ مِنَ الْفَرِيْضَةِ ثُمَّ يَكُوْنُ سَائِرُ عَمَلِهٖ عَلٰى ذٰلِكَ

Hadhrat Abu Hurairah (Radhiyallaho anho) narrates, "We heard the Prophet (Sallallaho alaihe wasallam) saying, 'The first among the doings of a person to be reckoned for on the Day of Judgement shall be his salaat. A person will succeed and attain his goal if his salaat is accepted, and he will fail and lose badly if it is rejected. If any deficiency is found in his fardh salaat, Allah will say (to the Angels): "Look for any nafl salaat in his account". Then the deficiency in his fardh salaat will be made good by nafl salaat. The rest of the religious practices (viz. Fast, Zakaat etc.) will then be reckoned for in the same manner."

This hadith shows that we should have adequate nafl salaat to our credit to make up any deficiency in our fardh salaat. It is a habit with many people to say. "It is enough to observe only the fardh salaat. nafl salaat is meant for the eminent. No doubt it is enough to offer fardh salaat properly, but is it so easy to observe it to the proper standard? Most probably, there will always be some deficiency in one respect or the other, and there is no way out to make up that deficiency except through nafl salaat.

There is another hadith which deals with this point more elaborately. It declares, "Salaat is the foremost duty enjoined by Allah and the first thing to be presented before Allah, and the first thing to be reckoned for on the Day of Judgement. If the fardh salaat is found wanting in quality, then its deficiency will be made good through nafl salaat. The fasts of Ramadhaan will be the next to be reckoned for and any deficiency therein will be made good through nafl Fasts. Then Zakaat shall be reckoned for in a similar manner. If after adding nafl the good deeds are found heavier in the scales, the person concerned shall be sent to Paradise, otherwise he shall meet his doom in Hell." Such was the practice of the Prophet (Sallallaho alaihe wasallam) that when anybody embraced Islaam at his hand, the first thing he taught him was salaat.

Hadith–IV

عَنْ عَبْدِ اللهِ بْنِ قُرْطٍ رَضِىَ اللهُ عَنْهُ قَالَ قَالَ رَسُوْلُ اللهِ ﷺ اَوَّلُ مَايُحَاسَبُ بِهِ الْعَبْدُ يَوْمَ الْقِيٰمَةِ الصَّلٰوةُ فَاِنْ صَلُحَتْ صَلُحَ سَآئِرُ عَمَلِهِ وَاِنْ فَسَدَتْ فَسَدَ سَآئِرُ عَمَلِهِ رواه الطبرانى

Hadhrat Abdullah bin Qurt (Radhiyallaho anho) narrates that he heard the Prophet (Sallallaho alaihe wasallam) saying "Salaat will be the first thing to be reckoned for on the Day of Judgement. If this is found satisfactory, then the rest of the deeds will also come out as such. If this is not so, then the remaining deeds are sure to be found wanting.

Hadhrat Umar (Radhiyallaho anho) during his caliphate had issued a proclamation to all the officers under him saying, "I regard salaat as the most important duty. A person who ensures salaat is likely to observe other injucctions of Islam as well; but if he discards salaat, he will more easily damage the rest of Islaam."

The above saying of the Prophet (Sallallaho alaihe wasallam) and the proclamation of Hazrat Umar (Radhiyallaho anho) are also corroborated by another hadith, "Satan is scared of a Muslim so long as he is mindful of his salaat; but no sooner he neglects the salaat than Satan descends on him and becomes hopeful of leading him astray, and then he can easily be lured to commit more serious wrongs and major sins. This is exactly what is meant by Almighty Allah when He says,

اِنَّ الصَّلٰوةَ تَنْهٰى عَنِ الْفَحْشَآءِ وَالْمُنْكَرِ

"Lo! salaat preserveth from lewdness and inequity"
(XXIX: 45)

Hadith V

عَنْ عَبْدِ اللهِ بْنِ اَبِيْ قَتَادَةَ رَضِىَ اللهُ عَنْهُ عَنْ اَبِيْهِ قَالَ قَالَ رَسُوْلُ اللهِ ﷺ اَسْوَأُ النَّاسِ سَرِقَةً اَلَّذِيْ يَسْرِقُ صَلٰوتَهُ قَالُوْا يَارَسُوْلَ اللهِ وَكَيْفَ يَسْرِقُ صَلٰوتَهُ قَالَ لَايُتِمُّ رُكُوْعَهَا وَلَاسُجُوْدَهَا رواه الدارمى

Hadhrat Abdullah bin Abu Qataadah (Radhiyallaho anho) narrates, "The Holy Prophet (Sallallaho alaihe wasallam) once said, 'The worst thief is one who steals from his salaat.' The companions inquired, 'How can one steal from his salaat? O, Prophet of Allah!' He replied, 'When one does not do his ruku and sajdah properly.'

There are many other Ahaadith conveying the same meaning. Stealing is a very disgraceful act and a thief is despised by everybody. What about a person who is declared, 'the worst thief', by no less a person than the Prophet himself?

Hadhrat Abu Darda (Radiyallaho anho) narrates, "Once the Prophet (Sallallaho alaihe wasallam) looked up towards the sky and said, 'The knowledge of Deen is soon to be taken away from this world.' Ziyaad (Radhiyallaho anho), who was also present there inquired, 'How can the knowledge of Deen be taken way, O, Prophet of Allah (Sallallaho alaihe wasallam), when we are teaching the Qur'an to our children and this process will continue in our posterity?' The Prophet (Sallallaho alaihe wasallam) said to him, 'Ziyaad! I always took you to be an intelligent person. Don't you see that the Jews and the Christians are also teaching their Bibles to their children? Has this prevented their deterioration?" One of Hadhrat Abu Darda's (Radhiyallaho anho) pupils says "After hearing this hadith from Hadhrat Abu Darda (Radhiyallaho anha), I went to Hadhrat Ubaadah (Radhiyallaho anho) and related the hadith to him." He said, "Abu Darda (Radhiyallaho anho) is quite right. May I tell you the first thing that will be taken away from this world? It is devotion in salaat. You will see that not a single person in the full congregation is saying his salaat with devotion." Hadhrat Huzaifah (Radhiyallaho anho), the confidante of the Prophet (Sallallaho alaihe wasallam), was also heard saying, "Devotion in salaat shall be the first thing to disappear."

It is said in a hadith, "Allah does not pay any attention to that salaat with which ruku and sajdah are not performed properly."

Another hadith says, "A person has been offering salaat for sixty years, but in fact not a single salaat of his is accepted by Allah. This is because he has been careless about his ruku in some salaats and about his sajdah in others."

A great stress is laid on the proper performance of salaat in the famous Epistles of Shaikh Ahmad Sirhindi (Rahmatullah alaih). His discourses on the subject cover a good portion of the Epistles. In one of them he writes, "It is necessary among other things that we should be particular about keeping the fingers of our hands together while in sajdah and separated while in ruku. These regulations are not without a purpose." He further writes, "To keep our glance at the place of sajdah while standing, on our feet while in ruku, on our nose while in sajdah, and on our hands while in Qa'dah, goes a long way in keeping the desired concentration in salaat." When such ordinary regulations, which are only mustahab, increase the value of our salaat, you can well imagine how much benefit we shall derive if we be particular of other regulations, which are either sunnat or otherwise more important.

Hadith–VI

عَنْ اُمِّ رُوْمَانَ رَضِىَ اللّٰهُ عَنْهَا وَالِدَةِ عَائِشَةَ رَضِىَ اللّٰهُ عَنْهَا قَالَتْ رَاٰنِىْ
اَبُوْبَكْرِنِ الصِّدِّيْقُ اَتَمَيَّلُ فِيْ صَلَاتِىْ فَزَجَرَنِيْ زَجْرَةً كِدْتُّ اَنْصَرِفُ مِنْ صَلٰوتِىْ
قَالَتْ سَمِعْتُ رَسُوْلَ اللّٰهِ ﷺ يَقُوْلُ اِذَا قَامَ اَحَدُكُمْ فِى الصَّلٰوةِ فَلْيَسْكُنْ اَطْرَافُهٗ

لَايَتَمَيَّلُ تَمَيُّلَ الْيَهُوْدِ فَاِنَّ سُكُوْنَ الْاَطْرَافِ فِيْ الصَّلٰوةِ مِنْ تَمَامِ الصَّلٰوةِ

اخرجه الحكيم الترمذى من طريق القاسم بن محمد

Hadhrat Umme Roomaan (wife of Abu Bakr) (Radhiyallaho anha) narrates, "Once I was offering my salaat, when I unknowingly started leaning sometimes to one side and sometimes to the other. Hadhrat Abu Bakr (Radhiyallaho anho) saw me doing this and reprimanded me so harshly that I was about to abandon my salaat with fear. He told me later that he had heard the Prophet (Sallallaho alaihe wasallam) saying, "When a person stands for salaat, he should keep his body at rest and he should not behave like the Jews, since to remain motionless is one of the complements of salaat."

Keeping the body at rest during salaat is enjoined in many ahaadith. In the beginning, it was a habit with the Prophet (Sallallaho alaihe wasallam) that he kept looking towards the heaven in expectation of Hadhrat Jibra-eel (Alayhis salaam) to bring him some revelation, so much so that his eyes would sometimes rise up unconsciously even during salaat. When the first two verses of Soorah XXIII (viz.,

قَدْ اَفْلَحَ الْمُؤْمِنُوْنَ ، اَلَّذِيْنَ هُمْ فِيْ صَلٰوتِهِمْ خَاشِعُوْنَ

(Successful indeed are the believers who are humble in their salaat) were revealed, he began to keep his gaze down while in salaat. It is also said about the companions that in the beginning they would sometime cast their glances here and there during their salaat but, after these verses were revealed, they gave up this practice. Explaining these verses, Hadhrat Abdullah bin Umar (Radhiyallaho anho) says, "When the Sahabah stood for salaat they never looked this side or that side. They remained attentive in salaat with their eyes fixed at the place of sajdah, totally absorbed in Allah, their Lord. Someone inquired from Hadhrat Ali (Radhiyallaho anho), 'What is devotion?' He replied, 'Concentration in salaat is included in devotion."

Hadhrat Ibn Abbas (Radhiyallaho anho) says, "Humble' (mentioned in the above verses) are those who fear Allah and remain motionless in salaat."

Hadhrat Abu Bakr (Radhiyallaho anho) narrates, "Once

the Prophet (Sallallaho alaihe wasallam) said, 'Seek refuge in Allah from sanctimonious devotion.' We inquired, 'What is sanctimonious devotion, O Prophet of Allah! (Sallallaho alaihe wasallam). He replied, 'To feign concentration, with nifaaq lurking in the heart.''

Hadhrat Abu Darda (Radhiyallaho anho) relates a similar hadith in which the Prophet (Sallallaho alaihe wasallam) is reported to have said, "Hypocritical devotion is that in which a person outwardly pretends concentration, while his heart is devoid of that."

Hadhrat Qataadah (Radhiyallaho anho) says, "For devotion in salaat, the heart should be full of Allah's fear, and the gaze should be kept down."

The Prophet (Sallallaho alaihe wasallam) once saw a person fondling his beard while in salaat. He remarked, "If his heart were blessed with devotion, then his entire body would be at rest."

Hadhrat Aa'ishah (Radhiyallaho anha) once inquired from the Prophet (Sallallaho alaihe wasallam) as to what his opinion was about the practice of looking around while in salaat. He said, "It is a damage to salaat caused by Satan."

Once the Prophet (Sallallaho alaihe wasallam) said, "People in the habit of looking up while in salaat must give up that habit, lest their gaze may become fixed and not return to them."

It has been said by many of the companions and their successors that devotion means tranquillity in salaat. The Prophet (Sallallaho alaihe wasallam) is reported (by many narrators) to have said, "Offer each salaat (with) such (devotion) as if it were the last salaat of your life."

Hadith–VII

عَنْ عِمْرَانَ بْنِ حُصَيْنٍ رَضِىَ اللهُ عَنْهُ قَالَ سُئِلَ النَّبِيُّ ﷺ عَنْ قَوْلِ اللهِ تَعَالٰى اِنَّ
الصَّلٰوةَ تَنْهٰى عَنِ الْفَحْشَاءِ وَالْمُنْكَرِ فَقَالَ مَنْ لَمْ تَنْهَهُ صَلٰوتُهُ عَنِ الْفَحْشَآءِ
وَالْمُنْكَرِ فَلَا صَلٰوةَ لَهُ أخرجه ابن أبي حاتم وابن مردويه كذا في الدرالمنثور

Hadhrat Imraan bin Husain (Radhiyallaho anho) narrates, Someone inquired of the Prophet (Sallallaho alaihe wasallam) about the meaning of the verse in Qur'an:

اِنَّ الصَّلٰوةَ تَنْهٰى عَنِ الْفَحْشَآءِ وَالْمُنْكَرِ

'Lo! Salaat restrains from shameful and unjust deeds. (XXIX: 45)

He replied, "Salaat is no salaat if it does not preserve one from lewdness and iniquity."

No doubt, salaat is a very valuable service and when offered properly, results in preservation from all undesirables. If this result is not achieved, then there is something lacking in the proper performance of salaat. There are many other ahaadith conveying this meaning. Hadhrat Ibn Abbas (Radhiyallaho anho) says, "Salaat has the power to check the inclination to sins."

Hadhrat Abul Aaliyah (Radhiyallaho anho) explaining the same verse of the Qur'an writes: "There are three essentials of salaat: Sincerity, Fear of Allah, and His remembrance. Salaat is no salaat if these three are missing. Sincerity heralds virtuous deeds, fear of Allah expels vices, and His remembrance is the Qur'an, which in itself is a guidance towards good and guard against evil."

Hadhrat Ibn Abbas (Radhiyallaho anho) reports that the Prophet (Sallallaho alaihe wasallam) once said, "Salaat that does not prevent from lewdness and iniquity instead of bringing close to Allah, takes away from Him."

Hadhrat Ibn Mas'ood (Radhiyallaho anho) narrates that he heard the Prophet (Sallallaho alaihe wasallam) saying, "A person who does not follow up his salaat, has actually offered no salaat. To follow up the salaat is to shun lewdness and iniquity."

Hadhrat Abu Hurairah (Radhiyallaho anho) narrates, "A person came to the Prophet (Sallallaho alaihe wasallam) and reported about a certain man, who was in the habit of offering salaat for the whole night and then committing a larceny before daybreak. The Prophet (Sallallaho alaihe wasallam) remarked, "His salaat will very soon wean him off that sin.' This shows that the evil habits can be got rid of by adhering to salaat with due sincerity. It is a difficult and lengthy affair to redeem each and every bad habit. On the contrary, it is easier and quicker to start offering salaat with proper care when through the blessings that follow it, bad habits are sure to disappear one by one." May Allah grant me strength to say my salaat properly!

Hadith–VIII

عَنْ جَابِرٍ رَضِیَ اللّٰہُ عَنْهُ قَالَ قَالَ رَسُوْلُ اللّٰہِ ﷺ اَفْضَلُ الصَّلٰوۃِ طُوْلُ الْقُنُوْتِ

أخرجه ابنْ أبي شيبة ومسلم والترمذي وابن ماجه كذا في الدر المنثور وفيه أيضا عن مجاهد في قوله تعالى وَقُوْمُوْا لِلّٰهِ قٰنِتِيْنَ قَالَ مِنَ الْقُنُوْتِ الرُّكُوْعُ وَالْخُشُوْعُ وَطُوْلُ الرُّكُوْعِ يَعْنِى طُوْلَ الْقِيَامِ وَغَضُّ الْبَصَرِ وَخَفْضُ الْجَنَاحِ وَالرَّهْبَةُ لِلّٰهِ وَكَانَ الْفُقَهَاءُ مِنْ اَصْحَابِ مُحَمَّدٍ ﷺ اِذَا قَامَ اَحَدُهُمْ فِى الصَّلٰوةِ يَهَابُ الرَّحْمٰنَ سُبْحَانَهُ وَتَعَالٰى اَنْ يَلْتَفِتَ اَوْ يَقْلِبَ الْحَصٰى اَوْ يَشُدَّ بَصَرَهُ اَوْ يَعْبَثَ بِشَيْءٍ اَوْ يُحَدِّثَ نَفْسَهُ بِشَيْءٍ مِنْ اَمْرِ الدُّنْيَا اِلَّا نَاسِيًا حَتّٰى يَنْصَرِفَ اخرجه سعيد بن منصور وعبد بن حميد وابن جرير ووابن المنذر وابن ابى حاتم والاصبهانى فى الترغيب والبيهقى فى شعب الايمان

Hadhrat Jabir (Radhiyallaho anha) narrates that he heard the Prophet (Sallallaho alaihe wasallam) saying, "The best salaat is one with prolonged rakaats." Mujahid while explaning the verse

وَقُوْمُوْا لِلّٰهِ قٰنِتِيْنَ

"And stand up with Qunoot to Allah (ii–238)" says Qunoot comprises all such things as proper bowing, devotion, long rakaat, keeping the eyes down, lowering of shoulders in submission and fear of Allah. Whenever a companion of the Holy Prophet (Sallallaho alaihe wasallam) stood for salaat, he would not look here and there or level the pebbles at the place of sajdah (while prostrating) or engage himself in any absurd act, or think of any worldly thing (except unintentionally), all for fear of Allah."

Many interpretations have been given to the word Qunoot, which occurs in the Qur'an in the verse mentioned in this hadith. According to one of the interpretations, Qunoot means silence. In the beginning of Islam, it was permissible to talk or to return greetings during salaat, but when this verse was revealed, talking during salaat was absolutely forbidden. Hadhrat Ibn Mas'ood (Radhiyallaho anho) says, "In the beginning whenever I visited the Prophet (Sallallaho alaihe wasallam), I would greet him with 'Assalamu alaikum' and he would reply with 'Wa alaikumus salaam' even if he were engaged in salaat. Once I visited him while he was in salaat and greeted him as usual, but he did not reply. I grew very anxious, fearing that his attitude might be due to Allah's displeasure for me. All sorts of anxious thoughts began to enter my mind. One moment, I would think the Prophet (Sallallaho alaihe wasallam) was angry with me and then some other saddening explanation would occur to me. When the Prophet (Sallallaho alaihe wasallam) finished his salaat he said, "Allah amends His commandments as He pleases. He has now forbidden any talking during salaat." He then recited the verse, 'And stand up with Qunoot to Allah' (II: 238) and said, salaat is now meant exclusively to hymn the glory, praise and sanctity of Allah."

Hadhrat Mu'aawiyah bin Hakam Salami (Radhiyallaho anho) says, "When I visited Madinah to embrace Islaam, I was taught many things. One of those was that I should say 'Yarhamukallaah' when anybody sneezed and exlaimed 'Alhamdulillaah'. As I was new in Islaam, I did not know that this was not to be done during salaat. Once we were all standing in salaat when somebody sneezed. I immediately shouted, 'Yarhamukallaah'. Everybody began to stare at me. As I did not know then that we were not to talk in salaat, I protested saying, 'Why are you all casting these angry looks?' They hushed me up with a gesture, but I could not understand their behaviour, although I decided to be quiet. When salaat was over, the Prophet (Sallallaho alaihe wasallam) called me. Neither did he beat or rebuke me, nor was he harsh to me. He simply said, 'It is not permitted to talk in salaat. Salaat is the occasion for praising the glory and magificence of Allah and reciting the Qur'an.' By Allah, I have never met, before or after, a teacher as affectionate as the Prophet (Sallallaho alaihe wasallam)."

Another interpretation is given by Hadhrat Ibn Abbas (Radhiyallaho anho) in which he says that Qunoot means devotion. The words of Mujahid given above are based on this interpretation. Hadhrat Abdullah bin Abbas (Radhiyallaho anho) says, "In the beginning, the Prophet (Sallallaho alaihe wasallam) used to tie himself up with a string while in Tahajjud, so that he might prevent sleep over-powering him. It was for this that the following verse was revealed in the Qur'an:

طٰهٰ مَآ اَنْزَلْنَا عَلَيْكَ الْقُرْاٰنَ لِتَشْقٰى

"We have not revealed unto thee (Muhammad) (Sallallaho alaihe wasallam) this Qur'an that Thou should be distressed." (XX: 2)

It is reported in many ahaadith that the Prophet's (Sallallah alaihi wasallam) feet would get swollen on account of standing for long hours during Tahajjud. Out of mere kindness and affection for his followers, he, however, advised them to be moderate in their worship, lest any excessiveness should lead to deflection. That is why we find him forbidding a woman from tying herself up for avoiding sleep during salaat.

We should remember that a salaat with long rakaat is surely better and more valuable, provided the endurance limits are not exceeded. After all, there is some meaning in the Prophet's (Sallallaho alaihe wasallam) offering such lengthy salaat that would give him swollen feet. When the companions requested him to reduce his toil in worship, as he had been assured of forgiveness in Soorah Fath:

لِيَغْفِرَلَكَ اللّٰهُ مَاتَقَدَّمَ مِنْ ذَنْبِكَ وَمَاتَاَخَّرَ

(That Allah may forgive thee of thy sins that which is past and that which is to come (XLVIII:2), he used to say, "Why should I not, then, be a grateful slave of Allah?"

It is stated in a hadith that when, the Prophet (Sallallaho alaihe wasallam) offered his salaat, his bosom would give a constant groaning sound, which resembled that of a grinding mill. In another hadith, this sound is likened to that of a boiling kettle. Hadhrat Ali (Radhiyallaho anho) narrates, "On the eve of Badr, I noticed that the Prophet (Sallallaho alaihe wasallam) stood under a tree, busy in salaat and crying before Allah all night long till daybreak." It is said in a number of ahaadith, "Allah is very much pleased with certain persons one of them is he who forsakes his bed shared with his dear and lovely wife and engages himself in Tahajjud on a winter night. Allah is very much pleased with him, takes pride in him, and in spite of being All-knowing inquires from the angels, 'What made this slave of mine forsake his bed and stand up like this?' The Angels reply, 'The hope of winning Thy Bounty and Grace, and the fear of Thy displeasure.' At this Allah says, 'Listen, I bestow upon him what he hopes for and grant him refuge from what he is afraid of."

The Prophet (Sallallaho alaihe wasallam) says, "None receives a better reward from Allah more than he who is blessed to offer two 'rakaats of salaat."

It has often been mentioned in the Qur'an and ahaadith that the Angels are perpetually engaged in worship.

There are some who shall remain in ruku and some in sajdah till eternity. Allah has combined all these postures of the Angels in our salaat, so that we may get our shares from each type of their worship. Recitation of the Qur'an in salaat is an addition over and above their worship. While salaat is the sum total of all the postures in the Angels' methods of worship, it gives out its best when it is offered by a person possessing angelic habits. That is why the Prophet (Sallallaho alaihe wasallam) says, "For (a good) salaat, keep your back and stomach light." The back of a person is said to be light when he has very few worldly encumbrances, and his stomach is light when he eats moderately to avoid indolence and laziness, which is a sure outcome of gluttony.

REQUISITES OF GOOD SALAAT SUGGESTED BY SOOFIA

The Soofia write: "There are twelve thousand virtues in salaat, which can be achieved through twelve points. If a person is to acquire full benefit from salaat, then, he must take care of these points. Sincerity is of course essential at every step. These points are as follows:

1. **Knowledge:** An action performed without knowledge is far inferior to the one done with full knowledge about it. We should therefore know:

(a) Which of the Islamic Practices are fardh and which are sunnat.
(b) What is fardh and what is sunnat in wudhu and salaat.
(c) How does Satan cause obstruction in the proper observance of salaat.

2. **Wudhu:** We must try to:

(a) Clean our heart of jealously and malice, just as we wash the other parts of our body.
(b) Keep ourselves clean of sins.
(c) Be neither wasteful nor abstemious in the use of water.

3. **Dress:** It should be:

(a) Got through honest living.
(b) Clean.

(c) According to the Sunnat, e.g. the ankles should not be covered.
(d) Simple, and should not display vanity and pride.

4. Time: We should be:

(a) Able to tell correct time at any moment.
(b) Always watchful about Azaan.
(c) Particular about the time of salaat, lest we should be too late for it.

5. Qiblah: There are three things to be ensured in facing Qiblah:

(a) We must face Qiblah physically.
(b) Have the heart in union with Allah, for He is the Qiblah of the heart.
(c) Be as attentive as a slave is before his master.

6. Intention: For this we need to be particular about three things:

(a) We must be definite as to what salaat we are offering.
(b) Remain constantly conscious of our presence before Allah, Who sees us.
(c) Have perfect faith that Allah know all that is in our hearts.

7. Takbeer Tahreemah: The essentials of 'Takbeer Tahreemah' are:

(a) To pronounce the words correctly.
(b) To raise both hands right up to the ears. This signifies that we have severed our connection with all, except Allah.
(c) To feel the greatness of Allah in our heart when we say Allaho Akbar.

8. Qiyaam: While in Qiyaam we should:

(a) Keep our gaze at the place of sajdah.
(b) Feel in our heart that we are standing before Allah.
(c) Not think of anything else.

9. Qiraat: The essentials of Qiraat are:

(a) To recite the Qur'an with Tajweed.
(b) To ponder on the meanings of what we recite.
(c) To bind ourselves to what we recite.

10. Ruku: The essentials of Ruku are:

(a) To keep the back quite straight i.e. the whole body above the legs should be in one straight line.
(b) To hold the knees firmly with fingers spread apart.
(c) To recite Tasbeeh with humility and devotion.

11. Sajdah: The essentials of Sajdah are:

(a) To place the hands flat and close to the ears.
(b) To keep elbows raised above the ground.
(c) To recite Tasbeeh with devotion.

12. Qa'dah: The essentials of Qa'dah are:

(a) To sit up on the left foot, keeping the right one erect.
(b) To recite Tashahhud with devotion, keeping the meaning in mind, for it contains greetings for the Prophet (Sallallaho alaihe wasallam) and prayer for the Muslim brethren.
(c) To consider the concluding Salaam a definite greeting to the Angels as well as the people on the right and on the left.

As has been said already, sincerity is the essence of all these points, which requires us:

1. To offer salaat with the sole purpose of pleasing Allah.
2. To understand that it is only through the grace and favour of Allah that we are able to offer salaat.
3. To hope for the reward promised by Allah.

SIGNIFICANCE OF WORDING OF SALAAT

Salaat is really a very blessed and auspicious observance. Every word uttered in it is imbued with Allah's greatness and sanctity. Thanaa, the opening prayer of salaat, contains extremely virtuous and devotional meaning viz:

(1) *Subhaanakallaahumma:*	O, Allah! I praise Thy Sanctity. Thou art free from all blemishes. Thou art above anything that is not the best.
(2) *Wa bihamdika:*	I praise Thy Glory. All virtues and beauties are admittedly for Thee and befit Thee.

(3) *Wa tabaarakasmuka:*	Thy name is blessed: and in fact so blessed that blesses everything over which it is mentioned.
(4) *Wa ta'aalaa jadduka:*	Thy eminence is most exalted. Thy magnificence is most sublime.
(5) *Wa laa ilaaha ghairuk:*	There is no god save Thee. None has ever been and none shall ever be fit to be worshipped save Thee.

Similary in ruku we recite "Subhaana rabbiyal azeem." which means:

> "My Magnificent and Almighty Allah is free from all blemishes. I express my humbleness and weakness before His Greatness by bowing my head before Him (for the bowing of head is the symbol of humbleness and submission, just as a stiff neck is the sign of haughtiness and pride). I submit before all Thy commandments and I take upon me Thy service. I am at Thy command. Thou art really very Great and I submit before Thy greatness."

Similary in sajdah we express our submission before Allah the Highest, and declare Him above all defects. Our head, which is considered as the most superb part of our body along with our eyes, ears, nose and tongue, is placed on ground before Him in the hope that He would show mercy and bestow His blessings on us. Standing with our hands folded before Him this was the first expression of our humbleness and submission. This was further augmented by the bending of our head in ruku and it reached its climax when we placed our head on the ground before Him. In fact the whole salaat is an indication of humbleness and submission, and therefore a means of advancement and success in the world and in the hereafter. May Allah through His Kindness arouse me and all the Muslims to offer such a salaat.

SALAAT OF FEW SAHAABAH, TAABI'EES AND SOOFIA

It is said about Hadhrat Hasan (Radhiyallaho anho) that whenever he performed wudhu, his face grew pale. When someone inquired from him its cause, he replied, "It is time to stand before the most Majestic and Irresistable Sovereign." On reaching the gate of the musjid he would say,

> "O Allah! Thy slave is at Thy door, O, the most Beneficent! Here is a sinner before Thee: Thou hast enjoined upon the good amongst us to overlook the faults of the bad. O Allah, Thou art Good and I am bad So for the sake of all that is most beautiful in Thee, overlook all that is ugly in me. O, The most Bountiful."

He would then enter the musjid.

Zainul Aabideen (Rahmatullah alaih) used to offer one thousand rakaats of nafl salaat daily. He never missed his Tahajjud, whether in journey or at home. His face grew pale when he performed his wudhu and he would tremble when he stood in salaat. Somebody asked him the reason for that. He said, "Don't you know before Whom I am going to stand?" Once when he was engaged in salaat, a fire broke out in his house. He continued his salaat most calmly. When asked about it, he remarked, "The fire of the hereafter kept me unmindful of the fire of this world." He once said, "The pride of a proud person surprises me. The day before, he was a drop of a dirty fluid and tomorrow he will be carrion, and still he is proud." He used to say, "It is strange that people do so much for the world, which is transitory, and do nothing for the hereafter, where they are to live for ever." He used to help the poor in the darkness of night, so that they should not even know who helped them. It came to light only after his death that no less than one hundred families were being supported by him.

It is said about Hadhrat Ali (Radhiyallaho anho) that the colour of his face would change and he would tremble at the approach of the hour of salaat. On being asked by someone he said, "This is the time for discharging the trust which the Heaven and the Earth and even the mountains were afraid to bear. I do not know if I shall be able to discharge it."

It is said of Hadhrat Abdullah bin Abbas (Radhiyallaho anho) that, when he heard the Azaan, he wept so much that his shawl would get wet with his tears, his veins would swell and his eyes would become red. Somebody said to him, "We do not see anything in the Azaan that should make you so nervous." He replied, "If people understood what the mu'azzin announced to them, they would give up sleep and forsake their comforts." He then explained to him the warning conveyed by each word of the Azaan.

A person narrates, "I happened to offer my Asr prayer with Zunnoon Misri (Rahmatullah alaih). When he uttered 'Allah' (in takbeer), he was so much struck with awe on account of Allah's Majesty, as though his soul had departed, and when he uttered 'Akbar' I felt my heart would burst with fear of Allah.

Uwais Qarni (Rahmatullah alaih), a famous saint and the most exalted of all the Taabi'ees, would spend his whole night sometimes in ruku and sometimes in sajdah.

Asaam (Rahmatullah alaih) once inquired from Haatim Zaahid Balkhi (Rahmatullah alaih) how he offered his salaat. He replied:

> "When the hour for salaat draws near, I perform my wudhu thoroughly and go to the place of salaat. When I stand for salaat, I visualise the Ka'bah in front of me, the Siraat under my feet, Paradise on my right, Hell on my left and the Angel of death over my head; and I think that this is my last salaat, so I may have no opportunity to say another; Allah alone knows what goes on in my heart at that time. Then I say 'Allaho Akbar' with full humility and recite the Holy Qur'an, pondering over its meaning. I do my ruku and sajdah with full humbleness and submission, and finish my salaat quite calmly, hoping that Allah will accept it through His mercy, and fearing that it may be rejected if it is judged on its merits."

Asaam (Rahmatullah alaih) asked him, "Since when have you been offering such salaat?" Haatim (Rahmatullah alaih) replied, "I have been doing it for the last thirty years." Asaam (Rahmatullah alaih) wept and said, "I have never been so fortunate as to offer a single salaat of this kind."

It is said that Haatim (Rahmatullah alaih) once missed his salaat with jamaat and felt for it too much. A couple of persons came to condole with him on this loss. He started weeping and then said, "If I had lost one of my sons, half the population of Balkh town would have come to me for condolence, but on the loss of my jamaat you are the only people condoling with me. It is only because people regard the afflictions in the Hereafter as lighter than the affliction of this world."

Sa'eed bin Musayyab (Rahmatullah alaih) says, "For

the last twenty years, I have never been out of the musjid at the time of the Azaan."

Muhammad bin Waasi' (Radmatullah alaih) says, "I love three things in this life; a friend who could warn me on my slips, bread sufficient to keep me alive, and salaat (with jamaat) such that Allah may condone its defects and give me reward for anything good in it.

Hadhrat Abu Ubaidah bin Jarraah (Radhiyallaho anho) was once leading the salaat. When the salaat was over, he said to the people, "Satan made a dangerous attack on me while I was leading the salaat. He made me think that as I was leading salaat, I am the best of all of you. I shall never lead the salaat again."

Maimoon bin Mahraan (Rahmatullah alaih) once reached the musjid when the jamaat was over. He recited 'Innaa lillaahi wa innaa ilaihi raaji-oon' and said, "The reward of this salaat with jamaat was dearer to me than sovereignty over Iraq."

It is said of the Companions that they would mourn for three days if they happened to miss the first takbeer and for seven days if they missed jamaat.

Bakr bin Abdullah once said, "You can speak to your Lord and Master any time you like." "How?" inquired somebody. He replied, "Perform your wudhu properly and stand up for salaat."

Aa'ishah (Radhiyallaho anha) says, "The Holy Prophet (Sallallaho alaihe wasallam) would be among us (family members) talking and listening, but on approach of salaat hour, he would all of a sudden behave as if he had never known us and would be completely absorbed in Allah.

It is said of Sa'eed Tannookhi (Rahmatullah alaih) that, as long as he remained in salaat, tears would flow from his eyes incessantly.

Somebody asked Khalaf bin Ayyoob (Rahmatullah alaih), "Do not the flies annoy you in your salaat?" His answer was: "Even the bad characters in society patiently bear the lashes of the police to boast of their endurance afterwards. Why should I be disturbed by mere flies, while standing in the presence of my Creator?"

It is said in 'Bahjatun nufoos' that one of the Sahabah was once offering Tahajjud when a thief came and took away his horse. He noticed it, but he did not break his salaat. Somebody asked him, "Why did you not break salaat and catch the thief?" He replied, "I was engaged in something far more valuable than the horse."

It is said about Ali (Radhiyallaho anho) that whenever an arrow got stuck into his body (in a battle), this was drawn out during his salaat. Once he got an arrow stuck into his thigh. This could not be extracted, in spite of several efforts, due to severe pain felt by him. When he was busy in his nafl salaat and prostrate in sajdah, the people drew out the arrow with force. When he finished his salaat, he asked the people who had collected around him, "Have you gathered to take out the arrow?" When they told him that it was already taken out, he informed them that he had no feeling of pain during the extraction.

Muslim bin Yasaar (Rahmatullah alaih), when he stood up for salaat, said to his family members, "You may keep on talking; I shall not be aware of what you talk."

It is said of Aamir bin Abdullah (Rahmatullah alaih) that he would not even hear the beating of a drum while in salaat, nor to speak of the talk of people around him. A person asked him, "Are you conscious of anything while in salaat?" He replied, "Yes, I am conscious of the fact that I have to stand one day before Allah, whence I shall either be sent to Paradise or Hell." The person said, "No, I do not mean that. Do you come to know of anything we talk around you?" He replied, "It is better that spears pass through my body rather than I grow conscious of your conversation while I am in salaat." He used to say, "My conviction in the things of the Hereafter is so perfect that it is impossible for it to improve, even if I happen to see those things with my physical eyes."

A pious man was asked, "Do you ever think of this world while you are in salaat?" He replied, "I never think of this world, either in salaat or out of it." Another such man was asked, "Do you think of anything while in salaat?" He replied, "Is there anything more attractive than salaat itself to think of?"

In 'Bahjatun Nufoos' it is written about a Shaikh that he had either been offering fardh or nafl salaat or been absorbed in Zikr without break, right from Zuhr to Fajr of the next day. After Fajr, while continuing Zikr, he was overpowered by slumber, when immediately he recited Istighfaar and the following prayer:

اعوذ بالله من عينٍ لاتشبع من النوم

"I seek refuge in Allah from the eye that does not get satiated with sleep."

It is said about another Shaikh that he would go to bed and try to sleep. But when he failed in his attempt, he would rise up and engage himself in salaat and would say, "O Allah! Thou knowest very well that it is the fear of the Fire of Hell that has caused my sleep to disappear."

There are so many stories about the pious people spending their nights praying in eagerness and love for Allah that these cannot possibly be covered in one book. We have in fact lost the taste for the pleasures of such pursuits so much that we have begun to doubt the veracity of such facts. But these have been related so frequently and continuously that if we doubt them we can as well doubt history, for frequency and continuity in narration about an event vouch safe its correctness without dispute.

Again we see with our own eyes people spending the whole night (sometimes even standing) for witnessing a show in a cinema or a theatre. They neither get tired nor does sleep overpower them. When such impious deeds, if indulged in, have such an attraction, then what makes us doubt that the spiritual pursuits can be so attractive and tasteful, while persons partaking in them are specially endowed with additional strength and endurance by Allah? The only reason for our doubt is our ignorance, which is like that of an immature child about the experiences of puberty. May Allah enable us to attain the heights where we may be able to taste the pleasures of His worship.

AN IMPORTANT NOTE

According to the Soofia, salaat is in fact a supplication to and speech with Allah, and therefore needs thorough concentration. In case of other observances, we need not be so attentive. For example, the essence of Zakaat is to spend money for the pleasure of Allah. Spending, in itself is so hard on a person that even if he does it inattentively he would feel the pinch of it. Similarly, fasting requires giving up eating and drinking and sexual satisfaction. All these restrictions are really very hard, even if not observed by proper attention and devotion. On the other hand, Zikr and recitation of the Qur'an are the chief constituents of Salaat. If these are not done intelligently and attentively, they can make neither supplication nor speech. They are just like the ravings of a person in high fever, which do not require any conscious effort nor carry any meaning for the listener. It is therefore necessary that we should be completely attentive when in salaat, otherwise our salaat will be like the talk of a person in his sleep, which carries no meaning for the listeners, nor any benefit accrues from it. In the same way, Allah pays no heed to a salaat that is offered inattentively and without concentration. But even if our salaat is not up to the mark, as compared with that of the eminent people in the past, we should not give up the practice. It is absolutely incorrect to think that there is no use offering a salaat unless it is perfect. To offer an imperfect salaat is far better than to give it up completely, as this shall result in punishments of a very drastic nature in the Hereafter. A school of Ulama have declared that person to be a kaafir who intentionally discards salaat (as discussed in full in Chapter I).

It is therefore imperative on all of us to make sincere and genuine efforts to do justice to our salaat and pray to Allah to grant us the ability to offer salaat similar to that of the eminent people in the past, so that we may have at least one salaat of that nature to our credit for presentation before Allah.

In the end, it may be pointed out that the Muhadditheen are rather liberal in accepting the authenticity of the ahaadith relating to the rewards of different religious observances. As for the stories about saints and pious people, these are a part of ordinary history and therefore on a different footing.

وَمَا تَوْفِيْقِىْ اِلَّا بِاللهِ عَلَيْهِ تَوَكَّلْتُ وَاِلَيْهِ اُنِيْبُ رَبَّنَا ظَلَمْنَا اَنْفُسَنَا وَاِنْ لَمْ تَغْفِرْلَنَا
وَتَرْحَمْنَا لَنَكُوْنَنَّ مِنَ الْخَاسِرِيْنَ رَبَّنَا لَاتُؤَاخِذْنَا اِنْ نَّسِيْنَا اَوْ اَخْطَاْنَا رَبَّنَا
وَلَاتَحْمِلْ عَلَيْنَا اِصْرًا كَمَا حَمَلْتَهُ عَلَى الَّذِيْنَ مِنْ قَبْلِنَا رَبَّنَا وَلَاتُحَمِّلْنَا مَالَا طَاقَةَ
لَنَا بِهِ ، وَاعْفُ عَنَّا وَاغْفِرْلَنَا وَارْحَمْنَا اَنْتَ مَوْلٰنَا فَانْصُرْنَا عَلَى الْقَوْمِ الْكَافِرِيْنَ
وَصَلَّى اللهُ تَعَالٰى عَلٰى خَيْرِ خَلْقِهٖ سَيِّدِ الْاَوَّلِيْنَ وَالْاٰخِرِيْنَ وَعَلٰى اٰلِهٖ وَاَصْحَابِهٖ
وَاَتْبَاعِهِمْ وَحَمَلَةِ الدِّيْنِ الْمَتِيْنِ بِرَحْمَتِكَ يَاَارْحَمَ الرَّاحِمِيْنَ

Virtues of ZIKR

Translation of the Urdu book Faza'il-e-Zikr

Virtues of Zikr

فَضَائِل ذکر

By:-

Shaikhul Hadith Maulana Muhammad Zakariyyah Kaandhlawi (Rah)

Translated by
Shafiq Ahmad

ادارہ اشاعتِ دینیات (پرائیویٹ) لمیٹڈ
idara IDARA ISHA'AT-E-DINIYAT (P) LTD.

VIRTUES OF ZIKR

By: Shaikhul Hadith
Maulana Muhammad Zakariyya Kaandhlawi (Rah)

Edition 2001

Published by:
IDARA ISHA'AT-E-DINIYAT (P) LTD.
168/2, Jha House, Hazrat Nizamuddin
New Delhi-110 013 (India)
Tel.: 6926832, 6926833
Fax: +91-11-6322787,4352786
Email: **sales@idara.com**
Visit us at: **www.idara.com**

Printed at:
Nice Printing Press, Delhi

VIRTUES OF ZIKR

CONTENTS

CHAPTER I VIRTUES OF ZIKR IN GENERAL

CHAPTER II. VIRTUES OF KALIMAH TAYYABAH

CHAPTER III VIRTUES OF THIRD KALIMAH

بِسْمِ اللهِ الرَّحْمٰنِ الرَّحِيْمِ

نَحْمَدُهٗ وَنُصَلِّيْ عَلٰى رَسُوْلِهِ الْكَرِيْمِ وَعَلٰى اٰلِهٖ وَاَصْحَابِهٖ وَاَتْبَاعِهٖ حَمَلَةِ الدِّيْنِ الْقَوِيْمِ

THE VIRTUES OF ZIKR

FOREWORD

IN THE NAME OF ALLAH, THE MOST GRACIOUS, THE MOST MERCIFUL

The sacred name of Almighty Allah carries the blessings, taste, sweetness, thrill, and peace of mind that is invariably experienced by one who has practised and remained absorbed in His zikr for a considerable time. This name brings joy to the heart and peace of mind. Almighty Allah has said Himself:

اَلَا بِذِكْرِ اللهِ تَطْمَئِنُّ الْقُلُوْبُ (سورة رعد ركوع ٤)

"Lo! the zikr of Allah provides satisfaction for the hearts."

Today there is a wave of discontentment in the whole world; and the letters that I receive daily contain mostly accounts of worries and anxieties. The object of this booklet is that people who lack peace of mind, whether in an individual or collective capacity, may be told how to overcome their malady and that the good and blessed persons may be benefitted by the general publication of the virtues of zikr of Almighty Allah. It is just possible that the study of this booklet may inspire some people to recite the sacred name of Allah with sincerity (ikhlaas) and this may prove useful to me (also) at the time when only good deeds will prove helpful. Of course, Almighty Allah can, through His sheer grace, forgive one who has no good deeds to his credit.

Besides this, the thing which prompted me to this undertaking was that Almighty Allah, through His extreme Benevolence and Grace has blessed my uncle, Hazrat Muhammad Ilyas Kandhlavi, who resides in Nizamuddin (Delhi) with a special insight and zeal for the work of Tableegh, the activities of which are no longer confined to India alone, but have reached Hijaaz as well. This movement is well known and needs no introduction. Its good results soon began to be visible in India and abroad generally, but especially so in the region of Mewat, as is well-known. The fundamental principles of this movement are basically very sound, good and strong, and are inherently fruitful and beneficial. One of the important principles is that those who are engaged in Tableegh work should be particular in practising zikr, and more so when they are actually busy in Tabligh work. After observing the wonderful results of this practice, I myself felt the necessity of writing this booklet. I was also ordered by my respected uncle that the virtues of zikr of Allah should be compiled and made available to them, so that those who so far practise it out of obedience to Allah may themselves feel an urge for doing so for the sake of its virtues, and thereby realise that zikr is a great wealth.

It is neither possible for a humble person like myself to compile a comprehensive treatise on the virtues of zikr, nor is it humanly possible to do full justice to this subject. I have however briefly described some narrations relating to this subject. I have divided the book into three chapters, of which the virtues of zikr in general are described in the first chapter, those of Kalimah Tayyibah in the second and those of the third Kalimah (known as Tasbeeh-Fatimah) in the third.

CHAPTER I

VIRTUES OF ZIKR IN GENERAL

Even if there were no ayat or hadith relating to zikr, we should not have forgotten to remember our real Benefactor, Whose blessings and favours on us at all times are unlimited, and have no parallel. It is but natural that we should remember our Benefactor, perform His zikr (remember Him) and thank Him. Countless virtues of zikr are described in the Qur'an and Ahaadith, and the sayings and deeds of our elders in support thereof are available for our benefit. No doubt, the blessings of the glorious zikr of Allah are unlimited and its effulgence is so sublime.

Here, I first describe a few ayaat (Verses from the Holy Qur'an) and then some ahaadith on the subject of His glorious zikr.

SECTION 1

Quranic Verses relating Zikr

(١) فَاذْكُرُوْنِيْٓ اَذْكُرْكُمْ وَاشْكُرُوْا لِيْ وَلَاتَكْفُرُوْنِ (البقرة ، ركوع ١٨)

1. Therefore remember Me, I will remember you. Give thanks to Me and reject not Me.

(٢) فَإِذَا اَفَضْتُمْ مِنْ عَرَفَاتٍ فَاذْكُرُوْا اللّٰهَ عِنْدَ الْمَشْعَرِ الْحَرَامِ وَاذْكُرُوْهُ كَمَا
هَدَاكُمْ وَاِنْ كُنْتُمْ مِنْ قَبْلِهِ لَمِنَ الضَّآلِّيْنَ (البقرة ركوع ٢٥)

2. When (during the Hajj) ye pass on in the multitude from Arafaat, remember Allah by the sacred monument. Remember Him as He hath guided you, although before this ye were of those gone astray.

(٣) فَإِذَا قَضَيْتُمْ مَنَاسِكَكُمْ فَاذْكُرُوْا اللّٰهَ كَذِكْرِكُمْ آبَاءَكُمْ اَوْ اَشَدَّ ذِكْرًا فَمِنَ
النَّاسِ مَنْ يَّقُوْلُ رَبَّنَا آتِنَا فِي الدُّنْيَا وَمَا لَهُ فِي الْآخِرَةِ مِنْ خَلَاقٍ ، وَمِنْهُمْ مَنْ
يَّقُوْلُ رَبَّنَا آتِنَا فِي الدُّنْيَا حَسَنَةً وَّفِي الْآخِرَةِ حَسَنَةً وَّقِنَا عَذَابَ النَّارِ ، اُوْلٰئِكَ
لَهُمْ نَصِيْبٌ مِمَّا كَسَبُوْا وَاللّٰهُ سَرِيْعُ الْحِسَابِ (بقره ٢٥ ع)

3. And when ye have completed your Hajj rites, then remember Allah as ye remember your fathers, or with a more lively remembrance. There are men who say, "Our Creator! Give unto us, Your bounties in this world," but they will have no portion in the Hereafter."

There are men (also) who say, "Our Creator! Give unto us in the world that which is good and in the Hereafter that which is good, and guard us from the doom of Fire." For them, there is in store a goodly portion (in both worlds) out of that which they have earned. Allah is swift at reckoning.

It is related in a hadith that the du'aa of three persons is not rejected rather it is surely accepted. (1) He who remembers Allah profusely (2) A wronged person (3) A ruler who avoids tyranny.

(٤) وَاذْكُرُوا اللهَ فِيْ أَيَّامٍ مَعْدُوْدَاتٍ (بقرة ٢٥ ع)

4. (During the Hajj) remember Allah all through the appointed days.

(٥) وَاذْكُرْ رَبَّكَ كَثِيراً وَسَبِّحْ بِالعَشِيِّ وَالْإِبْكَارِ (آل عمران ع ٤)

5. Remember thy Lord much, and praise Him in the early hours of night and morning.

(٦) اَلَّذِيْنَ يَذْكُرُوْنَ اللهَ قِيَاماً وَّقُعُوْدًا وَّعَلٰى جُنُوْبِهِمْ وَيَتَفَكَّرُوْنَ فِيْ خَلْقِ السَّمٰوٰاتِ وَالْاَرْضِ رَبَّنَا مَاخَلَقْتَ هٰذَا بَاطِلًا سُبْحَانَكَ فَقِنَا عَذَابَ النَّارِ (آل عمران ع ٢٠)

6. (Talking of the wise men, these are) such as remember Allah, standing, sitting, and reclining, and consider the creation of the Heavens and the Earth, and say, (after deliberation) "Our Lord! Thou has not created this in vain. Glory be to Thee! Preserve us from the doom of the Fire."

(٧) فَإِذَا قَضَيْتُمُ الصَّلٰوةَ فَاذْكُرُوا اللهَ قِيَامًا وَّقُعُوْدًا وَّعَلٰى جُنُوْبِكُمْ (النساء ١٥ ع)

7. When ye have performed the act of salaat, remember Allah, standing, sitting and reclining (We should remember Him in all circumstances.)

(٨) وَاِذَا قَامُوْآ اِلَى الصَّلٰوةِ قَامُوْا كُسَالٰى يُرَاءُوْنَ النَّاسَ وَلَايَذْكُرُوْنَ اللهَ اِلَّا قَلِيْلًا (النساء - ٢١ ع)

8. (The hypocrites) when they stand up to worship, they perform it languidly and to be seen by men, and are mindful of Allah but little.

(٩) إِنَّمَا يُرِيْدُ الشَّيْطَانُ اَنْ يُوْقِعَ بَيْنَكُمُ الْعَدَاوَةَ وَالْبَغْضَآءَ فِى الْخَمْرِ وَالْمَيْسِرِ وَيَصُدَّكُمْ عَنْ ذِكْرِ اللهِ وَعَنِ الصَّلٰوةِ ، فَهَلْ اَنْتُمْ مُنْتَهُوْنَ (مائدة - ١٢ع)

9. Satan seeketh only to cast among you enmity and hatred by means of strong drink and games of chance, and to turn you from remembrance of Allah, and from His worship. Will ye then leave off (these bad habits)?

(١٠) وَلَاتَطْرُدِ الَّذِيْنَ يَدْعُوْنَ رَبَّهُمْ بِالْغَدٰوةِ وَالْعَشِيِّ يُرِيْدُوْنَ وَجْهَهُ (انعام ع٦)

10. Send not away those who call their Lord at morning and evening, seeking His countenance (pleasure).

(١١) وَادْعُوْهُ مُخْلِصِيْنَ لَهُ الدِّيْنَ (اعراف - ٣ع)

11. And call upon Him, making your devotion purely for Him (only).

(١٢) اُدْعُوْا رَبَّكُمْ تَضَرُّعًا وَّخُفْيَةً اِنَّهُ لَايُحِبُّ الْمُعْتَدِيْنَ وَلَاتُفْسِدُوْا فِي الْاَرْضِ بَعْدَ اِصْلَاحِهَا وَادْعُوْهُ خَوْفاً وَطَمَعاً اِنَّ رَحْمَةَ اللهِ قَرِيْبٌ مِّنَ الْمُحْسِنِيْنَ (اعراف - ٧ع)

12. Call upon your Lord humbly and in secret. Lo! He loveth not transgressors. Work not confusion in the Earth after the fair ordering thereof, and call on Him in fear and hope. Lo! The mercy of Allah is nigh unto the good.

(١٣) وَلِلّٰهِ الْاَسْمَاءُ الْحُسْنٰى فَادْعُوْهُ بِهَا (اعراف ٢٢ ع)

13. Allah's are the fairest names. Invoke Him by them.

(١٤) وَاذْكُرْ رَبَّكَ فِي نَفْسِكَ تَضَرُّعاً وَخِيْفَةً وَدُوْنَ الْجَهْرِ مِنَ الْقَوْلِ بِالْغُدُوِّ وَالْاٰصَالِ وَلَاتَكُنْ مِنَ الْغَافِلِيْنَ (اعراف ٢٤)

14. And remember thy Lord within thyself humbly and with awe, below thy breath, at morn and evening. And be thou not of the neglectful.

(١٥) إِنَّمَا الْمُؤْمِنُوْنَ الَّذِيْنَ إِذَا ذُكِرَ اللّٰهُ وَجِلَتْ قُلُوْبُهُمْ وَإِذَا تُلِيَتْ عَلَيْهِ آيَاتُهُ زَادَتْهُمْ إِيْمَانًا وَّعَلٰى رَبِّهِمْ يَتَوَكَّلُوْنَ (انفال ع١)

15. "They only are the (true) believers whose hearts feel a tremor when Allah is mentioned, and when the revelations of Allah are recited unto them, they find their faith strengthened, and who trust in their Lord. Thereafter mentioning the observance of salaat by them it is stated "Such in truth are the believers, they shall enjoy dignified positions with their Lord and blessed with His forgiveness and generous sustenance."

(١٦) وَيَهْدِيْ إِلَيْهِ مَنْ اَنَابَ ، اَلَّذِيْنَ آمَنُوْا وَتَطْمَئِنُّ قُلُوْبُهُمْ بِذِكْرِ اللّٰهِ اَلَا بِذِكْرِ اللّٰهِ تَطْمَئِنُّ الْقُلُوْبُ (رعد - ٤ ع)

16. And He guideth unto Himself all who turn to Him in penitence: who have believed and whose hearts find satisfaction in the remembrance of Allah. Verily in the remembrance of Allah do hearts rest content!

(١٧) قُلِ ادْعُوا اللّٰهَ اَوِدْعُوْا الرَّحْمٰنَ اَيًّامَّا تَدْعُوْا فَلَهُ الْاَسْمَاءُ الْحُسْنٰى (اسراء ١٢ع)

17. Say (unto mankind): call upon Allah, or call upon the Beneficient. By whatever name you call upon Him, it is well. His are the most beautiful names.

(١٨) وَاذْكُرْ رَبَّكَ إِذَا نَسِيْتَ (كهف ٤ ع)

(وفي مسائلِ السُّلُوْكِ : فِيهِ مطلُوْبِيَّةُ الذِّكرِ ظاهِرٌ)

18. And remember thy Lord when thou forgettest.

(١٩) وَاصْبِرْ نَفْسَكَ مَعَ الَّذِيْنَ يَدْعُوْنَ رَبَّهُمْ بِالْغَدَاةِ وَالْعَشِيِّ يُرِيْدُوْنَ وَجْهَهُ
وَلَاتَعْدُ عَيْنَاكَ عَنْهُمْ تُرِيْدُ زِيْنَةَ الْحَيٰوةِ الدُّنْيَا وَلَاتُطِعْ مَنْ اَغْفَلْنَا قَلْبَهُ عَنْ ذِكْرِنَا
وَاتَّبَعَ هَوَاهُ وَكَانَ اَمْرُهُ فُرُطًا (كهف - ع٤)

19. Restrain thyself along with those who call upon their Lord at morning and evening, seeking His pleasure; and let not thine eyes overlook them, desiring the pomp of this worldly life; and obey not him whose heart We have made heedless of Our remembrance, who followeth his own lust and whose case has gone beyond all bounds.

(٢٠) وَعَرَضْنَا جَهَنَّمَ يَوْمَئِذٍ لِّلْكَافِرِيْنَ عَرْضًا ، الَّذِيْنَ كَانَتْ اَعْيُنُهُمْ فِيْ غِطَآءٍ عَنْ
ذِكْرِيْ (كهف - ١١ع)

20. On that day, We shall present Hell to the disbelievers, plain to view; those whose eyes had been under a veil from remembrance of Me.

(٢١) ذِكْرُ رَحْمَةِ رَبِّكَ عَبْدَهُ زَكَرِيَّا ، اِذْ نَادٰى رَبَّهُ نِدَاءً خَفِياً (مريم ع٣)

21. A mention of the mercy of thy Lord unto His servant Zakariyya; when he cried unto his Lord a cry in secret.

(٢٢) وَادْعُوْا رَبِّيْ عَسٰى اَلَّا اَكُوْنَ بِدُعَاءِ رَبِّيْ شَقِيًّا (مريم ع ٣)

22. And I shall pray unto my Lord. It may be (and I have every hope), that with prayer unto my Lord, I shall not be unblest.

(٢٣) اِنَّنِيْ اَنَا اللهُ لَااِلٰهَ اِلَّا اَنَا فَاعْبُدْنِيْ ، وَاَقِمِ الصَّلٰوةَ لِذِكْرِيْ ، اِنَّ السَّاعَةَ اٰتِيَةٌ
اَكَادُ اُخْفِيْهَا لِتُجْزٰى كُلُّ نَفْسٍۭ بِمَا تَسْعٰى (طٰهٰ - ١ع)

23. Lo! I, even I, am Allah. There is no God save Me. So serve Me and establish salaat for My remembrance. Lo!

the Hour is surely coming. But I will keep it hidden, that every soul may be rewarded for that which it striveth to achieve.

(٢٤) وَلَا تَنِيَا فِيْ ذِكْرِيْ (طٰهٰ – ١ع)

24. And be not faint in remembrance of Me. (This is a piece of advice for Prophet Moosa and Haroon (Alayhimas salaam).

(٢٥) وَنُوْحاً اِذْ نَادٰى مِنْ قَبْلُ (انبياء – ٦ ع)

25. And (mention) Nooh, (Alayhis salaam) when he cried of old; We heard his prayer (before times of Ibrahim (Alayhis salaam)

(٢٦) وَاَيُّوْبَ اِذْ نَادٰى رَبَّهُ اَنِّيْ مَسَّنِيَ الضُّرُّ وَاَنْتَ اَرْحَمُ الرَّاحِمِيْنَ (انبياء ٦ ع)

26. And (mention) Ayyoob (Alayhis salaam) when he cried unto his Lord, "Lo! adversity afflicteth me, and Thou are Most Merciful of all who show mercy.

(٢٧) وَذَاالنُّوْنِ اِذْ ذَّهَبَ مُغَاضِبًا فَظَنَّ اَنْ لَّنْ نَقْدِرَ عَلَيْهِ فَنَادٰى فِى الظُّلُمَاتِ اَنْ لَّآاِلٰهَ اِلَّا اَنْتَ سُبْحَانَكَ اِنِّيْ كُنْتُ مِنَ الظَّالِمِيْنَ (انبياء ٦ ع)

27. And Zun-Noon Younus (Alayhis salaam) when he went off in anger (displeased with his community) and deemed that We had no power over him; but he cried out in the darkness (of the whale) saying "There is no God save Thee: be Thou glorified! Lo! I have been a wrong-doer."

(٢٨) وَزَكَرِيَّآ اِذْ نَادٰى رَبَّهُ رَبِّ لَاتَذَرْنِيْ فَرْدًا وَّاَنْتَ خَيْرُ الْوَارِثِيْنَ (أنبياء – ٦ع)

28. And (mention) Zakariyya (Alayhis salaam) when he cried unto his Lord, "My Lord! Leave me not childless, though Thou art the best of inheritors."

(٢٩) اِنَّهُمْ كَانُوْا يُسَارِعُوْنَ فِيْ الْخَيْرَاتِ وَيَدْعُوْنَنَا رَغَبًا وَّرَهَبًا وَكَانُوْا لَنَا خَاشِعِيْنَ (أنبياء ٦ع)

29. Lo! they (the Prophets mentioned before) used to vie one with the other in good deeds, and they cried unto Us in longing and in fear, and were submissive to Us.

(٣٠) وَبَشِّرِ الْمُخْبِتِيْنَ ، اَلَّذِيْنَ اِذَا ذُكِرَ اللهُ وَجِلَتْ قُلُوْبُهُمْ (حج – ٥ع)

30. And give good tidings to the humble: whose hearts fear when Allah is mentioned.

(٣١) إِنَّهُ كَانَ فَرِيْقٌ مِّنْ عِبَادِيْ يَقُوْلُوْنَ رَبَّنَا آمَنَّا فَاغْفِرْلَنَا وَارْحَمْنَا وَاَنْتَ خَيْرُ
الرَّاحِمِيْنَ ، فَاتَّخَذْتُمُوْهُمْ سِخْرِيًّا حَتّٰى اَنْسَوْكُمْ ذِكْرِيْ وَكُنْتُمْ مِنْهُمْ تَضْحَكُوْنَ ،
اِنِّيْ جَزَيْتُهُمُ الْيَوْمَ بِمَاصَبَرُوْآ اَنَّهُمْ هُمُ الْفَائِزُوْنَ (مؤمنون – ٦ع)

31. (While talking to the unbeliever on the Day of Judgement, they will be asked whether they remember) Lo! There was a party of My servants who said, "Our Lord! we believe, therefore forgive us and have mercy on us, for Thou art best of all who show mercy."

But ye chose them for a laughing-stock, until this (past time) caused you to forget remembrance of Me, while ye laughed at them. Lo! I have rewarded them this day for as much as they were steadfast; and they verily are the triumphant.

(٣٢) رِجَالٌ لَّاتُلْهِيْهِمْ تِجَارَةٌ وَّلَابَيْعٌ عَنْ ذِكْرِ اللهِ (الاية) (نور – ٥ع)

32. (While praising men with perfect faith) Men whom neither merchandise nor sale beguileth from remembrance of Allah and constancy in prayer and paying to the poor their due.

(٣٣) وَلَذِكْرُ اللهِ اَكْبَرُ (عنكبوت ٥ع)

33. But verily, remembrance of Allah is the most important.

(٣٤) تَتَجَافٰى جُنُوْبُهُمْ عَنِ الْمَضَاجِعِ يَدْعُوْنَ رَبَّهُمْ خَوْفًا وَّطَمَعًا وَّمِمَّا رَزَقْنَاهُمْ
يُنْفِقُوْنَ ، فَلَاتَعْلَمُ نَفْسٌ مَّا اُخْفِيَ لَهُمْ مِنْ قُرَّةِ اَعْيُنٍ جَزَآءً بِمَا كَانُوْا يَعْمَلُوْنَ
(سجدة – ٢ع) في الدر عن الضحاك هم قوم لايزالون يذكرون الله وروى نحوه عن ابن عباس

34. (Those) who forsake their beds to call upon their Lord in fear and hope, and spend of what We have bestowed on them. No soul knoweth what joy is kept hidden for them as a reward for what they used to do.

Note: It is mentioned in a hadith that one who prays to Allah in the last portion of the night gains acceptance of Allah. If possible, you should remember Allah at this hour.

(٣٥) لَقَدْ كَانَ لَكُمْ فِىْ رَسُوْلِ اللهِ اُسْوَةٌ حَسَنَةٌ لِمَنْ كَانَ يَرْجُوْا اللهَ وَالْيَوْمَ الْآخِرِ وَذَكَرَ اللهَ كَثِيْرًا (احزاب – ع ٣)

35. Verily in the messenger of Allah ye have a good example for him who looketh unto Allah and the Last Day, and remembreth Allah much.

(٣٦) وَالذَّاكِرِيْنَ اللهَ كَثِيْرًا وَالذّٰكِرٰتِ اَعَدَّ اللهُ لَهُمْ مَّغْفِرَةً وَّاَجْرًا عَظِيْمًا (احزاب ع ٥)

36. (While talking of the virtues of the believers) And men who remember Allah much and women who remember; Allah hath prepared for them His forgiveness and a vast reward.

(٣٧) يٰاَيُّهَا الَّذِيْنَ اٰمَنُوْا اذْكُرُوْا اللهَ ذِكْرًا كَثِيْرًا ، وَسَبِّحُوْهُ بُكْرَةً وَّاَصِيْلًا (احزاب ٦ع)

37. O ye who believe! Remember Allah with much remembrance. And glorify Him morning and evening.

(٣٨) وَلَقَدْ نَادٰنَا نُوْحٌ فَلَنِعْمَ الْمُجِيْبُوْنَ (صافات ع٣)

38. And Nooh (Alayhis salaam) verily prayed unto Us, and We are the best Who grant prayers.

(٣٩) فَوَيْلٌ لِّلْقٰسِيَةِ قُلُوْبُهُمْ مِّنْ ذِكْرِ اللهِ اُولٰئِكَ فِيْ ضَلٰلٍ مُّبِيْنٍ (زمر – ٣ ع)

39. Then woe unto those whose hearts are hardened against remembrance of Allah. Such are clearly in error.

(٤٠) اَللّٰهُ نَزَّلَ اَحْسَنَ الْحَدِيْثِ كِتَابًا مُتَشَابِهًا مَّثَانِيَ تَقْشَعِرُّ مِنْهُ جُلُوْدُ الَّذِيْنَ يَخْشَوْنَ رَبَّهُمْ ثُمَّ تَلِيْنُ جُلُوْدُهُمْ وَقُلُوْبُهُمْ اِلٰى ذِكْرِ اللّٰهِ ذٰلِكَ هُدَى اللّٰهِ يَهْدِىْ بِهٖ مَنْ يَّشَاءُ (زمر ع ٣)

40. Allah hath (now) revealed the most beautiful message of the Qur'an, a Scripture consistent with itself, repeating (its teaching in various aspects). Whereat doth tremble the skins of those who fear their Lord, so that their flesh and their hearts soften to Allah's remembrance. Such is Allah's guidance, wherewith be guideth whom He will.

(٤١) فَادْعُوْا اللّٰهَ مُخْلِصِيْنَ لَهُ الدِّيْنَ وَلَوْ كَرِهَ الْكَافِرُوْنَ (مؤمن ٢ ع)

41. Therefore pray unto Allah, making devotion pure for Him (only), however much the disbelievers may be averse.

(٤٢) هُوَ الْحَيُّ لَا اِلٰهَ اِلَّا هُوَ فَادْعُوْهُ مُخْلِصِيْنَ لَهُ الدِّيْنَ (مؤمن ٧ ع)

42. He is the Living One, there is no Allah save Him. So pray unto Him, making devotion pure for Him (only).

(٤٣) وَمَنْ يَعْشُ عَنْ ذِكْرِ الرَّحْمٰنِ نُقَيِّضْ لَهُ شَيْطَانًا فَهُوَ لَهُ قَرِيْنٌ (زخرف ٤ ع)

43. And he whose sight is dim to the remembrance of the Beneficent, We assign unto him a devil who becometh his comrade.

(٤٤) مُحَمَّدٌ رَّسُوْلُ اللّٰهِ وَالَّذِيْنَ مَعَهٗ اَشِدَّآءُ عَلَى الْكُفَّارِ رُحَمَآءُ بَيْنَهُمْ تَرَاهُمْ رُكَّعًا سُجَّدًا يَبْتَغُوْنَ فَضْلًا مِنَ اللّٰهِ وَرِضْوَانًا سِيْمَاهُمْ فِيْ وُجُوْهِهِمْ مِنْ اَثَرِ السُّجُوْدِ ذٰلِكَ مَثَلُهُمْ فِى التَّوْرَاةِ وَمَثَلُهُمْ فِى الْاِنْجِيْلِ كَزَرْعٍ اَخْرَجَ شَطْاَهٗ فَاٰزَرَهٗ فَاسْتَغْلَظَ فَاسْتَوٰى عَلٰى سُوْقِهٖ يُعْجِبُ الزُّرَّاعَ لِيَغِيْظَ بِهِمُ الْكُفَّارَ وَعَدَ اللّٰهُ الَّذِيْنَ اٰمَنُوْا وَعَمِلُوْا الصَّالِحَاتِ مِنْهُمْ مَغْفِرَةً وَاَجْرًا عَظِيْمًا (فتح – ع ٤)

44. Muhammad (Sallallaho alaihe wasallam) is the messenger of Allah. And those with him are hard against

the disbelievers and merciful among themselves. Thou seest them bowing and falling prostrate (in worship), seeking bounty from Allah and His acceptance. Their mark is on their foreheads from the traces of prostration. Such is their likeness in the Torah and their likeness in the Gospel–like sown corn that sendeth forth its shoot and strengtheneth it and riseth firm upon its stalk, delighting the farmers–In the same manner, the Companions of the Prophet (Sallallaho alaihe wasallam) were weak in the beginning then grew in strength day by day, that He may enrage the disbelievers with (the sight of) them. Allah hath promised, unto such of them as believe and do good works, forgiveness and immense reward.

COMMENTARY

In these verses though the emphasis obviously is on the blessings occurring from ruku, sujood and salaat but there is also an indication about the blessings associated with the second part of the Kalimah viz. (Muhammadur Rasulullah).

Imam Raazi (Rahmatullah alaih) has related that in the treaty of Hudaibiyah, on the refusal and insistence of the unbeliever not to write 'Muhammad Rasulullah' and to substitute it by 'Muhammad bin Abdullah', Allah Ta'aalaa asserts that He himself bears testimony to the Prophethood of Muhammad (Sallallaho alaihe wasallam). When the Sender confirms personally about a particular person to be His messenger, then the non-acceptance by any number of people does not matter. To confirm this testimony, Allah Ta'aalaa made the statement 'Muhammadur Rasulullah' (Muhammad is a Prophet of Allah).

There are other important subjects in these verses. One of them relates to the glow on the face of a blessed person. It has been explained that a person who keeps a vigil at night for prayers develops such a glow on his face. Imaam Raazi (Rahmatullah alaih) considers it an established fact that if two persons keep awake at night, one spending it in sensual and idle pleasures and the other uses his time in reciting the Qur'an, learning religious knowledge and offering prayers, they will get up with different facial expressions the next morning. The latter described above will be because of his spiritual glow, will show himself quite a different person.

The third important thing is that Imaam Maalik (Rahmatullah alaih) and a group of scholars established kufr for those people who talk ill of the Sahaba and bear hatred against them.

(٤٥) اَلَمْ يَاْنِ لِلَّذِيْنَ اٰمَنُوْا اَنْ تَخْشَعَ قُلُوْبُهُمْ لِذِكْرِ اللهِ (حديد ع٢)

45. Is not the time ripe for the hearts of those who believe to submit to Allah's reminder?

(٤٦) اِسْتَحْوَذَ عَلَيْهِمُ الشَّيْطَانُ فَاَنْسَاهُمْ ذِكْرَ اللهِ اُوْلٰٓئِكَ حِزْبُ الشَّيْطَانِ اَلَآ اِنَّ
حِزْبَ الشَّيْطَانِ هُمُ الْخَاسِرُوْنَ (مجادلة – ٣ ع)

46. (Mentioning of the hypocrites.) The devil hath engrossed them and so hath caused them to forget remembrance of Allah. They are the devil's party. Lo! is it not the devil's party who will be the losers?

(٤٧) فَاِذَا قُضِيَتِ الصَّلٰوةُ فَانْتَشِرُوْا فِى الْاَرْضِ وَابْتَغُوْا مِنْ فَضْلِ اللهِ وَاذْكُرُوْا
اللهَ كَثِيْرًا لَعَلَّكُمْ تُفْلِحُوْنَ (جمعة – ٢ع)

47. And when the (Friday) prayer is ended, then disperse in the land and seek of Allah's bounty, (with the permission to engage yourself in worldly pursuits but even then) and remember Allah much, that ye may be successful.

(٤٨) يٰاَيُّهَا الَّذِيْنَ اٰمَنُوْا لَاتُلْهِكُمْ اَمْوَالُكُمْ وَلَا اَوْلَادُكُمْ عَنْ ذِكْرِ اللهِ وَمَنْ يَفْعَلْ
ذٰلِكَ فَاُوْلٰٓئِكَ هُمُ الْخَاسِرُوْنَ (منافقون – ٢ع)

48. O ye who believe! Let not your wealth nor your children distract you from remembrance of Allah. Those who do so, they are the losers. (These things will not last beyond the grave and Allah's remembrance will prove useful in the Hereafter.

(٤٩) وَاِنْ يَّكَادُ الَّذِيْنَ كَفَرُوْا لَيُزْلِقُوْنَكَ بِاَبْصَارِهِمْ لَمَّا سَمِعُوا الذِّكْرَ وَيَقُوْلُوْنَ
اِنَّهٗ لَمَجْنُوْنٌ (قلم – ٢ع)

49. And Lo! those who disbelieve would fain disconcert thee with their eyes when they hear the message (the Qur'an) and they say, "Lo! he is indeed mad."

Note: Using the eyes in this manner indicates their extreme enmity. Hasan Basri (Rahmatullah alaih) advises benediction on a person, affected by malignant looks, after reciting this verse.

(٥٠) وَمَنْ يُّعْرِضْ عَنْ ذِكْرِ رَبِّهٖ يَسْلُكْهُ عَذَابًا صَعَدًا (جن ع ١)

50. And whoso turneth away from the remembrance of His Lord; He will thrust him into ever-growing torment.

(٥١) وَاَنَّهٗ لَمَّا قَامَ عَبْدُ اللهِ يَدْعُوْهُ كَادُوْا يَكُوْنُوْنَ عَلَيْهِ لِبَدًا ، قُلْ اِنَّمَآ اَدْعُوْا رَبِّيْ وَلَآاُشْرِكُ بِهٖٓ اَحَدًا (جن ع ١)

51. And when the devotee of Allah (Muhammad Sallallaho alaihe wasallam) stood up in prayer to Him, they crowded on him, almost stifling him. Say (unto them, O Muhammad), I pray unto Allah only, and ascribe to Him no partner.

(٥٢) وَاذْكُرِ اسْمَ رَبِّكَ وَتَبَتَّلْ اِلَيْهِ تَبْتِيْلًا (مزمل – ع ١)

52. So remember the name of thy Lord and devote thyself to him with whole-hearted devotion. (All other attachments should be reversed at that time and devotion to Allah should dominate).

(٥٣) وَاذْكُرِ اسْمَ رَبِّكَ بُكْرَةً وَّاَصِيْلًا ، وَمِنَ الَّيْلِ فَاسْجُدْ لَهٗ وَسَبِّحْهُ لَيْلًا طَوِيْلًا ، اِنَّ هٰٓؤُلَاءِ يُحِبُّوْنَ الْعَاجِلَةَ وَيَذَرُوْنَ وَرَآءَهُمْ يَوْمًا ثَقِيْلًا (دهر ع ٢)

53. Remember the name of thy Lord at morning and evening; and worship Him (a portion) of the night, and glorify Him through long night in Tahajjud salaat. Lo! these people who oppose you, love the fleeting life, and put behind them (the remembrance of) a grievous day.

(٥٤) قَدْ اَفْلَحَ مَنْ تَزَكّٰى وَذَكَرَ اسْمَ رَبِّهٖ فَصَلّٰى (سورة أعلى ع ١)

54. He is successful who purifieth himself (of evil manners) and remembereth the name of his Lord, so prayeth.

Chapter 1
SECTION 2
AHAADITH ON ZIKR
(REMEMBRANCE OF ALLAH)

When the importance of zikr has been emphasised in so many verses of the Holy Qur'an, the number of ahaadith on this subject is naturally far too great; it is in proportion to the many voluminous books of ahaadith. The Holy Qur'an is one book of only 30 parts, but the books of ahaadith are many and each book contains a large number of ahaadith. For example, Bukhari Shareef alone consists of 30 voluminous parts, and similarly Abu Dawood Shareef has 32 parts. There is no book of ahaadith which does not contain several ahaadith on the subject of zikr, and it is, therefore impossible to quote all such ahaadith in this small booklet. Of course, a single verse of the Holy Qur'an or a hadith moves the faithful to good actions, but volumes of books would not move an unwilling person, who is like an ass carrying a load of books.

Hadith No 1

(١) عَنْ اَبِيْ هُرَيْرَةَ رَضِىَ للهُ تَعَالٰى عَنْهُ قَالَ قَالَ رَسُوْلُ اللهِ ﷺ يَقُوْلُ اللهُ تَعَالٰى اَنَا عِنْدَ ظَنِّ عَبْدِيْ بِيْ وَاَنَا مَعَهُ اِذَا ذَكَرَنِيْ فَاِنْ ذَكَرَنِيْ فِيْ نَفْسِهِ ذَكَرْتُهُ فِيْ نَفْسِيْ وَاِنْ ذَكَرَنِيْ فِيْ مَلَاءٍ ذَكَرْتُهُ فِيْ مَلَاءٍ خَيْرٍ مِنْهُمْ وَاِنْ تَقَرَّبَ اِلَىَّ شِبْرًا تَقَرَّبْتُ اِلَيْهِ ذِرَاعًا وَاِنْ تَقَرَّبَ اِلَيَّ ذِرَاعًا تَقَرَّبْتُ اِلَيْهِ بَاعًا وَاِنْ اَتَانِيْ يَمْشِيْ اَتَيْتُهُ هَرْوَلَةً

رواه أحمد والبخاري ومسلم والترمذي والنسائى وابن ماجه والبيهقى في الشعب وأخرج أحمد والبيهقى في الأسماء والصفات عن أنس بمعناه بلفظ ابن آدم إذا ذكرتنى في نفسك الحديث وفي الباب عن معاذ بن أنس عند الطبراني بإسناد حسن وعن ابن عباس عند البزار بإسناد صحيح والبيهقي وغيرهما وعن أبي هريرة عن ابن ماجة وابن حبان وغيرهما بلفظ : أنا مع عبدي إذا ذكرني وتحركت بي شفتاه كما في الدر المنثور والترغيب للمنذري والمشكواة مختصرا وفيه برواية مسلم عن أبى ذر بمعناه وفي الاتحاف علقه البخاري عن أبي هريرة بصيغة الجزم ورواه ابن حبان من حديث أبي الدرداء

Hadhrat Abu Hurairah (Radhiyallaho anho) narrated that Rasulullah (Sallallaho alaihe wasallam) has said, "Almighty Allah says, 'I treat my slave (man) according to his expectations from Me, and I am with him when he remembers Me. If he remembers Me in his heart, I remember him in My heart; if he remembers Me in a gathering, I remember him in a better and nobler gathering (i.e. of angels). If he comes closer to Me by one span, I go towards him a cubit's length, if he comes towards Me by a cubit's length, I go towards him an arm's length, and if he walks towards Me, I run unto him."

Note: There are several points elaborated in this hadith. The first point is that Allah deals with a man according to his expectations from Him. One should therefore always be hopeful of the mercy and benevolence of Almighty Allah and never be despondent of His blessings. Certainly, we are extremely sinful and justly deserve punishment on account of our evil deeds, yet in no case should we feel despondent of the mercy of Allah, as He may perhaps totally forgive us.

إِنَّ اللّٰهَ لَايَغْفِرُ اَنْ يُّشْرَكَ بِهٖ وَيَغْفِرُ مَادُوْنَ ذٰلِكَ لِمَنْ يَّشَاءُ

"Lo! Allah forgiveth not if a partner be ascribed unto Him and forgiveth all save that to whom He will."

But Almighty Allah may or may not forgive; that is why the Ulama say that true belief lies in between hope (of forgiveness of Allah) and fear (of His wrath). The Holy Prophet (Sallallaho alaihe wasallam) once visited a young Sahabi, who was breathing his last, and asked him how he was feeling. He replied, "O! Messenger of Allah, I am hopeful of the mercy of Allah, and yet I am afraid of my sins." Thereupon the Holy Prophet (Sallallaho alaihe wasallam) said "When the heart of a believer is filled with these two feelings of hope and fear, Almighty Allah fulfils his hope and saves him from what he is afraid of."

It is mentioned in one hadith that a believer thinks of his sin, as if he is sitting under a huge rock that is threatening to fall on him, while for a transgressor his sin is no more than a fly which is easily scared off, i.e., he takes his sins very lightly. In short, one should be appropriately afraid of ones sins, and at the same time remain hopeful of Allah's mercy.

Hadhrat Mu'aaz (Radhiyallaho anho) died of the plague and, in the moments of death's agony, he fainted many times. Whenever he regained consciousness for a moment, he would say, "Oh Allah! Thou knowest that I love Thee. By Thy Honour and Glory, Thou knowest this very well." Just before breathing his last, he said, "O Death, you are a welcome guest but have come at a time when there is nothing in the house to eat." Then he said, "O Allah! Thou knowest very well that I always feared Thee, and today I die hopeful of Thy forgiveness. O Allah! I enjoyed life, not in digging canals and planting gardens, but in remaining thirsty in the hot weather, in undergoing hardships for the sake of Islaam, and in taking part in the gatherings engaged in zikr under the supervision of the Ulama."

Some Ulama have written that the fulfilment of expectations promised by Almighty Allah in the aforesaid hadith is in its most general sense. It carries assurance not only in respect of forgiveness but also in respect of prayers, health, wealth and safety. For instance when a person prays to Allah and sincerely believes that Allah shall accept his prayer, then his prayer is actually accepted, but if he has doubt (that his prayer would not be accepted), it is not accepted. Thus, in another hadith it is stated that the prayer of a person is granted so long as he does not say that his prayer is not granted. The same is true in the case of all blessings relating to health, prosperity, etc. According to one hadith, if a destitute person discloses his hunger to everybody, he is not relieved of his poverty, but if he shows submission to Gracious Allah, his condition may soon change for the better. However, hoping for the better from Almighty Allah is one thing, and being over-confident of His help and forgiveness is another thing. Almighty Allah has warned us against such an attitude in several verses of the Holy Qur'an e.g.

وَلَا يَغُرَّنَّكُمْ بِاللّٰهِ الْغَرُوْرُ

"Let not the deceiver (the Satan) beguile you in regard to Allah" i.e. one should not be misled by the devil to commit sins just because Allah is the most Merciful and the Forgiver".

There is another verse,

اَطَّلَعَ الْغَيْبَ اَمِ اتَّخَذَ عِنْدَ الرَّحْمٰنِ عَهْدًا كَلَّا

"Hath he knowledge of the Unseen, or hath he made a pact with the Beneficent. No, never."

The second point in this hadith is "Whenever a slave of mine remembers Me, I am with him." In another hadith, it is stated, "So long as one's lips move in My remembrance I remain with him" i.e. Almighty Allah bestows His special care and mercy on him during all this time.

The third point is that Almighty Allah mentions him with a favour to the angels, which signifies the value of zikr. Firstly, this is because Allah created man such that inherently he is liable to be good as well as to go astray, as given below in Hadith No. 8. Submission on his part therefore deserves special appreciation. Secondly, at the time of Aadam's creation, the Angels (who have no instinct for doing evil) could not understand the creation of man and had contended that he would cause blood-shed and trouble in the world, while they are always there to praise and glorify Almighty Allah. Thirdly, man's worship of Allah and submission to His will is more commendable than that of the Angels, because he does so on account of his faith in the unseen which, however, is actually seen by the angels. It is to this fact that Allah refers in the Holy Book: "How would man not have worshipped if he had actually seen the Paradise and the Hell." It is for this reason that Almighty Allah praises the noble deeds of those who worship and glorify Him without seeing Him.

The fourth point contained in the above-mentioned hadith is that if a man increases his devotion to Almighty Allah, the increase in His mercy and kindness upon him is proportionately far greater. "Getting near" and "running" signify immediate increase in His blessings and mercy. Thus, it is upto a person that, if he wants to enjoy more kindness and favours from Almighty Allah, he should increase his devotion to Him.

The fifth point in the above mentioned hadith is that the Angels have been stated to be superior to man, while it is commonly known that man is the best creation of Allah. One reason for this has already been explained in the translation (of the hadith), that the angels are superior because they are innocent and are unable to commit sins. Secondly, they are superior because they are better than the majority of men, including even the majority of believers; and yet some selected Believers like the Prophets (Alaihimus salaam) are superior to the angels. There are other reasons as well, which are however left out in order to prevent the discourse from getting too long.

Hadith No. 2

(٢) عَنْ عَبْدِ اللهِ بْنِ بُسْرٍ رَضِىَ للهُ تَعَالٰى عَنْهُ اَنَّ رَجُلًا قَالَ يَارَسُوْلَ اللهِ اِنَّ شَرَائِعَ الْاِسْلَامِ قَدْ كَثُرَتْ عَلَيَّ فَاَخْبِرْنِى بِشَيْءٍ اَسْتَنُّ بِهِ قَالَ لَايَزَالُ لِسَانُكَ رَطْبًا مِنْ ذِكْرِ اللهِ

أخرجه ابن شيبة وأحمد والترمذي وحسنه وابن ماجه وابن حبان في صحيحه والحاكم وصححه والبيهقي كذا في الدر وفي المشكواة برواية الترمذي وابن ماجة وحكى عن الترمذي حسن غريب اهـ

قلت وصححه الحاكم وأقره عليه الذهبي وفي الجامع الصغير برواية أبي نعيم في الحلية مختصرا بلفظ : اَنْ تُفَارِقَ الدُّنْيَا وَلِسَانُكَ رَطْبٌ مِنْ ذِكْرِ اللهِ وَرَقَمَ لَهُ بِالضُّعْف وبمعناه عن مالك بن يخامر اَنَّ مُعَاذ بن جَبَلَ قال لَهُمْ اِنَّ آخِرُ كَلَامٍ فَارَقْتُ عَلَيْهِ رَسُوْلَ اللهِ ﷺ اَنْ قُلْتُ اَيُّ الأعمالِ اَحَبُّ إِلَى اللهِ؟ قال : أن تَمُوتَ وَلِسَانُكَ رَطْبٌ مِنْ ذِكْرِ اللهِ ، أخرجه ابن أبي الدنيا والبزار وابن حبان والطبراني والبيهقي كذا في الدر والحصن والحصين والترغيب للمنذري وذكره في الجامع الصغير مختصرا وعزاه إلى ابن حبان في صحيحه وابن السنى في عمل اليوم والليلة والطبراني في الكبير والبيهقي في الشعب وفي مجمع الزوائد رواه الطبراني بأسانيد

A Sahabi once said, "O, Rasulullah, (Sallallaho alaihe wasallam), I know that the commandments of Shareeat are many, but of these tell me the one that I may practise assiduously throughout my life." The Prophet, (Sallallaho alaihe wasallam), replied, "Keep your tongue always moist (i.e. busy) with the zikr of Allah." According to another hadith, Harat Mu'aaz (Radhiyallaho anho) has said, "Once at the time of my departure from Rasulullah (Sallallaho alaihe wasallam), I asked him to advise me of that action which is most pleasing to Almighty Allah: whereupon he replied, "At the time of your death, your tongue should be busy with zikr of Almighty Allah."

Note: By "my departure", Hadhrat Mu'aaz (Radhiyallaho anho) refers to the occasion when he was appointed by the Holy Prophet (Sallallaho alaihe wasallam) as the Governor of Yemen and sent there for teaching and propagating Islaam. It was at the time of that farewell that Rasulullah (Sallallaho alaihe wasallam) had given him some parting instructions.

By saying that "the commandments of Sharee-at are many", the Sahabi had meant that although observance of every commandment is imperative, to specialize and attain perfection in each and every one is difficult; and so he wanted that Rasulullah (Sallallaho alaihe wasallam), may recommend him something of over-riding importance which he might hold fast to, and practise at all times and in all conditions of sitting, standing or walking.

According to another hadith, a person who possesses the following four things is truly blessed, from the worldly as well as spiritual point of view:—

(i) A tongue ever absorbed in the zikr of Almighty Allah.

(ii) A heart filled with gratitude of Allah.

(iii) A body capable of undergoing hardships.

(iv) A wife who does not betray her husband's trust in respect of her chastity and his wealth.

The phrase "moist tongue" according to some Ulama means excessive utterance (of zikr) and, idiomatically, it is used to convey excessive glorification and praise. But in my (the author's) humble opinion it can have another meaning as well. It is always very sweet and pleasant to talk of one's beloved, as is the common feeling and experience of every lover. On this basis, the phrase "moist tongue" would, therefore mean that one should glorify with love the name of Almighty Allah, so as to feel love's sweetness in the mouth. I have observed many times that when some of my religious elders do zikr aloud, the flavour of the sweetness enjoyed by them is so transmitted to the listeners that their mouths also feel the sweetness and they share the ecstasy likewise. But this phenomenon is possible only where there is a genuine yearning for zikr, and the tongue is accustomed to excessive zikr. It is stated in one hadith that the proof of one's love for Almighty Allah lies in one's love for the zikr of Allah, and in the same way lack of zikr betrays lack of attachment with Almighty Allah.

Hadhrat Abu Darda (Radhiyallaho anho) said that those who keep their tongues wet with the zikr of Allah, will enter paradise smiling.

Hadith No. 3

(٣) عَنْ اَبِيْ الدَّرْدَاءِ رَضِىَ اللّٰهُ تَعَالٰى عَنْهُ قَالَ قَالَ رَسُوْلُ اللّٰهِ ﷺ اَلَا اُنَبِّئُكُمْ بِخَيْرِ اَعْمَالِكُمْ وَاَزْكَاهَا عِنْدَ مَلِيْكِكُمْ وَاَرْفَعِهَا فِيْ دَرَجَاتِكُمْ وَخَيْرٍ لَّكُمْ مِنْ اِنْفَاقِ الذَّهَبِ وَالْوَرَقِ وَخَيْرٍ لَّكُمْ مِنْ اَنْ تَلْقَوْا عَدُوَّكُمْ فَتَضْرِبُوْا اَعْنَاقَهُمْ وَيَضْرِبُوْا اَعْنَاقَكُمْ قَالُوْا بَلٰى قَالَ ذِكْرُ اللّٰهِ

أخرجه أحمد والترمذي وابن ماجه وابن أبي الدنيا والحاكم وصححه والبيهقي كذا في الدر والحصن والحصين قلت : قال الحاكم صحيح الاسناد ولم يخرجاه وأقره عليه الذهبى ورقم له في الجامع الصغير بالصحة وأخرجه أحمد عن معاذ بن جبل كذا في الدر وفيه أيضاً برواية أحمد والترمذي والبيهقي عن أبي سعيد سئل رسول الله ﷺ أيُّ العِبَادِ اَفْضَلُ دَرَجَةً عِنْدَ اللّٰهِ يَوْمَ الْقِيَامَةِ؟ قَالَ الذَّاكِرُوْنَ اللّٰهَ كَثِيْرًا ، قُلْتُ يَارَسُوْلَ اللّٰهِ وَمِنِ الْغَازِيْ؟ قَالَ : لَوْ ضَرَبَ بِسَيْفِهِ فِيْ الكُفَّارِ وَالْمُشْرِكِيْنَ حَتّٰى يَنْكَسِرَ وَيَخْتَضِبَ دَمًا لَكَانَ الذَّاكِرُوْنَ اللّٰهَ اَفْضَلَ مِنْهُ دَرَجَةً

Rasulullah (Sallallaho alaihe wasallam) once said to his companions, "Shall I tell you of something that is the best of all deeds, constitutes the best act of piety in the eyes of your Lord, will elevate your status in the Hereafter, and carries more virtue than the spending of gold and silver in the service of Allah or taking part in jihaad and slaying or being slain in the path of Allah." The Companions begged to be informed of such an act. The Prophet (Sallallaho alaihe wasallam) replied, "It is the zikr of Almighty Allah."

Note: This hadith is a generalized statement; otherwise, at times of specific need and emergency sadaqah (charity) and jihaad (fighting in the path of Allah), etc., become more desirable, as stated in some other ahaadith. These acts become more important during the hour of need, but the zikr is for all times and therefore generally more important and virtuous.

According to another hadith, Rasulullah (Sallallaho alaihe wasallam) is reported to have said, "for everything there is a purifier or cleanser. (For instance, soap is used for cleaning the body and the clothes, while a furnace is used for purifying iron). The zikr of Almighty Allah cleanses and purifies the heart, and provides the best protection against retribution in the Hereafter." This hadith describes zikr as the purifier of the heart, and as such it also established superiority of zikr over all other actions, because the value of every act of worship depends upon ikhlaas (sincerity of the intention), which in turn depends on the purity of heart. Therefore, according to some Sufis, the zikr in this hadith implies the zikr of the heart as against the zikr by the tongue. By the zikr of the heart, they mean that the heart remains always conscious of, and in communication with Almighty Allah. This state of the heart is doubtless superior to all kinds of worship, because when this state is attained, then omission of any kind of worship is just not possible. All parts of the human body, internal and external, are controlled by the heart and submit completely to the Being to Whom the heart is attached. The conduct of true lovers bears ample testimony to this fact.

There are many more ahaadith that describe the superiority of zikr over all other actions. Somebody enquired of Hazrat Salmaan (Radhiyallaho anho) as to what action of man is most virtuous. He replied, "Have you not read in the Holy Qur'an,

وَلَذِكْرُ اللهِ اَكْبَرُ

(certainly the zikr of Allah is most exalted)?"

Hadhrat Salmaan (Radhiyallaho anho) had referred here to the first ayat of Part 21 of the Holy Qur'an. The author of "Majaalisul Abraar", while commenting on this Hadith, has written that zikr of Allah is described to be superior to sadaqah, jihaad, and all forms of worship, because it is an end in itself, and all types of worship constitute only a means to achieve this end. zikr is of two kinds: one is done by word of mouth and the other is in the form of deep meditation and contemplation. It is the latter form of zikr that is implied in the hadith which states that meditation for one moment is better than doing worship for seventy years Hadhrat Suhail (Radhiyallaho anho) reported that Rasulullah (Sallallaho alaihe wasallam) has said, "The reward of the zikr of Allah is seven hundred thousand times more than that for spending wealth in the path of Allah."

Thus, in conclusion, it is evident that jihaad and sadaqah, etc., assume more importance and become more virtuous due to the need of the hour. The ahaadith which describe their superiority are therefore understandable. For instance, it is stated in one hadith that standing up for a short while in the path of Allah is more valuable than offering salaat at home for seventy years. Although salaat is unanimously admitted to be the best form of worship, yet taking part in jihaad at the time of an invasion by the infidels carries far greater reward.

Hadith No. 4

(٤) عَنْ اَبِيْ سَعِيْدِ الْخُدْرِيِّ رَضِىَ للهُ تَعَالٰى عَنْهُ اَنَّ رَسُوْلَ اللهِ ﷺ قَالَ لَيَذْكُرَنَّ اللهَ اَقْوَامٌ فِيْ الدُّنْيَا عَلَى الْفُرُشِ الْمُمَهَّدَةِ يُدْخِلُهُمُ اللهُ فِيْ الدَّرَجَاتِ الْعُلٰى أخرجه ابن حبان كذا في الدر قلت : ويؤيده الحديث المتقدم قريبا بلفظ ارفعها في درجاتكم وأيضا قوله صلى الله عليه وسلم سَبَقَ الْمُفَرِّدُوْنَ قَالُوْا وَمَا الْمُفَرِّدُوْنَ يَا رَسُوْلَ اللهِ قَالَ الذَّاكِرُوْنَ اللهَ كَثِيْرًا وَالذَّاكِرَاتُ رواه مسلم كذا في الحصن وفي رواية قال الْمُسْتَهْتِرُوْنَ فِيْ ذِكْرِ اللهِ يَضَعُ الذِّكْرُ عَنْهُمْ اَثْقَالَهُمْ فَيَأْتُوْنَ يَوْمَ الْقِيَامَةِ خِفَافاً رواه الترمذي والحاكم مختصرا وقال صحيح على شرط الشيخين وفي الجامع رواه الطبراني عن أبي الدرداء أيضا

Rasulullah (Sallallaho alaihe wasallam), said, "There are many a people who do zikr of Almighty Allah, while lying comfortably in their soft beds, and for this, they will be rewarded with the highest positions in Paradise by Almighty Lord."

Note: Generally, the greater the sufferings and hardships one undergoes in the cause of religion, the higher will be his status in the Hereafter. But the zikr of Allah is such a blessed act that, even if it is done in soft beds in this world, it will bring high rewards and elevated positions in the Hereafter. Rasulullah (Sallallaho alaihe wasallam) had said, "If you keep yourselves busy in zikr all the time, the angels will shake hands with you in your beds as well as on your way."

Once Rasulullah (Sallallaho alaihe wasallam) said, "The mufarrideen have gone far ahead." "Who are the mufarrideen?" enquired the Sahabah. Rasulullah (Sallallaho alaihe wasallam) replied, "Those who are intensely devoted to the zikr of Allah." On the basis of this hadith, the Sufis have stated that the kings and rulers should not be prevented from zikr of Allah, for they, by this means, can attain a lofty rank in the Hereafter.

Hadhrat Abu Darda (Radhiyallaho anho) says, "Glorify Almighty Allah during the time of prosperity and happiness, and it will help you in times of distress and trouble." Hadhrat Salmaan Faarsi (Radhiyallaho anho) said, "If a person remembers Allah in times of peace, pleasure and prosperity, then whenever he is in trouble and difficulty, the angels, being familiar with his voice, recognise him in his helplessness and intercede before Almighty Allah (for his forgiveness); but, if one who does not remember Allah in his time of pleasure and happens to pray for help at the time of difficulty, the angels find his voice to be quite unfamiliar and therefore do not intercede for him."

Hadhrat Ibn Abbas, (Radhiyallaho anho) said, "Paradise has eight gates, one of which is exclusively reserved for those who are engaged in zikr." It is said in one hadith, "A person who constantly does zikr of Allah is immune from hypocrisy in faith", and according to another hadith, "He is loved by Almighty Allah."

Once during his return journey to Madina Rasulullah (Sallallaho alaihe wasallam) said, "Where are those who have gone ahead." The Companions said, "The fast travellers have gone ahead"; then Rasulullah (Sallallaho alaihe wasallam) said, "Those who remain ahead are the persons who remain constantly absorbed in zikr. Whoever desires to enjoy himself in Paradise, should do zikr of Allah excessively."

Hadith No 5

(٥) عَنْ اَبِيْ مُوْسَى قَالَ قَالَ النَّبِيُّ ﷺ مَثَلُ الَّذِيْ يَذْكُرُ رَبَّهُ وَالَّذِيْ لَايَذْكُرُ رَبَّهُ مَثَلُ الْحَيِّ وَالْمَيِّتِ اخرجه البخاري ومسلم والبيهقي كذا في الدر والمشكوٰة

Rasulullah (Sallallaho alaihe wasallam) said, "The contrast between a person who glorifies Almighty Allah and one who does not remember Him is like that between the living and the dead."

Note:

Life is dear to all, and every one fears death. The Prophet (Sallallaho alaihe wasallam) meant to say that one who does not remember Allah, though bodily alive, is spiritually dead and his life is but worthless. A Persian couplet quoted here by the author means,
"(The lover says) My life (of loneliness) is no life; his is the life who lives in contact with the beloved."
Some scholars have stated that the example refers to the condition of the heart: the heart that remembers Allah is really alive, while the one that does not, is described as

dead. Some scholars say that the contrast is in respect of gain and loss. A man who harasses a zaakir is like one harassing a living being, and he will be avenged for this harassment and will suffer for it. One who ill-treats the neglectful, ill-treats a dead body, which cannot avenge itself. Some Sufis say that the hadith refers to the eternal life of the zaakireen, because those who glorify Allah constantly with sincerity never really die, but instead remain spiritually alive even after passing away from this world. The zaakireen also enjoy a special life after death, like the martyrs, mentioned in a verse of the Holy Qur'an:

بَلْ اَحْيَاءٌ عِنْدَ رَبِّهِمْ

Nay, they are alive in the eyes of their Sustainer.

Hakiem Tirmizi writes, "Zikr moistens the heart and softens it. A heart that is devoid of zikr becomes dry and hard, due to the excessive heat of lust and base desires. All parts of the body likewise become stiff and abstain from submission to Allah; if you try to bend them, they break like a dry piece of wood, which can be used as firewood only.

Hadith No. 6

(٦) عَنْ اَبِيْ مُوْسٰى قَالَ قَالَ رَسُوْلُ اللهِ ﷺ اَنَّ رَجُلًا فِيْ حِجْرِهٖ دَرَاهِمُ يَقْسِمُهَا وَاٰخَرُ يَذْكُرُ اللهَ لَكَانَ الذَّاكِرُ لِلّٰهِ اَفْضَلَ أخرجه الطبراني كذا في الدر وفي مجمع الزوائد رواه الطبراني في الأوسط ورجال وثقو

Rasulullah (Sallallaho alaihe wasallam) is reported to have said, "If a person has a lot of wealth and distributes it amongst the needy, while another person is only busy with the zikr of Allah, the latter, who is engaged in zikr, is the better of the two."

Note:

Spending in the path of Allah is a splendid virtue, but zikr of Allah is more virtuous. How lucky are those well-to-do persons who, in addition to spending for the pleasure of Allah, remain also devoted to His zikr.

According to one hadith, Almighty Allah also gives sadaqah every day, i.e. He showers His favours on the people, and everybody gets what he deserves, but the luckiest is the person who is favoured with the ability to do His zikr. People who are engaged in different occupations, such as trade, farming and service, should spare some time for zikr every day and thereby earn great rewards. It should not be difficult to devote an hour or two out of 24 hours, exclusively for this noble purpose.

A lot of our time is wasted in frivolous pursuits, and some of this can be easily spared for this most useful work.

In another hadith, the Prophet (Sallallaho alaihe wasallam) is reported to have said, "The wisest of all people are those who keep track of time, with the help of the sun, the moon, the stars, and the shadows, for doing zikr regularly." Nowadays we can determine time with the help of watches, yet one should be able to judge time with the help of these natural agents, so that no time gets wasted in case the watch stops or goes out of order. In another hadith, it is stated that the place where zikr is done, takes pride over other parts of the earth.

Hadith No. 7

(٧) عَنْ مُعَاذِ بْنِ جَبَلٍ رَضِىَ اللهُ عَنْهُ قَالَ قَالَ رَسُوْلُ اللهِ ﷺ لَيْسَ يَتَحَسَّرُ اَهْلُ الْجَنَّةِ اِلَّا عَلٰى سَاعَةٍ مَرَّتْ بِهِمْ لَمْ يَذْكُرُوا اللهَ تَعَالٰى فِيْهَا اخرجه الطبراني والبيهقي كذا في الدر وفي الجامع رواه الطبراني ورجاله في الكبير والبيهقي في الشعب في ورقم له بالحسن وفي مجمع الزوائد رواه الطبراني ورجاله ثقات وفي شيخ الطبراني خلاف وأخرج ابن أبي الدنيا والبيهقي عن عائشة رضى الله عنها بمعناه مرفوعًا كذا في الدر وفي الترغيب بمعناه عن أبي هريرة مرفوعًا وقال رواه أحمد بإسناد صحيح وابن حبان والحاكم وقال صحيح على شرط البخاري

The Holy Prophet (Sallallaho alaihe wasallam) said, "Those who are admitted into Paradise will not regret over anything of this world, except the time spent without zikr in their life."

Note:

After their entry into Paradise, when they will see the huge reward (as large as mountains) for remembering Allah once, they will feel extremely sorry over their loss caused by the time spent without zikr, as can be well imagined. In this world, there are such blessed persons who would not relish this life it is were spent without the zikr of Allah. Hafiz Ibn Hajar (Rahmatullah alaih) writes in his book "Munabbihaat" that Yahya bin Mu'aaz Raazi (Rahmatullah alaih) used to say in his supplication:

اِلٰهِيْ لَايَطِيْبُ اللَّيْلُ اِلَّا بِمُنَاجَاتِكَ وَلَايَطِيْبُ النَّهَارُ اِلَّا بِطَاعَتِكَ وَلَاتَطِيْبُ الدُّنْيَا اِلَّا بِذِكْرِكَ وَلَا تَطِيْبُ الْاٰخِرَةُ اِلَّا بِعَفْوِكَ وَلَا تَطِيْبُ الْجَنَّةُ اِلَّا بِرُؤيَتِكَ

O Allah! the night is no good unless spent in communion with You, the day is no good unless spent in worshipping You, this life is no good without Your zikr, the next life will be no good without forgiveness from You, and Paradise will not be enjoyable without beholding You.

Hadhrat Sirri (Rahmatullah alaih) says, "I saw Jurjani swallowing roasted barley flour. He told me that he had compared the time taken in chewing bread and in eating barley flour: eating bread took so much longer that he could say سُبْحَانَ اللهِ seventy times in that time. Therefore, he had not taken bread for forty years, and had lived by swallowing barley flour alone."

It is said about Mansoor bin Mu'tamar that he never spoke to anybody after Ishaa prayers for forty years. Similarly, it is said about Rabee' bin Hatheem that it was his practice for twenty years that he noted down what he talked during the day, and would check at night whether that talking was necessary or not. Those pious scholars were particular that every moment of their life was spent in zikr and in nothing else.

Hadith No 8

(٨) عَنْ اَبِيْ هُرَيْرَةَ وَاَبِيْ سَعِيْدٍ رَضِىَ اللهُ عَنْهُمَا اَنَّهُمَا شَهِدَا عَلٰى رَسُوْلِ اللهِ ﷺ اَنَّهُ قَالَ لَايَقْعُدُ قَوْمٌ يَذْكُرُوْنَ اللهَ اِلَّا حَفَّتْهُمُ الْمَلَائِكَةُ وَغَشِيَتْهُمُ الرَّحْمَةُ وَنَزَلَتْ عَلَيْهِمُ السَّكِيْنَةُ وَذَكَرَهُمُ اللهُ فِيْمَنْ عِنْدَهُ أخرجه ابن أبي شيبة وأحمد ومسلم والترمذي وابن ماجه والبيهقي كذا في الدر والحصن والمشكواة وفي حديث طويل لأبي ذر اُوْصِيْكَ بِتَقْوَى اللهِ فَاِنَّهُ رَاْسُ الْاَمْرِ كُلِّهِ وَعَلَيْكَ بِتِلَاوَةِ الْقُرْآنِ وَذِكْرِ اللهِ فَاِنَّهُ ذِكْرٌ لَّكَ فِي السَّمَآءِ وَنُوْرٌ لَكَ فِي الْاَرْضِ الحديث ذكره في الجامع الصغير برواية الطبراني وعبد بن حميد في تفسيره ورقم له بالحسن

Hadhrat Abu Hurairah (Radhiyallaho anho) and Hadhrat Abu Sa'eed (Radhiyallaho anho) both bore testimony to having heard from Rasulullah (Sallallaho alaihe wasallam), that the gathering engaged in zikr of Almighty Allah is surrounded by the angels on all sides, the grace of Allah and sakeenah (peace and tranquility) descend upon them, and Almighty Allah speaks about them, by way of appreciation, to His angels."

Hadhrat Abu Zar (Radhiyallaho anho) related that Rasulullah (Sallallaho alaihe wasallam) had said to him, "I advise you to fear Allah, as this is the root of all virtues; remain engaged in the recitation of Holy Qur'an and in zikr of Almighty Allah, which will earn you an appreciation in the Heavens and serve you as a light in this world; keep silent for most of the time, so that you speak nothing but good, as this will keep the Devil away from you and make it easy for you to perform your religious duties, abstain also from too much laughing, for laughing weakens the heart and deprives the face of its spiritual glow (luminosity), always take part in jihaad as this is the sign of piety for my ummah; like the poor and keep their company; compare your lot with persons lower than you, and never look upto those higher than you, otherwise you will forget the bounties of Almighty Allah and become ungrateful to Him; try to retain ties with your relatives though they may try to break them; do not hesitate to speak out the truth, though it may be bitter for others; always obey Almighty Allah in spite of adverse criticism, find fault with your own self, and never with others; do not criticise others for the shortcomings that you suffer from. O! Abu Zar (Radhiyallaho anho) there is no wisdom better than farsightedness, abstinence from the unlawful is the best act of piety, and good manners constitute true nobility."

Note:

The word 'sakeenah' according to various scholars means tranquility and peace, as well as Allah's special mercy, as explained in detail in my book Fazaa'il-i-Qur'an. For instance, Imam Nawawi (Rahmatullah alaih) states that sakeenah is a special favour consisting of tranquility, mercy, etc. and is brought down from the Heavens by the angels.

This appreciation, in the presence of the angels, by Almighty Allah for those engaged in zikr is for two reasons.

Firstly, it is because the angels (as mentioned under the first hadith) had submitted, at the time of the creation of Hadhrat Aadam (Alayhis salaam), that man would commit mischief in the world. Secondly, it is because the Angels are ever engaged in prayers, submission, and obedience to Almighty Allah, and are devoid of the very instinct for sin, whereas man has the instinct of obedience as well as of sin and (in addition) he is surrounded by things that lead him to negligence and disobedience, and has desires and lust ingrained in him. Therefore, prayers, submission and abstinence from sin, despite all his handicaps, are more praiseworthy and creditable on his part.

In one hadith, it is stated that, when Allah created Paradise, he told the angel Jibra-eel (Alayhis salaam) to go and visit it. On his return from Paradise, he reported, "O Lord! by Your Greatness, whoever comes to know of it, will do his best to enter it", that is to say, its pleasures, comforts, enjoyments and blessings are so intense that there will be no body who, after knowing and believing these, will not strive his utmost for admission into it. Almighty Allah then surrounded Paradise with hardships and made it compulsory to offer prayers, observe fasting, take part in jihaad, go for Haj, etc., for admission into it. Almighty Allah then sent Jibra-eel (Alayhis salaam) to visit it again. He saw these and then said, "O Allah! I fear that hardly anybody will be able to enter it." Similarly, after creating Hell, Almighty Allah ordered Jibra-eel (Alayhis salaam) to visit it. After witnessing the punishments, horrors, afflictions and tortures of Hell, he submitted, "I swear by Thy Grandeur that one who comes to know of the conditions in Hell will never dare go near it." Then Allah surrounded Hell with acts of indulgence, such as adultery, drinking wine, cruelty, disregard of the Divine commandments, etc., and then asked Jibra-eel (Alayhis salaam) to visit it again. He saw it and submitted, "My Lord! I fear that hardly anybody will be able to escape it." It is for this reason that, when a person obeys Almighty Allah and abstains from sins, he becomes praiseworthy with respect to his environments, and therefore Almighty Allah expresses His pleasure about him. The angels mentioned in this hadith and in so many other similar ahaadith belong to a special group who are duty-bound to visit the places and attend the meetings where people are engaged in zikr. This is supported by another hadith wherein it is stated that there is a class of angels who are scattered all over, and when and wherever any one of them hears zikr being recited he calls all his companions to come to that place, and partake of what they wanted. They throng to the place and they fill it up to the sky, as mentioned in Chapter II under item 14.

Hadith No. 9

(٩) عَنْ مُعَاوِيَةَ رَضِىَ اللّٰهُ عَنْهُ اَنَّ رَسُوْلَ اللّٰهِ ﷺ خَرَجَ عَلٰى حَلْقَةٍ مِنْ اَصْحَابِهٖ فَقَالَ مَااَجْلَسَكُمْ قَالُوْا جَلَسْنَا نَذْكُرُ اللّٰهَ وَنَحْمَدُهٗ عَلٰى مَاهَدَانَا لِلْاِسْلَامِ وَمَنَّ بِهٖ عَلَيْنَا قَالَ آللّٰهِ مَا اَجْلَسَكُمْ اِلَّا ذٰلِكَ قَالُوْا آللّٰهِ مَااَجْلَسَنَا اِلَّا ذٰلِكَ قَالَ اَمَا اِنِّيْ لَمْ اَسْتَحْلِفْكُمْ تُهْمَةً لَّكُمْ وَلٰكِنْ اَتَانِيْ جِبْرَئِيْلُ فَاَخْبَرَنِيْ اَنَّ اللّٰهَ يُبَاهِىْ بِكُمُ الْمَلَائِكَةَ أخرجه ابن أبي شيبة وأحمد ومسلم والترمذي والنسائى كذا في الدر والمشكوٰة

Once Rasulullah (Sallallaho alaihe wasallam) went to a group of Sahaba, (Radhiyallaho anhum) and said to them, "What for are you sitting here?" They replied, "We are engaged in the zikr of Almighty Allah, and are glorifying Him for His extreme kindness to us in that He has blessed us with the wealth of Islaam." Rasulullah (Sallallaho alaihe wasallam) said, "By Allah, Are you here only for this reason?" "By Allah!", replied the Sahaba, (Radhiyallaho anhum), "We are sitting here only for this reason." Rasulullah (Sallallaho alaihe wasallam) then said, "I asked you to swear not out of any misunderstanding, but because Jibra-eel (Alayhis salaam) came to me and informed me just now that Almighty Allah was speaking high about you before angels."

Note: Enquiry on oath by the Prophet (Sallallaho alaihe wasallam) was simply to ascertain whether there was any other special thing, besides zikr, which might be the cause of Allah's pride. It became definite that it was only because of the zikr of Almighty Allah that He was proud of them. How lucky were those people whose worship was accepted, and the news of Allah's recognition of the zikr on their part was revealed to them in this very earthly life through Rasulullah (Sallallaho alaihe wasallam). Certainly, their sublime deeds deserved all this appreciation. Their heroic deeds are briefly described in my book named Hikaayaat-e- Sahabah, (i.e. The Stories of Sahabah). Mulla

Ali Qari (Rahmatullah alaih) interprets the pride on the part of Almighty Allah to mean that He wants the angels to realize, "Despite the fact these humans are full of temptations, the Devil is after them, desires are inside them, the worldly needs chase them, and yet they are engaged in glorifying Almighty Allah, and so many deterrents cannot prevent them from doing zikr; and therefore your zikr and glorification, in the absence of any such handicaps is comparatively insignificant."

Hadith No 10

(١٠) عَنْ اَنَسٍ رَضِىَ اللّٰهُ عَنْهُ عَنْ رَسُوْلِ اللّٰهِ ﷺ قَالَ مَامِنْ قَوْمٍ اِجْتَمَعُوْا
يَذْكُرُوْنَ اللّٰهَ لَايُرِيْدُوْنَ بِذٰلِكَ اِلَّا وَجْهَهُ اِلَّا نَادَاهُمْ مُنَادٍ مِّنَ السَّمَآءِ اَنْ قُوْمُوْا
مَغْفُوْرًا لَّكُمْ قَدْ بَدَّلْتُ سَيِّئَاتِكُمْ حَسَنَاتٍ أخرجه أحمد والبزار وأبو يعلى والطبراني وأخرجه
الطبراني عن سهل بن حنظلية أيضًا وأخرجه البيهقى عَنْ عَبْدِ اللّٰهِ بِنِ مُغَفَّلٍ رَضِىَ اللّٰهُ عَنْهُ وَزَادَ
وَمَامِنْ قَوْمٍ اِجْتَمَعُوْا فِيْ مَجْلِسٍ فَتَفَرَّقُوْا وَلَمْ يَذْكُرُ اللّٰهَ اِلَّا كَانَ ذٰلِكَ عَلَيْهِمْ حَسْرَةٌ يَّوْمَ الْقِيَامَةِ
كذا في الدر وقال المنذري رواه الطبراني في الكبير والأوسط ورواته محتج بهم في الصحيح وفي الباب
عن أبي هريرة عند أحمد وابن حبان وغيرهما وصححه الحاكم على شرط مسلم في موضع وعلى شرط
البخاري في موضع أخرى وعزا السيوطى في الجامع حديث سهل إلى الطبراني والبيهقي في الشعب
والضيأ ورقم له بالحسن وفي الباب روايات ذكرها في مجمع الزوائد

Hadhrat Anas (Radhiyallaho anho) reported that Rasulullah (Sallallaho alaihe wasallam) had said, "When some people assemble for the zikr of Allah with the sole purpose of earning His pleasure, an angel proclaims from the sky, 'You people have been forgiven, your sins have been replaced by virtues." According to another hadith, "A gathering devoid of zikr of Allah, would be the cause of dismay and sorrow on the Day of Judgement." It means that the participants of such a gathering will repent that they earned no blessings and wasted their time for nothing; may be, it led them to afflictions. In another hadith, it is stated that the members of a gathering devoid of zikr of Allah and salawaat on Rasulullah (Sallallaho alaihe wasallam) are like those who get up from the dead body of an ass. According to another hadith, one should get the variour transgressions (unwittingly) committed in a gathering condoned by reciting the following prayer at the conclusion of the meeting:

سُبْحَانَ اللهِ وَبِحَمْدِهِ سُبْحَانَكَ اللّٰهُمَّ وَبِحَمْدِكَ اَشْهَدُ اَنْ لَّا اِلٰهَ اِلَّا اَنْتَ اَسْتَغْفِرُكَ وَاَتُوْبُ اِلَيْكَ

"Glory be to Allah with all kinds of praises. Glory be to Thee, O Allah! with all Thy Praise; I stand witness that there is no one to be worshipped except Thee. I seek Thy forgiveness and turn (for mercy) to Thee."

It is narrated in another hadith that any gathering devoid of Allah's zikr and salawaat will be a source of dismay and loss. Then, out of His sheer mercy, Allah may grant forgiveness, or He may demand an explanation and penalize. It is stated in another hadith, "Do proper justice to a gathering by remembering Allah profusely, show the way to wayfarers (if need be), and close your eyes or cast them down when you come across a forbidden thing.

Hadhrat Ali (Karamallaaho Wajhahoo) said, "Whosoever desires that his reward be weighed on the Day of Judgement in a large scale (i.e. his reward should be very big, as only weighty things, and not the small things, are weighed in big scales), should recite the following prayer at the end of a meeting:

سُبْحَانَ رَبِّكَ رَبِّ الْعِزَّةِ عَمَّا يَصِفُوْنَ وَسَلَامٌ عَلَى الْمُرْسَلِيْنَ وَالْحَمْدُ لِلّٰهِ رَبِّ الْعَالَمِيْنَ

(Glory) to Thy Lord–The Lord of Honour And Power. (He is free) from what they ascribe (to Him). And peace be on the apostles, and Praise to Allah, the Lord and Sustainer of the Worlds).

The above hadith also includes the happy tidings that the sins will be replaced by virtues. Even in the Holy Qur'an, at the end of surah al-Furqaan, Almighty Allah mentions the good qualities of the believers and then says:

فَاُولٰٓئِكَ يُبَدِّلُ اللهُ سَيِّاٰتِهِمْ حَسَنَاتٍ وَكَانَ اللهُ غَفُوْرًا رَّحِيْمًا

As for such, Allah will change their evil deeds to good deeds; and Allah is ever forgiving and most merciful.

The following are some comments made by the commentators on this verse:—

1. All sins would be forgiven and only virtues would remain (in the account); that no sin is left behind (in the account) is itself a big change.

2. Almighty Allah will enable them to do good deeds when otherwise they would have committed bad deeds, just as it is sometimes said, "the heat was replaced by the cold."

3. Their habits become related to virtues instead of vices, so much so that doing good deeds becomes their habit. Habits once formed become second nature, which does not change. The Persian proverb meaning that "The mountain can move, but not the habit" refers to this fact. This proverb is also derived from another hadith, "You may believe if you hear that a mountain has moved from its place, but do not believe if you are told that the habits of somebody have changed." This hadith implies that the change of a habit is more unlikely than a mountain changing its place. The question then arises what is meant when it is said that the Sufis and religious teachers reform the behaviour of their disciples. The answer is that habits do not change, but the relationship of habits changes. For instance, if a man's temperament is such that he is prone to anger, it is difficult for him to get rid of his hot temperament through the training and excercises under the supervision of the Shaikhs, but they would reform him in such a way that, whereas formerly his anger led him to show unjustified cruelty and haughtiness, it will now be directed against transgression of Allah's commandments. Hadhrat Umar (Radhiyallaho anho) at one time had left no stone unturned in molesting the Muslims, but after embracing Islaam and remaining in the company of Rasulullah (Sallallaho alaihe wasallam) he became correspondingly hard on the unbelievers and transgressors. So is the case with other aspects of one's conduct. This clarification leads us to the conclusion that

Almighty Allah shifts the direction of the conduct of such people from vices to virtues.

4 Almighty Allah guides him to repent for his sins. He recollects his old sins, repents over them and prays for forgiveness. Thus, for every sin previously committed, he gets the credit of one repentance, which constitues a devotion and a virtue.

5. If Allah is pleased with the good deeds of somebody, and through His sheer benevolence grants him virtues equal to his sins, there is nobody to question His authority. He is the Lord, He is the King, He is All powerful, His mercy is boundless. Who can close the door of His forgiveness? Who can stop His bounty? He gives everything from His own treasures. He will exhibit His powers and unlimited forgiveness on the Day of Judgement. Various scenes of reckoning on the Day of Judgement are described in ahaadith, as briefly given in the book, Bahjatun Nufoos. It is mentioned that reckoning will be conducted in different ways. "Some people will be examined in camera under the cover of (secret) Mercy; their sins will be recounted to them, they will be reminded of the occasion when each sin was committed by them and there will be no alternative for them but to confess all their sins. Due to the abundance of his sins, he will think that he is doomed, but the Lord will say, "I covered your sins during the worldly life and again I cover them now, and forgive them all." When such a person, along with others like him, will return from the place of reckoning, the people will see him and exclaim, "What a blessed person, he never committed any sin," because they will have no knowledge of his sins. Similarly, in another mode of reckoning, the people will have minor as well as major sins to their account. Then, Almighty Allah will order that their minor sins may be converted into virtues, at which they (in order to get more virtues) will exclaim that many of their sins are not mentioned in their account. In the same way, the modes of reckoning are also mentioned in ahaadith. An anecdote is mentioned in one hadith, wherein Rasulullah (Sallallaho alaihe wasallam) is reported to have said, "I recog-

nise the person who will be transferred from the Hell to the Paradise last of all. He will be summoned, and the angels will be directed that his major sins should not be mentioned and that only his minor sins should be read out, and he should be asked to give explanation for them. This trial will start, and his sins will be recounted to him with time and place. How can he deny them? He will confess them all. Almighty Allah will then order that for every sin he may be given one virtue. At this, the man will speak out at once, "There are still many sins that have not been mentioned so far." While narrating this part of the story, even Rasulullah (Sallallaho alaihe wasallam) smiled. Firstly, to be the last one to come out of the Hell, as mentioned in this narrative, does not mean a light punishment; secondly, it is not known as to who will be that lucky one whose sins will be converted into virtues. Hoping for the best from Almighty Allah and constantly begging for His mercy constitute the best form of submission. But one should never be over-complacent in this matter. However, the above-mentioned hadith shows that taking part in meetings of zikr with ikhlaas leads to replacement of sins by virtues. But this ikhlaas is possible only through the grace of Almighty Allah.

The main point contained in this hadith is that of ikhlaas (i.e. doing a thing only for the pleasure of Allah). That ikhlaas is the pre-requisite for all good deeds will be found in several other ahaadith in this book. In fact, the acceptance by Almighty Allah depends only on ikhlaas: every deed will be evaluated according to the degree of ikhlaas involved therein. According to the Sufis, ikhlaas on one's part requires that one's words, thoughts and deeds should be compatible. It will be found in one hadith that ikhlaas is that which prevents one from committing sin.

A story of a despotic king who was notorious for his tyranny and cruelty is related in the book "Bahjatun Nufoos." Once, a large consignment of wine was being brought for him in a ship. A pious man who happened to travel by that ship broke all the bottles or casks of wine except one, but nobody could stop him from that act. Everybody wondered how he dared to do this, for nobody had the courage to face the cruelty of the king. When the king was informed about it, he was surprised to learn how an ordinary person had the courage to do all that and also wondered why he left one cask intact. The man was called for, and interrogated. He replied, "My conscience had urged me to do this; you may punish me as you like." He was then asked why one cask was left unbroken? He replied, "At first I broke the casks of wine out of my religous sentiments, but when only one was left, my heart felt elated at having done something forbidden by religion. I then felt that breaking this last cask would be for the satisfaction of my ego. I, therefore, did not break it." Finding him selfless in what he did, the king ordered his release.

It is narrated in Ihyaa-ul Uloom that there was a pious man among the Israelites, who always remained busy in the worship of Allah. A group of people came to him and told him that a tribe living nearby worshipped a tree. The news upset him, and with an axe on his shoulder he went to cut down that tree. On the way, Satan met him in the form of an old man and asked him where he was going. He said he was going to cut a particular tree. Satan said, "You are not concerned with this tree, you better mind your worship and do not give it up for the sake of something that does not concern you." "This is also worship", retorted the worshipper. Then Satan tried to prevent him from cutting the tree, and there followed a bout between the two, in which the worshipper overpowered the Satan. Finding himself completely helpless, Satan begged to be excused, and when the worshipper released him, he again said, "Allah has not made the cutting of this tree obligatory on you. You do not lose anything if you do not cut it. If its cutting were necessary, Allah could have got it done through one of his many Apostles." The worshipper insisted on cutting the tree. There was again a bout between the two and again the worshipper overpowered the Satan. "Well, listen" said the Satan, "I propose a settlement that will be to your advantage." The worshipper agreed, and the Satan said, "You are a poor man, a mere burden on this earth. If you desist from this act, I will pay you three gold coins everyday. You will daily find them lying under your pillow. By this money you can fulfil your own needs, can oblige your relatives, help the needy, and do so many other virtuous things. Cutting the tree will be only one virtue, which will ultimately be of no use because the people will grow another tree." This proposal appealed to the worshipper, and he accepted it. He found the money on two successive days, but on the third day there was nothing. He got enraged, picked up his axe and went to cut the tree. The old man again met him on the way and asked him where he was going. "To cut the tree", shouted the worshipper. "I will not let you do it", said the Satan. An encounter ensured between the two, and this time the Satan had the upper-hand and overpowered the worshipper. The latter was surprised at his own defeat, and asked the former the cause of his success. The Satan replied, "At first, your anger was purely for earning the pleasure of Allah, and therefore Almighty Allah helped you to overpower me, but now it has been partly for the sake of the gold coins and therefore you lost." Truly speaking, a deed performed purely for the pleasure of Allah alone carries great force.

Hadith No. 11

(١١) عَنْ مُعَاذِ بْنِ جَبَلٍ رَضِىَ اللهُ عَنْهُ قَالَ قَالَ رَسُوْلِ اللهِ ﷺ مَا عَمِلَ اٰدَمِىٌّ عَمَلًا اَنْجٰى لَهُ مِنْ عَذَابِ الْقَبْرِ مِنْ ذِكْرِ اللهِ أخرجه أحمد كذا في الدر وإلى أحمد عزاه في الجامع الصغير بلفظ انجى له من عذاب الله ورقم له بالصحة وفي مجمع الزوائد رواه أحمد ورجاله رجال الصحيح إلا أن زيادًا لم يدرك معاذا ثم ذكره بطريق آخر وقال رواه الطبراني ورجاله رجال الصحيح قلت:وفي المشكواة عنه موقوفا بلفظ مَاعَمِلَ الْعَبْدُ عَمَلًا اَنْجٰى لَهُ مِنْ عَذَابِ اللهِ مِنْ ذِكْرِ اللهِ وقال رواه مالك والترمذي وابن ماجه اهـ قلت وهكذا رواه الحاكم وقال صحيح الاسناد وأقره عليه الذهبى وفي المشكواة برواية البيهقى في الدعوات عن ابن عمر مرفوعا بمعناه قال القارى : رواه ابن أبي شيبة وابن أبي الدنيا وذكره في الجامع الصغير برواية البيهقي في الشعب ورقم له بالضعف وزاد في اوله لِكُلِّ شَيْءٍ صِقَالَةٌ وصِقَالَةُ الْقُلُوْبِ ذِكْرُ اللهِ وفي مجمع الزوائد برواية جابر مرفوعا نحوه وقال رواه الطبراني في الصغير والأوسط ورجالهما رجال الصحيح اهـ

Rasulullah (Sallallaho alaihe wasallam) said, "No other action of a person can surpass zikr of Almighty Allah in saving him from the punishment in the grave."

Note:

How serious is the punishment in the grave can be realized only by those who have the knowledge of hadith on this subject. Whenever Hadhrat Uthman (Radhiyallaho anho) visited a grave, he would weep so much that his beard would become wet with tears. Some one asked him, "How is it that mention of Paradise and Hell does not make you weep so much as you do when you come across a grave?" He replied, "The grave is the first of the many stages of the Hereafter. For him who is successful or safe during this stage, the later stages will also be easy; while for a person who is not exempted in this stage, the later stages will be even more difficult." Then he quoted Rasulullah (Sallallaho alaihe wasallam) as having said, "I have not come across any sight more terrifying than that of the grave." Hadhrat Aa'ishah (Radhiyallaho anha) said, that Rasulullah (Sallallaho alaihe wasallam) used to pray after every Salaat for protection against the chastisement in the grave. Hadhrat Zaid (Radhiyallaho anho) reported Rasulullah (Sallallaho alaihe wasallam) to have said, "But for fear that you might give up burying your dead, I would have prayed to Almighty Allah to let you hear the torture of the grave. With the exception of men and jinns, all other creatures hear the punishment in the grave."

According to a hadith, once when Rasulullah (Sallallaho alaihe wasallam) was going on a journey, his she-camel took fright. Someone asked him what had happened to her. Rasulullah (Sallallaho alaihe wasallam) replied that somebody was being punished in the grave, and the cries of the punished had frightened the she-camel.

Once Rasulullah (Sallallaho alaihe wasallam) entered the mosque and saw that some people were laughing very loudly. He said to them, "If you had remembered death quite often, you would not have laughed like this. Not a day passes when the grave does not proclaim, "I am the house of wilderness, the house of loneliness, and the abode of worms and insects." When a true believer is buried in a grave, it welcomes him, saying, "You are welcome here, you have done well to have come here. Of all the people walking upon the earth, you were the dearest to me. Now that you have been made over to me, you will see my excellent behaviour." Then the grave expands to the farthest point of sight, and a door of paradise opens into it. Through this door comes the scented air of paradise. But when an unbeliever or a transgressor is buried, the grave says, "Your coming here is unwelcome and abominable. You had better not come here. Of all the people who have been walking upon me, I hated you the most. Today you have been made over to me, and you will see my treatment." Then it narrows down and presses him mercilessly, till his ribs pierce into each other as the fingers of the two hands interlock each other. Then ninety or ninety nine dragons are let loose upon him, and they will continue clawing at him till the Day of Resurrection. If one of those serpents or dragons were to blow on the earth, it will be rendered incapable of growing any grass till the Day of Judgement. Then Rasulullah (Sallallaho alaihe wasallam) continued, "The grave is either a garden out of Paradise or a pit out of Hell."

According to another hadith, Rasulullah (Sallallaho alaihe wasallam) happened to pass by two graves. He said, "The two persons buried in these graves are being punished, one for back-biting and the other for polluting his body with his urine." It is a pity that many of our so-called civilized people regard istinjaa (washing the private parts after urination) as an undignified act, and even redicule it. Some Ulama regard such pollution by urine as a major sin. Ibn Hajar Makki (Rahmatullah alaih) has stated that, according to an authentic hadith, the punishment in the grave is generally due to neglect of cleanliness from urine.

It is narrated in one hadith that interrogation in the grave will first be about (pollution with) urine. In short, the punishment of the grave is a very serious affair. Just as some types of sins lead to this affliction, in the same way certain virtuous acts provide special safeguard against it. It is stated in several ahaadith that the recitation of surah Tabarakal lazi every night guarantees security from the tortures in the grave, as well as from that in the Hell. The effectiveness of zikr in this respect is evident from the above-mentioned hadith.

Hadith No. 12

(١٢) عَنْ اَبِي الدَّرْدَاءِ رَضِيَ اللّٰهُ عَنْهُ قَالَ قَالَ رَسُوْلُ اللّٰهِ ﷺ لَيَبْعَثَنَّ اللّٰهُ اَقْوَامًا
يَّوْمَ الْقِيَامَةِ فِي وُجُوْهِهِمْ النُّوْرُ عَلٰى مَنَابِرِ اللُّؤْلُؤِ يَغْبِطُهُمُ النَّاسُ لَيْسُوْا بِاَنْبِيَاءِ
وَلَاشُهَدَاءَ فَقَالَ اَعْرَابِيٌّ حُلَّهُمْ لَنَا نَعْرِفُهُمْ قَالَ هُمُ الْمُتَحَابُّوْنَ فِي اللّٰهِ مِنْ قَبَائِلَ

شَتّٰى وَبِلَادٍ شَتّٰى يَجْتَمِعُوْنَ عَلٰى ذِكْرِ اللهِ يَذْكُرُوْنَهُ أخرجه الطبراني باسناد حسن كذا في الدر ومجمع الزوائد والترغيب للمنذري وذكر أيضا له متابعة برواية عمرو بن عبسة عند الطبراني مرفوعاً قال المنذري واسناده مقارب لا بأس به ورقم لحديث عمرو بن عبسة في الجامع الصغير بالحسن وفي مجمع الزوائد رجاله موثوقون وفي مجمع الزوائد بمعنى هذا الحديث مطولا وَفِيْهِ حُلَّهُمْ لَنَا يَعْنِىْ صِفْهُمْ لَنَا شَكِّلْهُمْ فَسُرَّ وَجْهُ رَسُوْلِ اللهِ ﷺ بِسُوَالِ الْاَعْرَابِىِّ الحديث قال رواه أحمد والطبراني بنحوه ورجاله وثقوا قلت وفي الباب عن أبي هريرة عند البيهقي في الشعب اِنَّ فِىْ الْجَنَّةِ لَعُمْدًا مِّنْ يَاقُوْتٍ عَلَيْهَا غُرَفٌ مِنْ زَبَرْجَدٍ لَهَا اَبْوَابٌ مُفَتَّحَةٌ تُضِىْءُ كَمَايُضِىْءُ الْكَوْكَبُ الدُّرِّىُّ يَسْكُنُهَا الْمُتَحَابُّوْنَ فِىْ اللهِ تَعَالٰى وَالْمُتَجَالِسُوْنَ فِىْ اللهِ تَعَالٰى وَالْمُتَلَاقُوْنَ فِىْ اللهِ كذا في الجامع الصغير ورقم له بالضعف وذكر في مجمع الزوائد له شواهد وكذا في المشكٰوة

Rasulullah (Sallallaho alaihe wasallam) had said, "Almighty Allah will, on the Day of Resurrection, resurrect certain groups of people in such a state that their faces will be radiant with light, they will be sitting on pulpits of pearls and others will envy their lot. They will neither be from among the Prophets nor from among the martyrs." Somebody asked the Prophet (Sallallaho alaihe wasallam) to let him have more details about these people, so that he may be able to recognize them. Rasulullah (Sallallaho alaihe wasallam) replied, "They will be the people who belong to different families and different places, but assemble at one place for the love of Almighty Allah and are engaged in His zikr."

It is said in another hadith, "In paradise there will be pillars of emerald supporting balconied houses made of rubies and with open doors on all the four sides. These will shine like brilliant stars, and will be occupied by those people who love each other for the sake of Allah, and who assemble at a place and meet each other only for His pleasure.

Nowadays, the religious devotees are criticized and ridiculed by everybody. The people may reproach them today as much as they like, but the reality will dawn on them in the Hereafter, when they will realize how these humble persons have been able to earn high fortunes and occupy such grand pulpits and such flats, whereas those who criticized and ridiculed them had earned nothing but misery and despair:

فَسَوْفَ تَرَىٰ إِذَا انْكَشَفَ الْغُبَارُ أَفَرَسٌ تَحْتَ رِجْلِكَ أَمْ حِمَارٌ

"Soon the dust-cloud will clear away, and it will be seen whether you are riding a horse or an ass."

How blessed, in the eyes of Almighty Allah, are the khanqahs (places where zikr is practised), which are the targets of abuse from all quarters, can best be judged from this hadith in their favour. It is mentioned in one hadith that the houses where zikr is practised shine unto the dwellers of the Heaven, as do the stars shine unto the inhabitants of the Earth. According to another hadith, sakeenah (a very special blessing) descends on the gathering engaged in zikr, the angels surround them, the divine mercy covers them, and Almighty Allah mentions them on His Throne.

Hadhrat Abu Razeen (Radhiyallaho anho) a Sahabi, narrated that Rasulullah (Sallallaho alaihe wasallam) had said, "Shall I tell you something that will strengthen your Imaan and earn you the blessings of Allah, the Great, in both the worlds? It is the gatherings of those who do zikr of Almighty Allah; you should make it a point to take part in them, and when you are alone, do as much zikr as you can."

Hadhrat Abu Hurairah (Radhiyallaho anho) has explained that the houses in which zikr is done appear to be as bright and shining as are the stars to the dwellers of the Earth. These houses are so bright because of their light of zikr, they shine like the stars. There are people who are endowed by Almighty Allah with spiritual insight and are capable of seeing this light in this very world. There are some who can recognise the spiritual persons and their houses from the special radiance emitted by them. Hadhrat Fudhail bin Iyaadh, (Rahmatullah alaih) a famous saint, has said that the houses in which zikr is practised shine like a lamp unto the dwellers of the Heavens. Sheikh Abdul Aziz Dabbaagh, a saint of recent times, was illiterate but he could clearly distinguish between the verses of the Qur'an, Hadith Qudsi, and Hadith Nabawi. He used to say that words coming out from the mouth of the speaker carry a distinguishing glow and that the words of Almighty Allah carry one kind of radiance and the words of Rasulullah (Sallallaho alaihe wasallam) carry another kind of radiance, while the words of others are devoid of these two types of radiance.

It is given in Tazkiratul Khaleel, the biography of Maulana Khaleel Ahmad (May Allah enlighten his grave) that Maulana Zafar Ahmad had related, "When Maulana Khaleel Ahmad, on the occasion of his fifth Hajj, entered the Masjidul Haraam for Tawaaful Qudoom, I was sitting in the company of Maulana Muhibbuddeen, who was one of the most trusted disciples of Maulana al-Haaj Imdaadullah Muhaajir Makki (May Allah enlighten his grave) and was well known for his gift of divine foresight. He was then engaged in his usual recitation of salawaat from a book, when all of a sudden he turned to me and said, "Who has entered the Haram? The whole of the Haram has been flooded with his radiance and light." I kept quiet. After a short while, Maulana Khaleel Ahmad after completing his tawaaf happened to pass by us. On seeing him Maulana Muhibbuddeen stood up, smiled and said, "Now indeed I see who has entered the Haram today!"

The virtues of assembling for the sake of zikr have been described in different ways in so many other ahaadith. In one hadith, it is stated that salaat and gatherings for zikr constitute the best ribaat. Ribaat stands for guarding the boundaries of Daarus Salaam (the Muslim territory) against invasion by the infidels.

Hadith No 13

(١٣) عَنْ اَنَسٍ رَضِىَ اللهُ عَنْهُ اَنَّ رَسُوْلَ اللهِ ﷺ قَالَ اِذَا مَرَرْتُمْ بِرِيَاضِ الْجَنَّةِ فَارْتَعُوْا قَالَ وَمَارِيَاضُ الْجَنَّةِ قَالَ حِلَقُ الذِّكْرِ أخرجه أحمد والترمذي وحسنه وذكره في المشكواة برواية الترمذي وزاد في الجامع الصغير والبيهقي في الشعب ورقم له بالصحة وفي الباب عن جابر عند ابن أبي الدنيا والبزار وأبي يعلى والحاكم وصححه البيهقى في الدعوات كذا في الدر وفي الجامع الصغير برواية الطبراني عن ابن عباس بلفظ مَجالس الْعِلْم برواية الترمذي عن أبي هريرة بلفظ المساجد محل حلق الذكر وزاد الرتع سُبْحَانَ اللهِ اَلْحَمْدُ لِلهِ لَآاِلٰهَ اِلَّا اللهُ اَللهُ اَكْبَرُ

Rasulullah (Sallallaho alaihe wasallam) said, "When you pass the gardens of Paradise, graze to your heart's content." Someone asked, "O Rasulullah! (Sallallaho alaihe wasallam), what is meant by the gardens of Paradise?" He replied, "Gatherings for performing zikr."

What is meant is that if somebody is lucky enough to get access to such gatherings, he should take full advantage of this, as these are the gardens of Paradise on this Earth.

The words, "graze to your heart's content", signify that, just as an animal grazing in a green pasture or garden does not give up grazing in spite of being driven or beaten by its owner, similarly a zaakir (one who practises zikr) should not get pulled away from the gatherings for zikr by the worldly anxieties and hindrances. The gatherings for zikr are likened to the gardens of Paradise, because just as there are no worries in the paradise, similarly gatherings of zikr are safeguarded against every kind of calamity.

It is stated in one hadith that the zikr of Almighty Allah cures all diseases of the mind, such as arrogance, jealousy, malice, etc. The author of 'Fawaa'id fis Salaah wal Awaa'id' has stated that constancy in zikr is a sure safeguard against all kinds of calamities. According to another hadith, Rasulullah (Sallallaho alaihe wasallam) has said, "I enjoin on you to do zikr of Allah profusely. It is like taking refuge in a fort against a strong enemy. One who practises zikr is as if it were in the company of Almighty Allah." Can there be any benefit greater than that of being in the company of the Almighty Lord? Moreover, it leads to satisfaction of the mind, it enlightens the heart and removes its callousness. In addition, there are many other material and spiritual benefits, which are enumerated, upto a hundred, by some Ulama.

A man came to see Hadhrat Abu Umaamah, (Radhiyallaho anho) and said to him, "I saw in a dream that whenever you went or came out, or sat or stood up, the angels prayed for you." Hadhrat Abu Umaamah (Radhiyallaho anho) replied, "If you wish you can also earn their prayers", and recited the ayat:

يَاأَيُّهَا الَّذِيْنَ آمَنُوْا اذْكُرُوا اللهَ ذِكْرًا كَثِيْرًا

"O you who believe! celebrate the praises of Allah and do this excessively and glorify Him morning and evening. He sends blessings on you, as also His angels that He may bring you out from the depths of darkness into light, and He is full of Mercy to the believers."

This ayat was quoted to show that the Mercy of Almighty Allah and the prayers of the angels can be earned through zikr. The more we remember Allah, the more He remembers us.

Hadith No 14

(١٤) عَنْ اِبْنِ عَبَّاسٍ رَضِىَ اللهُ عَنْهُ قَالَ قَالَ رَسُوْلُ اللهِ ﷺ مَنْ عَجزَ مِنْكُمْ عَنِ اللَّيْلِ اَنْ يُّكَابِرَهُ وَبَخِلَ بِالْمَالِ أنْ يُّنْفِقَهُ وَجَبُنَ عَنِ الْعَدُوِّ اَنْ يُّجَاهِدَهُ فَلْيُكْثِرْ ذِكْرَ اللهِ رواه الطبراني والبيهقى والبزار واللفظ له وفي سنده أبويحيى القتات وبقيته محتج بهم في الصحيح كذا في الترغيب قلت هو من رواة البخاري في الأدب المفرد والترمذي وأبي داود وابن ماجه وثقه ابن معين وضعفه آخرون وفي التقريب لين الحديث وفي مجمع الزوائد رواه البزار والطبراني وفيه القتات قد وثق وضعفه الجمهور وبقية رجال البزار رجال الصحيح

Rasulullah (Sallallaho alaihe wasallam) said, "One who is too weak to bear the strain of keeping awake at night (in the worship of Almighty Allah), is too miserly to spend his wealth in the path of Allah, and is too cowardly to take part in jihaad, is advised to remain engaged in the zikr of Allah."

This shows that deficiencies in respect of non-obligatory form of worship can be atoned through profuse zikr of Almighty Allah. Hadhrat Anas (Radhiyallaho anho) reported that Rasulullah (Sallallaho alaihe wasallam) had said, "Zikr of Allah is a sign of Imaan, and it ensures exemption from hypocrisy, and provides a safeguard against the devil and protection from the fire of Hell." Because of all these benefits, zikr has been regarded as more virtuous than many other forms of worship; it is specially effective in providing protection against the Devil. It is stated in one hadith that the Devil, in a kneeling position, clings to the heart of a man, and when the man remembers Almighty Allah the devil becomes helpless and frustrated and therefore draws back, but whenever he finds the man neglecting it he pollutes the heart with evil thoughts. It is for this reason that the Sufis advise practising zikr excessively, so that the heart remains free from evil thoughts and becomes strong enough to resist the Devil. The Sahaba (Radhiyallaho anhum) who had developed this inner strength through the blessed company of Rasulullah (Sallallaho alaihe wasallam) did not stand in such great need of exercising zikr, but with the passage of time after Rasulullah (Sallallaho alaihe wasallam) this resistive power of the heart became weaker and weaker; and the need to remedy this weakness through zikr became correspondingly greater. In the present age, the hearts have become so degenerate that no amount of treatment can restore their strength to compare with that of the Sahabah. Nevertheless, whatever improvement is effected is worthwhile at this time when the disease has taken the form of an epidemic.

It is related about a holy man that he prayed to Almighty Allah that he may be shown how Satan prevails upon the heart. He found that the Satan sits like a mosquito over the left side of the heart under the back of the shoulder and then advances his needle-like snout towards the heart. If he finds the heart buzy in zikr he withdraws at once, but if the heart is idle he injects the poison of evil and sinful thoughts into it. It is stated in one hadith that Satan keeps on sitting with the top of his nose over the heart, and if the heart is buzy in zikr he withdraws in disgrace, but if it is idle he makes a morsel of it.

Hadith No 15

(١٥) عَنْ اَبِىْ سَعِيْدِ نِ الْخُدْرِىِّ رَضِىَ اللّٰهُ عَنْهُ اَنَّ رَسُوْلَ اللّٰهِ ﷺ قَالَ اَكْثِرُوا ذِكْرَ اللّٰهِ حَتّٰى يَقُوْلُوْا مَجْنُوْنٌ رواه أحمد وأبو يعلى وابن حبان والحاكم في صحيحه وقال صحيح الاسناد وروى عن ابن عباس مرفوعا بلفظ اذكروا الله ذكرا يقول المنافقون إنكم مراءون رواه الطبراني ورواه البيهقي عن أبي الجوزاء مرسلا. كذا في الترغيب والمقاصد الحسنة للسخاوي وهكذا في الدر المنثور للسيوطي إلا أنه عزا حديث أبي الجوزاء إلى عبدالله بن أحمد في زوائد الزهد وعزاه في الجامع الصغير إلى سعيد بن منصور في سننه والبيهقي في الشعب ورقم له بالضعف وذكر في الجامع الصغير أيضا برواية الطبراني عن ابن عباس مسندا ورقم له بالضعف وعزا حديث أبي سعيد إلى أحمد وأبي يعلى في مسنده وابن حبان والحاكم والبيهقي في الشعب ورقم له بالحسن

Rasulullah (Sallallaho alaihe wasallam) is reported to have said, "Practise zikr so excessively that people may regard you as a maniac." It is stated in another hadith "Practise zikr so much that the hypocrite may regard you as insincere."

It is clear from this hadith that the taunts of madness and hypocrisy by the munaafiqs and by the foolish people should not make one give up the spiritual wealth of zikr. On the contrary, it should be done with such rapture and abundance that those people may take you to be actually mad and let you alone. They will consider you mad, only if you practise zikr excessively and loudly, and not if you do it quietly.

Ibn Katheer (Rahmatullah alaih) has narrated, on the authority of Hadhrat Abdullah bin Abbas (Radhiyallaho anho) "Nothing has been made obligatory by Almighty Allah without fixing maximum limit for it and excusing shortcomings in respect of it, except His zikr, for which no limit has been fixed and no person, as long as he is sane is exempted from it." Almighty Allah has ordered in the Holy Quran:

اُذْكُرُوا اللّٰهَ ذِكْرًا كَثِيْرًا

"Practise zikr of Allah excessively." A person should do zikr under all circumstances, whether by day or night; whether in the jungle or at sea; whether travelling or halting; whether in affluence or poverty; whether in sickness or health; whether loudly or quietly.

In his book 'Munabbihaat', Hafiz Ibn Hajar (Rahmatullah alaih) writes that Hadhrat Uthman (Radhiyallaho anho), while explaining the Quranic verse

وَكَانَ تَحْتَهُ كَنْزٌ لَّهُمَا

Beneath it there was a treasure for them

said that the treasure meant a golden tablet, on which were written the following seven lines:

(1) I wonder at the man who knows that he is to die and indulges in laughter.
(2) I wonder at the man who knows that this world will come to an end one day, but hankers after it.
(3) I wonder that a man who knows that everything is predestined should lament the loss of anything.
(4) I wonder that a man who believes in the reckoning in the Hereafter should amass wealth.
(5) I wonder that a man who has the knowledge of the fire of the Hell should commit any sin.
(6) I wonder that a man who believes in Almighty Allah should remember anybody other than Him.
(7) I wonder that a man who believes in Paradise should feel pleasure in anything of this world.

In some editions of that book, it is also added, "I wonder that a man who knows that Satan is his eternal enemy should obey and follow him."

Hafiz (Rahmatullah alaih) has also stated on the authority of Hadhrat Jaabir (Radhiyallaho anho) that Rasulullah (Sallallaho alaihe wasallam) once said, "Hazrat Jibra-eel (Alayhis salaam) laid so much stress on doing zikr that I felt that without zikr nothing can benefit whatsoever."

The above mentioned quotations show that one should practise zikr as much as possible; giving it up simply because others may call one mad or a hypocrite is fraught with serious loss to oneself. The Sufis have written that it is also a trap on the part of Satan that at first he discourages one from zikr on the plea of avoiding criticism by the people and, if he succeeds in this attempt, he is encouraged and exploits this fear of criticism for preventing the person from doing zikr forever. Although one should not do any good deed for the sake of a show, yet if anybody happens to see it one should not thereupon give it up.

Hadhrat Abdullah Zul Bajadeen (Radhiyallaho anho), a Sahabi, became an orphan in his childhood. He lived with his uncle, who looked after him well. He had embraced Islaam secretly and, when his uncle came to know of it, in his anger, he turned him out of the house stark naked. His mother was also displeased, but she took pity on him and gave him a sheet of coarse cloth, which he tore into two pieces, using one piece as a lower garment and the other as an upper covering for the body. He migrated to Madina, where he was always found before the house of Rasulullah (Sallallaho alaihe wasallam) and used to practise zikr very loudly. Hadhrat Umar (Radhiyallaho anho) remarked, "Is this man a hypocrite that he does zikr so loudly? "No" said Rasulullah (Sallallaho alaihe wasallam), "He is from amongst the Awwaabeen," i.e. those who ever turn to Almighty Allah. He died in the battle of Tabook. The Sahabah saw a lamp burning in the graveyard. On approaching it, they found Rasulullah (Sallallaho alaihe wasallam) standing in the grave and asking Hadhrat Abubakr and Hadhrat Umar (Radhiyallaho anhuma) to make over their brother to him. The two made over the dead body to him for burial. After the burial, the Prophet (Sallallaho alaihe wasallam) prayed, "O Allah! I am pleased with him, Thou be also pleased with him."

On seeing this scene, Hadhrat Ibn Masood (Radhiyallaho anho) wished that it should have been his corpse.

Hadhrat Fudhail (who was one of the great Sufis) stated, "To abstain from a virtuous act for fear of being seen by the people is in itself an act of hypocrisy, and a good action done with the intention to make a show amounts to Shirk (false worship)."

It is stated in one hadith that some persons are the keys to zikr, i.e. their very sight reminds and inspires other people to do zikr of Allah. According to another hadith, such people are the friends of Allah whose very sight makes others remember Almighty Allah. It is stated in one hadith, "The best amongst you are the people whose very sight reminds you of Allah." Similarly it is stated in another hadith, "The best amongst you are those whose sight makes you remember Almighty Allah, whose words add to your knowledge, and whose actions induce you to work for the love of the Hereafter." Of course, such a condition can be attained by one who practises zikr profusely. One who is himself indolent in this respect, his sight can hardly inspire others to remember Allah.

Some people regard zikr in loud voice as an innovation and forbidden in religion, but this view is due to lack of insight into the knowledge of hadith. Maulana Abdul Hay, (Rahmatullah alaih) has written a booklet 'Sabahatul Fikr' on this very subject, wherein he has quoted about fifty ahaadith in support of zikr in loud voice. However, it is subject to proper limitations, so as not to annoy anybody else.

Hadith No 16

(١٦) عَنْ اَبِيْ هُرَيْرَةَ رَضِىَ اللّٰهُ عَنْهُ قَالَ سَمِعْتُ رَسُوْلَ اللّٰهِ ﷺ يَقُوْلُ سَبْعَةٌ يُظِلُّهُمُ اللّٰهُ فِيْ ظِلِّهِ يَوْمَ لَاظِلَّ اِلَّا ظِلُّهُ اِمَامٌ عَادِلٌ وَشَابٌّ نَشَاءَ فِيْ عِبَادَةِ اللّٰهِ وَرَجُلٌ قَلْبُهُ مُعَلَّقٌ بِالْمَسَاجِدِ وَرَجُلَانِ تَحَابَّا فِيْ اللّٰهِ اِجْتَمَعَا عَلٰى ذٰلِكَ وَتَفَرَّقَا عَلَيْهِ وَرَجُلٌ دَعَتْهُ اِمْرَاَةٌ ذَاتُ مَنْصَبٍ وَّجَمَالٍ فَقَالَ اِنِّيْ اَخَافُ اللّٰهَ وَرَجُلٌ تَصَدَّقَ بِصَدَقَةٍ فَاَخْفَاهَا حَتّٰى لَاتَعْلَمَ شِمَالُهُ مَاتُنْفِقُ يَمِيْنُهُ وَرَجُلٌ ذَكَرَ اللّٰهَ خَالِيًا فَفَاضَتْ عَيْنَاهُ رواه البخاري ومسلم وغيرهما كذا في الترغيب والمشكوٰة وفي الجامع الصغير برواية مسلم عن أبي هريرة وأبي سعيد معا وذكر عدة طرقه أخرى

Rasulullah (Sallallaho alaihe wasallam) has said:

> "The following seven persons will be accommodated by Allah in the shade of His Mercy on the day when there will be no other shade except His: (1) A

just ruler (2) A young man who worships Allah in his youth (3) A person whose heart yearns for the musjid (4) Those two persons who love, meet and depart only for the pleasure of Allah. (5) A man who is tempted by a beautiful woman and refuses to respond for fear of Allah. (6) A person who gives alms so secretly that the charity of one hand is not known to the other hand. (7) A person who practises zikr of Allah in solitude, so that tears flow of his eyes."

The flowing of tears can mean deliberate weeping, due to repentance over one's past sins, but it may also mean a spontaneous outburst of tears due to overwhelming passion of love. Thaabit Banaani (Rahmatullah alaih) has quoted the words of a pious man, "I come to know when a prayer of mine is accepted." When asked as to how he comes to know of it, he said, "That prayer, at the time of which the hair on my body stand up, my heart starts beating rapidly and my eyes shed tears, is accepted by Allah." Among the seven persons mentioned in the foregoing hadith, is included also the person who weeps while doing zikr in solitude. He combines two sublime qualities: first ikhlaas, which makes him remember Allah in solitude, secondly the fear or love of Allah, which makes him weep. Both these things are extremely virtuous. According to a poet,

ہمارا کام ہے راتوں کو رونا یادِ دلبر میں
ہماری نیند ہے محوِ خیالِ یار ہو جانا

"My work is to weep at night in remembering my beloved; and my sleep is to remain absorbed in thoughts of my beloved."

In the Arabic text of the hadith (رَجُلٌ ذَكَرَ اللهَ خَالِيًا), (a person who remembers Allah when he is unoccupied), the word 'unoccupied' according to Sufis, has two meanings. It means in solitude, as is generally understood; but it also signifies the heart being free from all thoughts except of Almighty Allah, which constitutes the real solitude. The ideal is to have both forms of solitude, physical as well as mental. But if a person, even while in the company of others, has his heart free from all worldly thoughts and, being absorbed in the zikr of Allah, happens to weep thereby, he will also be rewarded as mentioned in this hadith, because the presence or absence of others makes no difference to him. His heart is free from the thoughts, not only of his companions, but also of everything other than Almighty Allah. The presence of others cannot distract him from his attention towards Allah.

To be able to weep for fear and love of Allah implies possession of great spiritual wealth. Fortunate is he who is blessed with it by Almighty Allah. It is stated in one hadith that a person who weeps for fear of Allah will not be sent to Hell till the milk goes back into the teats of an animal (which is impossssible). This implies that it is similarly impossible for such a person to go to Hell. According to another hadith, a person who weeps for fear of Allah will not be punished on the Day of Judgement.

It is stated in one hadith that the fire of Hell is forbidden for two eyes—one that sheds tears for fear of Allah, and the other that has remained awake in guarding the Muslims and Islaam against the infidels. In another hadith, it is stated that the fire of Hell is forbidden on the eye that has wept for fear of Allah, on the eye that has remained awake in the path of Allah, on the eye that has refrained from the unlawful and also on the eye that has been lost in the path of Allah.

Yet another hadith states that a person who remembers Allah in solitude is like one who goes all alone to fight against the infidels.

Hadith No 17

(١٧) عَنْ اَبِي هُرَيْرَةَ رَضِيَ اللّٰهُ عَنْهُ قَالَ قَالَ رَسُوْلُ اللّٰهِ ﷺ يُنَادِيْ مُنَادٍ يَوْمَ
الْقِيَامَةِ اَيْنَ اُولُوْا الْاَلْبَابِ قَالُوْا اَيَّ اُولِى الْاَلْبَابِ تُرِيْدُ قَالَ اَلَّذِيْنَ يَذْكُرُوْنَ اللّٰهَ
قِيَامًا وَّقُعُوْدًا وَّعَلٰى جُنُوْبِهِمْ وَيَتَفَكَّرُوْنَ فِيْ خَلْقِ السَّمٰوٰتِ وَالْاَرْضِ رَبَّنَا
مَاخَلَقْتَ هٰذَا بَاطِلًا سُبْحَانَكَ فَقِنَا عَذَابَ النَّارِ عُقِدَ لَهُمْ لِوَاءٌ فَاتَّبَعَ الْقَوْمُ لِوَاءَ
هُمْ وَقَالَ لَهُمْ اُدْخُلُوْهَا خَالِدِيْنَ أخرجه الأصبهاني في الترغيب كذا في الدر

Rasulullah (Sallallaho alaihe wasallam) said, "An announcer will call out on the Day of Judgement, 'Where are the wise ones?' People will enquire, 'Who are meant by the wise ones?' The reply will be, 'They are those who always remembered Allah, whether sitting, standing or reclining, and pondered over the creation of the Heaven and the Earth, and would say, "O Allah! Thou hast not created all this in vain. We glorify Thee; save us from the fire of Hell." Thereafter a flag will appear for them, and they will follow this flag and will be told to enter Paradise and stay for ever."

By "pondering over the creation of the Heaven and the Earth" is meant that they contemplate over the phenomena and secrets of the things created by Allah, and thereby strengthen their spiritual knowledge.

الٰہی یہ عالم ہے گلزار تیرا

The whole universe is like a garden planned and planted by Allah.

As narrated by Ibn Abid Dunyaa, Rasulullah (Sallallaho alaihe wasallam) once approached a group of Sahabah who were sitting in silence. He asked them what they were thinking about. The Sahabah replied that they were pondering over the wonderful creations of Allah. Rasulullah (Sallallaho alaihe wasallam) appreciated it and said "Do not ever meditate over the Self of Almighty Allah, (He is beyond comprehension), but do meditate over His creation"

Somebody once asked Hadhrat Aa'ishah (Radhiyallaho anha) to relate some remarkable thing about Rasulullah (Sallallaho alaihe wasallam). She replied, "There was nothing about him that was not remarkable. Once he came home at night and lay down in my bed. After a short while, he said 'Let me pray to my Lord! Saying this, he got up, performed wudhu and stood up in salaat, during which he wept so profusely that tears flowed onto his chest. Then he continued weeping in the same manner while performing ruku and sajdah. He spent the whole night like this, till Hadhrat Bilaal came to call the azaan for the morning prayer. I pleaded with him, 'Almighty Allah has promised you His forgiveness, then why did you weep so much?' He replied, "Should I not be a grateful slave of my Allah", and continued, "Why should I not pray and weep when these verses have been revealed to me today:

إِنَّ فِي خَلْقِ السَّمٰوٰتِ وَالْأَرْضِ ...... فَقِنَا عَذَابَ النَّارِ

"Lo! in the creation of heaven and earth, and in the difference of night and day, are tokens (of His sovereignty) for men of understanding such as remember Allah standing, sitting and reclining . . . .

Then he added, 'Destruction is for the person who, in spite of reading these verses, does not ponder over His creation."

Aamir bin Abdul Qais (Rahmatullah alaih) said, "I heard from the Sahabah not from one or two or three, but from many of them–that the light and radiance of faith lies in contemplation and meditation." Hadhrat Abu Hurairah (Radhiyallaho anho) narrated, from Rasulullah (Sallallaho alaihe wasallam) that a person lying on the roof of his house was looking at the sky and stars for some time, and then said, "I swear by Allah and I believe there is somebody who has created you all; O Allah! forgive me for my sins." Thereupon Allah's mercy turned towards him and he was forgiven. Hadhrat Ibn Abbas (Radhiyallaho anho) said that meditation for a short duration of time is better than worshipping throughout the night. Similarly, Hadhrat Anas, (Radhiyallaho anho) narrated that meditation over the creations of Allah is better than doing worship for eighty years. Somebody asked Hadhrat Umme Darda (Radhiyallaho anha) as to what had been the best kind of worship done by her husband, Hadhrat Abu Darda (Radhiyallaho anho). She replied it was meditation and contemplation. According to Abu Hurairah (Radhiyallaho anho) Rasulullah (Sallallaho alaihe wasallam) had said that meditation and contemplation for a short duration of time is better than worship for sixty years. It should not be deduced from the various quotations given above that meditation obviates the necessity of worship. If anybody neglects any form of worship, he is liable to the same penalty and punishment, as for a fardh or waajib if a fardh or waajib is abandoned, and so for a sunnat or mustahab if any of these is neglected.

Imam Ghazaali (Rahmatullah alaih) has written that meditation is held to be superior to zikr because, in addition to the essence of zikr, it includes two additional things, of which one is recognition of Allah, for which meditation is said to be the key, and secondly the love of Allah, which is induced by deep thinking. It is this meditation, which the Sufis call 'muraaqabah', and the virtue of which is narrated in many ahaadith.

Hadhrat Aa'ishah (Radhiyallaho anha) reported that Rasulullah (Sallallaho alaihe wasallam) had said silent zikr, which is not heard even by the angels, is rewarded seventy times over. When, on the Day of Resurrection, Allah will summon all the creation for reckoning, and the recording angels will bring the recorded accounts of all the people, Allah will ask them to verify if there is any more good deed to the credit of a certain individual. They will submit that they had not omitted anything from his recorded account. Allah will then say, there is yet one good to his credit, which is not known to the angels, and it is his zikr in silence. Baihaqi (Rahmatullah alaih) has quoted on the authority of Hadhrat Aa'ishah (Radhiyallaho anha) that the zikr that is not heard even by the angels is seventy times superior to the zikr that is heard by them. The following Persian couplet refers to the same thing:

میانِ عاشق و معشوق رمزے است
کراماً کاتبیں را ہم خبر نیست

Between the lover and the beloved, there is a code of communication that is not known even to the reporting angels.

How fortunate are the people who do not remain idle from zikr even for a moment. In addition to the reward that they will get for their outward prayers, their zikr and meditation throughout their life will earn for them seventy times extra reward. It is for this reason that the devil remains worried.

Hadhrat Junaid (Rahmatullah alaih) is stated to have seen Satan stark naked in a dream. He asked him whether he did not feel ashamed of the men around him. "Are these men?" replied the devil, "The men are those who are sitting in the mosque of Shonezia, who have worried me so much that my body has become lean and thin, and my heart is burnt." Hadhrat Junaid (Rahamatullah alaih) writes that he went to the mosque of Shonezia and saw that a few men sitting there were deeply absorbed in meditation. When they saw Hadhrat Junaid (Rahamatullah alaih) they told him not to be misled by the deceptive words of the wicked Satan. Similar to this, Masoohi (Rahmatullah alaih) has also written about a dream. On seeing Satan in naked condition, he asked him whether he did not feel ashamed of being naked in the midst of men. The Satan replied, "By

God! if they were men, I would not have toyed with them as do the boys with their playball. Real men are those who made me ill'', and he pointed to the group of Sufis. Abu Sa'eed Khazzaar (Rahmatullah alaih) also states that he once saw in a dream that Satan attacked him and he tried to beat him back with a stick, but the Satan did not care for this beating. Then he heard a heavenly voice saying that the devil is not scared away by the beating, he is only frightened by the spiritual light in one's heart.

Hadhrat Sa'od (Radhiyallaho anho) quoted Rasulullah (Sallallaho alaihe wasallam) to have said, "The best zikr is the silent one, and the best livelihood is that which just suffices'', (i.e. it should neither be too insufficient to make both ends meet, nor too abundant as to drive one to vanity and vice). In another hadith, Rasulullah (Sallallaho alaihe wasallam) is reported to have said, "Remember Allah through perfect zikr''. When somebody enquired; "What is perfect zikr.'' He replied, "Silent zikr.'' All the above quoted narrations establish the excellence of zikr in silence. We have also read the hadith that favours loud zikr, as of a mad man. Either form of zikr is important under different sets of conditions. It is for the Shaikh (religious guide) of a person to prescribe the best form of zikr for him at a particular time.

Hadith No. 18

(١٨) عَنْ عَبْدِ الرَّحْمٰنِ بْنِ سَهْلِ بْنِ حُنَيْفٍ قَالَ نَزَلَتْ عَلٰى رَسُوْلِ اللهِ ﷺ وَهُوَ فِيْ بَعْضِ اَبْيَاتِهِ وَاصْبِرْ نَفْسَكَ مَعَ الَّذِيْنَ يَدْعُوْنَ رَبَّهُمْ بِالْغَدٰوةِ وَالْعَشِيِّ فَخَرَجَ يَلْتَمِسُهُمْ فَوَجَدَ قَوْمًا يَّذْكُرُوْنَ اللهَ فِيْهِمْ ثَائِرُ الرَّاْسِ وَجَافُّ الْجِلْدِ وَذُوْا الثَّوْبِ الْوَاحِدِ فَلَمَّا رَاٰهُمْ جَلَسَ مَعَهُمْ وَقَالَ اَلْحَمْدُ لِلّٰهِ الَّذِيْ جَعَلَ فِيْ اُمَّتِيْ مَنْ اَمَرَنِيْ اَنْ اَصْبِرَ نَفْسِيْ مَعَهُمْ أخرجه ابن جرير والطبراني وابن مردويه كذا في الدر

Rasulullah (Sallallaho alaihe wasallam) was in his house when the verse

وَاصْبِرْ نَفْسَكَ مَعَ الَّذِيْنَ يَدْعُوْنَ رَبَّهُمْ بِالْغَدٰوةِ وَالْعَشِيِّ

Keep yourself bound to the company of those who invoke their Lord, morning and evening

was revealed to him. On this revelation, he went out in

search of such people; he found a group of men who were engaged in zikr. Some of them were with dishevelled hair, parched skins, and clad in a single cloth i.e. except for the loin cloth, the whole body was naked. On seeing them, Rasulullah (Sallallaho alaihe wasallam) sat down by them and said, "All praise is for Allah who has created in my ummah such people that I have been ordered to sit in their company."

According to another hadith, Rasulullah (Sallallaho alaihe wasallam) went out in search of them and found them in the farthest part of the mosque, where they were busy in zikr of Almighty Allah. He said, "All praise is for Allah Who has created, during my lifetime, such people that I have been ordered to sit with them." Then he continued, "My life and death is with you" (i.e. You are my companions in life and death.) It is mentioned in one hadith that a group of Sahabah, including Hadhrat Salmaan Faarsi (Radhiyallaho anho) were engaged in zikr of Allah, when Rasulullah (Sallallaho alaihe wasallam) came to them. They became all silent. In reply to his enquiry as to what they were doing, they submitted that they were practising zikr of Allah. Rasulullah (Sallallaho alaihe wasallam) said, "I saw that the mercy of Allah was descending upon you, and so I desired that I should join your company. Alhamdu lillah (All praise is for Allah)" he then continued, "Almighty Allah has raised such people in my ummah that He ordered me to sit in their company."

It is from such orders of Almighty Allah that the Sufis have deduced that the Shaikh should also sit with his disciples. In addition to the benefit, that will thereby accrue to the disciples, it will provide good excercise for the person of the Shaikh. In the effort to tolerate the vulgarities of the uncivilized and uninitiated people, his ego will undergo severe strain, and thereby he will develop humbleness in him. In addition to this, the get-together of the hearts is important for attracting the mercy and grace of Almighty Allah. It was for this reason that offering prayers in congregation was started, and this is why all the pilgrims (in uniform appearance) are made to pray to Allah together at the same time, in the valley of Arafat. This point has been repeatedly and specially stressed by Shah Waliullah (Rahmatullah alaih) in his book, Hujjatullaahil Baalighah.

All these virtues, as mentioned in many ahaadith, relate to the group of people who are engaged in zikr. On the other hand, if somehow one happens to be in a group of the negligent, and even there he keeps busy with zikr of Allah, great reward is also promised for him, as stated in many ahaadith. On such occasions, it is all the more necessary that one should remain absorbed in remembrance of Allah, so that he is immune from the evil effect of such company.

According to one hadith, a person who remains engaged in zikr, while in the company of the negligent is like one who remains steadfast in his allotted position in a jihaad (holy war), while his companions are fleeing for their lives. In another hadith, he is like one who fights the infidels single-handed, after his companions have fled away. He is also likened to a lamp in a dark house or a beautiful green tree in autumn, when all the trees have shed their leaves. Almighty Allah will show him beforehand his abode in the Paradise; all his sins, even if equal to the number of all men and animals, will be forgiven. All these rewards are subject to the condition that one remains engaged in zikr while in the company of the negligent; otherwise it is forbidden even to join in such meetings.

According to one hadith, one should keep away from those so-called friendly gatherings where there is nothing but idle talk and merrymaking. A pious man once took his negro maid-servant to the bazaar. He left her at a place and asked her to await for his return there; went about the market. When he returned, he was upset to find her missing. He went home, when he found the maid-servant was already there. She came to him and said, 'O Master! do not be angry with me in the haste; you left me in the midst of people who were absolutely negligent in the remembrance of Allah; I feared lest some calamity should befall them, or the Earth should devour them, and I too be buried along with them."

Hadith No. 19

(١٩) عَنْ اَبِيْ هُرَيْرَةَ رَضِىَ اللهُ عَنْهُ قَالَ قَالَ رَسُوْلُ اللهِ ﷺ فِيْمَا يَذْكُرُ عَنْ رَبِّهٖ تَبَارَكَ وَتَعَالٰى اُذْكُرْنِيْ بَعْدَ الْعَصْرِ وَبَعْدَ الْفَجْرِ سَاعَةً اَكْفِكَ فِيْمَا بَيْنَهُمَا أخرجه أحمد كذا في الدر

Rasulullah (Sallallaho alaihe wasallam) said that Almighty Allah says, "Do My zikr for some time after

Fajr salaat and after Asr salaat, and I will suffice for you during the intervening periods."

In one hadith it is stated, "Do zikr of Allah, He will look after your interests."

Note:

We work so hard for this worldly life, though not for the life Hereafter. We lose nothing if we remember Allah for a little while after Fajr and after Asr, because so many virtues have been mentioned for doing zikr at these two times. When Almighty Allah prómises His full help, what more is needed?

According to one hadith, Rasulullah (Sallallaho alaihe wasallam) has said, "I prefer sitting with those who remain busy in remembering Allah after Fajr prayer up to sunrise, to the noble act of setting four Arab slaves free; and similarly I prefer sitting with the group who remain busy in zikr of Allah after Asr salaat up to sunset to setting four slaves free." According to another hadith, if a person offers Fajr salaat in congregation and remains engaged in zikr of Allah until sunrise, and then offers two rakaats of nafl salaat, his reward will equal to that of a perfect Hajj and Umrah. Rasulullah (Sallallaho alaihe wasallam) is also stated to have said, "offering Fajr salaat in congregation, and then remaining busy in zikr until sunrise, is more precious to me than this world and all that it contains. Similarly, remaining busy in zikr with a group after Asr till sunset is preferred by me to this world and everything that it contains." It is for this reason that the time after Fajr and Asr prayers is specially reserved for zikr as a matter of routine by the Sufis. Especially, the time after Fajr prayer is also reserved for zikr, even by the Fuqahaa i.e. the Muslim jurists.

It is stated in the book 'Mudawwanah' on the authority of Imaam Maalik (Rahmatullah alaih) that it is makrooh (undesirable) to indulge in talking during the time between Fajr and sunrise. From amongst the Hanafees the author of Durrul Mukhtaar also regarded it undesirable to indulge in talking during this time. According to one hadith, if after Fajr prayer a person continues to sit in the same posture before talking, recites the following kalimah ten times, ten virtues will be recorded to his account, ten sins remitted, his position in Paradise raised by ten degrees, and he will be protected from the Devil and other undesirables throughout the day.

لَا اِلٰهَ اِلَّا اللّٰهُ وَحْدَهُ لَاشَرِيْكَ لَهُ لَهُ الْمُلْكُ وَلَهُ الْحَمْدُ يُحْيِ وَيُمِيْتُ وَهُوَ عَلٰى كُلِّ شَيْءٍ قَدِيْرٌ

Nobody is worthy of worship except Allah; He is one, and He has no partner. This world and the Hereafter belong to Him and He is worthy of all praise; life and death are controlled by Him, and He controls the destiny of everything.

According to another hadith, whosoever, after Fajr and Asr, recites three times the following prayer:

اَسْتَغْفِرُ اللّٰهَ الَّذِيْ لَا اِلٰهَ اِلَّا هُوَ الْحَيُّ الْقَيُّوْمُ وَاَتُوْبُ اِلَيْهِ

I seek pardon of Allah, except whom there is nobody worthy of worship and Who is living and eternal; I turn to Him.

All his sins, even if big like the sea, will be forgiven.

Hadith No. 20

(٢٠) عَنْ اَبِيْ هُرَيْرَةَ رَضِيَ اللّٰهُ عَنْهُ قَالَ سَمِعْتُ رَسُوْلَ اللّٰهِ ﷺ الدُّنْيَا مَلْعُوْنَةٌ وَمَلْعُوْنٌ مَافِيْهَا اِلَّا ذِكْرُ اللّٰهِ وَمَا وَالَاهُ وَعَالِمًا وَمُتَعَلِّمًا رواه الترمذي وابن ماجه والبيهقي وقال الترمذي حديث حسن كذا في الترغيب وذكره في الجامع الصغير برواية ابن ماجه ورقم له بالحسن وذكره في مجمع الزوائد برواية الطبراني في الأوسط عن ابن مسعود وكذا السيوطى في الجامع الصغير وذكره برواية البزار عن ابن مسعود بلفظ إِلَّا اَمْراً بِمَعْرُوْفٍ اَوْ نَهْيًا عَنْ مُنْكَرٍ اَوْ ذِكْرَ اللّٰهِ رقم له بالصحة

Rasulullah (Sallallaho alaihe wasallam) has said, "The world and all it contents, are accursed (i.e. are devoid of Allah's mercy), except the folowing three:

(1) zikr of Allah and everything that is near it,

(2) the (Religious) aalim, and,

(3) the student (the seeker of religious knowledge)."

The first may mean either the things near to zikr of

Allah, in which case all the things that are helpful in doing zikr, such as eating and drinking in reasonable quantities, and all other necessities of life, as also all forms of worship are implied therein; or it may mean the things near to Allah, in which case it will mean all forms of worship of Allah, and the zikr would mean special form of zikr. In both cases, 'ilm is included therein, because in the first case, it is 'ilm that leads one to zikr, and whereas an ignorant man cannot recognize Allah and in the second case because 'ilm (i.e. religious knowledge) is the best form of worship. In spite of this, the 'aalim and the student have been specially mentioned separately for emphasis. 'ilm, indeed, is a great wealth.

According to one hadith, "Learning 'ilm just for the pleasure of Allah is a proof of the fear of Allah, travelling in search of it is a worship, memorizing it is like glorifying Allah, making research in it is like jihaad, reading it is like charity, and teaching it to one's members of family promotes nearness to Allah. This is because 'ilm enables one to distinguish between right and wrong; it is the road sign indicating the way to Paradise; it provides consolation in wilderness and a companion while travelling, because reading a book serves this dual purpose. Further, it is like a companion to talk to in solitude, a guide during pain and pleasure, and a weapon for friends against foes. Because of this, Almighty Allah raises the position of Ulama, because they propagate the right, provide a lead for others, so that with their deeds, and their advice be sought and acted upon in all matters. The angels love to befriend them, and rub their wings over them to be blessed or to show love. All things, whether of land or in sea, including fish in the sea, beasts of the jungle, animals and even poisonous insects and reptiles like the snakes, pray for their forgiveness. All this is because 'ilm is a light for the heart as well as for the eyes; it urges one to be one of the best personalities of the ummat, and enables one to attain high position in this life as also in the Hereafter. Its study is as virtuous as fasting, and its memorising is like offering Tahajjud prayer. It promotes good relations; and it helps distinguish between right and wrong; it is a prerequisite for good deeds and controls them. The blessed are inspired by it and the accursed are deprived of it."

Though some authorities have questioned the overall authenticity of this hadith, yet the virtues mentioned herein are by parts corroborated by many other ahaadith. In fact, many additional virtues are mentioned in the books of ahaadith, let alone the foregoing accounting for the specific mention of the 'aalim' and the student in the fore-mentioned hadith.

Hafiz Ibn Qayyim (Rahmatullah alaih), a well-known muhaddith, has written an authentic book, named 'al-Waabilus Sayyib', on the virtues of zikr. He has stated therein that the virtues of zikr are more than one hundred and he has listed seventy nine of these, which are briefly given below in the same order. Some of these include multiple benefits, and for this reason their actual number is more than one hundred:

(1) Zikr keeps away the Satan and weakens his strength.

(2) It is the cause of Almighty Allah's pleasure.

(3) It relieves the mind of anxieties and worries.

(4) It produces joy and happiness in the heart.

(5) It strengthens the body and the mind.

(6) It brightens the face and the heart.

(7) It attracts one's sustenance.

(8) It invests the zaakirs with awe and sweetness so that the seeing eye is filled with awe and pleasure at his sight.

(9) It induces love for Allah, which in fact is the spirit of Islaam and the pivot of deen, and the source of success and salvation in the Hereafter. He who seeks access to the love of Almighty Allah should do zikr profusely. Just as reading and repetition is the door of knowledge, so zikr of Allah is the gateway to His love.

(10) Zikr involves muraaqabah (deep meditation), through which one reaches the stage of Ihsaan, wherein a person worships Almighty Allah as if he is actually seeing Him. (The attainment of this stage of Ihsaan is the ultimate objective of the Sufis).

(11) It helps realization of Allah so that by and by a stage is reached when he comes to regard

Almighty Allah as his sole Cherisher, Guardian and Master, and he turns unto Him, in all afflictions.

(12) It is the key to nearness to Almighty Allah; the greater the zikr, the greater the nearness to Allah, and greater the indifference to zikr, the greater the distance from Him.

(13) It opens the door of Ma'rifat (realization) of Allah.

(14) It makes one realize the greatness and grandeur of Almighty Allah, and strengthens the consciousness of his omni-presence.

(15) Zikr of Allah causes one's mention in the Court of Allah, as said in the Holy Book.

فَاذْكُرُوْنِىْ اَذْكُرْكُمْ

Remember me, and I will remember you,
and as stated in a hadith

مَنْ ذَكَرَنِىْ فِىْ نَفْسِهٖ ذَكَرْتُهٗ فِىْ نَفْسِىْ – الحديث

Whosoever remembers me in his heart, I remember him in My heart.

It has already been explained under other verses and ahaadith that, even if there were no other good points in zikr, except that mentioned above, this alone would have established its superiority over others. Nevertheless, there are many more virtues and benefits of zikr.

(16) It gives life to the heart. Hafiz Ibn Taimiyah (Rahmatullah alaih) says that zikr is as necessary for the heart as water for the fish. Imagine the condition of a fish out of water.

(17) It is food for the heart and the soul; depriving them of zikr is like depriving the body of its food.

(18) It cleanses the heart of its rust. It has been mentioned in an earlier hadith; everything rusts according to its nature; and the heart rusts with wordly desires and indifference, to purify it zikr is necessary.

(19) It safeguards against pitfalls and lapses.

(20) The heart of a neglectful person is tormented by a feeling of remoteness from Allah, and nothing other than zikr can rid the heart of this feeling.

(21) The words of zikr keep on moving round the Arsh of Almighty Allah, as stated in a hadith.

(22) If one remembers Allah in happiness, Almighty Allah remembers him in his afflictions.

(23) It is a means to deliverance from Allah's punishment.

(24) It causes Allah's peace and mercy to descend, while angels surround the person engaged in zikr.

(25) It saves the tongue from indulging in backbiting, loose talk, lies and abuses. It is a common experience that a man whose tongue remains engaged in zikr does not commit these absurdities. On the other hand, the tongue that is not used in zikr, falls an easy prey to all kinds of useless talk.

(26) The gatherings of zikr are gathering of angels, and gatherings without zikr are gatherings of Satan. A person is free to have a choice between the two, and verily man, by instinct, is drawn towards what is akin to his temperament.

(27) By virtue of zikr, the zaakir is blessed, as also the person sitting by him. Similarly the indolent person is accursed for his indolence, as also the person sitting by him.

(28) Zikr will save one from despair on the Day of Judgement. This is confirmed by one of the ahaadith which says that the gathering devoid of Allah's zikr will cause sorrow and losses on that day.

(29) If zikr is shared by tears and repentance in loneliness the zaakir will be blessed under the shadow of Allah's throne on the Day of Judgement, when hearts will jump to lips due to agony of intolerable heat of that day.

(30) Those who remain busy in zikr are better rewarded by Allah than those who remain busy in

du'aa and supplication. According to one hadith, Almighty Allah says that I will give better reward to one who is abstained by his engagements in zikr from making du'aa than all those who find time for making du'aa.

(31) In spite of the fact that zikr is the easiest form of worship (the movement of the tongue being easier than the movement of any other party of the body), yet it is the most virtuous form.

(32) Allah's zikr helps the plants of Paradise to grow.

(33) Of all actions the reward and forgiveness promised for zikr is the highest. According to one hadith if on any day a person repeats one hundred times the kalimah:

لَآ اِلٰهَ اِلَّا اللّٰهُ وَحْدَهُ لَاشَرِيْكَ لَهُ لَهُ الْمُلْكُ وَلَهُ الْحَمْدُ وَهُوَ عَلٰى كُلِّ شَيْءٍ قَدِيْرٌ

There is none worthy of worship except Allah, the One. There is no partner with Him; His is the kingdom, and for Him is all praise, and He is All-powerful to do everything,

he is rewarded as for freeing ten slaves, and in addition one hundred virtues are written to his account and one hundred sins are forgiven. He remains protected against the devil throughout the day, and none is considered as having acted better than him except one who has recited these words more often than him. Similarly, there are many other ahaadith proclaming the superiority of zikr over all other good deeds.

(34) Due to incessant zikr one is able not to forget one's soul. Forgetting one's soul leads to failure in both the worlds, because forgetting the remembrance of Allah leads to neglecting one's soul and all its best interests. Allah says in His book:

وَلَاتَكُوْنُوْا كَالَّذِيْنَ نَسُوْا اللّٰهَ فَاَنْسَاهُمْ اَنْفُسَهُمْ اُوْلٰئِكَ هُمُ الْفَاسِقُوْنَ (حشر ع٣)

And be not ye as those who forgot Allah and therefore He caused them to forget their souls. Such are the evil-doers.

Thus, when one forgets one's soul he becomes

careless and forgets his real interests which leads to his ruin just as a garden or field is invariably ruined when its owner fails to look after it. Protection against this ruin can only be provided by keeping one's tongue always busy in zikr, so that zikr should become as indispensable as water is at the extreme thirst, or food at the time of hunger, or the house and clothes for protection against extreme heat and cold. As a matter of fact, one should be more mindful of zikr than any of these material necessities, which at the most can result in physical death, which is a small loss as compared with the spiritual death.

(35) Zikr is the source of one's spiritual elevation whether done in bed or in the market, whether in good health or in sickness, or even when one is making most of the pleasures of life. Nothing but zikr can take a man to such spiritual heights, whereby his heart is so illuminated with the light of zikr that even asleep he is more wakeful than the neglectful person who is awake all through the night.

(36) The noor (radiance) of zikr remains with a person in his life as well as in his grave. It will go in front of him on the Siraat in the Hereafter. Almighty Allah says in the Quran:

اَوَ مَنْ كَانَ مَيْتًا فَاَحْيَيْنَاهُ وَجَعَلْنَا لَهُ نُوْرًا يَمْشِيْ بِهِ فِيْ النَّاسِ كَمَنْ مَّثَلُهُ فِى الظُّلُمٰتِ لَيْسَ بِخَارِجٍ مِنْهَا

Can he who was dead and whom We gave life, and a light whereby he can walk among men, be like him who is in utter darkness whence he cannot emerge.

The one mentioned first is the faithful, who believes in Allah and shines with the light of His love, zikr, and cognizance, while the second one is devoid of all these virtues. In reality this radiance is a great blessing and leads to perfect success. That is why Rasulullah (Sallallaho alaihe wasallam) used to beg for it in prolonged prayers, and prayed for noor for every part of his body. As mentioned in many ahaadith Rasulullah (Sallallaho alaihe wasallam) prayed that Almighty Allah may bless his flesh, bones, muscles, hair, skin, eyes and ears with noor, and that he may be surrounded with noor on all sides; he even prayed that he may be blessed with noor from top to bottom, and that his whole person may be made into noor. One's deeds will shine according to the noor in oneself, so much so that the good deeds of some people (while going upto heaven) will shine like the sun. Similar noor will be found in their faces on the Day of Judgement.

(37) Zikr is the basic principle of Tasawwuf (Sufism) and is invoked in all the schools of Sufism. A person who gets conversant with zikr enters the gateway to Almighty Allah, and one who enters this gateway is sure to reach Almighty Allah, from Whom he will get whatever he wants, for Allah's treasures are unlimited.

(38) There is not a corner in the heart of a man, which can not be filled but with zikr. When zikr controls the heart, not only does it fill up this corner, but also does it lead the zaakir to contentment which wealth would fail to produce and to respect among people, which the family or party would fail to bring about, and to such control over people as a sovereign would never dream of. On the other hand, the indolent comes to disgrace, in spite of all his wealth and riches, party, strength and powers.

(39) Zikr transform dispersion into concentration, and concentration into dispersion; and remoteness into nearness and nearness into remoteness. This means that one is relieved of one's troubles, worries and fears, and is blessed with peace of mind. His mistakes and sins are forgiven, and the devils who are after him are dispersed away. It makes him to remember that the Hereafter is not far away, and the worldly life has little attraction for him.

(40) Zikr does not allow one's heart to suffer from forgetfulness, which leads to ignore one's ultimate interest.

(41) Zikr is just like a tree, the fruit of which is realization of Almighty Allah. The more zikr is done, the stronger shall grow the root of this tree; and stronger the root of this tree, the more abundant the fruit it will bear.

(42) Zikr of Almighty Allah promotes nearness to Him and thereby earns His constant patronage. It is given in the Quran

اِنَّ اللّٰهَ مَعَ الَّذِيْنَ اتَّقَوْا

No doubt Allah is with those who fear Him.

It is stated in one hadith

اَنَا مَعَ عَبْدِيْ مَاذَكَرَنِيْ

I am with my slave who remembers Me.

According to another hadith, Allah says, "Those who remember Me are My men, and I do not deprive them of My mercy. When they repent, I am their friend, but when they do not repent. I am their physician. I put them to worries to condone their sins." Nearness to Almighty Allah resulting from zikr has no parallel. No words and no writing can describe this nearness. Its taste is known only to those who are blessed with it. (May Almighty Allah also bless me with the same).

(43) Zikr of Allah is as meritorious as liberating of slaves, and spending in charity, and jihaad in the path of Allah.
(Many virtues of this kind have already been described and more will further be narrated in this book).

(44) Zikr is the fundamental form of thanksgiving to Almighty Allah. One who does not do zikr cannot thank him. It is stated in hadith that Hadhrat Moosa (Alayhis salaam) had asked Almighty Allah "O My Lord! You have done me countless favours, teach me the manner in which I should thank you befittingly." Almighty Allah said, "The more zikr you do, the more thanks you offer." According to another hadith, Hadhrat Moosa (Alayhis salaam) is reported to have said, "O, Lord! how can I offer

thanks worthy of Your greatness." Almighty Allah replied, "Let your tongue always remain engaged in zikr."

(45) According to Almighty Allah, the best of the pious people are those who always remain busy in zikr, because piety leads to paradise, and zikr to the nearness to Allah.

(46) There is a sort of hardness in the human heart, which is not softened by anything except zikr.

(47) In fact, zikr is a remedy for all ills of the heart.

(48) Zikr of Allah is the root of His love, and neglecting zikr is the root of His enmity.

(49) Nothing is more effective than zikr in attracting Allah's blessings and in warding off His chastisement.

(50) Almighty Allah grants His grace to those who do zikr, and the angels pray for them.

(51) One who wants to remain in the gardens of Paradise, even in this life, should sit in the gatherings of zikr, because these are likened to the gardens of Paradise.

(52) Gatherings of zikr are also the gatherings of angels.

(53) In the presence of the angels, Almighty Allah praises those who do zikr.

(54) One who is constant in doing zikr will enter Paradise in high spirits.

(55) All good deeds have been ordained because of zikr.

(56) A good deed becomes superior to others of its kind because of zikr. Of the fasts, the one with more zikr is the best; Of the Hajj, one with excessive zikr is more virtuous. Similar is the case with other good deeds like jihaad etc:

(57) Zikr is a substitute of nafl salaat and other non-obligatory devotions. It is related in one hadith that the poor people once complained to Rasulullah (Sallallaho alaihe wasallam) of the higher reward available to the rich because of their

wealth. They said, "These rich men offer prayers and fast, just as we do, but they excel us by performing Umrah and Hajj, and taking part in jihaad on account of their wealth." Rasulullah (Sallallaho alaihe wasallam) replied, "Should I tell you something, so that none except one who practices it can excel you." He then advised them to recite after every salaat:

سُبْحَانَ اللّٰهِ اَلْحَمْدُ لِلّٰهِ اَللّٰهُ اَكْبَرُ

By this Rasulullah (Sallallaho alaihe wasallam) had indicated the importance of zikr, to be the substitute for various kinds of worship, like Umrah, Hajj, jihaad, etc.

(58) Zikr is very helpful to all other forms of worship. Excessive zikr creates love for various forms of worship, so that one starts taking delight in their performance and never feels bored or burdened while offering them.

(59) Zikr is a solution to all difficulties, and remedy for all handicaps. It lightens every burden, and relieves every affliction.

(60) Zikr dispels every fear of the heart. It has a special hand in inducing peace of mind and for relieving the heart of its fear. To free the heart of its fears and mind of its perplexity is one of the specific qualities of zikr. The greater, therefore, the amount of zikr, the greater freedom from fear.

(61) By zikr one is blessed with divine help that associates in all one's doings. That is why some time man's achievements surpass his powers, and he attains what was seemingly beyond his reach. This is perhaps the reason why Rasulullah (Sallallaho alaihe wasallam) advised his daughter Hadhrat Fatimah, (Radhiyallaho anha) to recite سُبْحَانَ اللّٰهِ اَلْحَمْدُ لِلّٰهِ thirty three times each and اَللّٰهُ اَكْبَرُ thirty four times before going to bed at night, when she approached him for a helper, complaining that she was over-worked by the labour of grinding wheat and doing other house-hold jobs. The Prophet

(Sallallaho alaihe wasallam) further said, "The recitation of these kalimahs is better for you than a servant."

(62) Those who are working for the life Hereafter are in a race, wherein the zaakirs shall remain ahead of all on account of their zikr. On the day of Judgement, says Umar Maula Ghufra (Rahmatullah alaih), when people will be rewarded for their good deeds, many shall repent why they neglected zikr when it was easiest of all good deeds and the highest in reward. In a hadith, Rasulullah (Sallallaho alaihe wasallam) is quoted to have said, "The mufarrideen have surpassed all." He was asked, "Who were the mufarrideen?" The Prophet (Sallallaho alaihe wasallam) replied, "Those who toil hard for zikr because it lightens their burdens."

(63) Those who do zikr are held truthful by Almighty Allah, and those who are testified as such by Almighty Allah cannot be raised among the liars on the Day of Judgement. It is quoted on the authority of Prophet (Sallallaho alaihe wasallam) that when a man utters,

لَآ اِلٰهَ اِلَّا اللّٰهُ وَاللّٰهُ اَكْبَرُ

Allah proclaims, "My slave has spoken the truth, and nobody is worthy of worship except I, and I am the Greatest of all."

(64) Zikr causes houses to be built in Paradise by the angels. When zikr is stopped, the angels also stop construction of houses. When asked why a particular construction was stopped by the angels, they reply, "The construction had to be stopped because funds for that were stopped. The fact is confirmed by a hadith, which says when a man recites سُبْحَانَ اللّٰهِ وَبِحَمْدِهٖ سُبْحَانَ اللّٰهِ الْعَظِيْمِ seven times, a tower is raised for him in Paradise.

(65) Zikr provides protection against Hell. If, due to any misdeed a zaakir deserves Hell, his zikr acts as a defence between him and the Hell, the more his zikr, the stronger will be this defence.

(66) The angels pray for the forgiveness of those who do

zikr. It is related on the authority of Hadhrat Amr bin Aas (Radhiyallaho anho) that when a man says سُبْحَانَ اللهِ وَبِحَمْدِهِ اَلْحَمْدُ لِلّٰهِ رَبِّ الْعٰلَمِيْنَ the angels pray to Almighty Allah for his forgiveness.

(67) The mountain or plain on which zikr is recited feels proud of it. According to a hadith, one mountain asks another if any zaakir has crossed over it during the day. If the reply is in the affirmative, it feels happy.

(68) Zikr guarantees immunity from hypocrisy, for Almighty Allah has described the hypocrite as لَا يَذْكُرُوْنَ اللهَ اِلَّا قَلِيْلًا They do not remember Allah except very rarely. It is also related on the authority of Ka'b Ahbaar (Radhiyallaho anho) that he who makes frequent zikr of Allah is free from hypocrisy.

(69) Compared with other good deeds, zikr carries a special taste, which is not to be found in any other action. Even if there were no other virtue to zikr, this fine taste alone would have been a sufficient reward to justify it. Maalik bin Deenaar (Rahmatullah alaih) has said that nothing surpasses the taste of zikr, which is the best and finest.

(70) The faces of those who do zikr remain bright in this life, and will carry a special radiance in the Hereafter.

(71) One who is frequently engaged in zikr, whether he is in or out of his house, whether he is stationary or travelling, he will find, on the Day of Judgement, a large number of witnesses in his favour. Almighty Allah has described the Day of Judgment as يَوْمَئِذٍ تُحَدِّثُ اَخْبَارَهَا The day when the Earth will tell all that it knows.

Rasulullah (Sallallaho alaihe wasallam) asked his companions if they knew what those news would be. They expressed their ignorance. Then Rasulullah (Sallallaho alaihe wasallam) said, "Whatever deed is done, good or bad, by any man or woman on the face of the Earth, the Earth will describe it all, with date, time and place." Hence, one who does zikr at many places will find many witnesses in his favour.

(72) As long as the tongue is busy in zikr, it cannot indulge in lies, backbiting or any other kind of evil talk. The tongue will engage itself in useless talk if it is not in zikr, because it cannot remain quiet. So is the case with the heart; if it is devoid of love for Almighty Allah, it will be filled with the love of worldly things.

(73) The devils are outright enemies of man and always create trouble for him and keep him surrounded. The miserable condition of one who remains surrounded by enemies can well be imagined, especially when the enemies are vindictive and everyone of them wants to surpass the other in troubling him. Nothing except zikr can protect him against these enemies. Many forms of du'aa are mentioned in the ahaadith, so that, if any of these is recited by a person, then Satan dare not come near him. If the same is recited at the time of going to bed, one remains safe from the Satan throughout the night. Hafiz Ibn Qayyim (Rahmatullah alaih) has also mentioned many such du'aas.

In addition to these, the author has also mentioned in detail under six headings the relative merits of zikr as also some of its virtues, which are specific to zikr alone. Then he has also given seventy five chapters on special du'aas, which are suited to specific times and occasions. For the sake of brevity, these have been excluded from this book. For those blessed with determination to act, the virtues of zikr detailed above are more than enough, and for those who are disinclined to act, thousands of such virtues would be of little avail.

وَمَا تَوْفِيْقِىْ اِلَّا بِاللهِ عَلَيْهِ تَوَكَّلْتُ وَاِلَيْهِ اُنِيْبُ

Whatever good I have done is through the grace of Almighty Allah; I, therefore, depend on Him and turn to Him.

CHAPTER II

KALIMAH TAYYIBAH

Kalimah Tayyibah, which is also called Kalimah Tauheed (utterance of Unity), has been mentioned in the Qur'an and the hadith far more frequently than anything else. Since all the saints and Prophets had been sent specifically with the primary aim of propagating the Unity of Allah, its excessive mention can well be understood. In the Holy Qur'an, this kalimah has been referred to by various names and in different contexts. It has been referred to as Kalimah Tayyibah (excellent utterance), (قول ثابت) (firm statement) (كلمة التقوى) (utterance of piety), (مَقَالِيْدُ السَّمٰوٰتِ وَالْأَرْضِ) (key of heaven and earth), etc; as will be found in the Qur'anic verses given in the following pages. Imaam Ghazaali (Rahmatullah alaih) has written in his book Ihyaa that it is (كلمة التوحيد) (utterance of Unity) (كلمة اخلاص) (utterance of sincerity) (كلمة التقوى) (utterance of piety) (كلمة طيّبة) (excellent utterance) (عُروة الوثقى) (strong rope) (دَعوة الحق) (call of truth) (ثمن الجنة) (price of paradise).

As this kalimah has been mentioned in various contexts in the Holy Qur'an, this chapter is divided into three parts. The first part includes those verses wherein the words of Kalimah Tayyibah do not occur, although it is implied therein. Each verse is followed by a brief explanation, as given by the Sahabah and by Rasulullah (Sallallaho alaihe wasallam) himself.

The second part consists of those verses which contain the text of Kalimah Tayyibah i.e. لَآاِلٰهَ اِلَّا اللّٰه in full, or slightly modified, such as لَآاِلٰهَ اِلَّا هُوَ. As the words of the kalimah occur in these verses, their translation has not been considered necessary. Only the surah and ruku, in which the ayat occurs, has been indicated. The third part includes the translation and explanation of those ahaadith that describe the virtues and importance of this kalimah

وَمَا تَوْفِيْقِىْ اِلَّا بِاللّٰهِ

(Whatever has been done is merely through Allah's grace).

PART I

This contains those ayaat in which the words of the Kalimah Tayyibah do not occur, although it is implied therein:

(١) اَلَمْ تَرَ كَيْفَ ضَرَبَ اللهُ مَثَلًا كَلِمَةً طَيِّبَةً كَشَجَرَةٍ طَيِّبَةٍ اَصْلُهَا ثَابِتٌ وَفَرْعُهَا فِي السَّمَاءِ ، تُؤْتِىْ اُكُلَهَا كُلَّ حِيْنٍ بِاِذْنِ رَبِّهَا وَيَضْرِبُ اللهُ الْاَمْثَالَ لِلنَّاسِ لَعَلَّهُمْ يَتَذَكَّرُوْنَ ، وَمَثَلُ كَلِمَةٍ خَبِيْثَةٍ كَشَجَرَةٍ خَبِيْثَةِ اجْتُثَّتْ مِنْ فَوْقِ الْاَرْضِ مَالَهَا مِنْ قَرَارٍ (ابراهيم – ع٤)

(1) Seest thou not how Allah explains through a parable. Good words are like a good tree that is firmly rooted and its branches reach the sky. It brings fruit at all times, under order from its Lord. So Allah explains through parables for men that they may take heed. The parable of evil words is like an evil tree. It is torn up by the root from the surface of the Earth. It has no stability.

Note:

Hadhrat Ibn Abbas (Radhiyallaho anho) has explained that the words "Kalimah Tayyibah" in this ayat mean the Kalimah Shahaadat

اَشْهَدُ اَنْ لَا اِلٰهَ اِلَّا اللهُ

which is like a tree with its roots in the hearts of the faithful and its branches spread out up to Heaven, by means of which the deeds of the faithful climb up to Heaven; and كلمة خبيثة (ugly utterance) is the utterance of Shirk, which prevents any good deed from being accepted. In another hadith, it is stated by Ibn Abbas (Radhiyallaho anho) that "bearing of fruit all the time" means that almighty Allah be remembered day and night.

It was narrated by Hadhrat Qataadah (Rahmatullah alaih) that somebody had said to Rasulullah (Sallallaho alaihe wasallam), "The rich are able to earn great rewards (by virtue of spending their wealth in charity)". Rasulullah

(Sallallaho alaihe wasallam) replied, "Tell me if anybody can reach the sky by piling up his goods one over the other. I tell you of something, which has its roots in the Earth and its branches spread out into the Heaven. It is recitation of the kalimah

لَآ اِلٰهَ اِلَّا اللهُ وَاللهُ اَكْبَرُ سُبْحَانَ اللهِ وَالْحَمْدُ لِلّٰهِ

ten times each after every salaat.

(٢) مَنْ كَانَ يُرِيْدُ الْعِزَّةَ فَلِلّٰهِ الْعِزَّةُ جَمِيْعًا ، اِلَيْهِ يَصْعَدُ الْكَلِمُ الطَّيِّبُ وَالْعَمَلُ الصَّالِحُ يَرْفَعُهُ

(2) Whosoever desires glory and power (should know) that glory and all powers belong to Allah; Unto Him good words ascend and He exalts all righteous deeds.

According to the majority of commentators, the Kalimah Tayyibah in this ayat means (لآاِلٰهَ اِلَّا الله), but some are of the opinion that it implies the kalimah of tasbeeh, as will be described in part II.

(٣) وَتَمَّتْ كَلِمَةُ رَبِّكَ صِدْقًا وَّعَدْلًا

(3) The word of thy Lord finds its fulfilment in truth and in justice.

According to Hadhrat Anas (Radhiyallaho anho), Rasulullah (Sallallaho alaihe wasallam) had said that the kalimah of the Lord means the kalimah لآاِلٰهَ اِلَّا الله. But many commentators are of the opinion that it means the Holy Qur'an.

(٤) يُثَبِّتُ اللهُ الَّذِيْنَ آمَنُوْا بِالْقَوْلِ الثَّابِتِ فِي الْحَيَاةِ الدُّنْيَا وَفِي الْآخِرَةِ وَيُضِلُّ اللهُ الظَّالِمِيْنَ ۚ وَيَفْعَلُ اللهُ مَايَشَاءُ (ابراهيم ع٤)

(4) Allah will confirm those who believe in words that stand firm, in this world and in the Hereafter, and Allah sends wrong doers astray. Allah does what He wills.

Hadhrat Baraa (Radhiyallaho anho) stated that Rasulullah (Sallallaho alaihe wasallam) had said, "At the time of interrogation in the grave, a Muslim bears witness to

لَآ اِلٰهَ اِلَّا اللّٰهُ مُحَمَّدٌ رَّسُوْلُ اللّٰهِ

and this is meant by the words (firm statement) in this ayat. Hadhrat Aa'ishah (Radhiyallaho anha) also corroborated that it refers to the interrogation in the grave. Hadhrat Ibn Abbas (Radhiyallaho anho) said, "When a Muslim is about to die, the angels come to him, greet him, and convey the glad tidings of paradise; after his death, they accompany him and join his funeral prayer; and after he is buried, they make him sit up when, in the grave, questioning starts. He replies

اَشْهَدُ اَنْ لَآ اِلٰهَ اِلَّا اللّٰهُ وَاَشْهَدُ اَنَّ مُحَمَّدًا رَّسُوْلُ اللّٰهِ

'I bear witness that there is nobody worthy of worship except Allah, and I bear witness that Muhammad is the messenger of Allah.'

This is what is implied in this ayat."

Hadhrat Abu Qataadah, (Radhiyallaho anho) also said that (قَوْلٌ ثَابِتٌ) (firm statement) refers to the Kalimah Tayyibah in this life, and the interrogation in the grave after death. Hadhrat Taa'oos (Rahmatullah alaih) also gave the same interpretation.

(٥) لَهُ دَعْوَةُ الْحَقِّ ، وَالَّذِيْنَ يَدْعُوْنَ مِنْ دُوْنِهِ لَايَسْتَجِيْبُوْنَ لَهُمْ بِشَيْءٍ اِلَّا كَبَاسِطِ كَفَّيْهِ اِلَى الْمَاءِ لِيَبْلُغَ فَاهُ وَمَا هُوَ بِبَالِغِهِ وَمَا دُعَاءُ الْكَافِرِيْنَ اِلَّا فِيْ ضَلٰلٍ (رعد ع٢)

(5) Unto Him is the real prayer. Those unto whom they pray besides Allah responds to them not at all. They are like those who stretch forth their hands for water to reach their mouths but it reaches them not. The prayer of disbelievers goes astray.

Note: According to Hadhrat Ali (Radhiyallaho anho) as well as Ibn Abbas (Radhiyallaho anho) and many others, the words دعوة الحق (propagation of truth) means this kalimah.

(٦) قُلْ يَآاَهْلَ الْكِتَابِ تَعَالَوْا اِلٰى كَلِمَةٍ سَوَاءٍ بَيْنَنَا وَبَيْنَكُمْ اَلَّا نَعْبُدَ اِلَّا اللّٰهَ وَلَانُشْرِكَ بِهٖ شَيْئًا وَّلَايَتَّخِذَ بَعْضُنَا بَعْضًا اَرْبَابًا مِنْ دُوْنِ اللّٰهِ فَاِنْ تَوَلَّوْا فَقُوْلُوْا اشْهَدُوْا بِاَنَّا مُسْلِمُوْنَ (آل عمران ع٧)

(6) Say: O, people of scriptures! Come to an agreement between us and you; that we shall worship none but Allah and that we shall ascribe no partner unto Him, and none of us shall take others for Lords beside Allah. And if you turn away, bear witness that we (at least) are Muslims.

Note: This sacred ayat is self-explanatory, in that the word kalimah in this ayat implies tauheed and the Kalimah Tayyibah. The same view-point has been categorically confirmed by Hadhrat Abu Aaliyah and Hadhrat Mujahid (Rahmatullah alaihima).

(٧) كُنْتُمْ خَيْرَ أُمَّةٍ أُخْرِجَتْ لِلنَّاسِ تَأْمُرُوْنَ بِالْمَعْرُوْفِ وَتَنْهَوْنَ عَنِ الْمُنْكَرِ وَتُؤْمِنُوْنَ بِاللهِ وَلَوْ آمَنَ اَهْلُ الْكِتَابِ لَكَانَ خَيْرًا لَّهُمْ مِنْهُمُ الْمُؤْمِنُوْنَ وَاَكْثَرُهُمُ الْفَاسِقُوْنَ (آل عمران ع ١٢)

(7) You are the best of people, evolved for mankind, enjoining what is right, forbidding what is wrong, and believing in Allah. If only the people of scriptures had faith, it were best for them; among them are some who have faith; most of them are transgressors.

Note: Hadhrat Ibn Abbas (Radhiyallaho anho) has stated تَأْمُرُوْنَ بِالْمَعْرُوْفِ (i.e. you enjoin the good) means that you enjoin the people to believe in لَاإِلٰهَ إِلَّا الله and obey Almighty Allah; and that this kalimah is by far the best and foremost of all the good things.

(٨) وَاَقِمِ الصَّلَاةَ طَرَفَيِ النَّهَارِ وَزُلَفًا مِّنَ اللَّيْلِ ، اِنَّ الْحَسَنَاتِ يُذْهِبْنَ السَّيِّئَاتِ ، ذٰلِكَ ذِكْرٰى لِلذَّاكِرِيْنَ (هود ع ١٠)

(8) Establish regular prayer at the two ends of the day and at the approaches of the night. Lo! good deeds annul ill deeds. This is a reminder for the mindful.

The explanation of this sacred ayat is to be found in many ahaadith according to which Rasulullah (Sallallaho alaihe wasallam) while refering to this ayat had said that good deeds wipe out the sins from one's account. Hadhrat Abu Zar (Radhiyallaho anho) says that he had once requested Rasulullah (Sallallaho alaihe wasallam) to give him some advice and Rasulullah (Sallallaho alaihe wasallam) replied, "Hold Almighty Allah in constant fear. If perchance you commit any sin, hasten at once to do some virtuous deed so that the sin is atoned, and it is written off." Then Abu Zar (Radhiyallaho anho) continues to say that he asked Rasulullah (Sallallaho alaihe wasallam) if this kalimah لَآاِلٰهَ اِلَّا اللّٰهُ was also counted amongst the virtues. At this, Rasulullah (Sallallaho alaihe wasallam) gave the reply that this kalimah is the highest of all virtues. It is likewise quoted from Hadhrat Anas (Radhiyallaho anho) that Rasulullah (Sallallaho alaihe wasallam) had said "Whosover, any time during the day or night, recites the kalimah لَآاِلٰهَ اِلَّا اللّٰهُ his sins are washed off his account."

(٩) اِنَّ اللّٰهَ يَاْمُرُ بِالْعَدْلِ وَالْاِحْسَانِ وَاِيْتَاءِ ذِي الْقُرْبٰى وَيَنْهٰى عَنِ الْفَحْشَاءِ وَالْمُنْكَرِ وَالْبَغْيِ ، يَعِظُكُمْ لَعَلَّكُمْ تَذَكَّرُوْنَ (نحل – ١٣ع)

(9) (a) Lo! Allah enjoineth justice and kindness and giving to kinsfolk. He forbids shameful deeds, injustice and rebellion. He instructs you in order that you take heed.

There are different versions regarding the interpretation of the word عَدْل (justice). In one version, Hadhrat Abdullah bin Abbas (Radhiyallaho anho) says that عَدْل (justice) means to believe that nobody is worthy of worship except Allah, while اِحْسَان (goodness) means to do one's obligations to Allah.

(١٠) يَاَيُّهَا الَّذِيْنَ آمَنُوْا اتَّقُوْا اللّٰهَ وَقُوْلُوْا قَوْلًا سَدِيْدًا ، يُصْلِحْ لَكُمْ اَعْمَالَكُمْ وَيَغْفِرْلَكُمْ ذُنُوْبَكُمْ وَمَنْ يُّطِعِ اللّٰهَ وَرَسُوْلَهٗ فَقَدْ فَازَ فَوْزًا عَظِيْمًا (احزاب – ٩ع)

(10) O, you who believe! Fear Allah and say words straight to the point, that He may make your conduct sound and forgive your sins. Whosoever obeys Allah and His Prophet (Sallallaho alaihe wasallam), he has attained the highest achievement.

Hadhrat Abdullah bin Abbas and Hadhrat Ikramah (Radhiyallaho anhuma) are both said to have been of the view that the meaning of قُوْلُوْا قَوْلًا سَدِيْدًا (and speak words straight to the right) is to recite the لَآاِلٰهَ اِلَّا اللّٰهُ kalimah. According to one hadith, three things constitute the best of all actions. The first is to do zikr of Allah under all circumstances, in happiness and in grief, in poverty and in affluence; the second is to conduct oneself with impartiality even when one's own interests are involved; and the third is to help one's brother with money.

(١١) فَبَشِّرْ عِبَادِ ، اَلَّذِيْنَ يَسْتَمِعُوْنَ الْقَوْلَ فَيَتَّبِعُوْنَ اَحْسَنَهُ اُولٰئِكَ الَّذِيْنَ هَدَاهُمُ اللّٰهُ وَاُوْلٰئِكَ هُمْ اُوْلُوا الْاَلْبَابِ (زمر ع٦)

(11) Give good tidings to my servants, who hear advice and follow the best thereof. Such are those whom Allah guideth, and such are men of understanding.

Hadhrat Ibn Umar (Radhiyallaho anho) said that Hadhrat Sa'eed bin Zaid, Hadhrat Abu Zar Ghifaari and Hadhrat Salmaan Faarsi (Radhiyallaho anho), all the three, used to recite the kalimah لَآاِلٰهَ اِلَّا اللّٰهُ even before they embraced Islaam, and by the words اَحْسَنَ الْقَوْل (the best utterance) what is exactly meant in this sacred ayat is this kalimah. Hadhrat Zaid bin Aslam (Radhiyallaho anho) had also said that this ayat relates to three persons who used to recite the kalimah لَآاِلٰهَ اِلَّا اللّٰهُ even in their days of ignorance, and they were Hadhrat Zaid bin Amr bin Nufail, Hadhrat Abu Zar Ghifaari and Hadhrat Salmaan Faarsi (Radhiyallaho anhum).

(١٢) وَالَّذِيْ جَآءَ بِالصِّدْقِ وَصَدَّقَ بِهِ اُوْلٰئِكَ هُمُ الْمُتَّقُوْنَ لَهُمْ مَّا يَشَآءُوْنَ عِنْدَ رَبِّهِمْ ذٰلِكَ جَزَآءُ الْمُحْسِنِيْنَ ، لِيُكَفِّرَ اللّٰهُ عَنْهُمْ اَسْوَ الَّذِيْ عَمِلُوْا وَيَجْزِيَهُمْ اَجْرَهُمْ بِاَحْسَنِ الَّذِيْ كَانُوْا يَعْمَلُوْنَ (زمر ع٤)

(12) He who brings the true thing and He who confirms it; such are the dutiful. They shall have all they wish from their Lord's bounty. Such is the reward of those who do good.

The persons who brought the message from Almighty Allah are the Prophets (Alaihimus salaatu was salaam) and the people who brought a message from Rasulullah (Sallallaho alaihe wasallam) are the Ulama (May Allah accept their efforts). Hadhrat Ibn Abbas (Radhiyallaho anho) is stated to have said that "the true thing" means the kalimah لَآاِلٰهَ اِلَّا اللّٰهُ According to some commentators, the words الَّذِى جَاءَ بِالصِّدْقِ (one who brought the true message from Allah) refers to Rasulullah (Sallallaho alaihe wasallam) and the words صَدَّقَ بِهٖ (those who confirmed it) refer to the believers.

(١٣) اِنَّ الَّذِيْنَ قَالُوْا رَبُّنَا اللّٰهُ ثُمَّ اسْتَقَامُوْا تَتَنَزَّلُ عَلَيْهِمُ الْمَلٰٓئِكَةُ اَلَّا تَخَافُوْا وَلَاتَحْزَنُوْا وَاَبْشِرُوْا بِالْجَنَّةِ الَّتِيْ كُنْتُمْ تُوْعَدُوْنَ ، نَحْنُ اَوْلِيٰٓؤُكُمْ فِى الْحَيٰوةِ الدُّنْيَا وَفِى الْاٰخِرَةِ ، وَلَكُمْ فِيْهَا مَاتَشْتَهِىٓ اَنْفُسُكُمْ وَلَكُمْ فِيْهَا مَاتَدَّعُوْنَ ، نُزُلًا مِنْ غَفُوْرٍ رَّحِيْمٍ (حٰم سجده ع٤)

(13) In the case of those who say, "Our Lord is Allah", and afterwards are steadfast, the angels descend upon them saying, "Fear not, nor grieve but hear good tidings of the Paradise which you were promised. We are your protecting friends in the life of the world and in the Hereafter. There you will have all that your souls desire, and then you will have what you pray for. A gift of welcome from the forgiving the Merciful."

Hadhrat Ibn Abbas (Radhiyallaho anho) said that the words (ثُمَّ اسْتَقَامُوْا) (then remained steadfast) means that they remained steadfast in their belief in the kalimah (لَآاِلٰهَ اِلَّا اللّٰهُ) Hadhrat Ibrahim and Hadhrat Mujahid (Rahmatullah alaihima) both supported the interpretation "they stuck to the kalimah (لَآاِلٰهَ اِلَّا اللّٰهُ) upto their death, and never indulged in Shirk of any kind"

(١٤) وَمَنْ اَحْسَنُ قَوْلًا مِّمَّنْ دَعَا اِلَى اللّٰهِ وَعَمِلَ صَالِحًا وَّقَالَ اِنَّنِيْ مِنَ الْمُسْلِمِيْنَ (حٰم سجده ع٧)

(14) Who is better in speech than one who calls (men) to Allah and doeth righteous deeds and says, "I am among those who bow in Islaam (the Muslims)."

Hadhrat Hasan (Radhiyallaho anho) said that the words (دَعَآ اِلَى اللّٰهِ) (invited towards Allah) refers to the calling of (لَآاِلٰهَ اِلَّا اللّٰهُ) by the muazzin. Aasim bin Hubairah (Rahmatullah alaih) advised, "After finishing azaan, one should recite

لَآاِلٰهَ اِلَّا اللّٰهُ وَاللّٰهُ اَكْبَرُ وَاَنَا مِنَ الْمُسْلِمِيْنَ

Nobody is worthy of worship except Allah; Allah is the greatest and I am from among the Muslims.

(١٥) هَلْ جَزَآءُ الْاِحْسَانِ اِلَّا الْاِحْسَانُ ، فَبِاَىِّ اٰلَآءِ رَبِّكُمَا تُكَذِّبَانِ (رحمٰن - ع٣)

(15) Is the reward of goodness ought save goodness? Which is it, of the favours of your Lord, that ye deny?

Hadhrat Ibn Abbas (Radhiyallaho anho) narrated that Rasulullah (Sallallaho alaihe wasallam) had said, "The meaning of this ayat is that Allah says, 'Can there be any other reward than Paradise in the Hereafter for one whom I blessed in his worldly life with the recitation of kalimah (لَآاِلٰهَ اِلَّا اللهُ).'' Hadhrat Ikramah and Hadhrat Hasan (Radhiyallaho anhuma) have also said that the reward of (لَآاِلٰهَ اِلَّا اللهُ) cannot be anything but Paradise.

(١٦) فَاَنْزَلَ اللهُ سَكِيْنَتَهٗ عَلٰى رَسُوْلِهٖ وَعَلَى الْمُؤْمِنِيْنَ وَاَلْزَمَهُمْ كَلِمَةَ التَّقْوٰى وَكَانُوْٓا اَحَقَّ بِهَا وَاَهْلَهَا (فتح - ع٣)

(16) Then Allah sent down His tranquility upon His Messenger and upon the believers and imposed upon them the word of self restraint, for they were entitled to it and worthy of it.

(كلمة تقوىٰ)(utterance of piety) in this hadith means kalimah Tayyibah as explained in many narrations. Hadhrat Abu Hurairah and Hadhrat Salama (Radhiyallaho anhuma) quoted Rasulullah (Sallallaho alaihe wasallam) as having said that it means (لَآاِلٰهَ اِلَّا اللهُ). The same view was expressed by Hadhrat Ubayy bin Kab, Hadhrat Ali, Hadhrat Umar, Hadhrat Ibn Abbas, Hadhrat Ibn Umar, and many other Sahabas, (Radhiyallaho anhum). Ataa Khurasani (Rahmatullahi alaihi) was of the view that it meant the whole Kalimah Tayyibah i.e. لَآاِلٰهَ اِلَّا اللهُ مُحَمَّدٌ رَّسُوْلُ اللهِ while Hadhrat Ali (Radhiyallaho anho) had said that it meant لَآاِلٰهَ اِلَّا اللهُ اللهُ اَكْبَرُ Tirmizi is stated to have quoted on the authority of Baraa (Radhiyallaho anho) that this implied: لَآاِلٰهَ اِلَّا اللهُ .

(١٧) قَدْ اَفْلَحَ مَنْ تَزَكّٰى (اعلىٰ)

(17) Those who purify themselves will prosper.

Hadhrat Jaabir (Radhiyallaho anho) has quoted Rasulullah (Sallallaho alaihe wasallam) to have said that تَزَكّٰى

(purified) means he declared his faith in لَآاِلٰهَ اِلَّا اللهُ مُحَمَّدٌ رَّسُوْلُ اللهِ and gave up idol-worship. According to Hadhrat Ikramah (Radhiyallaho anho) تَزَكّٰى means he proclaimed لَآاِلٰهَ اِلَّا اللهُ and this also was the viewpoint held by Ibn Abbas (Radhiyallaho anho)

(١٨) فَاَمَّا مَنْ اَعْطٰى وَاتَّقٰى ، وَصَدَّقَ بِالْحُسْنٰى ، فَسَنُيَسِّرُهٗ لِلْيُسْرٰى (ليل - ع ١)

(18) As for him who giveth and is dutiful (towards Allah) and believeth in goodness. Surely we will ease his way unto the state of ease.

(لليسرى) (state of ease) means Paradise, because it is Paradise where all kinds of comforts and facilities will be available. Its further elaboration is that Allah will so grace a man as to make good deeds easy for him, which will expedite his entry to Paradise. Many commentators are of the view that the above-mentioned ayat was revealed in favour of Hadhrat Abu Bakr (Radhiyallaho anho).

According to Hadhrat Ibn Abbas (Radhiyallaho anho) the word (الحسنى) (good thing) mentioned in this ayat means the kalimah (لَآاِلٰهَ اِلَّا اللهُ). Hadhrat Abu Abdur Rahmaan Salmi (Radhiyallaho anho) also shares this view. Hadhrat Imaam-e-A'zam (Rahmatullah alaih) quoting on the authority of Abu Zubair and Hadhrat Jaabir (Radhiyallaho anhuma) says that Rasulullah (Sallallaho alaihe wasallam) explained that (صَدَّقَ بِالْحُسْنٰى) means 'testified لَآاِلٰهَ اِلَّا اللهُ', while كَذَّبَ بِالْحُسْنٰى means 'refuted'.

(١٩) مَنْ جَاۤءَ بِالْحَسَنَةِ فَلَهٗ عَشْرُ اَمْثَالِهَا ، وَمَنْ جَاۤءَ بِالسَّيِّئَةِ فَلَايُجْزٰى اِلَّا مِثْلَهَا وَهُمْ لَايُظْلَمُوْنَ (انعام - ع ٢٠)

(19) He who does a good deed shall have ten times as much to his credit. He who does an evil deed will be awarded according to his evil. No wrong shall be done to them.

It is related when this ayat مَنْ جَاۤءَ بِالْحَسَنَةِ descended, someone asked Rasulullah (Sallallaho alaihe wasallam) if the reciting of (لَآاِلٰهَ اِلَّا اللهُ) was also counted among their virtuous deeds. The Prophet (Sallallaho alaihe wasallam) replied that it is the best of all virtues. Hadhrat Abdullah bin Abbaas and Hadhrat Abdullah bin Mas'ood (Radhiyallaho anhum) take (حسنة) (virtue) to mean (لَآاِلٰهَ اِلَّا اللهُ). Hadhrat Abu Hurairah (Radhiyallaho anho) also holds exactly the same view. Similar meanings were also narrated by Hadhrat Abu

Zar Ghifaari (Radhiyallaho anho) on the authority of Rasulullah (Sallallaho alaihe wasallam) who held that (لآاِلٰهَ اِلَّا اللّٰهُ) was the best amongst all virtuous deeds.

According to Hadhrat Abu Hurairah (Radhiyallaho anho), one good deed is counted ten times over as a general principle but, for the muhaajirs, compensation for one good deed is raised to seven hundred times.

(٢٠) حٰمٓ ، تَنْزِيْلُ الْكِتٰبِ مِنَ اللّٰهِ الْعَزِيْزِ الْعَلِيْمِ ، غَافِرِ الذَّنْبِ وَقَابِلِ التَّوْبِ شَدِيْدِ الْعِقَابِ ذِى الطَّوْلِ ، لَآ اِلٰهَ اِلَّا هُوَ ، اِلَيْهِ الْمَصِيْرُ (مومن — ع ١)

(20) The revelation of this Book is from Allah, exalted in power, full of knowledge, who forgives sin and accepts repentance, strict in punishment, and hath a long reach. There is no god save He; to Him is the final goal.

Note:

In an explanation of this ayat, Hadhrat Abdullah bin Umar (Radhiyallaho anho) states that Almighty Allah is the forgiver of sins, for one who says (لآاِلٰهَ اِلَّا اللّٰهُ) and acceptor of towbah for one who recites (لآاِلٰهَ اِلَّا اللّٰهُ), and is the dispensor of severe punishment for one who does not proclaim (لآاِلٰهَ اِلَّا اللّٰهُ). The words (لآاِلٰهَ اِلَّا اللّٰهُ) refute the Quraish, who did not believe in the Unity of Allah; (وَاِلَيْهِ الْمَصِيْرُ) implies that one who says (لآاِلٰهَ اِلَّا اللّٰهُ) will return to Allah for entry into Paradise, while one who refutes (لآاِلٰهَ اِلَّا اللّٰهُ) will return to Him for entry into Hell.

(٢١) فَمَنْ يَّكْفُرْ بِالطَّاغُوْتِ وَيُؤْمِنْ بِاللّٰهِ فَقَدِ اسْتَمْسَكَ بِالْعُرْوَةِ الْوُثْقٰى لَا انْفِصَامَ لَهَا (بقره — ع ٣٤)

(21) He who rejects false deities and believeth in Allah has grasped the firm hand-hold, which will never break.

Note:

Hadhrat Ibn Abbaas (Radhiyallaho anho) says that "grasping the firm handhold (عُرْوَةِ الْوُثْقٰى)" means proclaiming (لآاِلٰهَ اِلَّا اللّٰهُ). The same interpretation is also related from Sufyaan (Rahmatullah alaih).

CONCLUSION:

قلت وقد ورد في تفسير آيات آخر عديدة أيضا أن المراد ببعض الألفاظ في هذه الآيات كلمة التوحيد عند بعضهم فقد قال الراغب في قوله في قصة زكريا مصدقا بكلمة قيل كلمة التوحيد وكذا قال في قوله تعالى إنا عرضنا الأمانة الآية قيل هى كلمة التوحيد واقتصرت على مامر للاختصار

PART 2

This chapter includes such ayaat as contains the Kalimah Tayyibah in full or in part, or else its equivalent in different words but having the same meaning. The Kalimah Tayyibah (لَآاِلٰهَ اِلَّا اللّٰهُ) means that nobody is worthy of worship except Allah. The words (مَا مِنْ اِلٰهٍ غَيْرُهٗ) and لَآاِلٰهَ اِلَّا هُوَ and (لَانَعْبُدُ اِلَّا اللّٰهَ) also carry the same meaning. Similarly (لَانَعْبُدُ اِلَّا اِيَّاهُ) (We do not worship anybody other than Allah) and (اِنَّمَا هُوَ اِلٰهٌ وَّاحِدٌ) (He is the only one worthy of worship) also mean the same thing. There are other similar ayaat, which imply the same meaning as of Kalimah Tayyibah. The surah and ruku in which each such ayat occurs has been indicated below. In fact, the whole of the Holy Qur'an is an explanation of the Kalimah Tayyibah, because the basic objective of the Holy Qur'an and of the deen of Islam is towheed. It is to propagate towheed that the messengers of Allah were sent to people at different times. Towheed is the common objective of all the revealed religions, and for this reason the subject of towheed has all along been dealt with under different headings to establish its truth. The same towheed is therefore the object of Kalimah Tayyibah.

(١) وَاِلٰهُكُمْ اِلٰهٌ وَّاحِدٌ ، لَآاِلٰهَ اِلَّا هُوَ الرَّحْمٰنُ الرَّحِيْمُ (بقرة – ع١٩)

1. Your Allah is one Allah. There is no god save Him; Most Beneficent, The Merciful. (Baqarah–163)

(٢) اَللّٰهُ لَآاِلٰهَ اِلَّا هُوَ الْحَيُّ الْقَيُّوْمُ (بقرة – ع٣٤)

2. There is no god but He–The Living, The Eternal. (Baqarah–255)

(٣) اَللّٰهُ لَآاِلٰهَ اِلَّا هُوَ الْحَيُّ الْقَيُّوْمُ (آل عمران – ع١)

3. There is no god but He–The Living, The Eternal. (Aali Imraan–2)

(٤) شَهِدَ اللّٰهُ اَنَّهٗ لَآ اِلٰهَ اِلَّا هُوَ وَالْمَلٰٓئِكَةُ وَاُولُوا الْعِلْمِ (آل عمران – ع٢)

4. Allah Himself is witness, there is no god but He. The angels and the men of learning too are witness.
(Aali Imraan–18)

(٥) لَآ اِلٰهَ اِلَّا هُوَ الْعَزِيْزُ الْحَكِيْمُ (آل عمران – ع٢)

5. There is no god but He–The Exalted in Power, The Wise. (Aali Imraan–18)

(٦) وَمَا مِنْ اِلٰهٍ اِلَّا اللهُ ، وَاِنَّ اللهَ لَهُوَ الْعَزِيْزُ الْحَكِيْمُ (آل عمران – ع٢)

6. There is no god save Allah, and Allah is Exalted in Power, The Wise. (Aali Imraan–62)

(٧) تَعَالَوْا اِلٰى كَلِمَةٍ سَوَآءٍ بَيْنَنَا وَبَيْنَكُمْ اَلَّا نَعْبُدَ اِلَّا اللهَ (آل عمران – ع٧)

7. Come to an agreement between us and you, that we shall worship none but Allah. (Aali Imraan–64)

(٨) اَللهُ لَآ اِلٰهَ اِلَّا هُوَ ، لَيَجْمَعَنَّكُمْ اِلٰى يَوْمِ الْقِيٰمَةِ (نساء – ع١١)

8. Allah! There is no god but He; of surety, He will gather you together on the Day of Judgment. (Nisaa–87)

(٩) وَمَا مِنْ اِلٰهٍ اِلَّا اِلٰهٌ وَّاحِدٌ (مائده – ع١٠)

9. There is no god save One Allah. (Maa'idah–76)

(١٠) قُلْ اِنَّمَا هُوَ اِلٰهٌ وَّاحِدٌ (انعام – ع٢)

10. Say: In truth He is the One Allah. (An'aam–18)

(١١) مَنْ اِلٰهٌ غَيْرُ اللهِ يَاْتِيْكُمْ بِهٖ (انعام – ع٥)

11. Which god other than Allah could restore them to you
(An'aam–46)

(١٢) ذٰلِكُمُ اللهُ رَبُّكُمْ لَآ اِلٰهَ اِلَّا هُوَ (انعام – ع٥)

12. That is Allah, your Lord. There is no god save Him. (An'aam–102)

(١٣) لَآاِلٰهَ اِلَّا هُوَ ، وَاَعْرِضْ عَنِ الْمُشْرِكِيْنَ (انعام – ع١٣)

13. There is no god save Allah, and turn away from those who join gods with Allah. (An'aam–106)

(١٤) قَالَ اَغَيْرَ اللهِ اَبْغِيْكُمْ اِلٰهًا (اعراف – ع١٦)

14. He said: Shall I seek for you a god other than Allah. (A'raaf–140)

(١٥) لَآاِلٰهَ اِلَّا هُوَ يُحْيِ وَيُمِيْتُ (اعراف – ع٢٠)

15. There is no god save He (Allah). It is he that gives both life and death. (A'raaf–185)

(١٦) وَمَآ اُمِرُوْآ اِلَّا لِيَعْبُدُوْآ اِلٰهًا وَّاحِدًا ، لَآاِلٰهَ اِلَّا هُوَ (توبه – ع٥)

16. They were commanded to worship but One Allah. There is no god save He, Allah. (Taubah–31)

(١٧) حَسْبِيَ اللهُ لَآاِلٰهَ اِلَّا هُوَ ، عَلَيْهِ تَوَكَّلْتُ وَهُوَ رَبُّ الْعَرْشِ الْعَظِيْمِ (توبه – ع ١٦)

17. Allah is sufficient for me. There is no god save He (Allah). In Him I have put my trust. He is the Lord of the Tremendous Throne. (Taubah–129)

(١٨) ذٰلِكُمُ اللهُ رَبُّكُمْ فَاعْبُدُوْهُ (يونس – ع١)

18. This is Allah your Lord. Him, therefore, you should worship. (Yunus–3)

(١٩) فَذٰلِكُمُ اللهُ رَبُّكُمْ فَاعْبُدُوْهُ (يونس – ع٤)

19. Such is Allah, your real Sustainer. (Yunus–32)

(۲۰) قَالَ اٰمَنْتُ اَنَّهُ لَآاِلٰهَ اِلَّا الَّذِیٓ اٰمَنَتْ بِهِ بَنُوْٓا اِسْرَآئِيْلَ وَاَنَا مِنَ الْمُسْلِمِيْنَ

(یونس - ع۹)

20. He said, there is no god except Him (Allah), in Whom the Children of Israel believe, and I am of those who submit unto Him. (Yunus–90)

(۲۱) فَلَآ اَعْبُدُ الَّذِيْنَ تَعْبُدُوْنَ مِنْ دُوْنِ اللّٰهِ (یونس - ع۱۱)

21. I worship not what you worship other than Allah. (Yunus–104)

(۲۲) فَاعْلَمُوْٓا اَنَّمَآ اُنْزِلَ بِعِلْمِ اللّٰهِ وَاَنْ لَّآاِلٰهَ اِلَّا هُوَ (هود - ع۲)

22. Know you that this revelation is sent down in the knowledge of Allah, and there is no god save Him (Allah). (Hood–14)

(۲۳) اَنْ لَّاتَعْبُدُوْٓا اِلَّا اللّٰهَ (هود - ع۳)

23. That ye serve none but Allah. (Hood–26)

(۲۴ /۲۵ /۲۶) قَالَ يٰقَوْمِ اعْبُدُوا اللّٰهَ مَالَكُمْ مِّنْ اِلٰهٍ غَيْرُهٗ (هود - ع۵، ع۶، ع۸)

24, 25, 26) He said: "O my people, worship Allah; you have no other god but Him. (Hood–50–61–84)

(۲۷) ءَاَرْبَابٌ مُّتَفَرِّقُوْنَ خَيْرٌ اَمِ اللّٰهُ الْوَاحِدُ الْقَهَّارُ (یوسف - ع۵)

27. Are many lords differing among themselves better or the One Allah, the Irresistible? (Yusuf–39)

(۲۸) اَمَرَ اَلَّا تَعْبُدُوْٓا اِلَّا اِيَّاهُ (یوسف - ع۵)

28. He has commanded that you worship none but Him. (Yusuf–40)

(۲۹) قُلْ هُوَ رَبِّیْ لَآاِلٰهَ اِلَّا هُوَ (رعد - ع۴)

29. Say, "He is my Lord, there is no god but He (Allah).
(Ra'd–30)

(٣٠) وَلِيَعْلَمُوْآ اَنَّمَا هُوَ اِلٰهٌ وَّاحِدٌ (ابراهيم – ع٧)

30. And let them know that He (Allah) is only one god.
(Ibrahim–52)

(٣١) اَنَّهُ لَآاِلٰهَ اِلَّا اَنَا فَاتَّقُوْنِ (نحل – ع١)

31. There is no god but I, so do your duty unto Me.
(Nahl–2)

(٣٢) اِلٰهُكُمْ اِلٰهٌ وَّاحِدٌ (نحل – ع٣)

32. Your Allah is one Allah. (Nahl–22)

(٣٣) اِنَّمَا هُوَ اِلٰهٌ وَّاحِدٌ (نحل – ع٧)

33. He is just one Allah. (Nahl–5)

(٣٤) وَلَاتَجْعَلْ مَعَ اللهِ اِلٰهًا اٰخَرَ (بنی اسرائیل – ع٤)

34. And do not set up with Allah any other god.
(Bani Israa-eel–39)

(٣٥) قُلْ لَّوْ كَانَ مَعَهُ اٰلِهَةٌ كَمَا يَقُوْلُوْنَ (بنی اسرائیل – ع٥)

35. Say if there had been other gods with Him (Allah), as they say. (Bani Israa-eel–42)

(٣٦) فَقَالُوْا رَبُّنَا رَبُّ السَّمٰوٰتِ وَالْاَرْضِ لَنْ نَّدْعُوَا مِنْ دُوْنِهٖ اِلٰهًا (كهف – ع٢)

36. They said: 'Our Lord is the Lord of the Heavens and of the Earth. Never shall we call upon any god other than Him (Allah). (Kahf–14)

(٣٧) هٰٓؤُلَاءِ قَوْمُنَا اتَّخَذُوْا مِنْ دُوْنِهٖ اٰلِهَةً (كهف – ع٢)

37. There are people who chose other gods beside Him (Allah).
(Kahf–15)

(٣٨) يُوْحٰى اِلَيَّ اَنَّمَا اِلٰهُكُمْ اِلٰهٌ وَّاحِدٌ (كهف – ع١٢)

38. The revelation has come to me that your Allah is one Allah.
(Kahf–110)

(٣٩) وَاِنَّ اللهَ رَبِّىْ وَرَبُّكُمْ فَاعْبُدُوْهُ (مريم – ع٢)

39. Verily, Allah is my Lord and your Lord, so serve Him.
(Maryam–36)

(٤٠) اَللهُ لَآاِلٰهَ اِلَّا هُوَ (طه ع١)

40. Allah! there is no god but He (Allah). (Taha–8)

(٤١) اِنَّنِىْ اَنَا اللهُ لَا اِلٰهَ اِلَّا اَنَا فَاعْبُدْنِىْ (طه ع١)

41. Verily, I am Allah. There is no god but I. So Serve Me.
(Taha–14)

(٤٢) اِنَّمَا اِلٰهُكُمُ اللهُ الَّذِىْ لَآاِلٰهَ اِلَّا هُوَ (طه ع٥)

42. But the god of you all is the one Allah: There is no god but He.
(Taha–98)

(٤٣) لَوْ كَانَ فِيْهِمَا اٰلِهَةٌ اِلَّا اللهُ لَفَسَدَتَا (أنبياء ع٢)

43. If there were (in the Heavens and the Earth) other gods besides Allah, there would have been disorder in both of them.
(Ambiyaa–22)

(٤٤) اَمِ اتَّخَذُوْا مِنْ دُوْنِهٖ اٰلِهَةً (انبياء ع٢)

44. Have they taken for worship gods besides Him (Allah).
(Ambiyaa–24)

(٤٥) اِلَّا نُوْحِيْ اِلَيْهِ اَنَّهُ لَا اِلٰهَ اِلَّا اَنَا (انبياء ع٢)

45. It was revealed by Us (Allah) to him (The Apostle) that there is no god but I (Allah). (Ambiyaa–25)

(٤٦) اَمْ لَهُمْ اٰلِهَةٌ تَمْنَعُهُمْ مِنْ دُوْنِنَا (انبياء ع٥)

46. Or have they gods who can shield them from us? (Ambiyaa–43)

(٤٧) اَفَتَعْبُدُوْنَ مِنْ دُوْنِ اللهِ مَالَا يَنْفَعُكُمْ شَيْئًا وَّلَا يَضُرُّكُمْ (انبياء ع٥)

47. Do you worship besides Allah things that can neither be of any good to you, nor do you harm? (Ambiyaa–66)

(٤٨) لَا اِلٰهَ اِلَّا اَنْتَ سُبْحَانَكَ (انبياء ع٦)

48. There is no god save Thou: Glory be to Thee. (Ambiyaa–87)

(٤٩) اِنَّمَا يُوْحٰى اِلَيَّ اَنَّمَا اِلٰهُكُمْ اِلٰهٌ وَّاحِدٌ (انبياء ع٥)

49. What has come to me by revelation is that your Allah is one Allah. (Ambiyaa–108)

(٥٠) فَاِلٰهُكُمْ اِلٰهٌ وَّاحِدٌ فَلَهُ اَسْلِمُوْا (حج ع٥)

50. Your Allah is one Allah, submit unto Him. (Haj–34)

(٥١ /٥٢) اُعْبُدُوْا اللهَ مَالَكُمْ مِنْ اِلٰهٍ غَيْرُهُ (مؤمنون ٢ ع)

51–52. Worship Allah, you have no other god but Him (Allah). (Mu'minoon–23)

(٥٣) وَمَا كَانَ مَعَهُ مِنْ اِلٰهٍ (مؤمنون ٦ ع)

53. Nor is there any god along with Him. (Mu'minoon–91)

(٥٤) فَتَعَالَى اللّٰهُ الْمَلِكُ الْحَقُّ لَا اِلٰهَ اِلَّا هُوَ (مؤمنون ع٦)

54. Therefore Allah, Exalted, the True King! There is no god save Him (Allah). (Mu'minoon–114)

(٥٥) وَمَنْ يَّدْعُ مَعَ اللّٰهِ اِلٰهًا اٰخَرَ لَابُرْهَانَ لَهُ بِهِ فَاِنَّمَا حِسَابُهُ عِنْدَ رَبِّهِ (مؤمنون ع٦)

55. If any one invokes any other god besides Allah, he has no authority therefore. His reckoning is only with his Lord. (Mu'minoon–117)

(٥٦) ءَاِلٰهٌ مَّعَ اللّٰهِ (نمل ع٥)

56. Can there be another god besides Allah? (Naml–64)

(٥٧) وَهُوَ اللّٰهُ لَآاِلٰهَ اِلَّا هُوَ لَهُ الْحَمْدُ (قصص – ع٧)

57. And He is Allah. There is no god but He. To Him be praise. (Qasas–70)

(٥٨) مَنْ اِلٰهٌ غَيْرُ اللّٰهِ يَاْتِيْكُمْ بِلَيْلٍ (قصص ع٧)

58. Is there other than Allah, who can give you a night? (Qasas–70)

(٥٩) وَلَا تَدْعُ مَعَ اللّٰهِ اِلٰهًا اٰخَرَ لَا اِلٰهَ اِلَّا هُوَ (قصص ع٩)

59. And call not, besides Allah, on any other god. There is no god but He. (Qasas–88)

(٦٠) وَاِلٰهُنَا وَاِلٰهُكُمْ وَاحِدٌ (عنكبوت ع٥)

60. And our Allah and Your Allah is One. (Ankaboot–46)

(٦١) لَآ اِلٰهَ اِلَّا هُوَ فَاَنّٰى تُؤْفَكُوْنَ (فاطر ع١)

61. There is no god save Allah. How then are you deluded? (Faatir–3)

(٦٢) اِنَّ اِلٰهَكُمْ لَوَاحِدٌ (صٰفّٰت ع ١)

62. Lo! Thy Lord is surely One. (Saaffaat–4)

(٦٣) اِنَّهُمْ كَانُوْا اِذَا قِيْلَ لَهُمْ لَآاِلٰهَ اِلَّا اللّٰهُ يَسْتَكْبِرُوْنَ (صٰفّٰت ع ١)

63. For when it was said unto them: "There is no god save Allah," they were scornful. (Saaffat–35)

(٦٤) اَجَعَلَ الْآلِهَةَ اِلٰهاً وَّاحِدًا (ص ع ١)

64. Maketh he the gods One Allah? (Saad–5)

(٦٥) وَمَا مِنْ اِلٰهٍ اِلَّا اللّٰهُ الْوَاحِدُ الْقَهَّارُ (ص ع ٥)

65. There is no god save Allah, The One, The Irresistible. (Saad–65)

(٦٦) هُوَ اللّٰهُ الْوَاحِدُ الْقَهَّارُ (زمر ع ١)

66. He is Allah, The One, The Irresistable. (Zumar–4)

(٦٧) ذٰلِكُمُ اللّٰهُ رَبُّكُمْ لَهُ الْمُلْكُ لَآاِلٰهَ اِلَّا هُوَ (زمر ع ١)

67. Such is Allah. Your Lord and Cherisher. His is the Sovereignty. There is no god save Him. (Zumar–6)

(٦٨) لَآ اِلٰهَ اِلَّا هُوَ اِلَيْهِ الْمَصِيْرُ [مومن ف ء]

68. There is no god save Him, to Him is the final goal. (Mu'min–3)

(٦٩) لَآ اِلٰهَ اِلَّا هُوَ فَاَنّٰى تُؤْفَكُوْنَ (مومن ع ٧)

69. There is no god save Allah. How then are you deluded? (Mu'min–62)

(٧٠) هُوَ الْحَيُّ لَا اِلٰهَ اِلَّا هُوَ فَادْعُوْهُ (مومن ع٧)

70. He is the living (one). There is no god but He. Call upon Him. (Mu'min–65)

(٧١) يُوْحَىٰ اِلَيَّ اَنَّمَا اِلٰهُكُمْ اِلٰهٌ وَّاحِدٌ (حم سجدة ع١)

71. It is revealed to me that your god is One Allah. (Haameem-Sajdah–6)

(٧٢) اَلَّا تَعْبُدُوْا اِلَّا اللّٰهَ (حم سجدة – ع٢)

72. Worship Ye none but Allah. (Haameem Sajdah–14)

(٧٣) اَللّٰهُ رَبُّنَا وَرَبُّكُمْ (شورى ع٢)

73. Allah is our Lord and Your Lord. (Shooraa–15)

(٧٤) اَجَعَلْنَا مِنْ دُوْنِ الرَّحْمٰنِ اٰلِهَةً يُّعْبَدُوْنَ (زخرف ع٤)

74. Did we appoint gods to be worshipped besides the Beneficient? (Zukhruf–45).

(٧٥) رَبِّ السَّمٰوٰتِ وَالْاَرْضِ وَمَا بَيْنَهُمَا (دخان ع١)

75. The Lord of Heavens and the Earth and all between them. (Dukhaan–7)

(٧٦) لَآ اِلٰهَ اِلَّا هُوَ يُحْيٖ وَيُمِيْتُ (دخان ع١)

76. There is no god but He. It is He who gives life and gives death. (Dukhaan–8)

(٧٧) اَلَّا تَعْبُدُوْا اِلَّا اللّٰهَ (احقاف ع ٣)

77. Worship ye none other than Allah. (Ahqaaf–21)

(۷۸) فَاعْلَمْ اَنَّهُ لَآاِلٰهَ اِلَّا هُوَ (محمد ع۲)

78. Know, therefore, that there is no god but Allah. (Muhammad–19)

(۷۹) وَلَا تَجْعَلُوْا مَعَ اللهِ اِلٰهًا آخَرَ (ذاريات ع۳)

79. And set not any other god along with Allah. (Zaariyaat–51)

(۸۰) هُوَ اللهُ الَّذِيْ لَا اِلٰهَ اِلَّا هُوَ (حشر ع۱۳)

80. Allah is He besides Whom there is no other god. (Hashr–22)

(۸۱) اِنَّا بُرَآؤُا مِنْكُمْ وَمِمَّا تَعْبُدُوْنَ مِنْ دُوْنِ اللهِ (ممتحنة ع۱)

81. We are guiltless of you and all that you worship beside Allah. (Mumtahinah–4)

(۸۲) اَللهُ لَآاِلٰهَ اِلَّا هُوَ (تغابن ع۲)

82. Allah! There is no god but He. (Taghaabun–13)

(۸۳) رَبُّ الْمَشْرِقِ وَالْمَغْرِبِ لَآ اِلٰهَ اِلَّا هُوَ (مزمل ع۱)

83. He is the Lord of the East and the West; there is no god but He (Allah). (Muzzammil–9)

(۸٤) لَآ اَعْبُدُ مَاتَعْبُدُوْنَ وَلَا اَنْتُمْ عَابِدُوْنَ مَااَعْبُدُ (كافرون)

84. I worship not that which ye worship, nor will you worship that which I worship. (Kaafiroon–2-3)

(۸۵) قُلْ هُوَ اللهُ اَحَدٌ (اخلاص)

85. Say: He is Allah, The One and Only. (Ikhlaas)

The above are the eighty five verses, in which text of Kalimah Tayyibah or its equivalent in meaning has occurred. There are still many more verses, which equally convey the same sense and meaning of the Kalimah as I have stated in the beginning of this section. Tauheed is the fundamental basis of Deen, and therefore the more acquainted a man is with the requirements of Tauheed, the more steadfast he shall be in Deen. Tauheed in the Holy Qur'an has been described from various viewpoints and in various manners and aspects, so that it may penetrate through the very depths of the heart; so it firmly settles there, leaving no room for anything else to enter.

PART 3

Part 3 includes such ahadith which describe the virtues and blessings of reciting Kalimah Tayyibah. In the foregoing we have seen that there is plurality of ayaat on this subject, which goes to prove that the number of ahadith on this subject must be far more numerous. It is therefore difficult to record them all here. Only a few illustrative examples will be given here.

Hadith No 1

(١) عَنْ جَابِرٍ رَضِىَ اللّٰهُ عَنْهُ عَنِ النَّبِىِّ ﷺ قَالَ اَفْضَلُ الذِّكْرِ لَآاِلٰهَ اِلَّا اللّٰهُ وَاَفْضَلُ الدُّعَاءِ اَلْحَمْدُ لِلّٰهِ كذا فى المشكوة برواية الترمذى وابن ماجه و قال المنذرى رواه ابن ماجة والنسائى وابن حبان فى صحيحه والحاكم كلهم من طريق طلحة بن خراش عنه وقال الحاكم صحيح الاسناد قلت رواه الحاكم بسندين وصححهما واقره عليهما الذهبى وكذا رقم له بالصحة السيوطى فى الجامع

Rasulullah (Sallallaho alaihe wasallam) has said, "of all the azkaar (plural of zikr) the repetition of (لآاِلٰهَ اِلَّا اللّٰهُ) is the best, and of all the du'aas (اَلْحَمْدُ لِلّٰهِ) is the best."

That (لآاِلٰهَ اِلَّا اللّٰهُ) is the best of all azkaar is quite evident. It is described as such in many ahadith. In fact when the whole of Deen depends on this Kalimah Tauheed, there can hardly be any doubt that it is the highest of all azkaar. Again (اَلْحَمْدُ لِلّٰهِ) (Alhamdolillah) has been regarded as the best du'aa, because praising one who is the most benevolent person is in fact a form of begging. It is common experience that by writing a eulogy in praise of a man of wealth or of authority does not mean anything else than begging his favours or riches.

Hadhrat Ibn Abbaas (Radhiyallaho anho) says that one who recites (اَلْحَمْدُ لِلّٰهِ) should follow it by (لآاِلٰهَ اِلَّا اللّٰهُ) because in the Holy Qur'an the verse

فَادْعُوْهُ مُخْلِصِيْنَ لَهُ الدِّيْنَ

(Ask Allah with sincere devotion)

is followed by اَلْحَمْدُ لِلّٰهِ رَبِّ الْعٰلَمِيْنَ (All praise is for Allah Who is the Cherisher of all the universe).

Mulla Ali Qari (Rahmatullah alaih) has stated: "There is not the slightest doubt that Kalimah Tayyibah is by far the best and foremost of all azkaar because it is the root and fundamental basis of the Deen and the whole religion of Islam centres round it. It is for this reason that the Sufis and saints emphasise its importance and prefer it over all other azkaar and advise their followers to practise it as much as possible. Also, actual experience has shown that, the benefits following from Kalimah Tayyibah far outnumber those which result from other forms of zikr.

There is a well-known story of Sayyid Ali bin Maymoon Maghrabi. Once Shaikh Ulwan Hamawi, who himself was a great scholar, Mufti and teacher of his age, came for learning zikr. The Sayyid (Rahmatullah alaih) devoted special attention to him and made him give up all his routines, such as teaching and writing fatawa, and to take up zikr all the time. On this, the common people started freely indulging in fault finding and condemnation. They started a campaign of criticism that the Shaikh has now been lost to them and the people were being deprived of his benefits. A few days later, when the Sayyid (Rahmatullah alaih) came to know that Shaikh Ulwan was occasionally reciting the Holy Qur'an, he stopped him from this recitation also. At this, the people lost all sense and openly accused the Sayyid, (Rahmatullah alaih), of irreligiousness and perversion. After some time, when the Shaikh observed that the zikr has had its effect on his heart, the Sayyid (Rahmatullah alaih) allowed him to resume recitation of the Holy Qur'an. When he opened the Book, every word and aayat emerged with new meanings and significance he never thought of before. The Sayyid (Rahmatullah alaih) then told Shaikh Hamawi that he had not forbidden him from recitation, but in fact he had desired to develop in him spiritual awareness, which was a pre-requisite for this recitation of the Qur'an.

As this Holy Kalimah constitutes the fundamental basis of religion and the root of Imaan (faith), the greater the devotion to this Kalimah, the more firmly will Imaan be rooted. Imaan depends on this Kalimah, and the very existence of this world depends on it. According to a hadith, the Day of Judgment will not dawn as long as there exists on Earth a single man reciting the Kalimah لَآاِلٰهَ اِلَّا اللّٰه. This is reported in other ahadith also. So long as there lives a single man on Earth who remembers Almighty Allah, Qiyaamat (Doomsday) will not take place.

Hadith No. 2

(٢) عَنْ اَبِىْ سَعِيْدِنِ الْخُدْرِىِّ رَضِىَ اللّٰهُ عَنْهُ عَنِ النَّبِىِّ ﷺ اَنَّهُ قَالَ قَالَ مُوْسٰى عَلَيْهِ السَّلَامُ يَارَبِّ عَلِّمْنِىْ شَيْئًا اَذْكُرُكَ بِهِ وَاَدْعُوْكَ بِهِ قَالَ قُلْ لَآاِلٰهَ اِلَّا اللّٰهُ قَالَ يَارَبِّ كُلُّ عِبَادِكَ يَقُوْلُ هٰذَا قَالَ قُلْ لَآاِلٰهَ اِلَّا اللّٰهُ قَالَ اِنَّمَا اُرِيْدُ شَيْئًا تَخُصُّنِىْ بِهِ قَالَ يَامُوْسٰى لَوْ اَنَّ السَّمٰوٰتِ السَّبْعَ وَالْاَرْضِيْنَ السَّبْعَ فِىْ كِفَّةٍ وَلَآ اِلٰهَ اِلَّا اللّٰهُ فِىْ كِفَّةٍ مَالَتْ بِهِمْ لَآاِلٰهَ اِلَّا اللّٰهُ رواه النسائى وابن حبان والحاكم كلهم من طريق دراج عن ابى الهيثم عنه وقال الحاكم صحيح الاسناد كذا فى الترغيب قلت قال الحاكم صحيح الاسناد ولم يخرجاه واقره عليه الذهبى واخرج فى المشكوة برواية شرح السنة نحوه زاد فى منتخب الكنز ابايعلى والحكيم وابانعيم فى الحلية والبيهقى فى الاسماء و سعيد بن منصور فى سننه و فى مجمع الزوائد رواه ابويعلى ورجاله وثقوا وفيهم ضعف

Virtues of Zikr

Rasulullah (Sallallaho alaihe wasallam) is reported to have said: "Once the prophet Moosa (Alayhis salaam) prayed to Almighty Allah to teach him some forms of zikr for his remembrance. He was advised to recite (لآاِلٰهَ اِلَّا اللّٰهُ). He submitted: 'O my Lord! this zikr is recited by all the creation. Again came the reply: "Recite لآاِلٰهَ اِلَّا اللّٰهُ." He submitted: 'O my Sustainer, I want something special, exclusively meant for me." Then Almighty Allah said: 'If the seven heavens and the seven earths were placed in one pan of the Balance, and the Kalimah (لآاِلٰهَ اِلَّا اللّٰهُ) in the other, the latter will outweigh the former."

It is the usual way of Almighty Allah that what is required most is provided most. The more pressing the need for a thing, the more plentiful is the provision for the same. Looking at the most essential necessities of life, such as breathing, water and air, it will be observed that Almighty Allah has created them in great abundance. It is, however, Ikhlaas (purity of intention) that determines the value of things in the eye of Almighty Allah. The greater the Ikhlaas in an action the greater will be its weight and, likewise, less the Ikhlaas and devotion, the lesser the weight. For the attainment of this Ikhlaas, nothing is more effective than this Kalimah. That is why it is also known as purifier of hearts (جلاء القلوب). For its purifying effect, Sufis prescribe zikr of this Kalimah and advise its recitation as a daily routine, not only in hundreds but in thousands of times. Mulla Ali Qari (Rahmatullah alaih) writes that a disciple once complained to his Shaikh that, despite doing zikr, his heart remained inattentive. The Shaikh replied: "Go on with your zikr firmly, and thank Almighty Allah for His Grace that He enabled a part of your body, i.e. the tongue, to remain busy in His zikr, and pray to Allah for a devoted heart." A similar incident is related in Ihyaa-ul Uloom about Abu Usman Maghribi, who gave the same reply on a similar complaint made by one of his disciples, and he prescribed the same cure. As a matter of fact, zikr is the best remedy for indolence of the heart. Almighty Allah says in His Book, "If you show gratitude to Me, I will grant even more than before." Likewise the hadith says "zikr of Almighty Allah is a great blessing; and be thankful to Him in as much as He has enabled you to do His zikr."

Hadith No 3

(٣) عَنْ اَبِىْ هُرَيْرَةَ رَضِىَ اللّٰهُ عَنْهُ قَالَ قُلْتُ يَارَسُوْلَ اللّٰهِ مَنْ اَسْعَدُ النَّاسِ بِشَفَاعَتِكَ يَوْمَ الْقِيَامَةِ قَالَ رَسُوْلِ اللّٰهِ ﷺ لَقَدْ ظَنَنْتُ يَااَبَاهُرَيْرَةَ اَنْ لَّايَسْئَلَنِىْ عَنْ هٰذَا الْحَدِيْثِ اَحَدٌ اَوَّلَ مِنْكَ لِمَا رَاَيْتُ مِنْ حِرْصِكَ عَلَى الْحَدِيْثِ اَسْعَدُ النَّاسِ بِشَفَاعَتِىْ يَوْمَ الْقِيَامَةِ مَنْ قَالَ لَآاِلٰهَ اِلَّا اللّٰهُ خَالِصًا مِّنْ قَلْبِهِ اَوْ نَفْسِهِ

رواه البخارى وقد اخرجه الحاكم بمعناه وذكر صاحب بهجه النفوس فى الحديث اربعا و ثلثين بحثا

Hadhrat Abu Hurairah (Radhiyallaho anho) once enquired from Rasulullah (Sallallaho alaihe wasallam) as to who would be most benefitted by his intercession on the Day of Resurrection. Rasulullah (Sallallaho alaihe wasallam) replied, "Knowing your anxiety for the Ilm (knowledge) of ahadith, I could expect that none other than you would have asked this question earlier." Thereafter the Prophet (Sallallaho alaihe wasallam) told Abu Hurairah (Radhiyallaho anho) that the most blessed or the most benefitted by my intercession will be the person who proclaims (لآاله الا الله) with Ikhlaas (sincerity).

The meaning of good fortune here is to get something good through the Grace of Allah. That the person reciting the Kalimah with Ikhlaas will be most deserving to be benefitted by the intercession of Rasulullah (Sallallaho alaihe wasallam), can be interpreted in two ways. Firstly, such a person could be one who has just embraced Islaam with sincerity of heart, and has done no other good deed except the recitation of the Kalimah. Evidently he can be helped only by virtue of this intercession, because he has no deed to his credit. In this case, this hadith is corroborated by other ahadith, in which it is stated that the intercession will be for those guilty of major sins who shall have been sent to the Hell because of their sins, but by virtue of their recitation of the Kalimah Tayyibah they will be released through the intercession of Rasulullah (Sallallaho alaihe wasallam). Secondly, the most deserving people to be benefitted will be those who continually recite this Kalimah with sincerity and they have to their credit other good deeds as well. Being most fortunate means that they will be benefitted more than by anything else by the intercession of Rasulullah (Sallallaho alaihe wasallam) in raising their status in Paradise.

Allama Ainee (Rahmatullah alaih) has stated that Rasulullah (Sallallaho alaihe wasallam), will intercede in six different ways on the Day of Judgement. Firstly, it will be for relief from the intolerable distress and supense in the field of judgement, where all the people will be afflicted in various ways and will even prefer to be sent to Hell so that their present worries may come to an end. They will go to all the high-ranking Prophets, one by one, and beg them to intercede before Almighty Allah, but none of them will dare to do so. At last, Rasulullah (Sallallaho alaihe wasallam) will intercede, and this intercession will be in favour of all the people, including Jinn and mankind, believers and non-believers, all of whom will be benefitted by it, as explained in detail in the ahadith describing the Resurrection. Secondly, Rasulullah (Sallallaho alaihe wasallam) will intercede for mitigation of punishment to some nonbelievers, as mentioned in the hadith about Abu Talib. Thirdly, his intercession will be for the release from Hell of some of the Believers who have been thrown in there. Fourthly, it will be for the pardon from Hell of some Believers, who on account of their misdeed have deserved to be condemned to it. Fifthly, it will be in favour of some Believers for their admittance into Paradise, without requiring them to render account of their deeds. Sixthly, it will be for raising the status of the Believers in general.

Hadith No 4

(٤) عَنْ زَيْدِ بْنِ اَرْقَمْ رَضِىَ اللهُ عَنْهُ قَالَ قَالَ رَسُوْلِ اللهِ ﷺ مَنْ قَالَ لَآاِلٰهَ اِلَّا اللهُ مُخْلِصًا دَخَلَ الْجَنَّةَ قِيْلَ وَمَا اِخْلَاصُهَا قَالَ اَنْ تَحْجِزَهُ عَنْ مَحَارِمِ اللهِ

رواه الطبرانى فى الأوسط والكبير

Hadhrat Zaid bin Arqam (Radhiyallaho anho) narrates that Rasulullah (Sallallaho alaihe wasallam) had said that one who recites (لَآاِلٰهَ اِلَّا اللهُ) with Ikhlaas will enter Paradise. Somebody asked what was the sign of Ikhlaas. He explained that it prevents one from indulging in the forbidden things.

It is apparent that one who abstains from the forbidden things and professes faith in لَآاِلٰهَ اِلَّا اللهُ , will directly be admitted into the Paradise. But if one has indulged in some forbidden things and has been sent to Hell, even then through the blessing of this Kalimah he will, certainly someday, after undergoing punishment for his misdeeds, be transferred to Paradise. But if his misdeeds have led him to stray out of the fold of Islaam and Imaan, he will remain condemned in the Hell for ever.

Faqih' Abul Laith of Samarkand has written in his book Tanbeeh-ul-Ghaafileen, "It is imperative for everybody to hymn (لَآاِلٰهَ اِلَّا اللهُ) often, and also pray to Almighty Allah for steadfastness in Imaan, and abstain from sins; because there are many people whose sinful deeds destroy their Imaan and they die as non-believers. There can be no tragedy greater than that a man should be listed as a Muslim throughout his life, but on the Day of Resurrection his name should appear in the list of non-believers. This is indeed the greatest misfortune. One does not feel sorry for a person who has throughout worshipped in a church or a temple and in the Hereafter is listed among the non-believers, but it is a matter of great grief that he who had remained in the musjid should be counted as one of the non-believers. This happens, as a result of excessive sinning and secret indulgence in forbidden things. For instance, a person gets unlawful possession of something knowingly, but he consoles his conscience that he will restore it some day to its real owner, or will get it condoned by him, but he happens to die before he is able to do anything of the sort. There are some who divorce their wives, but even then, knowingly, they continue to cohabit with them, till death overtakes them. In such cases, one does not get a chance of doing Taubah (repentance) and consequently is completely deprived of his Imaan. May Almighty Allah save us from this!

اَللّٰهُمَّ احْفَظْنَا مِنْهُ

In the books of Hadith, the story of a young man who was unable to recite the Kalimah, when his end was near, is related. It was brought to the notice of Rasulullah (Sallallaho alaihe wasallam), who went to the young man and asked him what was the matter with him. He replied that he felt as if his mind was locked. On enquiry, it transpired that his mother was angry with him because of his misbehaviour. She was called by Rasulullah (Sallallaho alaihe wasallam) and when she came, he said to her: "If somebody kindles a big fire and wants to throw your son into it, will you recommend mercy for him?" "I will certainly do so", she replied. "If it is so, then forgive his sin", said Rasulullah (Sallallaho alaihe wasallam). At this she pardoned her son, and thereafter when the young man was asked to recite the Kalimah he readily did so. Rasulullah (Sallallaho alaihe wasallam) thanked Almighty Allah that, through his effort, the man was saved from the fire of Hell. There are hundreds of cases, like the one mentioned above, where the evil effect of the sins in which we get involved results in our worldly as well as spiritual loss.

The worthy author of Ihya-ul-Uloom has related that once Rasulullah (Sallallaho alaihe wasallam) delivered a sermon, in which he said: "One who recites (لَآاِلٰهَ اِلَّا اللهُ), in the manner that he does not mix it up, he becomes entitled to Paradise." Hadhrat Ali (Radhiyallaho anho) asked for the clarification of the meaning of mixing it up. Rasulullah (Sallallaho alaihe wasallam) said: "It is to love the worldly life and hanker after it. There are many who talk like the Prophets, but act like the arrogant people and tyrants. If one recites this Kalimah while not indulging in anything of this sort, he becomes entitled to Paradise."

Hadith No. 5

(٥) عَنْ اَبِیْ هُرَیْرَةَ رَضِیَ اللهُ عَنْهُ قَالَ قَالَ رَسُوْلُ اللهِ ﷺ مَاقَالَ عَبْدٌ لَآاِلٰهَ اِلَّا
اللهُ اِلَّا فُتِحَتْ لَهُ اَبْوَابُ السَّمَآءِ حَتّٰی یُفْضِیَ اِلَی الْعَرْشِ مَا اجْتَنَبَ الْكَبَائِرَ

Virtues of Zikr

رواه الترمذی وقال حدیث حسن غریب كَذا فی الترغیب وهكذا فی المشكوٰة لكن لیس فیها حسن بل غریب فقط قال القاری ورواه النسائی و ابن حبان وعزاه السیوطی فی الجامع الی الترمذی ورقم له بالحسن وحكاه السیوطی فی الدر من طریق ابن مردویه عن ابی هریرة ولیس فیه مَا اَجْتَنَبَ الْكَبَائِرِ وفی الجامع الصغیر بروایة الطبرانی عن معقل بن یسار لِكُلِّ شَیْءٍ مُّفْتَاحٌ وَمِفْتَاحُ السَّمٰوٰتِ قَوْلُ لَآاِلٰهَ اِلَّا اللّٰهُ ورقم له بالضعف

> Rasulullah (Sallallaho alaihe wasallam) said, "There is nobody who may recite (لَآاِلٰهَ اِلَّا اللّٰهُ) and the doors of the Heavens do not get opened to allow this Kalimah to reach the Arshi Ilaahi (Allah's throne), provided he abstains from the major sins."

The extreme excellence and acceptability of this Kalimah is proved by its going straight to the Arshi Ilaahi (throne of Allah). It has already been stated that its recitation, even with major sins, is not without benefit. Mulla Ali Qari (Rahmatullah alaih) says that the condition of being free from major sins is the key to quick acceptance and for the opening of all the doors of Heaven; otherwise the recitation of Kalimah is not without reward and acceptance, in spite of major sins. Some scholars have explained this hadith to mean that, after the death of such a person, all the doors of the Heavens are opened to welcome his soul. According to another hadith, two Kalimahs are such that one does not stop before reaching the Throne of Allah, and the other fills the Heaven and Earth with its light or reward: one is (لَآاِلٰهَ اِلَّا اللّٰهُ) and the other is (لَآاِلٰهَ اِلَّا اللّٰهُ).

Hadith No. 6

(٦) عَنْ يَعْلَى بْنِ شَدَّادٍ قَالَ حَدَّثَنِىْ اَبِىْ شَدَّادُ بْنُ اَوْسٍ وَ عُبَادَةُ بْنُ الصَّامِتِ رَضِىَ اللّٰهُ عَنْهُمَا حَاضِرٌ يُصَدِّقُ قَالَ كُنَّا عِنْدَ النَّبِىِّ ﷺ فَقَالَ هَلْ فِيْكُمْ غَرِيْبٌ يَعْنِىْ اَهْلَ الْكِتَابِ قُلْنَا لَا يَارَسُوْلَ اللّٰهِ فَاَمَرَ بِغَلَقِ الْاَبْوَابِ وَقَالَ ارْفَعُوْا اَيْدِيْكُمْ وَقُوْلُوْا لَآاِلٰهَ اِلَّا اللّٰهُ فَرَفَعْنَا اَيْدِيَنَا سَاعَةً ثُمَّ قَالَ اَلْحَمْدُ لِلّٰهِ اَللّٰهُمَّ اِنَّكَ بَعَثْتَنِىْ بِهٰذِهِ الْكَلِمَةِ وَوَعَدْتَّنِىْ عَلَيْهَا الْجَنَّةَ وَاَنْتَ لَاتُخْلِفُ الْمِيْعَادَ ثُمَّ قَالَ اَبْشِرُوْا فَاِنَّ اللّٰهَ قَدْ غَفَرَ لَكُمْ رواه احمد باسناد حسن والطبرانی وغیرهما كذا فی الترغیب قلت واخرجه

الحاكم وقال اسماعيل بن عياش احدائمة اهل الشام وقد نسب الٰی سوء الحفظ وانا علی شرطی فی امثاله وقال الذهبی راشد ضعفه الدارقطنی وغیره ووثقه رحیم اهـ وفی مجمع الزوائد رواه احمد والطبرانی والبزار و رجال موثقون اهـ

Hadhrat Shaddaad (Radhiyallaho anho) relates, while Hadhrat Ubaadah (Radhiyallaho anho) confirms, that once we were sitting with Rasulullah (Sallallaho alaihe wasallam) and he asked if there was any stranger (non-Muslim) in the gathering. We submitted that there was none. He then had the door closed and asked us to raise our hands and recite (لآاِلٰهَ اِلَّا اللهُ). We raised our hands for some time and recited the Kalimah. He then exclaimed (لآاِلٰهَ اِلَّا اللهُ) and said: "O Allah! You have sent me with this Kalimah. You have promised paradise for those who profess it, and Your promise never remains unfulfilled." Then he turned to us and said: "Be happy, Allah has blessed you with His forgiveness." Rasulullah (Sallallaho alaihe wasallam) had made sure that no stranger was present there, and he had got the door closed, because presumably he had every hope that those particular people would be forgiven by virtue of reciting the Kalimah, and he had no such hope in respect of non-believers."

The Sufis quote this hadith as an argument for making their disciples engage in zikr collectively. It is stated in Jaami-ul-Usool that there were instances when Rasulullah (Sallallaho alaihe wasallam) made his companions do zikr collectively and individually, and this Hadith is quoted as authority for doing zikr collectively. In that case, the closing of the door would be to help those present to concentrate their attention. The enquiry about the presence of any stranger might also be for the same purpose; it may not have distracted the Prophet (Sallallaho alaihe wasallam), but there was likelihood of others getting distracted.

Hadith No. 7

(٧) عَنْ اَبِیْ هُرَیْرَةَ رَضِیَ اللهُ عَنْهُ قَالَ قَالَ رَسُوْلُ اللهِ ﷺ جَدِّدُوا اِیْمَانَکُمْ قِیْلَ یَارَسُوْلَ اللهِ وَکَیْفَ نُجَدِّدُ اِیْمَانَنَا قَالَ اَکْثِرُوْا مِنْ قَوْلِ لَآاِلٰهَ اِلَّا اللهُ

رواه احمد والطبرانی واسناد احمد حسن کذا فی الترغیب قلت ورواه الحاکم فی صحیحه وقال صحیح الاسناد وقال الذهبی صدقة (الراوی) ضعفوه قلت هو من رواة ابی داوٗد والترمذی واخرج له البخاری

فی الادب المفرد وقال فی التقریب صدوق له اوهام وذکره السیوطی فی الجامع الصغیر بروایة احمد والحاکم ورقم له بالصحة وفی مجمع الزوائد رواه احمد واسناده جیدو فی موضع اٰخر رواه احمد والطبرانی ورجال احمد ثقات

Rasulullah (Sallallaho alaihe wasallam) said: "Keep on renewing your Imaan. "O Rasulullah! Sallallaho alaihe wasallam, how should we renew our Imaan?" enquired the Sahabah. "Recite (لَآاِلٰهَ اِلَّا اللهُ) very often", was the reply.

Note:

In one hadith, Rasulullah (Sallallaho alaihe wasallam) is reported to have said, "Like old clothes, the Imaan also gets worn out, hence keep on renewing it through supplication to Almightv Allah." That the Imaan gets old and worn out means that it loses strength and radiance on account of sins. Thus it is stated in one hadith that, when a man commits a sin, a dark spot appears on his heart. If he then does sincere Taubah (repentance), this spot gets washed away, otherwise it remains there. When he commits another sin, another black dot appears on the heart. Thus, on account of further sins, the black dots continue to increase, till ultimately the heart is all blackened and rusted, as decribed in the Qur'an in Surah Tatfeef."

كَلَّا بَلْ رَانَ عَلٰى قُلُوْبِهِمْ مَّاكَانُوْا يَكْسِبُوْنَ

Nay, but that which they have earned is rust upon their hearts.

When such a stage is reached, then the heart is no longer influenced by words. It is said in one hadith, "Four things cause ruination of the heart, namely, debating with stupid people, excessive sinning, excessive mixing with women, and remaining in the society of the dead." Somebody enquired, "What is meant by the dead in this case?" Rasulullah (Sallallaho alaihe wasallam) explained that it meant such wealthy persons who assume arrogance on account of their wealth.

Hadith No. 8

(٨) عَنْ اَبِىْ هُرَيْرَةَ رَضِىَ اللهُ عَنْهُ قَالَ قَالَ رَسُوْلُ اللهِ ﷺ اَكْثِرُوْا مِنْ شَهَادَةِ اَنْ لَّا اِلٰهَ اِلَّا اللهُ قَبْلَ اَنْ يُّحَالَ بَيْنَكُمْ وَبَيْنَهَا رواه ابو یعلی باسناد جید قوی کذا فی

الترغيب وعزاه فى الجامع الى ابى يعلى وابن عدى فى الكامل ورقم له بالضعف وزاد لقنوها موتاكم و فى مجمع الزوائد رواه ابو يعلى و رجاله رجال الصحيح غير ضمام وهو ثقة

Rasulullah (Sallallaho alaihe wasallam) said, "Recite (لآإِلٰهَ اِلَّا اللهُ) very often, before the time of death comes when you will not be able to say it."

Note:

It means that no deed is possible after death. This life is very short, but it is the only time for action and for sowing the seeds. This life after death is infinitely long, and we will there reap whatever we have sown here.

Hadith No. 9

(٩) عَنْ عَمْرٍو رَضِىَ اللهُ عَنْهُ قَالَ سَمِعْتُ رَسُوْلَ اللهِ ﷺ يَقُوْلُ اِنِّىْ لَاَعْلَمُ كَلِمَةً لَايَقُوْلُهَا عَبْدٌ حَقًّا مِّنْ قَلْبِهٖ فَيَمُوْتُ عَلٰى ذٰلِكَ اِلَّا حُرِّمَ عَلَى النَّارِ لَآاِلٰهَ اِلَّا اللهُ رواه الحاكم وقال صحيح على شرطها ورويا بنحوه كذا فى الترغيب

Rasulullah (Sallallaho alaihe wasallam) said, "I know of a Kalimah, such that if anybody recites it with sincerity of belief in it and then dies, Hell becomes forbidden for him. This Kalimah is (لآاِلٰهَ اِلَّا اللهُ)."

Note:

This subject matter has been related in many ahadith. If the person referred to in the above hadith has been a new convert to Islam, then there can be no doubt about the meaning, because it is unanimously agreed that on embracing Islaam all the sins committed as a non-Muslim are forgiven. But if it refers to an old Muslim, who recites the Kalimah with sincerity just before his death, even then it is hoped that Almighty Allah, through His sheer Grace, may forgive all his sins. Almighty Allah has Himself said that He may forgive whomsoever He likes, all his sins, except Shirk.

Mulla Ali Qari (Rahmatullah alaih) has stated that some scholars are of the view that these ahadith pertain to the very early period of Islaam when detailed commandments had not yet been revealed. Some scholars have stated that the hadith implies declaration of this Kalimah with proper discharge of one's obligations enjoined by it, as given under Hadith No 4 above. Hasan Basri (Rahmatullah alaih) and many others also held the same view. According to the considered view of Imam Bukhari (Rahmatullah alaih) Allah's promise holds good if the declaration of the Kalimah before death is with repentance, which is the essence of Taubah while, according to Mulla Ali Qari, the reciter will not be doomed to Hell for ever. Moreover, it is a matter of common observation that sometimes the inherent quality of a thing becomes ineffective due to some counterforce. For instance, a purgative may become ineffective if it is followed by a strong constipative drug, but that does not mean that the purgative has become devoid of its inherent effect; it has only not worked because of the strong counteracting agent.

Hadith No 10

(١٠) عَنْ مُعَاذِبْنِ جَبَلٍ رَضِىَ اللّٰهُ عَنْهُ قَالَ قَالَ رَسُوْلُ اللّٰهِ ﷺ مَفَاتِيْحُ الْجَنَّةِ شَهَادَةُ اَنْ لَّا اِلٰهَ اِلَّا اللّٰهُ رواه أحمد كذا في المشكوٰة والجامع الصغير ورقم له بالضعف وفي مجمع الزوائد رواه أحمد ورجاله وثقوا إلا أن شهرا لم يسمعه عن معاذ اهـ ورواه البزار كذا في الترغيب وزاد السيوطى في الدر ابن مردويه والبيهقي وذكره في المقاصد الحسنة برواية أحمد بلفظ مفتاح الجنة لا إله إلا الله واختلف في وجه حمل الشهادة وهى مفرد على المفاتيح وهى جمع على أقوال أوجهها عندي أنها لماكانت مفتاحا لكل باب من أبوابه صارت كالمفاتيح

Rasulullah (Sallallaho alaihe wasallam) said "Professing faith in (لَآاِلٰهَ اِلَّا اللّٰهُ) provides the keys to Paradise."

Note:

The Kalimah has been described as the keys of Paradise, because it serves as the key for opening every door and every part of Paradise; therefore, the Kalimah constitutes all the keys. Or else, it is called the keys, because the Kalimah itself is made up of two parts, one (لَآاِلٰهَ اِلَّا اللّٰهُ) and the other مُحَمَّدٌ رَّسُوْلُ اللّٰهِ. Thus, the Paradise may be said to open with these two keys. In these ahadith, wherever the Kalimah is stated to cause entry into Paradise or protection against Hell, it means the complete Kalimah comprising both the parts. In one hadith, it is said that the price of Paradise is (لَآاِلٰهَ اِلَّا اللّٰهُ).

Hadith No 11

(۱۱) عَنْ اَنَسٍ رَضِیَ اللّٰہُ عَنْہُ قَالَ قَالَ رَسُوْلُ اللّٰہِ ﷺ مَامِنْ عَبْدٍ قَالَ لَآاِلٰہَ اِلَّا اللّٰہُ فِیْ سَاعَۃٍ مِّنْ لَّیْلٍ اَوْ نَھَارٍ اِلَّا طُمِسَتْ مَافِی الصَّحِیْفَۃِ مِنَ السَّیِّئَاتِ حَتّٰی تَسْکُنَ اِلٰی مِثْلِھَا مِنَ الْحَسَنَاتِ رواه أبو يعلى كذا في الترغيب وفي مجمع الزوائد فيه عثمان بن عبدالرحمن فيه عثمان بن عبدالرحمن الزهري وهو متروك اهـ

Rasulullah (Sallallaho alaihe wasallam) said, "Whosoever recites (لَآاِلٰہَ اِلَّا اللّٰہُ) any time during day or night, his sins are remitted from his account and virtues are written instead."

Note:

The replacement of sins by virtues has been fully described under Hadith No 10 of Chapter 1, part 2, where various meanings of all the aayats and ahadith of this kind are given. According to every version, this hadith categorically states that sins are washed away from the account of a person's deeds, provided there is Ikhlaas, that is sincerity of intention. In any case, hymning the blessed name of Allah and excessive recitation of Kalimah Tayyibah also develops Ikhlaas. That is why this blessed Kalimah is also called the Kalimah of Ikhlaas."

Hadith No. 12

(۱۲) عَنْ اَبِیْ ھُرَیْرَۃَ رَضِیَ اللّٰہُ عَنْہُ عَنِ النَّبِیِّ ﷺ قَالَ اِنَّ لِلّٰہِ تَبَارَکَ وَتَعَالٰی عَمُوْدًا مِّنْ نُوْرٍ بَیْنَ یَدَیِ الْعَرْشِ فَاِذَا قَالَ الْعَبْدُ لَآاِلٰہَ اِلَّا اللّٰہُ اِھْتَزَّ ذٰلِکَ الْعَمُوْدُ فَیَقُوْلُ اللّٰہُ تَبَارَکَ وَتَعَالٰی اُسْکُنْ فَیَقُوْلُ کَیْفَ اَسْکُنُ وَلَمْ یُغْفَرْ لِقَائِلِھَا فَیَقُوْلُ اِنِّیْ قَدْ غَفَرْتُ لَہٗ فَیَسْکُنُ عِنْدَ ذٰلِکَ رواه البزار وهو غريب كذا في الترغيب وفي مجمع الزوائد فيه عبدالله بن إبراهيم بن أبي عمرو وهو ضعيف جداً اهـ قلت وبسط السيوطي في اللآلى على طرقه وذكر له شواهد

Rasulullah (Sallallaho alaihe wasallam) said, "There is a pillar of Noor (Divine Light) in front of the Arshi Ilaahi (the Throne of Allah). When somebody recites (لَآاِلٰہَ اِلَّا اللّٰہُ), this pillar starts shaking. When Allah asks it to stop shaking, it says, 'How can I stop, when the reciter of the Kalimah has not yet been granted forgiveness?'

Thereupon Allah says: 'Well, I have forgiven him', and then that pillar stops shaking.''

Note:

Some scholars of hadith have doubted authenticity of this hadith, but Allama Suyuti (Rahmatullah alaih) has written that this hadith (tradition) in different words has been narrated through many sources. According to some narrations, Almighty Allah also says, ''I have made him utter the Kalimah in order that I may grant him forgiveness.'' How kind and benevolent is Almighty Allah that He himself graces a person with the power to do this virtuous act, and then grants pardon on this basis to complete His extreme favour. In this connection a story told about Hadhrat Ataa (Rahmatullah alaih) is well known. He once happened to go to the market where a woman lunatic slave was on sale. He purchased her. At midnight she got up, performed her ablution, and began offering Salaat. During her prayers she wept so profusely that her breath was getting choked. Then she said: ''O my Lord! in the name of the love that You have for me, bestow Your Mercy on me.'' Hearing this, Ataa said ''O, slave woman, say: 'O Allah, in the name of the love that I have for You.''' Upon hearing this she got upset and said, ''By Allah! If He had not loved me, He would not have let you sleep and made me to stand in prayer as you see!'' Then she recited the following couplets:

اَلْكَرَبُ مُجْتَمِعٌ وَالْقَلْبُ مُحْتَرِقٌ   وَالصَّبْرُ مُفْتَرِقٌ وَالدَّمْعُ مُستَبِقٌ

كَيْفَ القَرَارُ عَلٰى مَنْ لَا قَرَارَ لَهُ   مِمَّا جَنَاهُ الهَوٰى والشَّوْقُ والْقَلَقٌ

يَارَبِّ اِنْ كَانَ شَيْءٌ فِيْهِ لِىْ فَرَجٌ   فَامْنُنْ عَلَيَّ بِهِ مَادَامَ بِىْ رَمَقٌ

My restlessness is increasing, and my heart is burning; patience has forsaken me, and my tears are flowing. How can one have peace of mind, when one is all upset by the pangs of love and restlessness. O Allah! if there is anything which can help me to get rid of my grief, please bestow it upon me as a favour! Then she said, 'O Allah! so far the deal between You and me was known to none, since it has ceased to be secret now, take me away from here. Saying this, she uttered a shriek and breathed her last. There have been many other incidents like this. It is a fact that only Almighty Allah grants the power to do good.

وَمَا تَشَآءُوْنَ اِلَّا اَنْ يَّشَآءَ اللّٰهُ رَبُّ الْعٰلَمِيْنَ

(And if Allah, the Sustainer of the Universe does not will it, you cannot even wish for anything).

Hadith No 13

(١٣) عَنْ اِبْنِ عُمَرَ رَضِیَ اللّٰهُ عَنْهُ قَالَ قَالَ رَسُوْلُ اللّٰهِ ﷺ لَيْسَ عَلٰی اَهْلِ لَآ اِلٰهَ اِلَّا اللّٰهُ وَحْشَةٌ فِیْ قُبُوْرِهِمْ وَ لَامَنْشَرِهِمْ وَكَاَنِّی اَنْظُرُ اِلٰی اَهْلِ لَآ اِلٰهَ اِلَّا اللّٰهُ وَهُمْ يَنْفُضُوْنَ التُّرَابَ عَنْ رُؤُسِهِمْ وَيَقُوْلُوْنَ اَلْحَمْدُ لِلّٰهِ الَّذِيْ اَذْهَبَ عَنَّا الْحَزَنَ

وفي رواية ليس على أهل لا إله إلا الله وحشةٌ عند الموت ولا عند القبر رواه الطبراني والبيهقى كلاهما من رواية يحيى بن عبدالحميد الحمانى وفي متنه نكارة كذا في الترغيب وذكره في الجامع الصغير برواية الطبراني عن ابن عمر ورقم له بالضعف وفي اسنى المطالب رواه الطبراني وأبويعلى بسند ضعيف وفي مجمع الزوائد رواه الطبراني وفي رواية ليس على أهل لا إله إلا الله وحشة عندالموت ولا عند القبر في الأولى يحيى الحمانى وفي الأخرى مجاشع بن عمرو كلاهما ضعيف اهـ وقال السخاوي في المقاصد الحسنة رواه أبويعلى والبيهقي في الشعب والطبراني بسند ضعيف عن ابن عمر اهـ قلت وماحكم عليه المنذري بالنكارة مبناه أنه حمل أهل لا إله إلا الله على الظاهر على كل مسلم ومعلوم أن بعض المسلمين يعذبون في القبر والحشر فيكون الحديث مخالفاً للمعروف فيكون منكرا لكنه إن أريد به المخصوص بهذه الصفة فيكون موافقا للنصوص الكثيرة من القرآن والحديث والسابقون السابقون أولئك المقربون ومنهم سابق بالخيرات باذن الله وسبعون ألفا يدخلون الجنة بغير حساب وغير ذلك من الآيات والروايات فالحديث موافق لها لامخالف فيكون معروفا لامنكرا وذكر السيوطى في الجامع الصغير برواية ابن مردويه والبيهقى فى البعث عن عمر بلفظ سابقنا سابق ومقتصدنا ناج وظالمنا مغفور له ورقم له بالحسن قلت ويؤيد حديث سبق المفردون المستهترون في ذكر الله يضع الذكر عنهم أثقالهم فيأتون يوم القيامة خفافا رواه الترمذي والحاكم عن أبي هريرة والطبراني عن أبي الددرداء كذا في الجامع ورقم له بالصحة وفي الاتحاف عن ابى رداء موقوفا الذين لاتزال السنتهم رطبة من ذكر الله يدخلون الجنة وهم يضحكون وفى الجامع الصغير برواية الحاكم ورقم له بالصحة السابق والمقتصد يدخلون الجنة بغير حساب ، والظالم لنفسه يحاسب حسابا يسيرا ثم يدخل الجنة

Virtues of Zikr

Rasulullah (Sallallaho alaihe wasallam) has said, "Those who believe in لَآ اِلٰهَ اِلَّا اللّٰهُ will neither have fear in the grave nor on the Day of Resurrection. It is as if I see the spectacle when they will rise from their graves, wiping dust from their heads and saying: 'All praise is for Allah, who has cast off (for good) all worry and fear from us.'"

It is stated in another hadith that those who profess لَآ اِلٰهَ اِلَّا اللهُ will experience no affliction at the time of death or in the grave.

Note:

Hadhrat Ibn Abbaas (Radhiyallaho anho) says: "Once Hazrat Jibraa-eel (Alayhis salaam) came to Rasulullah (Sallallaho alaihe wasallam): Rasulullah (Sallallaho alaihe wasallam) was very much worried, and Jibraa-eel said: 'Almighty Allah has sent His salaam to you and has enquired why you look so sad and worried!" Although Allah knows whatever is hidden in the hearts, yet by such enquiries Allah means to indicate honour, respect and favours. Rasulullah (Sallallaho alaihe wasallam) replied, "O Jibraa-eel! I am worried about my Ummat, as to how they will (fare) on the Day of Judgement!" "Is it about the non-believers or about the Muslims?" asked Jibraa-eel (Alayhis salaam). "About the Muslims," replied the Prophet (Sallallaho alaihe wasallam). Jibraa-eel (Alayhis salaam) then took the Prophet (Sallallaho alaihe wasallam) along to a graveyard where the people of the tribe of Banu Salama were buried; there he struck a grave with his wing and said قُمْ بِاِذْنِ اللهِ (stand up by the orders of Allah). Out of that grave, an extremely handsome man stood up, and he was reciting

لَآ اِلٰهَ اِلَّا اللهُ مُحَمَّدٌ رَّسُوْلُ اللهِ اَلْحَمْدُ لِلّٰهِ رَبِّ الْعَالَمِيْنَ

Hadhrat Jibraa-eel (Alayhis salaam) told him to go back to his place, which he did. Then he struck another grave with his wing. Out of it stood up an extremely ugly person with black face and worried eyes, who was saying, "Alas, there is nothing but sorrow, shame and horror!" Hadhrat Jibraa-eel (Alayhis salaam) told him to go back to his place, and then explained to Rasulullah (Sallallaho alaihe wasallam), "The people will rise up on the Day of Resurrection in the same state that they were at the time of their death."

In this hadith, the people of لَآ اِلٰهَ اِلَّا اللهُ apparently imply those who have close attachment for and remain busy with this Kalimah, just as milkman, shoeman, pearlman and iceman mean those who deal in and especially stock those particular things. Thus, there is no doubt whatsoever that the people of this Kalimah, will receive this extraordinary treatment. In Surah Faatir of the Holy Qur'an, three categories of this Ummat have been described; one category is named سابق بالخيرات (leaders in virtues), about whom it is stated in a hadith that they will enter Paradise without any reckoning. According to one hadith, a person who recites لآ اِلٰهَ اِلَّا اللّٰهُ one hundred times daily will on the Day of Resurrection be raised up with his face shining like the full moon. Hadhrat Abu Darda (Radhiyallaho anho) narrated that those whose tongues remain busy in the zikr of Allah will enter Paradise rejoicing.

Hadith No. 14

(١٤) عَنْ عَبْدِ اللّٰهِ بْنِ عَمْرِو بْنِ الْعَاصِ رَضِىَ اللّٰهُ عَنْهُ اَنَّ رَسُوْلَ اللّٰهِ ﷺ قَالَ اِنَّ اللّٰهَ يَسْتَخْلِصُ رَجُلًا مِّنْ اُمَّتِيْ عَلٰى رُءُوْسِ الْخَلَائِقِ يَوْمَ الْقِيَامَةِ فَيَنْشُرُ عَلَيْهِ تِسْعَةً وَّتِسْعِيْنَ سِجِلًّا كُلُّ سِجِلٍّ مِثْلُ مَدِّ الْبَصَرِ ثُمَّ يَقُوْلُ اَتُنْكِرُ مِنْ هٰذَا شَيْئًا اَظَلَمَكَ كَتَبَتِيَ الْحَافِظُوْنَ فَيَقُوْلُ لَايَارَبِّ فَيَقُوْلُ اَفَلَكَ عُذْرٌ فَيَقُوْلُ لَا يَارَبِّ فَيَقُوْلُ اللّٰهُ تَعَالٰى بَلٰى اِنَّ لَكَ عِنْدَنَا حَسَنَةً فَاِنَّهُ لَاظُلْمَ عَلَيْكَ الْيَوْمَ فَتُخْرَجُ بِطَاقَةٌ فِيْهَا اَشْهَدُ اَنْ لَّااِلٰهَ اِلَّا اللّٰهُ وَاَشْهَدُ اَنَّ مُحَمَّدًا عَبْدُهٗ وَرَسُوْلُهٗ فَيَقُوْلُ اُحْضُرْ وَزْنَكَ فَيَقُوْلُ يَارَبِّ مَاهٰذِهِ الْبِطَاقَةُ مَعَ هٰذِهِ السِّجِلَّاتِ فَقَالَ فَاِنَّكَ لَاتُظْلَمُ الْيَوْمَ فَتُوْضَعُ السِّجِلَّاتُ فِيْ كِفَّةٍ وَالْبِطَاقَةُ فِيْ كِفَّةٍ فَطَاشَتِ السِّجِلَّاتُ وَثَقُلَتِ الْبِطَاقَةُ فَلَايَثْقُلُ مَعَ اللّٰهِ شَيْءٌ رواه الترمذي وقال حسن غريب وابن ماجه وابن حبان في صحيحه والبيهقي والحاكم وقال صحيح على شرط مسلم كذا في الترغيب . قلت قال الحاكم في كتاب الإيمان وأخرجه أيضا في كتاب الدعوات وقال صحيح الاسناد وأقره في الموضعين الذهبي وفي المشكواة أخرجه برواية الترمذي وابن ماجة وزاد السيوطي في الدر فيمن عزاه إليهم أحمد وابن مردويه واللالكائى والبيهقي في البعث وفيه اختلاف في بعض الالفاظ كقوله في أول الحديث يُصاحُ بِرَجُلٍ مِنْ امتى عَلى رُءوسِ الخلائِقِ وفيه أيضا فيقول اَفَلَكَ عُذرٌ أو حسنةٌ فيُهابُ الرجل فيقول لا يارَبِّ فيقول بلى إن لك عندنا حسنةً الحديث وعلم منه أن الاستدراك في الحديث على محله ولاحاجة إذا إلى ما أوله القارى في المرقاة وذكر السيوطى مايؤيد الرواية من الروايات الاخر

Rasulullah (Sallallaho alaihe wasallam) said, "On the Day of Judgement, Almighty Allah will select a man from my Ummat and will call him in the presence of all mankind, and then 99 registers of his misdeeds, each register as long as one can see, will be opened before him. He will then be asked if he denies anything recorded in his account of deeds, or whether the angels who were appointed to record his deeds had been unjust to him in any respect. He will reply in the negative (i.e. he will neither deny anything nor blame the angels for any injustice to him). Then Allah will ask him if he can justify his misdeeds, but he will submit that he has no excuse to offer. Then Allah will say 'Well, there is indeed one virtue to your credit. Today no injustice will be done to you.' Then a small piece of paper with the Kalimah

اَشْهَدُ اَنْ لَآ اِلٰهَ اِلَّا اللّٰهُ وَاَشْهَدُ اَنَّ مُحَمَّدًا عَبْدُهٗ وَرَسُوْلُهٗ

written on it will be handed over to him, and he will be asked to go and get it weighed. He will submit that this small piece of paper will be of little avail as against so many lengthy registers. Allah will say, "This day, no injustice will be done to you." Then all the registers will be placed in one pan and the piece of paper in the other pan. The pan with the registers will fly up in the air on account of the excessive weight of that piece of paper. The fact is that nothing is weightier than the name of Allah."

Note:

It is a blessed result of Ikhlaas that a single recitation, with sincerity, of Kalimah Tayyibah can outweigh all the misdeeds recorded in so many registers. It is, therefore, necessary that one should not look down upon any Muslim and think oneself as superior to him. Who knows that Almighty Allah may accept from him some deeds that may suffice for his redemption, while nobody can be sure about himself whether any of his own deeds will be found worthy of acceptance. There is related in one hadith the story of two persons belonging to Bani Israa-eel. One of whom was worshipper and the other was a sinner. The worshipper always criticised the latter, who used to reply: "Leave me to my Creator." One day, the worshipper, in a fit of anger, said: 'By Allah! you will never be forgiven.' Almighty Allah assembled them unto His presence and pardoned the sinner because he always expected mercy from Him, but ordered punishment for the worshipper due to his swearing upon Allah. No doubt, the oath was serious and offended against the declaration of Allah in the verse

اِنَّ اللّٰهَ لَا يَغْفِرُ اَنْ يُّشْرَكَ بِهٖ وَيَغْفِرُ مَادُوْنَ ذٰلِكَ لِمَنْ يَّشَاءُ

(Almighty Allah will not forgive Kufr and Shirk but excepting that, He may forgive any sin as He may like). None else has the right to say that a certain person will not be forgiven, but this does not mean that we should not warn others against sins and undesirable things, and ask others to desist from these. At hundreds of places in the Holy Qur'an and in the books of hadith, there are warnings against not forbidding from evil. It is stated in many ahadith that the people who see a sin being committed and do not stop it, in spite of their having power to do so, will also share the punishment for that sin. This point has been discussed by me in detail in my book, Fazaaile Tabligh, which can be consulted if desired. There is, moreover, a note of caution. Whereas it is very wrong to condemn sinful Muslims as absolute dwellers of Hell, it is even more dangerous on the part of ignorant people to accept any person as their spiritual guide, in spite of his being devoid of good practices and his saying senseless and un-Islamic words. Rasulullah (Sallallaho alaihe wasallam) has said: "Whosoever respects an innovator in Islam is considered to have taken part in demolishing Islam." It is stated in several ahadith that in times to come, there will appear many imposters, cheats and liars, who will relate ahadith that you will have never heard before. Beware of such persons, lest they should mislead you and put you into trouble."

Hadith No. 15

(١٥) عَنْ اِبْنِ عَبَّاسٍ رَضِىَ اللّٰهُ عَنْهُ قَالَ قَالَ رَسُوْلُ اللّٰهِ ﷺ وَالَّذِىْ نَفْسِىْ بِيَدِهٖ لَوْ جِيْءَ بِالسَّمٰوٰتِ وَالْاَرْضِ وَمَنْ فِيْهِنَّ وَمَابَيْنَهُنَّ وَمَا تَحْتَهُنَّ فَوُضِعْنَ فِيْ كِفَّةِ الْمِيْزَانِ وَوُضِعَتْ شَهَادَةُ اَنْ لَّآاِلٰهَ اِلَّا اللّٰهُ فِىْ الْكِفَّةِ الْاُخْرٰى لَرَجَحَتْ بِهِنَّ

اخرجه الطبراني كذا في الدر وهكذا في مجمع الزوائد وزاد في أوله لَقِّنُوْا موتاكم شهادة أن لا إله إلا الله فمن قالها عند موته وجبت له الجنة قالوا يارسول الله فمن قالها في صحته قال تلك أوجب وأوجب ثم قال والذي نفسي بيده الحديث قال رواه الطبراني ورجاله ثقات إلا ان ابن أبي طلحة لم يسمع من ابن عباس

Rasulullah (Sallallaho alaihe wasallam) said: "I swear by Allah Who controls my life that if all the skies and the Earth, with all the people and all the things between them and all that may be within them, are placed together in one pan of the balance, and the faith in (لَآاِلٰهَ اِلَّا اللهُ) is put in the other pan, the latter will outweigh the former."

This subject matter has been described in many ahadith. It admits of no doubt that nothing can be equal to the blessed name of Allah. It is really a great misfortune and deprivation for those who take it lighty. However, the weight of this Kalimah is proportional to the Ikhlaas with which it is uttered. The greater the Ikhlaas, the weightier becomes the Kalimah. It is to cultivate this Ikhlaas that one has to remain in the service of the Sufis. According to one hadith, the above-mentioned saying of Rasulullah (Sallallaho alaihe wasallam) was in connection with another subject matter. He has said: "Persuade a dying person to recite (لَآاِلٰهَ اِلَّا اللهُ) because he who recites this Kalimah at the time of his death gets entitled to enter Paradise." The Sahaba enquired: "O Rasulullah! (Sallallaho alaihe wasallam) what about reciting it during good health?" He replied, "Then it is even more effective in obtaining entitlement to Paradise," and then stated, on oath, the hadith related above.

Hadith No. 16

(١٦) عَنْ اِبْنِ عَبَّاسٍ رَضِىَ اللهُ عَنْهُ قَالَ جَاءَ النَّحَّامُ بْنُ زَيْدٍ وَقُرَدُ بْنُ كَعْبٍ وَبَحْرِيُّ بْنُ عَمْرٍو فَقَالُوْا يَامُحَمَّدُ مَاتَعْلَمُ مَعَ اللهِ اِلٰهًا غَيْرَهُ فَقَالَ رَسُوْلُ اللهِ ﷺ لَآاِلٰهَ اِلَّا اللهُ بِذٰلِكَ بُعِثْتُ وَاِلٰى ذٰلِكَ اَدْعُوْا فَاَنْزَلَ اللهُ تَعَالٰى فِىْ قَوْلِهِمْ قُلْ أَيُّ شَيْءٍ اَكْبَرُ شَهَادَةً الاية

أخرجه ابن إسحاق وابن المنذر وابن أبي حاتم وأبوالشيخ كذا في الدر المنثور

There came to Rasulullah (Sallallaho alaihe wasallam) three non-Muslims who said to him: "O Muhammad! (Sallallaho alaihe wasallam) don't you recognise anybody, except Allah as worthy of worship?" In reply, Rasulullah (Sallallaho alaihe wasallam) recited (لَآاِلٰهَ اِلَّا اللهُ) (Nobody is worthy of worship except Allah), and added: "I have been deputed specifically for the propagation of this Kalimah, and to it I invite all mankind." It was in this connection that the verse قُلْ اَيُّ شَيْءٍ اَكْبَرُ شَهَادَةً (What thing is of most weight in testimony) was revealed."

Note:

The words of Rasulullah (Sallallaho alaihe wasallam) namely, "I have been deputed (as a prophet) specifically for the propagation of this Kalimah, and to it I invite all mankind" did not mean that only he had been sent on this special mission. In fact, all the Prophets had been deputed for the propagation of this Kalimah, and all of them had invited mankind to it. From Aadam (Alayhis salaam) to Rasulullah (Sallallaho alaihe wasallam) the last and the best of Prophets, there was not a single prophet who had not propagated this sublime Kalimah. So blessed and sublime is this Kalimah, that all the Prophets and all true religions propagated it, and served its cause. In fact, every true religion is based on this Kalimah. It is in support of this Kalimah that the Qur'anic verse قُلْ اَیُّ شَيْءٍ اَكْبَرُ شَهَادَةً ، (انعام ع ۲) has been revealed, in which Almighty Allah is a witness in favour of Rasulullah (Sallallaho alaihe wasallam). According to one hadith, when somebody recites (لَآ اِلٰهَ اِلَّا اللّٰهُ) then Almighty Allah testifies to it and says: "My slave has spoken the truth; there is nobody worthy of worship except I."

Hadith No. 17

(۱۷) عَنْ لَيْثٍ قَالَ قَالَ عِيسٰى بْنُ مَرْيَمَ عَلَيْهِ السَّلَامُ اُمَّةُ مُحَمَّدٍ (ﷺ) اَثْقَلُ النَّاسِ فِي الْمِيْزَانِ ذَلَّتْ اَلْسِنَتُهُمْ بِكَلِمَةٍ ثَقُلَتْ عَلٰى مَنْ كَانَ قَبْلَهُمْ لَآ اِلٰهَ اِلَّا اللّٰهُ

أخرجه الأصبهاني في الترغيب كذا في الدر

The Prophet Eesa (Jesus) (Alayhis salaam) had said: The deeds of the Ummat of Hadhrat Muhammad (Sallallaho alaihe wasallam) would be reckoned weightiest, on the Day of Judgement, because their tongues are accustomed to the recitation of a Kalimah, which was found too hard by the Ummats of other Prophets, and this Kalimah is لَآ اِلٰهَ اِلَّا اللّٰهُ.

Note:

It is a fact that the Ummat of Rasulullah (Sallallaho alaihe wasallam) is devoted particularly to this Kalimah, far more than any other Ummat. There have been hundreds of thousands, nay millions of Sufis (divine persons) every one of whom had hundreds of disciples, all of whom recited the Kalimah thousands of times daily as a matter of routine. It is stated in the book 'Jaami-ul-Usool' that the word 'Allah' should be repeated a minimum number of five thousand times daily and that there is no upper limit for this, and the Sufis are required to repeat (لَآاِلٰهَ اِلَّا اللّٰهُ) daily at least twenty five thousand times. This number varies according to the advice of the Mashaaikh. I have related all this in support of the above saying of Hadhrat Eesa (Jesus) (Alayhis salaam). Shah Waliullah (Rahmatullah alaih) has stated in his book al-Qowlul Jameel that his father as a beginner in Sufism used to recite (لَآاِلٰهَ اِلَّا اللّٰهُ) two hundred times in one breath.

Shaikh Abu Yazeed Qurtubi (Rahmatullah alaih) writes: "On learning that one who recites (لَآاِلٰهَ اِلَّا اللّٰهُ) seventy thousand times becomes safe from the fire of Hell, I completed this number once for my wife and then several times for my own self as a provision for the Hereafter. There used to live near us a young man who was known to be blessed with the power of Kashf (divine manifestation of unseen thing), even in respect of Paradise and Hell, but I hesitated to believe it. Once when this young man was dining with us, he uttered a cry of agony, his breathing became difficult and he exclaimed, 'I see my mother burning in fire of Hell.' When I saw him so perturbed, I thought of bestowing one of my complete seventy thousand recitations of the Kalimah in favour of his mother, so that the truth of what the young man said could be tested. I quietly did so in my heart, without telling anybody else about it. But as soon as I did this, the young man felt relieved and said, 'O Uncle! my mother has been relieved of the punishment of Hell! This incident proved useful to me in two ways: firstly, the blessing of reciting the Kalimah seventy thousand times was proved by actual experience, and secondly it was established that the young man was truly blessed with the power of Kashf.

This is but one of many such incidents in the lives of various individuals of this Ummat. The Sufis make their followers practise that no breath goes in or comes out without zikr of Allah. There are millions of people from the Ummat of Muhammad (Sallallaho alaihe wasallam) who have adopted this practice. There is, therefore, no denying the fact stated by Hazrat Eesa (Jesus) (Alayhis salaam) that their tongues are specially accustomed to the recitation of the Kalimah.

Hadith No. 18

(١٨) عَنْ اِبْنِ عَبَّاسٍ رَضِیَ اللّٰهُ عَنْهُ اَنَّ رَسُوْلَ اللّٰهِ ﷺ قَالَ مَكْتُوْبٌ عَلٰى بَابِ الْجَنَّةِ اِنَّنِیْ اَنَا اللّٰهُ لَآ اِلٰهَ اِلَّا اَنَا لَآاُعَذِّبُ مَنْ قَالَهَا أخرجه أبو الشيخ كذا في الدر المنثور

Rasulullah (Sallallaho alaihe wasallam) has said: "There is inscribed on the gate of Paradise اِنَّنِیْ اَنَا اللّٰهُ لَآ اِلٰهَ اِلَّا اَنَا لَآ اُعَذِّبُ مَنْ قَالَهَا (Only I am Allah, none except I am worthy of worship. Whosoever keeps reciting this Kalimah will not be punished by Me.)"

That punishment will be awarded for sins is mentioned in many other ahadith. As such, if the word punishment mentioned in the above hadith implies eternal punishment, then there is no doubt as regards the final atonement. But if any fortunate person recites this Kalimah with such sincerity of heart that he is altogether spared from punishment in spite of his sins, no one can question the mercy of Almighty Allah, as already stated under ahadith 9 and 14 of this chapter.

Virtues of Zikr

Hadith No. 19

(١٩) عَنْ عَلِيٍّ رَضِیَ اللّٰهُ عَنْهُ قَالَ حَدَّثَنَا رَسُوْلُ اللّٰهِ ﷺ عَنْ جِبْرَئِيْلَ عَلَيْهِ السَّلَامُ قَالَ قَالَ اللّٰهُ عَزَّ وَجَلَّ اِنِّیْ اَنَا اللّٰهُ لَآ اِلٰهَ اِلَّا اَنَا فَاعْبُدْنِيْ مَنْ جَاءَنِیْ مِنْكُمْ بِشَهَادَةِ اَنْ لَّآاِلٰهَ اِلَّا اللّٰهُ بِالْاِخْلَاصِ دَخَلَ فِيْ حِصْنِيْ وَمَنْ دَخَلَ فِيْ حِصْنِيْ اَمِنَ عَذَابِيْ أخرجه أبونعيم في الحلية كذا في الدر وابن عساكر كذا في الجامع الصغير وفيه أيضا برواية الشيرازي عن على ورقم له بالصحة وفي الباب عن عتبان ابن مالك بلفظ ان الله قد حرم على النار من قال لا إله إلا الله يبتغى بذلك وجه الله رواه الشيخان وعن ابن عمر بلفظ أن الله لا يعذب من عباده إلا المارد والمتمرد الذي يتمرد على الله وأبىٰ أن يقول لااله الا الله رواه ابن ماجه

Rasulullah (Sallallaho alaihe wasallam) related that he was told by Jibraa-eel (Alayhis salam) that Almighty Allah says: "Only I am Allah; there is none worthy of worship except I, hence worship only Me; whosoever will come to Me with firm faith in (لَآ اِلٰهَ اِلَّا اللّٰه) will enter My fort, and whosoever enters My fort will be safe from My punishment."

Note:

If the abovementioned blessing is on the condition that one does not commit major sins, as mentioned under Hadith No 5, then there is no ambiguity about it; but if recitation of the Kalimah, in spite of major sins, is implied, then the word 'punishment' implies eternal punishment. However, Allah's Mercy knows no bounds. It is mentioned in the Qur'an that Almighty Allah will not forgive the sin of Shirk (polytheism), but will forgive any other sin, as he may like. According to one hadith, Almighty Allah punishes only such persons who revolt against him and refuse to recite (لَآ اِلٰهَ اِلَّا اللّٰه). According to another hadith, the recitation of (لَآ اِلٰهَ اِلَّا اللّٰه) removes the wrath of Almighty Allah, as long as one refrains from attaching more importance to the worldly things as compared with the religion; but if one starts preferring the former over the religion, then recitation of (لَآ اِلٰهَ اِلَّا اللّٰه) proves of little use, because then Allah says: "You are not true to what you profess."

Hadith No. 20

(٢٠) عَنْ عَبْدِ اللّٰهِ بِنْ عَمْرٍو عَنِ النَّبِيِّ ﷺ قَالَ اَفْضَلُ الذِّكْرِ لَآ اِلٰهَ اِلَّا اللّٰهُ وَاَفْضَلُ الدُّعَآءِ اَلْاِسْتِغْفَارُ ثُمَّ قَرَأَ فَاعْلَمْ اَنَّهُ لَآ اِلٰهَ اِلَّا اللّٰهُ وَاسْتَغْفِرْ لِذَنْبِكَ الآية

أخرجه الطبراني وابن مردويه والديلمي كذا في الدر وفي الجامع الصغير برواية الطبراني مامن الذكر أفضل من لا إله إلا الله ولا من الدعاء أفضل من الاستغفار ورقم له بالحسن

Rasulullah (Sallallaho alaihe wasallam) said: "The best form of zikr is (لَآاِلٰهَ اِلَّا اللّٰه); and the best form of du'aa is Istighfaar (seeking forgiveness of Allah)"; then, in support thereof, he recited from Surah Muhammad, the verse

فَاعْلَمْ اَنَّهُ لَآ اِلٰهَ اِلَّا اللّٰهُ

So know that none is worthy of worship but Allah.

It is already given in Hadith No. 1 of this Chapter that (لَآاِلٰهَ اِلَّا اللّٰه) is superior to all other forms of zikr. The reason for this superiority, according to the Sufis, is that zikr has a special cleansing effect on the heart; by virtue of this zikr, the heart gets purified of all its maladies and, if supplemented by Istighfaar, this becomes most effective. It is stated in one hadith that when the fish had swallowed Hadhrat Yunus (Alayhis salaam) he recited the prayer

لَآ اِلٰهَ اِلَّآ اَنْتَ سُبْحَانَكَ اِنِّيْ كُنْتُ مِنَ الظَّالِمِيْنَ

and that whosoever supplicates Allah in these words will be granted his prayer. This subject has also been mentioned in Hadith No. 1 of this chapter, namely that the best form of supplication is stated to be (اَلْحَمْدُ لِلّٰهِ), whereas here it is stated to be Istighfaar. This apparent difference is according to the differing circumstances. For a pious man, (اَلْحَمْدُ لِلّٰهِ) is the best form of supplication, whereas a sinner should do Taubah and Istighfaar, and for him Istighfaar is naturally the most suitable supplication. For increase of benefits, praising and glorifying Allah is more effective, while for relieving the evils and hardships, Istighfaar proves to be more effective. There are also several other reasons for this difference.

Hadith No. 21

(٢١) عَنْ اَبِيْ بَكْرِ نِ الصِّدِّيْقِ رَضِيَ اللّٰهُ عَنْهُ عَنْ رَسُوْلِ اللّٰهِ ﷺ عَلَيْكُمْ بِلَآ اِلٰهَ اِلَّا اللّٰهُ وَالْاِسْتِغْفَارِ فَاَكْثِرُوْا مِنْهُمَا فَاِنَّ اِبْلِيْسَ قَالَ اَهْلَكْتُ النَّاسَ بِالذُّنُوْبِ وَاَهْلَكُوْنِيْ بِلَآ اِلٰهَ اِلَّا اللّٰهُ وَالْاِسْتِغْفَارِ فَلَمَّا رَاَيْتُ ذٰلِكَ اَهْلَكْتُهُمْ بِالْاَهْوَاءِ وَهُمْ يَحْسَبُوْنَ اَنَّهُمْ مُهْتَدُوْنَ أخرجه أبو يعلى كذا في الدر والجامع الصغير ورقم له بالضعف

As narrated by Hadhrat Abu Bakr (Radhiyallaho anho) Rasulullah (Sallallaho alaihe wasallam) had said: "Recite (لَآاِلٰهَ اِلَّا اللّٰهُ) and Istighfaar as frequently as you can, because Shaytaan says: "I ruin the people by inclining them to commit sins but they frustrate me through their recitation of (لَآاِلٰهَ اِلَّا اللّٰهُ) and Istighfaar. When I find this so, I mislead them to indulge in bid'at and thereby make them follow their base desires in the belief that they are still on the right path."

Note:—

The main object of Shaytaan is to inject poison into one's mind, as stated under Hadith No. 14 in part 2 of Chapter I, and he is successful in doing so only when the heart is not engaged in zikr, otherwise he has to retreat in disgrace. In fact, zikr of Allah purifies the heart. It is narrated in Mishkaat that Rasulullah (Sallallaho alaihe wasallam) had said: "For every thing there is a cleaner, and the heart is cleansed by means of zikr of Almighty Allah." The effect of Istighfaar is similar, as mentioned in many ahadith that it removes the dust and rust from the heart. Abu Ali Daqqaaq (Rahmatullah alaih) writes that when a person recites (لَآاِلٰه) with sincerity, his heart is cleansed of all dirt (as a mirror is cleaned with a wet cloth), and when he says (اِلاَّ الله), his heart shines with its light. It is clear that, under these circumstances, the whole effort of Shaytaan is bound to go waste.

Ruining through base desires, means that one may begin to consider wrong as right, and give religious sanctity to whatever he desires. This practice has been condemned in the Holy Qur'an at several places. At one place it is said:

اَفَرَئَيْتَ مَنِ اتَّخَذَ اِلٰهَهُ هَوٰهُ وَاَضَلَّهُ اللهُ عَلٰى عِلْمٍ وَّخَتَمَ عَلٰى سَمْعِهِ وَقَلْبِهِ وَجَعَلَ عَلٰى بَصَرِهِ غِشٰوَةً ، فَمَنْ يَّهْدِيْهِ مِنْ م بَعْدِ اللهِ ، اَفَلَا تَذَكَّرُوْنَ (جاثية ع٣)

Hast thou seen him who maketh his desire as a god and Allah sendeth him astray knowingly and sealeth up his hearing and his heart, and setteth on his sight a covering? Then who will lead him, after Allah (hath condemned him)? Will ye not then heed? (Surah XLV/23).

It is said at another place in the Holy Qur'an:

وَمَنْ اَضَلُّ مِمَّنِ اتَّبَعَ هَوٰهُ بِغَيْرِ هُدًى مِّنَ اللهِ ، اِنَّ اللهَ لَا يَهْدِى الْقَوْمَ الظّٰلِمِيْنَ (قصص ع٥)

Who geteth further astray than one who followeth his lust without guidance from Allah? Lo! Allah guideth not wrong-doing folk. (XXXVIII/50)

There are many other verses on the same subject. It is the most treacherous attack of Shaytaan that he presents an rreligious deed as a religious one, so that one does it as an ırticle of faith and hopes to get reward for it. As the person ›erforms it as a religious act, there is no likelihood of his loing Taubah. If somebody is habituated to obvious sins, ike adultery and theft, there is a possibility that he may do Taubah and give them up, but if somebody is doing a vrong thing under the impression that it is religious duty, he question of his doing Taubah does not arise. Rather, he vill get more involved in it day by day. This explains the vords of the Shaytaan: "I involved them in sins, but they rustrated my efforts through zikr, Taubah, and Istighfaar; hereupon I entrapped them in such a manner that their escape became impossible."

Thus, it is essential that in all matters of religion, guidance be sought from the ways of life of Rasulullah (Sallallaho alaihe wasallam) and of his Companions (Radhiyallaho anhum). Doing otherwise is devoid of virtue, and will entail sins.

Imam Ghazali (Rahmatullah alaih) has reported from Hasan Basri, (Rahmatullah alaih) a narrative that Shaytaan says: "I presented sinful deeds in an attactive form to the Muslims, but they nullified my efforts through Istighfaar. Then I presented before them vices in the garb of virtues, hus leaving no initiative for Istighfaar." Instances of such vices are self-made innovations in religious practices.

Wahb bin Munabbih (Rahmatullah alaih) says: "Fear Almighty Allah, who knows everything; you curse Shaytaan in the presence of others, but you quietly obey and befriend him." Some Sufis have narrated: "It is most unfortunate that, in spite of knowing Almighty Allah as our real benefactor, and acknowledging His favours, we should show disobedience to Him and obey Shaytaan, whom we know and believe to be most treacherous and our greatest enemy."

Hadith No 22

(٢٢) عَنْ مُعَاذِ بْنِ جَبَلٍ رَضِىَ اللّٰهُ عَنْهُ قَالَ قَالَ رَسُوْلُ اللّٰهِ ﷺ لَايَمُوْتُ
يَشْهَدُ اَنْ لَآ اِلٰهَ اِلَّا اللّٰهُ وَاَنِّيْ رَسُوْلُ اللّٰهِ يَرْجِعُ ذٰلِكَ اِلٰى قَلْبِ مُّوْقِنٍ اِلَّا دَ
الْجَنَّةَ وَفِيْ رِوَايَةٍ اِلَّا غَفَرَ اللّٰهُ لَهُ أخرجه أحمد والنسائى والطبراني والحاكم والترمذي في نو
الأصول وابن مردويه والبيهقي في الأسماء والصفات كذا في الدر وابن ماجه وفي الباب عن عمران با

من علم أن الله ربه وإني نبيه موقناً من قلبه حرمه الله على النار رواه البزار ورقم له في الجامع بالصحة
ه أيضا برواية البزار عن أبي سعيد من قال لا إله إلا الله مخلصا دخل الجنة ورقم له بالصحة

Rasulullah (Sallallaho alaihe wasallam) says: "Whosoever professes sincere belief in لا إله إلا الله محمد رسول الله at the time of his death, shall certainly enter Paradise." According to another hadith, "He shall certainly be pardoned by Almighty Allah."

Note:

Rasulullah (Sallallaho alaihe wasallam) is also reported to have said: "Listen to happy tidings, and convey them to others as well, that whosoever believes in لا إله إلا الله with sincerity of heart, shall enter Paradise." It is the Ikhlaas that is valued by Almighty Allah. A small deed done with Ikhlaas (sincerity) earns a great reward; but anything done for the sake of mere show or to please some people, will earn no good reward, but punishment from Almighty Allah. That is why a person who recites the Kalimah with sincerity of heart will certainly be pardoned and admitted into Paradise. It may or may not be that he undergoes some punishment for his sins before going to Paradise; but, if Almighty Allah is really pleased with particular deeds of a sinning believer, He may forgive all his sins in the very first instance. When Allah is so Merciful and Gracious, it is our greatest misfortune if we do not serve and obey Him in full. In short, great rewards are promised in these ahadith for one who believes in the Kalimah Tayyibah. Two possibilities are however there: he may have to suffer some punishment for his sins according to the general rule before being forgiven, or he may be forgiven forthwith without any punishment by Almighty Allah, out of sheer Mercy and Grace.

Yahya bin Akhtam (Rahmatullah alaih) is a Muhaddith. After his death, somebody saw him in a dream, and asked him how he had fared. He replied: "I appeared before Almighty Allah, and He said to me: 'You sinful old man, you did this and you did that', till all my sins were recounted one by one, and I was asked if I had any explanation in my defence. I submitted that no hadith to that effect had been conveyed to me. Then Allah asked: 'What hadith had been conveyed to you?' I submitted: "I was told by Abdur Razzaaq who was told by Muammar who was told by Zuhri who was told by Urwah who was told by ladhrat 'Aa-ishah (Radhiyallaho anha), who was told by Rasulullah (Sallallaho alaihe wasallam), who was told by ibraa-eel (Alayhis salaam), who was told by You: 'A person who grows to old age in Islam may have deserved punishment on account of his sins, yet as a token of respect or his old age, I pardon him', and You know that I am very old." Allah then said, Abdur Razzaaq spoke the truth, Muammar spoke the truth, Zuhri spoke the truth, Urwah spoke the truth, 'Aa-ishah (Radhiyallaho anha) spoke the truth, Rasulullah (Sallallaho alaihe wasallam) spoke the truth, Jibraa-eel (Alayhis salaam) spoke the truth, and what had said is true.' After that, it was ordered that I should be admitted into Paradise."

Hadith No 23

(٢٣) عَنْ اَنَسٍ رَضِىَ اللّٰهُ عَنْهُ قَالَ قَالَ رَسُوْلُ اللّٰهِ ﷺ لَيْسَ شَيْءٌ اِلَّا بَيْنَهُ وَ
اللّٰهِ حِجَابٌ اِلَّا قَوْلَ لَآ اِلٰهَ اِلَّا اللّٰهُ وَدُعَاءَ الْوَالِدِ أخرجه ابن مردويه كذا في الدر
الجامع الصغير برواية ابن النجار ورقم له بالضعف وفي الجامع الصغير برواية الترمذي عن ابن
ورقم له بالصحة التسبيح نصف الميزان والحمد لله تملأه ولا اله الا الله ليس لها دون الله حجاب
تخلص إليه

Rasulullah (Sallallaho alaihe wasallam) said: "There are obstacles in the way of every action before it reaches Almighty Allah, but recitation of (لَآ اِلٰهَ اِلَّا اللّٰه) and the prayer of a father in favour of his son go up to Him unchecked."

Note:

Going unchecked upto Almighty Allah means that these two actions are accepted without any delay. Whereas there are intermediate stages for other deeds before they reach Allah, these two things go to Him directly.

There is a story of a Kaafir king, who was extremely cruel and bigoted against the Muslims. It so happened that he was captured alive in a battle against the Muslims. As he had caused a lot of sufferings to the Muslims, they were naturally very revengeful. They put him in a cauldron placed on fire. At first, he besought his idol gods for help, but finding no response from them he became a Muslim and started continuous recitation of (لَآ اِلٰهَ اِلَّا اللّٰه). How sincerely and devotedly he must have been reciting can well be imagined. At once help came from Almighty Allah i the form of heavy rain, which extinguished the fire an cooled the cauldron. It was then followed by a powerfu cyclone which carried away the cauldron and dropped it i a city inhabited by non-believers. He was still engaged i the recitation of the Kalimah. The people there wer wonderstruck by this scene, and after listening to his whol story all them also embraced Islam.

Hadith No. 24

) عَنْ عُتْبَانَ بْنِ مَالِكٍ رَضِىَ اللهُ عَنْهُ قَالَ قَالَ رَسُوْلُ اللهِ ﷺ لَنْ يُّوَافِيَ عَبْدٌ
الْقِيَامَةِ يَقُوْلُ لَآ اِلٰهَ اِلَّا اللهُ يَبْتَغِىْ بِذَالِكَ وَجْهَ اللهِ اِلَّا حُرِّمَ عَلَى النَّارِ
ه أحمد والبخاري ومسلم وابن ماجه والبيهقي في الأسماء والصفات كذا في الدر

Rasulullah (Sallallaho alaihe wasallam) says: "On th Day of Resurrection, Hell would be forbidden for al those who had recited (لَآ اِلٰهَ اِلَّا اللهُ) with the sole aim o earning the pleasure of Allah."

Note:

That a person who recites Kalimah Tayyibah with sin cerity will, as a rule, be safe from the fire of Hell is con ditional on his being free from the major sins. Forbiddin of Hell for such a person may of course mean that his eter nal stay therein is forbidden; but who is there to questio Almighty Allah if he forbids Hell altogether for the sincer reciter of the Kalimah, in spite of his sins. Mention is mad in ahadith of such people whose sins will be enumerate by Almighty Allah on the Day of Judgement, so that the will feel sure of being doomed to heavy punishment, bu after their confession, Allah will say to them: 'I covere your sins in your worldly life, and I cover them now an pardon you.' Many similar cases have been related in aha dith. There is thus little wonder if all the reciters of the Ka limah may be treated in this way. There are many blessing and benefits in reciting the exalted name of Allah, so tha one should do it as often as possible. How lucky are thos blessed souls who understood the virtues of this Kalimah and devoted their lives fully to its recitation.

Hadith No 25

(٢٥) عَنْ يَحْيٰ بْنِ طَلْحَةَ بْنِ عَبْدِ اللهِ قَالَ رُؤِىَ طَلْحَةُ حَزِيْنًا فَقِيْلَ لَهُ مَالَكَ قَالَ اِنِّي سَمِعْتُ رَسُوْلَ اللهِ ﷺ يَقُوْلُ اِنِّىْ لَاَعْلَمُ كَلِمَةً لَايَقُوْلُهَا عَبْدٌ عِنْدَ مَوْتِهٖ اِلَّا نَفَّسَ اللهُ عَنْهُ كُرْبَتَهُ وَاَشْرَقَ لَوْنُهُ وَرَاٰى مَايَسُرُّهُ وَمَا مَنَعَنِيْ اَنْ اَسْاَلَهُ عَنْهَا اِلَّا الْقُدْرَةُ عَلَيْهِ حَتّٰى مَاتَ فَقَالَ عُمَرُ رَضِىَ اللهُ عَنْهُ اِنِّىْ لَاَعْلَمُهَا قَالَ فَمَا هِىَ قَالَ لَانَعْلَمُ كَلِمَةً هِىَ اَعْظَمُ مِنْ كَلِمَةٍ اَمَرَهَا عَمَّهُ لَآ اِلٰهَ اِلَّا اللهُ قَالَ فَهِىَ وَاللهِ هِىَ

أخرجه البيهقي في الأسماء والصفات كذا في الدر قلت أخرجه الحاكم وقال صحيح على شرط الشيخين وأقره عليه الذهبي وأخرجه أحمد وأخرج أيضا من مسند عمر بمعناه بزيادة فيهما وأخرجه ابن ماجه عن يحيى بن طلحة عن أمه وفي شرح الصدور للسيوطى وأخرج أبويعلى والحاكم بسند صحيح عن طلحة وعمر قالا سمعنا رسول الله ﷺ يقول إنى لاعلم كلمة الحديث

Once Hadhrat Talhah (Radhiyallaho anho) was seen sitting in a sad mood. Somebody asked him why he was so sad. He said: "I had heard from Rasulullah (Sallallaho alaihe wasallam) that he knew the words which, if recited by a dying person at the time of his death, brings him relief from the pangs of death, so that his face brightens and he dies in happiness. Unfortunately I could not enquire about those words from Rasulullah (Sallallaho alaihe wasallam), and therefore I am feeling unhappy." Hadhrat Umar (Radhiyallaho anho) said that he knew those words. Hadhrat Talhah (Radhiyallaho anha) joyously asked what those were and Hadhrat Umar (Radhiyallaho anho) said: "We know that no words are better than the Kalimah which was offered by Rasulullah (Sallallaho alaihe wasallam) to his uncle Abu Taalib and it is (لَآ اِلٰهَ اِلَّا اللهُ)." Hadhrat Talhah (Radhiyallaho anho) said "By Allah! it is this, By Allah! it is this."

Note:

It is related and implied in many ahadith that the Kalimah Tayyibah constitutes light and happiness through and through. Hafiz Ibn Hajar (Rahmatullah alaih) has stated in his book Munabbihaat: "There are five kinds of darknesses, for which there are five specific lights. The love of the world is a darkness, the light for it is a piety; sin is a darkness, the light for which is Taubah; the grave is a darkness, the light for which is the Kalimah (لَآ اِلٰهَ اِلَّا اللّٰهُ مُحَمَّدٌ رَّسُوْلُ اللّٰهِ) the next life is a darkness, the light for which is good deeds; and Pulsiraat is a darkness, the light for which is Faith."

Raabiah Adawiyyah (Rahmatullah alaiha) a well known woman saint, used to remain busy in salaat throughout the night, would sleep a little at the time of early dawn and would wake up abruptly just before the Fajr prayer, blaming herself and saying: "How long will you lie asleep; soon you will be in the grave, where you will sleep till the Doomsday." At the time of her death, she told her maid-servant that she should be buried in the patched woolen cloak, which she used to wear at the time of Tahajjud prayer, and that nobody should be informed or her death. After her burial according to her wishes, the maid-servant saw her in a dream wearing a very beautiful dress. When asked what happened to her old woolen dress, she replied that it had been deposited with her deeds. The maid servant requested her for some advice, and she replied: "Do zikr of Almighty Allah as much as you can; by virtue of this you will be worthy of envy in the grave."

Hadith No. 26

(٢٦) عَنْ عُثْمَانَ رَضِىَ اللّٰهُ عَنْهُ قَالَ اِنَّ رِجَالًا مِنْ اَصْحَابِ النَّبِىِّ ﷺ حِيْنَ تُوُفِّىَ
حَزِنُوْا عَلَيْهِ حَتّٰى كَادَ بَعْضُهُمْ يُوَسْوِسُ قَالَ عُثْمَانُ رَضِىَ اللّٰهُ عَنْهُ وَكُنْتُ مِنْهُمْ
فَبَيْنَا اَنَا جَالِسٌ مَرَّ عَلَيَّ عُمَرُ رَضِىَ اللّٰهُ عَنْهُ وَسَلَّمَ فَلَمْ اَشْعُرْ بِهِ فَاشْتَكٰى عُمَرُ
رَضِىَ اللّٰهُ عَنْهُ اِلٰى اَبِىْ بَكْرٍ رَضِىَ اللّٰهُ عَنْهُ ثُمَّ اَقْبَلَا حَتّٰى سَلَّمَا عَلَيَّ جَمِيْعًا فَقَالَ
اَبُوْبَكْرٍ رَضِىَ اللّٰهُ عَنْهُ مَاحَمَلَكَ عَلٰى اَنْ لَّاتَرُدَّ عَلٰى اَخِيْكَ عُمَرَ رَضِىَ اللّٰهُ عَنْهُ
سَلَامَهُ قُلْتُ مَافَعَلْتُ فَقَالَ عُمَرَ رَضِىَ اللّٰهُ عَنْهُ بَلٰى وَاللّٰهِ لَقَدْ فَعَلْتَ قَالَ قُلْتُ
وَاللّٰهِ مَاشَعُرْتُ اَنَّكَ مَرَرْتَ وَلَاسَلَّمْتَ قَالَ اَبُوْ بَكْرٍ رَضِىَ اللّٰهُ عَنْهُ صَدَقَ عُثْمَانُ
رَضِىَ اللّٰهُ عَنْهُ قَدْ شَغَلَكَ عَنْ ذٰلِكَ اَمْرٌ فَقُلْتُ اَجَلَ قَالَ مَاهُوَ قُلْتُ تَوَفَّى اللّٰهُ
تَعَالٰى نَبِيَّهُ ﷺ قَبْلَ اَنْ نَسْأَلَهُ عَنْ نَجَاةِ هٰذَا الْاَمْرِ قَالَ اَبُوْبَكْرٍ رَضِىَ اللّٰهُ عَنْهُ قَدْ
سَاَلْتُهُ عَنْ ذٰالِكَ فَقُمْتُ اِلَيْهِ وَقُلْتُ لَهُ بِاَبِىْ اَنْتَ وَاُمِّىْ اَنْتَ اَحَقُّ بِهَا قَالَ
اَبُوْبَكْرٍ رَضِىَ اللّٰهُ عَنْهُ قُلْتُ يَارَسُوْلَ اللّٰهِ مَانَجَاةُ هٰذَا الْاَمْرِ فَقَالَ رَسُوْلُ اللّٰهِ ﷺ

مَنْ قَبِلَ مِنِّىْ الْكَلِمَةَ الَّتِىْ عَرَضْتُ عَلٰى عَمِّىْ فَرَدَّهَا فَهِيَ لَهُ نِجَاةٌ

رواه أحمد كذا في المشكواة وفي مجمع الزوائد رواه أحمد والطبراني في الأوسط باختصار وأبويعلى بتمامه

At the time of the death of the Holy Prophet (Sallallaho alaihe wasallam), his companions were so much shocked and grieved that many of them became overwhelmed with frustration and doubts of various sorts. Hadhrat Uthman (Radhiyallaho anho) said: "I was also one of those who were given to frustration. Hadhrat Umar (Radhiyallaho anho) came to me and wished me salaam, but I was too absorbed to be aware of his coming. He complained to Hadhrat Abu Bakr (Radhiyallaho anho) that I was displeased with him, so much so that I did not respond even to his salaam. Then both of them came to me and wished me salaam, and Hadhrat Abu Bakr (Radhiyallaho anho) enquired of me the reason why I had not responded to Umar's salaam. Hadhrat Umar (Radhiyallaho anho) said: "Yes, I swear by Allah, most certainly you did". I denied having behaved like this, and told them I did not even know of his coming and wishing me salaam. Hadhrat Abu Bakr (Radhiyallaho anho) accepted my explanation, and said that it must have happened so, and that probably I must have been absorbed in some thought. I confessed that I was indeed absorbed in deep thought. Hadhrat Abu Bakr (Radhiyallaho anho) enquired what it was, and I submitted that I was worried because Rasulullah (Sallallaho alaihe wasallam) had died and we had failed to enquire from him the basic thing required for salvation. Hadhrat Abu Bakr (Radhiyallaho anho) said that he had made this enquiry from Rasulullah (Sallallaho alaihe wasallam). I got up, and praised him saying that only he was worthy of this honour, because he always exelled in matters of religion. Hadhrat Abu Bakr (Radhiyallaho anho) then said, I had asked Rasulullah (Sallallaho alaihe wasallam) what basic thing was necessary for salvation, and he had replied that whoever accepts the Kalimah that he had offered to his uncle Abu Talib at the time of his death (but which he rejected) will have salvation, and that this Kalimah leads to salvation."

Note:

All the Sahabah were so much upset and overwhelmed with grief and sorrow that even Hadhrat Umar (Radhiyallaho anho), in spite of his being so brave, held out his sword in his hand and proclaimed: "I will chop off the head of whosoever says that Rasulullah (Sallallaho alaihe wasallam) is dead. He has only gone to meet his Allah, as Hadhrat Moosa (Alayhis salaam) had gone on Mount Toor." Some of the Sahabas feared that the death of the Prophet (Sallallaho alaihe wasallam) meant the end of Islam, some thought that there was no longer any chance for the progress of Islam, whereas some were dumbfounded and could not even speak. It was only Hadhrat Abu Bakr (Radhiyallaho anho) who, in spite of his extreme love and attachment with Rasulullah (Sallallaho alaihe wasallam), remained firm, calm, and collected. He got up and delivered his forceful address, beginning with the verse وَمَا مُحَمَّدٌ اِلَّا رَسُولٌ , which means "Muhammad (Sallallaho alaihe wasallam) is but a messenger; many messengers have passed away before him. Will it be that when he dieth or is slain, ye will turn back on your heels? He who turneth back doth no harm to Allah, but Allah will reward the dutiful." This story has been briefly related by me in my book Stories of Sahabah.

Another point made in the above mentioned hadith is on what essential basic thing does salvation depend. It can be interpreted in two ways. Firstly, it may mean: The matters of Deen are many, but what is that on which all these things of Deen depend, and which is indispensable? According to this interpretation, the reply given above is clearly understood: The whole of Deen depends on the Kalimah which is the fundamental tenet of Islam. Secondly it can mean that there are hardships in the path of Deen viz. doubts crop up, the machinations of the devil are a constant source of trouble, worldly needs demand one's attention, etc.; how can these be overcome? In this case, the saying of Rasulullah (Sallallaho alaihe wasallam) would mean that frequent recitation of Kalimah Tayyibah will help overcome all these difficulties, for it develops sincerity of intention, it cleanses the heart, it causes defeat of the devil, and has many other benefits, as mentioned in all these ahadith. It is said in one hadith that the Kalimah (لَآ اِلٰهَ اِلَّا اللّٰهُ) wards off ninety nine kinds of calamities, the least of which is grief, which is a constant worry for a man.

Hadith No. 27

(٢٧) عَنْ عُثْمَانَ رَضِىَ اللّٰهُ عَنْهُ قَالَ سَمِعْتُ رَسُوْلَ اللّٰهِ ﷺ يَقُوْلُ اِنِّىْ لَاَعْلَمُ كَلِمَةً لَايَقُوْلُهَا عَبْدٌ حَقًّا مِّنْ قَلْبِهِ اِلَّا حُرِّمَ عَلَى النَّارِ فَقَالَهُ عُمَرُ بْنُ الْخَطَّابِ اَنَا اُحَدِّثُكَ مَاهِىَ هِىَ كَلِمَةُ الْاِخْلَاصِ الَّتِىْ اَعَزَّ اللّٰهُ تَبَارَكَ وَتَعَالٰى بِهَا مُحَمَّدًا ﷺ وَاَصْحَابَهُ وَهِىَ كَلِمَةُ التَّقْوٰى الَّتِىْ اَلَاصَ عَلَيْهَا نَبِىُّ ﷺ عَمَّهُ اَبَا طَالِبٍ عِنْدَ الْمَوْتِ شَهَادَةُ اَنْ لَّااِلٰهَ اِلَّا اللّٰهُ رواه احمد واخرجه الحاكم بهٰذا اللفظ وقال صحيح على شرطهما واقره عليه الذهبى واخرجه الحاكم برواية عثمان رضى الله عنه عن عمر رضى الله عنه مرفوعا انى لاعلم كلمة لايقولها عبد حقا من قلبه فيموت على ذٰلك الا حرمه الله على النار لَآ اِلٰهَ اِلَّا اللّٰهُ وقال هذا صحيح على شرطهما ثم ذكرله شاهدين من حديثهما

Hadhrat Uthman (Radhiyallaho anho) narrated that he had heard Rasulullah (Sallallaho alaihe wasallam) saying: "I know of a Kalimah which, if recited by a person with sincerity of heart, fobids the fire of Hell to touch him." Hadhrat Umar (Radhiyallaho anho) said: "Shall I tell you what that Kalimah is? It is the same Kalimah by virtue of which Almighty Allah honoured Rasulullah (Sallallaho alaihe wasallam) and his companions, it is the same Kalimah of piety that was offered by Rasulullah (Sallallaho alaihe wasallam) to his uncle Abu Taalib at the time of his death. It is لَآاِلٰهَ اِلَّا اللّٰهُ.

Note:

This well known story of Abu Taalib, the uncle of Rasulullah (Sallallaho alaihe wasallam) is given in the books of Hadith, Tafseer, and history. As he had been helping Rasulullah (Sallallaho alaihe wasallam) and the Muslims, Rasulullah (Sallallaho alaihe wasallam) went to him when he was about to die, and said: "O my uncle, recite (لَآ اِلٰهَ اِلَّا اللّٰهُ), even now, so that I may be able to intercede on your behalf on the Day of Judgement, and i may bear witness before Allah that you embraced Islam." Abu Taalib replied: "People will taunt me for having accepted the faith of my nephew for fear of death, otherwise I would have pleased you by reciting this Kalimah." Rasulullah (Sallallaho alaihe wasallam) returned from there deeply grieved. It was in this connection that the Qur'anic verse

اِنَّكَ لَا تَهْدِىْ مَنْ اَحْبَبْتَ (قصص ع٦)

was revealed, which means: "Lo! Thou guidest not whom thou lovest, but Allah guideth whom He will." It is evident from this incident that those who indulge in sins and bad deeds, and disobey Allah and His Prophet Rasulullah (Sallallaho alaihe wasallam), but think that they will get salvation by virtue of the prayer in their favour of some pious person are sadly mistaken. All power rests with Almighty Allah, to whom we should always turn and with whom we should establish our real connection. However, the company of pious men and their prayers and good wishes can help us in achieving this end.

Hadith No. 28

فَاَوْحَى اللهُ اِلَيْهِ مَنْ مُحَمَّدٌ فَقَالَ تَبَارَكَ اسْمُكَ لَمَّا خَلَقْتَنِيْ رَفَعْتُ رَأْسِىْ اِلٰى عَرْشِكَ فَاِذَا فِيْهِ مَكْتُوْبٌ لَآ اِلٰهَ اِلَّا اللهُ مُحَمَّدٌ رَّسُوْلُ اللهِ فَعَلِمْتُ اَنَّهٗ لَيْسَ اَحَدٌ اَعْظَمُ عِنْدَكَ قَدْرًا عَمَّنْ جَعَلْتَ اِسْمَهٗ مَعَ اِسْمِكَ فَاَوْحٰى اللهُ اِلَيْهِ يَاآدَمُ اِنَّهٗ آخِرُ النَّبِيِّيْنَ مِنْ ذُرِّيَّتِكَ وَلَوْلَا هُوَ مَاخَلَقْتُكَ أخرجه الطبراني والحاكم وأبونعيم والبيهقي كلاهما في الدلائل وابن عساكر في الدر وفي مجمع الزوائد رواه الطبراني في الأوسط والصغير وفيه من لم أعرفهم قلت ويؤيد آخر الحديث المشهور لولاك لما خلقت افلاك قال القاري في الموضوعات الكبير موضوع لكن معناه صحيح وفي التشرف معناه ثابت ويؤيد الأول ماورد في غير رواية من أنه مكتوب على العرش وأوراق الجنة لا اله الا الله محمد رسول الله كما بسط طرقه السيوطي في مناقب اللآلى في غير موضع وبسط له شواهد أيضا في تفسيره في سورة ألم نشرح

Rasulullah (Sallallaho alaihe wasallam) said: "After Hadhrat Aadam (Alayhis salaam) happened to commit the mistake as a result of which he was transferred from Paradise to this Earth, he used to spend all his time in weeping, praying and repenting, and once he looked up towards the Heaven and prayed: "O Allah! I beg Thy forgiveness in the name of Muhammad (Sallallaho alaihe wasallam)." "Who is Muhammad?" came the enquiry through Divine revelation. He replied: "When you had created me, I saw the words لَآ اِلٰهَ اِلَّا اللهُ مُحَمَّدٌ رَّسُوْلُ اللهِ written on Your Arsh, and since then I believed that no human being is superior to Muhammad (Sallallaho alaihe wasallam), whose name appeared along with Yours." In reply, it was revealed, "He is to be the last of all the prophets, and will be your descendant. If he were not to be created, you would not have been created."

Note:

How, at that time, Aadam (Alayhis salaam) prayed, wept and besought pardon has been described in many ahadith. Only those who have experienced the agony of the displeasure of a master can have some idea about the plight of Hadhrat Aadam (Alayhis salaam). On account of the displeasure of earthly masters, a servant gets very much worried, but in the case of Hadhrat Aadam (Alayhis salaam) it was the displeasure of the Lord of Lords, the Sustainer of the whole universe, and in short the anger of Allah the Great himself over one before whom the Angels were made to bow, and who enjoyed the position of a favourite. The higher the position of a favourite, the more he feels the wrath of the Master, provided he is not mean; and in this case a prophet was involved. Hadhrat Ibn Abbas (Radhiyallaho anho) narrated that Hadhrat Aadam (Alayhis salaam) wept so much that his weeping exceeded the total weeping by all the people of this world, and he remained in sajdah for forty years without lifting up his head even once. Hadhrat Buraidah (Radhiyallaho anho) also narrated that Rasulullah (Sallallaho alaihe wasallam) had said: "The weeping of Hadhrat Aadam (Alayhis salaam), if compared, will exceed the weeping by all the people of the world." It is stated in another hadith that his tears would outweigh the tears shed by all his descendants. Under these circumstances, in how many ways he must have lamented and repented can well be imagined. In addition, he even begged to be pardoned for the sake of Rasulullah (Sallallaho alaihe wasallam).

That the Kalimah لَآ اِلٰهَ اِلَّا اللّٰهُ مُحَمَّدٌ رَّسُوْلُ اللّٰهِ is written on the Arsh is corroborated by many other ahadith. Rasulullah (Sallallaho alaihe wasallam) had said: "When I entered Paradise, I saw three lines written in gold on both sides. In the first line was written

لَآ اِلٰهَ اِلَّا اللّٰهُ مُحَمَّدٌ رَّسُوْلُ اللّٰهِ

In the second was written

ما قَدَّمْنَا وَجَدْنَا وَمَا اَكَلْنَا رَبِحْنَا وَمَاخَلَفْنَا خَسِرْنَا

What we sent in advance (i.e. charity, etc.), we found, what we consumed we enjoyed, and what we left behind we lost),
and in the third line was written

أُمَّةٌ مُذْنِبَةٌ وَّرَبٌّ غَفُوْرٌ

(People are sinful, but the Lord is forgiving).

A saint relates: "I happened to visit a town in India, and there I came across a tree, the fruit of which resembles the almond and has a double shell. When it is broken, a rolled green leaf comes out with لَآ اِلٰهَ اِلَّا اللهُ مُحَمَّدٌ رَّسُوْلُ اللهِ inscribed on it in red. When I spoke about it to Abu Yaqoob, the hunter, he was not suprised at all, and told me that in Elah he had caught a fish, which had لَآ اِلٰهَ اِلَّا اللهُ inscribed on one ear and مُحَمَّدٌ رَّسُوْلُ اللهِ on the other.

Hadith No. 29

(٢٩) عَنْ اَسْمَاءَ بِنْتِ يَزِيْدَ بْنِ السَّكَنِ عَنْ رَسُوْلِ اللهِ ﷺ اَنَّهٗ قَالَ اِسْمُ اللهِ تَعَالٰى الْاَعْظَمُ فِيْ هَاتَيْنِ الْاٰيَتَيْنِ وَاِلٰهُكُمْ اِلٰهٌ وَّاحِدٌ لَآ اِلٰهَ اِلَّا هُوَ الرَّحْمٰنُ الرَّحِيْمُ وَالٓمّٓ اللهُ لَآ اِلٰهَ اِلَّا هُوَ الْحَيُّ الْقَيُّوْمُ أخرجه ابن شيبة وأحمد والدارمي وأبوداود والترمذي وصححه وابن ماجه وأبومسلم الكجي في السنن وابن الضريس وابن أبي حاتم والبيهقي في الشعب كذا في الدر

Hadhrat Asma (Radhiyallaho anha) relates that Rasulullah (Sallallaho alaihe wasallam) said: "The greatest name of Allah, which is generally known as Ismul-A'zam, is contained in the following two verses (provided these are recited with Ikhlaas)."

وَاِلٰهُكُمْ اِلٰهٌ وَّاحِدٌ لَآ اِلٰهَ اِلَّا هُوَ الرَّحْمٰنُ الرَّحِيْمُ (بقرة – ع١٩)

Note:

It is stated in several ahadith that whatever prayer is made after the recitation of Ismul-A'zam is granted by Allah. However, scholars differ in specifying the Ismul-A'zam, as is the case with some of the most sublime things that Almighty Allah keeps them partly secret. This results in difference of opinion about their specification. Thus, there is difference of opinion about Laylatul Qadr (Night of Power) and in respect of the special time of acceptance of prayer on Friday. This difference of opinion in such matters is a blessing in disguise, as explained in detail in my book on Fadhaail-e-Ramadhaan. Thus, there have been different narrations in respect of Ismul-A'zam; that given above is one of these. There have been ahadith too in regard to these two ayaat as follows:—

Hadhrat Anas (Radhiyallaho anho) reported that Rasulullah (Sallallaho alaihe wasallam) had said that no other verse falls so heavy on the most mischievous and wicked devils as the two ayats beginning with

وَاِلٰهُكُمْ اِلٰهٌ وَّاحِدٌ

According to Ibrahim bin Wasma, the recitation of the following ayats is very effective in cases of mental derangement, etc., and whosoever is particular in their recitation will be safeguarded against such maladies; and that these are written on the corner of the Arsh and cause relief to terrified children or those who fear of the evil eye.

وَاِلٰهُكُمْ اِلٰهٌ وَّاحِدٌ ..... الآية (بقرة ع١٩)

اللّٰهُ لَآ اِلٰهَ اِلَّا هُوَ الحَيُّ القَيُّوْمُ آية الكرسي

إنَّ رَبَّكُمُ اللّٰهُ الَّذِيْ ..... مُحْسِنِيْنَ (اعراف ع ٧)

(هُوَ اللّٰهُ الَّذِىْ لَآ اِلٰهَ هُوَ) ..... اَلْحَكِيْمُ سورة حشر

Allama Shami (Rahmatullah alaih) has quoted Imam Abu Hanifa (Rahmatullah alaih) as saying that Ismul-A'zam is the word "Allah". He has also stated that Allama Tahaawi as well as other scholars supported this view. The great mystics and Sufis also have reached the same conclusion, and that is why the zikr of this Holy word is practised more than anything else by their followers. The leader of the saints, Hadhrat Shaikh Abdul Qadir Jilani (may Allah enlighten his grave), is also of the same view that "Allah" is the Ismul-A'zam, provided at the time of its recitation, there is nothing but Allah in one's mind. He further advised that during its recitation ordinary people should think of His grandeur and fear Him, while the specialists in zikr should also concentrate on His attributes, and the selected few should have in their mind thoughts of nothing else except Almighty Allah. He also stated that it was for this reason that this blessed name is mentioned so many times, in fact two thousand three hundred and sixty times, in the Holy Qur'an.

Shaikh Ismail Farghaani (Rahmatullah alaih) relates: "I had, for a long time, a keen desire to learn this Ismul-A'zam, and for this purpose I had undergone great hardships: I would fast for days together, so much that sometimes I would fall senseless on account of severe hunger. One day, I was sitting in a mosque in Damascus, when two men entered there and stood besides me. To me they looked like angels. One of them said to the other: "Do you want to learn Ismul-A'zam?" "Yes", replied the other, "please tell me." On hearing this conversation, I became more attentive. The former said, "It is the word "Allah", provided it is recited with Sidqul-Lija (صدق لجا), which according to Shaikh Ismail (Rahmatullah alaih) is the state of mind comparable to that of a drowning person when there is nobody to save him, and he calls Almighty Allah for help with extreme sincerity. In order to learn the Ismul-A'zam one should possess high qualities as well as endurance and self-restraint. There is a story of a pious person who knew the Ismul-A'zam. Once a man came to him and begged that he should be taught the Ismul-A'zam: "You lack the required capability," said the pious person. "No, I am capable of learning it," said the supplicant. The pious person then asked him to go and sit at a particular place and then come back and relate to him his observations. The man went there and saw an old man who was bringing firewood on his donkey from the jungle. A policeman came from the other direction and started beating the old man and snatched away his firewood. The man was extremely enraged against the policeman and came back to report the whole incident before the pious person, and said that if he had known the Ismul-A'zam he would have prayed against that policeman. The pious man said: "I learnt the Ismul-A'zam from that very old man who was bringing the firewood."

Hadith No. 30

(٣٠) عَنْ اَنَسٍ رَضِىَ اللّٰهُ عَنْهُ قَالَ قَالَ رَسُوْلُ اللّٰهِ ﷺ يَقُوْلُ اللّٰهُ تَبَارَكَ وَتَعَالٰى
اَخْرِجُوْا مِنَ النَّارِ مَنْ قَالَ لَآاِلٰهَ اِلَّا اللّٰهُ وَ فِىْ قَلْبِهٖ مِثْقَالُ ذَرَّةٍ مِّنَ الْاِيْمَانِ اَخْرِجُوْا

مِنَ النَّارِ مَنْ قَالَ لَآاِلٰهَ اِلَّا اللّٰهُ اَوْ ذَكَرَنِىْ اَوْ خَافَنِىْ فِىْ مَقَامٍ

أخرجه الحاكم برواية المؤمل عن المبارك بن فضالة وقال صحيح الاسناد وأقره عليه الذهبى وقال الحاكم قد تابع أبوداود مؤملا على روايته واختصره

Rasulullah (Sallallaho alaihe wasallam) said that Almighty Allah will order on the Day of Judgement: "Take out of Hell all persons who professed (لَآ اِلٰهَ اِلَّا اللّٰهُ) and who had an iota of Imaan in their hearts; take all those who recited (لَآ اِلٰهَ اِلَّا اللّٰهُ) or remembered Me in any way or feared Me on any occasion."

Note:

The blessings that Almighty Allah bestows on account of this Kalimah can be imagined from the fact that if a hundred years old man, who practised Kufr and Shirk all his life, happens to recite this Kalimah once with Imaan and sincerity, he becomes a Muslim and all the sins committed by him are washed away; and if he happens to commit any sins after he had become a Muslim, even then, by virtue of this Kalimah, he will sooner or later be released from Hell.

Hadhrat Huzaifa (Radhiyallaho anho) who was a confidant of Rasulullah (Sallallaho alaihe wasallam) narrated that Rasulullah (Sallallaho alaihe wasallam) had once said: "A time will come when Islam will become weak and dim like the worn-out prints on an old cloth, when nobody will even know about fasting, Hajj or Zakaat, till one night even the Qur'an will be lifted from this world, so that no one will remember any ayat. At this time, old men and women will say that they had heard their elders reciting the Kalimah (لَآاِلٰهَ اِلَّا اللّٰهُ) and that they would recite it too." A pupil of Hadhrat Huzaifa enquired: "When there is no Hajj, Zakaat, fasting or any other fundamental of Islam, will the mere Kalimah then be of any use?' Hadhrat Huzaifa (Radhiyallaho anho) did not answer, but when his pupil repeated his enquiry a second and then a third time, he replied: "Sooner or later it will cause deliverance from Hell, deliverance from Hell, deliverance from Hell." He implied that the Kalimah will deliver from Hell after one has undergone the punishment for not observing the fundamentals of Islam. This is what is meant by above mentioned hadith that a person with even an iota of Imaan will be freed from Hell one day. It is also narrated in one hadith: "Whosoever recites the Kalimah لَآاِلٰهَ اِلَّا اللّٰهُ, it will come to his rescue one day, which may be after he has undergone some punishment."

Hadith No. 31

(٣١) عَنْ عَبْدِ اللهِ بْنِ عَمْرٍو قَالَ اَتَى النَّبِيَّ ﷺ اَعْرَابِيٌّ عَلَيْهِ جُبَّةٌ مِنْ طَيَالِسَةٍ
مَكْفُوفَةٌ بِالدِّيْبَاجِ فَقَالَ اِنَّ صَاحِبَكُمْ هٰذَا يُرِيْدُ يَرْفَعُ كُلَّ رَاعٍ وَابْنَ رَاعٍ وَيَضَعُ
كُلَّ فَارِسٍ وَابْنَ فَارِسٍ فَقَامَ النَّبِيُّ ﷺ مُغْضَبًا فَاَخَذَ بِمَجَامِعِ ثَوْبِهٖ فَاجْتَذَبَهٗ
وَقَالَ اَلَا اَرٰى عَلَيْكَ ثِيَابَ مَنْ لَّايَعْقِلُ ثُمَّ رَجَعَ رَسُوْلُ اللهِ ﷺ فَجَلَسَ فَقَالَ اِنَّ
نُوْحًا لَمَّا حَضَرَتْهُ الْوَفَاةُ دَعَا ابْنَيْهِ فَقَالَ اِنِّىْ قَاصٌّ عَلَيْكُمَا الْوَصِيَّةَ اٰمُرُكُمَا
بِاثْنَيْنِ وَاَنْهَاكُمَا عَنْ اثْنَيْنِ اَنْهٰكُمَا عَنِ الشِّرْكِ وَالْكِبْرِ وَاٰمُرُكُمَا بِلَآاِلٰهَ اِلَّا اللهُ
فِىْ الْكِفَّةِ الْاُخْرٰى كَانَتْ اَرْجَحَ مِنْهُمَا وَلَوْ اَنَّ السَّمٰوٰتِ وَالْاَرْضَ وَمَافِيْهِمَا
كَانَتْ حَلْقَةً فَوُضِعَتْ لَآاِلٰهَ اِلَّا اللهُ عَلَيْهَا لَقَصَعَتْهُمَا وَاٰمُرُكُمَا بِسُبْحَانَ اللهِ
وَبِحَمْدِهٖ فَاِنَّهُمَا صَلٰوةُ كُلِّ شَيْءٍ وَبِهِمَا يُرْزَقُ كُلُّ شَيْءٍ

أخرجه الحاكم وقال صحيح الاسناد ولم يخرجه للصعقب بن زهير فإنه ثقة قليل الحديث اهـ وأقره عليه
الذهبي وقال الصعقب ثقة ورواه ابن عجلان عن زيد بن أسلم مرسلًا اهـ قلت ورواه أحمد في مسنده
بزيادة فيه بطرق وفي بعض منها فإن السموات السبع والأرضين السبع كنَّ حلقة مُبهمة قصمَتْهنَّ
لَآاِلٰهَ اِلَّا اللهُ وذكره المنذري في الترغيب عن ابن عمر مختصرا وفيه لو كانت حلقة لقصمتهن حتى
تخلص إلى الله ثم قال رواه البزار ورواته محتج بهم في الصحيح إلا ابن إسحاق وهو في النسائى عن
صالح بن سعيد رفعه إلى سليمان بن يسار إلى رجل من الأنصار لم يسمه ورواه الحاكم عن عبدالله وقال
صحيح الاسناد ثم ذكر لفظه قلت وحديث سليمان بن يسار يأتي في بيان التسبيح وفي مجمع الزوائد
ورواه أحمد ورواه الطبراني بنحوه ورواه البزار من رواية حديث ابن عمر ورجال أحمد ثقات وقال في
رواية البزار محمد بن إسحاق وهو مدلس وهو ثقة

There came to Rasulullah (Sallallaho alaihe wasallam) a villager who was wearing a long silken robe bordered with silken lace, and said to the Sahaba: "This friend of yours wants to exalt every ordinary shepherd and his children, and to degrade every (noble) horseman and his children." Rasulullah (Sallallaho alaihe wasallam) got up in anger and pulling his robe by the lapel said to him: "Are you not dressed like a fool?" Then after going back to his seat, he added: "At the time of death, Hadhrat Nooh (Alayhis salaam) summoned his two sons and said to them: 'I recommend to you two things and warn you against two things. The two things against which I warn you are shirk and arrogance. And of the two things which I recommend, one is the Kalimah (لَآاِلٰهَ اِلَّا اللهُ), which weighs heavier than all the Universe together with all its contents; in fact the latter, if placed under it will get crushed and crumble on account of its weight; and the second is (سُبْحَانَ اللهِ وَبِحَمْدِهٖ), which two words constitute the prayer of all the creation, and by virtue of its blessings everything gets its sustenance.

Note:

The comments of Rasulullah (Sallallaho alaihe wasallam) on the clothes implied that the outward appearance provides an indication of one's inner self. When a person's outward behaviour is incorrect, his inner mind is bound to be defective as well. Hence every effort is to be made to improve the exterior because the interior is dependant on it, and the Sufis lay stress on outward cleanliness through Wudhu, etc., as a first step for attaining inner purity. Those who talk of internal improvement and ignore the external betterment are not right. The external betterment is as important as the internal one. One of the duaas of Rasulullah (Sallallaho alaihe wasallam) was:

اَللّٰهُمَّ اجْعَلْ سَرِيْرَتِيْ خَيْرًا مِّنْ عَلَانِيَتِيْ وَاجْعَلْ عَلَانِيَتِيْ صَالِحَةً

O Allah! make my interior better than my exterior, and make my exterior noble and good). Hadhrat Umar narrates that this duaa was recommended to him by Rasulullah (Sallallaho alaihe wasallam).

Hadith No 32

(٣٢) عَنْ اَنَسٍ رَضِىَ اللهُ عَنْهُ اَنَّ اَبَابَكْرٍ رَضِىَ اللهُ عَنْهُ دَخَلَ عَلَى النَّبِىِّ ﷺ وَهُوَ كَئِيْبٌ فَقَالَ لَهُ النَّبِىُّ ﷺ مَالِىْ اَرَاكَ كَئِيْبًا قَالَ يَا رَسُوْلَ اللهِ كُنْتُ عِنْدَ ابْنِ عَمٍّ لِّىْ الْبَارِحَةَ فُلَانٌ وَهُوَ يَكِيْدُ بِنَفْسِهٖ قَالَ فَهَلْ لَقَّنْتَهُ لَآاِلٰهَ اِلَّا اللهُ قَالَ قَدْ فَعَلْتُ يَارَسُوْلَ اللهِ قَالَ فَقَالَهَا قَالَ نَعَمْ قَالَ وَجَبَتْ لَهُ الْجَنَّةُ قَالَ اَبُوْبَكْرٍ يَارَسُوْلَ اللهِ كَيْفَ هِىَ لِلْاَحْيَاءِ قَالَ هِىَ اَهْدَمُ لِذُنُوْبِهِمْ هِىَ اَهْدَمُ لِذُنُوْبِهِمْ

رواه ابويعلى والبزار وفيه زائدة بن أبي الرقاد وثقه القواريري وضعفه البخاري وغيره كذا في مجمع الزوائد وأخرج بمعناه عن ابن عباس أيضا قلت وروى عن علي مرفوعا من قال إذا مرَّ المقابر السلام على أهل

لَآ اِلٰهَ اِلَّا اللّٰهُ من أهل لَآ اِلٰهَ اِلَّا اللّٰهُ كيف وجدتُّمْ قولَ لَآ اِلٰهَ اِلَّا اللّٰهُ إغْفِرْ لِمَنْ قال لَا اِلٰهَ اِلَّا اللّٰهُ وَاحْشُرْنَا في زمرة من قال لَا اِلٰهَ اِلَّا اللّٰهُ غُفرله ذنوب خمسين سنة قيل يارسول الله من لم يكن له ذنوب خمسين سنة قال لوالديه ولقرابته ولعامة المسلمين رواه الديلمي في تاريخ همدان والرافعى وابن النجار كذا في منتخب كنز العمال لكن روى نحوه السيوطي في ذيل اللآلي وتكلم على سنده وقال الاسناد كله ظلمات ورمى رجاله بالكذب وفي تنبيه الغافلين وروى عن بعض الصحابة من قال لَا اِلٰهَ اِلَّا اللّٰهُ مِنْ قلبه خالصا ،مِدًّها بالتَّعظيْم كفَّر الله عنه أربعة الاف ذنب من الكبائر قيل إن لم يكن له أربعة ألاف ذب قال يغفر من ذنوب أهله وجيرانه اهـ قلت وروى بمعناه مرفوعا لكنهم حكموا عليه بالوضع كما فى ذيل اللآلى نعم يؤيده الامر بدفن جوار الصالح وتاذيه بجوار السوء ذكره السيوطى فى اللآلى بطرق وورد السلام على اهل القبور بالفاظ مختلفة فى كنز العمال وغيره

Once Hadhrat Abu Bakr (Radhiyallaho anho) came to Rasulullah (Sallallaho alaihe wasallam) in a very sad mood. Rasulullah (Sallallaho alaihe wasallam) asked him: "You look very sad. What is the matter with you?" He replied: "My cousin died last night, and I was sitting near him when he breathed his last." "Did you persuade him to recite لَآ اِلٰهَ اِلَّا اللّٰهُ?" asked Rasulullah (Sallallaho alaihe wasallam); "Yes", said he. "Did he recite?" asked Rasulullah (Sallallaho alaihe wasallam). "Yes, he had recited it," said he. "Then certainly he will go to Paradise," said the Prophet (Sallallaho alaihe wasallam). "What do the living people get if they recite this Kalimah?" enquired Abu Bakr (Radhiyallaho anho). Rasulullah (Sallallaho alaihe wasallam) said twice: "This Kalimah will demolish and even eliminate their sins."

Note:

Stress is laid in many ahadith on reciting Kalimah near the dead and in the graveyard. It is said in one hadith that the Kalimah (لَآ اِلٰهَ اِلَّا اللّٰهُ) should be recited profusely during a funeral. In another hadith it is said that لَآ اِلٰهَ اِلَّا اَنْتَ (none is worthy of worship except Thee) will be the distinguishing mark of this Ummat, when they pass over the Siraat (the Bridge). In yet another hadith, it is related that when they will rise from their graves on the Day of Resurrection, they will be reciting.

لَآ اِلٰهَ اِلَّا اللّٰهُ وَعَلَى اللّٰهِ فَلْيَتَوَكَّلِ الْمُؤْمِنُوْنَ

(Nobody is worthy of worship except Allah, and on Him the faithful will rely). In a third hadith, it is said that their mark of distinction in the darkness of the Doomsday will be (لَآ اِلٰهَ اِلَّا اَنْتَ) .

The blessings of frequent recitation of the Kalimah frequently becomes apparent just before one's death, and in the case of some pious men, these blessings appear even earlier in their life. Abul Abbaas related: "I was lying sick in the town of Ashbila. I saw a large flock of huge birds of different colours, white, red, green, etc., which were spreading their wings all together and there were many men who were carrying something in big covered trays. I took them as gifts of death, and started reciting the Kalimah Tayyibah hurriedly. Then one of those men said to me that the time of my death had not yet come, and that this was a gift for another believer."

Just before his death, Hadhrat Umar bin Abdul Aziz (Rahmatullah alaih) asked those around him to make him sit up. After they did so, he said: "O Allah! You ordered me to do many things, which I could not do, and You forbade me certain things, but I disobeyed you in them." He repeated these words thrice, and then after reciting (لَآاِلٰهَ اِلَّا اللّٰهُ) began to stare in one direction. Somebody asked him what was he looking at He said: "There are green figures who are neither men nor Jinn", and then breathed his last.

Sombeody saw Zubaidah (Rahmatullah alaiha) in dream and asked her how she fared. She replied that she has been pardoned on account of reciting four Kalimahs.

لَآ اِلٰهَ اِلَّا اللّٰهُ اُفْنِیَ بِهَا عُمْرِیْ   لَآ اِلٰهَ اِلَّا اللّٰهُ اَدْخُلُ بِهَا قَبْرِیْ

لَآ اِلٰهَ اِلَّا اللّٰهُ اَخْلُوْ بِهَا وَحْدِیْ   لَآ اِلٰهَ اِلَّا اللّٰهُ اَلْقٰی بِهَا رَبِّیْ

(i) I will hold fast unto (لَآاِلٰهَ اِلَّا اللّٰهُ) until I die,
(ii) I will take (لَآاِلٰهَ اِلَّا اللّٰهُ) with me into my grave,
(iii) I will pass my time of solitude with (لَآاِلٰهَ اِلَّا اللّٰهُ),
(iv) I will take (لَآاِلٰهَ اِلَّا اللّٰهُ) with me when I appear before my Sustainer.

Hadith No 33

(٣٣) عَنْ اَبِیْ ذَرٍّ رَضِیَ اللّٰهُ عَنْهُ قَالَ قُلْتُ یَارَسُوْلَ اللّٰهِ اَوْصِنِیْ قَالَ اِذَا عَمِلْتَ
سَیِّئَةً فَاَتْبِعْهَا حَسَنَةً تَمْحُهَا قُلْتُ یَارَسُوْلَ اللّٰهِ اَمِنَ الْحَسَنَاتِ لَآاِلٰهَ اِلَّا اللّٰهُ قَا

هِيَ اَفْضَلُ الْحَسَنَاتِ رواه أحمد وفي مجمع الزوائد رواه أحمد ورجاله الثقات إلا أن شمر بن عطية حدثه عن أشياخه ولم يسم أحدا منهم قال السيوطي في الدر أخرجه أيضا ابن مردويه والبيهقي في الأسماء والصفات قلت وأخرجه الحاكم بلفظ ياأبا ذر اتّق الله حيث كنت واتبع السئة الحسنة تمحها وخالق الناس بخلق حسن وقال صحيح على شرطهما وأقره عليه الذهبي وذكره السيوطي في الجامع مختصرا ورقم له بالصحة

Hadhrat Abu Zar Ghifari (Radhiyallaho anho) submitted: "O, Rasulullah (Sallallaho alaihe wasallam) favour me with some advice." Rasulullah (Sallallaho alaihe wasallam) said: "When you happen to commit a sin, hasten to do a virtue in atonement, so that the ill effect of the sin may be washed away." Abu Zar (Radhiyallaho anho) then further enquired: "O Rasulullah! (Sallallaho alaihe wasallam) is recitation of (لآاِلٰهَ اِلَّا اللهُ) also a virtue?" "It is the best of all virtues," was the reply of Rasulullah (Sallallaho alaihe wasallam).

Note:

A minor sin, no doubt, is washed away by a virtuous deed, but a major one is wiped off, as a rule, through Taubah or of course through the Mercy of Almighty Allah, as explained earlier in this book. In either case, the wiped-out sin is neither written in the account of deeds nor mentioned anywhere else. So it is said in one hadith that when a man does Taubah, the Almighty Allah makes the scribing angels forget that sin. It is forgotten even by the hands and feet of the sinner, and even by the piece of land where it was committed, so that there is nobody to give evidence for that sin on the Day of Judgement, when the hands, feet, and other parts of the body of the person himself will stand witness for his good or bad deeds, as will be explained in Hadith No. 18 of Chapter 2 part 3.

The subject matter of the above mentioned hadith is supported by many other ahadith. There are many ahadith to the effect that Taubah from a sin washes it away, as if one had never committed it. Taubah means to repent and feel ashamed of the sin that has been committed, and make a firm resolution not to repeat it.

Rasulullah (Sallallaho alaihe wasallam) according to one hadith has said: "Do worship Allah only, and do not ascribe any partner to Him; be sincere in all your actions as if you are standing before Almighty Allah; consider yourself among the dead; remember Allah near every stone and every tree, so that there are many witnesses in your favour on the Day of Judgement; and if you happen to commit a sin, do some virtue immediately in atonement thereof, so that if the sin is committed in secret the virtue should also be done in secret, and if the sin is committed openly the virtue should also be done openly."

Hadith No 34

(٣٤) عَنْ تَمِيْمِ الدَّارِىْ رَضِىَ اللّٰهُ عَنْهُ قَالَ قَالَ رَسُوْلُ اللّٰهِ ﷺ مَنْ قَالَ لَآ اِلٰهَ اِلَّا اللّٰهُ وَاحِدًا اَحَدًا صَمَدًا لَمْ يَتَّخِذْ صَاحِبَةً وَّلَا وَلَدًا وَّلَمْ يَكُنْ لَّهُ كُفُوًا اَحَدٌ عَشَرَ مَرَّاتٍ كُتِبَتْ لَهُ اَرْبَعُوْنَ اَلْفَ حَسَنَةٍ اخرجه احمد قلت اخرج الحاكم شواهده بالفاظ مختلفة

Rasulullah (Sallallaho alaihe wasallam) has said: "Whosoever recites the following ten times will be rewarded with forty thousand virtues":

لَآ اِلٰهَ اِلَّا اللّٰهُ وَاحِدًا اَحَدًا صَمَدًا لَمْ يَتَّخِذْ صَاحِبَةً وَّلَا وَلَدًا وَّلَمْ يَكُنْ لَّهُ كُفُوًا اَحَدٌ

Note:

Great rewards are mentioned in the books of hadith for reciting Kalimah Tayyibah a certain number of times. It is said in one hadith: "When you offer an obligatory Salaat, then recite:

لَآ اِلٰهَ اِلَّا اللّٰهُ وَحْدَهُ لَا شَرِيْكَ لَهُ لَهُ الْمُلْكُ وَلَهُ الْحَمْدُ وَهُوَ عَلٰى كُلِّ شَيْءٍ قَدِيْرٌ

ten times, because its reward is equivalent to that of releasing a slave from bondage."

Hadith No 35

(٣٥) عَنْ عَبْدِ اللّٰهِ بْنِ اَبِىْ اَوْفٰى رَضِىَ اللّٰهُ عَنْهُ قَالَ قَالَ رَسُوْلُ اللّٰهِ ﷺ مَنْ قَالَ لَآ اِلٰهَ اِلَّا اللّٰهُ وَحْدَهُ لَاشَرِيْكَ لَهُ اَحَدًا صَمَدًا لَمْ يَلِدْ وَلَمْ يُوْلَدْ وَلَمْ يَكُنْ لَّهُ كُفُوًا اَحَدٌ كَتَبَ اللّٰهُ لَهُ اَلْفَىْ اَلْفِ حَسَنَةٍ

رواه الطبراني كذا في الترغيب وفي مجمع الزوائد فيه فائد أبو الورقا متروك

It is said in another hadith: "Whoever recites:

لَا اِلٰهَ اِلَّا اللّٰهُ وَحْدَهُ لَاشَرِيْكَ لَهُ اَحَدًا صَمَدًا لَمْ يَلِدْ وَلَمْ يُوْلَدْ وَلَمْ يَكُنْ لَهُ كُفُوًا اَحَدٌ

two million virtues will be written to his credit.

Note:

How great is the kindness and benevolence of Almighty Allah, that He bestows thousands and millions of virtues for the mere recitation of this Kalimah, which action does not involve hard labour or much time; but, unfortunately we are negligent and remain so much absorbed in our wordly pursuits that we never care to take advantage of these bounties. Almighty Allah grants at least ten times reward for every virtue, provided it is done with Ikhlaas, and then this reward multiplies further according to the degree of sincerity. Rasulullah (Sallallaho alaihe wasallam) has said: "When a person embraced Islam, all his previous sins are forgiven, and then every virtue is rewarded ten to seven hundred times, and even more than that as Almighty Allah may please, but a sin is indicated as a single deed and if it is forgiven by Allah it is not even mentioned in the account of deeds." According to another hadith, a virtue is noted in the account of a person as soon as he intends to do it, but when it is actually done its reward is increased from ten to seven hundred times, and even more, as Allah may please. There are many ahadith to this effect, that Allah's bounty knows no limits, provided a person tries to deserve it. The pious people keep this thing in view, and so they are not misled by any amount of worldly wealth.

اَللّٰهُمَّ اجْعَلْنِيْ مِنْهُمْ

(O Allah! make me one of them).

Rasulullah (Sallallaho alaihe wasallam) had said: "There are six kinds of deeds and four categories of people. Of the deeds, the first two kinds lead to definite results, two carry equivalent rewards while the reward is ten times for the fifth and seven hundred times for the remaining one. Of the first two kinds of deed, one is certain to lead to Paradise a person who is free from Shirk at the time of his death, and the other is certain to lead to Hell a person who is committed to Shirk at the time of his death; of the two kinds of deeds which bring equivalent rewards, one is to make firm intention for a virtuous deed (before its actual performance), and the other is to commit a sin which is also recorded as one only. The fifth is to do a noble deed, the reward for which is ten times, while the sixth is to spend wealth in the path of Allah, in which case the reward is enhanced seven hundred times.

Of the four categories of people, the first is of those who enjoy prosperity in this world but will face adversity in the Hereafter, the second is of those who face adversity in this world but will enjoy prosperity in the Hereafter; the people in the third category face adversity in both the worlds i.e. they are poor in this life and will be punished in the Hereafter, and the fourth category includes those who are well off in both the worlds.

A person came to Hadhrat Abu Hurairah (Radhiyallaho anho) and asked him if he had narrated that Almighty Allah multiplies the reward of some virtues one million times. He swore in confirmation that he had heard it exactly like that. According to another version, he had heard it from Rasulullāh (Sallallaho alaihe wasallam) that the reward of some virtues is two million times. Almighty Allah says in the Holy Qur'an (يُضَاعِفْهَا وَيُؤْتِ مِنْ لَّدُنْهُ اَجْرًا عَظِيْمًا) that He multiplies the virtues and grants from His treasure great rewards. Who can imagine the extent of the reward which has been described as great by Almighty Lord?

According to Imam Ghazali, (Rahmatullah alaih) the great reward will be possible only if we recite these words with full concentration on their meanings, because important attributes of Almighty Allah are described therein.

Hadith No 36

(٣٦) عَنْ عُمَرَ بْنِ الْخَطَّابِ رَضِيَ اللّٰهُ عَنْهُ عَنِ النَّبِيِّ ﷺ قَالَ مَا مِنْكُمْ مِّنْ اَحَدٍ يَّتَوَضَّأُ فَيُبْلِغُ اَوْ فَيُسْبِغُ الْوُضُوْءَ ثُمَّ يَقُوْلُ اَشْهَدُ اَنْ لَّآ اِلٰهَ اِلَّا اللّٰهُ وَاَشْهَدُ اَنَّ مُحَمَّدًا عَبْدُهٗ وَرَسُوْلُهٗ اِلَّا فُتِحَتْ لَهٗ اَبْوَابُ الْجَنَّةِ الثَّمَانِيَةُ يَدْخُلُ مِنْ اَيِّهَا شَآءَ

رواه مسلم وابو داود وابن ماجه وقالا فَيُحْسِنُ الْوُضُوْءَ زاد أبو داود ثم يرفع طرفه إلى السماء ثم يقول فذكره ورواه الترمذي كأبي داود وزاد

اللّٰهُمَّ اجْعَلْنِيْ مِنَ التَّوَّابِيْنَ وَاجْعَلْنِيْ مِنَ الْمُتَطَهِّرِيْنَ

الحديث وتكلم فيه كذا في الترغيب زاد السيوطى في الدر ابن أبي شيبة والدارمي

Rasulullah (Sallallaho alaihe wasallam) said, "When a person performs wudhu (ablution) properly (i.e. observing all its essentials as well as details) and then recites:

اَشْهَدُ اَنْ لَّآ اِلٰهَ اِلَّا اللّٰهُ وَاَشْهَدُ اَنَّ مُحَمَّدًا عَبْدُهٗ وَرَسُوْلُهٗ

(I bear witness that there is none worthy of worship except Allah, the One who has no partner, and also that Muhammad is His slave and prophet), all the eight gates of Paradise are thrown open for him, so that he may enter as he likes, through anyone of them.

One gate is enough for entering into Paradise, but opening of all the eight gates is a mark of special welcome and extreme favour. According to another hadith, a person who did not indulge in Shirk before his death, and never committed any unlawful murder, is allowed to enter paradise as he may like through any one of its gates.

Hadith No. 37

(٣٧) عَنْ اَبِى الدَّرْدَآءِ عَنِ النَّبِىِّ ﷺ قَالَ لَيْسَ مِنْ عَبْدٍ يَقُوْلُ لَآ اِلٰهَ اِلَّا اللّٰهُ مِائَةَ مَرَّةٍ اِلَّا بَعَثَهُ اللّٰهُ يَوْمَ الْقِيَامَةِ وَوَجْهُهٗ كَالْقَمَرِ لَيْلَةَ الْبَدْرِ وَلَمْ يُرْفَعْ لِاَحَدٍ يَوْمَئِذٍ عَمَلٌ اَفْضَلَ مِنْ عَمَلِهٖ اِلَّا مَنْ قَالَ مِثْلَ قَوْلِهٖ اَوْزَادَ

رواه الطبراني وفيه عبدالوهاب بن ضحاك متروك كذا في مجمع الزوائد قلت هو من رواة ابن ماجه ولا شك أنهم ضعفوه جداً إلا أن معناه مؤيد بروايات منها ماتقدم من روايات يحيى بن طلحة ولا شك أنه افضل الذكر وله شاهد من حديد أم هانى الآتى

A person who recites (لآاِلٰهَ اِلَّا اللّٰهُ) one hundred times a day, will on the Day of Resurrection, be raised with his face shining like the full moon, and none can surpass him in excellence on that day except one who recites this Kalimah more than he.

Many ahaadith and ayaat confirm that (لآاِلٰهَ اِلَّا اللّٰهُ) is a light for the heart as well as for the face. It has been observed that the pious people who are used to reciting this Kalimah excessively have a sort of brightness over their faces, even during their earthly life.

Hadith No. 38

(٣٨) عَنْ اِبْنِ عَبَّاسٍ رَضِىَ اللّٰهُ عَنْهُ عَنِ النَّبِىِّ ﷺ قَالَ اِفْتَحُوْا عَلٰى صِبْيَانِكُمْ اَوَّلَ كَلِمَةٍ بِلَآ اِلٰهَ اِلَّا اللّٰهُ وَلَقِّنُوْهُمْ عِنْدَ الْمَوْتِ لَآ اِلٰهَ اِلَّا اللّٰهُ فَاِنَّهُ مَنْ كَانَ اَوَّلُ كَلَامِهٖ لَآ اِلٰهَ اِلَّا اللّٰهُ ثُمَّ عَاشَ اَلْفَ سَنَةٍ لَمْ يُسْئَلْ عَنْ ذَنْبٍ وَّاحِدٍ

موضوع ابن محموية وأبوه مجهولان وقد ضعف البخاري إبراهيم بن مهاجر حكاه السيوطي عن ابن الجوزي ثم تعقبه بقوله الحديث في المستدرك أخرجه البيهقي في الشعب عن الحاكم وقال متن غريب لم نكتبه إلا بهذا الاسناد وأورده الحافظ بن حجر في أمالية ولم يقدح فيه بشيء إلا أنه قال إبراهيم فيه لين وقد أخرج له مسلم في المتابعات كذافي اللالآلى وذكره السيوطى في شرح الصدور ولم يقدح فيه بشيء قلت وقد ورد في التلقين أحاديث كثيرة ذكرها الحافظ في التلخيص وقال في جملة من رواها عن عروة بن مسعود الثقفى رواه العقيلي باسناد ضعيف ثم قال روى في الباب أحاديث صحاح عن غير واحد من الصحابة ورواه ابن أبي الدنيا في كتاب المحتضرين من طريق عروة بن مسعود عن أبيه عن حذيفة بلفظ لقّنوا موتاكم لا إله إلا الله فإنها تَهْدِمِ ماقبلها من الخطايا وروى فيه أيضا عن عمر وعثمان وابن مسعود وأنس وغيرهم اهـ وفي الجامع الصغير لقّنوا موتاكم لا إله إلا الله رواه أحمد ومسلم والأربعة عن أبي سعيد ومسلم وابن ماجه عن أبي هريرة والنسائى عن عائشة ورقم له بالصحة وفي الحصن إذا أفصح الولد فليعلّمه لااله الا الله وفي الحرز رواه ابن السنى عن عمرو بن العاص اهـ قلت ولفظه في عمل اليوم والليلة عن عمرو بن شعيب وجدت في كتاب جدي الذي حدَّثه عن رسول الله ﷺ قال إذا أفصح أولادكم فعلموهم لا اله الا الله لاتبالوا متى ماتوا وإذا اثْفروا فمروهم بالصلاة وفي الجامع الصغير برواية أحمد وأبي داود والحاكم عن معاذ من كان آخر كلامه لا إله إلا الله دخل الجنة ورقم له بالصحة وفي مجمع الزوائد عن علي رفعه من كان آخر كلامه لا اله الا الله لم يدخل النار وفي غير رواية مرفوعة من لقن عند الموت لا اله الا الله دخل الجنة

Rasulullah (Sallallaho alaihe wasallam) says, "Teach the Kalimah (لَآاِلٰهَ اِلَّا اللّٰهُ) to a child when he starts speaking and persuade a dying person to recite (لَآاِلٰهَ اِلَّا اللّٰهُ). He who has had his beginning with (لَآاِلٰهَ اِلَّا اللّٰهُ) and has his end with (لَآاِلٰهَ اِلَّا اللّٰهُ), he would not be required to account for any of his sins, even though he lives for thousand years, (i.e. either he would commit no sin, or if he happened to commit any sin, it would be written off by virtue of Taubah or through the sheer mercy of Almighty Allah).

Note:

The best way to persuade a dying man to recite the Kalimah is that those sitting near him should recite it, so that on hearing it he may also do the same. He should not be compelled to do it, because he is dying in agony. That a dying person should be persuaded to recite the Kalimah has been stressed in many ahaadith. In several ahaadith, Rasulullah (Sallallaho alaihe wasallam) is reported to have said, "The sins of a person who is blessed to recite the Kalimah at the time of death are washed off just as a building is washed away by flood water." According to other ahaadith, one who recites this blessed Kalimah before his death gets all his past sins forgiven. It is said in one hadith that a hypocrite is never able to recite it (at the time of his death). It is said in another hadith that we should give (لَآاِلٰهَ اِلَّا اللهُ) as provision to our deceased ones. According to a hadith, one who brings up a child till he is able to recite (لَآاِلٰهَ اِلَّا اللهُ) will not be required to render any account. In one hadith it is said, "When a person who has been steadfast in offering salaat is about to die, an Angel comes to him, drives away the Satan and persuades him to recite the Kalimah (لَآ اِلٰهَ اِلَّا اللهُ مُحَمَّدٌ رَّسُوْلُ اللهِ).

It is however often observed that this sort of persuasion proves useful only in case of those who are accustomed to the recitation of the Kalimah during their lifetime. A story is related about a person who used to trade in straw. When he was about to die, people tried to persuade him to recite the Kalimah, but he only cried out, "The price of this bundle is so much and of that is so much." Many such incidents, which had been actually observed, have been described in the book, "Nuzhatul Basaateen".

Sometimes, involvement in a sin prevents a dying person from reciting the Kalimah. The Ulama say that opium has seventy disadvantages, one of which is that the opium-user cannot recollect the Kalimah at the time of his death. On the contrary, brushing one's teeth (with miswaak) carries seventy benefits, one of which is that to recite Kalimah at the time of his death. It is related about one man that, when he was persuaded before his death to recite the Kalimah, he expressed his inability to recite, because he said, he used to cheat through underweighing. There is a story of another person who, when persuaded to recite the Kalimah, said, "I cannot say it, because I was tempted to cast sinful looks on a woman who had come to purchase a towel from my shop." Many such stories are related in the book, 'Tazkirah Qurtabyah'. In view of the foregoing, it is essential for a man to ask and seek Allah's help, forgiveness of his sins, and to recite the Kalimah at the time of one's death.

Hadith No. 39

(٣٩) عَنْ أُمِّ هَانِيءٍ رَضِيَ اللّٰهُ عَنْهَا قَالَتْ قَالَ رَسُوْلُ اللّٰهِ ﷺ لَآ اِلٰهَ اِلَّا اللّٰهُ لَايَسْبِقُهَا عَمَلٌ وَلَاتَتْرُكُ ذَنْبًا رواه ابن ماجه كذا في منتخب كنزالعمال قلت وأخرجه الحاكم في حديث طويل وصححه ولفظه قَوْلُ لَآاِلٰهَ اِلَّا اللّٰهُ لَايَتْرُكُ ذَنْبًا وَلَايَشْبَهُهَا عَمَلٌ اهـ وتعقب عليه الذهبى بأن زكريا ضعيف وسقط بين محمد وأم هانىء وذكره في الجامع برواية ابن ماجه ورقم له بالضعف

The Holy Prophet (Sallallaho alaihe wasallam) has said, "No deed can excel recitation of (لَآاِلٰهَ اِلَّا اللّٰهُ) and this Kalimah does not let any sin remain unwashed."

Note:

That no deed can excel professing this Kalimah is quite apparent, because without belief in this Kalimah no action carries any reward. It is the pre-requisite for the acceptance of Salaat, Fasting, Hajj and Zakaat, because unless there is Imaan, no action is acceptable. Recitation of Kalimah Tayyibah, which amounts to profession of faith, is not dependent on anything else. If a person has only Imaan and no other virtue in his account, sooner or later he is bound (through the grace of Allah) to get admission into Paradise. On the other hand, if a person does not possess Imaan, then no amount of good deeds will be sufficient for his salvation.

The second part of the above-mentioned hadith is that the Kalimah does not let any sin remain unwashed. It is unanimously agreed that if a person embraces Islam in his old age, and immediately after recitation of the Kalimah he happens to meet his death, then all his sins which he had committed as a disbeliever before his declaration of Imaan are remitted. If, however recitation of the Kalimah in an earlier stage is implied, then the hadith means that the Kalimah purifies and polishes the heart, and its excessive recitation will cleanse the heart, to such an extent that he must do Taubah, which will result in the forgiveness of his sins. According to one hadith, if a person is particular to recite لآاِلٰهَ اِلَّا اللّٰهُ before going to sleep and after getting up, even his wordly affairs will lead to the betterment of his life in the Hereafter, and he will be guarded against misfortune and trouble.

Hadith No. 40

(٤٠) عَنْ اَبِىْ هُرَيْرَةَ رَضِىَ اللّٰهُ عَنْهُ قَالَ قَالَ رَسُوْلُ اللّٰهِ ﷺ اَلْاِيْمَانُ بِضْعٌ وَّسَبْعُوْنَ شُعْبَةً فَاَفْضَلُهَا قَوْلُ لَآاِلٰهَ اِلَّا اللّٰهُ وَاَدْنَاهَا اِمَاطَةُ الْاَذٰى عَنِ الطَّرِيْقِ وَالْحَيَاءُ شُعْبَةٌ مِّنَ الْاِيْمَانِ رواه الستة وغيرهم بألفاظ مختلفة واختلاف يسير في العدد وغيره ، وهذا أخر ماأردت إيراده في هذا الفصل رعاية لعدد الأربعين والله الموفق لما يحب ويرضىٰ

Rasulullah (Sallallaho alaihe wasallam) has said, "Imaan has more than seventy (According to some, seventy seven) branches, of which the most important is the recitation of لآاِلٰهَ اِلَّا اللّٰهُ , and the least one is to remove some obstacle (stone, wood, thorn, etc) from the way; and modesty also is a special requisite of Imaan."

Note:

Modesty has been specially mentioned, because it serves as a safeguard against many sins like adultery, theft, dirty talk, nakedness, abusive language, etc. Similarly, the fear of bad reputation leads to virtuous acts: In fact, fear of getting a bad name in this as well as in the next life actuates a man towards all good deeds, including of course Salaat, Hajj, Zakaat, etc, and obedience in all respects to Almighty Allah. Thus, there is the well-known proverb, "Be shameless and do whatever you like." There is also one hadith to this effect

اِذَا لَمْ تَسْتَحْيِ فَاصْنَعْ مَاشِئْتَ

"If you do not feel ashamed, you will do whatever you like." The fact is that we abstain from misdeeds for fear of disgrace and shame. A sense of modesty and shame makes one think, "If I do not offer salaat, I will face disgrace in the Hereafter." But if one has lost all sense of shame, he will say "What does it matter if others call me low?"

According to the above-mentioned hadith, there are more than seventy branches of Imaan. In many ahadith, this number is given as seventy-seven. Scholars have written detailed commentaries on these seventy seven branches. Imam Abu Haatim bin Hibbaan (Rahmatullah alaih) wrote, "I contemplated on the meaning of this hadith for a long time. When I counted the forms of prayers, the number far exceeded seventy-seven. If I counted the things which are specially mentioned in the ahaadith as branches of Imaan, their number was less. The things counted as part of Imaan in the Holy Qur'an would also total less than this. I, however, found that the total of such things mentioned in both the Qur'an as well as the hadith, agreed with this number. I therefore concluded that the above-mentioned hadith implied all these things."

Qaadhi Iyaadh (Rahmatullah alaih) writes, some people have made special efforts to give details of these branches of Imaan by means of Ijtihaad, but failure to know all these details does not mean any defect in one's Imaan, as its basic principles (with their details) are so well known. Khattaabi (Rahmatullah alaih) says that full details of the exact number is known only to Allah and His Apostle, but they are there in the Islamic Code (Shariat), and therefore it does not matter if their details are not known.

Imaam Nawawi (Rahmatullah alaih) has written that the Prophet (Sallallaho alaihe wasallam) has said that Kalimah Tauheed i.e. (لا إله إلا الله) is the most important branch of Imaan. This proves that it is the highest thing in Imaan, and that no other branch of Imaan is superior to it. Thus, belief in Tauheed is the most important essential of Imaan and is incumbent on every believer. The least thing (in the order of merit) is the removal of anything that is likely to cause obstruction or inconvenience to any Muslim. The degree of importance of all the remaining essentials of Imaan lies in betweeen the two; it is enough to believe in them in a general way just as it is necessary to believe in the angels in a general way without knowing their names and details. Some Mohaddiths have however written books about their details. Abu Abdullah Haleemi (Rahmatullah alaih) wrote a book, Fawaaidul Minhaaj on this topic, Imam Bayhaqi (Rahmatullah alaih) and Shaikh Abdul Jaleel (Rahmatullah alaih) wrote books which they called Shu-abul Imaan. Ishaaq Qurtubi (Rahmatullah alaih) wrote

Kitabun Nasaa-'ih and Imam Abu Haatim wrote "Wasful Imaan wa Shu-abihi."

The commentators of Bukhari, the most tamous collection of ahaadith, have summarised the contents of these books at one place. The gist of this summary is that complete Imaan in reality consists of three components: firstly, confirmation by heart of all the essentials of Imaan, secondly, confirmation by word of mouth; and thirdly, confirmation by our physical actions. Thus, the branches of Imaan are divided into three categories, the first of which concern the intention, belief and action of the heart, the second concern the use of the tongue, and the third concern all the remaining parts of the body. All the things of Imaan are included in these three categories. The first category includes thirty articles of faith, as follows:

1. To believe in Allah—In His Being and His Attributes, and that He is One, has no partner, and that there is no one like Him.
2. To believe that all things except Him, were created afterwards by Him, and that only He has been there forever.
3. To believe in the Angels.
4. To believe in the revealed Books.
5. To believe in the Apostles of Allah.
6. To believe in Destiny, i.e. whether good or bad, it is ordained by Allah.
7. To believe in the life after death, including interrogation in the grave, punishment in the grave, resurrection, the Day of Judgement, rendering account of ones deeds, and passing over the Bridge of Siraat.
8. To believe in the existence of Paradise, and that (by the grace of Almighty Allah) the Believers will live in it forever.
9. To believe in the existence of Hell, with its severest punishments, and that it will last for ever.
10. To love Almighty Allah.
11. To love or hate other people for the pleasure of Allah (i.e. to love the pious and hate the disobedient ones). It includes, of course, loving the Sahabas, specially Muhajirs, Ansars, and descendants of Rasulullah (Sallallaho alaihe wasallam).

12. To love Rasulullah (Sallallaho alaihe wasallam), which include cherishing the highest esteem for him, offering Durood on him, and following the Sunnah i.e. his way of life.
13. To practise Ikhlaas, which includes avoiding show and hypocrisy.
14. To make Taubah i.e. to repent over one's sins from the core of the heart, and to be determined not to repeat them.
15. To fear Almighty Allah.
16. To hope and pray for the mercy of Allah.
17. Not to despair of Almighty Allah's mercy.
18. To remain thankful to Allah.
19. To be faithful in one's promise.
20. To exercise patience.
21. To show humility, which includes respect for the elders.
22. To show kindness and pity, which includes kindness to children.
23. To be resigned to one's fate.
24. To practise tawakkul i.e. to depend on Almighty Allah.
25. To refrain from self-praise and self-aggrandisement. This includes self reformation also.
26. Not to harbour rancour and jealousy against others.
27. To cultivate modesty.
28. To restrain one's rage.
29. Not to deceive, cheat or suspect others.
30. To expel from one's heart the love of the worldly things, including that for wealth and status.

According to Allamah Ainee, (Rahmatullah alaih) this list covers all the functions of the heart. If anything is found apparently missing, a little thought will show that it is covered by one item or the other of this list.

The second category includes the functions of the

tongue, and there are seven essentials in this respect, as follows:—

1. Recitation of Kalimah Tayyibah.
2. Recitation of the Holy Qur'an.
3. Acquisition of Ilm (religious knowledge).
4. Propagation of religious knowledge to others.
5. Duaa, i.e. supplication.
6. Zikr of Allah, including Istighfaar.
7. To abstain from loose and useless talk.

The third category includes bodily actions. In this respect, there are forty essentials which are divided into three parts. The first part which includes actions that relate to the self or person of an individual. These are sixteen, as follows:—

1. Observing cleanliness of body, clothes and place. The cleanliness of body includes wudhu and obligatory bath, purification from menstruation and post-birth blood.
2. Offering salaat, including fardh, nafl and qadhaa salaat. This would mean offering and fulfilling its pre-requisites.
3. Giving sadaqah (charity), which includes zakaat, Sadaqatul-Fitr, voluntary alms, feeding people, entertaining guests, and liberating slaves.
4. Fasting, obligatory as well non-obligatory.
5. Performing Hajj, obligatory or non-obligatory. It includes making Umrah and Tawaaf.
6. I'tikaaf (remaining in a mosque in full devotion), which includes search for Lailatul Qadr.
7. Leaving one's home for the defence of the Deen. This includes Hijrat (migration for the sake of Allah).
8. Fulfilling one's offerings.
9. Steadfastness in one's oaths.
10. Payment of atonement money, if due.

11. Covering the essential parts of the body, as required by Islam, during salaat and outside salaat.
12. Offering of sacrifice and taking care of animals to be offered.
13. Making arrangements for the funeral.
14. Payment of debt.
15. Rectitude in dealings, and abstaining from usury.
16. Giving correct evidence, and not concealing the truth.

The second part, which includes action involving treatment with one's relatives and others, has six essentials:—

1. Getting married as a safeguard against adultery.
2. To discharge obligation towards one's family members, servants and subordinates.
3. Good treatment towards one's parents, and being kind and obedient to them.
4. Bringing up one's children in a proper way.
5. Remaining on good terms with one's relatives.
6. Obeying one's elders, and following their advice.

The third part includes eighteen essentials, which relates to our social obligations to society in general:—

1. To rule one's domain with justice.
2. To support the right party.
3. To obey the rulers, provided their orders are not against religion.
4. To work for the betterment of mutual relations, including punishing the wrong-doers and making Jihaad against the rebels.
5. To help others in their noble deeds.
6. To enjoin the good and forbid the evil; it includes work and speech for propagation of religion.
7. To carry out the punishments enjoined by religion (for specific offences).
8. To take part in Jihaad i.e. to fight in the path of Allah. It includes guarding the defence lines.

9. To pay off our dues and return amaanats; this includes payment of Khums (payment of tax equal to one fifth of the booty).
10. To lend (to the needy) and to pay back the debt.
11. To discharge our obligations to our neighbours, and to be kind and helpful to them.
12. To be fair in one's business dealings; it includes savings and earnings in a lawful manner.
13. To be careful in expenditure; one should guard against extravagence as well as miserliness.
14. To make salaam and respond to the salaam.
15. To say يرحمك الله (May Allah have mercy on you) when somebody happens to sneeze.
16. Not to be the cause of trouble and loss to others.
17. To avoid idle and useless pursuits.
18. To clear troublesome obstructions from the way.

The seventy-seven branches of Imaan have been counted above. Some of these can be merged together, as for example earning and spending can be put together, under fair dealings. Careful consideration can enable one to cut down the total to seventy or sixty-seven, the numbers given in some ahaadith.

The above list has been prepared mainly from the commentary of Allamah Ainee (Rahmatullah alaih) on Bukhari Shareef, wherein these things are mentioned in their order of merit. Selection has been made also from other books, i.e. Fathul-Baari of Ibn Hajar and Mirqaat of Allamah Qari.

Scholars have written that the implied essentials of Imaan are as given above. One should ponder over these, and be thankful to Almighty Allah for the good qualities acquired already, because all goodness is possible only through His grace and mercy. In case of deficiency in respect of any quality, one should strive for it and keep on praying that Almighty Allah may grace him with His blessings.

وَمَا تَوْفِيْقِىْ اِلَّا بِاللهِ

CHAPTER III

(The Third Kalimah)

The virtues of the third Kalimah, i.e. (سُبْحَانَ اللهِ وَالْحَمْدُ لِلّٰهِ وَلَآ اِلٰهَ اِلَّا اللهُ وَاللهُ اَكْبَرُ) which, according to some narrations is also followed by (لَاحَوْلَ وَلَاقُوَّةَ اِلَّا بِاللهِ), are described in this chapter. These words are also known as Tasbihaati-Fatimah, because the Prophet (Sallallaho alaihe wasallam) had advised his most beloved daughter, Hadhrat Fatimah (Radhiyallaho anha) to recite these regularly, as will be described later on. As there are many verses of the Holy Qur'an and several ahadith in respect of this Kalimah, this chapter is divided into two parts. The first part contains the Qur'anic verses, and the second part the sayings of the Prophet (Sallallaho alaihe wasallam).

PART I

This part includes the verses of the Holy Book that relate to the Kalimah

(سُبْحَانَ اللهِ وَالْحَمْدُ لِلّٰهِ وَلَآ اِلٰهَ اِلَّا اللهُ وَاللهُ اَكْبَرُ)

As a rule, the greater the importance of the subject matter, the stress on the method of describing it, make it thoroughly understood. That is why the meanings and significances of these words have been explained in various ways in the Holy Qur'an.

The first of these phrases is (سُبْحَانَ اللهِ). It means that Almighty Allah is free from all defects and shortcomings, and it is a declaration of firm belief in His being so. Almighty Allah has ordered its recitation, and has also informed us that the angels and all other creation remain busy in reciting it. Such is also the case with the other words of this Kalimah, in that their significance and importance is stressed in so many ways in the Holy Qur'an.

(١) وَنَحْنُ نُسَبِّحُ بِحَمْدِكَ وَنُقَدِّسُ لَكَ (بقرة ع ٤)

1. (At the time of creation of man, the angels had said,) "We hymn Thy Praise, glorify and revere Thee."

(٢) قَالُوْا سُبْحَانَكَ لَاعِلْمَ لَنَا اِلَّا مَا عَلَّمْتَنَا اِنَّكَ اَنْتَ العَلِيْمُ الحَكِيْمُ (بقرة ع٤)

2. (When the angels were put to a test vis-a-vis the first man, they submitted,) "Glory be to Thee. We have no knowledge save that which Thou hast taught us; Thou art the Knower and the Wise."

(٣) وَاذْكُرْ رَبَّكَ كَثِيْرًا وَسَبِّحْ بِالْعَشِيِّ وَالْاِبْكَارِ (آل عمران ع٤)

3. Remember Thy Lord exceedingly, and praise (Him) in the early hours of night and morning.

(٤) رَبَّنَا مَاخَلَقْتَ هٰذَا بَاطِلًا سُبْحَانَكَ فَقِنَا عَذَابَ النَّارِ (أيضا ع٢٠)

4. (Wise men are those who remain busy in the zikr of Allah, and ponder over the wonders of Nature and say,) "O, Lord! Thou created this not in vain, Glory be to Thee; preserve us from the doom of fire."

(٥) سُبْحٰنَهُ اَنْ يَّكُوْنَ لَهُ وَلَدٌ (نساء ٢٣ع)

5. Far removed it is from His Transcendant Majesty that He should have a son.

(٦) قَالَ سُبْحَانَكَ مَايَكُوْنُ لِيَ اَنْ اَقُوْلَ مَالَيْسَ لِيْ بِحَقٍّ (مائدة – ١٦ع)

6. (On the day of judgement when Allah would enquire from Hadhrat Eesaa (Alayhis salaam) whether he had preached to his followers the faith in Trinity, he would say,) "Allah Be glorified; it was not for me to utter that which I had no right."

(٧) سُبْحَانَهُ وَتَعَالٰى عَمَّا يَصِفُوْنَ (انعام ١٢ ع)

7. Glorified be He and exalted high above (all) they (Unbelievers) ascribe unto Him.

(٨) فَلَمَّآ اَفَاقَ قَالَ سُبْحَانَكَ تُبْتُ اِلَيْكَ وَاَنَا اَوَّلُ الْمُؤْمِنِيْنَ (اعراف ١٧ ع)

8. (When on the mountain of Toor, Hadhrat Moosa, (Alayhis salaam) could not withstand even a glimpse of Allah's glory and became senseless), and when he woke up he said, "Glory unto Thee; I turn unto Thee repentant, and I am the first of true believers.

(٩) اِنَّ الَّذِيْنَ عِنْدَ رَبِّكَ لَايَسْتَكْبِرُوْنَ عَنْ عِبَادَتِهٖ وَيُسَبِّحُوْنَهٗ وَلَهٗ يَسْجُدُوْنَ
(اعراف ع٢٤)

9. Lo! those who are with thy Lord (i.e. angels) are not too proud to do Him service, but they praise Him and adore Him alone.

The Sufis have written that the mention of the negation of pride before anything else implies that to be free from pride is a pre-requisite for constancy in prayers, and that pride makes one neglectful in prayers.

(١٠) سُبْحَانَهٗ وَتَعَالٰى عَمَّا يُشْرِكُوْنَ (توبة ع٥)

10. Be He glorified above all that they (unbelievers) ascribe as partners (unto Him).

(١١) دَعْوَاهُمْ فِيْهَا سُبْحَانَكَ اللّٰهُمَّ وَتَحِيَّتُهُمْ فِيْهَا سَلَامٌ وَآخِرُ دَعْوَاهُمْ اَنِ
الْحَمْدُ لِلّٰهِ رَبِّ الْعَالَمِيْنَ (يونس ع١)

11. Their (i.e. of dwellers of Paradise) prayers therein will be "Glory be to Thee, Allah", and their greetings therein (among themselves) will be "Peace," and the conclusion of their prayer wil be "Praise be to Allah, Lord of the worlds."

(١٢) سُبْحَانَهٗ وَتَعَالٰى عَمَّا يُشْرِكُوْنَ (يونس ع٣)

12. Praised be He and exalted above all that ye (nonbelievers) associate with Him.

(١٣) قَالُوْا اتَّخَذَ اللّٰهُ وَلَدًا سُبْحٰنَهٗ هُوَ الْغَنِيُّ (يونس ع٧)

13. They say, Allah had taken (unto Him) a son. Glorified be He; He hath no needs.

(١٤) وَسُبْحَانَ اللهِ وَمَا اَنَا مِنَ الْمُشْرِكِيْنَ (يوسف ١٢ ع)

14. Glory be to Allah, and I am not of the idolators.

(١٥) وَيُسَبِّحُ الرَّعْدُ بِحَمْدِهِ وَالْمَلَائِكَةُ مِنْ خِيْفَتِهِ

15. And the thunder (angel) hymneth His praise, and (so do) the other angels for awe of Him. It is stated by the scholars that if anybody on hearing the thunder recites

سُبْحَانَ الَّذِيْ يُسَبِّحُ الرَّعْدُ بِحَمْدِهِ وَالْمَلٰٓئِكَةُ مِنْ خِيْفَتِهِ

he will be immune from the ill consequences of lightening. It is narrated in one hadith, "Make zikr of Allah when you hear the thunder of lightening, because it cannot harm one who is doing zikr." It is narrated in another hadith, "At the time of thunder say (تسبيح) (Subhanallah) and not (تكبير) (Allaho-Akbar).

(١٦) وَلَقَدْ نَعْلَمُ اَنَّكَ يَضِيْقُ صَدْرُكَ بِمَا يَقُوْلُوْنَ فَسَبِّحْ بِحَمْدِ رَبِّكَ وَكُنْ مِنَ السَّاجِدِيْنَ ، وَاعْبُدْ رَبَّكَ حَتّٰى يَأْتِيَكَ الْيَقِيْنُ (حجر ع ٦)

16. Well know We that thy bosom is at times oppressed by what they say. But hymn the praise of thy Lord, and be of those who make prostration (unto Him). And serve thy Lord until the inevitable (i.e. death) cometh unto thee.

(١٧) سُبْحَانَهُ وَتَعَالٰى عَمَّا يُشْرِكُوْنَ (نحل ع ١)

17. High be He exalted above all that they associate with Him.

(١٨) وَيَجْعَلُوْنَ لِلّٰهِ الْبَنَاتِ سُبْحَانَهُ وَلَهُمْ مَايَشْتَهُوْنَ (نحل ع ٧)

18. And they assign unto Allah daughters—be He glo-

rified, and unto themselves (they assign) what they desire.

(١٩) سُبْحٰنَ الَّذِىْ اَسْرٰى بِعَبْدِهٖ لَيْلًا مِّنَ الْمَسْجِدِ الْحَرَامِ اِلَى الْمَسْجِدِ الْاَقْصَى (بنی إسرائيل ع١)

19. Glorified be He who carried His servant by night from the inviolable place of worship, musjid of Kaaba, to the musjid Al-Aqsa (in Jerusalem).

(٢٠) سُبْحَانَهٗ وَتَعَالٰى عَمَّا يَقُوْلُوْنَ عُلُوًّا كَبِيْرًا (بنی إسرائيل ٥ ع)

20. Glorified is He and exhalted high above what they say.

(٢١) تُسَبِّحُ لَهُ السَّمٰوٰتُ السَّبْعُ وَالْاَرْضُ وَمَنْ فِيْهِنَّ (أيضا)

21. The seven heavens and earths, and all that is therein, Praise Him.

(٢٢) وَاِنْ مِّنْ شَيْءٍ اِلَّا يُسَبِّحُ بِحَمْدِهٖ وَلٰكِنْ لَّا تَفْقَهُوْنَ تَسْبِيْحَهُمْ (أيضا)

22. And there is not a thing but hymenth His praise, but ye understand not their praise.

(٢٣) قُلْ سُبْحَانَ رَبِّيْ هَلْ كُنْتُ اِلَّا بَشَرًا رَّسُوْلًا (أيضا ع١٠)

23. (In reply to the absurd demands of others) say, "My Lord is glorified, and I am naught save a mortal messenger."

(٢٤) وَيَقُوْلُوْنَ سُبْحَانَ رَبِّنَا اِنْ كَانَ وَعْدُ رَبِّنَا لَمَفْعُوْلًا (أيضاً ع١٢)

24. (When the Qur'an is recited before those scholars, they go down in prostration) and they say, "Glory to our Lord, verily the promise of our Lord must be fulfilled."

(٢٥) فَخَرَجَ عَلٰى قَوْمِهٖ مِنَ الْمِحْرَابِ فَاَوْحٰى اِلَيْهِمْ اَنْ سَبِّحُوْا بُكْرَةً وَّعَشِيًّا

(مريم ع١)

25. Then the (Prophet Zakariyya) (Alayhis salaam) came forth unto his people from the sanctuary, and signified to them, "Glorify your Lord at break of day and fall of night."

(٢٦) مَاكَانَ لِلّٰهِ اَنْ يَّتَّخِذَ مِنْ وَّلَدٍ سُبْحٰنَهُ (مريم ع ٢)

26. It befitteth not Allah that He should take unto Himself a son; glory be to Him.

(٢٧) وَسَبِّحْ بِحَمْدِ رَبِّكَ قَبْلَ طُلُوْعِ الشَّمْسِ وَقَبْلَ الغُرُوْبِ وَمِنْ آنَآىءِ اللَّيْلِ فَسَبِّحْ وَاَطْرَافَ النَّهَارِ لَعَلَّكَ تَرْضٰى (طه ع ٨)

27. Therefore (O, Muhammad Sallallaho alaihe wasallam, bear with what they say) and celebrate the praise of thy Lord ere the rising of the sun and ere the going down thereof. And glorify Him some hours of the night and at the two ends of the day, that thou mayst find joy (because of reward you could expect).

(٢٨) يُسَبِّحُوْنَ اللَّيْلَ وَالنَّهَارَ لَايَفْتَرُوْنَ (انبياء ع ٢)

28. They (The pious people) celebrate His (Allah's) praise night and day; they feel not tired.

(٢٩) فَسُبْحَانَ اللهِ رَبِّ الْعَرْشِ عَمَّا يَصِفُوْنَ (أيضا)

29. Glorified be Allah, the Lord of the Arsh (throne), from all that they ascribe (Unto Him).

(٣٠) وَقَالُوْا اتَّخَذَ الرَّحْمٰنُ وَلَدًا سُبْحَانَهُ (أيضا)

30. And they (mushrikeen) say, the Beneficent hath taken unto Himself a son! Be He glorified.

(٣١) وَسَخَّرْنَا مَعَ دَاوٗدَ الْجِبَالَ يُسَبِّحْنَ وَالطَّيْرَ (انبياء ع ٦)

31. And He subjugated the hills and the birds to Dawood; they hymn (His) praise along with Dawood.

(٣٢) لَآ اِلٰهَ اِلَّا اَنْتَ سُبْحَانَكَ اِنِّيْ كُنْتُ مِنَ الظَّالِمِيْنَ (انبياء ع٦)

32. (Younus Alayhis salaam cried in the darkness) There is no Allah save Thee, be Thou glorified. Lo! I have been a wrongdoer.

(٣٣) سُبْحَانَ اللهِ عَمَّا يَصِفُوْنَ (مؤمنون ع٢)

33. Glorified be Allah above all that they allege.

(٣٤) سُبْحَانَكَ هٰذَا بُهْتَانٌ عَظِيْمٌ (نور ع٢)

34. Glory to thee (all that they falsely allege against Hadhrat Aa-ishah, (Radhiyallaho anho) it is manifest untruth.

(٣٥) يُسَبِّحُ لَهُ فِيْهَا بِالْغُدُوِّ وَالْاٰصَالِ ، رِجَالٌ لَّاتُلْهِيْهِمْ تِجَارَةٌ وَّلَابَيْعٌ عَنْ ذِكْرِ اللهِ
وَاِقَامِ الصَّلٰوةِ وَاِيْتَاءِ الزَّكٰوةِ يَخَافُوْنَ يَوْمًا تَتَقَلَّبُ فِيْهِ الْقُلُوْبُ وَالْاَبْصَارُ (نور ع٥)

35. Therein do offer praise to Him, at morning and evening, men whom neither merchandise nor sale beguileth from remembrance of Allah and constancy in prayer and paying to the poor their dues; men who fear the day (i.e. Dooms-day) when the hearts and eyeballs will be upturned.

(٣٦) اَلَمْ تَرَ اَنَّ اللهَ يُسَبِّحُ لَهُ مَنْ فِي السَّمٰوٰتِ وَالْاَرْضِ وَالطَّيْرُ صٰٓفّٰتٍ كُلٌّ
قَدْ عَلِمَ صَلَاتَهُ وَتَسْبِيْحَهُ وَاللهُ عَلِيْمٌ بِمَا يَفْعَلُوْنَ (نور ع٦)

36. Hast thou not seen that Allah, He it is Whom all those in the Heavens and the Earth praise, and the birds in their flight. Each one knoweth verily its own (mode of) worship and praise; and Allah is aware of what they do.

(٣٧) قَالُوْا سُبْحَانَكَ مَاكَانَ يَنْبَغِيْ لَنَا اَنْ نَّتَّخِذَ مِنْ دُوْنِكَ مِنْ اَوْلِيَاءَ وَلٰكِنْ
مَّتَّعْتَهُمْ وَآبَائَهُمْ حَتّٰى نَسُوْا الذِّكْرَ وَكَانُوْا قَوْمًا بُوْرًا (فرقان ع٢)

37. (On the Day of Judgement when Allah will haul up the non-believers and those whom they worshipped, and enquire from the latter whether they had misled the former) they will say, "Be Thou glorified. It was not for us to choose any protectors besides Thee; but Thou did give them and their fathers ease, till they forgot the warning and became lost folk."

(٣٨) وَتَوَكَّلْ عَلَى الحَيِّ الَّذِيْ لَايَمُوْتُ وَسَبِّحْ بِحَمْدِهِ وَكَفٰى بِهِ بِذُنُوْبِ عِبَادِهِ خَبِيْرًا (فرقان ع١)

38. And trust thou in the Living One, Who dieth not, and hymn His praise. He is sufficient as Knower of His bondsman's sins.

(٣٩) وَسُبْحَانَ اللهِ رَبِّ الْعَالَمِيْنَ (نمل ع١)

39. Glorified be Allah, the Lord of the worlds.

(٤٠) سُبْحٰنَ اللهِ وَتَعَالٰى عَمَّا يُشْرِكُوْنَ (قصص – ع٧)

40. Glorified be Allah and exalted above all that they associated with Him.

(٤١) فَسُبْحَانَ اللهِ حِيْنَ تُمْسُوْنَ وَحِيْنَ تُسْبِحُوْنَ وَلَهُ الْحَمْدُ فِيْ السَّمٰوٰتِ وَالْاَرْضِ وَعَشِيًا وَّحِيْنَ تُظْهِرُوْنَ (روم – ع٢)

41. So, glory be to Allah when ye enter the night and when ye enter the morning. Unto Him be praise in heavens and Earth, and at the Sun's decline and at noonday.

(٤٢) سُبْحَانَهٗ وَتَعَالٰى عَمَّا يُشْرِكُوْنَ (روم – ع٤)

42. Praised and exalted be He above what they associate (with Him).

(٤٣) اِنَّمَا يُؤْمِنُ بِاٰيٰتِنَا الَّذِيْنَ اِذَا ذُكِّرُوْا بِهٖ خَرُّوْا سُجَّدًا وَّسَبَّحُوْا بِحَمْدِ رَبِّهِمْ وَهُمْ لَايَسْتَكْبِرُوْنَ (سجدة – ع٢)

43. Only those believe in Our revelation who, when they are reminded of them, fall down prostrate and hymn the praise of their Lord, and they are not proud and scornful.

(٤٤) يَاأَيُّهَا الَّذِيْنَ آمَنُوْا اذْكُرُوْا اللهَ ذِكْرًا كَثِيْرًا وَّسَبِّحُوْهُ بُكْرَةً وَّاَصِيْلًا (احزاب – ع٦

44. Ye who believe! Remember Allah with much remembrance, and glorify Him early in the morning and late in the evening.

(٤٥) قَالُوْا سُبْحَانَكَ اَنْتَ وَلِيُّنَا مِنْ دُوْنِهِمْ (سبا ع٣)

45. (On the Day of Judgement when the entire creation would be assembled, Allah will ask from the Angels whether you were being worshipped). They (Angels) will say, "Be Thou glorified, (and need no partner) Thou art our protector from them."

(٤٦) سُبْحَانَ الَّذِيْ خَلَقَ الْاَزْوَاجَ كُلَّهَا (يس ع٣)

46. Glory be to Him Who created all the pairs of things and beings.

(٤٧) فَسُبْحَانَ الَّذِيْ بِيَدِهٖ مَلَكُوْتُ كُلِّ شَيْءٍ وَّاِلَيْهِ تُرْجَعُوْنَ (يس – ع٥)

47. Therefore, glory be to Him in Whose hand is the domination over all things. Unto Him ye will be brought back.

(٤٨) فَلَوْلَا اَنَّهٗ كَانَ مِنَ الْمُسَبِّحِيْنَ لَلَبِثَ فِيْ بَطْنِهٖ اِلٰى يَوْمِ يُبْعَثُوْنَ (صافات – ع

48. And had he not been one of those who glorify Him, he would have tarried in its (fish's) belly till the day when they are raised up.

(٤٩) سُبْحَانَ اللهِ عَمَّا يَصِفُوْنَ أيضا

49. Glorified be Allah from that which they attribute unto Him.

(٥٠) وَاِنَّا لَنَحْنُ الْمُسَبِّحُوْنَ ايضا

50. Lo! indeed we (angels) are they who hymn His praise.

(٥١) سُبْحَانَ رَبِّكَ رَبِّ الْعِزَّةِ عَمَّا يَصِفُوْنَ وَسَلٰمٌ عَلَى الْمُرْسَلِيْنَ وَالْحَمْدُ لِلّٰهِ رَبِّ الْعٰلَمِيْنَ أيضا

51. Glorified be Thy Lord, the Lord of Majesty, from that which they attribute (unto Him). And peace be unto those sent as prophets, and praise be to Allah, the Lord of the worlds.

(٥٢) اِنَّا سَخَّرْنَا الْجِبَالَ مَعَهُ يُسَبِّحْنَ بِالْعَشِيِّ وَالْاِشْرَاقِ وَالطَّيْرَ مَحْشُوْرَةً كُلٌّ لَّهُ اَوَّابٌ (ص – ع ٢)

52. Lo! We subdued the hills to hymn the praises (of their Lord) with him (Prophet Dawood) (Alayhis salaam) at nightfall and sunrise. And the birds assembled, all with him, were turning unto Him (and hymn His Praises).

(٥٣) سُبْحٰنَهُ ، هُوَ اللّٰهُ الْوَاحِدُ الْقَهَّارُ (زمر – ع ١)

53. Be He glorified; He is Allah, the One, the Absolute.

(٥٤) سُبْحٰنَهُ وَتَعَالٰى عَمَّا يُشْرِكُوْنَ (زمر – ع ٧)

54. Glorified is He and exalted High above all that they ascribe as partners (unto Him).

(٥٥) وَتَرَى الْمَلٰئِكَةَ حَآفِّيْنَ مِنْ حَوْلِ الْعَرْشِ يُسَبِّحُوْنَ بِحَمْدِ رَبِّهِمْ وَقُضِيَ بَيْنَهُمْ بِالْحَقِّ وَقِيْلَ الْحَمْدُ لِلّٰهِ رَبِّ الْعٰلَمِيْنَ (زمر – ع ٨)

55. And thou (O! Muhammad Sallallaho alaihe wasallam) seest (on the Day of Judgement), the angels thronging round the Throne, hymning the praises of their Lord. And the assembled people are judged aright. And it will be said, Praise be to Allah, the Lord of the worlds.

(٥٦) اَلَّذِيْنَ يَحْمِلُوْنَ الْعَرْشَ وَمَنْ حَوْلَهٗ يُسَبِّحُوْنَ بِحَمْدِ رَبِّهِمْ وَيُؤْمِنُوْنَ بِهٖ
وَيَسْتَغْفِرُوْنَ لِلَّذِيْنَ اٰمَنُوْا رَبَّنَا وَسِعْتَ كُلَّ شَيْءٍ رَّحْمَةً وَّعِلْمًا فَاغْفِرْ لِلَّذِيْنَ تَابُوْا
وَاتَّبَعُوْا سَبِيْلَكَ وَقِهِمْ عَذَابَ الْجَحِيْمِ (مومن – ع ٥)

56. Those (angels) who bear the Throne, and all who are round about it, hymn the praise of their Lord, and believe in Him and ask forgiveness for all those who believe, saying: our Lord, Thy comprehensive reach is over all things in mercy and knowledge; therefore forgive those who repent and follow Thy way, and ward off from them the punishment of hell.

(٥٧) وَسَبِّحْ بِحَمْدِ رَبِّكَ بِالْعَشِيِّ وَالْاِبْكَارِ (مومن – ع ١)

57. And hymn the praise of thy Lord at fall of night and in the early dawn.

(٥٨) فَالَّذِيْنَ عِنْدَ رَبِّكَ يُسَبِّحُوْنَ لَهٗ بِاللَّيْلِ وَالنَّهَارِ وَهُمْ لَا يَسْئَمُوْنَ
(حم سجدة – ع ٥)

58. Those (angels) who are near to Allah glorify Him by day and by night, and they never feel tired.

(٥٩) وَالْمَلٰٓئِكَةُ يُسَبِّحُوْنَ بِحَمْدِ رَبِّهِمْ وَيَسْتَغْفِرُوْنَ لِمَنْ فِي الْاَرْضِ (شورى – ع ١)

59. And the angels hymn the praises of their Lord and ask forgiveness for those on the Earth.

(٦٠) وَتَقُوْلُوْا سُبْحَانَ الَّذِيْ سَخَّرَ لَنَا هٰذَا وَمَا كُنَّا لَهٗ مُقْرِنِيْنَ ، وَاِنَّا اِلٰى رَبِّنَا
لَمُنْقَلِبُوْنَ (زخرف – ع ١)

60. Glorified be He Who had subdued these (mounts) unto us, and we are not capable (of subduing them). And Lo! unto one Lord we shall return.

(٦١) سُبْحَانَ رَبِّ السَّمٰوٰتِ وَالْاَرْضِ رَبِّ الْعَرْشِ عَمَّا يَصِفُوْنَ (زخرف – ع ٧)

61. Glorified be the Lord of the Heavens and the Earth,

the Lord of the Throne, from what they ascribe (unto Him).

(٦٢) وَتُسَبِّحُوْهُ بُكْرَةً وَّاَصِيْلًا (فتح – ع ١)

62. And glorify Him at early dawn and at the close of the day.

(٦٣) فَاصْبِرْ عَلٰى مَايَقُوْلُوْنَ وَسَبِّحْ بِحَمْدِ رَبِّكَ قَبْلَ طُلُوْعِ الشَّمْسِ وَقَبْلَ الْغُرُوْبِ ، وَمِنَ الَّيْلِ فَسَبِّحْهُ وَاَدْبَارَ السُّجُوْدِ ق ع٣

63. Therefore (O Muhammad Sallallaho alaihe wasallam) bear with what they say, and hymn the praises of thy Lord before the rising and before the setting of the sun; and in the night time hymn His praise, and after the (prescribed) prostration (salaat).

(٦٤) سُبْحَانَ اللهِ عَمَّا يُشْرِكُوْنَ (طور ع ١)

64. Glorified be Allah from all that they ascribe as partners (unto Him).

(٦٥) وَسَبِّحْ بِحَمْدِ رَبِّكَ حِيْنَ تَقُوْمُ ، وَمِنَ الَّيْلِ فَسَبِّحْهُ وَاِدْبَارَ النُّجُوْمِ (ايضًا)

65. And hymn the praise of they Lord when thou uprisest. And in the night time hymn His praise, and also at the setting of the stars.

(٦٦ /٦٧) فَسَبِّحْ بِاسْمِ رَبِّكَ الْعَظِيْمِ (واقعة – ع ٢ ع ٣)

66. Therefore (O Muhammad Sallallaho alaihe wasallam), praise the name of the Lord, the Supreme.

(٦٨) سَبَّحَ لِلّٰهِ مَافِي السَّمٰوٰتِ وَالْاَرْضِ وَهُوَ الْعَزِيْزُ الْحَكِيْمُ (حديد – ع ١)

68. All that is in the Heavens and the Earth glorifieth Allah, and He is the Mighty, the Wise.

(٦٩) سَبَّحَ لِلّٰهِ مَا فِي السَّمٰوٰتِ وَمَا فِى الْاَرْضِ وَهُوَ الْعَزِيْزُ الْحَكِيْمُ (حشر ع١)

69. All that is in the Heavens and the Earth glorifieth Allah, and He is the Mighty the Wise.

(٧٠) سُبْحَانَ اللّٰهِ عَمَّا يُشْرِكُوْنَ (حشر – ع٣)

70. Glorified be Allah from all that they ascribe as partners (unto Him).

(٧١) يُسَبِّحُ لَهٗ مَافِي السَّمٰوٰتِ وَالْاَرْضِ وَهُوَ الْعَزِيْزُ الْحَكِيْمُ (حشر – ع٣)

71. All that is in the Heavens and the Earth glorifieth Him, and He is the Mighty, the Wise.

(٧٢) سَبَّحَ لِلّٰهِ مَافِي السَّمٰوٰتِ وَمَا فِى الْاَرْضِ الْمَلِكِ الْقُدُّوسِ الْعَزِيْزِ الْحَكِيْمِ

(صف ع١)

72. All that is in the Heavens and the Earth glorifieth Allah, and He is the Mighty, the Wise.

(٧٣) يُسَبِّحُ لِلّٰهِ مَافِي السَّمٰوَاتِ وَمَا فِي الْاَرْضِ الْمَلِكِ الْقُدُّوْسُ الْعَزِيْزِ الْحَكِيْمِ

(جمعة – ع١)

73. All that is in the Heavens and all that is in the Earth glorifieth Allah, the governing Lord, the Holy One, the Majesty, the Wise.

(٧٤) يُسَبِّحُ لِلّٰهِ مَا فِى السَّمٰوٰتِ وَمَا فِىْ الْاَرْضِ ، لَهُ الْمُلْكُ وَلَهُ الْحَمْدُ وَهُوَ
عَلٰى كُلِّ شَيْءٍ قَدِيْرٌ (تغابن – ع١)

74. All that is in the Heavens and all that is in the Earth glorifieth Allah; unto Him belongeth the sovereignty and unto Him belongeth praise, and He is able to do all things.

(۷۵ /۷٦) قَالَ اَوْسَطُهُمْ اَلَمْ اَقُلْ لَّكُمْ لَوْلَا تُسَبِّحُوْنَ ، قَالُوْا سُبْحَانَ رَبِّنَا اِنَّا كُنَّا ظٰلِمِيْنَ (قلم ع ۱)

75 & 76. The best among them said: did I not say unto you: why glorify ye not (Allah)?
They said: glorified be our Lord, indeed we have been guilty.

(۷۷) فَسَبِّحْ بِاسْمِ رَبِّكَ الْعَظِيْمِ (الحاقة – ع ۲)

77. So glorify the name of thy Supreme Lord.

(۷۸) وَاذْكُرِسْمَ رَبِّكَ بُكْرَةً وَّاَصِيْلًا ، وَمِنَ الَّيْلِ فَاسْجُدْ لَهُ وَسَبِّحْهُ لَيْلًا طَوِيْلًا (دهر – ع ۲)

78. Remember the name of thy Lord at morning and evening; and worship Him a portion of the night, and glorify Him through the long night.

(۷۹) سَبِّحِ اسْمَ رَبِّكَ الْاَعْلَى (اعلى)

79. Praise the name of thy Lord, the most High.

(۸۰) فَسَبِّحْ بِحَمْدِ رَبِّكَ وَاسْتَغْفِرْهُ اِنَّهُ كَانَ تَوَّابًا (نصر)

80. Then hymn the praise of thy Lord and seek forgiveness of Him. Lo! He is ever ready to show mercy.

In the eighty verses quoted above, there is either a clear commandment of Almighty Allah for hymning his glory, or else its importance is stressed. A thing that has been repeatedly mentioned and especially stressed by the Lord of Lords in His Holy Book is doubtless most virtuous. Along with the commandment for glorification of Almighty Allah, it has been stressed in many of the above mentioned verses to hymn His praise and recite (اَلْحَمْدُ لله). In addition to these verses, there are other ayaats as well, given below, which describe specifically the importance of hymning His praise and reciting (اَلْحَمْدُ لله) It is most significant that the Holy Book starts with the verse (اَلْحَمْدُ لله رَبِّ الْعٰلَمِيْنَ) which indicates the excellence of this sacred phrase.

(١) اَلحَمْدُ لِلّٰهِ رَبِّ الْعَالَمِيْنَ (فاتحة)

1. Praise be to Allah, Lord of the worlds.

(٢) اَلْحَمْدُ لِلّٰهِ الَّذِيْ خَلَقَ السَّمٰوٰتِ وَالْاَرْضَ وَجَعَلَ الظُّلُمَاتِ وَالنُّوْرَ ثُمَّ الَّذِيْنَ كَفَرُوْا بِرَبِّهِمْ يَعْدِلُوْنَ (انعام – ع ١)

2. Praise be to Allah, Who hath created the Heavens and Earth, and hath appointed darkness and light. Yet those who disbelieve ascribe rivals unto their Lord.

(٣) فَقُطِعَ دَابِرُ الْقَوْمِ الَّذِيْنَ ظَلَمُوْا وَالْحَمْدُ لِلّٰهِ رَبِّ الْعَالَمِيْنَ (انعام – ع ٥)

3. So, of the people who did wrong, the last remnant was cut off. Praise be to Allah Lord of the worlds.

(٤) وَقَالُوْا الْحَمْدُ لِلّٰهِ الَّذِيْ هَدَانَا لِهٰذَا وَمَا كُنَّا لِنَهْتَدِيَ لَوْ لَآ اَنْ هَدَانَا اللّٰهُ (اعراف ع٥)

4. And they say, all praise be to Allah, Who hath guided us to this; we could not have truly been led aright if Allah had not guided us.

(٥) اَلَّذِيْنَ يَتَّبِعُوْنَ الرَّسُوْلَ النَّبِيَّ الْاُمِّيَّ الَّذِيْ يَجِدُوْنَهُ مَكْتُوْبًا عِنْدَهُمْ فِي التَّوْرَاةِ وَالْاِنْجِيْلِ (اعراف ع١٩)

5. Those who follow the messenger, the prophet who can neither read nor write, whom they will find described in the Torah and Gospel (which are) with them. (Among the qualities described in the Torah, one is that his followers will praise Allah very much).

(٦) اَلتَّائِبُوْنَ الْعَابِدُوْنَ الْحَامِدُوْنَ السَّائِحُوْنَ الرَّاكِعُوْنَ السَّاجِدُوْنَ الْاٰمِرُوْنَ بِالْمَعْرُوْفِ وَالنَّاهُوْنَ عَنِ الْمُنْكَرِ وَالْحَافِظُوْنَ لِحُدُوْدِ اللّٰهِ وَبَشِّرِ الْمُؤْمِنِيْنَ (توبة – ع ١٤)

6. (While talking about the qualities of those who have sold to Him their lives and wealth, Allah says:) Triumphant are those who turn repentent (to Allah), those who serve (Him), those who praise (Him), those who fast, those who bow down, those who fall prostrate (in prayers), those who enjoin the right and who forbid the wrong, and those who keep the (ordained) limits of Allah; give glad tidings to the believers.

(٧) وَآخِرُ دَعْوَانَا عَنِ الْحَمْدُ لِلّٰهِ رَبِّ الْعَالَمِيْنَ (یونس – ع١)

7. And the conclusion of their prayer will be: Praise be to Allah, Lord of the worlds.

(٨) اَلْحَمْدُ لِلّٰهِ الَّذِیْ وَهَبَ لِیْ عَلَی الْكِبَرِ اِسْمٰعِيْلَ وَاِسْحٰقَ (ابراهيم ع٦)

8. Praise be to Allah, Who hath given me, in my old age, Ismail and Ishaaq. (Alyhimas salaam).

(٩) اَلْحَمْدُ لِلّٰهِ ، بَلْ اَكْثَرُهُمْ لَايَعْلَمُوْنَ (نحل ع١٠)

9. Praise be to Allah: But most of them know not.

(١٠) يَوْمَ يَدْعُوْكُمْ فَتَسْتَجِيْبُوْنَ بِحَمْدِهٖ وَتَظُنُّوْنَ اِنْ لَّبِثْتُمْ اِلَّا قَلِيْلًا
(بنی اسرائیل ع٧)

10. A day (the Resurrection day) when He will call you, and ye will obey and answer with His praise, and ye will think that ye have tarried but a little while (in the world and the grave).

(١١) وَقُلِ الْحَمْدُ لِلّٰهِ الَّذِیْ لَمْ يَتَّخِذْ وَلَدًا وَّلَمْ يَكُنْ لَّهٗ شَرِيْكٌ فِی الْمُلْكِ
وَلَمْ يَكُنْ لَّهٗ وَلِیٌّ مِّنَ الذُّلِّ وَكَبِّرْهُ تَكْبِيْرًا (ایضًا ع١٢)

11. And say; praise be to Allah, Who hath not taken unto Himself a son and Who hath no partner in the sovereignty, nor hath He (need of) any protecting friend through dependence. And magnify Him with all magnificence.

(١٢) اَلْحَمْدُ لِلّٰهِ الَّذِىْ اَنْزَلَ عَلٰى عَبْدِهِ الْكِتٰبَ وَلَمْ يَجْعَلْ لَّهٗ عِوَجًا (كهف ع١)

12. Praise be to Allah, Who hath revealed the scripture unto His slave, and has not placed therein any crookedness.

(١٣) فَقُلِ الْحَمْدُ لِلّٰهِ الَّذِىْ نَجّٰنَا مِنَ الْقَوْمِ الظّٰلِمِيْنَ (مومنون ع٢)

13. (Addressing Nooh Alayhis salaam) And say Praise be to Allah, Who hath saved us from the wrongdoing folk."

(١٤) فَقَالَا الْحَمْدُ لِلّٰهِ الَّذِىْ فَضَّلَنَا عَلٰى كَثِيْرٍ مِّنْ عِبَادِهِ الْمُؤْمِنِيْنَ (نمل ع٢)

14. (Prophets Sulaimaan and Dawood Alayhimas salaam) said, "Praise be to Allah", Who hath preferred us above many of His believing slaves.

(١٥) قُلِ الْحَمْدُ لِلّٰهِ وَسَلٰمٌ عَلٰى عِبَادِهِ الَّذِيْنَ اصْطَفٰى (نمل ع٥)

15. Say (O, Muhammad!) (Sallallaho alaihe wasallam) praise be to Allah, peace be on His slaves whom He hath chosen.

(١٦) وَقُلِ الْحَمْدُ لِلّٰهِ سَيُرِيْكُمْ اٰيٰتِهٖ فَتَعْرِفُوْنَهَا (نمل ع٧)

16. And say: Praise be to Allah, Who will show His portents, so that ye shall know them.

(١٧) لَهُ الْحَمْدُ فِى الْاُوْلٰى وَالْاٰخِرَةِ وَلَهُ الْحُكْمُ وَاِلَيْهِ تُرْجَعُوْنَ (قصص ع٧)

17. His is all praise in the former and the latter (state of life), and His is the command and unto Him ye will be brought back.

(١٨) قُلِ الْحَمْدُ لِلّٰهِ ، بَلْ اَكْثَرُهُمْ لَايَعْقِلُوْنَ (عنكبوت ع٦)

18. Say: Praise be to Allah. But most of them have no sense.

(١٩) وَمَنْ كَفَرَ فَاِنَّ اللّٰهَ غَنِىٌّ حَمِيْدٌ (لقمٰن ع ٢)

19. And whosoever refuseth-Lo! Allah is absolute, worthy of all praise.

(٢٠) قُلِ الْحَمْدُ لِلّٰهِ ، بَلْ اَكْثَرُهُمْ لَايَعْلَمُوْنَ (لقمٰن ع٣)

20. Say: Praise be to Allah. But most of them know not.

(٢١) اِنَّ اللّٰهَ هُوَ الْغَنِىُّ الْحَمِيْدُ (لقمٰن ع٣)

21. Lo! Allah, He is the Absolute, worthy of all praise.

(٢٢) اَلْحَمْدُ لِلّٰهِ الَّذِىْ لَهُ مَافِى السَّمٰوٰتِ وَمَا فِى الْاَرْضِ وَلَهُ الْحَمْدُ فِى الْاٰخِرَةِ (سبا ع١)

22. Praise be to Allah, unto Whom belongeth whatsoever is in the Heavens and whatsoever is in the Earth. For Him is the praise in the Hereafter.

(٢٣) اَلْحَمْدُ لِلّٰهِ فَاطِرِ السَّمٰوٰتِ وَالْاَرْضِ (فاطر ع١)

23. Praise be to Allah, the Creator of Heavens and the Earth.

(٢٤) يٰاَيُّهَا النَّاسُ اَنْتُمُ الْفُقَرَآءُ اِلَى اللّٰهِ ، وَاللّٰهُ هُوَ الْغَنِىُّ الْحَمِيْدُ (فاطر ع٣)

24. O, Mankind! You are the needy in your relation to Allah. And Allah: He is the absolute, worthy of all praise.

(٢٥) وَقَالُوْا الْحَمْدُ لِلّٰهِ الَّذِىْٓ اَذْهَبَ عَنَّا الْحَزَنَ ، اِنَّ رَبَّنَا لَغَفُوْرٌ شَكُوْرُ ۨالَّذِىْ اَحَلَّنَا دَارَ الْمُقَامَةِ مِنْ فَضْلِهِ ، لَايَمَسُّنَا فِيْهَا نَصَبٌ وَّلَايَمَسُّنَا فِيْهَا لُغُوْبٌ (فاطر – ع٤)

25. And they (virtuous ones) say: Praise be to Allah, Who hath put grief away from us. Lo! our Lord is forgiving, bountiful; Who, of His grace, has installed us in the mansion of eternity, where toil toucheth us not, nor can weariness affect us.

(٢٦) وَسَلَامٌ عَلَى الْمُرْسَلِيْنَ وَالْحَمْدُ لِلّٰهِ رَبِّ الْعٰلَمِيْنَ (صفّات ع ٥)

26. And peace be unto those sent (to warn), and praise be to Allah, Lord of the worlds.

(٢٧) اَلْحَمْدُ لِلّٰهِ ، بَلْ اَكْثَرُهُمْ لَايَعْلَمُوْنَ (زمر ع٣)

27. Praise be to Allah; but most of them know not.

(٢٨) وَقَالُوْا الْحَمْدُ لِلّٰهِ الَّذِىْ صَدَقَنَا وَعْدَهُ وَاَوْرَثَنَا الْاَرْضَ نَتَبَوَّأُ مِنَ الْجَنَّةِ حَيْثُ نَشَآءُ ، فَنِعْمَ اَجْرُ الْعٰمِلِيْنَ (زمر ع٨)

28. (After entry into Paradise) they would say, "Praise be to Allah, Who hath fulfilled His promise unto us, and hath made us inherit the land, sojourning in the garden where we will; so bounteous are the wages of (good) workers."

(٢٩) فَلِلّٰهِ الْحَمْدُ رَبِّ السَّمٰوٰتِ وَرَبِّ الْاَرْضِ رَبِّ الْعٰلَمِيْنَ (جاثية ع٤)

29. Then praise be to Allah, Lord of Heavens and Lord of the Earth, the Lord of the worlds.

(٣٠) وَمَانَقَمُوْا مِنْهُمْ اِلَّا اَنْ يُّؤْمِنُوْا بِاللّٰهِ الْعَزِيْزِ الْحَمِيْدِ الَّذِىْ لَهُ مُلْكُ السَّمٰوٰتِ وَالْاَرْضِ (بروج)

30. (Talking of an unbeliever ruler, who was tyrannising over the believers) And they had naught against them, save that they believed in Allah, Worthy of praise; Him unto Whom belongeth the Sovereignty of the Heavens and the Earth.

The ayaats given above describe the attributes of Allah and the virtues of reciting His praise, and contain persuasion and commandment for doing so. Those who hymn His praise have been eulogised in many of the ahadith. According to one hadith, the first to be called for admittance into Paradise will be those who used to hymn His praise under all circumstances, whether favourable or adverse. It is stated in another hadith that Almighty Allah likes recitation of His praises. As a matter of fact, it ought to be so, because He alone is worthy of real praise. Nobody else (really) deserves praise, because nobody has real control over anything, not even over his own person.

It is narrated in one hadith that the luckiest persons on the Day of Resurrection will be those who hymn Allah's praise excessively. According to one hadith, recitation of Allah's praise is in reality expression of one's gratitude to Him, and one who does not recite His praise has not expressed his thanks to Him. It is stated in one hadith that reciting Allah's praise on receipt of any bounty acts as a safeguard against its loss. Rasulullah (Sallallaho alaihe wasallam) is stated to have said, "Saying (اَلْحَمْدُ لِلّٰهِ) by anyone from my Ummat is more beneficial to him than his getting possession of the whole world."

It is narrated in one hadith that when Allah bestows a bounty on some one and thereupon that person recites His Praise, this act on his part surpasses the value of that bounty, however big it might be.

A Sahabi while sitting near Rasulullah (Sallallaho alaihe wasallam) happened to recite in a low voice

اَلْحَمْدُ لِلّٰهِ كَثِيْرًا طَيِّبًا مُّبَارَكًا فِيْهِ

The holy Prophet (Sallallaho alaihe wasallam) enquired as to who had recited that duaa. Thinking that he had done something which he should not have done at that time, the Sahabi kept quiet. Rasulullah (Sallallaho alaihe wasallam) assured that there was no harm in telling it, because it was not anything undesirable, after which the Sahabi admitted that the duaa had been uttered by him. Then Rasulullah (Sallallaho alaihe wasallam) said, "I saw thirteen angels, all of whom were trying to surpass each other in carrying this duaa to Almighty Allah."

And there is the well-known hadith, wherein it is stated that an undertaking, which may be very grand otherwise, will lack Allah's blessing unless praise of Allah is recited at the time of its commencement. Hence it is that every book is commenced with the praise of Almighty Allah.

It is narrated in one hadith that when a child dies, Almighty Allah asks the angels if they have taken out the soul of His bondman's child. On receiving the reply in the affirmative, He adds that they have taken out (so to say) a part of his heart. Almighty Allah then enquires "what did my bondsman say on that?' They say, "He praised You and recited (اِنَّا لِلّٰهِ وَاِنَّا اِلَيْهِ رَاجِعُوْنَ) (We belong to Allah, and to Him we shall return).,On this, Almighty Allah orders that a house for him should be built in Paradise, and that it should be named Bait-ul-Hamd (House of Praise). According to another hadith, Allah is greatly pleased with a person who says (اَلْحَمْدُ لِلّٰهِ) on eating a morsel of food or on getting a drink of water.

The third part of this Kalimah is (لَآاِلٰهَ اِلَّا اللّٰهُ) which has been described in detail in the last chapter. The fourth part is known as Kalimah Takbeer (اَللّٰهُ اَكْبَرُ) which means acclamation of His greatness and affirmation of His grandeur and His splendour. The importance of this fourth part of the Kalimah has also been described in many of the verses given already; there are other ayaat which specifically describe the greatness and grandeur of Almighty Allah. These are as follows:—

(١) وَلِتُكَبِّرُوا اللّٰهَ عَلٰى مَاهَدٰاكُمْ وَلَعَلَّكُمْ تَشْكُرُوْنَ (بقره ع ٢٣)

1. That ye should glorify Allah for having guided you, and that peradventure ye may be thankful.

(٢) عَالِمُ الْغَيْبِ وَالشَّهَادَةِ الْكَبِيْرُ الْمُتَعَالِ (رعد ع٢)

2. He is the knower of the invisible and the visible the Great, the most High.

(٣) كَذٰلِكَ سَخَّرَهَا لَكُمْ لِتُكَبِّرُوْا اللّٰهَ عَلٰى مَا هَدٰاكُمْ وَبَشِّرِ الْمُحْسِنِيْنَ

(حج ع٥)

3. Thus We made (the sacrificial animals) subject unto you that ye may glorify Allah, that He hath guided you. And give good tidings (O'Muhammad) (Sallallaho alaihe wasallam) to the doers of good deeds.

(٤ ، ٥) وَاَنَّ اللّٰهَ هُوَ الْعَلِيُّ الْكَبِيْرُ (حج ع ٨ ، لقمٰن ع ٣)

4 & 5. And indeed Allah, He is the High and the Great.

(٦) حَتَّى إِذَا فُزِّعَ عَنْ قُلُوبِهِمْ قَالُوا مَاذَا قَالَ رَبُّكُمْ قَالُوا الْحَقَّ ، وَهُوَ الْعَلِيُّ الْكَبِيرُ (سباع ٣)

6. (When the angels receive any commandment they get upset because of fear) Yet when fear is removed from their (angels) hearts (on descending of revelation), they say: "What was that which your Lord said?" They say: "The truth, and He is the Sublime, the Great."

(٧) فَالْحُكْمُ لِلّٰهِ الْعَلِيِّ الْكَبِيرِ (مومن ع ٢)

7. So, the command belongeth only to Allah, the Sublime, the Majestic.

(٨) وَلَهُ الْكِبْرِيَاءُ فِي السَّمٰوٰتِ وَالْأَرْضِ وَهُوَ الْعَزِيزُ الْحَكِيمُ (جاثيه ع ٤)

8. And unto Him (alone belongeth Majesty in the Heavens and the Earth, and He is the Mighty, the Wise.

(٩) هُوَ اللّٰهُ الَّذِىْ لَآ اِلٰهَ اِلَّا هُوَ ، اَلْمَلِكُ الْقُدُّوْسُ السَّلَامُ الْمُؤْمِنُ الْمُهَيْمِنُ الْعَزِيْزُ الْجَبَّارُ الْمُتَكَبِّرُ (حشر ع ٣)

9. He is Allah, other than Whom there is no God, the Sovereign Lord, the Holy One, Bestower of peace, the Keeper of Faith, the Guardian, the Majestic, the Compeller, the Superb.

The ayaats given above describe the greatness and grandeur of Almighty Allah, and contain commandment and persuasion for recounting it. In many of ahadith too commandment and persuasion for reciting Allah's Greatness has been stressed. It is stated in one hadith, "When you see that fire has broken out somewhere, hymn (اللّٰه اكبر) excessively, which will put out the fire." Another hadith also states that recitation of (اللّٰه اكبر) puts out the fire. It is said in one hadith that when a person says (اللّٰه اكبر) its Noor (Light) covers everything between the Earth and the sky. According to one hadith, Rasulullah (Sallallaho alaihe wasallam) has said, "Hadhrat Jibraa-eel (Alayhis salaam) conveyed to me the order for reciting the Greatness of Allah."

In addition to the ayaats and ahadith given above, Allah's greatness and His splendour has been desribed, and recitation of it has been stressed under different headings and in different words at many places in the Holy Qur'an. There are also many other ayaats, which do not contain the specific words of these Kalimah, but they imply these Kalimahs. Some of these ayaats are as follows:

(١) فَتَلَقّٰى اٰدَمُ مِنْ رَّبِّهٖ كَلِمٰتٍ فَتَابَ عَلَيْهِ ، اِنَّهٗ هُوَ التَّوَّابُ الرَّحِيْمُ (بقره ع ٤)

1. Then Aadam received from his Lord some words (of revelation), and His Lord turned towards him, for He is the Relenting, the Merciful.

There are different versions and explanations about the words refered to in this ayat. According to some of these versions, these words were as follows:

لَآ اِلٰهَ اِلَّا اَنْتَ سُبْحَانَكَ وَبِحَمْدِكَ رَبِّ عَمِلْتُ سُوْٓءًا وَظَلَمْتُ نَفْسِيْ فَاغْفِرْلِيْ
اِنَّكَ اَنْتَ خَيْرُ الْغَافِرِيْنَ ، لَآ اِلٰهَ اِلَّا اَنْتَ سُبْحَانَكَ وَبِحَمْدِكَ رَبِّ عَمِلْتُ سُوْٓءًا
وَظَلَمْتُ نَفْسِيْ فَارْحَمْنِيْ اِنَّكَ اَنْتَ اَرْحَمُ الرَّاحِمِيْنَ ، لَآاِلٰهَ اِلَّا اَنْتَ سُبْحَانَكَ
وَبِحَمْدِكَ رَبِّ عَمِلْتُ سُوْٓءًا وَظَلَمْتُ نَفْسِيْ فَتُبْ عَلَيَّ اِنَّكَ اَنْتَ التَّوَّابُ الرَّحِيْمُ

(a) (There is no Allah except Thee) You are above all shortcomings and are worthy of all kinds of praise. O! my Lord. I have acted viciously and wronged myself; therefore forgive me, surely you are the best of forgivers.

(b) There is no Allah except Thee. You are above all defects; you are worthy of all praise. O! my Lord, I have acted viciously and wronged myself; kindly show mercy upon me, surely You are most Compassionate, most Merciful.

(c) There is no Allah except Thee. You are above all defects and shortcomings, and are worthy of all praise. O! my Lord, I have acted viciously and wronged myself; relent towards me, as You are Relenting and Merciful.

There are other ahadith of similar nature, as narrated by Allamah Soyuti (Rahmatullah alaih) in 'Durrul Manthoor' wherein words meaning glorification and hymning praise of Allah occur.

(٢) مَنْ جَآءَ بِالْحَسَنَةِ فَلَهٗ عَشْرُ اَمْثَالِهَا وَمَنْ جَآءَ بِالسَّيِّئَةِ فَلَايُجْزٰى اِلَّا مِثْلَهَا وَهُمْ لَايُظْلَمُوْنَ (انعام ع ٢٠)

2. Whosoever bringeth a good deed will receive tenfold the like thereof, while whosoever bringeth an ill deed will be awarded like thereof, and they will not be wronged.

Rasulullah (Sallallaho alaihe wasallam) said, "There are two routines, which if followed by a Muslim will enable him to enter into Paradise. Both the routines are very easy, but there are very few people, who act according to them. One is to recite (سُبْحَانَ اللهِ ، اَلْحَمْدُ لِلّٰهِ ، اللهُ اَكْبَرُ) ten times after every obligatory salaat i.e. five times a day. In this way, one is able to glorify Allah one hundred and fifty times, and thereby earns one thousand and five hundred virtues every day. The second routine is to recite (اَللهُ اَكْبَرُ) thirty four times, (اَلْحَمْدُ لِلّٰهِ) thirty three times, and (سُبْحَانَ اللهِ) thirty three times at the time of going to bed every night. One glorifies Allah one hundred times in this way, and earns one thousand virtues thereby. Thus, the virtues earned during the day total two thousand and five hundred. On the Day of Judgement, when deeds will be weighed, will there be anybody who will have committed everyday two thousand and five hundred evil deeds, which can counter-act as many virtues?"

Although among the Sahaba, there was likely to be none who could have done two thousand and five hundred evil deeds during a day, yet in this age our daily misdeeds far exceed this number. Thus, it was extremely kind of Rasulullah (Sallallaho alaihe wasallam) to have told us the prescription for increasing our good deeds over our misdeeds. It is upto the patient to act upon it.

According to one hadith, the companions of Rasulullah (Sallallaho alaihe wasallam) asked him the reason why only a few people are able to act upon the above mentioned two things in spite of their being so easy. He replied that at night the devil makes one to sleep before he has recited it and at time of Salaat he reminds him of something which actuates him to get up and go away at once without having recited it.

According to one hadith Rasulullah (Sallallaho alaihe wasallam) said, "Is it not possible for you to earn even one thousand virtues every day? Someone enquired, "How can we earn one thousand virtues daily O' Rasulullah (Sallallaho alaihe wasallam?" He replied, "Recite (سُبْحَانَ الله) one hundred times, and you will have earned one thousand virtues."

(٣) اَلْمَالُ وَالْبَنُوْنَ زِيْنَةُ الْحَيٰوةِ الدُّنْيَا وَالْبَاقِيَاتُ الصّٰلِحٰتُ خَيْرٌ عِنْدَ رَبِّكَ ثَوَابًا وَّخَيْرٌ اَمَلًا (مريم ع٥)

3. Wealth and children are the ornaments of the earthly life. But good deeds that endure are better in thy Lord's sight for rewards, and better in respect of hope, (i.e. we should base our hope on good deeds instead of on our wealth and children.).

(٤) وَيَزِيْدُ اللهُ الَّذِيْنَ اهْتَدَوْا هُدًى ، وَالْبَاقِيَاتُ الصّٰلِحَاتُ خَيْرٌ عِنْدَ رَبِّكَ ثَوَابًا وَّخَيْرٌ مَّرَدًّا (مريم ع ٥)

4. Allah increaseth in right guidance those who walk aright, and the good deeds which endure are better in thy Lord's sight for reward, and better for ultimate resort.

Although الباقيات الصالحات (good deeds which endure for ever) include all good deeds which are rewarded for ever, yet according to some ahadith it implies these very Kalimahs. Rasulullah (Sallallaho alaihe wasallam) has said, "Hymn these (الباقيات الصالحات) excessively." Somebody enquired what this was. Rasulullah (Sallallaho alaihe wasallam) replied, "It is to recite Takbeer (اَللهُ اَكْبَرُ), Tahleel (لَا اِلٰهَ اِلَّا الله), Tasbeeh (سُبْحَانَ الله), Tahmeed (اَلْحَمْدُ لله) and (لَاحَوْلَ وَلَاقُوَّةَ اِلَّا بِالله)." According to another hadith, Rasulullah (Sallallaho alaihe wasallam) said, "Beware, (سُبْحَانَ اللهِ اَلْحَمْدُ لله لَااِلٰهَ اِلَّا اللهُ اَللهُ اَكْبَرُ) constitute (الباقيات الصالحات) (good deeds which endure for ever)." It is stated in one hadith that Rasulullah (Sallallaho alaihe wasallam) had said, "Beware, be on your guard." "Somebody enquired "O, Rasulullah (Sallallaho alaihe wasallam), is it against some impending invasion by some enemy?" "The Prophet (Sallallaho alaihe wasallam) replied, "No, arrange to guard yourself against the fire of hell, through the recitation of (سُبْحَانَ اللهِ اَلْحَمْدُ لِلّٰهِ لَآاِلٰهَ اِلَّا اللهُ اَللهُ اَكْبَرُ), because these Kalimahs will go forward to intercede for you on the Day of Judgement (or they will move you forward towards Paradise), these will guard you from behind, these will oblige and benefit you and these are the الباقيات الصالحات (good deeds which endure for ever)." Similarly, there are many other ahadith in support of this contention, as given in Durul Manthoor, by Allama Suyuti.

(٥) لَهُ مَقَالِيْدُ السَّمٰوٰتِ وَالْاَرْضِ (زمر ع ٦ ، شورى ع ٢)

5. To Him belong the keys of heavens and the earth.

It was narrated by Hadhrat Uthman (Radhiyallaho anho) that in reply to his enquiry about (مَقَالِيْدُ السَّمٰوٰتِ وَالْاَرْضِ) (keys of heavens and the earth), Rasulullah (Sallallaho alaihe wasallam) had said that it was

لَآاِلٰهَ اِلَّا اللهُ وَاللهُ اَكْبَرُ ، سُبْحَانَ اللهِ اَلْحَمْدُ لِلّٰهِ اَسْتَغْفِرُ اللهَ الَّذِىْ لَآاِلٰهَ اِلَّا هُوَ الْاَوَّلُ وَالْاٰخِرُ وَالظَّاهِرُ وَالْبَاطِنُ يُحْيِىْ وَيُمِيْتُ وَهُوَ حَىٌّ لَّايَمُوْتُ بِيَدِهِ الْخَيْرُ وَهُوَ عَلٰى كُلِّ شَيْءٍ قَدِيْرٌ

According to another hadith, the keys of heavens and the earth means (سُبْحَانَ اللهِ اَلْحَمْدُ لِلّٰهِ لَآاِلٰهَ اِلَّا اللهُ اَللهُ اَكْبَرُ) which had been sent down from the treasure of the Arsh i.e. Allah's Throne.

(٦) اِلَيْهِ يَصْعَدُ الْكَلِمُ الطَّيِّبُ وَالْعَمَلُ الصَّالِحُ يَرْفَعُهُ (فاطر ع ٢)

6. To Him go up their good kalimahs, and good deeds carry them there.

Hadhrat Abdullah bin Masood, (Radhiyallaho anho) said, "Whenever I recite some hadith, I also quote from the Holy Qur'an in support thereof. When a Muslim hymns

سُبْحَانَ اللهِ وَبِحَمْدِهِ اَلْحَمْدُ لِلّٰهِ لَآاِلٰهَ اِلَّا اللهُ اَللهُ اَكْبَرُ تَبَارَكَ اللهُ

an angel carefully takes the words, towards heaven in his wings, and whichever sky he crosses, its angels pray for the forgiveness of the reciter." This is supported by the above ayat (اِلَيْهِ يَصْعَدُ الْكَلِمُ الطَّيِّبُ). Hadhrat Ka'ab, (Radhiyallaho anho) had said that hymning of

سُبْحَانَ اللهِ اَلْحَمْدُ لِلّٰهِ لَآاِلٰهَ اِلَّا اللهُ اَللهُ اَكْبَرُ

goes buzzing round the Arsh and therein mentions the name of the reciter. Another Sahabi narrated a similar hadith.

PART II

This part deals with the ahadith in which Rasulullah (Sallallaho alaihe wasallam) mentioned the virtues of these kalimahs and recommended their recitation.

Hadith No 1

(١) عَنْ اَبِىْ هُرَيْرَةَ رَضِىَ اللّٰهُ عَنْهُ قَالَ قَالَ رَسُوْلُ اللّٰهِ ﷺ كَلِمَتَانِ خَفِيْفَتَانِ عَلَى اللِّسَانِ ثَقِيْلَتَانِ فِى الْمِيْزَانِ حَبِيْبَتَانِ اِلَى الرَّحْمٰنِ سُبْحَانَ اللّٰهِ وَبِحَمْدِهٖ سُبْحَانَ اللّٰهِ الْعَظِيْمِ رواه البخارى ومسلم والترمذى والنسائى وابن ماجه كذا فى الترغيب

Rasulullah (Sallallaho alaihe wasallam) said, "There are two kalimahs which are very light for the tongue (i.e. easy to utter) but very weighty in reward and very pleasing to Allah: These are (سُبْحَانَ اللّٰهِ وَبِحَمْدِهٖ سُبْحَانَ اللّٰهِ الْعَظِيْمِ) (Glory to Allah with all praises, Glory to Allah, the Majestic)."

Light for the tongue means that these kalimahs are so brief that no time is spent in their recitation and no difficulty is experienced in memorizing them. In spite of their being so easy, they will be found very weighty when good deeds will be weighed. Then the fact that they are dear to Allah more than anything else, surpasses all other advantages. Imam Bukhari (Rahmatullah alaih) concluded his book "Sahih Bukhari" with these two kalimahs, and the above mentioned hadith was given at the end of the book. According to one hadith, Rasulullah (Sallallaho alaihe wasallam) had said, "None of you should miss earning one thousand virtues every day. Hymn (سُبْحَانَ اللّٰهِ وَبِحَمْدِهٖ) one hundred times and you will get one thousand virtues. Through Allah's grace, your daily sins will be less than this number. Then the reward of your good deeds, other than reciting this kalimah, will be in addition." According to another hadith a person who recites (سُبْحَانَ اللّٰهِ وَبِحَمْدِهٖ) one hundred times in the morning and in the evening has all his sins forgiven, even if they exceed the foam on the sea. It is stated in one hadith that recitation of (سُبْحَانَ اللّٰهِ اَلْحَمْدُ لِلّٰهِ لَآ اِلٰهَ اِلَّا اللّٰهُ اَللّٰهُ اَكْبَرُ) causes the sins to fall off like the leaves of trees (during the winter season).

Hadith No 2

(٢) عَنْ اَبِىْ ذَرٍّ رَضِىَ اللّٰهُ عَنْهُ قَالَ قَالَ رَسُوْلُ اللّٰهِ ﷺ اَلَا اُخْبِرُكَ بِاَحَبِّ الْكَلَامِ اِلَى اللّٰهِ قُلْتُ يَارَسُوْلَ اللّٰهِ اَخْبِرْنِىْ بِاَحَبِّ الْكَلَامِ اِلَى اللّٰهِ فَقَالَ اِنَّ اَحَبَّ الْكَلَامِ اِلٰى اللّٰهِ سُبْحَانَ اللّٰهِ وَبِحَمْدِهِ رواه مسلم والنسائى والترمذى الا انه قال سُبْحَانَ رَبِّىْ وَبِحَمْدِهِ وقال حسن صحيح وعزاه السيوطى فى الجامع الصغير الى مسلم واحمد والترمذى ورقم له بالصحة وفى رواية لمسلم اَنَّ رَسُوْلَ اللّٰهِ صَلَّى اللّٰهُ عَلَيْهِ وَسَلَّمَ سُئِلَ اَيُّ الْكَلَامِ اَفْضَلُ قَالَ مَااَصْطَفَى اللّٰهُ لِمَلٰئِكَتِهِ اَوْ لِعِبَادِهِ سُبْحَانَ اللّٰهِ وَبِحَمْدِهِ كذا فى الترغيب قلت واخرج الاخير الحاكم وصححه على شرط مسلم واقره عليه الذهبى وذكره السيوطى فى الجامع برواية احمد عن رجل مختصرا ورقم له بالصحة

Hadhrat Abu Zar (Radhiyallaho anho) narrated that once Rasulullah (Sallallaho alaihe wasallam) had said, "Should I tell you what speech is most liked by Allah?" "Do tell me", said I. He said "It is (سُبْحَانَ اللّٰهِ وَبِحَمْدِهِ)." In another hadith, it is (سُبْحَانَ رَبِّىْ وَبِحَمْدِهِ). Another hadith relates, "The thing that Allah ordered His angels to hymn is undoubtedly the best one, and it is (سُبْحَانَ اللّٰهِ وَبِحَمْدِهِ).

It is mentioned in several ayaat given in Part I that the angels, those near the Arsh and all others, remain ever hymning the glory and praise of Almighty Allah, which is their sole occupation. This is why, when Allah created Aadam (Alayhis salaam) the angels submitted, "We hymn Thy praise and glorify Thee (نَحْنُ نُسَبِّحُ بِحَمْدِكَ وَنُقَدِّسُ لَكَ)," as given in the first ayat in Part I. According to one hadith, Rasulullah (Sallallaho alaihe wasallam) had said, "The heaven crackles due to the awe of Allah's greatness, as does a bedstead under a heavy weight, and the Heaven is justified in doing so. I swear by Allah, Who controls my life, that in the Heaven there is not an inch of space where some angel is not prostrating and hymning the glory and praise of Almighty Allah."

Hadith No. 3

(٣) عَنْ اِسْحٰقَ بْنِ عَبْدِ اللّٰهِ بْنِ اَبِىْ طَلْحَةَ عَنْ اَبِيْهِ عَنْ جَدِّهِ قَالَ قَالَ رَسُوْلُ اللّٰهِ ﷺ مَنْ قَالَ لَآاِلٰهَ اِلَّا اللّٰهُ دَخَلَ الْجَنَّةَ اَوْ وَجَبَتْ لَهُ الْجَنَّةُ وَمَنْ قَالَ سُبْحَانَ اللّٰهِ

وَبِحَمْدِهٖ مِائَةَ مَرَّةٍ كَتَبَ اللّٰهُ لَهٗ مِائَةَ اَلْفِ حَسَنَةٍ وَّاَرْبَعًا وَّعِشْرِيْنَ اَلْفَ حَسَنَةٍ قَالُوْا يَارَسُوْلَ اللّٰهِ اِذًا لَّايَهْلِكُ مِنَّا اَحَدٌ قَالَ بَلٰى اِنَّ اَحَدَكُمْ لَيَجِيْءُ بِالْحَسَنَاتِ لَوْ وُضِعَتْ عَلٰى جَبَلٍ اَثْقَلَتْهُ ثُمَّ تَجِيْءُ النِّعَمُ فَتَذْهَبُ بِتِلْكَ ثُمَّ يَتَطَاوَلُ الرَّبُّ بَعْدَ ذٰلِكَ بِرَحْمَتِهٖ رواه الحاكم و قال صحيح الاسناد كذا فى الترغيب قلت واقره عليه الذهبى

Rasulullah (Sallallaho alaihe wasallam) said, "Whosoever says (لَآاِلٰهَ اِلَّا اللّٰهُ) his admittance into Paradise is guaranteed, and whosoever hymns one hundred times, سُبْحَانَ اللّٰهِ وَبِحَمْدِهٖ he is credited with one hundred and twenty four thousand virtues." The Sahaba said, "O, Rasulullah! (Sallallaho alaihe wasallam) if such is the case, then nodoby will be doomed to destruction on the Day of Judgement because the virtues are sure to outweigh the sins." Rasulullah (Sallallaho alaihe wasallam) said, "Some people will even then be doomed to destruction because some people will have so many virtues that a mountain may crumble under their weight, but these will be just nothing in comparison with Allah's bounties. However, Almighty Allah, out of His extreme mercy and grace, will rescue them."

Note:

The largest number of virtues will look like nothing as compared with the bounties of Allah, shows that whereas virtues and sins will be weighed on the Day of Judgement, a person will also be called to account whether he had made proper use of Allah's bounties and had shown gratitude to Him. As a matter of fact, everything we have is granted by Almighty Allah, and for each thing we owe a duty, and it will be checked whether we have discharged this duty properly. Rasulullah (Sallallaho alaihe wasallam) had said, "

يَصْبِحُ عَلٰى كُلِّ سُلَامٰى مِنْ اَحَدِكُمْ صَدَقَةٌ (المشكوٰة)

برواية المسلم قلت ورواه ابو داود وابن ماجه

which means that it is obligatory on a person to give, every morning, a sadaqah (offering) in respect of every joint and bone. According to another hadith, there are three hundred and sixty joints in the human body, and it is obligatory on a person to give a sadaqah in respect of each joint. This is a token of gratitude to Almighty Allah, that after the night's sleep (which is akin to death) Almighty Allah gave him life again, with each part of the body in good order." The Sahabas (Radhiyallaho anhum) submitted, "Who can afford to do so many sadaqahs every day?" Rasulullah (Sallallaho alaihe wasallam) replied, "Saying (تسبیح) is a sadaqah, saying (تکبیر) is sadaqah, saying (لَآاِلٰهَ اِلَّا اللّٰه) is sadaqah, saying اللّٰهُ اَكْبَرُ is sadaqah, removing some obstacle from the way is sadaqah (and so on)." In short, he enumerated several such items of sadaqah. There are other ahadith like this, wherein Allah's bounties in one's own person are enumerated, and then there are, in addition, the bounties in respect of food, drink, comfort, and so many other blessings of Allah.

This subject is mentioned in the Holy Qur'an in Surah at-Takaathur: that on the Day of Judgement, one will be questioned about the bounties of Allah. Hadhrat Ibn Abbas stated that one will be reminded about the health of his body, of his ears, of his eyes, that Almighty Allah had bestowed all such bounties out of sheer mercy; and a person will be questioned how he used these for the service of Allah, or whether he used them like the animals for his own self. Thus in the Holy Qur'an in Surah Bani Israa-eel, Allah says,

اِنَّ السَّمْعَ وَالْبَصَرَ وَالْفُؤَادَ كُلُّ اُوْلٰٓئِكَ كَانَ عَنْهُ مَسْئُوْلًا

the hearing and the sight, and the heart; of each of them will be asked, i.e. everybody will be required to render account for the proper use of his ears, eyes, and heart. The holy Prophet, (Sallallaho alaihe wasallam) remarked that the bounties about which one will be questioned include peace of mind, which is a great blessing, and also physical health. Mujahid has stated that every worldly pleasure is a bounty, for which one will have to give account. Hadhrat Ali (Radhiyallaho anho) said that security is one of the bounties of Allah. A person asked Hadhrat Ali (Radhiyallaho anho) the meaning of the ayat

ثُمَّ لَتُسْئَلُنَّ يَوْمَئِذٍ عَنِ النَّعِيمِ

(then on the Day, you will be questioned about the bounties). He replied that one will be questioned about the wheat bread eaten and of cold water, as well as about the house in which one lived. It is stated in one hadith that, when this ayat was revealed, some Sahaba (Radhiyallaho anhum) said, "O, Rasulullah (Sallallaho alaihe wasallam), what are the bounties about which we shall be questioned? We get only half a meal and that too of barley bread." Then came the revelation, "Do you not put on shoes? Do you not drink cold water? These are also bounties of Allah." According to one hadith, when this ayat was revealed, some Sahabas said, "O, Rasulullah (Sallallaho alaihe wasallam), about what bounties shall we be questioned? We get only dates to eat and water to drink, and we have to remain always with our swords on our shoulders, ready to fight some enemy (on account of which even these two things cannot be enjoyed by us in peace)." Rasulullah (Sallallaho alaihe wasallam) replied, "The bounties are about to become available in the near future."

It is stated in one hadith that Rasulullah (Sallallaho alaihe wasallam) had said, "Of the bounties to be accounted for on the Day of Judgement, the first is the physical health, (i.e. whether we discharged our obligation in respect of it, and did any service for the pleasure of Allah) and the other is the cold drinking-water." Cold water is, in fact, a great gift of Allah, and is realised as such where it is not (readily) available. It is indeed a great blessing of Allah, but we never even acknowledge it to be as such; not to speak of thanking Almighty Allah for it and discharging our duty in respect of it.

It is said in one hadith, "The bounties to be accounted for include the piece of bread eaten to satisfy the hunger, the water drunk to quench the thirst, and the cloth used to cover the body."

Once at midday when it was very hot, Hadhrat Abu Bakr (Radhiyallaho anho) felt famished and went out of his house. Soon after his arrival in the mosque, Hadhrat Umar (Radhiyallaho anho) also reached there in similar condition, and asked him how he was there at that time. "My hunger has become unbearable", was the reply. Hadhrat Umar said, "By Allah, the same thing has compelled me to come out." The two were talking thus, when Rasulullah (Sallallaho alaihe wasallam) also came there, and asked them how they were there. They submitted, "Hunger made us restless and compelled us to come out here." Rasulullah (Sallallaho alaihe wasallam) said, "I have come here for the same reason." All the three then went to the house of Hadhrat Abu Ayub Ansari (Radhiyallaho anho). He was not in, and his wife welcomed them; she was overjoyed to have them in her house. Rasulullah (Sallallaho alaihe wasallam) enquired about Abu Ayub; she replied that he had gone out for something and would soon be back. After a little while, Hadhrat Abu Ayub (Radhiyallaho anho) also came back. On seeing them, he was overwhelmed with joy, and cut a big bunch of dates to entertain them. Rasulullah (Sallallaho alaihe wasallam) remarked, "Why did you cut the whole bunch. The raw and the half-ripe dates have also been cut thereby. You could have selected and plucked the ripe ones only." He submitted, "I plucked the whole bunch so that all kind of dates may be before you, and you may eat the kind you may like." (Sometimes, one likes the half ripe dates in preference to the ripe ones). Leaving the dates before them, he slaughtered a small goat, roasted some of its meat, and cooked the rest. Rasulullah (Sallallaho alaihe wasallam) took some bread and a piece of roasted meat, and giving it to Abu Ayub said, "Take this to Fatimah (Radhiyallaho anha); she also did not get anything to eat for several days." Hadhrat Abu Ayub (Radhiyallaho anho) hastened to comply with the orders and then returned. All of them ate to their hearts' content. Then Rasulullah (Sallallaho alaihe wasallam) said, "See, these are the bounties of Allah: the bread, the meat, the raw dates and the ripe ones." While uttering these words, tears came in his eyes and then he said, "By Allah! Who controls my life; these are the bounties about which one will be questioned on the Day of Judgement." Considering the circumstances under which these things had become available, the Sahabas felt perplexed and worried that account was required to be rendered for these things, which became available under such critical conditions of helplessness. Rasulullah (Sallallaho alaihe wasallam) said, "It is necessary to express our gratitude to Almighty Allah. When you put your hand on such things, say (بِسْمِ اللهِ) before starting to eat and

اَلْحَمْدُ لِلّٰهِ الَّذِیْ هُوَ اَشْبَعَنَا وَاَنْعَمَ عَلَیْنَا وَاَفْضَلَ

(All praise is for Allah who feasted us to the full, and did favour on us, and bestowed upon us plentifully) after you finish eating. Its recitation will suffice as your expression of gratitude." Many incidents of this nature are narrated under different headings in the books of hadith. Rasulullah (Sallallaho alaihe wasallam) said the same things when he happened to visit the house of Abul Haitham Maalik bin Tayhaan (Radhiyallaho anho) and once when he visited a Sahabi whose name was Waqfi (Radhiyallaho anho).

Once Hadhrat Umar (Radhiyallaho anho) came across a leper who was blind, deaf and dumb. He said to his companions, "Do you see any bounties of Allah on this person?" "Apparently none," they replied. "Can he not urinate easily?" said Umar (Radhiyallaho anho).

Hadhrat Abdullah bin Mas'ood (Radhiyallaho anho) said, "On the Day of Judgement there will be three courts. In one of these, the accounts of virtues will be scrutinized, in the second Allah's bounties will be counted, and in the third the sins will be accounted for. The virtues will be counterbalanced by the bounties of Allah, so the sins will remain outstanding and their disposal will depend on Allah's mercy."

All this means that a man is duty bound to show his gratitude to Almighty Allah for His unlimited favours at all times and under all conditions. Therefore, he should strive his utmost to earn as many virtues as possible and should not rest content at any stage, because it will be on the Day of Judgement that he will realize how many sins had been committed unknowingly through his eyes, nose, ears, and other parts of the body. The Prophet (Sallallaho alaihe wasallam) had said, "Everyone of you will have to appear before Almighty Allah, you will be face to face with Him, with no curtain in between. There will be no lawyer or interpreter to advocate your cause; there will be heaps of your deeds on either side. The fire of Hell will be in front of you, and therefore you should try your best to ward off this fire through sadaqah, (voluntary charity) which may be as paltry as a single date." It is stated in one hadith, "On the Day of Judgement, you will first be reminded how you were blessed with good health and were given cold water to drink" (which implies, whether you showed gratitude for these favours). According to another hadith, "You will not be allowed to move away from the court of Allah until you have answered five questions: (1) How did you spend your life? (2) How did you utilize your youth? (3) How did you earn your wealth? (4) How did you spend it? (i.e. whether earning and spending was in a lawful manner). (5) How did you act upon your acquired knowledge?''

Hadith No. 4

(٤) عَنْ اِبْنِ مَسْعُوْدٍ رَضِىَ اللهُ عَنْهُ قَالَ قَالَ رَسُوْلُ اللهِ ﷺ لَقِيْتُ اِبْرَاهِيْمَ لَيْلَةَ اُسْرِىَ بِىْ فَقَالَ يَا مُحَمَّدُ اِقْرَأْ اُمَّتَكَ مِنِّىْ السَّلَامَ وَاَخْبِرْهُمْ اَنَّ الْجَنَّةَ طَيِّبَةُ التُّرْبَةِ عَذْبَةُ الْمَاءِ وَاَنَّهَا قِيْعَانٌ وَاَنَّ غِرَاسَهَا سُبْحَانَ اللهِ وَالْحَمْدُ لِلّٰهِ وَلَآاِلٰهَ اِلَّا اللهُ وَاللهُ اَكْبَرُ رواه الترمذى والطبرانى فى الصغير والاوسط وزاد وَلَاحَوْلَ وَلَاقُوَّةَ اِلَّا بِاللهِ وقال الترمذى حسن غريب من هذا الوجه ورواه الطبرانى ايضا باسناد واه من حديث سلمان الفارسى رضى الله عنه و عن ابن عباس رضى الله عنه مرفوعًا مَنْ قَالَ سُبْحَانَ اللهِ وَالْحَمْدُ لِلّٰهِ وَلَآاِلٰهَ اِلَّا اللهُ وَاللهُ اَكْبَرُ غُرِسَ لَهُ بِكُلِّ وَاحِدَةٍ مِّنْهُنَّ شَجَرَةٌ فِىْ الْجَنَّةِ رواه الطبرانى واسناده حسن لابأس به فى المتابعات وعن جابر مرفوعا مَنْ قَالَ سُبْحَانَ اللهِ الْعَظِيْمِ وَبِحَمْدِهِ غُرِسَتْ لَهُ نَخْلَةٌ فِىْ الْجَنَّةِ رواه الترمذى وحسنه والنسائى الا انه قال شجرة وابن حبان فى صحيحه والحاكم فى الموضعين باسنادين قال فى احدهما على شرط مسلم وفى الأخر على شرط البخارى وذكره فى الجامع الصغير برواية الترمذى وابن حبان والحاكم ورقم له بالصحة و عن ابى هريرة اَنَّ النَّبِىَّ صَلَّى اللهُ عَلَيْهِ وَسَلَّمَ مَرَّبِهِ وَهُوَ يَغْرِسُ الحديث رواه ابن ماجة باسناد حسن والحاكم وقال صحيح الاسناد كذا فى الترغيب وعزاه فى الجامع الى ابن ماجة والحاكم و رقم له بالصحة قلت و فى الباب من حديث ابى ايوب مرفوعا رواه احمد باسناد حسن وابن ابى الدنيا وابن حبان فى صحيحه ورواه ابن ابى الدنيا والطبرانى من حديث ابن عمر ايضا مرفوعا مختصرا الا ان فى حديثهما الحوقلة فقط كما فى الترغيب قلت وذكر السيوطى فى الدر حديث ابن عباس مرفوعا بلفظ حديث ابن مسعود وقال اخرجه الترمذى وحسنه والطبرانى وابن مردويه قلت وذكره فى الجامع الصغير برواية الطبرانى ورقم له بالصحة وذكر فى مجمع الزوائد عدة روايات فى معنى هذا الحديث

The Holy Prophet (Sallallaho alaihe wasallam) says, ''When on the night of Mi'raaj I met Hadhrat Ibrahim (Alayhis salaam) he asked me to convey his salam to my Ummat and tell them that the soil of Paradise is very fine and fertile and there is very good water to irrigate it, but the land is all a virgin plain and its plants are

سُبْحَانَ اللهِ وَالْحَمْدُ لِلّٰهِ وَلَآاِلٰهَ اِلَّا اللهُ وَاللهُ اَكْبَرُ

so that one can plant there as much as he likes."

According to one hadith, the above Kalimah is also followed by لَا حَوْلَ وَلَاقُوَّةَ إِلَّا بِاللهِ . According to another hadith it was said, "A tree for every part of this Kalimah is planted in Paradise." It is stated in one hadith, "Whosoever recites سُبْحَانَ اللهِ وَبِحَمْدِهِ , a tree is planted for him in Paradise." It is stated in one hadith, "Rasulullah (Sallallaho alaihe wasallam) was going somewhere when he saw that Abu Hurairah (Radhiyallaho anho) was planting a tree. He asked him what he was doing. "I am planting a tree," was the reply. Thereupon Rasulullah, (Sallallaho alaihe wasallam) said, "Should I tell you about the best plantation? It is (سُبْحَانَ اللهِ اَلْحَمْدُ لِلّٰهِ لَآاِلٰهَ اِلَّا اللهُ اَللهُ اَكْبَرُ) ; the recitation of each of these Kalimahs causes a tree to grow for you in Paradise."

Hadhrat Ibrahim (Alayhis salaam) sent his salam through Rasulullah (Sallallaho alaihe wasallam) to this Ummat. The 'Alims' have written that whosoever hears this hadith, should say in return وَعَلَيْهِ السَّلَامُ وَرَحْمَةُ اللهِ وَبَرَكَاتُهُ (May peace be upon him as well as Allah's mercy and His blessings).

The second thing mentioned in the hadith is that the soil of Paradise is very fine and its water very sweet, which can be interpreted in two ways. Firstly, it is the description of that place that it is extremely fine, its soil (according to some ahadith) is of saffron and musk, and its water is very sweet, so that everybody loves to have a house there; and as it has all facilities for recreation and for planting gardens, etc., nobody likes to leave it. The second interpretation is that where there is fine soil and excellent water, there is always luxurious growth. In that case, it means that hymning (سُبْحَانَ اللهِ) once will cause a tree to be planted and then, by virtue of the fertile soil and excellent water, this tree will continue to grow by itself. Only the seed is required to be planted once; the growth afterwards is all automatic.

In this hadith, Paradise is stated to have a treeless and virgin soil. In other ahadith where Paradise has been described it is stated that there are all kinds of fruit trees in it, so much so that the literal meaning of the word Jannat (Paradise) is "garden". There is thus a sort of contradiction: the Ulama explain that originally Paradise is a treeless plain, but when it will be handed over to the various people they will find gardens and trees there, in accordance with their deeds. The second explanation by some Ulama is that the gardens in the Paradise will be awarded according to the deeds of good people, and as such it is the deeds that are said to have caused these trees to grow for them. The third explanation is that the smallest Paradise that anybody will get will be bigger than the whole world, and some parts of it are covered with original gardens and other parts of it are without growth, so that trees will get automatically planted there according to the Zikr and glorification done by its recipient. Hadhrat Maulana Gangohi, (Rahmatullah alaih) a great Shaikh and scholar, has stated in his book Kaukabud Durree that all the trees are available there in the form of a nursery, and are planted according to the good deeds, after which they continue to grow.

Hadith No. 5

(٥) عَنْ اَبِىْ اُمَامَةَ رَضِىَ اللّٰهُ عَنْهُ قَالَ قَالَ رَسُوْلُ اللّٰهِ ﷺ مَنْ هَالَهُ اللَّيْلُ اَنْ يُكَابِدَهُ اَوْ بُخِلَ بِالْمَالِ اَنْ يُّنْفِقَهُ اَوْ جُبُنَ عَنِ الْعَدُوِّ اَنْ يُّقَاتِلَهُ فَلْيُكْثِرْ مِنْ سُبْحَانَ اللّٰهِ وَبِحَمْدِهٖ فَاِنَّهَا اَحَبُّ اِلَى اللّٰهِ مِنْ جَبَلِ ذَهَبٍ يُّنْفِقُهُ فِىْ سَبِيْلِ اللّٰهِ)

رواه الفريابى والطبرانى واللفظ له وهو حديث غريب ولباس باسناده انشاء الله كذا فى الترغيب وفى مجمع الزوائد رواه الطبرانى وفيه سليمان بن احمد الواسطى وثقه عبدان وضعفه الجمهور والغالب على بقية رجاله التوثيق وفى الباب عن ابى هريرة رضى الله عنه مرفوعا اخرجه ابن مردويه وابن عباس ايضا عند ابن مردويه كذا فى الدر

Rasulullah (Sallallaho alaihe wasallam) said, "One who is unable to toil at night i.e., he cannot keep awake and pray at night, or is too miserly to spend money, or is too cowardly to take part in Jihaad (fighting in the path of Allah) should hymn (سُبْحَانَ اللّٰهِ وَبِحَمْدِهٖ) excessively, because this action is more valuable with Allah than spending in His path a mountain load of gold."

How great is the grace of Allah that even those who cannot bear hardship in the path of Allah are not deprived from earning virtues and huge rewards. One who cannot keep awake at night, cannot spend in Allah's path and cannot take part in religious fighting, because of cowardice, but still has value for Deen in his heart, and is anxious to improve his life in the Hereafter, is still eligible to earn

Allah's favours. It is one's extreme misfortune if he cannot do something even then.

Hadith No. 6

٦) عَنْ سَمُرَةَ بْنِ جُنْدُبٍ رَضِىَ اللّٰهُ عَنْهُ قَالَ قَالَ رَسُوْلُ اللّٰهِ ﷺ اَحَبُّ الْكَلَامِ
لَى اللّٰهِ اَرْبَعٌ سُبْحَانَ اللّٰهِ وَالْحَمْدُ لِلّٰهِ وَلَآاِلٰهَ اِلَّا اللّٰهُ وَاللّٰهُ اَكْبَرُ لَايَضُرُّكَ بِاَيِّهِنَّ
دَأْتَ رواه مسلم وابن ماجة والنسائى وزادوهن من القرآن ورواه النسائى ايضا وابن حبان فى صحيحه
ن حديث ابى هريرة رضى الله عنه كذا فى الترغيب وعزا السيوطى حديث سمرة الى احمد ايضا ورقم له
لصحة وحديث ابى هريرة الى مسند الفردوس للديلمى ورقم له ايضا بالصحة

Rasulullah (Sallallaho alaihe wasallam) said, "The words most liked by Almighty Allah consist of four Kalimahs, viz; (سُبْحَانَ اللّٰهِ اَلْحَمْدُ لِلّٰهِ لَآاِلٰهَ اِلَّا اللّٰهُ اَللّٰهُ اَكْبَرُ) which may be recited in any sequence. According to one hadith, these Kalimahs are also mentioned in the Holy Qur'an. These Kalimahs occur very frequently in the Holy Qur'an, wherein there is the commandment and persuasion for their recitation, as described in detail in Part I. In one hadith, it is stated, "Adorn the festivals of Eid with these words by their frequent recitation."

Hadith No. 7

٧) عَنْ اَبِىْ هُرَيْرَةَ رَضِىَ اللّٰهُ عَنْهُ قَالَ اِنَّ الْفُقَرَآءَ الْمُهَاجِرِيْنَ اَتَوْا رَسُوْلَ اللّٰهِ
ﷺ فَقَالُوْا قَدْ ذَهَبَ اَهْلُ الدُّثُوْرِ بِالدَّرَجَاتِ الْعُلٰى وَالنَّعِيْمِ الْمُقِيْمِ فَقَالَ مَاذَاكَ
لُوْا يُصَلُّوْنَ كَمَا نُصَلِّىْ وَيَصُوْمُوْنَ كَمَانَصُوْمُ وَيَتَصَدَّقُوْنَ وَلَانَتَصَدَّقُ
يُعْتِقُوْنَ وَلَانُعْتِقُ فَقَالَ رَسُوْلُ اللّٰهِ ﷺ اَفَلَآ اُعَلِّمُكُمْ شَيْئًا تُدْرِكُوْنَ بِهِ مَنْ
سَبَقَكُمْ وَتَسْبِقُوْنَ بِهِ مَنْ بَعْدَكُمْ وَلَايَكُوْنُ اَحَدٌ اَفْضَلَ مِنْكُمْ اِلَّا مَنْ صَنَعَ
لَ مَاصَنَعْتُمْ قَالُوْا بَلٰى يَا رَسُوْلَ اللّٰهِ قَالَ تُسَبِّحُوْنَ وَتُكَبِّرُوْنَ وَتُحَمِّدُوْنَ دُبُرَ
لِّ صَلٰوةٍ ثَلٰثًا وَّثَلٰثِيْنَ مَرَّةً قَالَ اَبُوْ صَالِحٍ فَرَجَعَ فُقَرَآءُ الْمُهَاجِرِيْنَ اِلٰى رَسُوْلِ
هِ ﷺ فَقَالُوْا سَمِعَ اِخْوَانُنَا اَهْلُ الْاَمْوَالِ بِمَا فَعَلْنَا فَفَعَلُوْا مِثْلَهُ فَقَالَ رَسُوْلُ اللّٰهِ
ﷺ ذٰلِكَ فَضْلُ اللّٰهِ يُؤْتِيْهِ مَنْ يَّشَآءُ متفق عليه و ليس قول ابى صالح الى اٰخره الا عند

مسلم و فى رواية للبخارى تُسَبِّحُوْنَ فِيْ دُبُرِ كُلِّ صَلوٰةٍ عَشْرًا وَّتُحَمِّدُوْنَ عَشْرًا وَتُكَبِّرُوْنَ عَشْرًا بَدَلَ ثَلٰثًا وَّ ثَلٰثِيْنَ كذا فى المشكوٰة و عن ابى ذر رضى الله عنه بنحو هذا الحديث فيه اِنَّ بِكُلِّ تَسْبِيْحَةٍ صَدَقَةٌ وَبِكُلِّ تَحْمِيْدَةٍ صَدَقَةٌ وَفِىْ بُضْعِ اَحَدِكُمْ صَدَقَةٌ قَالُوْا يَارَسُوْلَ اللهِ يَأْتِىْ اَحَدُنَا شَهْوَتَهُ يَكُوْنُ لَهُ فِيْهَا اَجْرٌ الحديث اخرجه احمد وفى الباب عن ابى الدرداء عند احمد

Once a group of poor Muhajirs came to Rasulullah (Sallallaho alaihe wasallam) and said, "O Rasulullah! (Sallallaho alaihe wasallam) only the rich attain to the higher spiritual grades, and the eternal bounties of Allah fall only to their lot." "How?" enquired Rasulullah (Sallallaho alaihe wasallam). They replied, "They offer salaat and observe fasting in the same manner as we do, but being rich they are able to perform other good deeds, like giving sadaqah and freeing slaves, which we being poor are unable to do." Rasulullah (Sallallaho alaihe wasallam) said, "Should I tell you something by acting upon which you may overtake your predecessors and surpass your successors, and nobody may be better than you unless he also acts upon the same thing." "Do tell us," said the Sahabas, (Radhiyallaho anhum). "Recite (سُبْحَانَ اللهِ ، اَلْحَمْدُ لِلّٰهِ ، اَللهُ اَكْبَرُ) thirty three times each after every salaat," said Rasulullah (Sallallaho alaihe wasallam). They acted upon his advice, but the rich of those days came to know of it and started doing the same. The poor again came to Rasulullah (Sallallaho alaihe wasallam) and complained, "Our rich brothers have come to learn what you told us, and are also acting upon it." Rasulullah (Sallallaho alaihe wasallam) then remarked, "It is Allah's favour which He bestows on whomsoever He likes; nobody can stop Him." According to another hadith, Rasulullah (Sallallaho alaihe wasallam) is also narrated to have said to them, "Allah has also favoured you with a substitute of sadaqah. Reciting (سُبْحَانَ اللهِ) once is sadaqah, saying (اَلْحَمْدُ لِلّٰهِ) once is sadaqah, intercourse with one's own wife is sadaqah." The Sahabas were astonished to hear this, and submitted, "O Rasulullah! (Sallallaho alaihe wasallam) indulgence with one's own wife is an act of satisfying one's lust, and you say this is also sadaqah. Rasulullah (Sallallaho alaihe wasallam) said, "Would it not be a sin to indulge in the unlawful?" "Yes", said the Sahabas. "In the same manner, doing the lawful amounts to sadaqah, and is virtuous", explained Rasulullah (Sallallaho alaihe wasallam). From this it is clear that to cohabit with one's own wife in order to save himself from adultery brings reward from Allah."

In another hadith, the reply of Rasulullah (Sallallaho alaihe wasallam) to the query by the Sahabas, (Radhiyallaho anhum) that intercourse with the wife is the satisfaction of one's lust, was "Just tell me if a child is born as a result thereof, and when he grows up to youth and becomes a centre of your expectation, he happens to die, will you not hope for a reward from Allah in lieu of this loss?" Their reply was in the affirmative, and then Rasulullah (Sallallaho alaihe wasallam) continued, "Why this expectation of reward? Did you create him? Did you guide him or did you sustain him? On the contrary, it was Almighty Allah who created him, guided him and sustained him. Similarly, you put your semen at the lawful place, then it is up to Allah to make it into a child or prevent it from becoming a child." In short, this hadith implies that the reward from Allah is for one's having become the cause of the birth of the child.

Hadith No. 8

(٨) عَنْ اَبِىْ هُرَيْرَةَ رَضِىَ اللّٰهُ عَنْهُ قَالَ قَالَ رَسُوْلُ اللّٰهِ ﷺ مَنْ سَبَّحَ اللّٰهَ فِىْ دُبُرِ كُلِّ صَلٰوةٍ ثَلٰثًا وَّثَلٰثِيْنَ وَحَمِدَ اللّٰهَ ثَلٰثًا وَّثَلٰثِيْنَ وَكَبَّرَ اللّٰهَ ثَلٰثًا وَّثَلٰثِيْنَ فَتِلْكَ تِسْعَةٌ وَّتِسْعُوْنَ وَقَالَ تَمَامُ الْمِائَةِ لَآاِلٰهَ اِلَّا اللّٰهُ وَحْدَهُ لَاشَرِيْكَ لَهُ لَهُ الْمُلْكُ وَلَهُ الْحَمْدُ وَهُوَ عَلٰى كُلِّ شَىْءٍ قَدِيْرٌ غُفِرَتْ خَطَايَاهُ وَاِنْ كَانَتْ مِثْلَ زَبَدِ الْبَحْرِ

رواه مسلم كذا فى المشكٰوة وكذا فى مسند احمد

Rasulullah (Sallallaho alaihe wasallam) said, "Whosoever hymns (سُبْحَانَ اللّٰهِ اَلْحَمْدُ لِلّٰهِ اَللّٰهُ اَكْبَرُ) 33 times each, and then once recites

لَآاِلٰهَ اِلَّا اللّٰهُ وَحْدَهُ لَاشَرِيْكَ لَهُ لَهُ الْمُلْكُ وَلَهُ الْحَمْدُ وَهُوَ عَلٰى كُلِّ شَىْءٍ قَدِيْرٌ

after every salaat, all his sins are forgiven, even though they may be (countless) like the foam in the sea."

Note:

That the sins are forgiven (by virtue of zikr) has already been discussed under several ahadith. According to the Ulamaa, it is only the minor sins that are forgiven. In this hadith, it is stated that three Kalimahs should be recited 33 times each, and then (لَآاِلٰهَ اِلَّا اللّٰهُ) only once. According to the next hadith, two of the three Kalimahs should be recited 33 times each and the third one i.e. (اَللّٰهُ اَكْبَرُ) 34 times. Hadhrat Zaid, (Radhiyallaho anho) is stated to have narrated, Rasulullah (Sallallaho alaihe wasallam) had ordered us to recite (سُبْحَانَ اللّٰهِ ، اَلْحَمْدُ لِلّٰهِ ، اَللّٰهُ اَكْبَرُ) thirty three times each after every salaat. An Ansari saw in a dream that a person advised reciting the three Kalimahs 25 times each and then (لَآاِلٰهَ اِلَّا اللّٰهُ) also 25 times. When Rasulullah (Sallallaho alaihe wasallam) was told about this dream, he permitted him to recite that way. According to one hadith (سُبْحَانَ اللّٰهِ ، اَلْحَمْدُ لِلّٰهِ ، اَللّٰهُ اَكْبَرُ) should be hymned 11 times each after every salaat, and in another hadith it is ten times each. In one hadith, the recitation of (لَآاِلٰهَ اِلَّا اللّٰهُ) is ten times and that of the other three Kalimahs is 33 times each. According to one hadith, each of the four kalimahs should be hymned hundred times each. All these ahadith are narrated in the book Hisnul Haseen. The apparent difference in these versions is due to the different circumstances of the persons who were advised by Rasulullah (Sallallaho alaihe wasallam). Those who were busy with other (important) things were advised the lesser number, and those who were free were advised a greater number. The religious authorities, however, advise that one should conform to the numbers narrated in the ahadith just as the quantity of a thing that is used as a medicine is also specified.

Hadith No. 9

(٩) عَنْ كَعْبِ بْنِ عُجْرَةَ رَضِىَ اللّٰهُ عَنْهُ قَالَ قَالَ رَسُوْلُ اللّٰهِ ﷺ مُعَقِّبَاتٌ لَّايَخِيْبُ قَائِلُهُنَّ اَوْ فَاعِلُهُنَّ دُبُرَ كُلِّ صَلٰوةٍ مَكْتُوْبَةٍ ثَلٰثٌ وَّثَلٰثُوْنَ تَسْبِيْحَةً وَثَلٰثٌ وَّثَلٰثُوْنَ تَحْمِيْدَةً وَاَرْبَعٌ وَّثَلٰثُوْنَ تَكْبِيْرَةً رواه مسلم كذا فى مشكوٰة وعزاه السيوطى فى الجامع الى احمد ومسلم والترمذى والنسائى ورقم له بالضعف وفى الباب عن ابى الدرداء عند الطبرانى

Rasulullah (Sallallaho alaihe wasallam) said, "The following words are such that one who recites them is

Virtues of Zikr

never disappointed. These are (سُبْحَانَ اللهِ اَلْحَمْدُ لِلّٰهِ اَللهُ اَكْبَرُ) which should be recited, 33, 33 and 34 times, respectively after every obligatory salaat."

Note:

These Kalimahs have been termed as (مُعَقِّبَاتٌ) (things that follow), either because these are recited after the salaat or because the recitation of these after sins results in washing them off, or because these are recited one after the other. Hadhrat Abu Darda (Radhiyallaho anho) narrated, "We have been directed to recite (سُبْحَانَ اللهِ) 33 times and (اَلْحَمْدُ لِلّٰهِ) 33 times and (لَآاِلٰهَ اِلَّا اللهُ) 34 times after every salaat."

Hadith No. 10

(۱۰) عَنْ عِمْرَانَ بْنِ حُصَيْنٍ رَفَعَهُ اَمَايَسْتَطِيْعُ اَحَدُكُمْ اَنْ يَعْمَلَ كُلَّ يَوْمٍ مِثْلَ اُحُدٍ عَمَلًا قَالُوْا يَارَسُوْلَ اللهِ وَمَنْ يَّسْتَطِيْعُ قَالَ كُلُّكُمْ يَسْتَطِيْعُ قَالُوْا يَا رَسُوْلَ اللهِ مَاذَا قَالَ سُبْحَانَ اللهِ اَعْظَمُ مِنْ اُحُدٍ وَّلَآاِلٰهَ اِلَّا اللهُ اَعْظَمُ مِنْ اُحُدٍ وَالْحَمْدُ لِلّٰهِ اَعْظَمُ مِنْ اُحُدٍ وَاللهُ اَكْبَرُ اَعْظَمُ مِنْ اُحُدٍ للكبير والبزار كذا فى جمع الفوائد واليهما عزاه فى الحصن ومجمع الزوائد وقال رجالها رجال الصحيح

Rasulullah (Sallallaho alaihe wasallam) once said, "Is there nobody amongst you who may be able to do, everyday, good deeds equal to Uhud (a mountain near Madinah)." The Sahaba (Radhiyallaho anhum) said, "O Rasulullah! who has the strength to do that?" "Everybody has the strength to do it," said Rasulullah (Sallallaho alaihe wasallam). "How is it?" enquired the Sahabas (Radhiyallaho anhum). He explained, "The reward of (سُبْحَانَ اللهِ) is greater than the mountain Uhud, that of (لَآاِلٰهَ اِلَّا اللهُ) is greater than Uhud, that of اَلْحَمْدُ لِلّٰهِ is greater than Uhud and that of (اَللهُ اَكْبَرُ) is greater than Uhud."

Note:

It is thus stated that the reward of each of these Kalimahs is greater than the mountain of Uhud, nay, it is greater than many such mountains. It is said in one hadith that the reward of (سُبْحَانَ اللهِ) and (اَلْحَمْدُ لِلّٰهِ) fills all the Heavens and the Earths. It is said in another hadith that the reward of (سُبْحَانَ الله) occupies half the scale-pan, the reward of (اَلْحَمْدُ لله) occupies the remaining half, and the reward of (اَللهُ اَكْبَرُ) fills the space between the Earth and the sky. It is stated in one hadith that Rasulullah (Sallallaho alaihe wasallam) had said, "

سُبْحَانَ اللهِ اَلْحَمْدُ لِلّٰهِ لَآاِلٰهَ اِلَّا اللهُ اَللهُ اَكْبَرُ

is more dear to me than all the things under the Sun." Mullah Ali Qari (Rahmatullah alaih) explained it to mean that it is more dear than spending in the path of Allah all that this world contains. It is said that once Hadhrat Sulaiman (Alayhis salaam) was going somewhere on his throne, when the birds spread their wings to protect him from the Sun, and the armies of men and Jinn were going with him. On seeing this, a worshippper praised Allah for the grandeur of this vast kingdom. Hadhrat Sulaiman (Alayhis salaam) remarked, "The credit in the account of deeds of a believer for reciting (سُبْحَانَ الله) once is more than the whole kingdom of Sulaiman Bin Dawood, because this kingdom is transitory but the reward of reciting (تسبیح) is everlasting."

Virtues of Zikr

Hadith No. 11

(١١) عَنْ اَبِیْ سَلَّامٍ مَوْلٰی رَسُوْلِ اللهِ ﷺ اَنَّ رَسُوْلَ اللهِ ﷺ قَالَ بَخٍّ بَخٍّ خَمْسٌ مَااَثْقَلَهُنَّ فِی الْمِیْزَانِ لَآاِلٰهَ اِلَّا اللهُ وَاللهُ اَكْبَرُ وَسُبْحَانَ اللهِ وَالْحَمْدُ لِلّٰهِ الحديث

اخرجه احمد فی مسنده ورجاله ثقات کما فی مجمع الزوائد والحاکم وقال صحیح الاسناد واقره علیه الذهبی وذکره فی الجامع الصغیر بروایة البزار عن ثوبان وبروایة النسائی وابن حبان والحاکم عن ابی سلمیٰ وبروایة احمد عن ابی امامة ورقم له بالحسن وذکره فی مجمع الزوائد بروایة ثوبان وابی سلمیٰ راعی رسول الله صلی الله علیه وسلم وسفینة ومولی لرسول الله صلی الله علیه وسلم لم یسم وصحح بعض طرقها

Once Rasulullah (Sallallaho alaihe wasallam) said, "Bakhkha! Bakhkha! How weighty in the scales are five things, viz. (لَآاِلٰهَ اِلَّا الله) , (اَللهُ اَكْبَرُ) , (سُبْحَانَ الله) , (اَلْحَمْدُ لِلّٰه) and exercise of patience (صبر) by the father (or the mother) over the death of his (or her) child."

The subject-matter of this hadith is narrated by many Sahabas (Radhiyallaho anhum) in so many other ahadith. The words (بخ بخ) (Bakhkha! Bakhkha!) are exclaimed at the time of extreme joy and pleasure. These things are of great joy and pleasure to Rasulullah (Sallallaho alaihe wasallam)

and therefore are stressed so much by him. Is it not therefore incumbent upon us who claim to love him that we should show extreme devotion to these Kalimahs, because doing so also amounts to showing respect, obedience, and gratitude to Him.

Hadith No. 12

(١٢) عَنْ سُلَيْمَانِ بْنِ يَسَارٍ عَنْ رَجُلٍ مِّنَ الْاَنْصَارِ اَنَّ النَّبِیَّ ﷺ قَالَ قَالَ نُوحٌ لِاِبْنِهٖ اِنِّیْ مُوْصِيْكَ بِوَصِيَّةٍ وَ قَاصِرُهَا لِكَیْ لَاتَنْسهَا اُوْصِيْكَ بِاِثْنَيْنِ وَاَنْهَاكَ عَنْ اِثْنَيْنِ اَمَّا الَّتِیْ اُوْصِيْكَ بِهِمَا فَيَسْتَبْشِرُ اللّٰهُ بِهِمَا وَصَالِحُ خَلْقِهٖ وَهُمَا يُكْثِرَانِ الْوُلُوْجَ عَلَى اللّٰهِ اُوْصِيْكَ بِلَااِلٰهَ اِلَّا اللّٰهُ فَاِنَّ السَّمٰوٰتِ وَالْاَرْضَ لَوْ كَانَتْ حَلْقَةً قَصَمَتْهُمَا وَلَوْ كَانَتَا فِیْ كِفَّةٍ وَزَنَتْهُمَا وَاُوْصِيْكَ بِسُبْحَانَ اللّٰهِ وَبِحَمْدِهٖ فَاِنَّهُمَا صَلٰوةُ الْخَلْقِ وَبِهَا يُرْزَقُ الْخَلْقُ وَاِنْ مِّنْ شَیْءٍ اِلَّا يُسَبِّحُ بِحَمْدِهٖ وَلٰكِنْ لَّاتَفْقَهُوْنَ تَسْبِيْحَهُمْ اِنَّهُ كَانَ حَلِيْمًا غَفُوْرًا وَاَمَّا اللَّتَانِ اَنْهَاكَ عَنْهُمَا فَيَحْتَجِبُ اللّٰهُ مِنْهُمَا وَصَالِحُ خَلْقِهٖ اَنْهَاكَ عَنِ الشِّرْكِ وَالْكِبْرِ

رواه النسائی واللفظ له والبزار والحاكم من حديق عبد الله بن عمرو رضی الله عنه وقال صحيح الاسناد كذا فی الترغيب قلت وقد تقدم فی بيان التهليل حديث عبد الله بن عمرو مرفوعا وتقدم فيه ايضا ما فی لباب وتقدم فی الايات قوله عز اسمه وَاِنْ مِّنْ شَیْءٍ اِلَّا يُسَبِّحُ بِحَمْدِهٖ الاية واخرج ابن جرير وابن ابی حاتم وابو الشيخ فی العظمة عن جابر مرفوعا اَلَا اُخْبِرُكُمْ بِشَیْءٍ اَمَرَ بِهٖ نُوْحُ نِ ابْنَهٗ اِنَّ نُوْحًا قَالَ لِاِبْنِهٖ يَابُنَیَّ اٰمُرُكَ اَنْ تَقُوْلَ سُبْحَانَ اللّٰهِ فَاِنَّهَا صَلٰوةُ الْخَلْقِ وَتَسْبِيْحُ الْخَلْقِ وَبِهَا يُرْزَقُ الْخَلْقُ اخرج احمد وابن مردويه عن ابن عمر مرفوعا اِنَّ نُوْحًا لَمَّا حَضَرَتْهُ الْوَفَاةُ قَالَ لِاِبْنَيْهِ اٰمُرُكُمَا سُبْحَانَ اللّٰهِ وَبِحَمْدِهٖ فَاِنَّهَا صَلٰوةُ كُلِّ شَیْءٍ وَبِهَا يُرْزَقُ كُلُّ شَیْءٍ كذا فی الدر

Rasulullah (Sallallaho alaihe wasallam) said, "Prophet Nooh (Alayhis salaam) said to his sons, "I give you a piece of advice and, in order that you may not forget it, I say it very briefly. I advise you for doing two things and forbid you from doing two things. The two things which I recommend are such that Almighty Allah and His noble creation are greatly pleased with them, and both of these have easy access to Almighty Allah. One of the two things is (لَااِلٰهَ اِلَّا اللّٰهُ), which if it were enclosed in the mighty sky, will break through it and reach Almighty Allah and, if all the heavens and the earth were placed in one pan of the balance and this kalimah were put in the other pan, the latter would outweight the former. The second thing that I recommend to you is the recitation of (سُبْحَانَ اللهِ وَبِحَمْدِهِ), which is the prayer of all the creation and by virtue of which all the creation get their sustenance. There is none among the creation that does not hymn glorification of Allah, but you do not understand their speech. And the two things from which I forbid you, are shirk (polytheism) and arrogance, because these two keep you away from Allah and His noble creation."

Note:

The subject matter of this hadith has also been discussed before when describing the virtues of (لَآ اِلٰهَ اِلَّا اللهُ). That all the creation hymn the glory of Allah is also mentioned in the aayaat of the Holy Qur'an. One of these aayaat is

وَاِنْ مِّنْ شَيْءٍ اِلَّا يُسَبِّحُ بِحَمْدِهٖ

(There is none among the creation who does not hymn His glory).

It is narrated in many ahadith that on the night of Mi'raaj, Rasulullah (Sallallaho alaihe wasallam) had heard all the Heavens hymning the glory of Allah.

Once Rasulullah (Sallallaho alaihe wasallam) happened to pass by a group of men who, though halted, were sitting on the backs of their horses and camels. He said to them "Do not use the backs of your animals as chairs and pulpits, as so many of them are better than their riders and do zikr of Allah more than the riders."

Hadhrat Ibn Abbas (Radhiyallaho anho) said that even the crops hymn the glory of Allah, and the owner gets the reward for it.

Once a bowl of food was presented to Rasulullah (Sallallaho alaihe wasallam), who remarked that the food was hymning the glory of Allah. Somebody asked if he understood its hymning. He replied in the affirmative, and then he asked that it be taken to a certain person who also, when the cup was brought to him, heard it hymning the glory of Allah; In the same way, another person also heard it. Somebody requested that all those present should be allowed to hear it. Rasulullah (Sallallaho alaihe wasallam) said, "If some one fails to hear it, others will think that he is a sinner." This sort of revelation is known as Kashf (كشف), which is bestowed on the Prophets, but the Sahabas (Radhiyallaho anhum) also were able to attain it as a result of their company with and their nearness to Rasulullah (Sallallaho alaihe wasallam). Hundreds of incidents can be cited as a proof thereof. Even the Sufis often develop this quality through their spiritual labour, as a result of which they are able to understand what the rocks and animals hymn and speak. But according to the authentic scholars, proficiency in this line is not necessarily proof of one's high spiritual attainment or nearness to Allah. Whoever labours and strives for this can develop it, irrespective of whether he attains nearness to Almighty Allah or not; therefore, the true religious authorities do not attach any importance to it. On the other hand, they regard it as harmful in the respect that the novice gets so much absorbed and involved into it that it acts as a hindrance to his spiritual progress. I know this about some disciples of Maulana Khalil Ahmad (Rahmatullah alaih) when they happened to develop a sort of Kashf that to prevent its further progress Maulana (Rahmatullah alaih), stopped them from doing all sorts of zikr. Moreover, the scholars avoid development of Kashf, because it leads to the disclosure to them of the sins of others, which is against their liking.

Allamah Sha'raani has related in his book "Meezaanul Kubra" about Hadhrat Imam Abu Hanifa (Rahmatullah alaih) that when he happened to see somebody performing ablution, he could also see the sins that were being washed away in the water, so much so that he could even distinguish whether the washed off sins were major or minor sins or merely undesirable deeds, just as one is able to see the material things. Once he happened to go into the place of wudhu in the main mosque of Koofa, where a young man was performing wudhu. After looking at the water used by him, he quietly advised him, "My brother! make taubah from disobeying your parents," which he did. Then he saw another person and said to him, "My brother! refrain from adultery, it is a major sin," and the man made taubah from adultery. He saw that the water used by yet another man indicated the sins of drinking and sinful amusement. He advised the man accordingly, who also made taubah then and there. Afterwards, Hadhrat Imam Abu Hanifa (Rahmatullah alaih) prayed, "O Allah! take away this thing from me. I do not want to see the shortcomings of other people." His prayer was accepted by Almighty Allah, and he got relieved of this power. It is related that it was during that earlier period that he had declared the water once used for wudhu to have become polluted; when he saw the dirt and bad smell of sins in it, he could not regard it otherwise. After he was relieved of this power, he also gave up declaring this water as polluted.

It is related of a disciple of our Shaikh Maulana Abdur Rahim Raipuri (Rahmatullah alaih), may Allah enlighten his grave, that for days together, he could not go out to answer the call of nature, because he found spiritual light prevailing all over. Similarly, there are hundreds and thousands of incidents proving beyond any doubt that those who are blessed with Kashf can see hidden things, according to the degree of their attainment.

Hadith No. 13

(١٣) عَنْ اُمِّ هَانِیْءٍ رَضِیَ اللّٰهُ عَنْهَا قَالَتْ مَرَّ بِیْ رَسُوْلُ اللّٰهِ ﷺ فَقُلْتُ يَارَسُوْ
اللّٰهِ قَدْ كَبُرْتُ وَضَعُفْتُ اَوْ كَمَا قَالَتْ فَمُرْنِیْ بِعَمَلٍ اَعْمَلُهٗ وَاَنَا جَالِسَةٌ قَا
سَبِّحِی اللّٰهَ مِائَةَ تَسْبِيْحَةٍ فَاِنَّهٗ تَعْدِلُ لَكِ مِائَةَ رَقَبَةٍ تُعْتِقِيْنَهَا مِنْ وُلْدِ اِسْمٰعِيْ
وَاَحْمَدِیْ اللّٰهِ مِائَةَ تَحْمِيْدَةٍ فَاِنَّهَا تَعْدِلُ لَكِ مِائَةَ فَرَسٍ مُسْرَجَةٍ مُلْجَمَةٍ تَحْمِلِيْ
عَلَيْهَا فِیْ سَبِيْلِ اللّٰهِ وَكَبِّرِیْ اللّٰهَ مِائَةَ تَكْبِيْرَةٍ فَاِنَّهَا تَعْدِلُ لَكَ مِائَةَ بَدَنَةٍ مُقَلَّ
مُتَقَبَّلَةٍ وَهَلِّلِیْ اللّٰهَ مِائَةَ تَهْلِيْلَةٍ قَالَ اَبُوْ خَلْفٍ اَحْسِبُهٗ قَالَ تَمْلَاُ مَا بَيْنَ السَّم
وَالْاَرْضِ وَلَايُرْفَعُ لِاَحَدٍ عَمَلٌ اَفْضَلُ مِمَّا يُرْفَعُ لَكَ اِلَّا اَنْ يَّاتِیَ بِمِثْلِ مَا اَتَيْ

رواه احمد باسناد حسن واللفظ له والنسائی ولم یقل ولایرفع الی اٰخره والبیهقی بتمامه وابن ابی الدنیا فجع
ثواب الرقاب فی التحمید والفرس فی التسبیح وابن ماجة بمعناه باختصار والطبرانی فی الکبیر بنح
احمد ولم یقل احسبه وفی الاوسط باسناد حسن بمعناه کذا فی الترغیب باختصار قلت رواه الح
بمعناه وصححه وعزاه فی الجامع الصغیر الی احمد والطبرانی والحاکم ورقم له بالصحة وذکره فی مج
الزوائد بطرق وقال اسانید هم حسنة وفی الترغیب ایضا عن ابی امامة مرفوعا بنحو حدیث البا
مختصرا وقال رواه الطبرانی ورواته رواة الصحیح خلاسلیم بن عثمان الفوزی یکشف حاله فانه لایحضر
الاٰن فیه جرح ولاعدالة ه وفی الباب عن سلمیٰ ام بنی ابی راف

قَالَتْ يَارَسُوْلَ اللهِ اَخْبِرْنِىْ بِكَلِمٰتٍ وَلَاتُكْثِرْ عَلَىَّ الحديث مختصرًا وفيه التكبير والتسبيح عشرًا عشرًا و اَللّٰهُمَّ اغْفِرْلِىْ عشرًا قال المنذرى رواه الطبرانى ورواته محتج بهم فى الصحيح ه قلت وبمعناه عن عمرو بن شعيب عن ابيه عن جده مرفوعا بلفظ مَنْ سَبَّحَ اللهِ مِاْئَةً بِالْغَدَاةِ وَمِائَةً بِالْعَشِىِّ كَانَ كَمَنْ حَجَّ مِائَةَ حَجَّةٍ الحديث ، وجعل فيه التحميد كمن حمل على مائة فرس والتهليل كمن اعتق مائة رقبة من ولد اسمٰعيل ذكره المشكوٰة برواية الترمذى وقال حسن غريب

Hadhrat Umme Haani (Radhiyallaho anha) related that once Rasulullah (Sallallaho alaihe wasallam) paid her a visit, when she said to him, "O Rasulullah! (Sallallaho alaihe wasallam) I have grown very old and weak. Tell me something that I may be able to do while sitting." Rasulullah (Sallallaho alaihe wasallam) said to her, "Hymn (سُبْحَانَ اللهِ) one hundred times and you will get a reward as if you set free one hundred Arab slaves; hymn (اَلْحَمْدُ لِلهِ) one hundred times, which will fetch you a reward as if you present a hundred horses, fully equipped, for the Jihaad; hymn (اَللهُ اَكْبَرُ) hundred times, which is as if you sacrificed a hundred camels for the sake of Allah; and hymn (لَآاِلٰهَ اِلَّا اللهُ) a hundred times, the reward of which will fill the whole space between the earth and the sky. There is no other commendable action that can surpass it." Hadhrat Salma (Radhiyallaho anha) the wife of Abu Raafe' (Radhiyallaho anho) had also requested Rasulullah (Sallallaho alaihe wasallam) to prescribe her some zikr which may not be very lengthy. Rasulullah (Sallallaho alaihe wasallam) advised her, "Recite (اَللهُ اَكْبَرُ) ten times, because Almighty Allah says in reply, "It is for Me," recite (سُبْحَانَ اللهِ) ten times, because Almighty Allah says in reply, "It is for Me", and then recite (اَللّٰهُمَّ اغْفِرْلِىْ) (O Allah! forgive me) ten times, because then Allah says, "Yes, I have forgiven you." If you recite (اَللّٰهُمَّ اغْفِرْلِىْ) ten times, Almighty Allah will also say each time, "I have forgiven you." What a brief and easy zikr has been proposed by Rasulullah (Sallallaho alaihe wasallam) for old and weak people, especially the women. It is very brief and involves no labour or going about, and yet what tremendous reward is promised for it. It is really a pity if we fail to earn this high reward.

Hadhrat Umme Sulaim (Radhiyallaho anha) has narrated that she also requested Rasulullah (Sallallaho alaihe wasallam) to prescribe for her something that she should recite before her supplication to Allah at the time of salaat, and that she was told, "Recite (سُبْحَانَ اللّٰهِ اَلْحَمْدُ لِلّٰهِ) and (اَللّٰهُ اَكْبَرُ) ten times each, and then pray for what you like, Allah will say; "Yes, Yes, I accept it." How simple and common are these words, that no effort is required to memorize them. We talk all sorts of rubbish throughout the day but if, while doing our business or sitting in the shop, or working on the field, we hymn this zikr as well, then along with work for the earthly life we can also earn a lot of wealth for the next life.

Hadith No. 14

(١٤) عَنْ اَبِىْ هُرَيْرَةَ رَضِىَ اللّٰهُ عَنْهُ قَالَ قَالَ رَسُوْلُ اللّٰهِ ﷺ اِنَّ لِلّٰهِ مَلٰٓئِكَةً يَطُوْفُوْنَ فِى الطُّرُقِ يَلْتَمِسُوْنَ اَهْلَ الذِّكْرِ فَاِذَا وَجَدُوْا قَوْمًا يَذْكُرُوْنَ اللّٰهَ تَنَادَوْا هَلُمُّوْا اِلٰى حَاجَتِكُمْ فَيَحُفُّوْنَهَا بِاَجْنِحَتِهِمْ اِلَى السَّمَآءِ فَاِذَا تَفَرَّقُوْا عَرَجُوْا وَصَعِدُوْا اِلَى السَّمَاءِ فَيَسْاَلُهُمْ رَبُّهُمْ وَهُوَ يَعْلَمُ مِنْ اَيْنَ جِئْتُمْ فَيَقُوْلُوْنَ جِئْنَا مِنْ عِنْدِ عِبَادٍ لَّكَ يُسَبِّحُوْنَكَ وَيُكَبِّرُوْنَكَ وَيَحْمَدُوْنَكَ فَيَقُوْلُوْنَ جِئْنَا مِنْ عِنْدِ عِبَادٍ لَّكَ يُسَبِّحُوْنَكَ وَيُكَبِّرُوْنَكَ وَيَحْمَدُوْنَكَ فَيَقُوْلُ هَلْ رَاَوْنِىْ فَيَقُوْلُوْنَ لَا فَيَقُوْلُ كَيْفَ لَوْ رَاَوْنِىْ فَيَقُوْلُوْنَ لَوْ رَاَوْكَ كَانُوْا اَشَدَّ لَكَ عِبَادَةً وَاَشَدَّلَكَ تَمْجِيْدًا وَاَكْثَرَ لَكَ تَسْبِيْحًا فَيَقُوْلُ فَمَايَسْاَلُوْنَ فَيَقُوْلُوْنَ يَسْاَلُوْنَكَ الْجَنَّةَ فَيَقُوْلُ وَهَلْ رَاَوْهَا فَيَقُوْلُوْنَ لَا فَيَقُوْلُ فَكَيْفَ لَوْ رَاَوْهَا فَيَقُوْلُوْنَ لَوْ اَنَّهُمْ رَاَوْهَا كَانُوْا اَشَدَّ عَلَيْهَا حِرْصًا وَاَشَدَّ لَهَا طَلَبًا وَاَعْظَمَ فِيْهَا رَغْبَةً قَالَ فَمِمَّ يَتَعَوَّذُوْنَ فَيَقُوْلُوْنَ يَتَعَوَّذُوْنَ مِنَ النَّارِ فَيَقُوْلُ وَهَلْ رَاَوْهَا فَيَقُوْلُوْنَ لَافَيَقُوْلُ فَكَيْفَ لَوْ رَاَوْهَا فَيَقُوْلُوْنَ لَوْ اَنَّهُمْ رَاَوْهَا كَانُوْا اَشَدَّ مِنْهَا فِرَارًا وَاَشَدَّ لَهَا مَخَافَةً فَيَقُوْلُ اُشْهِدُكُمْ اَنِّىْ قَدْ غَفَرْتُ لَهُمْ فَيَقُوْلُ مَلَكٌ مِّنَ الْمَلٰٓئِكَةِ فُلَانٌ لَيْسَ مِنْهُمْ اِنَّمَا جَاءَ لِحَاجَةٍ قَالَ هُمُ الْقَوْمُ لَايَشْقٰى بِهِمْ جَلِيْسُهُمْ رواه البخارى ومسلم والبيهقى فى الاسماء والصفات كذا فى الدر والمشكوٰة

Rasulullah (Sallallaho alaihe wasallam) had said:

"There is a class of angels who keep going about on the pathways, and wherever they find some people engaged in the zikr of Allah, they call each other and gather round them, and pile up over each other right upto the sky. When that assembly for zikr is over, the angels ascend to the Heavens and then Almighty Allah, in spite of knowing everything, asks them where they had come from? They submit that they have come from such and such group of His bondsmen, who were busy in hymning His Glory, His Grandeur, His Greatness and His Praise. Allah says, "Have those people seen Me?" "No, our Lord", confirm the angels. "How would they have acted if they had actually seen me?" "They would have busied themselves with even greater zeal in praying to You and in hymning Your praise and Glory," submit the angels. "What do they demand?" "They want Paradise", reply the angels. "Have they ever seen Paradise?" says Almighty Lord. "No our Lord" say the angels. "If they had seen it, how would they have acted?" says Almighty Allah. "Their zeal, yearning, and their prayers for it would have been even greater," submit the angels. "What were they seeking refuge from?" says Almighty Allah. "They were seeking refuge from Hell", say the angels. "Have they seen the Hell?" "They have not seen it." "How would they have acted if they had seen it?" says Allah. "They would have been more scared of it, and would have tried more for protection against it," say the angels. Then Almighty Allah says, "Allright then, all of you bear witness that I grant forgiveness to all those present in that assembly." One angel says, "O Allah! a person happened to be there only by chance; he had come for some other business and had not taken part in what they did." Almighty Allah says, "That group was so blessed that whosoever happened to sit with them, even by the way, is not deprived of the blessings (and thus he is also forgiven)."

It is described in several ahaadith that there is a group of angels who go about in search of assemblies and individuals engaged in zikr, and wherever they find them, they sit near them and listen to their zikr. This subject matter is already included in Hadith No. 8 in Chapter I, wherein it is also explained why Almighty Allah praises these persons in the presence of the angels.

The submission by an angel that there was, in that assembly, a person who had come there on his private business was only a statement of facts, because on that occasion those angels were acting as the witnesses that those people were engaged in prayers and zikr of Allah. That is why they had to clarify the position, lest there should be any objection. But it is the extreme benevolence of Allah that, because of the blessed people engaged in zikr, a man who is sitting near them by the way is not deprived of the blessings. Almighty Allah says in His Book:

يَآاَيُّهَا الَّذِيْنَ اٰمَنُوْا اتَّقُوْا اللّٰهَ وَكُوْنُوْا مَعَ الصّٰدِقِيْنَ (توبة ع ١٥)

"O you who believe! fear Almighty Allah and be with the truthful.

The Sufis say, "Remain with Almighty Allah, and if this is not possible, then be in the society of those persons who remain with Almighty Allah." Remaining with Almighty Allah means (as given in the book of Bukhari Shareef): Almighty Allah says, "By means of non-obligatory prayers, My bondman keeps on getting nearer and nearer to Me, till I make him My beloved, and at that stage I become his ears with which he listens, his eyes with which he sees, his hands with which he holds, his feet with which he walks; and whatever he begs of Me I grant him." That Allah becomes his hands and feet, etc., means that he performs his actions for earning the pleasure and love of Allah and that he does not do anything against the will of Allah. The books of history relate the lives of many sufis of this level. A booklet, known as 'Nuzhatul Basaateen' is specially devoted to the account of such Sufis.

Sheikh Abu Bakr Kattaani (Rahmatullah alaih) related, "Once, at the time of Hajj, there was a gathering in Mecca of some Sufis, the youngest among whom was Junaid Baghdadi (Rahmatullah alaih). In that gathering, there was a discussion on the subject of 'Love of Allah' and as to who is the lover of Allah! Many of them expressed their views on the subject, but Junaid Baghdadi (Rahmatullah alaih) kept quiet. He was pressed to say something. With his head bowed down and tears in his eyes, he said, "A lover (of Allah) is he who forgets his own self, remains engaged in Allah's zikr with due regard to all its requirements; sees Allah with the eyes of his heart, which is burnt by the heat of Allah's fear; Allah's zikr intoxicates him like a cup of wine, he speaks the word of Allah as if Almighty Allah speaks through his mouth; if he moves he does so under the command of Allah; he derives peace of mind only through obedience to Allah; and when such a stage is reached, his eating, drinking, sleeping, awaking and, in short, all his actions are for the pleasure of Allah; he neither pays any heed to the worldly customs, nor does he attach any importance to adverse criticism by the people."

Hadhrat Sa'eed bin Musayyib was a well known Tabi'ee, and is counted as a great Muhaddith. A person named Abdullah bin Abi Widaa-ah, who used to go to him very often, related as follows: "I could not go to him for a few days. Then when I went, Hadhrat Sa'eed asked me where I had been. I told him that my wife had died and that I remained busy on that account. He said, "Had you informed me, I could have also joined the funeral." When, after a little while, I got up to leave he said, 'Have you married again?" I replied, 'Who would marry a penniless person such as I am?" He said that he would arrange it, and there and then he read out the marriage sermon and solemnised my nikaah (marriage declaration) with his own daughter, fixing the mehr (jointure) at a paltry sum of eight or ten annas" (This small amount as mehr may be permissible according to them, as it is according to some Imams, but according to Imam Abu Hanifa (Rahmatullah alayh) a sum less than two rupees and eight annas is not permissible). "After the nikaah, I left the place. Only Almighty Allah knows how overjoyed I was; in my happiness, I was thinking where from to borrow the money for expenses to bring the wife to my house. I remained absorbed in these thoughts till it was evening. I was keeping a fast, and I broke it at sunset. After the evening prayer, I reached home and, lighting the lamp, I started eating my bread with olive oil, when somebody knocked at the door. Who is there? said I, "Sa'eed", came the reply. I started thinking which Sa'eed it was. It did not occur to me that it could be Hadhrat Sa'eed, because for forty years he had never been to any place except the mosque and his own house. I was surprised to see him standing outside, and submitted that he should have called for me. He replied, 'It was proper for me to come. I thought that since you have been married, you should not be alone in your house. I have, therefore, brought your wife to live with you. Saying this, he sent his daughter in, closed the door and went away. The girl, being overwhelmed with modesty, fell down on the ground. I bolted the door from inside, removed the bread and olive oil from near the lamp lest she should see it, climbed up on the roof of my house and called out to my neighbours. When people gathered, I told them that Hadhrat Sa'eed had given his daughter to me in marriage, and that he had just then himself brought her and left her in my house. They were all greatly surprised, and exclaimed, 'Is it true that she is already in your house? 'Yes,' confirmed I. The news spread and also reached my mother, who at once came there and said, 'If you touch her for three days, I will not see your face; in three days we will make all the preparations. After three days, when I met the girl, I found her extremely beautiful. She was a Hafiz of the Qur'an, very conversant with the Sunnat of the Prophet (Sallallaho alaihe wasallam) and well acquainted with her obligations to her husband. For one month, neither Hadhrat Sa'eed came to me, nor I went to him. After one month, when I went to him there was a big gathering. After wishing salaam to him, I sat down. When all others left, he asked me how I found my wife. I replied, 'She is most excellent, so that friends are pleased to see her and foes become envious,' He further said, 'If you find anything undesirable, you may use a stick to rectify it.' After I returned from there, he sent me through a special messenger a gift of twenty four thousand dirhams (which comes to about five thousand rupees). This girl had been demanded by King Abdul Malik bin Marwaan for marriage with his son, Waleed, who was the crown prince, but Hadhrat Sa'eed had declined the offer. In this way, he had incurred the wrath of King Abdul Malik, who on some other pretext got him punished with a hundred lashes in bitter cold, and then had a pitcher of cold water poured on him."

Hadith No. 15

(١٥) عَنْ اِبْنِ عُمَرَ رَضِيَ اللّٰهُ عَنْهُ قَالَ سَمِعْتُ رَسُوْلَ اللّٰهِ ﷺ يَقُوْلُ مَنْ قَالَ سُبْحَانَ اللّٰهِ وَالْحَمْدُ لِلّٰهِ وَلَآاِلٰهَ اِلَّا اللّٰهُ وَاللّٰهُ اَكْبَرُ كُتِبَتْ لَهُ بِكُلِّ حَرْفٍ عَشْرُ حَسَنَاتٍ وَمَنْ اَعَانَ عَلٰى خُصُوْمَةٍ بَاطِلٍ لَمْ يَزَلْ فِيْ سَخَطِ اللّٰهِ حَتّٰى يَنْزِعَ وَمَنْ حَالَتْ شَفَاعَتُهُ دُوْنَ حَدٍّ مِّنْ حُدُوْدِ اللّٰهِ فَقَدْ ضَادَّ اللّٰهَ فِيْ اَمْرِهِ وَمَنْ بَهَّتَ مُؤْمِنًا اَوْ مُؤْمِنَةً حَبَسَهُ اللّٰهُ فِيْ رَدْغَةِ الْخَبَالِ يَوْمَ الْقِيَامَةِ حَتّٰى يَخْرُجَ مِمَّا قَالَ وَلَيْس

بِخَارِجٍ رواه الطبرانى فى الكبير والاوسط ورجالهما رجال الصحيح كذا فى مجمع الزوائد قلت اخرجه ابو داود بدون ذكر التسبيح فيه

Rasulullah (Sallallaho alaihe wasallam) said, "Whosoever recites (سُبْحَانَ اللهِ اَلْحَمْدُ لِلّٰهِ لَآاِلٰهَ اِلَّا اللهُ اَللهُ اَكْبَرُ) will be rewarded with ten virtues for each letter thereof. Whosoever supports an unjust party in a dispute incurs the wrath of Allah, until he repents and does toubah. Whosoever intercedes to prevent infliction of punishment awarded according to Islamic law is considered to oppose Almighty Allah, and whosoever slanders a Muslim, man or woman, will in the Hereafter be imprisoned in Radghatul Khabal (a deep part of Hell), until he gets exonerated from this sin, which will hardly be possible there."

Backing an unjust cause has nowadays become our second nature. In spite of knowing that we are at fault, we become unjust and partial for the sake of our relatives and our party. We are not afraid of the wrath, displeasure, and punishment of Almighty Allah, when our relatives and friends are involved. Not to speak of telling them that they should desist from committing wrong, we cannot even keep quiet and remain neutral, but we go to the extreme in supporting them. If anybody puts up a claim against them, we try to oppose him. If a friend of ours commits theft, wrongs somebody, or indulges in adultery, we encourage and help him in all possible ways. Is this according to the dictates of our faith and religion? Is this according to Islam that we feel proud of? Do we not thus degrade our Islam in the eyes of others, and degrade ourselves before Almighty Allah? It is stated in one hadith that one who deals or fights with somebody on the basis of sectionalism (racialism) is not one of us. According to another hadith, sectionalism means to help one's own people in their wrong cause.

"Radghatul Khabal" is the mud formed by the blood and puss of those in Hell. How dirty and horrible would be that place where such people who do slander against the Muslims will be imprisoned. In this life, we take it very lightly to talk against whosoever we like, but we will realise the gravity of our offence in the Hereafter when we will be required to justify and prove whatever we have said here, and the proof given there will have to be acceptable from the Shariat point of view. Fluent talk based on lies will be of no avail there. What we talk here and what the actual reality is will all be known there. Rasulullah (Sallallaho alaihe wasallam) had said, "Sometimes one talks merely to amuse others, but because of it he is thrown into Hell to a depth which exceeds the distance between the earth and the sky. A slip of the tongue is fraught with more dangers than the slip of the foot." It is said in one hadith, "Whosoever reproaches somebody else for his sin will find himself involved in it before his death." Imam Ahmad (Rahmatullah alaih) explained that this hadith implies such sins from which the sinner has done toubah. Hadhrat Abu Bakr (Radhiyallaho anho) used to pull his tongue and say, "You are the cause of our woes." Ibn Munkadir, a famous Muhaddith, and a Taabi'ee was seen weeping when he was about to die. Someone asked why he wept. He replied, "I do not remember to have committed any sin, but I might have said something which, though ordinary in my opinion, may turn out to be something very serious before Almighty Allah."

Hadith No 16

(١٦) عَنْ اَبِىْ بَرْزَةَ الْاَسْلَمِىِّ رَضِىَ اللّٰهُ عَنْهُ قَالَ كَانَ رَسُوْلُ اللّٰهِ ﷺ يَقُوْلُ بِاٰخِرِهٖ اِذَا اَرَادَ اَنْ يَّقُوْمَ مِنَ الْمَجْلِسِ سُبْحَانَكَ اللّٰهُمَّ وَبِحَمْدِكَ اَشْهَدُ اَنْ لَّا اِلٰهَ اِلَّا اَنْتَ اَسْتَغْفِرُكَ وَاَتُوْبُ اِلَيْكَ فَقَالَ رَجُلٌ يَارَسُوْلَ اللّٰهِ اِنَّكَ لَتَقُوْلُ قَوْلًا مَاكُنْتَ تَقُوْلُهٗ فِيْمَا مَضٰى قَالَ كَفَّارَةٌ لِّمَا يَكُوْنُ فِى الْمَجْلِسِ رواه ابن ابى شيبة وابو داود والنسائى والحاكم وابن مردويه كذا فى الدر وفيه ايضا برواية ابن ابى شيبة عن ابى العالية بزياد علمنيهن جبرئيل عليه السلام

In the closing period of his life, whenever Rasulullah (Sallallaho alaihe wasallam) got up from a meeting, he used to recite

سُبْحَانَكَ اللّٰهُمَّ وَبِحَمْدِكَ اَشْهَدُ اَنْ لَّااِلٰهَ اِلَّا اَنْتَ اَسْتَغْفِرُكَ وَاَتُوْبُ اِلَيْكَ

"Glory to Thee, O Allah, with the highest of Praises; I bear witness that there is none worthy of worship except Thee, I seek Thy forgiveness and turn to Thee."

Someone said, "It is only nowadays that it has become customary with you to recite this prayer, but it was not so before." Rasulullah (Sallallaho alaihe wasallam) said, "It is the kaffaarah (atonement) of the meeting". According to another version Rasulullah (Sallallaho alaihe wasallam) had said, "These words constitute the kaffaarah of the meeting, and were taught to me by Hadhrat Jibraa-eel (Alayhis salaam)."

Hadhrat Aa-ishah (Radhiyallaho anha) also related, "Whenever Rasulullah (Sallallaho alaihe wasallam) got up from a meeting, he used to recite:

سُبْحَانَكَ اللّٰهُمَّ رَبِّیْ وَبِحَمْدِكَ لَآاِلٰهَ اِلَّا اَنْتَ اَسْتَغْفِرُكَ وَاَتُوْبُ اِلَيْكَ

When I asked him the reason for reciting this duaa so often, he said, "If a person recites it at the end of a meeting, then all his slips during the meeting are forgiven". We are all liable to do some irrelevant and useless talk during a meeting. This duaa is very brief, but whosoever recites either of the two versions of this duaa will get saved from the adverse results of that meeting. The Almighty Lord has provided so many facilities for our benefit.

Hadith No 17

(١٧) عَنِ النُّعْمَانِ بْنِ بَشِيْرٍ رَضِىَ اللّٰهُ عَنْهُ قَالَ قَالَ رَسُوْلُ اللّٰهِ ﷺ اَلَّذِيْنَ يَذْكُرُوْنَ مِنْ جَلَالِ اللّٰهِ مِنْ تَسْبِيْحِهِ وَتَحْمِيْدِهِ وَتَكْبِيْرِهِ وَتَهْلِيْلِهِ يَتَعَاطَفْنَ حَوْلَ الْعَرْشِ لَهُنَّ دَوِىٌّ كَدَوِىِّ النَّحْل يَذْكُرُوْنَ بِصَاحِبِهِنَّ اَلَا يُحِبُّ اَحَدُكُمْ اَنْ لَايَزَالَ لَهُ عِنْدَ اللّٰهِ شَيْءٌ يَذْكُرُبِهِ رواه احمد والحاكم وقال صحيح الاسناد قال الذهبى موسى بن سالم قال ابو حاتم منكر الحديث ولفظا الحاكم كَدَوِىِّ النَّحْلِ يَقُلْنَ لِصَاحِبِهِنَّ اَلَا يُحِبُّ اَحَدُكُمْ اَنْ لَايزال لهُ عِنْدَ اللهِ شَيْءٌ يُذْكَرُبِهِ رواه احمد والحاكم وقال صحيح الاسناد قال الذهبى موسى بن سالم قال ابو حاتم منكر الحديث ولفظ الحاكم كَدَوِىِّ النَّحْلِ يَقُلْنَ لِصَاحِبِهِنَّ واخرجه بسند اخر صححه على شرط مسلم واقره عليه الذهبى وفيه كدوى النحل يذكرون بصاحبهن

Rasulullah (Sallallaho alaihe wasallam) said, "When a person hymns the greatness of Allah, i.e. recites

سُبْحَانَ اللّٰهِ اَلْحَمْدُ لِلّٰهِ اَللّٰهُ اَكْبَرُ لَآاِلٰهَ اِلَّا اللّٰهُ

these kalimahs revolve round the Arsh with a low humming tone, and mention the name of the reciter. Do not you wish that there should be somebody near Almighty Allah to mention and recommend you before Him?" Persons who seek an approach to the rulers, and hanker after position, get overwhelmed with joy and feel so proud if they are praised before a governor, not to speak of the king or the minister or even the viceroy, even though such a recommendation does not result in any benefit to them. That no gain results is clear because even if they get some lift in status, they have to spend comparatively far more in getting it through such recommendation. In order to approach the high officials, some people squander their property, get involved in debt, incur the enmity of others and thus disgrace themselves in so many ways. All this is experienced during the election period.

On the other hand, just imagine the blessings and honour of one's name being mentioned before the Arsh of Almighty Allah, the Lord of Lords, who controls this world as well as the Hereafter, and in fact everything in all the universe, Who controls the hearts of the kings, Who grants success or failure, gain or loss; so that, all the people of the world including the rulers and the ruled, the kings and their subjects, cannot harm or help anybody against His will, they cannot give even a drop of water to anybody if He does not will it. No worldly wealth or honour can be compared to this blessing that one's name should be mentioned with favour before such a Supreme Lord. If a person attaches more importance to any worldly honour, he does a great wrong to himself.

Hadith No. 18

(١٨) عَنْ يُّسَيْرَةَ رَضِىَ اللّٰهُ عَنْهَا وَكَانَتْ مِنَ الْمُهَاجِرَاتِ قَالَتْ قَالَ لَنَا رَسُوْلُ اللّٰهِ ﷺ عَلَيْكُنَّ بِالتَّسْبِيْحِ وَالتَّهْلِيْلِ وَالتَّقْدِيْسِ وَاعْقِدْنَ بِالْاَنَامِلِ فَإِنَّهُنَّ مَسْئُوْلَاتٌ مُسْتَنْطِقَاتٌ وَلَاتَغْفَلْنَ فَتَنْسَيْنَ الرَّحْمَةَ رواه الترمذى وابى داود كذا فى المشكوٰة وفى المنهل اخرجه ايضا احمد والحاكم اه وقال الذهبى فى تلخيصه صحيح وكذا رقم له بالصحة فى الجامع الصغير وبسط صاحب الاتحاف فى تخريجه وَقَالَ عَبْدُ اللّٰهِ بْنُ عَمْرو رَضِىَ اللّٰهُ عَنْهُ رَأَيْتُ رَسُوْلَ اللّٰهِ صَلَّى اللّٰهُ عَلَيْهِ وَسَلَّمَ يَعْقِدُ التَّسْبِيْحَ رواه ابو داود والنسائى والترمذى وحسنه والحاكم كذا فى الاتحاف وبسط فى تخريجه ثم قال قال الحافظ معنى العقد المذكور فى الحديث احصاء العدد وهو

اصطلاح العرب بوضع بعض الانامل على بعض عقد انملة اخرى فالآحاد والعشرات باليمين والمئون والالاف باليسار اه

Hadhrat Yaseerah (Radhiyallaho anha) one of the Muhajir women, related that Rasulullah (Sallallaho alaihe wasallam) had said, "Make it a point to hymn (تسبیح) and (تهلیل) and to sanctify Allah through reciting the words (سُبْحَانَ الْمَلِكِ الْقُدُّوسِ) or (سُبُّوحٌ قُدُّوسٌ رَبُّ الْمَلٰئِكَةِ وَالرُّوحِ) and counting on your fingers, because the fingers will also be questioned, on the Day of Judgement, about the deeds performed by them and will speak out what they did. You should not neglect doing zikr of Allah, otherwise you would get deprived of His Mercy.

Note:

On the Day of Judgement, the body of a person, nay, his hands, feet, and every limb will be questioned about the good and bad actions performed by them, as stated in the Holy Qur'an at so many places. At one place, it is stated

يَوْمَ تَشْهَدُ عَلَيْهِمْ اَلْسِنَتُهُمْ وَاَيْدِيْهِمْ (الاية نور ع ٣)

The day when their tongues, hands and feet will stand witness against them about the sins they committed.

At another place, it is said:

وَيَوْمَ يُحْشَرُ اَعْدَآءُ اللّٰهِ اِلَى النَّارِ (الايات حم سجدة ع ٣)

At this place, the subject matter is decribed in several aayaat, which are translated as follows:

"On that Day (Day of Judgement), the enemies of Allah will be driven towards Hell. Then they will be checked at one place, till they have all reached near the Hell. At that time, their ears, eyes, skin, etc, will bear witness against them, (and will tell the sins committed through these by each person). At this, those people will (in utter surprise) say to them, "Why do you give witness against us?" (it was for you that, in the worldly life, we indulged in sins? These organs will reply, "Allah has given us speech, as He gave speech to all the things. It is He Who created you the first time, and unto Him you have returned."

There are many ahaadith that describe this sort of testimony. In one hadith, it is stated, "On the Day of Resurrection, the non-believer in spite of knowing his own sins will deny that he had ever committed them. He will be told that his neighbours stand witness against him. He will reply that the neighbours tell lies out of enmity against him. He will be told that his own kith and kin testify against him, but he will say that they are also false. Then his own limbs will be made to give evidence against him. According to one hadith, the thigh will be the first to testify the evil deeds committed by it.

It is stated in one hadith, "The last one to cross the Siraat Bridge will pass stumbling to this side and that side, as a child does when his father gives him a beating. The angels will ask him whether he would confess his sins if he were helped to cross it with ease. He will promise that he will tell the real truth, and he will swear by Allah that he will not hide any fact. The angels will make him stand erect and pass the Siraat Bridge. When he has crossed over, he will be asked by the angels to give his statement. Thinking that, if he confesses, he may be sent back to Hell, he will flatly deny having committed any bad deed. The angels will tell him that they can produce witnesses against him. He will look around, and as there will be nobody, he will think that since everybody has now reached his destination, no witness can be available against him, and therefore, he will agree to face witnesses. His own limbs will be asked to tell the truth, and when they start speaking he will be left with no alternative but to make a confession. Then he will say, "There are many serious sins that are still to be told." Almighty Allah will then say that he has been granted forgiveness.

It is thus a matter of necessity for us that we should make our limbs do as many good acts as possible. So that these may as well give witness in our favour. It is for this reason that Rasulullah (Sallallaho alaihe wasallam) had ordered (his followers) to count zikr on the fingers. For the same reason, it is ordered in another hadith that we should go to the mosque very frequently, so that the foot-prints will bear witness in our favour, and reward is granted for these.

How fortunate are the people against whom there is nobody to stand witness, either because no sins are committed or because these were washed off through toubah, etc, and who (on the other hand) have hundreds and thousands of witnesses to testify their good deeds and virtues. The easy way to become one of such people is: Firstly, if a sin happens to be committed, it should be got wiped out at once by means of toubah (because in this way the sin becomes extinct, as stated in Hadith No 33 of Section II, Chapter II) and secondly, the virtues should be accumulated in the account of deeds and there should be witnesses to testify to them, the limbs used for good deeds will all stand witness in one's favour.

Counting (of zikr) on the fingers by Rasulullah (Sallallaho alaihe wasallam) himself is mentioned in various words in several ahaadith. Hadhrat Abdullah bin Amr (Radhiyallaho anho) related that the Holy Prophet (Sallallaho alaihe wasallam) used to hymn Allah's glory with counting on his fingers.

In the hadith under discussion, there is warning against neglecting zikr of Allah, which deprives one of His Mercy. It is thereby learnt that the people who neglect zikr are ignored in respect of the Mercy of Almighty Allah. It is said in the Holy Qur'an, "You remember Me, then I will remember you (with My Mercy)." Almighty Allah has thus conditioned His granting of favours on doing His zikr. The Holy Qur'an says:

وَمَنْ يَّعْشُ عَنْ ذِكْرِ الرَّحْمٰنِ نُقَيِّضْ لَهُ شَيْطٰنًا فَهُوَ لَهُ قَرِيْنٌ وَاِنَّهُمْ لَيَصُدُّوْنَهُمْ
عَنِ السَّبِيْلِ وَيَحْسَبُوْنَ اَنَّهُمْ مُّهْتَدُوْنَ (زخرف ع ٤)

"And a person who intentionally closes his eyes against Allah's zikr (which may be recitation of the Qur'an or any other zikr), We appoint a devil on him, who remains with him all the time and who (with other such devils) keeps on misleading all such people (as have become blind to Allah's zikr), and yet they deem they are rightly guided."

It is stated in one hadith that a devil is appointed to remain with every person. In the case of a non-believer, he takes part in everything he does, he is with him even when he eats, drinks and sleeps. In the case of a believer he remains at some distance, but is always on the lookout for a chance to attack him unawares when he is not doing zikr of Allah. Allah says at another place in the Holy Qur'an:

يٰٓاَيُّهَا الَّذِيْنَ اٰمَنُوْا لَاتُلْهِكُمْ اَمْوَالُكُمْ وَلَآاَوْلَادُكُمْ عَنْ ذِكْرِ اللهِ (الى اخر السورة)
(منٰفقون ع٢)

"O, you who believe! Let not your wealth or your children (and other similar things) distract you from remembrance of Allah. Those who do so are the losers. And spend of that wherewith We have provided you, before death overtakes one of you and then he says, My Lord: if only Thou wouldst give me respite for a little while, then I would give alms and be amongst Thy good bondsmen, But Almighty Allah reprieves no soul when its time has come and Allah is aware of all that you do."

There are some people who do not neglect remembrance of Allah at any time. Hadhrat Shibli (Rahmatullah alaih) writes, "I happened to see a lunatic on whom some boys were throwing stones. I reprimanded the boys, who said, "This man claims that he sees Allah." I went near him and found that he was murmuring something. On listening to him attentively, I heared him saying, "You have done so well to have set these boys after me." I said to him, "These boys accuse you of something." "What do they say?" enquired he. I said, "They say that you claim to see Allah." He yelled a shriek and said, "O Shibli, I swear by Him, who has made me mad in His Love and Who keeps me wandering restlessly sometimes near Him and at times away from Him, if I were to lose sight of Him even for a while, my heart would burst into pieces on account of the pangs of separation." He said this, and ran away reciting the following couplet:

خَيَالُكَ فِىْ عَيْنِىْ وَذِكْرُكَ فِىْ فَمِىْ وَمَثْوَاكَ فِىْ قَلْبِىْ فَاَيْنَ تَغِيْبُ

Your appearance is constantly before my eyes, your remembrance is always on my tongue, your abode is in my heart, then where can you hide from me.

When Junaid Baghdadi (Rahmatullah alaih) was about to die someone advised him to recite the kalimah. He said, "I have never forgotten it any time; (you should remind it to someone who may have neglected it). When Hadhrat Mumshaad Dinwari (Rahmatullah alaih) was about to die some one prayed to Allah for the grant of such and such blessings to him in Paradise. He smiled, and said, "For the last thirty years, the Paradise with all its blessings has been appearing before me, but I have not even once diverted my attention from Almighty Allah towards it.''

When somebody reminded Hadhrat Royam (Rahmatullah alaih) at the time of his death, to recite the kalimah, he said, ''I have no acquaintance with anyone except Almighty Allah.'' When Hadhrat Ahmad bin Khidhrwayh was about to die, somebody asked him something. With tears in his eyes he said, ''For the last ninety five years, I have been knocking at a door which is now about to open. I am not aware whether it will mean good or bad fortune for me; I am too absorbed to talk to anybody at this time.''

Hadith No. 19

(١٩) وَعَنْ جُوَيْرِيَّةَ رَضِىَ اللّٰهُ عَنْهَا اَنَّ النَّبِىَّ ﷺ خرج مِنْ عِنْدِهَا بُكْرَةً حِيْنَ صَلَّى الصُّبْحَ وَهِىَ فِيْ مَسْجِدِهَا ثُمَّ رَجَعَ بَعْدَ اَنْ اَضْحٰى وَهِىَ جَالِسَةٌ قَالَ مَازِلْتِ عَلَى الْحَالِ الَّتِىْ فَارَقْتُكِ عَلَيْهَا قَالَتْ نعم قَالَ النَّبِىُ ﷺ لَقَدْ قُلْتُ بَعْدَكِ اَرْبَعَ كَلِمَاتٍ ثَلٰثَ مَرَّاتٍ لَوْوُزِنَتْ بِمَاقُلْتِ مُنْذُ الْيَوْمِ لَوَزَنَتْهُنَّ سُبْحَانَ اللّٰهِ وَبِحَمْدِهِ عَدَدَ خَلْقِهِ وَرِضَا نَفْسِهِ وَزِنَةَ عَرْشِهِ وَمِدَادَ كَلِمَاتِهِ رواه مسلم كذا فى المشكوٰة قال القارى وكذا اصحاب السنن الاربعة وفى الباب عَنْ صَفِيَّةَ قَالَتْ دَخَلَ عَلَىَّ رَسُوْلُ اللّٰهِ صَلَّى اللّٰهُ عَلَيْهِ وَسَلَّمَ وَبَيْنَ يَدَىَّ اربعة الاف نواة اسبح بهن الحديث اخرجه الحاكم وقال الذهبى صحيح وَعَنْ سَعْدِ بْنِ اَبِىْ وَقَّاصٍ رَضِىَ اللّٰهُ عَنْهُ اَنَّهُ دَخَلَ مَعَ النَّبِىِّ صَلَّى اللّٰهُ عَلَيْهِ وَسَلَّمَ عَلٰى اِمْرَأَةٍ وَبَيْنَ يَدَيْهَا نوىً اَوْ حَصًى تُسَبِّحُ بِهِ فَقَالَ اَلَااُخْبِرُكِ بِمَا هُوَ اَيْسَرُ عَلَيْكِ مِنْ هٰذَا اَوْ اَفْضَلُ سُبْحَانَ اللّٰهِ عَدَدَ مَاخَلَقَ فِى السَّمَاءِ وَسُبْحَانَ اللّٰهِ عَدَدَ مَاخَلَقَ فِى الْاَرْضِ وَسُبْحَانَ اللّٰهِ عَدَدَ مَابَيْنَ ذٰلِكَ وَسُبْحَانَ اللّٰهِ عَدَدَ مَاهُوَ خَالِقٌ وَاللّٰهُ اَكْبَرُ مِثْلَ ذٰلِكَ وَالْحَمْدُ لِلّٰهِ مِثْلَ ذٰلِكَ وَلَآاِلٰهَ اِلَّا اللّٰهُ مِثْلَ ذٰلِكَ وَلَاحَوْلَ وَلَاقُوَّةَ اِلَّا بِاللّٰهِ مِثْلَ ذَالِكَ رواه ابو داود والترمذى وقال الترمذى حديث غريب كذا فى المشكوٰة قال القارى وفى نسخة حسن غريب ه وفى المنهل اخرجه ايضا النسائى وابن ماجة وابن حبان والحاكم والترمذى وقال حسن غريب من هٰذا الوجه ه قلت وصححه الذهبى

Hadhrat Juwairiah (Radhiyallaho anha) related, ''When Rasulullah (Sallallaho alaihe wasallam) left my house for the morning prayer, I was sitting on the prayer-mat (busy in Allah's zikr). When he came back after Chaasht prayer (just before midday), I was still sitting in the same position. He asked me whether I had continued in that position right from the time he left in the morning. I replied in the affirmative. He then said, "After I left you, I recited four kalimahs three times which, if compared to all that you have recited since the morning, will be found to outweigh it. These kalimahs are:

سُبْحَانَ اللهِ وَبِحَمْدِهِ عَدَدَ خَلْقِهِ وَرِضَا نَفْسِهِ وَزِنَةَ عَرْشِهِ وَمِدَادَ كَلِمَاتِهِ

Glory and praise be to Allah equal in number to his creation, according to His will and pleasure, equal in weight to His Arsh and equal in dimensions to His World)."

Hadhrat Sa'ad (Radhiyallaho anho) accompanied Rasulullah (Sallallaho alaihe wasallam) to the house of a Sahabi woman, who had before her some datestones and pebbles, on which she was counting her zikr. Rasulullah (Sallallaho alaihe wasallam) said to her, "May I tell you something which may be easier (or better) than this?

سُبْحَانَ اللهِ عَدَدَ مَاخَلَقَ ....

I glorify Allah equal to the number of His creation in the Heaven, I glorify Allah equal to the number of His creation on the earth, and I glorify Allah equal to the number of His creation in between the two (i.e. between the Heaven and the Earth), and I glorify Allah equal to the number of things He is to create. Likewise I hymn (اَللهُ اَكْبَرُ) (اَلْحَمْدُ لِلّٰهِ) and (لَآاِلٰهَ اِلَّا اللهُ) each the same total number of times."

Mulla Ali Qari has written that the zikr in the words mentioned above is more rewarding because one concentrates on Allah's attributes mentioned therein, and then meditates over them. It is evident that the more one meditates and contemplates over the zikr one does, the better it is. For this very reason, the recitation of even a few aayaat of the Qur'an, with proper contemplation on what is read, is far better than considerably more recitation done without proper understanding.

Some Ulama consider that this zikr is superior because there is in it an expression of one's utter helplessness in respect of counting the praises and favours of Almighty Allah, which is the best form of submission to Him. It is for this reason that some Sufis say that we commit countless sins, but we recite the name of Allah a limited number of times by counting. This does not mean that we should not count zikr; if it were so, then counting in particular cases would not have been stressed in the ahaadith. In many of the ahaadith, special rewards are promised for doing a particular zikr a specific number of times. It really means that one should not feel contented after completing the specified number, and that after completing the zikr specified for particular timings of the day, one should still remain engaged in other various forms of zikr in one's vacant periods, because zikr is such a precious wealth that it should not be confined to any number or any other limitation.

These ahaadith also indicate the propriety of using a tasbeeh (i.e. a string of beads) for counting the zikr. Some people think this to be an innovation, but this is not correct, because Rasulullah (Sallallaho alaihe wasallam) saw others counting zikr on pebbles and date-seeds, but did not object to it, which proves its justification. Stringing or not stringing these together does not make any difference. Therefore all scholars and jurists have been using it. Maulana Abdul Hay wrote a book named Nuzhatul Fikr on this subject. According to Mullah Ali Qari (Rahmatullah alaih) also the above mentioned hadith provides a complete argument in favour of the commonly used string of beads, because Rasulullah (Sallallaho alaihe wasallam) saw his companions counting on date-seeds and pebbles, and did not disapprove it, which proves its justification, and stringing or not stringing the beads does not make any difference. Therefore, the statement of the people who call this practice an innovation is not reliable. In the terminology of the Sufis, the string of beads is called a scourge for Satan. Someone, once saw a tasbeeh (rosary) in the hands of Hadhrat Junaid Baghdadi (Rahmatullah alaih) at a time when he was at the height of his spiritual glory, and questioned him about it. He replied that he could not give up a thing by means of which he had attained nearness to Allah. It is narrated about many Sahabas (Radhiyallaho anhum) that they kept date-seeds and pebbles for counting zikr. It is related about a Sahabi named Abu Safiyyah (Radhiyallaho anho) that he used to count zikr on small pebbles or stones. It is related about Hadhrat Sa'ad bin Abi Waqqaas (Radhiyallaho anho) that he used (both) datestones as well as pebbles. Hadhrat Abu Sa'eed (Radhiyallaho anho) is also reported to have used pebbles for counting zikr. It is given in Mirqaat that Hadhrat Abu Hurairah (Radhiyallaho anho) used to count on a string with knots on it. It is mentioned in Sunan Abi Dawood (a book of ahaadith) that Hadhrat Abu Hurairah (Radhiyallaho anho) used to keep a bag full of date-stones and pebbles for counting zikr on these, and that when the bag would get empty, his maid-servant would put these back into the bag and place it near him again. The bag would get empty because the stones after counting were placed outside the bag, till all the stones would get finished, when the maid-servant would put the same stones again into the bag and place it near him. It is also narrated about Hadhrat Abu Darda (Radhiyallaho anho) that he had a bag containing Ajwah date-seeds, on which he would commence zikr after the morning prayer and would continue till all the seeds were finished from the bag.

Hadhrat Abu Safiyyah (Radhiyallaho anho) a slave of Rasulullah (Sallallaho alaihe wasallam) used to have a piece of skin with pebbles spread on it before him, and he would recite zikr on these from morning to mid-day, when this skin with pebbles used to be removed from there, then he would attend to his other needs. After the noon-prayer, the skin was again spread before him, and he would continue zikr on the pebbles till the evening.

The grandson of Hadhrat Abu Hurairah (Radhiyallaho anho) narrated that his grandfather used to have a string with two thousand knots in it, and that he would not go to bed until he had completed doing zikr on these. The daughter of Hadhrat Imam Husain (Radhiyallaho anho) narrated about Hadhrat Fatimah (Radhiyallaho anha) that she had a thread with knots, on which she used to count her zikr.

In the terminology of the Sufis, the tasbeeh is also known as muzakkirah (that which reminds), because when it is held in one's hand there is a sort of urge for doing zikr, and therefore it is termed as such. In this connection a hadith is also narrated through Hadhrat Ali (Radhiyallaho anho) that Rasulullah (Sallallaho alaihe wasallam) had said, "What a good muzakkirah (reminder) is the tasbeeh."

In this connection, a hadith is narrated by Maulana Abdul Hay (Rahmatullah alaih) "Every Sheikh teacher in my line right upto a pupil of Hadhrat Junaid Baghdadi had bestowed a tasbeeh on his pupil and recommended him to do zikr on it. The pupil of Hadhrat Junaid (Rahmatullah alaih) had stated 'On seeing a tasbeeh in the hand of my Sheikh, I enquired if he still needed the tasbeeh after having reached such a spiritual height. He replied that he had seen this tasbeeh in the hand of his Sheikh, Sirri Saqati (Rahmatullah alaih), and had put the same question to him, and Hadhrat Sirri Saqati (Rahmatullah alaih), had also replied that on seeing a tasbeeh in the hand of his Sheikh, Hadhrat Ma'roof Karkhi (Rahmatullah alaih), he had put the same question to his Sheikh Hadhrat Bishr Haafi, (Rahmatullah alaih) who said that he had also put the question to his Sheikh Umar Makki, (Rahmatullah alaih) who had also stated that he had asked the same question from his Sheikh Hadhrat Hasan Basri (Rahmatullah alaih) as to why he kept a tasbeeh in his hand in spite of his having attained such spritual heights, to which the Sheikh had replied, ''It had proved very useful in my initial stages of Tasawwuf and I had made progress by virtue of it; I do not want to leave it in the last stage, when I want to use my heart, tongue, hands, and everything in doing zikr of Almighty Allah.'' The Muhaddith however have questioned its use.

Hadith No. 20

(٢٠) عَنْ اِبْنِ اَعْبُدٍ قَالَ قَالَ عَلِیٌّ رَضِیَ اللّٰہُ اَلَا اُحَدِّثُكَ عَنِّیْ وَعَنْ فَاطِمَةَ بِنْتِ رَسُوْلِ اللّٰہِ ﷺ وَكَانَتْ مِنْ اَحَبِّ اَهْلِهٖ قُلْتُ بَلٰی قَالَ اِنَّهَا جَرَتْ بالرَّحٰی حَتّٰی اَثَّرَ فِیْ یَدَیْهَا وَاسْتَقَتْ بِالْقِرْبَةِ حَتّٰی اَثَّرَ فِیْ نَحْرِهَا وَكَنَسَتِ الْبَیْتَ حَتّٰی اغْبَرَّتْ ثِیَابُهَا فَاَتَی النَّبِیَّ ﷺ خَدَمٌ فَقُلْتُ لَوْ اَتَیْتِ اَبَاكِ فَسَأَلْتِهٖ خَادِمًا فَاَتَتْهُ فَوَجَدَتْ عِنْدَهٗ حُدَّاثًا فَرَجَعَتْ فَاَتَاهَا مِنَ الْغَدِ فَقَالَ مَاكَانَ حَاجَتُكِ فَسَكَتَتْ فَقُلْتُ اَنَا اُحَدِّثُكَ یَارَسُوْلَ اللّٰہِ جَرَتْ بِالرَّحٰی حَتّٰی اَثَّرَتْ فِیْ یَدِیْهَا وَحَمَلَتْ بِالْقِرْبَةِ حَتّٰی اَثَّرَتْ فِیْ نَحْرِهَا فَلَمَّا اَنْ جَاءَكَ الْخَدَمُ اَمَرْتُهَا اَنْ تَاتِیْكَ فَتَسْتَخْدِمَكَ خَادِمًا یَّقِیْهَا حَرَّمَا هِیَ فِیْهِ قَالَ اِتَّقِیْ اللّٰہَ یَافَاطِمَةُ وَ اَدِّیْ فَرِیْضَةَ رَبِّكِ وَاعْمَلِیْ عَمَلَ اَهْلِكِ فَاِذَا اَخَذْتِ مَضْجَعَكِ فَسَبِّحِیْ ثَلٰثًا وَّ ثَلٰثِیْنَ وَاحْمَدِیْ ثَلٰثًا وَّ ثَلٰثِیْنَ وَكَبِّرِیْ اَرْبَعًا وَّ ثَلٰثِیْنَ فَتِلْكَ مِائَةٌ فَهِیَ خَیْرٌ لَّكِ مِنْ خَادِمٍ

قَالَتْ رَضِيْتُ عَنِ اللهِ وَعَنْ رَّسُوْلِهِ اخرجه ابو داود وَفِيْ الْبَابِ عَنِ الْفَضْلِ بْنِ الْحَسَنِ الضَّمْرِيِّ اَنَّ اُمَّ الْحَاكِمِ اَوْ ضَبَاعَةَ ابْنَتَيِ الزُّبَيْرِ بْنِ عَبْدِ الْمُطَّلِبِ حَدَّثَتْهُ عَنْ اِحْدٰهُمَا اَنَّهَا قَالَتْ اَصَابَ رَسُوْلُ اللهِ ﷺ سَبْيًا فَذَهَبْتُ اَنَا وَ اُخْتِيْ وَفَاطِمَةُ بِنْتُ رَسُوْلِ اللهِ ﷺ فَشَكَوْنَا اِلَيْهِ مَانَحْنُ فِيْهِ وَسَأَلْنَاهُ اَنْ يَّأْمُرَ لَنَا بِشَيْءٍ مِّنَ السَّبِيِّ فَقَالَ رَسُوْلُ اللهِ ﷺ سَبَقَكُنَّ يَتَامٰى بَدْرٍ وَلٰكِنْ سَأَدُلُّكُنَّ عَلٰى مَاهُوَ خَيْرٌ لَّكُنَّ مِنْ ذٰلِكَ تُكَبِّرْنَ اللهَ عَلٰى اَثَرِ كُلِّ صَلٰوةٍ ثَلٰثًا وَّ ثَلٰثِيْنَ تَكْبِيْرَةً وَثَلٰثًا وَّثَلٰثِيْنَ تَسْبِيْحَةً وَ ثَلٰثًا وَّ ثَلٰثِيْنَ تَحْمِيْدَةً وَلَآاِلٰهَ اِلَّا اللهُ وَحْدَهُ لَاشَرِيْكَ لَهُ لَهُ الْمُلْكُ وَلَهُ الْحَمْدُ وَهُوَ عَلٰى كُلِّ شَيْءٍ قَدِيْرٌ رواه ابو داود وفى الجامع الصغير برواية ابن منده عن جليس كان يامر نسائه اذا ارادت احداهن ان تنام ان تحمد الحديث ورقم له بالضعف

Hadhrat Ali (Radhiyallaho anho) said to one of his disciples, "May I tell you a story relating to me and my wife, Fatimah (Radhiyallaho anha), the daughter of Rasulullah (Sallallaho alaihe wasallam) and the most beloved one in his family?" "Do tell us," replied the disciple. Hadhrat Ali said, "She used to grind the corn herself, as a result of which there were marks of calluses on her hands. She herself used to fetch the water in a skinbag, the string of which left an impression on her chest. She swept the house herself, so that her clothes remained dirty. Once Rasulullah (Sallallaho alaihe wasallam) received a few slaves, both men and women, and I persuaded Fatimah (Radhiyallaho anha) to go to her father and ask for a servant who could help her in her work. She went but, on seeing a big crowd with Rasulullah (Sallallaho alaihe wasallam), she came back. The next day, Rasulullah (Sallallaho alaihe wasallam) came to our house and asked her why she had gone to him the previous day. She kept silent (out of modesty), so I said, "O Rasulullah! (Sallallaho alaihe wasallam) her hands have become worn out on account of working the grindstone, the skinbag used by her for fetching water has left an impression on her chest, and her clothes remain dirty because of sweeping the house herself. Therefore, I had sent her to ask for a slave so that she would get some relief in her work. Rasulullah (Sallallaho alaihe wasallam) said, "O Fatimah! keep fearing Almighty Allah, discharge your duties to Him, do all the work in the house yourself and at the time of going to bed recite (سُبْحَانَ اللهِ) 33 times, (اَلْحَمْدُ لِلّٰهِ) 33 times and (اَللهُ اَكْبَرُ) 34 times, because it is better for you than a servant." She said, "I submit to the Will of Allah and the advice of His Prophet (Sallallaho alaihe wasallam)."

According to another hadith, a similar story is related by two cousins of Rasulullah (Sallallaho alaihe wasallam) who, along with his daughter, Fatimah (Radhiyallaho anha), went to him, and told him of their hardships and asked for a servant, Rasulullah (Sallallaho alaihe wasallam) replied to them, "As for giving you a servant, the orphans of the battle of Badr deserve preference over you; but I can tell you something that is better than a servant. After every Salaat, recite the three Kalimahs (i.e. tasbeeh, tahmeed and takbeer) thirty-three times each and then recite once

لَآاِلٰهَ اِلَّا اللهُ وَحْدَهُ لَاشَرِيْكَ لَهُ لَهُ الْمُلْكُ وَلَهُ الْحَمْدُ وَهُوَ عَلٰى كُلِّ شَيْءٍ قَدِيْرٌ

This will be more useful than a servant."

Rasulullah (Sallallaho alaihe wasallam) recommended this zikr especially to members of his household and his relatives. According to one hadith, he would advise his wives to recite (سُبْحَانَ الله) , (اَلْحَمْدُ لِله) and (اَللهُ اَكْبَرُ) 33 times each at the time of going to bed.

In the hadith under consideration, he recommended this zikr to face worldly labour and hardship. The reason is apparent that the worldly labour and hardship is not a matter of serious consequence for a Muslim; he is always anxious to provide for the comforts and joys in the life after death. It was therefore that Rasulullah (Sallallaho alaihe wasallam) diverted the attention of his dear ones from the hardships and worries of this life to making provision for the comforts in the Hereafter.

That this particular zikr is most rewarding in the Hereafter has been described in the hadith given in this chapter. The other reason why Rasulullah (Sallallaho alaihe wasallam) recommended these Kalimahs for zikr is that, in addition to spiritual and religious gains, these Kalimahs bring many worldly benefits as well. There are many things in the Book of Allah and in the sayings of Rasulullah (Sallallaho alaihe wasallam) which result not only in spiritual gains but also in worldly benefits. Thus, it is said in one hadith that during the time of Dajjaal the food of the believers will be the same as of the angels, i.e. reciting (سُبْحَانَ الله) etc., Almighty Allah will satisfy his hunger. This hadith proves that in this life also one can live upon the zikr of Allah, and without eating and drinking anything. When such proficiency can be acquired by the common believers at the time of Dajjaal, it is no wonder that the distinguished ones attain this blessing even at this time. This suggests that instances of some saints having lived without (or on insufficient) food for days together should not be disbelieved or refuted.

It is stated in one hadith that, when fire breaks out anywhere (اَللهُ اَكْبَرُ) should be recited excessively, because it is helpful in extinguishing the fire. It is written in the book His-nul Haseen that if somebody feels difficulty or weariness in doing some job and requires additional strength to overcome his shortcoming, he should recite (سُبْحَانَ الله) 33 times, (اَلْحَمْدُ لله) 33 times and (اَللهُ اَكْبَرُ) 34 times, before going to bed, or each of the three Kalimahs should be recited 33 times or any one of the three may be said 34 times.

Hafiz Ibn Taimiyah (Rahmatullah alaih) has deduced from the ahaadith, in which Rasulullah (Sallallaho alaihe wasallam) instead of giving a servant to Hadhrat Fatimah (Radhiyallaho anha) advised her to recite these Kalimahs, that one who does this zikr with constancy will not get tired while doing laborious jobs. Hafiz Ibn Hajar has stated that, even if he feels somewhat tired, it will not harm him in any way. Mulla Ali Qari stated that it had been well-tried that the recitation of this zikr before going to bed eliminates weariness and increases the strength.

Allamah Suyuti (Rahmatullah alaih) has written in his book Mirqaatus-Sa'ood that the fact that recitation of these Kalimahs is better than a servant is true in respect of the life in the Hereafter as well as in the worldly life; of course, the benefits that will accrue in the Hereafter as a result of this zikr cannot be compared to the meagre usefulness of a servant in this world, and also the strength acquired through doing this zikr enables one to accomplish more than is possible even with the help of a servant.

According to one hadith, Rasulullah (Sallallaho alaihe wasallam) has said, "There are two routines which if followed by a Muslim will enable him to enter Paradise. Both the routines are very easy, but there are very few people who act according to them. One is to recite these three Kalimahs ten times each after every salaat. In this way, one glorifies Allah one hundred and fifty times, and thereby earns one thousand and five hundred virtues every day. The second routine is to recite (سُبْحَانَ اللهِ) and (اَلْحَمْدُ لِلّٰهِ) 33 times each, and (اَللهُ اَكْبَرُ) 34 times before going to bed every day. In this way, one does one hundred good deeds, but actually earns one thousand virtues." Someone asked the reason why only a few people are able to act upon this? Rasulullah (Sallallaho alaihe wasallam) said, "At the time of salaat, the devil comes and reminds him of something, which actuates him to get up and go away, and at night the devil reminds him of other necessities, which makes him neglect to recite these Kalimahs."

In these ahaadith, there is one thing specially noteworthy: that Hadhrat Fatimah (Radhiyallaho anha) who would be the leader of women in Paradise, and the daughter of the leader of mankind in both the worlds, used to grind corn flour herself (as a result of which her hands developed calluses on them, would herself fetch the water in the skin waterbag, which left impressions on her chest and would sweep the house herself, so that her clothes remained dirty, and did all other household duties, like cooking meals and preparing bread, etc. Do our womenfolk perform that much labour, or even half of it, with their own hands? It is certainly not so, and our lives have little resemblance with the lives of those whom we profess to be our leaders. It ought to have been that we who claim to be the servants should put in more labour than our masters, but it is a matter of great disappointment that the actual position is quite the reverse.

فَاِلَى اللهِ الْمُشْتَكٰى وَاللهُ الْمُسْتَعَانُ

EPILOGUE

Virtues of Salaatut Tasbeeh and Method of Performing

Now I will describe something that is really very grand, and thereby conclude this part of the book. The Kalimahs mentioned above are very important and very useful from the wordly as well as spiritual points of view, as mentioned in the ahaadith given above. As these Kalimahs are very important and rewarding. Rasulullah (Sallallaho alaihe wasallam) prescribed a special prayer, which is known as Salaatut Tasbeeh (i.e. salaat of these Kalimahs). It is called Salaatut Tasbeeh, because these Kalimahs are recited 300 times during this salaat. Rasulullah (Sallallaho alaihe wasallam) greatly stressed this and persuaded the believers to offer this salaat, as is evident from the following ahaadith:

(١) عَنْ اِبْنِ عَبَّاسٍ رَضِىَ اللّٰهُ عَنْهُ اَنَّ النَّبِىَّ ﷺ قَالَ لِلْعَبَّاسِ بْنِ عَبْدِ الْمُطَّلِبِ
يَاعَبَّاسُ يَاعَمَّاهُ اَلَا اُعْطِيْكَ اَلَا اَمْنَحُكَ اَلَا اُخْبِرُكَ اَلَاافْعَلُ بِكَ عَشْرَ خِصَالٍ
اِذَا اَنْتَ فَعَلْتَ ذٰلِكَ غَفَرَ اللّٰهُ لَكَ ذَنْبَكَ اَوَّلَهُ وَاٰخِرَهُ قَدِيْمَهُ وَحَدِيْثَهُ خَطَأَهُ
وَعَمَدَهُ صَغِيْرَهُ وَكَبِيْرَهُ سِرَّهُ وَعَلَانِيَتَهُ اَنْ تُصَلِّىَ اَرْبَعَ رَكَعَاتٍ تَقْرَأُ فِيْ كُلِّ
رَكْعَةٍ فَاتِحَةَ الْكِتَابِ وَسُوْرَةً فَاِذَا فَرَغْتَ مِنَ الْقِرَاءَةِ فِيْ اَوَّلِ رَكْعَةٍ وَاَنْتَ قَائِمٌ
قُلْتَ سُبْحَانَ اللّٰهِ وَالْحَمْدُ لِلّٰهِ وَلَآاِلٰهَ اِلَّا اللّٰهُ وَاللّٰهُ اَكْبَرُ خَمْسَ عَشَرَةَ ثُمَّ تَرْكَعُ
فَتَقُوْلُهَا وَاَنْتَ رَاكِعٌ عَشْرًا ثُمَّ تَرْفَعُ رَأْسَكَ مِنَ الرُّكُوْعِ فَتَقُوْلُهَا عَشْرًا ثُمَّ
تَهْوِىْ سَاجِدًا فَتَقُوْلُهَا وَاَنْتَ سَاجِدٌ عَشْرًا ثُمَّ تَرْفَعُ رَأْسَكَ مِنَ السُّجُوْدِ
فَتَقُوْلُهَا عَشْرًا ثُمَّ تَسْجُدُ فَتَقُوْلُهَا عَشْرًا ثُمَّ تَرْفَعُ رَأْسَكَ فَتَقُوْلُهَا عَشْرًا
فَذٰلِكَ خَمْسٌ وَّسَبْعُوْنَ فِيْ كُلِّ رَكْعَةٍ تَفْعَلُ ذَالِكَ فِيْ اَرْبَعِ رَكَعَاتٍ اِنِ
اسْتَطَعْتَ اَنْ تُصَلِّيَهَا فِىْ كُلِّ يَوْمٍ مَرَّةً فَافْعَلْ فَاِنْ لَّمْ تَفْعَلْ فَفِىْ كُلِّ جُمُعَةٍ مَرَّةً
فَاِنْ لَّمْ تَفْعَلْ فَفِىْ كُلِّ شَهْرٍ مَرَّةً فَاِنْ لَّمْ تَفْعَلْ فَفِىْ كُلِّ سَنَةٍ مَرَّةً فَاِنْ لَّمْ تَفْعَلْ
فَفِىْ عُمُرِكَ مَرَّةً رواه ابو داود ، وابن ماجة والبيهقى فى الدعوات الكبير وروى الترمذى عن ابى رافع
نحوه كذا فى المشكوٰة قلت واخرجه الحاكم وقال هذا حديث وصله موسى بن عبد العزيز عن الحاكم بن

ابان وقد اخرجه ابوبكر محمد بن اسحق وابو داود وعبد الرحمن احمد بن شعيب فى الصحيح ثم قال بعد ماذكر توثيق رواتة واما ارسال ابراهيم بن الحكم عن ابيه فلايوهن وصل الحديث فان الزيادة من الثقة اولى من الارسال على ان امام عصره فى الحديث اسحٰق بن ابراهيم الحنظلى قد اقام هٰذا الاسناد عن ابراهيم بن الحكم ووصله اه قال السيوطى فى اللالى هذا اسناد حسن وما قال الحاكم اخرجه النسائى فى كتابه الصحيح لم نره فى شيء من نسخ السنن لاالصغرىٰ ولاالكبرىٰ

(1) Once Rasulullah (Sallallaho alaihe wasallam) said to his uncle, Hadhrat Abbaas, (Radhiyallaho anho), "O, Abbaas, my uncle! I want to make a special gift to you i.e. to tell you something special, so that if you act upon it Almighty Lord will forgive all your sins, whether old or new, intentional or unintentional, minor or major, open or secret. That action is to offer four rakaats of nafl salaat, and during each rakaat, after you have recited Surah Fatihah, and one more surah, then you should say:

سُبْحَانَ اللهِ وَ الْحَمْدُ لِلّٰهِ وَ لَآاِلٰهَ اِلَّا اللهُ وَ اللهُ اَكْبَرُ

15 times, while standing still, then repeat it 10 times when you are in ruku, 10 times when you rise from the ruku, 10 times in the first sajdah, 10 times when you rise from the first sajdah, 10 times in the second sajdah, and ten times when you sit up after the second sajdah. The total in each rakaat comes to 75 times. If possible, you should offer this salaat once everyday, and if you cannot do it daily, then offer it on every Friday, or once a month, or once a year or at least once in your lifetime."

(٢) وَعَنْ اَبِى الْجَوْزَاءِ عَنْ رَجُلٍ كَانَتْ لَهُ صُحْبَةٌ يَرَوْنَ اَنَّهُ عَبْدُ اللهِ بْنُ عَمْرٍو قَالَ قَالَ لِىَ النَّبِىُّ ﷺ اِئْتِنِى غَدًا اَحْبُوكَ وَاُثِيْبُكَ وَاُعْطِيْكَ حَتّٰى ظَنَنْتُ اَنَّهُ يُعْطِيْنِىْ عَطِيَّةً قَالَ اِذَا زَالَ النَّهَارُ فَقُمْ فَصَلِّ اَرْبَعَ رَكْعَاتٍ فَذَكَرَ نَحْوَهُ وَفِيْهِ وَقَالَ فَاِنَّكَ لَوْ كُنْتَ اَعْظَمَ اَهْلِ الْاَرْضِ ذَنْبًا غُفِرَلَكَ بِذٰلِكَ قَالَ قُلْتُ فَاِنْ لَمْ اَسْتَطِعْ اَنْ اُصَلِّيَهَا تِلْكَ السَّاعَةَ قَالَ صَلِّهَا مِنَ اللَّيْلِ وَالنَّهَارِ رواه ابو داود

(2) A Sahabi narrated, "Once Rasulullah (Sallallaho alaihe wasallam) said to me, 'Come to me tomorrow morning,

I will grant you something; I will give you a special gift.' I thought that I would be given some thing of material value. When I went to him he said to me 'Offer four rakaats of salaat after midday'. Then Rasulullah (Sallallaho alaihe wasallam) explained the method of offering this Salaat (as given in the last hadith). Rasulullah (Sallallaho alaihe wasallam) also told me that even if I were more sinful than all the other people of the world, my sins would be forgiven. I asked him what I should do if, for some reason, I am not able to offer this salaat at the given time. He told me to offer it whenever I could during day or night."

(٣) عَنْ نَافِعٍ عَنْ اِبْنِ عُمَرَ رَضِىَ اللّٰهُ عَنْهُ قَالَ وَجَّهَ رَسُوْلُ اللّٰهِ ﷺ جَعْفَرَ بْنَ اَبِىْ طَالِبٍ رَضِىَ اللّٰهُ عَنْهُ اِلٰى بِلَادِ الْحَبْشَةِ فَلَمَّا قَدِمَ اِعْتَنَقَهُ وَقَبَّلَهُ بَيْنَ عَيْنَيْهِ ثُمَّ قَالَ اَلَا اَهَبُ لَكَ اَلَا اُبَشِّرُكَ اَلَا اَمْنَحُكَ اَلَا اُتْحِفُكَ قَالَ نَعَمْ يَارَسُوْلَ اللّٰهِ قَالَ تُصَلِّىْ اَرْبَعَ رَكْعَاتٍ فذكر نحوه ، اخرجه الحاكم وقال اسناد صحيح لاغبار عليه وتعقبه الذهبي بان احمد بن داود كذبه الدار قطني كذا في المنهل وكذا قال غيره تبعا للحافظ لكن في النسخة التي بايدينا من المستدرك وقد صحت الرواية عن ابن عمران رسول الله صلى الله عليه وسلم علم ابن عمه جعفراً ثم ذكر الحديث بسنده وقال في اٰخره هذا اسناد صحيح لاغبار عليه وهكذا قال الذهبي في اول الحديث واٰخره ثم لايذهب عليه ان في هذا الحديث زيادة لاحول ولا قوة الا بالله العلي العظيم ايضا على الكلمات الاربع

(3) Rasulullah (Sallallaho alaihe wasallam) had sent his cousin, Hadhrat Ja'far, (Radhiyallaho anho) to Ethiopia. When he returned from there and reached Madina, Rasulullah (Sallallaho alaihe wasallam) embraced him, kissed him on his forehead, and said to him, "Shall I give you something, give you good tidings, give you a gift, grant you a present?" He replied, in the affirmative, and then Rasúllulah (Sallallaho alaihe wasallam) asked him to offer four rakaats in the manner explained already. In his hadith, the four kalimahs are also followed by

لَا حَوْلَ وَلَا قُوَّةَ اِلَّا بِاللّٰهِ الْعَلِيِّ الْعَظِيْمِ

(٤) وَعَنِ الْعَبَّاسِ بْنِ عَبْدِ الْمُطَّلِبِ رَضِىَ اللّٰهُ عَنْهُ قَالَ قَالَ رَسُوْلُ اللّٰهِ ﷺ اَلَا اَهَبُ لَكَ اَلَا اُعْطِيْكَ اَلَا اَمْنَحُكَ فَظَنَنْتُ اَنَّهُ يُعْطِيْنِيْ مِنَ الدُّنْيَا شَيْئًا لَمْ يُعْطِهِ

اَحَدًا مِّنْ قَبْلِىْ قَالَ اَرْبَعَ رَكْعَاتٍ فذكر الحديث وفي اٰخره غير انك اذا جلست للتشهد قلت ذلك عشر مرات قبل التشهد الحديث اخرجه الدارقطني في الافراد وابو نعيم في القربان وابن شاهين في الترغيب كذا في اتحاف السادة شرح الاحياء

(4) Hadhrat Abbaas (Radhiyallaho anho) narrated, "Rasulullah (Sallallaho alaihe wasallam) said to me 'Should I grant you a present, give you a gift, bestow something on you?' I thought that he wanted to give me some material thing such as had not been given to anybody else. Then he taught me the method of offering four rakaats, as explained above. He had also told me that when I sit for tahiyyaat I should repeat the kalimahs before reciting at-tahiyyaatu . . ."

(٥) قال الترمذي وقد روى ابن المبارك وغيره واحد من اهل العلم صلٰوة التسبيح وذكروا الفضل فيه حَدَّثَنَا اَحْمَدُ بْنُ عَبْدَةَ حَدَّثَنَا اَبُوْ وَهْبٍ سَاَلْتُ عَبْدَ اللهِ بْنِ الْمُبَارَكِ عَنِ الصَّلٰوةِ الَّتِىْ يُسَبَّحُ فِيْهَا قَالَ يُكَبِّرُ ثُمَّ يَقُوْلُ سُبْحَانَكَ اللّٰهُمَّ وَبِحَمْدِكَ وَتَبَارَكَ اسْمُكَ وَتَعَالٰى جَدُّكَ وَلَآ اِلٰهَ غَيْرُكَ ثُمَّ يَقُوْلُ خَمْسَ عَشَرَةَ مَرَّةً سُبْحَانَ اللهِ وَالْحَمْدُ لِلّٰهِ وَلَآاِلٰهَ اِلَّا اللهُ وَاللهُ اَكْبَرُ ثُمَّ يَتَعَوَّذُ وَيَقْرَأُ بِسْمِ اللهِ الرَّحْمٰنِ الرَّحِيْمِ ، وَفَاتِحَةَ الْكِتَابِ وَسُوْرَةً ثُمَّ يَقُوْلُ عَشَرَ مَرَّاتٍ سُبْحَانَ اللهِ وَالْحَمْدُ لِلّٰهِ وَلَآاِلٰهَ اِلَّا اللهُ وَاللهُ اَكْبَرُ ثُمَّ يَرْكَعُ فَيَقُوْلُهَا عَشْرًا ثُمَّ يَرْفَعُ رَأْسَهُ فَيَقُوْلُهَا عَشْرًا ثُمَّ يَسْجُدُ فَيَقُوْلُهَا عَشْرًا ثُمَّ يَرْفَعُ رَأْسَهُ فَيَقُوْلُهَا عَشْرًا ثُمَّ يَسْجُدُ الثَّانِيَةَ فَيَقُوْلُهَا عَشْرًا يُصَلِّىْ اَرْبَعَ رَكَعَاتٍ عَلٰى هٰذَا فَذَالِكَ خَمْسٌ وَّسَبْعُوْنَ تَسْبِيْحَةً فِيْ كُلِّ رَكْعَةٍ ثم قال قال ابو وهب اخبرني عبدالعزيز عن عبدالله انه قال يبدأ في الركوع سبحان ربي العظيم وفي السجدة بسبحان ربي الأعلى ثلاثا ثم يسبح التسبيحات قال عبد العزيز قلت لعبد الله بن المبارك ان سها فيها يسبح في سجدتي السهو عشرا عشرا قال لا انما هي ثلاث مائة تسبيحة اهـ مختصرا قلت وهكذا رواه الحاكم وقال رواته عن ابن المبارك كلهم ثقات اثبات ولا يتهم عبد الله ان يعلمه مالم يصح عنده سنده اهـ وقال الغزالي في الاحياء بعد ماذكر حديث ابن عباس المذكور وفي رواية اخرى انه يقول في اول الصلاة سبحانك اللهم ثم يسبح عشرة تسبيحة قبل القراءة وعشرا بعد القراءة والباقي كما سبق عشرا ولا يسبح بعد السجود الاخير وهذا هو الأحسن وهو اختيار ابن المبارك اهـ ، قال الزبيدي في الاتحاف ولفظ القوت هذه الرواية احب الوجهين الى اهـ ، قال الزبيدي اي لا يسبح في الجلسة الأولى بين الركعتين ولا في جلسة التشهد شيئا كما في القوت قال

وكذلك روينا في حديث عبد الله بن جعفر بن ابي طالب ان النبي صلى الله عليه وسلم علمه صلوٰة التسبيح فذكره اهـ ثم قال الزبيدي واما حديث عبد الله بن جعفر فاخرجه الدار قطني من وجهين عن عبد الله بن زياد بن سمعان قال في احدهما عن معاوية واسماعيل بن عبد الله ابنى جعفر عن ابيهما وقال في الأخرى عن عون بدل اسماعيل عن ابيهما قال قال لي رسول الله صلى الله عليه وسلم الا اعطيك فذكر الحديث وابن سمعان ضعيف وهذه الرواية هي التي اشار اليها صاحب القوت وهي الثانية عنده قال فيها يفتتح الصلوٰة فيكبر ثم يقول فذكر الكلمات وزاد فيها الحوقلة ولم يذكر هذا السجدة الثانية عند القيام ان يقولها قال وهو الذي اختاره ابن المبارك اهـ قال المنذري في الترغيب وروى البيهقي من حديث ابي جناب الكلبي عن ابي الجوزاء عن ابن عمرو (بن العاص) فذكر الحديث بالصفة التي رواها الترمذي عن ابن المبارك ثم قال هذا يوافق مارويناه عن ابن المبارك ورواه قتيبة عن سعيد عن يحيى بن سليم عن عمران بن مسلم عن ابي الجوزاء قال نزل على عبد الله بن عمرو العاص فذكر الحديث وخالفه في رفعه الى النبي صلى الله عليه وسلم ولم يذكر التسبيحات في ابتداء القراءة انما ذكرها بعدها ثم ذكر جلسة الاستراحة كما ذكرها سائر الرواة اهـ قلت حديث ابي الجناب مذكور في السنن على هذا الطريق، طريق ابن المبارك وما ذكر من كلام البيهقي ليس في السنن بهذا اللفظ فلعه ذكره في الدعوات الكبير وما في السنن انه ذكر اولا حديث ابي جناب تعليقا مرفوعا ثم قال قال ابو داود رواه روح بن المسيب وجعفر بن سليمان عن عمرو بن مالك النكرى عن ابي الجوزاء عن ابن عباس قوله وقال في حديث روح فقال حديث النبي صلى الله عليه وسلم اهـ وظاهر ان الاختلاف في السند فقط لافي الحديث وذكر شارح الاقناع من فروع الشافعية صلوٰة التسبيح واقتصر على صفة ابن المبارك فقط قال البجيرمي هذه رواية ابن مسعود والذي عليه مشائخنا انه لايسبح قبل القرائة بل بعدها خمسة عشر والعشرة في جلسة الاستراحة وهذه رواية ابن عباس اهـ مختصرا وعلم منه ان طريق ابن المبارك مروى عن ابن مسعود ايضا لكن لم اجد حديث ابن مسعود فيما عندي من الكتب بل المذكور فيها على مابسطه صاحب المنهل وشارع الاحياء وغيرهما ان حديث صلوٰة التسبيح مروى عن جماعة من الصحابة منهم عبد الله والفضل ابنا عباس وابوهما عباس بن عبد المطلب وعبد الله بن عمرو بن العاص وعبد الله بن عمر بن الخطاب وابو رافع مولى رسول الله صلى الله عليه وسلم وعلى بن ابي طالب واخوه جعفر بن ابي طالب وابنه عبد الله بن جعفر وام المؤمنين ام سلمة وانصاري غير مسمى وقد قيل انه جابر بن عبد الله قالٗ له الزبيدي وبسط في تخريج احاديثهم وعلم مما سبق ان حديث صلوٰة التسبيح مروى بطرق كثيرة وقد افرط ابن الجوزي ومن تبعه في ذكره في الموضوعات ولذا تعقب عليه غير واحد من ائمة الحديث كالحافظ ابن حجر والسيوطي والزركشي ، قال ابن المديني قد اساء ابن الجوزي بذكره اياه في الموضوعات كذا في اللآلى قال الحافظ ممن صححه او حسنه ابن منده والف فيه كتابا والآجري والخطيب ابو سعد السمعاني وابو موسى المديني وابو الحسن بن المفضل والمنذري وابن الصلاح والنووي في تهذيب الأسماء والسبكي وآخرون كذا في الاتحاف وفي المرقاة عن ابن حجر صححه الحاكم وابن خزيمة وحسنه جماعة اهـ قلت بسط السيوطي في اللآلي في تحسينه وحكى عن ابي منصور الديلمي صلوٰة التسبيح اشهر الصلوات واصحها اسنادا

(5) Hadhrat Abdullah bin Mubaarak and many other scholars, while narrating the virtues of this Salaatut Tasbeeh, also narrate the following method of offering, this salaat. "After reciting thanaa and before starting Surah Faatihah repeat these kalimahs fifteen times. Then start with (اَعُوْذُ بِاللهِ) and (بِسْمِ اللهِ) and, after completing Surah Faatihah and some surah, these kalimahs should be repeated ten times before the ruku, ten times during the ruku, ten times after rising from the ruku, ten times in each sajdah and ten times while sitting between the two sajdahs. This completes seventy five times in one rakaat (so that the kalimahs need not be recited in the sitting position after the two sajdahs. In the ruku (سُبْحَانَ رَبِّيَ الْعَظِيْمِ) and in sajdah (سُبْحَانَ رَبِّيَ الْاَعْلٰى) should be recited before reciting the kalimahs." (This method is also narrated to have been advised by Rasulullah (Sallallaho alaihe wasallam).

(1) The Salaatut Tasbeeh is a very important salaat, as is evident from the ahaadith given above, wherein Rasulullah (Sallallaho alaihe wasallam) enjoined it as a matter of great kindness and favour and stressed its importance. As such, the scholars, Muhadditĥs, jurists, and Sufis throughout the past centuries have been particular in offering this salaat. Haakim (Rahmatullah alaih) who is an authority on hadith, has written that the authenticity of this hadith is supported by the fact that, right from the second generation after the Sahabah to our times, all the great teachers of religion have been offering this salaat with constancy and have been advising the people to do so. Abdullah bin Mubaarak is also one of them. He was the teacher of the teachers of Imam Bukhari. Baihaqi (Rahmatullah alaih) stated that, even before Ibn Mubaarak, Abul Jauza (Rahmatullah alaih), an authentic Taabi'ee (one who had seen the Sahabah) and whose narrations are considered to be reliable, used to be very particular in offering this salaat. Daily, as soon as he heard the azaan for the noon prayer, he would go to the mosque and would complete this salaat before the noon salaat. Abdul Aziz bin Abi Rawwaad who was the teacher of Ibn Mubaarak, and who was a great devotee, saint, and pious man, stated that one who desires to go to Paradise should be very constant in offering Salaatut Tasbeeh. Abu Uthman Hairee (Rahmatullah alaih) who was a great saint, stated that nothing is as effective as Salaatut

Tasbeeh in providing relief from misfortunes and sorrows. Allama Taqi Subki (Rahmatullah alaih) stated, "This salaat is very important, and one should not get misled if some people happen to deny its importance. One who ignores it even after learning about its reward, is negligent in religious matters, fails to act like virtuous people, and should not be considered as a reliable person." It is stated in Mirqaat that Hadhrat Abdullah bin Abbaas (Radhiyallaho anho) used to offer this salaat every Friday.

(2) Some scholars do not accept this hadith to be authentic, because they cannot reconcile that there could be so much reward, especially forgiveness of major sins, for offering only four rakaats. But since it has been narrated by many Sahabas (Radhiyallaho anhum), its authenticity cannot be denied. However, according to many aayaat and other ahaadith, taubah is an essential condition for the forgiveness of major sins.

(3) In the ahaadith given above, two slightly different ways of offering this salaat have been described. One is that:

(سُبْحَانَ اللهِ اَلْحَمْدُ لِلّٰهِ لَآاِلٰهَ اِلَّا اللهُ وَاللهُ اَكْبَرُ)

should be recited fifteen times, after recitation of Surah Faatihah and one surah while standing, ten times after reciting (سُبْحَانَ رَبِّيَ الْعَظِيْم) in the ruku, ten times after rising from ruku, ten times after reciting (سُبْحَانَ رَبِّيَ الْاَعْلٰى) in each sajdah, ten times while sitting between the two sajdahs and ten times after the second sajdah, when after saying (اللهُ اَكْبَرُ) one should repeat it ten times before standing in the first and third rakaats and before reciting (التحيات) in the second and fourth rakaats. According to the second way of offering this salaat, the kalimahs should be recited fifteen times after reciting (سُبْحَانَكَ اللّٰهُمَّ) and before starting Surah Faatihah, ten times after reciting Surah Faatihah and a surah, and the rest is like the first method, except that it is not necessary to recite this kalimah after the second sajdah in any rakaat. The scholars have stated "It is better if this salaat is offered sometimes in one way and sometimes in the other way." As this salaat is not in general practice, a few instructions are mentioned below for the facility of those who offer it:

(1) In this salaat, no surah is particularly specified. Any

surah may be recited. But some scholars have stated that four out of the five surahs, namely Hadeed, Hashr, Saf, Jumu'ah, and Taghaabun should be recited. According to some ahaadith at least twenty aayaat should be recited. According to some, it should be any of the surahs, Asr, Kaafiroon, Nasr, and Ikhlaas.

اِذَا زُلْزِلَتْ ، وَالْعٰدِيَاتِ ، تَكَاثُرُ ، وَالْعَصْرِ ، كٰفِرُوْنَ ، نَصْر ، اِخْلَاص

(2) Counting should not be done by word of mouth, as this act will spoil the salaat. Counting on the fingers or by means of a string of beads is permissible but not desirable. The best way is that the fingers should be kept in their position, but should be pressed one by one for counting.

(3) If one forgets to recite the kalimah at any stage, he should make up the number in the next act of salaat, except that no such deficiency should be made up after rising from ruku, between the two sajdahs or after the second sajdah. In these three positions, one should recite the kalimahs as specified and then make up the deficiency in the next act. For instance, if one forgets recitation of the kalimah in the ruku one should make up this deficiency in the first sajdah. Similarly, the deficiency of the first sajdah should be made up in the second sajdah and that of second sajdah in the second rakaat while standing or, if one forgets to do so, then in the last rakaat while sitting and before reciting (التحيات).

(4) If for some reason, sajdatus sahw is required to be done, the kalimah is not to be recited then, because the number of 300 has already been completed. If however the total has been less than 300, the deficiency can be made up in sajdatus sahw as well.

(5) According to some ahaadith the following duaa should be recited after (التحيات) and before the salaam:

اَللّٰهُمَّ اِنِّىْ اَسْئَلُكَ تَوْفِيْقَ اَهْلِ الْهُدٰى وَاَعْمَالَ اَهْلِ الْيَقِيْنِ وَمُنَاصَحَةَ اَهْلِ التَّوْبَةِ
وَعَزْمَ اَهْلِ الصَّبْرِ وَجِدَّ اَهْلِ الْخَشْيَةِ وَطَلَبَ اَهْلِ الرَّغْبَةِ وَتَعَبُّدَ اَهْلِ الْوَرْعِ
وَعِرْفَانَ اَهْلِ الْعِلْمِ حَتّٰى اَخَافَكَ اَللّٰهُمَّ اِنِّىْ اَسْئَلُكَ مَخَافَةً تَحْجُزُنِيْ بِهَا عَنْ
مَعَاصِيْكَ وَحَتّٰى اَعْمَلَ بِطَاعَتِكَ عَمَلًا اَسْتَحِقُّ بِهٖ رِضَاكَ وَحَتّٰى اُنَاصِحَكَ فِيْ

التَّوْبَةِ خَوْفًا مِنْكَ وَحَتّٰى اُخْلِصَلَكَ النَّصِيْحَةَ حُبًّا لَّكَ وَحَتّٰى اَتَوَكَّلَ عَلَيْكَ فِي
الْاُمُوْرِ حُسْنَ الظَّنِّ بِكَ سُبْحَانَ خَالِقِ النُّوْرِ رَبَّنَا اَتْمِمْ لَنَا نُوْرَنَا وَاغْفِرْلَنَا اِنَّكَ
عَلٰى كُلِّ شَيْءٍ قَدِيْرٌ بِرَحْمَتِكَ يَااَرْحَمَ الرَّاحِمِيْنَ رواه ابو نعيم في الحلية من حديث ابن
عباس ولفظه اذا فرغت قلت بعد التشهد قبل التسليم اللهم الخ كذا الاتحاف وقال اورده الطبراني ايضا
من حديث العباس وفي سنده متروك اهـ قلت زاد في مرقاة في آخر الدعاء بعض الالفاظ بعد قول
خالق النور زدتها تكميلا للفائدة

"O Allah! I pray to you for granting me righteousness (as) of those who are on the right path, actions (as) of those who are true Believers, sincerity (as) of those who do taubah, constancy (as) of the contented ones, precaution (as) of those who fear You, yearning (as) of those who love You, devotion (as) of pious devotees, and knowledge (as) of religious scholars, so that I may fear You. O, Allah! grant me such fear as may prevent me from doing any wrong, so that, through submission to You, I may do such deeds as may earn for me your pleasure and your approval, and so that I may do taubah with sincerity out of Your fear, and I may become truely sincere out of Your love, and I may rely on You, because I may always hope for better (things) from You. O! The Creator of noor. You are above all defects. O! our Sustainer, grant us complete light (noor) and forgive us; no doubt You have complete control over everything. O! You, the Most Merciful, grant my prayer out of Your Mercy."

(6) Except the three forbidden times, this salaat can be offered at any time of the day or night. However, the more appropriate times, in order of perference, are: after midday, any time during the day, and any time during the night.

(7) According to some ahaadith, the third kalimah should also be followed by (لَاحَوْلَ وَلَاقُوَّةَ اِلَّا بِاللّٰهِ الْعَلِيِّ الْعَظِيْمِ) as also stated in Hadith No 3 given above. It is therefore better to recite it sometimes in addition to the third kalimah.

وآخِرُ دَعْوَانَا اَنِ الْحَمْدُ لِلّٰهِ رَبِّ الْعَالَمِيْنَ

ZAKARIYA KANDHALVI
Friday Night 26th Shawwal 1358 (Hijrah)

[illegible]

O Allah! I pray to you for granting me righteousness (as) of those who are on the right path, actions (as) of those who are true believers, sincerity (as) of those who do (tawbah) repentance, (as) of the contented ones, precaution (as) of those who fear You, yearning (as) of those who love You, devotion (as) of pious devotees and knowledge (as) of religious scholars, so that I may fear You. O Allah, grant me such fear as may prevent me from doing any wrong, so that through obedience to You I may do such deeds as may earn for me Your pleasure and Your approval, and so that I may do tawbah with sincerity out of Your fear, and I may become really sincere out of Your love, and I may rely on You in all affairs, I may always have hope for better (things) from You. O! The Creator of noor! You are above all defects. O! our Sustainer, grant us complete noor (and) forgive us, no doubt, You have complete control over everything. O! You, the Most Merciful, grant my prayer out of Your Mercy.

(6) Except the three forbidden times, Salaat-ut-Tasbeeh can be offered at any time of the day or night. However, the more appropriate times, in order of preference, are: after zawaal, any time during the day, and any time during the night.

(7) According to some ahadith, the third kalimah should also be followed by لاحول ولا قوة الا بالله, as also stated in Hadith No. 3 given above. It is therefore better to recite it sometimes in addition to the third kalimah.

وآخر دعوانا ان الحمد لله رب العالمين

ZAKARIYA KANDHALVI
Friday Night 20th Shawwal 1358 (Hijrah)

Virtues of TABLIGH

Revised translation of
the Urdu book *Faza'il-e-Tabligh*

فضائل تبلیغ

by
Shaikhul Hadith Maulana Muhammad Zakariyya Kaandhlawi

Virtues of Tabligh

translation revised by
Mazhar Mahmood Qureshi
Khwaja Ihsanul Haq

ادارہ اشاعتِ دینیات (پرائیویٹ) لمیٹڈ
idara.com
IDARA ISHA'AT-E-DINIYAT (P) LTD.

By: Shaikhul Hadith
Maulana Muhammad Zakariyya Kaandhlawi (Rah)

Edition 2001

Published by:
IDARA ISHA'AT-E-DINIYAT (P) LTD.
168/2, Jha House, Hazrat Nizamuddin
New Delhi-110 013 (India)
Tel.: 6926832, 6926833
Fax: +91-11-6322787,4352786
Email: **sales@idara.com**
Visit us at: **www.idara.com**

Printed at:
Nice Printing Press, Delhi

VIRTUES OF TABLIGH

CONTENTS

بِسْمِ اللهِ الرَّحْمٰنِ الرَّحِيْمِ

نَحْمَدُهُ وَنُصَلِّىْ عَلٰى رَسُوْلِهِ الْكَرِيْمِ

FOREWORD

IN THE NAME OF ALLAH, THE MOST GRACIOUS, THE MOST MERCIFUL

We praise Him, and we ask His blessings on His noble Prophet.

First, I give thanks to Allah, who has enabled me to write this booklet on Tabligh. One of the best of the Muslim scholars of this age has advised me to select a few verses of the Holy Qur'an and some sayings of the Holy Prophet (Sallallaho alaihe wasallam) on Tabligh, and explain the same. Since my humble services to such sincere believers can be a means of salvation for me, I present this useful pamphlet to every Islamic School, Islamic Association, Islamic Government, rather to every Muslim, and request them to serve the sacred cause of Tabligh in their own way. In fact, during this age there is a day-to-day decline in our devotion to religion, and objections against our true faith are raised not only by disbelievers, but also by the so-called 'Muslims'. The fardh and waajib observances are being neglected not only by the common Muslims, but by those also who hold important positions. Millions of Muslims have indulged in manifest false-worship, not to speak of neglecting prayers and fasting; yet they are never conscious of their practices which are against a pure allegiance to Allah. Trespassing the religious limits is very common, and mocking at the religious beliefs has become a fashion of the day. That is why the Muslim scholars have even begun to shun the common folk, and the result of this state of affairs is that ignorance about the teachings of Islam is increasing day by day. People offer the excuse that no one teaches them the religion of Islam with a keen interest, and the Muslim scholars have an excuse that no one listens to them attentively. But none of these excuses is valid before Allah. As a matter of fact, He will never accept the excuse of the common folk that they were ignorant about religious matters; for to learn religion, and to make a serious effort to acquire knowledge of its practices is the personal responsibility of every Muslim. Since ignorance of law is no excuse under any government, then why should it be accepted by the Lord of all rulers? They say, making excuses for crime is worse than crime itself. Similarly, the excuse of the scholars that no one listens to them does not hold water. They boast of representing the great spiritual leaders and divines of the past, but never consider how many troubles and hardships they bore to preach the true religion! Were they not pelted with stones? Were they not abused and oppressed to the extreme degree? But in spite of all these obstacles and hardships, they fulfilled their responsibilities about preaching, and they propagated the message of Islam regardless of any opposition.

Generally, the Muslims have limited Tabligh to the scholars only, whereas every Muslim has been commanded by Allah to stop people from doing forbidden things. If we admit for a moment that Tabligh is the duty of Muslim scholars only who do not perform it properly, then it is the particular duty of every Muslim to preach Islam. The emphasis that has been laid on Tabligh by the Qur'an and Hadith, will be proved by the Qur'anic verses and sayings of the Holy Prophet (Sallallaho alaihe wasallam) that are going to be quoted in the following pages. Therefore, you cannot confine Tabligh to scholars only, nor can it be an excuse for you to neglect the same. I would request every Muslim to devote his time and energy to Tabligh as much as he can:

هر وقت خوش که دست دهد مغتنم شمار

کس را وقوف نیست که انجام کار چیست

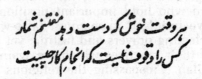

"Consider, the time at your disposal, a blessing;
for none knows what his end will be."

You need not necessarily be a perfect scholar to preach Islam and good morals to humanity. Whatever little knowledge of Islam you possess, you must impart it to others. Whenever a morally wrong or a forbidden thing is done in your presence, then as a Muslim it is your duty to stop the transgressor, as far as it lies in your power. I have described all the important things about Tabligh briefly in seven chapters, and I hope that every Muslim will benefit from them.

HAFIZ MOHAMMAD ZAKARIYYA
SHEIKH-UL-HADITH
MADRASAH MAZAHIR-UL-ULUM,
SAHARANPUR.

CHAPTER I

VERSES OF THE HOLY QUR'AN CONCERNING TABLIGH

First of all, I want to mention a few verses of the Holy Qur'an concerning Tabligh. From these verses, the readers can easily see how important Allah considers the preaching of Islam. I have come across as many as sixty verses on this particular subject, and Allah knows how many more verses could be found by another keen observer. I quote here a few of them for the benefit of every true believer.

(١) قَالَ اللهُ عَزَّ اِسْمُهُ وَمَنْ اَحْسَنُ قَوْلًا مِمَّنْ دَعَآ اِلَى اللهِ وَعَمِلَ صَالِحًا وَّقَالَ
اِنَّنِيْ مِنَ الْمُسْلِمِيْنَ

"And whose words can be better than his, who calls (people) towards Allah, and performs good deeds, and says: 'I am one of those who submit to Allah!'"

Certain commentators have written that whoever invites people to Allah through any means deserves the honour mentioned in the above verse. For instance, the prophets call people to Allah by means of miracles, and supernatural actions, the scholars invite them by preaching and arguments, the Muslim warriors (mujahids) call them by means of the sword; and the muazzins call them by means of the azaan. In short, whoever invites people to good deeds deserves this reward, whether he calls them to the formal observances of Islam or to the internal improvements of the spirit, like the mystics who stress the purification of the heart and the realization of Allah's attributes.

In the concluding verse quoted above some commentators say such a person should also be proud of the honour bestowed on him by Allah, of being categorised as a Muslim, and he should proclaim this honour in words.

Some other commentators interpret that he should not be proud of being a preacher, but should consider himself as an ordinary Muslim.

(٢) وَذَكِّرْ فَاِنَّ الذِّكْرٰى تَنْفَعُ الْمُؤْمِنِيْنَ (الذّٰرِيٰت ، ٥٥)

"(O Prophet! Sallallaho alaihe wasallam) preach to them (the Truth), for preaching proves very beneficial for the Believers."

The commentators have written that by preaching is meant instructing the believers through the verses of the Holy Qur'an, for these would guide them to the Right Path. But such a preaching can be useful for the disbelievers also, for thereby they may become believers. Alas! in this age, preaching is not performed regularly and properly. Generally the object of the preachers is to show off their ability and eloquence to the listeners, whereas the Holy Prophet (Sallallaho alaihe wasallam) has said:

"Whoever learns the art of declamation in order to attract the people towards himself, his prayers and observances, whether obligatory or optional, will not be accepted on the Day of Judgement."

(۳) وَاْمُرْ اَهْلَكَ بِالصَّلٰوةِ وَاصْطَبِرْ عَلَيْهَا لَانَسْئَلُكَ رِزْقًا نَحْنُ نَرْزُقُكَ وَالْعَاقِبَةُ لِلتَّقْوٰى (طٰهٰ ، ۱۳۲)

"And command your family to observe the prayers, and also perform these yourself regularly. We do not ask you for sustenance. We will give you sustenance; and the ultimate success is for the God-fearing."

Numerous traditions say that whenever anyone complained of poverty to the Holy Prophet (Sallallaho alaihe wasallam), he recited this verse, and advised him to perform his prayers regularly, as though pointing to the fact that regularity in prayers will lead to ample provision.

It has been stressed in this verse to do a thing yourself before giving instructions to other, because this is a more effective and successful method of preaching. That is why all the prophets themselves first did what they preached to others. Thus they became examples for their followers, who would not then think that the teaching of their religion are so difficult to carry out.

Moroever, Allah has promised ample provision for those who perform the prayers regularly, so that they should never feel that prayers can interfere with the earning of their livelihood, whether through trade, service, etc. Thereafter it is stated as a rule, that ultimate success and salvation will be attained by the God-fearing only.

(٤) يَابُنَيَّ اَقِمِ الصَّلَاةَ وَاْمُرْ بِالْمَعْرُوْفِ وَانْهَ عَنِ الْمُنْكَرِ وَاصْبِرْ عَلٰى مَآ اَصَابَكَ اِنَّ ذٰلِكَ مِنْ عَزْمِ الْاُمُوْرِ (لقمٰن ، ١٧)

"O son! Perform thy prayers regularly; and command people to do good deeds, and prevent them from forbidden things, and bear patiently whatever befalls you (in the preaching of Truth): undoubtedly this demands courage!" (Surah Luqmaan: 17)

In this verse, several important things for a Muslim have been mentioned, which can be a means for our salvation; but we have neglected these very badly. Not to speak of the lack of preaching the truth, we have neglected even the prayers, which is a basic principle of Islam, in fact the most important after faith. There are so many people who do not perform their prayers at all; but even those who do, hardly perform it with all its requisites, such as congregational prayers. It is the poor only who perform the prayers with congregation in the mosque, while the rich feel it below their dignity to be present in the mosque. Ah! my complaint is only to Allah!

آنچہ عار تست او فخر من است

"O careless person! What is an insult for you, is a matter of pride for me."

(٥) وَلْتَكُنْ مِنْكُمْ اُمَّةٌ يَدْعُوْنَ اِلَى الْخَيْرِ وَيَاْمُرُوْنَ بِالْمَعْرُوفِ وَيَنْهَوْنَ عَنِ الْمُنْكَرِ وَاُولٰئِكَ هُمُ الْمُفْلِحُوْنَ (اٰل عمران ، ١٠٤)

"O Muslims! there must be a group among you who would invite people to Good; and would command them to do good deeds, and would prevent them from forbidden things; and these are the people who will attain salvation." (Surah Aali Imraan: 105)

In this verse, Allah has clearly commanded the Muslims to prepare a group or party which would preach Islam throughout the world: but we see that the so-called Muslims have totally neglected this commandment. On the other hand, the non-Muslims, are preaching their religion day and night. For instance, parties of Christian missionaries have been specially assigned to propagate their religion in the whole world; similarly other communities are trying their best to preach their own religions. But the question is, is there such an organization among the Muslims? The answer, if not in the negative, cannot be in the affirmative either. If any individual or any party among the so-called Muslims arises for the preaching of Islam, unreasonable objections are raised against them, instead of giving them help and co-operation, whereas it is the duty of every true Muslim to help those who preach Islam, and to remove shortcomings where necessary; but these people neither do anything themselves to preach Islam, nor help those who have devoted their lives to this sacred cause. Thus the result is that even the sincere and unselfish preachers are disappointed, and give up their efforts in this regard.

(٦) كُنْتُمْ خَيْرَ أُمَّةٍ أُخْرِجَتْ لِلنَّاسِ تَأْمُرُوْنَ بِالْمَعْرُوفِ وَتَنْهَوْنَ عَنِ الْمُنْكَرِ وَتُؤْمِنُوْنَ بِاللّٰهِ (ال عمران ١١٠)

> "O Muslims! you are the best of peoples, who have been selected for the guidance of mankind; you enjoin them to do good deeds, and prevent them from forbidden things; and you have firm faith in Allah."
>
> (Surah Aali Imraan: 10)

That the Muslims are the best of all nations, has been asserted in certain sayings of the Holy Prophet (Sallallaho alaihe wasallam) also; and there are some verses of the Holy Qur'an that corroborate this. Even the above-mentioned verse bestows the honour of 'Best Nation' on us, provided we preach Islam, command people to do good and prevent them from evil.

The commentators have written that in this verse, the preaching of truth and prevention of evil has been mentioned before faith even, whereas faith (Imaan) is the root of all Islamic beliefs and actions. The reason is that faith has been a common factor among all the nations of the world, but the special thing that has particularly distinguished the Muslims is the mandate enjoining people to do good, and to prevent them from evil. So, this is the real basis for the superiority of the Muslims, whenever they fulfilled it; and since in Islam good actions are of little value without faith, it is therefore specifically mentioned at the end of the verse. In fact, the real object in this verse is to emphasise the importance of enjoining people to do good deeds, and this is the distinguishing feature of the Muslim Ummah. It is not sufficient to enjoin good and to prevent from evil only now and then, but this practice should continue at all times and on all occasions regularly. Reference to the task of preaching the truth are found in earlier religions, but the distinguishing merit of the Muslim Ummah lies in taking it up as a regular assignment. This is not a temporary work, but a permanent one.

(٧) لَاخَيْرَ فِيْ كَثِيْرٍ مِّنْ نَجْوَاهُمْ اِلَّا مَنْ اَمَرَ بِصَدَقَةٍ اَوْ مَعْرُوْفٍ اَوْ اِصْلَاحٍ بَيْنَ النَّاسِ وَمَنْ يَفْعَلْ ذٰلِكَ ابْتِغَاءَ مَرْضَاةِ اللهِ فَسَوْفَ نُؤْتِيْهِ اَجْرًا عَظِيْمًا (النساء ، ١١٤)

"In the talk of an assembly of common folk there is no good at all, except those who command people to give charity (to the poor) or instruct them to do good things, or make peace between people (they will be rewarded by Allah). And whoever does this only to please Allah, soon he will receive a great reward from Allah." (Surah Nisaa: 114)

In this verse, Allah has promised a great reward for those who preach truth; and how great and honourable can be the reward that has been called 'great' by Allah.

In this context, the Holy Prophet (Sallallaho alaihe wasallam) has said, "A man's words may be a burden (sin) for him, except those that he has spoken for giving instructions for good deeds, and preventing others from forbidden things, or for remembering Allah."

In another hadith, the Holy Prophet (Sallallaho alaihe wasallam) has said, "Shall I tell you a virtue better than optional prayer, fasting and charity?" His Companions said, "You must tell us that virtue, O Messenger of Allah!" (Sallallaho alaihe wasallam). He said: "To make peace between people, for hate and mutual conflict uproot good deeds, just as a razor removes the hair."

There are many more verses of the Holy Qur'an and sayings of the Holy Prophet (Sallallaho alaihe wasallam) that instruct us to make peace between people. What we mean to emphasise here is that to make peace between people is also another form of instructing them to do good and preventing them from evil. To introduce peace and cooperation in the society should therefore be given due importance.

CHAPTER 2

SAYINGS OF THE HOLY PROPHET (SALLALLAHO ALAIHE WASALLAM) CONCERNING TABLIGH

In this chapter, I will quote certain sayings of the Holy Prophet (Sallallaho alaihe wasallam) that explain the meaning of the above-mentioned verses of the Holy Qur'an. It is not the intention to encompass all the relevant ahaadith. If I quote all the verses and the ahaadith on this subject, I fear no one will read them, for now-a-days people hardly spare time for such things. So, to place before you how important Tabligh is in the eyes of the Holy Prophet (Sallallaho alaihe wasallam), and what serious consequences follow from its neglect, I give below a few sayings of the Holy Prophet (Sallallaho alaihe wasallam):

(١) عَنْ اَبِيْ سَعِيْدِ الْخُدْرِيِّ قَالَ سَمِعْتُ رَسُوْلَ اللهِ ﷺ يَقُوْلُ مَنْ رَّاٰى مِنْكُمْ مُنْكَرًا فَلْيُغَيِّرْهُ بِيَدِهٖ فَاِنْ لَّمْ يَسْتَطِعْ فَبِلِسَانِهٖ فَاِنْ لَّمْ يَسْتَطِعْ فَبِقَلْبِهٖ وَذٰلِكَ اَضْعَفُ الْاِيْمَانِ (رواه مسلم والترمذي وابن ماجه والنسائى كما في الترغيب)

It is reported by Abu Sa'eed Khudri (Radhiyallaho anho) that the Holy Prophet (Sallallaho alaihe wasallam) said: "Whoever sees a forbidden thing being done, he must prevent it by the use of his hand; and if he has no power for this action, then he should prevent it with his tongue; and if he cannot do this even, then he should at least consider it a vice in his heart, and this is a very low level of one's faith."

In another hadith, it has been said that if a person can prevent evil with his tongue then he should so prevent it; otherwise, he should at least think it evil in his heart and thus stand exonerated. Another hadith says that if anyone hates sin within his heart, he is a true believer, but this is the weakest form of faith. This topic has occurred in many other sayings of the Prophet. Now think well how many Muslims there are who act upon this hadith in a practical way. How many of us prevent evil forcibly, how many with the tongue, and how many seriously hate it within our heart? We have to take stock of ourselves on these issues.

(٢) عَنِ النُّعْمَانِ بْنِ بَشِيْرٍ قال مَثَلُ الْقَائِمِ فِيْ حُدُوْدِ اللهِ وَالْوَاقِعِ فِيْهَا كَمَثَلِ قَوْمٍ اِسْتَهَمُوْا عَلٰى سَفِيْنَةٍ فَصَارَ بَعْضُهُمْ اَعْلَاهَا وَبَعْضُهُمْ اَسْفَلَهَا فَكَانَ الَّذِيْ فِيْ اَسْفَلِهَا اِذَا اسْتَقَوْا مِنَ الْمَاءِ مَرُّوْا عَلٰى مَنْ فَوْقَهُمْ فَقَالُوْا لَوْ اَنَّا خَرَقْنَا فِيْ نَصِيْبِنَا خَرْقًا وَلَمْ نُؤْذِ مَنْ فَوْقَنَا فَاِنْ تَرَكُوْهُمْ وَمَا اَرَادُوْا اَهْلَكُوْا جَمِيْعًا وَاِنْ اَخَذُوْا عَلٰى اَيْدِيْهِمْ نَجَوْا وَنَجَوْا جَمِيْعًا (رواه البخاري والترمذي)

It has been reported by Nu'maan bin Basheer (Radhiyallaho anho) that the Holy Prophet (Sallallaho alaihe wasallam) said: "There are people who do not transgress the limits (laws) of Allah, and there are others who do so. They are like two groups who boarded a ship; one of them settled on the upper deck, and the other, on the lower deck of the ship. So, when the people of the lower deck needed water, they said: 'Why should we cause trouble to the people of the upper deck when we can easily have plenty of water by making a hole in our deck.' Now if the people of the upper deck do not prevent this group from such foolishness, all of them will perish – but if they stop them then they all will be saved." (Bukhari & Tirmizi)

Once the Companions of the Holy Prophet (Sallallaho alaihe wasallam) asked him: "O Messenger of Allah! (Sallallaho alaihe wasallam) can we people be destroyed even when there are certain pious God-fearing persons among us?" He answered: "Yes, when evil deeds predominate in a society."

Nowadays the Muslims are generally anxious about the decline and fall of this Ummah, and they suggest certain plans to stop this decline, but they never consider as to what is the main cause of our decline. They fail to identify the true reason of our spiritual and moral decline, particularly when the proper remedy has been told by Allah and the Holy Prophet (Sallallaho alaihe wasallam). It is a pity that because of the wrong diagnosis, incorrect remedies, including continued neglect of Tabligh, are leading to the further decline of the Ummah. In fact, the main cause of our decline is that we do not pay attention to Tabligh nor do we help those who devote themselves to this sacred mission.

(٣) عَنِ ابْنِ مَسْعُوْدٍ قَالَ قَالَ رَسُوْلُ اللهِ ﷺ: اَوَّلُ مَادَخَلَ النَّقْصُ عَلٰى بَنِيْ اِسْرَائِيْلَ اَنَّهُ كَانَ الرَّجُلُ يَلْقَى الرَّجُلَ فَيَقُوْلُ يَاهٰذَا اِتَّقِ اللّٰهَ وَدَعْ مَاتَصْنَعُ بِهٖ فَاِنَّهُ لَايَحِلُّ لَكَ ثُمَّ يَلْقَاهُ مِنَ الْغَدِ وَهُوَ عَلٰى حَالِهٖ فَلَايَمْنَعُهُ ذٰلِكَ اَنْ يَّكُوْنَ اَكِيْلَهُ وَشَرِيْبَهُ وَقَعِيْدَهُ فَلَمَّا فَعَلُوْا ذٰلِكَ ضَرَبَ اللّٰهُ قُلُوْبَ بَعْضِهِمْ بِبَعْضٍ ثُمَّ قَالَ لُعِنَ الَّذِيْنَ كَفَرُوْا مِنْ بَنِىْ اِسْرَائِيْلَ اِلٰى قَوْلِهٖ فَاسِقُوْنَ ثُمَّ قَالَ كَلَّا وَاللّٰهِ لَتَاْمُرُنَّ بِالْمَعْرُوْفِ وَلَتَنْهَوُنَّ عَنِ الْمُنْكَرِ وَلَتَاْخُذُنَّ عَلٰى يَدِ الظَّالِمِ وَلَتَاْطِرُنَّ عَلَى الْحَقِّ اَطْرًا (رواه أبو داود والترمذي كذا في الترغيب)

It has been reported by Ibn Mas'ood (Radhiyallaho anha) that the Holy Prophet (Sallallaho alaihe wasallam) said: "The decline and fall of Bani Israa-eel started thus: when the pious among them saw certain sins being committed by the transgressors, they forbade them from doing the same; but when the sinners did not repent, the pious because of their relationship and friendship continued to mix with them. So, when this state of affairs began to prevail, Allah caused their hearts to be accursed in the same manner." (i.e. the hearts were also affected with the disobedience of the transgressors). Then in support of this, the Holy Prophet (Sallallaho alaihe wasallam) recited a verse of the Holy Qur'an, which says: 'The disobedient and the transgressors among the Bani Israa-eel were accursed by Allah.' On this, the Holy Prophet (Sallallaho alaihe wasallam) emphatically instructed his Companions: "(To avoid such decline) you people must enjoin upon others to do good deeds and prevent them from doing forbidden things; you should restrain every tyrant from tyranny and invite him towards truth and justice."

Another hadith says that the Holy Prophet (Sallallaho alaihe wasallam) was reclining comfortably when, suddenly overcome with emotion, he sat up and said: "I swear by Allah that you people cannot attain salvation, unless you prevent the tyrants from tyranny."

Another hadith says that the Holy Prophet (Sallallaho alaihe wasallam) said: "You people must preach truth, and prevent the sinners from doing forbidden things, and check the tyrants, to bring them towards the right path, otherwise you will be accursed and your hearts will be corrupted, just as Allah did with Bani Israa-eel." The Holy Prophet (Sallallaho alaihe wasallam) read certain relevant verses of the Holy Qur'an to emphasize this subject. Bani Israa-eel were condemned because among other things, they did not prevent others from doing forbidden things.

Nowadays it is considered a virtue to be at peace with all, and to please everyone on every occasion. They say it is a requirement of good manners with the evildoers.

Obviously, this is a wrong policy, because at most there may be some religious sanction for keeping quiet in extreme case, but never for falling in line with the tyrants and transgressors. At the very least, every one must instruct those people to do good whom he easily can influence for instance: his subordinates, his servants, his wife, his children, and his relations. In such circumstances, to be absolutely silent about Tabligh is unpardonable before Allah.

Hadhrat Sufyaan Thowri says: "Whoever is very popular with his relations and neighbours, we suspect him to be compromising in preaching the true teachings of religion."

Numerous traditions say that when a sin is committed secretly, its harm is generally limited to the sinner only; but when a sin is committed openly, and those possessing the capability do not prevent it, then it ultimately affects all the people around.

Now everyone can see for himself, how many sins are committed before him every day, and he, in spite of having the power to prevent them neglects to do so. And it is a pity that, if anyone gets up to put the wrong down, the ignorant and shameless people oppose him instead of co-operating with him.

فَسَيَعْلَمُ الَّذِيْنَ ظَلَمُوْا اَيَّ مُنْقَلَبٍ يَّنْقَلِبُوْنَ

Those who do wrong will come to know by what a great reverse they will be overturned.

(٤) عَنْ جَرِيْرِ بْنِ عَبْدِ اللهِ قَالَ سَمِعْتُ رَسُوْلَ اللهِ ﷺ يَقُوْلُ: مَامِنْ رَجُلٍ يَكُوْنُ فِيْ قَوْمٍ يَعْمَلُ فِيْهِمْ بِالْمَعَاصِيْ يَقْدِرُوْنَ عَلٰى اَنْ يُغَيِّرُوْا عَلَيْهِ وَلَايُغَيِّرُوْنَ اِلَّا اَصَابَهُمُ اللهُ بِعِقَابٍ قَبْلَ اَنْ يَّمُوْتُوْا (رواه أبو داود وابن ماجه وابن حبان والاصبهاني وغيرهم كذا في الترغيب)

Hadhrat Jareer bin Abdullah (Radhiyallaho anho) says, "I heard the Messenger of Allah (Sallallaho alaihe wasallam) saying: "When a sin is committed before an individual or a group and they do not prevent it, in spite of having the capability, then Allah inflicts a severe punishment on them before their death." (Targheeb)

O my friends who desire the improvement of Islam and the Muslims! now you have clearly seen the causes of our decline. Not to speak of strangers, we generally do not prevent even our own family and our subordinates from wrong-doing. We do not even make up our minds to prevent evil, much less doing something practical about it. Whatever our own son does against the Commandments of Allah, we do not check him even; but if he takes some interest in politics, or mixes up in a certain political party, we are seriously anxious not only about him, but about our own safety and honour. Then we warn him and also think about some plans to be safe and secure from any harm; but on the other hand, when he transgresses against Allah's Commandments, we are never anxious about the life in the Hereafter, and about the Reckoning of the Day of Judgement.

Sometimes you know full well that your son is addicted to some idle pursuits and is very lax in his prayers, but you have no courage to prevent him from such habits, or to chastise him, although Allah has clearly commanded you to be severe in uprooting such evils and even sever relations with the transgressor. There is many a father who would be angry with his son, because he is lazy and does not attend to his studies or services or business properly, but is there anyone who is angry with his son, because he does not perform the fundamental observances of Islam?

As a matter of fact, the adverse effect of this negligence is not limited to the great loss in the Hereafter but it is a pity this evidently extends to our worldly affairs and interests also, which are so dear to us. This blindness of ours is horrible, for Allah says:

مَنْ كَانَ فِيْ هٰذِهٖ اَعْمٰى فَهُوَ فِي الْاٰخِرَةِ اَعْمٰى (بنی اسرائیل ، ۷۲)

"Whoever is blind in this world, he will be surely blind in the Hereafter."

And such transgressors have taken leave of their senses because

خَتَمَ اللّٰهُ عَلٰى قُلُوْبِهِمْ وَعَلٰى سَمْعِهِمْ وَعَلٰى اَبْصَارِهِمْ غِشَاوَةٌ وَ لَهُمْ عَذَابٌ عَظِيْمٌ
(البقرة ، ۷)

"Allah has sealed up their hearts, and on their ears and eyes there are veils (so they neither hear nor see the truth)."

(٥) رُوِیَ عَنْ انَسٍ رَضِیَ اللهُ عَنْهُ اَنَّ رَسُوْلَ اللهِ ﷺ قَالَ : لَاتَزَالُ لَا اِلٰهَ اِلَّا اللهُ تَنْفَعُ مَنْ قَالَهَا وَتَرُدُّ عَنْهُمْ الْعَذَابَ وَالنِّقْمَةَ مَالَمْ یَسْتَخِفُّوْا بِحَقِّهَا قَالُوْا یَارَسُوْلَ اللهِ مَاالْاِسْتِخْفَافُ بِحَقِّهَا قَالَ یَظْهَرُ الْاَمَلُ بِمَعَاصِیْ اللهِ فَلَایُنْکَرُ وَلَایُغَیَّرُ

(رواه الاصبهانی في ترغیب)

It has been reported by Hadhrat Anas (Radhiyallaho anho) that the Holy Prophet (Sallallaho alaihe wasallam) said: "So long as a person says "La ilaaha illallaah" (no one is worthy of worship but Allah), he receives spiritual benefits, and is saved from miseries and calamities, unless he neglects its rights." His Companions said: "O Messenger of Allah (Sallaho alaihe wasallam)! how are its rights neglected?" He answered: "When sins are committed openly, and the person who recites the kalimah does not prevent the sinners from wrongdoings." (Targheeb)

Now you can yourself consider how very often sins are committed during these times, yet there is no serious attempt to check or prevent them. In such a dangerous and ungodly atmosphere, the very existence of the Muslims in the world is a great blessing of Allah, otherwise we are inviting ruination through all possible means. Hadhrat Aaishah (Radhiyallaho anha) asked the Holy Prophet (Sallallaho alaihe wasallam), "When the punishment of Allah befalls the inhabitants of any locality, does it affect the pious, just as it affects the guilty?" The Holy Prophet (Sallallaho alaihe wasallam) answered: "Yes, it does affect all of them in this world, but at the Resurrection the pious will be separated from the guilty." Therefore, those people who are simply satisfied with their own piety, and do not participate in improving others should not rest assured that they are safe from the punishment of the Almighty. If any chastisement is inflicted by Allah, they too will be involved in it.

(٦) عَنْ عَائِشَةَ رَضِیَ اللهُ عَنْهَا قَالَتْ دَخَلَ عَلَیَّ النَّبِیُّ ﷺ فَعَرَفْتُ فِیْ وَجْهِهِ اَنْ قَدْ حَضَرَهُ شَیْءٌ فَتَوَضَّأَ وَمَا کَلَّمَ اَحَدًا فَلَصِقْتُ بِالْحُجْرَةِ اَسْتَمِعُ مَایَقُوْلُ فَقَعَدَ

عَلَى الْمِنْبَرِ فَحَمِدَ اللّٰهَ وَاَثْنٰى عَلَيْهِ وَقَالَ يَاَيُّهَا النَّاسُ اِنَّ اللّٰهَ تَعَالٰى يَقُوْلُ لَكُمْ مُرُوْا بِالْمَعْرُوْفِ وَانْهَوْا عَنِ الْمُنْكَرِ قَبْلَ اَنْ تَدْعُوْا فَلَااُجِيْبَ لَكُمْ وَتَسْاَلُوْنِى فَلَااُعْطِيَكُمْ وَتَسْتَنْصِرُوْنِى فَلَااَنْصُرَكُمْ فَمَازَادَ عَلَيْهِنَّ حَتّٰى نَزَلَ

(رواه ابن ماجه وابن حبان في صحيحه كذا في الترغيب)

Hadhrat Aa-ishah (Radhiyallaho anha) says: "Once the Holy Prophet (Sallallaho alaihe wasallam) entered the house and I guessed from his face that something of great importance had happened to him. He did not talk to anyone, and after making wudhu (ablution) he entered the mosque. I stood behind the wall to hear what he said. He sat at the pulpit and after praising Allah, he said, "O Muslims! Allah has commanded you to call people to good deeds, and prevent them from committing sins; otherwise a time will come when you will pray to Him, but He will not listen to you; you will ask your needs of Him, but He will not grant them; you will demand His help against your enemies, but He will not help you." After saying this, he came down from the pulpit "

Particularly those persons should consider this hadith well who want to fight the enemies of Islam, but neglect the performance of the requisites of Islam; they forget that the strength and stability of the Muslim Nation depends upon the propagation of Islam. Hadhrat Abu Darda (Radhiyallaho anho), who is a distinguished Companion of the Holy Prophet (Sallallaho alaihe wasallam) says: "You must command people to do good, and restrain them from evil; otherwise Allah will cause such a tyrant to rule over you, who will not respect your elders, and will not have mercy on your youngsters. Then you people will pray to Him, but He will not accept your prayer; you will ask Him for help, but He will not help you, you will seek His pardon but He will not pardon you; for Allah Himself says:

يَاَيُّهَا الَّذِيْنَ آمَنُوْا اِنْ تَنْصُرُوْا اللّٰهَ يَنْصُرْكُمْ وَيُثَبِّتْ اَقْدَامَكُمْ (محمد ، ٧)

"O Believers! if you help Allah, then will He help you, and will make your feet firm (against your enemies)."

Says Allah in another verse:

انْ يَنْصُرْكُمُ اللهُ فَلَاغَالِبَ لَكُمْ وَاِنْ يَّخْذُلْكُمْ فَمَنْ ذَاالَّذِىْ يَنْصُرُكُمْ مِّنْ بَعْدِهِ ، وَعَلَى اللهِ فَلْيَتَوَكَّلِ الْمُؤْمِنُوْن (آل عمران ، ١٦٠)

"O Believers! If Allah helps you, then no one can overpower you; and if He does not help you, then who can come to your help? and only in Allah should the Believers trust."

It has been reported by Hadhrat Huzaifah (Radhiyallaho anho) that the Holy Prophet (Sallallaho alaihe wasallam) said on oath:

"You must command people to do good deeds, and prevent them from doing forbidden things; otherwise Allah will inflict a severe punishment upon you, and then even your prayers will not be accepted by Him."

Here my respected readers should consider well how many times they violate the commandments of Allah; then they will know why their attempts to reform the nation fail, and why their prayers are of no avail, and they instead of sowing the seeds of progress, cause its decline.

(٧) عَنْ اَبِيْ هُرَيْرَةَ رَضِىَ اللهُ عَنْهُ قَالَ قَالَ رَسُوْلُ اللهِ ﷺ اِذَا عَظَّمَتْ اُمَّتِيْ الدُّنْيَا نُزِعَتْ مِنْهَا هَيْبَةُ الْاِسْلَامِ وَاِذَا تَرَكَتِ الْاَمْرَ بِالْمَعْرُوْفِ وَالنَّهْيَ عَنِ الْمُنْكَرِ حُرِمَتْ بَرَكَةَ الْوَحْيِ وَاِذَا تَسَابَّتْ اُمَّتِيْ سَقَطَتْ مِنْ عَيْنِ اللهِ
(كذا في الدر عن الحكيم الترمذي)

It has been reported by Abu Hurairah (Radhiyallaho anho) that the Holy Prophet (Sallallaho alaihe wasallam) said, "When my followers will begin to adore the worldly benefits, their hearts will be deprived of the dignity and love of Islam; and when they stop the preaching of truth, and preventing transgression, they will be deprived of the blessings of the Revelation; and when they will abuse each other, they will fall from the esteem of Allah." (Tirmazi)

The well-wishers of the nation should ponder why their efforts result in failure instead of success. If you people believe your Prophet (Sallallaho alaihe wasallam) and his teachings to be true and educative, then why do you take those things as useful that are declared harmful by him. He says such and such thing will aggravate your disease, but you think they will bring health to you. The Holy Prophet (Sallallaho alaihe wasallam) said:

> "None of you can be a true Muslim, unless his desires are subject to the religion that I have brought."

But contrary to this, you think that religion is an obstacle in the way of your individual and national progress on the lines of other nations. Says Allah in the Holy Qur'an:

مَنْ كَانَ يُرِيْدُ حَرْثَ الْآخِرَةِ نَزِدْلَهُ فِيْ حَرْثِهِ وَمَنْ كَانَ يُرِيْدُ حَرْثَ الدُّنْيَا نُؤْتِهِ مِنْهَا وَمَا لَهُ فِيْ الْآخِرَةِ مِنْ نَّصِيْبٍ (الشورٰى ، ٢٠)

> "Whoever desires the harvest of the Hereafter, We grant increase in his harvest; and whoever desires the harvest of this world we give him the fruit thereof but there is no portion for him in the Hereafter."

A hadith of this meaning says:

> "The heart of a Muslim whose object is the life Hereafter does not care for the worldly pleasures, yet the world is brought to his feet; on the other hand, whoever goes after the world, he is overpowered by miseries and calamities, yet he cannot receive more than his allotted portion."

The Holy Prophet (Sallallaho alaihe wasallam) read the above-mentioned verse, and said: Allah says: "O son of man! devote yourself to My worship, and I will free your bosom from the worldly anxieties and will remove your poverty, otherwise I will fill your heart with a thousand worries and will not remove your poverty."

These are the words of Allah and the Holy Prophet (Sallallaho alaihe wasallam), but you foolishly think that religion and the teachings of Mullahs (religious divines) are a hindrance in the path of your (worldly) progress. Don't you think that your worldly progress can be very helpful to the Mullahs, for then you would be in a better position to serve them. Then why should they oppose you, to their own loss? As a matter of fact, they are sacrificing their own worldly interests by speaking the truth, by preaching Islam, in order to bring you to the Right Path. When whatever your religion scholars tell you is in fact based on the teachings of the Holy Qur'an, then is it sensible for you to turn away from them? And if you deny them, then can you be a true believer? Your religious preachers might have some personal faults but, so long as they are conveying to you the commandments of Allah from the Holy Qur'an and the sayings of the Holy Prophet, (Sallallaho alaihe wasallam) you are bound to listen to them and to obey their instructions; and if you don't obey them, you have yourself to answer for your disobedience to Allah. Not even a fool would say that the official orders should not be obeyed, simply because they were communicated by a lowly servant.

Never make such a sweeping statement that those who have devoted themselves to the sacred cause of Islam hanker after worldly gains and interest. True preachers of Islam are never selfish, and never ask anything for themselves; the more they worship Allah, (and devote themselves to the work of religion) the less attention they pay to worldly offerings. Nevertheless, if they ask help of you, it will be entirely for the sake of religion (to preach Islam and the Holy Qur'an); and therein they find more satisfaction than in any personal cause. Then why should you hestitate to help them?

A question is generally raised stating that Islam does not prescribe giving up of worldly interests and in this connection the verses of the Holy Qur'an are often misunderstood, for instance, there is a verse that says:

رَبَّنَا آتِنَا فِي الدُّنْيَا حَسَنَةً وَّفِي الْآخِرَةِ حَسَنَةً وَّقِنَا عَذَابَ النَّارِ

"Our Lord! grant us good in this world, and good in the Hereafter; and save us from the chastisement of the Fire (of Hell)." (Al-Baqarah: 210)

Some ignorant people stress that in this verse the worldly good is favoured and appreciated by Islam, as much as the good in the Hereafter. In other words, there is no renunciation of the world in Islam. Such people claim to be perfect scholars after having seen only some translations of the Holy Qur'an. The true meanings of the Holy Qur'an can be properly understood by those only who have looked deep into its verses and are well-informed on this subject. Different interpretations of the above-mentioned verse that have been explained by the Companions of the Holy Prophet (Sallallaho alaihe wasallam) and the scholars of Islam are as follows:

Hadhrat Qatadah (Radhiyallaho anho) says: "By 'good in this world' is meant peaceful existence and necessary livelihood".

Hadhrat Ali (Karramallahu wajhahu) says that by 'good in this world' is meant a pious wife.

Hadhrat Hasan Basri (Rahmatullah alaih) says that by 'good in this world' is meant knowledge of Islam and prayer'.

Hadhrat Suddi (Rahmatullah alaih) says that by 'good in this world' is meant lawful earnings.

Hadhrat Ibn Umar (Radhiyallaho anho) says that by 'good in this world' is meant righteous children and goodwill of other human beings.

Hadhrat Ja'far (Radhiyallaho anho) says that by "good in this world" is meant good health, honest living, knowledge of the Holy Qur'an, victory over the enemies of Islam, and the company of the pious."

I would add that if "good in this world" meant our material progress, even then the emphasis in the verse is on praying to Allah for such a "good" but not on completely busying ourself in this pursuit. Asking from Allah, even if it be the mending of a shoe is in itself a part of religion. Besides, if it means honest living, or to be prosperous and self-sufficient, that too is not forbidden in Islam; by all means make your living in this world consistent with religion. The point is that our endeavours in the cause of religion should at least be as much as those for worldly gains, if not more, because Islam teaches us to value both this life and the Hereafter.

Please consider also the following verses of the Holy Qur'an, which lay more stress and importance on the life Hereafter:

مَنْ كَانَ يُرِيْدُ حَرْثَ الآخِرَةِ نَزِدْ لَهُ فِيْ حَرْثِهِ

"Whoever desires the harvest of the life Hereafter, We will certainly increase his harvest.

مَنْ كَانَ يُرِيْدُ العَاجِلَةَ عَجَّلْنَا لَهُ فِيْهَا مَانَشَاءُ لِمَنْ نُرِيْدُ ثُمَّ جعَلْنَا لَهُ جهَنَّمَ يَصْلٰهَا مَذْمُوْمًا مَّدْحُوْرًا ، وَمَنْ اَرَادَ الْآخِرَةَ وَسَعٰى لَهَا سَعْيَهَا وَهُوَ مُؤْمِنٌ فَاُوْلٰٓئِكَ كَانَ سَعْيُهُمْ مَشْكُوْرًا (بنى اسرائيل ، ١٩)

Whoever desires this present world (and its benefits), We shall soon grant him whatever he desires; then We will make Hell his destination, wherein he will be thrown headlong, with disgrace. And whoever desires the Hereafter, and makes an effort to attain it, and he is a true believer—those are the people whose efforts will be rewarded." (Bani Isra-eel: 18-19)

مِنْكُمْ مَنْ يُرِيْدُ الدُّنْيَا وَمِنْكُمْ مَنْ يُرِيْدُ الْآخِرَةِ (آل عمران ١٥٢)

"And amongst you are those who desire this world only; and amongst you are those who desire the life Hereafter." (Aali Imraan: 152)

ذٰلِكَ مَتَاعُ الْحَيَاةِ الدُّنْيَا وَاللّٰهُ عِنْدَهُ حُسْنُ الْمَآبِ (سورة آل عمران ، ١٤)

"These are the benefits of the life of this world; but with Allah is a very good abode." (Aali Imraan: 14)

قُلْ مَتَاعُ الدُّنْيَا قَلِيْلٌ وَالْآخِرَةُ خَيْرٌ لِّمَنِ اتَّقٰى (النساء ، ٧٧)

"(O Prophet! Sallallaho alaihe wasallam) say: "The benefit of this world is very little; but the life Hereafter is much better for those who fear Allah." (An-Nisaa: 77)

وَمَا الْحَيَاةُ الدُّنْيَا اِلَّا لَعِبٌ وَّلَهْوٌ وَلَلدَّارُ الْآخِرَةُ خَيْرٌ لِّلَّذِيْنَ يَتَّقُوْنَ (انعام ، ٣٢)

"The life of this world is nothing but a game and sport, and the House of the Hereafter is much better for the pious." (Al-An'aam: 32)

وَذَرِ الَّذِيْنَ اتَّخَذُوْا دِيْنَهُمْ لَعِبًا وَّلَهْوًا وَغَرَّتْهُمُ الْحَيَاةُ الدُّنْيَا (سورة انعام ، ٧٠)

"And leave aside those who have made a jest of their religion, and they have become puffed up with this worldly life." (Al-An'aam: 70)

تُرِيْدُوْنَ عَرَضَ الدُّنْيَا وَاللّٰهُ يُرِيْدُ الْآخِرَةَ (انفال ، ٦٧)

"You people desire the benefits of this present world only, but Allah desires the Hereafter (for you)."
(Al-Anfaal–67)

اَرَضِيْتُمْ بِالْحَيَاةِ الدُّنْيَا مِنَ الْآخِرَةِ فَمَا مَتَاعُ الْحَيَاةِ الدُّنْيَا فِي الْآخِرَةِ اِلَّا قَلِيْلٌ
(التوبة ، ٣٨)

Are you pleased with the worldly life instead of the Hereafter? But the benefits of the life of this world are as nothing, when compared to the Hereafter."
(At-Towbah–38)

مَنْ كَانَ يُرِيْدُ الْحَيَاةَ الدُّنْيَا وَزِيْنَتَهَا نُوَفِّ اِلَيْهِمْ اَعْمَالَهُمْ فِيْهَا وَهُمْ فِيْهَا
لَا يُبْخَسُوْنَ ، اُوْلٰٓئِكَ لَيْسَ لَهُمْ فِي الْآخِرَةِ اِلَّا النَّارُ وَحَبِطَ مَاصَنَعُوْا فِيْهَا وَبَاطِلٌ
مَّاكَانُوا يَعْمَلُوْنَ (هود ، ١٦)

"Whoever desires the life of this world, and all its adornments, we make their attempts therein fruitful, and nothing is decreased from their due. For them there is nothing but Fire in the Hereafter, whatever they performed (of some good deeds) in the world has been destroyed, for whatever they did was absolutely false."
(Hud–16)

وَفَرِحُوْا بِالْحَيَاةِ الدُّنْيَا وَمَا الْحَيَاةُ الدُّنْيَا فِي الْآخِرَةِ اِلَّا مَتَاعٌ (الرعد ، ٢٦)

"And they have become pleased with the worldly life only; but the worldly life, when compared to the Hereafter, is but a small benefit."
(Ar-Ra'd–26)

فَعَلَيْهِمْ غَضَبٌ مِنَ اللّٰهِ وَلَهُمْ عَذَابٌ عَظِيْمٌ ، ذٰلِكَ بِاَنَّهُمُ اسْتَحَبُّوا الْحَيَاةَ الدُّنْيَا
عَلَى الْآخِرَةِ (النحل ، ١٠٧)

"On them fell the wrath of Allah, and for them is a great chastisement. It is because they preferred the life of this world to the Hereafter."

(An-Nahl–107)

There are many other verses in which the life of this world and the Hereafter have been compared. I cannot mention all of them, but I have quoted a few of them as examples. Basically, the moral of all the verses is that those who prefer this world to the Hereafter will be losers in the long run. If you cannot properly deal with both the worlds, then the life Hereafter is preferable, and you should fulfil its requirements. I admit that this world and the requisites of the life here are unavoidable needs, yet note that no sensible person would keep sitting in the toilet, even though one is compelled to visit the toilet.

If we carefully study the Shariat, we will have to admit that it has prescribed a proper place for our worldly activities and religious duties. We have been commanded to devote one half of our time to the prayers, and we may spend the rest of our time in our worldly pursuits, whether we devote it to rest or to earning our living. According to this plan, we can maintain a balance between the two, and can carry out our duties about our religion as well as about our worldly life. So, if we devote ourselves wholly or mainly to the worldly requirements, then we are unjust and negligent. The sense of justice requires that we should be faithful to both, that is, to the requisites of life as well as to the hereafter, so that both are catered for because Islam does not advocate withdrawal from this world. This is what is meant by the verse:

رَبَّنَآ اٰتِنَا فِى الدُّنْيَا حَسَنَةً وَّفِى الْاٰخِرَةِ حَسَنَةً وَّقِنَا عَذَابَ النَّارِ (البقرة ، ٢٠١)

"O Lord! give us good in this world and in the Hereafter, and save us from the Fire (of Hell)."

(Al-Baqarah: 201)

In this chapter, my real object was to quote the sayings of the Holy Prophet (Sallallaho alaihe wasallam) about the Tabligh work. And the seven that I have quoted above are sufficient for true believers; as for the disbelievers, Allah says:

فَسَيَعْلَمُ الَّذِيْنَ ظَلَمُوْٓا اَيَّ مُنْقَلَبٍ يَّنْقَلِبُوْنَ

"Those who do wrong will come to know by what a (great) reverse they will be overturned."

Some sayings of the Holy Prophet (Sallallaho alaihe wasallam) indicate that there will come a time when everyone will follow his own wishes and temptations, and no one will pay heed to the teachings of religion or to the commandments of Allah. In those times, the Holy Prophet (Sallallaho alaihe wasallam) has advised us to mind our own business and to worship Allah, rather than deliver sermons to the people. But the divines of the nation say that such a period has not yet come; therefore, try your best to reform yourself and to instruct others, before such a time comes. We must avoid those shortcomings pointed out by the Holy Prophet (Sallallaho alaihe wasallam) above as these are the doors through which will occur corruption in our personal life as well as in the society. The Prophet (Sallallaho alaihe wasallam) has counted these shortcomings among the causes of our destruction.

اَللّٰهُمَّ احْفَظْنَا مِنَ الْفِتَنِ مَا ظَهَرَ مِنْهَا وَمَا بَطَنَ

"O Allah! save us from the trials of evil, whether it be external or internal."

CHAPTER 3

PRACTISE WHAT YOU PREACH

In this chapter it is intended to draw attention to a significant shortcoming. Just as most educated Muslims and scholars of the day have neglected the duty of Tabligh work, similarly there are those who preach Islam to others through speech and by writings, but they neglect practising what they say. In fact they, as preachers, should attend to reforming themselves more than to reform others. The Holy Prophet (Sallallaho alaihe wasallam) has strictly forbidden such persons to preach who are themselves guilty of transgression.

The Holy Prophet (Sallallaho alaihe wasallam) on the night of Mi'raaj (ascension) saw a group of persons whose lips were being clipped with fiery scissors. On asking who they were, Jibra-eel (Alayhis salaam) told him that these persons were preachers from among your followers who did not act on what they preached. A hadith says: "Some of the residents of Paradise will ask those in Hell: "How are you people here, whereas we followed your preachings, and thereby we got into Paradise?" They will answer: "We did not practise ourselves what we preached to others."

Another hadith says: "The punishment of Allah will descend more speedily upon the wicked scholars than on the common sinners. They will be astonished to see this, and will say: "Why is the punishment of Allah inflicted on us before the idolaters even?" They will be answered thus: "Those who transgressed in spite of having knowledge of religion are more guilty than those who had not this knowledge." The Muslim divines have written that the sermons of those who do not practise the religious observances themselves, cannot leave an impression on others. That is why the religious speeches, writings and the journals in this age fall flat on the listeners and the readers!

Says Allah in the Holy Qur'an:

اَتَأْمُرُوْنَ النَّاسَ بِالْبِرِّ وَتَنْسَوْنَ اَنْفُسَكُمْ وَاَنْتُمْ تَتْلُوْنَ الْكِتَابَ اَفَلَا تَعْقِلُوْنَ

(البقرة ، ٤٤)

"Do you command people to do good, but forget your own souls, although you read the Book? Do not you understand?"

The Holy Prophet says:

مَاتَزَالُ قَدَمَا عَبْدٍ يَّوْمَ الْقِيَامَةِ حَتَّى يُسْأَلَ عَنْ اَرْبَعٍ عَنْ عُمْرِهِ فِيْمَا اَفْنَاهُ وَعَنْ شَبَابِهِ فِيْمَا ابْلَاهُ وَعَنْ مَالِهِ مِنْ اَيْنَ اكْتَسَبَهُ وَفِيْمَ انْفَقَهُ وَعَنْ عِلْمِهِ مَاذَا عَمِلَ فِيْهِ

(ترغيب عن البيهقى)

"On the Day of Judgement, no one will be permitted to move away a single step until he is put these four questions: (1) How did you spend your period of life? (2) What use did you make of your youth? (3) How did you earn your wealth, and where did you spend it? (4) How far did you act upon your knowledge?"

Hadhrat Abu Darda (Radhiyallaho anho) is a distinguished Companion of the Holy Prophet (Sallallaho alaihe wasallam). He says: "The thing I fear most is the question that will be put to me on the Day of Judgement in the presence of all the people: Did you act upon the knowledge that you possessed?"

A certain Companion of the Holy Prophet (Sallallaho alaihe wasallam) asked him: "Who is the worst of all creatures?" He answered: "Don't ask me a question about bad things, but ask me a question about good things. The worst of all creatures are the wicked scholars, (i.e. those who do not practise what they say)."

Says the Holy Prophet (Sallallaho alaihe wasallam) in another hadith: "Knowledge is of two kinds: one, which remains on the tongue only and does not affect the heart and so is in fact an accusation from Allah; and the other which penetrates into the heart and revives the spirit: that is indeed useful." What we mean to say is that a Muslim should not acquire only that knowledge which concerns the formal observances, but also the spiritual knowledge which would purify his heart and enlighten his brain; otherwise it would be a cause for questioning on the Day of Judgement as to how far it was acted upon. Similar warnings are contained in several other ahaadith.

Therefore I would solemnly request all the missionaries and preachers to reform themselves outwardly and inwardly, and to practise themselves what they preach to others, otherwise mere preachment without practice cannot be accepted by Allah, as has been shown by various verses of the Holy Qur'an, as well as sayings of the Holy Prophet. I pray to Allah that He should enable me also to improve myself externally and internally and practise what I preach, for I entirely depend upon His favours to hide my deficiencies.

اِلَّا اَنْ يَّتَغَمَّدَنِى اللّٰهُ بِرَحْمَتِهِ الْوَاسِعَةِ

CHAPTER 4

THE IMPORTANCE OF IKRAAM IN TABLIGH

This chapter concerns another very important requirement for Tabligh, which through a little carelessness of the preachers, can do harm instead of good. For instance, when trying to prevent someone from wrongdoing, or save him from a bad habit, you should advise him privately and not openly disgrace him in the eyes of others; a Muslim's dignity is a valuable asset; as explained in the following sayings of the Holy Prophet (Sallallaho alaihe wasallam):

عَنْ اَبِيْ هُرَيْرَةَ رَضِىَ اللّٰهُ عَنْهُ مَرْفُوْعًا مَنْ سَتَرَ عَلٰى مُسْلِمٍ سَتَرَهُ اللّٰهُ فِىْ الدُّنْيَا
وَالْآخِرَةِ وَاللّٰهُ فِىْ عَوْنِ الْعَبْدِ مَاكَانَ الْعَبْدُ فِىْ عَوْنِ اَخِيْهِ

It has been reported by Abu Hurairah (Radhiyallaho anho) that the Holy Prophet (Sallallaho alaihe wasallam) said: "Whoever conceals the sins of a Muslim, Allah will conceal his sins in this world and in the Hereafter; and Allah helps His servant so long as he helps his brother Muslim." (Targheeb)

عَنْ ابْنِ عَبَّاسٍ رَضِىَ اللّٰهُ عَنْهُ مَرْفُوْعًا مَنْ سَتَرَ عَوْرَةَ اَخِيْهِ سَتَرَ اللّٰهُ عَوْرَتَهُ يَوْمَ
الْقِيَامَةِ وَمَنْ كَشَفَ عَوْرَةَ اَخِيْهِ الْمُسْلِمِ كشَفَ اللّٰهُ عَوْرَتَهُ حَتّٰى يَفْضَحَهُ بِهَا فِيْ
بَيْتِهِ (رواه ابن ماجه ترغيب)

It has been reported by Ibn Abbaas (Radhiyallaho anho) that the Holy Prophet (Sallallaho alaihe wasallam) said: "Whoever conceals the wrong-doings of a brother Muslim, Allah will conceal his wrong-doings on the Day of Judgement, and whoever will publicise the wrong-doings of a brother Muslim, Allah will disclose his wong-doings to the people, so much so that he will be disgraced sitting in his own house."

(Targheeb)

Similarly, there are many other traditions on this subject, therefore, the preachers of Islam should always have a great regard for conniving at faults and maintaining the dignity of brethren in Islam. Another hadith says: "Whoever does not help his brother Muslim, when he is being dishonoured, Allah will not pay heed to him when he himself is badly in need of help." Still another hadith says: "The worst form of usury is dishonouring a Muslim."

In numerous traditions like this, the dishonouring of a Muslim has been strictly forbidden; therefore, the missionaries should be particularly cautious on this subject. The correct method is to advise people secretly on the sins that come to knowledge secretly; and take corrective measures openly on the sins that are committed openly. Even the advice should be given in such a manner that the transgressor is not dishonoured, lest the advice produces the opposite effect. In short, the transgressors must be checked strictly, according to the commandments of Allah, but let us not forget the instructions given above to respect the dignity of every Muslim.

Moreover, a preacher must be polite and courteous when he addresses his audience; for ill temper and bitter words have just the opposite effect. A preacher spoke harshly to the Caliph Ma'moon ar-Rasheed. He said: "Please be polite and courteous to me, for Fir'own was a worse fellow than me, and Moosa (Alayhis salaam) was a much better person than you, but when he and Haroon (Alayhis salaam) were sent to instruct Fir'own, Allah said:

فَقُوْلَا لَهٗ قَوْلًا لَّيِّنًا لَعَلَّهٗ يَتَذَكَّرُ اَوْ يَخْشٰى (طٰه ، ٤٤)

"Speak to him in soft words, that he may turn to the Right Path, or perchance he may fear Me!" (Taahaa–44)

A youth (from the outlying regions) came to the Holy Prophet (Sallallaho alaihe wasallam), and said: "Please permit me to commit adultery." The Companions of the Holy Prophet (Sallallaho alaihe wasallam) took this very ill, and were enraged at his words; but the Holy Prophet (Sallallaho alaihe wasallam) said to him: "Come nearer to me. Would you like anyone to commit adultery with your mother?" He said: "Not at all." The Holy Prophet (Sallallaho alaihe wasallam) said: "Then other people will also never tolerate such a shameful act with their mothers." Then the Holy Prophet (Sallallaho alaihe wasallam) asked him the same question about his sister, aunt etc., and he answered each time in the negative. Then the Prophet (Sallallaho alaihe wasallam) put his hand on his chest and prayed: "O Allah! purify his heart, forgive his sins, and guard him against adultery." The reporters say that, after this, nothing was more hateful to him than adultery.

To be brief, the preachers should always be kind, polite and sympathetic towards their listeners, and should treat them as they would themselves like to be treated.

CHAPTER 5

IMPORTANCE OF IKHLAAS (SINCERITY) IN TABLIGH

I would particularly request the missionaries to base all their speeches, writings and actions on sincerity. Even a small good deed based on sincerity will be greatly rewarded by Allah, whereas without sincerity it will fetch no reward in this world or in the Hereafter.

اِنَّ اللهَ لَايَنْظُرُ اِلٰى صُوَرِكُمْ وَاَمْوَالِكُمْ وَلٰكِنْ يَنْظُرُ اِلٰى قُلُوْبِكُمْ وَاَعْمَالِكُمْ

(مشكواة عن مسلم)

Says the Holy Prophet (Sallallaho alaihe wasallam) in this context: "Allah does not look towards your faces, or towards your riches; but He sees (the sincerity of) your hearts, and the nature of your deeds."

(Mishkaat)

On another occasion, the Holy Prophet (Sallallaho alaihe wasallam) was asked as to what is the meaning of 'Eemaan'. He answered: "It means sincerity."

(Targheeb)

Hadhrat Mu'aaz (Radhiyallaho anho) was given command in Yemen. When he was about to depart, he asked for advice from the Holy Prophet (Sallallaho alaihe wasallam), who said: "Observe sincerity in all your religious beliefs and actions, for it will increase the reward of your good deeds." Another hadith says: "Allah accepts only those deeds of His servants, which are based on complete sincerity to Him."

قَالَ اللهُ تَعَالٰى: اَنَا اَغْنَى الشُّرَكَاءِ عَنِ الشِّرْكِ مَنْ عَمِلَ عَمَلًا اَشْرَكَ فِيْهِ مَعِى غَيْرِىْ تَرَكْتُهُ وَشِرْكَهُ ، وَفِىْ رِوَايَةٍ فَاَنَا مِنْهُ بَرِیٌّ فَهُوَ لِلَّذِيْ عَمِلَهُ

(مشكواة عن مسلم)

Another hadith says: "Allah has proclaimed: 'I am the most self-respecting and self-sufficient of all partners; therefore whoever brings forth a partner to Me in any action, I entrust him to the same partner, (and do not help him at all). Then I have no value for his actions, which are all given to the partner.'"

It has been stated in another hadith that it will be proclaimed on the Day of Judgement: "Whoever has brought forward a partner to Allah in any action, he should demand his reward from the same partner; for Allah is far above needing any partner."

Another hadith says:

مَنْ صَلَّى يُرَاءِىْ فَقَدْ اَشْرَكَ وَمَنْ صَامَ يُرَاءِىْ فَقَدْ اَشْرَكَ وَمَنْ تَصَدَّقَ يُرَاءِىْ
فَقَدْ اَشْرَكَ (مشكواة عن احمد)

"Whoever performs prayer for show, he becomes guilty of false worship; and whoever observes fasts for show, he also becomes guilty of false worship; and whoever gives alms for show, he also becomes guilty of false worship."

(Mishkaat)

To be guilty of false worship here means that he does not perform such good deeds sincerely to please Allah only, but by making a show of them he wants to win the favour and appreciation of human beings, which is to set up partners to Allah indirectly.

Another hadith says with this meaning:

اِنَّ اَوَّلَ النَّاسِ يُقْضَىٰ عَلَيْهِ يَوْمَ الْقِيَامَةِ رَجُلٌ اُسْتُشْهِدَ فَاُتِىَ بِهِ فَعَرَّفَهُ نِعْمَتَهُ
فَعَرَفَهَا فَقَالَ فَمَا عَمِلْتَ فِيْهَا؟ قَالَ قَاتَلْتُ فِيْكَ حَتَّى اُسْتُشْهِدْتُ قَالَ كَذَبْتَ
وَلٰكِنَّكَ قَاتَلْتَ لِاَنْ يُّقَالَ جَرِىٌّ فَقَدْ قِيْلَ ثُمَّ اُمِرَ بِهِ فَسُحِبَ عَلٰى وَجْهِهِ حَتّٰى
اُلْقِيَ فِى النَّارِ وَرَجُلٌ تَعَلَّمَ الْعِلْمَ وَعَلَّمَهُ وَقَرَأَ الْقُرْآنَ فَاُتِيَ بِهِ فَعَرَّفَهُ نِعَمَهُ فَعَرَفَهَا
قَالَ فَمَا عَمِلْتَ فِيْهَا قَالَ تَعَلَّمْتُ الْعِلْمَ وَعَلَّمْتُهُ وَقَرَأْتُ فِيْكَ الْقُرْآنَ قَالَ كَذَبْتَ
وَلٰكِنَّكَ تَعَلَّمْتَ الْعِلْمَ لِيُقَالَ اِنَّكَ عَالِمٌ وَقَرَأْتَ الْقُرْآنَ لِيُقَالَ هُوَ قَارِئٌ فَقَدْ قِيْلَ
ثُمَّ اُمِرَ بِهِ فَسُحِبَ عَلٰى وَجْهِهِ حَتّٰى اُلْقِيَ فِى النَّارِ وَرَجُلٌ وَسَّعَ اللّٰهُ عَلَيْهِ وَاَعْطَاهُ
مِنْ اَصْنَافِ الْمَالِ كُلِّهِ فَاُتِيَ بِهِ فَعَرَّفَهُ نِعَمَهُ فَعَرَفَهَا قَالَ فَمَا عَمِلْتَ فِيْهَا؟ قَالَ

مَاتَرَكْتُ مِنْ سَبِيْلٍ تُحِبُّ اَنْ يُنْفَقَ فِيْهَا اِلَّا اَنْفَقْتُ فِيْهَا لَكَ قَالَ كَذَبْتَ وَلٰكِنَّكَ فَعَلْتَ لِيُقَالَ هُوَ جَوَادٌ فَقَدْ قِيْلَ ثُمَّ اُمِرَ بِهِ فَسُحِبَ بِهِ عَلَى وَجْهِهِ ثُمَّ اُلْقِيَ فِي النَّارِ (مشكواة عن مسلم)

Certain categories of people will be called first of all for reckoning on the Day of Judgement. A martyr will be asked by Allah, "Did I not bestow such and such favours on you?" He will admit those boons and favours. Then Allah will ask him: "How did you make use of My favours?" He will answer: "I went to the Holy War to please You, and was killed therein." Allah will say: "You lie; you participated in the Holy War to be called a hero by people, and this has been done."

Then he will be thrown headlong into the fire of Hell. Next, a scholar will be called and the same questions will be put to him. In reply he will admit the favours of Allah. Then he will be asked: "How did you make use of My favours?" He will answer, "I acquired knowledge of Islam and taught it to others, simply to please You." Allah will say: "You lie: you attained knowledge in order to be called an aalim and recited the Holy Qur'an to be called a qaari." Then he too will be thrown headlong into the fire of Hell. Thereafter a rich man will be called, and the same questions will be put to him. He will say: "I always spent money to please Thee." Allah will say: "You lie; you spent money in order to be called a generous man, and this has been said." Then he will also be thrown headlong into the fire of Hell.

(Mishkaat)

Therefore, our preachers of Islam should always avoid show and vanity, and should render their services only to please Allah. They should follow the Sunnah of the Holy Prophet (Sallallaho alaihe wasallam), and should not desire to win fame, or favour and appreciation of people. If such a vain desire is suspected in their mind, they should seek the refuge of Allah, and should ask His pardon. May Allah grant us sincerity to serve His religion to the best of our efforts.

CHAPTER 6

RESPECT FOR LEARNING AND THE LEARNED IN ISLAM

In this chapter, I would make a few submissions to the Muslims in general that they may know how to respect the scholars and the preachers of Islam. Today it is usual to have unfounded misgivings and objections against the preachers and the learned men of the nation; this is very harmful from the religious point of view. In every circle and every institution of the world, there are good as well as bad people; and if there are a few bad persons among the scholars also, it is no wonder. Two important considerations are here noteworthy. Firstly, you should not form any definite opinion about the character of anyone, unless you have a solid proof about it.

Says Allah in the Holy Qur'an:

وَلَا تَقْفُ مَالَيْسَ لَكَ بِهِ عِلْمٌ اِنَّ السَّمْعَ وَالْبَصَرَ وَالْفُؤَادَ كُلُّ اُوْلٰئِكَ كَانَ عَنْهُ مَسْؤُلًا

"And do not take practical steps regarding anything, about which you have no knowledge; for everyone will be questioned as to how he used his ears and eyes and the heart."

And obviously it is unjust to reject the (good) advice of a preacher, simply because you have some unconfirmed doubts about him.

The Jews translated their scriptures into Arabic, and used to read them out to the Muslims; but the Holy Prophet (Sallallaho alaihe wasallam) was so cautious about giving his decision on this subject that he said: "O Muslims! you should neither confirm what they say, nor reject them; rather you should say: 'Whatever Allah has revealed, we believe in all that.'" In other words, he prohibited contradiction of even an unbeliever's narration without proper investigation. But contrary to this precept, we reject those instructions of preachers that are against our wishes, without any arguments on our part, and attack their reputation even when we know them to be righteous

Another thing that you must keep in mind is that even the righteous scholars and preachers of your nation are also human beings, and as such they too can have some weaknesses. The responsibility of their good or bad deeds really rests on them and the final reckoning belongs to Allah; but I hope that by His mercy and immense generosity He will forgive them for after all they have been serving His Religion and Faith at great personal sacrifice throughout their lives. In short, either to entertain doubts and objections against the religious preacher himself, or spread them amongst others, will take people away from religion and be the cause of geat distress for those who participate in such affairs.

The Holy Prophet (Sallallaho alaihe wasallam) has said:

اِنَّ مِنْ اَجْلَالِ اللهِ تَعَالٰی اِكْرَامُ ذِی الشَّيْبَةِ الْمُسْلِمِ وَحَامِلِ الْقُرْآنِ غَيْرِ الْغَالِیْ فِيْهِ وَلَا الْجَافِیْ عَنْهُ وَاِكْرَامُ ذِی السُّلْطَانِ الْمُقْسِطِ (ترغيب عن ابي داود)

"Whoever respects the following three, he really pays respect to Allah: (1) An aged Muslim, (2) One who teaches and preaches the Holy Qur'an without any excess, (3) And a ruler who is just to the people."

(Targheeb)

Also the following saying of the Holy Prophet (Sallallaho alaihe wasallam) tells us:

لَيْسَ مِنْ اُمَّتِيْ مَنْ لَمْ يُجِلَّ كَبِيْرَنَا وَيَرْحَمْ صَغِيْرَنَا وَيَعْرِفْ عَالِمَنَا (ترغيب)

"He is not among my followers, who does not respect our elders, is not merciful to our youngsters, and does not pay due reverence to our scholars."

عَنْ اَبِيْ اُمَامَةَ رَضِیَ اللهُ عَنْهُ عَنْ رَسُوْلِ اللهِ ﷺ قَالَ ثَلٰثٌ لَايَسْتَخِفُّ بِهِمْ اِلَّا مُنَافِقٌ ذُو الشَّيْبَةِ فِی الْاِسْلَامِ وَذُو الْعِلْمِ وَاِمَامٌ مُقْسِطٌ (ترغيب عن الطبراني)

"Whoever belittles the following three persons is not a Muslim but a hypocrite: first, an aged Muslim; second, a scholar (of religion); and third, a just ruler."

The Holy Prophet (Sallallaho alaihe wasallam) has also

said: "I fear particularly for three shortcomings in my followers. First, due to increasing worldly benefits and achievements, they will envy one another; second, discussion of the Holy Qur'an will become so common that even the ignorant will claim that they know the meanings of the Holy Qur'an, although many meanings are such that cannot be understood by anyone except the well versed scholars of that Book, who say: "We have a firm faith in it, and that it is from Allah", so how much more careful should be the common people; third, the religious scholars will be neglected and will not be patronized properly."

(Targheeb)

Many similar traditions are found in the books of hadith. It has been mentioned in 'Fataawa Aalamgiri' that the sort of derogatory words that are generally used today by the ignorant people about the scholars of Islam may seriously damage their faith. Therefore, people must be careful to avoid such words. Suppose for a moment there are no true and sincere scholars of Islam in the world (and the majority consists of corrupt people), even then nothing is gained by branding them as evil scholars. Rather, it is the religious and moral duty of every Muslim to form such an Islamic society that would give birth to sincere servants of Islam. Only when such a body of persons is in existence we should rest content.

Of course, there have always been some differences of opinion among the Muslim scholars, mostly about minor problems, for which they cannot be maligned. There is a hadith that says: "The Holy Prophet (Sallallaho alaihe wasallam) gave his shoes to Abu Hurairah (Radhiyallaho anho), and said: "Take my shoes as a sign, and proclaim among the Muslims that whoever will say 'La ilaha illallah, Mohammadur Rasul-ullah' from the bottom of his heart, he will certainly enter Paradise." Hadhrat Umar (Radhiyallaho anho) met Abu Hurairah (Radhiyallaho anho) in the way and asked him where he was going. He told him the message of the Holy Prophet (Sallallaho alaihe wasallam), yet Hadhrat Umar (Radhiyallaho anho) was annoyed, for he did not agree with such a proposition; therefore he hit the messenger in the chest, who fell back. Yet no one raised objections against Hadhrat Umar (Radhiyallaho anho), nor was any demonstration arranged against him because of this difference of opinion. Many differences of opinion existed among the Sahabah and later the four Imaams of Fiqh differed among themselves in numerous details.

There have been many minor differences of opinion about prayers among the four Imaams; I myself know of about two hundred, but this does not mean that their followers should doubt the faith of one another, and call each other 'infidel'. The fact is that the common people are mostly unaware of the finer points on which various scholars differ in their views; these differences are a blessing in disguise. As a matter of fact, good preachers and sincere servants of Islam do not attach any importance to such trifling things, but continue their attempt to bring people to the Right Path. We know that doctors differ among themselves and lawyers differ in their advice, nevertheless people continue to make use of their services. But those who are ignorant, selfish and lazy, they simply use their difference of views to raise objections against the religious scholars. Anyhow, it has been enjoined on every Muslim to listen to those scholars of the Holy Qur'an, whom he respects and knows to be the followers of the Sunnah, and should avoid reproaching those whom he does not like. Anyone who has no proper knowledge of Islam and the Holy Qur'an, has no right to raise objections against the scholars. The scholars of Islam should always keep this saying of the Holy Prophet (Sallallaho alaihe wasallam) in mind and act accordingly: "It is to waste knowledge to address those who are not fit for it."

In this corrupt age, when even the commandments of Allah and the sayings of the Holy Prophet (Sallallaho alaihe wasallam) are being criticised, I have no reason to wonder if the sermons of Muslim scholars are not heard and the Qur'an not followed. Says Allah in the Holy Qur'an.

وَمَنْ يَّتَعَدَّ حُدُوْدَ اللهِ فَأُولٰئِكَ هُمُ الظّٰلِمُوْنَ (البقرة ، ٢٢٩)

"And whoever transgresses the limits of Allah, surely these are the unjust."

CHAPTER 7

KEEPING COMPANY WITH THE RIGHTEOUS DIVINES

In this last chapter, which really completes the sixth one, I would remind the Muslims to follow the Sunnah of the Holy Prophet (Sallallaho alaihe wasallam), and to keep the company of those who devote themselves to Islam and remember Allah day and night, for this will make them steadfast in Islam. Even the Holy Prophet (Sallallaho alaihe wasallam) was commanded to keep such company; says the Holy Prophet (Sallallaho alaihe wasallam) on this subject:

اَلَا اَدُلُّكَ عَلٰى مِلَاكِ هٰذَا الْاَمْرِ الَّذِيْ تُصِيْبُ بِهٖ خَيْرَ الدُّنْيَا وَالْاٰخِرَةِ عَلَيْكَ
بِمَجَالِسِ اَهْلِ الذِّكْرِ ، الحديث (مشكوٰة)

"Shall I tell you a thing by which you can attain good in this world and the Hereafter? Remember, it is the company of those who remember and glorify Allah day and night." (Mishkaat)

Now it is up to you to search for and to recognize the true lovers of Allah and these are the followers of the Sunnah, for Allah has sent his beloved Prophet (Sallallaho alaihe wasallam) as a model for the guidance of the Muslims. Says Allah in the Holy Qur'an:

قُلْ اِنْ كُنْتُمْ تُحِبُّوْنَ اللّٰهَ فَاتَّبِعُوْنِيْ يُحْبِبْكُمُ اللّٰهُ وَيَغْفِرْلَكُمْ ذُنُوْبَكُمْ وَاللّٰهُ غَفُوْرٌ
رَّحِيْمٌ (اٰل عمران ، ٣١)

O Prophet (Sallallaho alaihe wasallam)! say: "If you people (really) love Allah, then follow me; so that Allah will love you, and will pardon your sins; and Allah is Forgiving, Merciful."

Therefore, whoever follows the Holy Prophet (Sallallaho alaihe wasallam) faithfully is nearer to Allah, and whoever does not follow him is far away from Allah and cannot win His favours. The commentators of the Holy

Qur'an have written that whoever claims to be a lover of Allah, but does not follow the Sunnah of the Holy Prophet (Sallallaho alaihe wasallam), he is a liar; for it is a requisite of love that everything associated with the beloved must be loved. A poet has quoted the words of the famous Qais-'Aamir, the lover of Laila:

امَرُّ عَلى الدِّيَارِ دِيَارِ ليلى   اُقَبِّلُ ذَا الْجِدَارَ وَذَا الْجِدَرَا
وَمَا حُبُّ الدِّيَارِ شَغَفْنَ قَلْبِي   وَلٰكِنْ حُبُّ مَنْ سَكَنَ الدِّيَارَا

"Whenever I pass through the city of Laila, I love every door and wall of it. Really I do not love the city as a city, but rather love the people in it who are associated with Laila." Another poet says:

تَعْصِي الْاِلٰهَ وَاَنْتَ تُظْهِرُ حُبَّهُ   وَهٰذَا لَعَمْرِيْ فِي الْفِعَالِ بَدِيْعُ
لَوْ كَانَ حُبُّكَ صَادِقًا لَاطَعْتَهُ   اِنَّ الْمُحِبَّ لِمَنْ يُحِبُّ مُطِيْعُ

"You pretend to be a lover of Allah, and yet you do not obey His commandments! And I swear, in practise this is strange. If you were a true lover, you would never disobey Him, for a lover always follows the orders of his beloved."

The Holy Prophet (Sallallaho alaihe wasallam) said: "All my followers will enter Paradise, but not those who have denied me." The Companions said: "Who would deny you?" He said: "Those who follow me would enter Paradise, but those who disobey me, they in fact deny me."

In another hadith, the Prophet (Sallallaho alaihe wasallam) has said, "No one of you can be a true Muslim unless his wishes are subordinate to that which I have brought, that is the Holy Qur'an."

(Mishkaat)

One can hardly believe that those who claim to be well-wishers of Islam and the Muslims would disobey Allah and His Prophet. When we say that such and such thing is against the Sunnah, they feel very annoyed; then how can they be among the followers of the Holy Prophet (Sallallaho alaihe wasallam)?

Sa'di (Rahmatullah alaih) has said:

خلافِ پیمبر کسے رہ گزید کہ ہرگز بمنزل نخواہد رسید

"Whoever treads a path contrary to the Sunnah of the Holy Prophet (Sallallaho alaihe wasallam), he will never reach his destination."

Therefore, whoever keeps the company of true lovers of Allah and followers of the Sunnah, in order to obtain spiritual benefits, he will certainly progress towards salvation.

On this particular subject, please consider the following sayings of the Holy Prophet (Sallallaho alaihe wasallam):

"Whenever you people pass through the Gardens of Paradise, partake of their fruits." The Companions asked: "What are the Gardens of Paradise?" The Holy Prophet (Sallallaho alaihe wasallam) answered: "The assemblies wherein knowledge of Islam and the Holy Qur'an is taught."

The Holy Prophet (Sallallaho alaihe wasallam) also said: "Luqmaan instructed his son in these words: "Keep the company of scholars, and listen attentively to the words of the wise, for therewith Allah revives the dead hearts, just as He revives the dead earth with heavy rains; and the wise alone understand the religion."

A Companion asked the Holy Prophet (Sallallaho alaihe wasallam) "Who can be the best companion for us?" He answered: "Such a person that, when you see him, you remember Allah; when you listen to him, your knowledge of Islam is increased; when you see his actions, you are reminded of the life Hereafter."

(Targheeb)

Again, "The most devoted servants of Allah are such that, when you see them you remember Allah." Says Allah in the Holy Qur'an:

يَاأَيُّهَا الَّذِيْنَ آمَنُوا اتَّقُوْا اللهَ وَكُوْنُوْا مَعَ الصَّادِقِيْنَ (التوبة ١١٩)

"O those who believe! Fear Allah, and be with the truthful (faithful) people!"

The commentators have written that by 'truthful' are meant the mystics and the true lovers of Allah, for whoever attaches himself to them and listens to their sermons, he attains very high standards of spirituality.

Sheikh Akbar has written: "You cannot get rid of the evil wishes of yourself, though you may strive for it for your whole life unless your desires are subjected to the commandments of Allah and the Sunnah of the Holy Prophet (Sallallaho alaihe wasallam). So, when you find a true lover of Allah, serve him well and follow his instructions as though you have no will of your own; obey him in all your spiritual, religious and personal problems, even those concerning your occupation, so that he may lead you to the right path and take you nearer to Allah."

Says the Holy Prophet (Sallallaho alaihe wasallam) "When a group of people remember Allah in a meeting, then the angels surround that gathering, Allah's mercy descends on them and Allah remembers them in the assembly of Angels." What honour can be greater for the believers than that Allah remembers and appreciates them? Says the Holy Prophet (Sallallaho alaihe wasallam): "An angel is sent to those who remember Allah sincerely, and he says 'Allah has forgiven your past sins, and has converted your bad deeds into good ones'."

In another hadith, the Holy Prophet (Sallallaho alaihe wasallam) says: "Any assembly of Muslims, who do not remember Allah, (do not) send salutations to His Messenger (Sallallaho alaihe wasallam), will face disappointment on the Day of Judgement."

There is a prayer of Hadhrat Dawood (Alayhis salaam) in the following words: "O Allah! if you see me neglecting the assembly of those who remember Thee, and attending the assembly of transgressors, then break my feet (that I may not be able to walk towards them)."

A poet has said,

جب اس کی صوت وصورت سے ہے محرومی تو بہتر ہے

مرے کانوں کا کر ہونا، اور آنکھیں کور ہو جانی

"When I do not listen to Him and see His face, it is better to be deaf and blind."

Hadhrat Abu Hurairah (Radhiyallaho anho) says: "An assembly wherein Allah is remembered and glorified, shines for the heavenly creatures, just as the stars shine for the earthly creatures."

Once, Hadhrat Abu Hurairah (Radhiyallaho anho) went to a bazaar and proclaimed to the people: "O brethren! You are sitting here, and the legacy of the Holy Prophet (Sallallaho alaihe wasallam) is being distributed in the mosque." The people ran to the mosque, but as nothing material was being distributed there, they returned disappointed. Hadhrat Abu Hurairah (Radhiyallaho anho) asked them. "After all what was being done there?" They answered: "A few people were reading the Holy Qur'an, and a few others were engaged in praising and glorifying Allah." He said: "This is what we call the legacy of the Holy Prophet (Sallallaho alaihe wasallam)."

Imam Ghazali (Rahmatullah alaih) has mentioned many similar traditions. Even the Holy Prophet (Sallallaho alaihe wasallam) has been commanded by Allah:

وَاصْبِرْ نَفْسَكَ مَعَ الَّذِيْنَ يَدْعُوْنَ رَبَّهُمْ بِالْغَدَاةِ وَالْعَشِيِّ يُرِيْدُوْنَ وَجْهَهُ وَلَاتَعْدُ عَيْنَاكَ عَنْهُمْ تُرِيْدُ زِيْنَةَ الْحَيٰوةِ الدُّنْيَا وَلَاتُطِعْ مَنْ اَغْفَلْنَا قَلْبَهُ عَنْ ذِكْرِنَا وَاتَّبَعَ هَوٰىهُ وَكَانَ اَمْرُهُ فُرُطًا (الكهف ٢٨)

"O Messenger! keep the company of those who pray to Allah every morning and evening, and they desire only His pleasure; and do not turn your eyes from them to the attractions and adornment of the worldly life; and do not follow him whose heart We have turned away from our remembrance, and who follows his desires, and (therefore) he has broken the limits (of true religion)."

Numerous traditions indicate that the Holy Prophet (Sallallaho alaihe wasallam) used to thank Allah for producing such pious people among his followers that he was commanded to keep their company. And in the same verse, the Holy Prophet (Sallallaho alaihe wasallam) has been commanded to avoid the company of those who are slaves of passion and tresspass the limits laid down by Allah. He has been instructed again and again not to follow their vain desires.

Now all those who blindly follow the ways of the ungodly and transgressing people of the non-believing nations should search their hearts and see how far they are true believers. Their imitating the pagans and the Christian has taken them far away from the Right Path;

ترسم نہ رسی بکعبہ اے اعرابی کیں رہ کہ تو میروی بترکستان است

"O ignorant desert dweller! I fear that you won't be able to reach the Kaaba; for the path that you tread leads to Turkistan."

مراد مانصیحت بود و کردیم

حوالت باخدا کردیم و رفتیم

وَمَا عَلَى الرُّسُلِ اِلَّا الْبَلَاغُ

My object was to advise you on religious matters, and I have done my duty. Now I entrust you to Allah, and bid farewell. Even the prophets were commanded only to preach the truth.

(Hafiz) Mohammad Zakariyya
Madrasah Mazahir-ul-Ulum
Saharanpur
5, Safar 1350
(21 June 1931)

Virtues of Ramadhaan

فضائلِ رمضان

by
Shaikhul Hadith Maulana Muhammad Zakariyya Saheb
of Saharanpur, India

Virtues of Ramadhaan

translated by
Yousuf Abdullah Karaan

ادارہ اشاعتِ دینیات (پرائیویٹ) لمیٹڈ
idara
IDARA ISHA'AT-E-DINIYAT (P) LTD.

FAZA'IL-E-RAMADHAAN

By: Shaikhul Hadith
Maulana Muhammad Zakariyya Kaandhlawi (Rah)

Edition 2001

ISBN:- 81-7101-328-7

Published by:
IDARA ISHA'AT-E-DINIYAT (P) LTD.
168/2, Jha House, Hazrat Nizamuddin
New Delhi-110 013 (India)
Tel.: 6926832, 6926833
Fax: +91-11-6322787,4352786
Email: **sales@idara.com**
Visit us at: **www.idara.com**

Printed at:
Nice Printing Press, Delhi

شَهْرُ رَمَضَانَ الَّذِىْ اُنْزِلَ فِيْهِ الْقُرْآنُ هُدىً لِّلنَّاسِ وَبَيِّنَاتٍ مِّنَ الْهُدىٰ وَالْفُرْقَانِ

CONTENTS

VIRTUES OF RAMADHAAN

CHAPTER—II LAYLATUL QADR
(The Night of Power)

CHAPTER—III I'TIKAAF (Seclusion)

FOREWORD

This book is a simple English translation of a famous book in Urdu by Shaikhul -Hadith Maulana Zakariyya of Saharanpur, India.

Maulana Zakariyya (May Allah have mercy on him and grant him a peaceful abode) was one of the world's greatest scholars on Hadith and was undoubtedly one of the greatest spiritual teachers of his age, having thousands of mureeds all over India, Pakistan, Malaya, South Africa, etc. He needs no introduction as an Aalim and spiritual guide since he is following in the footsteps of illustrious sons of Islaam such as Shaikhul-hind Maulana Mahmoodul -Hasan, Maulana Raipuri, Maulana Thanawy, Maulana Madani, Maulana Khalil Ahmad, Maulana 'Uthmaani and Maulana Ilyaas etc. His numerous works in Urdu and Arabic have benefitted millions and have spread far and wide as a result of the activities of the Tablighi Jamaa-ats all over the world.

Because of the beneficial nature of this book we felt that it should be translated into English. This humble effort is being placed before the English speaking public. May Allah accept this work and may it benefit us all. Our fervent duaa' is that Allah grant us the ability to serve Islaam and the Muslims at all times Aameen.

A humble appeal is made to all Tablighi Jamaa-ats and to the Imaams of musjids to read the contents of this book or to arrange for it to be read to congregations for about ten minutes daily, after the Maghrib or 'Ishaa' 'salaah in the weeks preceding Ramadhaan, and during the blessed month at a suitable time so that, In-shaa'Allah, as many Muslims as possible may be inspired to celebrate Ramadhaan in the most rewarding manner, Aameen.

Yusuf Karaan

بِسْمِ اللّٰهِ الرَّحْمٰنِ الرَّحِيْمِ

نَحْمَدُهٗ وَنُصَلِّىْ عَلٰى رَسُوْلِهِ الْكَرِيْمِ حَامِدًا وَّمُصَلِّيًا وَّمُسَلِّمًا

INTRODUCTION

All praise is for Allah and blessings be upon His chosen Messenger.

In the following pages I have quoted a few Ahaadith with the reference to the blessed month of Ramadhaan. The Holy Prophet (May Allah's choicest blessings be upon him) has urged us in these Ahaadith to mend our lives by acquiring the great virtues and blessings of this month. True appreciation would be that we fully carry out these teachings. Our negligence, in these days has become so marked that we neither act upon his advice nor pay any heed to it, so much so that very few of us even know about the great good we can obtain therefrom.

My object in collecting these Ahaadith in this book is to assist the Imaams of musjids, leaders of Taraaweeh 'salaah and other well-read Muslims who have the interest of our Deen at heart, to read out and explain this book in the musjid during the first few days of Ramadhaan (or before) so that through Allah's great mercy and the blessings of His beloved, we may pay due attention to it and receive Allah's blessings during this sacred month. This can lead us towards acting on His commands and keep us away from evil deeds.

Rasulullah صلى الله عليه وسلم said, "Should Allah guide one person aright through you, that shall be better for you than a red camel (something that is pricey, and also considered a most precious possession)."

Ramadhaan is for the Muslims a very great favour. This favour can only be considered as such if we appreciate it, otherwise Ramadhaan will come and go without us gaining anything.

It is stated in the Hadith "If my Ummah realise what Ramadhaan really is, they would wish that the whole year should just be Ramadhaan." Every person knows that fasting for a full year is a very difficult task, and only because of the great reward for Ramadhaan mentioned by Rasulullah صلی اللہ علیہ وسلم will they desire the full year to be Ramadhaan. In another Hadith we are told, "The fasting of Ramadhaan and fasting three days of every month keeps evil away from the heart."

The Sahaabah (companions) of Rasulullah صلی اللہ علیہ وسلم used to fast even during jihaad and on weary, tiresome journeys, inspite of having obtained permission from Rasulullah صلی اللہ علیہ وسلم to break their fast. In the end Rasulullah صلی اللہ علیہ وسلم had to prohibit them from fasting. So much did they exert themselves for not wanting to lose the blessings. Imaam Muslim reports that the Sahaabah were once on a journey for jihaad. It was extremely hot and due to poverty they did not even have a cloth for shade to protect themselves against the heat. In this condition they stopped at one place, while many of them used their hands for protection against the heat. In this condition too, many were fasting. They were so overcome with weakness that they could not bear the excessive heat and fell down. (Some Sahaabah fasted throughout the year).

There are many Ahaadith in which the blessings of Ramadhaan are explained. It is not possible for me to collect them all here, and if I am to enumerate and explain them all in detail then readers may become bored. However, now is the time to refresh our mind with them. After all one need not explain how disinterested we have become in our Deen. It is a self-evident truth.

I have mentioned only twenty-one Ahaadith in this book and have divided them into three chapters.

(a) Chapter one, on the Virtues of Ramadhaan *(Ten Ahaadith)*

(b) Chapter two, on Laylatul Qadr *(Seven Ahaadith)*

(c) Chapter three, on I'itikaaf *(three Ahaadith)*

At the end by way of ending this book, I have included one long Hadith. May Allah accept this work through His Grace and the blessings of His beloved Rasulullah, Muhammad صلی اللہ علیہ وسلم and grant me and all Muslims the hidaayah to derive benefit from it. Most surely He is the Good, The Generous and most kind. *Aameen.*

بِسْمِ اللّٰهِ الرَّحْمٰنِ الرَّحِيْمِ

CHAPTER ONE

THE VIRTUES OF RAMADHAAN

(١) عَنْ سَلْمَانَ رَضِىَ اللّٰهُ تَعَالٰى عَنْهُ قَالَ خَطَبَنَا رَسُوْلُ اللّٰهِ ﷺ فِى آخِرِ يَوْمٍ مِّنْ شَعْبَانَ فَقَالَ يَاۤاَيُّهَا النَّاسُ قَدْ اَظَلَّكُمْ شَهْرٌ عَظِيْمٌ مُبَارَكٌ شَهْرٌ فِيْهِ لَيْلَةٌ خَيْرٌ مِّنْ اَلْفِ شَهْرٍ ، شَهْرٌ جَعَلَ اللّٰهُ صِيَامَهُ فَرِيْضَةً وَقِيَامَ لَيْلِهِ تَطَوُّعًا مَنْ تَقَرَّبَ فِيْهِ بِخَصْلَةٍ كَانَ كَمَنْ اَدّٰى فَرِيْضَةً فِيْمَا سِوَاهُ وَمَنْ اَدّٰى فَرِيْضَةً فِيْهِ كَانَ كَمَنْ اَدّٰى سَبْعِيْنَ فَرِيْضَةً فِيْمَا سِوَاهُ ، وَهُوَ شَهْرُ الصَّبْرِ وَالصَّبْرُ ثَوَابُهُ الْجَنَّةُ وَشَهْرُ الْمُوَاسَاةِ وَشَهْرٌ يُزَادُ فِي رِزْقِ الْمُؤْمِنِ فِيْهِ ، مَنْ فَطَّرَ فِيْهِ صَائِمًا كَانَ مَغْفِرَةً لِذُنُوْبِهِ وَعِتْقَ رَقَبَتِهِ مِنَ النَّارِ وَكَانَ لَهُ مِثْلَ اَجْرِهِ مِنْ غَيْرِ اَنْ يُّنْقَصَ مِنْ اَجْرِهِ شَىْءٌ قَالُوْا يَارَسُوْلَ اللّٰهِ لَيْسَ كُلُّنَا يَجِدُ مَايُفَطِّرُ الصَّائِمَ فَقَالَ رَسُوْلُ اللّٰهِ ﷺ يُعْطِى اللّٰهُ هٰذَا الثَّوَابَ مَنْ فَطَّرَ صَائِمًا عَلٰى تَمْرَةٍ اَوْ شَرْبَةِ مَاءٍ اَوْ مَذْقَةِ لَبَنٍ وَهُوَ شَهْرٌ اَوَّلُهُ رَحْمَةٌ وَاَوْسَطُهُ مَغْفِرَةٌ وَآخِرُهُ عِتْقٌ مِّنَ النَّارِ مَنْ خَفَّفَ عَنْ مَمْلُوْكِهِ فِيْهِ غَفَرَ اللّٰهُ لَهُ وَاَعْتَقَهُ مِنَ النَّارِ وَاسْتَكْثِرُوْا فِيْهِ مِنْ اَرْبَعِ خِصَالٍ خَصْلَتَيْنِ تُرْضُوْنَ بِهِمَا رَبَّكُمْ وَخَصْلَتَيْنِ لَاغِنَاءَ بِكُمْ عَنْهُمَا فَاَمَّا الْخَصْلَتَانِ اللَّتَانِ تُرْضُوْنَ بِهِمَا رَبَّكُمْ فَشَهَادَةُ اَنْ لَّا اِلٰهَ اِلَّا اللّٰهُ وَتَسْتَغْفِرُوْنَهُ ، وَاَمَّا الْخَصْلَتَانِ اللَّتَانِ لَاغِنَاءَ بِكُمْ عَنْهُمَا فَتَسْئَلُوْنَ اللّٰهَ الْجَنَّةَ وَتَعَوَّذُوْنَ بِهِ مِنَ النَّارِ وَمَنْ سَقٰى صَائِمًا سَقَاهُ اللّٰهُ مِنْ حَوْضِى شَرْبَةً لَايَظْمَأُ حَتّٰى يَدْخُلَ الْجَنَّةَ رواه ابن خزيمة فى صحيحه وقال إن صح الخبر ورواه البيهقى ورواه أبوشيخ ابن حبان فى الثواب باختصار عنهما وفى أسانيدهم علي بن زيد بن جدعان ورواه ابن خزيمه أيضا والبيهقى باختصار عنه من حديث أبى هريرة وفى إسناده كثير بن زيد كذا فى الترغيب ص ٢٠٣ قلت علي بن زيد ضعفه جماعة وقال الترمذى صدوق وصحح له حديثا فى السلام وحسن له غير ما حديث وكذا كثير ضعفه النسائى وغيره وقال ابن معين ثقة وقال ابن عدى لم أر بحديثه بأسا وأخرج بحديثه ابن خزيمة فى صحيحه كذا فى رجال المنذرى ص ٧٠٤ لكن قال العينى الخبر منكر فتأمل)

HADITH NO. 1

Salmaan رضي الله عنه *reports, "On the last day of Sha-baan Rasulullah* صلى الله عليه وسلم *addressed us and said, 'O people there comes over you now a great month, a most blessed month in which lies a night more greater in virtue than a thousand months. It is a month in which Allah has made fasting compulsory by day. And has made sunnah the Taraaweeh by night. Whosoever intends drawing near to Allah by performing any virtuous deed, for such person shall be the reward like the one who had performed a fardh in any other time. And whoever performs a fardh, shall be blessed with the reward of seventy faraa-idh in any other time.*

This is indeed the month of patience, and the reward for true patience is Jannah (paradise). It is the month of sympathy with one's fellowmen. It is the month wherein a true believer's rizq is increased. Whosoever feeds another who fasted, in order to break the fast (at sunset), for the feeder there shall be forgiveness of sins and emancipation from the fire of Jahannam (hell), and for such feeder shall be the same reward as the one who fasted (who he fed) without that persons reward being decreased in the least."

Thereupon we said, "O messenger of Allah, not all of us possess the means whereby we can give a fasting person to break his fast." Rasulullah صلى الله عليه وسلم *replied, "Allah grants the same reward to the one who gives a fasting person to break the fast a mere date, or a drink of water, or a sip of milk."*

"This is a month, the first of which brings Allah's mercy, the middle of which brings His forgiveness and the last of which brings emancipation from the fire of Jahannam."

"Whosoever lessens the burden of his servants (bondsmen) in this month, Allah will forgive him and free him from the fire of Jahannam."

"And in this month four things you should continue to perform in great number, two of which shall be to please your Lord, while the other two shall be those without which you cannot do. Those which shall be to please your Lord, are that you should in great quantity bear witness that there is no deity to worship except Allah (i.e. recite

the Kalimah Tayyibah Laa Ilaaha illallaah) and make much Istighfaar (beg Allah's forgiveness with Astaghfirullaah)." And as for those without which you cannot do, you should beg of Allah, entrance into paradise and ask refuge in Him from Jahannam."

"And whoever gave a person who fasted water to drink, Allah shall grant that giver to drink from My fountain, such a drink whereafter that person shall never again feel thirsty until he enters Jannah."

Reported by ibn Khuzaimah in his 'Saheeh.

COMMENTARY

All the points which this Hadith draws attention have been further emphasised in numerous other Ahaadith on the great virtues of Ramadhaan. Quite a number of important points are brought to our notice.

Firstly, it should be noted that Rasulullah صلى الله عليه وسلم delivered this sermon at the end of the month of Sha-baan the obvious reason being that he intended to put into our minds the great importance of Ramadhaan so that we could remember and not allow one second of this month to go by without giving it the full importance it deserves. Thereafter attention is drawn to Laylatul Qadr, about which more is said later. Then attention is drawn to the fact that fasting has been made compulsory by Allah who also made sunnah the Taraaweeh 'salaah by night.

From this Hadith it is noted that the command for Taraaweeh prayers too comes from Allah Himself. Besides this in all the Ahadith wherein Rasulullah صلى الله عليه وسلم says, "I have made it sunnah", is mainly to emphasize its importance. All the authorities of the Ahlus sunnah wal Jamaa'ah are agreed upon the fact that Taraaweeh is sunnah. (Burhaan mentions that only the Rawaafidh deny this.)

Maulana Shaah Abdulhaq Dehlawi wrote in his book: "Maa Thabata Bis sunnah" that should the people of any town fail to perform Taraaweeh prayers, the Muslim ruler should make them do so by force.

Here one point should be noted. Many are of the opinion that one may listen to the full Qur'aan being recited in a certain musjid in eight or ten nights and then stop performing Taraaweeh with Jamaa-ah. Thereafter the virtue of the sunnah will have been attained. This is wrong. By doing this the one sunnah will be fulfilled and the other omitted. There are two things. Firstly, it is sunnah to hear the full Qur'aan being recited in the Taraaweeh in Ramadhaan. Secondly, it is sunnah to perform Taraaweeh with Jamaa-ah throughout Ramadhaan. Both should be performed with care.

As for those who are travelling and are unable to perform both sunnah, because of uncertainty as to where they will be, (at different places), then for them it is advisable that in the first few days of Ramadhaan they should have the full Quraan read in Taraaweeh so that the recitation is complete. Then they should attend Taraaweeh wherever they find the opportunity. In this way the Qur'aan will also be completed and their work will not be hampered.

Another point that is brought to our notice in the Hadith is that Rasulullah صلى الله عليه وسلم informed us that any nafl deed in Ramadhaan is rewarded as much as a fardh in normal times, and a fardh in Ramadhaan carries the reward of seventy faraa'idh at other times.

Our Faults

At this point we should ponder over our ibaadah. How much importance do we attach to it in Ramadhaan? How many nafl do we perform? As for fardh deeds, we observe how numerous people who after having eaten sah'ri get back into bed with the result that the Fajr 'salaah is neglected. Many perform it, but not with Jamaa'ah. It gives the impression that we give thanks to Allah for the food we had eaten for sah'ri by not performing the most important fardh or by not performing it with Jamaa'ah. Such a 'salaah has been termed defective. Rasulullah صلى الله عليه وسلم said that, "There is no 'salaah for those near the musjid except in the musjid".

In the kitaab 'Mazhaahire Haq' we find that there is no reward for the 'salaah for persons who do not perform 'salaah with Jamaa'ah without any valid reason or excuse.

Similarly, in numerous cases at the time of if'taar (boeka) Maghrib 'salaah is missed, and many who do not come to the musjid miss the Takbeer at the beginning or miss the first raka'ah. Many people hasten to get over the Taraaweeh 'salaah early and even perform the 'Ishaa' 'salaah before the time of 'Ishaa' commences. (Some do not pay any attention to 'salaah even in Ramadhaan.)

That is the way we look after our very important fardh 'salaah in Ramadhaan. Sometimes in the process of performing one fardh, three others are destroyed. How often do we see even the time of Zhuh-r 'salaah going by because we are asleep, while time of A'sr goes by because we are too busy buying, selling or cooking to prepare for if'taar.

If such is the case with the faraa'idh, then we can imagine how much less importance is given to the nafl actions. One finds that because of sleep, the time of 'salaatul Ishraaq (after sunrise) and 'salaatud Dhuhaa (before noon) go by. Then what about 'salaat Awwaabeen (just after Maghrib)? Here we find ourselves busy with If'taar and when thinking about Taraaweeh after about an hour this 'salaah too is wasted. Further we find that for 'salaatut Tahajjud the time is the same as that for sah'ri with the result that this too goes by. One may make a thousand excuses for not finding time for these nawaafil. These are all excuses for not performing these 'salaah.

We see that there are many who do find the time to do all these 'ibaadahs during these precious moments. I personally had observed my ustaaz Maulana Khalil Ahmad during many a Ramadhaan. He was a weak sickly person and of advanced age but inspite of these drawbacks he used to read one and a quarter juz of the Qur'an in nafl namaaz after Maghrib. Thereafter he used to have meals for about half an hour. After performing all other necessities in preparation for Taraaweeh 'salaah he used to stand in Taraaweeh for about two and a half hours when he was in India, and when he was in Madinah Munawwarah the duration was three hours. Thereafter he used to sleep about two or three hours (according to the season). Then he used to again recite the Qur'aan in Tahajjud 'saalah until about half an hour before Fajr. Then he ate sah'ri. From that time until Fajr he remained busy with reading the Qur'aan or reciting of wazifas. With the greyness of dawn he performed Fajr 'salaah, thereafter he remained in meditation (muraaqabah) until Ishraaq. Having performed Ishraaq he used to write his famous kitaab, 'Bazlul Majhood', commentary on

Abu Dawood. Then he normally attend to letters and dictating replies up to mid-day. Then he used to rest upto Zhuh-r 'salaah. Between Zhuh-r and A'sr he used to recite the Qur'aan.

From A'sr Namaaz until Maghrib he used to be busy with tasbeeh and answering the queries of those who visited him. When he completed 'Bazlul Majhood' then part of the morning used to be spent in tilaawah and studying some monumental religious works, especially Bazlul Majhood and Wafa al Wafa. This was his daily programme for nafl 'ibaadah throughout the year. In Ramadhaan however, he used to spend a bit more time in his 'ibaadah, making the rak'aats longer. For the ordinary person to observe the special programmes the other pious elders had for Ramadhaan would be difficult. Shaikhul Hind Maulana Mahmoodul Hasan (Rahmatullah alaihi) used to remain in nafl 'salaah from after Taraaweeh until Fajr, while also listening to the Qur'aan recited by various huffaazh one after the other.

Maulana Shah Abdurraheem Raipuri (d 1963) remained busy with tilaawah (recitation) of the Qur'aan day and night through Ramadhaan. There used to be no time for attending to correspondence or meeting visitors. Only his special ones were allowed to wait on him after Taraaweeh for a short period while he drank a cup of tea.

Advice

The reason for mentioning the manner in which these saintly ones spent their Ramadhaan is not that we may just read without deriving any benefit or pass a casual remark. It is written with the object that we in our way may build up courage and to the best of our ability endeavour to copy and follow their noble examples. Every pious elders programme had its particular speciality. How wonderful would it be if those who are not forced by wordly necessities, try their utmost to mend their religious life in this one month after having allowed eleven months of the year go by to destroy themselves.

As for those who have to be in their offices and be present at eight, nine or ten in the morning, what difficulty will it be for them if they at least in Ramadhaan, spend the time from Fajr until their hours of employment in reciting the Qur'aan. After all our wordly needs we do find time in spite of office hours.

For those engaged in farming, who normally are not bound to others nothing prevents them from reciting the Qur'aan on their farm or adjusting their daily routine. Then come the businessmen, shopkeepers and merchants. Nothing prevents them in Ramadhaan from reciting their Qur'aan during their shop hours or cutting short trading time in order to make time for recitation thereof. After all there is very strong link between Ramadhaan and the Tilaawah of the Qur'aan. Almost all Allah's great scriptures were revealed in this month. Similarly, in this month the Qur'aan was brought down from the Lowhul Mahfoozh to the Samaa'ud Dunyaa, from where it was revealed bit by bit to Rasulullah صلى الله عليه وسلم in a span of twenty three years.

Nabi Ibrahim (A.S.) received his scriptures on the first and third of this sacred month. Nabi Dawood (A.S.) received the Zaboor on the twelfth or eighteenth. Nabi Moosa (A.S.) received his Towrah on the sixth. Nabi Essa (A.S.) received the Injeel on the twelfth or thirteenth. From this we note the great connection between the divine scriptures and the month of Ramadhaan. For this reason, as much tilaawah of the Qur'aan as possible should be made during this month. Such was the habit of our saints. Jibraeel (A.S.) used to recite the whole Qur'aan to our Nabi Muhammad صلى الله عليه وسلم in the month of Ramadhaan. In some reports it is stated that Rasulullah صلى الله عليه وسلم used to recite and he (Jibraeel) used to listen. From joining these reports the 'ulama have said that it is mustahab to read the Qur'aan in such a manner that while one recites the other listens. Thereafter another recites while others listen. So recite the Qur'aan as much as possible. Whatever time remains thereafter should not be wasted.

Rasulullah صلى الله عليه وسلم drew our attention to four more things and advised that we should practice them as much as possible. They are the recitation of Kalimah 'Tayyibah, Istighfaar, begging for Jannah and seeking refuge from Jahannam. Therefore it must be regarded an honour to spend as much as available in these recitations. This will be the true appreciation of the teachings of Rasulullah صلى الله عليه وسلم. What is so difficult about keeping the tongue busy with the recitation of Durood ('salawaat) or Laa ilaaha illallaah while being engaged in our daily tasks?

In the same Hadith Rasulullah صلى الله عليه وسلم said a few more things, Ramadhaan is the month of patience. Hence even if great difficulty is experienced in fasting one should bear it with patience. One should not complain as people are fond of doing during hot days. If by chance sah-ri is missed then lamentations begin early in the day. Similarly, should difficulty be experienced at the same time of Taraweeh, it too should be borne with patience. Do not consider it a great calamity or trial, otherwise these deeds may be void of blessings. When we turn our backs on worldly things, forsake our very eating and drinking, then in the face of Allah's pleasure what are these difficulties?

Sympathy for the unfortunate

Further, the Hadith states that it is the month of sympathy, especially for the poor and destitute. Sympathy should be of a practical nature. When ten things are placed before us for if'taar, at least two or four of them should be set aside for the poor and needy. In fact they should be treated preferentially, if not then at least equally. They should certainly be remembered. In showing sympathy for the poor, as in all other matters, the Sahaabah R.A. were living examples, and in this, it is our duty to follow or at least try to follow them. In the matter of sacrifice and sympathy only the courageous can emulate the Sahaabah. There are numerous instances, if they are cited, will only leave one in astonishment.

Let us see the following example, Abu Jahm رضي الله عنه relates that: "During the battle of Yarmouk he went in search of his cousins, taking with him a water bag to give him to drink and also wash his wounds if he was found alive or wounded. He found him lying among the wounded. When I asked him whether he wanted some water, he indicated 'yes'. At that moment someone near him moaned. My cousin pointed to that person indicating that I should first quench the thirst of the neighbour. I went to him and found that he too needed water, but just as I was about to give him water, a third person groaned near him. The second one pointed to this third person meaning that I should give the third one to drink first. I went to the third person but before he could drink, I found out that he had passed away, whereupon I returned to the second one only to find that he too had passed away. When I came to my counsin, he too had become a martyr".

This is the type of sympathetic character our forefathers had. They preferred to die while thirsty rather than to drink before a strange Muslim brother. May Allah be pleased with them all and grant us ability to follow in their footsteps.

Roohul Bayaan quotes from Imaam Suyuti's Jaam'i 'Sagheer and Imam Sakhaawi's Maqaasid the narration of Hadhrat Umar that Nabi صلى الله عليه وسلم said, "At all times my ummah there will be five hundred chosen servants and forty abdaal (pious ones, totally devoted to Allah). When anyone of these passes away then immediately he is succeeded by another." The Sahaabah inquired, "What are exclusive deeds? Rasulullah صلى الله عليه وسلم replied, 'They overlook the injustices of the transgressors, and they show kindness to those who illtreat them, and from the sustenance provided for them by Allah, they engender sympathy and graciousness."

In another Hadith it is stated that whosoever feeds the hungry, clothes the naked, and grants shelter to the traveller, Allah shall save him from the terrors of Qiyaamah.

Yahya Barmaki used to grant Imaam Sufyaan Thowri one thousand Dirhams every month, whereupon Imaam Sufyaan used to prostrate himself before Allah praying "O Allah Yahya has seen sufficiently to my wordly needs. See You, through Your Great Mercy, to his necessities in the Hereafter." After the death of Yahya some people saw him in their dreams and on inquiring what had happened to him in the hereafter, he replied: "Through the prayers of 'Sufyaan I have been forgiven by Allah".

Further, Rasulullah صلى الله عليه وسلم mentioned the virtue of feeding a fasting person at the time of breaking the fast. In one Hadith it is reported that upon him who feeds a person to break the fast out of his halaal earnings, the angels confer mercy upon him during the nights of Ramadhaan, and on the night of Laylatul Qadr Jibraeel shakes hands with him. The signs of this is that his heart becomes soft while tears flow from his eyes.

Hammaad bin Salamah, a very famous Muhaddith used to feed fifty people every day during Ramadhaan at if'taar. (Roohul Bayaan)

Thereafter the Hadith of Rasulullah صلى الله عليه وسلم called the first section of Ramadhaan the coming of mercy, whereby it is meant that Allah's favour is with the believers. Those who are thankful to Allah for His bounties, receive even more. The Qu'raan says, "If you are thankful, I will surely grant you more." (Surah 14:7)

During the second section of Ramadhaan forgiveness begins to descend as a reward for the fasting during the first section. The last section of the Ramadhaan brings immunity from entrance in Jahannam. This is corroborated by many similar Ahaadith. In my personal opinion, Ramadhaan has been divided into three sections because people are normally of three different kinds. Firstly, there are those who have no burden of sins. For them Allah's Mercy and Bounties descend from the very beginning of Ramadhaan. Secondly, there are those whose burden of sins are not too heavy. For them forgiveness descends after one third of Ramadhaan has passed. Thirdly, there are the real sinners. For them forgiveness comes after having fasted the major section of Ramadhaan. As those who attained Allah's Mercy right at the beginning, they are the very fortunate ones because of the great amount of mercy they have received. (And Allah knows best).

Another point mentioned in the Ahaadith is that masters should be lenient to their servants in Ramadhaan because, after all, they too are fasting. Unnecessary hard work or too much of it will be a burden for them. So why should an extra worker not be hired when the work is too much? That of course only applies when the servant himself fasts, otherwise there is no difference for them between Ramadhaan and any other month.

Words cannot describe the position of the shameless oppressor who does not himself fast and drives his employees unnecessarily, and if there is any delay due to 'salaah or fasting he is outraged. Regarding such persons the Qur'aan states, "And soon the oppressor will come to know where his abode is. (In Jahannam)

Lastly, in the Hadith Rasulullah صلى الله عليه وسلم exhorted that four things should be repeated constantly. Firstly the recitation of Kalimah 'Tayyibah, which in the Ahaadith is called the highest form of thikr. In "Mishkaat" Abu Sa'iyd Khudri reports, "Once Nabi Moosa (Alayhis Salaam) begged of Allah to grant him a special prayer by which he can remember Allah and also (by which he could) ask

Him". Then Allah informed him to recite this kalimah. Sayyidina Moosa said, "O Allah, this is a verse recited by all your servants, I desire a special prayer". Allah replied, "O Moosa, if the seven heavens, the earth and all its occupants including the angels, except Myself are placed on one side of a scale and this kalimah on the other, then this kalimah will outweigh everything".

In another Hadith it is stated, "Should anyone sincerely recite this kalimah, the doors of Jannah open up for him immediately and nothing can stop him from reaching Allah's Throne". The only condition is that the reciter should refrain from major sins.

Allah's pattern is that He grants basic needs in abundance. We see all over the world that whatever is generally required is found in abundance. For example, water which is a basic necessity. How common has Allah, in His infinite mercy, made this basic necessity. And how rare has he made the unmeaningful use of alchemy. Similarly the Kalimah 'Tayyibah is the most excellent form of thikr. Allah has made it common to humanity, so that none is deprived of it. Hence if any person is deprived of it, it is only due to his misfortune. There are numerous Ahaadith regarding its virtues and for the sake of brevity they are not mentioned here.

The second of which a lot should be recited is Istighfaar. The Ahaadith report the virtue of Istighfaar and in one Hadith we read, "Whoever says much Istighfaar, Allah opens an exit for him from all difficulties and releases him from all sorrows. In a similar manner he receives rizq from unexpected sources". In another Hadith Rasulullah صلى الله عليه وسلم said that, "Every man is a sinner, but the best among the sinners are those who repent and seek forgiveness". We will soon mention a Hadith where in it is mentioned that, "When a man commits a sin, a black spot forms on his heart, but when he repents, it is washed away–if not, the black spot remains". Thereafter Rasulullah commanded us to beseech two things without which we cannot do, to beg Allah for entrance into Jannah and to seek refuge in Him from Jahannam.

May Allah grant you and I this good fortune.

(٢) عَنْ اَبِیْ هُرَيْرَةَ رَضِیَ اللّٰهُ تَعَالٰی عَنْهُ قَالَ قَالَ رَسُوْلُ اللّٰهِ ﷺ اُعْطِيَتْ اُمَّتِیْ
خَمْسَ خِصَالٍ فِیْ رَمَضَانَ لَمْ تُعْطَهُنَّ اُمَّةٌ قَبْلَهُمْ خُلُوْفُ فَمِ الصَّائِمِ اَطْيَبُ عِنْدَ
اللّٰهِ مِنْ رِّيْحِ الْمِسْكِ وَتَسْتَغْفِرُ لَهُمُ الْحِيْتَانُ حَتّٰی يُفْطِرُوْا وَيُزَيِّنُ اللّٰهُ عَزَّ وَجَلَّ
كُلَّ يَوْمٍ جَنَّتَهٗ ثُمَّ يَقُوْلُ يُوْشِكُ عِبَادِیَ الصَّالِحُوْنَ اَنْ يُّلْقُوْا عَنْهُمُ الْمَؤُنَةَ
وَيَصِيْرُوْا اِلَيْكِ وَتُصَفَّدُ فِيْهِ مَرَدَةُ الشَّيَاطِيْنِ فَلَايَخْلُصُوْا فِيْهِ اِلٰی مَاكَانُوْا
يَخْلُصُوْنَ اِلَيْهِ فِیْ غَيْرِهٖ وَيُغْفَرُ لَهُمْ فِیْ آخِرِ لَيْلِهٖ قِيْلَ يَارَسُوْلَ اللّٰهِ اَهِیَ لَيْلَةُ
الْقَدْرِ قَالَ لَا وَلٰكِنِ الْعَامِلَ اِنَّمَا يُوَفّٰی اَجْرُهٗ اِذَا قَضٰی عَمَلَهٗ رواه أحمد والبزار والبيهقى
ورواه أبوالشيخ ابن حبان فى كتاب الثواب إلا أن عنده وتستغفر لهم الملئكة بدل الحيتان ، كذا فى
الترغيب

HADITH NO. 2

Abu Hurayrah relates that Rasulullah ﷺ *said, "My Ummah were given five things for Ramadhaan which were not given to anyone except them. For them, the smell from the mouth of a fasting person is more sweeter to Allah than the fragrant smell of musk. On their behalf the fish in the sea seek forgiveness for the fasting persons until they break their fast. Allah prepares and decorates a special garden in Jannah everyday and then says (to it), "The time is near when faithful servants shall cast aside the great trials of the world and come to you". In this month (for them) evil-minded Shaytaan is chained so as not to reach unto those evils to which they normally reach during other months besides Ramadhaan. On the last night of Ramadhaan they are forgiven".*

The Sahaabah R.A. thereupon enquired, "O Messenger of Allah, is that last night Laylatul Qadr? Rasulullah ﷺ *replied, "No. But it is only right that a servant should be given his reward on having completed his service".*

Reported by Ahmad, Bazzaar and Bayhaqi

COMMENTARY

Rasulullah ﷺ mentions in Hadith five such presents from Allah which were not granted to the fasting people before Islaam. If only we can truly appreciate how great this bounty from Allah really is, and if only we could sincerely try to gain those special favours. Firstly, we are told that the smell from the mouth of a fasting one is more beloved and sweeter to Allah than the smell of musk. The commentators attach eight meanings to this. Of these, in my opinion, three are the most acceptable explanations; (a) Some are of the opinion that in the Hereafter Allah shall reward that smell from the mouth with fragrant smells more sweet and pleasing than musk. This is the obvious meaning. Durrul Manthoor has also concluded thus, therefore this appear to be the prefered explanation. (b) On the day of Qiyaamah, when we shall rise from the grave, a sweet smell shall emanate, from the mouth of those who fasted, which shall be better than musk. (c) The version which in my opinion is most acceptable, is the view that in the world the smell is more fragrant than musk. This shows the bond of love between Allah and His fasting creation.

We all know that even a bad smell from a person whom one loves truly and sincerely is in itself–regarded favourably by the lover, who in this case is Allah Himself. Allah wants to grant the fasting one complete closeness, that so he becomes like the beloved one. Fasting is one of the most accepted forms of 'ibaadah in Allah's sight. For this reason the Hadith states that the reward for every deed is carried by the angels, but Allah says, "The reward for fasting, I Myself will give, because it is for Me alone". Another version of the same Hadith according to some Mashaa'ikh (when read in a different way) says, "I Myself become his reward". And what greater reward can there be for the lover than to gain the beloved? In one Hadith we read, "Fasting is the door to all other forms of 'ibaadah". This means that through fasting the heart becomes enlightened through which one is encouraged towards all other 'i obaadah. This is the case only if fasting becomes fasting in the true sense of the word and all its requirements (as shall be explained later), and not just remaining hungry and thirsty.

NOTE: At this juncture I wish to draw attention to one point, because of this Hadith some Imaams (especially Imaam Shafi'iy) prohibited cleansing of the teeth with miswaak in the afternoon, whereas the Hanafis consider it to be mustahab at all times. The Imaam's reason is that through miswaak the smell from the teeth is removed. The odour referred to here is the smell resulting from the stomach being empty, having nothing to do with miswaak.

The second special favour is that fish in the sea make Istighfaar for the one who fasts. The aim here is to explain that many beings offer prayer on his behalf. This point has been mentioned in many Ahaadith. And in some Ahaadith it is mentioned that the Malaa'ikah (angels) make Istighfaar for them. My uncle Maulana Muhammad Ilyaas used to say that this is apparently so because Allah says in the Qur'aan, "Verily those who believe and do righteous deeds, Allah shall make them beloved (in this world)". One Hadith clarifies this, "When Allah loves a person, He says to Jibraeel A.S. 'I love this person, you should also love him'. Jibraeel A.S. then also loves that person and announces in the heavens. "That such a person is loved by Allah. You all should love him". Thereupon all the dwellers of the heavens begin to love him. Then, love for that person spreads on earth". Normally only those who are near to a person seem to love him but here that love spreads all over, even the animals in the jungle and the fish in the sea do the same. They all pray for him.

The third favour bestowed on the fasting ones is that Jannah becomes decorated for them. Another Hadith states that at the beginning of every year, the decoration and adornment of Jannah begins for the coming Ramadhaan. We know that when a well known person is expected to arrive, great care is taken in the preparations for his coming. At the time of marriage for example, preparations commence months in advance. Likewise it is with Ramadhaan.

The fourth favour is that the rebellious, evil sowing shayaa'teen are chained (detained), as a result of which evil is diminished. One would expect that because of the great desire for ibaadah in the blessed month of Ramadhaan, shay'taan would try just as hard to pull the faithful from their path so that much more evil would be committed. That is not the case. On the contrary we see so much less evil. How many drunkards do we not see, who, just because of the blessed month of Ramadhaan, do not drink. How many other evil doers do we not see casting aside evil just because of the blessed month of Ramadhaan. Committing sins during the month of Ramadhaan does not contradict the meaning of the Hadith, because the Hadith mentions only the rebellious shayaa'teen. Thus sin could be due to the influence of the non-rebellious shayaa'teen. In some Ahaadith the chaining of the shay'taan is not qualified, but this could be qualified by those Ahaadith in which the 'rebellious' shay'taan is mentioned. A question may arise here, that when the shayaa'teen are chained, how is it that we still see evil committed even though to a lesser degree? Our reply is that evil may not necessarily be caused by the Shayaa'teen. Having for eleven months lived in obedience to shay'taan's whims and wishes and because of the performance of deeds advised by him having become second nature to us, evil is done in and out of Ramadhaan. Thus even though shay'taan has been chained his influence in us has become so strong that we follow his path on our own.

Another answer to the question is Rasulullah صلى الله عليه وسلم said that, "When a person commits a sin, a black spot forms on his heart. When he sincerely repents, it is removed, otherwise it remains. When he again commits a sin another spot forms until his heart becomes completely black. Thereafter no good can reach his heart". With reference to this Allah says in the Qur'aan, "By no means. But on their heart is the stain (of the ill)". That their hearts have become totally rusted. In such cases these hearts have a natural inclination towards sin. This is the reason why many fearlessly commit one type of sin, but yet if confronted with another sin of similar magnitude then their hearts repudiate it. Whereas in sin these two misdeeds are equal similarly when these sins are constantly committed out of Ramadhaan the heart is tainted by them, thus resulting in these sins being committed without the presence of the shay'taan. My personal opinion is that not all shayaa'teen are chained. Only the most rebellious ones are. All of us can see in Ramadhaan it does not require a great amount of effort and exertion to do a good deed. Neither does it require great self control and sacrifice to avoid evil as in other times. Maulana Shaah Ishaaq was of the opinion that for the evil ones only the most rebellious shayaa'teen are chained whereas for the righteous ones all shayaa'teen are chained.

The fifth favour is that forgiveness is granted on the final night of Ramadhaan (see previous Hadith), because of this great favour the Sahaabah thought this night must be Laylatul Qadr. They knew the great blessings of that night and accordingly asked whether that was Laylatul Qadr.

The reply was that it was not. This is merely the favour granted for having given Ramadhaan its due right to the end.

(٣) عَنْ كَعْبِ بْنِ عُجْرَةَ رَضِىَ اللّٰهُ تَعَالٰى عَنْهُ قَالَ قَالَ رَسُوْلُ اللّٰهِ ﷺ اُحْضُرُوْا
الْمِنبَرَ فَحَضَرْنَا فَلَمَّا ارْتَقٰى دَرَجَةً قَالَ آمِيْنَ فَلَمَّا ارْتَقٰى الدَّرَجَةَ الثَّانِيَةَ قَالَ آمِيْنَ
فَلَمَّا ارْتَقٰى الدَّرَجَةَ الثَّالِثَةَ قَالَ آمِيْنَ فَلَمَّا نَزَلَ قُلْنَا يَارَسُوْلَ اللّٰهِ لَقَدْ سَمِعْنَا مِنْكَ
الْيَوْمَ شَيْئًا مَاكُنَّا نَسْمَعُهُ قَالَ اِنَّ جِبْرَئِيْلَ عَرَضَ لِىْ فَقَالَ بَعُدَ مَنْ اَدْرَكَ رَمْضَانَ
فَلَمْ يُغْفَرْ لَهُ قُلْتُ آمِيْنَ فَلَمَّا رَقِيْتُ الثَّانِيَةَ قَالَ بَعُدَ مَنْ ذُكِرْتَ عِنْدَهُ فَلَمْ يُصَلِّ
عَلَيْكَ قُلْتُ آمِيْنَ فَلَمَّا رَقِيْتُ الثَّالِثَةَ قَالَ بَعُدَ مَنْ اَدْرَكَ اَبَوَيْهِ الْكِبَرَ عِنْدَهُ اَوْ
اَحَدُهُمَا فَلَمْ يُدْخِلَاهُ الْجَنَّةَ قُلْتُ آمِيْنَ رواه الحاكم وقال صحيح الإسناد وكذا فى الترغيب
وقال السخاوى رواه ابن حبان فى ثقاته وصححه والطبرانى فى الكبير والبخارى فى برالوالدين له
والبيهقى فى الشعب وغيرهم ورجاله ثقات وبسط طرقه وروى الترمذى عن أبى هريرة بمعناه وقال ابن
حجر طرقه كثيرة كما فى المرقاة

HADITH NO. 3

Kaab bin Ujra relates, "Rasulullah ﷺ said, "Come near to the mimbar". And we came near to the mimbar. When he ascended the first step of the mimbar he said "Aameen". When he ascended the second step of the mimbar he said, "Aameen". When he ascended the third step he said, "Aameen". When he descended we said, "O Rasul of Allah, we have heard from you today something which we never heard before". He said, (When I ascended the first step) Jibra-eel A.S. appeared before me and said, "Woe to him who found the blessed month of Ramadhaan and let it pass by without gaining forgiveness", Upon that I said, "Aameen". When I ascended the second step, he said "Woe to him before whom thy name is mentioned and then does not read durood ('salaat alan Nabi) on you". I replied "Aameen". When I ascended the third step he said, "Woe unto the person in whose presence both parents or one of them attain old age, and (through failure to serve them) is not allowed to enter Jannah" I said "Aameen".

Reported by Haakim.

COMMENTARY

In his Hadith it appears that Jibra-eel A.S. expressed three curse upon which Rasulullah صلى الله عليه وسلم said, "Aameen" every time. In Durre Manthor it is reported that Jibra-eel commanded Rasulullah صلى الله عليه وسلم to say "Aameen". Being an angel of such a high stature, Jibra-eel instruction to Rasulullah صلى الله عليه وسلم to say "Aameen" upon curses. May Allah in His infinite mercy grant us help and save from these evils.

The first person finds himself in Ramadhaan, the month of blessing and righteousness, and still spends time in sin and disregards his duties and thus does not gain forgiveness. Ramadhaan is the month of Allah's Mercy and if this month is spent in evil and negligence, then how can he expect to be pardoned for his sins? If he cannot gain Allah's pleasure in Ramadhaan, then when will he? What doubt is there about his failure. Moreover, in Ramadhaan numerous opportunities are found for forgiveness.

The second unfortunate person is the one who hears Rasulullah's صلى الله عليه وسلم name mentioned and yet does not recite (durood) 'salaat alan Nabi on him. This has been mentioned in many other Ahaadith as well. For this reason some Ulama consider it to be waajib to read 'salaat alan Nabi (durood) whenever the name of Rasulullah صلى الله عليه وسلم is mentioned. Besides the curse in this Hadith many other warnings have been reported. In some Ahaadith the person who fails to do so is called an unfortunate and a miser.

At some places such people are even mentioned to be among those who are deserters and who have lost way to Jannah, or among those who will enter Jahannam, and those who are irreligious, and those who will not be allowed to look at the blessed face of Rasulullah صلى الله عليه وسلم. The Ulama give us different interpretations of these Ahaadith. The fact is that Rasulullah's صلى الله عليه وسلم warning to the one who fails to recite 'salaat alan Nabi (durood) is so severe that it is difficult to endure. And why not? After all, the favours bestowed upon this Ummah through Rasulullah صلى الله عليه وسلم are of such a nature that neither pens nor lectures can do justice in describing them. His favours on us are indeed so great that they truly justify the numerous warnings. On the other hand the reward for 'salaat alan Nabi (durood) is tremendous and to be deprived of this good act is indeed wickedness itself. The Hadith teaches us that, whosoever recites one 'salaat alan Nabi (durood) on Rasulullah صلى الله عليه وسلم on them Allah sends ten mercies and for them the Malaa'i-kah make duaa'. All their sins are forgiven, their rank is elevated, reward is received as much as Mount Uhad, and on their behalf Rasulullah صلى الله عليه وسلم shall make shafaa-at on the day of Qiyaamah. Further promises of reward are: Attaining Allah's pleasure and mercy, immunity against His anger, also safety from the terrors of Qiyaamah, and seeing one's promised place in Jannah even while on this earth. Many promises are mentioned for reciting 'salaat alan Nabi (durood) a certain number of times. Besides these there is the promise of not ever being troubled by poverty and need. Promise of achieving nearness to Rasulullah صلى الله عليه وسلم in Allah's court, the promise of help against enemies, the promise to cleanse the heart from hypocrisy and spiritual ailments and the promise of gaining the affection of others. Many glad tidings have been mentioned in the Hadith for the reciter of 'salaat alan Nabi (durood) in abundance. The 'Ulama of Fiq have said that it is fardh to recite 'salaat alan Nabi (durood) at least once in a life time, while it is waajib to recite it every time the name of Rasulullah صلى الله عليه وسلم is mentioned. Some say it is mustahab.

The third person is the one in whose presence one or both of his parents reach old age and yet is unable to gain Jannah through failure to serve them. This has been explained in many Ahaadith. The 'Ulama have stated that in every permissible act is it compulsory to obey ones parents' commands. One should not be disrespectful to them, but be humble even though one's father and mother be non-believers. Neither should one raise his voice above theirs, nor address parents by their first names. They should be given the preference to do anything before and ahead of you, (viz. eating, walking, sitting, etc.) when they have to be called towards good and prohibited from evil, it should be done with softness. If they refuse to accept, they should still be honoured and respected. And duaa' for their guidance should be made. In one Hadith it is related, "The best of doors entering Jannah is the father. If you wish, look after this and if you wish, destroy it". A Sahaabi رضي الله عنه inquired from Rasulullah صلى الله عليه وسلم "What are the fights that are due to parents?" He replied, "They are your jannah and jahannam". Their happiness is Jannah and their displeasure is Jahannam. Further it is stated in the Hadith that, "When an obedient son looks with love and devotion to his parents, the reward for that gaze shall be the same as for amaqbool (accepted)". In another Hadith it is stated that, "Apart from associating other gods with Allah, Allah forgives all as He pleases. However, He inflicts the punishments for disobedience to parents in this world before death". A Sahaabi رضي الله عنه said, "O Messenger of Allah, I want to go for Jihad". Rasulullah صلى الله عليه وسلم asked, "Is your mother alive?" He replied, "Yes". Rasulullah صلى الله عليه وسلم then said, "Serve her, Jannah lies beneath her feet for you". It is mentioned in the Hadith, "The pleasure of Allah lies in pleasing one's father, and Allah's displeasure lies in displeasing one's father". In numerous other Ahaadith the importance and virtue of this has been discussed. From the above it should not be deduced that where parents had not been properly treated and respected and are now dead, there is no other way out except Jahannam for the children. In Shari'ah there is a way out. The Hadith teaches us that in such cases one should make duaa' and Istighfaar for them, and by doing so, one will be counted among those who are obedient. Another Hadith states that the best one can do after one's father's death is to treat his friends and companions in a manner, just as the father would have done.

٤) عَنْ عُبَادَةَ بْنِ الصَّامِتِ رَضِىَ اللّٰهُ تَعَالىٰ عَنْهُ اَنَّ رَسُوْلَ اللّٰهِ ﷺ قَالَ يَوْمًا حَضَرَنَا رَمَضَانُ اَتَاكُمْ رَمَضَانُ شَهْرُ بَرَكَةٍ يَغْشَاكُمُ اللّٰهُ فِيْهِ فَيُنْزِلُ الرَّحْمَةَ يَحُطُّ الْخَطَايَا وَيَسْتَجِيْبُ فِيْهِ الدُّعَاءَ يَنْظُرُ اللّٰهُ تَعَالىٰ اِلىٰ تَنَافُسِكُمْ فِيْهِ وَيُبَاهِىْ كُمْ مَلٰئِكَتَهُ فَاَرُوْا اللّٰهَ مِنْ اَنْفُسِكُمْ خَيْرًا فَاِنَّ الشَّقِىَّ مَنْ حُرِمَ فِيْهِ رَحْمَةَ اللّٰهِ عَزَّ وَجَلَّ رواه الطبرانى ورواته ثقات إلا أن محمد بن قيس لايحضرنى فيه جرح ولا تعديل كذا فى الترغيب

HADITH NO. 4

'Ubaadah bin 'Saamit رضي الله عنه *reported that Rasulullah* صلى الله عليه وسلم *one day said when Ramadhaan had drawn near, "Ramadhaan, the month of blessing has come to you, wherein Allah turns towards you and sends down to you His special mercy, forgives faults, accept prayers, looks at your competitions for the greatest good and boasts to His mal-*

aa'ikah about you. So show to Allah your righteousness from yourselves. For verily the most pitiable and unfortunate one is the one who is deprived of Allah's mercy in this month".

Reported by 'Tabraani.

COMMENTARY

In this Hadith we read about the spirit of competition among the believers. One trying to do more good deeds than the other. In our own home, I am greatly pleased seeing how the womenfolk vie with each other, the one trying to recite more of the Qur'aan than the others, so that in spite of domestic responsibilities, fifteen to twenty juz of the Qur'aan is read by one daily. I mention this only with a sense of gratitude to Allah, mentioning His favour and not to boast. May Allah accept their and our deeds and increase our good deeds.

(٥) عَنْ اَبِىْ سَعِيْدِ ن الْخُدْرِىِّ رَضِىَ اللّٰهُ تَعَالٰى عَنْهُ قَالَ قَالَ رَسُوْلُ اللّٰهِ ﷺ اِنَّ للّٰه
تَبَارَكَ وَتَعَالٰى عُتَقَاءَ فِىْ كُلِّ يَوْمٍ وَلَيْلَةٍ يَعْنِىْ فِىْ رَمَضَانَ وَاِنَّ لِكُلِّ مُسْلِمٍ فِىْ كُلِّ
يَوْمٍ وَلَيْلَةٍ دَعْوَةً مُسْتَجَابَةً رواه البزار كذا فى الترغيب

HADITH NO. 5

Abu Saeed Khudri relates that Rasulullah ﷺ *said, "Everyday and night of Ramadhaan Allah sets free a great number of souls from Jahannam. And for every Muslim during everyday and night there is a time when his duaa' is certainly accepted.*

Reported by Bazzaar.

COMMENTARY

Apart from this Hadith, there are many others stating that the duaa' is accepted at the time of if'taar. Unfortunately at that time we are so engrossed in eating if'taar that we have no time for duaa', nor do we recall the duaa' of if'taar. The famous duaa' at if'taar is:

اَللّٰهُمَّ لَكَ صُمْتُ وَبِكَ آمَنْتُ وَعَلَيْكَ تَوَكَّلْتُ وَعَلٰى رِزْقِكَ اَفْطَرْتُ

"O Allah for you have I fasted, in You do I believe, and on You do I rely and now I break this fast with food coming from you".

In this Hadith book this duaa' is mentioned concisely.

Abdullah bin Amr bin Al Aas رضي الله عنه used to read the following duaa':

اَللّٰهُمَّ اِنِّیْ اَسْئَلُكَ بِرَحْمَتِكَ الَّتِیْ وَسِعَتْ كُلَّ شَیْءٍ اَنْ تَغْفِرَ لِیْ

'O Allah, I beg you, through your infinite mercy which surrounds all things, to forgive me".

In some books we read that Rasulullah صلى الله عليه وسلم used to say,

یَاوَاسِعَ الْفَضْلِ اِغْفِرْ لِیْ

"O You who are Great in bounties, forgive me".

Various duaa's are mentioned in the ahaadith. Remember that no special duaa' is fixed. This time (at if'taar) is one when duaa' is accepted. Submit before Allah your needs and if you remember, then make duaa' for me too. (The publishers also humbly request your duaa's).

(٦) عَنْ اَبِیْ هُرَیْرَةَ رَضِیَ اللّٰهُ تَعَالٰی عَنْهُ قَالَ قَالَ رَسُوْلُ اللّٰهِ ﷺ ثَلٰثَةٌ لَاتُرَدُّ دَعْوَتُهُمْ اَلصَّائِمُ حَتّٰی یُفْطِرَ وَالْاِمَامُ الْعَادِلُ وَدَعْوَةُ الْمَظْلُوْمِ یَرْفَعُهَا اللّٰهُ فَوْقَ الْغَمَامِ وَیُفْتَحُ لَهَا اَبْوَابُ السَّمَاءِ وَیَقُوْلُ الرَّبُّ وَعِزَّتِیْ لَاَنْصُرَنَّكَ وَلَوْ بَعْدَ حِیْنٍ

رواه أحمد فى حديث والترمذى وحسنه وابن خزيمه وابن حبان فى صحيحيهما كذا فى الترغيب

HADITH NO. 6

Abu Hurairah reports, Rasulullah صلى الله عليه وسلم *said, "There are three people whose duaa's are not rejected, the fasting person until he breaks the fast, the just ruler and the duaa's of the oppressed whose duaa' Allah lifts above the clouds and opens unto it the doors of the heavens, and Allah says, I swear by My honour, verily I shall assist you even though it may be after some time".*

Reported by Ahmad and Tirmizhi.

COMMENTARY

In Durre Manthoor it is reported from Aa-'ishah (R.A.) that when Ramadhaan arrived, the colour of Rasulullah's صلى الله عليه وسلم face used to change. He then used to increase 'salaah, became even more humble in his duaa's and had even more fear for Allah. According to another report he hardly ever lay down in bed until Ramadhaan came to an end. Further, in a Hadith it is stated that the Malaa'ikah bearing the throne are commanded in Ramadhaan to leave everything else and recite 'Aameen'' to the duaa' of those who fast. There are many Ahaadith stating that the duaa's during Ramadhaan in particular are accepted. When Allah has promised and His truthful Nabi صلى الله عليه وسلم has informed us, there should be no doubt whatsoever about the truth of these reports. Yet it is strange that in spite of this, we still find such people who apparently do not get what they make duaa' for. They ask and do not receive. This does not mean that their duaa's have been rejected. One should at this point understand the meaning of duaa' being answered.

Rasulullah صلى الله عليه وسلم informed us that when a muslim makes duaa' for anything from Allah, except for the severance of ties with relatives or for a sinful thing then he definitely receives one out of the following three things: Firstly he gets the exact thing for which he made duaa'. Secondly, if that is not received, Allah either removes from his some great calamity in exchange for that which he desired, or thirdly the reward for the thing for which he made duaa' is kept deposited for him in the Hereafter. Another Hadith states that on the day of Qiyaamah Allah will call His servant, and say to him, "O My servant, I used to command you to ask of me I had promised to answer. Did you beg of Me?'' The servant will answer, "Yes I did''. Then Allah shall reply, "You did not put forth any request which had not been accepted. You made duaa' that a certain calamity should be removed, which I did for you in the worldly life. You made duaa' that a certain sorrow should be case off you and the effect of that sorrow was even known to you. For that I have fixed for you such and such a reward''. Rasulullah صلى الله عليه وسلم says, that person shall again be reminded of each and every duaa', and he shall be shown how it had been fulfilled in the world or what reward had been stored for him in the hereafter. When seeing that, he shall wish that not a single duaa' of his should have been answered on earth, so that he could receive the full rewards only in the Hereafter.

Duaa' is indeed very important and to neglect it at any time causes us great loss. Even when the outward signs seem to indicate that our duaa' is not answered, courage should not be lost. At the end of this book, in the lengthy Hadith which we will be discussing, it is also apparent that Allah in answering duaa's, considers first of all our own good and welfare. Should Allah find that granting what we beseech of Him is beneficial, then He grants it, otherwise not. Actually it is Allah's favour that we do not always get what we ask for, since very often, because of our lack of understanding, we beg for things which are not beneficial at a particular time.

Once again I must draw your attention to the fact that men as well as women suffer from a disease of cursing their children in their anger and sorrows. Be very careful. In the sight of Allah there are certain times when whatever duaa' is made it is immediately answered. So here due to our stupidity, the child is cursed and when the effect of that same duaa' comes over the child and lands him into calamity, the parents go crying and wailing from side to side not even realising that this is the result of their own curse. Rasulullah صلى الله عليه وسلم commands us not to curse ourselves, our children, possessions, or servants.

It is just possible that this is the curse that is heard and answered at a time when all requests are granted, especially in Ramadhaan, which is filled with such special mustajjad (accepted) moments. Hence in this month great care should be taken. Sayyidana Omar رضي الله عنه reports from Rasulullah صلى الله عليه وسلم "The one who remembers Allah during Ramadhaan is forgiven and the one who makes duaa' to Allah is not forsaken".

Ibn Mas'ood رضي الله عنه reports that on every night of Ramadhaan a caller from the heavens calls out, "O you seeker of good come, come near, O you seeker of evil, turn away (from evil) and open your eyes". Thereafter that angel calls out, "Is there any seeker of forgiveness that he may be forgiven? Is there any one repenting so that his repentance shall be accepted? Is there anyone making duaa' that his duaa' may be granted? Is there anyone begging anything so that his plea may be fulfilled?"

Lastly it should be borne in mind that there are certain conditions on which duaa's are accepted. Among these is halaal food. Where haraam is consumed duaa' is not accepted. Rasulullah صلى الله عليه وسلم said, "Many a greatly troubled one in distress lifts up his hands to the heavens making duaa', crying, 'O Allah, O Allah'. However the food he eats is haraam, what he drinks is haraam, his clothes are of haraam and in such cases how can his duaa' be accepted?"

A story is related about a group of people in Kufa whose duaa' used to be always answered. Whenever a ruler was over them, they used to make duaa' for a curse upon him which quickly came to destroy him. When Hajjaaj became ruler there, he invited these people, among others, to a feast. After having eaten, he said, "Now I am not afraid of the duaa' for curse upon me from these people because haraam food has entered their stomachs". At this stage let us ponder over how much haraam is being consumed in these times when people are even trying to make permissible the earnings of interest money. We find our people go so far as to think that bribery and what is obtained from it is permissible, while our traders very often, when dealing with people, deceive them.

(٧) عَنِ ابْنِ عُمَرَ رَضِيَ اللهُ تَعَالٰى عَنْهُ قَالَ قَالَ رَسُوْلُ اللهِ ﷺ اِنَّ اللهَ وَمَلٰٓئِكَتَهٗ يُصَلُّوْنَ عَلَى الْمُتَسَحِّرِيْنَ رواه الطبرانى فى الأوسط وابن حبان فى صحيحه كذا فى الترغيب

HADITH NO 7

Ibn Umar رضي الله عنه relates Rasulullah صلى الله عليه وسلم said, "Verily Allah and His Malaa'ikah send mercy upon those who eat sah'ri (sower – suhoor)".

Reported by 'Tabraani.

COMMENTARY

How is Allah's favour upon us that even the partaking of sah'ri is a virtuous act which is enormously rewarded. There are so many Ahaadith in which the virtues of sah'ri are expounded and rewards mentioned. Allaama Ainy – commentator on Bukhaari gathered Ahaadith from seventeen Sahaabah on the excellence of sah'ri. All 'Ulama are agreed it is mustahab. Many are deprived of this great reward because of laziness. Some even finish Taraweeh and then eat, (which they regard as sah'ri) and get into bed. What great blessings do they loose! Sah'ri actually means partaking of food shortly before Fajr (ref: Qamoos). Some authorities say that the time for sah'ri commences after half of the night has passed (Mirquaat). The author of Kash-shaaf (Zamakhshari) divided the night into six portions stating that the last one of them is the time for sah'ri When the night (from sunset till dawn) lasts for twelve hours then the last two hours would be the correct time for sah'ri. It must also be remembered that to eat at the latest time is better and greater in reward than eating earlier, on condition that no doubt remains as to sah'ri had been eaten before or after the time of Fajr. The Ahaadith are full of the virtues of sah'ri. Rasulullah صلى الله عليه وسلم said, "The difference in our fasting with that of Ahulul-Kitaab (Jews and Christians) lies in partaking of food at sah'ri time, they do not".

It is mentioned in the Hadith, "Eat sah'ri because in it lies great blessings". It also mentioned, "In three things there are great blessings, in Jamaah (company), in eating thareed and in sah'ri". In this Hadith the use of the word jamaah is general, whereupon we deduce it to refer to 'salaah with jamaah and all those righteous deeds done together and Allah's help comes to them. (Thareed is a delicious type of food, in which dry baked bread is mixed with gravy containing meat). The third thing mentioned in the Hadith is sah'ri when Rasulullah صلى الله عليه وسلم used to invite any of the companions to eat sah'ri with him, he used to say, "Come and partake of blessed food with me". One Hadith says, "Eat sah'ri and strengthen yourself for fasting. And sleep in the afternoon (siesta) so as to gain assistance in waking up in the latter portion of the night (for 'ibaadah)". Abdullah bin Haarith reported that one of the Sahaabah said, "I once visited Rasulullah صلى الله عليه وسلم at such a time while he was busy partaking of sah'ri. Rasulullah صلى الله عليه وسلم then said, "This is a thing full of blessings which Allah has granted you. Never leave it".

Rasulullah صلى الله عليه وسلم has encouraged sah'ri in numerous Ahaadith, "Even though there be no food, then too one date should be eaten or a drink of water taken". Thus, when there definitely lies great blessings and reward in sah'ri, muslims should endeavour to gain as such as possible. However, in all things moderation is important, while going beyond the bonds of moderation is harmful. Neither should so little be eaten that one feels weak throughout the period of fasting, nor should so much be eaten that discomfort is felt in the digestive organs. Many a time we have been prohibited in the Hadith from filling the stomach excessively.

In his commentary on Saheeh Bukhaari, Ibn Hajar has mentioned various reasons for the blessedness of sah'ri.

(a) Because in it the sunnah is followed.

(b) Through sah'ri we oppose the ways of the Ahlul-Kitaab, which we are at all times called upon to do. They do not have sah'ri when fasting.

(c) It provides strength for ibaadah.

(d) It promotes more sincerity in ibaadah.

(e) It aids in eliminating bad temper which normally comes about as a result of hunger.

(f) It provides an opportunity to assist the needy at that early hour, especially a poor neighbour.

(g) Sah'ri is at a time when duaa's are accepted.

(h) At the time of sah'ri one gets the opportunity to remember Allah's, Thikr and lift up the hands to Him in duaa'.

These are a few of major reasons. There are others as well.

Ibn Daqeequl 'Iyd says that some 'Sufis are doubtful whether the eating of sah'ri is against the object of fasting or not. They maintain that the object of fasting is to stay away from food, drink and sexual desires, therefore sah'ri is against the object of fasting. In many opinion the amount to be eaten should be less at both sah'ri and if'taar, however this varies according to different persons and their activities. For example, for those students who are busy seeking knowledge of Deen, little food at sah'ri as well as if'taar, will be harmful. For them it is better not to have very little, because they seek Deeni knowledge which is very important (for the preservation and spread of Islaam). Similar is the case of those who are busy with thikr and other Deeni activities. Once Rasulullah صلى الله عليه وسلم announced to those proceeding to jihaad, "There is no virtue in fasting while travelling". That was in the month of Ramadhaan when some Sahaabah were busy with fardh fasting. This was because of jihaad. However if eating less does not cause laziness and weakness in doing important Deeni work, then there is no harm in eating less. Allaama Sharaani R.A. mentions in Sharh Iqna, "A convenant was made with us that we shall not fill our stomachs completely when eating especially in the nights of Ramadhaan". It is better that one should eat less in the nights of Ramadhaan than on other nights. After all, what type of fast is it after having filled oneself at sah'ri and i'ftaar? The Mashaa'ikh of 'Tariqah have said, "Whoever remains hungry in Ramadhaan, shall remain safe from the evil of shay'taan through the year until the next Ramadhaan". Numerous other Mashaa'ikh have also emphasized this point.

In the commentary of Ihyaa', Awaarif quotes that, Sahl bin Adullah Tastari used to eat only once in every fifteen days, while in Ramadhaan he ate only one morsel. In order to follow the sunnah he used to have a drink of water for sah'ri and i'ftaar. Shaikh Junaid R.A. was a man who always used to fast throughout the year. However, when noble friends used to visit him occasionally, he used to break his fast and eat with them saying, "The virtue of breaking fast and eating with (such noble) friends is not less than fasting (nafl).

Similarly we can mention the experiences of numerous saints, who through little food used to train their inner selves, but once again bear in mind, that it should not be carried out to such an extent that the religious activities and responsiblities are neglected as a result of weakness in the body.

(٨) عَنْ اَبِىْ هُرَيْرَةَ رَضِىَ اللّٰهُ تَعَالٰى عَنْهُ قَالَ قَالَ رَسُوْلُ اللّٰهِ ﷺ رُبَّ صَائِمٍ لَيْسَ لَهُ مِنْ صِيَامِهِ اِلَّا الْجُوْعُ وَرُبَّ قَائِمٍ لَيْسَ لَهُ مِنْ قِيَامِهِ اِلَّا السَّهْرُ

رواه ابن ماجه واللفظ له والنسائى وابن خزيمه فى صحيحه والحاكم وقال على شرط البخارى ذكر لفظهما المنذرى فى الترغيب بمعناه

HADITH NO. 8

Abu Hurayrah رضي الله عنه *relates that Rasulullah* صلى الله عليه وسلم *said, "Many are the ones who fast, attaining nothing by such*

fasting except for hunger, and many are the ones performing 'salaah by night attaining nothing by it, except for the discomfort of staying awake at night"

Reported by Ibn Majah and Nasa-iy.

COMMENTARY

With regard to this Hadith, the 'Ulama have mentioned three different interpretations. Firstly this Hadith may refer to those who fast during the day and then eat if'taar with such food which is haraam. All the reward received for fasting is destroyed because of the great sin of eating haraam, and nothing has been attained except hunger. Secondly, our Nabi صلى الله عليه وسلم may have meant those who fasted properly but during fasting, kept themselves busy with backbiting and slandering others (see later). Thirdly, the person referred to may be the one who, while fasting, did not stay away from evil and sin. Since Rasulullah صلى الله عليه وسلم sayings are concise, all forms of sin are included here. Likewise is the case of 'salaah all night but because of backbiting or other sinful act (e.g. allowing Fajr 'salaah to pass by) his noble act goes unrewarded.

(٩) عَنْ اَبِیْ عُبَیْدَةَ رَضِیَ اللّٰہُ تَعَالٰی عَنْهُ قَالَ سَمِعْتُ رَسُوْلَ اللّٰهِ ﷺ یَقُوْلُ
اَلصِّیَامُ جُنَّةٌ مَالَمْ یَخْرُقْهَا رواه النسائی وابن ماجه وابن خزیمه والحاكم وصححه على شرط البخاری
وألفاظهم مختلفة حكاها المنذری فی الترغیب

HADITH NO. 9

Abu 'Ubaidah رضي الله عنه *reports, "I have heard Rasulullah* صلى الله عليه وسلم *saying, "Fasting is a protective covering for a man, as long as he does not tear that protection".*

Reported by Nasa-iy, ibn Majah and ibn Khuzaymah

COMMENTARY

"Protective covering" here means such a covering whereby a man protects himself from his infamous enemy, shay'taan. This is what fasting does. In another Hadith we are told that fasting "saves one from Allah's punishment in the Hereafter". One Hadith mentions "that fasting saves one from Jahannam (hell)". Once somebody inquired from

Rasulullah صلى الله عليه وسلم "What causes the fast to break?" He replied: "Telling lies and backbiting".

This Hadith when read in conjunction with so many others, actually tells us to avoid such deeds. Such deeds cause fasting to be wasted. We are fond of indulging in unnecessary conversation to pass the time of fast. Some 'Ulama are of the opinion that the telling lies, backbiting, slander etc., actually does cause the fast to break just as eating and drinking does. However the vast majority of 'Ulama believe that the fast does not actually break but becomes void of blessings.

The Mashaa'ikh have mentioned six things about which care should be taken in fasting.

Firstly, one should keep the eyes away from any place where one is not supposed to look. They even go so far as to prohibit looking at one's own wife with desire. So how much more important is it to avoid looking at another woman with desire. Similarly one should avoid looking at any evil place or where evil is committed. Rasulullah صلى الله عليه وسلم said, "The evil eyes is an arrow of the shay'taan. Whosoever out of fear for Allah, prevents himself from looking at evil, Allah shall grant him such faith, the sweetness and ecstasy of which he will feel in the heart". The 'Sufis interpret the above saying about scenes which one should avoid looking at including such places and things which distract the mind from the rememberance of Allah.

Secondly, guarding the tongue against telling lies, unnecessary conversation, backbiting, arguments, swearing etc. In Bukhaari we read that fasting is a deterrent for the fasting person. For this reason those who fast should avoid all nonsensical talk, joking, arguments etc. Should anyone pick an argument, then say, "I am fasting". In other words, one should not start an argument and when someone else starts it then too one should avoid it. When the one who begins an argument is a reasonable person, then say to him "I am fasting". When the one who starts an argument is a foolish person then one should remind one's self that, "I am fasting and must not respond to such meaningless things". One must particularly abstain from backbiting and lies. During the time of our Nabi صلى الله عليه وسلم two women were fasting and suffered such extreme hunger that the fast became unbearable and both were on the point of death. The Sahaabah brought this to the notice of our Nabi

صلی اللہ علیہ وسلم who sent a bowl commanding them to vomit in it. When they both vomitted in the bowl, pieces of meat and fresh blood were found in it. The Sahaabah were greatly surprised, upon which our Nabi صلی اللہ علیہ وسلم said, "They fasted and avoided eating halaal food from Allah, but partook of haraam food by backbiting other people".

Something else that becomes clear from the aforegoing, that by backbiting, fasting becomes so much more difficult. For this reason both women almost died. Similar is the case with sinful acts. Experience shows that on the faithful God fearing ones, fasting has no adverse effect, whereas the wilful transgressors mostly find it difficult. If you wish the fast to be easy abstain from sins, especially backbiting. Allah says in the Qur'aan that backbiting is the (actual) eating of the flesh of one's brother. We find this description in the Hadith too. Once Rasulullah صلی اللہ علیہ وسلم on seeing a group of people said, "Pick your teeth", They replied; "We did not partake of meat today", Rasulullah صلی اللہ علیہ وسلم said, "A certain person's meat is sticking to your teeth". This meant that they were involved in backbiting. May Allah keep us safe from this evil because we are very neglectful of this. All are guilty of this. Backbiting is rife even in the assemblies of the religiously educated and those who are considered religious. What is most grieving is that we do not even consider it to be backbiting. If one suspects that one is guilty of backbiting then it is hidden by terming it a "relation of facts".

One of the Sahaabah inquired from Rasulullah صلی اللہ علیہ وسلم "What is backbiting?" Rasulullah صلی اللہ علیہ وسلم replied, "To mention something about your brother behind his back which he resents". The Sahaabah then said, "And is it still backbiting if that thing mentioned about him really is in him?" Our Nabi صلی اللہ علیہ وسلم said, "In that case (if that which was mentioned is really true) it is definitely backbiting. And if he is guilty of it then you have slandered him". Once Nabi صلی اللہ علیہ وسلم passed two graves. He said, "On both these inmates of the graves the punishment of the grave has descended. One is being punished because of backbiting, the other because of not having taken precautions when passing urine". Rasulullah صلی اللہ علیہ وسلم also said, "There are more than seventy kinds of evil in (using) interest. The mildest form of it is like having committed incest with your mother. And taking one Dirham of interest is a worse evil than having fornicated thirty-five times. The worst and most evil form of taking interest is the humiliation of a Muslim. In the Hadith we are sternly warned against backbiting and disgracing others. I very much wanted to write down here a number of Ahaadith on this subject because all our gatherings and conversations are generally filled with them (backbiting and slander). However I finally decide not to do so because the subject under discussion here is something else–not actually backbiting. So having just noted down these few, I once again make duaa' that Allah keep us safe from this evil. And I beg of my friends and brothers to pray for me too. We are all full of inner faults.

"Arrogance and pride, ignorance and negligence,
dislike and malice, evil thoughts,
lies and breaking of promises,
ostentation and hatred,
backbiting and animosity.
What sickness is there O Allah, that is not in me,
Heal me from every illness and grant me my necessity,
Verily I have a heart that is ailing,
Verily you are Healer of the sick".

Thirdly, according to the 'Sufis, what should be avoided is that the ears should be kept away from listening to anything makrooh. It is haraam to say or listen to anything which should not be said. Rasulullah صلى الله عليه وسلم said that in "backbiting both the backbiter and the listener are equal in sin".

Fourthly, the rest of the body should be kept away from sin and evil. Neither should the hands touch it, nor the feet made to walk towards it. Special care should be taken, especially at the time of if'taar. No such thing should enter it, about which there is any doubt as to its being haraam or halaal. When a person fasts, and at if'taar time breaks fast with haraam food, he becomes just like a sick person who takes medicine to cure himself of the sickness but also adds poison which destroys him.

Fifthly, after having fasted it is not advisable to fill the stomach completely even with halaal food at if'taar, because then, the object of fasting is defeated. Whereas fasting helps to diminish one's carnal desires, it also strengthens the angelic qualities of man and increases the illumination of the soul. For eleven months we have been eating and drinking. What harm is there if one eats less for only one month. We have a bad habit of filling our bellies at if'taar for what was not eaten during the day and also at sah'ri in preparation for the day, thus increasing our average consumption. Many such things are eaten which we normally do not eat at other times. In fact, during Ramadhaan we develop this type of bad habit.

Imaam Ghazaali R.A. asks the same question, "when the object of fasting is to conquer the dictates of Ibless and our carnal passions, then how can this possibly be done by eating excessively at if'taar and thus defeating the objects? Actually in that case we have only altered the time of eating and have not decreased our food intake. Moreover by having so many various types of delicacies which we do not have out of Ramadhaan and many people also have the habit of keeping special food items for Ramadhaan. Therefore after fasting the full day we consume even more than we do in normal times. The result is that instead of lessening the carnal desires, these are considerably increased. The real benefit of fasting comes as a result of actual hunger in the true spirit. Fasting has various worldly objectives and benefits as the observance of Shar'i injunction, which is the ultimate aim. Our Nabi صلى الله عليه وسلم said, "Shay'taan flows through the body of man like blood, so close up that path by remaining hungry". All the limbs are spiritually nourished when the body is starved and when the body is stuffed then all the limbs are spiritually starved.

Another object is that fasting gives us the chance of appreciating the plight of the poor and distitute and thus engender sympathetic feelings toward them. This could only be attained by remaining hungry and by filling the stomach with so much delicious food at sah'ri that one does not feel hungry until if'taar Once a person went to Bishr Haafi. He found the saint shivering from cold in spite of having warm clothes at his side. That person inquired, "Is this a time for taking off clothes?" Bishr replied; "There are numberious poor and needy ones, I am unable to sympathise with them. The most I could do is to be like them". The 'sufis plead for the same attitude in fasting and so do the Fuqaha's (Jurists). In Maraquil Falaah it is written, "Do not eat excessively at sah'ri as the prosperous ones do, for this is the way to lose the object of fasting". Allaama 'Tah'taawi writes, "enduring the pangs of hunger is a cause for increased reward". Similarly a feeling of sympathy is developed for the poor and hungry ones". Our Nabi صلى الله عليه وسلم himself said; "Allah does not dislike the filling of anything to the brim more than He dislikes the filling of the stomach". In another Hadith Rasulullah صلى الله عليه وسلم says, "A few morsels are sufficient to keep one fit". If anyone is bent on eating he should not overeat. The best amount for a person is that one third should be filled with food, one third with drink while the other third remains empty. After all there must have been some reason for which Rasulullah صلى الله عليه وسلم fasted continuously for many day on end, without eating anything in between. I had seen my ustaath Moulana Khalil Ahmed (R.A.) eating only slightly more than one thin (hand made) bread (roti) at if'taar and at sah'ri during the whole month of Ramadhaan. When any of his near ones used to urge him to eat more, he used to reply, "I am not hungry. Actually, I merely sat down to eat to be with my friends".

About Moulana Shaah Abdurraheem Raaipoori R.A., I have heard that in Ramadhaan, he used to fast for days on end, having only a few cups of tea without milk for sah'ri and if'taar apart from that nothing else. Once his most trusted follower (and Khalefah Moulana Shaah Abdulqaadir remarked with anxiety, "Hadhrat you will become quite weak, if you do not eat anything". To this Moulana Shaah Raaipoori replied; "Praise be to Allah, I am experiencing something of the ecstasy of Jannah". *(may Allah grant us all the ability to follow such pious ones. Aameen).*

The sixth point is that after fasting one should always have fear and anxiety as to whether one's fast had been accepted or rejected by Allah. This should be the case with all ibaadah. One never knows whether some such important thing may have left out about which no notice was takan. One should fear that Allah may reject one's deeds. Rasulullah صلى الله عليه وسلم said; "Many are the reciters of the Qur'aan who are being cursed by the Qur'aan". He also said, "On the day of Qiyaamah, one of those with whom Allah shall reckon first shall be a shaheed (martyr in the way of the Allah). Allah shall call him and reminding him of all Allah's favours bestowed upon him, which the shaheed shall admit. He shall then be asked; "What have you done by way of expressing gratitude for those favours?" The shaheed shall reply; "If fought in your way till I became a shaheed". Allah shall reply, "Not true. You fought so that you could be called a brave man. And so it was said". Thereafter it shall be commanded that he be pulled with his face on the ground and cast into Jahannam. Thereafter an aalim shall be called. He too shall reminded of Allah's favours and asked the same question. He shall reply, "O Allah, I strove to acquire knowledge, taught others and for Your sake I recited Qur'aan". Allah shall say, "Not true. You did all that merely to be said that you are learned and so it was said". Then it shall be commanded that he too be pulled face on the ground and cast into Jahannam. Thereafter a rich man shall be called. He too shall be reminded of Allah's favours. He too shall admit, and in reply to Allah's question as to what he did to express his gratitude, he shall reply, "I did not find any worthy cause wherein I did not spend out charitably for Your sake". Allah's reply shall come, "Not true. You did all that so that is may be said that you are very generous. And so it was said". Then it shall be commanded that he too be pulled face on the ground and cast into Jahannam. May Allah save us.

This is the result of ill-formed niyyahs. Numerous such instances are mentioned in the Hadith. The fasting person must at all times safeguard his niyyah and at the same time fear for its adulteration. He should also constantly make duaa' that Allah Ta'aala makes this a cause for His pleasure. It should also be borne in mind that regarding your act as not being worthy of acceptance is one aspect and your hopes for the infinite grace and mercy of Allah Ta'aala is another aspect. This latter aspect of Allah's graciousness is unique. At times He converts even misdeeds to be rewardful (due to other good deeds that follow the misdeed) then why be dispondent of reward for defective deeds? These six things are compulsory for all the righteous ones.

As for the exceptionally pious ones a seventh point is added. That is, during fasting, the heart should not be turned towards anyone else except Allah, so much that during the course of the fast it is a defect to worry whether there shall be something to eat for if'taar. Some Shaykhs even consider it a fault to think about food for if'taar or that one should endeavour to acquire something, because this shows lack of confidence in Allah's promise of sustenance. In the commentary of Ihya 'ulumid Deeni the author mentions, regarding some Mashaa'ikhs, that should anything arrive for if'taar before the time of if'taar, then it was given away fearing that the heart will now be set on the food for the rest of the day, which in turn would reduce the reliance on Allah. This can of course only be practiced by the exceptionally pious ones we cannot even imagine having such faith. Should we try to follow that, we may destroy ourselves.

The Qur'aan commands, "Fasting has been prescribed for you". The commentators of the Qur'aan say that from this verse it is deduced that fasting is made compulsory for every portion of the body. Thus, fasting of the tongue means abstaining from telling lies, etc. Fasting of the ears means not listening to evil. Fasting of the eyes means not to look at any form of evil and sin. Similarly fasting of the self means to be free from greed and all carnal desires. Fasting of the heart means casting away from it the love for worldly things. Fasting of the 'rooh' (spirit) means to abstain (in this world) from the pleasures of the Aakhirah. Fasting of the mind means avoiding thoughts about the presence of any other being besides Allah.

(١٠) عَنْ اَبِىْ هُرَيْرَةَ رَضِىَ اللهُ تَعَالٰى عَنْهُ اَنَّ رَسُوْلَ اللهِ ﷺ قَالَ مَنْ اَفْطَرَ يَوْمًا مِّنْ رَمَضَانَ مِنْ غَيْرِ رُخْصَةٍ وَلَامَرَضٍ لَمْ يَقْضِهِ صَوْمُ الدَّهْرِ كُلِّهِ وَاِنْ صَامَهُ

رواه أحمد والترمذى وأبوداود وابن ماجه والدارمى والبخارى فى ترجمة باب كذا فى المشكوٰة قلت وبسط الكلام على طرقه العينى فى شرح البخارى

HADITH NO. 10

Abu Hurayah رضي الله عنه *reports that Rasulullah* صلى الله عليه وسلم *said, "Whosoever eats on one day of Ramadhaan without a valid reason or excuse or genuine illness (acceptable in Shari-ah), shall never be able to compensate for that day even by fasting the rest of his life".*

Reported by Ahmad, Tirmizhi, Abu Dawood, and Ibn Majah.

COMMENTARY

The view of some 'ulama is that if anybody has without any valid excuse failed to fast any day of Ramadhaan and dishonoured it by eating etc, such a person can never compensate (duly fulfil the Qadhaa) for this violation. Even by fasting for the rest of one's life that person cannot compensate for this one day. Ali رضي الله عنه and others held the same view. However the vast majority of 'ulama maintain that where one did not fast one day of Ramadhaan, then only one fast will suffice as compensation. On the other hand, when a person has started to fast in Ramadhaan and then breaks it during the day without any valid excuse, then according to the Shari-ah, this person shall have to fast continuously for two months without a break in between. No matter what happens, the true virtue and blessings of Ramadhaan will never be attained. This is the meaning of the above Hadith ie. that where a day of Ramadhaan has been lost without excuse, any number of fasts by way of compensation will not bring back the true blessings of even one day of Ramadhaan.

This all is for those who keep the qadhaa fast. How unfortunate and misguided are those who deny the fast and do not observe it at all? Fasting is one of the fundamental pillars of Islam. Rasulullah صلى الله عليه وسلم has mentioned five principles of Islam. First and foremost is the oneness of Allah and Muhammad صلى الله عليه وسلم being a Rasul (Messenger of Allah) and thereafter the four famous pillars: Namaaz, Fast, Zakaat and Haj.

How many Muslims do we find who are counted amongst the Muslims, yet do not uphold even one of these five. In official papers and census they will be recorded as Muslims, whereas in Allah's sight they cannot be counted as such. Ibn Abbas (R.A.) relates in a Hadith stating, "Islam is based on three principles:–a. The Shahaadah, b. 'Salaah, c. Fasting. Whoever fails to uphold any of these is a disbeliever and it is permissible to give him capital punishment". As regard to the latter portion of this Hadith, the 'ulama have said that they only become disbelievers when together with failing to uphold any principle, they also deny its necessity, or its being a principle. No matter what interpretation is given, the fact remain that Rasulullah صلى الله عليه وسلم spoke against such people with utmost vehemence. Hence, those who fail to keep up the faraa'idh of the Deen should indeed fear Allah's wrath. No one can escape death, and the pleasure and comforts of this life are short lived.

Only obedience to His commands can save us. There are those ignorant ones who do not fast at all. So much worse is the position of those who do not only refuse to fast, but speak such words whereby they scoff and jeer at the month of fasting in sarcastic manner. This is something dangerous, bringing one to the brink of kufr. You may have heard them say, "Fasting is for those who have no food in their homes not for me". Or "What does Allah gain by having us suffer hunger?" Such words should never be uttered. It should be remembered that to scoff and jeer at, or poke fun at even the smallest part of our Deen becomes the cause of kufr (apostasy). Should any person not perform a single 'salaah in his life, not fast one single day, or fail to perform any fardh obligations in Islam, then that person does not become a kaafir, as long as one does not deny their being necessary. However one will certainly be punished for any fardh that has been neglected. But to scoff and jeer at any tiniest aspect of the Deen is kufr (apostasy), and can result in all good actions being invalidated. From this it can be seen how delicate this affair is. Such irresponsible utterances should never be made about fasting

CHAPTER TWO

LAYLATUL QADR

Amongst the nights of Ramadhaan there is one called "Laylatul Qadr" a night that is noted for its great blessings. The Qur'aan Kareem describes it as being greater in blessedness and spiritual virtue than a thousand months which in turn means that it is greater than eighty three years and four months.

Fortunate indeed is that person who attains the full blessings of this night by spending it in 'ibaadah of Allah, because he has then attained reward for 'ibaadah of eighty three years and four months and even more. Indeed the granting of this night to the faithful muslim is a great favour.

THE ORIGIN

Regarding this night, in a Hadith reported by Anas رضي الله عنه in Durre Manthoor Rasulullah صلى الله عليه وسلم is reported to have said; "Laylatul Qadr was granted to my ummah and not to any other ummah before this". Regarding the reason for the granting of Laylatul Qadr, various reasons are mentioned. One reason, according to some Ahaadith is given thus: Rasulullah صلى الله عليه وسلم used to look at the longer lives of the earlier people and was suddened when pondering over the much shorter lives of his own ummah. If his ummah had wished to compete with the people before them in the doing of righteous deeds, because of their shorter lives it would be impossible for them to either emulate or surpass them. To compensate for this difference in their life span, Allah in His infinite mercy granted them with this night of great blessing. This means that if any fortunate one of this ummah spends during his life time ten such nights in the worship of his maker, he would have gained the reward for 'ibaadah of eight hundred and thirty years and even more. Another report states that; Rasulullah صلى الله عليه وسلم once related to the sahaabah the story of a very righteous man from among the Bani Israa'iyl who used to spend one thousand months in jihaad. On hearing this, the sahaabah envied that person because they could not attain the same reward, whereupon Allah granted them the Night of Power as a recompense.

Still another report states that our Nabi صلى الله عليه وسلم once mentioned the names of the four most pious people from among the Bani Israa'iyl who each spent eighty years in Allah's sincere service, worshipping Him, and not sinning in the least. They were Nabi Ayyoob alayhis salaam, Zakariyya alayhis salaam, Hizqeel alayhis salaam and Yu'shaa alayhis salaam. The sahaabahs heard this with astonishment. Then Jibraeel aalyhis salaam appeared and recited Surah Qadr, wherein the blessing of this night was revealed.

Apart from these reports, there are others too, explaining the origin of the Night of Power. This type of difference in narration arises because, after occurrence of several incidents only one aayah is revealed. That aayah then is relevant to anyone of the incidents that took place. But no matter which of them we accept, the important fact that remains is that Allah has granted the ummah of Muhammad this night. This is a great favour and gift of Allah. To devote yourself on this night is also a blessing from Allah. How worthy of envy are those Mashaa'ikh who say they did not miss the 'ibaadah of one Laylatul Qadr since they became of age. Now, as to which night it is, here again approximately fifty different views of the 'ulama are mentioned. It is not easy for me to enumerate them all. But the most accepted versions, as well as further discussions on this night shall follow in the ensuing pages of this book. The numerous excellences of this night are mentioned in various books of Hadith. These will also be mentioned. For the reason that the Qur'aan Majeed itself mentions the night, we shall commence with a short commentary on Surah Qadr. (The translations are from A. Yusuf Ali).

بِسْمِ اللّٰهِ الرَّحْمٰنِ الرَّحِيْمِ اِنَّا اَنْزَلْنَاهُ فِيْ لَيْلَةِ الْقَدْرِ

"In the name of Allah the beneficient, the Merciful". "We have indeed revealed this (message) in the Night of Power". (Suratul Qadr: 1).

Reference here is made to the fact that on this special night, the Qur'aan was sent down from Al Lowhul Mahfuz (The preserved Tablet) to the heavens (above the earth). Because a great book like Qur'aan was revealed in this night is in itself sufficient to explain its excellence, needless to mention all other blessings and virtues which are included. In the very next verse by way of drawing and increasing our interest in the matter under discussion, a question is asked:

وَمَا اَدْرَاكَ مَالَيْلَةُ الْقَدْرِ

"And what will explain to you what the Night of Power is". (Suratul Qadr: 2).

In other words, the question asked here is: Have you any knowledge as to the greatness and the great importance of this night? Have you any knowledge as to the great favours and bounties that are placed in it? The next verse proceeds to enumerate some of that greatness:

لَيْلَةُ الْقَدْرِ خَيْرٌ مِّنْ اَلْفِ شَهْرٍ

"The Night of Power is better than a thousand months". (Suratul Qadr: 3).

The true meaning here is that reward for spending this night in 'ibaadah is better and more than having spent one thousand months 'ibadah, it is in fact more but as to how much more rewarding it is, we are not told here.

تَنَزَّلُ الْمَلآئِكَةُ وَالرُّوْحُ فِيْهَا بِاِذْنِ رَبِّهِمْ مِّنْ كُلِّ اَمْرٍ

"Therein come down the Angels and the Spirit by Allah's permission on every errand". (Suratul Qadr: 4)

A fine explanation is given in this verse by Imaam Raazi R.A. Commenting on this verse he explains that when man first appeared on earth, created by Allah as His vicegerent on earth, the Malaa'ikah looked on him with scorn. When Allah informed them of His intention of placing man on earth, they even ventured to ask: "Will you place in this earth one who shall commit evil therein and shed blood?"

Similarly, when his parents noted his original form as

a mere drop of mani (sperm), they too looked upon it with scorn and resentment, so much so, that they considered it as something which polluted clothing and had to be washed away. But later when Allah made that same despicable sperm into a fine form of man, they began to love and cherish him. So far have things now progressed that when on this Night of Power we see that same man worshipping Allah and adoring Him, those very same Malaa'ikah who had previously looked down on him with scorn, descend towards him, obviously repentant for the thoughts they had once harboured against him.

In this verse mention is made . . . "and the spirit". Reference is clearly to Jibraeelalayhis salaam. Commentators of the Qur'aan have given various versions of this word. Let us look at some of them:

(a) The vast majority of the commentators are agreed that Jibraeel alayhis salaam is meant here, and according to Imaam Raazi, (R.A.) this is the most correct meaning. Allah first makes mention of the Malaa'ikah and then because of Jibraeel's alayhis salaam status among them, special mention is made of him.

(b) Some commentators hold the view that "Spirits" here means one angel of such extra ordinary gigantic proportion that before him heavens and earth appear as almost nothing (as a morsel).

(c) Another group of commentators opine that "Spirit" here means one such group of Malaa'ikah who never appear and only on this night are they seen by other Malaa'ikah.

(d) Some commentators again believe that the "Spirit" here designates one such creation of Allah, which although it partakes of food and drink, still is neither man nor angel.

(e) There is also a view that "Spirit" here refers to 'Iysaa alayhis salaam who on this night comes down with the Malaa'ikah to view the righteous deeds of this ummah.

(f) The last view we wish to mention here is that "Spirit" means Allah's special mercy which comes in the wake of the angels descent. But already stated the first opinion is the most acceptable.

In this respect Imaam Bayhaqi R.A. reports a Hadith by Anas wherein Rasulullah صلى الله عليه وسلم is reported to have said, "On Laylatul Qadr Jibraeel alayhis salaam comes down with a group of angels and make duaa' for mercy for every one whom they find busy in 'ibadah". This same verse under discussion says,

بِإِذْنِ رَبِّهِمْ مِنْ كُلِّ أَمْرٍ

". . . By Allah's permission on every errand . . .".

The Author of Mazhaahire Haq writes that on this night ages ago the Malaa'ikah were created; on this night long ago the creation on Aadam alayhis salaam was begun as the matter from which he was created had been gathered; on this night trees were planted in Jannah and large number of Ahaadith bear witness to the fact that on this night duaa's are granted. Similary we read in the kitaab, Durre Manthoor, that according to a Hadith it was on this night that 'Iysaa alayhis salaam was lifted up bodily into the heavens and also it was on this night that the towbah (repentance) of Bani Israa-'iyl was accepted.

سَلَامٌ هِيَ حَتَّىٰ مَطْلَعِ الْفَجْرِ

"Peace be until the break of dawn".

(Suratul Qadr: 5).

Yes, this is the very embodiment of peace. Throughout its hours the Malaa'ikah recite salaam upon faithful believers adoring their Lord. As one group descends another ascends as is explained in the Ahaadith. Another interpretation is that it is a night of complete safety from evil and mischief.

These blessings remain throughout the night until the break of dawn and are not confined to any specific hour. And now having noted a few virtues of this night as explained in the words of Allah, there is no further need to quote any Ahaadith. However, since many virtues have been in numerous Ahaadith we mention a few here.

(١) عَنْ اَبِىْ هُرَيْرَةَ رَضِىَ اللهُ تَعَالٰى عَنْهُ قَالَ قَالَ رَسُوْلُ اللهِ ﷺ مَنْ قَامَ لَيْلَةَ لْقَدْرِ اِيْمَانًا وَّاحْتِسَابًا غُفِرَ لَهُ مَاتَقَدَّمَ مِنْ ذَنْبِهِ كذا فى الترغيب عن البخارى ومسلم

HADITH NO. 1

Abu Hurayrah رضي الله عنه *reports Rasulullah* صلى الله عليه وسلم *said, "Whoever stands in prayer and 'ibaadah on the night of Power with sincere faith and with sincere hope of gaining reward, his previous sins are forgiven".*

Reported in At Targheeb from Bukhaari and Muslim

COMMENTARY

In the above Hadith 'standing' refers to 'salaah as well as any other form of 'ibaadah, as for example thikr, tilaawah etc. The phrase '. . . *with sincere hope of gaining reward*', means that one should be sincerely occupied with 'ibaadah solely for the pleasure of Allah and to recieve reward from Him. This should not be done for others to see, or to deceive them. According to Khat'taabi it means that one should have complete faith in the promise that any deed shall be rewarded and thus one must stand before Allah with earnestness and enthusiasm. Neither should one think of this 'ibaadah as a burden, nor should there be any doubt about the reward which will be granted. After all it is a known fact that when one aims at a high goal and desire to have a great reward, while at the same time having complete certainty of receiving it, the burden of striving hard along an arduous path to attain that goal becomes easy. Similary the burden of standing for long hours becomes easy. This is the reason why those who had become spiritually elevated in Allah's sight find it easy to remain in 'ibaadah almost at all times.

It will be noted that the Hadith speaks about previous sins being forgiven. The 'ulamaa have said that this forgiveness are mentioned in the Hadith above and other Ahaadith, refers only to minor sins. Major sins can only be forgiven, according to the Qur'aan after sincere repentance, with the vow and promise never to return to such sins again. This is the reason why the 'ulamaa are unanimous that major sins are not forgiven except by sincere repentance. Hence whenever forgiveness of sins mentioned in the Ahaadith the 'ulamaa specify it to be minor sins.

My late father (May Allah bless him and grant him light in his resting place) used to say that the word 'minor' has been omitted here for two reasons.

Firstly, he says, a true muslim is one on whom major sins should not rest, because whenever a major sin has been commited, he will never rest or find peace until he has sincerely repented to Allah (begging) for forgiveness and promising not to do the same in future.

Secondly, my late father used to say, when such great and blessed days and nights come along, when a true muslim stands before Allah in prayer and adoration, hoping to gain reward, it is a fact that the true muslim in his conscience should feel greatly grieved for previous sins. This grief over sins and the resolution not to return to such acts are the most important requirements of towbah. This means that on such days and nights the repentance for major sins is automatic, (leaving only minor sins to be forgiven). It is best however that when a night like Laylatul Qadr comes along, one who has committed major sins should first of all verbally repent with a heart full of sincere longing for forgiveness so that Allah in His infinite mercy may forgive all forms of sins. And when you do, remember me too in your duaa's. (The publishers request the same).

(٢) عَنْ اَنَسٍ رَضِیَ اللّٰہُ تَعَالٰی عَنْهُ قَالَ دَخَلَ رَمَضَانُ فَقَالَ رَسُوْلُ اللّٰہِ ﷺ اِنَّ هٰذَ
الشَّهْرُ قَدْ حَضَرَكُمْ وَفِيْهِ لَيْلَةٌ خَيْرٌ مِّنْ اَلْفِ شَهْرٍ مَنْ حُرِمَهَا فَقَدْ حُرِمَ الْخَيْرَ كُلَّ
وَلَایُحْرَمُ خَيْرَهَا اِلَّا مَحْرُوْمٌ رواه ابن ماجه وإسناده حسن إنشاء الله كذا فى الترغيب وفى
المشكوٰة عنه إلا كل محروم

HADITH NO. 2

Anas رضي الله عنه *reports, "Once when Ramadhaan commenced, the Messenger of Allah* صلى الله عليه وسلم *said, 'A month has verily dawned over you wherein lies a night better than one thousand months. Whoever is deprived of its blessings has indeed deprived of (almost) all good. And none is deprived of its good except he who is completely unfortunate'".*

Reported by Ibn Majah.

COMMENTARY

Who can have doubt as to the misfortune of the person who deprives himself of the great good of Laylatul Qadr? (Who can doubt the misfortune of the one who misses all the bestowed favours? Indeed there are so many of us). There are those who during the course of their services and duties of employment have to stay awake throughout the year at night. What difficulty can there be for people like these, should they for the sake of gaining the reward of over eighty years 'ibaadah, stay awake at night for this month in the way of Allah's service?

For them the task should not be too difficult, but, because of lack of interest, there is no urge in the heart. If that was present, then not one night, but a thousand nights in worshipping Allah would become exceedingly easy.

It is that urge and desire that we must create. After all there must have been some reason why Rasulullah صلى الله عليه وسلم had performed such lengthy 'salaah that his feet even became swollen. This he did despite having firmly believed the promises and glad tidings which Allah had given him. We also profess to be his followers. Those who really appreciated these opportunities of 'ibaadah did what was necessary and set an example to the ummah. They left no room for the critics to say, "Who could do it better or who is more capable of following these examples". It is a matter of convincing the heart, that for those who desire doing things, the most difficult task presents no hardship. This could only be achieved by remaining with a recognised Shaikh for spiritual guidance.

Let us look at the example of the following illustrious sons of Islaam. One such man was 'Umar رضي الله عنه who, having performed his 'Ishaa' 'salaah used to return home and then remain in 'salaah throughout the night until the athaan was heard for fajr. Then there is the example of the pious Khaleefa Uthmaan رضي الله عنه who, after fasting the whole day (almost throughout the year) used to spend the whole night in 'salaah, apart from having a little sleep during part of the first third of the early night. It is well known about him that he used to recite the whole Qur'aan during one Rak-ah. In the Ihya 'Ulumid Deen by Imaam Ghazaali, Abu 'Taalib Makki makes mention about forty men from among the taabi'iy, who used to perform fajr 'salaah with the same wudhu with which they had performed their 'Ishaa' 'salaah. This has been reported by many authentic narrators.

Shaddaad رضي الله عنه was one of the sahaabah who used to lie awake throughout the night turning from side to side until fajir. Then he used to say, "O Allah, the fear for the fire of Jahannam has driven away sleep from my eyes". Aswad bin Yazeed رضي الله عنه apart from sleeping a little between Maghrib and 'Ishaa', used to remain in 'ibaadah throughout the night during Ramadhaan. Now let us look at a man like Sa'iyd ibn Musayyib رضي الله عنه it is said that he used to perform 'Ishaa' and fajr with the same wudhu for fifty years. Then there is the example of 'Sila bin Ashyam رضي الله عنه who after spending a whole night in Allah's worship, used to say at the break of day, "O Allah, I am not fit to beg of You Jannah but all I beseech from You now is that You save me from Jahannam".

Qataadah رضي الله عنه was a man who used to finish the recitation of the Qur'aan every three nights of Ramadhaan but during the latter ten nights he used to complete the whole Qur'aan every night. About Imaam Abu Haneefah R.A. it is well known that for forty years he performed Ishaa and the following morning's fajr 'salaah with the same wudhu. To doubt or disbelieve is the denial of true historical facts. When his companions inquired of him as to where he had obtained the strength for that, he replied, "It is in answer to a special duaa' which I made to Allah in the name of the blessedness of His special names". He merely slept a little in the afternoons about which he said, "In the Hadith we are advised to do that". In other words, even in the afternoon sleep he used to follow the sunnah. This same Imaam Abu Haneefah R.A. while reciting the Qur'aan used to cry so much that his neighbours used to feel pity for him. Once he wept the whole night, crying while reciting the following verse time and again:

بَلِ السَّاعَةُ مَوْعِدُهُمْ وَالسَّاعَةُ اَدْهٰى وَاَمَرُّ

"Nay the Hour (of Judgement) is the time promised for them (for their recompense) and that hour will be most grevious and bitter" (Suratul Qamar: 46).

Ibrahim Ibn Ad'ham R.A. went so far not to sleep in Ramadhaan neither by night nor by day. Imaam Shaafi'iy

R.A. used to recite the Qur'aan about sixty times in his 'salaah, in the days and nights of Ramadhaan. Apart from these few there were countless others saintly souls who used to act diligently on the injunctions of the verse:

وَمَا خَلَقْتُ الْجِنَّ وَالْاِنْسَ اِلَّا لِيَعْبُدُوْنِ

"I have only created jinn and human that they may serve Me". (Suratuth Thaariyaat: 56).

Nothing is difficult for those who have a will to practice. These are examples of those who have gone before. But today too there are many who with the same devotion, serve Allah and according to their own times turn night into day in the service of Allah. Even in these times of evil and iniquity there are those who in their saintly manner follow the example of Rasulullah ﷺ. Leisure and comfort should not prevent one from deligent devotion. Nor are wordly errand obstacles.

The Messenger of Allah ﷺ said, "Allah says, 'O son of Aadam, spend your time in my service and I shall enrich you with independence and freedom from want, and I remove poverty from you. Otherwise I shall fill you with obligations and duties while your poverty and needs shall not disappear". How true, and we see the truth of this daily.

(There are people who serve only Allah, while having no apparent means of earning anything and yet they need nothing. On the other hand we see people striving hard to earn wordly things and necessities. They become so engaged in their task that no time is left for 'ibaadah. Then too, inspite of spending all their time seeking material needs, they remain full of wordly desires, necessitres and obligations. Translator).

٣) عَنْ اَنَسٍ رَضِىَ اللّٰهُ تَعَالٰى عَنْهُ قَالَ قَالَ رَسُوْلُ اللّٰهِ ﷺ اِذَا كَانَ لَيْلَةُ الْقَدْرِ
لَ جِبْرَئِيْلُ فِىْ كَبْكَبَةٍ مِّنَ الْمَلَآئِكَةِ يُصَلُّوْنَ عَلٰى كُلِّ عَبْدٍ قَائِمٍ اَوْ قَاعِدٍ يَذْكُرُ
هٗ عَزَّ وَجَلَّ فَاِذَا كَانَ يَوْمُ عِيْدِهِمْ يَعْنِى يَوْمَ فِطْرِهِمْ بَاهٰى بِهِمْ مَلَائِكَتَهٗ فَقَالَ
مَلَائِكَتِىْ مَاجَزَاءُ اَجِيْرٍ وَفّٰى عَمَلَهٗ قَالُوْا رَبَّنَا جَزَاؤُهٗ اَنْ يُّوَفّٰى اَجْرُهٗ قَالَ
لَائِكَتِىْ عَبِيْدِىْ وَاِمَائِىْ قَضَوْا فَرِيْضَتِىْ عَلَيْهِمْ ثُمَّ خَرَجُوْا يَعُجُّوْنَ اِلَى الدُّعَاءِ

وَعِزَّتِىْ وَجَلَالِىْ وَكَرَمِىْ وَعُلُوِّىْ وَارْتِفَاعِ مَكَانِىْ لَأُجِيْبَنَّهُمْ فَيَقُوْلُ ارْجِعُوْا فَقَدْ غَفَرْتُ لَكُمْ وَبَدَّلْتُ سَيِّآتِكُمْ حَسَنَاتٍ قَالَ فَيَرْجِعُوْنَ مَغْفُوْرًا لَهُمْ رواه البيهقى فى شعب الايمان كذا فى المشكوٰة

HADITH NO. 3

Anas رضي الله عنه reports that Rasulullah صلى الله عليه وسلم said, "On the Night of Power Jibraeel A.S. decends to the earth with the group of angels, praying for blessings on every servant of Allah they see standing in worship or sitting and celebrating Allah's praises. Then on the day of 'I̲yd. Allah boasts about them to the angels, "O angels, what is the reward of that employee who had fully completed his service?" They reply, 'O our Sustainer, his reward should be given in full'. To this Allah replies; 'O My angels, verily My servants, the males among them as well as the females have performed the obligatory duty upon them, thereafter they set forth to the 'I̲ydgaah raising their voices in prayer to Me. I swear by My honour, by My Grace, by My High position of greatness, that I shall surely answer the prayer of those people". Thereafter Allah says (addressing the people) "Return, certainly I have forgiven your sins and have exchanged your evil deeds with righteous ones". Rasulullah صلى الله عليه وسلم said, "Those people then return (from the 'I̲ydgaah) in forgiven state.

Reported by Bayhaqi in Shu-a̲bul Iymaan.

COMMENTARY

In this H̲adith it is clearly mentioned that Jibraeel A.S. comes down with the angels. The author of Ghaaliyatul Mawaa-'ith̲z̲ quotes from the Ghunyah of Shaikh Abdul Qaadir Jilaani that in a H̲adith reported by Ibn Abbas (R.A.) it is mentioned that Jibraeel A.S., after his descent commands the angels to proceed to the house of every one busy with ibaadah, and to shake his hand. Thereupon the angels spead forth visiting every house whether big or small, whether in the jungle or on a ship wherein a believing worshipper resides, to shake his hand. However, certain houses are not entered. The house in which there is a dog or a pig. The house in which there is a person in state of Janaabah, which has resulted from adultery or fornication, and a house wherein pictures of men and animals are displayed. How unfortunate it is that many Muslim's houses do not have the angels entering simply because there are pictures of men and animals being displayed, solely for the sake of adding what appears to be a bit of adornmant.

Only one picture may have been hunged by one careless member of the household and the whole house (dwelling) is completely deprived of blessings.

(٤) عَنْ عَائِشَةَ رَضِىَ اللّٰهُ تَعَالٰى عَنْهَا قَالَتْ قَالَ رَسُوْلُ اللّٰهِ ﷺ تَحَرَّوْا لَيْلَةَ الْقَدْرِ فِى الْوِتْرِ مِنَ الْعَشْرِ الْاَوَاخِرِ مِنْ رَمَضَانَ مشکوٰة عن البخاری

HADITH NO. 4

Aa'ishah radhial-laahu an-haa reports that Rasulullah ﷺ *said, "Seek Laylatul Qadr among the odd numbered nights of the last ten days of the month of Ramadhaan".*

Reported in Mishkaat.

COMMENTARY

We come to the question: "When is Laylatul Qadr? The above Hadith commands us to seek it among the last ten nights of Ramadhaan. According to the vast majority of authorities, the last ten nights commence on 21st night. Such is the case that whether the month of Ramadhaan consists of 29 days or 30 days, one should seek Laylatul Qadr on the 21st, 23rd, 25th, 27th or 29th night. If the month is 29 days then too, these will be termed as the last ten (Akheer Asharah)

Ibn Hazm has a different opinion, saying that the word Asharah as used in the Hadith means ten. As such the above calculation will only be correct where the month of Ramadhaan consists of thirty days. However, when there are only twenty nine days in the month (as often happens), the last ten days in the month will commence with the 29th day and the night being the 20th night. According to this calculation it will mean that the unevenly numbered nights will be the 20th, 22nd, 24th, 26th and 28th night.

(With due respect to a greatly learned Aalim like Ibn Hazm, the majority of 'ulama do not agree with him, the reason being that I'itikaaf is sunnah during the last ten days of Ramadhaan). All the 'ulama are unimous that when Rasulullah went into I'itikaaf insearch of haq, he entered the Musjid to commence seclusion on the 21st night of Ramadhaan.

ADVICE

Though there is great possibility of Laylatul Qadr being on the odd nights from the 21st onwards, there does also exist the likelihood that it could fall during the last ten nights. The best advice one can give here is that one should spend each night from the twentieth onwards in ibaadah, so that one may be sure of having acquired the blessings of Laylatul Qadr. Ten or eleven nights is definitely not so difficult if one looks at the great reward that is granted.

(٥) عَنْ عُبَادَةَ بْنِ الصَّامِتِ رَضِیَ اللّٰهُ تَعَالٰی عَنْهُ قَالَ خَرَجَ النَّبِیُّ ﷺ لِيُخْبِرَنَا بِلَيْلَةِ الْقَدْرِ فَتَلَاحٰی فُلَانٌ وَفُلَانٌ فَرُفِعَتْ وَعَسٰی اَنْ يَّكُوْنَ خَيْرًا لَّكُمْ فَالْتَمِسُوْهَا فِی التَّاسِعَةِ وَالسَّابِعَةِ وَالْخَامِسَةِ مشكوة عن البخاری

HADITH NO. 5

'Ubaadah bin 'Saamit رضي الله عنه *said, 'Once Rasulullah* صلى الله عليه وسلم *came out to inform us the true date of Laylatul Qadr. (Unfortunately at that time) an argument took place between two muslim men, whereupon he said, "I came out in order to inform you as to when Laylatul Qadr was, but because two people argued (the fixing of the correct date) was taken away. Perhaps that is better for you. So seek it among the ninth, seventh and fifth nights".*

Reported in Mishkaat.

COMMENTARY

Three important points are referred to in this Hadith. Firstly, there is mention of an argument which resulted in the knowledge of Laylatul Qadr being withheld from us. Arguments are always the cause of loss of blessings. Once Rasulullah صلى الله عليه وسلم inquired of the companions, "Shall I inform you of some action that is better than 'salaah, fasting and charity?" The companions replied, "Certainly". Rasulullah صلى الله عليه وسلم then said, "Maintaining peaceful and good relations amongst yourselves is most virtuous for verily arguments among yourselves eliminates faith". This means that just as the razor removes hair from the head so does arguments amongst yourself remove faith.

This is indeed an illness among us. Even those among us who appear exceptionally religious and busy with thikr are victims of these arguments and strife. Firstly we should carefully study Rasulullah صلی اللہ علیہ وسلم saying, then check our conduct in which pride prevents us to submit towards natural conciliation. In the first chapter of this book (where the ettiquet of fasting is discussed) we read that Rasulullah صلی اللہ علیہ وسلم said, "To insult a muslim is the most despicable and obnoxious type of achievement. We often go to such extent that when we cross words with muslims in arguments, we do not even care for a muslim's or refrain from insults. In such cases no notice seems to be taken of the injunctions of Allah and His messenger. The Holy Qur'aan says,

"Argue not among yourselves, otherwise your courage will go and your strength depart, and be patient and persevering, for Allah is with those who patiently persevere".

(Surah Anfaal: 46)

It is now the duty of those who always seek to injure and destroy the honour and dignity of others to sit back and think how much harm they have done to themselves. They should think how much they have through these despicable deeds, themselves become despicable in Allah's sight and in the sight of those around them. The person who serves relationship with his brothers for more than three days and dies in this state will go straight to Jahannam. Rasulullah صلی اللہ علیہ وسلم said that on every Monday and Thursday the actions of servants are brought before Allah. Then through His Mercy (as a result of certain pious deeds) forgiveness is granted except to the idolators. However, regarding any two people between whom an argument had taken place, and friendship is cut off it shall be said "Leave their affair aside until such time that they become reconcilled".

Another Hadith states that when actions are presented before Allah, every Monday and Thursday, repentance is accepted from those who repent, and forgiveness is granted to those who seek pardon. As for those who had arguments, they are left as they are.

Another Hadith further teaches us that on Shabe-Bara'at (the night of the 15th Shabaan) the mercy of Allah is directed at all Allah's creation and forgiveness is freely granted except for two types of persons. One, a kaafir (disbeliever), and the one who harbours bad thoughts against others in another Hadith it is stated: There are three kinds of people whose 'salaah does not ascend one hand span above their heads for acceptance. Mentioned among these are the ones who argue among themselves.

In the above paragraphs I have digressed from the point under discussion. It was not my intention to mention all these Ahaadith on arguments. I merely did it to bring to our notice this great evil which we underestimate, so much so that even those whom we consider to be noble and righteous are guilty of it. To Allah is my plea, and He is the One we seek assistance from. On the other hand, be informed that this fighting, use of harsh words and cutting oneself off from another, will only be regarded as a crime and evil in Islaam, when done out of enmity and hatred over worldly matters. It is permissible to break off relations with somebody because of evil deeds or because of some religious matters (wherein he is in the wrong and blameable). Ibn Umar رضي الله عنه once quoted a saying of Rasulullah صلى الله عليه وسلم to which his son said something, which outwardly appears as if he objected to it. The result was that Ibn Umar رضي الله عنه never again spoke to that son for as long as he lived. There are numerous similar instances reported of the sahaabah.

Often we too cut off relations with people and claim that it is for the sake of the Deen. Allah as All-knowing, All-seeing and He alone knows the true state of affairs. He knows which relationships are broken off because of the Deen and which are cut off because of the hurt to our honour, pride and dignity.

The second point to which the Hadith under discussion draws attention is the fact that man should be satisfied and accept Allah's ruling in all matters. For example, even though it seems that the loss of the knowledge as to when Laylatul Qadr actually falls, is a great loss of blessing, it has to be accepted because it is from Allah. For this reason Rasulullah صلى الله عليه وسلم says, "It is better for us that way". One should ponder over this, Allah is at all times merciful to His servants.

Even when someone is overtaken by a great calamity because of his own evil deeds. He needs only appeal to His

Creator, admit his own weakness, and that same calamity becomes the cause for greater good. Nothing is impossible for Allah.

Our 'ulama have mentioned several advantages in not knowing the proper time for Laylatul Qadr. Firstly, had we known the actual time for this blessed night, there would have been so many who would not have served Allah at all during the year or on other nights. They would only wait for the prescribed night in which to perform their ibaadah. As things are now, one has to stay awake and be in ibaadah for quite a number of nights hoping that each night is perhaps the night. (This means more nights in Allah's service and reward for the same).

Secondly, there are among us those who just do not seem to be able to avoid evil. How extremely dangerous and unfortunate for them would it be, when in spite of knowing that such and such a night is Laylatul Qadr and then still spend it in sin and evil? Once Rasulullah صلى الله عليه وسلم, on entering the musjid saw one of the sahaabh sleeping on one side. He said to Ali رضي الله عنه : "Wake him up so that he can make wudhu". This Ali رضي الله عنه did and then addressed the Nabi صلى الله عليه وسلم thus, "O Messenger of Allah, you are always first to hurry towards any good deed. Why did you not wake him up yourself?" To this Rasulullah صلى الله عليه وسلم replied, "I fear on his behalf that this man may refuse, and refusal to my command is kufr. If he refused your command, it would not be kufr (disbelief). Similarly Allah in His mercy does not approve that in spite of knowing which night is the real one, one should still spend it in sin and evil.

Thirdly, there are amongst some who find it possible to spend one, two or three nights in ibaadah, while we do not know which is the night of Power. Now say for arguments sake, we did not know which night Laylatul Qadr would be and inspite of that, for one reason or another, within or outside our control, we allowed that night to go by without ibaadah, it is an almost certain fact that thereafter, for the rest of Ramadhaan, no other night would have been spent in ibaadah.

Fourthly, every night spent in ibaadah in search of Laylatul Qadr is a night for which a separate reward is granted.

Fifthly, We have read that Allah boasts to His angels about those believers who exert themselves in ibaadah during Ramadhaan. Now when they spend more nights in Allah's worship, more such chances of boasting arise.

In spite of not knowing when it is the night of Laylatul Qadr and although they have only a vague idea about its fixed time, still they exert themselves to the utmost in Allah's service night after night. If such is their exertion when they do not know then how more will they exert themselves when it is known to them?

There are sure to be advantages. Due to such blessings Allah often keeps certain things secret to Himself, as for example, the "Ismul Aazam" (the great name of Allah, whereby if we call upon Him, He answers). Similarly there is a special moment on the day of Jumu-ah when prayers are answered. This time too is not known with complete certainty. There are numerous other things which are included in this category. It is possible that because of the argument that took place the fixing of Laylatul Qadr during that Ramadhaan was caused to be forgotten. However, because of the other benefits the knowledge of the fixed date was no revealed.

The third point to which attention is drawn is that Laylatul Qadr should be sought among the 9th, 7th and 5th. By reading these in conjunction with the other Ahaadith, we come to know that this referes to the last ten nights of Ramadhaan. So which nights are these? If we start from the 20th, counting up, then these three nights are the 25th, 27th and 29th. If, on the other hand we start counting from the 29th down, where Ramadhaan has 29 days, these nights are the 21st, 23rd, and 25th. And in the case where the month has 30 days it would be 22nd 24th and 26th.

From the above one can see how much uncertainty there is about the correct date. Among the learned "ulama" there are approximately fifty different opinions. Because of this reason, some "ulama" have said that Laylatul Qadr does not occur on one and the same night every year. If in the one year it occurred on one night then the following year it occurred on another night. There are times when Rasulullah صلى الله عليه وسلم commanded the companions to search among a number of nights, whereas at other times again he used to fix a certain night.

Abu Hurayrah رضي الله عنه reports that once during a conversation with the companions, mention was made of Laylatul Qadr. Rasulullah صلى الله عليه وسلم asked "What is the date today?" They replied, "The 22nd of Ramadhaan. The Nabi صلى الله عليه وسلم said, "Search for Laylatul Qadr in the night following this day.

Abu Tharr رضي الله عنه reports that he inquired of Rasulullah صلى الله عليه وسلم whether Laylatul Qadr was only granted for the time of the duration of Rasulullah's صلى الله عليه وسلم life, or whether it continued to come after him. Rasulullah صلى الله عليه وسلم replied, "It continues until Qiyaamah". I then inquired "In which section of Ramadhaan does it come? The Nabi صلى الله عليه وسلم replied, "Search for it in the first ten and in the last ten days". Thereafter Rasulullah صلى الله عليه وسلم became busy with other work, I waited, and finding another chance inquired, "In which section of those ten does Laylatul Qadr come? Upon this Rasulullah صلى الله عليه وسلم became so angry with me as he had never been before or after, and he said, "If it had been Allah's object to make it known, would He not have informed? Search for it among the last seven nights, and ask no more". In another Hadith again Rasulullah صلى الله عليه وسلم is reported to have told one sahaabah that Laylatul Qadr was on 23rd night.

Ibn Abbaas رضي الله عنه related, "While sleeping once, somebody said to me in my dream, 'Rise up. This is Laylatul Qadr'. I woke up and proceeded in haste to Rasulullah صلى الله عليه وسلم. There I found him in 'salaah. That was the 23rd night". According to other reports again, the 24th is Laylatul Qadr. Abdullah ibn Mas'ood رضي الله عنه said, "Whoever remains all nights of the year in ibaadah can find Laylatul Qadr". (In other words the blessed night moves throughout the year and does not necessarily have to come in Ramadhaan only).

Ibn Mas'ood رضي الله عنه reports this view from Nabi صلى الله عليه وسلم. Durre Manthoor when this was mentioned to Ubay bin Kaab he said Abdullah ibn Mas'ood رضي الله عنه meant people will stay awake only on this night and become contented". Thereafter he swore by Allah that Laylatul Qadr comes on 27th. This is also the view held by numerous sahaabah as well as taabi-iyn.

Among the Imaams, the well known opinion of Imaam

Abu Hanifa R.A. is that Laylatul Qadr moves throughout the year, while another view of this is that it moves about throughout the month of Ramadhaan. His famous student followers, Imaam Muhammad and Imaam Abu Yousuf, however, were of the opinion that this night is fixed on one special night which is unknown, during the Holy month. While the Shaaf-i_y's believe that it occurs probably on 21st, Imaam Ahmad R.A. and Imaam Maalik R.A. hold view that it comes only among the odd nights of the last ten nights of Ramadhaan, moving from year to year and is not fixed. But as for the vast majority of 'ulama their hope lies in Laylatul Qadr coming annually on 27th night.

Ibn Arabi R.A. says, "In my opinion the view of those who believe that Laylatul Qadr comes on various nights throughout the year, is most correct, because twice have I seen it in Sha'baan once on the 15th, and once on 19th, and twice have I seen it in the middle ten nights of Ramadhaan, the 13th, and the 18th. And I have also seen it on every odd night of the last ten. For this reason I am certain that it could occur on any night of the year but comes mostly in Ramadhaan.

Shaah Waliyullah R.A. of Delhi believed that Laylatul Qadr comes twice every year: (a) One Laylatul Qadr is that one on which Allah's commands are revealed (to the angels). This is also the night on which the holy Qur'aan was sent down from the Al Lowhul Mahfuz to the heavens. This night does not come in Ramadhaan alone but moves and can come on any other night of the year. However, the night on which the Holy Qur'aan was revealed fell in Ramadhaan and mostly falls during Ramadhaan. (b) The second Laylatul Qadr is the one of tremendous spiritual value, when angels descend in large numbers, while shay'taans are held back, and a time when prayers and ibaadah are accepted. This comes only in Ramadhaan during the 'uneven' nights of the last ten days. (This view of Shaah Waliyullah used to be most acceptable to my late father).

Anyway, whether there are two Laylatul Qadrs or whether there is only one, the fact still remains that one has to search for it according to ones courage and ability. If not throughout the year, then in Ramadhaan. If that should prove difficult, then during the last ten days. When that too seems a bit too much to be expected, then only the odd numbered nights of the last ten days. When one has wasted these opportunities too, then by no means should the 27th be allowed to go by. If by Allah's blessings and your good fortune that is Laylatul Qadr, then in comparison all the prosperity and pleasures of the world would be meaningless. Thus, even though that may not be the much searched for night, then at least the reward for ibaadah is received.

The 'salaah of Maghrib and Esha throughout the year should be performed with Jamaa-ah; because if it is Laylatul Qadr the reward for both is so much more. It is a great blessing of Allah that when one endeavours for religious aims and cannot make a success, he is still rewarded for the effort. And inspite of this, there are those who do not leave a stone unturned in their services for Deen. On the contrary; in worldly affairs when one does not break even his efforts are also written off as a loss. Then too in this latter case numerous people spend their time, efforts and wealth in worldly things that are fruitless and without purpose, and do not hold any reward or consolation.

(٦) عَنْ عُبَادَةَ بْنِ الصَّامِتِ رَضِيَ اللهُ تَعَالىٰ عَنْهُ اَنَّهُ سَأَلَ رَسُوْلَ اللهِ ﷺ عَنْ لَيْلَةِ الْقَدْرِ فَقَالَ فِيْ رَمَضَانَ فِي الْعَشْرَةِ الْاَوَاخِرِ فَاِنَّهَا فِيْ لَيْلَةِ وِتْرٍ فِيْ اِحْدىٰ وَّعِشْرِيْنَ اَوْ ثَلٰثٍ وَّعِشْرِيْنَ اَوْ خَمْسٍ وَّعِشْرِيْنَ اَوْ سَبْعٍ وَّعِشْرِيْنَ اَوْ تِسْعٍ وَّعِشْرِيْنَ اَوْ آخِرِ لَيْلَةٍ مِّنْ رَمَضَانَ مَنْ قَامَهَا اِيْمَانًا وَّاحْتِسَابًا غُفِرَ لَهُ مَاتَقَدَّمَ مِنْ ذَنْبِهِ وَمِنْ اَمَارَاتِهَا اَنَّهَا لَيْلَةٌ بَلْجَةٌ صَافِيَةٌ سَاكِنَةٌ سَاجِيَةٌ لَاحَارَّةٌ وَّلَابَارِدَةٌ كَاَنَّ فِيْهَا قَمَرًا سَاطِعًا وَلَايَحِلُّ لِنَجْمٍ اَنْ يُّرْمىٰ بِهِ تِلْكَ اللَّيْلَةَ حَتّٰى الصَّبَاحَ وَمِنْ اَمَارَاتِهَا اَنَّ الشَّمْسَ تَطْلَعُ صَبِيْحَتَهَا لَاشُعَاعَ لَهَا مُسْتَوِيَةٌ كَاَنَّهَا الْقَمَرُ لَيْلَةَ الْبَدْرِ وَحَرَّمَ اللهُ عَلَى الشَّيْطَانِ اَنْ يَّخْرُجَ مَعَهَا يَوْمَئِذٍ

درّ منثور عن أحمد والبيهقى ومحمد بن نصر وغيرهم

HADITH NO. 6

'Ubaadah bin 'Saamit رضي الله عنه *reports that he asked Rasulullah* صلى الله عليه وسلم *about Laylatul Qadr. He replied, "It is in Ramadhaan during the last ten days, on the unevenly numbered nights, either the 21st, 23rd, 25th, 27th and 29th or the last night of the month of Ramadhaan. Whosoever stands in ibaadah on this night with sincere faith and with genuine hopes of gaining reward his previous sins*

will be forgotten. Among the signs of this night is that it is a serene, quite, shining night, not hot, nor cold and (as if through the amount of spiritual light) the moon remains clear, without any rays. No stars are flung (at the shayaa'teen) on that night until the break of dawn. Another sign is that the sun rises without any radiant beams of light, appearing rather like the moon in its fullness. On that day Allah prohibits the shayaa'teen from rising up with the sun".

Reported in Durru Manthoor.

COMMENTARY

Part of what has been mentioned in this Hadith has already been dealt with. Some signs are mentioned about the actual night. These signs are clear and need no further explanation. Apart from these signs, however, there are other signs too, as found in the Hadith and in the experience of those who had the fortune to encounter Laylatul Qadr. The sign that is, however, most common in the Hadith and generally witnessed is the rising of the sun 'without any radiant beams of light'. The other signs besides this are not necessarily always found. One sahaabi, Ab'da bin abi Lubaabah says, "On the evening of the 27th, I tasted the water of the sea and it was sweet". Ayoob bin Khaalid R.A. said, "When I once had to perform ghusl (bath) with sea water, then on tasting it found it sweet. This was on the 23rd night". Some of the Mashaa-ikh wrote that on the evening of Laylatul Qadr everything prostrates on the ground then return to their positions. These are however things that are only shown to the extremely pious ones and are not seen by the ordinary person.

(۷) عَنْ عَائِشَةَ رَضِىَ اللّٰهُ تَعَالٰى عَنْهَا قَالَتْ قُلْتُ يَارَسُوْلَ اللّٰهِ اَرَاَيْتَ اِنْ عَلِمْتُ اَىَّ لَيْلَةٍ لَيْلَةُ الْقَدْرِ مَااَقُوْلُ فِيْهَا قَالَ قُوْلِىْ اَللّٰهُمَّ اِنَّكَ عَفُوٌّ تُحِبُّ الْعَفْوَ فَاعْفُ عَنِّىْ رواه أحمد وابن ماجه والترمذى وصححه كذا فى المشكوٰة

HADITH NO. 7

Aa-isha radhiyallah anha reports, "O Messenger of Allah, when I find myself in Laylatul Qadr, what shall I say?" The Nabi صلی اللہ علیہ وسلم *replied, 'Say O Allah Thou art One*

who pardons, Thou lovest to pardon, so grant me forgiveness".

Reported by Ahmad, Ibn Majah and Tirmizhi.

COMMENTARY

This is indeed an all inclusive prayer, wherein one begs Allah in His infinite grace should forgive sins. What else would one require? Imaan Sufyaan Thowry R.A. used to say that to keep oneself busy on this night with duaa' is better than any other forms of ibaadah. Ibn Rajab R.A. says that one should not only remain busy with duaa', but should also take part in all other forms of 'ibaadah as well, such as the recitation of Qur'aan, 'salaah, duaa', prescribed devotions etc. This latter opinion is considered correct and close to what Rasulullah صلى الله عليه وسلم has said, as already mentiond in previous Ahaadith.

CHAPTER THREE

I'ITIKAAF (SECLUSION IN THE MUSJID)

The meaning of I'itikaaf is to seclude oneself in the musjid with the express niyyah (intention) of I'itikaaf. According to the Hanafi school of thought, there are three different types of I'itikaaf.

(a) Waajib I'itikaaf:
This I'itikaaf becomes compulsory when a person makes it obligatory upon himself. An example of this is, when a person makes a vow to Allah that if Allah fulfills a certain wish of his, he will undertake to perform so many days I'itikaaf. In this case the moment his wish is fulfilled, I'itikaaf becomes compulsory. A person may just make unconditional vow whereby he makes I'itikaaf waajib upon himself for certain number of days. This becomes a Waajib duty on him from that moment onwards.

(b) Sunnah I'itikaaf:
This was the general practice of Rasulullah and it means to seclude oneself inside the musjid for the last ten days of Ramadhaan.

(c) Nafl I'itikaaf:
There is no special time or specific number of days for Nafl I'itikaaf. A person may make niyyah for any number of days at any time, even for his whole life. Imaam Abu Haneefah R.A. however states that it must be for at least one full day.

Imaam Muhammad R.A. states that there is no limit on the minimum period of time. The fatwa is on this latter view. Therefore it is desirable for anyone entering a musjid to make the niyyah (intention) of I'itikaaf for the period that he will remain in the musjid. So while he is in ibaadah he also gains the reward of I'itikaaf.

(In view of the above, it is advisable that everyone entering the musjid to join the congregation prayer, should on entering the musjid, make the niyyah for I'itikaaf. In that case, it means that as long as he remains busy with 'salaah, thikr, listening to lectures or sermons, he also receives reward for the I'i̱tikaaf). I always observed that my late father used to make niyyah for I'i̱tikaaf while stepping into the musjid with his right foot. Occasionally, by way of teaching and reminding his followers, he used to raise his voice when reciting the niyyah.

OBJECTS AND ADVANTAGES OF I'I̱TIKAAF

The reward for I'i̱tikaaf is great. Rasulullah صلی اللہ علیہ وسلم constantly performed I'i̱tikaaf. The example of the one who resides in the musjid in I'i̱tikaaf is like a person, who having gone to a certain place for something, remains there until it is granted.

When someone comes begging to our door and then refuses to leave until he has been granted his request, I am sure that even the one with the hardest heart amongst us will eventually accede to his request. How much more merciful is Allah, Who even grants without reason.

Hence, when one isolates himself from all wordly things and goes to Allah's door, what doubt can there be for his plea to be accepted. And when Allah has favoured someone, others cannot describe the ecstacy and enrichment of such limitless treasures. How could a person ever describe what he has not obtained? However, can an underaged person describe adulthood? Nevertheless, this is a course in which one shall give nothing else besides total dedication or else be taken away for the final meeting of his creator. A̱llaama ibn Qayyim, on explaining the significance of I'i̱tikaaf, writes that actual aim of I'i̱tikaaf is to divert the heart from everything except Allah, and to join it with Allah alone, thereby forming a complete spiritual connection with the creator.

All worldly connections are thus cut off for the sake of gaining Allah's attention. All thoughts, desire, love and devotion become centred around Him. In consequence His love is attained–a love and friendship that will be the only friend in the loneliness of the grave. When a person has that, then who can possibly imagine the great ecstasy with which that time of the grave will be spent? In Maraquil Falaah, the author writes that I'i̱tikaaf, when properly and sincerely performed, is a most virtuous deed. One cannot possibly enumerate all the great advantages and benefits in it. In actual fact, what takes place in I'i̱tikaaf, is that the heart is drawn away from everything else except the Creator, while our whole life is actually laid down at His doorstep. One remains in 'ibaadah all the time. Even when one is asleep, one is still in His service, striving for nearness to Him. Allah says (according to a Hadith): "Whoever draws near to Me (the length of) one hand, then I draw nearer to him (the length of) two hands; and whoever draws near to Me by walking, I draw hear to him by running".

In I'itikaaf one goes to Allah's house and the most Kind Host always honours a guest who visits Him. The one in I'itikaaf also attains safety in Allah's fortress where no enemy can reach. Besides this there are numerous other virtues and distinctive featues of this important 'ibaadah.

WHERE TO PERFORM I'ITIKAAF

The best of places for I'itikaaf, for males, is the Musjidul Haraam in Mecca. The next best is the Musjidul Nabawi in Madina, and the next best is Baitul Mukaddas. Thereafter, comes the Jaam'i Musjid in one's own town, and last but not least, the musjid nearest to one's home. Imaam Abu Hanifah R.A. stipulate the musjid should be one wherein the five daily prayers are performed, while Imaam Abu Yousuf R.A. and Imaam Muhammad R.A. are agreed that any musjid according to the Shariah can be entered for I'itikaaf, even if there is no regular 'salaah with Jamaa-ah.

As for the females, they should perform I'itikaaf in the musjid inside their homes. Where, however, no musjid exists and the desire for I'itikaaf be there, one room of the house should be set aside for this purpose, I'itikaaf is in fact an easier task for women. A special section of the house, most commonly the prayer room, is set aside wherein they seclude themselves, remaining in 'ibaadah. The domestic duties can then be performed by daughters or servants, and the women in I'itikaaf, while remaining in a section of her own house, is spiritually rewarded for it. It is so very unfortunate that in spite of the ease, our women folk still remain deprived of the blessings of I'itikaaf. (*We here in South Africa are even more negligent of this sunnah, so much so, that many have not even heard of it–Translator*).

(١) عَنْ اَبِىْ سَعِيْدِ نِ الْخُدْرِىِّ رَضِىَ اللّٰهُ تَعَالٰى عَنْهُ اَنَّ رَسُوْلَ اللّٰهِ ﷺ اِعْتَكَفَ
الْعَشْرَ الْاَوَّلَ مِنْ رَمَضَانَ ثُمَّ اعْتَكَفَ الْعَشْرَ الْاَوْسَطَ فِىْ قُبَّةٍ تُرْكِيَةٍ ثُمَّ اَطْلَعَ
رَاْسَهٗ فَقَالَ اِنِّىْ اَعْتَكِفُ الْعَشْرَ الْاَوَّلَ اَلْتَمِسُ هٰذِهِ اللَّيْلَةَ ثُمَّ اعْتَكِفُ الْعَشْرَ
الْاَوْسَطَ ثُمَّ اُتِيْتُ فَقِيْلَ لِىْ اِنَّهَا فِى الْعَشْرِ الْاَوَاخِرِ فَمَنْ كَانَ اِعْتَكَفَ مَعِىَ
فَلْيَعْتَكِفِ الْعَشْرَ الْاَوَاخِرَ فَقَدْ اُرِيْتُ هٰذِهِ اللَّيْلَةَ ثُمَّ اُنْسِيْتُهَا وَقَدْ رَاَيْتُنِىْ اَسْجُدُ
فِىْ مَاءٍ وَطِيْنٍ مِنْ صَبِيْحَتِهَا فَالْتَمِسُوْهَا فِى الْعَشْرِ الْاَوَاخِرِ وَالْتَمِسُوْا فِىْ كُلِّ
وِتْرٍ قَالَ فَمُطِرَتِ السَّمَآءُ تِلْكَ اللَّيْلَةَ وَكَانَ الْمَسْجِدُ عَلٰى عَرِيْشٍ فَوَكَفَ
الْمَسْجِدُ فَبَصُرَتْ عَيْنَاىَ رَسُوْلَ اللّٰهِ ﷺ وَعَلٰى جَبْهَتِهٖ اَثَرُ الْمَاءِ وَالطِّيْنِ مِنْ
صَبِيْحَةِ اِحْدٰى وَّعِشْرِيْنَ مشكوٰة عن المتفق عليه باختلاف اللفظ

HADITH NO. 1

"Abu Sa'iyd Khudri رضي الله عنه *reports that Rasulullah* صلى الله عليه وسلم *once performed I'itikaaf for the first ten days of Ramadhaan. Thereafter he made I'itikaaf in a Turkish tent (inside the musjid) for the middle ten days. Thereafter he raised his head out of the tent and said, "Verily in search of Laylatul Qadr did I perform I'itikaaf for the first ten days, then for the middle ten days. Then someone (an angel) came and told me, "It is in the last ten days whosoever has made I'itikaaf with me should continue for the last ten days". I had indeed been shown that night and then made to forget, which it shall be. And verily did I see myself prostrating to Allah with my forehead on mud on the morning after the night. Seek Laylatul Qadr the last ten nights of Ramadhaan; seek it among uneven ones".*

Abu Sa'iyd رضي الله عنه *says; "That same night it rained. The roof on the musjid leaked, and I looked at Rasulullah's* صلى الله عليه وسلم *two eyes and on his forehead were remains of water and mud. This was on the morning of the 21st performing sujood in muddy clay".*

Reported in Mishkaat.

COMMENTARY

It used to be the general practice of Rasulullah صلى الله عليه وسلم to perform I'itikaaf in Ramadhaan. At times he used to remain in the musjid for the whole month and during the last year of his life he was in I'itikaaf for twenty days. Because he always secluded himself in the musjid for last ten days, the 'ulama consider it sunnah mu'akkadah to perform I'itikaaf for that period.

From the above Hadith it can be deduced that the major object behind I'itikaaf was to search for Laylatul Qadr. What better manner can there be than to be in I'itikaaf, because one is considered to be in 'ibaadah all the time, whether one is awake or asleep. Furthermore, one in I'itikaaf is free from all daily tasks and thus has all the time to devote to thikrullah, (the rememberance of Allah) and meditation. Throughout Ramadhaan Rasulullah صلى الله عليه وسلم exerted himself and increase his 'ibaadah and when the last ten days came along, he had no limit in exerting himself. He himself remained awake throughout the night and awakened his family for the same purpose. Aa-isha radhiyallahu anha reports:

> "During Ramadhaan Rasullullah tied his lungi tightly about him, staying awake all night and waking his family (for the purpose of 'ibaadah). 'Tied his lungi tightly about him' means either that he knew no limits in exerting himself in 'ibaadah; or that he gave due importance and preference to 'ibaadah, and avoided all forms of sexual contact.

(٢) عَنِ ابْنِ عَبَّاسٍ رَضِيَ للهُ تَعَالٰى عَنْهُ اَنَّ رَسُوْلَ اللهِ ﷺ قَالَ فِي الْمُعْتَكِفِ هُوَ
يَعْتَكِفُ الذُّنُوْبَ وَيُجْرٰى لَهُ مِنَ الْحَسَنَاتِ كَعَامِلِ الْحَسَنَاتِ كُلِّهَا
(مشكوٰة عن ابن ماجه)

HADITH NO. 2

Ibn Abbas رضي الله عنه relates that Rasullullah صلى الله عليه وسلم said, "The person performing I'itikaaf remains free from sins, and he is indeed given the same reward as those who do righteous deeds (inspite of not having done those deeds as a result of having been secluded in the musjid)".

Reported in Mishkaat from Ibn Majah.

COMMENTARY

(Note that one remaining secluded in the musjid is not allowed to depart from there for worldly needs. He may only set forth to the outside for the calls of nature, to perform ablution or ghusl or for attending Jumu-ah when that is not performed in the same musjid, after which he must return forthwith). Now this Hadith points to two great benefits of I'itikaaf.

Firstly one is saved from sin. It is true that it very often happens that one falls into sin without ever intended to do so. (The world all around us is full of temptations). To commit sin in the blessed month of Ramadhaan is indeed a great injustice to ourselves. By remaining secluded in the musjid, one complete avoids the temptation to sin. Secondly, it would appear outwardly that when one is secluded in the musjid, one is automatically at a disadvantage by not being allowed to perform certain good deeds like joining funeral prayers, attending burials visiting the sick, etc. That is not so, because according to this Hadith one is rewarded for these deeds even though not performing them. What a great favour from Allah! How great is Allah's bounty! By performing 'ibaadah one receives the reward of numerous other 'ibaadahs. In fact Allah Ta-aala seeks the slightest cause to bestow His blessings. His blessings could be received in abundance with a little effort and plea. If only we can understand and properly appreciate these favours. That proper appreciation and understanding can only enter our minds when we have the true love and interest for our Deen.

(May Allah grant us that Aameen).

٣) عَنِ ابْنِ عَبَّاسٍ رَضِىَ اللّٰهُ تَعَالٰى عَنْهُ اَنَّهُ كَانَ مُعْتَكِفًا فِىْ مَسْجِدِ رَسُوْلِ اللّٰهِ
ﷺ فَاَتَاهُ رَجُلٌ فَسَلَّمَ عَلَيْهِ ثُمَّ جَلَسَ فَقَالَ لَهُ ابْنُ عَبَّاسٍ يَافُلَانُ اَرَاكَ مُكْتَئِبًا
حَزِيْنًا قَالَ نَعَمْ يَاابْنَ عَمِّ رَسُوْلِ اللّٰهِ لِفُلَانٍ عَلَىَّ حَقٌّ وَلَا * وَحُرْمَةِ صَاحِبِ هٰذَا
الْقَبْرِ مَا اَقْدِرُ عَلَيْهِ قَالَ ابْنُ عَبَّاسٍ اَفَلَا اُكَلِّمُهُ فِيْكَ قَالَ اِنْ اَحْبَبْتَ قَالَ فَانْتَعَلَ
ابْنُ عَبَّاسٍ ثُمَّ خَرَجَ مِنَ الْمَسْجِدِ قَالَ لَهُ الرَّجُلُ اَنَسِيْتَ مَاكُنْتَ فِيْهِ قَالَ لَا
وَلٰكِنِّىْ سَمِعْتُ صَاحِبَ هٰذَا الْقَبْرِ ﷺ وَالْعَهْدُ بِهِ قَرِيْبٌ فَدَمِعَتْ عَيْنَاهُ وَهُوَ
يَقُوْلُ مَنْ مَّشٰى فِىْ حَاجَةِ اَخِيْهِ وَبَلَغَ فِيْهَا كَانَ خَيْرًا لَهُ مِنْ اِعْتِكَافِ عَشْرِ سِنِيْنَ
وَمَنْ اِعْتَكَفَ يَوْمًا اِبْتِغَاءَ وَجْهِ اللّٰهِ جَعَلَ اللّٰهُ بَيْنَهُ وَبَيْنَ النَّارِ ثَلٰثَ خَنَادِقَ اَبْعَدَ مِمَّا
بَيْنَ الْخَافِقَيْنِ رواه الطبرانى فى الأوسط والبيهقى واللفظ له والحاكم مختصرا وقال صحيح الإسناد وكذا
التر غيب وقال السيوطى فى الدر صححه الحاكم وضعفه البيهقى)

• هكذا فى النسخة التى بأيدينا بلفظ حرف النهى وهو الصواب عندى لوجوه ووقع فى بعض النسخ بلفظ ولاء بالهمزة فى آخره وهو تصحيف عندى من الكاتب وعليه قرائن ظاهرة

HADITH NO. 3

Ibn Abbaas رضي الله عنه reports that while he was once performing I'itikaaf in the musjidun Nabawi (Rasulullah's musjid), a certain man came to him, greated him and sat down. Ibn Abbaas said to him: "I see that you seem sad and troubled". The man replied: "Yes, O son of the uncle of Rasulullah, صلى الله عليه وسلم I am indeed troubled in that I have an obligation to fulfil to someone. I swear by the holiness of the inmate of this honoured resting place (Rasulullah's grave صلى الله عليه وسلم) that I am not able to fulfil this obligation". Ibn Abbaas رضي الله عنه inquired: "Shall I intercede with that person on your behalf?" The man replied: "By all means if you so wish". Ibn Abbaas put on his shoes and proceeded from the Musjid. The man, seeing this said: "Have you then forgotten that you are in I'itikaaf?" With tears filling his eyes Ibn Abbaas رضي الله عنه replied: "No, the time is still fresh in my mind, I heard the esteemed master of this tomb صلى الله عليه وسلم say, "Whoever sets forth in the way and makes an effort of settling a necessary affair on behalf of his brother, that service shall be better for him than to perform I'itikaaf for ten years, and whomsoever performs I'itikaaf for a day, thereby seeking the pleasure of Allah, Allah will open three trenches between him and the fire of hell, the width of each being the distance between heaven and earth".

Reported by 'Tabraani in Al Awsa't.

COMMENTARY

Two things are clear from this Hadith. In the first place we are told, that by way of reward for one day's I'itikaaf. Allah opens three trenches between him and the fire of Jahannam, the width of which being the distance between the heavens and the earth. Hence, for every additional day that I'itikaaf is performed so much more rewarded. In Kashful Ghummah, Allamah Sharaani relates a Hadith wherein Rasulullah صلى الله عليه وسلم said, "Whoever performs I'itikaaf for the final ten days of Ramadhaan, for him is the reward of two Haj and two Umrahs and whoever performs I'itikaaf from Maghrib until 'Ishaa' doing nothing except performing 'salaah and reciting the Qur'aan,' Allah will prepare a palace in Jannah".

In the second place, we are told that fulfilling the need of a brother brings a reward greater than ten years of I'itikaaf. For this reason Ibn Abbaas رضي الله عنه broke off his I'itikaaf. It was of course possible for him to continue it afterwards. (What he actually did was to leave the musjid to relieve some suffering of his brother, who was greatly troubled in the heart and mind). The 'Sufis say that Allah has sympathy with very few things as He has with a broken heart. It is for this reason that we have been sternly warned of the pleas to Allah of that person whose heart we hurt through an unjust treatment and persecution. Whenever Rasulullah صلى الله عليه وسلم appointed someone as a governor, amongst the many counsels he used to also say, "Be mindful of the plea of the oppressed".

Note that I'itikaaf breaks when one leaves the musjid even for the duty on behalf of fellow muslim. When that I'iti-kaaf is waajib, it will mean that it has to be performed all over again. Rasulullah never left the musjid except for the calls of nature and wudhu. As for Ibn Abbaas رضي الله عنه leaving the musjid to do some favour to a friend, it was in the same spirit that is reminiscent of that soldier lying near death on the battle field of Yarmouk, refusing to drink water until his neighbour had been given to drink. On the other hand, however, it is possible that Ibn Abbaas رضي الله عنه was performing nafl I'itikaaf, in which case it was permissible for him to break it off.

In conclusion I now wish to quote length Hadith. In many virtues are mentioned, and with this do I conclude this book.

(٤) عَنِ ابْنِ عَبَّاسٍ رَضِىَ لله تَعَالىٰ عَنْهُ اَنَّهُ سَمِعَ رَسُوْلَ اللهِ ﷺ يَقُوْلُ اِنَّ الْجَنَّةَ لَتُبَخَّرُ وَتُزَيَّنُ مِنَ الْحَوْلِ اِلَى الْحَوْلِ لِدُخُوْلِ شَهْرِ رَمَضَانَ فَاِذَا كَانَتْ اَوَّلُ لَيْلَةٍ مِّنْ شَهْرِ رَمَضَانَ هَبَّتْ رِيْحٌ مِنْ تَحْتِ الْعَرْشِ يُقَالُ لَهَا الْمُثِيْرَةُ فَتُصَفِّقُ وَرَقُ اَشْجَارِ الْجِنَانِ وَحَلَقُ الْمَصَارِيْعِ فَيُسْمَعُ لِذٰلِكَ طَنِيْنٌ لَمْ يَسْمَعِ السَّامِعُوْنَ اَحْسَنَ مِنْهُ فَتَبْرُزُ الْحُوْرُ الْعِيْنُ حَتَّى يَقِفْنَ بَيْنَ شُرَفِ الْجَنَّةِ فَيُنَادِيْنَ هَلْ مِنْ خَاطِبٍ اِلَى اللهِ فَيُزَوِّجُهُ ثُمَّ يَقُلْنَ الْحُوْرُ الْعِيْنُ يَارِضْوَانُ الْجَنَّةِ مَاهٰذِهِ اللَّيْلَةُ فَيُجِيْبُهُنَّ بِالتَّلْبِيَةِ ثُمَّ يَقُوْلُ هٰذِهِ اَوَّلُ لَيْلَةٍ مِّنْ شَهْرِ رَمَضَانَ فُتِحَتْ اَبْوَابُ الْجَنَّةِ عَلَى الصَّائِمِيْنَ مِنْ اُمَّةِ مُحَمَّدٍ ﷺ قَالَ وَيَقُوْلُ اللهُ عَزَّ وَجَلَّ يَارِضْوَانُ افْتَحْ اَبْوَابَ الْجِنَانِ

وَيَامَالِكُ اِغْلِقْ اَبْوَابَ الْجَحِيْمِ عَلَى الصَّائِمِيْنَ مِنْ اُمَّةِ اَحْمَدَ ﷺ وَيَاجِبْرَئِيْلُ
اِهْبِطْ اِلَى الْاَرْضِ فَصْفِدْ مَرَدَةَ الشَّيَاطِيْنِ وَغُلَّهُمْ بِالْاَغْلَالِ ثُمَّ اقْذِفْهُمْ فِى الْبِحَارِ
حَتّٰى لَايُفْسِدُوْا عَلٰى اُمَّةِ مُحَمَّدٍ حَبِيْبِىْ ﷺ صِيَامَهُمْ قَالَ وَيَقُوْلُ اللهُ عَزَّ وَجَلَّ فِىْ
كُلِّ لَيْلَةٍ مِّنْ شَهْرِ رَمَضَانَ لِمُنَادٍ يُّنَادِىْ ثَلٰثَ مَرَّاتٍ هَلْ مِنْ سَائِلٍ فَاُعْطِيَهُ سُؤْلَهُ
هَلْ مِنْ تَائِبٍ فَاَتُوْبَ عَلَيْهِ هَلْ مِنْ مُسْتَغْفِرٍ فَاَغْفِرَ لَهُ مَنْ يُّقْرِضُ الْمَلِىَّ غَيْرَ
الْعَدُوْمِ وَالْوَفِىَّ غَيْرَ الظَّلُوْمِ قَالَ وَ لِلّٰهِ عَزَّ وَجَلَّ فِىْ كُلِّ يَوْمٍ مِّنْ شَهْرِ رَمَضَانَ عِنْدَ
الْاِفْطَارِ اَلْفُ اَلْفِ عَتِيْقٍ مِّنَ النَّارِ كُلُّهُمْ قَدِ اسْتَوْجَبُوْا النَّارَ فَاِذَا كَانَ آخِرَ يَوْمٍ
مِنْ شَهْرِ رَمَضَانَ اَعْتَقَ اللهُ فِىْ ذٰلِكَ الْيَوْمِ بِقَدْرِ مَااَعْتَقَ مِنْ اَوَّلِ الشَّهْرِ اِلٰى
آخِرِهِ وَاِذَا كَانَتْ لَيْلَةُ الْقَدْرِ يَاْمُرُ اللهُ عَزَّ وَجَلَّ جِبْرَئِيْلَ فَيَهْبِطُ فِىْ كَبْكَبَةٍ مِّنَ
الْمَلَآئِكَةِ وَمَعَهُمْ لِوَاءٌ اَخْضَرُ فَيَرْكُزُ اللِّوَاءَ عَلٰى ظَهْرِ الْكَعْبَةِ وَلَهُ مِائَةُ جَنَاحٍ
مِنْهَا جَنَاحَانِ لَايَنْشُرُهُمَا اِلَّا فِىْ تِلْكَ اللَّيْلَةِ فَيَنْشُرُهُمَا فِىْ تِلْكَ اللَّيْلَةِ فَيُجَاوِزُ
الْمَشْرِقَ اِلَى الْمَغْرِبِ فَيَحُثُّ جِبْرَئِيْلُ عَلَيْهِ السَّلَامُ الْمَلَآئِكَةَ فِىْ هٰذِهِ الَّيْلَةِ
فَيُسَلِّمُوْنَ عَلٰى كُلِّ قَائِمٍ وَقَاعِدٍ وَمُصَلٍّ وَذَاكِرٍ وَيُصَافِحُوْنَهُمْ وَيُؤَمِّنُوْنَ عَلٰى
دُعَائِهِمْ حَتّٰى يَطْلُعَ الْفَجْرُ فَاِذَا طَلَعَ الْفَجْرُ يُنَادِىْ جِبْرَئِيْلُ مَعَاشِرَ الْمَلَآئِكَةِ
الرَّحِيْلَ فَيَقُوْلُوْنَ يَاجِبْرَئِيْلُ فَمَا صَنَعَ اللهُ فِىْ حَوَائِجِ الْمُؤْمِنِيْنَ مِنْ اُمَّةِ اَحْمَدَ ﷺ
فَيَقُوْلُ نَظَرَ اللهُ اِلَيْهِمْ فِىْ هٰذِهِ لِلَّيْلَةِ فَعَفَا عَنْهُمْ اِلَّا اَرْبَعَةً فَقُلْنَا يَارَسُوْلَ اللهِ مَنْ
هُمْ قَالَ رَجُلٌ مُدْمِنُ خَمْرٍ وَ عَاقٌّ لِوَالِدَيْهِ وَقَاطِعُ رَحِمٍ وَمُشَاحِنٌ قُلْنَا يَارَسُوْلَ اللهِ
مَا الْمُشَاحِنُ قَالَ هُوَ الْمُصَارِمُ فَاِذَا كَانَتْ لَيْلَةُ الْفِطْرِ سُمِّيَتْ تِلْكَ اللَّيْلَةُ لَيْلَةَ
الْجَائِزَةِ فَاِذَا كَانَتْ غَدَاةُ الْفِطْرِ بَعَثَ اللهُ عَزَّ وَجَلَّ الْمَلَآئِكَةَ فِىْ كُلِّ بِلَادٍ
فَيَهْبِطُوْنَ اِلَى الْاَرْضِ فَيَقُوْمُوْنَ عَلٰى اَفْوَاهِ السِّكَكِ فَيُنَادُوْنَ بِصَوْتٍ يَسْمَعُ مِنْ
خَلْقِ اللهِ عَزَّ وَجَلَّ اِلَّا الْجِنُّ وَالْاِنْسُ فَيَقُوْلُوْنَ يَااُمَّةَ مُحَمَّدٍ اُخْرُجُوْا اِلٰى رَبٍّ
كَرِيْمٍ يُعْطِى الْجَزِيْلَ وَيَعْفُوْا عَنِ الْعَظِيْمِ فَاِذَا بَرَزُوْا اِلٰى مُصَلَّاهُمْ فَيَقُوْلُ اللهُ عَزَّ
وَجَلَّ لِلْمَلَآئِكَةِ مَاجَزَاءُ الْاَجِيْرِ اِذَا عَمِلَ عَمَلَهُ قَالَ فَتَقُوْلُ الْمَلَآئِكَةُ اِلٰهَنَا
وَسَيِّدَنَا جَزَائُهُ اَنْ تُوَفِّيَهُ اَجْرَهُ قَالَ فَيَقُوْلُ فَاِنِّىْ اُشْهِدُكُمْ يَامَلَآئِكَتِىْ اِنِّىْ قَدْ

جَعَلْتُ ثَوَابَهُمْ مِنْ صِيَامِهِمْ شَهْرُ رَمَضَانَ وَقِيَامِهِمْ رِضَائِىْ وَمَغْفِرَتِىْ وَيَقُوْلُ
يَاعِبَادِىْ سَلُوْنِىْ فَوَعِزَّتِىْ وَجَلَالِىْ لَاتَسْئَلُوْنِىْ الْيَوْمَ شَيْئًا فِىْ جَمْعِكُمْ لِآخِرَتِكُمْ
اِلَّا اَعْطَيْتُكُمْ وَلَا لِدُنْيَاكُمْ اِلَّا نَظَرْتُ لَكُمْ فَوَعِزَّتِىْ لَاَسْتُرَنَّ عَلَيْكُمْ عَثَرَاتِكُمْ
مَارَاقَبْتُمُوْنِىْ وَعِزَّتِىْ وَجَلَالِىْ لَا اُخْزِيْكُمْ وَلَا اُفْضِحُكُمْ بَيْنَ اَصْحَابِ الْحُدُوْدِ
فَانْصَرِفُوْا مَغْفُوْرًا لَكُمْ قَدْ اَرْضَيْتُمُوْنِىْ وَرَضِيْتُ عَنْكُمْ فَتَفْرَحُ الْمَلَآئِكَةُ
وَتَسْتَبْشِرُ بِمَايُعْطِى اللّٰهُ عَزَّ وَجَلَّ هٰذِهِ الْاُمَّةَ اِذَا اَفْطَرُوْا مِنْ شَهْرِ رَمَضَانَ

كذا فى الترغيب وقال رواه الشيخ بن حبان فى كتاب الثواب والبيهقى واللفظ له وليس فى إسناده من أجمع على ضعفه قلت قال السيوطى فى التدريب قد التزم البيهقى أن لا يخرج فى تصانيفه حديثا يعلمه موضوعا الخ ، وذكر القارى فى المرقاة بعض طرق الحديث ثم قال : فاختلاف طرق الحديث يدل على أن له أصلا اهـ

HADITH NO. 4

Ibn Abbaas رضي الله عنه *says that he heard our Nabi* صلى الله عليه وسلم *say, Verily Jannah becomes perfumed with the sweetest fragance in Ramadhaan. From the beginning of the year till the end, it is being brightly decorated for the coming of this blessed month. And when the first night of Ramadhaan appears, a wind blows from beneath the Ar-sh (Throne). It is called Mutheerah, and causes the leaves of the trees of Jannah to rustle and door handles to sound, where by setting forth such a melodious sound as had never been heard before. The dark eyed damsels of Jannah then step forth till they appear in the centre of the balconies of Jannah, exclaiming: Is there anyone making duaa' to Allah for us that Allah may join us in marriage to him?" Then these damsels call out: "O Ridhwaan, keeper of Jannah, what night is this?" He replies: "Labbaik, this is indeed the first night of Ramadhaan, when the doors of Jannah are opened to those who observe the fast from among the ummah of Muhammad* صلى الله عليه وسلم*". Rasulullah* صلى الله عليه وسلم *further said, Allah says, "O Ridhwaan open the doors of Jannah, and O Maalik, (keeper of Jahannam) close the doors of Jahannam for those who fast from among the ummah of Ahmad "O Jibraeel proceed down to the earth and bind the rebellious shay'taans, put them in chains and cast them in the oceans so that they make no mischief, thereby spoiling the fast of the ummah of My beloved Muhammad* صلى الله عليه وسلم*"*

Allah commands a caller from the heavens to call out three times on every one of the nights of Ramadhaan: "Is there anyone begging of Me that I may grant him his desire? Is there anyone repenting to me that I may turn in mercy to him? Is there anyone begging for forgiveness that I may forgive him? Who is there who shall give a loan to the One whose wealth does not diminish, and the One who duly fulfills without unjust deductions".

Rasulullah صلی اللہ علیہ وسلم said further, "every day at the time of if'taar Allah sets free a thousand thousand (one million) souls from the fire of Jahannam, all of whom had already earned entrance into Jahannam. On the last night He sets free as many as had been set free throughout the month. On the night of Laylatul Qadr Allah commands Jibraeel A.S. to descend to the earth with the group of Malaa'ikah (angels). They descend carrying a green flag which is then planted on top of the Kabah. Jibraeel A.S. himself has one hundred wings, two of which are only spread out on this night. He spreads out these wings so that their width extends from East to West. Jibraeel A.S. then sends out the Malaa'ikah on this night in all directions to recite salaam upon each and everybody they find in prayer or sitting, performing 'salaah and celebrating the praise of Allah. They shake hands with them and say Aameen to all their duaa's until dawn breaks. When dawn comes Jibraeel A.S. calls out; Depart O Malaa'ikah of Allah depart".

The Malaa'ikah then inquire: "O Jibraeel but what did Allah do regarding the needs of the faithful ones from among the ummah of Ahmad صلی اللہ علیہ وسلم put before Him? Jibraeel A.S. replies: "Allah looked at them with mercy and pardoned them all except four kinds of people".

There upon we the sahaabahs inquired: "Who are they, O Rasulullah?" Rasulullah صلی اللہ علیہ وسلم replied, "They are the ones addicted to wine drinking, those disobedient to their parents, those who cut themselves from their near relatives and the "Mushaahin. We inquired, "O Rasulullah صلی اللہ علیہ وسلم who is a Mushaahin?" He said: Those who harbour ill-feelings in their hearts against their fellow brethren and break off relations with them".

"And then night of 'Iydul Fitr, the night that is called Laylatul Jaa'izah, (The night of prize giving), comes along. On the morning of 'Iyd Allah sends down the Malaa'ikah to all the lands of the earth where they take their positions

at access points of roads, calling out with a voice that is heard by all except man and jinn.

"O Ummah of Muhammad صلى الله عليه وسلم*, come forth from your houses towards a Lord that is noble and gracious, who grants much and pardons the major sins". When they proceed towards the places for their 'Iyd 'salaah, Allah says to the Malaa'ikah: "What indeed is the reward of that employee who had rendered his services?" The Malaa'ikah replies, "O Lord and master, it is only right that he should receive his reward in full for his services". Allah then says, "I call you to witness, O My Malaa'ikah, that for their having fasted during the month of Ramadhaan, and for their having stood before Me in prayer by night, I have granted to them as reward My pleasure and have granted them forgiveness. O My servants ask now of Me, for I swear by My honour and My greatness, that whatsoever you shall beg of Me this day in this assembly of yours for the needs of the Hereafter, I shall grant you; and whatsoever you shall ask for worldly needs, I shall look at you favourably. By My honour I swear, as long as you shall obey My commands, I shall cover your faults. By My Honour and My Greatness do I swear that I shall never disgrace you among the evil-doing ones and disbelievers. Depart now from here, you are forgiven. You have pleased Me and I am pleased with you.*

The Malaa'ikah on seeing this great reward bestowed by Allah upon the ummah of Muhammad صلى الله عليه وسلم *on the day of I'ydul Fitr become greatly pleased and happy".*

As reported in Targheeb.

"O Allah, make us also of those fortunate ones, Aameen".

COMMENTARY

The previous pages of this book already dealt with almost all that is contained in this last long Hadith. A few points need attention. We see here that there are a few people who are deprived of forgiveness in Ramadhaan and are unfortunate indeed in not being able to share the great gifts of Allah on the morning of 'Iyd. Among them are those who fight and argue among themselves and those disobedient to their parents.

Let us put one question to them: "You have displeased Allah and having done so, what other refuge do you have besides Allah?" We feel indeed sad that for some reason or other you have made yourselves the target for the curse of Allah, His Rasool صلى الله عليه وسلم and Jibraeel A.S. while at the same excluded from Allahs freely granted forgiveness. Who else can grant you refuge? Who and what can stand by your side when you carry the curse of Rasulullah صلى الله عليه وسلم ? Who can help you when Allah's close angel Jibraeel A.S. has made duaa' against you? While Allah is excluding you for His forgiveness and mercy. I implore you my dear brother (and sister) think about your position at this moment. Think and desist from all that draws you away from Allah. There is time to repair and repent and now is that time. To-morrow you shall have to stand before a Judge before whom no rank, honour, position and wealth shall avail you. A Judge before whom only actions shall count and Who is indeed aware of our every movement. Remember that Allah may forgive our faults as far as our relationship with Him is concerned, but will not forgive without penalty our faults in our relations with our fellowmen.

Rasulullah صلى الله عليه وسلم said, "The bankrupt one from among my Ummah is that person, who shall appear on the day of Qiyaamah, bringing with him righteous deeds like 'salaah, sown (fast) and charity. However he had also sworn at someone, falsely accused someone else and hurt someone, with the result that all these people shall come forward with the action against him, bearing witness against him. As a penalty, his good deeds shall be taken away and granted to the afflicted ones. And when his good deeds shall come to an end, in this manner, their sins shall be thrown upon him (when he is not able to pay the full penalty through lack of good deeds). Hence, in this manner he shall enter Jahannam'. So we see inspite of many good deeds his regret and sorry state is beyond description. *(O Allah save us from that).*

Another point is worth emphasising in this connection. Numerous times we have read about so many occasions and deeds which become the reason for forgiveness. The question now arises that when forgiveness is being granted why should it be granted time and again? In other words, once a person had been forgiven there are no sins left on him.

So why is forgiveness granted again? The answer is that when forgiveness comes to a person with sins on him, it will mean those sins are wiped off but when he has no sin it will mean that mercy and favour is granted to him. A further interesting point to note is that Allah time and again calls the Malaa'ikah to witness. The question may arise why is that so? Here one should bear in mind that the affairs of Qiyaamah at the time of reckoning have been set, so that a witness shall be brought forward to testify. Hence Ambiya A.S. shall be required to bring witnesses as to whether they had delivered the message. Very often our Nabi صلى الله عليه وسلم used to say, "Verily you shall be asked about me (and my mission). So bear witness that I did deliver the message."

In Bukhari we read a Hadith: "On the day of Qiyaamah Nooh A.S. shall be called and asked, "Did you deliver the message in the proper manner?" He shall reply, "Yes I did". Then his ummah shall be asked, "Did he deliver the message?" They shall reply,

مَاجَآءَنَا مِنْ بَشِيْرٍ وَّلَا نَذِيْرٍ

"No, neither did a bringer of glad tiding come to us nor did the warner". Thereupon Nooh A.S. A.S. shall be called to bring a witness. He shall call upon Muhammad and his Ummah. This Ummah shall be called forward and they shall testify (as to the truth of Nooh alayhis salaam's evidence).

In some versions of this Hadith this ummah shall be cross questioned, "How do you know that Nooh alayhis salaam did deliver the commands of Allah, (When you were not present at the time?") They shall reply, "Our Nabi صلى الله عليه وسلم informed us of that".

In this same manner all the Ambiyaa shall be questioned. For this the Qur'aan Karim says,

وَكَذٰلِكَ جَعَلْنَاكُمْ اُمَّةً وَّسَطًا لِّتَكُوْنُوْا شُهَدَآءَ عَلَى النَّاسِ

"Thus we made an ummah, justly balanced, that you might be witnesses over the nations".

(Suratul Baqarah: 143)

Imaama Raazi R.A. writes that on the day of Qiyaamah there shall be four types of witnesses:

1. The Malaa'ikah. The Qur'aan says:

وَجَاۤءَتْ كُلُّ نَفْسٍ مَّعَهَا سَآئِقٌ وَّشَهِيْدٌ ،

1.1. *"Not a word does he utter but there is a Sentinel by him ready (to note)".* (Surah Quaf: 18)

مَايَلْفِظُ مِنْ قَوْلٍ اِلَّا لَدَيْهِ رَقِيبٌ عَتِيْدٌ ،

1.2. *"And there will come forth every soul, with each will be (an angel) to bear witness".*

(Surah Quaf: 21)

وَاِنَّ عَلَيْكُمْ لَحَافِظِيْنَ كِرَامًا كَاتِبِيْنَ يَعْلَمُوْنَ مَاتَفْعَلُوْنَ

1.3. *"But verily over you (are appointed angels) to protect you, kind and honourable, writing down your deeds, that they know and understand all that you do".*

(Surah Infi'taar: 10, 11 & 12)

2. The Ambiyaa. The Qur'aan says:

وَكُنْتُ عَلَيْهِمْ شَهِيْدًا مَّادُمْتُ فِيْهِمْ

2.1. *"And I was a witness over them while I dwelt among them".* (Surah Al Maa-'idah: 117)

فَكَيْفَ اِذَا جِئْنَا مِنْ كُلِّ اُمَّةٍ بِشَهِيْدٍ وَّجِئْنَابِكَ عَلٰى هٰؤُلَآءِ شَهِيْدًا

2.2. *"And how shall it be when we shall bring forth every nation with its witness, and shall bring you forth, O prophet, as witness over these (the ummah)".* (Surah An Nisaa': 41)

3. The ummah of Muhammad ﷺ the following verse refers to this:

وَجِيْٓئَ بِالنَّبِيّٖنَ وَالشُّهَدَآءِ

3.1. *"The Prophets and the witnesses will be brought forward".* (Surah Az-zumar: 69)

4. The part of man's body. Thus the Qur'aan states:

اَلْيَوْمَ نَخْتِمُ عَلٰى اَفْوَاهِهِمْ وَتُكَلِّمُنَا اَيْدِيْهِمْ الآية

4.1. *"That day we set a seal on their mouths; but their hands will speak to us and their feet bear witness to all they did".* (Surah Yaaseen: 65)

The last H̲adith under discussion also brings out one joyous message to the fortunate ones. Allah says that He shall not disgrace and humiliate those who performed their duties in front of (and among) the unbelievers and evil doers. This is the enormous extent of Allah's grace and kindness and also the regard Allah shows for the status of the muslims. In addition for those who sought Allah's pleasure another of His blessing and favour is that their faults and sins on this occasion will also be covered.

A̲bdullah ibn 'U̲mar رضي الله عنه reports that Rasulullah صلى الله عليه وسلم said, "On the day of Qiyaamah Allah shall call a believer to draw near to Him. A curtain shall be drawn so that none may see. Allah shall then remind him of each and every fault of his which he shall be obliged to admit. Seeing the great amount of his faults, that person shall feel that he had indeed failed and shall perish. But then Allah say: "In the world did I cover your faults and today too do I hide them and forgive them for you". Thereafter his book of good deeds shall be given to him.

The contents of this H̲adith is contained in so many other Ah̲aadith as well. One should therefore be careful of not humiliating and attacking the righteous ones for their faults, because it is possible that their faults are forgiven. It is also possible that we may be the real loser through back-biting and jeering at those who in their own manner seek to please Allah. It is possible that Allah may cover their faults and forgive them through the blessings of their other good deeds, while we, who continue to backbite, scoff and jeer at them, may be the cause of our own destruction.

(May Allah in His Mercy pardon us all).

This H̲adith also states that the night before the day of

'Iyd is called the night of prize giving, the night when Allah gives the true reward. This night too should be properly appreciated. It is also common that once the announcement has been made that tomorrow is 'Iyd, majority of us even the pious, on this night enjoy ourselves in sleep, whereas this too is a night that should be spent in 'ibaadah, Rasulullah صلى الله عليه وسلم said, "Whoever remains awake (for 'ibaadah) on the nights preceding both 'Iyd's with the aim of gaining reward, his heart shall not die on that day when hearts shall die". The meaning here is that at the time when evil will have taken possession of all, his heart shall stay alive (guarded against evil). It may also refer to the time when the bugle shall be blown to herald the day of Qiyaamah. On that day his soul shall not become unconcious.

Rasulullah صلى الله عليه وسلم is also reported to have said, "Whoever stays awake for 'ibaadah on the following five nights, entrance into Jannah becomes waajib for him, Laylatul Tarwiyah: (the night preceding the eight of Zil Hijjah), Laylatul Arafah (the night preceding the ninth Zil Hijjah), Laylatul Nahr (the night preceding the tenth Zil Hijjah), the night preceding 'Iydul Fitr and the night preceding the fifteenth of Shabaan.

The jurists of Islaam have written that it is mustahab to remain in 'ibaadah on the nights preceding 'Iyd. It is reported in 'Maathabata bis sunnah from Imaam Shaa-iy R.A. that there are five nights in which duaa's are accepted: The night preceding Friday, the night preceding both 'Iyds, the first night of Rajab, and Laylatul Bara-a'h (fifteenth of Shabaan).

Among the pious in Islaam, it is said that because of the exceptional greatness of Friday night, one should spend this night in 'ibaadah during the month of Ramadhaan. But there are some Ahaadith wherein we have been prohibited from fixing only that night for 'ibaadah, it is best that one or two other nights should be joined with it.

I have now come to the end of this book, in conclusion, hoping that this shall be of benefit to those who seek Allah's pleasure. I beg and implore all readers to make duaa' for me, the humble writer of these pages, during those special hours of Ramadhaan. It is possible that because of your duaa's Allah Ta-aa'la bestows His happiness and love upon me too. Aameen.

Readers are humbly requested to also include in their duaa's the founder, past and present staff, pupils and associates of this Institute.

Muhammad Zakariyya Kandhlawy
Resident at Madrasah Mazahir Uloom
Saharanpur–U.P. India
27th Ramadhaan, 1349 Hijri.

Muslim Degeneration and its Only Remedy

Translation of the Urdu Book
Musalmano-Ki-Mawjoodah-pasti-ka-waahid-Ilaaj

مسلمانوں کی موجودہ
پستی کا واحد علاج

By:-
Maulana Ihtishamul Hasan Kaandhlawi (Rah)

Translated by
Malik Haq Nawaz

Muslim Degeneration
and its Only Remedy

ادارہ اشاعتِ دینیات (پرائیویٹ) لمیٹڈ
IDARA ISHA'AT-E-DINIYAT (P) LTD.

Muslim Degeneration & Its Only Remedy

By: Shaikhul Hadith
Maulana Ihtishamul Hasan Kaandhlawi (Rah)

Edition 2001

Published by:
IDARA ISHA'AT-E-DINIYAT (P) LTD.
168/2, Jha House, Hazrat Nizamuddin
New Delhi-110 013 (India)
Tel.: 6926832, 6926833
Fax: +91-11-6322787,4352786
Email: **sales@idara.com**
Visit us at: **www.idara.com**

Printed at:
Nice Printing Press, Delhi

نَحْمَدُهٗ وَنُصَلِّي وَنُسَلِّمُ عَلَى رَسُولِهِ الْكَرِيمِ

AUTHOR'S PREFACE

For the high devotion, keenness and perseverance of Hadhrat Mohammad Ilyas (Rahmat-Allah-Alaihi) and also due to the profound zeal shown by many other learned and pious personages among Muslims, a cohesive work is currently in progress for the propagation of Islam and the Islamic way of life. This fact is known to most of the well-informed Muslims of this period. Although an unworthy being for the high mission, I have been commanded by the distinguished gentlemen referred to above to write an account of this work, so as to bring out clearly the special features of propagation *(Tabligh)* and also to highlight the burning need for this, the Supreme Islamic activity, at this critical juncture, so that, as many Muslims as possible are able to understand and benefit from what is going on.

In obedience to their command, I have ventured to gather in this booklet a few thoughts and ideas, which are mere drops from the ocean of knowledge and enlightenment possessed by the above mentioned personalities. The collection really amounts to a handful of petals from the vast garden of the teachings of Islam, which I have hurriedly picked up for presentation to the readers. There may be mistakes and omissions in the presentation, for which I beg my readers to make allowance, and request them to be so kind as to amend or correct those mistakes if necessary, thereby earning my gratitude.

It is my earnest prayer that may Haq-Ta'ala (Shanahoo) by His special favours and kindnesses, and for the sake of the noble personages connected with this work, forgive me for my sins and not uncover my misdeeds, but He may graciously enable us all to lead a pious and virtuous life. May He bestow upon us the wealth of His own love, and grant us the approval to follow His own chosen faith of Islam. May He also give us the power to propagate Islam in strict obedience and loyalty to His dearest and the most distinguished Prophet, (Hadhrat Mohammad sallallaho alaihe wasallam).

MOHAMMAD EHTESHAM-UL-HASSAN (DELHI)
18 RIBIYYUSANI 1358 (HIJRI)

بِسْمِ اللّٰهِ الرَّحْمٰنِ الرَّحِيمِ

اَلْحَمْدُ لِلّٰهِ رَبِّ الْعٰلَمِينَ وَالصَّلٰوةُ وَالسَّلَامُ عَلٰى سَيِّدِ الْأَوَّلِينَ وَالْآخِرِينَ خَاتَمِ الْأَنْبِيَاءِ وَالْمُرْسَلِينَ مُحَمَّدٍ وَّآلِهِ وَأَصْحَابِهِ الطَّيِّبِينَ الطَّاهِرِينَ.

PAST HISTORY

About thirteen and a half centuries ago, when the world was sunk in the darkness of ignorance, sin and impiety, a light of true knowledge and guidance rose from the horizon of the rugged hills of Batha.* Its rays spread to the East, West, North and South; they reached every corner of the earth and within the short period of 23 years, the way was paved through that light for the mankind to move to such heights of glory as had never been attained before. It enlightened Muslims and created in them the urge for taking the right counsel, which would ultimately bring them their salvation. By following the right path and the guidance emanating from that light, the Muslims moved from success to success and attained the highest pinnacle of glory in history. For centuries, they ruled on this earth with such grandeur and strength that no contemporary power had the courage to challenge them and, if someone dared to do so, he did that at the risk of being annihilated. This is the historical truth, which cannot be erased. But, alas! this fact of history has only become a myth, an ancient tale, to narrate which may sound meaningless and ridiculous, particularly in the context of the present day life of Muslims, which obviously is a blot on the brilliant performance and achievements of their ancestors, the early followers of Islam.

THE DISEASE

The history, even up to the end of the thirteenth century Hijri, will reveal that the Muslims were the sole possessors of honour, dignity, power and grandeur, but when one turns his eyes away from the pages of the history books and looks at the Muslims of today, one sees the picture of a people sunk in misery and disgrace, a people who possess no real strength or power, honour or dignity, brotherhood or mutual love, and reflects no virtues or moral character worth the name. One cannot find any sign in them of those

* Name of hills around Mecca (Saudi Arabia).

noble deeds which at one time used to be the symbol of each and every Muslim. Now-a-days, there can hardly be a living person who can be said to have the purity or the sincerity of conscience. On the contrary, Muslims are sunk in vice and sin. They have wandered away so much from the path of virtue which at one time used to be their "hall-mark", that the enemies of Islam talk and discuss their affairs with delight, contempt and ridicule. Unfortunately, the matter does not end here. The Muslim youth of the new generation, which has been affected and influenced by the so-called modern trends or the Western way of life, take pleasure in laughing at the very ideals of Islam and openly criticize the sacred code of "Shariat" as being out of date and impracticable. One wonders at such behaviour and finds that a people, who once gave strength, happiness, honour and peace to the entire mankind, have now become completely demoralised, apathetic, shallow and helpless. Those who had once taught the world the golden lessons of etiquette and culture are today found wanting in these very adornments.

EARLIER ATTEMPTS TOWARDS IMPROVEMENT

For a long time, some distinguished thinkers and preachers of Islam have been seriously pondering over this unfortunate plight of their people and have been striving hard to reform the Muslim society, but alas!

مرض بڑھتا گیا جوں جوں دوا کی

(The treatment only aggravated the disease).

The situation is fast deteriorating and the future looks darker still. Inaction and complacency on our part in these circumstances will be an unforgiveable sin and crime. But, before deciding what is to be done, it will be necessary to look closely at the root cause of this sad state of affairs.

People have assigned several causes to this degeneration and have adopted numerous measures for arresting the rot, but unfortunately all efforts so far have only brought further frustration. Instead of improvement, despair and confusion have resulted, particularly so in the ranks of learned preachers and "ulema". The basic truth of all this is that the root cause of the real disease has not been diagnosed. Until this is done, no proper treatment can be prescribed or administered, hence no cure or improvement can be expected. Any step lacking proper diagnosis and correct treatment would amount to making a chronic situation more chronic, and further increase confusion and despair.

THE APPROACH

It is the proven claim of Islam that the "Shariat" is the Divine Code, which lays down a complete way of life outlining every possible measure for advancing and progressing on the path of true success and righteousness. It very clearly describes the proper course of action and indicates methods to check and re-orientate in the event of losing direction or going astray. In other words, "Shariat-e-Muhammadiah" assures its followers their spiritual and material well-being and advancement for their whole life in all situations, right up to the last day of life on this earth. Obviously, therefore, it would be futile to look for the cause and the cure for the prevailing degeneration outside the dictates of "Shariat". For this, of necessity, we must look closely into the "Quran-i-Hakim" which is the fountain source of "Shariat" and of all knowledge and guidance for the whole of mankind. In fact, it is the only source of wisdom for man. We ought to seek its help in finding out what our troubles are and how they are to be removed, if we really desire to attain full recovery. Once we come to know about that, we must cling to the solution and solemnly resolve to adopt it. Certainly, the wisdom and guidance from the "Quran" will never fail us, particularly at the critical juncture and in the difficult times through which we are passing nowadays. Let us look and search for the right solution in the "Quran" and "Sunnah"

THE DIAGNOSIS

The Creator of the universe, Allah Ta'ala, remains avowedly committed that the kingdom and His vicegerency on earth are only meant for the true Muslims (momineen).

This is clear from the following verse:

وَعَدَ اللّٰهُ الَّذِينَ آمَنُوا مِنكُمْ وَعَمِلُوا الصّٰلِحَاتِ لَيَسْتَخْلِفَنَّهُمْ فِي الْأَرْضِ (النور ٥٠)

"Allah has promised to those from amongst you who believe and do righteous deeds that He would surely make them His vicegerents on earth."

He has also given the assurances that true believers will always dominate over non-believers and that non-believers will be left without any friend or ally; as is clear from the following verse:

وَلَوْ قَاتَلَكُمُ الَّذِينَ كَفَرُوا لَوَلَّوُا الْأَدْبَارَ ثُمَّ لَا يَجِدُونَ وَلِيًّا وَلَا نَصِيرًا (الفتح ٢٢)

"And if these non-believers had given you a battle, they were sure to turn on their heels, and they would have found no protector and no helper."

Moreover, it is Allah Ta'ala's own obligation to grant every help to the true Muslims and it is also His promise that such people will always remain exalted and glorious. This is borne out by the following verses:

وَكَانَ حَقًّا عَلَيْنَا نَصْرُ الْمُؤْمِنِينَ (الروم ٤٧)

وَلَا تَهِنُوا وَلَا تَحْزَنُوا وَأَنْتُمُ الْأَعْلَوْنَ إِنْ كُنْتُمْ مُؤْمِنِينَ (آل عمران ١٣٩)

وَلِلَّهِ الْعِزَّةُ وَلِرَسُولِهِ وَلِلْمُؤْمِنِينَ (المنافقون ٨)

"And it is our bounden duty to render succour to the true believers."

"And do not give way to despair, and do not grieve, and you only shall dominate, if you are true believers."

"And honour is only for Allah, His Prophet (sallallaho alaihe wasallam) and those who believe."

The above Divine assertions clearly indicate that the way to regain honour, grandeur, exaltation, glory and virtues by Muslims, lies only in their being strictly faithful. If their relationship with Allah Ta'ala and the Holy Prophet (sallallaho alaihe wasallam) is strong and firm, they are destined to be masters of each and every things on this Earth. But if, on from the following verse:

وَالْعَصْرِ ، إِنَّ الْإِنْسَانَ لَفِي خُسْرٍ ، إِلَّا الَّذِينَ آمَنُوا وَعَمِلُوا الصَّالِحَاتِ وَتَوَاصَوْا
بِالْحَقِّ وَتَوَاصَوْا بِالصَّبْرِ (العصر ١ - ٣)

"And let Time be witness: verily man is in a great loss except, of course, those who believe and do righteous deeds and who rejoin truth and enjoin patience."

As already brought out, history proves that the early Muslims had been able to reach the highest summit of honour and glory, whereas the present day Muslims seem to have moved in the opposite direction. It is obvious from the above verses of the Quran that the first Muslims had attained that high position in life because of the purity and strength of their faith and the excellence of their character. Conversely, the deplorable condition of the present-day Muslims is the result of weakness in their faith and character, the opposite of what their forefathers possessed. Therefore, it will be right to say that today we are Muslims in name only! In this connection, the true Messenger of Allah Ta'ala Hadhrat Mohammad, (sallallaho alaihe wasallam), had prophesied:

سَيَأْتِي عَلَى النَّاسِ زَمَانٌ لَا يَبْقَى مِنَ الْإِسْلَامِ إِلَّا إِسْمُهُ وَلَا مِنَ الْقُرْآنِ إِلَّا رَسْمُهُ (مشكوة)

> "An era will come in the near future when Islam will exist merely in name and Quran will exist merely in phrase."

This is clearly applicable to the Muslims of the present time. In these circumstances, the points which need urgent investigation are:

(a) as the right type of faith, which can have the approval of Allah Ta'ala and His Apostle and which will bring us spiritual and material advancement, is not to be seen anywhere, what will be the means of acquiring that true faith; and

(b) what are the factors which have caused the extinction of that faith, and with it the true life of Islam, from our midst?

A study of the Holy Quran clearly reveals that the capacity to maintain the required level of the true faith of Islam, and the ultimate ascendance to exaltation and glory through it, are dependent on the fulfilment of a special task which has been so graciously assigned by Allah Ta'ala to the Muslims alone. It is for this that they have been given, in the Quran, the distinguished position, "Khair-ul-Umam" (the best of all peoples).

According to the faith of Islam, the main purpose behind the creation of this world was to establish and prove the Divinity, the Oneness, and the most exalted existence of Almighty Allah Ta'ala, and to reflect His unlimited Powers and boundless Attributes through man, who was to be guided by the light of true knowledge. It was impossible for man to conceive and utilize that knowledge without his first being purified of impiety and obscenity. Only after that purification, is he to be adorned with fine virtues, excellence of conduct and the eventual capacity to act righteously. It was for this purpose of bringing about this purity and power in the ranks of mankind that thousands of Prophets and Apostles had been deputed by Allah Ta'ala. The last in the series, came the "Sayyed-ul-Ambia wal Mursalin" (the greatest of all the Prophets) Mohammad (sallallaho alaihe wasallam). It was through him that man reached the high state of development of mind and body leading to the final stage of purity. It was then that mankind received the glad tidings in the following verse:

اَلْيَوْمَ أَكْمَلْتُ لَكُمْ دِينَكُمْ وَأَتْمَمْتُ عَلَيْكُمْ نِعْمَتِي (المائدة ٣)

"And today we have perfected your Religion for you and completed our bounty upon you."

The supreme purpose of man's creation had been fulfilled; good and evil had been clearly defined, a complete system of practical life had been revealed, the lineage of prophethood and apostlehood had been terminated, and lastely, the duties that were formerly discharged exclusively by the Prophets had devolved as a coliective mission upon the "Ummat-i-Mohammadia" (the Muslim people). This last fact has been clearly brought out in the following verses of the Holy Quran:

كُنْتُمْ خَيْرَ أُمَّةٍ أُخْرِجَتْ لِلنَّاسِ تَأْمُرُونَ بِالْمَعْرُوفِ وَتَنْهَوْنَ عَنِ الْمُنْكَرِ
وَتُؤْمِنُونَ بِاللّٰهِ (آل عمران ١١٠)

"O you (followers of Mohammad): you are the noblest of peoples, in that you have been brought out for (the benefit of) mankind. You enjoin the good and forbid the evil, and you believe in Allah."

وَلْتَكُن مِّنكُمْ أُمَّةٌ يَدْعُونَ إِلَى الْخَيْرِ وَيَأْمُرُونَ بِالْمَعْرُوفِ وَيَنْهَوْنَ عَنِ الْمُنكَرِ وَأُولَٰئِكَ هُمُ الْمُفْلِحُونَ (آل عمران ١٠٤)

"And it is but meet that amongst you there should be a group devoted to inviting people towards righteousness and enjoining the good and forbidding the evil, and it is only those who do this that prosper."

In the first verse, "Allah Ta'ala" has stated the reason why the Muslims are called "Khair-ul-Umam" (noblest of all peoples); it is because of spreading good and preventing evil. In the second verse, He has further clarified that only those people shall be exalted in life who fulfil that injunction. The command does not end here. It is stated in another place that the failure to accomplish this vital task will bring curse and gloom on its assignees. This inference is taken from the following verse:

لُعِنَ الَّذِينَ كَفَرُوا مِن بَنِي إِسْرَائِيلَ عَلَى لِسَانِ دَاوُدَ وَعِيسَى ابْنِ مَرْيَمَ ، ذَٰلِكَ بِمَا عَصَوا وَكَانُوا يَعْتَدُونَ ، كَانُوا لَا يَتَنَاهَوْنَ عَن مُّنكَرٍ فَعَلُوهُ ، لَبِئْسَ مَا كَانُوا يَفْعَلُونَ (المائدة ٧٨ - ٧٩)

"And those amongst the people of Israel who rejected Allah's commands were cursed by Allah through the tongues of Dawood and Isa, son of Mariam. And the curse was because they rebelled against Allah's commands and transgressed the limits and did not desist from the evil that they were doing; and verily it was a grievous lapse on their part."

A further explanation and clarification of the above verse of the Holy Quran can be seen from the following "Ahadis" (sayings of the Holy Prophet Mohammad (sallallaho alaihe wasallam).

(1) It has been narrated by Hadhrat Abdullah bin Masud (radi Allaho anho) that the Holy Prophet (sallallaho alaihe wasallam) was pleased to say:

(١) وَفِي السنن والمسند من حديث عبد الله بن مسعود قَالَ قَالَ رَسُولُ اللهِ صَلَّى اللهُ عَلَيْهِ وَسَلَّمَ: إِنَّ مَنْ كَانَ قَبْلَكُمْ كَانَ إِذَا عَمِلَ الْعَامِلُ فِيهِمْ بِالْخَطِيئَةِ جَاءَهُ النَّاهِيْ تَعْزِيرًا ، فَقَالَ يَا هذَا إِتَّقِ اللّهَ ، فَإِذَا كَانَ مِنَ الْغَدِ جَالَسَهُ وَآكَلَهُ وَشَارَبَهُ كَأَنَّهُ لَمْ يَرَهُ عَلَى خَطِيئَةٍ بِالْأَمْسِ ، فَلَمَّا رَأَى عَزَّ وَجَلَّ ذٰلِكَ مِنْهُمْ ضَرَبَ قُلُوبَ بَعْضِهِمْ عَلَى بَعْضٍ ، ثُمَّ لَعَنَهُمْ عَلَى لِسَانِ نَبِيِّهِمْ دَاوُدَ وَعِيسَى بْنِ مَرْيَمَ ، ذٰلِكَ بِمَا عَصَوا وَكَانُوا يَعْتَدُونَ ، وَالَّذِي نَفْسُ مُحَمَّدٍ بِيَدِهِ لَتَأْمُرُنَّ بِالْمَعْرُوفِ وَلَتَنْهَوُنَّ عَنِ الْمُنْكَرِ وَلَتَأْخُذُنَّ عَلَى يَدِ السَّفِيهِ وَلَتَأْطُرُنَّ عَلَى الْحَقِّ أَطْرًا أَوْ لَيَضْرِبَنَّ اللّهُ قُلُوبَ بَعْضِكُمْ عَلَى بَعْضٍ ثُمَّ يَلْعَنُكُمْ كَمَا لَعَنَهُمْ .

"Amongst peoples gone by, when somebody committed a sin, the other would reprimand him and would say: "Fear Allah"; but on the following day would befriend him and mix with him as if he had never seen him committing the sin. And when Allah saw them behaving thus, He confounded the hearts of some with those of some, and cursed them through the tongues of Dawood and Isa son of Mariam; and this because they rebelled against Allah and transgressed His limits."

I, Mohammad swear by Him, Who has control over my soul: you must enjoin the good and forbid the evil and force the ignorant wrongdoer into the path of rectitude; else Allah will confound your hearts and you will be cursed, as were some of the peoples gone by.

(٢) وفي سنن أبي داود وابن ماجة عَنْ جَرِيْرِ بْنِ عَبْدِ اللّهِ قَالَ سَمِعْتُ رَسُولَ اللّهِ صَلَّى اللّهُ عَلَيْهِ وَسَلَّمَ يَقُولُ: مَا مِنْ رَجُلٍ يَكُونُ فِي قَوْمٍ يَعْمَلُ فِيهِمْ بِالْمَعَاصِي يَقْدِرُونَ عَلَى أَنْ يُغَيِّرُوا عَلَيْهِ وَلَا يُغَيِّرُونَ إِلَّا أَصَابَهُمُ اللّهُ بِعِقَابٍ قَبْلَ أَنْ يَمُوتُوا

(2) Hadhrat Jareer (radi Allaho anho) has narrated that Hadhrat Mohammad (sallallaho alaihe wasallam) was pleased to say: "When an individual of a community sins, and the community, in spite of its authority over him, does not prevent him from sinning, Allah's punishment descends on them even before death, i.e., He subjects them to various tribulations in this very world."

(٣) وروى الأصبهاني عن أَنَسٍ أَنَّ رَسُولَ اللّهِ صَلَّى اللّهُ عَلَيْهِ وَسَلَّمَ قَالَ: لَا تَزَالُ لَا إِلَهَ إِلَّا اللّهُ تَنْفَعُ مَنْ قَالَهَا وَتَرُدُّ عَنْهُمُ الْعَذَابَ وَالنِّقْمَةَ مَالَمْ يَسْتَخِفُّوا بِحَقِّهَا ، قَالَ: يَظْهَرُ الْعَمَلُ بِمَعَاصِي اللّهِ فَلَا يُنْكَرُ وَلَا يُغَيَّرُ . (ترغيب)

(3) Hadhrat Anas (radi Allaho anho) has narrated that Hadhrat Mohammad (sallallaho alaihe wasallam) was pleased to say, "The Kalimah La ilaha Illallaho always benefits the individuals who proclaim it, and keeps away from them woes and troubles, unless, indeed, its rights are ignored." The companions inquired: "What does the ignoring of its rights mean?" Replied the Prophet: "It means that when sins are being committed openly they do not prevent or stop them."

(٤) عَنْ عَائِشَةَ قَالَتْ: دَخَلَ عَلَيَّ النَّبِيُّ صَلَّى اللّهُ عَلَيْهِ وَسَلَّمَ فَعَرَفْتُ فِي وَجْهِهِ أَنْ قَدْ حَضَرَهُ شَيْءٌ ، فَتَوَضَّأَ وَمَا كَلَّمَ أَحَدًا ، فَلَصِقْتُ بِالْحُجْرَةِ أَسْتَمِعُ مَا يَقُولُ ، فَقَعَدَ عَلَى الْمِنْبَرِ ، فَحَمِدَ اللّهَ وَأَثْنَى عَلَيْهِ ، وَقَالَ: يَا أَيُّهَا النَّاسُ إِنَّ اللّهَ تَعَالَى يَقُولُ لَكُمْ: مُرُوا بِالْمَعْرُوفِ وَانْهَوْا عَنِ الْمُنْكَرِ قَبْلَ أَنْ تَدْعُوا فَلَا أُجِيبَ لَكُمْ وَتَسْأَلُونِي فَلَا أُعْطِيَكُمْ ، وَتَسْتَنْصِرُونِي فَلَا أَنْصُرَكُمْ ، فَمَا زَادَ عَلَيْهِنَّ حَتَّى نَزَلَ . (ترغيب)

(4) Hadhrat Aisha (radi Allaho anha) says: "The Holy Prophet, (sallallaho alaihe wasallam) came to me and I could read from his noble countenance that something extraordinary had happened. He did not utter a single word but, having performed ablution, repaired straight to the mosque. I, too, stood by the wall of the mosque to hear what he had to say. The Prophet of Allah ascended the pulpit and, after the usual holy exordium, said: 'O people, Allah has ordained you to enjoin the good and forbid the evil, lest a time should come when you call and He may not respond, you ask for a favour and He may not grant it, and you call for help and He may refuse'."

(٥) عَنْ أَبِي هُرَيْرَةَ قَالَ: قَالَ رَسُولُ اللّهِ صَلَى اللّهُ عَلَيْهِ وَسَلَّمَ: إِذَا عَظَّمَتْ أُمَّتِي الدُّنْيَا نُزِعَتْ مِنْهَا هَيْبَةُ الْإِسْلَامِ ، وَإِذَا تَرَكَتِ الْأَمْرَ بِالْمَعْرُوفِ وَالنَّهْيَ عَنِ الْمُنْكَرِ حُرِمَتْ بَرَكَةَ الْوَحْيِ ، وَإِذَا تَسَابَّتْ أُمَّتِي سَقَطَتْ مِنْ عَيْنِ اللّهِ . (كذا في الدر عن الحكيم الترمذي)

(5) Hadhrat Abu Huraira (radi Allaho anho) has narrated:

"Said the Prophet (sallallaho alaihe wasallam): When my "Ummat" (followers) begin to attach more importance to the world and to regard it as a source of glory, the awe and importance of Islam will vanish from their hearts. When they give up the practice of enjoining good and forbidding evil, they will be deprived of the blessings of Revelation, and, when they begin to indulge in mutual recrimination, they will fall low in the eyes of Allah."

THE ROOT-CAUSE

From the above "Ahadis" it is clear, that the abandonment of the act of "Amir bil maruf wa nahi anil munkar" (enjoining the good and forbidding the evil) has usually been the root cause of "Allah Ta'ala's" anger and displeasure and His eventual wrath. And if the "Ummat-e-Mohammadiah" becomes guilty of that neglect and omission, the punishment to be given to them will be more severe than to the earlier people, because they would have failed to recognise their exclusive obligation and neglected to fulfil the sole mission in their life. For this reason, the Holy Prophet (sallallaho alaihe wasallam) has enjoined the act of "Amir bil maruf wa nahi anil munkar" (enjoining the good and forbidding the evil) "as the essence and the pivot of the faith of Islam" and the abandonment of that act as the cause of decay and decline of the faith.

In the "Hadis" of Abu Saeed Khudri, (radi Allaho anho) it is mentioned:

مَنْ رَاى مِنْكُمْ مُنكَرًا فَلْيُغَيِّرْهُ بِيَدِهِ ، فَإِنْ لَّمْ يَسْتَطِعْ فَبِلِسَانِهِ ، فَإِنْ لَّمْ يَسْتَطِعْ
فَبِقَلْبِهِ ، وَذٰلِكَ أَضْعَفُ الْإِيمَانِ . (مسلم)

"When anyone of you witnesses the commission of evil, he should use his hands to prevent it; and if he has not the power to do this, he should use his tongue; and if he has not the power to do even this, he should use the power of his heart; and this last represents the weakest degree of faith."

There is yet a clearer version of the same "Hadis" from Ibne Masud (radi Allaho anho):

مَا مِنْ نَبِيٍّ بَعَثَهُ اللّٰهُ قَبْلِي إِلَّا كَانَ لَهُ فِي أُمَّتِهِ حَوَارِيُّونَ وَأَصْحَابٌ يَأْخُذُونَ بِسُنَّتِهِ وَيَقْتَدُونَ بِأَمْرِهِ ، ثُمَّ إِنَّهَا تَخْلُفُ مِنْ بَعْدِهِمْ خُلُوفٌ يَقُولُونَ مَالَا يَفْعَلُونَ ، وَيَفْعَلُونَ مَالَا يُؤْمَرُونَ ، فَمَنْ جَاهَدَهُمْ بِيَدِهِ فَهُوَ مُؤْمِنٌ وَلَيْسَ وَرَاءَ ذٰلِكَ مِنَ الْإِيمَانِ حَبَّةُ خَرْدَلٍ . (مسلم)

It is usual for Allah to so arrange that every Prophet leaves behind a group of his companions who perpetuate His message, who follow it rigorously and preserve the holy message exactly in the form in which the Messenger left it. Then comes an epoch of mischief and error, an epoch that witnesses the birth of people who step aside from the path laid down by the Prophet. Their actions are at variance with their proclamations; their activities are not warranted by the holy law. So whosoever arises in defence of Truth and Law, and opposes the miscreants with his hands, is a true believer; he who cannot do this but uses his tongue, is a believer too; and he who cannot, do even this, but uses the power of his heart, is also a believer; but less than this, there is no degree of faith–(*Muslim*).

The vital importance of *Tabligh* (the task of propagation) has been further emphasized by Imam Ghazali, (rahmatullah alaih) in the following manner:

"There can be no doubt that the act of "amr bil maruf wa nahi anil munkar" is that solid pillar of Islam, on which each and every article of faith rests. It is for this very mission that Allah Ta'ala deputed all the Holy Prophets. If unfortunately, it is ignored or forgotten and its methods and practices are given up, one has to say that the very purpose of prophethood is totally defeated and rendered meaningless. Thereafter, the conscience, which is the capital wealth of man, will wither and degenerate. Indolence and dullness of mind will prevail. The highway to vice and arrogance will be opened up and barbarity will spread in the whole world. All achievements of man will become dangerous and even harmful. Human relationship will break down. Civilization will be ruined. Mankind will be reduced to utter moral destitution. But, the vivid realisation of all this will come only on the Day of Judgement, when the entire mankind will be under trial before the Almighty Allah Ta'ala and called upon to account for each and every action."

"Alas! alas! the fear has come true, that which was apprehended is before our eyes.

وَكَانَ أَمْرُ اللّٰهِ قَدَرًا مَقْدُورًا ، فَإِنَّا لِلّٰهِ وَإِنَّا إِلَيْهِ رَاجِعُونَ

The tower of knowledge and enlightenment has been demolished and its benefits and effects have been completely wiped out. Consequently, mutual contempt and humiliation are rampant. Nothing, of the sublime relationship between man and his Creator, is left in human hearts; on the contrary, man, like an animal, has become the slave of his passions. Indeed, not only is there a paucity of true Muslims in this world now, but it is practically impossible to meet anyone who is prepared to bear the inevitable privations for the sake of propagating Islam.

"Any Muslim who dares to take steps to remove the present state of ruin and devastation, endeavours to revive the act of propagation and comes forward to shoulder that heavy responsibility, will surely rank as the noblest and the most distinguished being among the whole of mankind."

He said this nearly eight hundred years ago, but his statement is very accurately applicable to us today.

We must ponder and calmly think out what is to be done in these circumstances. There are some well-known causes which seem to be responsible for the apathy and indifference that prevail today. These are discussed below.

CAUSES

FIRST

We generally believe that the act of *Tabligh* is the sole and special responsibility of the "ulema", even when the relevant injunctions of the Quran are clear and squarely apply to each and every living Muslim. The actions and the hard work of the Companions of the Holy Prophet (sallallaho alaihe wasallam), and all those distinguished Muslims who immediately followed them, bear definite testimony to the contention that each and every Muslim is responsible for the propagation of Islam *(Tabligh)*.

To assign the obligation of *Tabligh* (amr bil maruf wa nahi anil munkar) solely to the ranks of "ulema", and not to ourselves, is a sign of grave ignorance on our part. The duty of the "ulema" is to state the truth and to point out the right path. To enforce the righteousness among the people and to keep the people moving on the right path is the responsibility of all other Muslims. The following "Hadis" is a clear exhortation to this:

اَلَا كُلُّكُمْ رَاعٍ وَكُلُّكُمْ مَسْئُولٌ عَنْ رَعِيَّتِهِ ، فَالْأَمِيرُ الَّذِي عَلَى النَّاسِ رَاعٍ
عَلَيْهِمْ وَهُوَ مَسْئُولٌ عَنْهُمْ ، وَالرَّجُلُ رَاعٍ عَلَى أَهْلِ بَيْتِهِ وَهُوَ مَسْئُولٌ عَنْهُمْ ،
وَالْمَرْأَةُ رَاعِيَةٌ عَلَى بَيْتِ بَعْلِهَا وَوَلَدِهِ وَهِيَ مَسْئُولَةٌ عَنْهُمْ ، وَالْعَبْدُ رَاعٍ عَلَى مَالِ
سَيِّدِهِ وَهُوَ مَسْئُولٌ عَنْهُ ، فَكُلُّكُمْ رَاعٍ وَكُلُّكُمْ مَسْئُولٌ عَنْ رَعِيَّتِهِ . (بخاري -
مسلم)

"Lo! All of you are leaders and shall be questioned on the Day of Judgment in respect of your trust. So, the king is a head unto his subjects and shall be questioned in respect of them; the husband is a head unto his wife and shall be questioned in respect of her; the wife is a head unto her husband's house and the children, and shall be questioned in respect of them all; the slave is a watchman unto his master's effects and shall be questioned in respect of those. So you are all shepherds, and you shall be questioned in respect of that entrusted to you."

And similarly, in another place, a yet clearer version is given:

قَالَ: أَلدِّينُ النَّصِيحَةُ ، قُلْنَا: لِمَنْ؟ قَالَ: لِلّٰهِ وَلِرَسُولِهِ وَلِأَئِمَّةِ الْمُسْلِمِينَ

وَعَامَّتِهِمْ . (مسلم)

The Holy Prophet (sallallaho alaihe wasallam) said:

> "Religion is the act of counselling." (The Companions) enquired: "On whose part (to counsel)?" He said: "On the part of Allah, the Apostle, the leaders of the Muslims and the lay Muslims."

Even if we suppose, as an extreme case, that this task has to be carried out by the "Ulema" only, the present emergency and the critical situation demand that everyone of us should put his shoulder to the wheel and strive hard for the propagation of the "Kalimah" and the protection of the Muslim way of life.

SECOND

It is commonly believed that, if a person is firm and steadfast in his own faith (eeman), the infidelity of others will bring him no harm, because of the meaning attached to the following verse of Holy Quran:

يَا أَيُّهَا الَّذِينَ آمَنُوا عَلَيْكُمْ أَنْفُسَكُمْ لَا يَضُرُّكُمْ مَنْ ضَلَّ إِذَا اهْتَدَيْتُمْ (المائدة ١٠٥)

> "O you who believe! you are responsible for your own souls. He who goes astray cannot harm you, while you are on the path of righteousness."

In fact, the real meaning and sense of the above verse is not what is being apparently attached to it, because, in that case, the meaning would appear to be against the Divine wisdom and spirit and against the teachings of the "Shariat-i-Mohammadiah." It indicates that the collective life and progress and salvation of the Muslim society as a whole are the essence of Islam. The Muslim people must be considered like a single body having several limbs. When any limb receives an injury, the whole body suffers from the pain.

Mankind may progress to any limit and it may reach the highest pinnacle of glory in every sphere of life, yet there will be some who will go astray and become involved in impiety. In that event, the above verse re-assures the righteous people that as long as they remain steadfast and keep moving on the right path, no harm can be brought to them by those who decide to give up the right way of life.

Yet another point is that full enlightenment will be received only when all the rules of law of "Shariat-i-Mohammadiah" are accepted and practised, including all the Divine commands, which naturally cover "Amir bil maruf wa nahi anil munkar". This interpretation is supported by the following words of Hadhrat Abu Bakr (radi Allaho anho):

عَنْ أَبِي بَكْرِ الصِّدِّيْقِ قالَ: أَيُّهَا النَّاسُ إِنَّكُمْ تَقْرَءُونَ هذِهِ الآيَةَ: يَا أَيُّهَا الَّذِيْنَ آمَنُوا عَلَيْكُمْ أَنْفُسَكُمْ لَا يَضُرُّكُمْ مَّنْ ضَلَّ إِذَا اهْتَدَيْتُمْ ، فَإِنِّي سَمِعْتُ رَسُولَ اللّهِ صَلَى اللّهُ عَلَيْهِ وَسَلَّمَ يَقُولُ: إِنَّ النَّاسَ إِذَا رَأَوا الْمُنْكَرَ فَلَمْ يُغَيِّرُوهُ أَوْشَكَ أَنْ يَعُمَّهُمُ اللّهُ بِعِقَابِهِ .

> "O people! you are given to reading this verse: "O you who believe! you are responsible for your own souls; he who goes astray cannot harm you, while you are on the path of righteousness," but I have heard the Apostle of Allah saying that when people see something evil and do not seek to liquidate it, they will soon find themselves encompassed by the wrath of Allah."

The verse in question has been similarly interpreted by all the truly learned personages, such as Imam Nawavi (rahmat-ullah alaih), who explains in his "Sharah Muslim":

> "The consensus of opinion of the learned personages regarding the meaning of his verse is that, "when you have performed the duty enjoined on you, the remissness of those who refuse to profit by your counsel will not harm you," as says Allah Ta'ala:
>
> وَلَا تَزِرُ وَازِرَةٌ وِّزْرَ أُخْرى (فاطر ١٨)
>
> "(No one shall carry another man's burden)"; and of the several injunctions addressed to all, one is that

regarding enforcement of good and prevention of evil. Therefore when an individual has performed this duty, and the addressee proves refractory, the former shall not be penalised for it. He has performed his duty of "amr-o-nahi" and acceptance or rejection of it by the other party is not within his competence. Allah knows best."

THIRD

People of distinction as well as the common man, the learned and the ignorant, all alike, have become indifferent or even averse to the need for the reformation of society. They all seem to have resigned to the fate, that it is difficult, rather impossible these days, for the Muslims to make any progress to regain their lost glory. Whenever any scheme for improvement and reformation is presented to anyone, the usual reaction is: how can the Muslims progress in the circumstances when they have neither a state* of their own nor any power to rule, neither wealth nor any financial standing, no army and equipment of war nor any influence, they lack even in physical stamina, mutual agreement and unity of purpose. Even the religious people seem to have decided by themselves that, it being the fourteenth century "Hijri" and the people, having drifted so farther away from the prophetical teachings, the downfall of Islam and the Muslims is inevitable. They maintain that, in these circumstances, it will be useless to make any effort towards the reformation of Muslims.

It is true that the effects of the apostolic light become less and less as we are removed farther and farther away from it, but this does not mean that no effort is to be made to regenerate that light by enforcing "Shariat" and upholding and defending, with all our energies and power, the way of life taught by Hadhrat Mohammad (sallallaho alaihe wasallam).

For, had the Muslims before us thought so, there would have been no trace of Islam left anywhere by now, because there would have been no means through which the lessons and the teachings of "Shariat" could have reached us. Therefore, it will be fatal for us not to check the

* The original text was written in 1938 when the Muslims of the Indian subcontinent were not free and did not possess independent political power or authority.

present negative attitude towards Islam. We should adopt a vigorously positive line for our own sake and also for the sake of future generations. The time is moving fast, and so is the pace of deterioration in the religion of Islam. The situation demands a strong, quick and determined effort by one and all for arresting the rot and stopping further degeneration of the Muslim society.

As a rule, existence of true Islam depends entirely upon the perseverance and collective effort of its followers. Unfortunately, they seem to be deficient in these very requirements. We must appreciate that the "Quran" and "Hadis" are full of the lessons in calling the Muslims to be active and to persevere in the path of Allah. There is a "hadis" about a very pious person who may pray night and day all his life, but he cannot come to the level of one who strives and sacrifies his pleasure and comfort for the sake of guiding and helping people to move on the right path of Islam.

On this very point, many commands and injunctions in the "Quran" exist. It is clearly brought out that the one who strives hard in the path of Allah Ta'ala remains superior and exalted compared to all other; for example:

لَا يَسْتَوِي الْقَاعِدُونَ مِنَ الْمُؤْمِنِينَ غَيْرُ أُولِي الضَّرَرِ وَالْمُجَاهِدُونَ فِي سَبِيلِ اللَّهِ
بِأَمْوَالِهِمْ وَأَنْفُسِهِمْ ، فَضَّلَ اللَّهُ الْمُجَاهِدِينَ بِأَمْوَالِهِمْ وَأَنْفُسِهِمْ عَلَى الْقَاعِدِينَ
دَرَجَةً ، وَكُلًّا وَعَدَ اللَّهُ الْحُسْنَى ، وَفَضَّلَ اللَّهُ الْمُجَاهِدِينَ عَلَى الْقَاعِدِينَ أَجْرًا
عَظِيمًا ، دَرَجَاتٍ مِنْهُ وَمَغْفِرَةً وَرَحْمَةً ، وَكَانَ اللَّهُ غَفُورًا رَحِيمًا . (النساء ٩٥)

"The believers who, without a reasonable excuse, sit at home, cannot equal those who perform "jehad" in the path of Allah with their lives and wealth. Allah has raised the status of those who perform "jehad" with their lives and wealth as compared to those who stay at home. To the former, He has promised a blessed abode; Allah has exalted the "Mujahideen" over those who stay at home, with glorious reward: pompous ranks, His mercy and forgiveness; and Allah is Forgiving and Merciful."

Although the above verse refers to "jehad" (holy war) against the infidels and unbelievers in order to uphold the teachings of Islam and subdue and subjugate faithlessness and "shirk" and, although we are unfortunate in not having the opportunity of fulfilling that sublime task, we ought not to throw away any chance of doing something, howsoever small, in the direction of propagating the truth. Only then can we expect that one day our humble efforts and insignificant perseverance may gather momentum and impetus for bigger and higher performances.

وَالَّذِينَ جَاهَدُوا فِينَا لَنَهْدِيَنَّهُمْ سُبُلَنَا (العنكبوت ٦٩)

Undoubtedly Allah Ta'ala has promised to provide protection for the way of life propagated by Hadhrat Mohammad (sallallaho alaihe wasallam). But, human effort and perseverance have been defined as the only media for its promotion and advancement. The Companions of the Holy Prophet (sallallaho alaihe wasallam) strove untiringly for that purpose and, assuredly, they succeeded and were the recipients of high rewards. They had the honour of receiving Divine help and assistance. We, being their admirers and believers, ought to try and follow them and prepare ourselves for the propagation of the "Kalimah" and the message of Allah Ta'ala. Thus, we will also be favoured with Divine help and assistance:

إِنْ تَنْصُرُوا اللَّهَ يَنْصُرْكُمْ وَيُثَبِّتْ أَقْدَامَكُمْ (محمد ٧)

"If you (come forward to) help the religion of Allah Ta'ala, He shall help you and make you steadfast."

FOURTH

Most of us think that, as we ourselves do not possess the essential virtues and qualities of Islam, we are not competent to perform the duty of propagation of those qualities among others. This is a clear misunderstanding Since an obligation has to be fulfilled, particularly when we have been commanded by Allah Ta'ala for that task, there can be no question of denying obedience to it. We must set ourselves to work in obedience to Divine command. Our efforts then shall, "Insha Allah", gather greater strength and make us more determined and resolute. In this way, our sustained endeavour on proper lines will one day bring us the great honour of being dear to Allah Ta'ala. It is against the convention and the Sunnat of Allah Ta'ala that, if one perseveres and strives for His sake (religion), He would not, condescend to bestow favours and kindnesses because the person was not competent or fit for the task! This point is fully brought out in the following Hadis:

عَنْ أَنَسٍ قَالَ قُلْنَا يَا رَسُولَ اللّٰهِ لَا نَأْمُرُ بِالْمَعْرُوفِ حَتّٰى نَعْمَلَ بِهِ كُلِّهِ ، وَلَا نَنْهٰى عَنِ الْمُنْكَرِ حَتّٰى نَجْتَنِبَهُ كُلَّهُ ، فَقَالَ صَلَّى اللّٰهُ عَلَيْهِ وَسَلَّمَ: بَلْ مُرُوا بِالْمَعْرُوفِ وَإِنْ لَمْ تَعْمَلُوا بِهِ كُلِّهِ ، وَانْهَوا عَنِ الْمُنْكَرِ وَإِنْ لَمْ تَجْتَنِبُوهُ كُلَّهُ . (رواه الطبراني في الأوسط)

Hadhrat Anas (radiallaho anho) relates: "We inquired of the Holy Prophet: 'O Prophet of Allah, is it right that we should not enjoin virtue unless we practise all the virtues ourselves, and should not forbid the wrongs unless we ourselves completely abstain from them all? 'Nay,' said the Prophet, 'do enjoin others to practise good deeds even though you do not practise all of them, and do forbid evil actions even though you do not abstain from them all'."

FIFTH

Most of us take it for granted that the religious schools, the "Ulema", the saints who have their seats at various religious places (Khanqah), and the religious books and magazines are sufficient activities for the fulfilment of the mission of "Amr bil ma'ruf wa nahi anil munkar" (Tabligh). These efforts, they think, are enough to meet the requirements of Tabligh. Undoubtedly, the presence of all these is absolutely essential and one must look upon them with reverence and pay attention to their problems, as the traces of Islam that exist today owe their existence to these very institutions, but they are not enough to meet the situation even partially. The task is stupenduous, considering our present weaknesses and the extent of the problem. To be content with the existence of these few means will be a grave folly on our part.

Even to derive full benefit from these institutions, we have to create, within ourselves, a true and a deep respect for the faith of Islam and a burning desire to adopt it in our practical life. Up to fifty years back, people did possess real love, urge and passion for Islam, and there were visible signs and manifestations of Islamic way of life. In those days these institutions could perhaps meet the demand adequately. But, today all our sentiments and feelings for Islam are practically dead, because of the continuous onslaught on our faith and social structure by various foreign elements and forces. Alas! they have succeeded in their object! As, instead of love, we seem to possess a hidden inferiority complex towards our religion and faith! Obviously, therefore, we must act quickly and wrest the initiative from the hands of opposite forces and launch a strong counter-effort, whereby we are able to revive the dead spirit of each and every Muslim and rekindle in him the love and attachment for Islam. Only then can we derive full benefit from the existing religious institutions which, in turn, can serve the community in a befitting manner. Unless such steps are taken vigorously, the present state of complacency will spread deep and wide, and instead of these institutions, which are doing good in this limited way, may meet the fate of total extinction.

SIXTH

There is a great misunderstanding that, whenever one takes up the work of enjoining good and forbidding evil, he is not received well by the people. The people invariably treat him badly, using harsh and insulting language. Also, that sometimes people tend to adopt a mean and contemptuous attitude towards religious workers. This is true, but we are apt to forget the fact that the performance of the act of propagation means simply to follow in the footsteps of the Prophets of Allah Ta'ala, who were always the victims of the worst type of treatment. That is the usual and destined disposition of those who take to this mission! Indeed, all Prophets had to suffer untold miseries on account of this, as is clear from the following verse:

وَلَقَدْ أَرْسَلْنَا مِنْ قَبْلِكَ فِي شِيَعِ الْأَوَّلِينَ ، وَمَا يَأْتِيهِمْ مِنْ رَسُولٍ إِلَّا كَانُوا بِهِ يَسْتَهْزِءُونَ . (الحجر ١٠)

"And We sent down Prophets before you amongst people gone by, and no Prophet came to them but that they ridiculed him."

The Holy Prophet (sallallaho alaihe wasallam) once remarked:

"No Prophet has suffered more than me in the propagation of truth."

It is obvious therefore that there is no justification for giving rise to such misunderstanding. As we profess to be the followers of Hadhrat Mohammad (sallallaho alaihe wasallam) who himself had suffered in the performance of this very mission, but took everything cheerfully and with forbearance, we must also follow his sublime examples and show patience and calmness while performing the vital duty of "Tabligh"

SOLUTION

It has been clearly brought out in the preceding pages that the current disease in the body of Muslims has sprung from the extinction of the true spirit of Islam in our hearts. As a result, real sentiments and love for Islam are practically dead in us and our belief in it has dissipated. Obviously, when the very source becomes dry, the channels of virtue, good deeds and fine attributes, which can flow from it, are not to be seen any longer. This is exactly what is evident today. It has been fully discussed and brought out earlier that the only means for the building up of this source, and maintining a constantly proper flow of religious benefits from it, is the act of "Tabligh", which really and truly is the life-blood of Islam. Unless we are able to revive it, we cannot achieve anything in this life because no nation or people can rise to glory without having in them the high human attributes and character which only the religion of Islam can give.

We should now clearly feel the disease from which we suffer and judge the treatment which can bring the remedy. It is now up to us to set about the revival of the obligatory task of "Tabligh". It will be only then that we can hope to regenerate the true faith of Islam in the masses. By this means alone can we recognise and truly understand both Allah Ta'ala and His Holy Prophet, Hadhrat Mohammad (sallallaho alaihe wasallam), and will be able to clearly understand and finally submit to their commands and wishes. To achieve all this, we will have to adopt the exact methods and ways which are laid down and were demonstrated by the Holy Prophet (sallallaho alaihe wasallam) himself when he reformed the pagan Arabs. Allah Ta'ala says in the Quran:

لَقَدْ كَانَ لَكُمْ فِي رَسُولِ اللّٰهِ أُسْوَةٌ حَسَنَةٌ (الأحزاب ٢١)

"Indeed the Holy Prophet (sallallaho alaihe wasallam) is the perfect example for you to follow."

In this very connection, Hadhrat Imam Malik (rahmatullah alaihi) said:

لَن يُصْلِحَ آخِرَ هٰذِهِ الْأُمَّةِ إِلَّا مَا أَصْلَحَ أَوَّلَهَا

Reformation of the last (part) of this (Mohammad's) Ummat will not be possible except by adopting the method which was used in the beginning (by Hadhrat Mohammad sallallaho alaihe wasallam).

In the beginning, when the Holy Prophet (sallallaho alaihe wasallam) had started to call the people to Islam, he did not have a single supporter behind him nor had he any political power or possessions. The Pagan Arabs were arrogantly independent and self-opinionated. No one among them was prepared to listen to reason or truth or obey another person. They strongly disliked and were deadly opposed to the "Kalimah-tul-Haq", which the Holy Prophet (sallallaho alaihe wasallam) had the sole mission to teach. In these circumstances, one wonders what gave such invisible power and force to that one single man, who was wordly poor and without any means, that he eventually was able to draw the whole of the Arab nation towards him. First we ought to carefully think and see what was it towards which he beckoned the people; initially they refused, but came running towards him as soon as they perceived the light, and stood by him so close that they never left him again. It was the message of Eternal Truth to which he called!–that and only that (Truth), which was the Holy Prophet's (sallallaho alaihe wasallam) sole mission and aim in life–and which he so beautifully presented to the people! It is:

أَن لَّا نَعْبُدَ إِلَّا اللّٰهَ وَلَا نُشْرِكَ بِهِ شَيْئًا وَّلَا يَتَّخِذَ بَعْضُنَا بَعْضًا أَرْبَابًا مِّنْ دُونِ اللّٰهِ (آل عمران ٦٤)

"That we worship nothing but Allah, and associate none with Him as His compeer or rival, and none of us considers another god except Allah."

The propagation of that same very truth can bring the very same results again.

The Holy Prophet (sallallaho alaihe wasallam) forbade his followers from looking upon any 'Being' except Allah

Ta'ala for worship or obedience. Not only did he succeed in achieving his aim, but was able to cut all ties between his followers and every alien element, and bound his people in one uniform system of life from which they never tried to break away again. They really became the picture of:

اِتَّبِعُوا مَا أُنْزِلَ إِلَيْكُم مِّن رَّبِّكُمْ وَلَا تَتَّبِعُوا مِنْ دُونِهِ أَوْلِيَاءَ (الأعراف ٣)

"Follow that which has been sent to you from the Sustainer, and do not follow others (considering them) as Protectors except Allah Ta'ala."

This was the real lesson, which the Holy Prophet (sallallaho alaihe wasallam) had been commanded (by Allah Ta'ala) to teach and spread. It is further clear from the following verse:

أُدْعُ إِلى سَبِيلِ رَبِّكَ بِالْحِكْمَةِ وَالْمَوْعِظَةِ الْحَسَنَةِ وَجَادِلْهُمْ بِالَّتِي هِيَ أَحْسَنُ ، إِنَّ رَبَّكَ هُوَ أَعْلَمُ بِمَنْ ضَلَّ عَنْ سَبِيلِهِ وَهُوَ أَعْلَمُ بِالْمُهْتَدِينَ . (النحل ١٢٥)

"O Muhammad! invite people to your Lord with wisdom and better counsel, and argue with them in such wise as is best; verily your Lord knows the one who wanders astray from His path, and He knows those who are on the right path."

The highway marked for the progress of the Holy Prophet (sallallaho alaihe wasallam) and his followers is further declared in the following verses:

قُلْ هٰذِهِ سَبِيلِي أَدْعُوا إِلَى اللّٰهِ عَلَى بَصِيرَةٍ أَنَا وَمَنِ اتَّبَعَنِي وَسُبْحَانَ اللّٰهِ وَمَا أَنَا مِنَ الْمُشْرِكِينَ . (يوسف ١٠٨)

وَمَنْ أَحْسَنُ قَوْلًا مِّمَّنْ دَعَا إِلَى اللّٰهِ وَعَمِلَ صَالِحًا وَقَالَ إِنَّنِي مِنَ الْمُسْلِمِينَ . (حم السجدة ٣٣)

"O Muhammad! say, this is my path, and I invite you towards Allah Ta'ala knowingly, I and my followers too: and Allah is all pure and never will I join partners with Allah."

"And who is better in speech than one who invites you towards Allah Ta'ala, does good deeds and says, verily, I am of those who submit their will to Allah."

To call mankind to Allah Ta'ala and show the right path to all those who had gone astray was the only mission and the sole purpose of the Holy Prophet's (sallallaho alaihe wasallam) life. To serve this very purpose, thousands of prophets had been deputed before him. As Allah Ta'ala says:

وَمَا أَرْسَلْنَا مِنْ قَبْلِكَ مِنْ رَّسُولٍ إِلَّا نُوحِي إِلَيْهِ أَنَّهُ لَا إِلٰهَ إِلَّا أَنَا فَاعْبُدُونِ . (الأنبياء ٢٥)

"And We did not send any Prophet before you, but that We revealed upon him that verily there is no god but Me and so worship Me."

The sacred biography of Hadhrat Mohammad (sallallaho alaihe wasallam) and also those of other Prophets indicate one single aim as the sole mission of their lives: i.e., to believe in One True Allah Ta'ala and His one Divine Personality and His Attributes. This belief is the essence of the faith of Islam. It was to practise and demonstrate this very faith that man has been sent on this earth, as will be seen from this verse:

وَمَا خَلَقْتُ الْجِنَّ وَالْإِنْسَ إِلَّا لِيَعْبُدُونِ (الذاريات ٥٦)

"And We have not created the genii and human beings but to worship Me only."

We should by now ought to be able to understand the real purpose for the creation of man and the way we, particularly Muslims, should live; we also know the true disease from which we suffer and its treatment; it should, therefore, not be difficult then to find out how to apply that treatment and regain our lost vitality. If we bear in our mind all that has been discussed so far, and with that background act sincerely, any method adopted will "Insha Allah" prove to be beneficial and successful. However, a proven successful method is described.

COURSE OF ACTION

With the very limited knowledge and understanding that I have about such a vital matter as "Tabligh" (enjoining good and forbidding evil), a scheme of work and action is described below, for the improvement of Muslims and their progress in Islam. Actually, what I have to say is nothing else than a brief outline of the practical way of life which had been followed by our ancestors and early Muslims.

The FIRST and the FOREMOST thing to do is to change the aim of our life, from material motives and acquisition of wealth, to the propagation and spreading of Allah Ta'ala's "Kalimah" and Islam; to fix as a definite objective for ourselves, the enforcement of the commands and orders of Allah Ta'ala; and to sincerely resolve: I will obey every command of Allah Ta'ala, shall try to practise it in my daily life and will not disobey Allah Ta'ala in any circumstances. The fulfilment of this resolution must be made the main aim of life. We can plan and act on this broad base by adopting the following practical scheme and procedure:

(1) To memorise and correctly recite the "Kalimah":

لَا إِلٰهَ إِلَّا اللّٰهُ مُحَمَّدٌ رَّسُولُ اللّٰهِ

And to understand its literal meaning, as well as what it actually implies.

That is, to believe, to say, and to act on the faith that Allah Ta'ala is the only Power, the only Authority and the Sole Controller of all things, and it is He alone who is to be worshipped and obeyed, and it is He alone who grants success or failure in life. Success will depend on our truly adopting the way of life preached and taught by Hadhrat Mohammad (sallallaho alaihe wasallam) and our accepting him as true and last Prophet of Allah.

Having this as ideal, we begin to change our own life on the pattern requirements of the "Kalimah"

(2) To become punctual and regular in offering our prayers *(namaz)* five times a day. The performance of this most obligatory duty ought to be strictly in accordance with the procedure laid down by Hadhrat Mohammad (sal-

lallaho alaihe wasallam), to be performed in utmost humility and supplication. The greatness and superiority of Allah Ta'ala must be held uppermost in mind throughout the prayers, whilst maintaining the feelings of one's own humbleness and helplessness. In other words, "namaz" should be performed as if one was actually being presented to Allah Ta'ala in a manner befitting the Height of His Greatness and Glory. If the procedure of "namaz" is not known, it ought to be learnt properly with each detail committed to memory.

(3) To develop attachment of body and soul to the *Holy Quran* in the following manner:

(a) To recite daily a portion of the Quran, however small, with highest respect and reverence for the holy scripture and by understanding its meaning, if possible. If one is unable to understand the meaning, he may still recite the text with the purpose and hope that his salvation and progress depends on it. Simple recitation of the original words and lines is also a great blessing. If a person is unable to read, he ought to spend a litle time daily to learn to read.

(b) To ensure that one's own children as well as those of the neighbours and friends are taught the Holy Quran and other essential religious books as a first step in their learning.

(4) Some time should be devoted each day to *zikr*, which means concentrating on the Omnipotence, the Greatness, and the Attributes of Allah Ta'ala, and to offer DUROOD [prayers] for the Holy Prophet (sallallaho alaihe wasallam). In this connection, guidance should be sought from a "Sheikh-e-Tariqat" (a learned and saintly person), who should be carefully selected for his distinction in piety and his capacity to follow "Shariat" and "Sunnah". He may prescribe certain "Wazaif" (special verses) to be recited during the times of "Zikr". In case no such holy person can be contacted, it is suggested that the following "Wazaif" may be repeated a hundred times (one tasbih of 100 beads) each, both in the morning and in the evening:

(a) *Third Kalimah,*

سُبْحَانَ اللهِ وَالْحَمْدُ لِلّٰهِ وَلَا إِلٰهَ إِلَّا اللهُ وَاللهُ أَكْبَرُ وَلَا حَوْلَ وَلَا قُوَّةَ إِلَّا بِاللهِ الْعَلِيِّ الْعَظِيمِ

(b) *Durood* (praying blessings for the prophet).

(c) *Istighfar* (seeking forgiveness of Allah).

(5) Every Muslim must be considered as one's real brother and must always be given affection, sympathy and sincere attention at all times, particularly when he is in need. The fact that a person professes the faith of Islam automatically entitles him to brotherly respect and reverence from all Muslims, who must at all times refrain from causing him any physical or mental harm.

The above practices should be strictly enforced in one's own life and, at the same time, efforts should be made so that other people may follow them as well. The only and the best way to achieve this is to devote some time specially for learning and inculcating in oneself these fine Islamic qualities, and also persuading others to make similar efforts. Thus a joint and collective campaign will automatically ensure for the growth and expansion of Islam in its true form, which is the real and urgent need of the day.

It was exactly this type of work, which every Prophet of Allah Ta'ala had to do as his sole occupation. For the sake of this work, almost all Prophets had to bear untold miseries and perils. The worthy Companions of Hadhrat Mohammad (sallallaho alaihe wasallam), as well as many other distinguished Muslims of the early period of Islam, spent the whole of their lives in striving hard and struggling for the religion of Islam in this very manner. Most of them sacrificed their lives in the sacred path of Allah Ta'ala. It will be our misfortune and enormous loss if we do not devote a part of our lifetime, however small a period it may be, towards propagating and perpetuating Islam. We must confess that it is due to our negligence in this vital task that the Muslim society has reached its present state of low morale and virtual collapse and, therefore, we must rise and make manifold efforts.

Previously, the very purpose of being a Muslim was to be ready to lay down one's life, honour and wealth for upholding Islam and the *Kalimah*. In those days, if anyone did not do that, he was considered to be ignorant and a useless fellow. But alas! today, although we feel proud to be called Muslims, we remain totally unmoved by the fact that every particle of Islam is being destroyed one by one before our very eyes, and not a finger is moved to check this terrible loss. If we realise this we can appreciate that the propagation of Islam is our real mission in life, and therein lies our very existence as Muslims and also our success, glory and ultimate salvation. The opposite is also true that by neglecting this important task we suffer from moral degeneration and social degradation. The only remedy for this is that all of us must sincerely repent our lethargic and injurious past and take immediate steps to revive the act of *Tabligh* as our major occupation. It is only then that we can expect the mercy and compassion of Allah Ta'ala to flow, to bring us triumph and happiness both in this life and the hereafter.

This does not mean that we should give up everything else, i.e., our profession–trade or employment and take entirely to this work. It really means that, as we devote our whole-hearted attention and time to other material vocations, we should also attend to this work. As and when some persons find themselves ready to take up this sacred task, they should try to contact their friends or such persons in their neighbourhood who may already be engaged in this work and spend a few hours a week in their company. The next step will be to spend, under the guidance of those people, full three days every month outside in a locality or a village other than one's own. Later, but as early as possible, to pass one full month, or better still, forty days annually in some distant area in similar manner. Lastly, the real requirement in "Tabligh" is to spend continuously four months once in the lifetime, in a given place or area. All these periods are to be spent entirely in the pursuit of learning and propagation of the true faith of Islam and adopting the actual way of life under the Sacred code of "Shariat". Thus our efforts will become extensive and ultimately reach every person, rich and poor, employer and employee, Land-Lord and Peasant, learned and ignorant, to join hands in this work and become bound in the ties of true Islam as ordained by Allah Ta'ala and the Holy Prophet Mohammad (sallallaho alaihe wasallam).

PROCEDURE TO WORK

The most important factor in the task of Tabligh is the manner and the method of approach, which simply means to follow closely the lines adopted by the worthy Companions of the Holy Prophet (sallallaho alaihe wasallam) strictly in accordance with his teachings and practices. The method adopted by the Holy Prophet (sallallaho alaihe wasallam) was as follows:

A jamaat or group of at least ten men should be formed. One of them should be selected "amir" (leader). They should get together in a mosque, make ablutions and offer two *rakaat 'nafil' prayers. After this, all should supplicate together and beseech for Divine mercy, help and guidance for success in their efforts and remaining steadfast and resolute in their task of Tabligh. For all this time, "zikr" should be recited by all, and every precaution should be taken not to indulge in idle talk. On reaching the place for "Tabligh", once again the "jamaat" should supplicate and beseech for Allah Ta'ala's mercy and help in their mission. The place of Tabligh will be the vicinity of a mosque of the locality where the work is to be conducted. A part of the "jamaat" should be detailed to tour the locality calmly, and quietly inviting people to the mosque, where "ta'leem, (reading and teaching out of religious books) should be in progress and later the "namaz" (prayers) of the time should be offered. After this, one of the members of the "jamaat" should place before the people, in an affectionate and calm manner, the importance and urgency of reviving Islam in each and every Muslim as ordained by Allah Ta'ala and the Holy Prophet (sallallaho alaihe wasallam), giving out as simply as possible the cardinal points of Tabligh and the way to accomplish them. Finally, the people should be persuaded, again in a cordial manner, to join hands in this sacred task and come out to do the work of Tabligh like the Jamaat itself.

Later, some members of the "jamaat" may accompany the people to their homes, where the womenfolk should also be addressed and persuaded to do similar duty among women.

* In formal prayers, a rakaat means one complete action comprising standing, kneeling and bowing by placing the forehead on the ground, two "rakaat" means two such actions.

They should be told to be regular in their daily prayers. All this should be done without entering the private portion of any house. The women should also be told to strictly follow the cardinal points of "Tabligh" in their daily life and observe "pardah" in accordance with the "Shriat"

After this, all such people who may be prepared to join the work should be organized into a separate "jamaat", with and "amir" from among themselves. They should first be made to work under the guidance of the members of the original "jamaat". The important point to be remembered at this stage is that every person engaged on "Tabligh" must fully obey his "amir" and the latter, in turn, should ensure that his personal services and attention are available to each and every member of his Jamaat. He must see to every person's welfare, comforts and morale and, before taking any decision, he must consult all his colleagues. The following general principles of the work of "Tabligh" should be carefully noted at all times.

GENERAL PRINCIPLES

In its real form and sense, "Tabligh" is the most important type of worship of Allah Ta'ala and it amounts to a blessing of very high order. It literally means to follow in the footsteps of the Prophets. Truly, as the work is of a very superior character, it must be based on equally high principles, which ought to be strictly followed throughout. Each participant must feel that it is he who needs to improve himself rather than thinking of reforming others. During the course of work and, even away from it, he must try to behave as a perfect Muslim, as a faithful slave of Allah Ta'ala, constantly obeying and following the Divine commands of "Shariat" and always seeking Allah Ta'ala's mercy and pleasure. This is the basic requirement and the soul and foundation of the work of "Tabligh". Once it is deeply and firmly embedded in the hearts of workers, the other principles, rules and practices, some of which are narrated below, will become easy to follow:

(1) As far as possible, all expenses, including travelling, food etc., must be borne by each individual himself and, if he can afford, he may quietly assist those companions who may be in need.

(2) All fellow workers and companions in this work must be given full respect, shown tolerance, be cared for and encouraged at all times by one another. Such participation will prove a great blessing for the whole area where the "jamaat" may be working.

(3) Conversations, talks and discussions must be conducted in soft and persuasive tones, using simple and polite language. All types of displeasure with each other must be avoided. The "ulema-e-karam" (scholars of Muslim scripture) must be held in high respect and esteem as we usually display for the "Holy Quran" and "Hadis", because, it is through these learned personages that Allah Ta'ala has blessed us with the true knowledge of Islam and enlightenment. Any disrespect towards them, however insignificant, may amount to contempt of Islam itself, which in turn may provoke the wrath of Allah Ta'ala for the whole community.

(4) Leisure and free moments must be spent either in reading good religious books or in the company of pious and learned companions; by this means one will be able to learn many right things about the faith of Islam, about Allah Ta'ala and His apostle. Particular care must be taken of the time given to the "Tabligh" work itself, that nothing unimportant, useless or senseless is uttered, discussed or done.

(5) To endeavour to earn an honest and pure living, to be most careful and frugal in expenditure, and to constantly observe every single obligation, however big or small, towards one's family, relations and acquaintances.

(6) No controversial matters or points of secondary importance be discussed at any time. The total time must be devoted to bringing out the Divinity, Oneness and Omnipotence of Allah Ta'ala and to confine all talk to the main points of "Tabligh", which are in real sense the basic principles to be followed by each and every Muslim at all times.

(7) Every action, work and speech must be fused with sincerity and honesty of purpose, for an act, however small, but imbued with this quality is destined to bring high rewards and plenty of well-being. On the other hand, an insincere act, however big, will not bear any worthwhile fruit or benefit, either in this life or in the hereafter. Hadh-

rat Mu'az (Radi Allaho anho), who was appointed as Governor of Yemen, begged the Holy Prophet (sallallaho alaihe wasallam) to give him some special advice. The Holy Prophet (sallallaho alaihe wasallam) was pleased to say, "Be meticulously honest and sincere in matters of religion: a little done with sincerity is enough". There is yet another "Hadis" in the same connection, "Allah Ta'ala accepts only such actions and deeds which are performed purely for His pleasure and accord". In another place it is mentioned "Allah Ta'ala does not look at your face nor at your property, but only at your hearts and deeds". So the crux of the matter is that the work of "Tabligh" must be performed with all sincerity and honesty. No show or outward appearance is to be put on. The degree of success and progress will depend entirely on the depth of our sincerity.

SUMMARY AND CONCLUSION

A brief sketch of the work of "Tabligh", its importance and urgent need have been discussed. It now remains to be judged as to how all this can guide us and bring us the desired relief and benefits in these times, which are fraught with confusion, unrest and rivalries.

For this, once again, we have to seek guidance from the allwise "Holy Quran", which refers to the hard work and endurance for the faith of Islam as a highly profitable business, and puts it across in the following manner:

يَا أَيُّهَا الَّذِينَ آمَنُوا هَلْ أَدُلُّكُمْ عَلَى تِجَارَةٍ تُنْجِيكُمْ مِنْ عَذَابٍ أَلِيمٍ ، تُؤْمِنُونَ بِاللّٰهِ وَرَسُولِهِ وَتُجَاهِدُونَ فِي سَبِيلِ اللّٰهِ بِأَمْوَالِكُمْ وَأَنْفُسِكُمْ ، ذٰلِكُمْ خَيْرٌ لَّكُمْ إِنْ كُنْتُمْ تَعْلَمُونَ ، يَغْفِرْ لَكُمْ ذُنُوبَكُمْ وَيُدْخِلْكُمْ جَنّٰتٍ تَجْرِي مِنْ تَحْتِهَا الْأَنْهَارُ ، وَمَسَاكِنَ طَيِّبَةً فِي جَنّٰتِ عَدْنٍ ، ذٰلِكَ الْفَوْزُ الْعَظِيمُ ، وَأُخْرَى تُحِبُّونَهَا نَصْرٌ مِّنَ اللّٰهِ وَفَتْحٌ قَرِيبٌ ، وَبَشِّرِ الْمُؤْمِنِينَ . (الصّف ١٠ - ١٣)

> "O you who believe! shall I point out to you a trade that will shield you from a grievous doom? Believe in Allah and His Messenger, and perform "jehad" in His way with your wealth and lives. This is best for you, if you understand. Your Lord will forgive your sins, and you shall enter Paradise, under which ripple (beauteous) streams, and stately abodes in everlasting gardens; and this is great success . . .
>
> And another which you covet much, i.e., succour from Allah and victory near at hand; and give glad tidings to those who believe."

The above verse describes a trade, which if accepted promises deliverance from all types of afflictions and punishments. The trade is meant: to have a firm faith in Allah Ta'ala and His Apostle and to struggle hard in the path of Allah, without shirking to use one's life and wealth. This again points to the act of "Tabligh", which can ensure for us everlasting well-being and happiness. It is this simple work which will bring us great benefits, such as the forgiveness for all our sins, deliberate mistakes and shortcomings and high rewards in the life hereafter. So much for the success in the next life, which really is the greatest triumph for a Muslim, but there is also clear hint for this life too. We shall get what we cherish most, such as prosperity, divine help and success against all our adversaries!

In other words, Allah Ta'ala has demanded two things from us, firstly to have firm faith in Him and His Apostle, secondly, to struggle hard in His path, giving, if need be, our lives and all that we possess. In return for this, He has also promised two things: first a beautiful and peaceful abode in Heaven (Jannat) with an eternal life, and everlasting happiness: and second, glory and success in this life. The first demand on us is that of faith (eiman). This is exactly what the "Tabligh" is meant to bring to us, that we should all be endowed with the wealth of true faith. The second demand is that of striving in the path of Allah, which actually means "jehad". Jehad may normally mean fighting a war against oppressors and non-believers. In the practical sense, however, it means spreading of Kalimah of Allah and enforcing of Allah's Commandments, which is also the ultimate aim of "Tabligh".

It should be clear to us now that the happiness and success in the life after death is solely dependent on having firm faith in Allah Ta'ala and His Apostle, and in striving hard in the path laid down by Him. Similarly, the success and prosperity in this life too depend entirely on that very faith and on spending all our efforts in the path of Allah Ta'ala.

When we fulfil these basic requirements, firstly of faith in Allah Ta'ala and His Apostle, and secondly of struggling hard in their path, through these two attributes alone, we can adorn ourselves with high moral virtues and excellence of character. Only then can we fit to receive the promised vicegerency of Allah Ta'ala and His kingdom on earth, which are bound to come as is promised in the Holy Quran:

وَعَدَ اللّٰهُ الَّذِينَ آمَنُوا مِنْكُمْ وَعَمِلُوا الصَّالِحَاتِ لَيَسْتَخْلِفَنَّهُمْ فِي الْأَرْضِ كَمَا
اسْتَخْلَفَ الَّذِينَ مِنْ قَبْلِهِمْ ، وَلَيُمَكِّنَنَّ لَهُمْ دِينَهُمُ الَّذِي ارْتَضَى لَهُمْ وَلَيُبَدِّلَنَّهُمْ
مِنْ بَعْدِ خَوْفِهِمْ أَمْنًا ، يَعْبُدُونَنِي لَا يُشْرِكُونَ بِي شَيْئًا . (النور ٥٥)

"To those of you who believe and do righteous deeds, Allah promises that He will certainly give dominance to them in this world as He gave to those before you; and the religion that has been chosen for them shall be strengthened for them, and He will thereafter certainly transform their fear into tranquillity, provided they worship Me and associate none with Me."

The above verse portrays a forthright promise of kingdom, but through "eiman" (firm faith) and righteous deeds. This was actually fulfilled in the days of the Holy Prophet (sallallaho alaihe wasallam) and remained in effect right through the period on the "Khulfa-e-Rashidin" (the first four Caliphs after the Holy Prophet (sallallaho alaihe wasallam). Practically the whole of Arabia had become an Islamic State in the days of the Holy Prophet (sallallaho alaihe wasallam) himself and the rest of the countries (Muslim countries of today) mostly joined Islam during the period of "Khulfa-e-Rashdin" or immediately after their time. Later on too, the promise continued to be fulfilled in favour of a number of Muslim kings and "Khalifas" and it still awaits materialisation if someone fulfils the conditions, as is clear from the next verse:

فَإِنَّ حِزْبَ اللّٰهِ هُمُ الْغَالِبُونَ (المائدة ٥٦)

"Surely Allahs followers shall dominate"

In these few pages, an analysis of the present situation and a practical solution for improving it has been given; in fact the solution is nothing else than the actual Islamic way of life, which belonged to our forefathers and early Muslims.

CONCLUSION

In conclusion, it can be said that there is no way to gain honour, happiness, peace and tranquillity in this life other than to adopt and firmly hold on to the work and system of "Tabligh", for which everyone of us must use all his energies and wealth.

وَاعْتَصِمُوا بِحَبْلِ اللّٰهِ جَمِيعًا وَّلَا تَفَرَّقُوا (آل عمران ١٠٣)

"Hold fast to the rope of Allah and do not create dissensions."

FINAL APPEAL

This very system has actually been put into practice, in the recent past, in the territory of Mewat (an area of Alwar

State) and a few other districts around Delhi (India). The work in that region, has not yet reached the final stage; the progress of the local Muslims, however, has been quite marked. The blessing and benefits of the system of "Tabligh" are clearly visible and worth witnessing. If all Muslims collectively resolve to follow the noble example mentioned above and adopt the correct system of life, as described in this book, there is every hope that, through that effort, Allah Ta'ala may obviate all our miseries and adversities and we may be able to regain our faith, the power to do righteous deeds and the resultant honour, dignity and glory in this life and attain permanent salvation in the next. The Muslims can then set an example for the rest of the World to live in peace, tranquillity and happiness, which is the natural desire of every man on earth.

An attempt has been made to explain as early as possible the real purpose behind the writing of this book, which is to present to the readers the sketch of a practical way of life, which about thirty years ago had been initiated and vigorously followed by Hadhrat Maulana Mohammad Ilyas Sahib, "rahmatullah alaih". He had in fact dedicated all his life for this sacred purpose and mission. It is up to us, the Muslims of the present time, to understand our obligations towards Islam and fulfil them in our own interest and that of the coming generations and the mankind at large. The way is clear and well set. Let us begin the march and fix our minds on the final goal, which is to acquire the pleasure and approval of Allah Ta'ala.

میری قسمت سے الٰہی پائیں یہ رنگ قبول
پھول کچھ میں نے چنے ہیں انکے دامن کیلئے

وَآخِرُ دَعْوَانَا اَنِ الْحَمْدُ لِلّٰهِ رَبِّ الْعَالَمِيْنَ ، وَالصَّلٰوةُ وَالسَّلَامُ عَلٰى رَسُوْلِهٖ مُحَمَّدٍ
وَّآلِهٖ وَأَصْحَابِهٖ أَجْمَعِيْنَ ، بِرَحْمَتِهٖ يَا أَرْحَمَ الرَّاحِمِيْنَ

Nuh) and a few other districts around Delhi (India). The work in that region has not yet reached the final stage; the progress of the local Muslims, however, has been quite marked. The blessing and benefits of the system of 'Tabligh' are clearly visible and worth witnessing. If all Muslims collectively resolve to follow the noble footsteps mentioned above and adopt the correct system of life as described in this book, there is every hope that through that effort, Allah Ta'ala may remove all our miseries and adversities and we may be able to regain our faith, the power to do righteous deeds and the resultant honour, dignity and glory in this life and attain permanent salvation in the next. The Muslims can then set an example for the rest of the World to live in peace, tranquillity and happiness which is the natural desire of every human on earth.

An attempt has been made to explain as fully as possible the real purpose behind the writing of this book, which is to present to the readers the sketch of a practical way of life, which about thirty years ago had been initiated and vigorously followed by Hadhrat Maulana Mohammad Ilyas (rah) 'rahmatullahi alaih'. He had in fact dedicated all his life for this sacred purpose and mission. It is up to us, the Muslims of the present time, to understand our obligations towards Islam and fulfil them in our own interest and that of the coming generations and the mankind at large. The way is clear and well set. Let us begin the march and fix our minds on the final goal which is to acquire the pleasure and approval of Allah Ta'ala.

[illegible]

[illegible]

[illegible]

[illegible]

Six FUNDAMENTALS

چھ ٦ باتیں

By
Maulana Aashiq Ilaahi (Rah)

ادارہ اشاعتِ دینیات (پرائیویٹ) لمیٹڈ
idara.com IDARA ISHA'AT-E-DINIYAT (P) LTD.

Six FUNDAMENTALS

SIX FUNDAMENTS

By. Maulana Aashiq Ilaahi

Edition 2001

Published by:
IDARA ISHA'AT-E-DINIYAT (P) LTD.
168/2, Jha House, Hazrat Nizamuddin
New Delhi-110 013 (India)
Tel.: 6926832, 6926833
Fax: +91-11-6322787,4352786
Email: **sales@idara.com**
Visit us at: **www.idara.com**

Printed at:
Nice Printing Press, Delhi

بسم الله الرحمن الرحيم

In the name of Allah most Gracious, most Merciful.

First Lesson: Kalimah Tayyibah

لا إله إلا الله محمد رسول الله

Laa ilaaha illallaahu, Muhammadur-Rasulullaah.

This kalimah is just a sacred pledge of man with Allah. That is, when a believer solemnly reads this kalimah, he admits before Allah that he is His sincere and faithful servant, he will obey His commandments, and will avoid all the forbidden things. Therefore, one must keep in mind four important points about this kalimah: First, he should remember its words in the correct form. Second, he should remember its correct translation. Third, he should remember its exact meaning. Fourth, he should observe its practical requirements, and act accordingly!

Its Words and their Translation

This kalimah has two parts; first: "Laa ilaaha illallaah"; second, "Muhammadur-Rasulullaah"; and their translation is:

"No one is worthy of worship but Allah, and Muhammad is His true Messenger."

The Meaning of this Kalimah

When a believer admits that no one is worthy of worship but Allah, it necessarily means that he should worship none in the whole universe, but the Almighty, and should bring no partner to Him in worship, concerning all the principles of Islam. He should believe Him to be his sole guardian and Helper in distress, to be present everywhere, seeing and hearing everything in the world. He should trust in His guidance, and should faithfully obey His commandments; moreover, he should not follow the customs and usages, that are contrary to His commandments. In all the affairs of his life, he should follow the teachings of the Holy Qur'aan; he should hope for His mercy, and should fear His wrath; he should completely rely upon Him for his guidance!

The second part of the kalimah, that is, "Muhammadur, Rasulullaah" means, that after believing in the unity of Allah, when I would desire to follow the commandments of Allah, I cannot do so unless I keep Muhammad (Sallallaho alaihe wasallam) my instructor and guide to the Right Path. That is, I will worship Allah just as he has told me; he is a faithful and true messenger of Allah, who taught us nothing of his own will or desire. The obedience of Rasulullah (Sallallaho alaihe wasallam), is really the obedience of Allah, and love for him, is love for Allah; one must believe that to be obedient to him is an obligatory thing, and he should submit to his orders, without any objection. Whatever he has told us of the unseen things like angels, like Hell, Paradise the incidents in the grave, and the Resurrection, we must believe in them, though we could not understand them. We must believe that the method of living, which he has told us, and has behaved himself accordingly, is the method which has been appreciated by Allah; and anyone who acts contrary to it, does not tread the Right Path, and is not loved by Allah.

The Requisites of Kalimah Tayyibah

When a Muslim has firm faith in the kalimah, undoubtedly he becomes a true believer, and then he has to abandon all the forbidden things, and to observe the commandments of Allah. That is why Rasulullah (Sallallaho alaihe wasallam) has said, "The first effect of 'Laa ilaaha illallaah' is that it should prevent its reader from all the forbidden things." Therefore, the reader of such a sacred kalimah must observe the commandments of Allah on all occasions. He should keep them in mind in marriage, on death, on taking meals, on going to sleep, on waking up, on deals, and on all other occasions; he should faithfully observe the commandments of Allah, and should give up the forbidden things.

The Benefits of the Kalimah

This kalimah has many spiritual benefits. Rasulullah (Sallallaho alaihe wasallam) said, "The most distinguished zikr is 'Laa ilaaha illallaah'. Again he says, "Read the kalimah a hundred times every day, for it is the best compensation for one's sins, and no good deed is better than it." In another hadith he says, "Whoever reads 'Laa ilaaha illallaah' a hundred times in the morning, and a hundred times in the evening shall have the reward of one who has released ten slaves from the posterity of Ismaa-eel (Alayhis salaam)" In another hadith Rasulullah (Sallallaho alaihe wasallam) says, "Keep your faith fresh by reading and observing 'Laa ilaaha illallaah.'"

Second Lesson: Salaat

When a Muslim has firmly believed in Kalimah Tayyibah, he has made a sacred pledge to obey all the commandments of Allah; of which the first and foremost is salaat which must be observed by every adult, male or female, five times a day. In other words, those who perform the prayer regularly, after believing in the kalimah, they practically fulfil their promise with Allah, made through the kalimah; and those who are not regular at the prayer, they practically belie their promise with Allah, to be His faithful servants; of them said Rasulullah (Sallallaho alaihe wasallam) "Whoever abandoned the prayer intentionally, he become an infidel". In another hadith he says, "Whoever gave up the prayer, he will be raised among Qaaroon, Fir'own, his minister Haamaan, and the famous hypocrite Ubayy bin Khalaf, on the Day of Resurrection."

Next to the kalimah, prayer is the most distinguished of all good deeds. It has been mentioned in the hadith that the first thing brought to account on the Day of Judgement, will be the prayer. If one's prayer is perfect in every respect, he will certainly attain salvation, otherwise he will be deprived of all the boons and favours of Allah, and will suffer a great loss. Therefore, one should observe the prayer at the appointed times, with good wudu and complete devotion, that one may not be raised with the infidels, and should be delivered from the hell-fire.

Whatever is read in the Prayer (that is, 'Subhaanak-Allahumma' and Attahiyyaat etc.), should be remembered well, that no mistake should occur during the prayer. One must know the fardh, the sunnah, and all the conditions of prayer, so that it may be correct, and by having concentration, it should be performed well.

A great merit of the prayer is, that all the limbs of a

worshipper, namely, hands, feet, head, waist, nose, forehead, tongue etc., are wholly and solely devoted to Allah, that is, every part of a worshipper's body is engaged in an exercise of the obedience of Allah's commandments. If a Muslim performs the prayer with all its conditions, he is not likely to commit sin by any limb, on times other than the prayer. It has been mentioned in the Holy Qur'aan that the prayer prevents a Muslim from shameful and forbidden things. The believers have been commanded hundreds of times in the Holy Qur'aan to perform the prayer properly. In the hadith also the prayer has been enjoined and emphasised many a time. For instance, Rasulullah (Sallallaho alaihe wasallam) said, "One's sins from one prayer to another are forgiven by Allah".

In another hadith he says, "If one has a stream at one's door, and he has a bath in it, five times a day, he will have no dirt on his body; similarly if one performs the prayer five times a day, his sins will be pardoned by Allah, and he will be clean of them". In another hadith Rasulullah (Sallallaho alaihe wasallam) says, "When your children are seven years old, instruct them to perform the prayer, but when they are ten years old, beat them to perform the prayer."

Prayer with Congregation

Rasulullah (Sallallaho alaihe wasallam) says in a hadith, "The prayer with congregation is granted a reward twenty-seven times more than the prayer performed alone". It has also been mentioned in a hadith that Rasulullah (Sallallaho alaihe wasallam) intended to burn the houses of those who did not visit the musjid to perform the prayer with congregation, but he abstained from doing so, because of children and women. Ibn Mas'ood (Radhiyallaho anho) says, "During the time of Rasulullah (Sallallaho alaihe wasallam) only that hypocrite dared neglect the prayer who was a declared hypocrite." It has also been mentioned in a hadith that peforming the night prayer with congregation begets the reward of prayers till midnight; and performing the morning prayer with congregation, begets the reward of prayers during the whole night.

The right way to perform rukoo' and sajdah

Rasulullah (Sallallaho alaihe wasallam) says in a

hadith, "Allah does not look to the prayer of one, who does not keep his waist straight in the prayer (he prays lazily)". In another hadith he says, "The worst kind of theft is the theft of prayer". His Companions asked, "What is the theft of prayer?" He answered, "The theft of prayer is, not to perform the rukoo' (bending the knees) and sajdah (prostration) properly, with full time and attention."

A prayer out of time

Rasulullah (Sallallaho alaihe wasallam) said, "It is the prayer of a hypocrite to cause delay in prayers, and to wait for sun-set; so when it becomes dull, he gets up to perform it just as a custom, and he remembers Allah but little."

Third Lesson

Knowledge and Zikr

There are two important subjects in this lesson; first, knowledge, second, zikr (that is, remembrance of Allah). There are so many sayings of Rasulullah (Sallallaho alaihe wasallam) which stress the utility and distinction of these two things. For instance, a hadith says, "Beware! This world, and whatever is in it, is cursed by Allah, with the exception of prayers, and zikr, and the religious scholar, and the religious student".

Therefore, every Muslim should try his best to achieve the high standard of knowledge and zikr.

Knowledge

Only that knowledge is appreciated by Allah, which takes a man nearer to Him, and enables him, to observe His commandments. So much knowledge of the religion of Islam, as would purify and strengthen one's faith, is obligatory for every Muslim man and woman. When a servant of Allah has entirely submitted himself to Allah, and has promised to observe His commandments, it is indispensable for him to know all His commandments, and the method of worship. Yes, he should have a perfect knowledge of prayers, fasting, poor-rate, hajj; of mutual dealings in everyday life, the true Islamic culture, and other important aspects of Islamic way of living. Every Muslim should particularly know those basic things about Islam, the ignorance of which is likely to commit sins; and when he has got the knowledge of these things, he must observe them in a practical form, for it has been mentioned in a hadith, "Verily, the worst punishment of Allah will be inflicted on those on the Day of Judgement, who have been scholars of religion, but did not practice it themselves".

The distinction of a scholar and a student

Rasulullah (Sallallaho alaihe wasallam) has said in a hadith, "Anyone who shows the Right Path to a Muslim, is like one who has already observed Allah's commandments". Another hadith says, "A thousand worshippers are not so annyoing and deadly to Shaytaan, as one person who has achieved perfect knowledge about Islam". Another hadith says, "Anyone who died during the period of attaining knowledge about Islam, his class in Jannah will be only one stage below the Ambiyaa". Another hadith says, "The best person among you is he, who has learned the Holy Qur'an and then teaches it to other Muslims". Rasulullah (Sallallaho alaihe wasallam) says in another hadith, "May Allah keep that person fresh and healthy who listens to my instructions, and then delivers them to others, exactly as I have spoken".

To leave home for the sake of knowledge

Rasulullah (Sallallaho alaihe wasallam) has said, "Whoever left his home for the sake of knowledge (about the Holy Qur'aan and Islam), he will be honoured as one, who has entirely devoted himself to Allah".

The service and help for a student of Islam

It has been mentioned in a hadith, that Rasulullah (Sallallaho alaihe wasallam) while addressing his followers said, "Undoubtedly, the coming generation will follow you, for you have followed me. After me people will come to you from remote places to attain the knowledge of Islam. So, when they visit you, it is my will, that you should entertain them well". That is, when the student of Islam visit you, serve them properly, sit in their society, and be courteous to them.

The use of scholarly meetings

Rasulullah (Sallallaho alaihe wasallam) says in a hadith, "When certain people gather together in the House of Allah (that is a musjid), and they read the Book of Allah (i.e., the Holy Qur'aan) to one another, they are blessed with spiritual consolation and Allah's mercy, the Angels assemble around them, and Allah remembers them among His courtiers (Angels)".

Zikr

The second part of the third lesson is zikr. The highest degree of zikr is that a believer should be entirely devoted to Allah, and should never forget Him. This standard of zikr is achieved by constant spiritual exercise, and by continuous remembrance of Allah. Those who have realized the spiritual benefits of zikr, they do not neglect it for a single moment of their life. Rasulullah (Sallallaho alaihe wasallam) instructed a companion of his with the following words, "Keep your tongue always busy with the remembrance of Allah". In another hadith he says, "When some people gather together in an assembly, and then get up without remembering Allah, be sure that they sat around the dead body of an ass, and left it; therefore such an assembly will be a sorrow to them on the Day of Qiyaamah".

The true believers should remember Allah most often, and by contemplating the wonders of His creation, they should glorify Him, and thereby strengthen their love for Him. The more they remember Allah, the better will be their good deeds, the stronger their faith and knowledge. Then, they will have more and more love for Allah, and their service to Him will be more sincere and realistic. Particularly, during the Tabligh journey they should not forget Allah for a single moment. If all the daily prayers, which are mentioned in the hadith, viz, prayer for going to sleep and waking up, prayer at the end of a meeting, prayer for the beginning and the end of the meals, prayer for entering home and going out, prayer for starting a journey, and prayer for returning from it, prayer for riding an animal (or any other transport), prayer for entering a new town or a city etc., are remembered well, and are read on the relevant occasion, naturally the exercise of the remembrance of Allah can be improved to a great extent. No amount of time is sufficient for a sacred thing like zikr, yet most spare time should be devoted to the same; but the least thing that every Muslim can do, is to read the kalimah, and Durood Sharief, and Istighfaar (each a complete Tasbeeh) every morning and evening; moreover, a time should be fixed for the recitation of the Holy Qur'aan. Even some worldly loss can easily be tolerated for the boundless boons of Allah, that are going to be granted to a believer in the next life!

The preference of zikr

It has been mentioned in the hadith that zikr purifies and enlightens the heart. Another hadith says that nothing saves a Muslim from the chastisement of Allah, more than zikr. Another Hadith says that amongst the negligent, one who remembers Allah most often is like a glowing lamp in a dark house. A hadith of Bukhaari says, "One who remembers Allah, is remembered by Him among His courtiers (Angels)". Rasulullah (Sallallaho alaihe wasallam) in another hadith says, "Anyone who remembers Allah most often, is so much preferable to a person, who distributes a great amount of money in the way of Allah". (Targheeb)

Fourth Lesson

Honour for a Muslim

The gist of this lesson is that every Muslim should realise the rights of other Muslims, and should observe them practically, according to the order of the classes and ranks of his brethren in Islam. Particularly, he should have great regard for the honour of a Muslim, who deserves reverance by all means, for he has the light of faith in his heart. Rasulullah (Sallallaho alaihe wasallam) says in a hadith, "He is not one of us, who does not respect our elders, and does not show mercy to our youngsters and is not respectful to our scholars". Another hadith says, "Only a hypocrite could insult these three person; first, an aged Muslim; second, a religious scholar; third, a Muslim king, who observes justice".

According to the teachings of the Holy Qur'aan, and hadith, here are the most important qualities of a true believer. He should realise the rights of Allah's creatures, and should be polite and humble to them. He should like for others, what he likes for himself. He should not be envious of others, nor should he have malice about them. He must not be proud. He should be courteous and loving to all. He should be the first to greet a Muslim. He should be generous enough to pardon those who have offended him. He should go to visit the sick. He should respect all just as he respects himself. He should avoid back-biting. He should overlook the weaknesses of others. If anyone consults him, he should give him the right and honest counsel. He should give financial help to the poor and the needy. He should not rejoice in the misery of others. And the most distinguished and valuable service to a Muslim is that he should be instructed with a firm faith in Allah, in the Day of Judgement, and to be prepared for it with a lot of good deeds, so that he should be delivered of the chastisement thereon. Undoubtedly, this is the best service to a brother in Islam.

Islam has instructed all the Muslims with a collective life, and has enjoined unity to them, that they should provide peace and prosperity for one another. For instance, they have been instructed to put on their best clothes, and apply perfume to them for the Jumu'ah and the Eid prayers; they have been prevented from jumping over the necks of the worshippers, or to sit between two persons without their permission, or to remove anyone from his sitting place. Rasulullah (Sallallaho alaihe wasallam) says, "A true Muslim is he, who does not offend any other Muslim with his tongue or hand; and a true believer is he, who does not cause any loss to another believer". In another hadith Rasulullah (Sallallaho alaihe wasallam) says, "That person will not enter Jannah, whose neighbour is not safe from his offence".

These sayings of Rasulullah (Sallallaho alaihe wasallam) clearly indicate that a believer should behave so courteously towards others, that they should never fear trouble or a loss from his quarters.

In another hadith Rasulullah (Sallallaho alaihe wasallam) says, "Whoever helps a poor and miserable person, Allah will grant him seventy three rewards, of which only one would be sufficient to put his affairs aright in this world, and the other seventy two rewards will sublimate his ranks in the life hereafter". Another hadith says, "When a Muslim leaves his home to see another Muslim, seventy thousand angels see him off, and all of them bless him with the mercy of Allah". Rasulullah (Sallallaho alaihe wasallam) says about a co-traveller, "Only that person is your chief in a journey, who serves his companions best; no one can supercede such a person, except a martyr".

Fifth Lesson

Sincerity of Intention

This is also called the "correction of intention". That is, whenever a person intends to do something good, he must not be tempted by some wordly interest, but should do it purely for the pleasure of Allah, and to have its reward in the life hereafter. This purity of intention can be achieved only when he has a firm faith in the reward which Allah and Rasulullah (Sallallaho alaihe wasallam) have promised for our good deeds, and, therefore, the hope of this reward should be our motive in good deeds. That is why Rasulullah (Sallallaho alaihe wasallam) has said, "The reward for your deeds depends entirely on your intention, and everyone is paid in accordance with the nature of his intention". It means, that it is not merely the action which ensures a reward from Allah, but it is the sincerity of our intention, which will ensure it. If an action is void of good intention, and is undertaken for the sake of passion, or to please men, or to attain some wordly interest, then it is hollow, lifeless and deserves no reward from Allah. A hadith to this effect says, "All the deeds of men will be gathered together before Allah, on the Day of Qiyaamah; of them only the deeds which are purely done for Allah, will be separated, and the rest will be thrown into hell".

(Targheeb)

When certain good deeds are done purely for Allah, it is called "Ikhlaas" and whenever a believer intends to do something based on sincerity, the evil self, or the Shaytaan cause hinderances in his way. Therefore it is indispensable to sincerity that one should forsake the wordly temptations, and should believe in the everlasting boons and favour of the life hereafter. Those who have realized the value of sincerity, they apply it to their worldly affairs also. They observe the sincerity of intention in eating, drinking, sleeping, awaking, walking, earning their living etc., but this standard of sincerity cannot be achieved without the company of saints and devouts. As an example, our religious scholars have told us that by observing fasts, if someone desires its reward and good health at the same time; or, if by undertaking a pilgrimage, one wishes reward, recreation, and safety from the enemy; or, if by giving alms to a beggar, one has an intention to have its reward from Allah, appreciation from the onlookers, and to silence the beggar, then all the above-mentioned deeds will be void of sincerity. A companion of Rasululla (Sallallaho alaihe wasallam) asked him, "What is faith?" He replied, "Another name for faith is sincerity!" (Targheeb) In another hadith Rasulullah (Sallallaho alaihe wasallam) says, "Observe sincerity in your deeds, then even a few good deeds will have the reward of great virtue for you!" (Targheeb). Another companion of Rasulullah (Sallallaho alaihe wasallam) asked him, "One man participates in the holy war for the sake of riches, and another man participates in it for the sake of reputation, that he may be called a hero; say, O Messenger of Allah, who is fighting in the way of Allah?" He answered, "Only that person fights in the way of Allah, who wants to propagate and establish the truth told by Him (in the Holy Qur'aan)". (Bukhaari, Muslim)

Those who do not desire the pleasure of Allah by their deeds, but wish only the worldly achievements, they are certainly hypocrites, and this (hypocrisy) is a desease of the heart, which our spiritualists say, is the root of all evils. Once Rasulullah (Sallallaho alaihe wasallam) said to his companions, "The thing I fear most in your actions, is smaller polytheism". His companions asked, "What is smaller polytheism?" He answered, "Show (of one's good deeds!)" Another hadith says, "Whoever made a show of his prayer, or fasting, or charity, he committed polytheism". Another hadith says, "There is a pit of sorrow in Jahannam, of which Jahannam even seeks refuge, of Allah; those worshippers, who make a show of their worship, will be thrown into it".

Sixth Lesson

The spare time

A believer should spare as much time as possible; for the preachment of the commandments of Allah, even if he has to leave his home and family for this noble cause. During this stage of life one should exercise the previous six lessons, for a long experience has told us that by sticking to one's home and family and the business, one cannot learn or teach the principles of Islam, nor one can adopt the original and traditional Islamic culture, particularly in this age of materialism.

Therefore, one should get rid of worldly engagements, to serve Allah and His true religion. In this course, a believer should join the group of the preachers of Islam, and should call those to the right path, who are lost in this fleeting world, and have forgotten immortal life hereafter.

To call the wrong doing and negligent people to Allah, and to instruct them with His commandments, was really the duty of the Ambiyaa, which has now been entrusted to the Muslims. The true following of Rasulullah (Sallallaho alaihe wasallam) requires that every Muslim should devote himself to his service, and should sacrifice everything for the preachment of his true religion (Islam). Just as Rasulullah (Sallallaho alaihe wasallam) himself bore so many troubles for the sake of Islam, similarly every follower of his should also follow his footsteps.

The companions of Rasulullah (Sallallaho alaihe wasallam) had properly realised the requisites of Tabligh, and, therefore, they tolerated the troubles of this world, for the sake of the boons and favours of Allah in the next life. They gladly devoted themselves to the service of Allah, and preferred the needs of religion to the needs of worldly life. Sometimes, they ate leaves, or a single date, and walked barefoot on long journies, in the way of Allah. During the time of the Sahabah it was necessary to propagate Islam, and to spread it far and wide, but today we have to revive it; just as those believers performed their duty by the sacrifice of their lives, we should also follow their example.

Leaving one's home and family for the cause of Allah, has great rewards for the subject, in the next life, just as Rasulullah (Sallallaho alaihe wasallam) has clearly told us.

Rasulullah (Sallallaho alaihe wasallam) has said, "Whoever spends his morning or evening in the way of Allah, his reward will be much better then the whole world, and whatever is in it." (Bukhaari and Muslim). In another hadith he says, "The fire of Jahannam will not reach anyone whose feet become dusty whilst he is on the path of Allah."

When we instruct the servants of Allah with His commandments, it means we have fulfilled the duty of Tabligh, and have revived it, for Rasulullah (Sallallaho alaihe wasallam) has said, "When people see others committing sins, and do not prevent them from the same, soon Allah will inflict a punishment on them, which will affect the common folk, as well as the distinguished persons".

A hadith of Tirmizi Sharief says, "I swear by Allah, you must command people with good deeds, and prevent them from forbidden things, or soon Allah will inflict a severe punishment to you, and then your prayers even will not be heard by Him!"

A verse of the Holy Qur'aan says,

وَلْتَكُنْ مِّنْكُمْ أُمَّةٌ يَّدْعُوْنَ إِلَى الْخَيْرِ وَيَأْمُرُوْنَ بِالْمَعْرُوْفِ
وَيَنْهَوْنَ عَنِ الْمُنْكَرِ ۗ وَأُولٰٓئِكَ هُمُ الْمُفْلِحُوْنَ ○

"There must be a group among you, who should invite people to good, and should induce them to legal things, and should prevent them from illegal things; and certainly these will attain salvation".

Another verse says,

كُنْتُمْ خَيْرَ أُمَّةٍ أُخْرِجَتْ لِلنَّاسِ تَأْمُرُوْنَ بِالْمَعْرُوْفِ وَتَنْهَوْنَ
عَنِ الْمُنْكَرِ وَتُؤْمِنُوْنَ بِاللّٰهِ ؕ

"O Muslims! You are the best nation, who has been chosen for the guidance of other nations; you command people with virtue, and prevent them from vice, and have a firm faith in Allah!"

It has been reported by Abu Darda (Radhiyallaho anho) that Rasulullah (Sallallaho alaihe wasallam) said, "You must induce people to good deeds, and prevent them from bad ones, otherwise Allah will bring such a tyrant sovereign over you, who will not respect your elders, nor will he show mercy to your youngsters; then the prayers of your pious people even will not be granted by Allah; if you called Him, He will not pardon you!"

Seventh Lesson

To quit vanity

This lesson will explain the most important requisites of piety. A Muslim should spend every moment of his life in the achievement of the eternal boons of the life hereafter. He should not only avoid the sins, but also the vain and destructive customs of his age, which affect our religious principles and beliefs so badly. Though there may not be sin in so many deeds and hobbies, yet they are a sheer waste of time and energy, and we could do some other constructive things during that time. This is the characteristic of a true believer that he spends his time only in virtuous deeds, remembers Allah as much as possible, avoids all forbidden things, does not indulge in vanity, and is polite and humble towards other Muslims. If one does not avoid vain talk and vain deeds, one is likely to indulge in shameful sins. It has been mentioned in a hadith that when a companion of Rasulullah (Sallallaho alaihe wasallam) died, a Muslim said to him, "I deliver to you the happy news of Jannah!" When Rasulullah (Sallallaho alaihe wasallam) heard these words, he said, "You are giving him the happy news of Jannah, while you dont know he might have indulged in vain talk, or, have been a miser in spending a thing for the good of others, which does not decrease by use". This evidently means that one should be very cautious in talk, and should avoid vanity, for one's tongue is likely to talk nonsense.

Another hadith says, "A man does not slip so much by his feet, as by his tongue".

Another hadith says, "Sometimes a man speaks an offensive and sinful thing unconsciously, by which he is thrown into hell deeper than the distance between East and West!" (Bukhaari & Muslim)

Therefore, every believer should be cautious in his talk, and should spend every moment of his life in good deeds. He must avoid vanity, particularly, during the period when he has left home to learn his religion, or to preach the same.

Someone asked Luqmaan the philosopher, "How did you attain so much wisdom?" He answered, "Because I speak the truth, pay the securities to their owners, and avoid vanity!" (Muwatta Imaam Maalik)

Hadhrat Sahl Tastari says, "Anyone who desires that the qualities and signs of the truthful should be revealed to him, he must not eat anything but pure and legal, and should follow the Sunnah very strictly". (Ihya-ul-Uloom)

In another hadith Rasulullah (Sallallaho alaihe wasallam) said, "The perfection of one's faith in Islam, requires that one should give up vanity altogether".

The Holy Qur'aan mentions a great quality of true believers,

وَالَّذِيْنَ هُمْ عَنِ اللَّغْوِ مُعْرِضُوْنَ ○

"Those who do not indulge in vanity!"

N.B.–All the ahaadith, which have no references have been quoted from Mishkaat Sharief.

The requisites of a journey for Tabligh

1. When a believer has determined to undertake such a journey, he should say the following prayer,

اَللّٰهُمَّ بِكَ اَصُوْلُ وَبِكَ اَحُوْلُ وَبِكَ اَسِيْرُ

"O Allah! I attack the enemy with your help, I plan my work with Your help, and I walk on the earth with Your help".

2. When he has left home, he should read,

بِسْمِ اللّٰهِ تَوَكَّلْتُ عَلَى اللّٰهِ وَلَا حَوْلَ وَلَا قُوَّةَ اِلَّا بِاللّٰهِ

"I start my journey with the name of Allah, I entirely depend on Allah; the power to do good and to avoid evil is from Allah".

3. The group of preachers should have a leader in this journey, who can be another person than the leader of the group.
4. When he rides and puts his feet in the stirrup, he should say "Bismillaah" and when he sits on the back

of the animal, he should say "Alhamdu lillaah"; and then he should read this verse,

سُبْحٰنَ الَّذِیْ سَخَّرَ لَنَا هٰذَا وَمَا كُنَّا لَهٗ مُقْرِنِيْنَ ○
وَاِنَّآ اِلٰى رَبِّنَا مُنْقَلِبُوْنَ ○

"Glory be to Allah, who has subjected this animal to us, and we could not overpower it without His help; and at last we have to return to our Sustainer!"

"Then he should say "Alhamdu lillaah" thrice, and then "Allaahu Akbar" thrice, and then he should say,

سُبْحٰنَكَ اِنِّیْ ظَلَمْتُ نَفْسِیْ فَاغْفِرْلِیْ فَاِنَّهٗ لَا
يَغْفِرُ الذُّنُوْبَ اِلَّآ اَنْتَ

"O Allah! You are clear of evil; I have been unjust to my soul; therefore, forgive me, for no one pardons sins, but You!".

5. When he has ridden, and the animal walks, or, when he himself begins to walk, he should say,

اَللّٰهُمَّ اِنِّیْ اَعُوْذُ بِكَ مِنْ وَعْثَاءِ السَّفَرِ وَكَآبَةِ الْمُنْقَلَبِ وَالْحَوْرِ
بَعْدَ الْكَوْرِ وَدَعْوَةِ الْمَظْلُوْمِ وَسُوْءِ الْمَنْظَرِ فِی الْاَهْلِ وَالْمَالِ۔

"O Allah! I seek Your refuge from the hardships of this journey, and from the calamities of my return, and from failure after success, and from the ill prayers of the oppressed, and from loss of wealth and my family".

6. When he ascends some high place, he should say "Allaahu Akbar" thrice, and when he descends, he should say "Subhaanallaah" thrice; and when he passes

through a plain or a stream, he should say "Laa ilaaha illallaah" and "Allaahu Akbar" (Hisn)

7. When he has to walk on foot, he should be pleased to do so; rather he should prefer to walk on foot, for this is a Sunnah of Rasulullah (Sallallaho alaihe wasallam) and his companions. Hence, he should get himself used to the troubles of this journey, which is a source of Allah's boons and favours, in the next life.

8. If his foot slips somewhere, or hits some obstacle, he should say "Bismillah". (Hisn Haseen)

9. When he sets foot at some station or destination, he should say,

أَعُوْذُ بِكَلِمٰتِ اللّٰهِ التَّامَّاتِ مِنْ شَرِّ مَا خَلَقَ

"With the complete words of Allah, I seek refuge from the evil of whatever He has created".

10. When he enters some village or a city, he should say thrice,

اَللّٰهُمَّ بَارِكْ لَنَا فِيْهَا

"O Allah! let it be auspicious for us."

Then he should say this prayer,

اَللّٰهُمَّ ارْزُقْنَا جَنَاهَا وَحَبِّبْنَا إِلٰى أَهْلِهَا وَحَبِّبْ
صَالِحِيْ أَهْلِهَا إِلَيْنَا۔

"O Allah! Let us enjoy the fruits of this city, and infuse our love into the hearts of the people of this city, and cause the love of the pious of this city in our hearts".

(Hisn Haseen)

11. He should serve his companions as much as he can, and should take pride in it. It has been mentioned in a hadith, "Only that person is your leader in a journey, who serves you more than him, except a martyr".

(Mishkaat Sharief)

The duties of a leader

Here are the duties of a leader on a journey of religious preachment:

1. He should provide comfort for his companions. He should consult his companions, and if he disagrees with anyone on a certain topic, he should not discourage him, and should tell him the utility of another's opinion, whose counsel is more useful.
2. He should not be hard upon any companion, and should not speak to him in the tone of command.
3. He should behave towards his companions, according to their status.
4. If some of his companions are capable of speech, he should give them an opportunity to deliver a speech, and if somebody's speech is not according to the aims and objects of the group, he should prevent him from the same in such words, as would not displease or dishearten him.
5. He should prevent his companions from vain things in a polite and favourable manner.
6. He should instruct them with the morning and evening zikr, particularly when they are out for Tabligh work.
7. He himself should appoint a leader for preachment, a leader for mutual talk, and if he does not find any efficient person for this purpose, he himself should adopt this office.
8. During the journey even, he should instruct his companions to remember the Tabligh lessons well; he should advise them to remember the prayers for all occasions, by heart.
9. He should entrust the ignorant to the scholars, that they may learn prayers, etc., from them.
10. If he thinks it proper, he should distribute various duties among his companions. For instance, some of them should awake others for the Tahajjud prayer, some of them should lead them for Chaasht and Ishraaq prayers, and some of them should instruct others with morning and evening zikr.

11. If there is some friction among his companions, he should reconcile them.

12. He should instruct his companions again and again, with the fear of Allah, and preparation for the next life, and should solemnly advise them in the following words: "We have left our homes to reform ourselves, before we reform others. Our real aim and object during this journey is that being in the company of the pious, and the God-fearing, we should strengthen our relationship with them, should perform our prayers in the best possible manner. Thus we should remember Allah as much as possible, should serve one another sincerely, and should devote ourselves to all good deeds, preventing ourselves from forbidden things. All the time that we have devoted to Tabligh work, is not ours at all, but for the promotion and establishment of the true religion of Allah. Therefore, we should make much of this time, and should learn and teach our religion. We lost our lives in vanity, but at least now we should spend the rest of our life, just as a true Muslim would do. We should fulfil the requisites of this journey at their best".

Knowledge and zikr

1. The subject of the teachings of the Tablighi group is to have a comprehensive and reliable knowledge of Islam, and to preach the same to other Muslims so that they have a keen interest in Islam. Moreover, this group must know the promises and the commandments of Allah, and snould observe them practically.

2. In the education course of this group the prayer and the Holy Qur'aan have a great importance, but the time which is required to learn these things perfectly, cannot be acquired on this brief Tabligh journey. Therefore, the companions are expected to realize the importance of salaah and learning the Holy Qur'aan, during this journey, that they should devote more and more time to this subject, in the future.

3. The members of the group should also contemplate their past life, and they should be sorry for not devoting themselves to Tabligh work in the past, and they should seek Allah's forgiveness. And those who are

still ignorant of their religion, should be sorry for their negligence, and should repent for the future.

4. In all the spare time they should remember Allah; they should engage in zikr not only their tongue, but their heart also.
5. Those who know their religion, should teach it to others as a duty, and those who are still ignorant about it, should learn the same very attentively.
6. One cannot learn all the teachings of the religion only by studying the books, or by listening to the orators; knowledge of Islam and the practice thereof are indispensable to each other, and perfection in faith cannot be acquired without action. Therefore, one must practise what he knows, and should also instruct others with the same.
7. All the mistakes that one commits during the reading of the Holy Qur'aan, or the prayer, their correction should not be limited only to the teaching class, but one should try his best to correct them during his leisure at home.
8. All the members of the group should sit silent and respectfully in the class, while they are instructed, and should not pay attention to anything else; only the leader of education should correct their mistakes, but others should keep silent, and having regard for Allah and His Messenger, they should sit motionless, as if birds were sitting on their heads.
9. In the circle of instruction the following things should be observed very attentively.

    (a) The teachings of the Holy Qur'aan, particularly in relation with the principles of Islam; all the possible mistakes concerning ذ Thaal, ز Zaa, س Seen, ص Saud, ح Haa, ه Haa, ع Ayn, ء Hamzah, ت Taa, ط Tau, َ Fatha/Zabar etc., should be avoided with great care.

    (b) The words of Kalimah Tayyibah should be remembered properly, and their meaning should be understood thoroughly, so much so that everyone should believe that Islam is incomplete without putting the kalimah into practice.

(c) The basic conditions and requisites of salaah should be learnt well; whatever is read in salaah, should be remembered well; the reward of salaah should be stressed, and the punishment for neglecting it should be told again and again; moreover, the methods to attain concentration in salaah, should be practised.

(d) All the punishments that are mentioned in the Qur'aan and hadith, for neglecting the requisites of salaah, kalimah, reverence for a Muslim, Islamic knowledge, zikr, Tabligh work etc., should be told to the students; moreover the reward for observing them should also be explained, from reliable books.

(e) The important features of the life of Rasulullah (Sallallaho alaihe wasallam) should also be told to the class. For instance, how he observed the Prayers, and how he led his daily life. Thus, by studying the biography of Rasulullah (Sallallaho alaihe wasallam), and his companions, a Muslim should learn that in spite of troubles and obstacles, how they preached Islam far and wide, and how they dealt with their families and business, being true and just to everyone.

(f) All the members of the group should assist one another in learning their Tabligh lessons, viz., the kalimah, salaah, Islamic knowledge, zikr, honour for a Muslim, sincerity, setting aside time to do good deeds, and abstaining from useless things. And then, they should instruct each other to lead their life according to these lessons.

10. They should read one Tasbeeh of Durood Sharief, one of the kalimah, and one of Istighfaar, every morning and evening; and if they have good books of prayer like 'Dalaail-ul-Khairaat, Hizb-al-Aazam, Munaajaate Maqbool, they should also read them regularly.

11. They should spend all their leisure in the remembrance of Allah, and should keep their tongues busy with zikr.

The optional prayers

The "nawaafil" or the "optional prayers" should also be

observed during the Tabligh journey. The Ishraaq, the Chaasht, the Tahajjud, the Awwaabeen, the Nawaafil after fardh, and the sunnah prayer, should be observed very carefully. These prayers are generally neglected at home, but they can be performed during the journey, if you find leisure; yet all the persons in the Tabligh group must know that the duty of preachment is more important than the optional prayers. That is to say, preachment has a priorty over the nawaafil, and you can easily give up the latter for the former. Observe the requisites of Tabligh first and perform the nawaafil afterwards.

Gasht (To go around for an informal visit and the special visit)

1. The real object of going around for an informal visit or a special visit for the purpose of Tabligh is that the worldly and business places like bazaars, streets, and the markets should also be blessed and benefitted with the remembrance of Allah, and the faith of the group should strengthen the faith of others, and vice versa. Remember, this Tabligh work is exactly the following of the Tabligh work observed by Rasulullah (Sallallaho alaihe wasallam), who observed it by going around from home to home.

2. When you go around for an informal or a special visit, lower your gaze, and keep your tongue and heart busy with the remembrance of Allah. This attitude of yours will effect the hearts of others, to a great extent.

3. The going around for informal visits and special visits must be done before the Prayer time, and during your Gasht instruct others with the requisites of the kalimah and the principles of Islam; moreover, call the listeners to the prayer in the mosque, and ask them to join your Tabligh group.

4. Do not ask everyone to let you hear his kalimah, nor compell him to perform the prayer, for such an attitude would sometimes cause unfavourable results. That is why, you are advised to take the educated and influencial people of that locality with you, so that he should talk to them according to their reason and status.

5. Pray to Allah before you start Gasht, and call upon

Him with all humbleness, saying, "O Allah! We are weak and helpless, and nothing can be achieved without Your assistance; therefore, assist us in this sacred cause, and divert the hearts of Your servants, to Your true religion, and to the life hereafter, and let us be a medium for this service. O Allah! Accept this humble service of ours, and establish Your religion with it. O Allah! Save us from the evil of those, whom we contact in this work of Tabligh, and also save them from the evil of our self. Let them benefit from the good in our souls, and let us benefit from the good in their souls! (And one could say any other suitable du'aa, according to the occasion).

6. Do not be engaged in discussions with anyone, nor arrange any debate.

7. During your going around for an informal or special visit for Tabligh, take the local pious people with you, so that they can see the impiety and transgression of the people of their town with their own eyes, and should, consequently, join you in Tabligh work.

8. When you reach a certain city or village, meet the distinguished people thereof, and explain to them the method and the aims and objects of Tabligh, and stress the importance of religious preachment, and then invite them to join the group. By the distinguished people we mean the pious, or the wealthy persons, who are, one way or another, influential in their city, mohalla or village. One should be very cautious, reasonable, and to the point, while talking to them.

The invitation and the speech

1. Since your speech is not your real aim and object, and is merely a medium of instruction, one should rather stress the meaning and the purpose of your words, for the sake of Tabligh. Make yourself clear to your listeners, in simple and easy language. Do not adopt the style of common orators, and do not talk about things, which the listener would not understand. Rasulullah (Sallallaho alaihe wasallah) repeated every sentence of his thrice, that his audience should understand it easily. His words were spoken slowly and clearly, so that the listeners could count them.

2. In your speech you should explain the vanity of worldly objects, and then the greatness and immortality of the boons and enjoyments in the life hereafter. Instruct them to prepare for the life in the grave and to do good deeds for the same; and then attain peace and salvation on the Day of Qiyaamah; and then ask them to live a pious life, for this will save them from the punishment of Jahannam. Explain to them the impiety and negligence of the present Muslims, particularly the condition of local people, which you will come to know during the going around for the informal and special visits.
3. Tell them the spiritual and religious benefits of joining the Tabligh group, and invite them to the same.
4. Explain to them the punishment for not inducing people to good, and preventing them from evil, and tell them the reward of being faithful to Islam, during this era of sin and disobedience.
5. Do not adopt a tone of command and superiority, while instructing people.
6. In every speech, one should advice the audience to be practical about what they know of Islam.

Obedience to the leader

Every order of the leader should be obeyed, provided he does not ask you to commit a sin. Yes, obey him, though he is not so much educated as you are. Rasulullah (Sallallaho alaihe wasallam) has said in a hadith, "If a leader has been appointed to you, whose nose and ears are cut, you should obey him, when he instructs you with the Holy Qur'aan."

Sometimes the leader will bestow an honour, or the right of speech, on a person inferior to you in status; in such a case, you should not object to it, and raise no objection against him. Hadhrat Ubaadah bin Saamit (Radhiyallaho anho) says, "We took a pledge at the hands of Rasulullah (Sallallaho alaihe wasallam), that we should obey him in prosperity and in calamity, in pleasure and sorrow, and will not obey the suggestions of our evil self, against his wish, and will not prefer ourselves to others against his choice; that we shall not try to snatch leadership from another; that we will speak the truth, wherever we are; that we will not mind the criticism of anyone, while obeying the commandments of Allah".

(Mishkaat Sharief)

The etiquette of taking meals

1. Wash your hands before and after meals, and wash your mouth also.
2. Begin to take meals by saying; "Bismillaah wa'alaa barkatillaah".
3. Take your meals with your right hand.
4. Take the food that is in front of you, but if there are various things in the utensil from which you are eating, then you may take it from wherever you please.
5. Place the food on a table cloth and then partake from the food.
6. Do not eat from the centre of the utensil, for the blessing of Allah descends at that point.
7. Finish all the food in the utensil, and do not spare anything for the Shaytaan. When all the food is taken, the utensil prays to Allah for your delivery from Jahannam.
8. Lick your fingers before washing your hands, it is mentioned in a hadith, "One does not know in which particle of the food is the blessing of Allah."
9. Take your meals with three fingers of the right hand.
10. If a morsel falls on the table cloth, pick it up and eat it, and do not spare it for Shaytaan.
11. One should not lean on a cushion or arrogantly recline whilst eating.
12. Do not object to the quality of food; if you like it, take it otherwise don't take it, and keep silent.
13. All of you should take your meals, as a group, and not separately.
14. Hadhrat Anas (Radhiyallaho anho) says, "I saw Rasulullah (Sallallaho alaihe wasallam) taking his meals, in a squatting position."

15. If some companions are eating sweetmeats or dates together, do not take two pieces at a time, without their permission.

16. If you forget to read "Bismillaah" at the beginning of your meals, then say when you remember it, "Bismillaahi awwaluhu wa aakhiruhu", that is, with the name of Allah in the beginning and at the end of it.

17. Do not eat onions while you are in the mosque, and if you have eaten them out of the mosque, do not enter it, until such time that there is no odour left.

18. When you have taken your meals, say,

الحمد لله الذى أطعمنا وسقانا وجعلنا من المسلمين

Al<u>h</u>amdu lillaahil la<u>th</u>ee at-'amanaa wasaqaanaa waja-alanaa minal muslimeen.

"All praise is due to Allah, who has nourished us, and has quenched our thirst, and has assisted us to be Muslims."

19. First pick up the table cloth, and then get up.

20. Do not eat food which is too hot.

21. If you have eaten to your fill, do not get up before your companions, but keep eating slowly; and if you have to get up, excuse yourself, and ask them to continue.

22. If you drink water, milk or any other liquid say, "Bismillaah" at the beginning and "Alhamdulillaah" at the end.

23. Do not drink continuously in one gulp, like a camel.

24. Do not breathe in a utensil nor blow into it.

25. If the utensil is broken or chipped at a certain point then do not eat or drink from that point of the utensil.

26. Wash your mouth after drinking milk, and read this du'aa,

اللهم بارك لنا فيه وزدنا منه -

Allaahumma baarik lanaa feehi wa zidnaa minhu.

"O Allah! let it be a blessing for us and increase it for us".

All these etiquettes of taking food and drink have been quoted from Mishkaat Sharief.

The etiquette of going to sleep

1. Do not go to sleep without wudhu.
2. Clean the bed thrice before going to sleep.
3. Lie on the bed on your right side, place your right hand under your cheek, and read "Allahumma be'ismika amooto wa ahyaa". O Allah! In Your name do I die and live.
4. Read "Aayatul Kursi" and "Aamanar Rasoolu (up to the end of Surah) before going to sleep.
5. Read "Subhaanallah", "Alhamdulillaah" and "Allaahu-Akbar", thirty three times each, before going to sleep.
6. Read all the four Surahs, beginning with "Qul", then blow on your hands, and apply them to your whole body; do this thrice.
7. Read Surah "Alif laam meem sajdah" and "Tabarakalladhi beyadihil mulk" (up to the end of Surah) before going to sleep.
8. When awakening read,

الْحَمْدُ لِلّٰهِ الَّذِيْ أَحْيَانَا بَعْدَ مَا أَمَاتَنَا وَإِلَيْهِ النُّشُوْرُ۔

Alhamdu lillaahil lathee ahyaanaa ba'da maa amaatanaa wa ilayhin nushoor.

"All praise to Allah. He who revived us to life after giving us death and to Him we shall have to return."

9. Apply collyrium (surmah) to your eyes thrice, before going to sleep.
10. If you want to get up for the Tahajjud prayer, read, "Inalladhina aamanu" (Up to the end of Surah Kahaf). All

these etiquettes of sleeping have been quoted from the ahaadith.

Wudhu and Salaah

1. If the time of salaah is near, then have wudhu before proceeding on a journey, also take a Lota (utensil for the purpose of wudhu) and a six yard rope, to draw water from a well if the necessity arises.
2. The water from the station taps and that from the toilet in the train is clean. If this water is not available then only will Tayammum be permissible.
3. The time for Maghrib salaah begins after sunset and ends when the redness in the sky disappears. The general belief that Maghrib salaah cannot be performed a short while after the sunset is incorrect.
4. If the distance of your journey is more than forty eight miles (77,248 Kilometres) then instead of performing four fardh rak'aats you should perform only two.
5. Do not postpone any prayer during the journey, for a single postponement will render your journey useless. If you have forgotten a certain prayer, or its time has passed during your sleep, then perform it as soon as possible, if the prayers of a journey are performed after reaching home, then observe two rak'aat for Zuhr, As'r and Esha; on the other hand, if the prayers postponed at home, are performed during the journey, then observe them in a complete form (four rak'aats for Zuhr, As'r and Esha).
6. There are many Muslims on whom Qadha salaah for years was due, they are advised to perform these salaahs as soon as possible, whilst on a Tabligh journey the opportunities are numerous so perform as many qadha salaahs as possible, rather perform the fardh qadha, instead of the nawaafil. Remember that qadha salaah is only performed for the fardh and Wit'r salaahs.
7. The jamaat salaah (congregational prayer) is necessary even during the Tabligh journey. When it is time for salaah, say the adhaan (the call to prayer) and then perform the salaah with jamaat, and say takbeer before

the same. If all the members cannot perform the salaah in a group, then let them perform it in pairs.

8. If you are in a hurry, then you may omit the sunnats before and after the fardh salaah, but not those of the Faj'r salaah. And if you are not in a hurry, then perform all the Sunnats.

9. If you have put your luggage in a railway compartment or in a bus, and it is about to depart, then terminate the salaah. Perform the same salaah in the train or vehicle if it is possible.

10. To face the qiblah is necessary even in a railway compartment, therefore perform your salaah in the correct direction; and if you do not know the direction of the qiblah, nor is there anyone to show you, then establish the same by careful estimation. If the train or vehicle takes a turn, while you are performing the salaah, then turn yourself accordingly.

11. Even if the train is moving it is fardh for you to stand and complete your salaah. If you are healthy and strong enough to stand, then do not sit for the salaah. One can easily perform the salaah in the passage or in between the seats, moreover you can perform the salaah in pairs with jamaat in the space between the two rows of seats.

Miscellaneous

1. Every member of the Tabligh group is responsible for his expenditure during the journey.

2. Be courteous and polite to every Muslim whom you meet during your journey. Be courteous to the non-Muslims also, and show them Islamic manners. If you sometimes talk to them, tell them that humanity is generally negligent of Allah, therefore they must submit to Him for their salvation.

3. When you reach a certain destination, consult the local inhabitants, before you start your work of Tabligh.

4. When you reach a city or a town, or a village, do not stay anywhere except in the musjid, even though someone may insist on doing otherwise.

5. Extinguish the lamp or the light of the musjid where

you stay, at the normally fixed times, for it is not correct to use it for yourself only. Extinguish the lights after Esha salaah, when the musallies (worshippers) have departed; then light a candle of your own, if it be needed.

6. Do not ask for any bedding from the people of that place; anyhow help one another if there is a shortage of beds; nor ask for any utensils.

7. Fix a fee before engaging any labourer; if you employ any labourer without fixing a fee, then pay him his full remuneration. If you pay him less than the local rate, and he is unhappy, and kept asking for more, until he went away disappointed, then you will have to pay him on the Day of Qiyaamah. Remember, oppression or forced agreement concerning fixing a fee before engaging any labourer is not recognized; therefore if anyone gives up his right by oppression, then the oppressor can not be forgiven by that person.

8. Avoid every kind of useless talk during your Tabligh journey, and be cautious of everything you do. In short spend your time carefully during this journey, and pay special attention to the Tabligh work. Do not talk much, nor laugh unnecessarily, for it is mentioned in a hadith, "Too much talk hardens your heart, and too much laughing kills your heart, and the noor of your face is lessened.

9. Every action of yours must be based on sincerity, and you should not despair the reward from Allah. In whatever you do you must make a good niyyat (intention).

10. Make your return journey also a Tabligh journey, and on your way home, observe the same as you observed while going abroad.

11. All the requisites of Islamic etiquette that you learnt during the journey, and all the salaahs that you performed, should be maintained at home also. Humbleness in salaah, constant zikr service to humanity, sincerity and all the good actions that you practised during the journey, should be observed at home also, for the main object of this journey was to involve oneself in the practice of good deeds.

12. If you undertake a journey for worldly objects, and not purely for Tabligh work, even then observe Islamic etiquette and du'aas; perform your salaahs regularly, with Jama'at and if there are three companions, one of them should be made an ameer.

13. In such a Tabligh journey keep all the books of Tabligh with you, namely Hikaayaat-i-Sahaabah, Fadhaa'il Namaaz, Fadhaa'il Tabligh etc., and you should also have a miswak, lota (utensil for holding water for the purpose of wudhu), musallah (prayer mat), soap, thread and needle, table cloth, mud lump made for the purpose of istinja, matches, candle, comb, surmah daani (surmah dispenser), torch, staff (which could be used as a sutrah).

14. If the leader asks you to prepare food for the group, or to do some other service, obey his orders happily; and don't think that you will be deprived of the reward of Tabligh when your companions leave you with your task, for then you will deserve double reward, one for rendering service to your companions, and the other, for relieving your companions of their worry to enable them to do Tabligh work freely.

15. The Tabligh journey is a good period in which to practice Islamic routine; therefore, be helpful to one another, and promote unity. Don't insist on your own proposal, but only suggest it, and explain the merits. If your companions do not accept your proposal, then don't despair; If the proposal of somebody else is accepted by the group, and the result is not good, then don't say, "What did I suggest to you? Had you observed my counsel, you would have attained much good!"

16. During the informal or special visit, or during Taalim lessons, or at the time of da'wat don't discuss any controversial subject; but should rather invite people to the fundamentals of Islam and the Oneness of Allah, for when one understands the meaning of the kalimah, then he will want to know more about Imaan and Islam.

17. Remain in any city or village that you visit as long as its inhabitants can easily understand the main object of the work of Tabligh, and are prepared to observe all

the rules of Tabligh work. It is not correct to be at one place in the morning, at another in the evening; at one place at Zuh'r, and at another as As'r. One cannot do justice to Tabligh work, if you visit only a few persons, or deliver a speech in the musjid. Your attempt in this task can be successful and impressive only when you stay in a town for a required period.

18. When you return from a journey, and are nearing your city or village, say,

    آئِبُوْنَ تَائِبُوْنَ عَابِدُوْنَ لِرَبِّنَا حَامِدُوْنَ۔

    Aa-iboona, taa-iboona, 'aabidoona lirabbinaa haami-doon.

    "We are returning (to piety); we are repenting; we are worshipping Allah; and we are giving thanks to Allah!"

19. When you return from the journey, and enter your home, say,

    اَوْبًا اَوْبًا لِرَبِّنَا تَوْبًا لَّا يُغَادِرُ عَلَيْنَا حَوْبًا۔

    Owban, owban, lirabbinaa towban, laa yughaadiru alaynaa howban.

    "I have returned, I have returned to my Sustainer with repentence, which would cleanse us of every sin".

20. It is preferable to reach your town after sunrise; then perform two rakaats nafl in the local musjid, then talk to your Muslim brothers for a while, and then enter your home. Whenever Rasulullah (Sallallaho alaihe wasallam) returned from a journey he did so. (Mishkaat)

21. Whenever Rasulullah (Sallallaho alaihe wasallam) returned from a journey during the night, he did not enter his home, but on the next morning or evening. (Mishkaat).

22. It has been reported by Jaabir (Radhiyallaho anho) that Rasulullah (Sallallaho alaihe wasallam) said, "Whenever you return from a journey after sunset, and wish

to go home to your wife, then give her sufficient time to remove pubic hair and to comb the hair on her head (in order that she groom herself in preparation for your return). (Bukhaari & Muslim)

23. After returning from a journey, one should hastely rejoin the Tabligh workers, successful and fortunate is he who observes the requisites of this journey sincerely, and returns home with a great spiritual improvement.

Directives for the workers of Tabligh

(Selected from the sayings of Hadhrat Maulana Muhammad Ilyaas (Rahmatullah alaih)

1. The first and the main object of knowledge is that one should examine his actions; he should realize his duties and shortcomings, and should seek means to overcome them. Then if you only compare the actions of others according to your ilm then this pride destroys those who have ilm.

2. The real remembrance of Allah is that a Muslim should always obey the commandments of Allah, and should keep them in mind at all times. I instruct my own friend with the same zikr.

3. The main object of our jamaat is to teach the Muslims the original and complete religion taught by Rasulullah (Sallallaho alaihe wasallam). This is our real object; as for our Tabligh journeys in groups this is a preliminary means to carry out our work; the instruction of Kalimah Tayyibah and Salaah is the initiation of our course.

4. Our workers should remember that if their da'wat is not accepted anywhere, they should not be disappointed; they should remember that they generally are following the Sunnah of the Ambiyaa (Alayhimus salaam) and particularly the Sunnah of Rasulullah (Sallallaho alaihe wasallam). How many are there who go out in Allah's path, who bear hardships and yet are disgraced? On the other hand, if they are welcomed and honoured somewhere, they should think it to be a favour of Allah, and should have great regard for it. When they teach religion to those who pay heed to it, though they be commoners, they thank Allah for His favour.

5. Our workers should not desire for calamities from Allah. Should any misfortune befall them then, they should accept that to be the mercy of Allah, and a compensation for their sins, and as a means to raise their ranks.

6. In your explanation you should have the intention to please Allah only, and not your audience. In the Tabligh journey we should bear in mind that we have left our homes in obedience to Allah's command, and not by our own wish; therefore it is He who will assist us. When you have such an intention, you will not be angered by the ill treatment of the people to whom you talk, nor will you be discouraged.

7. It has become an undesirable custom, if our audience does not follow our instructions we regard ourselves to be loosers, whereas it is infact the loss to our listeners, because they have not obeyed the teachings of their religion, our success lies in performing our duty to deliver the truth. How can we be unsuccessful, by the negligence of others? Our duty is to present Islam in the best possible manner. Even the Ambiyaa (Alayhimus salaam) were not held responsible, if the audience did not follow them. You may learn a lesson from peoples rejection, that your approach to this work may not be perfect and faultless; therefore, you shall improve your future attempts and ask Allah for complete guidance.

8. If the Ulama and pious people of a town show no keenness and are not sympathetic towards the work of Tabligh, then do not doubt their sincerity, and don't develop any ill feeling about them in your heart, but you should realize that the object of the work is not apparent to them yet.

9. Wherever you go, you should visit the Ulama and pious people of that place, so that you can benefit from their knowledge and piety. You should not invite them to the work of Tabligh, for they know their duties best, and the benefits thereof; they will not understand the object of your work merely by explanation, therefore, they will naturally not confirm the same, and once they do not acknowledge, they shall insist on their denial, hence meet them only for your benefit, as long as you are in their town make an effort to follow your

lessons and principles very strictly; when the ulama and pious ones are informed of your activities, they will naturally be interested in your Tabligh work; thereafter in a very honourable and respectful manner explain to them your aims and objects.

10. One of the principles of Tabligh is that a speaker should be concise and to the point in his general address but very polite and courteous, when addressing a particular person; rather when he instructs a particular person, even then his address should be of a general nature. Whenever Rasulullah (Sallallaho alaihe wasallam) came to know of the wrong actions of a particular person, he disapproved of it in general terms and said, "What will the result of such a nation be, who commit wrong actions".

11. We are accustomed to be pleased with talk only; we merely talk about good deeds, and think that our words replace them; therefore, try to refrain from this habit.

12. Whatever good deeds you do, attribute them to Allah, and seek His forgiveness for verily you should keep in mind that whatever action you did was not the best, and that there was fault in its completion. Rasulullah (Sallallaho alaihe wasallam) used to seek Allah's forgiveness at the end of his salaah. The responsibility of Allah's work cannot be completed in anyway by His servants, and when we are busy with certain work this should not stop us from doing other work, and we should seek Allah's forgiveness and assistance at the completion of all good work.

13. All your Tabligh journeys will be worthless if you did not continue studying deeni ilm and regular zikrullah, hence, there is fear that negligence of these two essentials could be a cause of turmoil, and to be led astray. If you do not possess deeni ilm then Islam and Imaan is for name sake and customary, for no good deed is possible without sound Islamic knowledge, and knowledge without zikrullah is but darkness and no noor can be derived therefrom, and this is what our workers have neglected.

14. When a deeni explanation is made and also during the gasht the jamaat members are taught to remain in zik-

rullah and fikr. The reason for this is whilst an effort is made to explain the truth and at the same time many hearts in the group are occupied in endorsing with a firm belief, the same idea, this makes an impression on other hearts.

15. The proportion of zikrullah must be increased concertedly to outweigh the unfavourable and adverse conditions the jamaat encounters when going out for Tabligh. This will protect them from the evil effects of the human and jinn shayaateen.

16. Sincerity and good intention is the base of Tabligh work, and steadfastness of the abovementioned is very important. Therefore, Tabligh workers should at all times seek Allah's pleasure and obey His commands, the greater the extent there is in your sincerity and steadfastness, the greater will be your reward with Allah.

17. The end of your good actions should always be a confession of your weakness and negligence, and the fear of that deed not being accepted by Allah.

18. In our Tabligh work in addition to both sincerity and truthfulness, unity and mutual consultation is essential. Without these a great danger of committing errors prevails.

19. Those high positions which Rasulullah (Sallallaho alaihe wasallam) showed, that could be attained by love and dedication of deen and which was also attained by the Sahaabah (Radhiyallaho anhum) for their sacrifices and hardships which they underwent, you wish to attain that status by the mere leasurely reading of books. For those lofty favours and rewards that were obtained through total sacrifice, we should at least sweat a bit.

20. What benefit is there in remembering the duties which have been completed. One should plan the completion of the remainder of the mission, and assess the shortcomings of the work done.

21. Don't be contented with a person's accepting or understanding your message, be mindful of how many millions are left out to whom Allah's message did not reach. How many more are there who accepted and

were aware of your message but due to our negligence did not carry out Allah's command.

22. Many are of the view that to convey the message is Tabligh, this is a serious misunderstanding. The meaning of Tabligh is that a person should according to his ability and experience convey the message of deen in a manner, that there is hope for the people to accept what is being said. This was the method practiced by the Ambiyaa (Alayhimus salaam).

23. Those who go out for deeni work or for gasht, and their hearts are effected by meeting unmindful and negligent people or irreligious places should make good this loss by zikrullah and fikr of the Deen in seclusion.

24. Basically, every good deed is for the pleasure of Allah and to gain reward in the Hereafter. Worldly gains should also be mentioned for encouragement towards piety. At the beginning, some do religious work for worldly gain, but due to the blessing of the work they are later favoured by Allah with sincerity.

25. Plan, suggest and propose ways and means to call people towards Deen and doing the work of Deen. Approach them in a manner that will draw their attention, and attract them towards Deen.

26. The purpose to go out for Tabligh journeys is not merely to advice and guide others, infact the object is to reform ourselves and develop pleasant habits. Hence, during the journey we should be engaged at all times with zikrullah and aquiring deeni ilm. These should be practiced with the advice and guidance of our learned elders and Ameer (leader). Be mindful of these for your going out for Tabligh will be futile if these are neglected.

27. In this work of Tabligh firm establishment is more significant than expansion. The method of this is that with establishment, expansion must be simultaneous. Without travelling to villages, towns and countries, how could this work of Tabligh be established.

28. One of the principles of this Tabligh work is that one abstains from unilateral decisions and freedom of movement, and at all times abides to the guidance of the recognized learned elders.

29. The general practice of Tabligh workers is that they give full attention to the more prominent personalities, and are less attentive towards other pious and humble not well to do persons who offer their services. It must be understood that this is an approach totally for worldly gain. Keep in mind that the pious and humble who are very poor and needy, who offer their services out of dedication for guidance, are a blessing from Allah. Therefore honour and be grateful to them.

30. Womenfolk should assist the men and give them the opportunity to do religious work. Make their household duties lighter for them so that they may do religious work without any hinderance. If the women do not co-operate in this direction, they will be the victims of becoming a trap of Shaytaan.

31. It is very important when one goes out for Tabligh work that one remains occupied in the activities of the jamaat, and does not get involved in other things. The work schedule of the jamaat is as follows: (1) To go around meeting Muslims for the upliftment of Deen. (2) The acquiring of deeni ilm, and the development of a habit of constant zikrullah. (3) To be helpful, particularly to your close associates. (4) The correction of intention and working towards the development of Ikhlaas (sincerity) and exercising Ihtisaab, i.e. with a concerted effort of keeping ones self under serveilance for purity and clarity of niyyah. One must also regularly entrench the thought in your heart that ones going out is solely for the pleasure of Allah alone, therefore one will definately be blessed with the promise in the Qur'aan and hadith for dedication ornate with this refined quality. It is this Ikhlaas that is kept in check by Ihtisaab which is termed true Imaan, and is also the essence of all our deeds.

32. The Shaytaan's desire is to annul and destroy the progress and higher position which would be attained by being punctual with the faraa'idh, therefore all ones free moments must be spent in nafl zikr (optional zikr), so that the Shaytaan is unable to influence you into meaningless things which would result in harm.

33. One of the principles of Tabligh work is that you honour every Muslim and respect the Ulama.

34. Understand that when some companions intend returning home, don't desire or yearn to follow them, rather contain your heartfelt desire and continue with Tabligh work, for great virtues have been promised for the same. The example of those who contain their heartfelt desire and remain steadfast on this work is that of a fighter who remains fighting on the battlefield whilst his co-fighters disappear in retreat.

35. The condition preceeding the assured method of attaining Allah's assistance is that you should assist His true religion. If you offer assistance to His deen then difficulties and obstacles in life will turn into means for your pleasure in this world, and the earth and skies and whatever it contains will be of assistance to you. Those who after carrying out Allah's work despair the mercy and pleasure of Allah would be most unfortunate and wilfully transgressing His laws.

36. What is termed to be divine assistance and unforseen power is not bestowed initially but is disseminated at the appropriate occasion and time.

GLOSSARY FOR FAZAA'IL-E-A'MAAL

The original names and terms which are understood all over the Muslim World have been retained untranslated. These have been explained in the following glossary, so as to facilitate their correct pronunciation.

The symbol (') used in such words as 'Ja'far–Ka'abah' stand for the Arabic letter ( ). The symbol (') stands for prolonged 'a' sound in 'Qur'an'.

Transliteration	Arabic	Meaning
"A"		
Aameen	امِيْن	'Amen' (May Allah accept it)
Abdaal	ابْدَال	A specific rank among Saints
Aabid	عابِدْ	A worshipper
Abu Dawood	ابُوْ داوُدْ	A book on Hadith compiled by Imam Abu Dawood
Aadam	ادَمْ	Adam the Prophet
Ahad	احَدْ	The Only One
Ahaadith	احَادِيْث	Plural of Hadith
Ah Ha (Urdu)	آها (اردو)	Exclamation of joy
Ahlul Kitaab	اهْلُ الكِتَاب	The people of the Book (Jews & Christians etc.)
Ahqaaf	احْقَافْ	Name of a Surah of Holy Qur'an
Al-aan	الْآن	Now
Al-An'aam	الْاَنْعَام	Name of a Surah of the Holy Qur'an
Alayhis salaam	عَلَيْهِ السَّلَامُ	Peace be upon him
Alayhimus salaam	عَلَيْهِمُ السَّلَامُ	Peace be upon him
Alayhimus salaato was salaam	عَلَيْهِمُ الصَّلٰوةُ وَالسَّلَامُ	Blessings and peace be upon them
Al-Baqarah	الْبَقَرة	Name of a Surah of the Holy Qur'an
Al-Ghinaa	الْغِنٰى	Another name for Surah Waqiyah
Al-Haajj	الْحَاجّ	One who has performed Hajj
Al-Hamd	الْحَمْدُ	A name of first surah of Holy Qur'an
Al-Hamdulillah	الْحَمْدُ لله	Praise be to Allah
Al-Haallul-Murtahil	الْحَالُ الْمُرْتَحِلُ	One who alights and then starts again on a journey
Alif Laam Meem	الٓمٓ	The Abbreviated letters called Al-Muqatt'at revealed at the beginning of various Surahs of Holy Qur'an
Aalim	عالِم	A Scholar of Islam
Aali Imraan	آل عِمْرَان	A Surah of the Holy Qur'an
Al Jalaalain	الْجَلالَيْن	Name of a Commentary on the Qur'an
Al-Khaatimul Mufattih	الْخَاتِمُ الْمُفَتِّحُ	One who concludes and then opens
Allah	الله	Name of Creator of Universe

Allaho Akbar	اللّٰهُ اَكْبَرُ	Allah is the Greatest of all
Allah Ta'ala	اللّٰهُ تَعَالٰى	Allah the Exalted
Allahumma Lakal-Hamd	اَللّٰهُمَّ لَكَ الْحَمْدُ	Allah! Thine is the praise
Allamah	عَلَّامَه	Highly Learned Person
Al-Mala-ul'Ala	اَلْمَلَأُالْاَعْلٰى	First category of angels in Heaven
Al-Mirqaat	اَلْمِرْقَاة	A book of Hadith
Amaanat	اَمَانَت	Trust
Amr bil ma'roof wan nahi anil munkar	(اَمْر بِالْمَعْرُوْف وَنَهْى عَنِ الْمُنْكَر)	Enjoining the good and forbidding the evil
Ambar	عَنْبَرُ	A kind of giant fish
Ambiyaa	اَلْاَنْبِيَآءُ	The Prophets (Name of a Surah of the Holy Qur'an)
Ameer	اَلْاَمِيْرُ	The Leader
Ameerul Mo'mineen	اَمِيْرُ الْمُؤْمِنِيْن	Commander of the Faithful
Ankaboot	اَلْعَنْكَبُوْت	Name of a Surah of the Holy Qur'an
Anwaar	اَنْوَار	Plural of 'Nur'
Aqeeq	اَلْعَقِيْقُ	A Camel market near Madinah
Aqlim	اِقْلِيْم	Continent
A'raaf	اَلْاَعْرَاف	Name of a Surah of the Holy Qur'an
Arabic	اَلْعَرَبِى	The language of the Arabs
Arsh	اَلْعَرْش	The Throne (of Allah)
Arshi Ilaahi	عَرْشِ اِلٰهِى (فارسى)	The Throne of Allah
Asaasul Qur'aan	اَسَاسُ الْقُرْاٰن	Another name for the first Suran Viz Fatihah, of the Holy Qur'an.
Asbaabun nuzool	اَسْبَابُ النُّزُوْل	The particular circumstances of revelation of diff ent verses of the Holy Qur'an
Asfiyaa	اَلْاَصْفِيَاءُ	Plural of 'Safi' (The Sincere)
As-haabus suffah	اَصْحَابُ الصُّفَّة	Men of 'Suffah' devoting full time devotees arou the Prophet
Asmaa-ur rijaal	اَسْمَاءُ الرِّجَال	Biographical Study of Narrator of Ahaadith
Asr	اَلْعَصْرُ	The time (Also name of Salaat) between afterno and Sunset
Assalaamu alaikum	اَسَّلَامُ عَلَيْكُمْ	Peace be upon you (greeting of Muslims)
Astaghfirullaah	اَسْتَغْفِرُ اللّٰهِ	I seek Forgiveness of Allah
Aathaar	آثَار	Sayings of the Sahabah
At-Takaathur	اَلتَّكَاثُرُ	Name of a Surah of the Holy Qur'an
At-Targheeb	اَلتَّرْغِيْب	A book on Hadith compiled by Al-Munziri
Aayat	اٰيَةٌ	A verse of the Holy Qur'an
Aayaat	اٰيَاتٌ	Plural of 'Ayat'
Aayatul Kursi	اٰيَتُ الْكُرْسِى	The name of the 154th verse of Surah of the H Qur'an
Azaan	اَذَانُ	The call for 'Salaat'
Azkaar	اَذْكَارُ	Plural of 'Zikr'
Azkhar	اَذْخَرُ	A kind of bush

"B"

Bahjatun-Nufoos	بَهجَةُ النُّفُوس	A book on religion
Bahrul Uloom	بَحرُ الْعُلُوْم	A name of book on religion
Baihaqi	بَيْهَقِى	A book on Hadith compiled by Baihaqi
Baitul-Hamd	بَيتُ الْحَمْد	House of Praise (in Hereafter)
Baitul-Maal	بَيتُ الْمَال	Treasury of Muslims
Baitul Maqaddas	بَيتُ الْمُقدَّس	Holy Mosque in Jerusalem
Bay-atush-Shajarah	بَيعَةُ الشَّجرَة	(Oath of Allegiance beneath the Tree at Hudabia).
Baandi	باندى (اردو)	A slave girl
Bani Aamir	بَنِىْ عَامِر	Clan of Aamir
Bani Israa-eel	بَنِىْ اِسْرَائِيْل	Progeny (clan) of Israel
Banu Quraizah	بَنُوْ قُرَيْظَة	Clan of Quraizah (Jew progeny)
Banu Salamah	بَنُوْ سَلْمَة	Clan of Salamah
Banu Sulaim	بَنُوْ سُلَيْم	Clan of Sulaim
Banu Thaqeef	بَنُوْ ثَقِيْف	Clan of Thaqeef
Barakah	بَرَكَةٌ	Blessings
Bazlui Majhood	بَذْلُ الْمَجْهُوْد	A book of commentary on Ahadith
Bid'at	بِدْعَةٌ	Innovation in religion
Bismillah	بِسْمِ الله	In the name of Allah
Bismilla-hir-Rahma-nir-Rahim	(بِسْمِ اللهِ الرَّحْمٰنِ الرَّحِيْم)	In the name of Allah, the Beneficent, the Merciful
Bakh Bakh	بَخٍ بَخٍ	How wonderful!
Bukhari	بُخارِىْ	The book of Hadith compiled by Imam Bukhari
Bukhari Sharif	بُخارِىْ شَرِيْف	Bukhari
Buthan	بُطْحَان	Hilly track near Madina

"C"

Chaasht	چاشت (فارسى)	Time (for non-obligatory Salaat) before Noon
Chillah	چِلّه	Forty days
Chishtiat	چِشْتِيت	Chishti school of thought in Sufism

"D"

Da'if	ضَعِيْف	Weak (in reporting of Hadith)
Dajjaal	دَجَّال	Islamic Anti-Christ
Daarus salaam	دَارُ السَّلام	Muslim Territory
Dhil Hijjah	ذِىْ الْحَجَّة	12th month of Islamic Calendar
Deen	دِيْنٌ	Religion
Dinaar	دِيْنَارٌ	A unit of currency in the days of the Prophet
Dirham	دِرْهَمٌ	A small unit of currency in the days of the Prophet
Durood	دُرُوْد (فارسى)	Seeking blessings of Allah on the Prophet
Du'aa	دُعَاء	A supplication; to ask something from Allah

Dukhaan	دُخان	Name of a Surah of Holy Qur'an
Dunuww	دُنُو	Nearness
Durrul Mukhtar	دُرّ مُختار	A book on Fiqah
Durrul Manthur	دُرّ منثور	A commentary on the Qur'an

"E"

Eesa, Eisa	عیسٰی	Prophet Jesus
Ehsan	احسان	Goodness (Also a stage in Sufism)
Eid	عید	Muslim religious Festival
Eidgah	عید گاه (فارسی)	A place where 'Eid' prayers are offered

"F"

Fajr	فجر	Dawn (Morning Salaat)
Faqih	فقیه	Jurist
Faraaidh	فرائض	Plural of 'Fardh'
Fardh	فرض	Obligatory religious practices
Fardh-e-Kifayah	فرض کفایة	Collectively obligatory (that which if fulfilled by a part of the community absolves the rest)
Faasiq	فاسق	Evil-Doer
Fathul Bari	فتح الباری	A commentary on Sahih Bukhari
Fatwa	فتوی	Religion-legal verdict
Fatawa Alamgiri	فتاویٰ عالمگیری	Book of decisions compiled in the period of King Aurangzeb Alamgir the great Mughal ruler in Indian History
Faatir	فاطر	Name of a surah of the Holy Qur'an
Fawaid Fis-Salaat	فوائد فی الصلوٰة	A book on virtues of Salaat
Fawaidul Minhaj	فوائد المنهاج	A book on religion
Fazail-e-Ramadhan	فضائل رمضان	Virtues of Ramadhan
Fazail-e-Tabligh	فضائل تبلیغ	Virtues of 'Tabligh'
Feel	فیل	Elephant – Name of a Surah of the Qur'an
Fiqh	فقه	Jurisprudence
Fitna(h)	فتنة	Evil, Disorder
Fitan	فتن	Plural of 'Fitnah'
Fuqaha	فقهاء	Plural of 'Faqih'

"G"

Ghadan	غدا	Tomorrow
Ghayy	غی	Deception (a pit in Hell)
Ghibta(h)	غبطه	In sense of Emulation
Ghunya(h)	غنیه	A book on tasawwuf by Abdul Qadir Jilani

"H"

Hadith	الْحَدِيْثُ	Saying of the Prophet
Hadith Qudsi	الْحَدِيْثُ الْقُدسِىْ	Saying of Allah, narrated by the Prophet
Hafiz	حَافِظٌ	One who remembers the Qur'an by heart
Haj, Hajj	اَلْحَجُّ	Pilgrimage to Holy Mecca
Haji (Al-Hajj)	الْحَاج	One who performs 'Hajj'
Hujjatullaahil Baalighah	حُجَّةُ اللهِ البَالِغه	A book on religion written by Shah Waliullah
Hakimul Ummah	حَكِيْمُ الْاُمَّةِ	The sage of Muslims
Halaal	حَلال	Lawful
Ha'mim Sajdah	حٰمٓ سَجْدَه	Name of a Surah of the Holy Qur'an
Hanafiyyah	حَنَفِيَّة	A school of Islamic Jurisprudence named after Imam Abu Hanifah
Haq Ta'ala Shanaho	حَق تَعَالٰى شَانُهُ	Allah the Exalted
Haraam	حَرَامٌ	Forbidden, religiously unlawful
Hasan	حَسَنٌ	Good, correct (specially when speaking about the authenticity of Hadith)
Haram (mosque)	اَلْمَسْجِدُ الْحَرَامُ	Holy Ka'aba(h) in Mecca
Hasad	حَسَدٌ	Jealousy
Hashr	اَلْحَشْرُ	Name of a Surah of the Holy Qur'an
Hasanaat	حَسَنَاتٌ	Good deeds; blessings
Hadhrat	حَضْرت	Respected elder
Hijrat	هِجْرَةٌ	Migration in the Path of Allah
Hijri	هِجْرِى	The calendar of Islam, starting with the migration of the Prophet from Mecca to Madinah
Hibrul-Ummat	حِبْرُ الْاُمَّة	The most learned man of Islam
Hisn-e-Haseen	حِصْن حَصِين	A book of supplications based on Hadith
Hood	هُوْدٌ	Name of surah of the Holy Qur'an
Huffaaz	حُفَّاظٌ	Plural of 'Hafiz'
Hujjat-ul-Islam	حُجَّةُ الْاِسْلام	An authority on Islam
Huqb	حُقُبٌ	Eighty years (of the Hereafter)

"I"

Ibaadah	عِبَادَةٌ	Worship
Iblees	اِبْلِيْس	Devil, Satan
Ibn	اِبْنٌ	Son of
Ibn Katheer	اِبْنُ كَثِيْرٌ	A book of commentary on the Qur'an
Ibrahim	اِبْرَاهِيْمُ	Prophet Abraham
Iftaar	اِفْطَارٌ	Breaking the fast
Ihya	اِحْيَآءُ	A book on religion by Imam Ghazali
Ihyaa Uloomid Deen	اِحْيَآءُ عُلُوْمُ الدِّيْنِ	-do-
Ijmaa	اِجْماع	Consensus of opinion

Ikhlaas (surah)	إخلاص	Name of Surah of the Qur'an
Ikhlaas (lit)	إخلاص	Sincerity
Ikraam	إكرام	Respect for others
Ilm-e-Wahbi	عِلمٌ وَهبِى	Divine gifted knowledge
Ilmul Aqaa-id	عِلمُ العَقائِد	Knowledge of fundamentals of Faith
Ilm-ul Badee'	عِلمُ البَدِيع	Knowledge of rhetoric
Ilm-ul-Bayaan	عِلمُ البَيان	Knowledge of figures of speech
Ilm-ul-Fiqh	عِلمُ الفِقه	Knowledge of Islamic jurisprudence
Ilm-ul-Ma'aani	عِلمُ المَعانِى	Knowledge of semantics
Ilm-ul-Qira'at	عِلمُ القِراءة	Knowledge of the art of pronunciation
Imaan	إيمان	Faith (in religion)
Injeel	انجيل	The Gospel
Innaa lillaahi wa	انّا لله وانّا	A verse of the Qur'an recited in grief and (Lit: verily
innaa ilayhi raaji-oon	اليه راجعون	we are for Allah and will return to Him)
Insha Allah	انشاء الله	If Allah Wishes
i'raab	إعراب	Vowel points
Isha, ishaa	عشاء	Salaat during early parts of night
Islam	اسلامٌ	The religion of Muslims
Ism-i-Azam	اسم اعظم (فارسى)	The most glorious name of Allah
Istighfaar	استغفار	Seeking forgiveness of Allah
Istinja	استنجاء	Cleaning after urination or moving the bowels
I'tikaaf	اعتكاف	Devotional seclusion in a mosque for a fixed period
Iza Zulzelat	اذا زلزلت	Name of a Surah of the Qur'an
Izar	إزار	Loose trousers

"J"

Jahannam	جهنّم	Hell
Jahri	جهرى	Loud recitation of Holy Qur'an (in Salaat)
Jamaat	جماعت	Congregation, congregational Salaat
Jami-ul-Usool	جامع الأصول	A book on Hadith
Jamhur	جمهور	General body of Ulama
Jannah, Jannat	جنّة	Paradise
Jannat-ul-Firdous	جنّة الفردوس	The highest category of Paradise
Jehaad	الجهاد	Religious War
Jibraa-eel	جبرئيل	Angel 'Gabriel'
Jumu'ah	جمعة	Friday (or Friday Prayers)
Juz	جزء	Part
Jam-ul-Fawaid	جمع الفوائد	A book on Hadith

"K"

Ka'ba(h)	كعبة	The structure (namely House of Allah) to which Muslims face during Salaat (prayer)

Kaamil	كَامِلٌ	Perfect thing
Kabaa'ir	كَبَائِرُ	Major Sins
Kaafir	كَافِرٌ	Non-believer
Kaafiroon	اَلْكَافِرُوْنَ	Name of a Surah of the Holy Qur'an
Kahf	كَهْف	A Surah of the Holy Qur'an
Kakh Kakh	كَخٍ كَخٍ	Exclamation of Displeasure
Kalimah, Kalimah Tayyibah	كَلِمَةٌ طَيِّبَةٌ	The pure Kalimah, i.e. assertion of the oneness of Allah
Kalimatul Haq	كَلِمَةُ الْحَقِّ	Righteous Kalimah or Phrase
Kanzul Ummaal	كَنْزُ الْعُمَّالُ	A book on Hadith compiled by Muttaqi
Karramallaaho wajhahu	كَرَّمَ اللهُ وَجْهَهُ	May Allah grace him
Kashf	كَشْفٌ	Intuitional illumination of the unseen
Kashful Ghumah	كَشْفُ الْغُمَّةُ	A book on Hadith
Khairul-Umam	خَيْرُ الْأُمَمْ	The best of all the peoples
Khalifah	خَلِيْفَةُ	Caliph
Khalil	خَلِيْلٌ	Friend (appellation of the Prophet Abraham)
Khawarij	خَوَارِجْ	A sect who opposed Hazrat Ali
Khazaf	خَذَفْ	A game which the children play by throwing pebbles with their thumb and fingers
Khilafat	خِلَافَتْ	Caliphate
Khutbah	خُطْبَةْ	Sermon
Kimia-e-Saadat	كِمْيَائِى سَعَادَتْ	A book on religion by Imam Ghazali
Kiraman Katibeen	كِرَامًا كَاتِبِيْنَ	Two angels who write down each and every deed of a man
Kitabul Azkaar	كِتَابُ الْأَذْكَارِ	A book of supplications
Kitaabun Nasaa'i	كِتَابُ النَّسَائِىْ	A book on Hadith compiled by Imam An-Nasaa'i
Kitaabush Shuab	كِتَابُ الشُّعَبْ	A book on Hadith by Imam Baihaqi
Kufr	كُفْرٌ	Non-believing
Kusair	كُسَيْرٌ	Broken thing

"L"

Laa ilaaha illallaaho	لَاإِلٰهَ إِلَّا اللهُ	There is no God save Allah (see Kalimah Tayyabah)
Labbaik	لَبَّيْكَ	I am present (Hajj's special slogan)
Laa ilaaha illallaaho Muhammadur Rasulullah	لَاإِلٰهَ إِلَّا اللهُ مُحَمَّدٌ رَّسُوْلُ اللهِ	There is no God save Allah, and Muhammad is the messenger of Allah
Lailat-ul-Qadr	لَيْلَةُ الْقَدْرُ	The Night of Power (most blessed night of Ramadhan)
Lam Lam	لَمْ لَمْ	A valley in Hell
Laat	لَاتْ	Goddess of the Arab idolaters
Lowhul Mah'fooz	لَوْحِ مَحْفُوْظ	Protected Tablet in the Heavens
Lu'ali Masnu'ah	اَللَّآلِىْ الْمَصْنُوْعَةُ	Title of a book of fabricated Ahadith

"M"

Ma'rifat	مَعْرِفَتْ	Spiritual Realisation (of Allah)
Maa Thabata Bis Sunnah	ماثَبَتَ بالسُّنَّة	A book on Hadith
Madd	مَدّ	Prolongation of 'a' vowel sound
Maghrib	مَغْرِبْ	Sunset; also Salaat just after sun set
Ma'iyat	مَعِيَّتْ	Togetherness
Majalis-ul-Abrar	مَجَالِسُ الأبْرَارِ	A book of preaching
Majoos	مَجُوسْ	Fire Worshippers
Makrooh	مَكْرُوهْ	Disliked (action)
Mala'ikah	مَلائِكَةٌ	The Angels
Maqbool	مَقْبُولْ	Accepted or responded
Maraqi-ul-Falaah	مراقیء الفلاح	A book on Fiqh
Martaba-e-Ihsan	مَرْتَبہء اِحْسَان	A stage in Sufism
Maryam	مَرْيَمْ	Mary. Also name of a Surah of the Qur'an
Masjid-Al-Aqsa	مَسْجِدُ الْاَقْصٰى	Holy Mosque at Jerusalem
Masjid-e-Nabawi	مَسْجِدِ نَبَوِیْ	Holy Mosque of the Prophet at Madinah
Mashaa'ikh	مَشَائِخْ	Shaikhs (Religious divines)
Mathaani	مَثَانِی	From 19th to 38th Surahs of Qur'an (Maryyam to Saad)
Maulana	مَوْلانا	Our master (term of respect used for religious scholar)
Maulvi	مَوْلَوِیْ	A religious scholar
Ma'wal Masaakeen	مأوَی الْمَسَاكِيْن	The refuge of the poor
Mazahir-e-Haq	مَظاهِرِ حَقْ	A commentary on Mishkaat
Mazahir ul Uloom	مظاهِرُ الْعُلُوْمِ	Name of a Madrassah in Saharanpur (India)
Ma'aaz Allah	معاذ الله	God forbid
Mehrab	مِحْرَاب	Nave/Niche in the wall of the mosque/facing Qiblah
Mi'raaj	مِعْرَاجْ	The Ascent of the Prophet towards Heavens
Mi'een	مِئِيْن	From 8th to 18th Surahs of Qur'an (Anfaal to Kahaf)
Mirqaat	مِرْقَاة	A commentary on Mishkat
Mimbar	مِمْبَرْ	Pulpit
Mishkaat	اَلْمِشْكوٰة	A book of Ahadith
Miswaak	مِسْوَاكْ	Green twig of tree used to brush the teeth
Mu'atta	مؤَطا	A book of Ahadith compiled by Imam Malik
Momin	مُؤْمِنٌ	A believer
'Momin		Name of a Surah of the Qur'an
Mominoon	اَلْمُؤْمِنُوْن	Name of a Surah of the Qur'an
Moosa	مُوْسٰی	Prophet Moses
Mudrikah	مُدْرِكه	Faculty of understanding
Muezzin	مُؤَذِّنْ	One who calls 'Asaan'
Mufassal	مُفَصَّل	From 39th to the last Surah of the Qur'an (Zumer to An-Nas)

Mufarrid	مُفرِّدٌ	Who remembers Allah abundantly
Muhaddith	مُحَدِّث	A great Scholar of Hadith
Muhadditheen	مُحدِّثِيْنَ	Plural of 'Muhadith'
Muhajir	مُهاجِرْ	Immigrant from Mecca to Madinah before the fall of Mecca
Muhajireen	مُهاجِرِيْن	Plural of 'Muhajir'
Muhammad	سُوْرَه مُحمَّدْ	Name of a Surah of the Holy Qur'an
Mujahid	مُجاهِدْ	One who strives in the path of Allah
Mujahideen	مُجاهِدِيْن	Plural of 'Muhjahid'
Mu'jam Kabir	مُعْجَمْ كبِيْرْ	A book on Hadith compiled by Tabarani
Mumtahina	اَلْمُمْتَحِنه	Name of a Surah of the Holy Qur'an
Munafiq	مُنافِقْ	Hypocrite
Munafiqin	مُنافِقِيْنَ	Plural of 'Munafiq'. Also name of a Surah of the Holy Qur'an
Munajat-e-Maqbul	مُناجات مقْبُوْل	A book of Islamic supplications
Mun'ema	مُنْعِمَة	Another name of 'Surah-e-Waquiah
Munkar Nakeer	مُنْكرْ نكِيْرْ	Two Angels who interrogate about the faith of the deceased in the grave
Munabbihaat	مُنبِّهاتْ	A book of preaching
Muraaqabah	مُراقبه	Meditation
Mushrik	مُشْرِكْ	One who ascribes partners unto Allah
Mushrikin	مُشْرِكِيْنَ	Plural of 'Mushrik'
'Muslim' **Muslim Sharif**	صَحِيْحْ مُسْلِمْ مُسْلِمْ شرِيْف	A book on Hadith compiled by Imam Muslim
Mustahabb	مُسْتَحبٌ	That which is desirable
Mustahabbat	مُسْتَحبَّاتٌ	Plural of 'Mustahab'
Mustajaab	مُسْتَجابٌ	That which will be accepted.
Mutheera	مُثِيْرَة	The fragrant air of Paradise
Muzammil	مُزَمّلٌ	Name of a Surah of the Holy Qur'an

"N"

Nubuwwat	نُبُوَّة	Prophethood
Nafl	نَفل	Non-obligatory, optional
'Nahl'	نَحْل	Name of a Surah of the Holy Qur'an
Namaaz **Namaz**	نَماز (فارسی)	Salaat (Muslim worship)
Nasikh-o-Mansukh	ناسِخْ وَ مَنْسُوْخ	Commandments that have subsequently been abrogated or replaced by another
Nawaafil	نَوافِلْ	Plural of 'Nafl'
Nawwar Allahu Marquadahu	نَوَّرَ اللهُ مَرْقدَهُ	May Allah enlighten his grave
Nuzhatul Basateen	نُزْهَتُ الْبَساتِيْن	A book of religious stories
Nifaq	نِفاق	Hypocrisy

Niyyah	نِيَّتْ	Intention
Nur	نُوْرٌ	Light, Effulgence
Nuzul	نُزُوْل	Revelation of the Qur'an

"O"

Ooqiyyah	اَوْقِيَه	A unit of weight

"P"

Pul Sirat	پُل صِرَاط (اردو)	Bridge over Hell in the Hereafter
Purdah, Pardah	پَرْدَه (اردو)	Veil or curtain

"Q"

Qa'adah	قَعْدَه	Sitting posture in the Salaat after every two rakaat
Qadha	قَضَاءٌ	Religious practise performed after due time
Qari	قَارِئ	One who recites the Qur'an correctly
Qaniteen	قَانِتِيْنَ	The obedient
Qisas	قِصَاصٌ	Retaliation
Qiblah	قِبْلَه	Direction in which one faces; direction of Kaabah
Qintaar	قِنْطَار	Equal to 12 000 Dirhams (or Dinars)
Qir'at	قِرَاءَة	Recitation of the Qur'an
Qiyaamah	قِيَامَة	The Day of Judgement
Qiyaam	قِيَامُ	Standing posture in the Salaat
Qiyaam-ul-Lail	قِيَامُ الَّيْلِ	Standing in prayers during night
Qunoot	قُنُوْت	Obedience to Allah
'Qunoot'	قُنُوْت	Special Invocation in 'Witr' Salaat
Quran-i-Hakim	قُرْآنِ حَكِيْم	Glorious Qur'an
Qurb	قُرْب	Nearness
Quresh (Qureysh)	قُرَيْشٌ	A famous tribe of Arabs to which the Prophet belonged
Qurraa	قُرَّاءٌ	Plural of 'Qari'
Qutbul Irshad	قُطْبُ الْاِرْشَادِ	A title meaning 'great servant'
Qutbus Sakha	قُطْبُ السَّخَاءِ	Highly generous person

"R"

Rabat	رِبَاطٌ	Guarding the boundries of Islamic Territory
Radhiyallaaho Anho	رَضِيَ اللهُ عَنْهُ	May Allah be pleased with him
Radhiyallaaho Anha	رَضِيَ اللهُ عَنْهَا	May Allah be pleased with her
Rafi'ah Khafidha	رَافِعَه خَافِضَة	That which raise lowly and humble the proud (Day of judgement)
Raahib	رَاهِبٌ	A man (of the previous Ummah)
Rahmatullah Alaih	رَحْمَةُ اللهِ عَلَيْهِ	Blessing of Allah be upon him

Rayhaan	رَيْحَانْ	Sweet smelling flowers
Rak'at, Rak'ah	رَكْعَة	A unit of prayer, involving Qiyam, one ruku and two sajdahs
Rakaat	رَكعَات	Plural of 'Rakat'
Ramadhan	رَمَضَان	The month of Fasting
Rasulullah	رَسُوْلُ الله	The Messenger of Allah
Raawi	رَاوِى	Narrator (of a Hadith)
Rahmat	رَحْمَة	Allah's Mercy
Ridhwaan	رِضْوَانْ	Angel in charge of Paradise
Riwayat	رِوَايَة	Narration of Hadith
Rizq	رِزْقٌ	Provisions
Radghatul Khabal	رَوْغَةُ الْخَبَال	A place in hell filled with mud in the form of blood and pus of its dwellers
Rohban	رُهْبَانْ	Plural of 'Rahib'
Rohbaniat	رَهْبَانِيَّة	Monasticism
Roti (Urdu)	روٹى	Bread
Rozah (Urdu)	روزه	Fast
Ruku	رُكُوْع	1. A section of the Qur'an 2. Second posture of Salaat

"S"

Saad	صٓ	Name of a Surah of Holy Qur'an
Saaffaat	صٰفّٰت	A Surah of Holy Qur'an
Sab'ul Mathaani	سَبْعِ مَثَانِى	Another name of Surah Fatehah
Sab'ut Tuwal	سَبْعِ طُوَل	The first seven (long) Surahs of the Holy Qur'an
Sadaqah	صَدَقَة	Alms
Safar	صَفر	Second month according to Hijri (Islamic) calendar
Saghair	صَغَائِرْ	Plural of Saghir (Small) i.e. Minor sins
Sahabi	صَحَابِىْ	A companion of the Prophet
Sahaba(h)	صَحَابَة	Plural of 'Sahabi'
Sahih	صَحِيْح	Authentic
Sahih Bokhari	صَحِيْح بُخَارِىْ	A book on Hadith compiled by Imam Bokhari
Sajdah	سَجْدَة	Prostration (especially in Salaat)
Sajdah Sahw	سَجْدَة سَهْو	Prostration performed to atone for minor errors in the Salaat
Sakeenah	سَكِيْنَه	Tranquillity
Salaat, Salat	صَلٰوة	Islamic way of worshipping Allah
Salaatul-Awwabeen	صَلٰوةُ الْاَوَّابِيْن	Non-obligatory Salaat just after Maghrib Salaat
Salaat ul Ishraq	صَلٰوةُ الْاِشْرَاق	Non-obligatory Salaat a little after sunrise
Salaat ut Tasbeeh	صَلٰوةُ التَّسْبِيْح	Special non-obligatory Salaat involving special praise of Allah
Salaat-ud-Duha	صَلٰوةُ الضُّحٰى	Non-obligatory Salaat before noon
Sallallaho alaihe Wasallam	صَلَّى اللهُ عَلَيْهِ وَسَلَّم	Blessing and peace be upon him from Allah

Sama ud Dunya	سَمَاءُ الدُّنْيَا	Heaven immediately above the earth
Saq	سَاق	Calf of the leg
Sarf	صَرْفٌ	Etymology – A branch of Grammar
Sayyidul Ambia	سَيِّدُ الأنبياء	The leader of all the Prophets (Mohammad)
wal Mursalin	وَالمُرْسَلِيْن	
Sehry	سَحَرِى	Meal before dawn to keep fast
Sha'baan	شَعْبَان	8th month of Islamic Calendar
Shafaa'at	شَفَاعَتْ	Intercession
Shahid	شَهِيْدْ	A martyr
Sharah Iqna	شَرْحِ اقْنَاع	A commeniary on Hadith
Shahwat	شَهْوَة	Passion, Desire
Shaikh	شَيْخٌ	Religious Divine
Shaqiy	شَقِىّ	Wretched
Sharaab	شَرَابٌ	Liquor, Drink
Sharah Muslim	• شَرْحِ مُسْلِم	A commentary on Muslim Sharif (A book of Hadith)
Sharahu Ihyaul Uloom	شَرْحِ احياء العُلُوْم	Commentary on Imam Ghazali's book named Ihyaul Uloom
Sharahus Sunnah	شَرْحِ السُّنَّة	A commentary on Hadith
Shari'at, Shari'ah	شَرِيْعَة	Code of Islamic laws
Shaytaan	شَيْطَان	Satan (Devil)
Shayateen	شَيَاطِيْن	Plural of 'Shaytaan'
Shirk	شِرْك	Setting up partners with Allah
Shu'bul Imaan	شعب الأيمان	Sections of Imaan
Shura	الشُّوْرَى	Name of a surah of the Qur'an
Shuruh-e-Hisn	شُرُوْح حِصْن	Commentaries on Hisne Haseen
Sirat	صِرَاط	Way, path
Sirri	سِرِّى	Quiet (recitation of Qur'an in Salaat)
Soofia	صُوْفِيه	Plural of 'Sufi'
Sowm	صَوْمُ	Fast
Sowar	سُوَر	Plural of 'Surah'
Subhaanakallahumma	سُبْحَانَكَ	O Allah, Thine is the Glory
Subhaanallah	اللّهم	Glory to Allah
Subhana Rabbiyal	سُبْحَانَ الله	Glory to my Lord, the Great
Azim	سُبْحَان	
Subhanahu wa	رَبِّىَ الْعَظِيْم	Glorious and sacred (Allah)
Taqaddas	سُبْحَانَهُ وَتَقَدَّسَ	
Suffah	صُفّه	A raised platform in the Mosque of the Prophet at Madinah
Sufi	صُوْفِى	A Mystic
Sajdah	سَجْدَة	Prostration
Sujood	سُجُوْد	Plural of Sajdah
Sulook ilallah	سُلُوْك الى الله	Path of the Mystic towards Allah
Sunan	سُنَن	Plural of 'Sunnat'

Sunnah Muakkadah	سُنّت مؤكّده	Regular Practice of the Prophet
Sunnat, Sunnah	سُنّت	Practice of the Prophet
Surah	سُوْرَةٌ	A chapter of the Holy Qur'an
Surah Al-Furqan	سُوْرَةُ الْفُرْقَان	Name of a Surah in the Qur'an
Surah Al-Hadid	سُوْرَةُ الْحَدِيْد	-do-
Surah-e-Alif-Lam-Mim-Sajdah	سُوْرَةُ الٓمّ سجْدَةُ	-do-
Surah Kauser	سُوْره كوْثر	-do-
Surah Al-Qamar	سُوْرَةُ الْقمر	-do-
Surah Ar-Rahmaan	سُوْرَةُ الرَّحْمٰن	-do-
Surah Baqarah	سُوْرَةُ الْبقرة	-do-
Surah Faatihah	سُوْره فاتحه	-do-
Surah Faatir	سُوْره فاطر	-do-
Surah Ibrahim	سُوْره ابْراهيْم	-do-
Surah Ikhlaas	سُوْره اخلاص	-do-
Surah Mulk	سُوْرَةُ الْمُلك	-do-
Surah Qadr	سُوْرَةُ الْقدر	-do-
Surah Tabarak-Al-Lazi	سُوْره تبارك الّذىٰ	-do-
Surah Ta Ha	سُوْره طٰه	-do-
Surah Waqi-ah	سُوْره واقعه	-do-
Surah Was-Saffat	سُوْرَةُ والصّٰفّت	-do-
Surah Yaaseen	سُوْره يٰسٓ	-do-

"T"

Ta'aam	طعام	Food, Meal
T'awwudh	تعوّذ	Seeking Allah's refuge against Satan
Taabi'ee	تابعىٰ	A Muslim who has seen or met any one of the Sahabah
Taabi'een	تابعيْن	Plural of the 'Tabai'.
Tabligh	تبْليْغ	Preaching Islam
Taghabun	التّغابن	Name of a Surah of the Holy Qur'an
Tahajjud	تهجّد	Non-obligatory Salaat between Midnight and the dawn
Tahlil	تهْليْل	Recitation of "Kalimah Tayyabah"
Tahmeed	تحميْد	Recitation of words on praise of Allah viz Alhamdo-Lillah
Tahzibul-Kamal	تهْذيْب الكمال	A book on names of narrators of Hadith
Tajalli	تجلّىٰ	Radiance
Tajweed	تجويد	Reciting the Holy Qur'an with proper intonation
Takbeer	تكبيْر	Recitation of words Allah-o-Akbar (Allah is Greatest)
Takbir Tahrima	تكبيْر تحريمه	Saying Allah-o-Akbar at the commencement of Salaat

Ta'lim	تعْلِيم	Teaching
Talqih	تلْقِيْح	A book of religion
Tambih-ul-Ghafileen	تنبِيْهُ الْغَافِلِين	A book of sermons
Tanqih-ur-Ruwat	تنْقِيْحُ الرُّوَاة	A critical review of narrators of Hadith
Taraweeh	تَرَاوِيْح	A sunnat salaat offered (in congregation) after Isha during Ramadhan
Targheeb	تَرْغِيْب	A book on religion by Munziri
Tarteel	تَرْتِيْل	Careful recitation of the Qur'an with due regard to the rules
Tasawwuf	تَصَوُّف	Sufi-ism
Tasbeeh	تَسْبِيْح	1. Glorifying Allah 2. Rosary
Tasbihat-e-Fatima	تَسْبِيْحَاتِ فَاطِمَه	Recitation of Subhan-ullah 33 times, Alham-do-lillah 33 times, and Allaho-Akbar 34 times after every Salaat, initially enjoined by the Prophet on his daughter Fatima
Tashahhud	تَشَهُّد	A prayer recited while sitting (Qa'adah) after every two rakaat of Salaat
Tashdid	تَشْدِيْد	Doubling of letters in Arabic words
Taubah	تَوْبَه	Repentance
Tauheed	تَوْحِيْد	Faith in Allah as the Sole Lord
Tawaf-i-Qudoom	طَوَافِ قُدُوْم	Circumambulation of (going round) the Ka'bah on first arriving in Mecca
Tawakkul	تَوَكُّل	Reliance on Allah
Tazkirah-e-Qurtubiyyah	تَذْكِرَه قُرْطِبِيَّه	A book on religion
Tazkiratul-Khalil	تَذْكِرَةُ الْخَلِيْل	A biography of Maulana Khalil Ahmad, a saint and scholar of Saharanpur (India)
Thareed	ثَرِيْد	A kind of food made with gravy and bread
Thawab	ثَوَاب	Spiritual Reward
Tabrani	طَبْرَانى	A book of Hadith compiled by Imam Tabarani
Tilawat, Tilawah	تِلاوَة	Recitation of the Holy Qur'an
Tirmizi	تِرْمِذِى	A collection of Hadith by Imam Tirmizi
Toor	طُوْر	A mountain in the valley of Sina
Turanj	تُرَنْج	Citron

"U"

Ulama-e-Kiram	عُلَمَاءُ	Plural of 'Aalim' (Scholar of Islam)
Umm	اُمّ	Mother
Ummah, Ummat	اُمَّتْ	Followers of a Prophet (viz Muslims)
Ummul Momineen	اُمّ الْمُؤْمِنِيْن	Mother of the believers (any wife of Holy Prophet)
Umrah	عُمْرَه	Circumambulation (going round) of Ka'bah and other rites on a visit to Mecca
Usul-e-Fiqh	اُصُوْلِ فِقْه	Principles of Islamic Jurisprudence
Ummat-i-Mohammadi	اُمَّتِ مُحَمَّدِيَه	The followers of Mohammad

Ustaz	اُسْتَاذ	Teacher
Urdu	اُرْدُو	The national language of Pakistan

"V"

Vail	وَيْلٌ	Pit of Grief

"W"

Wa-Alaikumus-Salam	وَعَلَيْكُمُ السَّلَامُ	Response to the greeting of Muslims saying 'and peace be upon you too'
Wajib	وَاجِبٌ	Almost obligatory
Wabeham dika	وَبِحَمْدِكَ	And with Thy praise
Watabarakasmuka	وَتَبَارَكَ اسْمُكَ	and Blessed be Thy Name
Wata-Ala-Jaddoka	وَتَعَالٰى جَدُّكَ	and exalted is Thy Greatness
Wa-La-Ilaha-Ghairuk	وَلَآاِلٰهَ غَيْرُكَ	and there is none worth of worship except Thee
Wasful Imaan-Lish-Shu'abi	وَصْفُ الْاِيْمَان لِلشَّعْبِىْ	A book on religion
Wazifa	وَظِيْفَه	Specified task, position, Scholarship, maintenance allowance, profession
Witr	وِتْرُ	Compulsory Salaat of 3 Rakaat following Isha
Wudhu	وُضُوْ	Ablutions

"Y"

Yarhamo Kallah	يَرْحَمُكَ اللهُ	Allah's Mercy be upon you
Yusuf	يُوْسُفْ	Name of a Surah of the Qur'an and name of a Prophet
Yunus	يُوْنُس	Name of a Surah of the Qur'an and name of a Prophet

"Z"

Zakaat	زَكٰوة	Obligatory charity payable on wealth
Zaariyaat	ذٰرِيَاتٌ	Name of a Surah of the Holy Qur'an
Zikrullah	ذِكْرُ اللهِ	Remembrance of Allah
Zilqadah	ذِىْ قَعْدَة	11th month (according to the lunar appearance) of Hijri Calendar
Zubab	ذُبَابُ	Ominous, flies
Zuhur	ظُهر	Afternoon
Zumar	زُمَرْ	Name of a Surah of the Holy Qur'an